Psychological Science

Psychological Science

Modeling Scientific Literacy

SECOND EDITION

Mark Krause
Southern Oregon University

Daniel Corts
Augustana College

Boston   Columbus   Indianapolis   New York   San Francisco   Hoboken
Amsterdam   Cape Town   Dubai   London   Madrid   Milan   Munich   Paris   Montréal   Toronto
Delhi   Mexico City   São Paulo   Sydney   Hong Kong   Seoul   Singapore   Taipei   Tokyo

VP, Product Development: Dickson Musslewhite
Executive Editor: Erin Mitchell
Senior Development Editor: Mary Piper Hansen
Editorial Assistant: Danique Robinson
Program Manager: Reena Dalal
Program Team Lead: Amber Mackey
Project Manager: Sherry Lewis
Project Team Lead: Denise Forlow
VP Product Marketing, Business & Arts: Maggie Moylan Leen
Director of Field Marketing: Jonathan Cottrell
Senior Product Marketer: Lindsey Prudhomme Gill
Executive Field Marketer: Kate Stewart
Marketing Assistant, Field Marketing: Paige Patunas

Marketing Assistant, Product Marketing: Jessica Warren
Senior Operations Specialist: Diane Peirano
Operations Manager: Mary Fischer
Associate Director of Design: Blair Brown
Interior Designer: Kathryn Foot
Cover Designer: Maria Lange
Cover Art: HONGQI ZHANG/123RFscol22/123RF and scol22/123RF
Digital Media Project Management: Caroline Fenton, Pamela Weldin
Full-Service Project Management/Composition: Integra
Cover Printer: Phoenix Color/Hagerstown
Printer/Binder: RR Donnelley

Acknowledgements of third party content appear on pages 642–649, which constitutes an extension of this copyright page.

Library of Congress Cataloging-in-Publication Data

Krause, Mark A. (Mark Andrew),
   Psychological science : modeling scientific literacy/Mark Krause, Southern Oregon University, Daniel Corts, Augustana College.—Second edition.
      pages cm
   Revised edition of Psychological science, 2014.
   ISBN 978-0-13-410158-3
   1. Psychology.   2. Psychology—Study and teaching.   I. Corts, Daniel Paul, 1970-   II. Title.
   BF121.K723 2016
   150—dc23

                                                                                          2015023381

10 9 8 7 6 5 4 3 2 1

Student Edition
ISBN 10:   0-13-410158-8
ISBN 13: 978-0-13-410158-3

Ála Carte Edition
ISBN 10:   0-13-422561-9
ISBN 13: 978-0-13-422561-6

*For Andrea and Finn. Both of you fuel
my passion and motivation for this endeavor.
I cannot thank you enough.*

Mark Krause

---

*To Kim, Sophie, and Jonah, for your patience,
understanding, and forgiveness during all
the hours this project has occupied me.*

Dan Corts

Brief Contents

Contents

About the Authors

Dr. Mark Krause received his Bachelor's and Master's degrees at Central Washington University, and his PhD at the University of Tennessee in 2000. He completed a post-doctoral appointment at the University of Texas at Austin where he studied classical conditioning of sexual behavior in birds. Following this, Krause accepted a research fellowship through the National Institute of Aging to conduct research on cognitive neuroscience at Oregon Health and Sciences University. He has conducted research and published on pointing and communication in chimpanzees, predatory behavior in snakes, the behavioral and evolutionary basis of conditioned sexual behavior, and the influence of testosterone on cognition and brain function. Krause began his teaching career as a doctoral candidate and continued to pursue this passion even during research appointments. His teaching includes courses in general psychology, learning and memory, and behavioral neuroscience. Krause is currently a professor of psychology at Southern Oregon University, where his focus is on teaching, writing, and supervising student research. His spare time is spent with his family, cycling, reading, and enjoying Oregon's outdoors.

Dr. Daniel Corts discovered psychology at Belmont University where he received his B.S. He completed a PhD in Experimental Psychology at the University of Tennessee in 1999 and then a post-doctoral position at Furman University for one year where he focused on the teaching of psychology. He is now professor of psychology at Augustana College in Rock Island, IL where he has taught for over 15 years. His research interests in cognition have lead to publications on language, gesture, and memory, and he has also published in the area of college student development. Corts is increasingly involved in applied work, developing programming and assessments related to K-12 educational programming and teacher preparation. Corts is enthusiastic about getting students involved in research and has supervised or coauthored over 100 conference presentations with undergraduates. Corts has served as the local Psi Chi advisor for a dozen years and has served on the Board of Directors for several years, including his current term as President. In his spare time, he enjoys spending time with his two children, traveling, camping, and cooking.

From the Authors

Welcome to the second edition of *Psychological Science: Modeling Scientific Literacy!* It is a great privilege for us to offer an updated and revised version of our textbook. Much has happened in psychology since the first edition and we are excited to present the latest and greatest that our field has to offer. Of course, equally if not more important to keeping up with the science is ensuring that our readers find our book accessible, interesting, and hopefully inspiring. To this end we have, as authors should, put ourselves in the mindset of a college student first encountering this material and re-read the entire book. There is no better way to begin the process of revising and improving a textbook. In the second edition we have continued our emphasis on helping the reader organize and assess their thinking and learning about the material. Each module includes learning objectives of increasing depth (knowing, understanding, analyzing and applying) and end of module quiz and chapter items assessing learning at each level. Also new to this edition are journal prompts in each module which prime students to think deeply about specific topics, take a stance on an issue, or apply a concept to oneself.

We firmly believe that a well-rounded college education requires a healthy dose of science. This is true regardless of an individual's personal and career goals. To this end, *Psychological Science* is written from the perspective of scientific literacy—the ability not only to define scientific terminology, but also to understand how it functions, to critically evaluate it, and to apply it to personal and societal matters. Scientific literacy comprises four interrelated components:

1. **knowledge:** what do we know about a phenomenon?
2. **scientific explanation:** how does science explain the psychological process we are examining?
3. **critical thinking:** how do we interpret and evaluate all types of information, including scientific reporting?
4. **application:** how does research apply to your own life and to society?

Psychological Science presents students with a model for scientific literacy; this model forms the core of how this book is written and organized. We believe a scientific literacy perspective and model will prove useful in addressing two course needs we often hear from instructors—to provide students with a systematic way to categorize the overwhelming amount of information they are confronted with, and to cultivate their curiosity and help them understand the relevance, practicality, and immense appeal of psychological science.

Psychological Science models the processes of scientific thinking. As was the case in the first edition, the elements of scientific literacy are explicitly demonstrated once per module, and implicitly throughout. We are very excited to introduce a new feature for the second edition: the Scientific Literacy Challenge. At the end of each chapter students can practice applying scientific and critical thinking to an important, contemporary issue. We tackle such topics as free-range parenting, cognitive enhancement drugs, college admissions testing, and brain training websites. Students are asked to read author created blog entries, editorials, or advertisements about these topics and evaluate them from a scientific literacy perspective through journal prompts, and multiple-choice, matching and true/false questions.

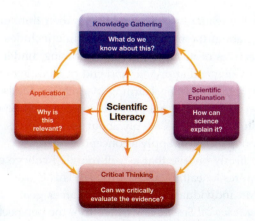

We thank the many instructors and students who have helped us craft this model and apply it to our discipline, and we look forward to your feedback. Please feel free to contact us and share your experiences with the 2nd edition of *Psychological Science.*

Mark Krause
krausema@sou.edu

Daniel Corts
danielcorts@augustana.edu

What's New?

The Scientific Literacy Challenge described above is an exciting new feature of the second edition. We also updated module openers to include contemporary and relevant examples, and updated research, and in some cases replaced, topics covered in the Working the Scientific Literacy Model features within each module. Naturally, the topics we cover involve ongoing and exciting research. Therefore, each chapter has been updated accordingly, and, in many places, we have added new topics we felt deserve inclusion in our book. For example:

- Chapter 1, "Introducing Psychological Science" includes additional instruction on critically thinking about sources. Students learn to evaluate a message by considering the author or speaker, the purpose of the article, the publisher or presenter, and other factors that affect the reliability and quality of the message. Interactive exercises help students understand the ways in which psychology may be expanded into other fields, such as sports psychology.

- Chapter 2, "Reading and Evaluating Scientific Research" provides additional tools to think about and understand the outcomes of research. The coverage of correlational methods is supplemented by instruction on how to think about what it means to be a small, medium, or large correlation. Similar improvements have been made to the discussion on how to understand group differences in experimental and quasi-experimental research.

- Chapter 3, "Biological Psychology" now begins by asking students to think about Paleo diets as a way to introduce evolutionary psychology. There is a new section introducing epigenetics. Citations and coverage have been expanded on topics of genomics, neurogenesis and brain plasticity, and brain imaging technology.

- Chapter 4, "Sensation and Perception" includes new interactive features for applying signal detection theory and monocular depth cues, and updated research and coverage of subliminal perception, multi-tasking, phantom limb therapies, and object recognition.

- Chapter 5, "Consciousness" includes a new Working the Scientific Literacy Model feature on the neurocognitive theory of dreaming, updated coverage on how marijuana and other drugs affect cognition, new research on dream sleep and memory, and the therapeutic effects of hypnosis and meditation.

- Chapter 6, "Learning" includes updated coverage on applications of classical conditioning; including taste aversions, advertisement, drug tolerance, in-text activities for practicing concepts of classical and operant conditioning, updated research and expanded personal application opportunities on topics of cognitive and long-term learning, a revised Working the Scientific Literacy Model feature to balance coverage of research on video game playing and violent behavior.

- Chapter 7, "Memory" has more coverage of applications including strengthening memories and the reliability of eyewitness testimony.

- Chapter 8, "Thought and Language" makes more connections between the often very abstract theories of reasoning and daily experience. For example, students can learn about individual differences in the reliance on representativeness, and how these differences relate to interest in superstition, the paranormal, and conspiracy theories.

- Chapter 9, "Intelligence and Aptitude, and Cognitive Abilities" includes updated citations and research, especially when covering intelligence and the brain. Also, students can engage in a debate on whether colleges and universities should consider personality tests as a supplement to or even a replacement for traditional college aptitude tests.

- Chapter 10, "Life Span Development" includes updated coverage of preterm infant development, child cognitive development, expanded and updated coverage of adolescent sexuality, brain development, and identity.

- Chapter 11, "Motivation and Emotion" includes updated research on sex and the brain, and sexual orientation, neural and psychological bases of hunger and eating, effects of loneliness and mental and physical health, and an in-text activity on achievement motivation.

- Chapter 12, "Personality" includes updated coverage of cultural and evolutionary influences on personality, practice application activities for the Big 5, cultural variation, and psychodynamic views on personality, updated discussion on scientific research on suppression and critical analysis of Freud's views on personality.

- Chapter 13, "Psychological Disorders" has been updated throughout to reflect *DSM 5* revisions and recent prevalence statistics when available.

- Chapter 14, "Therapies" includes a new Working the Scientific Literacy Model feature about the use of mobile apps designed to improve mental health, updated coverage of topics such as empirically supported treatments, precision medicine and cultural factors related to drug treatments, effects of nutrients such as Omega-3 fatty acids on health, and reduced emphasis on outdated anti-depressant drugs and expanded coverage of potential new treatments (e.g., low-dose ketamine).

- Chapter 15, "Social Psychology" has updated and modified coverage of stereotypes and person perception. This reflects increased national awareness of the use of force by law enforcement, an extremely important topic that is also very engaging for students.

- Chapter 16, "Health, Stress, and Coping" has updated coverage on the effects of media exposure on health related behaviors (smoking), social contagion effects occurring via social media (Facebook), effects of stress on cognitive processes, posttraumatic growth, effects of exercise and nutrition on cognitive functioning.

- Chapter 17, "Industrial and Organizational Psychology" includes substantial updates to sections on selection and assessment. There is increased linkage between the sections on employee affect and leadership through an interactive investigation of how money may or may not be a useful motivator for employees.

Content and Features

Students in the general psychology course are inundated with many disparate pieces of information at a time when they are still developing the skills and strategies for organizing and making sense of that information. How do Working the Scientific Literacy Model and supporting features in *Psychological Science* address this issue?

Modules

Chapters are divided into modules to make it easier for students to organize content as well as to self-test and review their learning at regular intervals. For instructors, the modular content makes it easy to customize their delivery based on their preferred syllabus.

Learning Objectives

Learning Objectives are organized around an updated Bloom's taxonomy that aims to guide students to higher-level understanding. Summaries of the key points related to these objectives are provided at the end of each module. Objectives are listed at four levels of increasing complexity: know, understand, apply, and analyze.

Module Summaries

The major terms, concepts, and applications of the modules are reviewed in the Module Summaries. The summaries also return to and address the original Learning Objectives from the beginning of the module and include application questions. **Answers to end-of-module and end-of-chapter assessment can be found in the Instructor's Manual.**

Module 2.1 Principles of Scientific Research

Learning Objectives

2.1a Know . . . the key terminology related to the principles of scientific research.

2.1b Understand . . . the five characteristics of quality scientific research.

2.1c Understand . . . how biases might influence the outcome of a study.

2.1d Apply . . . the concepts of reliability and validity to examples.

2.1e Analyze . . . whether anecdotes, authority figures, and common sense are reliably truthful sources of information.

Several years ago, the Society for Neuroscience invited the Dalai Lama, the spiritual leader of Tibetan Buddhism, to their annual emerging science meeting to discuss the practice of meditation. For most people, meditation is understood to be a mystical, subjective, nonscientific practice embraced by individuals outside the scientific community. It is likely that no more than a hundred—if not fewer—of the Society's 30,000 plus members had a professional, scientific interest in the subject. Why, then, would the Society invite the Dalai Lama to speak about a topic that was clearly not based in science? Several hundred Society members were so opposed to the Dalai Lama's talk that they signed a petition to cancel his scheduled appearance. But according to the Dalai Lama, the members' opposing opinions about the value of meditation are rooted in the same thing: an almost complete lack of understanding of the practice. Without the benefit of careful observations and measurement, there really is no scientific way of saying whether meditation is worthwhile. Therefore, it is precisely this lack of understanding why scientists should be interested in meditation. In recent years, neuroscientists such as Richard Davidson and Antoine Lutz of the University of Wisconsin have confirmed that meditation does have numerous benefits. They have also developed models for how specific brain functions translate the practice of meditation into physical and psychological well-being. In Chapter 1, we argued that critical thinkers should be skeptical. Why, then, would the Society invite the Dalai Lama to speak about a topic that was clearly not based in science? Several hundred Society members demonstrated. However, we also argued that critical thinkers should be curious and that their opinions should be modified to fit the evidence—something that Davidson, Lutz, and colleagues are working toward. In this chapter we turn to the process of gathering and evaluating evidence.

32

40 Chapter 2

Module **2.1** Summary

2.1a Know . . . the key terminology related to the principles of scientific research:

anecdotal evidence
appeal to authority
appeal to common sense
convenience samples
demand characteristics
double-blind study
ecological validity
generalizability
Hawthorne effect
objective measurements
operational definition
peer review
placebo effect
population
random sample
reliability
replication
sample
self-reporting
single-blind study
social desirability
validity
variable

2.1b Understand . . . the five characteristics of quality scientific research.

These characteristics include (1) that measurements are objective, valid, and reliable; (2) the research can be generalized; (3) it uses techniques that reduce bias; (4) the findings are made public; and (5) the results can be replicated. For example, objective, valid, and reliable measurements make it possible for other scientists to test whether they could come up with the same results if they followed the same procedures. Psychologists mostly study samples of individuals, but usually they are more concerned about describing principles that generalize to a broader population. Single- and double-blind procedures are standard ways of reducing bias. Finally, the process of publishing results is what allows scientists to share information, evaluate hypotheses that have been confirmed or refuted, and, if needed, replicate other researchers' work.

2.1c Understand . . . how biases might influence the outcome of a study.

Demand characteristics affect how participants respond in research studies. Understandably, they often attempt to portray themselves in a positive light, even if that means not answering questions or behaving in a fully truthful manner. Researchers can also influence the outcomes of their own studies, even unintentionally.

2.1d Apply . . . the concepts of reliability and validity to examples.

Reliable and valid measures are essential to scientific research. Table 2.1 on page 35 provided an opportunity to apply your knowledge. In the first example, Dr. Tatum had to improve reliability; although her physiological instruments measured what they were supposed to (validity), they lacked reliability because they were inconsistent. In another example, Dr. Nielsen questioned the validity of his checklist for observing happiness in children. Although his team achieved consistent results (reliability), there was some question over whether it truly measured happiness, or perhaps just activity level.

2.1e Analyze . . . whether anecdotes, authority figures, and common sense are reliably truthful sources of information.

To evaluate evidence, you should ask several questions. First, is support for the claim based on the words or endorsement of an authority figure? Endorsement by an authority is not necessarily a bad thing, as someone who is an authority (expert) at something should be able to back up the claim. But the authority of the individual alone is not satisfactory, especially if data gathered through good scientific methods do not support the claim. Second, is someone supplying anecdotal evidence? As convincing as a personal testimony may be, anecdotal evidence is not sufficient for backing any claim that can be scientifically tested. Common sense also has its place in daily life, but by itself is insufficient as a final explanation for anything. Explanations based on good scientific research should override those based on common sense.

jects. By examining and reporting an average effect for that group, psychologists can get a much better sense of how individuals are likely to behave. But how large of a group is it possible to study? Ideally, it would be best to study an entire **population**—*the group that researchers want to generalize about.* In reality, the task of finding all population members, persuading them to participate, and measuring their behavior is impossible in most cases. Instead, psychologists typically study a **sample**—*a select*

Key Terms

Key Terms are defined within the narrative, helping students place them in context, and are then listed again within the Module Summaries. A complete glossary is also included at the end of the text.

REVEL™

Fully digital and highly engaging, REVEL offers an immersive learning experience designed for the way today's students read, think, and learn. Enlivening course content with media interactives and assessments, REVEL empowers educators to increase engagement with the course, and to better connect with students: **pearsonhighered.com/revel.**

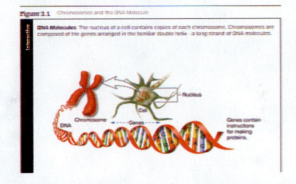

Module Quizzes
End-of-Chapter Quizzes

Quizzes appear at the conclusion of modules and chapters. These quizzes contain multiple-choice questions that enable students to assess their comprehension and better prepare for exams. Like the Learning Objectives, the Module Quizzes assess understanding at the four levels of Bloom's taxonomy and are marked accordingly. **Answers to quizzes can be found in the Instructor's Manual.**

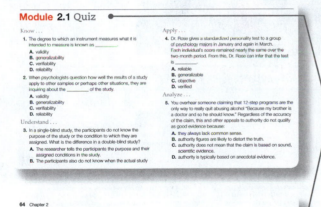

Scientific Explanation

How can science explain it?

This element of scientific literacy encompasses a basic understanding of research methodology and thinking about problems within a scientific framework. *Psychological Science* integrates and reinforces key research methodology concepts throughout the book. This interweaving of methodology encourages students to continue practicing their scientific thinking skills. As noted in the *National Science Education Standards*, learning science is more than accumulating facts; that is, students learn to ask questions, construct explanations, test those explanations, and communicate their ideas to others.

Module **2.1**   Principles of Scientific Research

Learning Objectives

2.1a Know . . . the key terminology related to the principles of scientific research.

2.1b Understand . . . the five characteristics of quality scientific research.

2.1c Understand . . . how biases might influence the outcome of a study.

2.1d Apply . . . the concepts of reliability and validity to examples.

2.1e Analyze . . . whether anecdotes, authority figures, and common sense are reliably truthful sources of information.

Module Opening Vignettes

Each module opens with a short vignette emphasizing the personal and societal relevance of certain topics to be covered.

Several years ago, the Society for Neuroscience invited the Dalai Lama, the spiritual leader of Tibetan Buddhism, to their annual emerging science meeting to discuss the practice of meditation. For most people, meditation is understood to be a mystical, subjective, nonscientific practice embraced by individuals outside the scientific community. It is likely that no more than a hundred—if not fewer—of the Society's 30,000 plus members had a professional, scientific interest in the subject. Why, then, would the Society invite the Dalai Lama to speak about a topic that was clearly not based in science? Several hundred Society members were so opposed to the Dalai Lama's talk that they signed a petition to cancel his scheduled appearance. But according to the Dalai Lama, the members' opposing opinions about the value of meditation are rooted in the same thing: an almost complete lack of understanding of the practice. Without the benefit of careful observations and measurement, there really is no scientific way of saying whether meditation is worthwhile. Therefore, it is precisely this lack of understanding why scientists should be interested in meditation. In recent years, neuroscientists such as Richard Davidson and Antoine Lutz of the University of Wisconsin have confirmed that meditation does have numerous benefits. They have also developed models for how specific brain functions translate the practice of meditation into physical and psychological well-being. In Chapter 1, we argued that critical thinkers should be skeptical, as many Society members demonstrated. However, we also argued that critical thinkers should be curious and that their opinions should be modified to fit the evidence—something that Davidson, Lutz, and colleagues are working toward. In this chapter we turn to the process of gathering and evaluating evidence.

Myths in Mind

Many commonly held beliefs people have about behavior before taking a psychology course are half-truths or outright falsehoods. This feature sets the record straight in a concise and informative way. The selected examples are likely to have personal relevance to many readers and deal with important scientific issues.

Myths in Mind

We Are Born With All the Brain Cells We Will Ever Have

Until the 1960s neuroscientists were unaware that new nerve cells could generate once an organism was born. This conclusion made perfect sense because no one had ever seen new neurons form in adults, and severe neurological damage is often permanent. Advances in brain science have challenged this belief (Gage, 2000). Researchers have observed *neurogenesis*, which is the formation of new nerve cells, in several brain areas of rodents, monkeys, and humans (Braun & Jessberger, 2014). The growth of a new cell, including neurons that populate a few different brain regions as well as some glial cells, starts with stem cells, which are unique types of cells that do not have a special- ized, genetically programmed function. When a stem cell divides, the resulting cells can become part of just about anything—bone, kidney, or brain tissue. What determines the type of nerve cell that develops and its migratory path within the brain is the stem cell's external chemical environment (Williams, Holman, & Klein, 2014). Our increased understanding of neurogenesis has raised some exciting possibilities; perhaps scientists can discover how to trigger neural growth in parts of the nervous system that do not naturally undergo neurogenesis throughout the life span. Developments in neural stem-cell research can bring added hope for recovery from brain injury and disease.

In recent years, an increasing number of instructors have begun to focus on telling students how psychological science fits within the scientific community. Psychology serves, in essence, as a hub science. Through this emphasis on scientific literacy in psychology, students begin to see the practicality and relevance of psychology and become more literate in the fields that our hub science supports.

Critical Thinking

Can we critically evaluate the evidence?

Many departments are focusing to an increasing extent on the development of critical thinking, as these skills are highly sought after in society and the workforce. Critical thinking is generally defined as the ability to apply knowledge, use information in new ways, analyze situations and concepts, and evaluate decisions. To develop critical thinking, the module objectives and quizzes are built around an updated Bloom's taxonomy. Objectives are listed at four levels of increasing complexity: know, understand, apply, and analyze. The following features also help students organize, analyze, and synthesize information. Collectively, these features encourage students to connect different levels of understanding with specific objectives and quiz questions.

Sensation and Perception 117

Working the Scientific Literacy Model

Object Recognition

Objects in our world can be seen from many different perspectives—that is, they can be seen from near or far, under varying levels of light, and from different angles. Given the numerous variations in how objects can be sensed, how is it that we still perceive them in the same, unified way?

What do we know about object recognition?

Despite the diverse ways that an object can be sensed, it is still perceived as the same object. This observation highlights what is called **perceptual constancy**, *the ability to perceive objects as having constant shape, size, and color despite changes in perspective.* What makes perceptual constancy possible is our ability to make relative judgments about shape, size, and lightness. For shape constancy, we judge the angle of the object relative to our position (see Figure 4.16). Color constancy allows us to recognize an object's color under varying levels of illumination. For example, a bright red car is recognized as bright red when in the shade or in full sunlight. Size constancy is based on judgments of how close an object is relative to one's position as well as to the positions of other objects. Also, our perception of objects involves distinguishing them individually, and identifying objects that appear frequently or rarely. As it turns

Figure 4.17 Find the T Among This Scattered Array of Offset Ls

It should not take you long to find the T. However, if a T was only actually mixed with Ls 2% of the time you were asked to locate one, you would likely miss it quite often.

out, the process of identifying objects can be much more complicated than just seeing and naming them.

How can science explain how object recognition occurs?

Psychologists who specialize in visual perception have attempted to identify conditions in which we are likely to succeed or fail to perceive objects. It turns out that the frequency with which we encounter objects is closely related to our perception of them.

To see how, view the stimulus in Figure 4.17. Scattered around the dark background are offset Ls. One of the objects, however, is actually a T. It is easy to spot and only

Working the Scientific Literacy Model

Working the Scientific Literacy Model, introduced in Chapters 1 and 2, and then featured in each module in the remaining chapters, fully integrates the model of scientific literacy. Core concepts are highlighted and students are walked through the steps of knowledge gathering, approaching the problem from a scientific standpoint, using critical thinking, and revealing applications.

Module 4.5 Scientific Literacy Challenge: Distracted Drivers

Cell phones made their first appearance in the retail market as car phones. Units had to be mounted in the interior of a vehicle and wired into its electrical system; they were literally part of the car. Ironically, there is now evidence suggesting that a car is the *last* place a cell phone should be. You have probably heard arguments in favor of banning drivers from using cell phones, and most states have enacted laws to curb their usage—especially for texting.

Before you start this activity, take a minute to write your thoughts about using a cell phone while driving.

JOURNAL PROMPT

Do you think cell phone use while driving should be legal, banned outright, or only permitted as hands-free devices for drivers? What experiences, assumptions, or statistics have influenced your opinion?

What do we know about distracted driving?

Read the following letter from a consumer advocacy group. Make sure you understand the boldfaced terms and concepts from Chapter 4 and that you have a clear sense of what the writer is claiming.

An Open Letter to Congress

By Vanessa Fowler, President, Federation of American Drivers

Dear Representative,

I am writing on behalf of the 320,000 members of the Federation of American Drivers (FAD) who, as a group, are concerned about a major threat to public safety: "Distracted drivers," who are responsible for more than 3,000 traffic deaths annually, and more than 420,000 significant injuries. Drivers face a barrage of sights and sounds that **divide attention**. Only a portion of these are relevant to driving; the rest are distractions, and few are as powerful and ubiquitous as the cell phone. FAD's position is that cell phone use should be completely banned for drivers of any age, any vehicle, on any public roadway. While several US states and territories have taken steps in that direction, far too few have enacted a complete ban.

Many people assume that the problem with cell phone use is limited to texting or conversations that require at least one hand off the wheel. However, data show that preoccupied hands are not the problem. The real issue is that cell phone use—including texting, talking, or using apps—demands that the user **selectively attends** to the task, which can block out virtually everything else. For drivers, that means blocking out the traffic, instruments on the dashboard, and pedestrians or cyclists. Scientists have shown that people are so good at selecting what to attend to that they can experience **inattentional blindness**. In other words, a driver can be unaware of something they are looking directly at, simply because their attention is on their phone.

The FAD is advocating a very strict position on cell phones, one that they know will meet a lot of resistance. Read on to see what kinds of evidence they cite to support their argument.

Scientific Literacy Challenge

At the end of each chapter, students can practice applying scientific and critical thinking to an important, contemporary issue such as free-range parenting, cognitive enhancement drugs, college admissions testing, and brain training websites. Students are asked to read author created blog entries, editorials, or advertisements about these topics and evaluate them from a scientific literacy perspective through journal prompts and multiple-choice, matching, and true/false questions.

Application

Why is this relevant?

Psychology is a highly relevant, modern science. To be scientifically literate, students should relate psychological concepts to their own lives, making decisions based on knowledge, sound methodology, and skilled interpretation of information.

For Instructors

SCIENTIFIC LITERACY is a key course goal for many introductory psychology instructors.

Learning science is an active process. How do we help instructors model scientific literacy in the classroom and online in a way that meets the needs of today's students?

Organization

Instructors consistently tell us one of the main challenges they face when teaching the introductory psychology course is organizing engaging, current, and relevant materials to span the breadth of content covered. How do we help organize and access valuable course materials?

Revel

Reading has been the cornerstone of education since the advent of the printing press. Yet despite our world becoming ever more technologically interconnected, the ways in which learners and educators interact with the written word have remained largely static. With REVEL from Pearson, a new learning experience can begin. Through our interactions with customers around etexts, videos, and powerful reporting tools, we arrived at REVEL—an immersive learning experience that enlivens familiar and respected course content with media interactives and assessments. Designed for the way today's students read, think, and learn, REVEL empowers educators to increase engagement in the course, to better connect with students, and to break through to learning reimagined.

Writing Space

Better writers make great learners—who perform better in their courses. To help you develop and assess concept mastery and critical thinking through writing, we created Writing Space.

It's a single place to create, track, and grade writing assignments, provide writing resources, and exchange meaningful, personalized feedback with students, quickly and easily, including auto-scoring for practice writing prompts. Plus, Writing Space has integrated access to Turnitin, the global leader in plagiarism prevention.

Learning Catalytics

Learning Catalytics is a "bring your own device" student engagement, assessment, and classroom intelligence system. It allows instructors to engage students in class with real-time diagnostics. Students can use any modern, web-enabled device (smartphone, tablet, or laptop) to access it.

Instructor's Manual

The Instructor's Manual (ISBN 0134403045) includes suggestions for preparing for the course, sample syllabi, and current trends and strategies for successful teaching. Each chapter offers integrated teaching outlines, lists the key terms for each chapter for quick reference, and provides an extensive bank of lecture launchers, handouts, and activities, as well as suggestions for integrating third-party videos and web resources. The electronic format features click-and-view hotlinks that allow instructors to quickly review or print any resource from a particular chapter. This resource saves prep work and helps maximize classroom time. Chapter and module quiz answers can also be found in the Instructor's Manual.

Standard Lecture PowerPoint Slides (ISBN 0134377850) are available online at http://www.pearsonhighered.com/irc, with a more traditional format with excerpts of the text material, photos, and artwork.

Create a Custom Text

For courses with enrollments of at least 25 students, instructors can create their own textbook by combining chapters from best-selling Pearson textbooks or reading selections in a customized sequence. To begin building a custom text, visit www.pearsoncustomlibrary.com.

Instructors can also work with a dedicated Pearson Custom editor to create the ideal text—publishing original content or mixing and matching Pearson content. Contact a Pearson publisher's representative to get started.

ASSESSMENT

Instructors consistently tell us that assessing student progress is a critical component to their course and one of the most time-consuming tasks. Vetted, good-quality, easy-to-use assessment tools are essential. We have been listening and we have responded by creating the absolutely best assessment content available on the market today.

Test Bank

The Test Bank (ISBN 0134377842) contains more than 3,000 questions, many of which were class-tested in multiple classes at both 2-year and 4-year institutions across the country prior to publication. Item analysis is provided for all class-tested items. All questions have been thoroughly reviewed and analyzed line-by-line by a development editor and a copy editor to ensure clarity, accuracy, and delivery of the highest-quality assessment tool. All conceptual and applied multiple-choice questions include rationales for each correct answer and the key distracter. The item analysis helps instructors create balanced tests, while the rationales serve both as an added guarantee of quality and as a time-saver when students challenge the keyed answer for a specific item. The Test Bank includes a two-page Total Assessment Guide, an easy-to-reference grid that organizes all test items by learning objective and question type.

In addition to this high-quality Test Bank, a second bank containing more than 2,000 questions is available for instructors looking for more variation. It has also been class-tested, with item analysis available for each question.

The Test Bank also comes with Pearson MyTest, a powerful assessment generation program that helps instructors easily create and print quizzes and exams. Questions and tests can be authored online, providing instructors with the ultimate in flexibility and the ability to efficiently manage assessments wherever and whenever they want. Instructors can easily access existing questions and then edit, create, and store them using simple drag-and-drop and Word-like controls. The data for each question identifies its difficulty level and the text page number where the relevant content appears. In addition, each question maps to the text's major section and Learning Objective. For more information, go to www.PearsonMyTest.com.

BlackBoard Test Item File and WebCT Test Item File: For instructors who need only the test item file for their learning management system, we offer the complete test item file in BlackBoard and WebCT format. Go to the Instructor's Resource Center at **http://www.pearsonhighered.com/irc.**

Total Assessment Guide
Chapter 1: Introducing Psychological Science
Krause and Corts

Total Assessment Guide Topic		Chapter 1 Introducing Psychological Science		
		Factual	Conceptual	Applied
Chapter Quiz	Multiple Choice	1, 4, 7, 13	3, 5-6, 8-9, 12, 14	2, 10, 11, 15
MODULE 1.1: THE SCIENCE OF PSYCHOLOGY				
	True or False		1-7	
	Essay		1	
KNOW...the key terminology of this module	Multiple Choice	1, 12-13, 35	3, 4, 31	2, 7, 11, 30
	Short Answer	3		
UNDERSTAND...the steps of the scientific method	Multiple Choice	6, 8-9, 15-16		5, 10
	Short Answer		1	
UNDERSTAND...the concept of scientific literacy	Multiple Choice	24, 28	23, 26	25, 27, 29
	Short Answer			
APPLY...the biopsychosocial model to behavior	Multiple Choice		22	20-21
	Short Answer			
APPLY...the steps in critical thinking	Multiple Choice		32, 34	33, 36-37
	Short Answer		2	
ANALYZE...the use of the term *scientific theory*	Multiple Choice	14, 18	17	19
	Short Answer			
MODULE 1.2: HOW PSYCHOLOGY BECAME A SCIENCE				
	True or False		8-17	
	Essay		2-3	
KNOW...the key terminology of psychology's history	Multiple Choice	38, 43, 48, 51, 55, 60, 62, 68, 73, 78-79, 88	40, 47, 87, 90	52, 54, 63
	Short Answer	6-8	4	
UNDERSTAND...how various philosophical and scientific fields became major influences on psychology	Multiple Choice	46, 49-50, 53, 56-57, 61, 64-67, 69, 70-7, 75-77, 84, 86, 91-92, 95-97, 99-102	74, 81-82, 85, 93, 104	58-59, 80, 83, 94, 98, 105
	Short Answer			
APPLY...your knowledge to distinguish among the different specializations and schools of thought in psychology	Multiple Choice	89, 103, 107	106, 108	
	Short Answer			
ANALYZE...how the philosophical ideas of empiricism and determinism are applied to human behavior	Multiple Choice	45	42, 44	39,41
	Short Answer			

Select questions
Select the questions you wish to add and click the Add button or Add and Close button. Click a question name to preview it.

Learning Objectives ▽

☑ **View Questions by Learning Objective**

☐ Name

☐ 2.1 Basic: Describe the basic characteristics of the scientific method in psychology

☐ 2.1 Developing: Analyze how primary behavioral research adheres to scientific principles

☐ 2.1 Advanced: Design research that adheres to the principles of the scientific method

☐ 2.2 Basic: Describe various general research methods, including advantages and disadvantages of use

☐ 2.2 Developing: Select and apply general research methods to address appropriate kinds of research questions

☐ 2.2 Advanced: Evaluate the effectiveness of a general research method in addressing a research question

APA Assessments

A unique bank of assessment items allows instructors to assess student progress against the American Psychological Association's Learning Goals and Outcomes. These assessments have been keyed to the APA's latest progressive Learning Outcomes (basic, developing, advanced).

For access to all instructor supplements for *Psychological Science: Modeling Scientific Literacy*, go to www.pearsonhigh ered.com/irc and follow the directions to register (or log in if you already have a Pearson user name and password). Once you have registered and your status as an instructor is verified, you will be emailed a log-in name and password. Use your log-in name and password to access the catalog.

Click on the "online catalog" link, click on "psychology" and then "introductory psychology," and finally select the Krause/Corts, *Psychological Science* text. Under the description of each supplement is a link that allows you to download and save the supplement to your desktop.

You can also request hard copies of the supplements through your Pearson sales representative. If you do not know your sales representative, go to www.pearsonhigh ered.com/replocator and follow the directions to identify him or her.

For technical support for any of your Pearson products, you and your students can contact http://247 .pearsoned.com.

Development Story

Psychological Science reflects the countless hours and extraordinary efforts of a team of authors, editors, and reviewers that shared a vision for not only a unique introductory psychology textbook, but also the most comprehensive and integrated supplements program on the market. Over 300 manuscript reviewers provided invaluable feedback for making the text as accessible and relevant to students as possible. Each chapter was also reviewed by a panel of subject matter experts to ensure accuracy and currency. Over 200

focus group participants helped guide every aspect of the program, from content coverage to the art style and design, to the configuration of the supplements. Over 200 students class tested the full manuscript and Test Bank to ensure the best content possible and over 500 students compared the manuscript to their current textbooks and provided suggestions for improving the prose and design. We thank everyone who participated in ways great and small, and hope that you are as pleased with the finished product as we are!

List of Reviewers

AL
Aimee Callender
Auburn University

Amy Skinner
Stillman College

Gina Mariano
Troy University

Harold E. Arnold
Judson College

Lisa Hager
Spring Hill College

Royce Simpson
Spring Hill College

Susan Anderson
University of South Alabama

AR
Albert K. Toh
University of Arkansas, Pine Bluff

Aneeq Ahmad
Henderson State University

Bernita Patterson
University of Arkansas, Pine Bluff

Bonnie Nichols
Arkansas Northeastern College

Christopher Long
Ouachita Baptist University

Elisabeth Sherwin
University of Arkansas at Little Rock

Guyla Davis
Ouachita Baptist University

Jason E. Warnick
Arkansas Tech University

Karen Yanowitz
Arkansas State University

Kathy Brownlee
Henderson State University

Kenith V. Sobel
University of Central Arkansas

Richard Clubb
University of Arkansas, Monticello

Robert J. Hines
University of Arkansas, Little Rock

Shawn Charlton
University of Central Arkansas

Sonya Stephens Robinson
Cossatot Community College

Travis Langley
Henderson State University

Travis P. McNeal
Harding University

AZ
Aaron Tesch
University of Arizona

Belinda Stevens
Pima Community College

Calleen A. Morris
Arizona State University

Jennifer Moore
Mesa Community College

Jorge Pierce
Mesa Community College

Pamela Sulger
Pima Community College

Patricia Marchok
Paradise Valley Community College, Phoenix

Robert Short
Arizona State University

Ron Jorgenson
Pima Community College

Suzy Horton
Mesa Community College

CA
Angela Sadowski
Chaffey College

Brenda Smith
Westmont College

Cari Cannon
Santiago Canyon College

Catherine Salmon
University of Redlands

Christina Aldrich
Folsom Lake College

Christopher Gade
UC Berkeley

Debra Berry Malmberg
California State University, Northridge

Diane K. Eperthener
California University of Pennsylvania

Eileen Roth
Glendale Community College

Fred Leavitt
California State University, East Bay

Inna Ghajoyan
California State University, Northridge

John Slosar
Chapman University

Kathleen Taylor
Sierra College

Kenneth Guttman
Citrus College

Kimberly Brinkman
San Joaquin Valley College

Lisa Harrison
California State University, Sacramento

Margaret Lynch
San Francisco State University

Matthew Bell
Santa Clara University

Melissa Gonzales
San Joaquin Valley College

Michelle Pilati
Rio Hondo College

Patricia Bellas
Irvine Valley College

Richard Kandus
Mt. San Jacinto College

Steven Isonio
Golden West College

Teesha Barry
San Joaquin Valley College

CO

Bethany Fleck
Metropolitan State College
of Denver

Brian Parry
Mesa State College

Frederick Coolidge
University of Colorado,
Colorado Springs

John Walsh
University of Colorado

Lisa Routh
Pikes Peak Community College

Peggy Norwood
Community College of Aurora

Randi Smith
Metropolitan State College
of Denver

Roger Drake
Western State College
of Colorado

CT

Daniel Barrett
Western Connecticut State
University

Melanie Evans
Eastern Connecticut State
University

Robert Beck
Northwestern Connecticut
Community College

Ruth Sharf
Yale University, School of
Medicine

DC

Morgan Slusher
Community College
of Baltimore County

DE

Gerard Hoefling
Drexel University and
University of Warsaw Poland
and University of Delaware

John D. Rich, Jr.
Delaware State University

FL

Alexander Marvin
Seminole State College of
Florida

Alicia Pfahler
Santa Fe College

Bita Sarah Haynes
Florida State College at
Jacksonville

Chelsea Hansen
Midlands Technical College

Christina S. Morris
Seminole State College

Dana L. Kuehn
Florida State College at
Jacksonville

Deletha Hardin
University of Tampa

Gary Bothe
Pensacola Junior College

Greg Fleming
Keiser University, Lakeland

James J. Jakubow
Florida Atlantic University

Jeanne L. O'Kon
Tallahassee Community College

Joanna Salapska-Gelleri
Florida Gulf Coast University

Kathleen Bey
Palm Beach Community
College, Central

Lawrence Siegel
Palm Beach State College

Michele Camden
Seminole State College
of Florida

Pamela Hall
Barry University

Peter Gram
Pensacola Junior College

Susana Barsky
Florida State College,
Jacksonville-Downtown
Campus

Theresa Foster
Santa Fe College

Thomas Westcott
University of West Florida

GA

Adam Goodie
University of Georgia

Chantal Tusher
Georgia State University

Chris Goode
Georgia College and State
University

Christopher K. Randall
Kennesaw State University

Clayton Teem
Gainesville College

Dan Fawaz
Georgia Perimeter College

David Brackin
Young Harris College

David Monetti
Valdosta State University

Deb Briihl
Valdosta State University

Diane Kreutzer
Georgia Perimeter College

Erica Gannon
Clayton State University

Heather Kleider
Georgia State University

Kristen Diliberto-Macaluso
Berry College

Michael Hoff
Dalton State College

Pam Marek
Kennesaw State University

Rose Arriaga
Georgia Institute of Technology

HI

Tanya Renner
Kapi'olani Community College

IA

Cynthia Bane
Wartburg College

James Rodgers
Hawkeye Community College

Jennifer Meehan
Brennom Kirkwood
Community College

Judith Wightman
Kirkwood Community College

ID

Elizabeth Morgan
Bosie State University

IL

Allen Huffcutt
Bradley University

Dawn M. McBride
Illinois State University

Derek Montgomery
Bradley University

Don Kates
College of Dupage

Dr. Eric Rogers
The College of Lake County

Elham Bagheri
Augustana College

Eva Mika
Loyola University, Lakeshore

James Sichlau
Lincoln Land Community
College

Jane Rose
Augustana College

Jeffrey Wagman
Illinois State University

Jill Yamashita
Saint Xavier University

Joel Nadler
Southern Illinois University,
Edwardsville

John Binning
Illinois State University

John Skowronski
Northern Illinois University

Joleen Schoulte
Augustana College

Joseph Ferrari
DePaul University

Lisa Fozio-Thielk
Waubonsee Community
College

Marjorie A. Getz
Bradley University

Mark Watman
South Suburban College

Michael Dudley
Southern Illinois University,
Edwardsville

Raymond Phinney
Wheaton College

Renee Engeln-Maddox
Northwestern University

Robert Currie
Judson College

Suzanne Bell
DePaul University

Terry Shapiro
Saint Xavier University

Valeri Farmer-Dougan
Illinois State University

IN

Karl Nelson
Indiana University Northwest

Kristin C. Flora
Franklin College

Mandy Gingerich Hege
Butler University

Sherry Schnake
Saint Mary-of-the-Woods
College

KS

Michael Rader
Johnson County Community
College

Stephani Johns-Hines
Cowley County Community
College

KY

Brian Cusato
Centre College

Cecile Marczinski
Northern Kentucky
University

Dawn McLin
Big Sandy Community
and Technical College

Janet B. Dean
Asbury University

Jennifer Sellers
Green Mountain College

Melissa Burns-Cusato
Centre College

Richard Miller
Western Kentucky University

Sabra Jacobs
Big Sandy Community and
Technical College

Veronica Tinsley
Brescia University

LA

Erin Dupuis
Loyola University

Lisa Schulte
Xavier University of Louisiana

Sandra Price
Delgado Community College

MA

Christopher Hakala
Western New England College

Elizabeth Davis
Suffolk University

Eric B. Weiser
Curry College

Jennifer A. Rivers
Elms College

Nate Kornell
Williams College

Robin Locke Arkerson
University of Massachusetts,
Dartmouth

Sarah Rose Cavanagh
Assumption College

Summer Williams
Westfield State University

MD

Christopher Bishop
Bowie State University

Cynthia Koenig
St. Mary

Katrina Kardiasmenos
Bowie State University

Marcia McKinley
Mount Saint Mary's University

Megan Bradley
Frostburg State University

Mike Kerchner
Washington College

ME

Christine L. B. Selby
Husson University

Jennifer Coane
Colby College

John Broida
University of Southern Maine

Kenneth Elliott
University of Maine at Augusta

Michael A. Burman
University of New England

Rachelle Smith
Husson University

Trude Cooke Turner
Community College of
Baltimore County, Essex

MI

Boris Ben Bates
Wayne State University

Gordon Hammerle
Adrian College

Justin W. Peer
University of
Michigan-Dearborn

Kari L. McArthur
Hillsdale College

Linda Jackson
Michigan State University

Marcus Dickson
Wayne State University

Renée L. Babcock
Central Michigan University

MN

Ben Denkinger
Augsburg College

Cory Butler
Southwest Minnesota State
University

Dennis Stewart
University of Minnesota,
Morris

Emily Stark
Minnesota State University,
Mankato

John Johanson
Winona State University

Keilah Worth
St. Catherine University

Kristie Campana
Minnesota State University

Marc Mooney
Augsburg College

Marilyn Swedberg
Fergus Falls Campus and
Minnesota State Community
and Technical College (M State)

Mark Covey
Concordia College

Mary Bodvarsson
St. Cloud State University

Richard Coelho
Lansing Community College

Stephanie Gaskin
Concordia College

MO

Christina M. Brown
Saint Louis University

David Kreiner
University of Central
Missouri

David McDonald
University of Missouri,
Columbia

Debra Zierenberg
Jefferson College

Julie Tietz
Cottey College

Peter J. Green
Maryville University

MS

Linda Fayard
Mississippi Gulf Coast
Community College

Lindsay R. Trent
University of Mississippi

Melissa Lea
Millsaps College

Michael Bordieri
University of Mississippi

Scott Drury
Delta State University

William Goggin
University of Southern
Mississippi

MT

Flora McCormick
University of Montana,
College of Technology

Fred W. Whitford
Montana State

NC

Christopher B. Mayhorn
North Carolina State University

Jason C. Allaire
North Carolina State University

Jennifer Bowler
East Carolina University

Jutta Street
Campbell University

Martha Low
Winston-Salem State University

Nancie Wilson
Southwestern Community
College

Pam Bradley
Sandhills Community College

Sarah Estow
Guilford College

Walter Charles
North Carolina Central
University

NE

Joseph Benz
University of Nebraska
at Kearney

Laura Gaudet
Chadron State College

Linda Petroff
Central Community College

Molly Wernli
College of Saint Mary

Wayne Briner
University of Nebraska
at Kearney

NH

Jayne Allen
University of New Hampshire

Jennie Brown
Franklin Pierce University

Mike Mangan
University of New Hampshire

NJ

Gary Kose
Long Island University
of Brooklyn

Gary Lewandowski
Monmouth University

Gerard La Morte
Rutgers University, Newark

Lynne Schmelter-Davis
Brookdale Community
College

Margaret Maghan
Rutgers University, Newark

Nicholas Salter
Ramapo College of
New Jersey

Robert Becklen
Ramapo College of
New Jersey

Tim VanderGast
William Paterson University

NM

Ron Salazar
San Juan College

NV

Evelyn Doody
College of Southern Nevada

Ned Clayton Silver
University of Nevada,
Las Vegas

NY

Amy Masnick
Hofstra University

Andreas Wilke
Clarkson University

Brenda Anderson
Stony Brook University

Candice S. Faulring
Genesee Community College

Caroline Olko
Nassau Community College

Celia Reaves
Monroe Community College

Cheryl Bluestone
Queens College, CUNY

Cheryl Dickter
Union College

Claire Rubman
Suffolk County Community
College

Dale Doty
Monroe Community College

David S. Malcom
Fordham University

Elizabeth Gaudino-Goering
Nassau Community College

Ellen Banks
Daemon College

Howard Sisco
New York City College of
Technology

Howard Steele
New School for Social
Research

James Hobbs
SUNY Ulster

Jean Kubeck
New York City College of
Technology

Jeffrey Baker
Monroe Community College

Jennifer Kyle
Borough of Manhattan
Community College, CUNY

Jennifer Yanowitz
Utica College

John Mavromatis
St. John Fisher College

Kaneez Naseem
Monroe College

Karen Wolford
Oswego, SUNY

Kathryn Caldwell
Ithaca College

Keith Shafritz
Hofstra University

Laurence Nolan
Wagner College

Maria LePadula
New York City Institute of
Technology

Marie-Joelle Estrada
University of Rochester

Martha Leah Chaiken
Hofstra University

Melody Berkovits
Queens College, CUNY

Michelle Bannoura
Hudson Valley Community
College

Pamela Lusk
Genesee Community College

Paul Schulman
Institute of Technology, SUNY

Phyllis Freeman
SUNY New Paltz

Ryan Thibodeau
St. John Fisher College

Sandra Hunt
College of Staten Island, CUNY

Susan Scharoun
Le Moyne College

Suzan Tessier
Rochester Institute of
Technology

Timothy M. Franz
St. John Fisher College

Victoria Cooke
Erie Community College

William Dragon
Cornell University

William Price
North County Community
College

Yasmine Kalkstein
Mount Saint Mary College

OH

Albert Smith
Cleveland State University

Alicia Doerflinger
Marietta College

Ana M.H. Kehrberg
Muskingum University

Barbara Oswald
Miami University

Bobby Beavers
Sinclair Community College

Carolyn Kaufman
Columbus State Community
College

Colleen Stevenson
Muskingum University

Darlene Earley Andrews
Southern Ohio State
Community College

David Baker
University of Akron

Dennis Shaffer
Ohio State University,
Mansfield

Dinah Meyer
Muskingum University

Elizabeth O'Dell
Owens Community College

Elizabeth Swenson
John Carroll University

Jessica Hillyer
Kenyon College

Philip Mazzocco
The Ohio State University
at Mansfield

Wayne Shebilske
Wright State University

OK

Alicia MacKay
Tulsa Community College

Jared Edwards
Southwestern Oklahoma State
University

John Hensley
Tulsa Community College, Metro

OR

Chris Koch
George Fox University

Deana Julka
University of Portland

Jeremy Miller
Willamette University

Melissa Witkow
Willamette University

R.H. Ettinger
Eastern Oregon University

Sue Leung
Portland Community College

Timothy Hackenberg
Reed College

Zip Krummel
Columbia Gorge Community
College

PA

Barbara Radigan
Community College
of Allegheny County

Bonnie Green
East Stroudsburg
University

Catherine Chambliss
Ursinus College

Cathy Sigmund
Geneva College

David Widman
Juniata College

Emily Keener
Slippery Rock University

Greg Loviscky
Penn State University

Jennifer Engler
York College of
Pennsylvania

Karen Rhines
Northampton Community
College

Mark McKellop
Juniata College

Melissa Terlecki
Cabrini College

Natasha Tokowicz
University of Pittsburgh

Rahan Ali
Penn State University

Robin Musselman
Lehigh Carbon Community
College

Ryan Leonard
Gannon University

RI

Allison Butler
Bryant University

Lisa Weyandt
University of Rhode Island

SC

Amanda Morgan
University of South Carolina

Amy M. Kolak
College of Charleston

Chad Galuska
College of Charleston

Daniel Bellack
Trident Technical College

Echo Leaver
University of South Carolina,
Aiken

Karen Thompson
Columbia College

Laura Negel May
University of South Carolina
Aiken

Maureen Carrigan
University of South Carolina,
Aiken

Michelle Caya
Trident Technical College

Nancy Simpson
Trident Technical College

Penny S. Edwards
Tri-County Technical College

Salvador Macias
University of South Carolina,
Sumter

SD

Brady Phelps
South Dakota State University

TN

Angelina MacKewn
University of Tennessee at
Martin

Chris S. Dula
East Tennessee State University

Colin Key
University of Tennessee at
Martin

Dick Pelley
Tennessee Wesleyan College

Gayle J. Beck
University of Memphis

Jameson K. Hirsch
East Tennessee State
University

Karen Baker
Lambuth University

Kristin L. Walker
East Tennessee State
University

Liz Moseley
Cleveland State Community
College

Lonnie Yandell
Belmont University

Marvin W. Lee
Tennessee State University

Michelle Merwin
University of Tennessee
at Martin

Patricia B. Hinton
Hiwassee College

Tiffany D. Rogers
University of Memphis

TX

Barb Corbisier
Blinn College

Bryan Neighbor
Southwestern University

Carl Scott
University of St. Thomas

Christopher Smith
Tyler Junior College

Denise Aspell
Northwest Vista College

Erin Young
Texas A&M University

Jack Chuang
San Jacinto College

Judith Easton
Austin Community College

Kraig Schell
Angelo State University

Kyle Baumbauer
Texas A&M Univeristy

Laura Cavicchi
Northwest Vista College

Mark Hartlaub
Texas A&M University,
Corpus Christi

Matt Diggs
Collin College

Mike Devoley
Lone Star College,
Montgomery

Pamela Brouillard
Texas A&M University,
Corpus Christi

Patricia Foster
Stephen F. Austin State
University

Patrick Carroll
University of Texas, Austin

Perry Collins
Wayland Baptist University

Perry Fuchs
University of Texas,
Arlington

Randall E. Osborne
Texas State University,
San Marco

Raquel Henry
Lone Star College, Kingwood

Stacy Walker
Lone Star College Kingwood

Stella Lopez
University of Texas,
San Antonio

Susan Hornstein
Southern Methodist
University

Vanessa Miller
Texas Christian University

Victoria Van Wie
Lone Star College, CyFair

Wanda Clark
South Plains College

Wendy Domjan
University of Texas, Austin

UT

Azenett Garza
Weber State University

David Yells
Utah Valley University

Grant Corser
Southern Utah University

Jann Belcher
Utah Valley University

Joseph Horvat
Weber State University

Kerry Jordan
Utah State University

Theresa Kay
Weber State University

VA

Bernice Carson
Virgina State University

Charles J. Huffman
James Madison University

Cynthia Lofaso
Central Virginia Community
College

Darling G. Villena-Mata
Northern Virginia Community
College, Woodbridge

David Daniel
James Madison University

Donald Devers
Northern Virginia Community
College, Annandale

Georgeana Stratton
Northern Virginia Community
College

Jennifer Mailloux
University of Mary Washington

John Wasserman
George Mason University

Leona Johnson
Hampton University

Margaret P. Russi
Northern Virginia Community
College

Mary Ann Schmitt
Northern Virginia Community
College, Manassas

Ron Boykin
Northern Virginia Community
College, Alexandria

Rosalyn King
Northern Virginia Community
College, Loudon

Theresa Tuttle
ECPI College of Technology

VT

Brigit Bryant
Le Moyne College

Larry P. Rudiger
University of Vermont

WA

Clara Cheng
American University

Gerrod W. Parrott
Georgetown University

John Wright
Washington State University

Pamela Costa
Tacoma Community College

Sandy Neal
Centralia College

Sue Frantz
Highline Community College

WV

Christopher W. LeGrow
Marshall University

WI

Barbara Beaver
University of Wisconsin,
Whitewater

Kathy Immel
University of Wisconsin,
Fox Valley

Loretta Veers
Marshfield High School

William Elmhorst
Marshfield High School

WY

Scott Freng
University of Wyoming

CANADA

Geoffrey S. Navara
Trent University

Jeffrey Adams
Trent University

Steven Smith
University of Winnipeg

Acknowledgments

The fact that there are two names on the cover is quite an understatement. If you were to look behind the scenes, you would find scores of people working a variety of roles to see this project to completion. Many of those individuals lead the team at Pearson Education including our Executive Editor, Erin Mitchell and our Program Manager, Reena Dalal who has proven both incredibly knowledgeable and completely unflappable. To our diligent Developmental Editors, Lai Moy and Mary Piper Hansen, we thank you for your guidance and patience. A major thank you to Sherry Lewis, project manager, for vigilantly keeping us on track from beginning to end. These are just a few of the names you will find in the credits, but only the tip of the iceberg. In addition to our friends in publishing, we have received steadfast support from those we see everyday. This ranges from the colleagues in our departments to those who matter most—our families. We are particularly grateful for our children and spouses who have been gracious enough to share our time with such a time-intensive project. Finally, no textbook could purport to represent as vast a discipline as psychology without the expertise of a wide range of professionals. Dozens of reviewers provided this expertise by suggesting recently published research and ways of presenting information to students. Thanks to our reviewers for their past contributions and we hope that you, as well as those who are new to the project, will continue to offer suggestions or comments by writing to Mark Krause (krausema@sou.edu) and Daniel Corts (danielcorts@augustana.edu).

Chapter 1
Introducing Psychological Science

Module 1.1 The Science of Psychology

Learning Objectives

1.1a Know . . . the key terminology of the scientific method.

1.1b Understand . . . the steps of the scientific method.

1.1c Understand . . . the concept of scientific literacy.

1.1d Apply . . . the biopsychosocial model to behavior.

1.1e Apply . . . the steps in critical thinking.

1.1f Analyze . . . the use of the term *scientific theory*.

Her (2013) is not your typical love story. Theodore (played by Joaquin Phoenix) falls in love with Samantha (Scarlett Johansson). They are perfect for each other, it would seem. But here is the conflict: Samantha is not a person; she is an artificial intelligence software designed to behave less like a machine and more like a living, breathing human being. Although the plot of *Her* is based on science fiction, encountering a "being" like Samantha may be closer to reality than you think. Ellie, for instance, is a computer-generated avatar developed by scientists at the University of Southern California. Ellie is designed to carry on conversations with you—sometimes seemingly meaningful ones. By detecting subtle changes in your facial expressions, speech patterns, and posture, Ellie is able to respond with vocal changes and gestures as a caring human would. If you feel a bit down, you will find that Ellie's expression may change as she listens; her voice may soften and she may even mention that you seem a bit upset. Many who have spoken with Ellie have been surprised that a technology comprising a series of algorithms can seem so empathetic.

So what do these virtual women have to do with your psychology course? The nonfictional Ellie demonstrates how scientific inquiry can reveal some pretty reliable facts about how people think, feel, and behave. Her fictional counterpart Samantha entertains by showing us how fascinating these thoughts and feelings can be. We hope you will learn both in this chapter.

Psychology is a vast discipline; in fact, we might do better to consider it to be a collection of disciplines, composed of many overlapping fields of study. Two unifying qualities allow us to group all these fields into the single category of *psychological science*. First, psychology involves the study of behavior that, broadly defined, can include perceptions, thoughts, and emotions. Second, psychologists employ the *scientific method* in their work. On these grounds, we can define **psychology** *as the scientific study of behavior, thought, and experience.*

The Scientific Method

What exactly does it mean to be a scientist? A person who haphazardly combines chemicals in test tubes may look like a chemist; a person who dissects a frog just to see its organs may appear to be a biologist—but neither is engaged in science. For a specific type of activity to be considered *scientific* or a field of study to be considered a *science*, application of the scientific method is a must. The **scientific method** *is a way of learning about the world through collecting observations, proposing explanations for the observations, developing theories to explain them, and using the theories to make predictions about future occurrences or behaviors.* It revolves around the concepts of hypothesis and theory and how they interact to produce a discipline-based body of knowledge (see Figure 1.1).

HYPOTHESES: MAKING PREDICTIONS A **hypothesis** (plural: hypotheses) *is a testable prediction about processes that can be observed and measured.* By *testable*, we mean that observations and measurements can be shown whether the prediction was correct or, equally important, whether it

"All swans are white" is a falsifiable statement. A swan that is not colored white will falsify it. Falsification is a critical component of scientific hypotheses and theories.

was false—a quality known as *falsifiability*. People claiming to be scientific regularly ignore falsifiability. Imagine a horoscope reads, "It's time for you to keep quiet and postpone important calls or e-mails." That is not really a testable prediction for a number of reasons, including the fact that it does not describe a specific consequence or a time frame in which a problem might arise. Therefore, if you did make that important call, it would be impossible to show the prediction was false. In contrast, a good scientific hypothesis is stated in more precise, and publicly relevant, terms, such as the following:

> People become less likely to help a stranger if there are others around.
>
> Cigarette smoking causes cancer.
>
> Exercise relieves depression.

Unlike the astrologer's prediction, each of these hypotheses can be supported or rejected through scientific testing. Astrology is an easy target for criticism. We bring it up only because it provides an opportunity to clarify what a scientific hypothesis is and also to highlight a key difference between science and **pseudoscience**, *which refers to ideas that are presented as science but do not actually use basic principles of scientific thinking or procedure.* Alarmingly, approximately one in four Americans believes astrology has at least some scientific basis despite a total lack of evidence or support from trained scientists (National Science Foundation, 2010).

EXPLAINING PHENOMENA Hypotheses are essential to creating and refining scientific theories. A **theory** *is a well-tested explanation that combines a range of observations into a coherent whole.* Figure 1.1 shows how hypothesis testing eventually leads back to the theory from which it was based. Theories are built from hypotheses that are repeatedly tested and confirmed; in turn, good theories eventually become accepted explanations of behavior

Figure 1.1 The Scientific Method

Scientists use theories to generate hypotheses. Once tested, hypotheses are either confirmed or rejected. Confirmed hypotheses lead to new ones and strengthen theories. Rejected hypotheses are revised and tested again, and can potentially alter an existing theory.

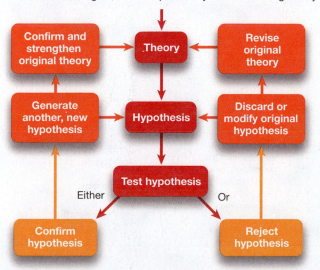

or other natural phenomena. Similar to hypotheses, an essential quality of scientific theories is that they are *falsifiable*; like hypotheses, they can be proved false with new evidence. As Figure 1.1 shows, falsifying a theory means that it either needs to be modified to account for new findings, or in some cases, replaced by an entirely new theory. In this way, science becomes self-correcting; bad ideas typically do not last long before being discovered and replaced.

The scientific term *theory* is specific and essential to understanding how explanations differ from common sense. Make sure that as you read this text you keep in mind *scientific* theory, rather than these common misusages:

- **Theories are not the same thing as opinions or beliefs.** Yes, it is certainly true that everyone is entitled to his or her own opinions. But the phrase "That's just your theory" is neither the scientific meaning of "theory," nor a valid scientific argument.
- **All theories are not equally plausible.** Groups of scientists might adopt different theories for explaining the same phenomenon. For example, several

Figure 1.2 The Biopsychosocial Model

Psychologists view behavior from multiple perspectives. A full understanding of human behavior comes from analyzing biological, psychological, social, and cultural factors.

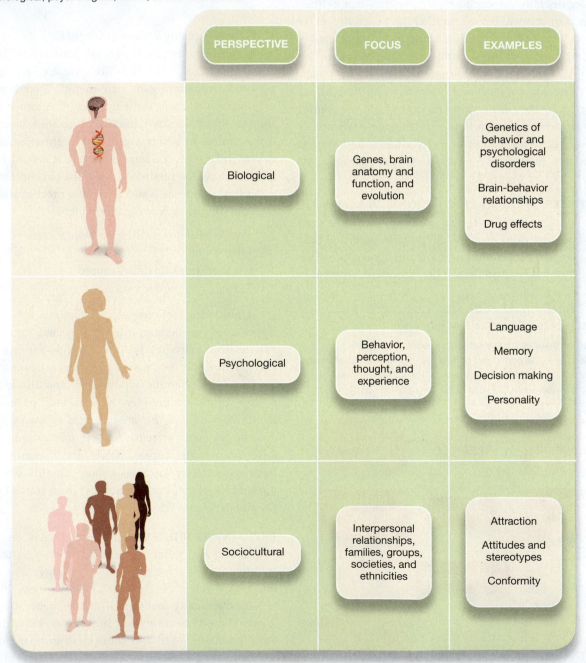

theories have been proposed to explain why people become depressed. This does not mean that all are equally valid. There are good theories, and there are not-so-good theories; the good ones generate successful hypotheses as shown in Figure 1.1.

- **The quality of a theory is not evaluated by the number of people who believe it to be true.** According to a 2013 Pew Research Center Survey, only one third of Americans believe in the theory of evolution by natural selection, despite the fact that it is the most plausible, rigorously tested theory of biological change and diversity.

Testing hypotheses and constructing theories are both part of all sciences. In addition, each science, including psychology, has its own unique way of approaching its subject matter. As the study of behavior, thought, and experience, psychology examines the individual as a product of multiple influences, including biological, psychological, and social factors.

THE BIOPSYCHOSOCIAL MODEL Defining psychology as the scientific study of behavior, thought, and experience may sound pretty straightforward, but thinking and behaving are complex subjects with complex explanations. One psychologist might study a single type of cell in the nervous system, whereas another might examine the cultural customs and beliefs that shape daily life for millions of people—all this to explain the same overarching question: Why do we behave the way we do?

Because our thoughts and behaviors have multiple influences, psychologists adopt multiple perspectives to understand them. The **biopsychosocial model** *is a means of explaining behavior as a product of biological, psychological, and sociocultural factors* (see Figure 1.2). Biological influences on our behavior include brain structures, hormones, and drug effects. On the other end of the spectrum, your family, peers, and immediate social situation also determine how you think, feel, and behave, as do beliefs about social characterisitcs such as ethnicity, gender, or socioeconomic status. These influences constitute the sociocultural part of the model. In between biology and culture, we can examine how a person's thoughts, experiences, emotions, and personality constitute his or her psychological makeup.

The biopsychosocial model is a reminder that behavior can be fully explained only if multiple perspectives are incorporated.

Building Scientific Literacy

A major aim of this text is to help students develop **scientific literacy**, *which is the ability to understand, analyze, and apply scientific information.* Our focal topic is psychology, but these same skills are applicable to other

Figure 1.3 A Model of Scientific Literacy
Scientific literacy involves four different skills: gathering knowledge about the world, explaining it using scientific terms and concepts, thinking critically, and applying this knowledge to relevant, real-world situations.

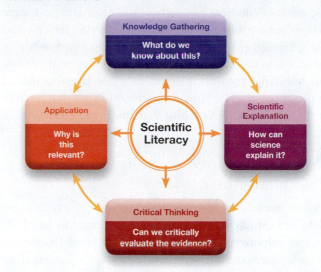

scientific fields. As shown in Figure 1.3, our model of scientific literacy reveals several key components, starting with the ability to learn new information, new terminology, and concepts. However, knowledge of terminology alone does not make one scientifically literate; one must also be able to provide explanations that incorporate the scientific terms and concepts of the discipline one is studying (in this case, psychology). Being scientifically literate means being able to read and interpret new terminology, and knowing when and where to go to find out more. It also means being able to apply this ability to real-world situations and to use one's critical thinking skills to evaluate information and claims.

Working the Scientific Literacy Model

How We Learn and Remember

To give you a chance to develop scientific literacy skills, we will revisit this model regularly and apply its four components to a specific psychological topic—a process we call *working the model.* We can demonstrate this process with a topic that is familiar to many: using flashcards to study vocabulary terms.

What do we know about studying with flashcards?

Many college courses require that you learn key-term definitions and factual information such as dates, and students often study with flashcards to master this information.

Most students prefer what is called *massing*—they break up a large pile of cards into smaller groups and move through each mass of cards separately. Another approach is *spacing*—leaving the cards in one big stack and moving through them one at a time. In contrast to massing, spacing means more time passes between each card and more new terms are introduced before any specific card repeats itself. The larger the deck, the more spacing there is before returning to the first card. Most students prefer the massing technique because it seems to allow them to master words more quickly. However, science shows that the two are not equally effective, and that spacing is generally the better of the two.

How can science explain this difference?

To find out which study method works best, psychologist Nate Kornell (2009) conducted an experiment in which 20 student volunteers agreed to study according to his instructions. Students studied one list of words with massing (four sets of five cards each) and another list with spacing (one set of 20 words). As shown in Figure 1.4, the volunteers studied each word four times, regardless of study method. At the end of the study period, Kornell administered a memory test and discovered that the volunteers could remember more words from the spaced condition than the massed condition. Interestingly, almost all students still preferred massing.

Can we critically evaluate this conclusion?

There is no such thing as a perfect study; no single experiment will fully answer scientific questions about studying with flashcards or any other topic. Although it is the researcher's job to conduct the best studies possible, it is up to you, the reader, to think critically about them. We provide advice on critical thinking later in this chapter, and once you read Chapter 2, you will be better prepared to assess the quality of the research. For now, start by asking your-

self questions about the outcome: Why do students prefer the less effective method? You should think about ways in which this may or may not apply to other situations: Does spacing work better for other types of studying, like learning to solve math problems? You should notice that being critical means asking for limitations and shortcomings without being overly emotional or hostile. This prevents us from wholeheartedly accepting faulty claims, but we should not hastily dismiss any single study either. Instead, we give time for researchers to build evidence with additional studies.

How is this finding relevant?

Ideally, you will be inspired to apply the findings from Kornell's experiment to your own experiences as a student—whether studying for your psychology or other courses. But to really make use of spacing, you might have to convince yourself to trust the data, especially if you are like the students in Kornell's study and find yourself preferring the massing technique, despite the evidence that more strongly supports the efficacy of spacing!

Keep in mind there is still much to learn about "working the model": The next section focuses on critical thinking skills and how to use them; Chapter 2 walks you through the specific methods for conducting and evaluating scientific research. You will get a chance to "work" the scientific literacy model again in Chapter 2, and then again in the remaining chapters.

Critical Thinking, Curiosity, and a Dose of Healthy Skepticism

On page 5, as shown in the scientific literacy model, critical thinking is an important element of scientific literacy. **Critical thinking** *involves intentionally analyzing and evaluating beliefs, claims, or judgments.* Psychologists often do this by assessing research in terms of how it relates to theory and how well it follows scientific principles.

Figure 1.4 Massed Versus Spaced Practice

In both conditions of Kornell's experiment, volunteers studied each vocabulary word four times. In the massed condition, shown at left, the individual cards were studied closer together whereas in the spaced condition, at right, they were studied further apart. Spaced learning results in better memory for vocabulary terms.

You have a total of 20 terms to learn.　　　　You have a total of 20 terms to learn.

Massing: Studying a deck of five cards four times in a row. This masses study for an individual card, such as card A in the drawing above.

Spacing: Leaving all 20 cards in one stack and studying the whole deck four times in a row. This spaces the studying for each card, such as card A in the drawing above. However, in both conditions, card A will be studied the same number of times (four).

As such, critical thinking is something you develop and practice rather than something with which you are born (Halpern, 1996).

In addition to analytical and evaluative skills, critical thinking requires a certain set of attitudes or dispositions, namely curiosity, skepticism, and self-reflection. As psychologists, we are always *curious*. We ask questions about all kinds of behaviors, not just the unusual or problematic, which many of us tend to do, but also about everyday activities and experiences (*How do we remember where we left our car keys?*).

We also approach matters with cautious and healthy *skepticism*. Because we are constantly being told about products that will radically improve our lives or about political positions that are supposedly in everyone's best interests, it is important to raise questions. Being skeptical can be challenging, especially when a product or campaign promise fits our assumptions of the truth or what we hope to be the truth—eventually, though, we have to challenge our own assumptions, even if it risks being proved wrong. Consider again Kornell's research on flashcards: Students overwhelmingly prefer massing, so you may assume massing works best; but if you challenge this assumption, you may actually find a technique that works better. Ultimately, curiosity and skepticism lead us to be *reflective*. In other words, they help us to reconsider what we think we know, to understand what we know, and to explore why we believe what we believe. Sometimes, the best outcome is to understand what we cannot be certain of, and to tolerate ambiguity when the evidence is inconclusive.

KEY PRACTICES TO CRITICAL THINKING Now that you have an idea of what critical thinking entails, it is time to learn the skills and put them to use. Researchers have identified six key practices of a critical thinker:

1. **Be curious.**   Look for opportunities to ask questions, even when they are not obvious. Here are two ways to approach curiosity. First, rather than wait until something goes wrong to be curious (*Why did he develop depression?*), ask questions while things are going well (*How did he succeed in the face of all that hardship?*). Second, watch out for narrow-minded questions that already presume to have an answer (*Why are they all criminals?* This question assumes knowledge of "they.") Instead ask open and objective questions (*Is that group more likely to engage in crime? If so, why?*). Remember that most aspects of behavior are complex; there is usually no single right answer to a question, but rather a complex set of answers.

2. **Examine the evidence.** Examining the evidence is key to science and critical thinking. Bear in mind that common sense is not evidence, and in fact, it will often lead you astray. Therefore, you should look for evidence that is reliable, objective, and relevant. You

will be even better equipped to do this after reading Chapter 2, which focuses on scientific processes.

3. **Examine assumptions and biases.** Assumptions and biases too quickly lead us to accept claims that support our expectations and to discount those that do not. Recall that in Kornell's flashcard experiment, the majority of his volunteers preferred massing. We have found that students in our own classes also prefer massing, and as such, they too quickly discount Kornell's rather strong evidence that spacing is better. Fortunately, this particular example does not have severe consequences. However, at their worst, biases and conflicts of interest can lead people to willfully mislead others, sometimes even with fabricated data and claims that they know are not true.

4. **Avoid overly emotional thinking.** Emotions can tell us what we value, but they do not always help us make critical decisions. By all means, emotions should guide decisions about a relationship, career, and so on. However, emotions can lead to some wrong answers, which, at their worst, can have grave consequences. For example, many young parents have opted not to vaccinate their children out of a fear that vaccines may lead to autism. This emotional decision ignores the fact that there is no credible scientific evidence for this threat, and in fact, the most influential medical study to support a purported vaccine–autism link was eventually exposed as a fraud and retracted by the research journal that published it (Godlee, Smith, & Marcovitch, 2011). Critical thinkers acknowledge their emotions, but they carefully discern the situations when emotional-based decisions may not be appropriate.

5. **Tolerate ambiguity.** Most complex issues do not have clear-cut answers, but they do have lots of *ifs*, *buts*, and *it depends*. For example, for many years the medical community advised the public to avoid eating fats based on the evidence that fats were associated with weight gain and heart disease. However, the same scientific community now encourages us to include certain fats, such as those that come from olive oil or avocados. Although this change seems contradictory, ongoing research will sometimes lead to changes in prior beliefs. This case is just one among many where the apparent contradiction includes an "if." In other words, fats are viewed more favorably, but only *if* they are rich in substances such as omega-3 acids.

6. **Consider alternative viewpoints.** Finally, make sure you are open to alternative viewpoints. This does not mean that everyone's opinion is equally correct, but you can often learn from the perspective of others. You may even discover that emotions, assumptions, and biases have been affecting your own thinking without your awareness, or that others have better evidence than you do!

Table 1.1 Critical Thinking

Practice applying critical thinking skills to the scenario:

Magic Mileage is a high-tech fuel additive that actually increases the distance you can drive for every gallon by 20%, although costing only a fraction of the gasoline itself!! Wouldn't you like to cut your fuel expenses by one-fifth? Magic Mileage is a blend of complex engine-cleaning agents and patented "octane-booster" that not only packs in extra miles per gallon but also leaves your engine cleaner and running smooth while reducing emissions!

1. How might this appeal lead to overly emotional thinking?
2. Can you identify assumptions or biases the manufacturer might have?
3. Do you have enough evidence to make a judgment about this product?

These six practices will help you to develop critical thinking habits and skills. To further hone these habits and skills, also consider what does *not* constitute critical thinking. Critical thinking is neither a belief nor a faith, nor is it meant to make everyone arrive at the same answer. In fact, complex issues often remain ambiguous, and a plausible answer may not always be possible. Although critical thinking means respecting others' viewpoints, the nature of the scientific method may lead you to discover that some of those ideas are incorrect. Critical thinking does not mean being negatively or arbitrarily critical; it means intentionally examining knowledge and beliefs, as well as how conclusions about them are obtained. It also means carefully examining the sources of information. You can practice applying critical thinking to the scenario in Table 1.1.

JOURNAL PROMPT

Critical Thinking: What is a common belief people tend to have in which critical thinking is especially lacking? Describe the belief and explain why you think people hold it.

CRITICAL THINKING ABOUT SOURCES Not all sources of information are equal and trustworthy. Therefore, it is important that you pay especial attention to the sources' purpose, openness, accuracy, and comprehensiveness *before, during,* and *after* you read or research information.

- **Purpose:** Make sure you can identify the purpose of the article you are reading. Obviously, this will help you establish whether it is relevant to your needs, but it will also help with other elements of critical thinking, such as determining bias. For example, imagine you are interested in dining out at a new restaurant. If you are counting your calories (*purpose*), you will likely examine fact-based data about the calorie value of each entree (*source*), but if you are wondering whether you will enjoy the food (*purpose*), you will more likely rely on opinion-based reviews (*source*). You would not read a rave review to find out the calorie value of the entrees because, chances are, the information you find will be biased, inaccurate, or irrelevant. There are parallels to this example in all sorts of domains, from

buying a new car to deciding how to be a better parent. When considering the relationship between purpose and source, ask yourself:
- Is this an opinion piece (e.g., an editorial or a campaign statement)?
- Is this a straightforward report of facts (news) or description (e.g., encyclopedia entry)?
- Is this an advertisement?

- **Bias and Openness:** Determine whether the source has a social or political agenda, or perhaps financial motives for presenting information in a certain way. For example, if you have encountered a YouTube video highlighting the terrible conditions endured by factory-raised pigs. You watch pigs being kicked, shoved into tiny pens, or denied fresh water. You would not be surprised to discover that an animal rights group produced it, but you would probably be shocked if it were created by an association of hog farmers. It is no surprise that groups with specific agendas and interests will produce media that suit their needs rather than present and assess all sides to the story. Knowing this, you should always ask yourself:
- Who are the publishers, advertisers, and other supporters of this source? What do these groups stand to gain when the source presents the information?
- Are multiple opinions or options represented, or should they be?
- What is being left out?
- Does the source appear thoughtful, or is there extensive use of exaggeration, sweeping generalizations, or emotional language?

- **Accuracy and credibility:** Responsibly written articles present accurate and precise information that can be traced back to credible sources. Imagine you encounter an article warning people of the dangers of marijuana on memory and reasoning skills, but you notice that the author has no background in drug research and only cites anecdotes rather than scientific evidence. You would be wise to disregard that article and instead look for a source written by someone with an appropriate background and provides verifiable data to support the opinions. When considering the accuracy and credibility of a source, ask yourself:

- Are the authors listed?
- Are claims supported with citations, footnotes, or references?
- Is it up to date?
- Do multiple sources agree? (Make sure they are not citing the same original source or sponsored by the same ads or organizations.)
- If someone is cited as an authority, are they still providing sound evidence? Are they speaking within their realm of expertise?

Myths in Mind

Abducted by Aliens!

Independent reports of alien abductions often resemble events and characters depicted in science fiction movies.

Occasionally we hear claims of alien abductions, ghost sightings, and other paranormal activity. Countless television shows and movies, both fictional and documentary, reinforce the idea that these events can and do occur. Alien abductions are often the most complicated and far-fetched stories, yet many people can provide extremely detailed accounts of being kidnapped and examined. So what should we believe about alien abductions?

Scientific and critical thinking involves the use of the *principle of parsimony*, which means that the simplest of all competing explanations (the most "parsimonious") of a phenomenon should be the one we accept. Is there a simpler explanation for alien abductions? Probably so. First, historical reports of abductions typically spike just after the release of science fiction movies featuring space aliens. Details of the reports often follow specific details seen in these movies (Clancy, 2005). Second, people who claim to have been abducted are likely to experience *sleep paralysis* (waking up and becoming aware of being unable to move—a temporary state that is not unusual) and hallucinations while in the paralyzed state (McNally et al., 2004). Finally, people who report being abducted tend to fantasize more than the average person and they also have more *false memories* (vivid and convincing memories about events that did not happen; Lynn & Kirsch, 1996). Taken together, these lines of research lead to a plausible explanation: abductions could be false memories incorporating elements of media with the experience of sleep paralysis; all of these events are easily observable. In contrast, finding physical evidence of aliens is not. Following the principle of parsimony typically leads to real, though sometimes less spectacular, answers.

Module **1.1** Summary

1.1a Know . . . the key terminology of the scientific method:

biopsychosocial model
critical thinking
hypothesis
pseudoscience
psychology
scientific literacy
scientific method
theory

1.1b Understand . . . the steps of the scientific method.

The basic model in Figure 1.1 guides us through the steps of the scientific method. Scientific theories generate hypotheses, which are specific and testable predictions. If a hypothesis is confirmed, new hypotheses may stem from it, and the original theory receives added support. If a hypothesis is rejected, the original hypothesis may be modified and retested, or the original theory may be modified or rejected.

1.1c Understand . . . the concept of scientific literacy.

Scientific literacy refers to the process of how we think about and understand scientific information. The model for scientific literacy was summarized in Figure 1.2. Working the model involves answering a set of questions:

- What do we know about a phenomenon?
- How can science explain it?
- Can we critically evaluate the evidence?
- Why is this relevant?

You will see this model applied to concepts in each chapter and module of this text. This includes gathering knowledge, explaining phenomena in scientific terms, engaging in critical thinking, and knowing how to apply and use your knowledge.

1.1d Apply . . . the biopsychosocial model to behavior.

This is a model we will use throughout the text. As you consider each topic, think about how biological factors (e.g., the brain and genetics) are influential. Also consider how psychological factors such as thinking, learning, emotion, and memory are relevant. Social and cultural factors complete the model. These three interacting factors influence our behavior.

1.1e Apply . . . the steps in critical thinking.

To be useful, critical thinking is not just a concept to memorize but rather a skill to use and apply. Remember, critical thinking involves (1) being curious, (2) evaluating the evidence, (3) examining assumptions and biases, (4) avoiding emotional thinking, (5) tolerating ambiguity, and (6) considering alternative viewpoints. The activity in Table 1.1 was designed to help you apply some critical thinking. Here are the answers we came up with.

Apply Activity: Table 1.1, p. 08

1. The appeals to your wallet and to your environmental conscience sound great, but it might be too good to be true!

2. The manufacturer is trying to make money. That does not make the company evil, but it might lead its marketing staff to exaggerate the benefits offered by its products.

3. We do not have any evidence that the product works, just the manufacturer's claim. Until you find the evidence, you must tolerate ambiguity; you cannot say if it is effective or not.

1.1f Analyze . . . the use of the term *scientific theory*.

The term *theory* is often used very casually in the English language, sometimes synonymously with *opinion*. Thus, it is important to analyze the scientific meaning of the term and contrast it with the common-use alternatives. A scientific theory is an explanation for a broad range of observations, integrating numerous findings into a coherent whole. Remember, theories are not the same thing as opinions or beliefs, all theories are not equally plausible, and strange as it may sound, a measure of a good scientific theory is not determined by the number of people who believe it to be true.

Module 1.1 Quiz

Know . . .

1. A testable prediction about processes that can be observed and measured is referred to as a(n)_____.
   A. theory
   B. hypothesis
   C. opinion
   D. hunch

Understand . . .

2. A theory or prediction is falsifiable if:
   A. it has been proven false.
   B. it is impossible to test.
   C. there can be evidence for it or against it.
   D. if and only if it comes from pseudoscience.

3. Scientific literacy does not include _____.
   A. gathering knowledge
   B. accepting common-sense explanations
   C. critical thinking
   D. applying scientific information to everyday problems

Apply . . .

4. Huang is considering whether to take a cholesterol-reducing medicine that has been recommended by his physician, so he inquires about its effectiveness and safety. His physician explains that the government agency that oversees medications—the Food and Drug Administration (FDA)—has approved the medication after dozens of scientific studies had been conducted on their usefulness and safety. Which aspect of critical thinking does this best represent?
   A. Huang is examining the nature and source of the evidence.
   B. Huang is simply curious.
   C. Huang is not considering alternative viewpoints.
   D. Huang is avoiding overly emotional thinking.

Analyze . . .

5. The scientific meaning of the word *theory* is different from how it is most often used in nonscientific language because
   A. it describes an explanation based on a variety of well-tested, objective observations rather than speculation.
   B. it simply reflects the opinions of a particular scientist instead of the facts.
   C. it is phrased in such a way that it cannot be proven incorrect.
   D. it can be proven.

Module **1.2** How Psychology Became a Science

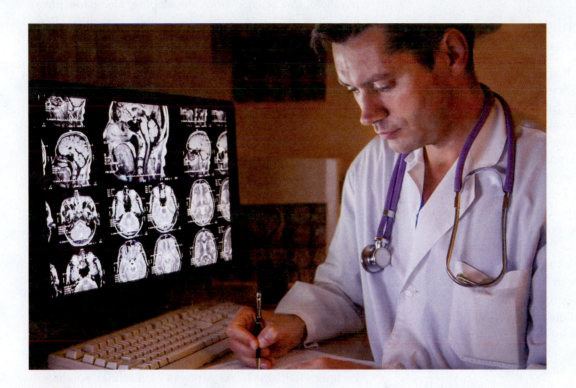

Learning Objectives

1.2a Know . . . the key terminology of psychology's history.

1.2b Understand . . . how various philosophical ideas and scientific fields became major influences on psychology.

1.2c Apply . . . your knowledge to distinguish among the different specializations and schools of thought in psychology.

1.2d Analyze . . . how the philosophical ideas of empiricism and determinism are applied to human behavior.

Domenico Mattiello garnered a great deal of respect and admiration in more than 30 years as a pediatrician, but it was all lost the instant investigators charged him with lewd conduct, including making sexual advances toward young children in his care. In his trial, lawyers did not deny the charges, but argued Mattiello's defense with medical records and brain scans. There was no doubt that he suffered a large and growing brain tumor or that the tumor was associated with changes in personality and behavior. So the legal question was raised: Did Mattiello commit the crimes or was the tumor guilty?

The premise of this legal defense should be familiar. Most judicial systems address questions about competence to stand trial, the ability to discern right from wrong, and other

inherently psychological questions. Underlying this legal question is the concept of free will—a topic that has been fundamental to philosophy for thousands of years. Increasingly, data from psychological research is used to influence how judges and jurors wrestle with the tough cases. It is interesting to note that although brain-based explanations are frequently useful, they often have little influence in people's assumptions about free will in everyday life (Nahamis, Sheperd, & Reuter, 2014). In this module, we will examine how many fascinating topics originating in ancient philosophy have developed into scientific questions explored by modern scientific techniques. These age-old topics, along with many new ones, make up psychological science today.

Modern psychology is built on many ideas and investigative techniques that have emerged over centuries of scholarly thought. In this module we put psychological questions and our attempts to answer them into historical context and see how these questions have influenced the current field of psychology.

Psychology's Philosophical and Scientific Origins

Science is more than a body of facts to memorize or a set of subjects to study. Science is actually a philosophy of knowledge that stems from two fundamental beliefs: empiricism and determinism.

Empiricism is a philosophical tenet that knowledge comes through experience. In everyday language, you might hear the phrase "Seeing is believing," but in the scientific sense, empiricism means that knowledge about the world is based on careful observation, not common sense or speculation. Whatever we see or measure should be observable by anyone else who follows the same methods. In addition, scientific theories must be rational explanations of how the observations fit together. Thus, although the empiricist might say, "Seeing is believing," thinking and reasoning about observations are just as important.

Determinism is the belief that events are governed by lawful, cause-and-effect relationships. This is easy enough when we discuss natural laws such as gravity; we probably all agree that if you drop a heavy object, it will fall. But does the lawfulness of nature apply to the way we think and feel? Does it mean that we do not have control over our own actions? This interesting philosophical debate is often referred to as *free will versus determinism*. Although we certainly feel as if we are in control of our own behaviors—that is, we sense that we have free will—there are some compelling reasons (such as Mattiello's brain-based legal defense) to believe that our behaviors are determined. The level of determinism or free will psychologists attribute to humans is certainly debated, and to be a psychologist, you do not have to believe that every single thought, behavior, or experience is determined by natural laws. But psychologists certainly do recognize that behavior is determined by both internal (e.g., genes, brain chemistry) and external (e.g. the presence of others) influences.

Psychological science is both empirical and deterministic. Our understanding of behavior comes from observing what we can see and measure, and behavior is caused by a multitude of factors. However, psychology arrived at this point only in the latter half of the 1800s—much later than the well-established sciences of physics, astronomy, and chemistry. Why did it take psychology so long to become scientific? One of the main reasons is *zeitgeist*, a German word meaning "spirit of the times." **Zeitgeist** *refers to a general set of beliefs of a particular culture at a specific time in*

history. It can be used to understand why some ideas take off immediately, whereas other perfectly good ideas may go unnoticed for years. The historical timeline of psychology shown in Figure 1.5 reflects the major viewpoints that have become a part of psychology over the past three centuries.

There are several ways zeitgeist may have prevented psychological science from developing alongside physical sciences. For example, philosophers such as Rene Descartes had no problem conceiving of the human body as a natural, lawfully behaving machine (human anatomy could be scientific). However, viewing human reasoning as the result of predictable physical laws was troubling, and many people resisted applying science to thought. Doing so would seem to imply the philosophy of **materialism**: *the belief that humans, and other living beings, are composed exclusively of physical matter*. Accepting this idea would mean that we are nothing more than complex machines that lack a self-conscious, self-controlling soul. The opposing belief, that there are properties of humans that are not material (a mind or soul separate from the body), is called *dualism*. Therefore, although thinking about the mind and behavior remained philosophical for generations, scientific methods were generating great discoveries in other fields.

INFLUENCES FROM PHYSICS: EXPERIMENTING WITH THE MIND The initial forays into scientific psychology were conducted by physicists and physiologists. One of the earliest explorations was made by Gustav Fechner (1801–1887). As a physicist, Fechner was interested in the natural world of moving objects and energy. These interests turned psychological when he began raising questions about human perception of the physical world. He called this **psychophysics**, *the study of the relationship between the physical world and the mental representation of that world*.

As an example of psychophysical research, imagine you are holding a 1-pound weight in your right hand and a 5-pound weight in your left hand. What if a researcher places a 1/4-pound weight in each hand, resting on top of the weight that is already there? Although both weigh the same amount physically—1/4 of a pound—the weight in your right hand will in some sense be psychologically heavier because it is a greater proportion of the original weight. Through psychophysical experiments like these, Fechner developed an equation to precisely calculate the perceived change in weight, and then extended this formula to apply to changes in brightness, loudness, and other perceptual experiences.

INFLUENCES FROM EVOLUTIONARY THEORY: THE ADAPTIVE FUNCTIONS OF BEHAVIOR Around the same time Fechner was doing his experiments, Charles Darwin (1809–1882) was studying the variety of plants and animals around the world. Darwin noticed that animal groups that were isolated from one another often differed

Figure 1.5 Major Events in the History of Psychology

Late 1700s: Franz Mesmer develops techniques to treat mental illness, including the use of hypnosis.

Around 1850: Gustav Fechner pioneers the study of psychophysics.

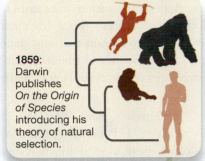

1859: Darwin publishes *On the Origin of Species* introducing his theory of natural selection.

1861: Physician Paul Broca discovers a brain area associated with the production of speech, now known as Broca's area, establishing that regions of the brain are specialized to serve different functions.

1879: Wilhelm Wundt establishes the first psychological laboratory in Leipzig, Germany, and two years later he establishes the first journal in psychology.

1883: G. Stanley Hall establishes his laboratory at Johns Hopkins University in Baltimore—the first psychology laboratory in the United States.

1880s: Francis Galton introduces and develops the study of anthropometrics.

1885: Hermann Ebbinghaus begins his scientific study of memory.

1890: William James, founder of the functionalist approach, publishes *Principles of Psychology*.

1892: The American Psychological Association (APA) is established.

AMERICAN PSYCHOLOGICAL ASSOCIATION

1936: Kurt Lewin authors *Principles of Topological Psychology*, which introduces the social psychological formulation that the behavior of individuals is influenced by their social environment.

1929: Psi Chi is founded as the National Honor Society in psychology to recognize and support excellence in academic psychology.

1913: John B. Watson writes "Psychology as the Behaviorist Views It," establishing behaviorism as the primary school of thought in American psychology.

1912: Max Wertheimer establishes the field of gestalt psychology.

1911: Edward Thorndike demonstrates the basic principles of instrumental learning, forming the basis for the study of operant conditioning.

1905: Alfred Binet develops the first intelligence test.

Early 1900s: Ivan Pavlov demonstrates the basic principles of classical conditioning.

1904: Mary Calkins is elected the first female president of the American Psychological Association.

1900: Sigmund Freud writes *The Interpretation of Dreams*, a key book in the development of psychoanalysis.

1896: Lightmer Witmer established the first psychological clinic at the University of Pennsylvania.

1894: Margaret Washburn is the first female to receive a PhD in psychology.

1938: B. F. Skinner writes the *Behavior of Organisms*, which furthers the cause of behaviorism.

1951: Carl Rogers writes *Client-Centered Therapy*, which helps establish humanistic psychology.

1967: Ulrich Neisser publishes *Cognitive Psychology*, which introduces a major new subfield of psychology.

1971: B. F. Skinner publishes *Beyond Freedom and Dignity*, stirring controversy over radical behaviorism.

1978: Herbert Simon wins the Nobel Prize in economics for research in cognitive psychology (there is no Nobel Prize dedicated to psychology).

1988: Establishment of the American Psychological Society, now known as Association for Psychological Science (APS).

1990s: President George H. W. Bush proclaims the 1990s to be "The Decade of the Brain," and there is unprecedented growth in neuroscience and biological psychology.

2000: Eric Kandel, Arvid Carlsson and Paul Greengard win the Nobel Prize for physiology or medicine for their discoveries of the cellular basis of memory.

2003: The Human Genome Project is completed.

2013: The American Psychiatric Association publishes the fifth edition of the *Diagnostic and Statistical Manual of Mental Disorders*, 52 years after the 1st edition was released.

Charles Darwin proposed the theory of natural selection to explain how evolution works.

by only minor variations in physical features. These variations seemed to fine-tune the species according to the particular environment in which they lived, making them better equipped for survival and reproduction. Darwin's theory of evolution by natural selection was based on his observations that the genetically inherited traits that contribute to survival and reproductive success are more likely to flourish within the breeding population. This theory explains why there is such a diversity of life on Earth.

What does evolution have to do with psychology? As Darwin pointed out in *The Expression of the Emotions in Man and Animals* (1872), behavior is shaped by natural selection, just as physical traits are. Darwin noted that for many species, including humans, survival and reproduction are closely related to an individual's ability to recognize some expressions as threats and others as submission. To Darwin, it appeared that emotional expressions and other behaviors were influenced by natural selection as well. Even before Darwin, humans had selectively bred animals to behave in certain ways (i.e., artificial selection of traits, rather than natural selection). Sheep dogs make good herders, whereas their pit bull cousins do not. Retrievers and pointers are good at hunting with humans, but how long would a toy poodle last in this context? Darwin's recognition that behaviors, like physical traits, are subject to hereditary influences and natural selection was a major contribution to psychology.

INFLUENCES FROM MEDICINE: DIAGNOSES AND TREATMENTS Medicine contributed a great deal to the biological perspective in psychology, as well as **clinical psychology**, *which is the field of psychology that concentrates on the diagnosis and treatment of psychological disorders.* One

interesting area of medical study was brain localization, the idea that certain parts of the brain control specific mental abilities and personality characteristics. Physicians noted that when a specific area of the brain was damaged, the correlated function was affected as in these two interesting examples:

- Physician Paul Broca studied a patient named Tan. Tan received this name because it was the only word he could speak, despite the fact that he could hear and understand perfectly well. Broca identified an area of the left side of Tan's brain that was damaged and claimed to have found where speech production was localized; that area of the brain is now known as *Broca's area*.

- Motivated by Broca's work, Karl Wernicke identified *Wernicke's area* in 1874. Patients with damage to Wernicke's area could speak in sentences that sounded normal, but with unusual or made-up words. Patients who regained some of their speech later reported that, although they could hear just fine, no speech—not even their own—made sense during the recovery period.

Additional medical influences on psychology came from outside of mainstream practices. Working in Paris, physician Franz Mesmer, believed that prolonged exposure to magnets could redirect the flow of metallic fluids in the body, thereby curing disease and insanity. Although his claim was rejected outright by the medical and scientific communities, some of his patients seemed to be cured after being lulled into a trance. Modern physicians and scientists attribute these cures to belief in the treatment— what we now call *a placebo effect*. This practice also caught the attention of an Austrian physician named Sigmund Freud (1856–1939), who began to use the related concept of *hypnosis* to treat his own patients. Freud believed hypnosis cured several patients of *hysterical paralysis*—a condition in which an individual loses feeling and control in a specific body part, despite the lack of any known neurological damage or disease.

Freud's belief in his successes contributed to his theory of **psychoanalysis**, *which is a method of explaining how behavior and personality are influenced by primitive drives and unconscious thought processes.* Freud acknowledged that conscious experience includes perceptions, thoughts, and a sense of self. However, he also believed in an unconscious mind driven to fulfill self-serving sexual and aggressive impulses. Freud proposed that because these urges were unconscious, they could exert influence in strange ways, such as restricting the use of a body part (psychosomatic or hysterical paralysis). When a person is hypnotized, dreaming, or perhaps medicated into a trancelike state (Freud had a fondness for cocaine during a period of his career), the psychoanalyst could have direct access into the

Sigmund Freud developed the concept of an unconscious mind and its underlying processes in his theory of psychoanalysis.

individual's unconscious mind. Once Freud gained access, he could attempt to determine and correct any desires or emotions he believed were causing the unconscious to create the psychosomatic conditions.

Although Freud neglected to conduct scientific experiments to test his ideas about human behavior, his legacy can be seen in some key elements of scientific psychology. First, many modern psychologists make inferences about unconscious mental activity, just as Freud had advocated. Second, the use of medical ideas to treat disorders of emotions, thought, and behavior—an approach known as the *medical model*—can be traced to Freud's influence. Third, Freud incorporated evolutionary thinking into his work; he emphasized how physiological needs and urges relating to survival and reproduction can influence our behavior. Finally, Freud placed great emphasis on how early life experiences influence our behavior as adults—a perspective that comes up many times in this text.

THE INFLUENCE OF SOCIAL SCIENCES: MEASURING AND COMPARING HUMANS   A third influential force came out of the social sciences of economics, sociology, and anthropology. Sir Francis Galton (1822–1911) combined the mathematical methods of economics with discussions of social class and ethnicity and made them relevant to psychology. Shortly after Galton's cousin, Charles Darwin, introduced his theory of evolution, Galton wondered why intelligence and achievement seemed to run in some families and not in others—particularly those who have

languished in poverty for generations. Is it possible that psychological traits can be inherited? For Galton, yes—it seemed natural that people who succeed in academics and business would inherit psychological traits that lead to high achievement. Galton was convinced by his own family lineage: his cousin Darwin was a great naturalist and his uncle Erasmus was a celebrated physician and writer. Galton himself began to read at age 2. You will see that many of Galton's beliefs and biases are no longer popular today, but several of his key contributions continue to influence research methods in psychology:

- Galton developed a psychological measure of *eminence*—a combination of ability, morality, and achievement—which he claimed was based on heredity. One observation helped to support this claim: The closer one relative is to another, the more similar are the traits they share. Although eminence is no longer used as a measure, modern psychology continues to emphasize the importance of measuring traits and behaviors and doing so accurately.

- Galton's statistical methods are the foundation of *correlation*, a mathematical representation of how two variables might go together. For example, wealth and academic achievement go together, as reflected in the calculation of correlation statistics.

- Galton pioneered the study of **nature and nurture relationships**, *the inquiry into how* heredity *(nature) and* environment *(nurture) influence behavior and mental processes.* He came down decidedly on the nature side, rejecting the likelihood that social conditions influenced eminence. Although we continue to explore nature and nurture, the focus is now on how they interact to produce individual abilities and traits.

Ultimately, Galton wanted his research to improve society—and so he attempted to scientifically justify *eugenics*, which literally translates as "good genes." He argued that his society—19th-century England—should encourage intelligent, talented individuals to have children, whereas criminals, those with disabilities, and other races should be kept out of the English gene pool. Modern psychologists continue to conduct research that they hope will improve society; however, we now understand the benefits of improving the social and educational conditions for children (nurture) and the futility and injustice of eugenics (an extreme view of nature).

Galton originated a lot of the methods and questions found in modern psychology, but you would be hard-pressed to find current research arguing for eugenics. Ironically, one of his contributions has been to serve as an example of how *not* to employ those very same methods. The eugenics movement was based on supporting preexisting beliefs rather than testing their validity and usefulness. Scientists are not perfect now, but definitely more cautious about creating falsifiable hypotheses. Also, remember that critical thinkers are willing to be proven wrong, and they always examine preexisting biases.

The Beginnings of Contemporary Psychology

As you now know, before psychology became its own discipline, there were scientists working across different fields who were converging on a study of human behavior. It is possible that physicists could have gone on studying psychophysics, physicians could have continued studying brain injuries, and biologists could have kept studying evolutionary influences on behavior. By modern standards, Darwin, Fechner, and others had produced psychological research, but it was not referred to as such because the field had not yet formed. Nevertheless, progress toward a distinct discipline of psychology was in the works.

STRUCTURALISM AND FUNCTIONALISM: THE BEGINNINGS OF PSYCHOLOGY Wilhelm Wundt (1832–1920) is credited with establishing the first psychology laboratory. His primary research method was *introspection* (to "look within"), which required a trained volunteer to experience a stimulus and then report each individual sensation he or she could identify. For example, if the volunteer were given a steel ball, he would likely report the sensations of cold, hard, smooth, and heavy. To Wundt, these basic sensations were mental atoms that combined to form the molecules of experience. Wundt also developed reaction time methods as a way of measuring mental effort. In one such study, volunteers watched an apparatus in which two metal balls swung into each other to make a clicking sound. The volunteers required about one-eighth of a second to react to the sound, leading Wundt to conclude that mental activity is not instantaneous, but rather it requires a small amount of effort measured by the amount of time it takes to react. What made Wundt's work distinctly psychological was his focus on measuring mental events and examining how they were affected by his experimental manipulations.

Wundt's student, Edward Titchener, brought the introspection method to the United States and began mapping the structure of human consciousness. **Structuralism** *was an attempt to analyze conscious experience by breaking it down into basic elements and to understand how these elements work together*. Titchener chose the term *elements* deliberately as an analogy with the periodic table in the physical sciences. He believed that mental experiences were made up of a limited number of sensations, which

German scientist Wilhelm Wundt is widely credited as the father of experimental psychology.

William James was a highly influential American psychologist who took a functionalist approach to explaining behavior.

were analogous to elements in physics and chemistry. According to Titchener, different sensations can form and create complex compounds, just like hydrogen and oxygen can combine to form water (H_2O).

US scholar William James (1842–1910) authored the first textbook in psychology, *The Principles of Psychology*, which was published in 1890. In it, James emphasized **functionalism**, *the study of how behavior and thought function in organisms' adaptation to their environments*. In contrast to structuralism, which looks for permanent, unchanging elements of thought, functionalism examines how our brains and behaviors have been shaped by the physical and social environment that our ancestors encountered. These ideas can be found today in the field of *evolutionary psychology*.

Although some of those techniques, such as Wundt's introspection, are no longer used, by the turn of the 20th century, it was clear that the discipline of psychology was here to stay. With that sense of permanence in place, the second generation of psychologists could focus on refining the subject matter and the methods and turning psychology into a widely accepted scientific field.

THE RISE OF BEHAVIORISM   Early in the 20th century, biologists became interested in how organisms learn to anticipate their bodily functions. One of the first to do so was Professor Edwin Twitmyer (1873–1943), a US psychologist interested in reflexes. His work involved a contraption with a rubber mallet that would regularly tap the patellar tendon just below the kneecap; this, of course, causes a kicking reflex in most individuals. To make sure his volunteers were not startled by the mallet, the contraption would ring a bell right before the mallet struck the tendon. As is often the case in experiments, the technology failed after a number of these bell-ringing and hammer-tapping combinations: The machine rang the bell, but the hammer did not come down on the volunteer's knee. But the real surprise was that the volunteer's leg kicked anyway! Because the sound of the bell successfully predicted the hammer, the ringing soon had the effect of the hammer itself, a process now called *classical conditioning*. The study of conditioning would soon become a focus of **behaviorism**, *which is an approach that dominated the first half of the 20th century of US psychology and had a singular focus on studying only observable behavior*, with little to no reference to mental events or instincts as possible influences on behavior.

Unfortunately for Twitmyer, his research was coolly received at the American Psychological Association meeting and the credit for discovering classical conditioning typically goes to a Russian physiologist named Ivan Pavlov (1849–1936). Pavlov's Nobel Prize–winning research showed that dogs could learn to salivate to a tone

Ivan Pavlov (on the right) explained classical conditioning through his studies of salivary reflexes in dogs.

if the tone has a history of sounding just before the delivery of food (Module 6.1).

Credit for the rise of behaviorism in the United States typically goes to John B. Watson (1878–1958). As research accumulated on the breadth of behaviors that could be conditioned, Watson began to believe that all behavior could ultimately be explained through conditioning. This emphasis on learning also came with stipulations about what could and could not be studied in psychology. Watson was adamant that only observable changes in the environment and behavior were appropriate for scientific study. Methods such as Wundt's introspection, he said, were too subjective to even consider. And, in stark contrast to Galton's eugenics, Watson believed anything was possible with controlled conditioning:

> Give me a dozen healthy infants, well-formed, and my own specified world to bring them up in and I'll guarantee to take any one at random and train him to become any type of specialist I might select—doctor, lawyer, artist, merchant-chief and, yes, even beggar-man and thief, regardless of his talents, penchants, tendencies, abilities, vocations, and race of his ancestors. (Watson, 1930, p. 82)

After an indiscretion involving a female graduate student, Watson lost his university job, but found his new career in advertising. Advertisers at the time assumed they should inform people about the merits of a product. Watson, however, discovered a consumer's knowledge about a product really was not that important, so long as he or she had positive emotions associated with it. Thus, Watson's company developed ads that employed behaviorist principles to form associations between a product's

B.F. Skinner revealed how rewards affect behavior by conducting laboratory studies on animals.

brand image and positive emotions. If Pavlov's dogs could be conditioned to salivate when they heard a tone, what possibilities might there be for conditioning humans in a similar way? Modern advertisers want the logos for their brands of snacks or the trademark signs for their restaurants to bring on a specific craving, and some salivation along the way. We have Watson and his colleagues to thank for this phenomenon.

Taking up the reins from Watson was B. F. Skinner (1904–1990), another behaviorist who had considerable influence over US psychology for several decades. Like Watson, Skinner believed that psychology was the study of behavior and not of the unobservable mind. His approach differed from Watson's and was based on the relatively straightforward observation that organisms repeat behaviors that bring rewards and avoid those that do not. Typically, these studies occurred with animals held in small chambers in which they could manipulate a lever to receive rewards such as food and water. The experimenter would control when rewards were available, and the animal's task was to learn the reward schedule. Though we are clearly different from pigeons in many ways, behaviorists determined that many of the principles in animal learning can apply to humans as well.

Watson's and Skinner's concept of behaviorism met with resistance from many psychologists. If our behavior is controlled by external stimuli and rewards, then this leaves little room for free will. Many of those who resisted believed that humans could rise above their instinctive drives for rewards.

HUMANISTIC PSYCHOLOGY EMERGES In response to the deterministic views in behaviorism, psychoanalysis, and eugenics, a new psychological perspective arose in the 1950s. **Humanistic psychology** *focuses on the unique aspects of each individual human, each person's freedom to act, his or her rational thought, and the belief that humans are fundamentally different from other animals.* Figures such as Carl Rogers (1902–1987) and Abraham Maslow (1908–1970) focused on the positive aspects of humanity, the meaning of personal experience, and the factors that lead to a productive and fulfilling life. Both Rogers and Maslow believed that humans strive to develop a sense of self and are motivated to personally grow and fulfill their potential. This is in stark contrast to the psychoanalytic tradition, which focused on disorders and animal instincts. The humanistic perspective also contrasted with behaviorism in proposing that humans had the freedom to act and a rational mind to guide the process.

THE COGNITIVE REVOLUTION Whereas behaviorism dominated psychology in the United States, many European psychologists were more open to studying *cognition*—mental processes such as memory and perception. Starting in the late 1800s, German psychologist Hermann Ebbinghaus (1850–1909) produced reams of data on remembering and forgetting. The results of his studies produced numerous forgetting curves, graphs that show that most of what a person learns will be forgotten rapidly, but then forgetting slows to a crawl. The forgetting curve remains a staple of modern psychology, and you will read more about Ebbinghaus in Module 7.2.

Another precursor to cognitive psychology was **Gestalt psychology**, *an approach emphasizing that psychologists need to focus on the whole of perception and experience, rather than its parts.* (*Gestalt* is a German word that refers to the complete form of an object; see Figure 1.6.) This contrasts with the structuralist goal of breaking experience into its individual elements. For example, if Wundt were to hand you an apple, you would not think, "Round, red, has a stem…" unless he

Figure 1.6 The Whole Is Greater than the Sum of its Parts

The Gestalt psychologists emphasized humans' ability to see whole forms. For example, you probably perceive a sphere in the center of this figure, even though it does not exist on the page.

asked you to. Instead, you would likely think, "This is an apple." This simple observation led Gestalt psychologists to argue that perception and thought occur at higher, more organized levels than Wundt believed. To them, Wundt's structuralism made about as much sense as understanding water only by studying its hydrogen and oxygen atoms.

In the 1950s, the scientific study of cognition was becoming accepted practice in US psychology. The recent invention of the computer gave psychologists a useful analogy for understanding the mind (the software of the brain). Linguists argued that grammar and vocabulary were far too complex to be explained in behaviorist terms; the alternative was to propose abstract mental processes. There was a great deal of interest in memory and perception as well, but it was not until 1968 that these areas of research were given the name "cognitive psychology" by Ulrich Neisser (1928–2012). These events ushered in a new era of psychology in which studies of mental processes and experiences flourished. *Cognitive psychology* is a modern psychological perspective that focuses on processes such as memory, thinking, and language.

SOCIOCULTURAL PERSPECTIVES IN PSYCHOLOGY

As structuralism and functionalism were taking shape in the late 1800s and early 1900s, psychologists were starting to examine how other people influence individual behavior. A US psychologist, Norman Triplett (1861–1931), conducted one of the first formal experiments in this area, observing that cyclists ride faster in the presence of other people than when riding alone. Triplett published the first social psychology research in 1892, and a few social psychology textbooks appeared in 1908.

Despite the early interest in this field, studies of how people influence the behavior of others did not take off until the 1940s. Interest in social and cultural perspectives grew out of collaborations between sociologists (who studied populations of humans) and psychologists (who were studying individuals), in part to try to make sense of the brutality of World War II. They attempted to understand how normal individuals could be transformed into ruthless prison camp guards, how political propaganda affected people, and how society might address issues of ethnic prejudice.

Kurt Lewin (1890–1947) is often cited as the founder of modern *social psychology*. Trained as a Gestalt psychologist, Lewin shifted his attention to race relations in the United States. After studying relations between individuals of different groups, he made an observation that is still well known among social psychologists: Behavior is a function of the individual and the environment, or $B = f\{I,E\}$. What Lewin meant was that all behaviors could be predicted and explained through understanding how an individual with a specific set of traits would respond in a context that involved a specific set of conditions. Take two individuals as an example: One tends to be quiet and engages in solitary activities such as reading, whereas the other is talkative and enjoys being where the action is. Now put them in a social situation, such as a wedding reception or a funeral. How will the two behave? Given the disparity between the individuals and between the two settings, we would suspect different behaviors would emerge.

The trends that emerged during this period laid the foundation for modern perspectives and theories in psychology. Psychology had become a clearly established discipline with established university departments, professional organizations, and academic journals. Although modern technology, such as brain scans and computing, would likely baffle psychology's founders, we believe they would find the results of modern research absolutely relevant to their own research questions. In the next module, we will explore the settings in which this broad array of psychologists are encountered and what they contribute to society.

JOURNAL PROMPT

The Diversity of Psychology: Students are often surprised to learn the breadth of approaches that psychologists take to understanding behavior. Describe the most unexpected piece of information you learned about psychology in reading this module.

Table 1.2 Areas of Specialization within Psychology

Apply your knowledge to distinguish among different specializations in psychology. You should be able to read a description of a psychologist on the left and match that individual's work to a specialization on the right.

1. I am an academic psychologist who studies various methods for improving study habits. I hope to help people increase memory performance and become better students. I am a(n) _____.	a. social psychologist
2. My work focuses on how the presence of other people influences an individual's acceptance of and willingness to express various stereotypes. I am a(n) _____.	b. cross-cultural psychologist c. cognitive psychologist
3. I have been studying how childrearing practices in Guatemala, the United States, and Cambodia all share some common elements, as well as how they differ. I am a(n) _____.	d. humanistic psychologist e. evolutionary psychologist
4. I am interested in behaviors that are genetically influenced to help animals adapt to their changing environments. I am a(n) _____.	
5. I help individuals identify problem areas of their lives and ways to correct them, and guide them to live up to their full potential. I am a(n) _____.	

Answers: 1) C, 2) A, 3) B, 4) E, 5) D

Module 1.2 Summary

1.2a **Know . . . the key terminology of psychology's history:**

behaviorism
clinical psychology
determinism
empiricism
functionalism
Gestalt psychology
humanistic psychology
materialism
nature and nurture relationships
psychoanalysis
psychophysics
structuralism
zeitgeist

1.2b **Understand . . . how various philosophical ideas and scientific fields became major influences on psychology.**

The philosophical schools of determinism, empiricism, and materialism provided the background for a scientific study of human behavior. The first psychologists were trained as physicists and physiologists. Fechner, for example, developed psychophysics, whereas Titchener looked for the elements of thought. Darwin's theory of natural selection influenced psychologist William James's idea of functionalism, which is the search for how behaviors may aid the survival and reproduction of the organism.

1.2c **Apply . . . your knowledge to distinguish among the different specializations and schools of thought in psychology.**

Psychology is a broad field that arose from the combination of multiple influences. These factors are reflected by the diverse interests and perspectives in modern psychology, such as cognitive and social psychology. Table 1.2 provided an opportunity to match terms to examples.

1.2d **Analyze . . . how the philosophical ideas of empiricism and determinism are applied to human behavior.**

Psychology is based on empiricism, the belief that all knowledge—including knowledge about human behavior—is acquired through the senses. All sciences, including psychology, require a deterministic viewpoint. Determinism is the philosophical tenet that all events in the world, including human actions, have a physical cause. Applying determinism to human behavior has been met with resistance by many because it appears to deny a place for free will.

Module 1.2 Quiz

Know . . .

1. In philosophical terms, a materialist is someone who believes that:
   A. money buys happiness.
   B. species evolve through natural selection.
   C. personality can be measured by feeling for bumps on the surface of the skull.
   D. everything that exists, including human beings, are composed exclusively of physical matter.

Understand . . .

2. Charles Darwin revolutionized biology by offering natural selection as an explanation for how physical characteristics of species evolved. How has his work influenced contemporary psychology?
   A. It shows that the biological approach to studying psychology is most important.
   B. Natural selection has encouraged people to think more scientifically in general.
   C. Evolutionary thought shows that psychology must be limited to the study of humans.
   D. Darwin applied his theory to behaviors such as emotional expressions, showing that natural selection is an important factor in understanding psychology.

3. A distinct feature of behaviorism is its:
   A. search for the deeper meaning of human existence.
   B. search for patterns that create a whole that is greater than its parts.
   C. use of introspection.
   D. exclusive emphasis on observable behavior.

Apply . . .

4. Jana uses research about how we cope with stress in order to help people with psychological disorders. Jana is probably _____.
   A. an empiricist   C. a clinical psychologist
   B. a supporter of eugenics   D. a phrenologist

Analyze . . .

5. The field of psychoanalysis arose from speculation that biological forces, rather than rational thinking, controlled behavior. This is in stark contrast to the humanistic psychologists who emphasized each individual's ability to control his or her life. On which philosophical element of psychology do these two schools of thought disagree?
   A. determinism   C. nature or nurture
   B. structuralism   D. functionalism

Module **1.3**   Putting Psychology to Work: Careers in Psychology and Related Fields

⌄ Learning Objectives

1.3a Know . . . the key terminology of psychological professions.

1.3b Understand . . . the various professional settings occupied by psychologists.

1.3c Understand . . . the distinctions among mental health professions in their approaches and educational requirements.

1.3d Apply . . . your knowledge to identify the job title of a psychologist based on their work.

1.3e Analyze . . . the claim that psychologists could contribute to virtually any field of work.

When you picture a psychologist at work, do you imagine one operating a huge chainsaw and cutting a hole through three feet of ground-level ice? What if the psychologist happened to be in Antarctica studying the behavior of seals and was creating the hole so that he could capture a glimpse of what these animals were doing beneath the ice? This would describe at least part of the career of Jesse Purdy, a psychology professor who spent many months in Antarctica recording the social behavior of Weddell

seals. When not cutting holes through ice and observing seals, Purdy teaches psychology courses to undergraduate students and conducts research on a quirky animal called the **cuttlefish***, a close relative of the octopus. This probably sounds like a far cry from what the stereotypes of psychologists suggest Purdy is sup-posed to do. Granted, this example is not exactly mainstream, but it does attest to the wide range of topics and settings where you will find psychologists at work.*

Professions in Psychology

Psychology is a broad discipline with many applications in the workplace. You will see a wide variety of job titles and descriptions in this module, including some jobs that are not labeled as *psychology* but are closely aligned to it. Despite the diverse roles described here, remember that these are applications of psychology, which means they involve a scientific approach to behavior and thought. Those who earn a doctoral degree in psychology work in a variety of settings, with the most common being in mental health settings, or engaged in research and teaching at colleges and universities (Figure 1.7).

RESEARCH AND TEACHING   *Research psychologists* typically work at universities, in corporations, in the military, and in governmental agencies (such as the National Institutes of Health and Mental Health). Many psychologists working in these different settings focus on applying basic principles of psychology to real-world settings. **Applied psychology** *uses psychological knowledge to address problems and issues across various settings and professions, including law, education, clinical psychology, and business organization and management.* Some applied psychologists do both basic and applied work; it really depends on where a psychologist is employed.

Your psychology instructor is employed (at least part of the time) in academic psychology. *Academic psychologists* work at colleges and universities, and most combine teaching with conducting research, although some do only one or the other. Psychologists working in academics are not likely to refer to themselves as academic psychologists, however. For example, most instructors of psychology courses would describe themselves by their specialization, as in "I am a social psychologist" or "I am a developmental psychologist."

PSYCHOLOGICAL HEALTH AND WELL-BEING Generally when most people hear the word *psychology*, they think first of mental health. In fact, the depiction of a psychologist with notepad in hand listening attentively to a client has become an all-too-common caricature, reinforcing the belief that psychologists are in the business of analyzing people. Clearly, the mental health field is the largest sector of employment for individuals with advanced degrees in psychology. However, helping professions are not limited to individuals with psychology degrees, as shown in Table 1.3. In fact, we call mental health jobs the *helping professions* because *helping* is what they all have in common, not the specific educational criteria, degrees, or occupational roles.

Multiple job descriptions are necessary for differentiating the distinct treatments considered the most effective for each individual helping profession. For example, **psychiatry** *is a branch of medicine concerned with the treatment of mental and behavioral disorders.* As physicians, psychiatrists can and are likely to prescribe drugs such as antidepressants. Clinical and counseling psychologists, however, treat mental health concerns and disorders with psychological approaches. Social workers are likely to emphasize the social context of the individuals in treatment, such as the family's dynamics, socioeconomic status, and community.

The educational levels required of each helping profession vary depending on the role. Psychologists may work with a master's degree in most states, but many go on to pursue doctorates, which provide greater career opportunities. This might include the typical graduate degree for a scientific discipline, the Doctor of Philosophy (Ph.D.), which combines training in scientific research and practice. However, there is also a specialized Doctor of Psychology (Psy.D.) degree that focuses almost exclusively on the practice of psychology.

As you can see, mental health providers can be found in many settings and provide numerous services to people in need. The caricature of a psychologist as an analyst breaks down even more when we expand our discussion of what psychologists do.

Psychologists can specialize to practice in specific contexts. **Forensic psychology** *encompasses work in the criminal justice system, including interactions with the legal system and its professionals.* The field is often glorified in movies and TV as criminal profiling and investigation, but it is actually a practical profession involving little of what is portrayed in these shows. The relatively few criminal profilers work with the FBI and larger law enforcement agencies to develop a set of characteristics that are statistically

Figure 1.7 Where Professional Psychologists Work
Primary employment settings for PhD recipients in psychology.

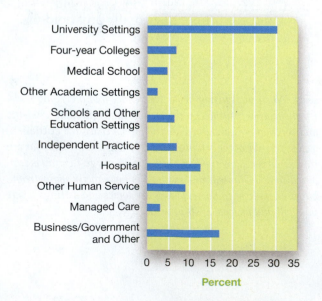

Table 1.3 Employment in Psychology

Common occupations in the area of mental health, their educational requirements, and the basic roles for each position.

Job Title	Education	Role
Clinical psychologist or Counseling psychologist	Ph.D. or Psy.D.	Diagnosis and treatment of psychological disorders
Neuropsychologist	Ph.D. or Psy.D.	Diagnosis and evaluation of individuals with neurological damage
School psychologist	Ed.D., Ph.D., or master's	Diagnosing behavioral problems and learning disabilities; working in schools to develop personalized programs to help students
Community psychologist	Ph.D. or Psy.D.	Providing basic mental health services to the community with a focus on education and prevention
Licensed Mental Health Counselor	Master's in Psychology or Marriage & Family Therapy	Providing individual and group counseling for individuals and families experiencing mental health problems
Licensed clinical social worker	Master's in social work (MSW)	Counseling individuals and families experiencing mental health and social problems; engaging in community organizations and providing social services
Forensic psychologist	Ph.D. or Psy.D.	Psychology related to judiciary or criminal issues, such as evaluating an individual's competency to stand trial
Psychiatrist	Medical doctor, M.D.	Diagnosis and treatment of psychological disorders with an emphasis on a medical perspective
Psychiatric nurse	Nursing degree, RN	Working as part of a comprehensive treatment team to manage medical and behavioral treatments on a regular basis
Behavioral health technician; case manager	Bachelor's degree	Assisting with treatment on either an inpatient or outpatient basis, respectively

related to a criminal's methods. You would more likely see forensic psychologists working in prisons, training and evaluating police officers, or assisting with jury selections and evaluating whether defendants are able to stand trial.

School psychology *involves working with students who have special needs, such as those with emotional, social, or academic problems.* Practitioners might address ways to change troubling or disruptive behavior, or a cognitive disability that interferes with learning, such as dyslexia. School psychologists may spend a lot of time observing a child's behavior or administering special psychological tests to identify learning disabilities. These professionals rarely work alone; instead, they are more often part of students' educational teams, which include their parents, teachers, and counselors.

Most of the helping professions we have described have two things in common: (1) graduate degrees (more school after college!) and (2) licensure or certification as approved by individual states. More school and licensing tests may or may not sound appealing; certainly many individuals prefer to start their careers immediately after college rather than going for another degree. With a bachelor's degree, individuals can work in treatment settings on a more basic level. For example, case managers make regular contact with individuals to ensure they are complying with treatment (e.g., taking medication as prescribed) and make sure their clients are in touch with public and private services that may help them. Behavioral health technicians have similar tasks, except they are for the short term (usually less than 30 days) and on an inpatient basis.

HEALTH AND MEDICAL PROFESSIONS In addition to providing for mental health, an increasing number of psychologists are focusing on physiological health in the field known as **health psychology** *(or behavioral medicine), the study of how individual, biological, and environmental factors affect physical health.* Health psychologists identify the behaviors and personality traits that put people at risk and that, when combined with an unfortunate genetic heritage or infection, lead to disease. For example, overeating, poor food choices, and a sedentary lifestyle have been linked to diabetes and a variety of cardiovascular ailments. Psychological traits such as pessimism and hopelessness are correlated with impaired immune functioning and lower recovery rates from major surgeries, diseases, or accidents. Working long hours at a high-stakes job while sacrificing rich and meaningful relationships can affect one's health as well. Thus, psychologists who work in the health fields might be seen as the behavioral counterparts to practitioners of traditional medicine. Whereas physicians treat the physiological aspects of a disease, psychologists help to change the related behaviors. Health psychology is the focus of Chapter 16.

PSYCHOLOGY IN THE CORPORATE WORLD One of the fastest-growing fields within psychology is **industrial and organizational (I/O) psychology**, *which is a branch of applied psychology in which psychologists work for businesses and other organizations to improve employee productivity and the organizational structure of the company or business.*

I/O psychologists may develop tests to hire workers who have the best chance at succeeding, they may assist work teams to improve communication and responsibility, and they may help organizations with the management of change. This approach to psychology is covered in depth in Chapter 17.

Closely related to I/O psychology is *human factors psychology*, which is the study of how people interact with tools, physical spaces, or products. This is the high-tech branch of applied psychology; a great deal of human factors work applies principles of sensation and perception to complex work environments such as aircraft cockpits or laparoscopic surgical devices. Human factors psychologists may study human–computer interaction to develop user-friendly software and other products. Similarly those who practice environmental psychology study factors that improve working and living conditions, but they do so by establishing how the environment affects individuals or groups. Results from this type of research may be used in the design of working and living spaces to foster communication, to reduce distractions, and to prevent or reduce strain, stress, and fatigue.

Many undergraduates who major in psychology go on to marketing and advertising. (In Module 1.2, we mentioned that psychologist Watson made a successful career for himself in advertising.) What does marketing have to do with psychology? A great deal, it turns out. Marketing involves a lot of research on what consumers prefer, what buyers expect, and what makes shoppers choose one product over another. Marketing professionals conduct surveys and experiments on preferences, such as the taste tests we see reported on television commercials.

JOURNAL PROMPT

Specializations in Psychology: If you were to enter the field of psychology, which area of specialization described in this module would you most likely choose? Why?

I'M NOT PLANNING ON A CAREER IN PSYCHOLOGY …

Not wanting to become a psychologist is fine, too; the world needs many types of professionals. Based on recent trends, only a small percentage of this year's nearly 100,000 bachelor-level psychology graduates will go on to work in psychological fields—far more (approximately 40%) will go on to work in business settings (Magaletta et al., 2010). But students who major or minor in psychology will be able to apply what they have learned in many different types of work. Because of psychology's emphasis on research methods, psychology majors turn out to be excellent problem solvers and critical thinkers. Also, psychology majors learn many principles of human behavior, ranging from individual cognition to group dynamics. These skills are needed for marketers, managers, and teachers (see Figure 1.8). So an understanding of behavior works to your advantage regardless of which career you eventually choose.

Even if this is the only course you take in psychology, we hope you enjoy it. We also hope that you come to understand more than just a few principles about human behavior. We anticipate that you will become more aware of the evidence people use when they make claims about behavior. Remember, as members of a capitalist society, our warning is *caveat emptor*—"Buyer, beware!"

Figure 1.8 Work Settings for People Earning Master's and Bachelor's Degrees in Psychology

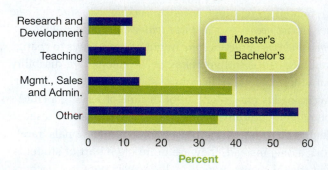

Table 1.4 Matching Psychologist Titles and Roles

Identify the appropriate job title for each psychologist in the table. For every job description on the left, there is one correct title on the right.

1. I am employed at a state penitentiary and work closely with parole officers to make sure parolees have a psychological treatment plan to address substance abuse, anger management, impulsiveness, and other problems. I am a(n) _____.	a. health psychologist b. psychiatrist c. forensic psychologist d. human factors psychologist e. I/O psychologist
2. I conduct research for the military to ensure that computer systems in aircraft are as user friendly as possible. I am a(n) _____.	
3. I went to medical school and then began working at a hospital, where I treat severe psychological disorders with medications and some psychotherapy. I am a(n) _____.	
4. I am an independent consultant, and I try to help businesses identify and hire the best possible executives. I am a(n) _____.	
5. Although I did not go to medical school, I have been working with heart surgery patients to help them adjust to life after surgery. This involves psychotherapy to deal with emotions and stress, as well as helping the patients adopt healthier behaviors. I am a(n) _____.	

Answers: 1) C, 2) D, 3) B, 4) E, 5) A

Module **1.3** Summary

1.3a   Know . . . the key terminology of psychological professions:

applied psychology
forensic psychology
health psychology
industrial and organizational (I/O) psychology
psychiatry
school psychology

1.3b   Understand . . . the various professional settings occupied by psychologists.

Psychologists work at universities as researchers and teachers. Of course, many psychologists work in the mental healthcare fields. They can be found in business and industry working in specialized roles geared toward promoting important factors such as team building, efficiency, and personnel matters. Professionals in the field also conduct applied work as specialists in human factors and environmental psychology. Schools employ psychologists for their specialized training in learning, thinking, and development. Some psychologists work in forensics and primarily work in court and law enforcement settings.

1.3c   Understand . . . the distinctions among mental health professions in their approaches and educational requirements.

The many different titles among those working in the mental health professions can be explained in terms of

education background and specific roles within the work setting. Typically, an advanced degree (Ph.D. or Psy.D.) and a state license is required for clinical psychologists, and, in the case of psychiatry, an M.D. is required. Many therapists and counselors who work directly with clients or patient populations have master's degrees in clinical, counseling, or school psychology and social work. Some jobs requiring a bachelor's degree involve work with clients in mental health settings, such as case managers or psychiatric nurses.

1.3d   Apply . . . your knowledge to identify the job title of a psychologist based on their work.

Table 1.4 provided you an opportunity to apply your knowledge. Remember when you encounter someone who describes their job as a "psychologist," you only know that they use scientific principles to understand thought and behavior. That is only the first part of the story, though. Clinical or counseling psychologists work toward improving mental health, I/O psychologists work in business settings, and other psychologists work in schools, medical centers, and of course, higher education institutions.

1.3e   Analyze . . . the claim that psychologists could contribute to virtually any field of work.

Data show that most psychologists are employed in mental health settings or in academics. However, fields such as I/O psychology, human factors, and environmental psychology have allowed psychologists to apply their knowledge to just about any field you can imagine.

Module **1.3** Quiz

Know . . .

1. A professional who would study how stress affects the heart is a(n) _____ psychologist.
   - **A.** environmental
   - **B.** health
   - **C.** clinical
   - **D.** I/O

Understand . . .

2. A psychologist works for a large automobile manufacturer in designing new models each year. Her job is to ensure that the display panel and controls such as turn signals, cruise control, and air conditioning are easy to understand and use without causing distractions to the driver. Her work illustrates _____ psychology.
   - **A.** health
   - **B.** forensic
   - **C.** school
   - **D.** human factors

3. A major difference between most clinical psychologists and psychiatrists is that:
   - **A.** all clinical psychologists can prescribe medications.
   - **B.** all psychiatrists can prescribe medications.
   - **C.** to be a clinical psychologist, you must obtain a doctorate degree.
   - **D.** to be a psychiatrist, you need to obtain only a master's degree.

Apply . . .

4. You meet someone on the bus who is a psychiatrist. From this, you may safely assume that:
   - **A.** she completed medical school.
   - **B.** she is likely to be analyzing you right now.
   - **C.** her work involves profiling criminals.
   - **D.** she most likely conducts research and teaches at a university.

Analyze . . .

5. Psychologists could be involved in virtually any field of work because:
   - **A.** they study how people behave in multiple situations, including how they carry out the tasks associated with their jobs.
   - **B.** there are not enough jobs, so psychologists usually cannot find work in their own field.
   - **C.** they are more likely to change careers than most other professions.
   - **D.** it is unlikely that they have the social skills needed when working cooperatively with others.

Module 1.4 Scientific Literacy Challenge: Imagery in Sports

Here, and at the end of every chapter, you will find an activity in which a claim has been made about a psychological phenomenon. These claims will come in the form of fictitious blog posts, editorials, advice columns for specific jobs, such as a business consultant, and an advertisement. As you work through the activity, you will review some key concepts from the chapter and practice recognizing, understanding, and critiquing scientific information.

Chapter 1 defined psychology and described the ideas about research and critical thinking that psychologists share. We also learned that psychologists are interested in numerous topics, which leads to a diverse field with many different specializations, one of which is sports psychology.

Before you start this activity, take a minute to write about how you think a sports psychologist might be helpful to an athlete.

JOURNAL PROMPT

Physical ability is clearly important to strong athletic performance. But what mental abilities help an athlete succeed? Choose a particular sport as an example to support your answer.

What do we know about sports psychology?

Read the following magazine article excerpts written by Tom Bolen, a university gymnastics team coach. Make sure you understand the key terms and concepts from Chapter 1 in bold type.

A Workout, To Go

By Tom Bolen, Head Coach, UEN Gymnastics
from *Physical Educator's Monthly*

For a long time, I believed that time away from the gym was time lost for my gymnasts, with the exception of basic stretching and conditioning exercises. However, I have recently come across some interesting methods that can put "down time" to good use; these methods are based on the concept of mental imagery, which has been studied in a number of ways. In **clinical psychology**, mental imagery can be used as a method to reduce anxiety. If an individual is afraid of spiders, for example, a psychologist can guide the individual through a series of steps that involve a mental picture of a spider along with relaxation techniques. **Cognitive psychologists** and neuroscientists have found that imagining body movements uses some of the same brain areas that are involved in actually making the movements. In a sense, imagining might be a little like practice without actually using your muscles.

Observations like these have stimulated a lot of discussion in a field I only learned about recently: Sports psychology. This is a field of **applied psychology** that takes a scientific approach to understanding the thoughts and behaviors that go into athletic performance. They claim that using imagery in sports is valuable because it can help reduce nervousness before a competition or performance. It can also be used to practice motor movements when an athlete is away from the gym or when their muscles are exhausted.

Coach Bolen has done his homework and knows what sports psychology is. Does he know what scientific evidence supports its practice? Let's read on.

How do scientists study imagery in sports psychology?

In this section, Coach Bolen introduces what he has learned about the science of sports psychology. As you read, look for terms and concepts related to scientific research, especially the ideas introduced in the highlighted phrases.

I was interested in applying sports psychology to my own gymnastics team, so I visited Professor Sykes, a psychologist on our campus specializing in athletic training. In her opinion, mental imagery can be a very important part of practice. If that is true, then we should expect to find that athletes who begin to use imagery should improve more than those who do not work imagery into their routine. Professor Sykes showed me an article from the scientific journal *Frontiers in Neuroscience* in which students were randomly assigned to one of three conditions before using a simulated driving course. One group imagined *themselves driving* a car through a slalom course (a first-person, "internal" perspective); another group imagined *watching someone else* driving through the course (an "external" perspective), while a third group did not use mental imagery at all. Researchers found that the groups all finished a simulated driving course in the same time, but the first-person perspective group averaged significantly fewer errors than the other two groups. The same article reported similar findings using a running slalom course and a downhill skiing slalom course. Dr. Sykes showed me two other studies where imagery helped improve golf putting in one, and the accuracy of serves for tennis players in another.

Hopefully you spotted the references to important scientific concepts. Test yourself by completing this short quiz, referring back to the article to find the answers.

1. The author provided a hypothesis when he stated that
   a. if the professor is correct, then athletes who use imagery should improve more than those who do not.
   b. the groups made the same number of errors made in the slalom course.
   c. the groups used first-person perspective, external perspective, or no imagery.
   d. imagery helps.

2. The prediction that one group of athletes will do better than another if they used imagery may prove to be incorrect. Is acknowledging this possibility an important part of scientific thinking?
   a. Yes, but only because the experiment supported it.
   b. Yes, scientific theories and hypotheses are falsifiable.
   c. No, because scientific statements are based on opinions.
   d. No, because scientists will not make claims without knowing that they are true.

3. What can a scientifically literate individual assume about a study published in a scientific journal, such as *Frontiers in Neuroscience*?
   a. The study was presented by a credible source.
   b. The experimenters were so satisfied with their results that they decided to pay someone to publish it.
   c. The editor of the journal hired some psychologists to write about their research.
   d. The claims about imagery are really just the psychologists' opinions.

Answers: 1. *a* **2.** *b* **3.** *a*

Our coach knows that visualization is scientifically supported. Let's see how he uses his critical thinking skills to get him closer to making a decision.

How should we think critically about using imagery in sports psychology?

Remember that critical thinking involves curiosity and reasonable levels of skepticism. Critical thinkers continue to ask questions while evaluating the quality of the answers they find. As you read the next paragraph, search for the signs of critical thinking, including those areas which have been highlighted for you.

> I tend to get excited about new ideas and within minutes I had dreamed up all kinds of ways to revamp our training. Thankfully, I had a more objective, scientifically based form of evidence to check my enthusiasm. Professor Sykes and I were unable to locate any studies that specifically examined imagery in competitive gymnastics, so we cannot say for sure that it will help with the types of activities I am working on. Still, the results of the research are promising for two reasons. First, in multiple laboratory experiments the imagery groups have outperformed control groups, so we can be confident that imagery can improve performance. Second, researchers are beginning to understand what types of imagery are best, so psychologists know *how* athletes should use imagery. Professor Sykes cautions that imagery cannot replace practice, but there is a good chance that it can supplement our physical training regimen.

The statements below will help you identify several aspects of critical thinking. Match the following critical thinking statements to the highlighted passages that illustrate them. Note that one or more of these may not appear in the article.

1. The author addressed overly emotional thinking.
2. The author examined the nature and quality of the evidence.
3. The author appears to tolerate the ambiguity rather than insist on certainty.
4. The author questioned whether Professor Sykes or the experimenters she described might be biased.

1. Yellow 2. Blue 3. Green 4. Not Addressed

The coach demonstrated several important aspects of critical thinking. Read on to find out how sports psychology is relevant to Coach Bolen's team.

How is imagery in sports psychology relevant?

Sports psychology is relevant to athletes who are looking for ways to optimize their performance, recover from injuries, and handle stress, among other things. Read how Coach Bolen is applying sports psychology at the end of his article and then share any newly formed thoughts you may have about sports psychology in the writing activity that follows.

> Based on what my staff and I have learned, we decided that it would be worthwhile to incorporate imagery training into our routine. We are only a month into it, so we cannot say if it is helping our athletes. However, I can provide some things to think about if you are considering doing the same. First, hiring a sports psychology consultant can eat into already strained budgets, and second, meetings about visualization will take up precious training time, at least for the first couple of months. But again, if our performance improves, I will consider it well worth the time, money, and effort.

SHARED WRITING

Based on the information the author gathered about imagery and sports psychology, and considering the sources the information came from, do *you* think he should make the investment of time and money in hiring a sports psychologist to teach his gymnasts visualization methods? Explain which elements of the article had the strongest effect on your opinion.

Chapter 1 Quiz

1. Psychology can be considered a collection of many related fields of study. What is one of the features that all of these fields have in common?
   - **A.** The use of the scientific method
   - **B.** The study of mental illness
   - **C.** The belief that the unconscious mind determines human behavior
   - **D.** The use of introspection

2. How would you apply the biopsychosocial model to a news report claiming that anxiety is caused by being around other people who are anxious?
   - **A.** Recognize that the news report considers all portions of the biopsychosocial model.
   - **B.** Recognize that psychologists do not regard biological factors when it comes to anxiety.
   - **C.** Recognize that the only effective treatment of anxiety must be drug based.
   - **D.** Recognize that the news report only considers one portion of the biopsychosocial model.

3. Which of the following is true about the concept of scientific literacy?
   - **A.** Only trained scientists are considered scientifically literate.
   - **B.** Scientific literacy is the ability to answer basic science questions without looking up their answers.
   - **C.** A person who can understand, analyze, and apply scientific information is demonstrating scientific literacy.
   - **D.** Knowledge of scientific terminology is the most important part of scientific literacy.

4. _____ is the belief that knowledge comes through observation and experience.
   - **A.** Determinism
   - **B.** Parsimony
   - **C.** Skepticism
   - **D.** Empiricism

5. How did physiologists and physicists, like Gustav Fechner, contribute to the development of psychology as a science?
   - **A.** They studied the relationship between the physical world and the mental representation of that world.
   - **B.** They demonstrated that the brain was responsible for consciousness.
   - **C.** They identified the locations of specific functions within the brain.
   - **D.** They extended Darwin's theory of evolution to behavior and cognitive abilities.

6. The belief that the unconscious mind has an influence on a person's behavior is part of which early approach to psychology?
   - **A.** Structuralism
   - **B.** Functionalism
   - **C.** Psychoanalysis
   - **D.** Behaviorism

7. The question of nature and nurture relationships centers on how _____ (nature) and _____ (nurture) influence behavior and mental processes.
   - **A.** environment; heredity
   - **B.** heredity; environment
   - **C.** emotion; logic
   - **D.** logic; emotion

8. Why was the perspective adopted by Wilhelm Wundt and his followers called structuralism?
   - **A.** They wanted to identify the major brain structures.
   - **B.** Their primary goal was to understand the physiology of the mind.
   - **C.** They focused their efforts on analyzing the elements of the nervous system.
   - **D.** Their primary focus was on describing the structure of conscious experience.

9. Which school of psychology questioned whether psychologists should study the mind, which was thought to be unobservable?
   - **A.** Psychoanalysis
   - **B.** Behaviorism
   - **C.** Gestalt psychology
   - **D.** Humanism

10. You attend a lecture by a psychologist who uses terms such as *free will* and *life's meaning*. Which psychological perspective is most consistent with the points the psychologist presented?
    - **A.** Behaviorism
    - **B.** Humanistic psychology
    - **C.** Functionalism
    - **D.** Psychodynamics

11. Natalia is in search of the deeper meaning of her life and would like to learn more about her potential as a human being. Which of the following types of psychologists would likely be most useful to her?
    - **A.** Humanistic
    - **B.** Gestalt
    - **C.** Behaviorist
    - **D.** Social

12. The Gestalt psychologists, with their focus on perception and experience, are closely linked to modern-day _____ psychologists.
    - **A.** developmental
    - **B.** social
    - **C.** cognitive
    - **D.** evolutionary

13. Francis Galton made a significant contribution to psychology by introducing methods for studying how heredity contributes to human behavior. Which alternative explanation was Galton overlooking when he argued that heredity accounts for these similarities?
    A. The primary importance of the nature side of the nature versus nurture debate
    B. The fact that people who share genes live together in families, so they tend to share environmental privileges or disadvantages
    C. A materialistic account of behavior
    D. The concept of dualism, which states that the mind is separate from the body

14. _____ psychologists are generally interested in how the behavior of individuals can be influenced by other people.
    A. Social
    B. Gestalt
    C. Behavioral
    D. Humanistic

15. Dr. Fernwood is a research psychologist. The main focus of her research is the use of psychological knowledge to find ways to reduce bullying in schools. Dr. Fernwood's research could be described as _____ psychology.
    A. basic
    B. forensic
    C. applied
    D. I/O

Chapter 2
Reading and Evaluating Scientific Research

Module 2.1 Principles of Scientific Research

Learning Objectives

2.1a Know . . . the key terminology related to the principles of scientific research.

2.1b Understand . . . the five characteristics of quality scientific research.

2.1c Understand . . . how biases might influence the outcome of a study.

2.1d Apply . . . the concepts of reliability and validity to examples.

2.1e Analyze . . . whether anecdotes, authority figures, and common sense are reliably truthful sources of information.

Several years ago, the Society for Neuroscience invited the Dalai Lama, the spiritual leader of Tibetan Buddhism, to their annual emerging science meeting to discuss the practice of meditation. For most people, meditation is understood to be a mystical, subjective, nonscientific practice embraced by individuals outside the scientific community. It is likely that no more than a hundred—if not fewer—of the Society's 30,000 plus members had a professional, scientific interest in the subject. Why, then, would the Society invite the Dalai Lama to speak about a topic that was clearly not based in science? Several hundred Society members were so opposed to the Dalai Lama's talk that they signed a petition to cancel his scheduled appearance. But according to the Dalai Lama, the members' opposing opinions about the value of meditation are rooted in the same thing: an almost complete lack of understanding of the practice. Without the benefit of careful observations and measurement, there really is no scientific way of saying whether meditation is worthwhile. Therefore, it is precisely this lack of understanding why scientists should be interested in meditation. In recent years, neuroscientists such as Richard Davidson and Antoine Lutz of the University of Wisconsin have confirmed that meditation does have numerous benefits. They have also developed models for how specific brain functions translate the practice of meditation into physical and psychological well-being. In Chapter 1, we argued that critical thinkers should be skeptical, as many Society members demonstrated. However, we also argued that critical thinkers should be curious and that their opinions should be modified to fit the evidence—something that Davidson, Lutz, and colleagues are working toward. In this chapter we turn to the process of gathering and evaluating evidence.

Perhaps the single most important aspect of scientific research is that it strives for objectivity. *Objectivity* assumes that certain facts about the world can be observed and tested independently from the individual (e.g. a scientist) who describes them. Everyone—not just the experts—should be able to agree on these facts given the same tools, the same methods, and the same context. Achieving objectivity is not a simple task, however. As soon as people observe an event, their interpretation of it becomes *subjective*, meaning that their knowledge of the event is shaped by prior beliefs, expectations, experiences, and even their mood. A scientific, objective approach to answering questions differs greatly from a subjective one. Most individuals tend to regard a scientific approach as one that is rigorous and demands proof. Although these are not inaccurate characterizations of scientific thinking and research, there is more to explore.

JOURNAL PROMPT

Qualities of Good Measurement: Imagine a class of students completed a 50-item multiple-choice test. Like the measures used in research, we hope that it is objective, valid, and reliable. How might we tell if it meets these three criteria?

The Five Characteristics of Quality Scientific Research

During the past few centuries, scientists have developed methods to help bring us to an objective understanding of the world. Whether you are reading about psychology or any other scientific field, the quality of scientific research should be judged based on the following five characteristics:

1. It is based on measurements that are objective, valid, and reliable.
2. It can be generalized.
3. It uses techniques that reduce bias.
4. It is made public.
5. It can be replicated.

As you will soon read, these five characteristics of quality research overlap in many ways. However, they are distinct enough and certainly important enough to consider each individually.

SCIENTIFIC MEASUREMENT: OBJECTIVITY, RELIABILITY, AND VALIDITY The foundation of scientific methodology is the use of **objective measurements**, *the measure of an entity or behavior that, within an allowed margin of error, is consistent across instruments and observers.* For example, imagine a team of psychologists is interested in how long it takes children of different ages to solve a specific word puzzle. Each time a child comes in for the test, a researcher will grab one of the stopwatches from their supply cabinet and carefully record the number of

seconds from when the child starts until the puzzle is complete. These scientists are using an objective measurement because they trust that they can accurately measure time regardless of the individual researcher (the observer) or the specific stopwatch they pick up (the instrument). To the extent that we can meet these criteria, we can say that weight has been measured objectively.

The term **variable** *refers to the object, concept, or event being measured.* The word *variable* reflects the fact that we only study things that vary; they might change over time or appear differently from situation to situation. This variability is what makes science interesting. For example, studying a variable like happiness would be dull if everyone was equally happy all the time, and in every situation. But happiness is a variable, and we can compare groups of people to see if we can understand why it varies.

Psychological science could involve an almost infinite number of variables and a substantial number of these can be recorded through behavioral measures: watching for specific actions and counting them; measuring for how long or how often they occur; noting their effects on the individual and on others; and so on. In addition, researchers have developed a wide range of *instruments*—devices and techniques for making objective measurements of variables. Instruments related to brain imaging allow scientists to measure differences in brain structures or the amount of energy generated in specific brain regions during a variety of tasks. Other instruments might involve computer software that can present words or images and record how long it takes for volunteers to respond to them.

Another common measurement method used by psychologists is **self-reporting**, *a method in which responses are provided directly by the people who are being studied, typically through face-to-face interviews, phone surveys, paper-and-pencil tests, and Web-based questionnaires.* Self-report instruments may include a survey that asks respondents to rate their agreement with a set of statements using, say, a scale of 1 to 7. It may inquire about shyness, mood, or political orientation. Other familiar instruments include tests designed to measure achievement and intelligence, for example, the SAT or ACT, which many high school students complete as part of their college application process.

Any method used by a researcher needs to include carefully defined terms. How would you define personality, shyness, or cognitive ability? This is the type of question a researcher would want to answer very carefully, not only for planning and conducting a study, but also when sharing the results of that research. **Operational definitions** *are statements that carefully describe the concepts being studied as well as the procedures and instruments being used to record observations* (Figure 2.1). To understand the importance of operational definitions, consider a study on the effects of meditation on stress (Creswell et al., 2014). What concepts, variables, and instruments should

Figure 2.1 Operational Definitions

A variable, such as the level of intoxication, can be operationally defined in multiple ways. This figure shows operational definitions based on physiology, behavior, and self-report measures.

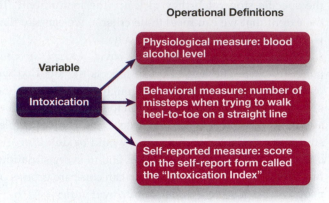

Operational Definitions

be involved in this study, and how might researchers begin to operationally define them? Figure 2.2 shows a summary of the variables used in this experiment. Note that the operational definitions in this summary provide a lot of detail, but the full, published report will provide even more detailed information. Ideally, the goal is to craft operational definitions that will allow other researchers to reproduce the experiment with the exact same variables as in the original study—such that when they do, the study yields the same results.

Operational definitions help ensure that researchers use measures that are as objective as possible. The quality of an instrument or method of observation is also judged by reliability and validity. A measure demonstrates **reliability** *when it provides consistent and stable answers across multiple observations and points in time.* In psychological research, several observers might watch the

same individuals to record instances of aggressive behavior. To achieve high reliability, researchers must carefully train the judges how to apply the operational definition. What specifically does someone have to do to be considered "aggressive"? What is considered not aggressive? Reliability criteria are not only important for judges; they also apply to mechanical instruments used for measurement, such as stopwatches, brain imaging equipment, and questionnaires. All of these instruments need to be consistent in their recordings.

Closely related to reliability is the concept of **validity**—*the degree to which an instrument or procedure actually measures what it claims to measure.* What if a psychologist claimed to measure intelligence based on shoe size? He could give a very clear operational definition of how to measure shoe size, and his measure should be very reliable—a simple tape measure should give the same answer (or close to it) each time a specific foot is measured. But no matter how consistently a tape measure yields a size 6 as a 6, or an 8 as an 8, it is not a valid measure of intelligence. Rather than shoe size, valid measures of intelligence might include problem solving and logical thinking—abilities that actually constitute the definition of intelligence. See Table 2.1 to practice distinguishing reliability and validity.

GENERALIZABILITY OF RESULTS Personal testimony can be very persuasive and compelling. Indeed, just a few people claiming great health improvements with meditation can tempt consumers to believe it is effective for everyone. Unfortunately, such testimonies are problematic: Although something may appear to be true for an individual (*Patrick was able to sleep better after taking up meditation*), it may not work for everyone else. In fact, we do not even know for sure that it worked for the person

Figure 2.2 Sample Research Report from an Experiment on Meditation and Stress

Meditation was operationally defined as three 25-minute training sessions using a specific set of pre-recorded instructional programs. Researchers provided information on where to find more details about these programs. Stress was operationally defined as the Trier Social Stress Test. This procedure involves three main elements:

1. Volunteers were required to make a self-presentation speech in front of two evaluators. The speech lasted five minutes, during which the volunteer tried to convince the evaluators that they should be hired for a job.
2. In addition, volunteers experienced cognitive stress through five minutes of challenging arithmetic. They were asked to count out loud, backward by 17, starting at the number 2083.
3. During both tasks, the evaluators remained cold and aloof, and interrupted to point out mistakes.

Stress responses were measured through two biological variables and one self-report. These were operationally defined as follows:

- Saliva samples were collected during specific afternoon hours before and after the stress test and then analyzed for cortisol, which is produced by the adrenal glands in response to stress.
- Blood pressure was measured continuously throughout the procedure.
- A paper-and-pencil rating scale was used as the instrument to measure perceptions of stress. Information on the specific type of scale is contained in the article and there is a reference for where to find more details in other research.

Table 2.1 Applying the Concepts of Reliability and Validity

Try this activity to see how well you can apply these concepts. Read the following descriptions and determine whether each scenario involves an issue with reliability or validity. When you finish, compare your answers with those provided in the module summary, objective 2.1d, on page 40.

1. Dr. Tatum is doing very standard physiological recording techniques on human participants. Each morning she checks whether the instruments are calibrated and ready for use. One day, she discovered that the instrumentation was way off the mark, and would surely give very inconsistent readings compared to previous days. Would this affect the reliability or validity of her research? Explain.

2. Dr. Nielson uses a behavioral checklist to measure happiness in the children he studies at an elementary school. Every time he and his associates compare their ratings, they find high levels of agreement on each child's happiness. Another group of psychologists observes the same children in an attempt to identify which children are energetic and seek excitement and which tend to be calm and more thoughtful. It turns out that the same children whom Dr. Nielson identifies as happy are also the children whom the second group of psychologists identify as energetic. Now Dr. Nielson wonders if he is really measuring happiness, or is he actually measuring energy level? Do you think it is a problem of reliability or validity? Explain.

making the claim (*Patrick's sleep quality might have improved by pure coincidence*). When we apply information and findings from one person to another, we are *generalizing*. In psychological research, **generalizability** *refers to the degree to which one set of results can be applied to other situations, individuals, or events.*

One way to increase the possibility that research results will generalize is to study a large group of subjects. By examining and reporting an average effect for that group, psychologists can get a much better sense of how individuals are likely to behave. But how large of a group is it possible to study? Ideally, it would be best to study an entire **population**—*the group that researchers want to generalize about.* In reality, the task of finding all population members, persuading them to participate, and measuring their behavior is impossible in most cases. Instead, psychologists typically study a **sample**—*a select group of population members.* Once the sample has been studied, then the results may be generalized to the population as a whole.

To ensure that findings within a sample generalize to a larger population, psychologists prefer to use random sampling whenever possible. In a **random sample**, *every individual of a population has an equal chance of being included.* If you wanted to study the population of students at your school, for example, the best way to obtain a true random sample would be to have a computer generate a list of names from the entire student body. Your random sample—a subset of this population—would then be identified, with each member of the population having an equal chance of being selected regardless of class standing, gender, major, living situation, and other factors. Obtaining a true random sample can be extremely difficult to do. In practice, psychologists are more likely to settle for **convenience samples**, *which are samples of individuals who are the most readily available*—perhaps even students in a psychology course.

Random sampling can help research results generalize across individuals, but research should generalize across specific contexts as well. In some situations, the generalizability of research findings can be influenced by where the research takes place. There are two primary research settings: *Laboratory research* includes any study conducted in an environment controlled by the researcher, whereas *naturalistic research* takes place where the behavior would typically occur. As you will see in the next module, many psychologists prefer to conduct their research in the controlled setting of the laboratory so that they can see how specific conditions influence behavior. However, the artificial nature of the laboratory can sometimes interfere with normal behavior, which in turn would affect the generalizability of the findings. **Ecological validity** *is the degree to which the results of a study can be applied to or repeated in the natural environment.* For example, imagine researchers discovered that a two-week meditation–training regimen improved the ability to concentrate during high-pressure tasks in the laboratory. Specifically, these tasks involved solving complex visual puzzles within strict time limits and the additional pressure of noisy alarms sounding whenever they made a mistake. That would certainly make for a high-pressure situation, but does it actually relate to the types of workplace situations in which we might want to help workers concentrate? If similar effects were found on the job—perhaps fewer errors made by air-traffic controllers or emergency-room surgeons—then researchers could claim that their laboratory research techniques were ecologically valid.

SOURCES OF BIAS IN PSYCHOLOGICAL RESEARCH
While creating objective, reliable, and valid measures is important in quality research, various types of bias can be introduced by the researchers doing the measuring as well as by the people or animals being observed. The **Hawthorne effect** *is a term used to describe situations in which behavior changes as a result of being observed.* Over the past century, psychologists have identified some common sources of bias that can affect research studies, including biases on the part of those who are conducting the experiments (researcher bias), and biases created by participants of studies who are aware that their behavior is under investigation (subject bias).

In the 1920s, researchers in the Chicago area studied the relationship between productivity and working conditions at the Western Electric Company's Hawthorne Works. When the researchers introduced some minor change in working conditions, such as adjustments in the lighting, the workers were more productive for a period of time. When they changed another variable in a different study—such as having fewer but longer breaks—productivity increased again. What was not obvious to the researchers was that any change in factory conditions brought about increased productivity, presumably because the changes were always followed by close attention from the factory supervisors (Adair, 1984; Parsons, 1974). Thus, research results are influenced by both the expectations of those who are observed, as well as those doing the observing.

Demand Characteristics and Participant Behavior

Results of psychological studies should provide uncontaminated views of behavior. In reality, however, people who participate in psychological studies typically enter the research environment with a curiosity about the subject of the study. Researchers need to withhold as much detail as possible to get the best, least biased results possible.

What do we know about how bias affects research participants?

When studying human behavior, a major concern is **demand characteristics**, *inadvertent cues given off by the experimenter or the research context suggest how participants are expected to behave.* Demand characteristics can range from very subtle to obvious influences on the behavior of research participants (Orne, 1962). They can lead to **socially desirable responding** (also known as social desirability), *which means that research participants try to present themselves in the most favorable way*—the most charitable or least prejudiced, for example. This type of bias is particularly relevant when the study involves face-to-face contact between the researcher and the volunteers.

Demand characteristics may be very subtle, but at times may seem rather obvious. For example, imagine you walk into a laboratory and a psychologist asks you to put on a heavy backpack. She then shows you a ramp and asks you to estimate how steep the ramp is. You would probably assume that these two events were related, and so the experimenter must want to know whether a heavy backpack will affect your judgment of the ramp. Even in this simple example demand characteristics have great potential to influence your response.

How can science test the effects of demand characteristics on behavior?

Using this same scenario with the backpack, psychologists have tested exactly how demand characteristics affect people's judgments (Durgin et al., 2009). In this experiment, undergraduate students were assigned to one of three groups. Group 1 did not wear a backpack during a task; Group 2 wore a 25-pound backpack with no explanation as to why; Group 3 wore a 25-pound backpack and was told that its contents consisted of electrical recording equipment that would measure the muscle activity of their ankles. To increase the believability of this procedure, actual electrodes with wires running to the backpack were attached to the ankles of members of the third group. One at a time, each participant was taken to the room that contained a ramp and was asked to judge how steep the ramp was before and after they stepped onto it. After completing the procedure, the participants responded to a survey that included a question about what they believed to be the purpose of the study.

The researchers found that volunteers in Group 2—those who wore the backpack without any explanation as to why—judged the ramp to be steeper than did members of the other two groups. On the survey, these same students reported that the purpose of the experiment was probably to determine how wearing a backpack affects steepness judgments. Students in Group 1 (who did not wear the backpack) and most importantly, those in Group 3 (who thought the backpack had a specific purpose) did not report this belief. Clearly, demand characteristics affected both the participants' perceptual judgment of slope as well as their beliefs about the purpose of the experiment (Durgin et al., 2009).

How can we critically evaluate the issue of bias in research?

While demand characteristics can influence the volunteers in a study, other types of bias can affect the researcher's behavior. Some classic examples of how expectations can influence results come from the research of Rosenthal and colleagues. In one study, they told teachers in 18 different classrooms that a group of children had "unusual" potential for learning, when in reality they were just a random selection of students (Rosenthal & Jacobson, 1966). After eight months of schooling, the children singled out as especially promising showed significant gains, not just in grades, but in intelligence test scores, which are believed to be relatively stable. Thus, the observers (i.e., teachers) found exactly the results they expected.

Experimenter bias can even be found when people work with animals. When research assistants were told they were handling "bright" rats, it appeared that the animals learned significantly faster than when the assistants were told they were handling "dull" rats. Because it is unlikely that these laboratory animals were influenced by demand characteristics—the rats were not trying to figure out what the researchers wanted—the most likely explanation for this difference is that researchers made subtle changes in how they observed and recorded behavior (Rosenthal & Fode, 1963).

Why is this relevant?

Given the time, energy, and monetary cost of conducting research, it is critical that results are as free from contamination as possible. Because of this, scientists that test new drugs or other treatments regularly give one group of volunteers an inactive substance (the placebo) so that they can be compared to a group given the active drug. This allows researchers to compare the effects of taking a drug and simply believing you are taking a drug; in many cases, the belief is enough to produce a **placebo effect**, *a measurable and experienced improvement in health or behavior that cannot be attributable to a medication or treatment*. Placebo effects have been reported time and again—not just with drugs, but with other medical and surgical treatments as well.

TECHNIQUES THAT REDUCE BIAS One of the best techniques for reducing subject bias—especially social desirability—is to provide anonymity and confidentiality to the volunteers. *Anonymity* means that each individual's responses are recorded without any name or other personal information that could link a particular individual to specific results. *Confidentiality* means that only the researcher will see the results. Ensuring anonymity and confidentiality are important steps toward gathering honest responses from research participants. Similarly, participant anxiety about the experiment can be reduced when researchers provide full information about how they will eventually use the data. If volunteers know that the data will not be used to diagnose psychiatric problems, affect their grades, or harm them in some other way, then their concerns about the study will be less likely to affect their performance.

Researchers can reduce biased responding from participants by using what are called blind procedures (see Figure 2.3). In a **single-blind study**, *the participants do not know the true purpose of the study, or else do not know which type of treatment they are receiving (for example, a placebo or a drug)*. In this case, the subjects are "blind" to the purpose of the study. Of course, a researcher can introduce bias as well, so an even more effective technique is a **double-blind study**, *in which neither the participant nor the experimenter knows the exact treatment for*

Figure 2.3 Single- and Double-Blind Procedures

In research, being "blind" means that individuals in an experiment do not know which group they were assigned to—a must in an experiment. This constraint can be applied just to the participants (a single-blind study), or, preferably, to both the participants and the researchers (a double-blind study).

Single-blind   Double-blind

any individual. To carry out a double-blind procedure, the researcher must arrange for an assistant to conduct the observations or, at the very least, the researcher must not be told which type of treatment a person is receiving until after the study is completed. Blinding techniques serve to reduce subject and experimenter bias, so ideally researchers should use them whenever possible.

Which kinds of biases might enter into the claims that meditation reduces stress? First, if a researcher stood to make money from showing the effectiveness of a specific meditation training manual or DVD, he or she could introduce bias into the study; even the most honest researchers could be unintentionally lenient when setting up or evaluating their observations. From the volunteer's perspective, just knowing the scientists believe meditation will help with stress reduction might be enough to lower blood pressure or cortisol levels, even without actually practicing meditation. Of course, we cannot be sure that these events would happen in an actual experiment, but a double-blind procedure would go a long way toward preventing them. Thus, before we give credence to a study's claims about meditation or any other subject, we would want to confirm that it was conducted with a double-blind procedure in place.

SHARING THE RESULTS One of the most important aspects of scientific research (as with any other scholarly endeavor) is making the results public. In Module 1.1, we discussed the scientific method and described the relationship between testing hypotheses and building

theories, which are central components of the scientific process. Sharing results is what allows this process to occur among groups of researchers working in different laboratories. In addition, a very important aspect of science is having the opportunity to repeat someone else's study to confirm or reject that researcher's observations and findings. Such processes are made possible by scholarly publications.

Psychology's primary mode of communication is through academic journals. Journals resemble magazines in that they are periodicals with a number of articles by different authors. Unlike magazines, however, journal articles are written by scientists to describe and explain their research or to review multiple studies on a single topic. Articles provide more than just the observations, however. They must include detailed descriptions of all the elements addressed so far in this module: the hypotheses, measures, instruments, samples, techniques to reduce bias, and so on. You will not find journals or research books in your average mall bookstore because they are too specialized for the general market, but you will find hundreds of them if you check with your school's librarians.

Before research findings can be published, they go through **peer review**—*a process in which papers submitted for publication in scholarly journals are read and critiqued by experts in the specific field of study.* Peer review involves two main tasks. First, an editor receives the manuscript from the researcher and determines whether it is appropriate subject matter for the journal. If so, then the editor sends copies of the manuscript to a select group of peer reviewers—"peer" in this case refers to another professional working within the same field of study. These reviewers critique the methods and results of the research and make recommendations to the editor regarding the merits of the research. In this process, the editors and reviewers serve as gatekeepers for the discipline, which helps increase the likelihood that the highest quality research is made public.

Science is an objective, ongoing, and self-correcting process. The finest, most interesting published research study can quickly become obsolete if other scientists cannot reproduce it. **Replication** *is the process of repeating a study and finding a similar outcome each time.* As long as an experiment uses sufficiently objective measurements and techniques, and if the original hypothesis was correct, then similar results should be achieved by later researchers who perform the same types of studies. Results are not always replicated in subsequent investigations, however. In the big picture, peer review and replication are self-corrective measures for all disciplines, because they ensure that published results did not occur through carelessness, dishonesty, or coincidence.

Subjective Thinking: Anecdotes, Authority, and Common Sense

In the preceding section, you read about what makes for quality research, and it is generally safe to assume that the opposite characteristics detract from the quality of research. Good research uses valid, objective measures; poor research uses subjective measures that are less valid, less reliable, and, therefore, less likely to be replicable. However, there are a few other issues to scrutinize whenever you hear someone make a scientific-sounding claim. How can we determine what to believe and how confident to be?

Poor evidence comes most often in one of three varieties: anecdotes, appeals to authority, and common sense. In an advertisement for a weight-loss pill, you might see a statement that an individual lost 200 pounds! This information is just **anecdotal evidence**—*an individual's story or testimony about an observation or event that is used to make a claim as evidence.* In this case, there is no way of knowing whether the diet was responsible for the person's weight loss; the outcome could have been due to any number of things, such as changes in food intake and lifestyle that were not part of the diet plan. In fact, you do not even know if the anecdote itself is true: The "before and after" photos could easily be manipulated.

The second kind of bogus evidence is the **appeal to authority**—*the belief in an expert's claim even when no supporting data or scientific evidence is present.* Expertise is not actually evidence; the term "expert" describes the person making the claim, not the claim itself. It is entirely possible that the expert is mistaken, dishonest, overpaid, or misquoted. True experts are good at developing evidence, so if a claim cites someone's expertise as evidence, then you should be perfectly comfortable asking whether the expert has peer-reviewed data to support the claim. True experts also understand that you have every right to be skeptical, so there is no harm in considering what the expert stands to gain by arguing for certain ideas and beliefs.

Finally, the purported evidence may consist of an **appeal to common sense**—*a claim that appears to be sound, but lacks supporting scientific evidence.* For example, many people throughout history assumed the world was the stationary center of the universe (see Figure 2.4). The idea that the Earth could orbit the sun at blinding speeds was deemed nonsense—the force generated would seemingly cause all the people and objects to be flung into space!

In addition to common sense, beliefs can originate from other potentially unreliable sources. For example, *appeals to tradition* ("We have always done it this way!") as well as their opposite, *appeals to novelty* ("It is the latest thing!"), can lead people to believe the wrong things. Claims based on common sense, tradition, or novelty maybe worthy of consideration, but whether something is true cannot be evaluated by these standards alone.

Figure 2.4 Beware of "Common Sense" Explanations

For centuries, it was obvious that Earth was at the center of the universe, with the sun and nearby planets orbiting around our planet—at least the Earth did not seem to be moving. Scientific explanations now tell us differently.

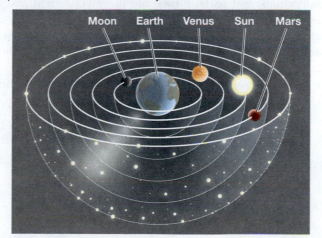

Module **2.1** Summary

2.1a Know . . . the key terminology related to the principles of scientific research:

anecdotal evidence
appeal to authority
appeal to common sense
convenience samples
demand characteristics
double-blind study
ecological validity
generalizability
Hawthorne effect
objective measurements
operational definition
peer review
placebo effect
population
random sample
reliability
replication
sample
self-reporting
single-blind study
social desirability
validity
variable

2.1b Understand . . . the five characteristics of quality scientific research.

These characteristics include (1) that measurements are objective, valid, and reliable; (2) the research can be generalized; (3) it uses techniques that reduce bias; (4) the findings are made public; and (5) the results can be replicated. For example, objective, valid, and reliable measurements make it possible for other scientists to test whether they could come up with the same results if they followed the same procedures. Psychologists mostly study samples of individuals, but usually they are more concerned about describing principles that generalize to a broader population. Single- and double-blind procedures are standard ways of reducing bias. Finally, the process of publishing results is what allows scientists to share information, evaluate hypotheses that have been confirmed or refuted, and, if needed, replicate other researchers' work.

2.1c Understand . . . how biases might influence the outcome of a study.

Demand characteristics affect how participants respond in research studies. Understandably, they often attempt to portray themselves in a positive light, even if that means not answering questions or behaving in a fully truthful manner. Researchers can also influence the outcomes of their own studies, even unintentionally.

2.1d Apply . . . the concepts of reliability and validity to examples.

Reliable and valid measures are essential to scientific research. Table 2.1 on page 35 provided an opportunity to apply your knowledge. In the first example, Dr. Tatum had to improve reliability; although her physiological instruments measured what they were supposed to (validity), they lacked reliability because they were inconsistent. In another example, Dr. Nielsen questioned the validity of his checklist for observing happiness in children. Although his team achieved consistent results (reliability), there was some question over whether it truly measured happiness, or perhaps just activity level.

2.1e Analyze . . . whether anecdotes, authority figures, and common sense are reliably truthful sources of information.

To evaluate evidence, you should ask several questions. First, is support for the claim based on the words or endorsement of an authority figure? Endorsement by an authority is not necessarily a bad thing, as someone who is an authority (expert) at something should be able to back up the claim. But the authority of the individual alone is not satisfactory, especially if data gathered through good scientific methods do not support the claim. Second, is someone supplying anecdotal evidence? As convincing as a personal testimony may be, anecdotal evidence is not sufficient for backing any claim that can be scientifically tested. Common sense also has its place in daily life, but by itself is insufficient as a final explanation for anything. Explanations based on good scientific research should override those based on common sense.

Module **2.1** Quiz

Know . . .

1. The degree to which an instrument measures what it is intended to measure is known as _____.
   - **A.** validity
   - **B.** generalizability
   - **C.** verifiability
   - **D.** reliability

2. When psychologists question how well the results of a study apply to other samples or perhaps other situations, they are inquiring about the _____ of the study.
   - **A.** validity
   - **B.** generalizability
   - **C.** verifiability
   - **D.** reliability

Understand . . .

3. In a single-blind study, the participants do not know the purpose of the study or the condition to which they are assigned. What is the difference in a double-blind study?
   - **A.** The researcher tells the participants the purpose and their assigned conditions in the study.
   - **B.** The participants also do not know when the actual study begins or ends.
   - **C.** The researcher also does not know which condition the participants are in.
   - **D.** The participants know the condition to which they have been assigned, but the researcher does not.

Apply . . .

4. Dr. Rose gives a standardized personality test to a group of psychology majors in January and again in March. Each individual's score remained nearly the same over the two-month period. From this, Dr. Rose can infer that the test is _____.
   - **A.** reliable
   - **B.** generalizable
   - **C.** objective
   - **D.** verified

Analyze . . .

5. You overhear someone claiming that 12-step programs are the only way to really quit abusing alcohol "Because my brother is a doctor and so he should know." Regardless of the accuracy of the claim, this and other appeals to authority do not qualify as good evidence because:
   - **A.** they always lack common sense.
   - **B.** authority figures are likely to distort the truth.
   - **C.** authority does not mean that the claim is based on sound, scientific evidence.
   - **D.** authority is typically based on anecdotal evidence.

Module 2.2   Scientific Research Designs

Learning Objectives

2.2a   Know . . . the key terminology related to research designs.

2.2b   Understand . . . what it means when variables are positively or negatively correlated.

2.2c   Understand . . . how experiments help demonstrate cause-and-effect relationships.

2.2d   Apply . . . the terms and concepts of experimental methods to understand research examples.

2.2e   Analyze . . . the pros and cons of descriptive, correlational, and experimental research designs.

Penguins are fascinating creatures to watch—some would even say adorable. In the past decade, they have been the stars of such Hollywood films as Happy Feet, Mr. Popper's Penguins, *and most recently, the* Penguins of Madagascar. *But if you want to know what real-life penguins are like, you should watch some of Yvon LaMaho's footage of emperor penguins. As a scientist, LaMaho wants to get a factual account of how these birds communicate, eat, and interact. However, like humans, penguins just do not act naturally when people are staring at them, taking notes. For this reason, LaMaho and colleagues developed robotic penguins that can move unobtrusively among flocks, gathering video footage as they go. It took several attempts before the team could design a penguin that looked real enough to be accepted by the flocks. Remote physiological sensors show that the robots can move among the penguins without triggering any stress reactions—the*

way human observation has done—and the rewards have been impressive. Scientists have been able to capture footage of behaviors never before witnessed by humans, such as of a female emperor penguin laying her single egg.

Psychologists always begin their research with a *research question,* such as "What is the most effective way to study?" or "What causes us to feel hungry?" or "How does attitude affect health?" When they develop a study to answer the question, they also make a prediction about the outcome they expect—the hypothesis. To guide this process, psychologists call on a variety of methods called research designs. Research designs guide investigators in (1) organizing the study, (2) making observations, and (3) evaluating the results. Because several types of designs are available, psychologists must choose the one that best addresses the research question and that is most suitable to the subject of their research. Before we examine different research designs, we will focus on the characteristics that all of them have in common.

- *Variables.* Recall from Module 2.1 that a variable is a property of an object, organism, event, or something else that can take on different values. For the penguins described previously, stress level can be a variable; any penguin will experience more stress at some times and less stress at others.
- *Operational definitions.* Operational definitions are the details that define the variables for the purposes of a specific study. For LaMaho's penguins, the operational definition of stress should include precise statements such as "a 10% increase in heart rate."
- *Data.* When scientists collect observations about the variables of interest, the information they record is called *data*. For example, data might consist of an individual bird's heart rate for one minute before, during, and after the approach of a human observer.

These characteristics of research designs are important regardless of the design that is used, and the same is true for the five elements of good research you read about in Module 2.1. Next, we will review the different types of designs that allow us to put these principles of research into practice.

Descriptive Research

The beginning of any new line of research must involve descriptive data. Descriptive research is not an attempt to explain a subject—telling why it happened; instead, it is an opportunity to present observations about the characteristics of the subject. Here are a few examples of descriptive research questions:

- How many words can the average two-year-old speak?
- How many hours per week does the typical college student spend on homework?
- What proportion of the population will experience depression or an anxiety disorder at some point in their lives?

As you can see, research questions address the appearance of a behavior, its duration or frequency, its prevalence in a population, and so on. To answer those questions, researchers usually gather data using one or more of the following designs: case studies, naturalistic observation, and surveys and questionnaires.

A **case study** *is an in-depth report about the details of a specific case.* As such, case studies are particularly useful in describing symptoms of psychological disorders and detailed descriptions about specific successes or failures in treatment. For example, researchers of one study described one individual's experience of a certain type of anxiety disorder and the steps used in therapy to treat the anxiety over a 16-week period (Elkins & Moore, 2011). They were able to document how and when changes in anxiety levels occurred and how the treatment affected other aspects of the individual's life. This level of detail would not be available if the authors had not focused on a single case. A drawback to this method is a low level of generalizability: A single case may not apply to others, so there is no guarantee that the findings can be generalized to other individuals and situations.

An alternative approach is to observe people or animals in their natural settings. When psychologists engage in **naturalistic observation**, *they unobtrusively observe and record behavior as it occurs in the subject's natural environment.* Most students have seen the television programs of scientists in search of animals in the wild—Yvon LaMaho's penguins starred in their own documentary called *Penguin: Spy in the Huddle* (2014). This certainly is a form of observation, but there is more to it than just informally watching animals in the wild. When a scientist conducts naturalistic observation research, she is making systematic observations of specific variables according to operational definitions. Naturalistic observation is also much wider in scope than the nature-programming images would suggest. In fact, one pair of psychologists managed to conduct their research in a bar: They observed the interplay of alcohol consumption and aggressive behavior (Graham & Wells, 2004). The lesson here is that naturalistic observation can occur anywhere that behavior occurs, and it can apply to any behavior imaginable. But remember—researchers still have to pay attention to specific variables, use operational definitions, and in some cases, develop robots that can sneak cameras into a flock of birds.

A final means of observation is self-reports, which include surveys and questionnaires (which we introduced in our discussion of objective measurements in Module 2.1). These methods measure individuals' attitudes, opinions, beliefs, and abilities. Despite the range in topics and techniques, the common element about these methods is that the individuals speak for themselves. The observations are provided by the people who are being studied rather than by the psychologist(s) who are studying them.

Correlational Research

Psychologists doing descriptive research almost always record information about more than one variable when they are collecting data. In these situations, the researchers may look for an association among the variables; they will ask whether the variables tend to occur together in some pattern, or if they tend to occur at opposite times. **Correlational research** *involves measuring the degree of association between two or more variables.* For example, consider these two questions:

- What are the high school graduation rates in each county of your state?
- What are the typical family incomes in each county of your state?

These two questions ask for very different types of information, but their answers may be related. Is it likely that counties with higher graduation rates also tend to have higher income levels? By asking two or more questions—perhaps through a survey—researchers can start to understand the associations among variables. Correlational research may involve any of the descriptive research designs mentioned earlier, but the data are evaluated in such a way that we can see relationships between variables. Perhaps the simplest way to do this is to present the observations in a graph called a *scatterplot*. In Figure 2.5 (a), you can see the data for education and income. The dots show a pattern that slopes upward and to the right, indicating that people with more education tend to have greater income. That correlation is not surprising, but it illustrates one of the two main characteristics that describe correlations:

- Correlations take a *direction*. They may be positive (Figure 2.5(a)), meaning that both variables occur together (such as education and income), or they may be negative (Figure 2.5(b)), meaning that the more of one variable, the less of the other (such as more sleep being associated with lower irritability).
- Correlations have a *magnitude* or *strength*. This magnitude is described in terms of a mathematical measure called the *correlation coefficient*. Correlation coefficients range from −1.0 to +1.0, but the closer it is to the absolute value of 1.0, the stronger the relationship. Figure 2.5(c) shows a zero correlation (no association between education and sleep), while the correlation coefficients for scatterplots (a) and (b) are closer to +1.0 and −1.0, respectively.

One key point to remember is that the correlation coefficient is a measure of association only—it is not a measure of causality. In many cases, a correlation gives the impression that one variable causes the other, but that relationship cannot be determined from correlational research. For example, psychologist Rod Martin (2004) has strong evidence that a sense of humor is associated with good health—this is an example of a positive correlation. But that does not mean that humor is responsible for the good health. Perhaps humor does cause some

Figure 2.5 Correlations are Depicted in Scatterplots

Here we see two variables that are positively correlated (a) and negatively correlated (b). In the example of a zero correlation (c), there is no relationship between the two variables.

(a)

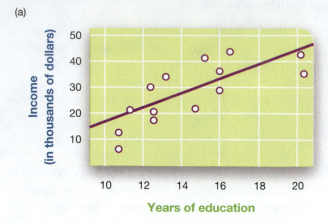

(b)

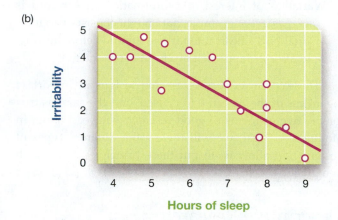

(c)

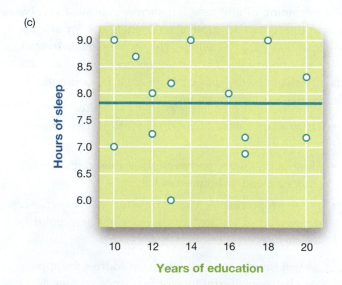

degree of health, but it is also possible that being healthy allows individuals to enjoy humor more fully. It is also quite possible that neither variable causes the other, but rather a third variable causes both good health and a good sense of humor.

Myths in Mind

Beware of Illusory Correlations

Chances are you have heard the following claims:

- Crime and emergency room intakes suddenly increase when there is a full moon.
- Opposites attract.
- Competitive basketball players (and even gamblers) get on a "hot streak" where one success leads to the next.

Many common beliefs such as these are deeply ingrained in our culture. They become even more widely accepted when they are repeated with such frequency. It is difficult to argue with a hospital nurse or police officer who swears that full-moon nights are the busiest and craziest of all. The conventional, reserved, and studious man who dates a carefree and spirited woman confirms that opposites attract. And, after LeBron James has hit a few amazing shots, of course his chances of success just get better and better as the game wears on.

But do they? Each of these three scenarios is an example of what are called *illusory correlations*—relationships that really exist only in the mind, rather than in reality. It turns out that well-designed studies have found no evidence that a full moon leads to, or is even related to, bizarre or violent behavior (Lilienfeld & Arkowitz, 2009). People who are attracted to each other are typically very similar (Buston & Emlen, 2003). Also, although some games may be better than others, overall the notion of a "hot streak" is not a reality in basketball or in black-jack (Caruso et al., 2010; Gilovich et al., 1985). On a more serious note, the sometimes hurtful stereotypes that people hold about others are often based on illusory correlations (Sherman et al., 2009).

Why do these illusory correlations exist? Instances of them come to mind easily and are more memorable than hum-drum examples of "normal" nights in the ER, perfectly matched couples, and all of the times LeBron James misses a shot, even in his best games. However, just because examples are easy to imagine, it does not mean that they represent the patterns in reality.

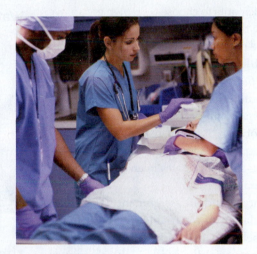

Contrary to popular opinion, a full moon is statistically unrelated to unusual events or increased emergency room visits.

JOURNAL PROMPT

Correlations and Causation: Several studies have reported strong correlations between the number of fast-food restaurants in an area and the rate of obesity; this is true at the city, state, and even national level. Does this mean that fast food causes obesity? That obesity leads people to purchase more fast food? Or is there some other variable that might explain the correlation?

Experimental Research

Experimental designs improve on descriptive and correlational studies because they are the only designs that can provide strong evidence for cause-and-effect relationships. Like correlational research, experiments have a minimum of two variables, but there are two key differences between correlational research and experiments: the random assignment of the participants and the experimenter's control over the variables being studied. As you will see, these unique features are what make experimental designs so powerful.

THE EXPERIMENTAL METHOD   The first unique element of experiments is **random assignment**, *a technique for dividing samples into two or more groups.* For the sake of illustration, consider the example from earlier in this module, about meditation helping people cope with stress. To test whether meditation causes the reduction in stress hormones and blood pressure, we would need to conduct an experiment. In this scenario, two groups could be formed, with participants randomly assigned to each group. Random assignment allows us to assume the two groups will be roughly equal.

Figure 2.6 Elements of an Experiment

 If we wanted to test whether humor causes a reduction in stress, we would first need to randomly assign people in our sample to either the experimental or control condition, perhaps by the flip of a coin. The dependent variable, the stress levels, would be measured following exposure to either humorous or neutral material. To test whether the hypothesis is true, the average stress scores in both groups would be compared.

Hypothesis: Humor causes a reduction in stress.

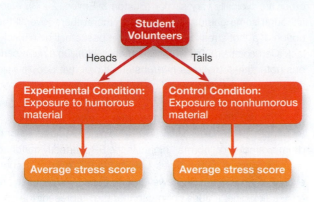

If we allowed the participants to choose their own group, we could not be sure that the two groups were similar to start with. When groups are not randomly assigned, any number of **confounding variables**—*variables outside of the researcher's control that might affect the results*—could potentially enter the picture. Numerous confounds are possible, and identifying which are most influential will depend on the nature of the study. In studies involving humans, researchers typically cannot control the genes an individual has inherited, the person's mood when he or she participates in an experiment, or the individual's personality.

Now, let us see how random assignment works with experimental manipulation of a variable (Figure 2.6). We need to distinguish between two types of variables. The first is the **dependent variable**, *which is the observation or measurement that is recorded during the experiment and subsequently compared across all groups.* In our example, the dependent variable is how participants respond to stress, and it is believed to depend on whether the participants

are exposed to the other. This second type of variable is the **independent variable**, *the variable that the experimenter manipulates to distinguish between the two groups.* In our example, it would be meditating compared with no meditation. The **experimental group** *is the group in the experiment that is exposed to the independent variable, which in this specific example would be a group of volunteers trained to meditate.* A **control group** *does not receive the treatment and, therefore, serves as a comparison.* In our example, the control group would not be involved in meditation. What if the experimental group showed reduced stress compared to the control group? Assuming that the experiment was well designed and all possible confounds were accounted for, the researchers could conclude that the independent variable—exposure to humor—is responsible for the difference. To review and reinforce these concepts, watch the following video Scientific Research Methods, which defines independent and dependent variables and control and experimental groups, and explains how experiments are designed and conducted.

Watch SCIENTIFIC RESEARCH METHODS

THE QUASI-EXPERIMENTAL METHOD   Random assignment and manipulation of a variable are required for experiments. They allow researchers to make the case that differences between the groups originate from the independent variable. In some cases, though, random assignment

Table 2.2 Strengths and Limitations of Different Research Designs

Method	Strengths	Limitations
Naturalistic observation	Allows for detailed descriptions of subjects in environments where behavior normally occurs	Poor control over possibly influential variables
Surveys/questionnaires	Quick and often convenient way of gathering large quantities of self-report data	Poor control; participants may not answer honestly, written responses may not be truly representative of actual behavior
Case studies	Yields detailed information, often of rare conditions or observations	Focus on a single subject limits generalizability
Correlational study	Shows strength of relationships between variables	Does not allow researcher to determine cause-and-effect relationships
Experiment	Tests for cause-and-effect relationships; offers good control over influential variables	Risk of being artificial with limited generalization to real-world situations

Table 2.3 Applying Your Knowledge of Research Terms to Understand Research Designs

1. Dr. Vincent randomly assigns participants to exercise versus no exercise conditions and, after 30 minutes, measures mood levels. In this case, exercise level is the _____ variable and mood is the _____ variable.

2. Dr. Harrington surveyed students on multiple lifestyle measures. He discovered that as the number of semesters that college students complete increases, their anxiety level increases. If number of semesters and anxiety increase together, this is an example of a(n) _____ correlation. Dr. Harrington also found that the more time students spent socializing, the less likely they were to become depressed. The increase in socializing and decrease in depression is an example of a(n) _____ correlation.

Answers: 1. independent; dependent; 2. positive; negative

is not possible. **Quasi-experimental research** *is a research technique in which the two or more groups that are compared are selected based on predetermined characteristics, rather than random assignment.* For example, you will read about many studies in this text that compare men to women. Obviously, in this case, one cannot flip a coin to randomly assign people to one group or the other. Also, if you gather one sample of men and one sample of women, they could differ in any number of ways that are not necessarily relevant to the questions you are studying. As a result, all sorts of causes could account for any differences that would appear: genetics, gender roles, family history, and so on. Thus quasi-experiments are actually correlational studies—they can point out relationships among preexisting groups and certain variables, but they cannot determine what it is about those groups that lead to the differences.

There are many decisions to make when designing a research study and each method has its pros and cons (Table 2.2). For example, naturalistic research allows psychologists to see behavior as it normally occurs, but it makes experimental control very difficult—some would argue impossible. Conversely, to achieve true random assignment while controlling for any number of confounding variables, the situation may be made so artificial that the results of the study do not apply to natural behavior. Nevertheless, each method has its own advantages, and luckily psychologists do not have to settle on only one. Most interesting topics have been studied using a variety of possible designs, measures, samples, and so on. When a theory's predictions hold up to dozens of tests using a variety of designs, we can be much more confident of its accuracy. Gain a bit of practice applying research terminology in Table 2.3.

Module **2.2** Summary

2.2a   Know . . . the key terminology related to research designs:

case study
confounding variable
control group
correlational research
dependent variable
experimental group
independent variable
naturalistic observation
quasi-experimental research
random assignment

2.2b   Understand . . . what it means when variables are positively or negatively correlated.

When two or more variables are positively correlated, their relationship is direct—they increase or decrease together. For example, income and education level are positively correlated. Negatively correlated variables are inversely related—as one increases, the other decreases. Substance abuse may be inversely related to cognitive performance—higher levels of substance abuse are associated with lower cognitive ability.

2.2c   Understand . . . how experiments help demonstrate cause-and-effect relationships.

Experiments rely on randomization and the manipulation of an independent variable to show cause and effect. At the beginning of an experiment, two or more groups are randomly assigned—a process that helps ensure that the two groups are roughly equivalent. Then, researchers manipulate an independent variable; perhaps they give one group a drug and the other group a placebo. At the end of the study, if one group turns out to be different, that difference is most likely due to the effects of the independent variable.

2.2d   Apply . . . the terms and concepts of experimental methods to understand research examples.

When you hear about a specific study in the media, or read about research in this text, be sure to think about the methods used. In order to analyze and think critically about the results, you will need to identify the type of study by applying the relevant terminology. Table 2.3 on this page provides an opportunity to practice.

2.2e **Analyze . . . the pros and cons of descriptive, correlational, and experimental research designs.**

Descriptive methods have many advantages, including observing naturally occurring behavior and providing detailed observations of individuals. In addition, when correlational methods are used in descriptive research, we can see how key variables are related. Experimental methods are used to test for cause-and-effect relationships. One drawback is that laboratory experiments may be limited in how far their results may generalize to real-world situations.

Module **2.2** Quiz

Know . . .

1. When psychologists observe behavior and record data in the environment where it normally occurs, they are using _____.
   A. case studies
   B. naturalistic observation
   C. the supervisory method
   D. artificial observation

2. The process of setting up two or more groups in an experiment is called _____.
   A. correlation
   B. observation
   C. random assignment
   D. selection

Understand . . .

3. What does it mean to say that two variables are negatively correlated?
   A. An increase in one variable is associated with a decrease in the other.
   B. An increase in one variable is associated with an increase in the other.
   C. A decrease in one variable is associated with a decrease in the other.
   D. The two variables have no relationship.

Apply . . .

4. A researcher sets up an experiment to test a new antidepressant medication. One group receives the treatment, and the other receives a placebo. The researcher then measures depression using a standardized self-report measure. What is the independent variable in this case?
   A. Whether the individuals scored high or low on the depression measure
   B. Whether the individuals received the treatment or a placebo
   C. Whether the individuals were experiencing depression before the study began
   D. Whether the individuals' depression decreased or increased during the study period

Analyze . . .

5. A researcher is able to conduct an experiment on study habits in his laboratory and finds some exciting results. What is one possible shortcoming of using this method?
   A. Results from laboratory experiments do not always generalize to real-world situations.
   B. Experiments do not provide evidence about cause-and-effect relationships.
   C. It is not possible to conduct experiments on issues such as study habits.
   D. Laboratory experiments do not control for confounding variables.

Module 2.3   Ethics in Psychological Research

Learning Objectives

2.3a Know . . . the key terminology of research ethics.

2.3b Understand . . . the importance of reporting and storing data.

2.3c Understand . . . the ethical guidelines that apply to research with humans or other species.

2.3d Apply . . . the ethical principles of scientific research to examples.

2.3e Analyze . . . the role of using deception in psychological research.

In 1932, 399 African American men from Tuskegee, Alabama, were recruited to participate in a medical study sponsored by the United States Public Health Service (USPHS). At the time, the USPHS was interested in observing the long-term effects of syphilis, a disease involving chronic degeneration of the nervous system, dementia, and, if left untreated, death. But, they needed human subjects. These men, who were mostly poor, uneducated, and lacked access to health care, volunteered. In exchange, the recruiting physicians promised them free medical care, transportation to the clinics, and a square meal for their participation. When these men volunteered, they were suffering from early symptoms of syphilis, but they did not know because they were never told. Instead, they were told they were suffering from "bad blood." Less than 10 years into this study, researchers elsewhere discovered that

penicillin could treat the disease effectively. By 1947, the drug became well established as a cure and widely available. Yet, the USPHS elected not to treat any of their volunteers. By the time the study ended in 1974, 28 of the men had died from the disease and 100 others suffered from problems related to it (Cave & Holm, 2003; Thomas & Quinn, 1991). The Tuskegee Syphilis Study, as it has come to be known, is an often-cited example of unethical research on human beings. Since this study, the rights of volunteers have changed dramatically. What separates unethical from ethical research? In the past three decades, much more attention has been given to this issue at all levels of society, by international health agencies, federal and local governments, professional organizations (such as the American Psychological Association), and the institutions that host and fund research.

All scientists share a core set of ethical responsibilities; they are expected to be honest with data and to give credit to those who develop new ideas. Psychologists, like many other scientists, study living, sensing organisms and are compelled to minimize any pain or discomfort that might be involved. In working with people, psychologists must consider additional ethical issues, particularly related to the participant's mental and emotional safety and comfort. Procedures discussed here are critical not only to ensure the individual well-being of the study participants, but also to maintain a positive and trustworthy image of the scientists who conduct research. This video, Ethics and Psychological Research, further describes the regulations and procedures that researchers need to follow to protect the health and dignity of research participants.

Watch ETHICS AND PSYCHOLOGICAL RESEARCH

JOURNAL PROMPT

Applying Research Ethics: Part of the scientific process involves withholding details of the study from participants. Is this an acceptable practice? Is deceiving research participants justified?

Promoting the Welfare of Research Participants

The Tuskegee study is an extreme case—extreme in terms of the harm to the victims, the disregard for their well-being, and its 40-year duration. Unfortunately, it is not the only such case in recent history. Such unethical treatment of research participants have led scientific groups around the world to develop codes of conduct to protect the human and animal subjects in research. In the United States, all institutions that engage in research with humans, including colleges and universities, are required to have an **institutional review board (IRB)**, *a committee of researchers and officials at an institution charged with the protection of human research participants.* The IRB is intended to protect individuals in two main ways: (1) The committee weighs potential risks to the volunteers against the

possible benefits of the research, and (2) it requires that volunteers agree to participate in the research.

WEIGHING THE RISKS AND BENEFITS OF RESEARCH
The majority of scientific research involves little risk of physical or emotional consequences. However, some research involves exposing individuals to brief periods of mild stress, such as placing a hand in a tub of freezing water, or engaging them in brief periods of exercise. Other studies present physical risks, for example, exposing participants to the virus that causes the common cold, or making small cuts in their skin to study factors that affect healing. More consideration needs to go into exposing participants to potential social risks, however, as humans are social beings with friends and families with social networks to maintain and reputations to uphold. As such, information about one's history of substance abuse, criminal records, medical records, and even information as seemingly benign as opinions about teachers or supervisors, need to be treated with sensitivity. Thus, when participants are asked questions about such topics, researchers emphasize anonymity and confidentiality (as addressed in Module 2.1). Similarly, research can present psychological risks, and so researchers need to justify how any negative emotional consequences of participating in a study are reasonable in light of what can be learned.

In general, we must think about the concept of risk broadly. In other words, everyone involved in the research process—the researcher, the IRB, and the potential volunteer—must determine whether the study's inherent risks are worth what can potentially be learned if the research goes forward. The psychologists who undertake such research tend to be motivated by several factors—including the desire to help others, the drive to satisfy their intellectual curiosity, and even their own livelihood and employment. Potential volunteers can be swayed by incentives, such as money. Others may fail to understand what their participation entails. In these cases, the IRB serves as a third party that weighs the risks and benefits of research without being personally invested in the outcome.

OBTAINING INFORMED CONSENT In addition to weighing the risks versus the benefits of a study, researchers must ensure that human volunteers truly are *volunteers.* Recall that the human subjects at Tuskegee were volunteers only in the sense that they voluntarily sought treatment for their "bad blood." These men did not know they had syphilis. And if they did, did they volunteer to have their disease go *untreated*? Had the men known the true nature of the study, it is doubtful that any would have continued to participate. Current practice is based on the concept of **informed consent**: *A potential volunteer must*

Figure 2.7 Informed Consent

Research participants must provide informed consent before taking part in any study. As shown here, the participant must be made aware of the basic topic of the study as well as any possible risks.

Informed Consent Statement

You are invited to participate in a research study assessing your attitudes and behaviors related to alcohol. We ask that you read this document before agreeing to participate in this study. Although the legal drinking age is 21, participants do not need to be of age, nor do they need to be regular drinkers. Participants must be at least 18 years of age and be willing to anonymously share opinions about alcohol. The study takes 30 minutes to complete. There are no risks associated with this study.

If you agree to be in this study, you will be asked to complete a survey and rate 40 statements about alcohol and alcohol use in your life. You may refuse to answer any questions and may withdraw from the study without penalty at any time. This research project has been reviewed and approved by the Institutional Review Board.

Thank you for your time.

__ I give consent to participate in this study

Participant Signature: _____ Date: _____

__ I do not wish to participate in this study

be informed (know the purpose, tasks, and risks involved in the study) and give consent (agree to participate based on the information provided) without pressure.

To be truly informed about the study, volunteers should be informed of, at minimum, the following details (see also Figure 2.7):

- The topic of the study
- The nature of any stimuli (e.g., images, sounds, smells) to which they will be exposed
- The nature of any tasks (e.g., tests, puzzles) they will complete
- The approximate duration of the study
- Any potential physical, psychological, or social risks involved
- The steps that the researchers have taken to minimize those risks

Ethical guidelines often help to negotiate conflicting interests, and in psychological research the main conflict is between the need for informed consent and the need for "blinded" volunteers. Recall from Module

2.1 that in the best experimental designs the participants do not know exactly what the study is about, because such information may lead to subject bias. In these cases, researchers use **deception**—*misleading or only partially informing participants of the true topic or hypothesis under investigation.* The participants are given enough information to evaluate their own risks. In medical research situations, however, deception can be much more serious. For example, as you learned in Module 2.1, patients who are being tested with an experimental drug may be randomly chosen to receive a placebo. After participating in the research study, participants must undergo a full **debriefing,** *meaning that the researchers should explain the true nature of the study, and especially the nature of and reason for the deception.*

Once participants are informed, they must also be able to give consent. Again, meeting this standard is trickier than it sounds. To revisit the men of Tuskegee, consider what their alternatives were. The men belonged to a socioeconomic group that had little access to health care; thus, even if they had been fully informed about the nature of the study, they might not have believed that they had any other options. Such issues affect the nature of consent, so modern psychological research includes the following elements in determining whether full consent is given:

- *Freedom to choose.* Individuals should not be at risk for financial loss, physical harm, or damage to their reputation if they choose not to participate.
- *Equal opportunities.* Volunteers should have choices. For example, if the volunteers are introductory psychology students seeking course credit, they must have non-research alternatives available to them for credit should they choose not to participate in a study.
- *The right to withdraw.* Volunteers should have the right to withdraw from the study, at any time, without penalty. The right to give informed consent stays with the participants throughout the entire study.
- *The right to withhold responses.* Volunteers responding to surveys or interviews should not have to answer any question that they feel uncomfortable answering.

Usually, these criteria are sufficient for ensuring full consent. Sometimes, however, psychologists are interested in participants who cannot give their consent that easily. If researchers are studying children or individuals with mental disabilities, some severe psychiatric disorders, or certain neurological conditions, then a third party must give consent on behalf of the participant. This usually amounts to a parent or next-of-kin and, of course, all the rules of informed consent still apply. You can apply principles of research ethics to the scenarios in Table. 2.4.

Table 2.4 Applying Research Ethics

Read the following two scenarios and identify why they may fail to meet ethical standards. Compare your answers to those provided in the Module Summary, Objective 2.3d on page 53.

Dr. Nguyen wants to expose individuals first to a virus that causes people to experience colds, and then to varying levels of exercise to test whether exercise either facilitates or inhibits recovery. She is concerned that people will not volunteer if they know they may experience a cold, so she wants to give them the informed consent after completing the study.

Researchers set up a study on sexuality that involves answering a series of questions in an online survey. At the end of each page of the survey, the software checks whether all of the questions are answered; it will not continue if any questions are left blank. Students cannot advance to the end of the survey and receive credit for participation until they answer all the questions.

The Welfare of Animals in Research

Many people who have never taken a psychology course view psychology as the study of human behavior, possibly because most psychological research does involve humans. But research with animals is just as important to psychological science for many reasons. One of the most significant reasons is that scientists can administer treatment to animals that could never be applied to humans. Animal models have proved highly beneficial to modern research on medical treatments and vaccines. In addition, genetic research requires species with much shorter life spans than our own so that several successive generations can be observed. Finally, scientists can manipulate the breeding of laboratory animals to meet the needs of their experimental procedures. Selective breeding allows researchers to study highly similar groups of subjects, which helps control for individual differences based on genetic factors.

Many ethical standards for animal research were developed at the same time as those for human research. In fact, colleges and universities have established committees responsible for the ethical treatment of animals, which are in some ways similar to IRBs that monitor human research. To be sure, there are differences in standards applied to human research and animal research; for example, we obviously do not ask for informed consent from animals. Nevertheless, similar procedures have been put in place to ensure that risk and discomfort are managed in a humane way, and that the pain or stress an animal may experience can be justified by the potential scientific value of the research.

Researchers and animal welfare committees emphasize three main areas of ethical treatment. The first is the basic care of laboratory animals—that is, providing appropriate housing, feeding, and sanitation for the species. The second is minimization of any pain or discomfort experienced by the animals. Third, although it is rare for a study to require discomfort, when it is necessary, the researchers must ensure that the pain can be justified by the potential benefits of the research.

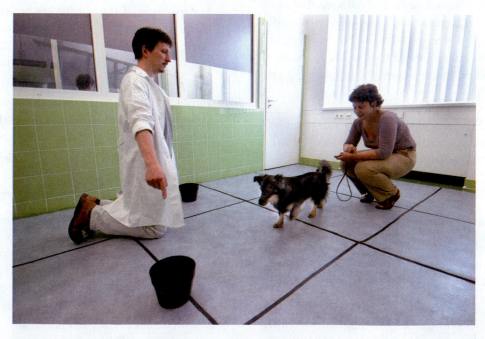

Many psychologists use animals in their research, so ethical codes have been extended to cover nonhuman species.

Ethical Collection, Storage, and Reporting of Data

Ethical research does not end when the volunteers go home. Researchers have continuing commitments to the participants, such as the requirement to maintain the anonymity, confidentiality, and security of the data. Once data are reported in a journal or at a conference, they should be kept for a reasonable amount of time—generally, three to five years is acceptable. The purpose of keeping data for a lengthy period relates to the public nature of good research. Other researchers may request access to the data to reinterpret it, or perhaps examine the data before attempting to replicate the findings. It might seem as though the confidentiality requirement conflicts with the need to make data public, but this is not necessarily true. For example, if the data are anonymous, then none of the participants will be affected if and when the data are shared.

In addition to keeping data safe, scientists must be honest with their data. Some researchers experience great external pressure to obtain certain results. These pressures may relate to receiving tenure at a university; gaining funding from a governmental, industrial, or non-profit agency; or providing evidence that a product (for example, a medical treatment for depression) is effective. Unfortunately, cases of scientific misconduct sometimes arise when individuals fabricate or manipulate their data to fit their desired results. These cases seem to be rare and, due to the public aspect of good research, other scientists are likely to find that the study cannot be replicated in such instances. It is also possible to minimize the pressures by requiring researchers to acknowledge any potential conflicts of interest, which might include personal financial gain from an institution or company that funded the work. If you look at most published journal articles, you will see a footnote indicating which agency or organization provided the funds for the study. This annotation is not just a goodwill gesture; it also informs the public when there is the potential for a company or government agency to influence research.

Module **2.3** Summary

2.3a Know . . . the key terminology of research ethics:

debriefing
deception
informed consent
institutional review board (IRB)

2.3b Understand . . . the importance of reporting and storing data.

Making data public allows scientific peers, as well as the general public, to have access to the details of research studies. This information includes details about participants, the procedures they experienced, and the outcome of the study. Furthermore, the requirement that data be stored allows fellow researchers to verify reports as well as examine the study for any possible misconduct. Fortunately, such cases are rare.

2.3c Understand . . . the ethical guidelines that apply to research with humans or other species.

Humans must be able to give fully informed consent, meaning that they understand the risks and benefits of participating and are freely volunteering. Note that some people (such as young children) may not fully understand, while others (such as prisoners) may not feel like they have a choice. Further efforts should be used to protect their safety and privacy. There are times when scientists need to control genetic and environmental variables that cannot be ethically controlled in samples of humans. In these cases, researchers may use animals as long as they can demonstrate the importance of the experiment and reduce the animals' discomfort to the greatest extent possible.

2.3d Apply . . . the ethical principles of scientific research to examples.

If you are ever asked to participate in psychological research, you should receive informed consent information before you begin. If the researcher fails to do so, you should ask for it, and then apply your knowledge of research ethics to make sure you can give fully informed consent. Table 2.4, Applying Research Ethics, gave you an opportunity to apply your knowledge from a slightly different perspective—the perspective of someone evaluating research. Be sure to review what you learned for practice. The exercise in the table raised two questions, and the answers we have are as follows: Scenario 1 is not really informed consent if the volunteers are exposed to risks before signing the consent form. The "informed" part of informed consent means that individuals are fully informed about risks they may experience as a result of participating in the study. Scenario 2 is unethical because it requires volunteers to answer all of the questions in a survey. Participants generally have the right to quit at any time, or to decline to answer any specific questions they choose. This issue is particularly important with sensitive topics such as sexuality.

2.3e Analyze . . . the role of using deception in psychological research.

It is often the case that fully disclosing the purpose of a study before people participate in it would render the results useless. Thus, specific details of the study may not provided during informed consent (although all potential risks are disclosed). When deception of any kind is used, researchers must justify that the benefits of doing so outweigh the costs.

Module 2.3 Quiz

Know . . .

1. The Institutional Review Board (IRB) is a committee that determines:
   A. whether a hypothesis is valid.
   B. whether the benefits of a proposed study outweigh its potential risks.
   C. whether a study should be published in a scientific journal.
   D. whether animal research is overall an ethical practice.

Understand . . .

2. Which of the following is not a requirement for informed consent?
   A. Participants need to know the nature of the stimuli to which they will be exposed.
   B. Participants need to understand any potential physical, psychological, or social risks involved in the research.
   C. Participants need to have a face-to-face meeting with the researcher before volunteering.
   D. Participants need to know the approximate duration of the study.

3. Researchers should store their data after they present or publish it because:
   A. other researchers may want to examine the data before conducting a replication study.
   B. it helps maintain the anonymity of the participants.
   C. the process of informed consent requires it.
   D. research participants may want to examine it.

Apply . . .

4. After completing a naturalistic observation study, a researcher does not quite have enough evidence to support her hypothesis. If she decides to go back to her records and slightly alters a few of the observations to fit her hypothesis, she is engaging in _____.
   A. scientific forgery
   B. scientific misconduct
   C. correcting the data
   D. ethical behavior

Analyze . . .

5. In a memory study, researchers have participants study a list of words, and then tell them it was the wrong list and that they should forget it. This deception is meant to see how effectively participants can forget something they have already studied. If the researchers plan to debrief the participants afterward, would this design meet the standards of an ethical study?
   A. No, it is not okay to mislead individuals during the course of a study.
   B. Yes, given that the participants are not at risk and that they will be debriefed, this seems to be an ethical study.
   C. No. The participants are likely to become angry when they learn about the deception, and research should not cause negative emotions.
   D. Yes, because participants fully understood all important aspects of the study and so debriefing is not even necessary.

Module **2.4** A Statistical Primer

Learning Objectives

2.4a Know . . . the key terminology of statistics.

2.4b Understand . . . how and why psychologists use significance tests.

2.4c Apply . . . your knowledge to interpret the most frequently used types of graphs.

2.4d Analyze . . . the choice of central tendency statistics based on the shape of the distribution.

2.4e Analyze . . . the conclusions that psychologists can reach based on significance tests.

Would you be surprised to learn that even infants and toddlers can think about probability, the foundation of statistics? Professor Allison Gopnik (2010) writes about some interesting experiments showing just how statistically minded young children are. For example, consider the illustration below. If a researcher reached in and randomly selected five balls, would you be more surprised if they were all red or all white? If you are as smart as an infant, you would be more surprised if they were all red. In another experiment, Gopnik's research team placed blue and yellow blocks into a fancy contraption. Yellow blocks appeared to make the machine light up two

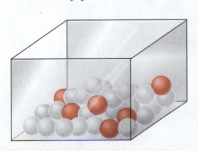

out of three times, whereas the blue blocks only seemed to work two out of six times. When asked to "make the machine light up," preschoolers selected the yellow blocks, which had a higher probability of working. If eight-month-olds and preschoolers can think statistically, adults should also be able to do so!

The analysis of scientific data typically begins with organizing numbers into ways that can be summarized and visualized; this provides an overall picture of trends and the outcome of the research. In addition, researchers analyze the data with statistical procedures to determine whether the outcomes confirm or refute a hypothesis. How do psychologists use statistics to describe their observations? How are statistics useful in testing the results of experiments?

Descriptive Statistics

Once research data have been collected, psychologists use **descriptive statistics**, *a set of techniques used to organize, summarize, and interpret data.* In most research, the statistics used to describe and understand the data are of three types: frequency, central tendency, and variability.

FREQUENCY Often, the first step in understanding data is to prepare a graph. This depiction of the data allows researchers to see what is often called the *distribution*, the location of where the scores cluster on a number line and to what degree they are spread out. In Figure 2.8, you can see what you probably already know is a bar graph. Researchers often present data in a type of bar graph called a *histogram*. Like other bar graphs, the vertical axis shows the **frequency**, *the number of observations that fall within a certain category or range of scores.* These graphs are generally very easy to interpret: The higher the bar, the more scores that fall into the specific range. For example, if you look on the horizontal axis in Figure 2.8, you will see a column of test scores corresponding to people who scored around 500 on the test. Looking over to the vertical axis, you will see there were four individuals in that range. Histograms are a great way to present data but, as you will soon read, we can present the same data with a smooth line called a curve.

It is usually easy to describe the distribution of scores from a histogram. By examining changes in frequency across the horizontal axis—basically by describing the heights of the bars—we can learn something about the variable. Where would you say the most scores cluster together? And how would you describe the way they spread out?

Figure 2.8 Graphing Psychological Data

The frequency of standardized test scores forming a normal curve.

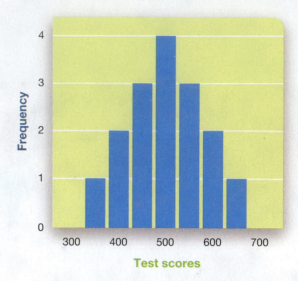

Although there are specific mathematical ways of answering these questions, we are still safe in making an estimate based on the graph: The scores appear to cluster around 500 and they spread out between 350 and 650. Remember that we are just making estimates, so we can describe this spread as a symmetrical curve, meaning that the left half is the mirror image of the right half. A **normal distribution** (sometimes called the bell curve) is *a symmetrical distribution with values clustered around a central, mean value.*

Many variables wind up in a normal distribution, such as the scores on most standardized tests or the

Figure 2.9 Skewed Distributions

Positively and negatively skewed distributions are clustered on one side and spread out on the other.

This negatively skewed distribution shows the class grades on a relatively easy quiz.

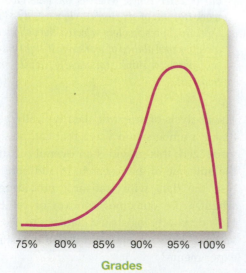

This positively skewed distribution shows that most students finished the quiz in less than 6 minutes— while a small number of students took up to 14 minutes.

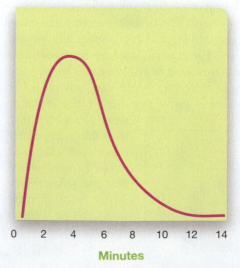

average amount of sleep adult humans get each night. Other variables have what is known as a skewed distribution, like the ones shown in Figure 2.9. A **negatively skewed distribution** *occurs when the curve has an extended tail to the left of the cluster.* A **positively skewed distribution** *occurs when the long tail is on the right of the cluster.* Most of the time, skews occur because there is an upper or lower limit to the data. For example, a person cannot take less than 0 minutes to complete a quiz, so a curve depicting times to complete a quiz cannot continue indefinitely to the left, beyond the zero point. In contrast, just one person could take a very long time to complete a quiz, causing the right side of the curve to extend far to the right.

CENTRAL TENDENCY   When we identified the portion of the graph where the scores seem to cluster together, we were estimating **central tendency**—*a measure of the central point of a distribution.* Psychologists choose to calculate central tendency by using one of three measures. The **mean** *is the arithmetic average of a set of numbers.* In Figure 2.10, you can see that the mean is $30,000, which is exactly in the center of the histogram.

A second measure of central tendency is the **median**, *the 50th percentile*—the point on the horizontal axis at which 50% of all observations are lower, and 50% of all observations are higher. The third and final measure of central tendency is the **mode**, *which is the category with the highest frequency* (that is, the category with the most observations). In the histogram showing a normal distribution of incomes, the mode is the same as the mean and median—$30,000 has the highest frequency, which, as seen in Figure 2.10, is 3. However, the mean and the median usually give us more information about the **central tendency** (*that is, where the scores cluster*), so the mode is typically only used when dealing with categories of data. For example, when you vote for a candidate, the mode represents the candidate with the most votes, and (in most cases) that person wins.

Notice that in Figure 2.11 the mean, median, and mode are the same. This is not always the case, but it is true for perfectly symmetrical curves. In contrast, if the histogram spreads out in one direction—in Figure 2.11, it is positively skewed—we are usually better off calculating central tendency by using the median. Notice what happens when you start to add extremely wealthy households to the data set: The tail extends to the right and the mean is pulled in that direction. The longer the tail, the more the mean is pulled away from the center of the curve. By comparison, the median stays relatively stable, so it is a better choice for describing central tendency when dealing with skewed data.

The mean, median, and mode are three favored measures of central tendency. Although you have often heard (and probably used) the terms "average" and "typical," you may not have realized that there were three ways to

---

Figure 2.10 Central Tendency in Symmetrical Distributions

This symmetrical histogram shows the annual income of nine randomly sampled households. Notice that the mean, median, and mode are all in the same spot—this is charactersitic of normal distributions.

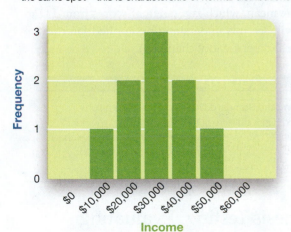

The graph shows that these nine households have the following incomes:

$10,000
$20,000
$20,000
$30,000
$30,000
$30,000
$40,000
$40,000
$50,000

Total = $270,000

Mean income per household:
$270,000 ÷ 9 = $30,000

Median (halfway between the lowest and highest numbers):
$30,000 (10, 20, 20, 30—30—30, 40, 40, 50)

Mode (most frequent number): $30,000

Figure 2.11 Central Tendency in Skewed Distributions

The mean is not always the ideal measure of central tendency. In this example, the mode and the median are actually more indicative of how much money most people make.

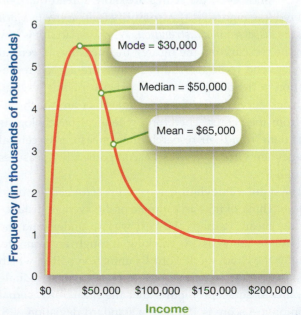

Mode = $30,000
Median = $50,000
Mean = $65,000

Figure 2.12 Applying Your Knowledge

This histogram shows the grades from a quiz in a statistics course. Complete the questions below and check your answers on page 60 under Objective 2.4c.

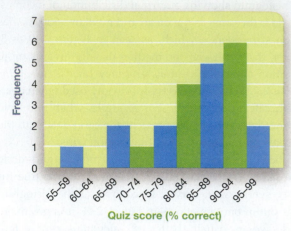

Questions:

1. What is the shape of this distribution? Normal, negatively skewed, or positively skewed?
2. What grade range is the mode for this class?
3. How many people earned a grade in the "B" range (between 80 and 89)?

Figure 2.13 Visualizing Variability

Imagine that these curves show how two classes fared on a 20-point quiz. Both classes averaged scores of 15 points. However, the students in one class (depicted in red) scored much more similarly to one another compared to students in another class (depicted in black), whose scores showed greater variability. The class represented by the black line would have a higher standard deviation.

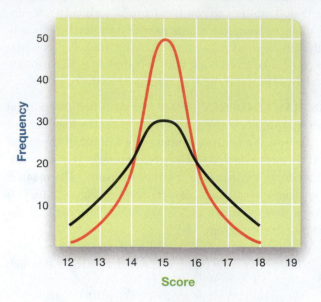

represent the middle of a distribution. Keep in mind that the function of these statistics is to describe an entire distribution based on a single number. When you hear someone say, "The typical value is…," remember to stop and investigate whether the measure the researcher chose to report is appropriate for that particular type of distribution.

VARIABILITY Measures of central tendency help us summarize a group of individual cases with a single number by identifying a cluster of scores. In some distributions, however, the scores are more spread out than clustered (see Figure 2.13). **Variability** *is the degree to which scores are dispersed in a distribution.* When variability is low (as in the red curve in the figure), the measures of central tendency tend to be the same, so they are a good representation of the distribution. But when variability is high (the black curve in the figure), some data are much farther from the center. Therefore, whenever psychologists report data from their research, their measures of central tendency are virtually always accompanied by measures of variability.

The **standard deviation** *is a measure of variability around the mean.* Think of it as an estimate of the average distance from the mean. Perhaps the best way to understand the standard deviation is by working through an example. Consider the Graduate Record Examination (GRE), which is a standardized test for admission into many graduate programs. If someone reports that the mean GRE verbal reasoning test score is 150 with a standard deviation of 8,

you should infer that 150 is in the middle of the pack and most people are within about 8 points on either side of the mean. (More technical calculations would tell us that roughly two-thirds of all individuals would score within 8 points of the mean, which is a range of scores from 142 to 158. (You will see this understanding applied later in the intelligence and personality chapters.)

JOURNAL PROMPT

Understanding the Standard Deviation: Imagine a survey question asked "On a scale from 1 to 10, how would you like to have a root canal?" Would you expect that to have a large standard deviation (a lot of variability) or small standard deviation (very consistent answers among individuals)?

Hypothesis Testing: Evaluating the Outcome of the Study

So far, you have learned about central tendency and variability, and perhaps you noticed that you cannot get the full description of what a distribution of scores looks like without one measure of each. You cannot tell where the scores cluster together without central tendency, and you cannot tell how much scores spread out without a measure of variability. Therefore, if a researcher winds up with normally distributed data—that is, the data appear in the bell-curve shape—she will report both the mean and the standard deviation for each sample studied.

Figure 2.14 Testing a Simple Hypothesis

To conduct an experiment on whether texting reduces loneliness, students would be randomly assigned to either text-messaging or no-text-messaging groups. Their average scores on a loneliness scale would then be compared.

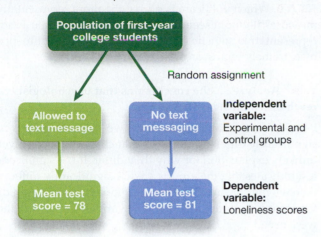

After researchers have described their data, the next step is to test whether the data support their hypothesis. Imagine, for example, that we wanted to test whether text messaging reduces feelings of loneliness in first-year college students. For three days, randomly selected students who regularly send text messages are assigned to one of two groups: those who can text and those who cannot. After three days, the students fill out a survey measuring how lonely they have felt. The diagram in Figure 2.14 shows us the key elements of such an experiment. Individuals are sampled from the population and randomly assigned to either the experimental or control group. The independent variable consists of the two groups, which includes texting or no texting. The dependent variable is the outcome—in this case, loneliness, with larger scores indicating greater loneliness. As you can see, the mean loneliness score of the group who could text message is three points below the mean of the group who did not text message. So, based on this information, are you willing to say that texting causes people to feel less lonely? Or have we left something out?

What we do not know from the diagram is the variability of test scores. We just emphasized that central tendency and variability should always be reported together, so we should add standard deviation to the mix before we determine whether there are differences between groups. On the one hand, it is quite possible that the scores of the two groups look like graph (a), which appears in the interactive. In that situation, the means are three points apart and the standard deviation is very small, so the curves have very little overlap. On the other hand, the scores of each group could have a broad range and therefore look like graph (b). In that case, the group means are three points apart, but the groups overlap so much—the standard deviations are very high—that they seem virtually identical. How, then, would researchers know if the difference in scores is enough to support their hypothesis? They would rely on the concept of statistical significance. If the outcome is like that for the groups on the left, where there is very little overlap, the difference is likely to have statistical significance. **Statistical significance** *implies that the means of the groups are farther apart than you would expect them to be by random chance alone.* If this study was replicated several times, members of the group who could text message would almost always report feeling less lonely. But now imagine that the outcome is like the one on the right of the figure, where the scores overlap a great deal. That outcome would be nonsignificant, which means that if we did the study again, the outcomes for the groups might very well be reversed—the group who did not text message might have a lower average loneliness score. Given how much overlap there is between the two distributions, small differences in mean scores will not be significantly different.

When we are describing these examples as significant or not significant, we are just making estimates based on the appearances of the scores. To determine whether their results are significant, researchers analyze data using a **hypothesis test**—*a statistical method of evaluating whether differences among groups are meaningful, or could have been arrived at by chance alone.* The results of a hypothesis test will tell us if the two groups are significantly different (different because of the independent variable) with a certain degree of probability.

Module **2.4** Summary

2.4a   Know . . . the key terminology of statistics:

central tendency
descriptive statistics
frequency
hypothesis test
mean
median

mode
negatively skewed distribution
normal distribution
positively skewed distribution
standard deviation
statistical significance
variability

2.4b **Understand . . . how and why psychologists use significance tests.**

Significance tests are statistics that tell us whether differences between groups or distributions are meaningful. For example, the averages of two groups being compared may be very different. However, how much variability there is among individuals within each of the groups will determine whether the averages are significantly different. In some cases, the averages of the two groups may be different, yet not statistically different because the groups overlap so much. This possibility explains why psychologists use significance tests—to test whether groups really are different from one another.

2.4c **Apply . . . your knowledge to interpret the most frequently used types of graphs**

Scientific literacy goes beyond just reading words, it also involves looking at images. Graphs are often used to summarize important data in a format that is relatively easy to read as long as you know what to look for. Be sure to review the activity in Figure 2.12 where you had a chance to apply your knowledge to examples. The correct answers are: **1.** Negatively skewed, **2.** 90–94, **3.** 9.

2.4d **Analyze . . . the choice of central tendency statistics based on the shape of the distribution.**

For example, incomes are positively skewed. Suppose one politician claims the mean income level is $40,000, while the other claims that the median income level is $25,000. Which politician is giving the more representative measure? It would seem that the median would be a more representative statistic because it is not overly influenced by extremely high scores.

2.4e **Analyze . . . the conclusions that psychologists can reach based on significance tests.**

If a significance test reveals that two or more groups are significantly different, it means that chance alone is a very unlikely explanation for why they differ. If the significance test indicates that the groups are not significantly different, then we can conclude that the individuals tested do not differ according to the independent variable for which they were tested.

Module 2.4 Quiz

Know . . .

1. The _____ always marks the 50th percentile of the distribution.
   A. mean
   B. median
   C. mode
   D. standard deviation

Understand . . .

2. A hypothesis test is conducted after an experiment to:
   A. determine whether the two groups in the study are exactly the same.
   B. determine how well the two groups are correlated.
   C. see if the groups are significantly different, as opposed to being different due to chance.
   D. summarize the distribution using a single score.

Apply . . .

3. A histogram is created that presents data on the number of mistakes participants in a study made on a memory test. The vertical axis indicates:
   A. the frequency of errors made.
   B. the total number of participants.
   C. the gender of the participants.
   D. the mean number of errors made.

Analyze . . .

4. In a survey of recent graduates, your college reports that the mean salaries of the former students are positively skewed. What are the consequences of choosing the mean rather than the median or the mode in this case?
   A. The mean is likely to provide a number that is lower than the largest cluster of scores.
   B. The mean is likely to provide a reliable estimate of where the scores cluster.
   C. The mean is likely to provide a number that is higher than the largest cluster of scores.
   D. The mean provides the 50th percentile of the distribution, making it the best choice to depict this cluster of scores.

5. Imagine an experiment where the mean of the experimental group is 50 and the mean of the control group is 40. Given that the two means are obviously different, is it still possible for a researcher to say that the two groups are not significantly different?
   A. Yes, the two groups could overlap so much that the difference was not significant.
   B. Yes, if the difference was not predicted by the hypothesis.
   C. No, because the two groups are so far apart that the difference must be significant.
   D. No, in statistics a difference of 10 points is just enough to be significant.

Module 2.5   Scientific Literacy Challenge: Self-reports

Chapter 2 defined the major research designs in psychology and described how researchers strive for the best possible methods. One critical feature of research is the use of objective measurements, such as behavioral observations and physiological responses. Another common measure is self-reporting, where individuals respond to written questions to characterize their behaviors, thoughts, beliefs, and feelings. However, not everyone is satisfied that self-reports can provide quality scientific data. Before you start this activity, take a minute to write about the value of self-report measures.

JOURNAL PROMPT

If a psychologist is researching what people believe or how they feel about a certain topic, should they just ask their research participants? What are some of the pros and cons to relying on self-reports for research?

What do we know about self-reports?

Read the excerpts of this opinion piece written by a psychologist and published in a psychology newsletter. Here, the psychologist questions whether researchers can trust self-reports; that is, can we simply ask people why they think and behave the way they do? Make sure you understand the terms and concepts in boldface from Chapter 2 and that you have a clear sense of what the writer is claiming.

The Climate Is Changing, and So Should Our Methods

By Felicia Mann, PhD

from *Psychology and Public Policy Newsletter*

When I try to gather some basic data on public opinion, I am often perplexed by the disparate, sometimes contradictory, results the pollsters find. For example, I have seen polls ranging from 17% to 67% agreement with the scientific consensus that human activity is responsible for climate change. These differences might reflect problems with reaching a **random sample** of respondents, but some people attribute the differences to the wording of **self-report** items. The cognitive psychologist in me is fascinated by language comprehension, so I decided to investigate the latter possibility further.

Before I continue, I should say that I am confident pollsters care about the **reliability** and **validity** of their surveys. I am confident that they know that elements of the wording, the question order, or even the affiliation of the survey author can be **demand characteristics**, shaping the responses people provide. However, I also know that a researcher's **bias** can lead him or her to unintentionally write questions, proofread their surveys, and interpret answers in a way that suits his or her own opinions. Therefore, I am proposing what seems to me to be a simple but very effective safeguard against bias: Scientifically test the quality of your self-report questions before you go to the public with them.

Clearly Dr. Mann understands how self-reports can lead to invalid conclusions. Let's look at how she applies scientific research to increase their validity and reliability.

How do scientists study self-reports?

In this section, the author introduces what she has learned from the scientific study of self-report methods. As you read it, make sure you understand the highlighted portions, which address the key elements of quality research, including the highlighted selections which contain clues to the quiz that follows.

> To see how this suggestion might be put into effect, let's return to the topic of climate change. Some of my colleagues actually tested the effects of wording in an experiment using the following question:
>
> *You may have heard about the idea that the world's temperature may have been going up [changing] over the past 100 years, a phenomenon sometimes called global warming [climate change]. What is your personal opinion regarding whether or not this has been happening?*
>
> Notice that individuals could be randomly assigned to hear one version of this question that used the terms "going up" and "global warming." Alternatively, some were randomly assigned to hear the terms in brackets instead: "changing" and "climate change." The difference between the two is that the former version emphasizes that the world is a hotter place than in the past. That's a tough sell when you are experiencing record cold temperatures. The alternative is that patterns are changing. That is easier to accept, especially if you have record highs, record lows, and record numbers of tropical storms on a regular basis. This was reflected in the results: 74% agree that there is *climate change* whereas only 67% agree that we're experiencing *global warming*. That may not seem like a huge difference, but look at the results from registered Republicans: 60% agreed with *climate change* whereas only 44% agreed with *global warming*. Interestingly, there was no such disparity for Democrats, who tend to agree with conclusions that scientists have drawn about client change.
>
> My colleagues and I have published other experiments showing that wording can influence how people respond to questions in other ways. People respond differently when they learn that the funding agency for the research being conducted has a known commitment to a specific political party (e.g., Democrat or Republican). When we ask about significant events, people judge what counts as "significant" based on whether we ask about the past week or past year. People will even give strong opinions for or against policies that do not exist, despite the fact that "I am not familiar with this policy" is a valid response option.

How well did you spot the references to important scientific concepts? Test yourself by completing this short quiz, referring back to the article to find the answers.

1. In the study of opinions about climate change, the dependent variable was
   a. the number of weather-related records set in a given year
   b. whether respondents had heard of global warming and/or climate change
   c. whether they believe the change "has been happening"
   d. whether they were given the term "global warming" or "climate change"
2. In the study of opinions about climate change, the independent variable was
   a. the number of weather-related records set in a given year
   b. whether respondents had heard about global warming and/or climate change before the poll
   c. whether they believe they change "has been happening"
   d. whether they were given the term "global warming" or "climate change"
3. You can tell that the main study is an experiment because
   a. it involved random assignment to one of two or more conditions
   b. the experimenters measured a dependent variable
   c. the experimenters reported a statistically significant difference in percentages
   d. the experimenters were able to compare Republicans vs. Democrats

Answers: 1. *c* 2. *d* 3. *a*

Dr. Mann was able to cite several studies that demonstrate how the wording or format of a question can affect the way a person responds. But does that mean that self-reports are totally unreliable? Let's read how Dr. Mann critically evaluates the research.

How should we think critically about the research on self-report methods?

Remember that critical thinkers continue to ask questions while evaluating the quality of the answers they find. As you read the next paragraph, be sure to look for signs of critical thinking.

> These are experiments, so we have compelling evidence that wording really does cause people to interpret and respond to questions in different ways. I have every reason to believe there are other elements of wording that can affect responses, but we do not know of them yet. We do not know for sure whether similar effects would apply to other scientific concepts. Does it matter if you ask about "evolution" or "natural selection?" Most of the general public are not going to understand the distinction between the terms, but I suspect we would find that wording counts.

The statements below will help you identify some critical thinking skills you should practice and common errors you should be able to recognize and avoid. Match the following statements to the highlighted passages that illustrate them. Note that not all of these items are included in the article.

1. The author is demonstrating curiosity by raising questions.
2. The author addressed whether the studies provide evidence of cause and effect.
3. The author states that some ambiguity remains.
4. The author identifies sources of bias.

1. Blue 2. Yellow 3. Green 4. Not included

Read on to learn about the recommendations for applying this information to improve self-report surveys and polls.

How is this research relevant?

It can be challenging to write high-quality questions for self-report measures, but failing to do so can produce invalid and unreliable results. Dr. Mann cites research showing that there are patterns in how the wording on a survey influences responses. Read about her suggestions to reduce wording problems and then share any newly formed thoughts you may have about self-reports in the writing activity that follows.

> In summary, I think polls are very important for understanding public policy. In fact, self-reports are essential to various academic fields as well, including my own field of psychology. We cannot do away with self-reports any more than we can convince every member of the public that global warming—I mean climate change—is real. What we *can* control is the quality of wording in self-report questions. I believe the best way to do this is to conduct brief experiments on the wording before collecting data; even a very brief study with two focus groups would do. For example, use the model described above to test two different wordings of the same basic question. If you find a difference in your results, you should probably ask both questions in your poll, and make sure to include both the answer and the responses when sharing your results.

SHARED WRITING

After reading this article, are you more confident or less confident in the results of polling and other forms of self-report data?

Chapter 2 Quiz

1. By studying a _____, scientists hope that they can generalize the results of their investigation to the _____.
   A. sample; population
   B. population; sample
   C. convenience sample; random sample
   D. random sample; convenience sample

2. Which of the following is an example of demand characteristics affecting an experiment?
   A. An experimenter draws the wrong conclusions from a study because she did not use the correct statistical analysis.
   B. A participant changes his response to a question because he has the feeling that the experimenter wants him to do so.
   C. An experimenter stops using a test because it does not appear to be reliable.
   D. A participant in a double-blind experiment believes she is in the control group.

3. Why it is a bad idea to draw conclusions from anecdotal evidence?
   A. Such conclusions usually go against common sense.
   B. Anecdotes are reliable only if they come from experts, which they rarely do.
   C. Anecdotes are a single-blind technique, not a double-blind method.
   D. There is no way to know if the anecdote is correct or if it will generalize to other people and situations.

4. What does a correlation coefficient of −0.94 indicate about two variables?
   A. The variables are weakly associated, with both increasing together.
   B. The variables are strongly associated, with both increasing together.
   C. The variables are weakly associated, with one increasing as the other decreases.
   D. The variables are strongly associated, with one increasing as the other decreases.

5. Most people would agree that anxiety can lead to sleep loss. However, Dr. Jenkins believes that sleep deprivation can also cause increased anxiety. Which research method would allow him to test a cause–effect relationship between the two?
   A. Naturalistic observation
   B. Experimental
   C. Correlational
   D. Survey

6. Which of the following statements describes the amount of cognitive and emotional risk to participants allowed in psychological research today?
   A. Any amount of risk is acceptable.
   B. No amount of risk is acceptable.
   C. A little risk is always acceptable, but more than minimal risk is never acceptable.
   D. The amount of acceptable risk depends in part on the likely benefits from the study.

7. The use of deception in psychological research is:
   A. not a serious issue.
   B. never acceptable.
   C. generally acceptable when absolutely necessary for the research.
   D. acceptable only in nonhuman research.

8. Under which of the following circumstances would the mean be the best measure of central tendency to use?
   A. The data have a normal distribution.
   B. The data are positively skewed.
   C. The data are negatively skewed.
   D. The mean is always the best measure of central tendency.

9. A teacher notices that on the last science test, some students did very well, while other students performed poorly or had grades in the middle of the pack. If she wanted to measure how "spread out" all of the scores were, which descriptive statistic could she use?
   A. Median
   B. Mode
   C. Standard deviation
   D. Mean

10. Keisha performs an experiment with two randomly assigned groups of school children. The first group is allowed 15 minutes of recess play before a math test, while the second group watches a video before the test. When she analyzes the test scores, she finds that there is a statistical difference between the groups, with the recess group scoring higher on average. Which conclusions can be drawn from this result?
    A. The difference between the scores for the two groups is probably due to random chance.
    B. The difference between the scores for the two groups is likely due to their differing pretest activities, and did not happen by chance.
    C. Students who are good at math prefer recess to watching a video.
    D. Students who are good at math prefer watching a video to recess.

11. Ann is convinced that corporal punishment (e.g., spanking) is a good way to discipline a child because she knows a child whose behavior improved because of it. Whether or not you agree with her, Ann is using a flawed argument. Which type of evidence is she using?
    A. Anecdotal
    B. Objective
    C. Generalizable
    D. An appeal to authority

12. Any property of an organism, event, or something else that can take on different values is called _____.
    A. an operational definition
    B. data
    C. a variable
    D. a case study

13. Imagine Dr. Martin finds that a sense of humor is positively correlated with psychological well-being. From this, we can conclude that:
    A. humor causes people to be healthier.
    B. health causes people to be funnier.
    C. people who have a good sense of humor tend to be healthier.
    D. people who have a good sense of humor tend to be less healthy.

14. Claiming that something is true because "it should be obvious" is really just _____.
    A. anecdotal evidence
    B. an appeal to common sense
    C. an appeal to authority
    D. generalizability

15. The _____ is a measure of variability around the mean of a distribution.
    A. mean
    B. median
    C. mode
    D. standard deviation

Chapter 3
Biological Psychology

Module 3.1 Genetic and Evolutionary Perspectives on Behavior

Learning Objectives

3.1a Know . . . the key terminology related to genes, inheritance, and evolutionary psychology.

3.1b Understand . . . how twin and adoption studies reveal relationships between genes and behavior.

3.1c Apply . . . evolutionary explanations to behavior.

3.1d Analyze . . . claims that scientists have located a specific gene that controls a single trait or behavior.

You may have heard about the Paleo or "stone age" diet, which plays up the stereotype of the meat-eating caveman. Proponents argue that this diet of the Paleolithic-era (which ended about 10,000 BCE) is ideal because it comprises foods that our body evolved to digest and use, not foods that arose with the advent of agriculture (e.g., wheat) and the domestication of livestock (e.g., sources of dairy). Paleo supporters argue that because the Paleo diet succeeded in sustaining the modern human lineage, why not return to it? This argument has a flaw: Our ancestors ate a variety of plant foods in addition to meat, and their life span on the Paleo diet was much shorter than that of individuals in modern society; this suggests that the contemporary diet (without the highly processed foods) may actually be better. Nevertheless, the evolutionary premise of the argument can still be hypothesized and scientifically tested. Let's consider, for example, the ability to digest dairy into adulthood, "lactase persistence," which likely evolved in the last 10,000 years (Bersaglieri et al., 2004; Itan et al., 2009). Evidence from anthropological studies

correlating the rise of specific digestive enzymes (lactase) with domestication and herding practices support this premise. In societies in which livestock provided a relatively safe and reliable source of nutrition (especially in Europe), more than 90% of the current population has the genes supporting this dietary adaptation. The reverse is true for individuals of non-European cultures (such as those of eastern Asia). More than 90% of these cultural groups remain "lactose-intolerant"; without this digestive enzyme, these groups have not adapted behaviorally, so dairy remains an uncommon staple of their diets. This evidence shows that evolutionary processes can influence not just bodily processes, but also our behaviors and cultural customs. Psychologists have applied this same evolutionary perspective to other human behaviors and characteristics such as dating and mating, emotion, personality, friendships, and even mental disorders. Evolutionary psychologists, therefore, examine the interplay between the environment and genes in determining our behavior. They reason that the brain, just like any other bodily system, has evolved to adapt to environmental pressures. Two fundamental questions we address here are: How can we determine the role that genes play in behavior? and What traits do we have that are especially relevant to survival and reproduction?

Heredity and Behavior

Examples of genetic influences easily come to mind when we consider physical traits because we tend to share our eye color, facial characteristics, stature, and skin coloration with our parents. Psychological research tells us that traits and behaviors are influenced by genes just as physical characteristics are. This research typically involves either comparing people of differing levels of relatedness (e.g., identical versus fraternal twins) or studying specific genes at the molecular level. Before we delve into this issue, let's briefly review some basic concepts of genetics.

THE GENETIC CODE Most of the billions of cells in the human body include a nucleus that houses most of our genetic code (some additional DNA is located in a cellular structure called the mitochondrion). **Genes** *are the basic units of heredity; they are responsible for guiding the process of creating the proteins that make up our physical structures and regulate development and physiological processes throughout the life span.* Genes are organized along **chromosomes,** *which are large molecules in the cellular nucleus that include the structures shaped like a double helix that are lined with all of the genes an individual inherits.* Humans have approximately 30,000 genes distributed across 23 pairs of chromosomes, half contributed by the mother and half from the father (see Figure 3.1).

Genes, which are comprised of **DNA (deoxyribonucleic acid),** *are the physical and functional units of heredity.* Each gene has a unique combination of amino acids that code for proteins that serve a specific function. Genes instruct cells how to behave, which type of molecules to produce, and when to produce them. Traits that show genetic variation, such as eye color, the shape and size of facial

features, and even personality, do so because of differences in the amino acids that comprise each gene, as well as through interactions with the environment.

The term **genotype** *refers to the genetic makeup of an organism.* The unique set of genes that comprise every chromosome represents the genotype of the individual, whereas the **phenotype** *consists of the observable characteristics, including physical structures and behaviors.* Distinguishing between the genotype and the phenotype is important when it comes to understanding how genes and traits are related. The genotype represents what was inherited, whereas the phenotype represents the physical and behavioral manifestation of the genotype through interactions with the environment.

Genes come in pairs, one inherited from each parent, aligned along the chromosomes. Genes at a given location on a pair of chromosomes can have different variations called *alleles*. If both alleles at a given location of the chromosome are the same, they are *homozygous*. If the alleles differ, they are *heterozygous*. The combination of gene pairs, or alleles, distributed across the chromosomes is the basis for much of the unique physical and behavioral variation we see among individuals. In other words, the unique genotype each person inherits gives rise to a unique phenotype. For example, your genotype determines whether you have the ability to taste a bitter substance called *phenylthiocarbamide (PTC)*. The laboratory test for whether you can taste PTC (the phenotype) is performed by placing a small tab of paper soaked in the substance on the tongue. Non-tasters cannot taste anything other than the tab of paper, whereas tasters can find it overwhelming. Even without the lab test, you can judge fairly accurately whether you're a taster or a non-taster based on your reaction to Brussels sprouts and cabbage, which also contain PTC; tasters are often taken aback by the bitterness of Brussels sprouts, whereas non-tasters get a sense for the other flavors (whether they actually like the vegetable is

Figure 3.1 Chromosomes and the DNA Molecule

In human cells, DNA is aligned along 23 paired chromosomes. Numbers 1–22 are common to both males and females. Chromosome 23 is sex linked, with males having the XY pattern and females the XX pattern. The nucleus of a cell contains copies of each chromosome. Chromosomes are composed of the genes arranged in the familiar double helix—a long strand of DNA molecules.

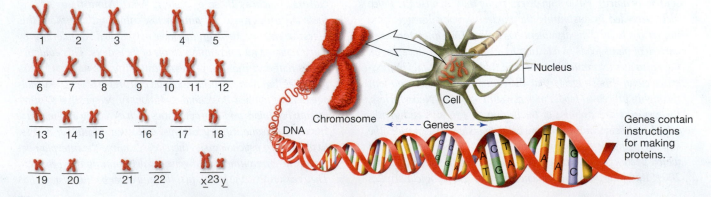

Biological Psychology **69**

Figure 3.2 Genetic Inheritance

Whether someone tastes the bitter compound PTC depends on which copies of the gene he or she inherits. Shown here is the statistically probable outcome of two heterozygous (Tt) parents with four children.

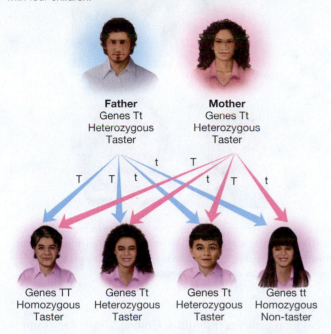

Father
Genes Tt
Heterozygous
Taster

Mother
Genes Tt
Heterozygous
Taster

Genes TT
Homozygous
Taster

Genes Tt
Heterozygous
Taster

Genes Tt
Heterozygous
Taster

Genes tt
Homozygous
Non-taster

another matter). Tasters have inherited at least one copy of the dominant allele for tasting (abbreviated capital "T") from either parent. People can also inherit a recessive copy of this gene (t). Those who report tasting PTC are either homozygous dominant (TT) or heterozygous (Tt). Non-tasters are homozygous recessive (tt); they've inherited a recessive allele from both parents (see Figure 3.2).

Human behavior is highly complex, and it is rare that normal behavior, or even disorders of the brain, can be explained as simply as in the PTC example. Although it is a helpful example, understanding the genetic contributions to characteristics such as personality, intelligence, and psychological disorders requires an understanding of gene and environmental interactions.

BEHAVIORAL GENETICS: TWIN AND ADOPTION STUDIES For centuries, the clearest evidence that behavioral characteristics could be inherited came from animal breeding, in which animals such as dogs were reared to be hunters, herders, protectors, or companions. Because we cannot use the methods of dog breeders to study humans, some alternatives are required. **Behavioral genetics** *is the study of how genes and environment influence behavior.* Behavioral genetic methods applied to humans typically involve comparing people of different levels of relatedness, such as parents and their offspring, siblings, and unrelated individuals, and measuring resemblance for a specific trait of interest.

Twins present an amazing opportunity to conduct natural experiments on how genes influence behavior. One method commonly used in twin studies involves comparing identical and fraternal twins. **Monozygotic twins** *come from a single ovum (egg), which makes them genetically identical.* An ideal comparison group, **dizygotic twins** (*fraternal twins*), *which come from two separate eggs fertilized by two different sperm cells, share the same womb.* Researchers around the world have studied the genetic and environmental bases of behavior by following different sets of twins for many years, or even decades.

Behavioral geneticists use twin studies to calculate **heritability**—*a statistic, expressed as a number between zero and one, that represents the degree to which genetic differences between individuals contribute to individual differences in a behavior or trait found in a population.* A heritability of 0 means that genes do not contribute to individual differences in a trait, whereas heritability of 1.0 indicates that genes account for all individual differences in a trait. Heritability estimates usually fall somewhere in between these two values. The estimated heritability for problems with depression and anxiety is approximately 0.76 for 3-year-old identical twin pairs (Boomsma et al., 2005). This tells us that 76% of individual differences in depression and anxiety at age 3 can be attributed to genetic factors in the population that was studied. Given that experiences inevitably accumulate with time, we sometimes see heritability estimates change as people age (Kendler et al., 2011). In the Boomsma et al. (2005) study, the heritability of anxiety and depression went from 0.76 at age 3 to 0.48 at age 12 for the identical twin pairs. This finding reminds us that the environment constantly interacts with genes.

Behavioral geneticists also study adopted children to examine genetic and environmental influences on behavior. If adopted children are more like their biological parents than their adoptive parents on measures of traits such as personality and intelligence, we might conclude that these traits have a strong genetic component. If the children are more like their adoptive, genetically unrelated parents, a strong case can be made that environmental factors outweigh the biological predispositions. Interestingly, young adopted children are more similar to their adoptive parents in intelligence levels than they are to their biological parents. By the time they reach 16 years of age, however, adopted adolescents score more similarly to their biological parents than their adoptive parents in tests of intelligence (Plomin et al., 1997; see also Plomin & Deary, 2014). Compare this finding to that from the study described in the preceding paragraph: For intelligence, heritability estimates seem to increase with age, whereas the opposite is true for depression and anxiety. To see heritability explained visually, watch the video Genes, Heritability, and Genetic Concordance, describing DNA and how we inherit traits from our biological parents.

Watch GENES, HERITABILITY, AND GENETIC CONCORDANCE

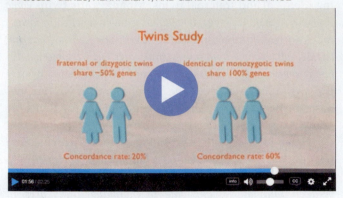

BEHAVIORAL GENOMICS: THE MOLECULAR APPROACH Twin and adoption studies provide estimates of heritability, but they do not tell us how traits are inherited or anything specific about the relationship between genes and behavior (see Johnson et al., 2009). To make this determination, researchers go straight to the source of genetic influence—to the genes themselves. **Behavioral genomics** *is the study of DNA and the ways in which specific genes are related to behavior.* The technology supporting behavioral genomics is relatively new, but once it became available, researchers initiated a massive effort to identify the components of the entire human genome—*the Human Genome Project.* This project, which was completed in 2003, resulted in the identification of approximately 30,000 genes. Imagine the undertaking: determining the sequences of the billions of amino acids making up the genes, including where each gene begins and ends, and how they are all arranged on the chromosomes. The Human Genome Project itself did not directly provide a cure for a disease or an understanding of any particular behavior. Instead, it has led to an abundance of new techniques and information about where genes are located, and it opened the door for an entirely new era of

Identical twins are genetically the same, whereas fraternal twins are no more closely related than full siblings from different pregnancies. However, fraternal twins do share much of the same prenatal and postnatal environment if they are reared together.

behavioral genetics (Plomin & Crabbe, 2000). For example, researchers can now examine genes that are present among individuals diagnosed with a disorder that are not present in others. Now that the human genome is sequenced, the next wave of research effort has been devoted to identifying the functions of the genes that were identified (Kellis et al., 2014).

The molecular approach also offers new ways of examining gene and environment interactions. **Epigenetics** *examines how gene expression (switching genes off and on) is influenced by interactions with the environment.* Here, "the environment" consists of both external events occurring outside of the body, as well as internal physiological processes that can influence gene expression. For example,

Myths in Mind

Single Genes and Behavior

Just Google the phrase "scientists find gene for" and you will wind up with more hits than you would ever have time to sift through. Although it is true that behavior, both normal and abnormal, can be traced to individual genes, typically combinations of genes influence behavior. When it comes to complex characteristics such as personality or disorders like Alzheimer's disease and schizophrenia, there is little chance that any single gene could account for them (Karch & Goate, 2014; Singh et al., 2014). A person's intelligence and his or her predisposition to alcoholism, anxiety, shyness, and depression are all examples of traits and conditions with genetic links, but they all involve multiple genes.

Another misconception is that a single gene can affect only one trait. In reality, the discovery that a particular gene predisposes someone to alcoholism does not mean that this gene is *only* relevant to alcohol addiction; it most likely affects other traits as well. For example, genes that are present in people who abuse alcohol are also more likely to be found in individuals who have a history of other problems such as additional forms of drug dependence and antisocial behavior. In other words, there is a "shared genetic liability" (Dick, 2007).

When you encounter a headline beginning "Scientists Find Gene For...," don't read it as "Scientists Found *THE* Gene

For...," It would be wise to carefully read on to fully understand what is being reported. It is likely that the news describes the work of scientists who found another one of the many genes involved in a disorder or behavior, or in the case of Alzheimer's disease, a gene that is a risk factor and not the sole cause.

Knowing about genes gives us some idea as to why individuals differ. Another issue, explored in the next section, is how these individual differences contribute to behaviors that lead to survival and reproductive success.

genetic females inherit two copies of the X chromosome, but do not express X-linked traits in duplicate. This is because epigenetic processes dampen or switch off the effects of one of the X chromosomes that resides in each cell. Epigenetic processes have been invoked to explain obesity and some cancers and the quality of cardiovascular health across generations. Epigenetics also accounts for how gene and environment interactions lead to physical and behavioral differences among individuals. For example, as identical twins develop they accumulate differences in behavior, physical appearance, and disease susceptibility because of epigenetic processes that switch on and off the genes related to those characteristics.

The technological sophistication of genomic research, as well as greater familiarity with simple examples of inheritance (e.g., being a taster or non-taster of PTC) has led to the common misconception that a single gene can be responsible for a complex trait, disorder, or disease. Although a single gene has been identified as a risk factor for Alzheimer's disease, not everyone who inherits it develops the disease. There is not just one, all-controlling gene for Alzheimer's disease; the same is true for many other conditions. A common misconception about genes and behavior is discussed in Myths in Mind.

Evolutionary Insights into Human Behavior

The animal kingdom's amazing behavioral diversity has long been of interest to scientists. Genes provide the basis for why species differ and why each individual within a species is unique. The best scientific explanation for how this diversity originated remained elusive until Charles Darwin, the 19th-century British naturalist, arrived at a theory for why the anatomical and behavioral traits of animals often seem so fitted to their respective environments. Darwin even applied his ideas to human behavior, and his influence is evident in the specialized field called *evolutionary psychology*.

EVOLUTIONARY PSYCHOLOGY As pointed out at the beginning of the module, evolutionary psychologists view modern human cognition and behavior as an outcome of the survival and reproductive challenges faced by our early ancestors. Just as evolutionary processes have modified the physical systems that support circulation, digestion, movement, and respiration, they have also molded

the circuitry and workings of the brain. Heritable traits, both physical and behavioral, pass from one generation to the next through sexual reproduction. Some of these traits—called *adaptations*—contribute to survival, health, and sexual behavior. Individuals with these adaptive traits are more likely to pass on their genes to the next generation compared to individuals with traits that do not contribute, or perhaps even hurt, chances for survival and reproduction. Thus, if you had the means to identify and count specific genes within a population, you would see that some of them become more and more widespread over time. This is a major part of the process of **evolution**, *the change in the frequency of genes occurring in an interbreeding population over generations.*

Why do some genes become more frequent and others less so in breeding populations? Darwin's answer was natural selection, and it is arguably the most important and scientifically validated principles in all of science. **Natural selection** *is the process by which traits become more or less common in a population of interbreeding individuals as a function of their contributions to reproductive success.* In the grand scheme of things, evolutionary change is gradual; the effects of natural selection on a trait unfold over numerous generations (see Figure 3.3). For example, at the beginning of this module we described how a gene that codes for the lactase enzyme has become increasingly common among human populations that consume the milk of domesticated animals. This is a remarkable case of how rapidly both genes and behavior can change in response to the environment and illustrates the complex relationship between biological and cultural processes.

Evolutionary Psychology and Attraction

How do natural selection and evolution apply to human behavior? According to evolutionary psychologists, the human brain contains specialized adaptations for performing certain cognitive and behavioral functions (Cosmides & Tooby, 2013). In particular, behavior and physical traits linked to sexual reproduction play a crucial role in the evolutionary process. The face, and how facial symmetry relates to attraction, is an illustrative case.

Figure 3.3 How Traits Evolve

Evolution through natural selection requires both that a trait be heritable (i.e., passed down through reproductive means) and that certain individuals within a breeding population have a reproductive advantage for having the trait.

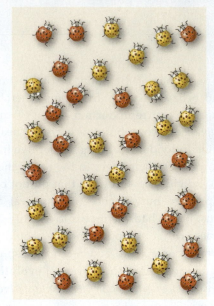 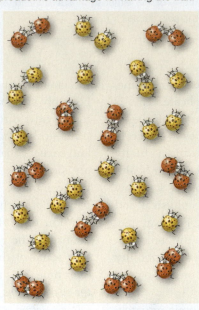 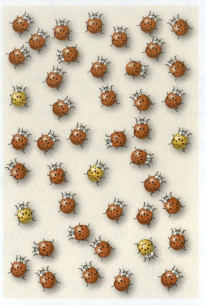

Suppose coloration is a genetically inherited trait in lady bugs.

Suppose a bird that preys on these lady bugs can see the yellow ones better. This brings about a survival and reproductive advantage to red lady bugs that have red-colored offspring.

Genes for red coloration should spread through the population because natural selection favors red lady bugs over yellow lady bugs.

What do we know about attraction and symmetry?

The external features of the human body and face are genetically programmed to be symmetrical, meaning that each side is a mirror image of the other. Even so, the genetic programming for facial symmetry is rarely perfect, and environmental factors such as illness may cause asymmetry of facial features. The eyes may be slightly offset or the chin may be slightly skewed to one side. Psychologists have tested our responses to deviations from symmetry and their effects on perceptions of physical attractiveness.

How can science provide evidence that we prefer symmetry?

The face is a focal point of our social interactions, and thus is a major focus of research on symmetry. People can detect even the subtlest asymmetries, and they rate symmetrical faces as more attractive than asymmetrical ones (Gangestad et al., 1994; Little et al., 2011). Studies of facial symmetry and attraction ask participants to complete tasks much like the one shown on the next page.

Clearly, the photos are of the same individual and each photo may have looked identical on superficial examination. However, if you look more closely, you likely noticed that the sizes of the eyes are asymmetrical in both photos on either side of the center one. Ratings by both males and females indicate that they prefer symmetrical faces of either sex (Rhodes et al., 2009). Other research on symmetry has shown that hormones and the context of the relationship influence attractiveness ratings. Women who are in the follicular phase (peak fertility) of their menstrual cycle find male symmetry more attractive if the context for which they base their ratings is a short-term relationship, but when evaluating attractiveness for a long-term partnership they are less discerning when it comes to facial symmetry (Little & Jones, 2012).

Can we critically evaluate the importance of symmetry?

Physical characteristics are useful for determining whether we might want to approach someone, ask for a date, and at the very least spend a bit of time with the person. Beyond this level of commitment, other characteristics become increasingly important. Symmetry likely plays a role in how we initially respond to others. In the long term, it is likely to be of less importance than other qualities. After dating

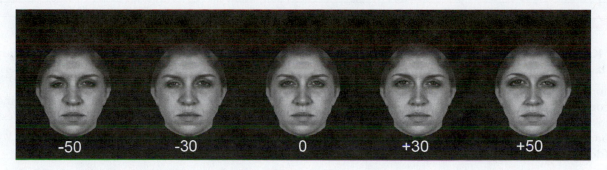

Which face do you prefer of these five? You likely chose the middle face because it has the highest level of symmetry. People can detect this quality without even having to study faces very closely.

someone for a month or so, we begin to wonder whether our partner will be faithful or a cheater, a saver or a spender, or nurturing or uncaring toward children. These are questions we ask ourselves about long-term mates, and whose answers we could not decipher from scrutinizing facial symmetry.

Critics and evolutionary psychologists alike point out that not all behaviors and physical traits are necessarily adaptive, either as they are expressed today or as they were expressed by our distant ancestors (Andrews et al., 2002; Gould & Lewontin, 1979). In other words, not all traits provide an evolutionary advantage. For example, baldness runs in families even though it is unlikely that this characteristic promotes survival and reproductive fitness. Similarly, we cannot assume that all behavioral traits, such as the ability to detect facial asymmetries, have an adaptive function relating to survival and reproductive fitness.

Why is this relevant?

How does research on facial symmetry apply to real-world situations? In evolutionary terms, symmetry is hypothesized to be a physical display of mate quality because it signals that the individual is genetically healthy (Lie, Rhodes, & Simmons, 2008). Also, with the rise of online dating sites, some people begin their searches for a mate by looking at photographs. However, facial symmetry corresponds to other traits people evaluate as well—this even includes dancing ability. Scientists have discovered that men who have symmetrical facial features are also better dancers, as rated by women who watch their moves (Brown et al., 2005). Dancing ability is probably easier to detect visually than subtle facial asymmetries. Thus, the attractiveness of having some good dance moves does not just signal good rhythm, but also a more symmetrical face.

JOURNAL PROMPT

Evolution of Behavior: Select one of the following behaviors and explain it from an evolutionary perspective. This means that you will explore how the behavior would have affected survival and reproductive success among early human ancestors. (1) The ability to throw overhand with great precision; (2) A preference for a mate who is young and healthy; (3) The ability to use spoken and gestural language.

CULTURAL AND ENVIRONMENTAL CONTRIBUTIONS TO BEHAVIOR Evolutionary psychologists have opened up new ways of studying and interpreting human behavior, but the field has also generated some controversy. For instance, studies pointing to gender differences in cognitive abilities and sexual motivation have led to debates about what those differences mean and how they arise (Joel, 2011; Petersen & Hyde, 2010). Scientists do not dispute that evolution and natural selection have played important roles in shaping the modern human mind, but they disagree over whether differences among individuals and groups are *hard-wired* in the brain or reflect sociocultural and personal experiences. For example, researchers can produce lower math test scores among women just by having them read a passage claiming a genetic basis for gender differences before taking a math test (a process known as *stereotype threat*). This simple suggestion results in increased activity in brain areas associated with emotional and social processing, and thereby reduces activity in regions involved in mathematical problem-solving (Krendl et al., 2008; Forbes & Leitner, 2014; but see Dunst et al., 2013 for opposing evidence). Similarly, researchers have been able to prevent or reduce gender differences on math problem-solving by providing female role models and educating test takers about how stereotypes can hurt performance (Johns et al., 2005; Stout et al., 2011). In other words, some gender differences may occur not because of genetic differences, but simply because people believe that gender differences exist.

Module **3.1** Summary

3.1a   **Know . . . the key terminology related to genes, inheritance, and evolutionary psychology:**

behavioral genetics
behavioral genomics
chromosomes
dizygotic twins
DNA (deoxyribonucleic acid)
epigenetics
evolution
genes
genotype
heritability
monozygotic twins
natural selection
phenotype

3.1b   **Understand . . . how twin and adoption studies reveal relationships between genes and behavior.**

Both methods measure genetic, environmental, and inter- active contributions to behavior. Twin studies typically compare monozygotic twins (genetically identical) and dizygotic twins (full siblings sharing the prenatal environ- ment). Adoption studies compare adopted children with their adoptive and biological parents. These designs allow researchers to determine heritability, a number between 0 and 1 that estimates the degree to which individual dif- ferences in a trait are due to genetic factors. A heritability of 1.0 would mean that genes contribute to 100% of indi- vidual differences. Many human characteristics, including intelligence and personality, have heritability estimates typically ranging between 0.40 and 0.70.

3.1c   **Apply . . . evolutionary explanations to behavior**

Applying evolutionary thinking to human behavior re- quires us to consider that modern-day behavior reflects how natural selection has impacted the human brain over thousands of generations. In this module you saw how humans respond to variations in facial symmetry, which influences attraction and, in turn, reproduction. Re- searchers suggest that our preference for facial symmetry may be an evolved specialization for detecting whether a potential partner is physically and genetically healthy.

3.1d   **Analyze . . . claims that scientists have located a specific gene that controls a single trait or behavior.**

As you learned in this module, most psychological traits, as well as disorders such as Alzheimer's disease, involve multiple genes, some of which are not yet discovered (see the Myths in Mind feature.)

Module **3.1** Quiz

Know . . .

1. The chemical units that provide instructions on how specific proteins are to be produced are called _____.
    A. chromosomes
    B. genes
    C. genomes
    D. autosomes

2. Evolution is best defined as:
    A. a gradual increase in complexity.
    B. a change in gene frequency over generations.
    C. solving the challenge of survival by adapting.
    D. a progression toward a complex human brain.

Understand . . .

3. A major question addressed by comparing monozygotic and dizygotic twins, or comparing adopted children with their adoptive and biological parents, is:
    A. To what degree has natural selection influenced human evolution?
    B. Does a single gene or do multiple genes influence complex behavior?
    C. Are psychological disorders homozygous or heterozygous conditions?
    D. To what extent do genes, the environment, and their interaction influence behavior?

Apply . . .

4. In evolutionary terms, why are symmetrical facial features important?
    A. They indicate health and, most likely, good genes.
    B. They guarantee offspring survival.
    C. They make romantic relationships more satisfying.
    D. Without them, there is no other way to decide whether you have found a quality mate.

Analyze . . .

5. If you read a news article titled "Scientists discover gene associated with ability to learn," what is a likely response a psychologist would post to the comment section?
    A. "Finally, *THE* gene for learning has been discovered!"
    B. "This is one of many different genes associated with something complex like learning."
    C. "This will once and for all prove that learning is 100 percent genetically determined."
    D. "Learning is something that happens when we interact with the environment, so there is probably an error in the study."

Module 3.2   How the Nervous System Works: Cells and Neurotransmitters

Learning Objectives

3.2a Know . . . the key terminology associated with nerve cells, hormones, and their functioning.

3.2b Understand . . . how nerve cells communicate.

3.2c Understand . . . the ways that drugs and other substances affect the brain.

3.2d Apply . . . your knowledge of neurotransmitters to predict drug effects.

3.2e Analyze . . . the claim that we are born with all the nerve cells we will ever have.

A bite from an Australian species of snake called the taipan can kill an adult human within 30 minutes. In fact, it is recognized as the most lethally venomous species of snake in the world (50 times more potent than the also fatal venom of the king cobra). The venom of the taipan is neurotoxic, meaning that it specifically attacks cells of the nervous system. First, drowsiness sets in, and control of the head and neck muscles begins to weaken. Victims then experience progressive difficulty with swallowing, followed by tightness of the chest and paralysis of breathing. If enough venom was injected and treatment is not available, coma and then death are inevitable. Not all snake venom is neurotoxic, however. Rattlesnake venom damages virtually any tissue in the vicinity of the bite as well as those tissues it reaches within the bloodstream. Not exactly comforting news, but it helps to illustrate that neurotoxic venom is enormously dangerous because it disrupts the functioning of cells that make up the nervous system. These cells and the nervous system that is built from them are the topics of this module.

The nervous system acts as a complex communications network, transmitting and receiving information throughout the body. It signals pain, pleasure, and emotion; it controls our reflexive responses as well as our voluntary movements such as reaching and walking; and it even regulates such basic processes as breathing and heart rate. In this module, we explore how nerve cells function individually as well as how they are able to transmit and receive information throughout the network of the nervous system.

Neural Communication

You already know that your body is composed of many different types of cells. Psychologists are most interested in **neurons**, *which are one of the major types of cells found in the nervous system and are responsible for sending and receiving messages throughout the body.* Billions of these cells are receiving and transmitting messages during our waking and sleeping hours.

Neurons vary in size and shape, but most have the same key structures that serve to receive and transmit messages (Figure 3.4). For starters, the **cell body** (also known as the *soma*) *is the part of a neuron that contains the nucleus that houses the cell's genetic material.* Genes in the cell body code for the proteins that form the chemicals and structures that allow the neuron to function. **Dendrites**, *the small branches radiating from the cell body, receive messages from other cells and transmit the message toward the cell body.* The **axon** *is the structure that transports information from the neuron to neighboring neurons in the form of electrochemical reactions.* At the end of the axon are axon terminals. Located within the axon terminals are **neurotransmitters**, *the chemicals that function as messengers allowing neurons to communicate with each other.* Many different types of neurotransmitters exist, and each has different

Figure 3.4 Structures of the Neuron

Each part of a nerve cell is specialized for a specific task.

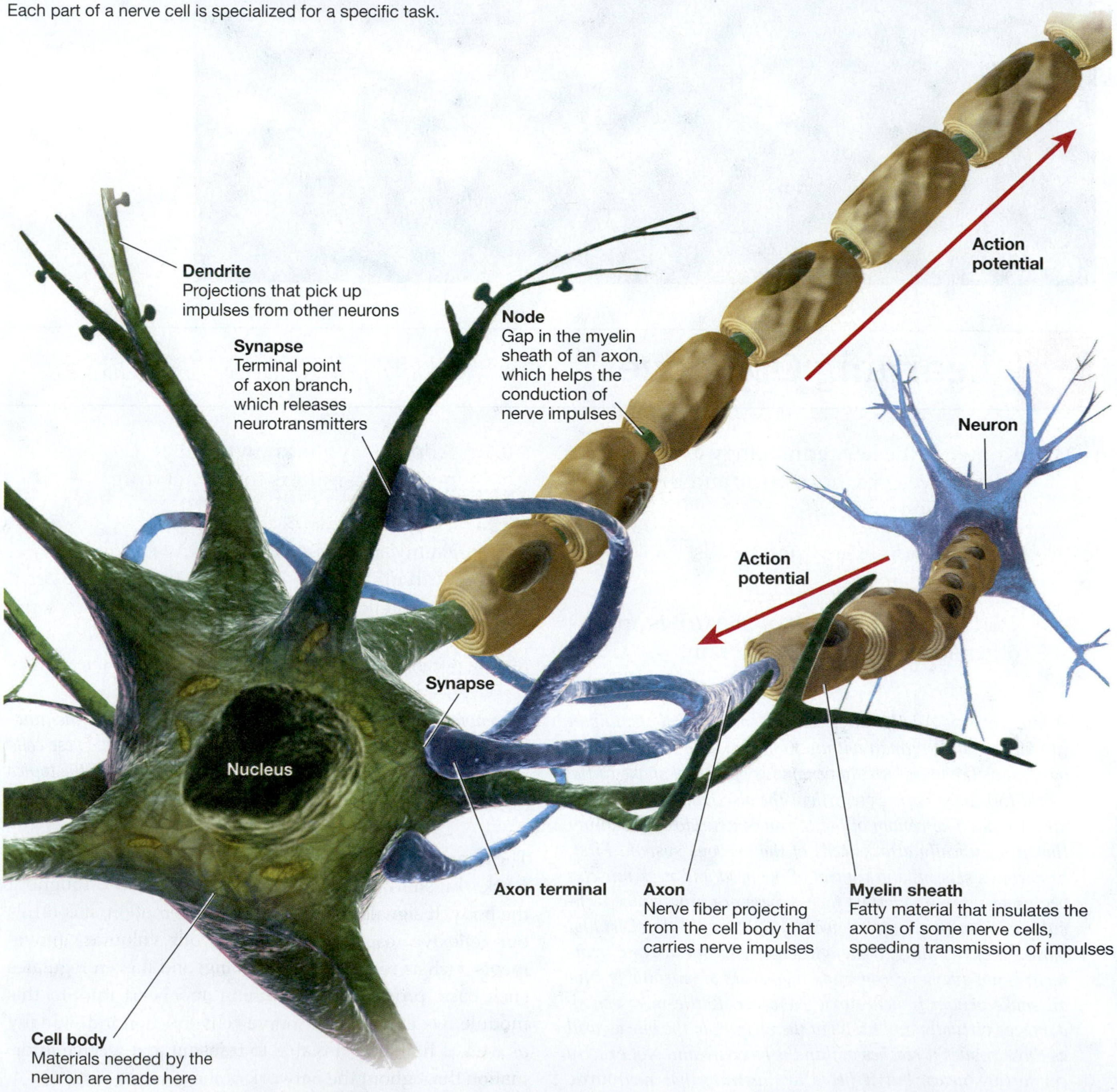

Dendrite
Projections that pick up impulses from other neurons

Synapse
Terminal point of axon branch, which releases neurotransmitters

Node
Gap in the myelin sheath of an axon, which helps the conduction of nerve impulses

Action potential

Neuron

Action potential

Nucleus

Synapse

Axon terminal

Axon
Nerve fiber projecting from the cell body that carries nerve impulses

Myelin sheath
Fatty material that insulates the axons of some nerve cells, speeding transmission of impulses

Cell body
Materials needed by the neuron are made here

functions—something we will explore later in more detail. Neurotransmitters are released across **synapses**, *the microscopically small spaces that separate individual nerve cells.*

Not all neurons are the same—they differ in form and function. *Sensory neurons* gather information from the bodily senses, such as touch or pain, and bring the messages toward the spinal cord and brain. In contrast, *motor neurons* carry messages away from the brain and spinal cord and toward muscles in order to control their flexion and extension. *Interneurons* modulate the connections between sensory and motor nerves. They can either excite or inhibit activity between sensory and motor nerves. The different roles played by these cells are illustrated simply in a spinal reflex arc (similar to the one you experience when your doctor taps your knee to test your patellar reflex; Figure 3.5).

GLIAL CELLS Glial cells *are specialized cells involved in protecting brain cells, removing wastes, and synchronizing activity of the billions of neurons within the nervous system.* Glial cells actually outnumber neurons in the brain by a ratio of approximately 10:1. Their structure differs from those of the sensory and motor nerves, and they perform different functions. Before these cells were better understood it was believed that their primary function was to hold neurons together (the word *glia* is derived from the Greek word for glue). We now know that the activity of neurons is highly dependent on interactions with glial cells.

One important function of glial cells is to form **myelin**, *a fatty sheath* (like the plastic around an electrical cord) *that insulates axons from one another, and increases the speed and efficiency of neural communication.* To illustrate the importance of myelin, we can examine the dysfunction of nervous systems without it. *Multiple sclerosis* is a disease in which the immune system does not recognize myelin and attacks it—a process that can devastate the structural and functional integrity of the nervous system. When myelin breaks down in multiple sclerosis, the resulting symptoms include numbness or tingling sensations caused by the disruption of sensory nerve cell signals that should otherwise reach the brain. Multiple sclerosis is also characterized by problems with voluntary, coordinated movement, owing to the breakdown of myelin that supports motor nerves.

As you can see, each part of an individual neuron and the different glial cells perform important functions. Ultimately, however, it is the networking of nerve cells that allows messages to be transmitted within the brain and rest of the body. The actual transmission of these messages is made possible by a combination of electrical and chemical activity.

Figure 3.5 Sensory and Motor Neurons

Sensory neurons carry information toward the spinal cord and the brain, whereas motor neurons send messages to muscles of the body. The interneuron links the sensory and motor neurons with both excitatory and inhibitory effects. This is the pathway of a simple withdrawal response to a painful stimulus.

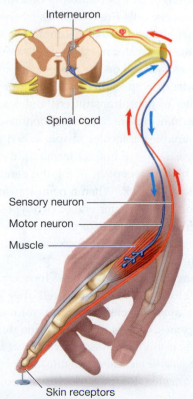

Interneuron

Spinal cord

Sensory neuron

Motor neuron

Muscle

Skin receptors

JOURNAL PROMPT

Functions of Brain Cells: Describe in your own words the functions of both neurons and glial cells.

THE NEURON'S ELECTRICAL SYSTEM: RESTING AND ACTION POTENTIALS The inner and outer environments of a neuron differ in their concentrations of charged atoms called *ions*. In other words, the neuron is polarized. The **resting potential** *of a neuron refers to its relatively stable state during which the cell is not transmitting messages.* At its resting potential, the outside of the neuron has a relatively high concentration of positively charged ions, whereas the interior of the axon has a relatively high concentration of negatively charged ions (and proteins). This difference in charge between the inside and outside of the cell leaves the inside of the axon with a negative charge of approximately −70 millivolts (mV). When stimulated the neuron springs into action, a process referred to as *neural firing* (Figure 3.6).

What causes a neuron to fire? When a neuron is stimulated, the pores of its membrane surface allow positively charged ions to rush in. If a sufficient number of positively charged ions enter the cell, they will alter the charge to be greater than −70 mV. Each neuron has a specific threshold that must be reached before it will fire. If a threshold of, say, −55 mV is reached, the neuron then initiates an **action**

Figure 3.6 Electrical Charge of the Inner and Outer Regions of Nerve Cells

The inner and outer environments of a nerve cell at rest differ in terms of their electrical charge. During the resting potential, there is a net negative charge. When a nerve cell is stimulated, generating an action potential, positively charged ions rush inside the cell membrane. After the cell has fired, the positively charged ions are channeled back outside the nerve cell as it returns to resting state.

 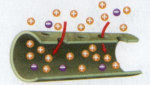 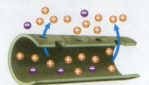

Resting potential.

Positively charged ions rush into the cell during an action potential.

After the nerve has fired the positively charged ions are pumped back out of the cell.

potential, *which is a wave of electrical activity that originates at the base of the axon and rapidly travels down its length.* The action potential moves down the length of the axon as positively charged ions rush through the membrane pores. During the action potential the net charge of the cell goes from negatively to positively charged (see Figure 3.7). At each point of the axon the pores slam shut as soon as the action potential occurs, and the positively charged ions are rapidly pumped back out of the cell, which helps the neuron return to a resting state.

When the action potential reaches the axon terminals at the end of the cell, neurotransmitters are released into the **synaptic cleft**, *the minute space between the terminal button and the dendrite*, and bind to receptors on the dendrites of neighboring neurons. Meanwhile, the action potential is followed by a **refractory period**, *which is a brief period in which a neuron cannot fire*. Within a couple of milliseconds, however, the neuron returns to its resting potential and can fire again if stimulated.

When stimulated, a given neuron always fires at the same intensity and speed. This activity adheres to the **all-or-none principle**: *Individual nerve cells fire at the same strength every time an action potential occurs.* Neurons do not "sort of" fire or "over fire," they just fire. That neurons behave this way may seem odd, because we might assume that intense sensations correspond to strong action potentials. In reality, according to the all-or-none principle, action potentials are always the same magnitude and speed. The strength of a sensation is determined by the rate at which nerve cells fire as well as by the number of nerve cells that are stimulated. A stimulus is experienced intensely because a greater number of cells are stimulated, and the firing of each cell occurs repeatedly.

Neurons tend to specialize in sending or receiving a limited number of neurotransmitters, and many different types of neurotransmitters have been identified; each type has its own unique molecular shape. When neurotransmitters are released at the axon terminal, they cross the synapse and bind to receptors lining the dendrites, much like a key fits into a lock. When a neurotransmitter binds to the receptor, it will trigger one of two types of reaction in the receiving neuron: *excitatory*, which increases action potentials, or *inhibitory*, which decreases the likelihood of action potentials.

After neurotransmitter molecules have bound to postsynaptic receptors of a neighboring cell, they are released back into the synaptic cleft where they may be broken down by enzymes. Others might go through **reuptake**, *a process whereby neurotransmitter molecules that have been released into the synapse are reabsorbed into the axon terminals of the presynaptic neuron.* Reuptake serves as a sort of natural

Figure 3.7 Time Course and Phases of a Nerve Cell Going from Resting Potential to Action Potential

Nerve cells fire once the threshold of excitation is reached. During the action potential positively charged ions rush inside the cell membrane, creating a net positive change within the cell. Positively charged ions are then forced out of the cell as it returns to its resting potential.

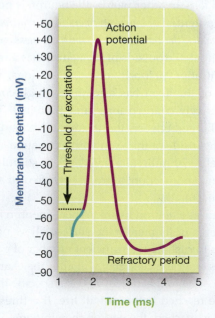

Figure 3.8 Major Events at the Synapse

As the action potential reaches the axon terminals, neurotransmitters (packed into spherically shaped vesicles) are released across the synaptic cleft. The neurotransmitters bind to the postsynaptic (receiving) neuron. In the process of reuptake, some neurotransmitters are returned to the presynaptic neuron via reuptake proteins. These neurotransmitters are then repackaged into synaptic vessicles.

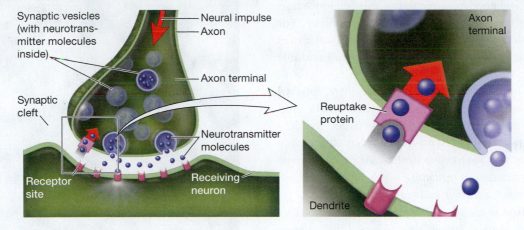

Watch NEUROTRANSMITTERS

recycling system for neurotransmitters (Figure 3.8). It is also a process that is modified by many commonly used drugs. To put all the pieces of action potential together, watch the following video Neurotransmitters.

TYPES OF NEUROTRANSMITTERS   The various classes of neurotransmitter differ in molecular structure and, therefore, to the type of receptor they can bind to and excite or inhibit. The *monoamines* are one class of neurotransmitter. Each of the monoamines has its own unique function, although there is some degree of overlap. For example, monoamine neurotransmitters mood, and such the major antidepressant drugs on the market influence their activity. **Dopamine** *is a monoamine neurotransmitter involved in such varied functions as mood, control of voluntary movement, and processing of rewarding experiences.* Dopamine

Myths in Mind

We Are Born With All the Brain Cells We Will Ever Have

Until the 1960s neuroscientists were unaware that new nerve cells could generate once an organism was born. This conclusion made perfect sense because no one had ever seen new neurons form in adults, and severe neurological damage is often permanent. Advances in brain science have challenged this belief (Gage, 2000). Researchers have observed *neurogenesis*, which is the formation of new nerve cells, in several brain areas of rodents, monkeys, and humans (Braun & Jessberger, 2014). The growth of a new cell, including neurons that populate a few different brain regions as well as some glial cells, starts with *stem cells*, which are unique types of cells that do not have a special-

ized, genetically programmed function. When a stem cell divides, the resulting cells can become part of just about anything—bone, kidney, or brain tissue. What determines the type of nerve cell that develops and its migratory path within the brain is the stem cell's external chemical environment (Williams, Holman, & Klein, 2014). Our increased understanding of neurogenesis has raised some exciting possibilities; perhaps scientists can discover how to trigger neural growth in parts of the nervous system that do not naturally undergo neurogenesis throughout the life span. Developments in neural stem-cell research can bring added hope for recovery from brain injury and disease.

release in conjunction with such varied pleasurable activities as exercise, gambling, eating, or taking drugs serves to increase the value we associate with these activities. For this reason dopamine is sometimes referred to as a "pleasure" or "feel good" chemical, but this reference fails to capture the complexity of the neurotransmitter. For example, people who are dependent on stimulant drugs continue to take them despite the fact that the pleasurable effects of the drugs cease (Berridge et al., 2009).

Serotonin *is a monoamine neurotransmitter involved in regulating mood, sleep, and appetite.* Researchers suggest that there may be some association between low levels of serotonin and those who suffer from depression. **Norepinephrine** *is a monoamine synthesized from dopamine molecules that is involved in regulating stress responses, including increasing arousal, attention, and heart rate.*

Acetylcholine *is one of the most widespread neurotransmitters within the nervous system, found throughout the brain and at the junctions between nerve cells and skeletal muscles; thus its role in movement.* Recall the neurotoxic snake venom discussed at the beginning of this module: Its toxins disrupt activity of acetylcholine transmission at neuromuscular junctions. Different snakes carry slightly different types of neurotoxic venom. Some types of venom block acetylcholine release at the presynaptic terminals, preventing its release into the synapse. Another type of venom blocks the receptors on the postsynaptic cell, preventing acetylcholine from binding to them (Lewis & Gutmann, 2004). Either way, the effects are devastating. In addition to movement, acetylcholine activity in the brain is associated with arousal and attention.

GABA (gamma-amino butyric acid) *is a primary inhibitory neurotransmitter of the nervous system, meaning that it prevents neurons from generating action potentials.* It accomplishes this feat by reducing the negative charge of neighboring neurons even further than their resting state of −70 mV. When GABA binds to receptors, it causes an influx of negatively charged ions to enter the cell, which is the opposite net effect of what happens when a neuron is stimulated. As an inhibitor, GABA facilitates sleep

Extracts from the seeds of some poppy flowers contain opium. Morphine and one of its derivatives, heroin, can be synthesized from these seeds.

and reduces arousal of the nervous system. In contrast, **glutamate** *is an excitatory neurotransmitter in the nervous system that, among other things, is critical to the processes of learning and memory.* Repeated glutamate release at synapses facilitates long-term changes in the physiology of neighboring cells, which increases their chances of firing together. Cells that form this type of glutamate-triggered physiological connection support memory formation. The major types of neurotransmitters and some of their major functions are summarized in Table 3.1.

Some brain chemicals, such as *neuropeptides*, have highly specialized functions. For example, **endorphin** *functions to reduce pain and induce feelings of pleasure.* Produced by the pituitary gland and the hypothalamus, endorphin is released into the bloodstream during events

Table 3.1 Major Neurotransmitters and Their Functions

Neurotransmitter	Some Major Functions
Acetylcholine	Movement, attention
Dopamine	Control of movement, reward-seeking behavior, cognition and attention
Norepinephrine	Memory, attention to new or important stimuli, regulation of sleep and mood
Serotonin	Regulation of sleep, appetite, mood
Glutamate	Excites nervous system, memory and autonomic nervous system reactions
GABA (gamma-amino butyric acid)	Inhibits brain activity, lowers arousal, anxiety, and excitation, facilitates sleep
Substance P	Pain perception

such as strenuous exercise, sexual activity, or injury. It acts on portions of the brain that are attuned to reward, reinforcement, and pleasure, inhibiting the perception of pain and increasing feelings of euphoria. Morphine—a drug derived from the poppy plant—binds to endorphin receptors (the term *endorphin* translates to *endogenous [internal] morphine*). Morphine molecules fit into the same receptor sites as endorphins, and therefore, produce the same pain-killing and euphoric effects.

The African naked mole rat lacks substance P activity, so it does not appear to experience pain when it comes into contact with a stimulus such as capsaicin.

Working the Scientific Literacy Model

Pain and Substance P

Another neuropeptide with a highly specialized function, and one that opposes that of endorphin, is called substance P.

What do we know about substance P?

Substance P *is a chemical involved in the experience of pain found in sensory nerves of the brain and spinal cord.* When tissue on the skin surface is damaged, sensory nerves carry messages to the brain. In turn, the brain releases substance P, giving rise to the perception of pain. You may already be familiar with the effect, if not the name, of *capsaicin*, the pain-inducing compound found on many types of chili peppers. Capsaicin stimulates release of substance P, which produces painful sensations of heat despite the lack of any physical injury. As you are probably aware, pain does not come just from eating peppers, but also from their coming in contact with the skin, particularly thin skin such as that around the eyes.

How can science explain what substance P does?

Much of what is known about substance P comes from a surprising source: the African naked mole rat. This animal seems oblivious to pain: It shows no behavioral response when capsaicin is applied to the skin surface. In contrast, humans, mice, and many other mammalian species show clear signs of pain and irritation. The lack of a pain response in naked mole rats has led to some fascinating discoveries. Researchers who have studied these animals have found that they do, in fact, have the same types of sensory neurons that register pain in other mammals. In addition, naked mole rats have the type of receptor on their postsynaptic neurons that substance P can bind to. Yet, they do not show any signs of pain when these nerves are stimulated (Smith et al., 2010). Evidence suggests that the pain pathway within the spinal cord

of naked mole rats has been modified via evolution to prevent stimulation of these cells to be "experienced" as pain (Park et al., 2008).

Can we critically evaluate this research?

How could an animal survive without a pain response, which is an important adaptive means of avoiding bodily harm? People who are born with a rare condition called *congenital insensitivity to pain* lack the ability to perceive pain, and even in early childhood acquire significant damage to the skin, joints, eyes, and other body regions. Because they lack a pain response, these individuals do not take action to prevent physical damage to the body. It would seem that naked mole rats would have a similar problem. However, evolving a nervous system that dampens pain signals allows this animal to benefit from exploiting a subterranean habitat that is high in carbon dioxide and ammonia, both of which stimulate neurons that route pain signals to the brain, but not for naked mole rats (Brand, Smith, Lewin, & Park, 2010).

Why is this relevant?

Millions of people in the United States suffer from chronic pain. In addition to compromising the well-being of affected individuals, problems with pain translate into reduced work productivity, increased healthcare costs, and, for some people, an increased risk of developing dependence or addiction to prescription painkillers. By better understanding the physiological basis of pain, including the information gathered on naked mole rats, researchers may be able to develop more effective drugs and other techniques to help alleviate pain.

Figure 3.9 Drug Effects at Synapses

Drugs can act as agonists by facilitating the effects of a neurotransmitter, or as antagonists by blocking these effects.

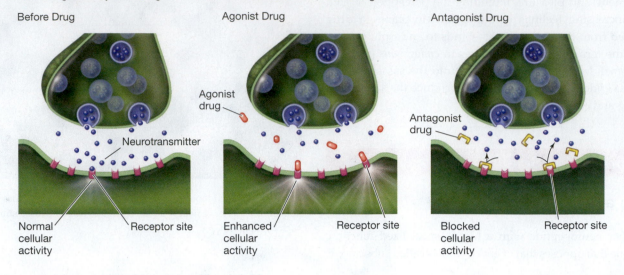

Before Drug

Agonist Drug

Antagonist Drug

Agonist drug

Antagonist drug

Neurotransmitter

Normal cellular activity — Receptor site

Enhanced cellular activity — Receptor site

Blocked cellular activity — Receptor site

DRUG EFFECTS ON NEUROTRANSMISSION Drugs of all varieties, from prescription to recreational, affect the chemical signaling that takes place between nerve cells (Figure 3.9). **Agonists** *are drugs that enhance or mimic the effects of a neurotransmitter's action.* The well-known drug nicotine is an acetylcholine agonist, meaning that it stimulates the receptor sites for this neurotransmitter. The antianxiety drug alprazolam (Xanax) is a GABA agonist; it causes relaxation by increasing the activity of this inhibitory neurotransmitter. Drugs can behave as agonists either directly or indirectly. A drug that behaves as a direct agonist physically binds to receptors at the postsynaptic cells. A drug that acts as an indirect agonist facilitates neurotransmission by increasing the release and availability of neurotransmitters. For example, drugs that block the process of reuptake, such selective serotonin reuptake inhibitors (SSRIs)—which are used in treatment of depression—are indirect agonists.

Drugs classified as **antagonists** *inhibit neurotransmitter activity by blocking receptors or preventing synthesis of a neurotransmitter.* You may have heard of the cosmetic medical procedure known as a Botox injection. Botox, which is derived from the nerve-paralyzing bacterium that causes botulism, blocks the action of acetylcholine by binding to its postsynaptic receptor sites (Dastoor et al., 2007). Blocking acetylcholine could lead to paralysis of the heart and lungs; however, when small amounts are injected into tissue around the eyes, the antagonist simply paralyzes the muscle activity that leads to wrinkles. When muscles are not used, they cannot stretch the skin; hence the reduction in wrinkling when acetylcholine activity is blocked. To practice applying the concepts of drug agonist and antagonist, see Table 3.2.

Hormones and the Endocrine System

Neurotransmitters are not the body's only chemical messenger system. **Hormones** *are chemicals secreted by the glands of the endocrine system.* With help from the nervous system, the endocrine system contributes to *homeostasis*, which is the balance of energy, metabolism, body temperature, and

Table 3.2 Applying the Concepts of Drug Agonist and Antagonist

Read the descriptions of events at synapses and identify whether the drug is an agonist or antagonist
1. A drug binds to the presynaptic cell membrane and prevents dopamine from re-entering, leaving extra dopamine in the synapse to bind with the postsynaptic cell.
2. A drug that affects the cell nucleus and prevents the synthesis (building) of new substance P neurotransmitters.
3. A drug that mimics the effects of glutamate and therefore increases stimulation of postsynaptic cells that glutamate neurotransmitters bind to.
4. A drug that prevents the reuptake of serotonin into the presynaptic cell.
5. A drug that blocks the release of GABA from presynaptic terminals.

Answers: 1. dopamine agonist, 2. Substance P antagonist, 3. glutamate agonist, 4. serotonin agonist, 5. GABA antagonist

other basic bodily functions. The **hypothalamus** *is a brain structure that regulates basic biological needs and motivational systems.* The hypothalamus stimulates the **pituitary gland**, which is *the master gland of the endocrine system that produces hormones and sends commands about hormone production to the other glands of the endocrine system.* Specialized chemicals called *releasing factors* are secreted by the hypothalamus and stimulate the pituitary to release specific hormones (Figure 3.10).

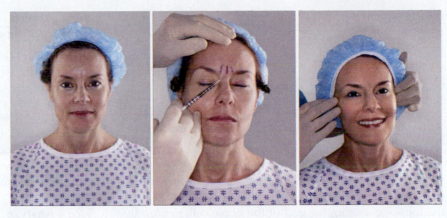

Botox injections paralyze muscles, which can increase youthful appearance in areas such as the face.

The body's response to stress nicely illustrates how the nervous and endocrine systems are related. In psychological terms, stress is defined as an imbalance between perceived demands and the resources available to meet those demands. Such an imbalance might occur if you suddenly realize your midterm exam is tomorrow at 8:00 AM. Your resources—time and energy—may not be enough to meet the demand of succeeding on the exam. The hypothalamus, however, sets chemical events in motion that physically prepare the body for stress. It signals the pituitary gland to release a hormone into the bloodstream that in turn stimulates the **adrenal glands**, *a pair of endocrine glands located adjacent to the kidneys that release stress hormones, such as cortisol and epinephrine.* Cortisol and epinephrine help mobilize the body during stress.

Sex hormones, such as testosterone and estrogen, are manufactured in the gonads and function in both long-term developmental processes such as growth and reproductive function, and are also involved in more immediate or short-term processes such as sexual arousal. Also, an often-overlooked role of sex hormones is in their ability to support cognitive activity such as learning and memory (Janowsky, 2006).

Figure 3.10 The Endocrine System

Glands throughout the body release and exchange hormones. The hypothalamus interacts with the endocrine system to regulate hormonal processes.

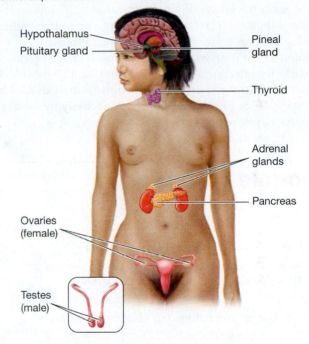

Module 3.2 Summary

3.2a Know . . . the key terminology associated with nerve cells, hormones, and their functioning:

acetylcholine
action potential
adrenal glands
agonists
all-or-none principle
antagonists
axon
cell body
dendrite
dopamine

endorphin
GABA (gamma-amino butyric acid)
glial cells
glutamate
hormones
hypothalamus
myelin
neuron
neurotransmitters
norepinephrine
pituitary gland
refractory period

resting potential
reuptake
serotonin
substance P
synapses
synaptic cleft

3.2b   Understand . . . how nerve cells communicate.

Nerve cells fire because of processes involving both electrical and chemical factors. A stimulated nerve cell goes from resting potential to action potential following an influx of positively charged ions inside the membrane of the cell. As the message reaches the end of the nerve cell, neurotransmitters are released into synapses and bind to neighboring postsynaptic cells. Depending on the type of neurotransmitter, the effect can be either inhibitory or excitatory.

3.2c   Understand . . . the ways that drugs and other substances affect the brain.

Drugs can be agonists or antagonists. A drug is an agonist if it enhances the effects of a neurotransmitter. This outcome occurs if the drug increases the release of a neurotransmitter, blocks reuptake, or mimics the neurotransmitter by binding to the postsynaptic cell. A drug is an antagonist if it blocks the effects of a neurotransmitter. Antagonists block neurotransmitter release, break down neurotransmitters in the synapse, or block neurotransmitter activity by binding to postsynaptic receptors.

3.2d   Apply . . . your knowledge of neurotransmitters to predict drug effects.

Drugs are developed to either increase the activity of a neurotransmitter (agonists) or decrease it (antagonists). When describing the effects of a drug either term typically follows the name of the neurotransmitter(s) it affects; for example "acetylcholine antagonist" or "dopamine agonist." Knowing how to apply this terminology will help you understand how the drug affects neurotransmission, and, therefore, behavior (see Table 3.2 Applying the Concepts of Drug Agonist and Antagonist).

3.2e   Analyze . . . the claim that we are born with all the nerve cells we will ever have.

In this module, a Myths in Mind feature (page 79) addressed the question of whether we are born with all of the nerve cells we will ever have. Although scientists once believed this to be true, we now know that neurogenesis, which is the growth of new neurons, takes place in several parts of the brain. One of these regions is the hippocampus, which is involved in learning and memory (see Module 3.3). In many other areas of the brain, neurogenesis has not been observed. Nevertheless, during normal development, neurons make new connections with neighboring cells. This process also occurs following damage to nerve cells, such that surviving nerve cells form new connections left vacant by damaged neurons.

Module 3.2 Quiz

Know . . .

1. A positive electrical charge that is carried away from the cell body and down the length of the axon is a(n) _____.
   A. refractory period
   B. resting potential
   C. action potential
   D. dendrite

Understand . . .

2. A neuron will fire when the ions inside the cell body are:
   A. at equal balance inside and outside of the cell.
   B. shifted to a threshold greater than the resting potential.
   C. shifted to a threshold less than the resting potential.
   D. in the refractory period.

3. A(n) _____ is a drug that blocks the actions of a neurotransmitter.
   A. agonist
   B. antagonist
   C. stop agent
   D. endorphin

Apply . . .

4. To reverse the effects of neurotoxic venom from a snakebite, which of the following actions would likely be most effective?
   A. Give the patient a high dose of dopamine.
   B. Give the patient a substance that would allow the body to resume transmission of acetylcholine.
   C. Give the patient a drug that would increase GABA transmission.
   D. Give the patient an acetylcholine antagonist.

Analyze . . .

5. An advertisement claims that we need to take care of our brains because once we are born we will never be able to grow new nerve cells, and that all changes that take place in the brain are the result of the formation and loss of connections between cells. What is a scientifically accurate response to this advertisement?
   A. It is false because neurogenesis occurs in several brain regions after we are born.
   B. It is false because with the help of new drugs it is possible to create new nerve cells in the human brain.
   C. It is true because all changes that occur in the brain once we are born are the result of new connections forming and cells dying.
   D. It is true, but only for people who have behavioral problems.

Module **3.3**   Structure and Organization of the Nervous System

Learning Objectives

3.3a Know . . . the key terminology associated with the structure and organization of the nervous system.

3.3b Understand . . . how studies of split-brain patients reveal the workings of the brain.

3.3c Apply . . . your knowledge of brain anatomy to predict which abilities might be affected when a specific area is injured, or when attempting to map out the functioning of healthy brains.

3.3d Analyze . . . what we can learn by mapping psychological functions in the brain.

How would you like to have a thought-controlled robot? On your laziest day, you could just think about turning off the alarm clock and a robotic arm would do it for you. It turns out that such a device is closer to reality than science fiction. Neuroscientists such as Nicholas Hatsopoulos have developed techniques to respond to the brain's electrical activity with robotic arms and other devices. This type of technology has some important applications. Currently, Hatsopoulos and his colleagues are trying to help people with quadriplegia— paralysis of the arms and legs—regain some of their independence. One of their devices reads the electrical signals of the brain and transfers these data to control the cursor of a computer as a mouse normally would (Hatsopoulos & Donoghue, 2009; Willett et al., 2013).

In this module, we translate our knowledge of individual nerve cells into an understanding of how they work as an integrated whole. We move from the microscopic world of cells and molecules to the nervous system that is built from them.

Divisions of the Nervous System

The nervous system is an intricate and highly complex network of nerve cells that coordinates both voluntary and involuntary activity in every region of the body. We begin by examining the two largest divisions: the peripheral and central nervous systems (Figure 3.11).

Figure 3.11 Divisions of the Nervous System

The nervous system can be divided into several different components, each with a specific set of structures and functions.

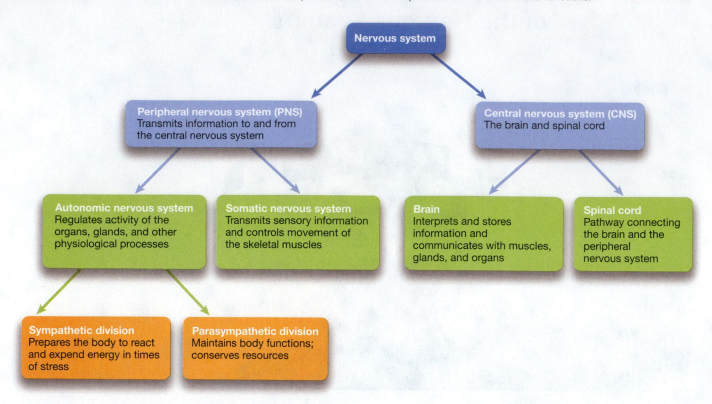

THE PERIPHERAL NERVOUS SYSTEM   The **peripheral nervous system (PNS)** *transmits signals between the brain and the rest of the body and is divided into two subcomponents, the somatic system and the autonomic system.* The **somatic nervous system** *consists of nerves that receive sensory input from the body and control skeletal muscles, which are responsible for voluntary and reflexive movement.* Any voluntary behavior, such as coordinating the movements needed to reach, walk, or move a computer mouse, are governed by the somatic nervous system.

The **autonomic nervous system** *is the portion of the peripheral nervous system responsible for regulating the activity of organs and glands.* It includes two subcomponents: the sympathetic and parasympathetic nervous systems. The **sympathetic nervous system** *is responsible for increasing physiological arousal to prepare the body for action (elevated heart rate, dilated pupils, and decreased salivary flow).* Bumping into someone you are attracted to or barely avoiding an accident while driving will result in sympathetic arousal. In this process, blood is directed toward your skeletal muscles, heart rate and perspiration increase, and digestive processes are slowed; each of these responses helps to direct energy where it is most needed. In contrast, the **parasympathetic nervous system** *helps maintain homeostatic balance in the presence of change; following sympathetic arousal, it works to return the body to a baseline, nonemergency state.* Generally speaking, the parasympathetic nervous system does the opposite of what the sympathetic nervous system does to maintain that balance (Figure 3.12).

THE CENTRAL NERVOUS SYSTEM   The **central nervous system (CNS)** *consists of the brain and the spinal cord.* Your behavior, personality, memories, and conscious awareness all emanate from the CNS. Its most prominent feature is the brain; a 3-pound structure made up of approximately 100 billion individual cells and a countless number of synapses, making it arguably the most complex known entity in the universe. The CNS integrates with the PNS to form a bodily network consisting of pathways regulating the activity of glands, muscles, and organs, as well as pathways that relay sensory information back to the CNS.

The Brain and Its Structures

The structures of the brain are organized in a hierarchical fashion. The human brain, as well as that of other animals, can be subdivided into three main regions: the hindbrain, the midbrain, and the forebrain. This system of dividing the brain may tempt you to view it as a mass of separate compartments, so keep in mind that even these divisions rely on each other and communicate through highly integrated circuitry. Our survey of the brain covers some, but not all, of the key structures and their specialized functions.

Figure 3.12 The Autonomic Nervous System

The sympathetic and parasympathetic divisions of the autonomic nervous system control and regulate responses by the glands and organs of the body.

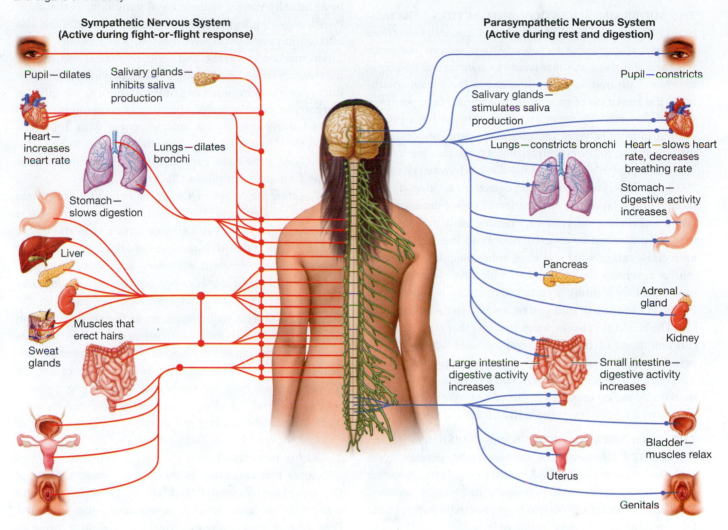

Sympathetic Nervous System
(Active during fight-or-flight response)

Pupil—dilates

Salivary glands—inhibits saliva production

Heart—increases heart rate

Lungs—dilates bronchi

Stomach—slows digestion

Liver

Muscles that erect hairs

Sweat glands

Parasympathetic Nervous System
(Active during rest and digestion)

Pupil—constricts

Salivary glands—stimulates saliva production

Lungs—constricts bronchi

Heart—slows heart rate, decreases breathing rate

Stomach—digestive activity increases

Pancreas

Adrenal gland

Kidney

Large intestine—digestive activity increases

Small intestine—digestive activity increases

Bladder—muscles relax

Uterus

Genitals

THE HINDBRAIN: SUSTAINING THE BODY   The **hindbrain** *consists of structures that are critical to controlling basic, life-sustaining processes* (Figure 3.13). At the top of the spinal cord is a region called the **brain stem**, *which consists of the medulla and the pons.* Nerve cells in the *medulla* connect with the body to perform basic functions such as regulating breathing, heart rate, sneezing, salivating, and even vomiting—all those actions your body does with little conscious control on your part. The *pons* helps regulate sleeping and dreaming. The *reticular formation* consists of several clusters of cells within the brain stem that send signals upward into the cortex, a higher brain center we will describe shortly, to influence attention and alertness. The reticular formation also communicates with cells in the spinal cord involved with movement.

   Another structure of the hindbrain, the **cerebellum** (Latin for "little brain") *is the lobe-like structure at the base of the brain that is involved in the details of movement, maintaining balance, and learning new motor skills.* Although

Figure 3.13 Hindbrain and Midbrain Structures

Structures in the hindbrain are responsible for basic functions that sustain the body and regulate sleep and arousal (pons and medulla). The cerebellum is involved in maintaining balance and coordinated movement, timing of movements, and many other functions. The midbrain includes structures that control basic sensory responses and voluntary movement.

Cerebellum

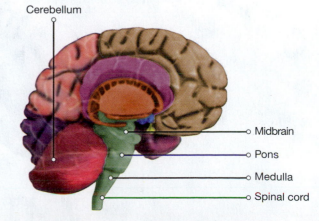

Midbrain

Pons

Medulla

Spinal cord

you use other parts of your brain to plan movements, the cerebellum specializes in their coordination and timing (Yamazaki & Tanaka, 2009).

THE MIDBRAIN: SENSATION AND ACTION The **midbrain** *resides just above the hindbrain and consists of structures that function in relaying messages between sensory and motor areas and also nerve cells that project to motivational systems of the brain.* One midbrain structure called the *tectum* coordinates the sensation of motion with actions. Have you ever walked down a city street and been startled by a pigeon darting in front of you? The pigeon's tectum responded to the impending collision with an object (you) moving toward it, and the pigeon almost instantly swerved away (Wu et al., 2005). Similarly, your own tectum detected a sudden, darting motion and relayed the information to motor areas of your brain. Depending on your experiences with pigeons, you may have flinched or covered your head before you were even conscious of what you were doing. Regions within the midbrain serve a similar function with information that we hear (auditory stimuli). Your reflexive ability to identify the location of sounds around you occurs within the midbrain.

The midbrain also includes neurons that contain dense concentrations of dopamine receptors and activity. These neurons send messages to higher brain centers involved in the control of movement. Parkinson's disease—a condition marked by major impairments in voluntary movement—is caused by a loss of dopamine-activated cells in the midbrain.

THE FOREBRAIN: EMOTION, MEMORY, AND THOUGHT The **forebrain**, *the most visibly obvious region of the brain, consists of multiple interconnected structures that are critical to such complex processes as emotion, memory, thinking, and reasoning.* We will begin our exploration of the forebrain by looking deep inside of it.

One set of structures comprises the **basal ganglia**, *which are involved in facilitating planned movements, skill*

learning, and are also integrated with the brain's reward system (Figure 3.14). People who are practiced at a given motor skill, such as playing an instrument or riding a bicycle, have actually modified their basal ganglia to better coordinate engaging in the activity. The basal ganglia are also affected in people who have Tourette's syndrome—a condition marked by erratic and repetitive facial and muscle movements (called tics), exaggerated eye blinking, and frequent noise making such as grunting, snorting, or sniffing. Contrary to popular belief, shouting of obscenities is actually relatively uncommon among people with Tourette's syndrome. The excess dopamine that appears to be transmitted within the basal ganglia contributes to many of the classic Tourette's symptoms (Baym et al., 2008).

Another major set of forebrain structures comprises the **limbic system**, *an integrated network involved in emotion and memory* (Figure 3.14). One key structure in the limbic system is the almond-shaped **amygdala**, *which facilitates memory formation for emotional events, mediates fear responses, and appears to play a role in recognizing and interpreting emotional stimuli, including facial expressions.* In addition, the amygdala connects with structures in the nervous system that are responsible for adaptive fear responses, such as freezing in position when a possible threat is detected. Just below the amygdala is another limbic region called the **hippocampus** (Greek for "seahorse"—something it physically resembles), *which is critical for learning and memory, particularly the formation of new memories* (Squire, Wixted, & Clark, 2007; see Module 7.1).

Richly networked with the limbic system is a set of structures that functions as our reward system. Parts of the reward system were first discovered decades ago, and somewhat incidentally, when researchers James Olds and Peter Milner were using electrical stimulation techniques to map out various brain functions in rats. Over the course of their work, they observed that stimulation to a

Figure 3.14 The Basal Ganglia and Limbic System

The basal ganglia function in both voluntary movement and processing of rewards. Structures in the limbic system include the limbic cortex, hippocampus, and amygdala, which play roles in regulating motivation, memory, and emotion.

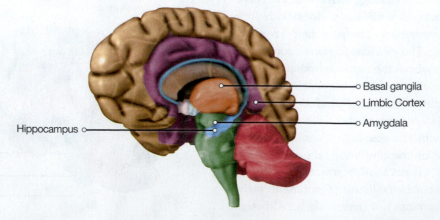

region called the *septum* caused an animal to return and stay in the location it had been standing when the stimulation was first delivered. The rat seemed to have learned that something rewarding would happen if it remained in that location. To explore this observation further, Olds and Milner (1954) placed rats individually into a chamber that included a lever that, when pressed, would deliver electrical stimulation to the septum. Self-induced stimulation to this particular area appeared highly rewarding to the rats. In fact, the rats did nothing but press the bar so long as it brought them the reward of stimulation. Subsequent research has confirmed that activity in the reward centers, in particular a region called the *nucleus accumbens*, accompanies many pleasurable experiences, including sexual excitement and satisfying a food craving (Avena et al., 2008) Many potentially addictive drugs are also known to target dopamine transmission in the nucleus accumbens and related reward center structures.

You have already encountered the hypothalamus (which translates to "below the thalamus") in Module 3.2. The hypothalamus serves as a sort of thermostat, maintaining the appropriate body temperature, and it regulates drives such as aggression and sex by interacting with the endocrine system. In fact, regions of the hypothalamus trigger orgasm for both females and males (Meston et al., 2004; Peeters & Giuliano, 2007).

The **thalamus** *is involved in relaying sensory information to different regions of the brain*. Most of the incoming sensory information, including what we see and hear, is routed through the thalamus and then proceeds to more specialized regions of the brain for further processing. Many of these regions include the highly complex and advanced cerebral cortex.

THE CEREBRAL CORTEX The **cerebral cortex** *is the convoluted, wrinkled outer layer of the brain that is involved in multiple higher functions, such as thought, language, and personality*. This highly advanced, complex structure has increased dramatically in size as the primate brain has evolved (Kouprina et al., 2002; Hofman, 2014). Figure 3.15 shows a slice of the brain revealing contrasting light and dark regions. The dark region is called *gray matter* and is composed of cell bodies and dendrites; the white region is composed of myelinated axons that interconnect the different structures of the brain. Within the brain are spaces called *ventricles*, which are filled with cerebrospinal fluid, a solution that helps to eliminate wastes and provides nutrition and hormones to the brain and spinal cord. Cerebrospinal fluid also cushions the brain from impact against the skull. In Figure 3.16, you can see that crossing the midline of the brain is a densely concentrated bundle of nerve cells called the **corpus callosum**, *a collection of neural fibers connecting the two hemispheres*.

Figures 3.15 Gray and White Matter of the Brain

The cerebral cortex includes both gray matter and white matter, which consist of myelinated axons. Also seen here are the ventricles of the brain. These cavities are filled with cerebrospinal fluid that provides nourishment and exhange of chemicals with the brain as well as structural protection.

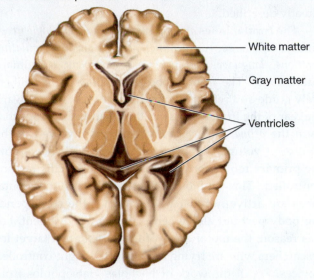

Figure 3.16 The Corpus Callosum

The left and right hemispheres of the brain are connected by a thick band of axons called the corpous callosum.

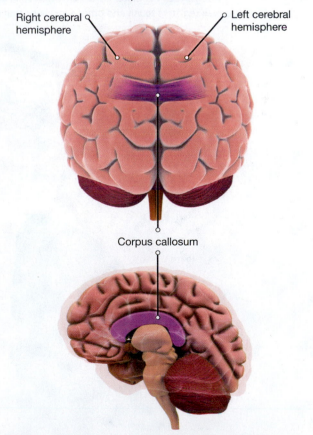

The cerebral hemispheres consist of four major areas, known as *lobes*: the frontal, parietal, occipital, and temporal lobes (Figure 3.17). Each of the cerebral lobes has a particular set of functions. Nerve cells from each of the four lobes are interconnected, however, and are also networked with regions of the midbrain and hindbrain already described.

The **frontal lobes** *are important in numerous higher cognitive functions, such as planning, decision making, regulating emotions, language, and voluntary movement* (Goldman-Rakic, 1996). The frontal lobes also allow us to deliberately guide and reflect on our thought processes. Toward the rear of the frontal lobes is a thick band of neurons that form the *primary motor cortex*, which is involved in the control of voluntary movement. Figure 3.18 shows how the primary motor cortex maps onto the specific regions controlled. This and other motor areas of the frontal lobes are active not just when moving the corresponding body part but also when planning a movement. For this reason, the motor areas of the cortex are a target for researchers who are trying to develop thought-controlled devices. Recall the work of Nicholas Hatsopoulos from the beginning of the module: In their experimental procedures, Hatsopoulos and his colleagues have implanted microchips into the motor cortex of healthy monkeys and

Figure 3.17 The Four Lobes of the Cerebral Cortex
The cerebral cortex is divided into the frontal, parietal, occipital, and temporal lobes.

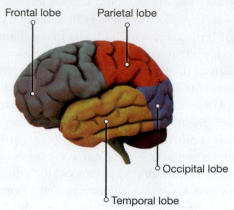

quadriplegic humans. They can then train the monkeys to make specific movements or ask their human volunteers to do the same. Recordings of motor cortex activity show reliable and predictable neural activity associated with specific types of movements. Using those electrical signals from the motor cortex, the research team has been able to develop thought-controlled robotic arms and computer navigation systems.

Figure 3.18 The Body as Mapped on the Motor Cortex and Somatosensory Cortex
The regions of the motor cortex are involved in controlling specific body parts. The somatosensory cortex registers touch and other sensations that correspond to the body region depicted.

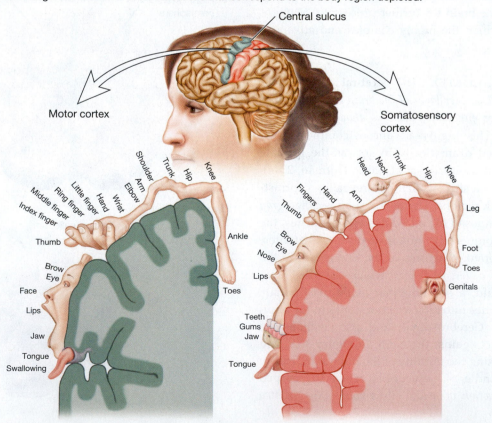

The **parietal lobes**, *located behind the frontal lobes, are involved in our experiences of touch and bodily awareness.* Adjacent to the primary motor cortex and at the front edge of the parietal lobe is the *somatosensory cortex*—a band of densely packed nerve cells that register touch sensations. Figure 3.18—a map of the body that corresponds to the somatosensory cortex—depicts differences in sensory sensitivity of the bodily regions. For instance, the volume of nerve cells in the somatosensory cortex corresponding to the face and hands is proportionally greater than the volume of cells devoted to less sensitive regions like the torso and legs. Regions within the parietal lobes also function in bodily awareness, and performing mathematical and visuospatial tasks.

The **occipital lobes** *are located at the rear of the brain, where visual information is processed* (vision is covered in more detail in Module 4.2). The **temporal lobes** *are located at the sides of the brain near the ears and are involved in hearing, memory, language, and some higher-level aspects of vision such as object and face recognition.*

Our sketch of the cerebral cortex thus far has been focused on specialized regions within the four lobes. However, we have yet to discuss the right and left hemispheres, which have further levels of specialization.

Hemispheric Specialization

Although they appear to be mirror images of each other, the two sides of the cortex often perform different functions, a phenomenon called *hemispheric specialization.* Speaking in general terms, the right hemisphere is specialized for cognitive tasks that involve visual and spatial skills, recognition of visual stimuli, and musical processing. In contrast, the left hemisphere is more specialized for language and math (Corballis, 1993; Gazzaniga, 1967, 2000). These specializations have led to the myth that creative artists and those who rely on intuition are literally "right-brained," whereas logical and analytical types are supposedly "left-brained." In reality, poets and engineers alike use both hemispheres in their work.

The left-brained and right-brained labels are clearly simplified ways of describing personality and interests. However, abundant evidence indicates that the two hemispheres are specialized to perform different functions. Language provides a great example: Almost all right-handed people and approximately two-thirds of left-handed individuals show language dominance in the left hemisphere. Some of the first evidence of this

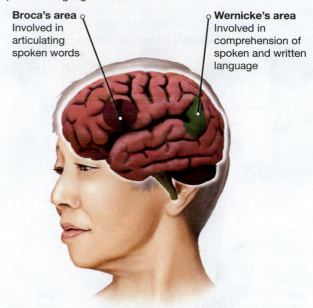

Figure 3.19 Hemispheric Specialization

Broca's area and Wernicke's area are associated with different aspects of language function.

Broca's area Involved in articulating spoken words

Wernicke's area Involved in comprehension of spoken and written language

specialization came in the mid-1800s, when French surgeon Paul Broca conducted a postmortem examination of a patient who had been unable to speak for the last three decades of his life. Broca identified an area of the man's left frontal lobe that was severely damaged and reasoned that it played a major role in speech (see Figure 3.19). Countless studies have confirmed that this area, now called *Broca's area*, is responsible for complex grammar and speech production. Another language region, *Wernicke's area*, is located in the left temporal lobe, extending into the adjacent parietal lobe and is involved in the comprehension of speech (discussed in more detail in Module 8.3).

Our understanding of hemispheric specialization expanded greatly through work with split-brain patients. In the 1960s, physicians hoping to curtail severe epileptic seizures in their patients used a surgical procedure to treat individuals who were not responding to other therapies. The surgeon would sever the corpus callosum, leaving a patient with two separate cerebral hemispheres. This surgery, which is used sparingly today, is not as drastic as it might sound. To some extent, patients think and behave remarkably normal after the operation, but there are some noticeable and curious changes that arise from the isolated functioning of each hemisphere. For example, if an object appears far enough to one side of your field of vision, it will only stimulate the visual centers in the opposite side of the brain. For most of us, that is not an issue because the two hemispheres quickly share that information. But what do you suppose would happen if they could not communicate?

Figure 3.20 A Split-Brain Experiment

This woman has had a split-brain operation. She is able to verbalize which objects match when they are placed to her right side, because language is processed in the left hemisphere. She cannot verbalize the matching objects at the left, but can identify them by pointing.

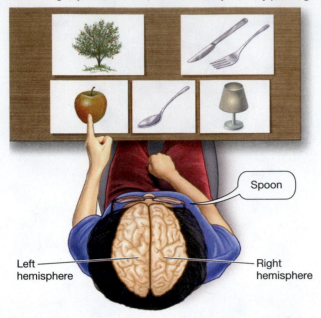

Spoon

Left hemisphere

Right hemisphere

To see how a split-brain experiment would work see Figure 3.20. Imagine the person pictured had split-brain surgery. On the one hand, she is able to match the two objects to her right and can verbalize the match, because the left side of her visual system perceives the objects and language is processed in the left hemisphere of the brain. On the other hand, a visual stimulus presented on the left side of the body is processed on the right side of the brain. As you can see, when the object is presented to the left side of the split-brain patient, the individual does not verbalize which of the objects match, because her right hemisphere is not specialized for language and cannot label the object. If asked to point at the matching object, however, she is able to do so. Thus, she is able to process the information using her right hemisphere, but cannot articulate it with language.

Split-brain surgery is rare, and it would be unthinkable to use it as an experimental procedure—how could you randomly assign a healthy person to have his or her cortex split in two? One alternative method that has been used with healthy individuals is called *Wada testing* (named after the researcher, Juhn Atsushi Wada, who devised the technique). Researchers begin by injecting a sedative into an artery on one side of the body. As the sedative travels upward into the brain, it sedates only one half of the cortex. This creates a temporary state in which one half of the cortex is doing all the work, so researchers can test for a specific ability—such as language or mathematics—in only one hemisphere.

Studies of split-brain patients show that the cerebral hemispheres are specialized for different functions. Again, these are general terms; it is easy to get caught up in thinking of these generalities as absolutes. The reality is that most cognitive functions are spread throughout multiple brain regions spanning both cerebral hemispheres.

Working the Scientific Literacy Model

Neuroplasticity and Recovery from Brain Injury

One truth of neuroscience is that the brain is a highly complex organ with numerous specialized regions. However, there is room for change. Although the brain is genetically programmed to be organized in specific ways, it still has a remarkable property called **neuroplasticity**, *which is the capacity of the brain to change and rewire itself based on individual experience*. In this video, you will see how the human brain grows and develops throughout the life span and how the brain can remarkably repair itself after being damaged.

Watch THE PLASTIC BRAIN

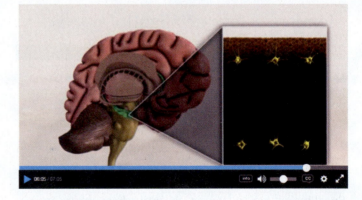

What do we know about neuroplasticity?

An example of neuroplasticity can be found in the brains of adults who received music training as children. The brains of musicians differ from nonmusicians in regions involved in controlling hand movements and in hearing. Experiments have confirmed that the musical training results in changes in brain anatomy and function (Gaser & Schlaug, 2003; Schlaug et al., 1995).

Neuroplasticity is also important when it comes to recovery from injury. Traumatic brain damage from strokes and accidents is often permanent because the generation of new neurons seems to be limited to a few specific areas. However, thanks to neuroplasticity, there is a chance that existing areas can be modified to accommodate the injury. For this reason, physicians and therapists attempt to capitalize on neuroplasticity in their treatments. For example, the loss of speech production may occur in the aftermath of a stroke. At least partial recovery is often possible by facilitating neuroplasticity. But how is this done?

How can science explain how neuroplasticity contributes to stroke recovery?

Researchers have discovered a remarkable technique for facilitating stroke recovery. Many patients who have suffered strokes and experience spoken language deficits actually sing using fluent, articulated words, even though they cannot speak those same phrases. Based on this observation, neurologists and speech therapists have developed Melodic Intonation Therapy (MIT) to restore speech function through singing (Norton et al., 2009). In a study of this technique, patients who had suffered strokes underwent intensive MIT sessions, singing long strings of words using just two pitches, while rhythmically tapping their left hand to the melody (see Figure 3.21).

The patients underwent 80 or more sessions lasting 1.5 hours each day, 5 days per week. Remarkably, this therapy has worked for multiple patients; after these intensive therapy sessions, they typically regain significant language function (Schlaug et al., 2009). The therapy does not "heal" damaged nerve cells in the left hemisphere at Broca's area. Rather, language function is taken over by areas of the right hemisphere that reorganize as a result of the therapy (Wan et al., 2014). In case you are wondering why the patients tapped the fingers of their left hand, it is because speech itself involves complex motor movements, so much so that it is sometimes difficult to speak without moving the hands. Therefore, researchers propose the tapping may facilitate the recovery process through engaging the motor system.

MIT is just one example of what neuroplasticity research has taught us, and language is only one of many abilities that can be affected through brain damage. Further insight into neuroplasticity comes from animal studies in which scientists have shown remarkable recovery following brain damage. Researchers are attributing much of the recovery they observe to chemicals called *trophic factors*. These substances are most likely responsible for nerve cell recovery in humans and other animals, and therefore show potential for medical treatments in the future.

Can we critically evaluate this research?

Is the success of MIT therapy the result of language function moving to a "vacancy" in the right hemisphere—an area of the brain waiting for something to do? Definitely not; there is no vacant or idle space in the brain, despite the myth that we use only 10% of our brain. In fact, the right hemisphere does appear to be involved in some aspects of expressive language (this should serve as a reminder not to overemphasize hemispheric specialization). For example, the ability to understand metaphors and other figurative language draws on the right hemisphere (Schmidt et al., 2007). This may help explain why language can, with great effort, move from left- to right-hemispheric processing. Nonetheless, there are certainly limits to how much neuroplasticity can help repair a damaged brain or modify a healthy one. Age at the time of injury influences recovery, with younger people tending to have more favorable outcomes. Sensory and motor experiences before and after an injury, diet, and stress also influence the degree to which neural plasticity occurs (Kolb et al., 2013).

Why is this relevant?

Melodic intonation therapy for patients who have suffered strokes and have lost language function is not yet commonplace. For decades, other forms of speech therapy have been the primary methods for helping patients recover. Given the promising results obtained to date, MIT will hopefully be added to existing speech therapy programs. The results of MIT offer a remarkable example of neuroplasticity and may pave the way for therapies needed to restore other functions.

Figure 3.21 Melodic Intonation Therapy

During melodic intonation therapy, patients are asked to sing phrases of increasing complexity.

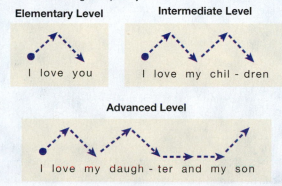

Windows to the Brain: Measuring and Observing Brain Activity

In the early days of brain research, scientists had to rely almost exclusively on case studies, such as those used by Broca in his discovery of one of the brain's language centers. Doctors and researchers typically identified symptoms of living patients and then conducted postmortem dissections to see which brain abnormalities might have been responsible for the problems. Alternatively, they made detailed observations of patients before and after brain surgery, often for tumor removal. There was no way to image the brain of a living, breathing patient or research participant.

Today, perfectly healthy college students can walk into brain imaging research centers found on many college campuses and have their brains scanned during research studies. Researchers not only take detailed pictures of their brains but are also able to measure actual brain activity. In this section, we review several methods for examining healthy, normally functioning brains, as well as the brains of individuals who have experienced major injuries or disease.

ELECTROPHYSIOLOGY   The electrical activity of nerve cells can be recorded using highly sensitive devices. An **electroencephalogram (EEG)** *measures patterns of brain activity with the use of multiple electrodes attached to the scalp.* The neural firing of the billions of cells in the brain can be detected with these electrodes, amplified, and depicted in an electroencephalogram (EEG). An EEG can tell us a lot about general brain activity during sleep, during wakefulness, and while patients or research participants are engaged in a particular cognitive activity (see Figure 3.22). The convenience and relatively in-expensive nature of EEGs, compared to other modern methods, make them appealing to researchers. EEGs also detect neural activity at the exact moment it oc-curs, which makes for precise measures of brain activity. However, this technique does not give researchers access to actual images of the brain.

BRAIN IMAGING   To obtain actual images of the brain, researchers turn to techniques such as **positron emission tomography (PET) scans**, *in which a low level of radioactive glucose is injected into the blood, and its movement to regions of the brain engaged in a particular task is measured (active nerve*

cells use up the glucose at a faster rate than do resting cells). This technique allows researchers to monitor brain activity while a person performs a task such as reading or viewing emotionally charged stimuli. The greatest strength of PET scans is that they show metabolic activity of the brain. A drawback is that glucose uptake in the brain is a relatively slow process, so there is a long delay between the pre-sentation of a stimulus and a brain response that the PET scan can detect. This is a problem when you want to see moment-by-moment changes in the activity of the brain.

Magnetic resonance imaging (MRI) *is a technology designed to acquire highly detailed images of brain anatomy via exposure to a strong (and harmless) magnetic field.* As you sit reading these words, millions of hydrogen atoms in your brain are spinning around in random directions. If you were to enter an MRI machine, the atoms would align and spin in the same direction because of the application of a magnetic field by the imaging device. Radio waves are then passed through the brain, disrupting the alignment of the atoms. These disruptions produce a signal that can be translated into a detailed, three-dimensional image of the brain.

Like PET, a certain type of MRI allows us to observe ac-tual brain activity. Blood cells carry oxygen to active nerve cells. **Functional MRI (fMRI)** *measures changes in blood flow, which is correlated with neural activity, throughout the brain.* Thus, fMRI can be used to examine the underlying brain activity of specific psychological processes (Figure 3.23).

Figure 3.23 Functional Magnetic Resonance Imaging

Functional MRI technology allows researchers to determine how blood flow, and hence brain activity, changes as study participants or patients perform different tasks. In this image, the colored areas depict increases in blood flow to the left and right temporal lobes, relative to the rest of the brain, during a cognitive task.

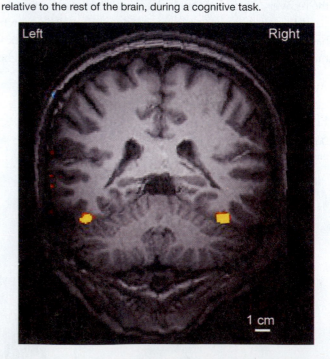

Figure 3.22 Measuring Brain Activity

The electroencephalogram measures electrical activity of the brain by way of electrodes that amplify the signals emitted by active regions.

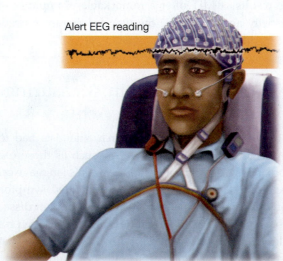

Another imaging technique, called **magnetoencephalography (MEG)**, *measures the magnetic fields created by the electrical activity of nerve cells in the brain.* With this technology, highly sensitive devices that measure magnetic fields surround the skull and record changes in brain activity. MEG records the electrical activity of nerve cells just a few milliseconds after it occurs, which allows researchers to record brain activity at nearly the instant a stimulus is presented. This is advantageous relative to PET and fMRI, which measure the slower processes of glucose consumption and blood flow, respectively.

LESIONING AND BRAIN STIMULATION A number of methods have been developed that, in effect, impair a portion of the brain to see how it affects behavior. The oldest method based on this idea is brain **lesioning**—*a technique in which researchers intentionally damage an area in the brain* (a lesion is abnormal or damaged brain tissue). Researchers interested in how the human brain works obviously cannot perform this procedure in experiments (they cannot randomly assign humans to experience brain damage), although many patients have been generous enough to become research participants after stroke, injury, or brain surgery.

Less drastic techniques affect brain activity only temporarily; in fact, some can be applied to humans with no ill effects. The Wada test, used to study hemispheric specialization, is one example. Researchers also study brain function using **transcranial magnetic stimulation (TMS)**, *a procedure in which an electromagnetic pulse is delivered to a targeted region of the brain.* Pulses delivered repeatedly at a low frequency cause a temporary disruption of brain activity (Figure 3.24). In contrast, high-frequency delivery of TMS stimulates, rather than impairs, the targeted brain region. Not only is this approach a tool for researching the brain, it can also be used to treat serious psychological problems. For example, TMS has been used to stimulate underactive areas associated with depression (Gaynes et al., 2014). In addition, researchers have found that the magnetic stimulation provided by TMS may be helpful in promoting stroke recovery by stimulating damaged nerve cells (Schlaug et al., 2008).

Figure 3.24 Brain Stimulation

Transcranial magnetic stimulation involves targeting a magnetic field to a very specific region of the brain. Depending on the amount of stimulation, researchers can either temporarily stimulate or disable the region.

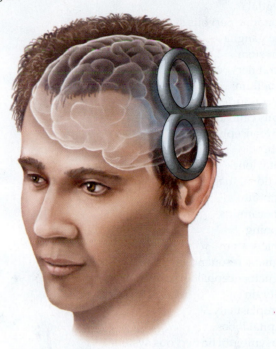

For example, patients who have damage to the left motor cortex may lose their ability to control regions on the right side of the body. TMS directed at the left motor cortex can help these patients regain some movement.

Brain stimulation techniques can also be used to supplement behavioral therapies, such as melodic intonation therapy, for stroke recovery. When brain stimulation and MIT are combined, recovery is often stronger in comparison to MIT alone (Vines, Norton, & Schlaug, 2011).

There are many different technological options for studying brain anatomy and functioning. Table 3.3 provides an overview of how these techniques work.

Table 3.3 Windows to the Brain: Measuring and Observing Brain Activity

Electroencephalogram (EEG)	Involves the use of multiple electrodes attached to the scalp. These record the strength, pattern, and location of the brain's electrical activity.
Positron emission tomography (PET) scans	Begins with the injection of radioactive glucose that can be traced as it fuels neuronal activity. The busiest cells use the most glucose and therefore emit the strongest radioactive signals.
Magnetic resonance imaging (MRI)	Applies electromagnetic energy to align hydrogen atoms in the brain. Then, another burst of energy disrupts the orientation of those atoms. The shift in the ions' positions and activity can be detected and used to map the structure of a brain.
Functional magnetic resonance imaging (fMRI)	Applies electromagnetic energy to trace the flow of oxygen-rich blood in the brain. The busiest brain cells use the most oxygen, and therefore emit the strongest signals.
Magnetoencephalography (MEG)	Measures the magnetic fields produced by the electrical activity of nerve cells.
Lesioning	Examines the changes in psychological function associated with damage to specific areas of the brain.
Transcranial magnetic stimulation (TMS)	Applies electromagnetic energy to a specific, targeted area of the brain to either disrupt or stimulate its activity.

Module 3.3 Summary

3.3a   Know . . . the key terminology associated with the structure and organization of the nervous system:

amygdala
autonomic nervous system
basal ganglia
brain stem
central nervous system (CNS)
cerebellum
cerebral cortex
corpus callosum
electroencephalogram (EEG)
forebrain
frontal lobes
functional magnetic resonance imaging (fMRI)
hindbrain
hippocampus
lesioning
limbic system
magnetic resonance imaging (MRI)
magnetoencephalography (MEG)
midbrain
neuroplasticity
occipital lobes
parasympathetic nervous system
parietal lobes
peripheral nervous system (PNS)
positron emission tomography (PET) scan
somatic nervous system
sympathetic nervous system
temporal lobes
thalamus
transcranial magnetic stimulation (TMS)

3.3b   Understand . . . how studies of split-brain patients reveal the workings of the brain.

Studies of split-brain patients were important in that they revealed that the two hemispheres of the brain are specialized for certain cognitive tasks. For example, studies of split-brain patients showed that the left hemisphere is specialized for language. These studies were carried out before other brain imaging techniques became available.

3.3c   Apply . . . your knowledge of brain anatomy to predict which abilities might be affected when a specific area is injured, or when attempting to map out the functioning of healthy brains.

As you learned in this module, scientists and surgeons often perform detective work to figure out how behavior and mental activity map onto brain structure and anatomy, or vice versa. By knowing the nature of a brain injury, one can make predictions about what behavior might be impaired. Conversely, observing behavioral changes after an injury allows one to make predictions about the location of the injury. When working with healthy brains, scientists can use imaging technologies to explore brain structure and function relationships, as summarized in Table 3.3.

3.3d   Analyze . . . what we can learn by mapping psychological functions in the brain.

Unlike early techniques such as case studies, the technology of mapping psychological functions in the brain allows us to see detailed images of both the structure and activity of the brain. The technology also helps scientists tackle important clinical and mental health issues. At the beginning of this module, we described a technology that links brain activity with motor movements. Researchers are able to detect planned movements by monitoring electrical patterns in the motor cortex, and then use this information to provide the impaired individual with motor control. Current technology can also be used to help with stroke recovery or disorders such as depression, as has been done using transcranial magnetic stimulation (TMS). However, it is important to keep in mind that brain mapping is most helpful if we have an understanding of behavior.

Module 3.3 Quiz

Know . . .

1. The central nervous system consists of which of the following?
   - **A.** The brain and the nerves controlling digestion and other automatic functions
   - **B.** The brain and the voluntary muscles
   - **C.** The brain and the spinal cord
   - **D.** The somatic and autonomic systems

2. The region of the brain that plays a critical role in relaying sensory information to different brain regions is called the:
   - **A.** hippocampus
   - **B.** temporal lobe
   - **C.** thalamus
   - **D.** basal ganglia

Understand . . .

3. Why would a person who has undergone a split-brain operation be unable to name an object presented to his left visual field, yet could correctly point to the same object from an array of choices?
   - **A.** Because his right hemisphere perceived the object but does not house the language function needed for naming it
   - **B.** Because the image was processed on his left hemisphere, which is required for naming objects
   - **C.** Because pointing is something done with the right hand
   - **D.** Because the right hemisphere of the brain is where objects are seen

Apply . . .

4. Damage to the somatosensory cortex would most likely result in which of the following impairments?

   A. Inability to point at an object
   B. Impaired vision
   C. Impaired mathematical ability
   D. Lost or distorted sensations in the region of the body corresponding to the damaged area

Analyze . . .

5. A drawback of PET scans compared to newer techniques, such as MEG, is that:

   A. PET is slower, which means it is more difficult to measure moment-to-moment changes in brain activity.
   B. PET is faster, which makes it difficult to figure out how brain activity relates to what someone sees or hears.
   C. PET is too expensive for practical use.
   D. PET is slower, and it does not provide a picture of the brain.

Module 3.4 Scientific Literacy Challenge: Is Football Too Dangerous?

Superbowl XLIX was the most-watched television broadcast in US history, attracting more than 114 million viewers. Statistics like that suggest that it could be the most popular form of entertainment in the country (although Katy Perry did attract an additional 3 million viewers during her halftime show). So why is there a movement to do away with football, particularly at the junior high and high school levels?

Before you continue to the activity, take a moment to consider your current feelings about football.

JOURNAL PROMPT

What kinds of evidence do you think it would take to have football banned in the United States? Do you think there is a chance that, because of injury risks, football will be taken out of the schools?

What do we know about the risks of football?

In the editorial that follows, you will read about one journalist's opinions on the dangers of football. As you read, pay attention to your initial reactions to these opinions because they are likely shaped by your preexisting attitudes. Maybe you're a football player yourself or a devoted fan. Or you may care little about football, or perhaps even come from a part of the world where US football is never played. The writer's ability to sway your opinion will depend in part on how you feel about football now. As you read, pay close attention to the types of information the author is considering, and notice the key terms and concepts covered in Chapter 3.

Football Does Not Belong in Our Schools

Lionel Matthews, city editor

On Wednesday night, I was saddened to read that another metro area high school football player died. During practice Monday afternoon, the 16-year old (whose name is being withheld) ducked down behind the defensive line and lunged forward to make a tackle. Instead, he hit helmet-to-helmet with a 210-pound fullback charging at full speed. The runner was fine, but **MRIs (magnetic resonance imaging brain scans)** revealed severe damage to the tackler's **cortex**, with bleeding and swelling around his

frontal and left **temporal lobes**, which bore the brunt of the impact. He lay on the field unconscious, and would not wake again. He was not the first player in the country to die this season. Three other high school footballers died in just the past week, and two others died the previous month. In all of these cases, head trauma was to blame.

No one would deny that these deaths are tragic, but some would argue that they are rare, freak accidents. If I cannot convince them otherwise, here is another problem to consider: Dozens of retired NFL players testified that the effects of concussions compound over time and lead to permanent brain damage. If science confirms that this is the result of a career in football, then I question why we would ever let young men suit up in the first place.

We now know that there have been a number of deaths among high school football players just this year, and that these deaths were the result of severe brain injuries. The editor also claims that less-severe brain injuries can add up over time, but we have yet to see the evidence for that. Next, we will read about the science of head injuries applied to football.

How do scientists study the risks of football?

Scientists who study brain injury include psychologists (often specializing in neuropsychology), biologists, and physicians (often specializing in neurology). As you read about what they have learned, pay attention to any terms and concepts from Chapter 2 that describe quality scientific research, including the highlighted selections that contain clues to the quiz that follows.

Does long-term football playing really lead to permanent brain damage? Here are a few important findings to consider:

- Retired NFL players between 30 and 50 years of age are 20 times more likely to have early signs of dementia or Alzheimer's than the rest of the population in that age range.

- A study of 34 retired players showed they experienced significantly higher scores on the Beck Depression Inventory (a standard test of depressive symptoms) than 29 control participants who had not experienced concussions. Additionally, the level of depression was correlated with the number of football-related head injuries. Further research found the rate of depression among retired players to be as much as 25%, compared with 10% in the rest of the population.

- A study published in the *American Journal of Geriatric Psychiatry* had volunteers complete a problem-solving task during an fMRI scan. The scan showed abnormal frontal lobe functioning in a group of 13 retired NFL players, while the 69 non-football players they were compared to were free of brain injury. Furthermore, the players who were sidelined with head injuries most often showed the greatest abnormality.

Hopefully you spotted the references to the important scientific concepts. Test yourself by completing this short quiz referring back to the article to find the answers.

1. A study published in the *American Journal of Geriatric Psychiatry* compared retired NFL players to nonplayers. What type of research design is this?
   a. Experimental
   b. Case study
   c. Natural observation
   d. Quasi-experimental

2. The author states that one study used the Beck Depression Inventory to assess depression. Scores on this test are a(n) _____ of depression.
   a. independent variable
   b. operational definition
   c. replication
   d. case study

3. One study found that the NFL players have higher than average levels of dementia. In this study, the dependent variable was
   a. number and severity of the symptoms of dementia.
   b. whether someone played in the NFL.
   c. the age of the volunteers.
   d. not mentioned.

Answers: 1. d 2. b 3. a

How should we think critically about the risks of football?

Remember that critical thinking involves curiosity and reasonable levels of skepticism. Critical thinkers continue to ask questions while evaluating the quality of the answers they find. As you read the next paragraph, be sure to look for signs of critical thinking.

These are only a few of the many studies documenting that a football career is associated with cognitive, motor, and mood problems. Football's defenders point out that these are correlational, not experimental findings. This is not surprising, because clearly nobody wants to, or would be allowed to, randomly assign people to concussion or control conditions. Given that similar problems are found among people who experience multiple head injuries in other areas (boxing, military-related injuries), it does seem head trauma is at fault. The alternative seems unlikely: It is difficult to imagine that this correlation comes from people who already have brain damage choosing to pursue football. Knowing the extent of damage that is possible—even likely—it is both fascinating and terrifying to me that people still let their children play football. The only reason I can imagine is because of the emotional engagement with the sport. Some people just love football, and no amount of evidence will change that.

The statements below will help you identify several aspects of critical thinking. Match the following critical thinking statements to the highlighted passages that illustrate them. Note that not all of these items are included in the article.

1. The author has evaluated the *generalizability* of the study to the population he is writing about (teenaged football players).
2. The author addressed whether the studies provide evidence of cause and effect.
3. The author considered alternative viewpoints or explanations.
4. The author acknowledged the ethical limits of this research.

1. Not included 2. Blue 3. Yellow 4. Green

After thinking about the evidence, Mr. Matthews wraps up his editorial by showing how the data might apply to the schools in his community.

How is this information relevant to the editor's position on football injuries?

If Mr. Matthews is correct that football really is that much of a risk to high school players, then there is a great deal of relevance. Read how he makes that connection in his editorial, and then explore any newly formed thoughts you may have about football and concussions.

> So, while I am advocating for eliminating football altogether, I have to acknowledge that I am in the minority. How then can we address the problem? One solution is to start by protecting our youth and ban football from our schools, but there may be alternatives. Perhaps if football players were not so heavily armored, they might be a bit more careful about running headfirst into each other. I am not optimistic about that option either. It may be that our best bet is for stricter rules: rules guiding how players can initiate contact, the length of games, number of full-contact practices and the like. I would consider any of those a small success because, at this point, I am willing to take any step in the right direction.

SHARED WRITING

Review your original thoughts on the hazards of football. Given the research results provided in the bullet points, do you think the author makes a convincing argument? Do you think your prior beliefs and opinions about football shape your agreement or disagreement with the editorial?

Chapter 3 Quiz

1. When behavioral geneticists use adoption studies to estimate the heritability of a behavior, the adoptive family can be thought of as representing _____, whereas the biological family can be thought of as representing

   _____.
   A. adaptive behavior; maladaptive behavior
   B. maladaptive behavior; adaptive behavior
   C. nature; nurture
   D. nurture; nature

2. In general, the _____ of a neuron receives messages from other cells. The neuron can then pass the message onto another neuron via its _____.
   A. axon; dendrites
   B. dendrites; axon
   C. myelin; cell body
   D. cell body; myelin

3. What is a synapse?
   A. The site where a "message" is transmitted from one nerve cell to another
   B. A chemical substance that is released by a transmitting neuron
   C. A fatty coating that increases the rate at which messages travel through neurons
   D. The part of the neuron that keeps it alive

4. Reggie suffered brain damage in a car accident. As a result, he can no longer breathe on his own and needs the help of a respirator. Which structure of his brain was most likely damaged?
   A. pons
   B. medulla
   C. cerebellum
   D. reticular formation

5. Dr. Stearns studies what happens behaviorally when she temporarily impairs a brain region. Which method is she most likely using?
   A. functional MRIs
   B. PET scans
   C. transcranial magnetic stimulation
   D. brain lesioning

6. A person who is homozygous for a trait:
   A. always has two dominant copies of a gene.
   B. always has two recessive copies of a gene.
   C. has identical copies of the gene.
   D. has different copies of the gene.

7. If a researcher wanted to identify an actual gene that put people at risk for developing depression, she would most likely use which of the following methods?
   A. Behavioral genomics
   B. A comparison of monozygotic and dizygotic twins
   C. An adoption study
   D. Calculation of heritability

8. Imagine you hear a report about a heritability study that claims trait X is "50% genetic." Which of the following is a more accurate way of stating this?
   A. Fifty percent of individual differences of trait X within a population are due to genetic factors.
   B. Only half of a population has the trait.
   C. The trait is homozygous.
   D. More than 50% of similarities of trait X within a population are the result of genetic factors.

9. Which of the following is a function of glial cells?
   A. Glial cells slow down the activity of nerve cells.
   B. Glial cells manufacture myelin.
   C. Glial cells suppress the immune system response.
   D. Glial cells contain the nucleus that houses the cell's genetic material.

10. Sensory and motor nerves differ in that:
    A. only sensory neurons have dendrites.
    B. only motor neurons have axons.
    C. sensory neurons carry messages away from the brain, and motor neurons carry information toward the brain.
    D. Sensory neurons carry messages toward the central nervous system and motor neurons carry information away from the central nervous system.

11. People who experience a loss of pain sensation in the middle of exercise are likely having a rush of _____.
    A. adrenaline
    B. norepinephrine
    C. pituitary
    D. endorphin

12. A major difference between the somatic and autonomic branches of the nervous system is that:
    A. the somatic nervous system controls involuntary responses, and the autonomic nervous system controls voluntary movement.
    B. the somatic nervous system is located in the brain, and the autonomic nervous system is located peripherally.
    C. the somatic nervous system controls voluntary movement, and the autonomic nervous system controls involuntary responses.
    D. the somatic nervous system controls involuntary movement, and the autonomic nervous system controls voluntary responses.

13. Producing words generally involves the _____ cerebral hemisphere region called _____ area.
    A. right; Broca's
    B. left; Broca's
    C. right; Wernicke's
    D. left; Wernicke's

14. The brain imaging technique that involves measuring blood flow in active regions of the brain is called:
    A. magnetic resonance imaging.
    B. functional magnetic resonance imaging.
    C. PET scan.
    D. transcranial magnetic stimulation.

15. The branch of the autonomic nervous system that prepares the body for quick action in an emergency is the _____ division.
    A. central
    B. secondary
    C. sympathetic
    D. parasympathetic

Chapter 4
Sensation and Perception

Module 4.1   Sensation and Perception at a Glance

Learning Objectives

4.1a Know . . . the key terminology of sensation and perception.

4.1b Understand . . . what stimulus thresholds are.

4.1c Understand . . . the methods of signal detection theory.

4.1d Apply . . . your knowledge of signal detection theory to examples.

4.1e Analyze . . . claims that subliminal advertising can influence your behavior.

We rarely seem to expect the unexpected. A case in point: Joshua Bell, one of the world's most talented violinists, performed a live concert at a Washington, D.C., subway station. He collected approximately $32 for his performance—quite a modest sum considering that just two days before, people had paid hundreds of dollars to hear him play with the Boston symphony. Only a handful of the more than 1,000 subway passersby stopped to listen to him, and the majority did what people typically do in this situation—they hurried by without stopping to listen or to pitch any coins into his collection. After 45 minutes of playing Bach, Joshua Bell returned his $3.5 million, 18th-century violin to its case and walked away.

This informal, yet remarkable experiment tells us a little bit about Joshua Bell, but it speaks volumes about what the

1,000 other people are like. One lesson is that context plays an extremely important role in what people sense and perceive. No one expects one of the best living violinists to be playing in a subway. Also, many commuters are so busy and focused they fail to notice amazing events going on around them. It is enough to make you wonder what else we are missing. The study of sensation and perception can offer some clues. Two questions we address in this module are What role does attention play in perception? and What are the principles that guide perception?

Sensation and perception are different, yet integrated processes. To illustrate this point, take a look at the Necker cube in Figure 4.1. After staring at it for several seconds,

Figure 4.1 The Necker Cube

Stare at this object for several seconds until it changes perspectives.

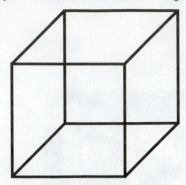

you likely noticed that the perspective changed: The cube seemingly flipped its orientation on the page. Although the cube remains constant on the page and in the way it meets the eye, it can be perceived in different ways. The switching of perspectives is a perceptual phenomenon that takes place in the brain.

Sensing the World Around Us

The outside world is a cacophony of light, sound, and natural and artificial chemicals. The body has an amazing array of specialized processes that allow us to absorb this information. The first step is **sensation**, *the process of detecting external events by sense organs and turning those events into neural signals*. At the sensory level, the sound of someone's voice is simply vibrations in the air, and the sight of a person is a combination of shape, color, and motion. **Perception** *involves attending to, organizing, and interpreting stimuli that we sense*. Perception includes recognizing the sounds as a human voice and understanding that the colors, shape, and motion together make up the image of a human being.

Sensation gives way to the beginnings of perception when specialized sensory receptors—structures that respond to external events—are stimulated (summarized in Table 4.1). **Transduction** *is the process in which physical or chemical stimulation is converted into a nerve impulse that is relayed to the brain*. For example, when patterns of light reach receptors at the back of the eye, they are converted into nerve impulses that travel to numerous brain centers where color and motion are perceived, and objects are identified.

Generally speaking, our sensory receptors are most responsive upon initial exposure to a stimulus. When you first walk into a crowded restaurant or when you exit a dark movie theater, the sound and light you encounter initially seem intense. Eventually the sensation becomes less intense even if the stimulation remains the same. **Sensory adaptation** *is the reduction of activity in sensory receptors with repeated exposure to a stimulus*. Sensory adaptation provides the benefit of allowing us to adjust to our surroundings and shift our focus and attention to other events.

STIMULUS THRESHOLDS How loud does someone have to whisper to be heard? If you touch a railroad track, how sensitive are your fingers to vibrations from a distant train? One early researcher, physicist and philosopher, William Gustav Fechner (1801–1887), coined the term **psychophysics**—*the field of study that explores how physical energy such as light and sound and their intensity relate to psychological experience*. Fechner and other early psychophysicists were interested in some basic questions about perceptual experience and sought to understand general principles of perception. A popular approach was to measure the minimum amount of a stimulus needed for detection, and the degree to which a stimulus must change in strength for the change to be perceptible.

See if you can estimate human sensory abilities in the following situations (based on Galanter, 1962):

- If you were standing atop a mountain on a dark, clear night, how far away do you think you could detect the flame from a single candle?

- How much perfume would need to be spilled in a three-room apartment for you to detect the odor?

On a clear night, a candle flame can be detected at 30 miles away. One drop of perfume is all that is needed for detection in a three-room apartment. Each of these values represents an **absolute threshold**—*that is, the minimum amount of energy or quantity of a stimulus required for it to be reliably detected at least 50% of the time it is presented* (Figure 4.2). The minimum amount of pressure, sound, light, or chemical required for detection varies among individuals and across the life span. Also, as you are surely aware, some species-related differences are quite amazing. The family dog may startle, bark, and tear for the door

Table 4.1 Stimuli Affecting Our Major Senses and Corresponding Receptors

Sense	Stimuli	Type of Receptor
Vision (Module 4.2)	Light waves	Light-sensitive structures at the back of the eye
Hearing (Module 4.3)	Sound waves	Hair cells that respond to pressure changes in the ear
Touch (Module 4.4)	Pressure, stretching, or piercing of the skin surface	Different types of nerve endings that respond to pressure, temperature changes, and pain
Taste (Module 4.4)	Chemicals on the tongue and in the mouth	Cells lining the taste buds of the tongue
Smell (Module 4.4)	Chemicals contacting mucus-lined membranes of the nose	Nerve endings that respond selectively to different compounds

Figure 4.2 Absolute Thresholds

The absolute threshold is the level at which a stimulus can be detected 50% of the time.

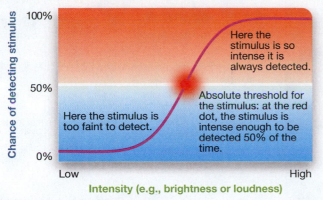

Here the stimulus is so intense it is always detected.

Absolute threshold for the stimulus: at the red dot, the stimulus is intense enough to be detected 50% of the time.

Here the stimulus is too faint to detect.

before you can even detect a visitor's approach, and a cat can detect changes in shadows and light that go unnoticed by humans. There is no magic or mystery in either example: These animals simply have lower absolute thresholds for detecting sound and light.

Another measure of perception refers to how well an individual can detect whether a stimulus has changed. A **difference threshold** *is the smallest detectable difference between stimuli*. When you add salt to your food, for example, you are attempting to cross a difference threshold that your taste receptors can register. Whether you actually detect a difference, known as a *just-noticeable difference*, depends on the intensity of the original stimulus. The more intense the original stimulus, the more of it that must be added for the difference threshold to be reached. If you add one pinch of salt to a plate of French fries that already had one pinch sprinkled on them, you can probably detect the difference. However, if you add one pinch of salt to fries that already had four pinches applied, you probably will not detect as much of a difference. When measured in terms of perception, a single pinch of salt does not always equal one pinch.

Sensory adaptation is one process that accounts for why we respond less to a repeated stimulus—even to something that initally seems impossible to ignore.

Whether someone perceives a stimulus is determined by self-report—that is, by an individual reporting that she either did or did not detect a stimulus. Someone may claim to see a faint candlelight just because he expects to see it. More importantly, think of a radiologist trying to detect tumors in a set of images, or a lifeguard who is supposed to listen to calls for help. How do we confirm whether these stimuli were truly perceived, or that the individuals were just guessing?

SIGNAL DETECTION **Signal detection theory** *predicts that whether a stimulus is perceived depends on both sensory experience and judgment made by the subject.* Thus, the theory requires us to examine two processes: a sensory process and a decision process. In a typical signal detection experiment conducted in the laboratory, the experimenter presents a faint stimulus or no stimulus at all (the sensory process), and the subject is asked to report whether it was present (the decision process).

Factors such as your expectations, arousal level, and motivation all influence whether you are able to detect a weak stimulus. If you are lost in the woods, you may be better able to notice the sound of someone's voice, the far-off growl of a bear, or the sound of a car on the road than if you are hiking with friends on a well-known trail—even if the surrounding noise level is the same. Is the heightened sensitivity due to enhanced functioning of your ears (the sensory process) or because you are more motivated to detect sounds (the decision process)? Research shows that motivational changes are likely to affect the decision process so that you assume every snapping twig is a bear on the prowl (see Figure 4.3).

Figure 4.3 Signal Detection Theory

Signal detection theory recognizes that a stimulus is either present or absent (by relying on the sensory process) and that the individual either reports detecting the stimulus or does not (the decision process). The cells represent the four possible outcomes of this situation. Here we apply signal detection theory to a man alone in the woods.

Figure 4.4 Applying Signal Detection Theory

Imagine a radiologist is examining an image to determine whether the patient has a tumor (positive result), or does not have a tumor (negative result). Identify which of the four events (A–D) goes within the correct box; that is, identify it as a hit, a miss, a false alarm, or a correct rejection.

Hit:	False alarm:
Miss:	Correct rejection:

A. There is no tumor; the radiologist concludes that the test is negative for a tumor.

B. There really is a tumor; the radiologist concludes that the test is negative for a tumor.

C. There really is a tumor; the radiologist concludes that the test is positive for a tumor.

D. There is no tumor; the radiologist concludes the test is positive for a tumor.

Hit: C	Miss: B
False alarm: D	Correct rejection: A

Answers:

According to signal detection theory, the sensory judgment process has four possible outcomes. You may be correct that you heard a sound (a *hit*), or correct that you did not hear a sound (a *correct rejection*). Of course, you will not always be correct in your judgments—sometimes you will think you heard something that is not there. Psychologists refer to this type of error as a false alarm; as would be the case if you believed you heard a bear when there were none around. Alternatively, you could experience a miss, such as when a bear sneaks up behind you but you fail to detect its presence. Practice applying signal detection theory to the example in Figure 4.4.

Thus far we have focused on sensation and perception for stimuli that we are aware of perceiving, regardless of whether they are actually present (hits) or absent (misses). Although not perceived, a weak stimulus *could* have a psychological effect even though it resides below the level of conscious awareness—a phenomenon that brings to mind the saga of subliminal messages.

The study of thresholds and signal detection gives us answers to some very basic questions about how we sense and perceive our environment. Perception, however, can be a very rich experience; to explain it we need a more complex set of principles.

Perceiving the World Around Us

To perceive figures, our perceptual systems make sense of ambiguity and fill in information where it seems to be missing. Figure 4.5 illustrates this principle well. We are compelled to see contours where there are none; our brain fills in the nonexistent square. The contours are referred to as subjective contours because they are not physically "there" (except in your brain). Which principles guide this and other perceptual processes?

Figure 4.5 The Kanizsa Square

Can you see a square? Our perceptual systems fill in contours where there are not any to help us perceive familiar shapes.

GESTALT PRINCIPLES OF PERCEPTION In the mid-20th century, a German school of psychology emerged that sought to describe how we perceive form. *Gestalt psychology* is based on the belief that "the whole is greater than the sum of its parts." That is, on their own, the individual parts of a stimulus may have little meaning, but when combined as a whole they take on a significant, perceived form. Gestalt psychologists identified several key principles to describe how we organize features that we perceive. One Gestalt principle, referred to as *figure–ground*, tells us that objects or "figures" in our environment tend to stand out against a background. In Figure 4.6a do you see a vase or two faces in profile? We sense (detect) neither a vase nor two faces—just a pattern of reflected light picked up by our eye. We perceive (interpret) two objects, but which is figure and which is ground is ambiguous. The figure–ground principle applies to hearing as well. When you are holding a conversation with one individual in a crowded party, you are attending to the figure (the voice of the individual) against the background noise (the ground).

Other key Gestalt principles include proximity, similarity, continuity, and closure (Figure 4.6b–e).

Myths in Mind

Setting the Record Straight on Subliminal Messaging

You may have heard claims that flashing persuasive images on television and movie screens can have strong influences on behavior. But does subliminal perception—meaning perception below conscious thresholds—really exist? And if so, does it really control our motivations, beliefs, and behaviors?

The answer to the first question is yes, we can perceive events without being aware of them. This phenomenon has been demonstrated in cognitive psychology experiments (Van den Bussche et al., 2009; Zajonc, 2001). To get a subject to register a stimulus unconsciously, a researcher might present a picture such as an angry face for a fraction of a second, immediately followed by what is called a *masking stimulus*, which could be a colored square. The colored square masks the picture of the angry face, meaning that it keeps the face outside of conscious awareness. Although people are not consciously aware of seeing an angry face, the emotional centers of their brain respond to the angry face, but not a face with a neutral expression (Critchley et al., 2000; Sweeny et al., 2009). It appears that perception can occur without our awareness, but with detectable effects on the nervous system.

Can subliminal messages lead us to purchase items we would not otherwise buy—an often-cited example of subliminal messaging? There is little evidence supporting this claim. Flashing a subliminally perceived message on a screen can have a temporary effect on thinking. When thirsty research participants watched a drink advertisement that included a subliminal flash of the word "thirst" on the screen, they found the ad to be more persuasive than did nonthirsty people who watched the same ad

Do you see a cigarette advertisement in this photo? There is not an obvious one, but you may be reminded of Marlboro cigarettes as you look at this race car. Critics have accused sponsors of this Formula One car of using the barcode design to create an image similar to Marlboro Red cigarettes. Inquiries into attempts at subliminal advertising over this issue ensued.

(Strahan, et al., 2002; see also Newell & Shanks, 2014). Advertisements certainly do affect our behavior, but it is far-fetched to interpret their effects as a form of unconscious "mind control". On the positive side, subliminal messages can be used to help people overcome negative stereotypes. Senior citizens who were repeatedly exposed to positive subliminal messages about aging (e.g., words such as "spry" presented on a screen) showed a reduction in negative beliefs about aging and improved physical functioning over an eight-week period in comparison to control participants exposed to neutral subliminal stimuli (Levy et al., 2014).

Figure 4.6 Gestalt Principles of Form and Perception

(a) Figure and ground. (b) Proximity helps us group items together so that we see three columns instead of six rows. (c) Similarity occurs when we perceive the similar dots as forming alternating rows of yellow and red, not as columns of alternating colors. (d) Continuity is the tendency to view items as whole figures even if the image is broken into multiple segments. (e) Closure is the tendency to fill in gaps so as to see a whole object.

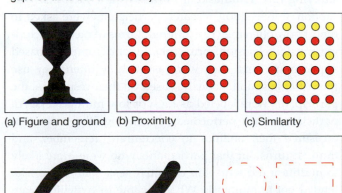

(a) Figure and ground   (b) Proximity   (c) Similarity

(d) Continuity   (e) Closure

The illusions and figures in Figure 4.6 reveal some common principles that guide how we perceive the world. We can take this exploration a step further by discussing the cognitive processes that underlie these principles.

TOP-DOWN AND BOTTOM-UP PROCESSING Sometimes our existing knowledge determines how we perceive a stimulus. **Top-down processing** *occurs when knowledge and expectations guide what is immediately perceived.* For example, we can perceive the center of Figure 4.7 as either

Figure 4.7 Top-Down Processing

Is the center item the letter B or the number 13?

A

12   13   14

C

Animals and insects take advantage of figure–ground ambiguity to camouflage themselves from predators. Can you see the walking stick insect in this photo?

the number 13 or the letter B, depending on whether you look down from the letter A, or across from the number 12—a top-down influence. Similarly, walking into a crowded room to locate a friend is a top-down process because you have a person's face in mind, which guides your perceptual expectations.

At other times, we first perceive the details of a stimulus, and then build up toward a recognizable whole. This is **bottom-up processing**: *constructing a whole stimulus or concept from bits of raw sensory information*. As you might expect, bottom-up processing would occur when you encounter something that is unfamiliar or difficult to recognize. Driving a car in a foreign country for the first time would engage bottom-up processing as you attempt to make sense of what different traffic signals and road signs mean.

The way we perceive the world is often a combination of both top-down and bottom-up processing (Beck & Kastner, 2009)—it is difficult to imagine not having some kind of expectation about an experience, and even more difficult to imagine perception without some kind of raw sensation. *Parallel processing* refers to the simultaneous use of top-down and bottom-up processing (Rumelhart & McClelland, 1986). It is what allows us to attend to multiple features of what we sense. Regardless of whether we perceive the world from a bottom-up, top-down, or combined direction, we must pay attention to the relevant features.

Working the Scientific Literacy Model

Attention, Perception, and Task Performance

Attention allows us to focus on a particular task, and maintaining this focus requires that we block out irrelevant stimuli. However, circumstances, including those of our own making, compel us to spread our attention across multiple tasks and stimuli. Given the enormous number of distractions we contend with every day, and the impact such distractions can have on our performance as well as personal safety, psychologists have sought to better understand the relationship between perception, attention, and task performance.

What do we know about attention, perception, and task performance?

Selective attention *involves focusing on one particular event or task at a time*: studying, driving, listening to music, or watching a movie, for example. In contrast, **divided attention** *involves attending to several stimuli or tasks at once*. Simultaneously playing a video game and holding a conversation involves divided attention. Whether people engage their selective or divided attention systems depends on several factors, including familiarity and complexity of the tasks at hand, mental energy level, and accurate self-evaluation: Are you a "good multitasker" or a "bad multitasker"? Psychologists have sought to better understand the attentional requirements of multitasking and how it affects performance (Pashler, 1994).

How can science explain the relationship between attention and performance?

Psychologists have adopted some interesting methods for studying how multitasking influences attention and perception. In one study, research participants were asked to report how often they use different forms of media, including music, television, print, phone, and computer-based applications; next, they were asked how often they use these media simultaneously. Based on their responses, the participants were labeled as high or low multitaskers. All participants then performed several cognitive tasks that measured their abilities to concentrate, remember, and think. It turns out that participants who were more likely to multitask did worse on cognitive tests than those who tended not to multitask. When it came to switching from one task to another, high multitaskers actually performed worse than low multitaskers because they were more easily distracted by irrelevant information (Ophir et al., 2009). It appears that those who multitask the most are the ones who should do it least.

Although some distractions may not be under our control, much of the time we choose to make them available and engage with them (e.g., leaving the smart phone on and nearby at all times, or keeping several unrelated applications open on the computer). The choice to multitask is related to our beliefs about our multitasking abilities. But just because a person believes she is a good multitasker does not make it so. Researchers found that college students underestimate how poor their own personal multitasking abilities are, even though these same students also report that multitasking in general is a bad idea (i.e., for other people) (Finley, Benjamin, & McCarley, 2014).

Can we critically evaluate this research?

Does this evidence mean that we should completely isolate ourselves from any possible distraction when working or studying? On the one hand, it certainly suggests that we should at least minimize distracters and the urge to multi-task. On the other hand, psychologists have found that the brain is designed to effectively do more than one cognitive task at a time, provided the two tasks can be processed by different brain structures. For example, one brain imaging study revealed that when participants engaged in one mental task, the left side of the frontal lobe would activate. When a second, very similar, task was added, the right frontal lobe would activate and performance would not suffer (Charron & Koechlin, 2010). Thus, the brain is able to multitask up to a point. However, only a very small proportion of people (estimated 2.5%) are referred to as "supertaskers" because they show no decrement in performance on tasks that typically interfere with each other (Watson & Strayer, 2010). Ultimately, multitasking while trying to learn new information, such as listening to music while reading text material or texting while listening to a classroom lecture, is not advised.

Why is this relevant?

Perhaps you engage with various media while studying or performing some other task: You post on Instagram, send an instant message, live stream music on your computer, or text and check your Facebook account. You are used to this. As such, you may believe that being allowed to engage in these activities during exams will improve your performance on them. In one observational experiment of a 180-minute study period, researchers found that students spent, on average, 73 minutes listening to music and 25 minutes engaged in any of 35 other distractions

(Calderwood, Ackerman, & Conklin, 2014). In light of the research just discussed, these observations would suggest that multitasking during both learning (studying) and remembering (exam taking) can impair cognitive performance. Thus, while it may seem unlikely, professors who forbid the use of headphones during exams are looking out for your best interests.

Lack of focused attention has an impact on safety as well. Close to 20% of car crashes resulting in injury have implicated distraction as the cause (National Highway and Traffic Safety Administration, 2010). The government website distraction.gov reveals more sobering statistics, including that 71% of teens and young adults have sent text messages while driving and 78% have read them. They also estimate that in 2012, more than 420,000 people were injured by a distracted driver.

MISSING THE OBVIOUS: INATTENTIONAL BLINDNESS Missing the obvious can be surprisingly easy—especially if you are focused on just one particular aspect of your environment. **Inattentional blindness** *is a failure to notice clearly visible events or objects because attention is directed elsewhere* (Mack, 2003; Neisser, 1979; Simons & Chabris, 1999). Inattentional blindness shows that when we focus on a limited number of features, we might not pay much attention to anything else—not even a world-renowned violinist performing in a subway station, as described at the beginning of this module.

Imagine you are asked to watch a video of students dressed in white T-shirts actively moving around while passing a ball to one another. Your task is to count the number of times the ball is passed. To complicate matters, there are also students in black T-shirts doing the same thing with another ball, but you are instructed to ignore them. This is a top-down task because you are to selectively attend to a single set of events. If this sounds easy—it is. In an experiment asking participants to do just this, most were able to accurately count the number of passes, give or take a few.

But what if a student wearing a gorilla suit walked through the video, stopped, pounded her chest, and walked off screen? Who could miss that? Surprisingly, about half the participants failed to even notice the gorilla (Simons & Chabris, 1999). You can imagine how shocked the participants were when they watched the film again without selectively attending to one thing and realized they had completely missed the gorilla. Inattentional blindness shows that when we focus on a limited number of features, we might not pay much attention to anything else.

Perhaps you were already familiar with the video of the "invisible gorilla" demonstration just described (if not you can readily find versions of it online). Daniel Simons found that, unsurprisingly, 100% of students who had previously seen the demonstration spotted the gorilla when asked to watch the video again, but 56% who had not yet seen the demonstration missed the gorilla. However, the original video was edited such that the color of the curtain in the background changed, as did the number of ball throwers wearing black. Only 14% of students who were familiar with the demonstration, and all of whom noticed the gorilla, reported seeing either of the unexpected changes in curtain color or the change in the number of players wearing black (Simons et al., 2010). Interestingly, 29% of students who had been unfamiliar with the video noticed at least one of the two changes.

Inattentional blindness has important implications for eyewitness reporting. People who witness events such as auto accidents or criminal behavior may offer faulty or incomplete testimony. This is not necessarily because they have failed to remember, or have been willfully deceitful, but because they have failed to notice the events. In another follow up to the gorilla study, psychologist Christopher Chabris and colleagues asked study participants to follow and focus on the behavior of a confederate (a research assistant—unbeknownst to the participants) across campus. When following the confederate at night, only 35% of the participants noticed a staged fight right in their pathway; during the daytime only 56% noticed (Chabris et al., 2011).

Demonstrations of inattentional blindness can be eye opening, amusing, and rightly lead us to question what else we might be missing. Alternatively, the phenomenon illustrates how effective we can be at attending to something while effortlessly blocking out distractions. To see an inattentional blindness experiment in action, watch this YouTube video called Magic in the Laboratory, posted by Dr. Anthony Barnhart, or "Magic Tony."

Watch MAGIC IN THE LABORATORY

Our ability to sustain attention draws from multiple sensory modalities, including, of course, vision, and also hearing and even touch. In Module 4.2 we explore specifically how the visual system works.

Psychologist Anthony Barnhart conducts experiments on attention using simple magic tricks as stimuli. In this study, participants watched a video of him placing two napkins on the table, the one on his right covering a coin (as shown in the first two photos). After covering each napkin with a coffee cup, he reveals that the coin is no longer under the napkin on the right—it has moved to the left. As the trick unfolds, Barnhart records participant's eye movements to measure what they spend the most time watching. The compiled results are shown the third photo, with the red area indicating the greatest level of attention. This image shows the crucial moment where he slides the coin from one side to another; most participants did not notice because they were focused on the cup—an instance of inattentional blindness (Barnhart & Goldinger, 2014).

Module **4.1** Summary

4.1a **Understand . . . the key terminology of sensation and perception:**

absolute threshold
bottom-up processing
difference threshold
divided attention
inattentional blindness
perception
psychophysics
selective attention
sensation
sensory adaptation
signal detection theory
top-down processing
transduction

4.1b **Understand . . . what stimulus thresholds are.**

Stimulus thresholds can be either absolute (the minimum amount of energy to notice a stimulus) or based on difference (the minimum change between stimuli required to notice they are different).

4.1c **Understand . . . the methods of signal detection theory.**

Signal detection theory involves testing whether a participant perceives stimuli by measuring hits (stimulus was presented and detected), misses (stimulus was presented and undetected), false alarms (stimulus was not presented and reported as present), and correct rejections (stimulus was not presented and not perceived).

4.1d **Apply . . . your knowledge of signal detection theory to examples.**

In the activity "applying signal detection theory" in Figure 4.4, you had the chance to apply the theory to scenarios that might occur when a radiologist examines an image for the presence of a tumor. When applying signal detection theory to any scenario, we need to consider that there will be a sensory process (either a stimulus was or was not present) and a decision rule (a statement that the stimulus was or was not detected). This yields the four possibilities of a hit, miss, false alarm, or correct rejection.

4.1e **Analyze . . . claims that subliminal advertising can influence your behavior.**

As you read in the Myths in Mind feature, we certainly can perceive stimuli below the level of awareness, and this perception can affect our behavior in some ways. As for the often-repeated claim that subliminal advertising can control consumer behavior, it seems safe to conclude that it alone will not cause you to mindlessly part with your money.

Module **4.1** Quiz

Know . . .

1. _____ is the study of how physical events relate to psychological experiences of those events.
   A. Sensation
   B. Sensory adaptation
   C. Perception
   D. Psychophysics

Understand . . .

2. The minimum stimulation required to detect a stimulus is a(n) _____, whereas the minimum required to detect the difference between two stimuli is a(n) _____.
   A. just noticeable difference; difference threshold
   B. absolute threshold; difference threshold
   C. difference threshold; absolute threshold
   D. just noticeable difference; absolute threshold

3. Signal detection theory improves on simple thresholds by including the influence of:
   A. psychological factors, such as expectations.
   B. engineering factors, such as how well a set of speakers is designed.
   C. whether an individual has hearing or visual impairments.
   D. the actual intensity of the stimulus.

Apply . . .

4. Walking on a crowded downtown sidewalk, Ben thinks he hears his name called, but when he turns around, he cannot find anyone who might be speaking to him. In terms of signal detection theory, mistakenly believing he heard his name is an example of a _____.
   A. hit
   B. miss
   C. bogus hit
   D. false alarm

Analyze . . .

5. Which statement accurately describes the conclusions psychologists have drawn about the effects of subliminal messages on behavior?
   A. Subliminal messages have no effect whatsoever.
   B. Research shows subliminal messages might have mild effects on behavior and thinking.
   C. Research shows that subliminal ads are powerful.
   D. Psychologists have not yet conducted studies to form an answer.

Module 4.2 The Visual System

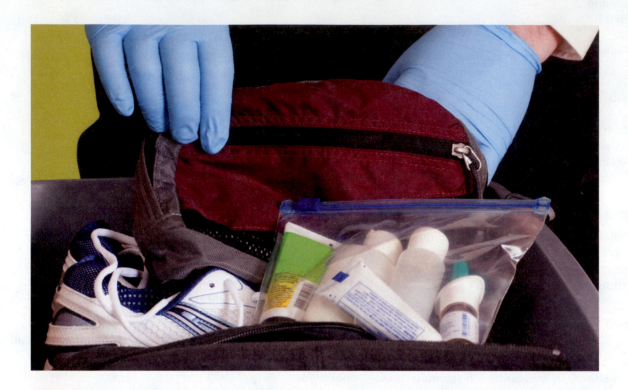

Learning Objectives

4.2a Know . . . the key terminology relating to the eye and vision.

4.2b Understand . . . how visual information travels from the eye through the brain to give us the experience of sight.

4.2c Understand . . . the theories of color vision.

4.2d Apply . . . your knowledge to describe how we perceive depth in our visual field.

4.2e Analyze . . . how we perceive objects and faces.

A few years ago, Gregory Hinkle of West Virginia passed through airport security with a loaded gun, only to return to the security checkpoint and turn it in after realizing the lapse. (He was charged with a misdemeanor.) Amazing as it may sound, these incidents are often accidental—passengers simply forget that they packed a weapon. More importantly, you might wonder how a gun could pass through security screening in the first place. According to monthly reports by the Transportation Security Authority (TSA), baggage screeners regularly intercept weapons, including guns. In fact, during the calendar year of 2014, TSA employees detected 2,100 guns. Another question that is much more difficult to answer is how many undetected weapons make it through security—and why do such lapses happen? TSA

employees have the same perceptual systems as the rest of us. Even though they have technology at their disposal and training to enhance detection of certain objects, they are still susceptible to the same types of errors that we all make. Among the questions we address in this module are 1) How do we recognize and perceive objects? and 2) Why do errors such as failing to perceive a dangerous object at security checkpoints occur?

The world is a visual place to most humans. Traffic signs and road maps, for example, are all visually based. Likewise, museums, restaurant menus, and computer screens were designed to be absorbed through sight. In this module, we explore how vision works—starting out

Figure 4.8 Light Waves in the Electromagnetic Spectrum

(a) The electromagnetic spectrum: When white light is shined through a prism, the bending of the light reveals the visible light spectrum. As you can see, we sense only a narrow band of this spectrum. (b) Wavelength is measured by amplitude and distance.

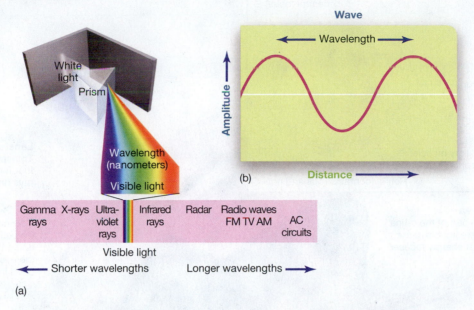

(a)

(b)

The Human Eye

as patterns of light entering the eye, and ending up as a complex, perceptual experience. We begin with an overview of the basic physical structures of the eye and brain that make vision possible, and then discuss the experience of seeing.

The Human Eye

The human eye senses an amazing array of information, and then relays it back to the brain for complex, perceptual processing. To ensure that this process occurs correctly, the eye needs numerous specialized structures.

HOW THE EYE GATHERS LIGHT The term "light" actually refers to radiation that occupies a relatively narrow band of the electromagnetic spectrum, shown in Figure 4.8a. Light travels in waves that vary in terms of two different properties: length and amplitude. The term *wavelength* refers to the distance between peaks of a wave—differences in wavelength correspond to different colors on the electromagnetic spectrum. As you can see from Figure 4.8a, long wavelengths correspond with the reddish colors and short wavelengths with the bluish colors. Also, the amplitude (or height; see Figure 4.8b) of the peaks of a wave give different experiences. Low-amplitude waves correspond with dim colors, and high-amplitude waves with bright colors.

Some organisms, such as bees, can see in ultraviolet, and some reptiles can sense infrared light. The prism in Figure 4.8a separates out the basic colors of the spectrum. We do not typically see such pure coloration as depicted in this figure. Rather, what we see is based on a mixture

of wavelengths that vary by hue (colors of the spectrum), intensity (brightness), and saturation (colorfulness, or density) (see Figure 4.9).

THE STRUCTURE OF THE EYE The eye consists of specialized structures that gather up the complex mixture of hue, intensity, and saturation (Figure 4.10). These structures

Figure 4.9 Hue, Intensity, and Saturation

Colors vary by hue (color), intensity (brightness), and saturation (colorfulness or "density").

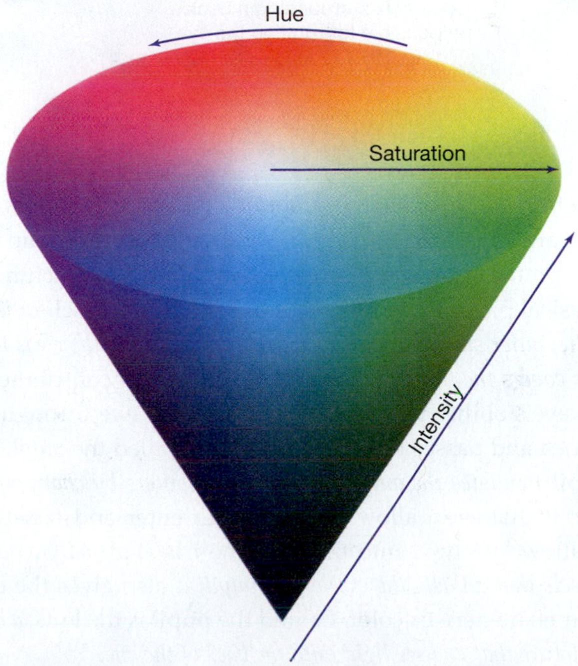

Figure 4.10 The Human Eye and Its Structures

Notice how the lens inverts the image that appears on the retina (see inset). The visual centers of the brain correct the inversion.

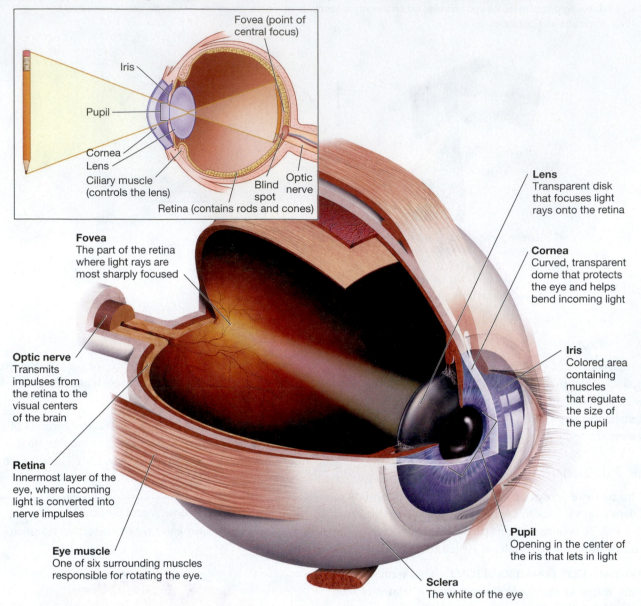

Fovea (point of central focus)

Iris

Pupil

Cornea
Lens

Ciliary muscle (controls the lens)

Blind spot

Optic nerve

Retina (contains rods and cones)

Fovea
The part of the retina where light rays are most sharply focused

Optic nerve
Transmits impulses from the retina to the visual centers of the brain

Retina
Innermost layer of the eye, where incoming light is converted into nerve impulses

Eye muscle
One of six surrounding muscles responsible for rotating the eye.

Lens
Transparent disk that focuses light rays onto the retina

Cornea
Curved, transparent dome that protects the eye and helps bend incoming light

Iris
Colored area containing muscles that regulate the size of the pupil

Pupil
Opening in the center of the iris that lets in light

Sclera
The white of the eye

function to regulate the amount of light that enters the eye, and organize light into a pattern that the brain can interpret. The eye is a sensitive and delicate structure, so physical protection of this organ is crucial. The **sclera** *is the white, outer surface of the eye* and the **cornea** *is the clear layer that covers the front portion of the eye* and also contributes to the eye's ability to focus. Light enters the eye through the cornea and passes through an opening called the *pupil*. The **pupil** *regulates the amount of light that enters by changing its size*; it dilates to allow more light to enter and constricts to allow less light into the eye. The **iris** *is actually a round muscle that adjusts the size of the pupil*; it also gives the eyes their characteristic color. Behind the pupil is the **lens**, *a clear structure that focuses light onto the back of the eye.*

THE RETINA: FROM LIGHT TO NERVE IMPULSE The **retina** *lines the rear inner surface of the eye and consists of specialized receptors that absorb light and send signals related to the properties of light to the brain.* The specialized receptors of the retina are called *photoreceptors.* Two general types of photoreceptors line the retina—rods and cones— each of which responds to different characteristics of light. **Cones** *are photoreceptors that are sensitive to the different wavelengths of light that we perceive as color.* The **fovea** *is the central region of the retina that contains the highest concentration of cones*; its functioning explains why objects in our direct line of vision are the clearest and most colorful relative to objects in the periphery. **Rods** *are photoreceptors that occupy peripheral regions of the retina; they are highly*

Figure 4.11 Distribution of Rods and Cones on the Retina
Cones are concentrated at the fovea, the center of the retina, whereas rods are more abundant in the periphery.

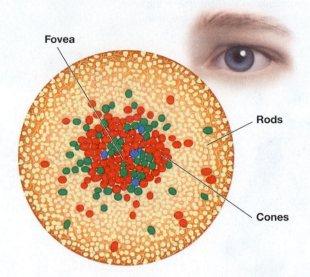

Figure 4.13 Blind Spot Demonstration
To find your blind spot, close your left eye and, with your right eye, fix your gaze on the + in the green square. Slowly move the page toward you. When the page is approximately 6 inches away, you will notice that the black dot on the right disappears because of your blind spot. Not only does the black dot disappear, but its vacancy is replaced by yellow: The brain "fills it in" for you.

sensitive under low light levels. As we move away from the fovea, the concentration of cones decreases and the concentration of rods increases (see Figure 4.11).

THE OPTIC NERVE Light stimulates chemical reactions in the rods and cones, and these reactions initiate neural signals that pass through an intricate network of cells in the retina, which in turn send impulses to the brain. The initial steps of the visual pathway are shown in Figure 4.12. Each eye has an **optic nerve**, *a cluster of neurons that gather sensory information, exit at the back of the eye, and connect with the brain.*

Figure 4.12 Arrangement of Photoreceptors in the Retina
Bipolar and ganglion cells collect messages from the light-sensitive photoreceptors and converge on the optic nerve, which then carries the messages to the brain.

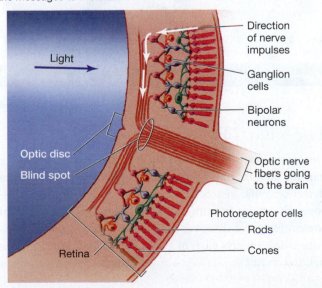

This nerve presents a challenge to the brain. Because it travels through the back of the eye, it creates an area on the retina with no rods or cones, called the *optic disc.* The result is a *blind spot*—a space in the retina that lacks photoreceptors. Discover your own blind spot by performing the activity described in Figure 4.13.

THE VISUAL PATHWAYS TO THE BRAIN The information contained in the cells of the optic nerve travels to numerous brain regions. The first major destination is the optic chiasm, the point at which the optic nerves cross at the midline of the brain (see Figure 4.14). For each optic nerve, about half of the nerve fibers travel to the same side of the brain, and half of them travel to the opposite side. Fibers from the optic nerves first connect with the visual area of the thalamus at a region called the *lateral geniculate nucleus* (LGN). The LGN then sends messages to the visual cortex, located in the occipital lobe, where the complex processes of visual perception begin (Figure 4.14).

How does the visual cortex make sense of all this incoming information? It starts with a division of labor among specialized cells. One set of cells in the visual cortex are referred to as *feature detection cells*; they respond selectively to simple and specific aspects of a stimulus, such as angles and edges (Hubel & Wiesel, 1962). Researchers have been able to map which feature detection cells respond to specific aspects of an image by investigating the visual cortex in lab animals (Figure 4.15). Feature detection cells of the visual cortex are thought to be where visual input is organized for perception, but further processing is required as well and involves additional neural pathways. From the visual cortex, information about shapes and contours is sent to other cortical areas. For example, the *ventral stream* is a pathway extending from the visual cortex to the temporal lobe and is where object recognition occurs. The

Figure 4.14 Pathways of the Visual System in the Brain

The optic nerves route messages to the visual cortex. At the optic chiasm, some of the cells remain on the same side and some cross to the opposite side of the brain. This organization results in images appearing in the left visual field being processed on the right side of the brain, and images appearing in the right visual field being processed on the left side of the brain.

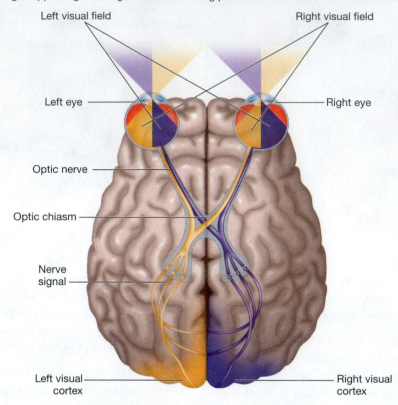

Figure 4.15 Measuring the Activity of Feature Detection Cells

Scientists can measure the activity of individual feature detector cells by inserting a microscopic electrode into the visual cortex of an animal. The activity level will peak when the animal is shown the specific feature corresponding to that specific cell.

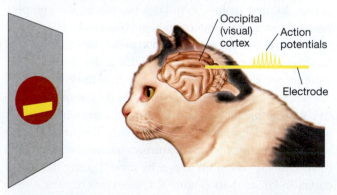

Watch THE VISUAL SYSTEM

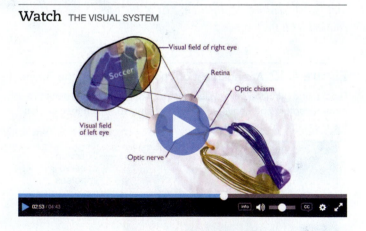

dorsal stream extends from the visual cortex to the parietal lobe of the cortex and is where depth and motion are perceived. To see the visual system in action and better understand how light passes through the eye to the brain, watch the following video, The Visual System.

The Visual Experience

Our visual experiences are not limited to the lines of various angles and orientations that stimulate feature detection cells. Instead, they are rich, meaningful experiences that arise from higher brain centers of the cerebral cortex. Here we discover how we recognize and experience whole objects such as people, cars, houses, and your pet dog or cat.

Working the Scientific Literacy Model

Object Recognition

Objects in our world can be seen from many different perspectives—that is, they can be seen from near or far, under varying levels of light, and from different angles. Given the numerous variations in how objects can be sensed, how is it that we still perceive them in the same, unified way?

What do we know about object recognition?

Despite the diverse ways that an object can be sensed, it is still perceived as the same object. This observation highlights what is called **perceptual constancy**, *the ability to perceive objects as having constant shape, size, and color despite changes in perspective*. What makes perceptual constancy possible is our ability to make relative judgments about shape, size, and lightness. For shape constancy, we judge the angle of the object relative to our position (see Figure 4.16). Color constancy allows us to recognize an object's color under varying levels of illumination. For example, a bright red car is recognized as bright red when in the shade or in full sunlight. Size constancy is based on judgments of how close an object is relative to one's position as well as to the positions of other objects. Also, our perception of objects involves distinguishing them individually, and identifying objects that appear frequently or rarely. As it turns

Figure 4.17 Find the T Among This Scattered Array of Offset Ls

It should not take you long to find the T. However, if a T was only actually mixed with Ls 2% of the time you were asked to locate one, you would likely miss it quite often.

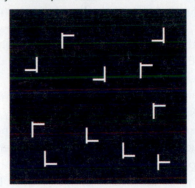

out, the process of identifying objects can be much more complicated than just seeing and naming them.

How can science explain how object recognition occurs?

Psychologists who specialize in visual perception have attempted to identify conditions in which we are likely to succeed or fail to perceive objects. It turns out that the frequency with which we encounter objects is closely related to our perception of them.

To see how, view the stimulus in Figure 4.17. Scattered around the dark background are offset Ls. One of the objects, however, is actually a T. It is easy to spot and only

Figure 4.16 Perceptual Constancies

(a) We perceive the door to be a rectangle despite the fact that the two-dimensional outline of the image on the retina is not always rectangular. (b) Color constancy: We perceive colors to be constant despite changing levels of illumination. (c) Size constancy: the person in the red shirt appears normal in size when in the background. A replica of this individual placed in the foreground appears unusually small because of size constancy.

(a)

(b)

(c)

takes a second or so to locate. Using this type of display, the experimenters flashed a mixture of Ls repeatedly, each time varying their locations. From time to time, the Ts appeared at a random location among the Ls and participants had to determine if any Ts were visible: The Ts appeared either 50% of the time for some participants, or 2% of the time for others. Those participants who were exposed to the Ts 2% of the time failed to detect them far more often than those who could have seen them 50% of the time (Rich et al., 2008).

Ts and offset Ls are great for laboratory experiments, but consider how this finding may apply to real-life situations, such as at airline security checkpoints. Wolfe and colleagues (2007) obtained photos of screen shots from the U.S. Department of Homeland Security that included luggage with typical travel objects, as well as luggage that included knives and guns. Participants were familiarized with what clothing, sunglasses, keys, and toys, as well as guns and knives, looked like on a security-screening device.

Similar to the experiment with Ls with the occasional T mixed in, the participants often failed to detect guns or knives if they occurred only 2% of the time, compared to 50% of the time (Wolfe et al., 2007). The rare event of a weapon in a suitcase makes these objects *less* likely to be perceived. Furthermore, little improvement in detecting infrequently placed weapons occurred when participants worked in teams. In summary, when something does not occur very often, you will have more difficulty spotting it.

Can we critically evaluate this evidence?

You might think that knives and guns would be even more noticeable when they appear among common objects such as clothing, hairdryers, and magazines. Sometimes the very reason we perceive objects is because they stick out like a sore thumb. This idea may have occurred to you when reading about the research we just described. However, the key issue here is that the more frequent an event is (e.g., a safe suitcase), the less likely an infrequent event (a weapon) will be detected.

Despite the similar findings of these two studies, we might still wonder about the generalizability of this research. In particular, we might question whether volunteers in the studies put forth as much effort as TSA baggage screeners, who have much more at stake. Follow-up work with newly trained TSA screeners showed that they too were more likely to miss infrequent events than frequent events that they had been trained to detect (Wolfe et al., 2013).

Why is this relevant?

Clearly, this research has applications beyond our own everyday experiences, although it is certainly still insightful on a personal level. You may be wondering whether people can be trained to overcome the tendency to miss out on infrequent events such as a knife or a gun in a suitcase. It turns out that monitoring and feedback under conditions in which weapons are found frequently improves people's ability to detect these events when they are infrequent (Wolfe et al., 2007). Another important application of this work is in interpretation of medical diagnostic imaging results, such as X-rays and MRIs. If the findings from these studies apply to medical settings, then we might expect that less frequent events such as tumors or other problematic symptoms would be less likely to be detected by a radiologist (Drew, Võ, & Wolfe, 2013).

JOURNAL PROMPT

Missing the Obvious: Even trained observers often miss seemingly obvious threats during airport security screenings and in medical diagnostic imaging. In what other situations might people miss what would *seem* to be obvious?

FACIAL RECOGNITION AND PERCEPTION One of the most important sources of social information comes from the human face—which explains why we have a natural inclination to quickly perceive faces. In fact, there is a region of the brain, located within the temporal lobe, that is specialized for facial recognition. Specific genetic problems or damage to this area can result in failure to recognize people's faces (a condition called *prosopagnosia*, or face blindness). People with face blindness are able to recognize voices and other defining features of individuals, but not faces. Some people with face blindness can find ways to compensate for the condition, such as developing heightened abilities to use voice recognition and other nonfacial cues, and some patients benefit from therapies designed specifically to help people perceive and remember faces (DeGutis et al., 2014; Hoover et al., 2010).

Face blindness also raises interesting questions about when perception and awareness occur. Although they cannot recognize faces consciously, people who are face blind may still exhibit involuntary physiological reactions to pictures of family members, but not to pictures of unfamiliar faces (Tranel & Damasio, 1985; Simon et al., 2011). In addition, people with face blindness can make judgments about famous faces more readily than about unfamiliar faces, and may even show activity in the face-processing region of the temporal lobe (Avidan & Behrmann, 2008; Eimer, Gosling, & Duchaine, 2012). These studies suggest that people with face blindness are able to distinguish among faces even if they are unaware that they are doing so. Although this is a rare clinical condition, it does help us understand some basic processes that are involved in perceiving faces. In the absence of this condition, the human

Figure 4.18 Seeing Faces

At left is a painting of turnips and other vegetables by the Italian artist Giuseppe Arcimboldo. The image at right is the same image rotated 180 degrees—does it resemble a human face?

brain seemingly insists on seeing faces, even when they are least expected (see Figure 4.18).

Perception and recognition of faces starts with the very basics. For example, our brain has the reasonable expectation that faces will appear upright. When a face is presented upside down, our ability to recognize the face and facial expressions diminishes (Figure 4.19). In one experiment, participants correctly recognized different faces 81% of the time when viewed upright, but the level of accuracy fell to 55% when the same faces were inverted (Freire et al., 2000). Also, we are especially attentive to the eyes when looking at faces (Bubic, Susac, & Palmovic, 2014).

Although objects and faces monopolize our visual experiences, we must also determine where they are in location to ourselves. Without this ability, we would not know how far to reach for an object, nor would we know how to navigate our environment.

DEPTH PERCEPTION Every pattern of light that hits your retina is two-dimensional, so we know that depth perception occurs in your brain. The words on this page, for example, lie on a two-dimensional surface—but look toward a more complex scene you will experience many cues for perceiving depth.

Binocular depth cues *are distance cues that are based on the differing perspectives of both eyes.* One type of binocular depth cue that we use, called **convergence**, *occurs when the eye muscles contract so that both eyes focus on a single object.*

Figure 4.19 The Face Inversion Effect

After viewing both upside-down photos of Beyonce, you probably noticed a difference between the two pictures. Now turn your page upside-down and notice how the distortion of one of the faces is amplified when viewed from this perspective.

We use convergence as a depth cue for objects that are relatively close up (e.g., 30 feet away or less).

One reason why humans have such a fine-tuned ability to see in three dimensions is that both of our eyes face forward. This arrangement means that we perceive objects from slightly different angles, which in turn enhances depth perception. For example, choose an object in front of you, such as an extended finger, and focus on that object with one eye while keeping the other eye closed. Then open your other eye to look at the object (and close the eye you were just using). You will notice that the position of your finger or object appears to change. This effect demonstrates **retinal disparity** (also called binocular disparity), *the difference in relative position of an object as seen by both eyes, which provides information to the brain about depth*. Your brain relies on cues from each eye individually and from both eyes working in concert—that is, in stereo. Most primates, including humans, have *stereoscopic vision*, which results from having overlapping visual fields.

Monocular cues *are depth cues that we can perceive with only one eye*. One such cue, called *accommodation*, takes place when the lens of your eye curves to allow you to focus on nearby objects. Close one eye and focus on a nearby object, and then slightly change your focus to an object that is farther away; the lens changes shape again so the next object comes into focus (see Figure 4.20a). *Motion parallax* is another monocular depth cue; it is used when you or your surroundings are in motion (Figure 4.20b). For example, as you sit in a moving vehicle and look out

of the passenger window, you will notice objects closer to you, such as the roadside, parked cars, and nearby buildings, appear to move rapidly in the opposite direction of your travel. By comparison, far-off objects such as foothills and mountains in the distance appear to move much more slowly, and in the same direction as your vehicle. The disparity in the directions traveled by near and far-off objects provides a monocular cue about depth.

Another kind of monocular depth cue, called *pictorial cues*, are used by many visual artists to create a sense of depth. This can be a very challenging task when working with a two-dimensional surface. To understand how artists work, view the painting by Gustave Caillebotte in Figure 4.21. In this painting, you will notice that the artist used numerous cues to depict depth.

Monocular and binocular depth cues combine to give us very detailed depth perception. Each individual eye adjusts so that depth can be perceived, and the eyes working together create even a greater sense of depth. In addition to depth, our visual experiences are greatly enriched by our ability to see color.

COLOR PERCEPTION   Our experience of color is based on how our visual system perceives different wavelengths on the electromagnetic spectrum. Color is not a characteristic of objects themselves, but rather an interpretation of these wavelengths by the visual system. As you learned earlier, the cones of the retina are specialized for responding to different wavelengths of light that correspond to different colors. However, the experience of color occurs in

Figure 4.20 Two Monocular Depth Cues

a) Accommodation. From the top left image light comes distant object, and the lens focuses the light on the retina. From the bottom left image the lens changes shape to accommodate the light when the same object is moved closer. (b) Motion parallax. Looking out the train window, objects close to you race past quickly and in the opposite direction that you are headed. At the same time, distant objects appear to move slowly and in the same direction that you are traveling.

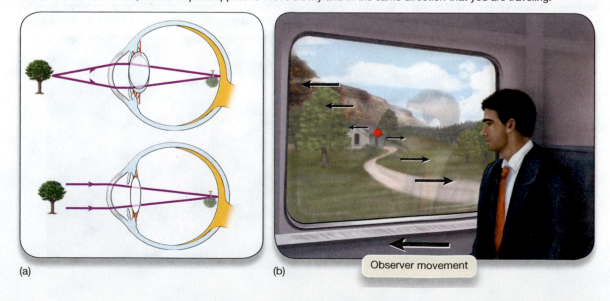

(a)   (b)   Observer movement

Figure 4.21 Applying Pictorial Depth Cues

Notice how each of the pictorial depth cues listed below are used in the painting.

Linear perspective: Parallel lines stretching to the horizon appear to move closer together as they travel farther away. This effect can be seen in the narrowing of the streets and the converging lines of the sidewalks and top of the building in the distance.

Interposition: Nearby objects block our view of far-off objects, such as the umbrellas blocking the view of buildings behind them.

Light and shadow: The shadow cast by an object (such as the lamp post) allows us to detect both the size of the object and the relative locations of objects. In addition, closer objects reflect more light than far-away objects.

Texture gradient: Objects that are coarse and distinct at close range become fine and grainy at greater distances. In the painting, for example, the texture of the cobblestone street varies from clear to blurred as distance increases.

Height in plane: Objects that are higher in our visual field are perceived as farther away than objects low in our visual field. The base of the main building in the background of the painting is at about the same level as the man's shoulder, but we interpret this effect as distance, not as height.

Relative size: If two objects in an image are known to be of the same actual size, the larger of the two must be closer. This can be seen in the various sizes of the pedestrians.

---

the brain. Exactly how this system works has long been a source of scientific debate.

One theory suggests that three different types of cones exist, each of which is sensitive to different wavelengths on the electromagnetic spectrum. These three types of cones were initially identified in the 18th century by physicist Thomas Young and again in the 19th century by scientist Hermann von Helmholtz. The relative responses of the three types of cones allow us to perceive many different colors on the spectrum (see Figure 4.22). For example, yellow is perceived by combining the stimulation of red- and green-sensitive cones, whereas light that stimulates all three cones equally is perceived as white. The **trichromatic theory (or Young-Helmholtz theory)** *maintains that color vision is determined by three different cone types that are sensitive to short, medium, and long wavelengths of light.* Modern technology has been used to measure the amount of light that can be absorbed in cones and confirmed that each type responds to different wavelengths.

Not all color experiences can be explained by the trichromatic theory. Stare at the image in Figure 4.23 for about a minute and then look toward a white background. After switching your gaze to a white background, you will see the colors of red, white, and blue, which are the opponent colors of green, black, and yellow. This negative afterimage is so named because you see one color after another color is removed. This demonstration suggests that we see color in terms of opposites, rather than combinations of activity by different cones in the retina as described by the trichromatic theory.

Figure 4.22 Trichromatic Theory of Color Vision

According to this theory, humans have three types of cones that respond maximally to different regions of the color spectrum. Color is experienced by the combined activity of cones sensitive to short, medium, and long wavelengths.

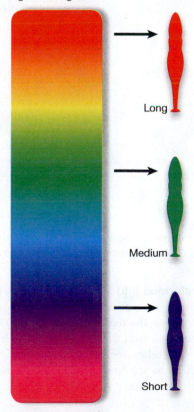

Figure 4.23 The Negative Afterimage: Experiencing Opponent-Process Theory

Stare directly at the white dot within the flag above and avoid looking away. After about a minute, immediately shift your focus to a white background. What do you see?

In the 19th century, Ewald Hering proposed the **opponent-process theory**, *which states that we perceive color in terms of opposite ends of the spectrum: red to green, yellow to blue, and white to black.* The experience of color takes place because of activity within specialized neurons networked with the retina. A cell that is stimulated by red is inhibited by green, for example, whereas a cell stimulated by blue inhibits yellow. These cells are responsible for either exciting or inhibiting cells that are responsive to different wavelengths.

The workings of the trichromatic theory concern different types of cone photoreceptors, while the opponent-process theory focuses on the existence of specialized nerve cells for perceiving color. Both the trichromatic and opponent-process theories are correct—and both are required to explain how we see color.

Module 4.2 Summary

4.2a Know . . . the key terminology relating to the eye and vision:

binocular depth cues
cones
convergence
cornea
fovea
iris
lens
monocular cues
opponent-process theory
optic nerve
perceptual constancy
pupil
retina
retinal disparity
rods
sclera
trichromatic theory

4.2b Understand . . . how visual information travels from the eye through the brain to give us the experience of sight.

Light is transformed into a neural signal by photoreceptors in the retina. This information is then relayed via the optic nerve through the thalamus and then to the occipital lobe of the cortex. From this location in the brain, neural circuits travel to other regions for specific levels of processing, such as to the temporal lobe, where object and facial recognition occur.

4.2c Understand . . . the theories of color vision.

The two theories reviewed in this module are the trichromatic and opponent-process theories. According to trichromatic theory, the retina contains three different types of light-sensitive cones. Color is experienced as the net combined stimulation of these receptors. The trichromatic theory is not supported by phenomena such as the negative afterimage. Opponent-process theory, which emphasizes how color perception is based on excitation and inhibition of opposing colors (e.g., red–green, blue–yellow, white–black), explains negative afterimages. Taken together, both theories help explain how we perceive color.

4.2d Apply . . . your knowledge to describe how we perceive depth in our visual field.

Numerous cues gives us the perception of depth. As to which one might apply in any given situation the first question you should ask: *Is it possible to perceive depth with just one eye using this cue, or are both eyes required*? If both eyes are required, binocular depth cues of convergence (for close-up objects) and retinal disparity account for the experience of depth. Cues requiring just one eye, monocular depth cues, complement binocular cues and occur when we experience motion parallax, and, of course are evident in the cues that visual artists use to convey depth. Figure 4.21 illustrated how pictorial, monocular depth cues can be used.

4.2e   Analyze . . . how we perceive objects and faces.

These tasks are accomplished by specialized perceptual regions of the temporal lobe. Perceptual constancies allow us to recognize objects even though their shape, size, and color may appear to change because their orientation, distance, and lightness in relation to the viewer are not always the same. Facial recognition is a distinct perceptual process, which is supported by evidence from people who are face blind but are otherwise successful at recognizing objects.

Module 4.2 Quiz

Know . . .

1. Cones are predominantly gathered in a central part of the retina known as the _____.
   - **A.** fovea
   - **B.** photoreceptor
   - **C.** blind spot
   - **D.** optic chiasm

Understand . . .

2. A familiar person walks into the room. Which of the following choices places the structures in the appropriate sequence required to recognize the individual?
   - **A.** Optic chiasm, visual cortex, photoreceptors, optic nerve
   - **B.** Visual cortex, optic chiasm, photoreceptors, optic nerve
   - **C.** Photoreceptors, optic nerve, optic chiasm, visual cortex
   - **D.** Photoreceptors, optic chiasm, optic nerve, visual cortex

3. Light waves from a blue shirt stimulate different photoreceptors than light waves coming from a red shirt. The fact that we see these shirts as two different colors can be explained by _____.
   - **A.** trichromatic theory
   - **B.** hyperopia
   - **C.** opponent process theory
   - **D.** motion parallax

Apply . . .

4. Michelle looks out of the train window and judges that one cactus is farther away than another because it appears to be moving more slowly. Michelle is relying on _____ to make this judgment.
   - **A.** binocular cues
   - **B.** motion parallax
   - **C.** texture gradient
   - **D.** trichromatic theory

Analyze . . .

5. Some people claim to be unable to perceive faces, yet scientists think that they may be able to do so unconsciously. What is the evidence for this?
   - **A.** Individuals with face blindness can guess the names that go with faces from pictures without knowing why.
   - **B.** Individuals with face blindness recognize faces but believe they are imposters.
   - **C.** Individuals with face blindness have physiological responses to familiar faces that they do not have for strangers.
   - **D.** When asked to make up names for faces, individuals with face blindness are often correct.

Module **4.3** The Auditory System

Learning Objectives

4.3a Know . . . the key terminology relating to the ear and hearing.

4.3b Understand . . . different characteristics of sound and how they correspond to perception.

4.3c Understand . . . theories of hearing.

4.3d Apply . . . your knowledge of sound localization.

4.3e Analyze . . . the assumption that deafness is something people are motivated to "overcome."

What would the soundtrack to your life sound like? Although each of us has our own musical preferences, some songs have the power to evoke similar emotions in large groups. Stadiums pump out songs that unite and energize fans; DJs at school dances or clubs select songs that fit the themes of friendship, love, and relationships; and even in the workplace certain types of music can harmonize people focusing on a common goal. Daniel Levitin, a psychologist and musician, believes that we are hard-wired not just to hear music, but to feel a significant emotional connection to it. Each of our lives' soundtracks would probably be different, but Dr. Levitin argues that human identity has music at its core, and that *common themes in music include love, friendship, knowledge, religion, relationships, and joy (Levitin, 2008; Rentfrow et al., 2012). So how does the auditory system perceive something complex like music? And, conversely, how might the ability to hear be lost?*

In this module we will explore characteristics of sound, the physical structures involved in the sensation of sound, and the pathways that handle its perceptual processing. In addition, we will consider how hearing can become impaired, what can done about it, and discuss some issues associated with deafness.

Figure 4.24 Characteristics of Sound: Frequency and Amplitude

The frequency of a sound wave (cycles per second) is associated with pitch, while amplitude (the height of the sound wave) is associated with loudness.

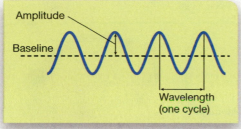

(a) Long-wavelength (low-frequency) sound

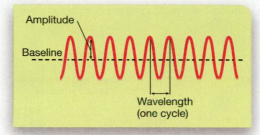

(b) Short-wavelength (high-frequency) sound

Sound and the Structures of the Ear

The function of the ear is to gather sound waves, and the function of hearing is to inform you about the nature of the sound source, such as someone calling your name, the phone, an alarm, or a vehicle coming toward you. How do people gain so much information from sound, the invisible yet audible vibrations resulting from mechanical pressure and displacement of air?

SOUND   Sound waves have two important characteristics: frequency and amplitude (see Figure 4.24).

Frequency refers to wavelength and is measured in hertz (Hz), the number of cycles a sound wave travels per second. **Pitch** *is the perceptual experience of sound wave frequencies.* High-frequency sounds, such as tires screeching on the road, have short wavelengths and a high pitch. Low-frequency sounds, such as those produced by a bass guitar, have long wavelengths and a low pitch. The *amplitude* of a sound wave determines its loudness: High-amplitude sound waves are louder than low-amplitude waves. To put it simply, our ears are specialized structures for gathering information about the frequency and amplitude of sound waves. Loudness—a function of sound wave amplitude—is typically expressed in units called decibels (dB). Table 4.2 compares decibel levels ranging from nearly inaudible to injury inducing.

THE HUMAN EAR   The human ear is divided into outer, middle, and inner regions (Figure 4.25). The most noticeable part of your ear is the *pinna,* the outer region that helps channel sound waves to the ear and allows you to determine the source or location of a sound. The *auditory canal* extends from the pinna to the eardrum. Sound waves cause the eardrum to vibrate. even very minute sounds, such as a faint whisper, produce vibrations of the eardrum. The middle ear consists of three tiny moveable bones, called *ossicles* (known individually as the hammer, anvil, and stirrup). The eardrum is attached to these bones, so any movement of the eardrum due to sound vibrations results in movement of the ossicles.

The ossicles attach to an inner ear structure called the **cochlea**—*a fluid-filled membrane coiled in a snail-like shape and contains the structures that convert sound into neural impulses.* Converting sound vibrations to neural impulses is possible because of hair-like projections that line the basilar membrane of the cochlea. The pressing and pulling action of the ossicles causes the fluid within the

Table 4.2 Decibel Levels for Some Familiar Sounds

Sound	Noise Level (DB)	Effect
Jet engines (near)	140	We begin to feel pain at about 125 dB
Rock concerts (varies)	110–140	
Thunderclap (near)	120	Regular exposure to sound over 100 dB for more than one minute risks perma-
Power saw (chainsaw)	110	nent hearing loss
Garbage truck/Cement mixer	100	No more than l5 minutes of unprotected exposure is recommended for sounds between 90 and 100 dB
Motorcycle (25 ft)	88	85 dB is the level at which hearing damage (after eight hours) begins
Lawn mower	85–90	
Average city traffic	80	Annoying; interferes with conversation; constant exposure may cause damage
Vacuum cleaner	70	Intrusive; interferes with telephone conversation
Normal conversation	50–65	Comfortable hearing levels are under 60 dB
Whisper	30	Very quiet
Rustling leaves	20	Just audible

Figure 4.25 The Human Ear

Sound waves travel from the outer ear to the eardrum and middle ear, and then through the inner ear. The cochlea of the inner ear is the site at which transduction takes place through movement of the tiny hair cells lining the basilar membrane. The auditory cortex of the brain is a primary brain region where sound is perceived.

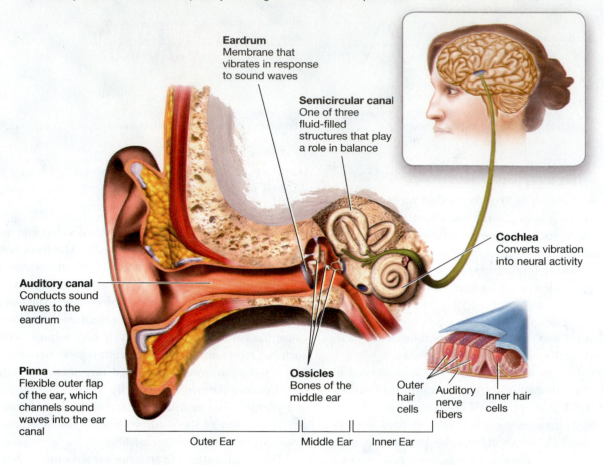

Eardrum
Membrane that vibrates in response to sound waves

Semicircular canal
One of three fluid-filled structures that play a role in balance

Cochlea
Converts vibration into neural activity

Auditory canal
Conducts sound waves to the eardrum

Pinna
Flexible outer flap of the ear, which channels sound waves into the ear canal

Ossicles
Bones of the middle ear

Outer hair cells

Auditory nerve fibers

Inner hair cells

Outer Ear   Middle Ear   Inner Ear

cochlea to move, displacing these tiny hair cells. When hair cells move, they stimulate the cells that comprise the auditory nerves. The *auditory nerves* are composed of bundles of neurons that fire as a result of hair cell movements. These auditory nerves, in turn, send signals to the auditory cortex, located within the temporal lobe. The *semicircular canal* is a set of fluid filled structures that are a part of the vestibular system, which is involved in balance.

The Perception of Sound

It is quite remarkable that we are able to determine what components make up a sound, and determine where the sound comes from, by simply registering and processing sound waves. In this section, we examine how the auditory system accomplishes these two tasks, starting with the ability to locate a sound in the environment.

SOUND LOCALIZATION: FINDING THE SOURCE Accurately identifying and orienting toward a sound source has some obvious adaptive benefits. In nature,

failure to do so could result in an animal becoming someone's dinner. In human terms it could result in a comparable disaster. **Sound localization**, *the process of identifying where sound comes from, is handled by a midbrain structure called the inferior colliculus.*

There are two ways that we localize sound. First, we take advantage of the slight time difference between a sound hitting both ears to estimate the direction of the source. If your friend shouts your name from your left side, the left ear gets the information just a fraction of a second before the right ear. Second, we localize sound by using differences in the intensity in which sound is heard by both ears—a phenomenon known as a *sound shadow* (Figure 4.26). If the source of the sound is to your left, the left ear will experience the sound more intensely than the right because the right ear will be in the sound shadow. The inferior colliculi (plural), located in the midbrain, detect differences in the times when sound reaches the left versus the right ear, as well as the intensity of the sound between one side and the other, allowing us to identify where it is coming from.

Figure 4.26 How We Localize Sound

To localize sound, the brain computes the small difference in time at which the sound reaches each of the ears. The brain also registers differences in loudness that reach each ear.

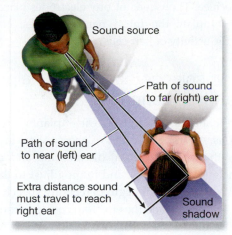

Sound source

Path of sound to far (right) ear

Path of sound to near (left) ear

Extra distance sound must travel to reach right ear

Sound shadow

PITCH PERCEPTION To explain how we perceive pitch, we will begin in the cochlea and work toward brain centers that are specialized for hearing. Not all hair cells along the basilar membrane are equally responsive to sounds within the 20 to 20,000 Hz range of human hearing. High-frequency sounds stimulate hair cells closest to the ossicles, whereas lower-frequency sounds stimulate hair cells toward the end of the cochlea (Figure 4.27). According to the **place theory of hearing**, *how we perceive pitch is based on the location (place) along the basilar membrane that sound*

stimulates. Place theory works well to explain hearing at higher frequencies, but hair cells for detecting lower frequencies are not so conveniently arranged at the end the cochlea.

Another determinant of how and what we hear is the rate at which the ossicles press into the cochlea, sending a wave of activity down the basilar membrane. According to the **frequency theory (of hearing)**, *the perception of pitch is related to the frequency at which the basilar membrane vibrates.* A 70-Hz sound, at 70 cycles per second, stimulates the hair cells 70 times per second. Thus, 70 nerve impulses per second travel from the auditory nerves to the brain, which interprets the sound frequency in terms of pitch (Figure 4.27). However, we quickly reach an upper limit on the capacity of the auditory nerves to send signals to the brain: Neurons cannot fire more than 1,000 times per second. Given this limit, how can we hear sounds exceeding 1,000 Hz?

The answer lies in the *volley principle*. A single neuron cannot fire more than 1,000 times per second, but a group of neurons could certainly accomplish this feat. According to the volley principle, groups of neurons fire in alternating (hence the term "volley") fashion. A sound measuring 5,000 Hz can be perceived because groups of neurons fire in rapid succession, such that their message is of sufficient magnitude.

Currently, the place, frequency, and volley concepts are all needed to explain our experience of hearing. Place theory is most applicable to high-pitched noises. Frequency theory, in combination with the volley principle, better

Figure 4.27 The Basilar Membrane of the Cochlea and Theories of Hearing

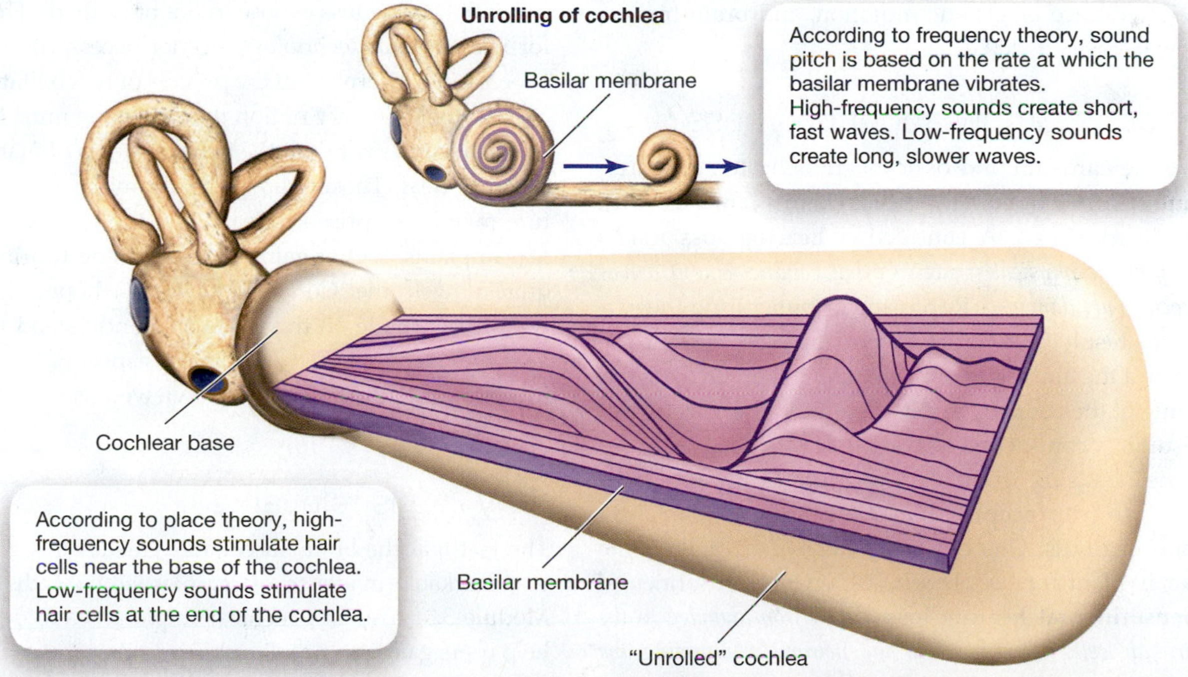

Unrolling of cochlea

Basilar membrane

According to frequency theory, sound pitch is based on the rate at which the basilar membrane vibrates. High-frequency sounds create short, fast waves. Low-frequency sounds create long, slower waves.

Cochlear base

According to place theory, high-frequency sounds stimulate hair cells near the base of the cochlea. Low-frequency sounds stimulate hair cells at the end of the cochlea.

Basilar membrane

"Unrolled" cochlea

explains how we hear low-pitched noises. When we hear complex stimuli, such as music, the place, frequency, and volley principles are likely all functioning at the sensory level. Perceiving music, voices, and other important sounds occurs in specialized regions of the brain.

The **primary auditory cortex** *is located within the temporal lobe of the cortex and is involved in perceiving what we hear.* The auditory cortex is organized in very similar fashion to the cochlea. Cells within different areas across the auditory cortex respond to specific notes—a phenomenon called *tonotopic organization.* For example, high musical notes are processed at one end of the auditory cortex, and progressively lower notes are heard as we move to the opposite end (Wang et al., 2005). The auditory cortex and surrounding areas are responsible for perceiving and interpreting sound. At the beginning of this module, we discussed the important emotional information conveyed by music. Not surprisingly, music perception also involves the emotional brain centers, such as those found in the limbic system (see Module 3.3; Bhatara et al., 2011; Koelsch et al., 2013).

JOURNAL PROMPT

Hearing Tones: In your own words summarize the place, frequency, and volley theories of pitch perception and explain why all three are needed.

Working the Scientific Literacy Model

Deafness

Hearing is not an experience that all people have. Some people are born without it, but hearing loss or complete deafness can also be brought on by factors such as aging, inheritance or genetic mutation, and brain trauma (Aggarwal & Saeed, 2005).

What do we know about deafness?

Because the eardrum and ossicles are delicate structures, exposure to loud sounds or physical injury can cause permanent hearing loss. A **conduction hearing loss** *results when any of the physical structures that conduct sound waves to the cochlea are damaged.* Rupturing or puncturing the eardrum will result in conduction hearing loss, even if the cochlea and the auditory nerves remain intact. Breakage or hardening of the connective tissue between the ossicles can also result in a conduction hearing loss.

Some amazing technological advances have been developed to help people overcome hearing loss, or even profound deafness. One especially notable advance is the cochlear implant for people who experience sensorineural loss. **Sensorineural hearing loss** *results from damage to the cochlear hair cells (sensory) and the neurons comprising the auditory nerve (neural).* Cochlear implants are small electronic devices that consist of a microphone, speech processor, and electrodes (Figure 4.28). The speech processor is affixed behind the ear, and a wire is routed through the skull and into the cochlea. Thousands of tiny electrodes placed along the wire stimulate the intact nerve endings, effectively replacing the activity of hair cells.

How can science be used to help people with hearing loss?

The process of adjusting to cochlear implants can be slow and arduous. At first, the sound of people speaking, or any sound for that matter, can be disorienting and unpleasant. As the auditory system and brain adjust to the input, people with implants can begin perceiving speech sounds. Researchers have tracked the effects of cochlear implants on language development in children. In one study, researchers tracked children who received cochlear implants over a three-year period to assess how well they expressed and understood language. Prior to cochlear implantation, the children (who were younger than five at the beginning of the study) were acquiring words at a very low rate, as would be predicted given their hearing impairment. At the end of the three-year study period, the children had greatly improved in both language comprehension and expression (Niparko et al., 2010; Ganek et al., 2012). Success with cochlear implants is not restricted to children. Elderly adults can also benefit from these devices (Carlson et al., 2010).

Can we critically evaluate this information?

Given that cochlear implants have become increasingly common, it may come as a surprise to learn that many people with hearing loss choose to not have them. The reasons for rejecting this technology do not necessarily reflect the expense or concern about the process of rehabilitation, however. Rather, the very notion that someone must be able to hear is inconsistent with the belief systems of many people who are deaf. Those who are not familiar with Deaf culture may be surprised to learn that the very idea of cochlear implants, and of gaining or regaining hearing, can be quite unwelcome. Conversely, we can hopefully identify with Deaf people on this issue and understand the resistance anyone would have if a major aspect of their cultural identity were misunderstood or viewed as something that necessitated changing.

Why is this relevant?

The fact that the brain successfully makes this adjustment is remarkable evidence of its plasticity (as discussed in Module 3.3). The first cochlear implants were designed to help users gain or regain the ability to detect speech sounds.

Figure 4.28 A Cochlear Implant

The sound processor and microphone are located just above the pinna. A wire with micro-electrodes attached is routed through the cochlea.

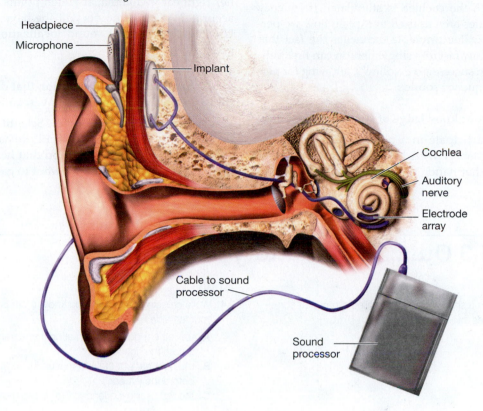

Unfortunately, other sounds, such as music or even the sound of a person's voice from a telephone, can be very unpleasant to implant users. These problems may occur because hearing-related areas of the auditory cortex are under-stimulated and, therefore, become rewired to perform other brain functions. Newer devices have been designed that allow some users the opportunity to enjoy music again. In addition, intensive speech therapy and family support are essential for successful use of cochlear implants. Successful surgeries have even been performed on infants.

Module 4.3 Summary

4.3a Know . . . the key terminology relating to the ear and hearing:

cochlea
conduction hearing loss
frequency theory
pitch
place theory of hearing
primary auditory cortex
sensorineural hearing loss
sound localization

4.3b Understand . . . different characteristics of sound and how they correspond to perception.

Sound can be analyzed based on its frequency (the number of cycles a sound wave travels per second) as well as on its amplitude (the height of a sound wave). Our experience of pitch is based on sound wave frequencies. Amplitude corresponds to loudness: The higher the amplitude, the louder the sound.

4.3c Understand . . . theories of hearing.

Theories of how we hear involve the physical location of the cochlea that is stimulated (place theory) and the frequency at which the cochlea is stimulated (frequency theory). Both theories are required to explain how we perceive sound. The volley principle reconciles the fact that there is a limit to how fast any single neuron can fire: Multiple neurons fire in succession ("volley"), allowing for perception of high frequency sounds.

4.3d Apply . . . your knowledge of sound localization.

Get a friend to participate in a quick localization demonstration. Have her sit with her eyes closed, covering her right ear with her hand. Now walk quietly in a circle around your friend, stopping occasionally to snap your fingers. When you do this, your friend should point to where you are standing, based solely on the sound. If her right ear is covered, at which points will she be most accurate? At which points will she have the most errors? Use the principles of sound localization to make your predictions.

4.3e Analyze . . . the assumption that deafness is something people are motivated to "overcome."

As you learned in the Working the Scientific Literacy Model feature, many members of Deaf culture have little desire to change and reject the assumption that hearing and speaking are something they should want to gain.

Module 4.3 Quiz: The Auditory System

Know . . .

1. The _____ is a snail-shaped, fluid-filled organ that converts sound waves into a neural signal.
   A. ossicle
   B. pinna
   C. cochlea
   D. outer ear

Understand . . .

2. The amplitude of a sound wave determines its loudness; _____-amplitude sound waves are louder than _____-amplitude waves.
   A. low; high
   B. short; tall
   C. wide; narrow
   D. high; low

3. _____ explains pitch perception in terms of the rate at which hair cells of the cochlea are stimulated in proportion to sound wave cycles.
   A. Place theory
   B. Frequency theory
   C. The volley principle
   D. Switch theory

Apply . . .

4. While crossing the street, you know a car is approaching on your left side because:
   A. the left ear got the information just a fraction of a second before the right ear.
   B. the right ear got the information just a fraction of a second before the left ear.
   C. the right ear experienced the sound more intensely than the left ear.
   D. both ears experienced the sound at the same intensity.

Analyze . . .

5. Cochlear implants are an amazing technology, offering people with hearing loss the option to regain much of their ability to hear again. What is an important societal concern regarding this technology?
   A. People with "bionic" ears may acquire unfair advantages in endeavors such as music performance.
   B. The belief that hearing loss is a physical defect is a judgment that is rejected by many in the Deaf community.
   C. Knowing that this technology is available has already led to people becoming less concerned about how they care for their hearing, as they know they can get implants if damage occurs.
   D. The implants are impossibly expensive and therefore not really available to anyone.

Module 4.4 Touch and the Chemical Senses

Learning Objectives

4.4a Know . . . the key terminology of touch and chemical senses.

4.4b Understand . . . how pain is sensed and perceived.

4.4c Understand . . . the relationship between smell, taste, and food flavor experience.

4.4d Apply . . . your knowledge about touch to describe the acuity of different areas of skin.

4.4e Analyze . . . the relationship between sensation and perception through the phenomenon of phantom limb experiences.

Would you ever describe your breakfast cereal as tasting pointy or round? Probably not. Touch, taste, and smell are integrated into our experiences with food, yet we can identify the separate components associated with what is tasted, smelled, and felt through the texture of food. A rare condition called synesthesia results in blended sensory experiences, such that affected individuals might actually hear colors or feel sounds. For the rare individuals who experience this condition, even letters or numbers may have a color associated with them. To illustrate this effect, find the number 2 below:

555555555555555555555
555555555555555555555
555555555555555525555555
555555555555555555555

People who have a type of synesthesia in which words or numbers have unique colors associated with them find the 2 faster than people without synesthesia. One person stated that the 2 was especially easy to find because it appears orange to him— all he had to find was the number that differed in color (Blake et al., 2005). Synesthesia can also involve blending taste and touch, which certainly can influence dining experiences. People may avoid oatmeal because it tastes mushy, but can you imagine avoiding a food because it tastes "pointy," or relishing another food because of its delicate hints of corduroy? Synesthesia occurs in an estimated 1 in 500 people. For the 499 others, touch, taste, and smell are distinct senses. Two questions we address in this module are 1) How are experiences of touch, taste and smell distinct? and 2) In addition to food textures, what else involves touch?

Generally speaking, vision and hearing are the senses that we seem to use the most and, therefore, have occupied the majority of interest in psychological science. In this module, we will explore the senses of touch, taste, and smell. Our putting them together in a single module is not meant to diminish their importance, however. Our quality of life, and possibly survival, would be severely compromised without these senses.

The Sense of Touch

The surface of our skin is equipped to respond to numerous types of stimulation. Generally speaking, pressure, temperature, and pain are three types of stimulation—but we can be even more specific. Pressure upon the skin can be barely detectable or cause bruising. It can also involve stretching the skin, as felt when you receive a backrub or when you run your hand over the surface of an object to feel its unique texture. Temperature ranges from freezing cold to boiling hot, and many other types of stimulation may cause pain. Our experiences of touch are attributable to the actions of several types of receptors located just beneath the surface of the skin, and also in the muscles, joints, and tendons.

HOW WE PERCEIVE TOUCH Sensitivity to touch varies across different regions of the body. One simple method of testing sensitivity, or acuity, is to use the two-point threshold test shown in Figure 4.29. Regions with high acuity, such as the fingertips, can detect the two separate, but closely spaced pressure points of the device, whereas less sensitive regions such as the lower back will perceive the same stimuli as only one pressure point. Body parts such as the fingertips, palms, and lips are highly sensitive to touch, compared to regions such as the calves and lower back.

Exploring objects in our environment by touch is an active process (Klatzky & Lederman, 2011). Merely laying your hand on the surface of an object does little to help identify it. What we need is an active exploration that stimulates receptors in the hand. **Haptics** *is the active, exploratory aspect of touch sensation and perception.* Active touch involves feedback. For example, as you handle an object, such as a piece of fruit, you move your fingers over its surface to identify whether any faults may be present. Your fingertips help you determine whether the object is the appropriate shape and detect bruising or abnormalities that may make it unsuitable. For some people, recognizing objects by haptics is hampered by damage to the somatosensory cortex, a condition called *tactile agnosia.* A person with this condition would struggle to identify common objects and even wooden blocks of common geometric shapes.

Haptics allows us not only to identify objects, but also to avoid damaging or dropping them. Fingers and hands coordinate their movements using a complementary body sense called **kinesthesis**, *the sense of bodily motion and position.* Receptors for kinesthesis reside in the muscles, joints, and tendons. These receptors transmit information about movement and the position of your muscles, limbs, and joints to the brain (Figure 4.30). As you handle an object, your kinesthetic sense allows you to hold it with the coordination and resistance needed to avoid dropping it.

Figure 4.29 Two-Point Threshold Device for Measuring Touch Acuity

The more sensitive regions of the body can detect two points even when they are spaced very close together. Less sensitive parts of the body have much larger two-point thresholds.

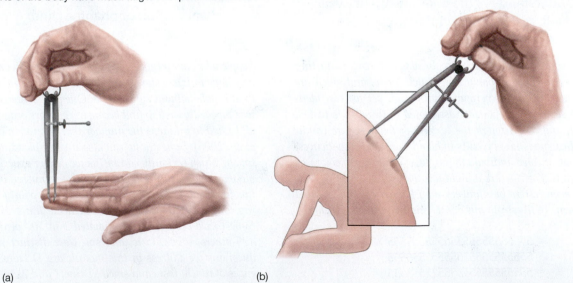

(a)   (b)

Figure 4.30 The Sense of Kinesthesis

Receptors in muscles and at the joints send sensory messages to the brain, helping us maintain awareness and control of our movements. Muscle spindles and Golgi tendon organs are sensory receptors that provide information about changes in muscle length and tension.

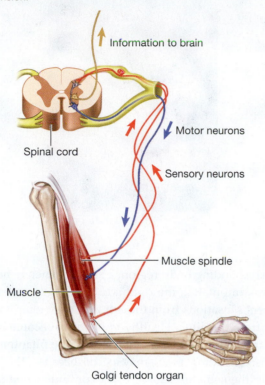

Information to brain

Spinal cord

Motor neurons

Sensory neurons

Muscle spindle

Muscle

Golgi tendon organ

FEELING PAIN   Painful stimulation is sensed across the bodily surface and in places within it, but pain is perceived by the brain. **Nociception** *is the activity of nerve pathways that respond to uncomfortable stimulation.* Our skin, teeth, cornea, and internal organs contain nerve endings called *nociceptors,* which are receptors that initiate pain messages that are routed to the central nervous system (see Figure 4.31). Nociceptors come in varieties that respond to various types of stimuli—for example, to sharp stimulation, such as a pin prick, or to extreme heat or cold (Julius & Basbaum, 2001).

Two types of nerve fibers transmit pain messages. Fast fibers register sharp, immediate pain, such as the pain felt when your skin is scraped or cut. Slow fibers register chronic, dull pain, such as the lingering feelings of bumping your knee into the coffee table. Pain messages first travel to cells in the spinal cord, then move upward to a point where sensory messages branch off to two regions of the brain. One region, the hypothalamus, as you learned in Module 3.3, regulates arousal and emotional responses, which certainly are a part of the experience of pain. The other region, the somatosensory cortex, registers the pain sensations occurring over the entire surface of the body. (Other regions of the cortex are also involved in the experience of pain.)

Pain varies from mild to severe and from acute (brief) to chronic. How do we explain differences in pain experiences? One long-held theory of pain perception is **gate-control theory**, *which explains our experience of pain as an interaction*

Figure 4.31 Cross Section of Skin and Free Nerve Endings

The nerve endings that respond to pain reside very close to the surface of the skin and, as you are likely aware, are very sensitive to stimulation.

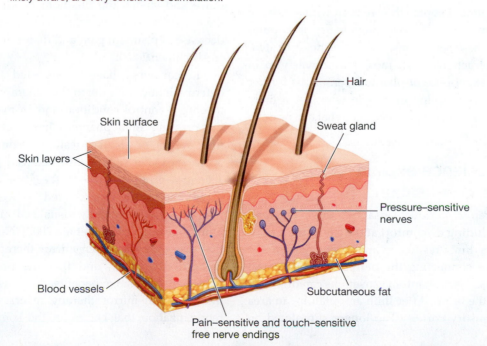

Hair

Skin surface

Sweat gland

Skin layers

Pressure–sensitive nerves

Blood vessels

Subcutaneous fat

Pain–sensitive and touch–sensitive free nerve endings

between nerves that transmit pain messages and those that inhibit these messages. According to this theory, cells in the spinal cord regulate how much pain signaling reaches the brain. Thus, the spinal cord serves as a "neural gate" that pain messages must pass through (Braz et al., 2014; Melzack & Wall, 1965, 1982). The spinal cord contains small nerve fibers that conduct pain messages and larger nerve fibers that conduct other sensory signals, such as those associated with rubbing, pinching, and tickling sensations. Stimulation of the small pain fibers results in the experience of pain, whereas the larger fibers inhibit pain signals. Thus the large fibers close the gate that is opened by the smaller fibers. According to gate-control theory, if you stub your bare toe, rubbing the area around the toe may alleviate some of the pain, because the large fibers carrying the message about touch inhibit the firing of smaller fibers carrying pain signals. Likewise, putting ice on a wound reduces pain by overriding the signals transmitted by the small fibers.

Figure 4.32 A Mirror Box

In this case, a woman who has lost her left arm can experience some relief from phantom pain by moving her intact hand, such as by unclenching her fist. In turn, she will experience relief from phantom pain corresponding to her left side.

Working the Scientific Literacy Model

Phantom Limb Sensations

The experience of pain is complex and involves many different biological and subjective factors. Pain is also the source of some deeper mysteries in psychological science and medicine, such as why people experience pain from a region of the body that has been amputated.

What do we know about phantom limb sensations?

Phantom limb sensations are frequently experienced by amputees, who report pain and other sensations coming from the absent limb. People who are born with a missing limb and those who lose a limb through injury or amputation experience these sensations. Amputees describe itching, muscle contractions, and, most unfortunately, pain sensations. The experience of phantom sensations further compromises the well-being of people who lose a limb. Why do people have this experience and what can be done to help them?

How does science explain phantom limb sensation?

Patients often report various sensations following limb amputation, including discomfort at the site of the amputation. Losing a limb results in major changes in the neural pathways connecting the peripheral and central nervous systems. Also, phantom sensations can originate entirely within the brain. After limb amputation, an area of the somatosensory cortex is no longer stimulated by

its corresponding body region. Thus, if someone has her left arm amputated, the right somatosensory cortex that registers sensations from the left arm no longer has any input from this limb. Healthy nerve cells become hypersensitive when they lose connections. The phantom sensations, including pain, may occur because the nerve cells in the somatosensory cortex continue to be active, despite the absence of any input.

One ingenious treatment for phantom pain involves the mirror box (Figure 4.32). This apparatus uses the reflection of the amputee's existing limb, such as an arm and hand, to create the visual appearance of having both limbs. Amputees often find that watching themselves move and stretch the phantom hand, which is actually the mirror image of the intact hand, results in a significant decrease in phantom pain and discomfort (Ramachandran & Altschuler, 2009).

Researchers have conducted experiments to determine how well mirror box therapy works compared to both a control condition and to mentally visualizing the presence of a phantom hand. Over the course of four weeks of regular testing, people who used the mirror box had significantly reduced pain compared to a control group who used the same mirror apparatus, except the mirror was covered, as well as compared to the people who mentally visualized moving the missing limb (Figure 4.33; Chan et al., 2007). Notice in Figure 4.33 that everyone was given mirror therapy after the fourth week of the study, and that the procedure seems to have lasting, positive benefits. Work using brain imaging indicates that mirror therapy reverses the maladaptive reorganization that occurs in the somatosensory cortex

Figure 4.33 Mirror Box Therapy Compared to Mental Visualization and a Control Condition

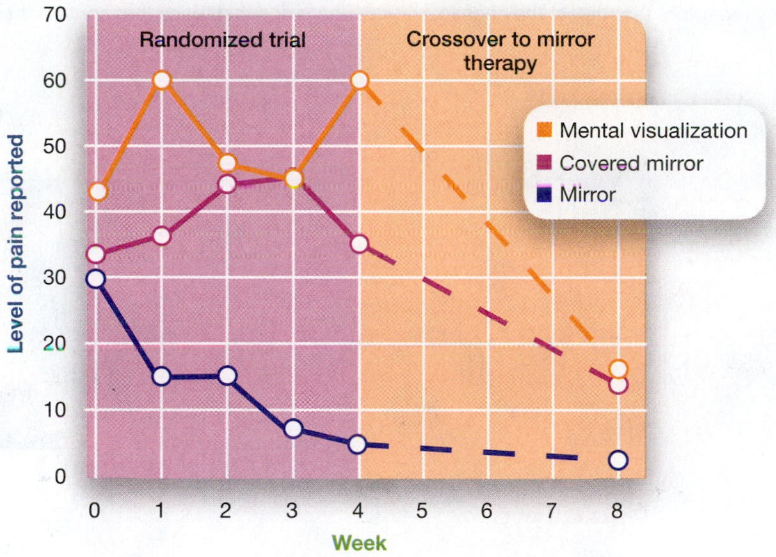

Can we critically evaluate the research on phantom limbs?

The mirror box may seem primarily applicable to people who have lost an arm or hand. What about regaining sensations and movements following loss of a leg? Researchers and engineers have devised a "virtual" mirror box that provides leg amputees with assistance in adjusting to a leg prosthesis. The technology involves virtual reality equipment used in conjunction with a treadmill. The technology helps patients adjust their gait by using visual feedback to synchronize the motor movements of the intact and prosthetic leg (Barton et al., 2014).

Why is this relevant?

Mirror box therapy is clearly a useful application of scientific knowledge for the well-being of people experiencing a major life-changing condition. Nevertheless, loss of limbs due to amputation is relatively rare compared to other conditions that compromise limb mobility. For example, stroke and other types of brain injury can also result in lost limb functionality and phantom pain sensation, and mirror therapy has also proven helpful to this population of patients (Yoon et al., 2014).

The Chemical Senses: Taste and Smell

The chemical senses are a combination of both taste and smell. Although they are distinct sensory systems, both

following amputation, which is thought to be a major source of the discomfort (Foell et al., 2014).

begin the sensory process when chemical compounds activate receptors at the tongue, mouth, and nose.

THE GUSTATORY SYSTEM: TASTE The **gustatory system** *functions in the sensation and perception of taste.* Food and drink are the most common types of taste stimuli that come to mind. Specifically, the receptors involved in taste sensations are chemical compounds that are water soluble (dissolvable).

Taste is perhaps one of our more indulgent senses. Most of our experiences with the sense of taste involve eating, and rarely do we seek out foods we do not want to put in our mouths. Losing the sense of taste can severely diminish one's quality of life. In the United States, approximately 200,000 people visit their doctors for taste-related disorders each year (National Institutes of Health [NIH], 2009). But our sense of taste does not merely serve the purpose of providing pleasure; rather, it is also useful for identifying potentially poisonous substances in the food we eat. Imagine if you were not able to detect the awful taste of sour, spoiled milk or rancid meat. Thus, taste is adaptive in that it helps ensure that we nourish our bodies and avoid illness.

Taste is registered primarily on the tongue, where roughly 9,000 taste buds reside. On average, approximately 1,000 taste buds are also found on the sides and roof of the mouth (Miller & Reedy, 1990). Sensory neurons that transmit signals from the taste buds respond to different types of stimuli, but most tend to respond best to a particular taste. Our experience of taste reflects an overall pattern of activity across many neurons, and generally comes from stimulation of the entire tongue rather than just specific, localized regions. The middle of

Figure 4.34 Papillae and Taste Buds

The tongue is lined with papillae (the bumpy surfaces). Within these papillae are your taste buds, the tiny receptors that detect the chemical components of substances that contact them.

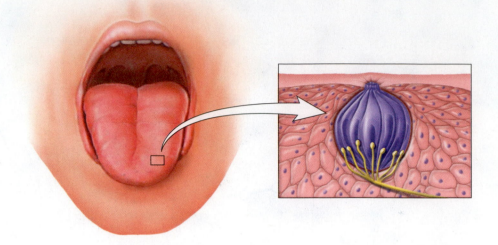

the tongue has very few taste receptors, giving it a similar character to the blind spot on the retina (Module 4.2). Taste receptors replenish themselves every 10 days throughout the life span—the only type of sensory receptor to do so.

Receptors for taste are located in the visible, small bumps (*papillae*) that are distributed over the surface of the tongue. The papillae are lined with taste buds. Figure 4.34 shows papillae, taste buds, and an enlarged view of an individual taste bud and a sensory neuron that sends a message to the brain. The bundles of nerves that register taste at the taste buds send the signal through the thalamus and on to higher-level regions of the brain, including the gustatory cortex, which is a deep-seated structure located in the interior of the cortex. Another region, the secondary gustatory cortex, processes the pleasurable experiences associated with food.

Approximately 2,500 identifiable chemical compounds are found in the food we eat (Taylor & Hort, 2004). When combined, these compounds give us an enormous diversity of taste sensations. The *primary tastes* include salty, sweet, bitter, and sour. In addition, a fifth taste, called umami, has been identified (Chaudhari et al., 2000). Umami, sometimes referred to as "savoriness," is a Japanese word that refers to tastes associated with seaweed, the seasoning monosodium glutamate (MSG), and protein-rich foods such as meat, milk and aged cheese.

Why do we identify some foods as strong or rich tasting? For one thing, the number of taste buds present on the tongue influences the psychological experience of taste. Although approximately 10,000 taste buds is the average number found in humans, there is wide variation among individuals. Some people may have many times

this number. *Supertasters*, who account for approximately 25% of the population, are especially sensitive to bitter tastes such as those of broccoli and black coffee. They typically have lower rates of obesity and cardiovascular disease, possibly because they tend not to prefer fatty and sweet foods. Figure 4.35 shows the number of papillae,

Figure 4.35 Density of Papillae, and Hence Taste Buds, in a Supertaster and in a Normal Taster

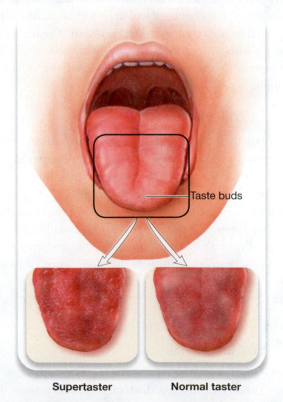

Taste buds

Supertaster   **Normal taster**

and hence taste buds, possessed by a supertaster compared to those without this ability.

Closely related to taste is our sense of smell, which senses the chemical environment via a different mode than does taste.

THE OLFACTORY SYSTEM: SMELL The **olfactory system** *is involved in smell—the detection of airborne particles with specialized receptors located in the nose.* Smell works in concert with taste to give us the experience of flavor. Without smell, a slice of onion might be difficult to discriminate from a slice of apple: The textures of these two foods are quite similar, but for some people their taste buds alone may not be sufficient to discriminate one from the other. The experience of smell makes food enjoyable, but also helps us to identify harmful substances, helps us to recognize individuals, and can warn us of danger.

Our sensation of smell begins with nasal air flow bringing in molecules that bind with receptors at the top of the nasal cavity. Within the nasal cavity is the **olfactory epithelium**, *a thin layer of cells that are lined by sensory receptors called cilia*—tiny hair-like projections that contain specialized proteins that bind with the airborne molecules that enter the nasal cavity (Figure 4.36). The cilia transmit messages to neurons that converge on the olfactory bulb, which serves as the brain's central region for processing smell. The olfactory bulb connects with several regions of the brain through the olfactory tract, including the limbic system (emotion) as well as regions of the cortex where the subjective experiences of pleasure and disgust occur.

Our perceptual experiences of smell begin with the encoding of sensory information by cells that comprise the olfactory epithelium. The cilia shown in Figure 4.36 contain specialized proteins that bind to inhaled compounds (Buck, 1996). This is a complex process, because there are thousands of molecules of differing shapes that correspond to particular odors. Despite the fact that humans have only 1,000 different types of odor receptors, we can detect approximately 10,000 different odors because odor molecules can stimulate several receptors simultaneously. It is the pattern of the stimulation, involving more than one receptor, that gives rise to the experience of a particular smell (Buck & Axel, 1991).

Figure 4.36 The Olfactory System

Lining the olfactory epithelium are tiny cilia that collect airborne chemicals, sending sensory messages to the nerve fibers that make up the olfactory bulb.

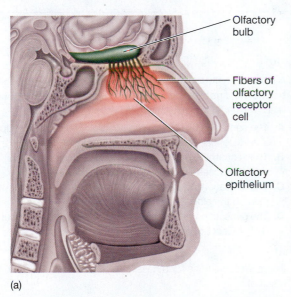

(a)

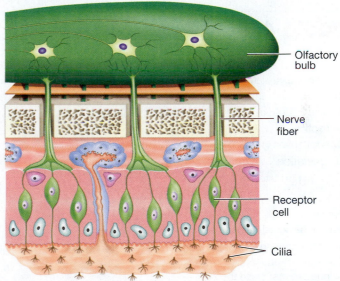

(b)

Module 4.4 Summary

4.4a   Know . . . the key terminology of touch and chemical senses:

gate-control theory
gustatory system
haptics
kinesthesis
nociception
olfactory epithelium
olfactory system

4.4b   Understand . . . how pain is sensed and perceived.

According to gate-control theory, small nerve fibers carry pain messages from their source to the spinal cord, and then up to the central nervous system. However, large nerve cells that register other types of touch sensations (such as rubbing) can override signals sent by small pain fibers.

4.4c   Understand . . . the relationship between smell, taste, and food flavor experience.

Both senses combine to give us flavor experiences. Contact with food activates patterns of neural activity among nerve cells connected to the taste buds, and food odors activate patterns of nerve activity in the olfactory epithelium. The primary and secondary gustatory cortex and the olfactory bulb are involved in the perceptual experience of flavor.

4.4d   Apply . . . your knowledge about touch to describe the acuity of different areas of skin.

You can try this yourself by creating a two-point threshold device like the one shown earlier in Figure 4.29. We fashioned one out of a straightened paper clip we could hold up to a ruler. Set the two points about ¼ inch apart and gently apply them to different parts of the body—your fingertips, your elbow, your cheek. Which parts of your body are sensitive enough to feel both points, and on which parts does it feel like a single object is touching you? Now try the experiment again with the two points closer together. Can you detect a change in acuity?

4.4e   Analyze . . . the relationship between sensation and perception through the phenomenon of phantom limb experiences.

Sensations are events that occur at the interface between a physical stimulus and specialized receptors of the body. Perception of those events occurs in the brain. Phantom limb experiences reveal a complex aspect of perception, which is that when sensory input from the missing limb stops, the brain itself manufactures a sensation that clearly should not be there. Mirror-box therapy relies on our dominant sense of vision to reinterpret the altered sensory experience the brain has after limb amputation.

Module 4.4 Quiz

Know . . .

1. The sense associated with actively touching objects is known as _____.
   A. tactile agnosia
   B. haptics
   C. nociception
   D. gestation

Understand . . .

2. At the sensory level _____ are the specialized structures that are the basis for pain sensations, and _____ helps explain the actual perceptual experience of pain.
   A. nociceptors: gate-control theory
   B. papillae: frequency theory
   C. nociceptors: place theory
   D. haptics: gate-control theory

3. The perceptual experience of flavor originates from:
   A. taste cues alone.
   B. olfactory cues alone.
   C. olfactory and taste cues together.
   D. haptic and olfactory cues together in the cerebral cortex.

Apply . . .

4. A student gently touches a staple to her fingertip and to the back of her arm near her elbow. How are these sensations likely to differ? Or would they feel similar?
   A. The sensation would feel like two points on the fingertip but is likely to feel like only one point on the arm.
   B. The sensations would feel identical because the same object touches both locations.
   C. The sensation would feel like touch on the fingertips but like pain on the elbow.
   D. The sensation would feel like two points on the arm but is likely to feel like only one point on the fingertip.

Analyze . . .

5. Phantom sensations for a missing limb are most likely the result of:
   A. continuous firing of nerve cells at the site of the actual amputation.
   B. attempts to gain attention by people who have been injured.
   C. the eyes insisting that the limb is still present and sending a confusing signal to the brain.
   D. increased sensitivity of the region of the sensory cortex that formerly registered sensations form the missing limb.

Module **4.5** Scientific Literacy Challenge: Distracted Drivers

Cell phones made their first appearance in the retail market as car phones. Units had to be mounted in the interior of a vehicle and wired into its electrical system; they were literally part of the car. Ironically, there is now evidence suggesting that a car is the *last* place a cell phone should be. You have probably heard arguments in favor of banning drivers from using cell phones, and most states have enacted laws to curb their usage—especially for texting.

Before you start this activity, take a minute to write your thoughts about using a cell phone while driving.

JOURNAL PROMPT

Do you think cell phone use while driving should be legal, banned outright, or only permitted as hands-free devices for drivers? What experiences, assumptions, or statistics have influenced your opinion?

What do we know about distracted driving?

Read the following letter from a consumer advocacy group. Make sure you understand the boldfaced terms and concepts from Chapter 4 and that you have a clear sense of what the writer is claiming.

An Open Letter to Congress

By Vanessa Fowler, President, Federation of American Drivers

Dear Representative,

I am writing on behalf of the 320,000 members of the Federation of American Drivers (FAD) who, as a group, are concerned about a major threat to public safety: "Distracted drivers," who are responsible for more than 3,000 traffic deaths annually, and more than 420,000 significant injuries. Drivers face a barrage of sights and sounds that **divide attention**. Only a portion of these are relevant to driving; the rest are distractions, and few are as powerful and ubiquitous as the cell phone. FAD's position is that cell phone use should be completely banned for drivers of any age, any vehicle, on any public roadway. While several US states and territories have taken steps in that direction, far too few have enacted a complete ban.

Many people assume that the problem with cell phone use is limited to texting or conversations that require at least one hand off the wheel. However, data show that preoccupied hands are not the problem. The real issue is that cell phone use—including texting, talking, or using apps—demands that the user **selectively attends** to the task, which can block out virtually everything else. For drivers, that means blocking out the traffic, instruments on the dashboard, and pedestrians or cyclists. Scientists have shown that people are so good at selecting what to attend to that they can experience **inattentional blindness**. In other words, a driver can be unaware of something they are looking directly at, simply because their attention is on their phone.

The FAD is advocating a very strict position on cell phones, one that they know will meet a lot of resistance. Read on to see what kinds of evidence they cite to support their argument.

How do scientists study distracted driving?

Research on driving takes many forms. It may come from traffic safety records, as did the figures cited previously, or from actual driving tests, driving on closed tracks, or even in driving simulators housed in laboratories. To find out how results from these different methods match up, read more of the letter below, and pay close attention to the highlighted portions that emphasize terms and concepts in scientific research.

> To get a sense of how dangerous a distracted driver with a cell phone can be, consider these traffic statistics: Drivers talking on cell phones—hands free or handheld—are 4 times more likely to be involved in a crash, and are involved in 21% of all crashes. Over 300,000 people are injured in cell-phone related distracted driver accidents each year.
>
> Anyone who doubts that cell phones can be distracting should examine the Virginia Tech Transportation Institute data (VTTI, it is freely available to the public online). The research team collected thousands of hours of real-time data from instruments mounted in vehicles (with the driver's consent) that recorded their behavior and important aspects of the car's operation, such as speed. This study produced scores of interesting results, one of which is that the average time a driver glances at their phone is about four seconds. That is the equivalent of driving over the length of a football field at 55 miles per hour with your eyes closed.
>
> In most cases, it is too dangerous to conduct experiments on distracted driving in real-world traffic. However, sophisticated driving simulations allow scientists more control of their studies without any risk. One such experiment at the University of Utah demonstrated that when an individual was randomly assigned to complete a driving challenge while on a cell phone versus when legally intoxicated (i.e., a blood alcohol level of .08). The results were similar whether it was a handheld or hands-free call.

There is not much room to write statistics in a letter, but Ms. Fowler managed to describe the breadth of evidence for FAD's cause. Test yourself to see how many scientific concepts you understood in this section.

1. What type of research design did the VTTI use?
   a. random assignment
   b. quasi independent
   c. natural observation
   d. experimental

2. Which finding described in the article provides the best evidence that cell phones *cause* accidents?
   a. An experiment showed that participants drove a simulator worse when using a cell phone than when intoxicated.
   b. Cell phones distract a driver's vision for about 4 seconds.
   c. 300,000 people are injured by distracted drivers every year
   d. 21% of all crashes involved a cell-phone distracted driver

3. Participants in the driving simulator could probably figure out the researchers' hypothesis when they were told they would be asked to drink alcohol before driving. This might influence behavior through
   a. demand characteristics
   b. heuristics
   c. coercion
   d. placebo effect

Answers: 1. c 2. a 3. a

Now that we have seen some of the evidence, let's engage in critical thinking.

How can we think critically about distracted drivers?

Remember that critical thinkers continue to ask questions while evaluating the quality of the answers they find. As you read the next paragraph, search for the signs of critical thinking.

In my experience, whenever FAD presents real-world data, such as statistics on the frequency of traffic accidents, the first argument against our position that cell phones are dangerous is that we cannot be sure that phone use caused the accidents. To counter this criticism, we can look at experiments involving driving simulators, which show strong evidence that cell phone use causes accidents. Then, the arguments we face suggest that a simulator is nothing like real traffic. Of course it is not real traffic, but the tasks are so similar that researchers can regularly use simulations to predict how drivers will perform on the road. Needless to say, some people are very resistant to the evidence. We have found that on most occasions, the only argument to allow drivers to use cell phones is, *I use my hands-free phone all the time, and I've never had an accident.* That is a natural reaction, but it is not a sound argument.

The statements below will help you identify several aspects of critical thinking. Match the following statements to the highlighted passages that illustrate them. Note that not all of these items are included in the article.

1. The letter urges readers not to appeal to authority.
2. The writer examines the quality of the evidence regarding ecological validity.
3. The writer examines the quality of the evidence regarding causality and ecological validity.
4. The writer identifies the use of weak anecdotal evidence.

1. Not included 2. Yellow 3. Green 4. Blue

This represents a good start on addressing the issue with critical thinking. Now, read on to see how this evidence might be applied.

How is distracted driving relevant?

Here, you can read how Ms. Fowler suggests we apply the research to traffic laws. When you finish, share any newly formed thoughts you may have about distracted driving in the writing activity that follows.

In summary, FAD is arguing for a total ban on cell phone use for drivers, and we suggest equal penalties for driving under the influence of a phone. Unlike the legal toleration of blood alcohol levels up to .08, we believe the legal limit for phone use should be zero. Equating drunk driving with cell phone use would expand your state's laws to exclude hands-free calls. We also believe that legal action is required because a sizeable number of distracted drivers deny they are contributing to the problem, citing their own accident-free history as evidence. Car manufacturers only worsen the problem by continuing to provide means of connecting phones to the car's audio system, and we believe this should become illegal as well. Even with legal restrictions, people will continue to engage in distracted driving, but at least a ban would provide some means of enforcement.

SHARED WRITING

Do you find the evidence against phone use while driving to be compelling? Do you believe it is enough to support a complete ban or not? Please explain how your opinion may or may not have changed as a result of reading the letter.

Chapter 4 Quiz

1. Which of the following requires the greatest amount of cognitive processing?
   A. Transduction
   B. Sensation
   C. Perception
   D. Sensory adaptation

2. When Keith had to give a presentation to the entire class, his classmate Daniel decided to wear a large fake mustache to make Keith laugh. To Daniel's disappointment, when Keith gave his presentation, he seemed completely unaffected, despite looking at Daniel several times. Afterward, Keith said that he was so focused on the presentation that he didn't even notice the mustache! This scenario is an example of:
   A. inattentional blindness.
   B. a blind spot.
   C. top-down processing.
   D. sensory adaptation.

3. At which structure does the transduction of light into a neural signal occur in the visual system?
   A. Retina
   B. Cornea
   C. LGN
   D. Lens

4. Which of the following statements is correct regarding the trichromatic and opponent-process theories of color vision?
   A. Research suggests that the trichromatic theory is incorrect.
   B. Research suggests that the opponent-process theory is incorrect.
   C. Both theories are correct; they simply describe color processing at different steps in the visual system.
   D. Researchers are still uncertain about which of the two theories is correct.

5. Which of the following depth cues requires two eyes?
   A. Motion parallax
   B. Retinal disparity
   C. Linear perspective
   D. Relative size

6. The place theory of hearing states that:
   A. the place or location from which a sound is coming is identified based on the difference in intensity between the two ears.
   B. the location along the basilar membrane that is stimulated by sound determines how we perceive the sound's pitch.
   C. the same frequency sound will have a different sound depending on the location of the sound source relative to the head.
   D. the primary auditory cortex is located in the same place in all human brains.

7. Cochlear implants are electronic hearing devices that can "replace" the functioning of which part of the auditory system when it is damaged?
   A. The pinna
   B. The eardrum
   C. The hair cells
   D. The ossicles

8. Sally is a ballet dancer. Although she often practices with her eyes closed, she is always aware of exactly where her arms and legs are and how her knees and elbows are bent. This is an example of which bodily sense?
   A. Nociception
   B. Gustation
   C. Haptics
   D. Kinesthesis

9. Which Gestalt principle refers to the perceptual rule that lines and other objects tend to be continuous, rather than abruptly changing direction?
   A. Figure–ground
   B. Continuity
   C. Proximity and similarity
   D. Psychophysics

10. Your professor allows students to listen to music while taking an exam. According to the research on multitasking, these students will most likely perform:
    A. better than if they were not listening to music.
    B. worse than if they were not listening to music.
    C. differently depending on each particular student's ability to multitask.
    D. the same as if they were not listening to music.

11. The _____ in the thalamus is where the optic nerves from the left and right eyes converge.
    A. fovea
    B. optic chiasm
    C. lateral geniculate nucleus
    D. retina

12. Which of the following is not considered a monocular depth cue?
    A. Interposition
    B. Linear perspective
    C. Convergence
    D. Motion parallax

13. _____ hearing loss results from damage to the cochlear hair cells and the neurons making up the auditory nerve.
    A. Temporary
    B. Conduction
    C. Sensorineural
    D. Puncturing

14. Neurons cannot fire fast enough to keep up with high-pitched sound waves. Therefore, they alternate firing according to the _____.
    A. place theory
    B. frequency theory
    C. volley principle
    D. switch theory

15. After eating grape lollipops, you and a friend notice that your tongues have turned blue. With the change in color, it is easy to notice that there are many more papillae on your friend's tongue. Who is more likely to be a supertaster?
    A. You are, because you have fewer, and therefore more distinct, papillae.
    B. Your friend is, because she has many more papillae to taste with.
    C. You are, because less dye stuck to your tongue, allowing you to taste more.
    D. It could be either of you because super tasting is unrelated to the number of papillae.

Chapter 5
Consciousness

Module 5.1 Biological Rhythms of Consciousness: Wakefulness and Sleep

Learning Objectives

5.1a Know . . . the key terminology associated with sleep, dreams, and sleep disorders.

5.1b Understand . . . how the sleep cycle works.

5.1c Understand . . . theories of why we sleep.

5.1d Apply . . . your knowledge to identify and practice good sleep habits.

5.1e Analyze . . . different theories about why we dream.

Smashing through a window in your sleep seems perfectly plausible if it occurs as part of a dream. Mike Birbiglia did just this—but in his case, it was both dream and reality. Birbiglia is a comedian whose show, Sleepwalk with Me, *is full of stories of personal and embarrassing moments, including one about jumping through a second-story, hotel-room window while asleep. He awoke upon landing, picked his bloodied, half-naked self up, and then limped to the hotel front desk to notify personnel of what happened. Indeed such a story seems to have come straight out of a dark comedy, but the truth is, Birbiglia suffers from a troubling sleep problem called REM sleep behavior disorder. This is a serious condition in which people act out their dreams in potentially dangerous and injurious ways. As it turns out, jumping through windows is not unusual for people with this disorder (Schenck et al., 2009). Although Mike's injury was self-inflicted, other people with* the condition have been known to hit or choke their bed partners. In this module, we examine two important questions: Why do we sleep and dream? What are some common and unusual sleep disorders, and why do they occur?

Consciousness *is a person's subjective awareness, including thoughts, perceptions, experiences of the world, and self-awareness.* Every day we go through many changes in consciousness; our thoughts and perceptions are constantly adapting to new situations. In some cases, when we are paying close attention to something, we seem to be more in control of conscious experiences. In other situations, such as when we are daydreaming, consciousness seems to wander. These changes in our subjective experiences make consciousness one of the most curious areas

Table 5.1 Theories of Why We Sleep

Restoration and repair: Sleep allows the body to restore energy and repair wear and tear on the body. Lack or absence of sleep leads to *sleep deprivation*, which can affect immune system functioning, cause cognitive impairments, and lead to mood problems (Bollinger et al., 2010; Harvey, 2011; Prince & Able, 2013; Lasselin et al., 2014).

Preservation and protection: Sleep helps preserve energy by lowering metabolism and reducing energy expenditure during times when searching for food is least likely to be productive. Sleep may also protect organisms from harm, as supported by observations of animals that sleep in hidden places and during times of the day when they are most vulnerable to predators (Berger & Philips, 1995; Siegel, 1995).

Brain plasticity and function: Sleeping and dreaming have cognitive benefits. Memories are consolidated during sleeping and dreaming, and adaptive changes in synaptic connections between neurons take place during sleep (Frank & Cantera, 2014). Conversely, sleep deprivation disrupts functioning of the hippocampus, which is a critical brain region for memory (Prince & Abel, 2013).

of psychological study. We begin this module by exploring the alternating cycles of consciousness—sleeping and waking.

What Is Sleep, and Why Do We Need It?

Humans spend approximately one-third of their lives sleeping. What happens during sleep can be just as fascinating as what happens during wakefulness. A basic question to begin with is *why do we need to sleep?* The answer is a complex one and likely includes the combined need to restore and repair the body; to preserve energy and protect the body from harm; and to maintain brain plasticity and function (Table 5.1).

The capacity to sleep requires a complex nervous system that can regulate an animal's activities during lightness and dark. Our cycle between wakefulness and sleep is based on a cyclic pattern controlled by various neural and hormonal fluctuations.

CIRCADIAN RHYTHMS Life involves patterns—patterns that cycle in days, weeks, months, or years. Organisms have evolved biological rhythms that are neatly adapted to environmental cycles. **Circadian rhythms** *are internally driven daily cycles of approximately 24 hours affecting physiological and behavioral processes.* They involve the tendency to be asleep or awake at specific times, to feel hungry during some parts of the day, and even the ability to concentrate better at certain times (Lavie, 2001; Verwey & Amir, 2009).

Think about your own circadian rhythms: When are you most alert? At which times of day do you feel the most tired? Night-shift workers and night owls aside, we tend to get most of our sleep when it is dark outside because our circadian rhythms are regulated by daylight interacting with our nervous and endocrine (hormonal) systems. One key brain structure in this process is the *suprachiasmatic nucleus* (SCN) of the hypothalamus. Once the SCN receives messages about light levels from the retina in the eye, the SCN then communicates signals about the light levels to the pineal gland (Figure 5.1).

Figure 5.1 Pathways Involved in Circadian Rhythms

Cells in the retina send messages about light levels to the suprachiasmatic nucleus, which in turn relays the information to the pineal gland, which secretes melatonin.

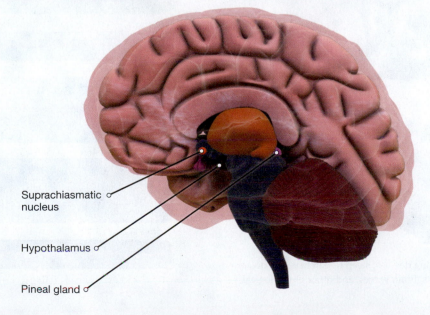

Suprachiasmatic nucleus

Hypothalamus

Pineal gland

For some people, however, the brain does not properly process light stimuli. For example, people with blindness as a result of retinal damage cannot transmit light stimuli to the SCN and pineal gland. Thus, their circadian rhythms do not synchronize to day–night cycles. However, their cycles can be adjusted using doses of *melatonin*, a hormone released by the pineal gland that helps to control a person's day–night cycle (Sack et al., 2000).

THE STAGES OF SLEEP We have already seen how sleep fits into the daily rhythm, but if we take a closer look, we will see that sleep itself has rhythms. **Polysomnography** *refers to a set of objective measurements used to examine physiological variables during sleep.* Some of the devices used in polysomnography are familiar, such as one to measure respiration and a thermometer to measure body temperature. In addition, electrical sensors attached to the skin measure muscle activity around the eyes and other parts of the body. However, sleep cycles themselves are most often defined by the *electroencephalogram* (EEG), a device that measures brain waves (also described in Module 3.3).

The output of an EEG is a waveform that shows brain wave *frequencies*—the number of up-down cycles every second—and their *amplitude*—the height and depth of the up-down cycle. *Beta waves*—high-frequency, low-amplitude waves—are characteristic of wakefulness. Their irregular nature reflects the bursts of activity in different regions of the cortex, and they are often interpreted as a sign that a person is alert. As the individual begins to shift into sleep, the waves start to become slower, larger, and more predictable; these *alpha waves* signal that a person may be daydreaming, meditating, or starting to fall asleep.

The EEG signals during sleep move through four different stages (Figure 5.2):

Stage 1: Brain waves slow down and become higher in amplitude; these are known as *theta waves*.

Stage 2: Brain waves continue to slow down but show periodic bursts of EEG activity in the form of *sleep spindles* and *K complexes*.

Stage 3: Brain waves continue to slow down and assume a new form called *delta waves*.

Stage 4: Brain waves continue to slow down in the form of delta waves; this is the deepest stage of sleep when the sleeper will be difficult to awaken.

At stage 4, the sleep cycle reverses toward stage 1 patterns, but does not go all the way back. Instead, we move into **REM sleep**—*which is a unique stage of sleep characterized by quickening brain waves, inhibited body movement, and rapid eye movements (REM).* This stage is sometimes known as

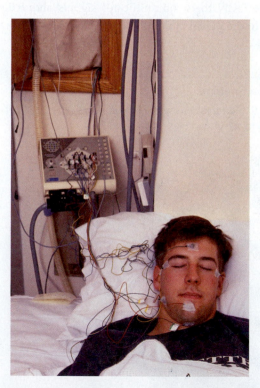

Using physiological recording devices, sleep researchers and doctors can monitor eye movements, brain waves, and other physiological processes.

Figure 5.2 EEG Recordings During Wakefulness and Sleep

Brain waves, as measured by the frequency and amplitude of electrical activity, change over the course of the normal circadian rhythm. Beta waves are predominant during wakefulness, but give way to alpha waves during periods of calm and as we drift into sleep. Theta waves are characteristic of stage 1 sleep. As we reach stage 2 sleep, the amplitude (height) of brain waves increases. During deep sleep (stages 3 and 4), the brain waves are at their highest amplitude. During REM sleep, they appear similar to the brain waves occurring when we are awake.

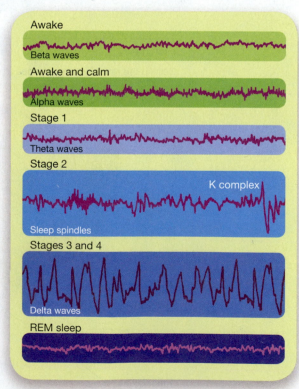

Figure 5.3 Order and Duration of Sleep Stages Through a Typical Night

Our sleep stages progress through a characteristic pattern. The first half of a normal night of sleep is dominated by deep, slow-wave sleep. REM sleep increases in duration relative to deep sleep during the second half of the night.

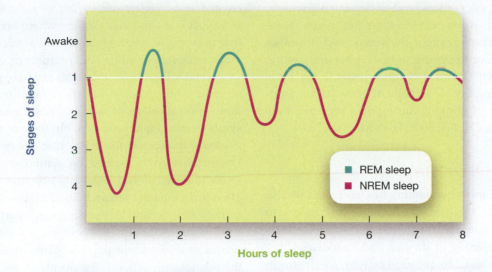

paradoxical sleep because the EEG waves appear to represent a state of wakefulness, despite the fact that we remain asleep. The REM pattern is so distinct that the first four stages are known collectively as *non-REM (NREM) sleep*. At the end of the first REM phase, we cycle back toward deep sleep stages and then back into REM sleep again every 90 to 100 minutes.

The sleep cycle through a typical night of sleep is summarized in Figure 5.3. As shown in the figure, the deeper stages of sleep (3 and 4) predominate during the earlier portions of the sleep cycle, but gradually give way to longer REM periods.

REM sleep appears to be critical to a good night's sleep. In fact, the lack of REM sleep may be the most negative aspect of sleep deprivation, rather than the actual amount of lost sleep time. If you usually sleep for 8 hours but end up only sleeping for 3, you can recover from this deficit the next time you sleep with only the normal 8 hours. Your time in REM sleep, however, will increase considerably—a phenomenon called *REM rebound*, when our brains spend more time in the REM stage following a period of deprivation.

With age our circadian rhythms and sleep cycle patterns change (Figure 5.4; Farajnia et al., 2014). Researchers

Figure 5.4 Sleep Requirements Change with Age

People tend to spend progressively less time sleeping as they age. The amount of a certain type of sleep, REM sleep, declines the most.

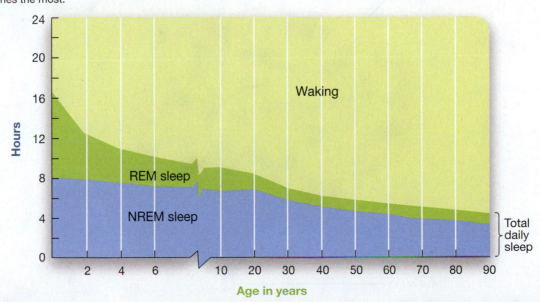

have found that we need much less sleep, especially REM sleep, as we move from infancy into early childhood; this trend continues into adulthood. Moreover, people generally experience a change in *when* they prefer to sleep. In our teens and 20s, many of us tend to become night owls, staying active and awake while others are asleep. Later in adulthood, we former night owls may find ourselves reversing this preference: going to bed earlier and getting up earlier. Research shows that these patterns are more than just preferences: People actually do show higher alertness and cognitive functioning during their preferred time of day (Cavallera & Giudici, 2008; Diaz-Morales, 2007).

Theories of Dreaming

The curious experience of dreaming has fascinated people for centuries, and it is not uncommon for cultures to search dreams for deep meaning. Here we touch on efforts to decipher the meaning of dreams and also discuss the more scientifically testable question of why we dream in the first place.

THE PSYCHOANALYTIC APPROACH Many Western beliefs about the meaning of dreams come from the psychoanalytic perspective of Sigmund Freud, who in 1899 published his classic work, *The Interpretation of Dreams.* Freud believed that our dreams reflect the significant issues we face in our waking state. To resolve these issues, one would need to describe one's dream to an analyst, who in turn would interpret the symbolism of these dreams in the

context of the individual's ongoing daily conflicts. Dreams comprise two types of content: The **manifest content** *of a dream consists of its imagery and storylines.* The **latent content** *of a dream consists of the actual symbolic meaning of its imagery and storylines, typically reflecting subconscious sources of anxiety.* It is in this latent content where Freud believed the true meaning of dreams resides, and as such, he advocated *dream work,* the recording and interpreting of dreams.

Freud's ideas live on in the popular press, and they resonate with mystical beliefs about dreaming. Indeed, there is no shortage of books offering insight into dream symbolism and interpretation, but there is also no scientific evidence to support the claim that dreams are symbolic. Dream analysis is focused on symbolism that is subjectively interpreted and lacks any objective measurements. Therefore, modern research focuses on the neurological activity that occurs during dreaming, particularly during REM sleep. Although symbols are no longer a focus of dream analysis, some psychologists continue to explore the relationship between the events of one's waking state and the manifest content of one's dream state.

THE ACTIVATION–SYNTHESIS HYPOTHESIS The **activation–synthesis hypothesis** *suggests that dreams arise from brain activity originating from bursts of excitatory messages from the brain stem.* This electrical activity is accompanied by the telltale signs of eye movements and EEG activity during REM sleep; moreover, the burst of activity activates perceptual areas of the brain, producing imaginary sights and sounds, as well as emotional areas (Figure 5.5).

Figure 5.5 The Activation-Synthesis Hypothesis of Dreaming

The pons, located in the brain stem, sends excitatory messages through the thalamus to the sensory and emotional areas of the cortex. The images and emotions that arise from this activity are synthesized into the bizarre and often vivid experience of dreaming. Inhibitory signals are also relayed from the pons down the spinal cord, which prevents movement during dreaming.

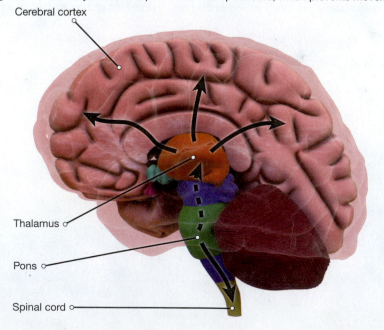

Cerebral cortex

Thalamus

Pons

Spinal cord

Thus, brain stem activity initiates the *activation* component of the model. The *synthesis* component arises as the brain attempts to organize bursts of neural activity in the absence of conscious guidance (Hobson et al., 2000). Because the imagery, sounds, and events are randomly activated, the storyline of a dream typically seems disjointed and bizarre. This would be similar to receiving a message composed of randomly selected and strung-together words. Likely, you would have to struggle to make sense of it.

Working the Scientific Literacy Model

Searching for Meaning in Dreams

If dreaming originates from brain stem activity, as the activation-synthesis hypothesis predicts, then it may seem pointless to mine them for any meaning or relevance to our lives. However, many dream scientists are revisiting the topic and asking again whether dream content might actually be meaningful, maybe they are not just the haphazard synthesis of brain stem activity. To investigate this possibility, psychologists are taking advantage of new technologies and testing whether there are meaningful aspects of dream content.

What do we know about the search for meaning in dreams?

Our dreams are often vivid replays of events and thoughts that occupy our conscious awareness during wakefulness, or are at least unusual renditions of them. Consistent with this observation is the **neurocognitive hypothesis of dreaming**, *which maintains that dreaming is not a completely random by-product of brain stem activity but rather reflects waking preoccupations and emotional experiences*. This hypothesis emphasizes the fact that higher brain centers are activated during dreaming and relevant daily events are present in dream content (see Domhoff, 2001; Hobson, 2005).

How can science explain the relevance of dreams to events during wakefulness?

The neurocognitive hypothesis has been tested with a range of tools from neural-imaging with both healthy and injured brains, to analyses of dream journals. Across methods, one finding that seems to support the neurocognitive hypothesis is the highly similar pattern of brain activity that occurs during both REM-stage dreaming and mind wandering during wakefulness. The frontal and temporal lobes of the brain, in particular areas involved in thinking about oneself, memory, and emotion, are active during both

dream sleep and mind wandering. Unlike mind wandering, however, brain regions involved in controlling attention and setting goals are relatively inactive during sleep. It is as if higher-level brain centers forego enough self-control to allow dreams to run their course, while maintaining enough emotion and sense of self to be remembered in the same way as actual experiences. Based on these brain-based observations, dreaming could be described as an "intensified" version of mind wandering (Fox et al., 2013).

Studies of dream journals also lend support to the neurocognitive hypothesis. One compelling example comes from the dream journals of college students written in the fall of 2001 (Propper et al., 2007). After the 9/11 terrorist attacks on the World Trade Center and Pentagon, the students continued journaling. They recorded a gradually increasing number of dreams involving objects and events related to the attacks, as well as more dreams in which threatening events occurred. Interestingly, the students who watched and listened to the most media coverage of the events reported more attack-related themes and imagery in their dreams (Figure 5.6). Similar results have been found in other cases of emotional events such as divorce. The amount of waking concern about an ex-spouse correlates with the number of times that individual appears in a divorcee's dreams (Cartwright et al., 2006).

Other support of the neurocognitive hypothesis comes from research on sleep-study participants. Volunteers spend the night sleeping in a laboratory, where researchers

Figure 5.6 The Influence of the September 11, 2001 Terrorist Attacks on Dream Content

This graph shows the number of dreams containing specific types of content related to the attacks. Specific references include images of box cutters, planes, and the World Trade Center. Thematic references include general images of disasters, crashes, or tall buildings. Threats involve direct threats and life-threatening situations. The fourth column of the graph summarizes the number of dreams that contained any of these three types of content.

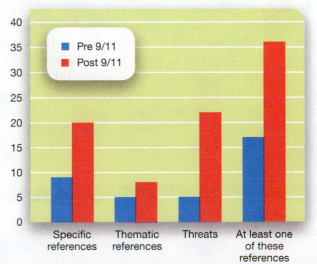

can monitor brain waves for signs of REM sleep and then awaken participants for a quick interview about any dreams they might have experienced. What these studies demonstrate is that dream content gradually becomes increasingly complex and story-like as we reach adolescence and into adulthood—something not supported by the activation-synthesis hypothesis. For example, when 9- to 11-year-olds are awakened during REM sleep only 20% to 30% of them report dreaming, whereas close to 80% of adults do so. Children younger than 5 years old report remembering only simple images or thoughts, such as that of an animal or of eating (Domhoff, 2001).

Can we critically evaluate this evidence?

It can seem bewildering to have multiple theories about the same basic behavior, such as dreaming. However, understanding different possibilities can help us understand the details and limitations of the evidence. Here, it might seem like the neurocognitive hypothesis of dreaming has revived Freud's theory of symbolic dreaming. Although the neurocognitive hypothesis certainly attaches more significance to dreaming than does the activation-synthesis hypothesis, it does so in a straightforward way. Specifically, saying that the content of a dream is related to wakefulness is not the same thing as saying that an image of one thing (*manifest* content) expresses a deep, symbolic, and emotional need residing beneath conscious awareness (*latent* content).

Why is this relevant?

If dreaming plays a role in processing information we experienced while awake, then the benefits of a good night's rest may go beyond restoring and repairing the body. Sleep researchers have discovered that dreaming during both REM and non-REM stages of sleep aids in the consolidation of memories (Payne & Kensinger, 2010; Wamsley, 2014; Wamsley & Stickgold, 2011). This aspect of dreaming is important to college students: Pulling an all-nighter before an exam may seem like a necessity, but dream research reminds us that the need to study should be balanced by the need to sleep. The best advice, then, is to study and sleep *every* night, not just the night before the exam. Scientific research has shown that dreaming plays an important role in cognitive activity. However, avoid taking to heart popular media claims that dreams have symbolic meaning. These claims are not based on scientific evidence.

JOURNAL PROMPT

Dreaming: Which theory of dreaming do you think best explains your own dream experiences? If you do not remember dreams, which theory seems the most plausible? For either answer, explain.

Insomnia can arise from worrying about sleep. It is among the most common of all sleep disorders.

Disorders and Problems with Sleep

Throughout this module, we have seen that sleep is essential; without it individuals are vulnerable to cognitive, emotional, and physical problems. Given this relationship, it is no wonder that so many people seek help getting better sleep for a variety of sleep disorders.

INSOMNIA   The most widely recognized and most common sleeping problem is **insomnia**, *which is a disorder characterized by an extreme lack of sleep.* Although the average adult may need 7 to 8 hours of sleep to feel rested, substantial individual differences exist. For this reason, insomnia is defined not in terms of the hours of sleep, but rather in terms of the degree to which a person feels rested during the day. This understanding is reflected in the American Psychiatric Association's criteria for insomnia shown in Table 5.2.

Although insomnia is thought of as a single disorder, there are different ways it can manifest. *Onset insomnia* occurs when a person has difficulty falling asleep, *maintenance insomnia* occurs when an individual cannot easily return to sleep after waking in the night, and *late insomnia* is a situation in which a person wakes up too early—sometimes hours too early—and cannot return to sleep. Insomnia disorder stems from internal sleep disturbances, rather than by external stimuli over which one has little control, such as a neighbor's persistent car alarm. Insomnia may accompany other problems such as depression and anxiety, and abuse of substances ranging from caffeine and nicotine to drugs such as marijuana, ecstasy, or cocaine (Schierenbeck et al., 2008). A sleep specialist is trained to determine the source of insomnia and to consider many possible contributing factors in diagnosing

Table 5.2 Sample of the American Psychiatric Association's Criteria for Insomnia Disorder

1. The person has at least 3 months of difficulty initiating or maintaining sleep.
2. Sleep problems occur despite having adequate opportunity to sleep.
3. Sleep difficulty is present at least 3 nights each week.
4. Sleep loss causes distress or impairment in social, occupational, and other areas.

SOURCE: Adapted from American Psychiatric Association (2013). *Diagnostic and Statistical Manual of Mental Disorders* (5th ed.).

and treating the problem. As we will discuss next, a number of other sleep-related disturbances can lead to insomnia. To get a sense of whether you are getting enough sleep see Table 5.3.

NIGHTMARES AND NIGHT TERRORS Certainly, a downside to dreaming is the experience of **nightmares**, *which are particularly vivid and disturbing dreams that occur during REM sleep.* Almost everyone—as many as 85% to 95% of adults—can remember having bad dreams that have negative emotional content, such as feeling lost, sad, or angry, within a 1-year period (Levin, 1994; Schredl, 2003). Not everyone recalls disturbing dreams, however, and data from numerous studies indicate that nightmares are correlated with psychological distress. As discussed with regard to the neurocognitive hypothesis of dreaming, people who are distressed when they are awake are likely to experience distress when they are asleep. This relationship was illustrated in a study of San Francisco and Arizona residents that began before a massive earthquake occurred in 1989. Although both groups began the study reporting similar rates of disturbed dreaming, residents of San Francisco reported a sharp increase in nightmares

following the earthquake; residents of Arizona were not directly affected by the disaster and showed no such changes (Wood et al., 1992).

Even worse than nightmares, some people experience **night terrors**, *which are intense bouts of panic and arousal that awaken the individual, typically in a heightened emotional state.* A person experiencing a night terror may call out or scream, fight back against imaginary attackers, or leap from the bed and start to flee before waking up. Night terrors differ from dreams because they occur during NREM sleep and most people who experience them typically do not recall any specific dream content. Night terrors are more common in young children than in adults, and they increase in frequency during periods of stress (Schredl, 2001).

MOVEMENT DISTURBANCES To sleep well, an individual needs to remain still. During REM sleep the brain prevents movement by sending inhibitory signals down the spinal cord. A number of sleep disturbances, however, involve movement and related sensations. For example, **restless legs syndrome** *is a persistent feeling of discomfort in the legs and the urge to continuously shift them into different positions* (Smith & Tolson, 2008). This

Table 5.3 Application Activity: Are You Getting Enough Sleep?

Try completing the Epworth Sleepiness Scale to make sure you are getting enough sleep.

Use the following scale to choose the most appropriate number for each situation:
0 = would never doze or sleep   1 = slight chance of dozing or sleeping
2 = moderate chance of dozing or sleeping   3 = high chance of dozing or sleeping

If you score 10 points or higher, you are probably not getting enough sleep. Check Table 5.4 to learn about techniques to overcome sleep difficulties.

Situation	Chances of Falling Asleep
Sitting and reading	0 1 2 3
Watching TV	0 1 2 3
Sitting inactive in a public place	0 1 2 3
Being a passenger in a motor vehicle for an hour or more	0 1 2 3
Lying down in the afternoon	0 1 2 3
Sitting and talking to someone	0 1 2 3
Sitting quietly after lunch (no alcohol)	0 1 2 3
Stopped for a few minutes in traffic while driving	0 1 2 3
Your total score	

SOURCE: Johns, M. W. (1991). A new method for measuring daytime sleepiness: The Epworth Sleepiness Scale. Sleep, 14 (6), 540–545.

disorder affects approximately 5% to 10% of the population and occurs at varying levels of severity. For those individuals who are in constant motion, sleep becomes difficult. They awake periodically at night to reposition their legs, even though in some cases they do not remember waking the next day.

A more severe and potentially dangerous condition is **REM sleep behavior disorder**, which was introduced in the beginning of this module. *People with this condition do not show the typical restriction of movement during REM sleep; in fact, they appear to be acting out the content of their dreams* (Schenck & Mahowald, 2002). Imagine what happens when an individual dreams of being attacked, the dreamed response of defending oneself or even fighting back can be acted out. Not surprisingly, this action can awaken some individuals. Because it occurs during REM sleep, however, some individuals do not awaken until they have hurt themselves or someone else (Schenck et al., 2009), as occurred with Mike Birbiglia.

Somnambulism, or *sleepwalking, is a disorder that involves wandering and performing other activities while asleep.* It is more prevalent during childhood. Sleepwalking is not necessarily indicative of any type of sleep or emotional disturbance, although it may put people in harm's way. People who sleepwalk are not acting out dreams, and they typically do not remember the episode. (For the record, it is not dangerous to wake up a sleepwalker, as is commonly thought. At worst, the person will be disoriented.)

SLEEP APNEA **Sleep apnea** *is a disorder characterized by the temporary inability to breathe during sleep* (*apnea* literally translates to "without breathing"). Although a variety of factors contribute to sleep apnea, this condition appears to be most common among overweight and obese individuals, and it is roughly twice as prevalent among men as among women (Lin et al., 2008; McDaid et al., 2009).

In most cases of apnea, the airway becomes physically obstructed, at a point anywhere from the back of the nose and mouth to the neck (Figure 5.7). Therefore, treatment for mild apnea generally involves dental devices that hold the mouth in a specific position during sleep. Weight-loss efforts should accompany this treatment in most cases because weight is a contributing factor for many individuals with sleep apnea. In moderate to severe cases, a continuous positive airway pressure (CPAP) device can be used to force air through the nose, keeping the airway open through increased air pressure (McDaid et al., 2009).

Sleep apnea can also be caused by the brain's failure to regulate breathing. This failure can happen for many reasons, including damage to or deterioration of the medulla of the brain stem, which is responsible for controlling the chest muscles during breathing. Despite this, sleep apnea is rarely fatal. Low blood oxygen levels elicit a gasping reflex and resumed oxygen flow.

Figure 5.7 Sleep Apnea

One cause of sleep apnea is the obstruction of air flow, which can seriously disrupt the sleep cycle.

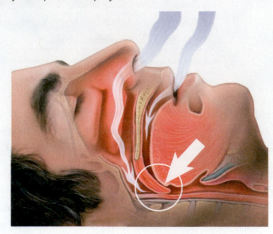

NARCOLEPSY Although movement disorders, apnea, and night terrors can all lead to insomnia, another condition is characterized by nearly the opposite effect. **Narcolepsy** *is a disorder in which a person experiences extreme daytime sleepiness and even sleep attacks.* These bouts of sleep may last only a few seconds, especially if the person is standing or driving when she falls asleep and is jarred awake by falling, a nodding head, or swerving of the car. Even without such disturbances, the sleep may last only a few minutes or more, so it is not the same as falling asleep for a night's rest.

Narcolepsy differs from more typical sleep in a number of other ways. People with a normal sleep pattern generally reach the REM stage after more than an hour of sleep, but a person experiencing narcolepsy is likely to go almost immediately from waking to REM sleep. Also, because REM sleep is associated with dreaming, people with narcolepsy often report vivid dreamlike images even if they did not fully fall asleep.

Why does narcolepsy occur? Scientists have investigated a hormone called *orexin* that functions to maintain wakefulness. Individuals with narcolepsy have deficient levels of orexin in the brain, resulting in greater difficulty maintaining wakefulness (Nakamura et al., 2011). Orexin deficiency associated with narcolepsy may be based on genetics because familial risk factors are high for first-degree relatives (Wing et al., 2011). Also, there is strong evidence that narcolepsy is an autoimmune disease (Arango et al., 2014).

SLEEP STATE MISPERCEPTION It may come as a surprise, but one sleep problem involves estimating how long you have slept. **Sleep state misperception (SSM)** *is a condition in which a person underestimates her amount of sleep on a regular basis.* People experiencing SSM are sometimes said to have *paradoxical insomnia*; they believe they cannot sleep enough, but there is no physiological or medical evidence to support that belief (American Academy of Sleep Medicine, 2005; Trinder, 1988). In fact, many people experience SSM without any detriment to their daily functioning. Thus, the problem with SSM is primarily the distress a person feels about having insomnia, even though the individual may not actually have insomnia. The opposite condition—**positive sleep state misperception**—*occurs when individuals regularly overestimate their sleep*. This form of misperception produces slightly more problems in that the individual begins to show signs of sleep deprivation—severe afternoon sleepiness and attention problems—and does not connect these symptoms with poor sleep (Trajanovic et al., 2007).

Think about the difficulty underlying sleep misperception: If you are unconscious when you are asleep, how are you supposed to monitor how long you are sleeping? Yet when researchers compare people's self-rated estimates of how much they sleep with more objective measures—through polysomnography—it turns out that most individuals are relatively accurate. This, however, is not the case in people with SSM. In other words, most sleepers can provide reasonably accurate estimates of their amount of sleep using cues such as the time they went to bed, the time it took to fall asleep, the amount of waking during the night, and the time they first awoke.

OVERCOMING SLEEP PROBLEMS There are many myths and anecdotes about what helps people overcome sleep problems. For some people, relief can be as simple as a snack or a warm glass of milk; it can certainly be difficult to sleep if you are hungry. Others might have a nightcap—a drink of alcohol—in hopes of inducing sleep, although the effects can be misleading. Alcohol may make you sleepy, but it disrupts the quality of sleep, especially the REM cycle, and may leave you feeling unrested. Fortunately, most people respond well to psychological interventions.

By practicing good sleep hygiene—healthy sleep-related habits—people can typically overcome sleep disturbances in a matter of a few weeks (Morin et al., 2006; Murtagh & Greenwood, 1995). The techniques shown in Table 5.4 are effective for many people who prefer self-help methods, but effective help is also available from psychologists, physicians, and even the Internet (Ritterband et al., 2009; van Straten & Cuijpers, 2009).

Although research supports the use of cognitive and behavioral techniques, people often turn to drugs to help them sleep. A number of over-the-counter sleep aids, as well as prescription drugs, are available. For most of the 20th century, these prescription drugs included sedatives such as barbiturates (Phenobarbital) and benzodiazepines (e.g., Valium). Benzodiazepines are *GABA agonists*; they magnify the inhibitory effects of the GABA (gamma-aminobutyric acid) neurotransmitter at synapses, thereby slowing brain activity and inducing sleep. (A more detailed discussion of drugs and their effects on consciousness appears in Module 5.3.) Although these drugs managed to put people to sleep, people also quickly developed a *tolerance* to them; they required increasingly higher doses to get the same effect. This eventually led to *dependency*; they could not sleep without them (Pallesen et al., 2001). Even though benzodiazepines are generally safer than barbiturates, the risk of dependence and worsening sleep problems makes them suitable only for short-term use—generally for a week or two—and only after sleep hygiene efforts have failed.

Ambien (zolpidem) is a top-selling sleep drug recognizable because of the occasional headlines reporting of people engaging in peculiar, self-injurious, or violent behavior while under its influence. Ambien, like benzodiazepines, are GABA agonists. The initial version of Ambien helped people fall asleep, but its sleep-inducing effects wore off too quickly and its side effects on behavior were troubling. An extended-release version of Ambien

Table 5.4 Nonpharmacological Techniques for Improving Sleep

1. Use your bed for sleeping only, not for working or studying. (Sexual activity is an appropriate exception to the rule.)

2. Do not turn sleep into work. Putting effort into falling asleep generally leads to arousal instead of sleep.

3. Keep your clock out of sight. Watching the clock increases pressure to sleep and worries about getting enough sleep.

4. Get exercise early during the day. Exercise may not increase the amount of sleep, but it may help you sleep better. Exercising late in the day, however, may leave you restless and aroused at bedtime.

5. Avoid substances that disrupt sleep. Such substances include caffeine (in coffee, tea, many soft drinks, and other sources), nicotine, and alcohol. Illicit drugs such as cocaine, marijuana, and ecstasy also disrupt healthy sleep.

6. If you lie in bed worrying at night, schedule evening time to deal with stress. Write down your worries and stressors for approximately 30 minutes before bedtime.

7. If you continue to lie in bed without sleeping for 30 minutes, get up and do something else until you are about to fall asleep and then return to bed.

8. Get up at the same time every morning. Although this practice may lead to sleepiness the first day or two, eventually it helps set the daily rhythm.

9. If you still have problems sleeping after 4 weeks, consider seeing a sleep specialist to get tested for sleep apnea, restless legs syndrome, or another sleep problem that may require more specific interventions.

SOURCE: "Non-Pharmacological Techniques for Improving Sleep" Based on recommendations from the American Psychological Association, 2004.

has been designed to help extend sleep and reduce some of its troubling side effects. It should be noted that dosage recommendations for Ambien were developed using only males as subjects (unfortunately a common practice in drug development and testing). Thus, reports of adverse effects of the drug affected a disproportionate number of females compared to males—a problem that went on for 20 years before the Federal Drug Administration (FDA) required dosages for females be cut by half. This problem

demonstrates how biological processes between the sexes differ. More importantly, it highlights the need to consider these differences in medical and neuroscientific research.

Modern sleep drugs are generally thought to be much safer in the short term, and many have been approved for long-term use as well. However, few modern drugs have been studied in placebo-controlled experiments, and even fewer have actually been studied for long-term use (e.g., for more than a month; Krystal, 2009).

Module 5.1 Summary

5.1a Know . . . the key terminology associated with sleep, dreams, and sleep disorders:

activation–synthesis hypothesis
circadian rhythms
consciousness
insomnia
latent content
manifest content
narcolepsy
neurocognitive hypothesis of dreaming
nightmares
night terrors
polysomnography
positive sleep state misperception
REM sleep
REM sleep behavior disorder
restless legs syndrome
sleep apnea
sleep state misperception (SSM)
somnambulism

5.1b Understand . . . how the sleep cycle works.

The sleep cycle consists of a series of stages going from stage 1 through stage 4, cycles back down again, and is followed by a REM phase. The first sleep cycle lasts approximately 90 minutes. Deep sleep (stages 3 and 4) is longest during the first-half of the sleep cycle, whereas REM phases increase in duration during the second-half of the sleep cycle.

5.1c Understand . . . theories of why we sleep.

Sleep theories include rest and restoration, preservation and protection, and brain plasticity and function. According to the rest and restoration view, we sleep so that the body can recover from the stress and strain that occurs

during wakefulness. According to the preservation and protection view, sleep has evolved as a way to reduce activity and provide protection from potential threats, and to reduce the amount of energy intake required. Changes in synaptic connections and memory consolidation during sleep support the brain plasticity and function theory. Evidence supports each theory, so it is likely that there is more than one reason for sleep.

5.1d Apply . . . your knowledge to identify and practice good sleep habits.

After reading this module you hopefully found several helpful ideas. Completing the "Are you getting enough sleep" activity in Table 5.3 on page 151 provides an estimate about one important aspect of good sleep habits: Getting enough of it. Perhaps you also found some useful suggestions on making improvements by exploring non-pharmacological methods in Table 5.4.

5.1e Analyze . . . different theories about why we dream.

Dreams have fascinated psychologists since Sigmund Freud's time. From his psychoanalytic perspective, Freud believed that the manifest content of dreams could be used to uncover their symbolic, latent content. Contemporary scientists are skeptical about the validity of this approach, given the lack of empirical evidence to support it. The activation–synthesis hypothesis eliminates the meaning of dream content, suggesting instead that dreams are just interpretations of haphazard neural activity in the sleeping brain. The neurocognitive hypothesis integrates findings from brain research, developmental studies of dreaming, and the analysis of dream content to suggest that dreams involve complex brain activity involving numerous higher regions and are relevant to waking experience.

Module **5.1** Quiz

Know . . .

1. _____ is a condition in which a person's breathing becomes obstructed or stops during sleep.
   A. Somnambulism
   B. Sleep state misperception
   C. Narcolepsy
   D. Sleep apnea

Understand . . .

2. Which of the following is the most likely order of sleep stages during the first 90 minutes of a night of rest?
   A. Stages 1-2-3-4-1-2-3-4-REM
   B. Stages 1-2-3-4-REM-1-2-3-4
   C. Stages 1-2-3-4-3-2-REM
   D. Stages REM-4-3-2-1

3. The neurocognitive theory of dreaming proposes that:
   A. dreaming creates complex thoughts that we become aware of upon awakening.
   B. dreaming involves activation of higher brain centers that show similar patterns seen during mind wandering.
   C. the symbols in our dreams represent unconscious urges related to sex and aggression.
   D. we cannot solve complex problems until we have dreamed about them.

Apply . . .

4. Which of the following is not good advice for improving your quality of sleep?
   A. Use your bed for sleeping only—not homework or watching TV.
   B. Exercise late in the day to make sure you are tired when it is time to sleep.
   C. Avoid drinking caffeine, especially late in the day.
   D. Get up at the same time every morning to make sure you develop a reliable pattern of sleep and wakefulness.

Analyze . . .

5. Scientists are skeptical about the psychoanalytic theory of dreaming because the _____ of a dream is entirely subject to interpretation.
   A. latent content
   B. sleep stage
   C. activation
   D. manifest content

Module 5.2 Altered States of Consciousness: Hypnosis, Meditation, and Disorders of Consciousness

Learning Objectives

5.2a Know . . . the key terminology associated with hypnosis, meditation, déjà vu, and disorders of consciousness.

5.2b Understand . . . the competing theories of hypnosis.

5.2c Apply . . . your knowledge of hypnosis to identify what it can and cannot do.

5.2d Analyze . . . claims that hypnosis can help with memory recovery.

5.2e Analyze . . . the effectiveness of meditation for use in therapy.

Have you ever walked into a room for the first time and suddenly had the eerie feeling that, although it was not possible, you had been there before? In a sense, you may have been—albeit not in a past life or through some supernatural means. Psychologists can actually induce this experience, called déjà vu. *In fact, Dr. Anne Cleary does it quite easily in her research. She asks her research participants to study pictures of settings such as bowling alleys, landscapes, and rooms from houses. Later, she shows them the same pictures, along with new pictures that vaguely resemble the originals. These latter pictures induce a déjà vu-like experience (Cleary et al., 2009). The same thing happens when she does this experiment using music; songs can also induce déjà vu (Kostic & Cleary, 2009). These experiments not only help explain the uncanny déjà vu experience, they also stimulate additional fascination about our consciousness*

experiences. For example, how is information processed in the background of our awareness? And what other various states of consciousness do people experience while awake?

Consciousness varies by degree, much lies between being awake versus being asleep. Humans have a remarkable ability to alter where on this continuum they want to reach. Techniques such as hypnosis and meditation are ways of inducing what many regard as an altered state of consciousness. Experiences such as déjà vu highlight the strange, subjective world of conscious experience. Also, injury or illness can temporarily or permanently change a person's level of consciousness. In this module, we examine these topics about consciousness.

Hypnosis

Chances are that you have seen hypnosis featured in films, television shows, or live stage performances. The caricature of a pocket watch swung back and forth before an increasingly subdued subject endures, though it promotes just one of many misunderstandings about hypnosis. **Hypnosis** *is a procedure of inducing a heightened state of suggestibility*; hypnosis is not a trance, as is often portrayed in the popular media (Kirsch & Lynn, 1998). The hypnotist simply suggests changes, and the subject is more likely (but not certain) to comply as a result of the hypnosis.

Although one could conceivably make suggestions about almost anything, hypnotic suggestions generally are most effective when they fall into one of three categories:

- *Ideomotor suggestions* are related to specific actions that could be performed, such as adopting a specific position.

- *Challenge suggestions* indicate actions that are not to be performed, so that the subject appears to lose the ability to perform an action.

- *Cognitive-perceptual suggestions* are to remember or forget, or to experience altered perceptions such as reduced pain sensations (Kirsch & Lynn, 1998).

Regardless of the category, hypnotic suggestions will not completely change an individual. In other words, a hypnotist could suggest to someone that the individual's sore hand no longer hurts, thereby helping to diminish the pain. In contrast, the hypnotist could not suggest that an honest person rob a bank and expect the subject to comply.

People who have not encountered scientific information about hypnosis are often skeptical that hypnosis can actually occur or are reluctant to be hypnotized themselves (Capafons et al., 2008; Molina & Mendoza, 2006). This is probably not surprising given the vast misunderstandings about hypnosis. For all these reasons, it is important to establish a scientific view of the phenomenon.

THEORIES OF HYPNOSIS   The word *hypnosis* comes from the Greek *hypno*, meaning "sleep". In reality, scientific research tells us that hypnosis is nothing like sleep. For example, it is possible to experience hypnosis during periods of high alertness, including during physical exercise (Wark, 2006). So, if hypnosis is not sleep, what is it?

Dissociation theory *explains hypnosis as a unique state in which consciousness is divided into two parts: an observer and a hidden observer*. It may sound magical, but this kind of divided state is actually quite common. Take any skill that you have mastered, such as driving a car or playing an instrument. When you began, it took every bit of your conscious awareness to focus on the correct movements; you were a single, highly focused observer of your actions. After extensive practice, you could do it

Stage hypnotists use the human plank demonstration with their subjects. They support an audience volunteer on three chairs. To the audience's amazement, when the chair supporting the mid-body is removed, the hypnotized subject does not fall (even when weight is added, as shown in the photo). However, nonhypnotized subjects also do not fall. (Please do not try this at home—there is a trick behind it!)

automatically while you observed and paid attention to something else. Although we call the familiar behavior automatic, there is still a hidden observer, that is, a part of you that is paying attention to the task. According to dissociation theory, hypnosis splits awareness in a similar way. At one level, the hypnotized individual is focused intently on the suggestions, while at another level of consciousness she is attending to something else (Hilgard, 1994).

Another perspective, **social-cognitive theory**, *explains hypnosis by emphasizing the degree to which beliefs and expectations contribute to increased suggestibility*. This perspective is supported by experiments in which individuals are either told that they will be able to resist ideomotor suggestions or that they will not be able to resist them. In these studies, people tend to conform to what they have been told to expect, which is a result that cannot be easily explained by dissociation theory (Lynn et al., 1984; Spanos et al., 1985). Similarly, research on hypnosis as a treatment for pain shows that response expectancy—whether the individual believes the treatment will work—plays a large role in the actual pain relief experienced (Milling, 2009; Montgomery et al., 2010).

APPLICATIONS OF HYPNOSIS   Since hypnosis is a state of heightened suggestibility, why not use it to suggest that an individual in psychotherapy stop thinking depressing thoughts or encourage confronting anxiety-provoking situations? Interestingly, hypnosis has been applied to these and other clinical problems (Kihlstrom, 2013; Spiegel, 2013). For example, the most frequently used, scientifically supported psychotherapy for depression is known as *cognitive-behavioral therapy* (CBT; see Module 14.2). Psychotherapy research studies have shown that hypnosis combined with CBT (an approach known as *cognitive hypnotherapy*) is equally effective as, and perhaps even more effective than, CBT alone (Alladin & Alibhai, 2007; Kirsch, Montgomery, & Sapirstein, 1995). In addition, if you have any anxiety about an oral presentation that lies in your future, cognitive hypnotherapy has been shown to reduce public speaking anxiety (Schoenberger et al., 1997).

Hypnosis is far from a cure-all, however. For example, researchers found that hypnotherapy combined with a nicotine patch is more effective as a smoking cessation intervention than the patch alone. Nonetheless, only one-fifth of the individuals receiving this kind of therapy managed to remain smoke-free for a year (Carmody et al., 2008; see also Barnes et al., 2010). Moreover, the individuals receiving hypnotherapy for depression improved only 5% to 8% more on several measures of depressive symptoms than those who received traditional CBT. A general conclusion regarding hypnosis in therapy is that it shows promise, especially when used in conjunction with other evidence-based psychological or medical treatments.

Perhaps the most practical use for hypnosis is in the treatment of pain (Jensen & Patterson, 2014). If researchers can demonstrate its effectiveness in this application, it may be a preferred method of pain control given painkillers' potential side effects and risk of dependence, not to mention that hypnosis treatments for medical procedures cost only half as much as drugs (Lang et al., 2000). What does the scientific evidence say about the use of hypnosis in treating pain? A review of 18 individual studies found that approximately 75% of all individuals experienced adequate pain relief with this approach beyond that provided by traditional analgesics or no treatment (Montgomery et al.,

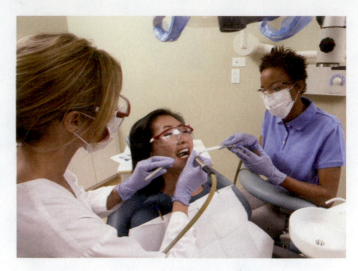

Under hypnosis, people can withstand higher levels of pain for longer periods of time, including the discomfort associated with dental procedures.

2000). What happened to the other 25%? Perhaps the failure of the treatment in this group is attributable to the fact that some people are more readily hypnotized than others. Both dissociation and social-cognitive theories may help explain the success of hypnotherapy in treating and preventing pain. Mentally distancing yourself (dissociating) from the physical source of pain, along with the expectation that hypnosis can lead to reduced pain, may both help dampen the experience (Jensen & Patterson, 2014).

Meditation and Déjà Vu

Hypnosis relies on suggestibility, but there are other variations in conscious experience, including those that are intentionally initiated by the individual and those that seem to catch us off guard. Here we will examine meditation and déjà vu.

Myths in Mind

Recovering Lost Memories Through Hypnosis

Hypnosis has long been used in psychotherapy, and it has many potential benefits in this setting. However, before the limitations of hypnosis were fully understood, professionals working in the fields of psychology and law regularly used it with the hope of uncovering lost memories. What a powerful tool this would be for a psychologist—if a patient could remember specifics about trauma or abuse, it could greatly help the individual's recovery. Similarly, law enforcement and legal professionals could benefit by learning the details of a crime recovered through hypnosis—or so many assumed.

As you have read, hypnosis puts the subject into a highly suggestible state. This condition leaves the individual vulnerable to prompts and suggestions by the hypnotist. A cooperative person could certainly comply with suggestions and create a story that, in the end, is entirely false. This has happened time and again. In reality, hypnosis does not improve memory (Kihlstrom, 1997; Loftus & Davis, 2006). Today, responsible psychologists do not use hypnotherapy to uncover or reconstruct lost memories. Also, testimony based on hypnosis sessions alone cannot be submitted as evidence in most US courts. Test your understanding of what hypnosis can and cannot do in Table 5.5.

Table 5.5 What Can Potentially be Done with Hypnosis?

Answer the following statements with true or false.

Hypnosis can:
1. temporarily increase physical strength
2. help someone quit smoking
3. alter perceptual experiences
4. improve memory for details of a crime scene
5. be used to recover traumatic memory
6. help someone relax
7. reduce pain sensations

Answers: 1. False 2. True 3. True 4. False 5. False 6. True 7. True

Working the Scientific Literacy Model

Meditation

Meditation is practiced in many forms by members of almost every known culture. You may be familiar with some: sitting meditation (or *zazen* in Zen Buddhism), breathing meditation (or *qi-gong* in Taoism), transcendental meditation (as practiced in Hinduism), and mindfulness (as practiced in Buddhism). Although these practices may seem beyond the realm of scientific study, researchers have found ways to study and understand them.

What do we know about meditation?

Meditation *is any procedure that involves a shift in consciousness to a state in which an individual is highly focused, aware, and in control of mental processes.* Although meditation includes some centuries-old practices, scientific interest in it is only a few decades old. Modern researchers have cautioned that we do not know exactly what meditation can accomplish (Sedlmeier et al., 2012), but thus far there is much promise in its results (Ricard, Lutz, & Davidson, 2014). Several approaches to meditation have emerged, including *Mindfulness-Based Stress Reduction (MBSR)*, which was developed to teach and promote mindfulness as a way of improving well-being and reducing negative experiences. Mindfulness-based interventions are generally well received by patients and can significantly reduce everyday levels of stress, depression, and anxiety, as well as more chronic psychiatric disorders such as severe social anxiety (Chiesa & Serretti, 2010; Olivo et al., 2009).

How can science explain the effects of meditation?

In one study, people who suffered severe social anxiety volunteered to undergo MBSR training (Goldin & Gross, 2010). Prior to the training, the participants' symptoms of social anxiety were assessed. They were also given brain scans while being fed statements such as "I am ashamed of my shyness," "People always judge me," to monitor how the brain's emotional-processing regions responded to such statements. After this initial assessment, the participants attended eight weekly MBSR training sessions, along with a half-day meditation retreat that involved focused breathing exercises, bodily awareness, relaxation, and other methods for sustaining a meditative state.

Following the meditation training, the participants improved in their overall well-being, including showing reduced anxiety and depression, and increased self-esteem (Figure 5.8). Also, the participants received a second brain scan in which their reactions to negative statements about themselves were monitored. The emotional centers of the brain that were previously activated by these statements were less responsive at this follow-up test (Goldin & Gross, 2010). MBSR has even been shown to be more beneficial than aerobic exercise (which is still strongly encouraged) in reducing anxiety (Goldin et al., 2012).

Figure 5.8 Meditation Reduces Negative Emotions

On the left side of the graph, notice that ratings of negative emotions decreased from before MBSR (blue bar) to after (red bar). In contrast, no real difference was apparent when volunteers simply distracted themselves from negative feelings, as shown by the blue and red bars on the right.

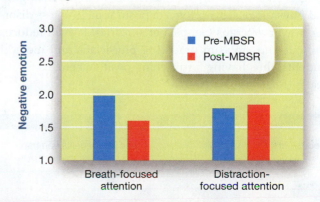

Can we critically evaluate this information?

As these results suggest, a growing body of research supports the use of meditation as a clinical intervention. Before this practice is adopted more widely for use in treating social anxiety, however, it would be important to address several issues. First, although participants in the study were tested for social anxiety before and after MBSR, there was no control group, which is essential for fully evaluating any form of therapy. Much of the work on meditation includes what is called a "wait-list control group," which is a group that initially does not receive the treatment under evaluation until after the research is completed. This is a normal procedure for ensuring ideal research methodology, as well as for fulfilling an ethical obligation to research participants who are initially randomly assigned to a group that does not receive a treatment. Also, the studies indicate that meditation can make improvements across a wide assortment of variables, but this does not mean that meditation is a cure. Instead, meditation should be seen as just one component of a treatment program that may also include medications, psychotherapy, or other interventions, depending on the specific problem.

Why is this relevant?

Stress, anxiety, and depression may seem like a wide range of symptoms to be treated by one type of intervention, but they actually share a similar theme. Each of these conditions can be worsened with continual dwelling on the problem, belief that it is unresolvable, and emphasis on its negative effects. This kind of focus can turn even a minor problem into a catastrophe. What meditation can do is to teach us awareness of the problem and to accept it in a nonjudgmental manner, which are important cognitive factors in reducing symptoms (Perlman et al., 2010). It is also extremely cost-effective (free).

In addition to reducing stress, anxiety, and depression, mindfulness meditation has a strong record of reducing pain, in both short-term experiments (e.g., Zeidan et al., 2010) and in long-term studies with patients who suffer with chronic pain (Grant & Rainville, 2009; Grant, 2014). It has been successfully used to reduce both psychological and physiological symptoms of posttraumatic stress disorder in war veterans (Seppälä et al., 2014). It even reduces burnout and stress in practicing physicians and medical students, thus having far-reaching positive benefits to our health (Regehr et al., 2014).

JOURNAL PROMPT

Meditation: Do you meditate? If so describe any benefits you have experienced from doing so. If not, would you consider starting? Why or why not?

DÉJÀ VU At the beginning of this module, we introduced the mysterious conscious experience known as **déjà vu**, *which is a distinct feeling of having seen or experienced a situation that is impossible or unlikely to have previously occurred.* You may have experienced it yourself; studies indicate that most people have had at least one episode (Brown, 2003). It generally begins with an individual entering a new situation or having a subtle shift of attention, and then the feeling of *I've been here before*, of experiencing the exact same event, sets in.

One neurological explanation for déjà vu comes from studies of temporal lobe epilepsy. Some individuals with temporal lobe epilepsy experience déjà vu regularly, right at the onset of a seizure (Guedj et al., 2010; O'Connor & Moulin, 2008). Could it be that structures within the temporal lobes are responsible for the intense experience of familiarity? This seems likely. The temporal lobes include a structure known as the hippocampus. As you will read in Module 7.1, this structure and the surrounding regions—the parahippocampal area—are important for memory. Brain scans show that individuals prone to temporal lobe epilepsy-induced déjà vu have decreased activity in the parahippocampal regions (Guedj et al., 2010).

Another neurological explanation for déjà vu derives from the fact that the brain contains multiple perceptual pathways. As explained in Module 4.2, the visual system transmits information from the eyes to the left and right hemispheres of the brain. The brain then processes information about what objects are and where they are located in separate pathways. It is possible that déjà vu arises when visual information in one of these pathways is processed a split second earlier than in the other pathway (Brown, 2003). This explanation is very difficult to test, however, and it is certainly contradicted by the finding that people who are blind can also experience déjà vu (O'Connor & Moulin, 2006).

Researchers have also examined déjà vu at the cognitive level, focusing on the memory experiences of familiarity and recognition (O'Connor & Moulin, 2010). Consider the experience of walking through a grocery store and encountering an acquaintance. Even if you have never seen her in a store before, you can still experience the familiarity of her face as well as something about the context from which you know her. Perhaps déjà vu arises in a situation characterized by both a strong sense of familiarity and an equally strong sense of a previous encounter (Cleary, 2008). Some interesting correlations to support this interpretation exist. For example, people who travel frequently are more prone to the déjà vu experience, as are people who report more dreams (Brown, 2003). These individuals have access to many scenes and situations in memory, which increases the likelihood that they will find something familiar. At the same time, they often have good reason to suspect that they have never experienced something before because they are in an entirely new location.

Disorders of Consciousness

It is difficult, if not impossible, to imagine a life without consciousness. However, someone who has dealt with a patient on life support, and certainly the rare individuals who recover from extended periods of lost consciousness, can provide vivid accounts of what it is like.

We should distinguish among three disorders of consciousness identified by medical personnel: coma, persistent vegetative state, and minimally conscious state. A **coma** *is a state marked by a complete loss of consciousness.* Coma may be temporarily medically induced and controlled with anesthetic drugs, but here we are considering what can happen after a serious brain injury or trauma. A patient who is in coma resides in a state that, at least on the surface, looks like sleep—the eyes are closed and the body remains still (except for some reflexes). However, a coma differs from sleep in that some brain stem reflexes are suppressed (e.g., the pupils no longer dilate and contract with changes in brightness).

If a patient in a coma improves slightly, the individual may enter a **persistent vegetative state (PVS)**, *which is a state of minimal to no consciousness in which the eyes may be open, and the individual will develop sleep–wake cycles without clear signs of consciousness.* For example, patients who are in a PVS do not appear to focus on objects in their visual field, nor do they track movement. There is hope for recovery if the patient improves within the first few months of PVS, but the chances for recovery decrease sharply between 6 and 12 months (Wijdicks, 2006).

The least severe of these disorders is the **minimally conscious state (MCS**), *which is a disordered state of consciousness marked by the ability to show some behaviors that suggest at least partial consciousness, even if on an inconsistent basis* (Giacino et al., 2002; Hirschberg & Giacino, 2011). These behaviors must last long enough or be produced with some consistency to be distinguishable from basic reflexes, which are thought to be possible even without awareness. For example, MCS may be diagnosed if a patient can follow simple instructions, intentionally reach for or grasp objects, provide yes/no answers either verbally or through gestures (regardless of whether they are correct), produce any intelligible speech, or at least perform nonreflexive, voluntary movement of the eyes in response to command (Estraneo et al., 2014).

At what point should or could an unconscious individual be removed from life support? Medical professionals frame their ethical decision-making process by keeping these disorders of consciousness in mind. For many, the primary challenge is determining whether the patient is conscious or has a chance of regaining consciousness. One approach is to consider the prognosis for individuals in a PVS. If they do not recover within 12 months, it is unlikely that they will ever recover. Critics disagree with this contention, arguing that there are some signs of consciousness, even in a PVS. For example, some people in a PVS have shown rudimentary responses to language. There have been cases of neurological changes in response to one's name (Staffen et al., 2006) as well as the emotional tone of a speaker's voice (Kotchouby et al., 2009). Still other individuals have responded to verbal instructions to imagine themselves completing activities such as playing tennis; their functional magnetic resonance imaging (fMRI) scans revealed neural activity similar to that of non-PVS controls (Owen & Coleman, 2008; Owen et al., 2006; Vogel et al., 2013). These patients cannot respond with gesture or speech, so they are classified as being in a PVS rather than a MCS. Clearly, their brain activity is responding in some hopeful ways, but is it a sign of consciousness? The answer remains elusive because another person's consciousness can only be inferred; it cannot be directly measured.

Module **5.2** Summary

5.2a Know . . . the key terminology associated with hypnosis, meditation, déjà vu, and disorders of consciousness:

coma
déjà vu
dissociation theory (of hypnosis)
hypnosis
meditation
minimally conscious state (MCS)
persistent vegetative state (PVS)
social-cognitive theory (of hypnosis)

5.2b Understand . . . the competing theories of hypnosis.

Dissociation theory states that hypnosis involves a division between observer and hidden observer, whereas social-cognitive theory states that beliefs and expectations about hypnosis heighten the subject's willingness to follow suggestions.

5.2c Apply . . . your knowledge of hypnosis to identify what it can and cannot do.

If you completed the "What can be done with hypnosis?" activity in Table 5.5 on page 159, you hopefully now have a good sense of what can and cannot be accomplished with

162 Chapter 5

it. Of course, there must be a willing participant who *can* be hypnotized (not all people can be). From there, a good hypnotist can use the technique for therapeutic benefit in some areas. In popular culture, the benefits of hypnosis are often exaggerated.

5.2d Analyze . . . claims that hypnosis can help with memory recovery.

Scientific evidence suggests that hypnosis is not a valid technique for recovering buried memories, but is effective at opening up the subject to suggestion from the hypnotist or therapist. The heightened state of suggestion may result in the construction of memories for events that have not occurred.

5.2e Analyze . . . the effectiveness of meditation for use in therapy.

People who meditate often find that this practice helps reduce symptoms of depression, stress, and anxiety and provides pain relief. For serious conditions, meditation typically needs to be accompanied by additional therapies or treatments to provide relief.

Module 5.2 Quiz

Know . . .

1. _____ suggestions specify that certain actions cannot be performed while hypnotized.
    A. Ideomotor
    B. Challenge
    C. Cognitive-perceptual
    D. Dissociation

Understand . . .

2. Dr. Morales claims that hypnosis is a distinct state of consciousness in which there is a "hidden" observer. It appears that she is endorsing the _____ theory of hypnosis.
    A. social-cognitive
    B. psychoanalytic
    C. dissociation
    D. hypnotherapy

Apply . . .

3. Hypnosis has been shown to be moderately successful as a therapy for alleviating symptoms and problems in all of the following except:
    A. addiction.
    B. pain therapy.
    C. autism.
    D. depression and anxiety.

Analyze . . .

4. Which of the following statements best describes the scientific consensus about recovering memories with hypnosis?
    A. Memories "recovered" through hypnosis are highly unreliable and should never be used as evidence in court.
    B. If the memory is recovered by a trained psychologist, then it may be used as evidence in court.
    C. Recovering memories through hypnosis is a simple procedure, and so the findings should be a regular part of court hearings.
    D. Memories can be recovered only in individuals who are highly hypnotizable.

5. What is known about the effects of meditation on pain perception?
    A. Beliefs about meditation are mostly superstition.
    B. Some forms of meditation such as mindfulness-based stress reduction are effective in controlling chronic pain.
    C. All forms of meditation have proven effective at reducing pain.
    D. Meditation is not an effective method for controlling pain.

Module **5.3** Drugs and Conscious Experience

 ## Learning Objectives

5.3a Know . . . the key terminology related to different categories of drugs and their effects on the nervous system and behavior.

5.3b Understand . . . drug tolerance and dependence.

5.3c Apply . . . your knowledge about drugs to identify their physical and psychological effects.

5.3d Analyze . . . conclusions drawn from studies on the effects of long-term drug abuse.

Could taking a drug-induced trip be a way to cope with traumatic stress or a life-threatening illness? A variety of medications for reducing anxiety or alleviating depression are readily available. However, a few doctors and psychologists have suggested that perhaps a 6-hour trip on psychedelic "magic" mushrooms (called **psilocybin***) could be helpful to people dealing with difficult psychological challenges.*

In the 1960s, a fringe group of psychologists insisted that psychedelic drugs were the answer to all the world's problems. The outcast nature of this group and the ensuing "war on drugs" prompted mainstream psychologists to shelve any ideas that a psychedelic drug or something similar could be used in a therapeutic setting. This perception appears to be changing, however. Roland Griffiths from Johns Hopkins University has been conducting studies on the possible therapeutic benefits

of psilocybin mushrooms. Patients with cancer who were experiencing depression volunteered to take psilocybin as a part of Griffiths's study. Both at the end of their experience and 14 months later, they reported having personally meaningful, spiritually significant experiences that improved their overall outlook on life (Griffiths et al., 2008). This study would best be described as preliminary because additional studies involving controls and follow-up evaluations are needed. It is likely that such investigations will be forthcoming, as Griffiths is one of several researchers who are now exploring the possibility that psilocybin and similar drugs could be used in therapy.

Every human culture uses drugs. It could even be argued that every human uses drugs, depending on your definition of the term. Many of the foods that we eat contain the same types of compounds found in mind-altering drugs. For example, nutmeg contains compounds similar to those found in some psychedelic substances, and chocolate contains small amounts of the same compounds found in amphetamines and marijuana (Wenk, 2010). Of course, caffeine and alcohol—both of which are mainstream parts of our culture—are also drugs. The difference between a drug and a nondrug compound seems to be that drugs are taken because the user has an intended effect in mind. **Psychoactive drugs** *are substances that affect thinking, behavior, perception, and emotion.* From a scientific viewpoint, psychoactive drugs are categorized based on their effects on the nervous system. Drugs can speed up the nervous system, slow it down, stimulate its pleasure centers, or distort how it processes the world.

Commonly Abused Illicit Drugs

Illicit drugs refer to those drugs whose manufacture, sale, and possession are illegal. As you will see, the boundary between illicit recreational drugs and legal prescription drugs can be razor-thin at times. Many common prescription medications are chemically similar, albeit safer, versions of illicit drugs. It often comes as a surprise to learn that the very substances that people can become addicted to, or whose possession and use can even land them in prison today, were once ingredients in everyday products.

STIMULANTS **Stimulants** *are a category of drugs that speed up the nervous system, typically enhancing wakefulness and alertness.* Cocaine, one of the most commonly abused stimulants, is synthesized from coca leaves, most often grown in South American countries such as Peru and Colombia. Some people who harvest these plants take the drug in its simplest form; they chew on the leaves and experience a mild increase in energy. However, illicit cocaine appears in other forms as well. It is typically snorted and absorbed into the bloodstream through the nasal passages, or if prepared as crack cocaine, is smoked from a pipe.

Amphetamines, another group of stimulants, come in a variety of forms. Some are prescription drugs, such as methylphenidate (Ritalin) and modafinil (Provigil), which are typically prescribed for attention-deficit/hyperactivity

Cocaine was once used as an inexpensive, over-the-counter pain remedy. A concoction of wine and cocaine was popular, and the drug was also added to cough syrups and drops for treating toothaches.

disorder (ADHD) and narcolepsy, respectively. Other abused stimulants, mostly methamphetamine, are not prescribed drugs. Methamphetamine may be even more potent than cocaine when it comes to addictive potential and is notorious for causing significant neurological as well as external physical problems. First, methamphetamine addiction can lead to neglect of basic dietary and hygienic care. Second, the drug is often manufactured from a potent cocktail of substances including hydrochloric acid and farm fertilizer; it is probably not surprising that these components can have serious side effects on appearance and health.

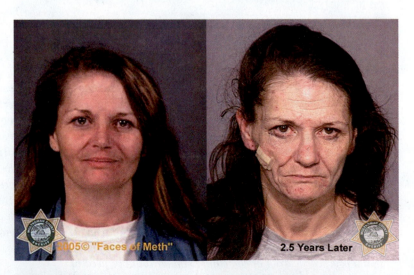

Theresa Baxter was 42 when the picture on the left was taken. The photo on the right was taken 2½ years later; the effects of methamphetamine are obvious and striking.

Figure 5.9 Stimulant Effects on the Brain

(a) Like many addictive drugs, cocaine and amphetamine stimulate the reward centers of the brain, including the nucleus accumbens and ventral tegmental area. (b) Cocaine works by blocking reuptake of dopamine, and methamphetamine works by increasing the release of dopamine at presynaptic neurons.

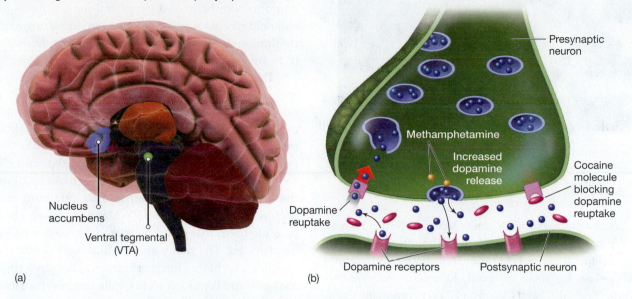

(a)

(b)

Stimulants such as cocaine and methamphetamine affect neural activity in the reward centers of the brain (Figure 5.9a). Cocaine, for example, blocks reuptake of dopamine by binding to presynaptic terminals. By blocking reuptake of dopamine, cocaine allows excess amounts of this neurotransmitter to remain in the synapse and continue binding with postsynaptic receptors (Figure 5.9b). Methamphetamine increases presynaptic release of dopamine and norepinephrine and also slows their reuptake. Watch this brief video, Stimulant Effects on the Brain, to see how stimulants affect the process of neurotransmitter reuptake.

Watch STIMULANT EFFECTS ON THE BRAIN

The drug **ecstasy (MDMA)** *(or "Molly") is typically classified as a stimulant but also has hallucinogenic effects.* It was developed in the early 1900s as a compound to use for developing various prescription drugs. Many decades later, in the 1980s, it was labeled a "club drug" because of its frequent appearance at rave parties. Ecstasy heightens physical sensations and is known to increase social bonding and compassion among those who are under its influence. These are actually the same effects that have made it a candidate for prescription use to treat mood and anxiety disorders and in relationship counseling. Whether this becomes the norm will depend on many factors, including answers to ongoing questions about negative side effects (Parrott, 2014). Heat stroke and dehydration are major immediate risks associated with ecstasy abuse, especially when the drug is taken in a place where there is a high level of physical exertion from dancing in an overheated environment.

HALLUCINOGENS **Hallucinogenic drugs** *are substances that produce perceptual distortions.* Depending on the type of hallucinogen consumed, these distortions may be visual, auditory, and sometimes tactile in nature, such as the experience of crawling sensations against the skin. Hallucinogens also alter how people perceive their own thinking. For example, deep significance may be attached to what are normally mundane objects, events, or thoughts. Commonly used hallucinogens include lysergic acid diethylamide (LSD), which is a laboratory-made (synthetic) drug. Hallucinogenic substances also occur in nature, such as psilocybin (a mushroom) and mescaline (derived from the peyote cactus). Hallucinogens can have long-lasting effects, more than 12 hours for LSD, for example. These drugs may also elicit powerful emotional experiences that range from extreme euphoria to fear, panic, and paranoia. The two most common hallucinogens, LSD and psilocybin, both act on the transmission of serotonin.

Salvia divinorum is a type of sage plant that grows naturally in Central and South America. Users of the herb combine juices from the leaves with tea for drinking, or the leaves are chewed or smoked.

Short-acting hallucinogens have become increasingly popular for recreational use. The effects of two of these hallucinogens—ketamine and dimethyltryptamine (DMT)—last for about an hour. Ketamine (street names include "Special K" and "Vitamin K") was originally developed as a surgical anesthetic to be used in cases in which a gaseous anesthetic could not be applied, such as on the battlefield. Ketamine induces dreamlike states, memory loss, dizziness, confusion, and a distorted sense of body ownership (Morgan et al., 2010). This synthetic drug blocks receptors for glutamate, which is an excitatory neurotransmitter that is important for, among other things, memory.

DMT is a short-acting hallucinogen that occurs naturally in such different places as the bark from trees native to Central and South America and on the skin surface of certain toads. DMT is even found in small, naturally produced amounts in the human nervous system (Fontanilla et al., 2009). The function of DMT in the brain remains unclear, although some researchers have speculated that it plays a role in sleep and dreaming, and even out-of-body experiences (Barbanoj et al., 2008; Strassman, 2001).

Another hallucinogen, *Salvia divinorum*, grows in Central and South America and when smoked or chewed induces a highly intense but short-lived effect. Intake of salvia leads to dissociative experiences—a detachment between self and body (Sumnall et al., 2010). Salvia is used by the Mazatec people of Mexico during spiritual rituals. The use of salvia for different reasons is on the rise among North Americans and Europeans, particularly among younger people (Nyi et al., 2010).

MARIJUANA Marijuana *is a drug comprising the leaves and buds of the Cannabis plant that produces a combination of hallucinogenic, stimulant, and relaxing (narcotic) effects.* It is among the most commonly used drugs in the United States.

The buds of *Cannabis* plants contain a high concentration of a compound called tetrahydrocannabinol (THC).

THC binds to cannabinoid receptors, which are distributed across various regions of the brain. Researchers had long puzzled over which natural brain chemical is mimicked by THC. It turns out that anandamide, a neurotransmitter found in both brain and peripheral nerves, binds to cannabinoid receptors and is involved in regulating circadian rhythms and sleep, memory, and possibly other functions (Edwards et al., 2010; Vaughn et al., 2010).

The drug induces feelings of euphoria, relaxation, and heightened and sometimes distorted sensory experiences. One immediate effect of marijuana is memory impairment, likely because the drug disrupts neurotransmitter activity supporting memory formation in the hippocampus (Ranganathan & D'Souza, 2006), and chronic cannabis use is associated with decreased volume of the hippocampus, which can lead to long-term memory problems (Ashtari et al., 2011). Many questions about the possible harm that could be caused by marijuana remain unanswered. The many studies that have addressed the question of whether long-term use has negative effects on the brain and cognition yield conflicting results. However, one consistent result is that heavy marijuana use during adolescence, a critical period of brain development, can have negative effects on brain functioning and some aspects of cognitive activity (Batalla et al., 2013; Crane et al., 2013).

The use of marijuana for medicinal purposes has seen a rapid increase in recent years. Many claims about the medicinal benefits of *Cannabis* have not been adequately tested using proper experimental methodology. As with any drug, results of carefully executed studies that have been conducted on *Cannabis* show mixed benefits. For example, drugs derived from *Cannabis* help reduce some neurological problems such as pain and muscle spasms, but evidence is inconclusive regarding movement disorders such as Parkinson's or Huntington's disease and Tourette's syndrome (Koppel et al., 2014; Ware et al., 2010). *Cannabis* can benefit patients undergoing chemotherapy by preventing nausea caused by the procedure, and because the drug stimulates hunger responses to help reduce weight loss in patients with acquired immune deficiency syndrome (Borgelt et al., 2013). Time and effort will determine the extent of the medicinal benefits of *Cannabis*, which, like any other drug, will require evaluating any problematic side effects.

OPIATES Opiates *(also called narcotics) are drugs such as heroin and morphine that reduce pain and induce extremely intense feelings of euphoria.* These drugs bind to endorphin receptors in the nervous system. Endorphins ("endogenous morphine") are neurotransmitters that reduce pain and produce pleasurable sensations—effects magnified by opiates. Naturally occurring opiates are derived from certain species of poppy plants that are primarily grown in

Asia and the Middle East. Opiate drugs are common in medical and emergency department settings. For example, the drug fentanyl is used in emergency departments to treat people in extreme pain. A street version of fentanyl, known as "China White," can be more than 20 times the strength of more commonly sold doses of heroin.

Treating opiate addiction can be incredibly challenging. People who are addicted to opiates and other highly addictive drugs enter a negative cycle of having to use these drugs simply to ward off withdrawal effects, rather than to actually achieve the sense of euphoria they may have experienced when they started using. Methadone is an opioid (a synthetic opiate) that binds to opiate receptors but does not give the same kind of high that heroin does. A regimen of daily methadone treatment can help people who are addicted to opiates avoid painful withdrawals as they learn to cope without the drug. In recent years, newer alternatives to methadone have been found to be more effective and need to be taken only a few times per week.

Another opioid, oxycodone (OxyContin), has helped many people escape and avoid severe pain with few problems. Unfortunately, this drug has high abuse potential. It is often misused, especially by those who have obtained it through illegal means (i.e., without a prescription).

Legal Drugs and Their Effects on Consciousness

So far we have covered drugs that are, for the most part, produced and distributed illegally. Some prescription drugs can also have profound effects on consciousness and, as a consequence, are targets for misuse.

SEDATIVES **Sedative drugs**, *sometimes referred to as "downers," depress activity of the central nervous system.* Barbiturates were an early form of medication used to treat anxiety and promote sleep. High doses of these drugs can shut down the brain stem regions that regulate breathing, so their medical use has largely been discontinued in favor of safer drugs. Barbiturates have a high potential for abuse, typically by people who want to lower inhibitions, relax, and try to improve their sleep. (Incidentally, these agents do not really improve sleep. Barbiturates actually reduce the amount of REM sleep.)

Newer forms of sedative drugs, called *benzodiazepines,* include prescription drugs such as Xanax, Ativan, and Valium. These drugs increase the effects of the inhibitory neurotransmitter GABA in brain regions associated with emotion and arousal. The major advantage of benzodiazepine drugs over barbiturates is that they do not specifically target the brain regions responsible for breathing and, even at high doses, are unlikely to be fatal. However, people under the influence of any kind of sedative are

at greater risk for injury or death as a result of accidents caused by their diminished attention, reaction time, and motor control.

PRESCRIPTION DRUG ABUSE Prescription drugs are now second only to marijuana as the substances most commonly abused by illicit users (Substance Abuse and Mental Health Services Administration [SAMHSA], 2013). A massive number of prescription drugs are available on the market, including stimulants, opiates, and sedatives. In 2009, 7 million Americans reported having used prescription drugs for nonmedical reasons within the month before the survey. This number is actually higher than the number of users of cocaine, heroin, hallucinogens, and inhalants (e.g., paints, glues, gasoline) combined (Volkow, 2010). Users typically opt for prescription drugs because they are legal (when used as prescribed), pure (i.e., not contaminated or diluted), and relatively easy to get. Prescription drugs are typically taken at large doses, and administered in such a way to get a quicker, more intense effect, for example, by crushing and snorting stimulants such as Ritalin or injecting liquefied oxycodone (see Figure 5.10).

ALCOHOL Alcohol is by far the most commonly used drug. It can be found in nearly every culture, although some frown on its use more than others. Alcohol use is a part of cherished social and spiritual rituals, but it is also associated with violence and accidents. It has the power to change societies, in some cases for the worse. For example, several decades ago, "problem drinking" was not an issue for the Carib people of Venezuela. During specific yearly festivals, alcohol was brewed and consumed in limited amounts. Otherwise it was not a part of daily life. In more recent years, the influence of Western civilization has led to the emergence of problems with alcohol abuse and alcoholism in this group of people. It is estimated that 87%

Figure 5.10 Ritalin and Cocaine

Stimulants like methylphenidate (Ritalin) affect the same areas of the brain as cocaine, albeit with different speed and intensity. The red-colored areas of these PET scans indicate areas of increased activation in response to each drug.

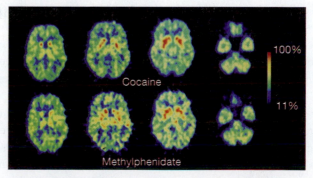

of Carib males are problem drinkers (e.g., engage in excessive binge-drinking, having blackouts; Seale et al., 2002). Most societies regard alcohol as an acceptable form of drug use, though they may attempt to limit and regulate its use through legal means. Customs and social expectations also affect usage. For example, drinking—especially heavy drinking—is considered more socially acceptable for men than for women.

Alcohol initially targets GABA receptors in the brain and subsequently affects opiate and dopamine receptors. Stimulation of opiate and dopamine receptors accounts for the euphoria associated with lower doses as well its rewarding effects. Alcohol facilitates the activity of GABA. The net effect is to depress the central nervous system, which helps explain the impairments in balance and coordination associated with consumption of alcohol. But if alcohol increases the release of an inhibitory brain chemical, why do people become less inhibited when they drink? One function of the frontal lobe of the cortex is to inhibit behavior and impulses, and alcohol appears to impair the frontal lobe's ability to serve in its regular capacity—in other words, it inhibits an inhibitor.

The lowered inhibitions associated with alcohol may help people muster the courage to perform a toast at a wedding, but many socially unacceptable consequences are also associated with alcohol use. Alcohol abuse has been linked to health problems, sexual and physical assault, automobile accidents, missing work or school, unplanned pregnancies, and contracting sexually transmitted diseases. These effects are primarily associated with heavy consumption. Underage drinkers are at higher risk for binge-drinking, typically defined as consuming five drinks at a setting for males and four drinks for females.

Researchers have determined that college students drink significantly more than their peers who do not attend college (Carter et al., 2010). In one study, nearly half of the college student participants binge-drank, one-third drove under the influence, 10% to 12% sustained an injury or were assaulted while intoxicated, and 2% were victims of date rape while drinking (Hingson et al., 2009). Alcohol abuse in our society is widespread, especially during times of celebration (Glindemann et al., 2007), so it might seem as if colleges have few options at their disposal to reduce reckless drinking on campus. Psychologists Kent Glindemann, Scott Geller, and their associates, however, have conducted some interesting field studies in fraternity houses at their university. For example, in two separate studies, these researchers measured the typical blood alcohol level at fraternity parties. They then offered monetary awards or entry into a raffle for fraternities that could keep their average blood alcohol level below 0.05 at their next party (0.08 is the legally defined level of intoxication). The interventions proved to be successful in both studies, with blood alcohol levels being significantly reduced from baseline levels (Fournier et al., 2004; Glindemann et al., 2007).

Reducing Binge-Drinking: How effective do you think monetary incentives would be in curbing binge-drinking in college students that you know or know of? What is another strategy that might curb excessive drinking?

Habitual Drug Use

Now that we know how drugs are classified based on their short-term effects, we can turn to the long-term effects of drug use. Society frowns on drug abuse, and to a great extent this attitude derives from the belief that drugs can have negative long-term consequences. As you will see, some evidence supports these beliefs.

SUBSTANCE ABUSE, TOLERANCE, AND DEPENDENCE Abuse, tolerance, and dependence are interacting facets of substance use. Substance abuse occurs when an individual experiences social, physical, legal, or other problems associated with drug use. **Tolerance** *occurs when repeated use of a drug results in a need for a higher dose to get the intended effect.* People build up a tolerance to most drugs, including alcohol. Coffee drinkers, for example, are well aware of the phenomenon of tolerance: First-time drinkers may become completely wired and unable to sleep the subsequent night, whereas veteran coffee drinkers can drink a cup of coffee and fall asleep immediately.

Dependence *refers to the need to take a drug to ward off unpleasant physical withdrawal symptoms; it is often referred to as addiction.* Caffeine withdrawal can involve head and muscle aches and impaired concentration. Although a hangover after a night of binge-drinking can certainly make a person miserable, withdrawal from long-term alcohol abuse is much more serious. A person who is dependent on alcohol can experience extremely severe, even life-threatening withdrawal symptoms, including nausea, increased heart rate and blood pressure, and hallucinations and delirium.

A growing body of evidence reveals a genetic component to some addictions, such as alcoholism (Foroud et al., 2010). Current research is aimed at understanding which genes may be responsible and how their actions render people susceptible to alcoholism. Such research suggests that genes are probably not fully responsible, however, because the alcoholism rate is low among groups that prohibit drinking (e.g., for religious reasons; Chentsova-Dutton & Tsai, 2007; Haber & Jacob, 2007). In addressing this issue from a psychological perspective, researchers have determined that factors such as early experience with alcohol and impulsive personality traits are linked to increased likelihood of substance abuse and addiction (Zernicke et al., 2010).

Psychological and Physical Effects of Drugs

The short-term effects of drugs obviously involve changes in cognition and behavior. The effects on emotions and perception are a large part of what motivates substance abuse in the first place. However, many of the substances we have covered so far are illegal, or at least their use is highly controlled because a significant portion of society is worried about the long-term effects of these substances.

What do we know about the psychological and physical effects of drugs?

Depending on the drug, the day or days after its use may involve lingering effects, depression, or further cravings. But what about chronic, long-term use of substances such as marijuana, cocaine, or prescription drugs? How does habitual drug use affect the brain and body? Researchers conducting animal and human studies are tracking the long-term effects of drug use to answer these questions.

How can science explain the long-term effects of drug use?

Research seeking to answer this question often combines tests of cognitive ability, such as memory and reasoning, with one of many different forms of brain imaging. This dual approach allows researchers to determine what, if any, long-term mental impairments are associated with drug use, and which part(s) of the brain may be impaired. As a result of this work, we now know that long-term exposure to methamphetamine and ecstasy can cause significant damage to nerve cells that transmit dopamine, norepinephrine, and serotonin (Yamamoto et al., 2010). These brain chemicals are important for regulating cognition, emotion, learning, sleep, and many other functions.

To test whether amphetamine abuse alters brain function, researchers have compared people with long histories of methamphetamine addiction and abuse with healthy control participants. Compared to the healthy participants, people with a history of abusing methamphetamine have structural abnormalities within the frontal lobes, which reduced the brain's ability to inhibit both impulsive behavior and irrelevant thoughts (Kohno et al., 2014; Tobias et al., 2010). The ability to inhibit cognitive processes can be measured through the Stroop task (Figure 5.11), which challenges a person's ability to

Figure 5.11 The Stroop Task

The Stroop task requires subjects to read aloud the color of the letters of these sample words. The task measures one's ability to inhibit a natural tendency to read the word, rather than identify the color. Chronic methamphetamine users have greater difficulty with this task than do non-users.

BLUE	GREEN	YELLOW
PINK	RED	ORANGE
GREY	BLACK	PURPLE
TAN	WHITE	BROWN

avoid reading a word in favor of identifying its color. Methamphetamine abusers had greater difficulty with this task than non-users, and they also had reduced activity in the frontal lobes, likely because of the damage described previously (Salo et al., 2010).

Can we critically evaluate this information?

"Methamphetamine Kills Brain Cells" might make for a compelling headline, and it certainly may be true. Even so, there are often multiple possible causes of brain damage in drug abusers. Notably, people who abuse drugs such as methamphetamine and ecstasy rarely just use one drug. Most users also abuse other drugs such as marijuana, alcohol, and possibly other stimulants. Thus, it may be these other drugs, or something about their combination, that accounts for any observed cognitive impairments and brain damage (Gouzoulis-Mayfrank & Daumann, 2006). Also, damaged nerve cells and other neurological problems are not necessarily the consequences of drug use. The relationship may go the other way around; people with certain types of neurological problems may be more likely to abuse drugs. Nevertheless, controlled animal studies indicate that the brain damage found in human drug users is likely caused by the toxicity of the drugs (Yamamoto et al., 2010).

In addition, the physical and emotional problems associated with addiction to drugs such as methamphetamine can be reversed, provided the individual is fortunate enough to survive the period of abuse and remains completely abstinent from any further use. When this is the case, recovering methamphetamine addicts show significant, positive increases in neurological and emotional functioning. In fact, they can recover to levels comparable to healthy people with no history of drug abuse (Iudicello et al., 2010).

Table 5.6 The Major Categories of Drugs and Their Effects on Behavior and Brain Chemistry

Drugs	Psychological Effects	Chemical Effects	Tolerance	Likelihood of Dependence
Stimulants: cocaine, amphetamine, ecstasy	Euphoria, increased energy, lowered inhibitions	Increase dopamine, serotonin, norepinephrine activity	Develops quickly	High
Marijuana	Euphoria, relaxation, distorted sensory experiences, paranoia	Stimulates cannabinoid receptors	Develops slowly	Low
Hallucinogens: LSD, psilocybin, DMT, ketamine	Major distortion of sensory and perceptual experiences. Fear, panic, paranoia	Increase serotonin activity; blocks glutamate receptors	Develops slowly	Very low
Opiates: heroin	Intense euphoria, pain relief	Stimulate endorphin receptors	Develops quickly	Very high
Sedatives: barbiturates, benzodiazepines	Drowsiness, relaxation, sleep	Increase GABA activity	Develops quickly	High
Alcohol	Euphoria, relaxation, lowered inhibitions	Primarily facilitates GABA activity; also stimulates endorphin and dopamine receptors	Develops gradually	Moderate to high

Why is this relevant?

What does a poor performance on the Stroop task tell us about cognitive functioning? This task measures the ability to focus attention and inhibit one way of thinking (to read) in favor of another (to name colors). The ability to focus attention and think flexibly is an important component of decision making and impulse control. Knowledge about the physical damage wrought by drugs helps psychologists and physicians know what to expect from treatment, and it raises awareness about the significant problems caused by drug use. Of course, it can apply to your own situation as well: If you or someone you know regularly abuses drugs, it is important to remember that there are serious risks associated with drug use.

In this module we have explored numerous drugs and their effects. To help organize and summarize this information, Table 5.6 provides a summary of the information we have covered.

Module **5.3** Summary

5.3a **Know . . . the key terminology related to different categories of drugs and their effects on the nervous system and behavior:**

dependence
ecstasy (MDMA)
hallucinogenic drugs
marijuana
opiates
psychoactive drugs
sedative drugs
stimulants
tolerance

5.3b **Understand . . . drug tolerance and dependence.**

Tolerance is a physiological process in which repeated exposure to a drug leads to a need for increasingly larger dosages to experience the intended effect. Dependence occurs when the user takes a drug to avoid withdrawal symptoms.

5.3c **Apply . . . your knowledge about drugs to identify their physical and psychological effects.**

Prescription, legal, and illegal recreational drugs come in many forms and have numerous effects on the nervous system and behavior. Table 5.6 provides an overview that will help summarize and apply your knowledge to predict the effects of drugs of a given category.

5.3d **Analyze . . . conclusions drawn from studies on the effects of long-term drug abuse.**

In this module, we summarized the short-term effects of the major drug categories. The long-term effects will depend on the drug. In this module, we focused on the long-term effects of methamphetamine, which can include damage to nerve cells that transmit norepinephrine, serotonin, and dopamine, as well as loss of white matter. Cognitive deficits, such as those involving monitoring thought processes, also occur. However, because drug users often have a history of abusing multiple drugs, it is difficult to isolate the effects of a single drug. Carefully controlled studies involving animal subjects do indeed confirm that there are long-term negative behavioral and neurological effects of chronic drug exposure.

Module 5.3 Quiz

Know . . .

1. _____ are drugs that increase nervous system activity.
   A. Hallucinogens
   B. Narcotics
   C. Psychoactive drugs
   D. Stimulants

2. Drugs that depress the activity of the central nervous system are known as _____.
   A. stimulants
   B. sedatives
   C. hallucinogens
   D. GABAs

Understand . . .

3. When does drug tolerance occur?
   A. When an individual needs increased amounts of a drug to achieve the desired effect
   B. When individuals do not pass judgment on drug abusers
   C. When an individual experiences withdrawal symptoms
   D. When an individual starts taking a new drug for recreational purposes

Apply . . .

4. Research shows that one effective way to decrease problem drinking on a college campus is to:
   A. hold informative lectures that illustrate the dangers of drinking.
   B. give up—there is little hope for reducing drinking on campus.
   C. provide monetary incentives for student groups to maintain a low average blood alcohol level.
   D. threaten student groups with fines if they are caught drinking.

Analyze . . .

5. What is the most accurate conclusion we can draw from research on the long-term effects of drug use on brain and behavior?
   A. It tends to be harmful, is never reversible, and animal research confirms this.
   B. It tends to be harmful, the effects can be reversed, and animal research confirms this.
   C. It may be harmful but we can never know how exactly because drug users tend to use many different drugs and animal research is rarely done to study drug abuse.
   D. Long-term use is rarely harmful. Behavioral and brain problems are always present before a person even begins using drugs.

Module 5.4   Scientific Literacy Challenge: Cognitive Enhancers

The pressure to perform in school can be intense. Taking several classes at once brings with it constant stress to meet deadlines and perform on one exam after the next. Many college students (and professionals in the workforce) turn to *nootropics*, substances ranging from nutritional supplements to prescription stimulants that are thought to enhance cognitive performance.

Before you start this activity, take a minute to write your thoughts on using drugs to enhance cognitive performance.

JOURNAL PROMPT

Are there any circumstances in which you would take a prescription drug to help you perform better in school? What about herbal or "all-natural" substances? Explain the factors that would make you more or less willing to try cognitive enhancers.

What do we know about cognitive enhancers?

Imagine you have two major exams and a term paper due in a couple of days. Given that you have not even started preparing, plus you still have to go to work, you know that it is going to be a rough stretch. Then, you come across an advertisement for a cognitive enhancement supplement called Nootropia. Notice that the advertisement includes some bold-faced terms that were covered in Chapter 5.

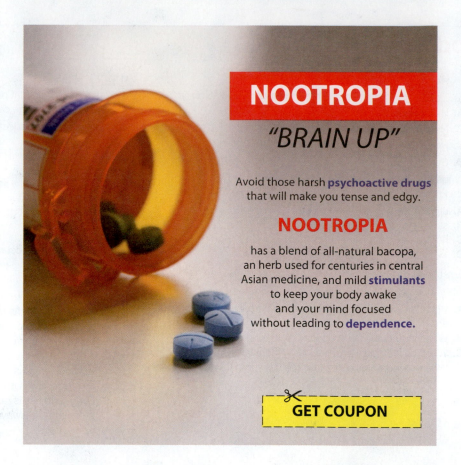

If this supplement really works, you could be on your way to easy As . . . or at least some Bs. But are the ingredients in Nootropia really effective? And if so, is it safe? Let's take a look at how scientists study cognitive enhancers, paying special attention to the highlighted selections, which contain clues to the quiz that follows.

How do scientists study cognitive enhancers?

A web search using the terms *nootropic* or *cognitive enhancer* will turn up a lot of hits for specific cognitive enhancer products and personal commentaries about them. If someone wanted to investigate whether they work and to learn about any risks associated with using cognitive enhancers, such as bacopa, they should seek reputable sources such as a major scientific organization or publication. Because we know that experiments that involve random assignment and control groups are ideal for testing hypotheses, it's wise to include a term such as *randomized placebo-controlled experiment* in a search for *bacopa*. Here is some of the information we found. As you read it, make sure you pay attention to the highlighted phrases, which feature concepts related to scientific research.

One study had participants randomly assigned to a 0-mg dosage (placebo), a 300-mg, or 600-mg daily dosage of bacopa. They completed several tests on a monthly basis, including a sustained attention test that involved pressing a button as quickly as possible when matching figures appeared on a computer screen. There were also tests of memory for words and images. At the end of the first month, the 300-mg group showed improved performance in attention speed, memory speed, and ability to maintain attention. The 600-mg group showed some improvements, but the placebo group showed no changes.

Another study used randomly assigned doses of 0 mg (placebo), 320 mg, and 640 mg in a sample of 24 healthy individuals. Their middle condition (320-mg dosage) was associated with improvement on the Cognitive Demand Battery (CDB), which includes arithmetic and attention span tasks. In addition, they examined cardiovascular activity and self-reports of stress and fatigue but found no differences among conditions.

Although two studies should not be seen as definitive, they do reach similar conclusions. Plus, they appear to share some commonalities. Were you able to identify qualities of good science in these examples? Test yourself with these questions:

1. What are the independent variables in these two studies?
   a. the cognitive tests
   b. whether participants were healthy or had dementia
   c. the dosages of bacopa
   d. whether participants showed changes in performance
2. What procedure used in these studies indicates that they were true experiments?
   a. The dosages were randomly assigned to groups of participants.
   b. The two studies produced somewhat similar results.
   c. One of the conditions in each group seemed to improve.
   d. They both involve dependent variables
3. In experiments like these, one way to address demand characteristics is to include
   a. a placebo condition.   c. more than one cognitive test.
   b. more than one dosage.   d. a large sample of volunteers.

Answers: 1. *c* 2. *a* 3. *a*

Now that we have seen some of the evidence, let's engage in some critical thinking.

How do we think critically about cognitive enhancers?

It turns out that there is some scientific evidence that bacopa, the key ingredient in Nootropia, enhanced cognitive performance. However, anyone considering using it should think critically about the evidence before consuming it.

Check your critical thinking skills by matching the tenets of critical thinking with the six statements related to the research you read.

1. Tolerate ambiguity.
2. Examine the nature and source of the evidence.
3. Avoid overly emotional thinking.
4. Examine assumptions and biases—both yours and those of your information sources.
5. Consider alternative viewpoints.
6. Be curious and ask questions.

a. Bacopa may have some effect, but I wonder if there are any side effects I should worry about?
b. These studies appear to be randomized, controlled experiments published in peer-reviewed journals.
c. I know the company that makes Nootropia has something at stake. I wonder if the researchers are impartial to the outcome of the study? Do they stand to gain financially if the drug works?
d. I desperately need cognitive enhancers just to make it through the week, but that doesn't mean I should just start popping supplements I know very little about.
e. The research shows that this particular supplement *may* improve attention and perhaps memory. On the other hand, there is still a lot we don't know, such as whether this would actually help a student do better on tests.
f. Maybe instead of taking a supplement, I could find a way to study more effectively.

Answers: 1. *e* 2. *b* 3. *d* 4. *c* 5. *f* 6. *a*

This represents a good start on addressing the product Nootropia with critical thinking. Now, read on to see how this evidence might be applied.

How is the research on cognitive enhancers relevant?

Sometimes it is easy to determine if a supplement is worth taking or if it is harmful. Read these suggestions for how Nootropia might be used in real-world applications and then share any newly formed thoughts you may have about cognitive enhancers in the writing activity that follows.

Imagine how beneficial this type of supplement or drug could be in medical treatments. There are a variety of disorders that involve cognitive problems, including degenerative conditions such as Alzheimer's disease. If cognitive enhancers could be used to treat degenerative brain diseases, they could greatly improve the quality of life for millions of people. Although the challenges of being a student are nowhere near those of people living with a serious disorder, nootropics might be appealing to healthy college students hoping to boost cognitive performance.

SHARED WRITING

Before beginning this activity did you agree or disagree that there are circumstances in which you would use cognitive enhancers to help with school work? Share whether your thoughts remained unchanged or were altered as a result of applying scientific and critical thinking about these drugs.

Chapter 5 Quiz

1. REM sleep is sometimes referred to as paradoxical sleep because:
   A. the more sleep deprived a person is, the less REM sleep she experiences.
   B. REM sleep is not really a sleep stage.
   C. electrical activity in the brain completely shuts down during REM sleep.
   D. EEG activity in the brain during REM is similar to EEG activity during an awake state.

2. Which of the following statements supports the "preservation and protection" hypothesis of sleep?
   A. People tend to require more sleep after a hard day of work.
   B. Sleep deprivation can lead to impaired cognitive abilities.
   C. Jet lag is usually worse when traveling east than it is when traveling west.
   D. Many small animals sleep during the day, when they could be easily seen by a predator.

3. Carmella tells her friend that last night she dreamed she was asking her boss for a promotion. If Carmella's friend believes in the activation–synthesis hypothesis of dreaming, which of the following is she likely to say about the dream?
   A. "The latent content of the dream is more important than the manifest content."
   B. "The dream is the result of random activity in the brain and has no deep symbolic meaning."
   C. "The dream indicates that your brain is trying to figure out how to get you promoted."
   D. "The dream is your brain's way of forming new memories."

4. Which of the following is the most common and widely recognized sleep problem:
   A. sleep apnea
   B. insomnia
   C. sleep-state misperception
   D. somnambulism

5. Hypnosis is best thought of as:
   A. a trance.
   B. a state of increased suggestibility.
   C. mind control.
   D. a myth.

6. Which of the following statements is true about the use of hypnosis to recover memories?
   A. It is generally ineffective, but poses no risks and is harmless.
   B. Research has shown hypnosis to be an effective way to recover memories.
   C. Research indicates that hypnosis does not work, and that it can potentially create false memories.
   D. While some debate persists regarding the technique's effectiveness, most US courts accept testimony obtained from a person who is placed under hypnosis.

7. Which of the following definitions accurately describes the state of coma?
- **A.** A prolonged state of consciousness similar to non-REM sleep
- **B.** A state marked by a complete loss of consciousness
- **C.** A disordered state of consciousness marked by the ability to show some behaviors that suggest at least partial consciousness, even if on an inconsistent basis
- **D.** A state of minimal consciousness, where the patient's eyes may be open, and he or she experiences a sleep–wake cycle

8. Opiates create their euphoric effects by stimulating receptors for:
- **A.** GABA.
- **B.** endorphins.
- **C.** anandamide.
- **D.** dopamine.

9. Repeated use of drugs over a period of time can result in a need for a higher dose to get the intended effect. This condition is known as:
- **A.** addiction.
- **B.** dependence.
- **C.** withdrawal.
- **D.** tolerance.

10. Large, periodic bursts of brain activity that occur during stage 2 sleep are known as _____.
- **A.** beta waves
- **B.** sleep spindles
- **C.** delta waves
- **D.** alpha waves

11. Déjà vu is the experience of:
- **A.** having been in a situation that is impossible or unlikely to have previously occurred.
- **B.** forgetting a previous perception.
- **C.** failing to perceive the obvious.
- **D.** being somewhere familiar but not remembering it.

12. What is one neurological explanation offered for déjà vu?
- **A.** Visual information may be processed in two brain regions, albeit slightly faster in one area than in the other.
- **B.** There is a déjà vu center in the brain.
- **C.** Déjà vu occurs when the brain waves recorded from two regions of the brain are similar.
- **D.** Déjà vu occurs only in people who have problems with temporal lobe functioning.

13. Drugs that are best known for their ability to alter normal visual and auditory perceptions are called _____.
- **A.** hallucinogens
- **B.** narcotics
- **C.** psychoactive drugs
- **D.** stimulants

14. A sleep disorder marked by sudden drowsiness and sleepiness is referred to as _____.
- **A.** somnambulism
- **B.** narcolepsy
- **C.** sleep-state misperception
- **D.** insomnia

15. Which of the following states refers to the experience of being completely aware of one's surroundings, focused and in control of mental processes?
- **A.** déjà vu
- **B.** hypnotized
- **C.** intoxicated
- **D.** meditative

Chapter 6
Learning

Module 6.1 Classical Conditioning: Learning by Association

Learning Objectives

6.1a Know . . . the key terminology involved in classical conditioning.

6.1b Understand . . . how responses learned through classical conditioning can be acquired and lost.

6.1c Understand . . . the role of biological and evolutionary factors in classical conditioning.

6.1d Apply . . . the concepts and terms of classical conditioning to new examples.

6.1e Analyze . . . claims that artificially sweetened beverages are a healthier choice.

Are soft drink consumers drinking themselves fat? Certainly, those individuals who drink a lot of sugary beverages are at greater risk of doing so, but what about the people who appear to be making the more prudent choice of a diet soda? How can we go wrong if the nutrition label reads "zero calories"? These artificially sweetened beverages are marketed as products that help people limit their sugar intake and trim down. However, as you will see later in this module, trends toward increased consumption of diet beverages have not corresponded with weight loss—if anything, it has led to the reverse. Psychologists have conducted experiments to figure out why people who drink artificially sweetened beverages may actually gain weight, and the results suggest that the neural and digestive

systems of diet soda drinkers may have "learned" an unhealthy lesson. This may come as a surprise to you, given that people typically think of learning as a deliberate process. In fact, classical conditioning, the topic of this module, often takes place without our even knowing it. How does this take place? And what other types of behaviors can be learned both with and without our knowing it is happening?

Learning *is a process by which behavior or knowledge changes as a result of experience.* It enables us to do many things that we clearly were not born to do, from the simplest tasks, such as flipping a light switch, to the more complex, such as playing a musical instrument.

To many people, the term "learning" signifies the activities that students do, such as reading, listening, and taking tests. This process, which is known as *cognitive learning*, is just one type of learning, however. Another way that we learn is by *associative learning*, which is the focus of this module. You probably associate certain holidays with specific sights, sounds, and smells, or foods with specific flavors and textures. We are not the only species with this capacity—even animals with relatively simple nervous systems, such as earthworms, learn by association. Here we will explore the processes that account for how associations form. Research on associative learning has a long history in psychology, dating back to Ivan Pavlov (1849–1936), a Russian physiologist and winner of the 1904 Nobel Prize for his work on digestion.

Pavlov's Dogs: Classical Conditioning of Salivation

After many years of studying the canine digestive system, Pavlov turned his attention to psychological questions about the complexity of the brain, how it adapts over time, and how nervous system activity gives rise to thought. He approached these issues by studying how automatic, reflexive responses could be affected by experience. For example, it had long been known that dogs (and other animals) salivate when they anticipate food—Pavlov himself had observed this many times (his lab assistants referred to the responses as "psychic secretions"). But could a dog actually *learn* to react this way?

To study how associations are formed, Pavlov developed a laboratory method that he could use again and again. These experiments generally involved presenting a brief sound generated by a device such as a metronome to individual dogs, and then immediately following the sound with the presentation of meat power. After presenting this pairing several times, the metronome (hereafter referred to as "tone") by itself could elicit salivation (see Figure 6.1). Pavlov's experiments began a long tradition of inquiry into what is now called **classical conditioning**—*learning that occurs when a neutral stimulus elicits a response that was originally caused by another stimulus.* In Pavlov's experiments, the neutral stimulus was the tone because it initially did not elicit any sort of response. It wasn't until

Figure 6.1 Associative Learning

Although much information may pass through the dog's brain, in Pavlov's experiments on classical conditioning an association was made between the tone and the food. (Pavlov used a metronome as well as other devices for presenting sounds. In this module, we use the term "tone" to represent the stimulus that was paired with food in his experiments.)

after the tone was presented along with the meat powder that it could elicit salivation.

The key to classical conditioning is the formation of an association between events, and a change in behavior as a result of this association. A *stimulus* is an external event or cue that elicits a response. When a stimulus, such as food, water, pain, or sexual contact, is "unconditioned," that means it produces a natural response in the absence of learning. Thus, an **unconditioned stimulus (US)** *is a stimulus that elicits a reflexive response without learning.* An **unconditioned response (UR)** *is a reflexive, unlearned reaction to*

an unconditioned stimulus. The link between the US and UR is, by definition, unlearned. In Pavlov's experiment, meat powder elicited unconditioned salivation in his dogs (see the top panel of Figure 6.2). Other examples of US–UR relationships include flinching (UR) in response to a loud sound (US), and blinking (UR) in response to a puff of air to the eye (US).

Recall that a defining characteristic of classical conditioning is that a neutral stimulus comes to elicit a response. It does so because the neutral stimulus is paired with, and therefore predicts, an unconditioned stimulus.

Figure 6.2 Pavlov's Salivary Conditioning Experiment

Food elicits the unconditioned response of salivation. Before conditioning, the tone elicits no response by the dog. During conditioning, the tone repeatedly precedes the food. After conditioning, the tone alone elicits salivation.

Before conditioning
Unconditioned stimulus (US) food

Unconditioned response (UR) salivation

Before conditioning
Neutral stimulus (NS) metronome

No salivation

During conditioning
Neutral stimulus (NS) metronome

Unconditioned stimulus (US) food

Unconditioned response (UR) salivation

After conditioning
Conditioned stimulus (CS) metronome

Conditioned response (CR) salivation

In Pavlov's experiment, the metronome was *originally* a neutral stimulus because it did not elicit a response, least of all salivation (see Figure 6.2). A **conditioned stimulus (CS)** *is a once neutral stimulus that elicits a conditioned response because it has a history of being paired with an unconditioned stimulus.* A **conditioned response (CR)** *is the learned response that occurs to the conditioned stimulus.* After being repeatedly paired with the US, the once neutral tone in Pavlov's experiment became a conditioned stimulus (CS) because it elicited the conditioned response of salivation. To establish that conditioning has taken place, the tone (CS) must elicit salivation in the *absence* of food (US; see the bottom panel of Figure 6.2).

A common point of confusion is the difference between a conditioned response and an unconditioned response. In Pavlov's experiment they are both salivation. What differentiates the two is the stimulus that elicits them. Salivation is a UR if it occurs in response to a US (food). Salivation is a CR if it occurs in response to a CS (the tone). A CS can have this effect only if it becomes *associated* with a US. To help you apply this terminology, practice with the examples in Table 6.1.

Processes of Classical Conditioning

Classically conditioned responses typically involve reflexive actions, but they are still quite flexible. Conditioned responses may be very strong and reliable, which is likely if the CS and the US have a long history of being paired together. Conditioned responding may diminish over time, or it may occur with new stimuli with which the response has never been paired. We now turn to some processes that account for the flexibility of classically conditioned responses.

ACQUISITION, EXTINCTION, AND SPONTANEOUS RECOVERY Learning involves a change in behavior due to experience, which can include acquiring a new response. **Acquisition** *is the initial phase of learning in which a response is established;* thus, in classical conditioning, acquisition is the phase in which a neutral stimulus is repeatedly paired with the US. In Pavlov's experiment, the conditioned salivary response was *acquired* with numerous pairings of the tone and food (see Figure 6.3). A critical part of acquisition is the predictability with which the CS and the US occur together. In Pavlov's experiment, conditioning either would not occur or would be very weak if food was delivered only sometimes (i.e., inconsistently) when the tone was presented. Even once a response is fully acquired, there is no guarantee it will persist forever.

In both natural situations and in the laboratory, the CS and the US may not always occur together. **Extinction** *is the loss or weakening of a conditioned response when a conditioned stimulus and unconditioned stimulus no longer occur together.* For the dogs in Pavlov's experiment, if a tone is presented repeatedly and no food follows, then salivation should diminish until eventually it may not occur at all (Figure 6.3). Extinction makes sense from a biological perspective: If the tone is no longer a reliable predictor of food, then salivation becomes unnecessary. However, even after extinction occurs, a once established conditioned response can return, and often does so very quickly.

Spontaneous recovery *is the reoccurrence of a previously extinguished conditioned response, typically after some time has passed since extinction.* Pavlov and his assistants studied the phenomenon of extinction—but also noticed that salivation would reappear when the dogs were later returned

---

Table 6.1 Applying Classical Conditioning

Read the following scenarios and identify the CS, CR, US, and UR in each one.

1. Cameron and Tia went to the prom together, and during their last slow dance the DJ played the theme song for the event. During the song, the couple kissed. Now, several years later, whenever Cameron and Tia hear the song, they feel a rush of excitement.
   a. The song
   b. The kiss
   c. Rush of excitement when kissing
   d. Rush of excitement when hearing the song

2. Harry has visited his eye doctor several times due to problems with his vision. One test involves blowing a puff of air into his eye. After repeated visits to the eye doctor, Harry starts blinking as soon as the instrument is being applied.
   a. Instrument that delivers the puff of air
   b. Blinking in response to the puff of air
   c. Blinking in response to the instrument
   d. Puff of air

3. Sarah went to a new restaurant and experienced the most delicious meal she has ever tasted. The restaurant starts advertising on the radio, and now every time an ad comes on, Sarah finds herself craving the meal she had enjoyed so much.
   a. Response to ingesting the meal
   b. Response to the song
   c. The meal
   d. The song

Answers: 1. a = CS, b = US, c = UR, d = CR; 2. a = CS, b = UR, c = CR, d = US; 3. a = UR, b = CR, c = US, d = CS

Figure 6.3 Acquisition, Extinction, and Spontaneous Recovery

Acquisition of a conditioned response occurs over repeated pairings of the CS and the US. If the US no longer occurs, conditioned responding diminishes—a process called *extinction*. Often, following a time interval in which the CS does not occur, conditioned responding rebounds when the CS is presented again—a phenomenon called *spontaneous recovery*.

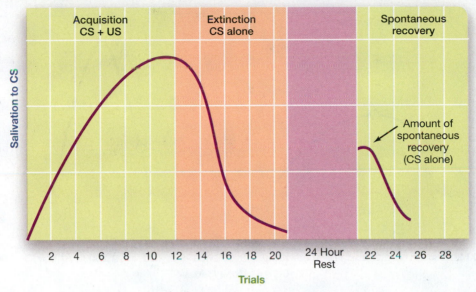

to the experimental testing room where acquisition and extinction trials had been conducted. The dogs would also salivate again in response to a tone, albeit less so than at the end of acquisition (Figure 6.3). Why would salivation spontaneously return after the response had supposedly extinguished? Psychologists are not fully sure why, but the fact that responses can be spontaneously recovered suggests that extinction does not result in what we typically think of as "forgetting." Rather, the opposite seems to be occurring—namely, extinction involves learning something *new* (Bouton, 2010). In Pavlov's experiment, for example, the dogs learned that in the experimental setting, the tone was no longer a reliable stimulus for predicting food. But perhaps with the passage of time, or in a place other than the experimental setting, it may still signal that food is on the way.

Extinction and spontaneous recovery are evidence that classically conditioned responses can change once they are acquired. Further evidence of flexibility of conditioned responding can be seen in some other processes of classical conditioning, including generalization and discrimination learning.

STIMULUS GENERALIZATION AND DISCRIMINATION
Stimulus **generalization** *is a process in which a response that originally occurs to a specific stimulus also occurs to different, though similar stimuli.* In Pavlov's experiment, dogs salivated not just to the original tone (CS), but also to very similar tones (see Figure 6.4). Generalization allows for flexibility in learned behaviors, although it is certainly possible for behavior to be *too* flexible. Salivating in response

to *any* sound would be wasteful because not every sound correctly predicts food. Thus, Pavlov's dogs also showed **discrimination**, *which occurs when an organism learns to respond to one original stimulus but not to new stimuli that may be similar to the original stimulus* (Figure 6.4). Learning to discriminate different stimuli is a critical aspect of learning. At times we need to learn to discriminate very similar stimuli, such as when learning to play the piano. The middle of a piano, A middle C, is about 261hz, and the adjacent keys are B (247hz) and C-sharp/D-flat (277Hz). These keys sound very similar, especially to someone who is just learning how to play piano. Alternatively, different preset ring tones on smart phones are very different, making discrimination learning easier.

Applications of Classical Conditioning

Now that you are familiar with the basic processes of classical conditioning, we can begin to explore its applications. Classical conditioning is relevant to many behaviors and phenomena, such as emotional learning, advertising, drug tolerance, aversions to certain foods, and as we will see, why diet beverages are seemingly ineffective at promoting weight loss.

CONDITIONED FEAR AND ANXIETY Classical conditioning plays a significant role in our emotional responses. The sweating of your palms, the butterflies in your stomach, a racing heart, and other sensations that accompany both positive and negative feelings result

Figure 6.4 Stimulus Generalization and Discrimination

A conditioned response may generalize to other similar stimuli. In this case, salivation occurs not just to the 1,200 Hz tone used during conditioning, but to other tones as well. Discrimination learning has occurred when responding is elicited by the original training stimulus, but much less so, if at all, to other stimuli.

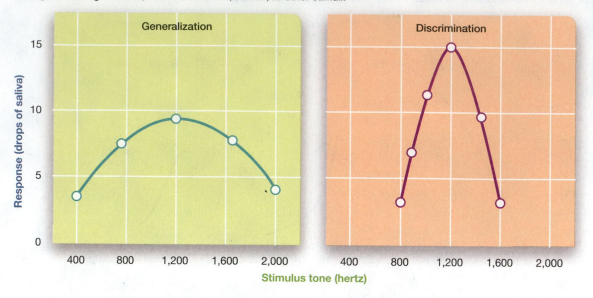

from sympathetic nervous system activity (see Modules 3.3, 11.3). Many of the stimuli that elicit these emotional responses do so because we have learned to respond that way (LeDoux, 2012).

Even fears that may seem innate, such as of snakes or spiders, are acquired and modified through conditioning; however, we do seem likely to fear some things more than others. To study this, psychologists paired photographs of snakes (the CS) with a mild electric shock (the US). The shock can produce several unconditioned responses, such as increased palm sweat, also known as the skin conductance response. Following several pairings between snake photos and shock in an experimental setting, the snake photos alone (the CS) elicited a strong increase in skin conductance responses (the CR). For comparison, participants were also shown pictures of nonthreatening stimuli (flowers) that were paired with the shock. Much less intense conditioned responding developed in response to pictures of flowers, even though the pictures had been paired with the shock an equal number of times as the

Psychologists have long been fascinated by an attempt made by John B. Watson to condition the infant "Little Albert" to fear rats. This early study is thought to be an important and original demonstration of how fears are conditioned. Here, Watson tests Albert's response to a mask.

Figure 6.5 Biologically Prepared Fear

Physiological measures of fear are highest in response to photos of snakes after the photos are paired with an electric shock—even higher than the responses to photos of guns. Flowers—something that humans generally do not need to fear in nature—are least effective when it comes to conditioning fear responses.

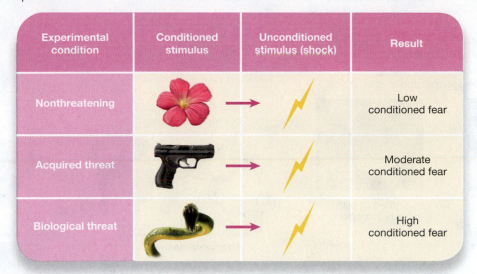

Experimental condition	Conditioned stimulus	Unconditioned stimulus (shock)	Result
Nonthreatening			Low conditioned fear
Acquired threat			Moderate conditioned fear
Biological threat			High conditioned fear

snakes and shock (Figure 6.5; Öhman & Mineka, 2001). Thus, it appears we are predisposed to acquire a fear of snakes, but not flowers.

This finding may not be too surprising, but what about other potentially dangerous objects such as guns? In modern times, guns are far more often associated with death or injury than snakes, and certainly flowers. When the researchers paired pictures of guns (the CS) with the shock (the US), they found that conditioned arousal to guns among participants was less than that to snake photos, and comparable to that of harmless flowers. In addition, the conditioned arousal to snake photos proved longer lasting and slower to extinguish than the conditioned responding to pictures of guns or flowers (Öhman & Mineka, 2001).

Given that guns and snakes both have the potential to be dangerous, why is it so much easier to learn a fear of snakes than a fear of guns? The term **preparedness** *refers to the biological predisposition to rapidly learn a response to a particular class of stimuli* (Seligman, 1971; Domjan et al., 2004), such as the finding that we learn to fear snakes more readily than either flowers or guns. Preparedness helps make sense of these research findings from an evolutionary perspective. Over time, humans have evolved a strong predisposition to fear an animal that has a long history of causing severe injury or death (LoBue, 2014; Van Le et al., 2013). The survival advantage has gone to those who were quick to learn to avoid such animals. The same is not true for flowers (which do not attack humans) or guns (which are relatively new in our species' history).

Fear conditioning procedures have been used to address clinical and mental health questions. For example, scientists have conducted some fascinating experiments on people diagnosed with *psychopathy*, meaning they are notorious for being self-centered and manipulative, and show little, if any, empathy or remorse (see Module 13.2). In one study, a sample of people diagnosed with psychopathy looked at brief presentations of human faces (the CS) followed by a painful stimulus (the US). What *should* have happened is that participants would acquired a negative emotional reaction (the CR) to the faces, but they did not. Instead, these individuals showed very little physiological arousal, their emotional brain centers remained quiet, and overall they did not seem to mind looking at pictures of faces that had been paired with pain (Birbaumer et al., 2005; see also Rothemund et al., 2012). A control group comprised of people who showed no signs of psychopathy did not enjoy this experience. Following several pairings between CS and US, they showed increased physiological arousal and activity of the emotion centers of the brain, and understandably reported disliking the experience of the experiment (Figure 6.6).

CONDITIONED TASTE AVERSIONS Have you ever eaten something that made you ill? Chances are you cannot stand to even look at it now. This is a **conditioned taste aversion**, *the acquired dislike or disgust of a food or drink because it was paired with illness* (Garcia et al., 1966). Figure 6.7 explains how one's previous negative experience with a specific food or drink can later trigger a conditioned response (taste aversion)— upon just the mere sight or smell of it.

Figure 6.6 Fear Conditioning and the Brain

During fear conditioning, a neutral stimulus (NS) such as a tone or a picture of a human face is briefly presented followed by an unconditioned stimulus (US), such as a mild electric shock. The result is a conditioned fear response to the CS. A procedure like this has been used to compare fear responses in people diagnosed with psychopathy with control participants. The brain images show that those with psychopathy (right image) have very little responding in their emotional brain circuitry when presented with the CS. In contrast, control participants show strong activation in their emotional brain centers (left image) (Birbaumer et al., 2005).

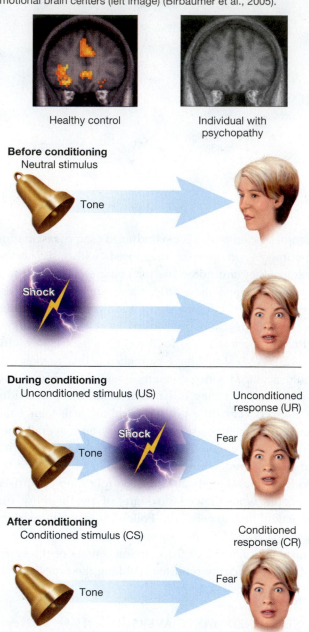

Healthy control   Individual with psychopathy

Before conditioning
Neutral stimulus

Tone

Shock

During conditioning
Unconditioned stimulus (US)   Unconditioned response (UR)

Tone   Shock   Fear

After conditioning
Conditioned stimulus (CS)   Conditioned response (CR)

Tone   Fear

Taste aversions may develop in a variety of contexts, such as through illness associated with food poisoning, chemotherapy, or intoxication. Also, as is the case with fear conditioning, only certain types of stimuli are amenable to conditioned taste aversions. When we develop an aversion to a particular food, the relationship typically

Figure 6.7 Conditioned Taste Aversions

Classical conditioning can account for the development of taste aversions. Falling ill after eating a particular food can result in conditioned feelings of nausea in response to the taste, smell, or texture of the food.

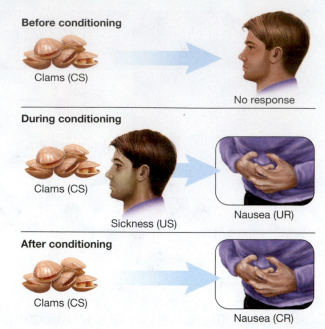

Before conditioning

Clams (CS)   No response

During conditioning

Clams (CS)   Sickness (US)   Nausea (UR)

After conditioning

Clams (CS)   Nausea (CR)

involves the flavor of the food and nausea, rather than the food and *any* stimulus that may have been present during conditioning. For example, if you were listening to a particular song and eating yogurt when you became sick, your aversion would develop to the sight, thought, and most definitely taste of yogurt, but not to the song that was playing. Thus, we can see that humans are biologically prepared to associate food, but not sound, with illness (Garcia et al., 1966).

Conditioned taste aversions are unique in several ways, such as the relatively long delay between tasting the food or beverage (the CS) and sickness (the US). Symptoms from food poisoning may not occur for hours after eating, but most conditioning happens only if the CS and the US occur very closely to each other in time. Another peculiarity is that taste aversions are learned very quickly—a single CS–US pairing is typically sufficient. These special characteristics of taste aversions are extremely important for survival. The flexibility offered by a long window of time separating CS and US, as well as the requirement for only a single exposure, raises the chances of acquiring an important aversion to the offending substance.

JOURNAL PROMPT

Classical Conditioning: Describe a personally relevant example of classical conditioning that you have experienced. Identify the CS, US, CR, and UR.

Conditioning and Advertising

Each day hundreds of companies and, depending on the season, political campaigners compete for your attention in the hope of winning your wallet, your vote, or both. Classical conditioning plays a surprisingly significant role in how people respond to advertisements (Allen & Shimp, 1990; Schachtman, Walker, & Fowler, 2011).

What do we know about classical conditioning in advertising?

The negative attack ads shown by political rivals rely on similar principles of fear conditioning already described. In contrast, advertisers often use principles of classical conditioning to elicit positive responses in their viewers. Psychologists use the term *evaluative conditioning* to describe the conditioning that occurs through advertisements. Here "evaluative" refers to the conditioned response, which is a positive (like) or negative (dislike) evaluation of a stimulus, typically a brand or product.

How can science help explain the role of classical conditioning in advertising?

To help visualize how classical conditioning can work in advertising, examine Figure 6.8, in which the CS (a product—in this case, a popular brand of perfume) is paired with a US (a photo of people in a provocative pose). This example alone does not provide scientific evidence that classical conditioning accounts for why people might be inclined to buy the product. Psychologists, however,

Figure 6.8 Classical Conditioning in Advertisements

Attractive people and sexual situations are a common theme in advertising. By pairing products, brand names, and logos (CSs) with provocative imagery (the US), advertisers hope that viewers become conditioned so that the CSs alone will elicit positive feelings—especially when potential consumers are making decisions.

have studied this phenomenon in the laboratory to unravel the mysteries of advertisers' appeals. In one study, researchers created a fictitious product they called "Brand L toothpaste." This CS appeared in a slide show several times, along with attractive visual scenery (the US). The participants who experienced the CS and US paired together had positive evaluations of Brand L compared to participants from a control group who viewed the same slides but in an unpaired fashion (Stuart et al., 1987). Further studies show that both positive and negative evaluations of stimuli can be conditioned in laboratory conditions that mimic what people experience in everyday exposure to advertisements (Olson & Fazio, 2001; Stahl et al., 2009).

Can we critically evaluate this information?

Are companies being sneaky and deceitful when they use classical conditioning as a strategy to influence consumer behavior? As discussed in Module 4.1, the effects of subliminal advertising are greatly exaggerated. In reality, images flashed on a screen for a fraction of second can go undetected, yet still elicit subtle emotional and physiological responses. However, this effect alone is not likely powerful enough to control spending behavior. The imagery in advertisements, by comparison, is presented for longer than a fraction of a second, giving viewers time to consciously perceive it. The effect is that you might choose a particular shampoo or body spray because you remember liking the advertisements. Therefore, although classical conditioning in advertisement affects emotional responding, and can contribute to the persuasive effect of messages, it is not causing us to blindly follow suggestions to purchase products (Stahl et al., 2009).

Why is this relevant?

Advertisements are often perceived as being geared toward instilling and retaining consumer loyalty to products. Another view, of course, is that ads seek to part you and your money. As a thoughtful consumer, you should take a moment to at least ask *why* you are drawn toward a given product. Our emotional responses are not necessarily good guides for decision making, though they certainly play a strong role. When it comes to deciding whether to make a purchase, you might ask yourself whether the sexy or humorous advertisement for the product is influencing your decision. Alternatively, is your purchase driven by the true value of the product and an actual need for it? Likewise, when you see political advertisements, consider their positive or negative emotional content. Making a reasoned decision about a candidate is preferable to making one based exclusively on emotional responses.

DRUG USE AND TOLERANCE Classical conditioning plays an important role in drug craving and tolerance (see Module 5.3). Cues that accompany drug use can become conditioned stimuli that elicit cravings (Lovibond & Colagiuri, 2013; Sinha, 2009). For example, to smokers a cigarette lighter, the smell of tobacco smoke, or the presence of another smoker can elicit cravings. Researchers have sought to better understand the role that conditioning plays in drug-taking behavior to help people with addictions and reduce potentially lethal interactions with drugs.

One can build a tolerance for many common drugs—that is, the desired effect lessens with repeated use, and this leads users to increase the dosage. One form of tolerance known as *conditioned drug tolerance* develops as the body begins associating environmental cues that accompany drug use with the drug itself. For example, a heroin user who always shoots up in the same room may also follow a specific set of injection rituals using a specific set of paraphernalia each time: These cues become the conditioned stimuli (CS). An increase in the physiological processes that metabolize the drug—adaptive responses that prepare the body for something potentially dangerous—become the conditioned responses (CR). Importantly, these conditioned responses actually dampen the effects of the drug once it is administered—their function is to prepare the body for something (in this case a drug) that disrupts normal physiological functions. Over repeated trials of administering the drug, the conditioned responses counteract the drug effects and the normal dosage no longer provides the anticipated high. Eventually, more of the drug is needed to attain the desired effect (Siegel, 2005).

This phenomenon can have fatal consequences for drug abusers, as psychologist Shepard Siegel demonstrated (1984). Over a period of time Siegel conducted interviews with patients who were hospitalized for overdosing on heroin. Eventually a pattern emerged from the

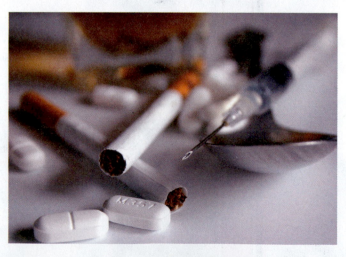

Physiological reactions to drugs are influenced by stimuli that are associated with administration of the drug.

interviews. Several reported that when they overdosed they had strayed from the ritual they typically followed when taking the drug; for example, they might have been in a different environment or injected themselves in a different part of their body. Their standard environmental cues (or CSs) were missing, leaving these individuals' bodies unprepared for even a *normal* dose of heroin. Without CSs to trigger CRs, even a *normal* dose of the drug can be lethal. This finding has been confirmed in animal studies: Siegel and his associates (1982) found that conditioned drug tolerance and overdosing can also occur with rats. When rats received heroin in an environment different from where they experienced the drug previously, mortality was double that in control rats that received the same dose of heroin in their normal surroundings (64% versus 32%). Knowing how conditioning contributes to responses to drugs can help combat problems involving abuse and overdose.

THE PARADOX OF DIET BEVERAGES Consumption of diet beverages has risen over the last several decades, but so has obesity. Figure 6.9 establishes a relationship between the two variables, but of course does not tell us what is causing either one of the variables to increase. However, classical conditioning may help explain why diet drinks are seemingly ineffective in helping people lose weight, as described at the beginning of this module (Swithers et al., 2009; Swithers & Davidson, 2005).

Through mechanisms linking the nervous and digestive systems, humans actually become conditioned to the foods and drinks that they consume, including those that contain real sugar. Sweet tastes send a message to the body that a large number of calories is on the way. For example, the taste of a candy bar is a conditioned stimulus (CS) that tells the body that a high-calorie food item (the US) is soon to arrive in the gut. This relationship is an important

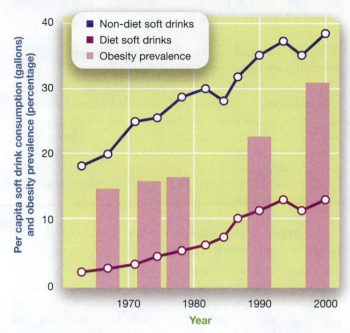

Figure 6.9 Diet Soda's Consumption's Association with Increased (not Decreased) Prevalence of Obesity

one for the body to learn, as it helps maintain an energy balance—eventually your body tells you it is time to stop eating sweets and switch to something else, perhaps with fewer calories. Artificially sweetened beverages disrupt the feedback relationship between the sugary sweet CS and high-calorie food US. The artificially sweetened taste of a diet soda is not followed by a high dose of calories that your body "expects." So how does the body respond? It continues to send out hunger messages: Your gut "tells" you to make up for the calories by opening up a bag of cookies or potato chips. This linkage may very well help explain why, by themselves, artificially sweetened beverages do not promote weight loss (Davidson, Sample, & Swithers, 2014).

Module **6.1** Summary

6.1a **Know . . . the key terminology involved in classical conditioning:**

acquisition
classical conditioning
conditioned response
conditioned stimulus
conditioned taste aversion
discrimination
extinction
generalization
learning

preparedness
spontaneous recovery
unconditioned response
unconditioned stimulus

6.1b **Understand . . . how responses learned through classical conditioning can be acquired and lost.**

Acquisition of a conditioned response occurs with repeated pairings of the CS and the US. Once a response is acquired, it can be extinguished if the CS and the US no longer occur together. During extinction, the CR diminishes, although it may reappear under some circumstances. For example, if enough time passes following extinction, the CR may spontaneously recover when the organism encounters the CS again.

6.1c Understand . . . the role of biological and evolutionary factors in classical conditioning.

Not all stimuli have the same potential to become strong CSs. Responses to biologically relevant stimuli, such as snakes, are more easily conditioned than are responses to stimuli such as flowers or guns. Similarly, avoidance of potentially harmful foods is critical to survival, so organisms can develop a conditioned taste aversion quickly (in a single trial) and even when ingestion and illness are separated by a relatively long time interval.

6.1d Apply . . . the concepts and terms of classical conditioning to new examples.

Although seemingly straightforward in concept, applying classical conditioning to examples can be challenging. The activity "applying classical conditioning" in Table 6.1 provided opportunities for practice. How did you do?

Some rules of thumb to apply to examples: Remember that a stimulus is something that elicits a behavior, and a response is the behavior itself—*always*. Also, the "un" in unconditioned stimulus (US) and unconditioned response (UR) tells us that no learning is required for the US to elicit the UR. Food (the US) elicits salivation (the UR) and no learning is required here. However, when a conditioned (or "learned") stimulus is paired with the US, it alone elicits a conditioned (learned) response.

6.1e Analyze . . . claims that artificially sweetened beverages are a healthier choice.

Because of classical conditioning, the digestive system responds to the flavor of the artificially sweetened (CS) beverage as though a high-calorie food source (the US) is on the way. When the low-calorie beverage reaches the digestive system, the gut has already prepared itself for something high in calories (the CR). As a consequence, hunger messages continue to be sent to the brain. Because the "diet" beverage does not deliver on the promise of high calories, the person experiences an increased level of hunger.

Module 6.1 Quiz

Know . . .

1. The learned response that occurs to the conditioned stimulus is known as the _____.
   - A. conditioned response
   - B. conditioned stimulus
   - C. unconditioned response
   - D. unconditioned response

Understand . . .

2. In classical conditioning, the process during which a neutral stimulus becomes a conditioned stimulus is known as _____.
   - A. extinction
   - B. spontaneous recovery
   - C. acquisition
   - D. discrimination

3. Why are humans biologically prepared to fear snakes and not guns?
   - A. Guns kill fewer people than do snakes.
   - B. Guns are not a natural phenomenon, whereas snakes do occur in nature.
   - C. Snakes are more predictable than guns.
   - D. Although also potentially involved in injury, guns are a more recent addition to our evolutionary history.

Apply . . .

4. Sylvia used to play with balloons. When she tried to blow up a balloon last week, it popped in her face and gave her quite a scare. Now, blowing up a balloon is so scary that Sylvia will not try it. In this example, the pop is a(n) _____ and the balloon is a(n) _____.
   - A. conditioned stimulus; unconditioned stimulus
   - B. unconditioned stimulus; conditioned stimulus
   - C. unconditioned response; conditioned response
   - D. conditioned response, unconditioned response

Analyze . . .

5. Which is the best explanation based on classical conditioning for why diet beverages do not prevent people from gaining weight?
   - A. Diet beverages actually have more calories than regular beverages.
   - B. The artificially sweetened beverages seem to stimulate hunger for high-calorie foods.
   - C. People who drink diet beverages typically eat more food than those who drink only water.
   - D. Diet drinks elicit conditioned emotional reactions that lead people to overeat.

Module **6.2**   Operant Conditioning: Learning Through Consequences

Learning Objectives

6.2a Know . . . the key terminology associated with operant conditioning.

6.2b Understand . . . the role that consequences play in increasing or decreasing behavior.

6.2c Understand . . . how schedules of reinforcement affect behavior.

6.2d Apply . . . your knowledge of operant conditioning to examples.

6.2e Analyze . . . the effectiveness of punishment on changing behavior.

Since the age of 24, Patient E had been a regular gambler, betting on horses, primarily. Patient E had also been diagnosed with bipolar disorder, and in his mid-30s, his therapist prescribed a common antidepressant to help treat it (Gaboriau et al., 2014). Shortly thereafter, Patient E's seemingly harmless penchant for betting on horses transformed from a regular habit to an irresistible, pathological urge. Soon, his gambling went out of control. His marriage began falling apart, as did, predictably, his financial situation. At the advice of his therapist, Patient E discontinued the drug and his pathological gambling ceased (Jones & George, 2011).

When we think about the common side effects of drugs, the urge to gamble is last to come to mind. As highly unusual as it is, cases like that of Patient E's have been found even

among people with no history of regular gambling. Today's medical literature now includes many examples of how antidepressants, which alter dopamine and serotonin activity, can lead to problematic gambling (though it is very rare). But what does this case study have to do with learning? Patient E's case illustrates an important relationship between brain chemistry and what the brain perceives as actual rewards. We learn that certain types of behavior produce rewards; but the dopamine- and serotonin-altering effects of the antidepressant led Patient E to experience gambling itself as rewarding, so much so, that he could not resist its urge—even as his marriage and finances fell apart—which are typically regarded as punishment. Unfortunately, E was not responding to these problems as such. It was not until after he ceased taking the drug that he was able to accurately perceive the negative consequences of his gambling behavior and to learn to stop it. Psychologists have spent decades unraveling how the availability of rewards influences our behavior, as well as how the circuitry and chemistry of our brain supports our seeking rewards out and relishing in their attainment. In this next module we examine what has come of this research, as well as how both reward and punishment affect our behavior.

We tend to repeat the actions that bring rewards and avoid those that lead to punishment. This is a straightforward statement about behavior, but one that oversimplifies the complex dynamics that occur between our actions and their consequences—as we saw in the case of Patient E. **Operant conditioning** *is a type of learning in which behavior is influenced by consequences.* The term *operant* is used because the individual *operates* on the environment before consequences can occur. In contrast to classical conditioning, which typically involves reflexive responses, operant conditioning involves voluntary actions such as speaking or listening, starting and stopping an activity, and moving toward or away from something. The consequences of our behavior, that is, whether it is reinforced or punished, determine our operant behavior. Table 6.2 summarizes the key differences between operant and classical conditioning.

Table 6.2 Major Differences Between Classical and Operant Conditioning

	Classical Conditioning	Operant Conditioning
Target response is …	Automatic	Voluntary
Reinforcement is …	Present regardless of whether a response occurs	A consequence of the behavior
Behavior mostly depends on …	Reflexive and physiological responses	Skeletal muscles

Processes of Operant Conditioning

The concept of *contingency* is important to understanding operant conditioning; it simply means that a consequence depends upon an action. Earning good grades is generally contingent upon studying effectively. Excelling at athletics is contingent upon training and practice. The consequences of a particular behavior can be either reinforcing or punishing (see Figure 6.10).

REINFORCEMENT AND PUNISHMENT Reinforcement *is a process in which an event or reward that follows a response increases the likelihood of that response occurring again.* We can trace the scientific study of the effects of reinforcement on behavior to Edward Thorndike's experiments with cats. Thorndike measured the time it took cats to learn how to escape from puzzle boxes (see Figure 6.11). He observed that over repeated trials cats were able to escape more rapidly because they learned which responses worked (such as pressing a pedal on the floor of the box).

From his experiments, Thorndike proposed the *law of effect*—the idea that responses followed by satisfaction will occur again, and those that are not followed by satisfaction become less likely. Within a few decades after the publication of Thorndike's work, the famous behaviorist, B. F. Skinner, began conducting his own studies on the systematic relationship between reinforcement and behavior. As was the case with Thorndike, much of Skinner's work took place in the laboratory using nonhuman subjects, namely pigeons. In the search for general principles of learning, it mattered less which species of animal was used, as certainly pigeons were easier to keep, feed, and control than human subjects.

Many of the basic principles of operant conditioning stem from laboratory studies conducted on nonhuman species placed in an apparatus, such as the one pictured

Figure 6.10 Reinforcement and Punishment

The key distinction between reinforcement and punishment is that reinforcers, no matter what they are, increase behavior. Punishment involves a decrease in behavior, regardless of what the specific punisher may be. Thus, both reinforcement and punishment are defined based on their effects on behavior.

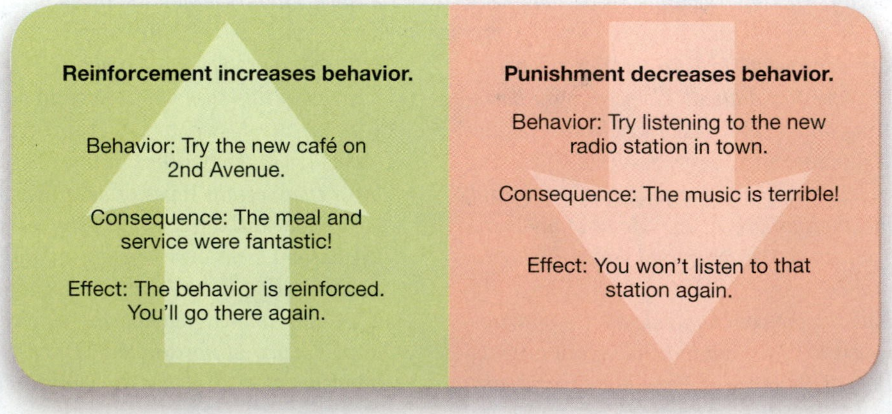

Reinforcement increases behavior.

Behavior: Try the new café on 2nd Avenue.

Consequence: The meal and service were fantastic!

Effect: The behavior is reinforced. You'll go there again.

Punishment decreases behavior.

Behavior: Try listening to the new radio station in town.

Consequence: The music is terrible!

Effect: You won't listen to that station again.

Figure 6.11 Thorndike's Puzzle Box and the Law of Effect

Thorndike conducted experiments in which cats learned an operant response that was reinforced with escape from the box and access to a food reward (a). Over repeated trials, the cats took progressively less time to escape, as shown in the learning curve (b).

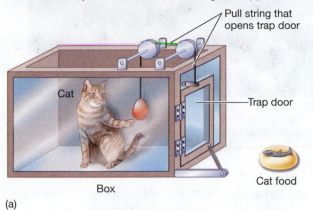

Pull string that opens trap door

Cat

Trap door

Box

Cat food

(a)

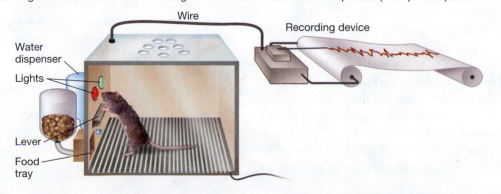

(b)

in Figure 6.12. *Operant chambers*, sometimes referred to as Skinner boxes, include a lever or key that the subject can manipulate. Pushing the lever may result in the delivery of a reinforcer, such as food. In operant conditioning terms, a **reinforcer** *is a stimulus that is contingent upon a response and increases the probability of that response occurring again.* Using operant chambers, researchers record the animal's rate of responding over time (a measure of learning), and typically set a criterion for the number of responses that must be made before a reinforcer becomes available. As we will discuss later in this module, animals and humans are quite sensitive to how many responses they must make, or how long they must wait, before they will receive a reward. View an example of a pigeon being trained in an operant chamber in the following video, Pigeon in the Skinner Box.

Watch PIGEON IN THE SKINNER BOX

01:26 / 02:14

Figure 6.12 An Operant Chamber

The operant chamber is a standard laboratory apparatus for studying operant conditioning. The rat can press the lever to receive a reinforcer such as food or water. The lights can be used to indicate when lever pressing will be rewarded. The recording device measures cumulative responses (lever presses) over time.

Wire

Recording device

Water dispenser

Lights

Lever

Food tray

Animals pressing levers in operant chambers to receive rewards may *seem* artificial. However, our environment is full of devices that influence our operant responses. Behavior in operant chambers can be remarkably consistent with what is found in real-world settings.

After studying Figure 6.12, you might wonder whether observations made with this apparatus could possibly apply to real-world situations. In fact, similar machinery can be found in all sorts of non-laboratory settings. People pull levers on slot machines, press buttons on vending machines, and punch keys on telephones and keyboards. Researchers use machinery such as operant chambers to help them control and quantify learning, but the general principles of operant conditioning apply to life outside and away from these contraptions.

Reinforcement involves increased responding, but decreased responding is also a possible outcome of an encounter with a stimulus. **Punishment** *is a process that decreases the future probability of a response.* Thus, a **punisher** *is a stimulus that is contingent upon a response and results in a decrease in behavior.* Like reinforcers, punishers are not defined based on the stimuli themselves, but rather in terms of their effects on behavior. We will explore some topics related to punishment in this module, but because reinforcement has held a more central place in operant conditioning, we will elaborate on reinforcement more extensively. One key characteristic of reinforcement learning is that it is motivated by the satisfaction of various types of drives.

PRIMARY AND SECONDARY REINFORCERS Reinforcement can come in many different forms. On the one hand, it may consist of stimuli that are inherently reinforcing, such as food, water, shelter, and sexual contact. These **primary reinforcers** *consist of reinforcing stimuli that satisfy basic motivational needs.* On the other hand, many stimuli that we find reinforcing, such as money or good grades, are reinforcing only after we first *learn* that they have value. **Secondary reinforcers** *consist of reinforcing stimuli that acquire their value through learning.* The pursuit of secondary reinforcers can be an all-consuming affair for some; certainly the attainment of success and money

is not a trivial motivator. But not all secondary reinforcers are created equal. Money and good grades can (hopefully) help secure the primary reinforcers we seek and require. But then consider many of the fantasy sports fans obsessed with post-game point totals or video gamers avidly seeking high rankings and experience points (XPs). Unlike primary reinforcers like food and water, secondary reinforcers do not lead to satiation and therefore can become endlessly reinforcing. People who passionately pursue either money or fantasy football glory are similarly influenced by brain circuitry designed to acquire rewards.

Both primary and secondary reinforcers satisfy our drives, but what underlies the motivation to seek these reinforcers? The answer is complex, but research points to a specific brain circuit that includes a structure called the *nucleus accumbens* (see Module 5.3). The nucleus accumbens becomes activated during the processing of all kinds of rewards, including primary ones such as eating and having sex, or using cocaine and smoking a cigarette, as well as secondary rewards. Individual differences in brain chemistry associated with the reward may account for why individuals differ so much in their drive for reinforcers. For example, scientists have discovered that people who are prone to risky behaviors such as gambling and alcohol abuse are more likely to have inherited particular copies of genes that code for dopamine and other reward-based chemicals of the brain (Blum et al., 2014). Perhaps the reward centers of gamblers and others who engage in high-risk behaviors are not sufficiently stimulated by natural rewards, making them more likely to engage in behaviors that will give them the rush that they crave.

POSITIVE AND NEGATIVE REINFORCEMENT AND PUNISHMENT Behavior can be reinforced because it brings a reward or, alternatively, because it results in the removal of something unpleasant. **Positive reinforcement**

Table 6.3 Distinguishing Types of Reinforcement and Punishment

	Consequence	Effect on Behavior	Example
Positive reinforcement	Stimulus is added or increased.	Increases the response	A child gets an allowance for making her bed, so she is likely to do it again in the future.
Negative reinforcement	Stimulus is removed or decreased.	Increases the response	The rain no longer falls on you after opening your umbrella, so you are likely to do it again in the future.
Positive punishment	Stimulus is added or increased.	Decreases the response	A pet owner scolds his dog for jumping up on a house guest, and now the dog is less likely to do it again.
Negative punishment	Stimulus is removed or decreased.	Decreases the response	A parent takes away TV privileges to stop the children from fighting.

is the strengthening of behavior after potential reinforcers such as praise, money, or nourishment following that behavior (see Table 6.3). With positive reinforcement, a stimulus is added to a situation (the "positive" in positive reinforcement indicates the *addition* of a reward).

Negative reinforcement *involves the strengthening of a behavior because it removes or diminishes a stimulus* (Table 6.3). (In this context, the word "negative" indicates the removal of something.) Much of what we do is for the purposes of avoiding or getting rid of something aversive (unpleasant); these actions serve as examples of negative reinforcement. For instance, taking aspirin is negatively reinforced because doing so eliminates a headache. Similarly, asking someone behind you in a movie theater to stop kicking your seat may remove the annoyance, thereby reinforcing you and encouraging you to repeat this behavior in future situations.

Negative reinforcement is a concept some frequently find confusing because it seems unusual that something aversive could be involved in the context of reinforcement. Recall that reinforcement (whether positive or negative) always involves an increase in the strength or frequency of responding. The term "positive" in this context simply means that a stimulus is introduced or increased, whereas the term "negative" means that a stimulus has been reduced or avoided.

Negative reinforcement can be further classified into two subcategories. **Avoidance learning** *is a specific type of negative reinforcement that removes the possibility that a stimulus will occur*. Examples of avoidance learning include taking a detour to circumvent traffic congestion on a particular road, and paying bills on time to avoid late fees. In these cases, negative situations are avoided. In contrast, **escape learning** *occurs if a response removes a stimulus that is already present*. Covering your ears upon hearing overwhelmingly loud music is one example. You cannot avoid the music, because it is already present, so you escape the aversive stimulus. The responses of taking a detour and covering your ears both increase in frequency because they have effectively removed or

diminished the offending stimuli. In the laboratory, operant chambers, such as the one pictured in Figure 6.12, often come equipped with a steel grid floor that can be used to deliver a mild electric shock; responses that remove (escape learning) or prevent (avoidance learning) the shock are negatively reinforced.

As with reinforcement, various types of punishment are possible. **Positive punishment** *is a process in which a behavior decreases because an unpleasant stimulus was introduced as a consequence of the behavior* (Table 6.3). For example, some cat owners use a spray bottle to squirt water when the cat hops on the kitchen counter or scratches the furniture. Remember that the term "positive" simply means that a stimulus is added to the situation—in these cases, the stimuli are punishers because they decrease the frequency of a behavior.

Behavior may also decrease as a result of the removal of a stimulus. **Negative punishment** *occurs when a behavior decreases because it removes or diminishes a particular stimulus* (Table 6.3). Withholding a child's privileges as a result of an undesirable behavior is an example of negative punishment. A parent who "grounds" a child does so because this action removes something of value to the child. If effective, the outcome of the grounding will be to decrease the behavior that got the child into trouble.

Keeping the terminology of reinforcement and punishment straight can require some practice. See Table 6.4 for some practice examples.

EXTINCTION, STIMULUS CONTROL, GENERALIZATION, AND DISCRIMINATION If you read Module 6.1, you know how extinction, generalization, and discrimination apply to classical conditioning. Similar phenomena occur with operant conditioning. In operant conditioning, **extinction** *refers to the weakening of an operant response when reinforcement is no longer available.*

Reinforcement is often only available under certain conditions and circumstances. A pigeon in an operant chamber may learn that pecking is reinforced only when the chamber's light is switched on, so there is no need to

Table 6.4 Applying Terms of Reinforcement and Punishment

The concepts of positive and negative reinforcement and punishment are often the most challenging when it comes to this material. Read the following scenarios and determine whether positive reinforcement, negative reinforcement, positive punishment, or negative punishment explains the change in behavior.

1. Steven is caught cheating on multiple examinations. As a consequence, the school principal suspends him for a three-day period. Steven likes being at school and, when he returns from his suspension, he no longer cheats on exams. Which process explains the change in Steven's behavior?

2. Tamika earns As in all of her math classes. Throughout her schooling, she finds that the personal and social rewards for excelling at math continue to motivate her. She eventually completes a graduate degree and teaches math. Which process explains her passion for math?

3. Automobile makers install sound equipment that produces annoying sounds when a door is not shut properly, lights are left on, or a seat belt is not fastened. The purpose is to increase proper door shutting, turning off of lights, and seat belt fastening behavior. Which process explains the behavioral change these sounds are designed to make?

4. Hernan bites his fingernails and cuticles to the point of bleeding and discomfort. To reduce this behavior, he applies a terrible-tasting topical lotion to his fingertips; the behavior stops. Which process explains Hernan's behavioral change?

Answers: 1. negative punishment, 2. positive reinforcement, 3. negative reinforcement, 4. positive punishment

continue pecking when the light is turned off. This illustrates the concept of a **discriminative stimulus**—*a cue or event that indicates that a response, if made, will be reinforced.* A behavior—in this case, pecking—is under *stimulus control* when a discriminative stimulus reliably elicits a specific response. As with the pigeon in the operant chamber, much of human behavior is under stimulus control. Your

@tuxedotrio

Training a cat to use the toilet involves shaping. One recommendation is to start by placing the litter pan next to the toilet, and gradually raise it by placing objects beneath it until it is at the level of the seat. This would need to happen over the course of several "trials" (cat potty breaks). Training the cat to sit on the seat and even flush the toilet when done is a delicate matter. If you are thinking of doing this, there are many online resources that will provide the details. Good luck!

cellphone specifically "dings" each time a text message comes through. The ding is the discriminative stimulus that tells you there is an incoming text message. Behavior is reinforced each time you respond.

The processes of generalization and discrimination influence whether organisms respond to discriminative stimuli. Generalization is observed in operant conditioning just as in classical conditioning, albeit with some important differences. In operant conditioning, *generalization* occurs when an operant response occurs in the presence of a new stimulus that is similar to the stimulus present during original learning. Children who have a history of being reinforced by their parents for tying their shoes, for example, are likely to demonstrate this same behavior when a teacher or other adult asks them to do so. *Discrimination* occurs when an operant response is made to one stimulus but not another one—even though it may be very similar. Perhaps you have learned that reinforcement is associated with only specific behaviors. For example, your behavior of stopping in response to a red traffic light has been reinforced in the past. You would not expect the same reinforcement for stopping at a green traffic light, even though these stimuli are often located closely to each other, and are often the same shape, brightness, and size.

Table 6.5 differentiates among the processes of extinction, generalization, and discrimination in classical and operant conditioning.

Applications of Operant Conditioning

You should now have a sense of how much our behavior is influenced by rewards and punishment. In this section, we focus on some specific applications of operant conditioning.

SHAPING Rats placed in operant chambers do not automatically go straight for the lever and begin pressing it to obtain food rewards. Instead, they must first learn that

Table 6.5 Comparing Extinction, Generalization, and Discrimination in Classical and Operant Conditioning

Process	Classical Conditioning	Operant Conditioning
Extinction	A CS is presented without a US until the CR no longer occurs.	Responding gradually ceases if reinforcement is no longer available.
	Example: A tone occurs but is no longer followed by shock, and therefore no longer elicits fear responses.	**Example:** Losing an Internet connection leads to fewer attempts at refreshing the Web browser because there is no reinforcement for doing so.
Generalization	A different CS that resembles the original CS used during acquisition elicits a CR.	Responding occurs to a stimulus that resembles the original discriminative stimulus used during learning.
	Example: Salivating to a metronome ticking at a similar but not identical rate as the one used during conditioning.	**Example:** Finding your first taste of Indian food pleasing, and subsequently trying other dishes with similar ingredients.
Discrimination	A CR does not occur in response to a different CS that resembles the original CS.	There is no response to a stimulus that resembles the original discriminative stimulus used during learning.
	Example: Feeling nauseous in response to tomato juice, because of a previously bad experience with it, but having no aversion to other types of juice.	**Example:** A dog runs to the door upon hearing the doorbell, but stays put to a different doorbell sound coming from the television.

lever pressing accomplishes something. Getting a rat to press a lever can be done by reinforcing behaviors that *approximate* lever pressing, such as standing up, facing the lever, standing while facing the lever, placing paws upon the lever, and pressing downward. **Shaping** *is a procedure in which a specific operant response is created by reinforcing successive approximations of that response.* Shaping is done in step-by-step fashion until the desired response—in this case, lever pressing—is learned. Skilled behavioral psychologists can string together long sequences of behavior using shaping techniques.

Shaping procedures, such as the educational method called *applied behavior analysis* (ABA), has some incredibly useful applications. Specifically, ABA can improve the quality of life for people living with autism (Granpeesheh et al., 2009). From a very early age, individuals with autism are typically under-responsive to social cues, such as facial expressions indicating joy or sadness. This impairment can hinder the development of many skills, ranging from the most basic (such as saying hello or goodbye to others) to the more complex (such as sharing and playing with toys). Psychologists who specialize in ABA can develop strategies that address challenges such as these. To do so, they use a system of close observation, prompting, and reinforcement to shape the target behaviors.

SCHEDULES OF REINFORCEMENT Typically, behavior is rewarded according to some kind of schedule. Skinner and his colleagues recognized the importance of **schedules of reinforcement**—*rules that determine when reinforcement is available* (Ferster & Skinner, 1957). Reinforcement may be available at highly predictable or irregular times. Also, reinforcement may be based on how often someone engages in a behavior, or on the passage of time.

Vending machines should deliver a snack every time the correct amount of money is deposited. With such **continuous reinforcement**, *every response made results in reinforcement*, and learning initially occurs rapidly.

Other reinforcers that we work to achieve do not come with such regularity; we also encounter situations where reinforcement is available only some of the time. Texting a friend may not always get a response for some period of time, or at all. With **partial (intermittent) reinforcement**, *only a certain number of responses are rewarded, or a certain amount of time must pass before reinforcement is available.* Ratio schedules of reinforcement are based on the number of responses that occur, and interval schedules of reinforcement are based on the passage of time. There are four types of partial reinforcement schedules and each has a different effect on rates of responding (Figure 6.13):

- **fixed-ratio schedule**, *reinforcement is delivered after a specific number of responses have been completed.* For example, a rat may be required to press a lever 10 times to receive food. Similarly, an employee working on commission may receive a bonus only after selling a specific number of items.

- **variable-ratio schedule**, *the number of responses required to receive reinforcement varies according to an average.* Slot machines at casinos operate on variable-ratio reinforcement schedules. The odds are that the slot machine will not give anything back, but sometimes a player will win a modest sum. Of course, hitting the jackpot is very infrequent. The variable nature of the reward structure for playing slot machines helps explain why responding on this schedule can be vigorous and persistent. Slot machines and other games of chance hold out the *possibility* that at some point players will be rewarded, but the unpredictable reward structure tends to promote strong response levels—in other words, a lot of money deposited into the machine.

- **fixed-interval schedule**, *reinforces the first response occurring after a set amount of time passes.* If your psychology professor gives you an exam every three weeks, your reinforcement for studying is on a

Figure 6.13 Schedules of Reinforcement

(a) Four types of reinforcement schedule are shown here: fixed ratio, fixed interval, variable ratio, and variable interval. Notice how each schedule differs based on when reinforcement is available (interval schedules) and on how many responses are required for reinforcement (ratio schedules). (b) These schedules of reinforcement affect responding in different ways. For example, notice the vigorous responding that is characteristic of the variable ratio schedule, as indicated by the steep upward trajectory of responding.

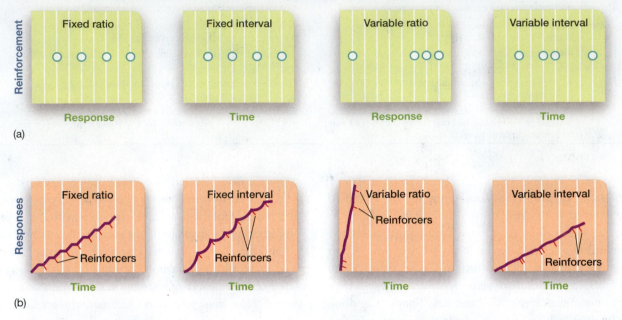

fixed-interval schedule. In Figure 6.13, notice how the fixed-interval schedule shows that responding drops off after each reinforcement is delivered (as indicated by the tick marks). However, responding increases because reinforcement is soon available again. This schedule may reflect how you devote time to studying for an upcoming exam—studying time tends to decrease after an exam, and then builds up again as another test looms.

- **variable-interval schedule**, *first response is reinforced following a variable amount of time*. The time interval varies around an average. For example, if you were watching the nighttime sky during a meteor shower, you would be rewarded for looking upward at irregular times. A meteor may fall on average every 5 minutes, but there will be times of inactivity for a minute, 10 minutes, 8 minutes, and so on.

As you can see from the Figure 6.13, ratio schedules tend to generate relatively high rates of responding. This outcome makes sense in light of the fact that, in ratio schedules, reinforcement is based on how often we engage in the behavior (something we have some control over) versus how much time has passed (something we do not control). For example, checking for new emails every minute does not *cause* emails to arrive sooner than hoped. In contrast, a sales person who is on a variable-ratio schedule

is reinforced with greater frequency if she approaches a lot of customers in a given period of time.

One general characteristic of schedules of reinforcement is that partially reinforced responses tend to be very persistent. For example, although people are only intermittently reinforced for putting money into a slot machine, a high rate of responding is maintained and may not decrease until after a great many losses in a row (or the individual runs out of money). The effect of partial reinforcement on responding is especially evident during extinction. Being partially reinforced can lead to very persistent responding even if, unbeknownst to the organism, reinforcement is no longer available. The **partial reinforcement effect** *refers to a phenomenon in which organisms that have been conditioned under partial reinforcement resist extinction longer than those that are reinforced continuously.*

Working the Scientific Literacy Model

Reinforcement and Superstition

By definition, reinforcement strengthens behavior, and as we have seen, it takes multiple forms and is available through various schedules. Although we cannot always identify which specific behavior actually prompted the reinforcer, we persist in the behavior because we believe it will be reinforced. In other words, we behave superstitiously.

What do we know about superstition and reinforcement?

Humans all over the world maintain superstitious beliefs—namely that specific rituals or good luck charms can improve their chances of success (Fluke, Webster, & Saucier, 2014). The most common variety of superstitious belief involves *negative illusions*, where the removal of an unpleasant experience, such as hiccups, is falsely attributed to an irrelevant action (such as plugging your ears while drinking water through a straw) (Aeschelman, Rosen, & Williams, 2003). Psychologists believe that operant conditioning plays a role in how people acquire superstitious beliefs (Matute & Blanco, 2014). Superstition is frequently displayed by athletes; for example, they may wear a (sometimes unwashed) "lucky jersey" during an important game, or they might perform a set of pre-game rituals before heading out into the field. Former Cleveland Indians outfielder Kevin Rhomberg believed that if someone touched him, he would be cursed with bad luck unless he touched that person back. This quirk *may* have been accepted by his teammates, but it also included the opposing players. When Rhomberg was tagged out, he could be seen pursuing the defensive player in order to touch him, which was especially awkward when it meant chasing him all the way to the dugout (Rhomberg's professional career spanned 41 games).

How can science explain superstition?

Decades ago, B. F. Skinner (1948) tested whether pigeons could acquire something analogous to superstitious behavior if they were offered reinforcement that was not tied to a particular response. In this study, pigeons received food every 15 seconds regardless of what they were doing. Over time, the birds started engaging in "superstitious" behaviors. The pigeons repeated the behaviors that happened to occur just before reinforcement, such as scratching, head-bobbing, or standing on one foot. A pigeon that happened to be turning in a counterclockwise direction when reinforcement was delivered repeated this seemingly senseless behavior.

Psychologists have conducted controlled studies to see whether superstition had any effect on performance outcomes. In one investigation, college students, 80% of whom believed in "good luck," were asked to participate in a golf-putting contest. Members of one group were told they were playing with "the lucky ball," and members of the other were told they would be using "the ball everyone has used so far." Those who were told they were using the lucky ball performed significantly better than those who were not (Damisch et al., 2010). Other studies, such as those involving memory and anagram games, yielded similar results. Participants who brought along a good luck charm performed better than those who did not bring one.

Can we critically evaluate these findings?

Superstitious beliefs, though irrational on the surface, may enhance individuals' belief that they can perform successfully at a task. Sometimes these beliefs can even enhance performance, as the golf-putting experiment revealed. These findings, however, are best applied to situations where the individual has some control over an outcome, such as taking an exam or playing a sport. People who spend a lot of time and money gambling are known to be quite superstitious, but it is important to distinguish between games of chance versus skill in this setting. "Success" at many gambling games is due entirely, or predominantly, to chance. Thus, the outcomes are immune to the superstitious beliefs of the players.

Why is this relevant?

Three out of four people in the United States believe in paranormal phenomena, and many of these beliefs are based on superstition (Moore, 2005). Superstitious beliefs can be harmless, and in some cases even helpful to individuals, but problems arise when they creep into decisions that impact medical, economic, and other societal issues. Superstitious beliefs are related to pseudoscience, which as discussed in Module 1.1 are ideas presented as science but lack basic scientific thinking or procedure. Back pain treatments make a great case in point. Forty percent of primary treatments for back pain are based on claims made by people who practice alternative medicine (White House Commission on Complementary and Alternative Medicine Policy, 2002). One characteristic of back pain is that, in general, there is a high probability of it temporarily subsiding without any treatment at all. Thus, someone who tries an alternative treatment for the pain is prone to falsely believing that a remedy works, when in actuality the pain went away for some other reason.

JOURNAL PROMPT

Superstition: Describe a superstition you have, or if none comes to mind a superstition held by someone you know. Explain a possible role that operant conditioning may have played in acquiring the superstition.

Table 6.6 Punishment Tends to Be Most Effective When Certain Principles Are Followed

Principle	Description and Explanation
Severity	Should be proportional to offense. A small fine is suitable for parking illegally or littering, but inappropriate for someone who commits assault.
Initial punishment level	The initial level of punishment needs to be sufficiently strong to reduce the likelihood of the offense occurring again.
Contiguity	Punishment is most effective when it occurs immediately after the behavior. Many convicted criminals are not sentenced until many months after they have committed an offense. Children are given detention that may not begin until hours later. Long delays in punishment are known to reduce its effectiveness.
Consistency	Punishment should be administered consistently. A parent who only occasionally punishes a teenager for breaking her curfew will probably have less success in curbing the behavior than a parent who uses punishment consistently.
Show alternatives	Punishment is more successful, and side effects are reduced, if the individual is clear on how reinforcement can be obtained by engaging in appropriate behaviors.

APPLYING PUNISHMENT Punishment is the intuitive flipside to reinforcement, but the two processes actually work quite differently. For example, people tend to be more sensitive to the unpleasantness of punishment than they are to the pleasures of reward. Psychologists have demonstrated this asymmetry in laboratory studies with college students who were asked to play a computerized game that offered them two response options yielding one of two outcomes: a monetary reward or a monetary loss. In one study participants showed that losing money ($100) is three times more punishing (it felt more like a loss of $300) than gaining money is reinforcing (Rasmussen & Newland, 2008).

The use of punishment, especially when it is physical, raises some ethical concerns. A major, globally debated issue is whether corporal punishment (e.g., spanking) is acceptable to use with children. In fact, more than 20 countries, including Sweden, Austria, Finland, Demark, and Israel, have banned the practice in both school and the home. Interestingly, very few people in the United States publicly advocate spanking. This is certainly the case among psychologists. Even so, spanking remains a very common practice. In one study approximately two-thirds of participating families reported spanking their three-year-old child at least once in the past month (Taylor et al., 2010). Parents often use this tactic because it can work: Spanking is generally a very effective punisher when it is used for immediately stopping a behavior (Gershoff, 2002). However, one reason why so few psychologists advocate spanking is because it is associated with some major side effects. In multiple studies, spanking has been associated with poorer parent–child relationships, poorer mental health for both adults and children, delinquency in children, and increased chances of children becoming victims or perpetrators of physical abuse in adulthood (Gershoff & Bitensky, 2007; Gershoff et al., 2012).

Do these findings suggest that corporal punishment should be abandoned altogether? Although few psychologists recommend spanking, further research has shown that the negative side effects are more likely if punishment is particularly severe, such as slapping children in the face. Other research indicates that less harsh forms of corporal punishment, such as light spanking, are effective and unlikely to bring about negative side effects (Kazdin & Benjet, 2003). It is difficult to confirm whether spanking directly causes long-term negative mental health issues. There are many variables in play. However, meta-analysis of research in this area indicates weak or nonexistent relationships between corporal punishment and long-term problems (Ferguson, 2013). A final important point is that although punishment may suppress an unwanted behavior temporarily, it alone does not teach which behaviors are appropriate. As a general rule, punishment of any kind is most effective when combined with reinforcement of an alternative, suitable response. Table 6.6 offers some general guidelines for maximizing the effects of punishment and minimizing negative side effects.

Module **6.2** Summary

6.2a Know . . . the key terminology associated with operant conditioning:

avoidance learning
continuous reinforcement
discriminative stimulus
escape learning
extinction
fixed-interval schedule
fixed-ratio schedule
negative punishment
negative reinforcement
operant conditioning
partial (intermittent) reinforcement
partial reinforcement effect
positive punishment
positive reinforcement
primary reinforcer
punisher
punishment
reinforcement
reinforcer
schedules of reinforcement
secondary reinforcer
shaping
variable-interval schedule
variable-ratio

6.2b Understand . . . the role that consequences play in increasing or decreasing behavior.

Positive and negative reinforcement increase the likelihood of a behavior, whereas positive and negative punishment decrease the likelihood of a behavior. Positive reinforcement and punishment involve adding a stimulus to the situation, whereas negative reinforcement and punishment involve removal of a stimulus.

6.2c Understand . . . how schedules of reinforcement affect behavior.

Schedules of reinforcement can be fixed or variable, and can be based on intervals (time) or ratios (the number of responses). In contrast to continuous reinforcement, intermittent schedules tend to elicit vigorous responding. Our tendency to link our behavior to reinforcement is particularly evident when it comes to superstition—where a ritual is believed to bring about reinforcement, regardless of whether it actually does.

6.2d Apply . . . your knowledge of operant conditioning to examples.

The activity "applying terms of reinforcement and punishment" in Table 6.4 provided some opportunity to practice. Some rules of thumb: Does the response in question increase or decrease as a result of the consequence? If the behavior increases, then reinforcement is involved. Does it increase because something pleasurable is made available after the behavior occurs? Then this is an example of positive reinforcement. If responding results in something unpleasant being taken away, then negative reinforcement is involved. Punishment occurs when the response decreases as a result of a consequence. Adding a stimulus (e.g., scolding) to decrease a behavior describes positive punishment, and removing a stimulus (e.g., taking away privileges) to decrease a behavior describes negative punishment.

6.2e Analyze . . . the effectiveness of punishment on changing behavior.

Many psychologists recommend that people rely on reinforcement to teach new or appropriate behaviors. The issue here is not that punishment does not work, but rather that there are some notable drawbacks to using punishment as a means to change behavior. For example, punishment may teach individuals to engage in avoidance or aggression, rather than developing an appropriate alternative behavior that can be reinforced.

Module 6.2 Quiz Operant Conditioning

Know . . .

1. _____ removes the immediate effects of an aversive stimulus, whereas _____ removes the possibility of an aversive stimulus from occurring in the first place.
   A. Avoidance learning; escape learning
   B. Positive reinforcement; positive punishment
   C. Negative reinforcement; negative punishment
   D. Escape learning; avoidance learning

Understand . . .

2. As a consequence for misbehaving, many teachers use "timeout." How does this consequence affect students' behavior?
   A. It adds a stimulus that is rewarding to decrease bad behavior.
   B. It takes away a stimulus that is rewarding to decrease bad behavior.
   C. It adds a stimulus that is punishing to increase bad behavior.
   D. It takes away a stimulus that is punishing to increase bad behavior.

3. Pete cannot seem to stop checking the change slots of vending machines. Although he usually does not find any money, occasionally he finds a quarter. Despite the low levels of reinforcement, this behavior is likely to persist due to _____.
   A. escape learning
   B. the partial reinforcement effect
   C. positive punishment
   D. generalization

Apply . . .

4. Frederick trained his parrot to open the door to his cage by pecking at a lever three times. Frederick used a _____ schedule of reinforcement to train the desired behavior.
   A. variable interval
   B. variable-ratio
   C. fixed interval
   D. fixed-ratio

Analyze . . .

5. Which statement is most accurate in regard to using spanking as a form of corporal punishment?
   A. Spanking *can* be an effective method of punishment but carries risks of additional negative outcomes.
   B. Spanking is an effective method of punishment and should always be used.
   C. Spanking is not an effective method of punishment, so it should never be used.
   D. The effects of spanking have not been well researched, so it should not be used.

Module 6.3   Cognitive and Observational Learning

Learning Objectives

6.3a Know . . . the key terminology associated with cognitive and observational learning.

6.3b Understand . . . the concept of latent learning and its relevance to cognitive aspects of learning.

6.3c Apply . . . principles of learning to make your own learning experiences more effective.

6.3d Analyze . . . the claim that viewing violent media increases violent behavior.

Are you smarter than a chimpanzee? For years psychologists have asked this question about all of us, but in a more nuanced way. More specifically, they have tested the problem-solving and imitative abilities of chimpanzees and humans to help us better understand what sets us apart, and what makes us similar to other animals. Chimps and humans both acquire many behaviors from observing others, but imagine if you pitted a typical human preschooler against a chimpanzee. Who do you think would be the best at learning a new skill just by watching someone else perform it? Researchers Victoria Horner and Andrew Whiten asked this question by showing 3- and 4-year-old children how to retrieve a treat by opening a puzzle box, and then they demonstrated the task to chimpanzees. But there was one trick

thrown in: As they demonstrated the process, the researchers added in some steps that were unnecessary to opening the box. The children and chimps both figured out how to open it, but the children imitated all the steps—even the unnecessary ones—while the chimps skipped the useless steps and went straight for the treat (Horner & Whiten, 2005). What can we conclude from these results? Maybe it is true that both humans and chimps are excellent imitators, although it appears the children imitated a little too well, while the chimps imitated in a smarter manner. Certainly, we both share an ability to learn through observation—which is a complex cognitive ability. Here we ask what role do cognitive factors play in learning? And which processes are required for imitation to occur?

The types of learning covered in Modules 6.1 and 6.2 emphasized relatively simple relationships between stimuli and responses, and avoided making reference to an organism that was doing the *thinking* part of the learning process. When John Watson, B. F. Skinner, and other behavioral psychologists of the time were conducting their research, they assumed that "thought" was unnecessary for a scientific account of how stimuli and responses are related. However, since the 1950s and continuing today, psychologists have incorporated cognitive processes such as thinking and remembering into theories and explanations for how we learn (Spence, 1950; Holland, 2008).

Cognitive Perspectives on Learning

Since the mid-20th century and the rise of the cognitive perspective, psychologists began advocating that mental phenomena (e.g., expectation, attention) supported learning. The traditional behaviorists focused on stimulus input and response output. However, the cognitivists sought to test hypotheses that residing between stimulus and response was an organism with a capacity to think—that is, stimulus inputs and cognitive processes both played a causal role in determining how organisms behaved. Although once at polar opposites, behavioral and cognitive approaches to learning are now quite integrated, as evidenced in modern studies of learning (Kirsch et al., 2004; Rescorla, 1988, 1991).

THE PAST PREDICTS THE FUTURE: COGNITIVE PROCESSES AND CONDITIONING Cognitive accounts of classical and operant conditioning maintain that learning in animals and people involves the development of new *expectancies*, or, beliefs that something will happen in the future. A cognitive account of operant conditioning states that the organism learns to expect that a certain response will result in a specific outcome or reinforcer (e.g., *If I order Chinese food from Restaurant X, I expect that it will be delivered in 20 minutes or less*, which in turn reinforces ordering food from this particular restaurant). In classical fear conditioning the organism expects that when one stimulus occurs (e.g., a tone), another will follow (shock).

Pavlov's experiments illustrated how classical conditioning involves pairing a conditioned stimulus such as a tone with an unconditioned stimulus of food, resulting in the conditioned response of salivation to the tone alone (Module 6.1). When it comes to the real world, however, learning is rarely so simple. Tones might occur in the absence of food, and food might be available with or without tones. Classical conditioning occurs if an organism recognizes that there is a consistent relationship between the two stimuli. In other words, an association can form if the conditioned stimulus is a *reliable* predictor of the unconditioned stimulus (Rescorla, 1968; Rescorla & Wagner, 1972). It seems that humans are sensitive to the degree to which stimuli are associated and respond only if there is consistency in their relationship. The same is true for rats. Rats show more fear in response to a tone that occurs with shocks 100% of the time than do rats that experience tones and shocks that occur together only 50% of the time (see Figure 6.14).

LATENT LEARNING Much of human learning involves absorbing information and then demonstrating what we have learned through a performance task, such as taking a quiz. Psychologist Edward Tolman proposed that humans, and even rats, express **latent learning**—*learning*

Figure 6.14 CS-US Relationships Predict Conditioning

In 12 trials (see top figure), Rat A hears a tone that is followed by a shock every time. Rat B also receives 12 shocks, but hears the tone preceding it in only 50% of the trials. Even though tones are always followed by shocks for both rats, Rat A will show a stronger conditioned response to the tones (bottom figure).

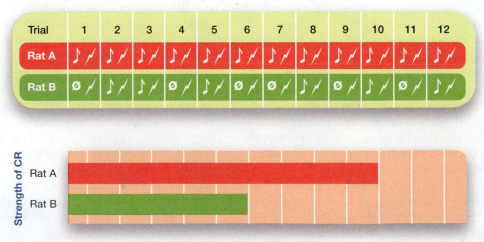

that is not immediately expressed by a response until the organism is reinforced for doing so. Tolman and Honzik (1930) demonstrated latent learning in rats running a maze (see Figure 6.15). The first group of rats could obtain food if they navigated the correct route through the maze. They were given 10 trials to figure out an efficient route to the end of the maze, where food was always waiting. A second group was allowed to explore the maze, but did not have food available at the other end until the 11th trial. A third group (a control) never received any food while in the maze. It might seem that only the first group—the one that was reinforced on all trials—would learn how to best shuttle from the start of the maze to the end. After all, it was the only group that was consistently reinforced. This is, in fact, what happened—at least for the first 10 trials. Tolman and Honzik discovered that rats that were finally rewarded on the 11th trial quickly performed as well as the rats that were rewarded on every trial (see Figure 6.15). It appears that this second group of rats was learning after all, but only demonstrated their knowledge when they received reinforcement worthy of quickly running through the maze.

If you put yourself in the rat's shoes—or perhaps paws would be more appropriate—you will realize that humans experience latent learning as well. Consider a familiar path you take to work or school. There is probably a spot along the route that you have never visited, simply because there is no reason—perhaps it is a vacant storefront. But imagine you discover one day that a fantastic and inexpensive new restaurant opened up in that spot. You would have no trouble finding it in the future because you have an understanding of the general area. Tolman and Honzik assumed that this process held true for their rats, and they further hypothesized that rats possess a *cognitive map* of their environment, much like our own cognitive map of our surroundings. This classic study is important because it illustrates that humans (and rats) acquire information in the absence of immediate reinforcement and that we can use that information when circumstances allow.

SUCCESSFUL LONG-TERM LEARNING AND DESIRABLE DIFFICULTIES
Unlike rats, we have the ability to think about and reflect on strengths and weaknesses in how we learn. Specifically, we can identify what works and what does not work and adjust our learning strategies accordingly.

While we have remarkable *capacities* to keep track of what we have learned and know, as well as what we do not yet know, we do not always tap into these capacities very well. All too often we study and learn in ways that provide only short-term effects, and very little improvement over time (Schmidt & Bjork, 1992; Bjork, Dunlosky, & Kornell, 2013). We have at least three expectations about our individual learning:

- We want clarity about what to learn or do.
- We want very noticeable results.
- We want it all to happen very fast.

Figure 6.15 Learning without Reinforcement

Tolman and Honzik (1930) placed rats in the start box and measured the number of errors they made en route to the end box. Rats that were reinforced during the first 10 days of the experiment made fewer errors. Rats that were reinforced on day 11 immediately made far fewer errors, which indicates that they were forming a cognitive map of the maze, even though reinforcement was not available during the first 10 trials for this group.

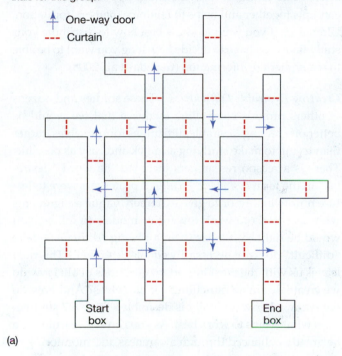

(a)

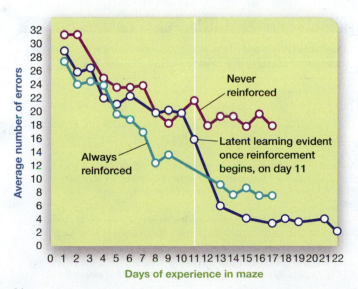

(b)

Let's say you have a vocabulary quiz for your German language class in the next few hours, but you haven't been studying for it—even though you have known about it for a week. Chances are you will cram for it. You might read through the items of your study guide repeatedly, testing yourself as you go. You might learn the first set of words easily, so you move quickly on to the next set; you continue this way with each set of words you get right. This approach *might* get you through the quiz you need to take in the next hour, but it probably will not help you get through a conversation with a native speaker when you fly out to Germany next week.

We like techniques such as cramming because they are easy and quick, and they seem to be effective. In reality, though, they merely trick us into thinking that we have learned more—or better—than we have. In other words, getting results fast usually causes us to overestimate how well we will remember things in the long run. To really remember and understand something, learning should be a little more difficult—but it should be the right kind of difficult (Bjork & Bjork, 2011; Schmidt & Bjork, 1992). *Desirable difficulties* are situations that make acquiring new knowledge more challenging and with benefits that are less obvious in the short term. At the same time, desirable difficulties promote long-term learning and the ability to apply the information to new and unique situations. Next, we will discuss two applications of desirable difficulties.

Organization Versus Rearrangement At the end of the term students typically complete course evaluations that almost always ask whether the professor was clear. Students tend to like their course work laid out clearly and logically, so a question about clarity seems to make sense. But is clarity *always* a good thing? In one study, half of the students in a college course received lecture outlines that fit the lecture perfectly, whereas the other half of the students received outlines that were scrambled. After the lecture, students were quizzed on their retention for the material. On recognition and cued-recall tests, the students with the organized notes did better. So does that mean students are right in wanting perfect clarity? Not necessarily. On the hard questions—which required inferring the meaning of material or solving

problems—the students with the scrambled lecture notes performed better. In other words, the scrambled notes led to more effortful studying and, therefore, more meaningful learning (Mannes & Kintsch, 1987; see also Rohrer, 2012).

Total Time Versus Distributed Practice Students are invariably busy people, and most probably engage in some degree of procrastination; this in turn leads to cramming. So which of the following result in better learning: Studying 4 hours the night before an exam or studying in four 1-hour sessions in the days leading up to the exam? In nearly 200 scientific articles describing more than 300 experiments, distributing study time has proven much better than cramming (Cepeda et al., 2006). There is not a clear consensus among psychologists as to why this is so, but spreading out study sessions across time seems to provide more opportunities to link concepts together and helps to reinforce memory formation. Ultimately, if you want to know best how to distribute your study time, you have to decide how long you want to be able to remember the information (Cepeda et al., 2008).

Creating Desirable Difficulties These studies and dozens of others provide compelling evidence that we would be better off creating desirable difficulties for ourselves, rather than trying to make studying as quick and easy as possible. There is a reason researchers included the word "desirable" in the term *desirable difficulty*: If professors were to lecture unintelligibly, or to give extremely vague assignments with no criteria to work toward or models to follow, you would be right to criticize them for being "difficult"—here "difficult" does not necessarily equal "desirable." This then leaves us with the most important questions of all: How do we create desirable difficulties for ourselves? And how do we know when a difficulty is desirable? Table 6.7 summarizes what seems to work best. As you can see, learning can be greatly enhanced through awareness and monitoring of your own experiences.

JOURNAL PROMPT

Desirable Difficulties: How would you implement the concepts and strategies of desirable difficulties to improve your own learning?

Table 6.7 Three Tips for Creating Desirable Difficulties to Promote Learning

Determine the purpose of learning.	On the one hand, if you are learning a three-item grocery list, there is no need to make it difficult. On the other hand, if you are learning a skill for a hobby (e.g., playing guitar) or if you need to remember information for your job (e.g., rules for filing reports), then you will probably want to achieve a thorough understanding.
Consider changing the order.	If you are learning a song on an instrument, do not start at the beginning every time—start halfway through, or one-fourth of the way. If you are learning vocabulary through flashcards, shuffle the order of the words. To learn about more complex ideas—perhaps how nerve cells work—approach the process from a different order each time.
Distribute your learning.	Practicing or studying for four hours can produce varying results, depending on how you spend those four hours. Longer-lasting learning will result if your learning is distributed over a few short study sessions, rather than cramming all at once. Also, you might try the spacing effect: gradually increase the intervals between learning sessions, but start with short ones.

Observational Learning and Imitation

Not all learning requires direct experience. So much of what humans and many nonhuman species learn comes from observing others. And this is a good thing. Can you imagine if modern surgeons had to learn by trial and error? Who on earth would volunteer to be the first patient?

Observational learning *involves changes in behavior and knowledge that result from watching others*. Humans have elaborate cultural customs and rituals that spread through observation. The cultural differences we find in dietary preferences, clothing styles, athletic events, holiday rituals, music tastes, and so many other customs exist because of observational learning. Socially transmitting behavior is an efficient approach; indeed, it is the primary way that adaptive behavior spreads so rapidly within a population, even in nonhuman species (Heyes & Galef, 1996; Gariépy et al., 2014). Before setting off in search of food, rats smell the breath of other rats. They will then search preferentially for food that matches the odor of their fellow rats' breath.

Human children are also very sensitive to social cues about what they should avoid. Curious as they may be, even young children will avoid food if they witness their parents reacting with disgust toward it (Stevenson et al., 2010). For observational learning to occur, and for behavior to be successfully transmitted from one person to the next, some key processes need to be in place.

PROCESSES SUPPORTING OBSERVATIONAL LEARNING Albert Bandura identified four processes involved in observational learning: *attention* to the act or behavior, *memory* for it, the *ability to reproduce it,* and the *motivation* to do so (Figure 6.16). Without any one of these processes, observational learning would be unlikely—or at least would result in a poor rendition of the behavior. Furthermore, research indicates that observational learning is most effective when we first observe, practice immediately, and continue practicing soon after acquiring the response. For example, one study found that the optimal way to develop and maintain motor skills is by repeated observation before and during the initial stages of practicing (Weeks & Anderson, 2000). It appears that watching someone else helps us practice effectively, and allows us to see how errors are made. When we see a model making a mistake, we know to examine our own behavior for similar mistakes (Blandin & Proteau, 2000).

Even rats have a special way of socially transmitting information. Without directly observing what other rats have eaten, rats will smell the food on the breath of other rats and then preferentially search for this food. To humans, this practice may not seem very appealing—but for rats, using breath as a source of information about food may help them survive. By definition, a breathing rat is a living rat, so clearly the food the animal ate did not kill it. Living rats are worth copying.

Figure 6.16 Processes Involved in Observational Learning
For observational learning to occur, several processes are required: attention, memory, the ability to reproduce the behavior, and the motivation to do so.

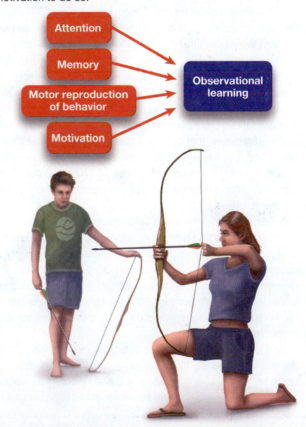

In addition to observational learning, observational punishment is also possible, but appears to be less effective at changing behavior than reinforcement. Witnessing others experience negative consequences may decrease one's chances of copying someone else's behavior. Even so, people are sometimes surprisingly bad at learning from observational punishment. Seeing the consequences of smoking, drug abuse, and other risky behaviors does not seem to prevent many people from engaging in the same activities.

One of the primary mechanisms that allows observational learning to take place is **imitation**—*re-creating a motor behavior or expression, often to accomplish a specific goal.* From a very young age, infants imitate the facial expressions of adults (Meltzoff & Moore, 1977). Later, as they mature physically, toddler and children readily imitate motor acts produced by a model, such as a parent,

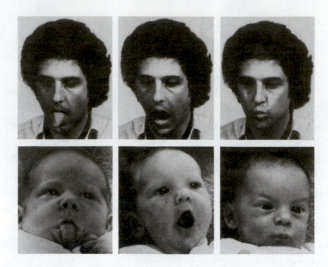

At just a few days of age infants will imitate the facial expressions of others (Meltzoff & Moore, 1977).

Myths in Mind

Teaching Is Uniquely Human

Teaching is a significant component of human culture and a primary means by which information is learned in classrooms, at home, and many other settings. But are humans the only species with the ability to teach others? Some intriguing examples of teaching-like behavior have been observed in nonhuman species (Thornton & Raihani, 2010; Skerry et al., 2013). Prepare to be humbled.

Teaching behavior was discovered in ants (Franks & Richardson, 2006)—probably among the last species we might suspect would demonstrate this complex ability. Nevertheless, it was discovered that "teacher" ants gave "pupil" ants feedback on how to locate a food source. In another example, field researchers studying primates discovered the rapid spread of potato washing behavior in Japanese macaque monkeys (Kawai, 1965). Imo—perhaps one of the more ingenious monkeys of the troop—discovered that potatoes could be washed in salt water, which also may have given them a more appealing taste. Potato washing behavior subsequently spread through the population, especially among the monkeys that observed the behavior in Imo and her followers.

Transmission of new and unique behaviors typically occurs between mothers and their young (Huffman, 1996). Chimpanzee mothers, for example, actively demonstrate to their young the special skills required to crack open nuts (Boesch, 1991). Also, mother orcas appear to show their offspring how to beach themselves (Rendell & Whitehead, 2001), a behavior that is needed for the type of orca that feeds on seals that congregate along the shoreline.

In each of these examples, it is possible that the observer animals are imitating the individual who is demonstrating a behavior. These observations raise the possibility that teaching may not be a uniquely human endeavor.

Primate researchers have documented the spread of potato washing in Japanese macaque monkeys across multiple generations. Monkeys appear to learn how to do this by observing experienced monkeys from their troop.

Is this killer whale teaching her offspring to hunt for seals? Researchers have found evidence of teaching in killer whales and a variety of other nonhuman species.

teacher, or friend. This ability seems to be something very common among humans.

Recall that at the beginning of this module, we raised the topic of human imitation—namely, how children, in contrast to chimpanzees, may imitate *beyond* what is necessary. Psychologists have found that both children from industrialized regions of Australia and children from remote non-industrialized communities in Africa over-imitate the actions of adults who model how to open a contraption using a variety of sticks, switches, and knobs. The adult demonstrating the actions involved in opening the box added irrelevant, unnecessary steps to the process—many of which the children were compelled to imitate (Nielsen & Tomaselli, 2010). Perhaps humans are so wired and motivated to learn from others that evolution has given us, but not nonhumans, the tendency to over-imitate.

MEDIA EFFECTS ON LEARNING AND BEHAVIOR The topic of observational learning raises questions about the effects that modern media (e.g., television, music, video games, Internet) may have on our behavior. A classic study by social psychologist Albert Bandura (1961, 1963) was among the earliest attempts to formally conduct an experiment to find out whether children who observe the aggressive acts of others are in turn more prone to behave aggressively.

Groups of children watched an adult or cartoon character attack a "Bobo" doll, while another group of children watched adults who did not attack the doll. Children who watched adults attack the doll did likewise when given the opportunity, in some cases even imitating the specific attack methods used by the adults. The other children did not attack the doll. This provided initial evidence that viewing aggression makes children at least temporarily more prone to committing aggressive acts toward an inanimate object

Bandura's work was a good starting point, but many questions remain as to whether the words and behavior of celebrities, or the fictional characters we control in video games influence our behavior. Policies for ratings systems and warnings for movies, television, music, and video games stem from the combined efforts of parents, politicians, the judicial system, and the entertainment industry. The efforts made by these parties clearly indicate strong concerns that media exposure directly affects behavior.

Working the Scientific Literacy Model

Video Gaming and Behavior

"Grand Theft Auto," "Manhunt," "Mortal Kombat."… These are just a few of the violent video games that have soared in popularity, as well as both negative and positive attention. News media, as well as some politicians, have been quick to

name violent video games as a major cause of the brutal violence that has occurred in the real world. This is, however, not a new concern. Video games were blamed for causing societal decay long before the advent of the extreme graphic violence, HD visual displays, and the explosive audio that make today's video games appear so realistic. Ever since, psychological scientists have been attempting to answer complex questions about the relationship between video gaming and behavior.

What do we know about video gaming and behavior?

First, consider some observations about video game use. Gaming is no longer just a child or adolescent obsession. It has become an adult obsession too, with some people spending more money on gaming than they do on theater tickets. Among the most popular video games are the extremely violent ones such as "Call of Duty: Modern Warfare" and, as earlier noted, "Grand Theft Auto" (the fifth version generated $1 billion in sales just three days after its release). Given the popularity of these games, and the amount of time people spend playing them, it comes as little surprise that many people are quick to conclude that violent video game playing is *causing* people, particularly younger children and adolescents, to behave violently. Recall the 1999 school shootings at Columbine High School: The two people who murdered 12 students and one teacher were fans of "Doom," a first person-shooter game popular during that time. Recall also the 2012 school shootings in Newton, Connecticut: Adam Lanza, who murdered 20 school children and six adults, was also a player of violent video games. The news media, politicians, and even the National Rifle Association (NRA) were quick to suggest that violent video games played a significant role in these horrible acts. There is a lot at stake when it comes understanding any potential effects that video gaming has on behavior.

How can science explain whether gaming affects aggression or violence?

All too often we overlook the possibility that the games individuals choose to play *reflects* their personality and behavior, rather than causes it. And so researchers ask, are violent video games the *cause*, or are they an *effect*, of aggressive behavior? Bandura's early work on how children's behavior is affected when they observe aggression has been followed by decades of experiments and correlational studies—all of which have attempted to answer this question.

In one study undergraduate students were randomly assigned to play either a violent video game (e.g., "Mortal Kombat") or a nonviolent one (3-D pinball) alone for 20 minutes. After each group played their assigned game, they

In Albert Bandura's experiment, children who watched adults behave violently toward the Bobo doll were aggressive toward the same doll when given the chance—often imitating specific acts that they viewed.

then sat down in a room to complete a questionnaire. In the background, the experimenters played an audio recording of a staged fight in which one of the parties was heard being physically injured. Those who had just played the violent video game were slower to leave the room to help the injured party; they also rated the fight as less severe than those who played the nonviolent game (Bushman & Anderson, 2009). Experimenters using a similar methodology have concluded that violent video gaming can actually desensitize gamers to violence (Anderson & Bushman, 2001; Bushman & Anderson, 2007).

Can we critically evaluate this research?

It is quite a stretch to suggest that these findings could account for such real-world violence as school shootings. Another way to address a complex question such as this one is to compile the dozens of experiments conducted into a *meta-analysis*, which allows researchers to test many different possible variables. For example, much of the experimental work on the relationship between video gaming and violence was conducted on college students. However, a more pressing concern has been on whether younger children, who are possibly more vulnerable to the effects of media exposure, are negatively affected by violent video game play. One recent meta-analysis that tested this and other variables revealed very weak or non-existent relationships between violent video gaming and

aggression, helping behavior, depression, and attention deficit problems among youths and adults (Ferguson, in press). Even in instances where exposure to violent media and aggressive behavior are correlated, at least two very important questions remain. First, does exposure to violence *cause* violent behavior or desensitization to violence? Second, does early exposure to violence turn children into violent adolescents or adults? Unfortunately, there are no simple answers to either question, due in large part to investigators' reliance on correlational designs, which are typically used for studying long-term effects. Recall that correlational studies can establish only that variables are related, but cannot determine that one variable (media) causes another one (violent behavior). Scholars continue to debate this issue and often arrive at different interpretations and conclusions (Ferguson & Kilburn, 2009; Gentile et al., 2014; Groves, Anderson, & DeLisi, 2014). However, it is likely that news media and other nonscientific sources frequently overstate the role that violent video games could possibly play in aggressive or violent acts by young people.

Why is this relevant?

Many organizations have stepped in to help parents make decisions about which type of media their children will be exposed to. The Motion Picture Association of America has been rating movies, with violence as a criterion, since 1968. Violence on television was being monitored and debated even before the film industry took this step. Since the 1980s, parental advisory stickers have been appearing on music with lyrics that are sexually explicit, reference drug use, or depict violence. Even more recently, due to a drastic upsurge in their popularity and sophistication, video games have been labeled with parental advisory stickers. The financial interests of the entertainment industry and the more relevant concerns of parents are at stake. In 2011 the US Supreme Court ruled that regulating violent video game sales violates free speech protections, and also that scientific study has not yet given sufficient basis for concluding that violent gaming is harmful to young people (*Brown v. Entertainment Merchants Association*; Ferguson, 2012). This issue will likely remain hotly debated for many years to come.

Module **6.3** Summary

6.3a   Know . . . the key terminology associated with cognitive and observational learning:

imitation
latent learning
observational learning

6.3b   Understand . . . the concept of latent learning and its relevance to cognitive aspects of learning.

Behavioral psychologists of decades ago argued that learning cannot occur in the absence of reinforcement. However, Tolman and Honzik showed that rats can form "cognitive maps" of their environment. They found that even when no immediate reward was available, rats still learned about their environment.

6.3c   Apply . . . principles of learning to make your own learning experiences more effective.

Understanding and using the concepts and suggestions described in this module should reap rewards. Be sure to review the strategies described in Table 6.7 and also apply them to your own experiences by responding to the journal prompt about desirable difficulties found in this section.

6.3d   Analyze . . . the claim that viewing violent media increases violent behavior.

Psychologists agree that observational learning occurs and that media can influence behavior. Many studies show a correlational (noncausal) relationship between violent media exposure and aggressive behavior. Also, experimental studies, going all the way back to Albert Bandura's work of several decades ago, indicate that exposure to violent media can at least temporarily increase aggressive behavior. However, there is no consensus that violent media, such as video games, cause or are even strongly associated with aggression and violence.

Module **6.3** Quiz

Know . . .

1. _____ create(s) situations that make acquiring new knowledge more challenging and with benefits that are less obvious in the short term.
   A. Classical conditioning
   B. Operant conditioning
   C. Latent learning
   D. Desirable difficulties

2. Observational learning:
   A. is the same thing as teaching.
   B. involves a change in behavior as a result of watching others.
   C. is limited to humans.
   D. is not effective for long-term retention.

Understand . . .

3. Contrary to some early behaviorist views, _____ suggests that learning can occur without any immediate behavioral evidence.
   A. classical conditioning
   B. operant conditioning
   C. latent learning
   D. desirable difficulties

Apply . . .

4. To learn most effectively, you should _____ your study time and study material in _____ order.
   A. distribute; a different
   B. distribute; the same
   C. mass (cram); a different
   D. mass (cram); the same

Analyze . . .

5. Which is the most accurate conclusion from the large body of research that exists on the effects of viewing media violence?
   A. Viewing aggression directly causes increased aggression and desensitization to violence.
   B. Viewing aggression does not cause increased aggression and desensitization to violence.
   C. Viewing aggression is related to increased aggression and desensitization to violence.
   D. Viewing aggression is not related to increased aggression and desensitization to violence.

Module **6.4** Scientific Literacy Challenge: Corporal Punishment

There are situations in which learning theory is used to exert influence over behavior, from training your dog to encouraging employees to be more productive. But how do we select the most effective ways to influence behavior, and how far is too far? Here we examine corporal punishment (spanking) and whether there is sufficient enough evidence supporting it as an effective way to raise well-behaved, psychologically healthy children.

Before you start this activity, write a paragraph or two about your own childhood experiences.

JOURNAL PROMPT

How did your parents and other caregivers reinforce good behavior and discourage inappropriate behavior? What was most effective in shaping your behavior?

What do we know about corporal punishment?

The following article was written by a staff reporter for a major newspaper. Although she does not claim to be a psychologist or other type of scientist, the story requires that she first introduce the controversial topic of corporal punishment and then report on key data regarding its effectiveness and outcomes. As you read, pay close attention to the relevant boldfaced key terms from Chapter 6.

> ### Canadian Medical Journal Seeks to Repeal Nation's "Spanking Law"
>
> **By Celina Holiday, staff reporter**
>
> The editors of the *Canadian Medical Association Journal* (CMAJ), one of Canada's biggest medical journals, are arguing to repeal the nation's "spanking law." The law, which protects parents who use corporal punishment, has been in effect for 120 years. But John Fletcher, the editor-in-chief of CMAJ, cited a recent meta-analysis of research associating spanking with various negative outcomes. In his statements, Fletcher called physical **punishment** an "anachronistic excuse for poor parenting" and argued that aggression is not "an appropriate response to frustration." In contrast, **positive reinforcement** can be used to **shape** more appropriate behavior while modeling a calmer, more rational approach to discipline. If Fletcher and his colleagues have their way, Canada would join the more than 30 countries that have already banned corporal punishment in the home.

It is important to note that Fletcher is addressing only one type of discipline: corporal punishment. He is not trying to argue against punishment or discipline in general. Read on to find out what led Fletcher and his colleagues to this opinion.

How do scientists study the effects of corporal punishment?

This is not the first time people have publically spoken out against corporal punishment. When it does come up, there are usually some very strong opinions on both sides of the debate. That being the case, Fletcher and the other editors of CMAJ, as well as the staff reporter covering the issue, will need to provide some very convincing evidence. As you read on, make sure to pay close attention to the highlighted portions that emphasize scientific concepts.

Fletcher reiterated the importance of scientific evidence in his call to ban corporal punishment. In the peer-reviewed research, many studies reach the same conclusion: spanking is not very effective in changing behavior patterns and it is associated with negative consequences such as increased risk for legal problems and mental illness. As an example, one survey compared the responses of individuals in the probation system with other members of the general public who did not have a record of probation or incarceration. That study reported substantial evidence linking corporal punishment with depression, substance abuse, and aggressive behavior. In fact, individuals on probation were nearly three times as likely to report being disciplined with spanking during childhood. Further, more severe punishments were related to more severe substance abuse issues. "Surely any bias should be toward protecting children, who are the most vulnerable," writes Fletcher.

Although this is certainly not all of the evidence available to researchers or the general public about corporal punishment, it should capture the main points of the journal editors' and reporter's argument. See if you can identify the key scientific concepts in the article, and then test yourself with the quiz below.

1. One study showed that the severity of punishments were related to the severity of substance abuse. This implies that the researchers used a _____ design to find this result.
   a. correlational
   b. experimental
   c. natural observation
   d. random assignment
2. On the newspaper's website, one reader left the comment, "I wouldn't be surprised about people being so against physical punishment if you were talking about beating your kids, but a little spanking isn't going to turn anyone into a monster." If the reporter had included _____, this reader would better understand the long-term effects of spanking.
   a. the dependent variable
   b. the operational definition of corporal punishment
   c. the sample
   d. the independent variable
3. When the researchers compared two groups of people—those who received corporal punishment as children versus those who did not—they were conducting a quasi-experiment. Why do you suppose they did not conduct a true experiment?
   a. It would take too long to study.
   b. A true experiment would not tell them anything more than a quasi-experiment could.
   c. They would not be able to find a large enough population to study.
   d. It would be unethical to randomly assign children to the necessary experimental conditions (e.g., at least one in which the participants would be spanked).

Answers: 1. a 2. b 3. d

A meta-analysis, which Fletcher presented to make his case, can provide a great deal of support for an argument because it summarizes not one, but dozens of studies. Still, we should not accept the argument that corporal punishment causes lasting harm without thinking critically about the evidence, as we will do next.

How do we think critically about corporal punishment?

The reporter concludes by adding various views on corporal punishment. As shown in the paragraph below, not everyone she interviewed thought critically about the issue, however.

> There certainly are those who have come out in defense of the law. As one lawmaker put it, "Parents know what they are doing, it doesn't take a doctor to tell them how to raise their kids." A great deal of public opinion is on his side as well, with one of the most common responses to the polls being "I was spanked as a child, and I turned out alright." But if you think those arguments have appeal, don't tell that to Terence Burke of the Child Safety Alliance of West Ontario: "The research shows that spanking your kids will cause them to have problems later. For some, that feels like depression, and for others, it means doing drugs."

The reporter has found a variety of opinions, but public opinion is not always based on critical thinking. The statements below will help you identify some critical thinking skills you should practice, and common errors you should be able to recognize and avoid. Match the following statements to the highlighted passages that illustrate them.

1. An individual confuses correlation with cause and effect.
2. Many people rely too much on anecdotal evidence.
3. Someone ignores the evidence and makes an appeal to common sense.

1. Yellow 2. Blue 3. Green

It appears that individuals this reporter quoted let their prior opinions shape how they interpret the evidence. Some are too eager to ignore the data, which are quite strong, while another over-interpreted the data, assuming cause-and-effect. Let's read on to see how the research on corporal punishment is relevant.

How is corporal punishment relevant?

The research on corporal punishment is obviously relevant for parents, but it's also relevant for anyone working with children, such as teachers and camp counselors, who may need to use discipline to ensure they are safe and well-behaved. Read how this reporter sums up Fletcher and his colleagues' beliefs, then share any newly formed thoughts you may have about corporal punishment.

> The medical journal editors will concede that it remains unknown as to whether corporal punishment actually causes so many negative outcomes, but they do have overwhelming evidence for its correlation with psychological and legal problems. "Ask 50 people in jail or on probation about their punishments as kids and compare it to another 50 people without a record," Fletcher suggests. "It's been done a hundred times. The same group of people always reports corporal punishment at home; usually two or three times as often."
>
> That may be the case, but as long as corporal punishment is protected by law, the individual parent—that could even mean you—gets to decide how best to discipline a child.

SHARED WRITING

After reading this article, are you persuaded that corporal punishment can cause psychological and legal problems? If you had a say in the legal case, what would you do?

Chapter 6 Quiz

1. In classical conditioning, a(n) _____ becomes a(n) _____, which elicits a response.
   A. neutral stimulus; conditioned stimulus
   B. neutral stimulus; unconditioned stimulus
   C. unconditioned stimulus; conditioned stimulus
   D. unconditioned stimulus; neutral stimulus

2. Most mornings, Misoo listens to her favorite song as she gets ready for work, which includes putting in her contacts. One afternoon, Misoo hears her favorite song playing, and her eyes start watering—something that usually happens only when she put her contacts in. If this is an example of classical conditioning, what is the unconditioned stimulus?
   A. Eye watering
   B. Misoo's contacts
   C. Contact lenses applied to the eye
   D. Getting ready for work

3. An important distinction between classical and operant conditioning is that:
   A. classical conditioning involves voluntary responding, while operant conditioning involves involuntary responding.
   B. classical conditioning involves reinforcement, while operant conditioning involves punishment.
   C. classical conditioning involves cognitive learning, while operant conditioning involves associative learning.
   D. responding does not affect the presentation of stimuli in classical conditioning, but in operant conditioning responding has consequences.

4. The word "negative" in the term negative reinforcement refers to:
   A. the removal of a stimulus.
   B. an unwanted conditioned behavior.
   C. the use of punishment.
   D. the use of inappropriate stimuli.

5. A rat is conditioned to press a lever for food. One day a food pellet jams in the automatic feeder and the rat no longer receives food after pressing the lever. After a few minutes, the rat eventually stops pressing the lever. This is an example of:
   A. negative reinforcement.
   B. extinction.
   C. classical conditioning.
   D. avoidance learning.

6. All other things being equal, an animal trained on which of the following schedules of reinforcement should experience extinction most quickly when the reinforcement is removed?
   A. Fixed-interval schedule
   B. Continuous schedule
   C. Variable-ratio schedule
   D. Variable-interval schedule

7. In general, studying is more effective when:
   A. desirable difficulties are present.
   B. the information is organized in outlines that can quickly be reviewed several times.
   C. the total amount of studying time is short.
   D. all of the studying occurs in one long session.

8. A once neutral stimulus that elicits a conditioned response because it has a history of being paired with an unconditioned stimulus is known as a(n) _____.
   A. unconditioned response
   B. conditioned stimulus
   C. conditioned response
   D. unconditioned response

9. A dental drill can become an unpleasant stimulus, especially for people who may have experienced pain while one was used on his teeth. In this case, the pain elicited by the drill is a(n) _____.
   A. conditioned response
   B. unconditioned stimulus
   C. conditioned stimulus
   D. unconditioned response

10. What is the reoccurrence of a previously extinguished conditioned response, typically after some time has passed since extinction?
    A. Extinction
    B. Spontaneous recovery
    C. Acquisition
    D. Discrimination

11. Your dog barks every time a stranger's car pulls into the driveway, but not when you come home. Reacting to your car differently is a sign of _____.
    A. discrimination
    B. generalization
    C. spontaneous recovery
    D. acquisition

12. A television advertisement for beer shows young people at the beach drinking and having fun. Based on classical conditioning principles, the advertisers are hoping you will buy the beer because the commercial elicits:
    A. a conditioned emotional response of pleasure.
    B. a conditioned emotional response of fear.
    C. humans' natural preparedness toward alcohol consumption.
    D. a taste aversion to other companies' beers.

13. A basic need such as food may be used as a _____ reinforcer, whereas a stimulus whose value must be learned is a _____ reinforcer.
    A. primary; continuous
    B. secondary; shaping
    C. primary; secondary
    D. continuous; secondary

14. Shaping is the process of:
    A. reinforcing a series of responses that approximate the desired behavior.
    B. decreasing the likelihood of a behavior.
    C. reinforcing the basic motivational needs of a subject.
    D. punishing a series of responses that you want to increase.

15. _____ is the replication of a motor behavior or expression, often to accomplish a specific goal.
    A. Observational learning
    B. Latent learning
    C. Imitation
    D. Cognitive mapping

Chapter 7
Memory

Module 7.1 Memory Systems

 ## Learning Objectives

7.1a Know . . . the key terminology of memory systems.

7.1b Understand . . . which structures of the brain are associated with specific memory tasks and how the brain changes as new memories form.

7.1c Understand . . . the methods psychologists use to study the components of memory.

7.1d Apply . . . your knowledge of the brain basis of memory to predict what types of damage or disease would result in certain types of memory loss.

7.1e Analyze . . . the claim that humans have multiple memory systems.

Hugh Armstrong, 72, was vacationing with his family in New Hampshire in the summer of 2012. One morning, he went out for a walk near Stinson Lake but then never returned. He went missing for more than 2 weeks. All he remembers is wandering out of the woods with no idea who he was or where he should go. He hitchhiked and walked for 1,000 miles south of the state, eventually stopping in Pennsylvania to help a local farmer pitch hay. The farmer drove him to Virginia after Hugh told him he thought he was from North Carolina

and possibly from Asheville. In Asheville, Hugh still had no recollection of his former life, until he overheard someone in a local McDonald's say the name "Emma"; he realized he had a niece with that name. Although bits and pieces of memory returned, not enough returned to help him reestablish his identity. Eventually, a deputy spotted Hugh walking along a highway at 1:30 AM and was able to identify him from a missing persons report. Hugh was approximately 240 miles away from his home located just outside of Raleigh. Deputies contacted his wife and daughter, and as soon as they drove up to the sheriff's department, Hugh recognized the car. When his wife stepped out, he immediately smiled and said, "That's my wife!" Hugh's story is definitely an unusual one, and it leads many to ask how someone might forget the most fundamental things about himself.

You have probably heard people talk about memory as if it were a single ability:

- I have a terrible memory!
- Isn't there some way I could improve my memory?

But have you ever heard people talk about memory as if it were several abilities?

- One of my memories works well, but the other is not so hot.

As you will learn in this module, memory is actually a collection of several systems that store information in different forms for differing amounts of time (Atkinson & Shiffrin, 1968).

The Atkinson-Shiffrin Model

In the 1960s, Richard Atkinson and Richard Shiffrin reviewed what psychologists knew about memory at that time and constructed the memory model that bears their name (Figure 7.1). The first thing to notice about the Atkinson-Shiffrin model is that it includes three memory stores. **Stores** *retain information in memory without using it for any specific purpose*; they essentially serve the same purpose as hard drives serve for a computer. The three stores include sensory memory, short-term memory (STM), and long-term memory (LTM), which we will investigate in more detail later. In addition, **control processes** *shift information from one memory store to another*; these processes are represented by the arrows in the model.

Information enters the sensory memory store through vision, hearing, and other senses, and the control process we call *attention* selects which information it will pass on to STM. To keep information in STM, it is repeated in a process called *rehearsal*. Some of this information then goes through **encoding**, *the process of storing information in the LTM system*. **Retrieval** *brings information from LTM back into STM*; this happens when you become aware of existing memories, such as what you did last week. In this module, we are primarily concerned with the various types of memory stores, so next we will examine each one in detail.

SENSORY MEMORY   **Sensory memory** *is a memory store that accurately holds perceptual information for a brief amount of time*—how brief depends on which sensory system we talk about. Sensory memory holds *iconic memory*, the visual form of sensory memory, for about 0.5 to 1 second. *Echoic memory*, the auditory form of sensory memory, is held for considerably longer, but still only about 5 seconds (Cowan et al., 1990). Because these forms of memory last for such a brief period, precise techniques and measurements are required to study them, such as the partial-report technique (see Figure 7.2; Sperling, 1960).

Sensory memory is not just a curious laboratory finding; rather, it functions to hold information long enough for us to determine what to pay attention to (the first control process in the Atkinson-Shiffrin model). If not for iconic sensory memory, our visual experience would probably be similar to that of looking around a room with a strobe light flashing; everything would appear to be a series of isolated and still images. Instead, iconic sensory memory holds images long enough to provide smooth, continuous perceptions. Echoic memory is equally important. Have you ever experienced the "What? Oh!" phenomenon? Someone asks you a question and you say, "What?" only to realize that you still have the person's voice in echoic memory, and suddenly you say "Oh!" and answer the question.

Figure 7.1 The Atkinson-Shiffrin Model

Memory is a multistage process. Information flows through a brief sensory memory store into short-term memory, where rehearsal keeps the information active until it is encoded in long-term memory for permanent storage. Memories are retrieved from long-term memory and brought into short-term storage for further processing.

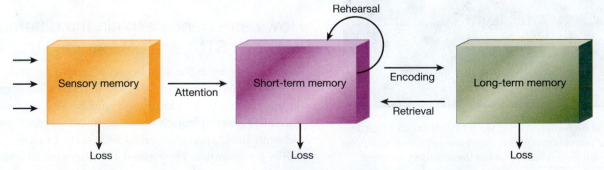

Figure 7.2 A Test for Iconic Sensory Memory

Sperling's participants viewed a grid of letters flashed on a screen for a split second, then attempted to recall as many of the letters as possible. In the whole report condition (a), they averaged approximately four items, usually from a single row. However, the partial report condition (b) indicated that participants could remember far more than four letters, as long as they were cued within 1–2 seconds before the memory faded. Participants could usually name any row of four items, depending on the row they were cued to recite.

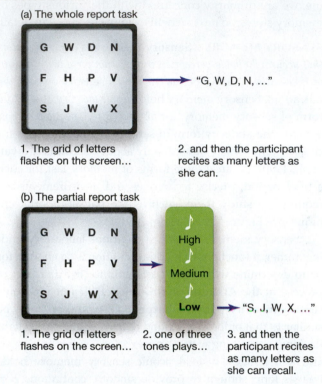

(a) The whole report task

1. The grid of letters flashes on the screen...

2. and then the participant recites as many letters as she can.

(b) The partial report task

1. The grid of letters flashes on the screen...

2. one of three tones plays...

3. and then the participant recites as many letters as she can recall.

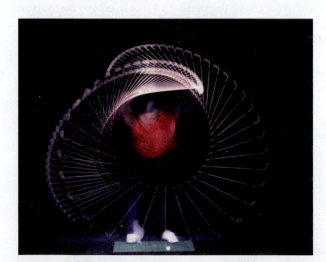

Each time the strobe light flashes, we get a distinct still image. In more typical perceptual experiences, we see continuous movement rather than still images because of our iconic sensory memory.

Distinguishing Short-Term from Long-Term Memory Stores

Sperling's research identified a brief memory system, one that you may have never noticed that you had. After we pay attention to specific stimuli in sensory memory, selected information moves into two types of longer-lasting memory systems, the short-term and long-term memory stores.

What do we know about short-term and long-term memory stores?

A major distinction in memory systems is between **short-term memory (STM)**, *a memory store with limited capacity and duration (less than a minute)*, and **long-term memory (LTM)**, *a memory store that holds information for extended periods of time, if not permanently*. The distinction between STM and LTM can be revealed with a simple experiment. Imagine everyone in your psychology class studied a list of 15 words and then immediately tried to recall the words in the list. The serial position curve—the U-shaped graph in Figure 7.3—shows what the results would look like according to **the serial position effect**: *In general, most people will recall the first few items from a list and the last few items, but only an item or two from the middle*. This finding holds true for many types of information, ranging from simple strings of letters to the ads you might recall after watching the Super Bowl (Laming, 2010; Li, 2010).

The first few items are remembered relatively easily (known as the *primacy effect*) because they have begun the process of entering LTM. They then begin to produce **proactive interference**—*that is, the first information learned (e.g., in a list of words) occupies memory, leaving fewer resources free to remember the newer information*. Yet, we also remember the last few items because they still reside in our STM—a pattern referred to as the *recency effect*. The last few items on the list create **retroactive interference**—*that is, the most recently learned information overshadows some preceding memories that have not yet made it into LTM*.

How can science explain the difference between STM and LTM stores?

The evidence from the serial position curve suggests that STM and LTM are distinct systems. To further support this argument, however, scientists should be able to spot the different systems through brain scans. This is exactly what Deborah Talmi and colleagues (2005) set out to look for in one of their studies. They asked 10 volunteers to undergo

Figure 7.3 The Serial Position Effect

Memory for the order of events is often superior for initial items (the primacy effect) and later items (the recency effect). The serial position effect provides evidence of distinct short-term and long-term memory stores.

memory testing during functional magnetic resonance imaging (fMRI) brain scans. These participants studied a list of 12 words presented one at a time on a computer screen. Next, the computer screen flashed a word and the participants had to determine whether the word was from their study list. Researchers were mostly concerned about the brain activity that occurred when the volunteers correctly recognized words. When volunteers remembered information from early in the serial position curve, the hippocampus was active (this area is associated with the formation of LTM, as you will read about later). By comparison, the brain areas associated with sensory information—hearing or seeing the words—were more active when people recalled items at the end of the serial position curve. Thus, the researchers believed they have isolated the effects of two different neural systems that, working simultaneously, produce the serial position curve.

Can we critically evaluate the distinction between STM and LTM?

You may remember from Module 1.1 of Chapter 1 that parsimony is an important scientific principle; it suggests that we should not use more complex explanations if a simpler one garners the same amount of support from experiments. This is certainly relevant when researchers suggest that there might be two types of memory when one system would be much simpler. So, in addition to the serial position effect, what justifies a multisystem approach? Certainly the neuroscience data from Talmi and colleagues contribute to the multistore argument. But there are other types of data as well. For example, when individuals make errors in recalling lists of words, they almost always make rhyming mistakes for the last few items. It appears that they have not had time to store meaning yet. In contrast, people do the opposite for items closer to LTM; they tend

to make mistakes involving meaning, such as substituting a synonym. Evidence like this is different from what a brain scan can show, and yet it contributes more support to the idea of a multisystem model.

Why is this relevant?

This information about multiple memories and the serial position effect also applies to healthy memory functioning, so consider what implications it has for you as a student. If you studied the key terms from this module in alphabetical order, which ones would you be most likely to forget? We might expect that you would remember the first few words (thanks to the primacy effect) as well as the last few words (thanks to the recency effect). Your knowledge of the terms in the middle of the list would suffer, however. Fortunately, we are not doomed to fall victim to serial position effects: Perhaps you could avoid the problem by constantly shifting the order in which you study the key terms.

The Working Memory Model: An Active STM System

Imagine you are driving a car when you hear the announcement for a radio contest—*the 98th caller at 1-800-555-HITS will win $98*! As the DJ shouts out the phone number, you do not have a pen or a phone handy, and traffic is swarming, so what do you do? You will probably try to remember the number by using **rehearsal**, *or repeating information (in this case, the number) until you do not need to remember it anymore*. Psychological research, however, demonstrates that remembering is much more than just repeating words to yourself. In fact, memory is now viewed as a complex system involving several processes.

Working memory *is a model of short-term remembering that includes a combination of memory components that can temporarily store small amounts of information for a short period of time*. This includes new information such as the specific phone number that will win $98 for you, as well as keeping track of the traffic patterns. Working memory can also draw from older information that is stored in a relatively stable way: the fact that you know what a phone is, how to operate one, and that $98 translates into roughly eight large pizzas.

The working memory model for short-term remembering can be subdivided into three storage components (Figure 7.4), each of which has a specialized role (Baddeley, 2012; Jonides et al., 2005):

- The **phonological loop** *is a storage component of working memory that relies on rehearsal and stores information as sounds (known as an auditory code)*. It engages some

Figure 7.4 Components of Working Memory Work Together to Manage Complex Tasks

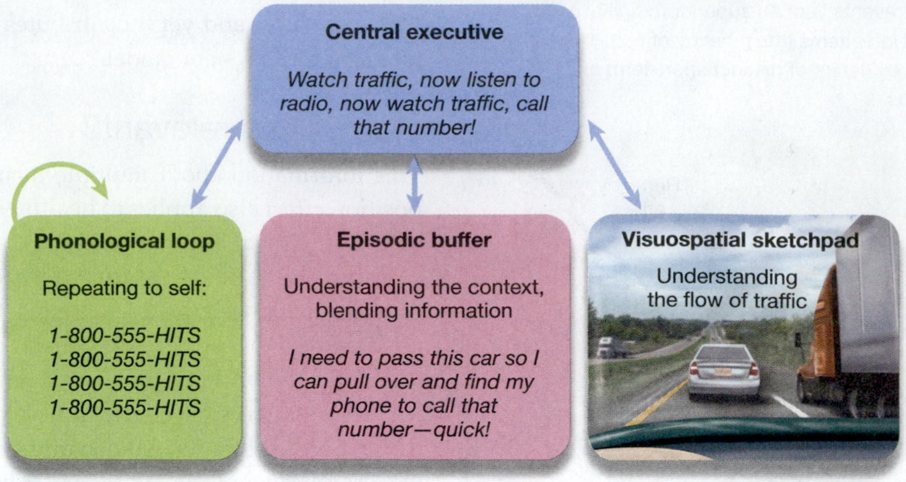

Central executive

Watch traffic, now listen to radio, now watch traffic, call that number!

Phonological loop

Repeating to self:

*1-800-555-HITS
1-800-555-HITS
1-800-555-HITS
1-800-555-HITS*

Episodic buffer

Understanding the context, blending information

I need to pass this car so I can pull over and find my phone to call that number—quick!

Visuospatial sketchpad

Understanding the flow of traffic

portions of the brain that specialize in speech and hearing, and it can be active without affecting memory for visual and spatial information.

- The **visuospatial sketchpad** *is a storage component of working memory that maintains visual images and spatial layouts in a visuospatial code.* It keeps you up to date on where objects are around you and where you intend to go. To do so, the visuospatial sketchpad engages portions of the brain related to perception of vision and space and does not affect memory for sounds.

- Recent research suggests that working memory also includes an **episodic buffer**—*that is, a storage component of working memory that combines the images and sounds from the other two components into coherent, story-like episodes.* These episodes include the relevant information to make sense of the images and sounds, such as "I was driving to a friend's house when I heard the radio DJ give a number to call."

Finally, working memory includes one component that is not primarily used for storing information. Instead, the **central executive** *is the control center of working memory; it coordinates attention and the exchange of information among the three storage components.* It does so by seeking out what is relevant to the person's goals, interests, and prior knowledge. For example, when you see a series of letters from a familiar alphabet, it is easy to remember the letters by rehearsing them in the phonological loop. In contrast, if you were to look at letters or characters from a foreign language—perhaps you are visiting Seoul and you do not know Korean—you may not be able to convert them to sounds; thus you would assign them to the visuospatial sketchpad instead (Paulesu et al., 1993). Regions within the frontal lobes of the brain are responsible for carrying out these tasks for the central executive.

So how does this system work for you when you cannot pull your car over immediately to place the 98th call? Most of us would rely on our phonological loop, repeating the number to ourselves until we can call. Meanwhile, our visuospatial sketchpad is remembering where other drivers are in relation to our car, even as we look away to check the speedometer, the rearview mirror, or the volume knob. Finally, the episodic buffer binds together all this information into episodes, which might include information such as "I was driving to school," "the DJ announced a contest," and "I wanted to pull over and call the station." In the middle of all this activity is the central executive, which guides attention and ensures that each component is working on the appropriate task.

Psychologists have long been curious about the dimensions of memory, asking questions about how much information a memory store can hold and for how long. As you will see, measuring memory is not as simple as counting off seconds on a stopwatch. How much and how long one can remember are affected by the specific information that is being remembered. Therefore, as we address questions of how much and how long, we will need to understand the methods used to make these measurements.

THE DIMENSIONS OF STM The capacity of STM was summed up by one psychologist as *The Magical Number 7 ± 2* (Miller, 1956). In his review, Miller found study after study in which participants were able to remember seven units of information, give or take a couple. Another researcher made the analogy between STM and a juggler who can keep seven balls in the air before dropping any of them. Similarly, STM can rehearse only seven units of information at once before forgetting something (Nairne, 1996).

This point leads to an important question: What, exactly, is "a unit of information"? It turns out that, whenever possible, we expand our memory capacity with

chunking, *organizing smaller units of information into larger, more meaningful units.* Consider these examples:

1. O B A N C N C H C S N C B N S
2. N B C H B O C B S A B C C N N

If we randomly assigned one group of volunteers to remember the first list, and another group to remember the second list, how would you expect the two groups to compare? Before answering, make sure you look carefully at both lists. Volunteers reading list 2 have the advantage of being able to apply patterns that fit their background knowledge; specifically, they can chunk these letters into five groups based on major television networks:

2a. NBC HBO CBS ABC CNN

In this case, chunking reduces 15 bits of information to a mere 5. Now think back to the example of the radio contest. Can you remember the 11-digit phone number? If so, it is almost certainly because you remembered it in 3 chunks, just as the DJ presented it: (*1-800*), (*555*), and (*HITS*).

THE PHONOLOGICAL LOOP The Magical Number 7 provides a good estimate of STM capacity in general, but to focus more precisely on phonological memories, we must consider how long it takes to pronounce the items. Based on the word-length effect, we know that people remember more one-syllable words (*sum, pay, bar,…*) than four- or five-syllable words (*helicopter, university, alligator,…*) in a short-term task (Baddeley et al., 1975). Despite the fact that both bar and alligator are single chunks of information, you remember more chunks if they are single syllables. Research indicates that working memory can store as many syllables as can be rehearsed in about 2 seconds.

Now that we have explored how much information STM can hold, let's move on to how long STM can hold it. The *Brown-Peterson test* (Brown, 1958; Peterson & Peterson, 1959) was one of the first techniques for measuring the duration of STM. This test relies on two main elements—meaningless stimuli and interference. In this test, to ensure that participants are relying solely on working memory and not chunking, they must first read a trigram (an unpronounceable series of three letters—the meaningless stimuli) that is not associated with anything in LTM. Immediately after reading each trigram, they must then read a three-digit number—counting backward by threes each time. This interference prevents rehearsal. The participants continue to do this until the experimenter says, "Stop." With these particular kinds of stimuli and interference, most of the forgetting takes place within 15 to 18 seconds. Thus, the duration of the phonological memory is believed to be approximately 15 seconds.

THE VISUOSPATIAL SKETCHPAD When using the Brown-Peterson task for phonological memory, researchers present test materials that do not sound like familiar words.

Figure 7.5 Working Memory Binds Visual Features into a Single Chunk

Working memory sometimes stores information such as shape, color, and texture as three separate chunks, like the three pieces of information on the left. For most objects, however, it stores information as a single chunk, like the box on the right.

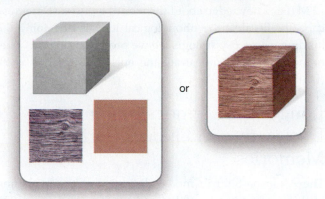

Likewise, psychologists studying visual and spatial memory often use images that do not resemble familiar objects. Recall that the phonological store can be gauged at several levels—that is, in terms of the number of syllables, the number of words, or the number of chunks. Similarly, items stored in visuospatial memory can be counted based on shapes, colors, and textures. This leads to an important question: Can a smooth, square-shaped, red block count as one chunk? Or do texture, shape, and color of the block act as three separate bits of information? Research has consistently shown that a square-shaped block painted in two colors is just as easy to recognize as the same-shaped block painted in one color (Vogel et al., 2001). Therefore, visuospatial working memory may use a form of chunking. However, this process of combining visual features into a single unit goes by a different name, *feature binding* (see Figure 7.5).

After visual feature binding, visuospatial memory can accurately retain approximately four whole objects, regardless of how many individual features one can find on those objects. Perhaps this is evidence for the existence of a second magical number—four (Awh et al., 2007; Vogel et al., 2001).

To put feature binding into perspective, consider the amount of visual information available to you when you are driving a car. If you are at the wheel, watching traffic, you probably would not look at a car in front of you and remember images of red, shiny, and smooth. Instead, you would simply have these features bound together in the image of the car, and you would be able to keep track of three or four such images without much problem as you glance at the speedometer and then back to the traffic around you.

THE EPISODIC BUFFER The episodic buffer seems to hold 7 to 10 pieces of information, which may be combined with other memory stores. This aspect of its operation can be demonstrated by comparing memory for prose (words strung into sentences) to memory for unrelated words. When people are asked to read and remember meaningful prose, they usually remember 7 to 10 more words than when reading a random list of unrelated words. Some portion of working memory is able to connect the prose with LTM (i.e., knowledge about the world) to increase memory capacity. Because the phonological loop is not doing the binding, some psychologists have proposed that this phenomenon may demonstrate the episodic buffer at work (Baddeley, 2012).

Long-Term Memory Systems: Declarative and Nondeclarative Memories

The Atkinson-Shiffrin model discussed at the beginning of this module suggests that humans have only one LTM system. However, just as working memory has subcomponents, LTM can be divided as well. First, we can distinguish between memories that one is aware of versus those that do not require awareness (Figure 7.6). Some have referred to this distinction as the difference between "knowing how and knowing that." Specifically, **declarative memories** *are memories that we are consciously aware of and can be verbalized, including facts about the world and one's own personal experiences.* These memories include a vast range of information, from knowing that you had breakfast this morning to knowing that a penguin is a bird, albeit a funny kind of bird.

Nondeclarative memories *include actions or behaviors that you can remember and perform without awareness.* For example, these memories might consist of **procedural memories**: *patterns of muscle movements (motor memory) such as how to walk, play piano, or shift gears while driving.* Classical conditioning (described in Module 6.1) is another type of nondeclarative memory because people can be classically conditioned without awareness. Although declarative and nondeclarative memories are distinct types of memory, both are involved in the same day-to-day events. You might know how to ride a bike, which is an example of a nondeclarative procedural memory, but knowing that bikes are two-wheeled vehicles is a declarative memory.

Declarative memory comes in two varieties (Tulving, 1972). **Episodic memories** *are declarative memories for personal experiences that seem to be organized around "episodes" and are recalled from a first-person ("I" or "my") perspective.* **Semantic memories** *are declarative memories that include facts about the world.* Going back to the bicycle example, your semantic memory is your knowledge of what a bike is, whereas episodic memory is the memory of when you first (or last) rode a bike, a specific ride that was enjoyable to you, or the time you rode into a fence. These memories involve bicycles, but episodic memories are specific instances about you and your bike.

Scientific evidence that semantic and episodic memories are distinct comes from several different sources. First, as people get older, their episodic memory declines more rapidly than their semantic memory (Craik & Rose, 2012). Older people are more likely to forget the story from a novel their book club discussed last year than they are to forget something like the names of state capitals. Psychologists have even studied cases like Hugh Armstrong's (discussed at the beginning of this module) in which an individual has lost episodic memory, yet his semantic memory store remained.

Although some technical debates focus on the difference between knowing *how* and knowing *that*, most psychologists agree that declarative memory can be divided into episodic and semantic levels. Such a distinction helps us better understand how memories break down following brain trauma or through conditions such as Alzheimer's disease, as we will address later in this chapter.

Figure 7.6 Varieties of Long-Term Memory

Long-term memory can be divided into different systems based on the type of information that is stored.

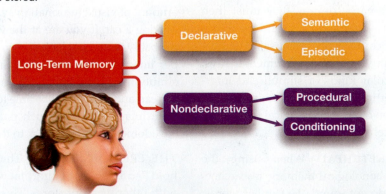

The Cognitive Neuroscience of Memory

The research on the cognitive neuroscience of memory is not independent of what you have read so far; as you may recall from the research on the serial position effect, memory models generally account for both what is remembered as well as how the brain supports the memory. In addition, the models help us understand what happens when memory breaks down after brain injuries or through disease.

THE BRAIN BASIS OF MEMORY   Memories begin at the microscopic level with **long-term potentiation (LTP)**, *an enduring increase in connectivity and transmission of neural signals between nerve cells that fire together.*

Although it is long-term by name, LTP is not necessarily permanent, and by itself, it cannot account for memories that may last days, weeks, or even years. Lasting memories require **consolidation**, *the processes that convert short-term memories into long-term memories in the brain.* When LTP continues long enough or, even better, often enough, the neurons will adapt and make the changes more permanent through a process called *cellular consolidation* (Mednick et al., 2011). Without the consolidation process, the changes of LTP either revert back to normal or are replaced by new patterns, effectively preventing further encoding. To demonstrate this effect, researchers administered laboratory rats a drug that allowed LTP, but blocked the biochemical actions that lead to consolidation. The animals were able to learn a task for a brief period, but they were not able to form long-term memories. By comparison, rats in the placebo group went through the same tasks and formed long-term memories without any apparent problems (Squire, 1986).

LTP is just the beginning of, not the permanent home for, the new memory. Instead, long-term declarative memories are distributed throughout the cortex of the brain (Paller, 2004). The move from temporary storage to LTM involves a limbic system structure called the *hippocampus* and the process of *systems consolidation* (Figure 7.7; Mednick et al., 2011). The hippocampus appears to maintain LTP until the acquired information can form multiple connections resulting in a memory spread across a vast network of cells (Shimamura, 2014). Interestingly, once memories reach this long-term stage, neither the original site of LTP nor the hippocampus appear to be necessary to store that memory.

Figure 7.7 The Hippocampus

The hippocampus resides within the temporal lobe and is critical for memory processes.

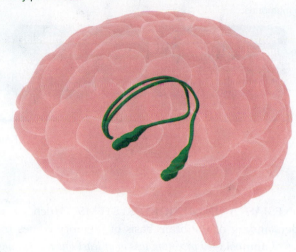

The hippocampus seems to bridge the short-term storage of LTP and the long-term storage following consolidation. This has been observed in many laboratory studies including the study by Deborah Talmi and colleagues (2005); they found that older memories, but not the newest ones, activated the hippocampus. Without a functioning hippocampus, information would never make it to LTM. This is the case for binge drinkers (someone consuming four or five drinks in one sitting) because alcohol's effects on the hippocampus are quite pronounced. Individuals who experience blackouts will have virtually no recollection of what happened while they were intoxicated, yet show no effects on those memories that had already been consolidated prior to the blackout (Schummers & Browning, 2001; White, 2003).

Researchers in London found that the hippocampi of cab drivers, who navigate the complex maze of the city, are larger than the hippocampi of non-cab drivers (Maguire et al., 2000). It is not certain whether people with a larger hippocampus are more likely to take up cab driving, or whether the cab driving increases the size of the hippocampus. Nevertheless, this finding underscores the importance of the hippocampus in memory processes.

Figure 7.8 Retrograde and Anterograde Amnesia

The term *amnesia* can apply to memory problems in both directions. It can wipe out old memories, and it can prevent consolidation of new memories.

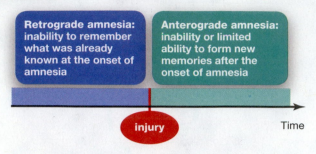

AMNESIAS AND MEMORY SYSTEMS Much of our understanding of the brain basis of memory comes from cases of **amnesia**—*a profound loss of at least one form of memory.* Cases of amnesia vary greatly in terms of severity and duration. They also vary according to which parts of the brain are affected, so understanding memory models also helps explain why some systems can be severely affected, whereas others seem to function as usual.

Retrograde amnesia *is a condition in which memories for the events preceding trauma or injury are lost* (Figure 7.8). The amnesia is most devastating for recent events, that is, events for which consolidation has just begun. For example, someone who experienced a concussion during a football game might remember the day before just fine, but have no recollection of what happened that morning. In contrast, anterograde amnesia is the inability to form new memories for events occurring after a brain injury. Imagine a person who experienced anterograde amnesia after a stroke 10 years ago. Even with deliberate effort, he may not be able to form new memories, not even for significant events. For example, someone living with anterograde amnesia may not recall that he has moved to an assisted living facility or that there is now a different president of the United States.

Case studies allow for detailed descriptions of specific phenomena, and the most famous amnesia patient in psychology is Henry Molaison (referred to as H. M. until his passing in 2008). In 1953 surgeons removed H. M.'s hippocampus and some surrounding regions to quell his epileptic seizures. In the ensuing five decades following his surgery dozens of studies have been conducted on H. M. that have contributed to our understanding of the brain basis of memory and memory-related disorders.

Knowing that the hippocampus facilitates consolidation, you should anticipate that H. M. experienced profound **anterograde amnesia**—he was virtually *unable to move information from STM to LTM* (Figure 7.8). To a lesser extent, he experienced retrograde amnesia for more recent memories from adulthood, but not his earlier years. One intriguing aspect of H. M.'s memory was that his amnesia severely affected his declarative memory, and yet could learn to solve puzzles that test nondeclarative memory. One puzzle involved tracing a shape using only the mirror image of his hand to guide his movements, which he was able to learn to do even though he could not remember the task or any of his testing sessions (episodic memory; Gabrieli et al., 1993). H. M. retained some ability to form semantic memories. For example, he was able to remember the names of celebrities who rose to fame after his surgery, although even in this case he required quite a bit of repetition and the use of first names as cues (O'Kane, Kensinger, & Corkin, 2004).

The takeaway is this: Memory models help us understand or even predict the memory loss following brain damage; the most severely affected is episodic memory followed by semantic memory. Meanwhile, nondeclarative memories may not be affected at all. Also, we know the hippocampus is critical to the consolidation of declarative memories. If it is injured, one result will be moderate retrograde amnesia, that is, memories for events undergoing consolidation process will be weak or lost. In contrast, older events that have already moved into cross-cortical storage will be stored as long-term memories. Practice applying the terms "retrograde" and "anterograde" amnesia to examples in Table 7.1.

Table 7.1 Read the Following Scenarios and Predict What and How Memory Loss Will Occur in Each.

Refer to the summary objective 7.1d on page 225 to check your answers.

Dr. Richard trains a rat to navigate a maze, and then administers a drug that blocks the biochemical activity involved in long-term potentiation. What will happen to the rat's memory? Will it become stronger? Weaker? Or is it likely the rat will not remember the maze at all?

In another study, Dr. Richard removes a portion of the rat's hippocampus the day after it learns to navigate a maze. What will happen to the rat's memory? Will it become stronger? Weaker? Or will it be unaffected by the procedure?

Module 7.1 Summary

7.1a   Know . . . the key terminology of memory systems:

amnesia
anterograde amnesia
central executive
chunking
consolidation
control process
declarative memory
encoding
episodic buffer
episodic memory
long-term memory (LTM)
long-term potentiation (LTP)
nondeclarative memory
phonological loop
proactive interference
procedural memory
rehearsal
retrieval
retroactive interference
retrograde amnesia
semantic memory
sensory memory
serial position effect
short-term memory (STM)
stores
visuospatial sketchpad
working memory

7.1b   Understand . . . which structures of the brain are associated with specific memory tasks and how the brain changes as new memories form.

The hippocampus is critical to the formation of new declarative memories. LTP at the level of individual nerve cells is the basic mechanism underlying this process. LTM stores are distributed across the cortex. Working memory uses the parts of the brain associated with visual and auditory perception, as well as the frontal lobes (for functioning of the central executive).

7.1c   Understand . . . the methods psychologists use to study the components of memory.

To test someone's memory, researchers generally present some information and, after a delay, ask research participants to tell or show them how much they can remem-

ber. However, to get at specific components of memory, researchers have to introduce new variables or procedures into the process. For example, in the Brown-Peterson task, participants study meaningless sets of letters to prevent chunking (using LTM) and they count backward by threes to prevent rehearsal. Thus, these steps isolate STM from other components of memory.

7.1d   Apply . . . your knowledge of the brain basis of memory to predict what types of damage or disease would result in certain types of memory loss.

In this module, you have learned about the distinction between STM and LTM, and the distinction between episodic and semantic memory. Once you understand how brain structures correspond to these aspects of memory, you should be able to apply your knowledge to understanding amnesia. Recall that damage to the hippocampus would most likely disrupt the formation of long-term, declarative memories. Here are the answers to the questions posed in Table 7.1.

1. If Dr. Richard blocks LTP, then the rat is unlikely to form any long-term memories. At best, they will be weak memories, and the rat will only partially remember the maze.
2. A damaged hippocampus can lead to anterograde amnesia. However, if the damage happens after the rat has committed the maze path to memory, then memory for this specific information should be unaffected by the procedure.

7.1e   Analyze . . . the claim that humans have multiple memory systems.

Consider all the evidence from biological and behavioral research, not to mention the evidence from amnesia. Data related to the serial position effect indicate that information at the beginning and end of a list is remembered differently, and even processed and stored differently in the brain. Also, evidence from amnesia studies suggests that LTM and STM can be affected separately by brain damage or disease. Most psychologists agree that these investigations provide evidence supporting the existence of multiple storage systems and control processes.

Module 7.1 Quiz

Know . . .

1. Which elements of memory do not actually store information, but instead describe how information may be shifted from one type of memory to another?
   A. Serial position effects
   B. Recency effects
   C. Primacy effects
   D. Control processes

Understand . . .

2. Chris suffered a stroke that damaged part of his hippocampus. He is likely to experience some memory loss, especially related to:
   A. retrieving semantic memories.
   B. forming new episodic memories.
   C. rehearsal.
   D. nondeclarative memories.

3. When psychologists ask research participants to remember combinations of letters (such as TJD), why might they have participants engage in distracting tasks such as counting backward by threes?
   A. Counting backward prevents rehearsal, so researchers can see how long an unrehearsed memory trace will last.
   B. Researchers try to make the participants forget.
   C. Counting backward can facilitate episodic binding.
   D. Researchers are actually interested in backward-counting ability.

Apply . . .

4. Bibi suffered a head injury during an automobile accident and was knocked unconscious. When she woke up in a hospital the next day, she could tell that she was in a hospital room, and she immediately recognized her sister, but she had no idea why she was in the hospital or how she got there. Which memory system seems to be affected in Bibi's case?
   A. Semantic memories
   B. Episodic memories
   C. Nondeclarative memories
   D. Working memories

Analyze . . .

5. Brain scans show that recently encountered items are processed in one area of the brain, whereas older items are stored in a different area. Which concept does this evidence support?
   A. Multiple memory stores
   B. A single memory store
   C. Complex control processes
   D. Retrieval

Module **7.2**   Encoding and Retrieving Memories

 ## Learning Objectives

7.2a Know . . . the key terminology related to forgetting, encoding, and retrieval.

7.2b Understand . . . how the type of cognitive processing employed can affect the chances of remembering what you encounter.

7.2c Apply . . . what you have learned to improve your ability to memorize information.

7.2d Analyze . . . whether emotional memories are more accurate than nonemotional ones.

Sixty-three seconds is all the time Nelson Dellis needs to memorize a shuffled deck of cards. How many times have you heard someone say they are bad at names? Dellis once memorized 193 names—in 15 minutes! In Module 7.1 you read that the typical person can manage around seven chunks of information, plus or minus two, in STM. For Dellis, that is just child's play. His STM capacity reaches as high as 98 digits. As it happens, Dellis has won the USA Memory Championship—the Olympics of memory games—four years since 2011 (he only made it to second place in 2013). If you are surprised that there are memory championships, then you will probably be more surprised to learn that most memory athletes do not believe that they inherited a special memory talent. Instead, they attribute their amazing performance *to specific skills and strategies that they have built up over years of practice. The basic principles of how memories are formed, as well as strategies for improving memory that college students and memory Olympians alike can use, are the central topics of this module. What causes some memories to be strong, and others to be weak? How can we improve our memory abilities?*

In this module, we explore various factors that influence the encoding and retrieval of memories. Although we cannot promise that you will make it to the Championship, we can offer research-based advice on improving your own memory—tips that every student can put to use.

Figure 7.9 The Limits of Maintenance Rehearsal

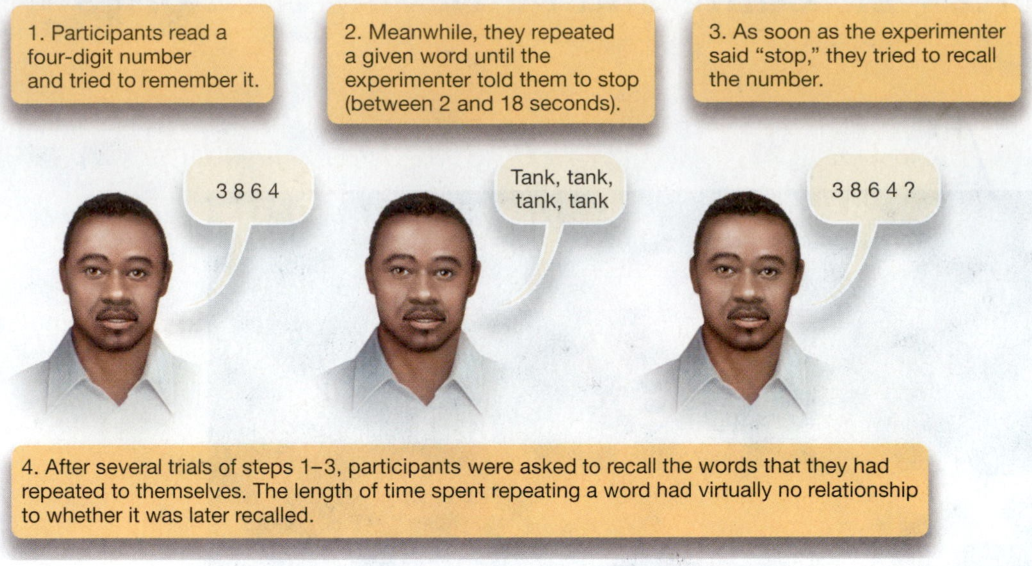

1. Participants read a four-digit number and tried to remember it.

2. Meanwhile, they repeated a given word until the experimenter told them to stop (between 2 and 18 seconds).

3. As soon as the experimenter said "stop," they tried to recall the number.

3 8 6 4

Tank, tank, tank, tank

3 8 6 4 ?

4. After several trials of steps 1–3, participants were asked to recall the words that they had repeated to themselves. The length of time spent repeating a word had virtually no relationship to whether it was later recalled.

Encoding and Retrieval

The most familiar aspects of memory are encoding, storage, and retrieval—the processes by which we acquire new memories and then recall them at a later time. In Module 7.1, you learned that encoding is the process of transforming sensory and perceptual information into memory traces, and retrieval is the process of accessing memorized information and returning it to STM. In between these two is the concept of **storage**, *which refers to the time and manner in which information is retained between encoding and retrieval*.

REHEARSAL: THE BASICS OF ENCODING Common sense suggests that there are two essential steps to encoding new memories: (1) rehearsing information for a significant length of time, and (2) intentionally trying to remember. These beliefs are evident among students who try to learn vocabulary terms by reading flashcards with key terms and definitions over and over: They rehearse the information and they intend to learn it (Figure 7.9). This type of rehearsal—often called *learning by rote*—works some of the time, but is it really the most effective way to remember? Probably not (Craik & Watkins, 1973).

Unfortunately, rehearsal itself is not very effective. Decades of research have made it clear that it is not how long we rehearse information, but rather *how* we rehearse it that determines the strength of a memory. Individuals who just repeatedly read flashcards are engaged in **maintenance rehearsal**—*prolonging exposure to information by repeating it*—which does relatively little to facilitate encoding. By comparison, **elaborative rehearsal**—*prolonging*

exposure to information by thinking about its meaning— significantly improves the process of encoding. For example, repeating the word "bottle," and then imagining what a bottle looks like, why you might need one, and how you would use it, is an elaborative technique. Although maintenance rehearsal helps us remember for a short time, elaborative rehearsal improves long-term learning and remembering. You can probably see how the two types of rehearsal are relevant to your studying. Students who simply repeat key terms and their definitions are employing maintenance rehearsal and are less likely to do well on an exam. The wise strategy is to try to elaborate on the material rather than just repeat it.

Working the Scientific Literacy Model

Levels of Processing

Elaborative and maintenance rehearsal strategies indicate that the more meaningful we make information as we learn it, the more likely we are to remember it. The different ways in which information is encoded and retrieved can be understood by considering what are called *levels of processing (LOP)*.

What do we know about levels of processing?

The LOP framework of memory begins with the understanding that encoding is most directly related to *how* information is initially processed. Additionally, but less important, is how often the information is encountered or how long one is exposed to it (Craik & Lockhart, 1972). Differences in processing can be described as a continuum from shallow processing (which is similar to maintenance rehearsal) to deep processing (which is more similar to elaborative rehearsal). Deep processing is generally the preferred method of encoding information because it is associated with better retention and retrieval.

How can science explain the LOP effect?

Psychologists study LOP effects on encoding with experimental procedures that manipulate how people process information (Craik & Tulving, 1975). For example, research participants may answer questions that require processing at various levels, ranging from very shallow (e.g., "Does this word rhyme with *dust?...TRUST*") to very deep processing (such as "Is this word a synonym for *locomotive?...TRAIN*"). At first, the participants focus solely on answering the questions; they do not expect a memory test. Later, when they are asked to recall the target words such as *trust* or *train*, they remember many more deeply processed words than shallow words. In one study, the differences ranged from recalling as few as 14% of the shallow words to 96% of the deeply processed words. In essence, they were almost 7 times more likely to recall a deep-processed word than one that was processed at only a shallow level.

Does LOP affect short-term and long-term memories in the same way? Rose and his colleagues (2010) adapted the traditional LOP task to focus on working memory processes. In their study, participants viewed a target word such as *leg* followed by a comparison screen with two words—*arm* and *beg*—written in two different colors. This procedure was repeated for a whole list of target words. The LOP was the important part of this experiment: Researchers instructed volunteers before the study began to process the comparison words in one of three ways. They were instructed to find the word that was the same color as the target word (shallow processing), to find the word that rhymed with the target word (intermediate processing), or to find the word that was meaningfully related to the target word (deep processing). Depending on the instructions they received, the volunteers processed the information at levels ranging from shallow (comparing colors) to deep (comparing meanings). If you understand the definition of LOP, you should be able to anticipate these researchers' hypothesis and results: Rose et al. (2010) predicted that more deeply processed words would be recalled from LTM, but not working memory. As you can see in Figure 7.10, the results confirmed their hypothesis.

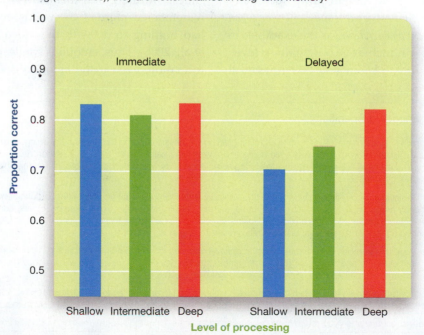

Figure 7.10 Levels of Processing Affects Long-Term but not Short-Term Memory

When tested immediately after studying words, levels of processing do not seem to affect memory. In contrast, when there is a gap between studying words and being tested, levels of processing are important. When words are encoded based on their meaning (semantics), they are better retained in long-term memory.

Can we critically evaluate this evidence?

The LOP framework has been enormously influential on memory research over the past 40 years. However, critics claim that it is simply circular reasoning, meaning that the idea of LOP does not really answer questions about memory, but rather simply provides a label. For example, one might ask, "How do we know what counts as deep processing?" We might then answer, "Whatever makes memories last longer." This response seems satisfactory at first, but what if we then ask, "What makes memories last longer?" We could simply answer, "Deep processing." To get around this problem, researchers must focus on identifying exactly what counts as deep processing and why.

How is LOP relevant?

There are all sorts of ways to think deeply about information while working, studying, or whenever you might rely on good memory. The simplest might be the self-reference effect: When you think about information as it relates to you or how it is useful to you, you will remember it better (Symons & Johnson, 1997). If the material you are learning does not apply well to you, try finding connections among the items or think of multiple ways of expressing the same information because both require you to focus on meaning.

ENCODING SPECIFICITY Encoding and retrieval might seem like opposites; one brings information in and the other takes it out, but the two processes work especially well together when they share something in common. This is illustrated by the **encoding specificity principle**, *which predicts that retrieval is most effective when it occurs in the same context as encoding.* As the examples in Table 7.2 show, context can include mood, activity level, or even characteristics of the room you are in, even if

Figure 7.11 Context-Dependent Learning

Divers who encoded information on land had better recall on land than underwater. Divers who encoded information underwater had the reverse experience, demonstrating better recall underwater than when on land.

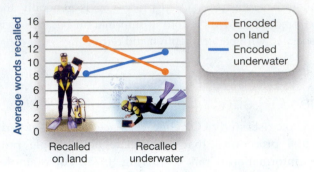

these factors are completely unrelated to the information you are learning (see Figure 7.11).

Emotional Memories

LOP describes how thinking affects retention, but emotions can also do the same. Emotions seem to lead to strong and vivid memories through cognitive and biological mechanisms (Talmi, 2013). You no doubt have your own emotional memories that you think about often and perhaps even share with others. In that sense, emotional memory is just another variety of deep processing. But emotion also influences memory biologically, without any elaborative processing. For example, in one study, participants studied a list of words and were then randomly assigned to watch a video of oral surgery (the emotional condition) or instructions on how to brush your teeth effectively (*not* the emotional condition). After the slideshow, the group members who viewed the surgery remembered more of the words even though the words had nothing to do with the video (Figure 7.12; Nielson et al., 2005). Thus, emotions can lead to stronger memory formation, even if the emotion does not lead to deeply

---

Table 7.2 Varieties of Encoding Specificity

- *Context-Dependent Learning.* Retrieval is more effective when it takes place in the physical setting (context) as encoding. In one experiment, members of a scuba club volunteered to memorize word lists—half while diving underwater, and half while on land. After a short delay, the divers were tested again, but some had switched locations. Those who were tested in the same context as where encoding took place remembered approximately 40% more items than those who switched locations (see Figure 7.11; Godden & Baddeley, 1975).

- *State-Dependent Learning.* Retrieval is more effective when your physiological state matches what you experienced during encoding. Lang and colleagues demonstrated this by presenting a group of students with a memory task in the presence of snakes or spiders, knowing that the volunteers had phobias about them. Volunteers who were in this anxiety-provoking situation both during the test *and* during the recall task did better than groups who performed either the encoding task or the retrieval task in a relaxed state (Lang et al., 2001).

- *Mood-Dependent Learning.* People remember better if their mood at retrieval matches their mood during encoding. Volunteers in one study studied images in an unpleasant or neutral mood, and then attempted to remember them in either the same or a different mood. The results indicated that if the type of mood at encoding and retrieval matched, then memory was superior (Robinson & Rollings, 2003).

- *Context-dependent forgetting* occurs when switching from one context, state, or mood to another leads you to draw a blank. Almost everyone has walked into a room to retrieve something—maybe a specific piece of mail or a roll of tape—only to find that they have no idea what they intended to pick up.

- The *context reinstatement effect* occurs when you return to the original location, state, or mood and the memory suddenly comes back.

Figure 7.12 Does Emotion Enhance Memory for Events?

Both groups remembered approximately the same percentage of words at pretest, and then watched dentistry videos unrelated to the word lists. The group whose members watched the more emotional video recalled more of the words in the end (Nielson et al., 2005).

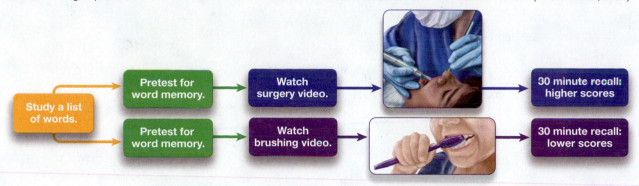

processing the original event. This link between emotions and memory may lie in the limbic system, which includes the hippocampus and amygdala. Brain imaging shows that emotional memories often activate the amygdala, whereas nonemotional memories generated at the same time do not (Sharot et al., 2007). The increased activity in the neighboring hippocampus leads to greater consolidation for whatever information might be present, even if it is just a video about brushing your teeth.

As you thought about the linkage between emotion and memory, you might have begun to recall some of your own emotional memories. Perhaps you even have a **flashbulb memory**—*an extremely vivid and detailed memory about an event and the conditions surrounding how one learned about the event* (Brown & Kulik, 1977). These can certainly be personal memories, such as the memory of where you were and what you were doing when you learned a loved one died. However, most research examines events that affect an entire society, such as the terrorist attacks of September 11, 2001 (Hirst et al., 2009). Flashbulb memories are studied over years, and so these examples may seem like the distant past to our youngest readers. However, you can probably identify

moments from the past few years that are likely to stay with you for life. For example, fans of actor Robin Williams are likely to have flashbulb memories surrounding his death in the summer of 2014. One defining feature of flashbulb memories is that people are highly confident that their recollections are accurate. But is this confidence warranted?

Forgetting and Remembering

Few people actually appreciate memory problems as much as the philosopher Friedrich Nietzsche—usually not known for looking on the bright side—who said, "The advantage of a bad memory is that one enjoys several times the same good things for the first time."

THE FORGETTING CURVE: HOW SOON WE FORGET... It might seem odd that the first scientific research on remembering actually looked at the opposite: how quickly people forget. However, this approach does make sense: Without knowledge of forgetting, it is difficult to ascertain how well we can remember. Hermann Ebbinghaus began this work by using himself as a subject and hundreds of nonsense syllables as the material. He would learn lists

Myths in Mind

The Accuracy of Flashbulb Memories

Although flashbulb memories are detailed and individuals reciting the details are highly confident of their accuracy, it might surprise you to learn that they are not necessarily more accurate than any other memories. For example, on September 12, 2001, one group of researchers asked their students to describe the moment they heard about the 9/11 terrorist attacks the day before. For a comparison event, they asked students to describe something memorable from the preceding weekend, just 2 or 3 days before the attacks. Over several months, the students were

asked to recall details of both events. Although the accuracy of their memories was fading at the same rate for both events, the students only recognized the forgetting related to the mundane events. They remained highly confident in their memories of September 11, when, in fact, those memories were not any more accurate (Talarico & Rubin, 2003). The same pattern has been found for other major flashbulb events, such as the 1986 Space Shuttle Challenger explosion and the verdict in the O. J. Simpson murder trial (Neisser & Harsch, 1992; Schmolk et al., 2000).

Figure 7.13 Ebbinghaus's Forgetting Curve

This graph reveals Ebbinghaus's results showing the rate at which he forgot a series of nonsense syllables. You can see that there is a steep decline in performance within the first day and that the rate of forgetting levels off over time.

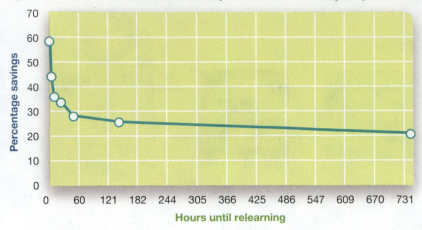

of these syllables until he could recite them twice without error, and then would give himself various amounts of time before testing his memory.

So, how soon do we forget? For Ebbinghaus, it was about half of a list in the first hour. If Ebbinghaus had continued to forget at that rate, the rest of the list should be lost after 2 hours. However, after a day, he could generally remember one-third of the material, and he could still recall between one-fifth and one-fourth of the words after a week. The basic pattern in his test results has come to be known as a *forgetting curve* (Figure 7.13). It clearly shows that most forgetting occurs right away, and that the rate of forgetting eventually slows to the point where one does not seem to forget at all. These results have stood the test of time; more than 200 articles replicated Ebbinghaus's forgetting curve in the century after they were first published (Rubin & Wenzel, 1996).

MNEMONICS: IMPROVING YOUR MEMORY SKILLS
Nietzsche made a good point about forgetting, but for those things we really need to remember, a number of ways to improve our memories exist; chances are you know some of them already. This section focuses on a few **mnemonics**—*techniques that are intended to improve memory for specific information*—that you can begin using right away.

First, an **acronym** *is a pronounceable word whose letters represent the initials of an important phrase or set of items.* For example, the word "scuba" came into being with the invention of the self-contained underwater breathing apparatus. The **first letter technique** *uses the first letters of a set of items to spell out words that form a sentence.* It is like an acronym, but it tends to be used when the first letters do not spell a pronounceable word (see Figure 7.14). One well-known example is "Every Good Boy Does Fine" for the five lines on the treble clef in musical notation: E G B D and F. Another way to remember these five lines is to use

the acronym "FACE"; F-A-C-E represent the four spaces (or letters) that come between E, G, B, D, and F.

These types of mnemonic techniques work by chunking, that is, by organizing the information into a pattern that makes more sense than the original information (chunking was discussed in Module 7.1). Acronyms have a meaning of their own, so the learner gets the benefit of both elaborative rehearsal and deeper processing.

A number of mnemonic devices are based on the premise of dual coding. **Dual coding** *occurs when information is stored in more than one form*—such as a verbal description and a visual image, or a description and a sound—and it regularly produces stronger memories than the use of one form alone (Paivio, 1991). Most children growing up in the United States learned the alphabet with the help of a song. In fact, even adults find themselves humming portions of that song when alphabetizing documents in a file cabinet. Although there are a number of ways to use images to improve verbal memory, we will focus on just

Figure 7.14 The First Letter Technique

Students of biology often use mnemonics, such as this example of the first letter technique, which helps students remember the taxonomic system.

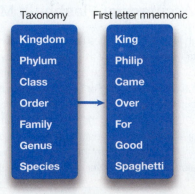

The method of loci relies on mental imagery of a familiar location or path, like this path that students take to class three times a week.

one here—the **method of loci**, *a mnemonic that connects words to be remembered to locations along a familiar path*. To use the method of loci, one must first imagine a route that has landmarks or easily identifiable spaces such as the things you pass on your way from your home to a friend's house. Once the path is identified, the learner takes a moment to visually relate the first word on the list to the first location encountered. For example, one study of waitstaff found that typical servers could recall as many as 20 dinner orders by linking the entree with a table location (method of loci), and acronyms for salad dressings (RaVoSe for a party of three would be ranch, vinegar and oil, and sesame in that order). Waiters, as well as memory researchers, will tell you that the worst thing restaurant patrons can do is switch seats because it completely disrupts the mnemonic devices used by the waiter (Bekinschtein et al., 2008).

Although these mnemonic devices can help with rote memorization, they may not necessarily improve your understanding of material. Researchers have begun to examine other memory boosters that may offer more benefits to you as a student as you prepare for exams. Recall from Module 6.3 that *desirable difficulties* can aid learning. These techniques make studying slower and more effortful, but result in better overall remembering. They include spacing out your studying rather than cramming, and studying material in varying orders.

One popular approach to studying is to use flashcards, and psychologists have identified some right ways and some wrong ways of using them. First, using the spacing effect is the right way. Applying this to flashcards means it is better to use one big stack rather than several smaller stacks; using the entire deck helps take advantage of the effect of spacing the cards. One potential problem stems from students' tendency to drop flashcards as soon as they believe they learn the material. In reality, doing so seems to reduce the benefits of overlearning the material (making it more difficult to forget) and spacing out cards in the deck (Kornell, 2009; Kornell & Bjork, 2007). No matter how you study, you should take advantage of the **testing effect**, *the finding that taking practice tests can improve exam performance, even without additional studying* (Arnold & McDermott, 2013). In fact, researchers have directly compared testing to additional studying and have found that in most cases, testing actually improves memory more (Roediger et al., 2010).

JOURNAL PROMPT

Memory in School: Think of a class other than your current psychology course. Describe how you would use the different memory phenomena and techniques (e.g., LOP, mnemonics) to maximize your preparation and memorization of the material.

Module 7.2 Summary

7.2a Know . . . the key terminology related to forgetting, encoding, and retrieval:

acronym
dual coding
elaborative rehearsal
encoding specificity principle
first letter technique
flashbulb memory
maintenance rehearsal
method of loci
mnemonics
storage
testing effect

7.2b Understand . . . how the type of cognitive processing employed can affect the chances of remembering what you encounter.

Generally speaking, the deeper the processing, the more likely something is to be remembered. Greater depth of processing may be achieved by elaborating on the meaning of the information, through increased emotional content, and through coding in images and sounds simultaneously.

7.2c Apply . . . what you have learned to improve your ability to memorize information.

The best way is to give it a try. One mnemonic device that might be helpful is the method of loci. Have someone create a shopping list for you while you prepare yourself by imagining a familiar path (perhaps the route you take to class). When you are ready to learn the list, read a single item on the list and imagine it at some point on the path. Feel free to exaggerate the images in your memory; each item could become the size of a stop sign or might take on the appearance of a particular building or tree that you pass by. Continue this pattern for each individual item until you have learned the list. Then try what Ebbinghaus did: Test your memory over the course of a few days. How do you think you will do?

7.2d Analyze . . . whether emotional memories are more accurate than nonemotional ones.

Both personal experiences and controlled laboratory studies demonstrate that emotion enhances memory. However, as we learned in the case of flashbulb memories, even memories for details of significant events decline over time, although confidence in memory accuracy typically remains very high.

Module 7.2 Quiz

Know . . .

1. Prolonging exposure to information by repeating it to oneself is referred to as _____.
    - **A.** maintenance rehearsal
    - **B.** storage
    - **C.** elaborative rehearsal
    - **D.** recall

Understand . . .

2. According to the levels of processing approach to memory, thinking about synonyms is one method of _____ processing that promotes stronger memories.
    - **A.** shallow
    - **B.** deep
    - **C.** parallel
    - **D.** state-dependent

3. One study had participants view tapes of dental surgery after studying a word list. This study concluded that:
    - **A.** emotional videos have no effect on memory.
    - **B.** emotional videos can enhance memory, but only for material related to the video itself.
    - **C.** emotional videos can enhance memory even for unrelated material.
    - **D.** emotional videos can enhance memory for related material, while reducing memory for unrelated material.

Apply . . .

4. If you wanted to remember a grocery list using the method of loci, you should:
    - **A.** imagine the items on the list on your path through the grocery store.
    - **B.** match rhyming words to each item on your list.
    - **C.** repeat the list to yourself over and over again.
    - **D.** tell a story using the items from the list.

Analyze . . .

5. Which statement best sums up the status of flashbulb memories?
    - **A.** Due to the emotional strain of the event, flashbulb memories are largely inaccurate.
    - **B.** Recall for only physical details is highly accurate.
    - **C.** Both emotion and physical details are remembered very accurately.
    - **D.** Over time, memory for details become less accurate, just as they do for non-flashbulb memories.

Module 7.3 Constructing and Reconstructing Memories

Learning Objectives

7.3a Know . . . the key terminology used in discussing how memories are organized and constructed.

7.3b Understand . . . how schemas serve as frameworks for encoding and constructing memories.

7.3c Understand . . . how psychologists can produce false memories in the laboratory.

7.3d Apply . . . what you have learned to judge the reliability of eyewitness testimony.

7.3e Analyze . . . the arguments in the "recovered memory" debate.

Imagine you saw a photograph of yourself in a situation you knew you had never been in—perhaps riding in a hot-air balloon when you were 5 or 6 years old. Would you believe the picture? More importantly, would you remember riding in the balloon, even though it never happened? Psychologist Kimberly Wade and her colleagues have been asking these questions and found some surprising answers. In summary, people who view doctored photographs and videos usually believe what they see and quite often begin to remember the imaginary event. These false memories bring up some intriguing questions. How is it possible to remember events that never happened? Do these false memories represent memory problems, or are they just a normal part of remembering?

JOURNAL PROMPT

Clarity and Accuracy: Some of our memories appear crystal clear and we seemingly relive details with perfect accuracy. Why are some memories like this, but others fade? And are highly vivid memories always accurate memories?

Memory is dynamic. Unlike photographs, memories can change. Cognitive psychologist Ulric Neisser once recounted what he was doing on December 7, 1941, the day Japan attacked Pearl Harbor. Neisser was in the den listening to a baseball game on the radio when a reporter interrupted with the news (Neisser, 2000). Or was he? He had certainly constructed a distinct memory, but he was clearly wrong: Baseball season had already been over for 2 months. In this module, we will explore how memories are constructed, and describe how even the experts among us can have inaccurate memories.

How Memories Are Organized and Constructed

Think about the last time you read a novel or watched a film. What do you recall about the story? If you have a typical memory, you will forget the proper names of locations and minor characters quickly, but you will be able to remember the basic plot for a long time (Squire, 1989; Stanhope et al., 1993). The plot may be referred to as the gist of the story and it impacts us much more than characters' names, which are often just details. As it turns out, much of the way we store memories depends on our tendency to remember the gist of things.

THE SCHEMA: AN ACTIVE ORGANIZATION PROCESS

In this section, we will focus on the concept of a **schema**, *an organized cluster of memories that constitutes one's knowledge about events, objects, and ideas.* Whenever we encounter familiar events or objects, these schemas become active, and they allow us to know what to expect, what to pay attention to, and what to remember. Because we use these patterns automatically, it may be difficult to understand what they are, even though you have been using them your whole life. Here is an example; just read the following passage one time.

> *The procedure is quite simple. First, you arrange things into different groups. Of course, one pile may be sufficient, depending on how much there is to do. If you have to go somewhere else due to lack of facilities, that is the next step; otherwise, you are pretty well set. It is important not to overdo things. That is, it is better to do too few things at once than too many. At first the whole procedure will seem complicated. Soon, however, it will become just another facet of life. After the procedure is completed, one arranges the materials into different groups again. Then they can be put into their appropriate places. Eventually they will be used once more, and the whole cycle will have to be repeated.* (Bransford & Johnson, 1973)

If you were to write down the details of the paragraph solely from memory, how well do you think you would do? Most people do not have high expectations for themselves because the paragraph is so vague. That vagueness is due to a lack of schemas. However, after we tell you the passage is about laundry, you will have a fitting schema in place. If you read the paragraph a second time, you should see that it is easier to understand.

Schemas are products of culture and experience (e.g., Ross & Wang, 2010). For example, individuals within a culture tend to have schemas related to gender roles; men

and women are each assumed to engage in certain jobs and to behave in certain ways. Even if an individual realizes that these schemas are not 100% accurate (in fact, they can be far from accurate in some cases), he or she is likely to engage in schematic processing when paying attention and recalling related material.

As further demonstration of how schemas influence memory, Heather Kleider and colleagues conducted a study in which they had participants view photographs of a handyman engaged in schema-consistent behaviors (e.g., working on plumbing) as well as in a few schema-inconsistent tasks (e.g., folding a baby's clothing). Along with these photos were images of a mother doing the same two tasks. Immediately after viewing the photographs, participants were quite successful at remembering correctly who had performed which actions (Kleider et al., 2008). However, after 2 days, what types of memory mistakes do you think the researchers found? As you can see from Figure 7.15, individuals began making mistakes consistent with schemas about gender and occupations.

CONSTRUCTING MEMORIES Schemas involve a collection of ideas and memories that tell us what to expect in a situation. Research shows that instead of remembering a bunch of accurate details (which would be very time consuming), we remember events using **constructive memory**, *a process by which we first recall a generalized schema and then add in specific details* (Scoboria et al., 2006; Silva et al., 2006).

Schemas also tell us what is relevant and important in a situation. Here is an interesting true story to illustrate

Figure 7.15 Schemas Affect How We Encode and Remember

In this study, memory was accurate when tested immediately, as shown by the small proportion of errors on the "immediate" side of the graph. After two days, however, participants misremembered seeing the schema-inconsistent tasks in line with stereotypes. For example, they misremembered the homemaker stirring cake batter even if they had actually seen the handyman do it.

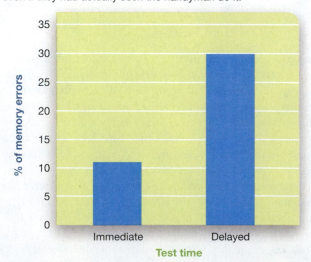

how schemas and details interact to construct memories. It actually happened to a student of ours: Imagine you are visiting an unfamiliar city in the United States. As you explore a park downtown, you round a corner and find an elephant standing in your path. What is an elephant doing in the middle of downtown?! If you have any knowledge of US cities, then your schemas will tell you what the landscape and buildings of a typical downtown probably look like. Any buildings, high rises, roads, and parks you see are all *schema consistent*. You are just as confident that pigeons and squirrels are consistent with your schema as well, but that free-roaming elephants are not—indeed, they are schema inconsistent, and quite surprising at that.

This example shows that schemas influence the construction of memories in two ways:

1. *Organization*. When we encounter a new situation, some objects and events will undoubtedly fit our schemas (i.e., our expectations) better than others. When the new information makes sense—that is, when it fits our schema—it can be easier to recall, yet it may be more difficult to recognize or report the exact details.
2. *Distinctiveness*. When we encounter new information, some of it will not fit our schemas. If the new information stands out as weird or unusual, it will be easy to recall. If it does not fit our schema, but is not all that unusual, it will likely be forgotten (Silva et al., 2006).

The effects of organization would be easy to spot if we asked you to recall your encounter with the elephant. Schemas would help you freely recall normal things: There was a walking path, there were grass and shrubbery around, and there were tall buildings on the right and a creek on the left. All of these general ideas are correct, and they would be easy to remember because they fit your schema. In contrast, when presented with several details, such as pictures of downtown, you might have difficulty recognizing the exact buildings you passed by on your trip.

Distinctiveness also has obvious effects. Like our student, you would definitely remember the elephant—that was the central point of the story—but there are bound to be other distinctive sights along the way that do not come to mind at all. Perhaps you encountered a discarded shoe on the side of the bike path, or you saw a sign that had been vandalized. Although you probably will not recall those schema-inconsistent objects, if prompted with questions or perhaps a picture, you might very well recognize them.

Here, you can see that schemas and details work together. To use the metaphor of memory construction, the schema provides the framework and structure, and the details are the walls and windows that make each event memorable. Incidentally, as the student continued to round the corner, he saw signs advertising a circus, along with a lot full of large trucks. With the circus schema in place, the encounter immediately made sense to him—the elephant was simply being let out for some exercise.

False Memories: Constructing Memories of What Never Happened

One of the most intriguing aspects of cognition is **false memory**, *remembering events that did not occur, or incorrectly recalling details of an event*. Oddly enough, false memories do not arise from memory malfunction. Instead, they show how normal memory processes developed to be efficient rather than 100% accurate. Every time we reconstruct a memory, there is a possibility that we are getting some of the details incorrect, even those about which we are extremely confident. To better understand how we create false memories, researchers have conducted experiments designed to increase or decrease the occurrence of false memories. Over the past 30 years, a number of methods have emerged that reliably produce false memories, and often very profound memories at that.

Participants in one study viewed the photo on the left and later were asked about the "yield sign," even though they saw a stop sign. This small bit of misinformation was enough to get many participants to falsely remember seeing a yield sign. Similarly, participants who first viewed the photo on the right could be led to misremember seeing a stop sign with a single misleading question.

THE MISINFORMATION EFFECT   A classic method in false memory research involves the **misinformation effect**, *which happens when information occurring after an event becomes part of the memory for that event*. In the original studies pioneered by Elizabeth Loftus (1975), students viewed films of staged events such as a car crash. In the experimental conditions, participants were asked about an object that was not in the video, such as "the stop sign." Later, when asked if they had seen a stop sign, participants in the experimental group were likely to say yes. As this experiment demonstrates, one can change the details of a memory just by phrasing a question in a certain way.

THE DRM PARADIGM   The Deese-Roediger-McDermott (DRM) paradigm, named after the psychologists who developed it, is probably the most straightforward procedure used in false memory research (see Figure 7.16). In the **DRM procedure**, *participants study a list of highly related words called semantic associates* (which means they are associated by meaning). The word that should be most obviously a part of this list is missing; this missing word is called the *critical lure*. If after studying the list of semantic associates the person then recalls the word that was actually missing, this experience in false memory is called an *intrusion*.

The fact that people make intrusion errors is not particularly surprising. However, the strength of the effect is surprising. In routine studies, the DRM lures as many as 70% of the participants. The most obvious way to reduce this effect would be to simply explain the DRM procedure and warn participants that intrusions may occur. Although this approach has proved effective in reducing intrusions, false memories still occur (Gallo et al., 1997). Obviously, intrusions are difficult to prevent, but not because memory is prone to mistakes. In fact, memory is generally accurate and extremely efficient, given the millions of bits of information we encounter every day. Instead, the DRM effect reflects the fact that normal memory processes are constructive.

Figure 7.16   The DRM Paradigm

The words on the left side are all closely related to the word "bread"—but "bread" does not actually appear on the list. People who study this list of words are very likely to misremember that "bread" was present.

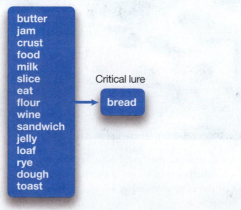

butter
jam
crust
food
milk
slice
eat
flour
wine
sandwich
jelly
loaf
rye
dough
toast

Critical lure
bread

IMAGERY AND FALSE MEMORIES   Researchers have found that the more readily and clearly we can imagine events, the more certain we are that the memories are accurate. Based on this evidence, it was not surprising when researchers found that images could be used to lead to false memories in several different ways. One technique known as *guided imagery* involves a researcher giving instructions to participants to imagine certain events. For example, in one study, volunteers were asked to imagine a procedure in which a nurse removed a sample of skin from a finger while their peers in the control condition read a passage about the procedure but were not asked to imagine it happening. Despite the fact that removing skin from a finger is not a documented medical procedure and thus certainly never occurred, individuals in the experimental group still reported that this event had actually happened to them more often than those in the control group (Mazzoni & Memon, 2003).

Imagination inflation *refers to the increased confidence in a false memory of an event following repeated imagination of the event*. To study this effect, researchers created a list of events that may or may not have happened to the individuals in their study (e.g., got in trouble for calling 911, found a $10 bill in a parking lot). The volunteers were first asked to rate their confidence that the event happened. In sessions held over a period of days, participants were asked to imagine these events, until finally they were asked to rate their confidence again. For each item they were asked to imagine, repeated imagination *inflated* their confidence in the memory of the event (Garry et al., 1996; Garry & Polaschek, 2000).

Perhaps the strongest piece of evidence for image-based false memories comes from doctored images, such as the one mentioned at the beginning of this module. In another similar case, researchers asked volunteers to provide pictures of themselves from early childhood participating in some event. They were then asked to provide an explanation of the event, the location, and the people and objects in the photo. The researchers took one of the pictures and digitally cut and pasted it into a balloon ride. On three occasions the participants went through the set of pictures, the true originals plus the doctored photo, in a structured interview process (the kind designed to help police get more details from eyewitnesses). By the end of the third session, half the participants had some memory for the balloon ride event, even though it never occurred (Wade et al., 2002).

Other researchers have gone so far as to create false video evidence of an event (Nash et al., 2009). For this method, a volunteer was videoed watching a graduate student perform one action. Researchers then edited in another video of the graduate student performing a second action, one that the volunteer never witnessed. Now imagine you were shown a video of yourself watching an action you had not seen before—would you believe it?

In one study of false memory, true photos were obtained from volunteers' families (left), and were edited to look like a balloon ride (right). About half of the volunteers in this study came to recall some details of an event that never happened.

In fact, a significant portion of the individuals not only believed they saw the second action, but they also actually formed memories of events they had never witnessed.

As you can see, it is relatively easy to create false memories. In fact, they can happen all the time and without our awareness. There are some obvious situations—such as *eyewitness testimony*—when we would like to be able to distinguish between true and false memories. Recent work in neuroscience is beginning to make progress in this area. For example, psychologists have found that when people recount information that is true, the visual and other sensory areas of the brain become more active. When revealing falsely remembered information, these regions are much less active; the brain is not drawing on mental imagery because it was not there in the first place (Stark et al., 2010). Of course, being convinced you went on a hot-air balloon ride that never happened is of little consequence. As mentioned previously, false memories can become problematic, as you'll see in the next section.

THE DANGER OF FALSE REMEMBERING Our ability to organize and construct memories helps us store large amounts of information, yet it also leaves us vulnerable to false memory. A number of personal and social dangers are associated with the confusion between true and false memories. The worst effects of false remembering on individuals have been the well-documented occurrence of false memories of early childhood abuse. These events stem from a belief in **recovered memories**, *memories of a traumatic event that are suddenly recovered after blocking the memory of that event for a long period of time, often many years*. This idea that we suppress traumatic memories is popularly known as *repression* from Freudian psychoanalysis (you will read more about this topic in Module 12.3). This school of thought suggests that if a repressed memory can be recovered, then a patient can find ways to cope with

the trauma. Some therapists espouse this view and use techniques such as hypnosis and guided imagery to try to unearth repressed memories, though the practice is far less accepted and practiced than in previous decades.

Recovered memories, like many other types of LTM, are difficult to study because one can rarely determine if they are true or false. The **recovered memory controversy** *is a heated debate among psychologists about the validity of recovered memories* (Patihis et al., 2014). On one side of the controversy are some clinical mental health workers (although certainly not the majority) who regularly attempt to recover memories they suspect have been repressed. On the opposing side are the many psychologists who are very skeptical that repression occurs at all and assert that any so-called recovered memory is actually a false memory. This perspective argues that the techniques that might help "recover" a memory bear a striking resemblance to those that are used to create false memories in laboratory research; they often involve instructions to remember, attempts to form images, and social reinforcement for reporting memories. Similarly, experiments described in Module 5.2 show that, rather than improving access to repressed memories, hypnosis significantly increases false remembering. A neutral party would be correct to point out that, beyond controlled studies, it is virtually impossible to tell what is a true memory versus a false memory without corroborating evidence. Therefore, the debate will likely continue for some time.

What is the danger in a false memory of childhood abuse? The example of Beth Rutherford illustrates the worst that can happen. In the early 1990s, Rutherford sought the help of her church counselor to deal with personal issues. During their sessions the counselor repeatedly told her that she fit the profile of a sexual abuse survivor and geared each session toward the recovery of the memories they believed to be repressed. As a result of these efforts, Rutherford eventually constructed a false memory in which her father, a minister, had raped her. The memories were further elaborated so that she remembered becoming pregnant and that her father had forced her to undergo an abortion using a coat hanger. You can imagine what kind of effects this had on the family. Her father was forced to leave his position, and his reputation was left in shambles. Although it can be difficult to prove some false memories, this incident is particularly disturbing because it could have been supported by medical evidence. However, it clearly was not: When a medical investigation was finally conducted, absolutely no evidence was found that Beth had ever been raped or that she had ever been pregnant (Loftus, 1997).

This case is not an isolated one, although fortunately such gravely serious instances remain rare. Even so, the recovered memory controversy is a serious topic of debate for psychologists. On the one hand, if repression occurs, and if repressed memories affect mental health, then it would be helpful to use memory recovery techniques. On the other hand, most memory recovery techniques are based on the same techniques that cognitive psychologists use to create false memories, especially imagery. Thus, the risk for wrongful accusations when this course is pursued is high.

Working the Scientific Literacy Model

Eyewitness Testimony

Research and anecdotes about how memory can fail us raise serious legal issues, particularly in criminal investigations and proceedings in which individuals' freedoms and the public safety are at stake. Police officers, judges, jury members, plaintiffs, and defendants all rely to some extent on testimony that is based on memories for critical events and details of a crime. Knowing that memory is never perfect, how much should we trust eyewitness testimony?

What do we know about eyewitness testimony?

The identification of the suspect(s) in a crime is perhaps the most basic and critical piece of information; thus, despite the chances of false remembering, eyewitnesses are too important to disregard. As you have likely seen in television and film portrayals, there are different ways that lineups are conducted. A group of individuals might be aligned side by side (along with *foils*—people who could not have possibly committed the crime), and the witness is asked to decide whether the suspect is present by identifying him. What the screenwriter and director often overlook, however, is that lining people up at the same time—a process known as the *simultaneous lineup*—can actually encourage

mistaken identifications. An alternative procedure that appears to minimize undue influence on witness memory and decision making is called *sequential lineup*—a process in which suspects are viewed one at a time.

How can science explain eyewitness testimony?

What are the pros and cons of simultaneous and sequential lineups? Scholars such as Dr. Gary Wells have conducted numerous laboratory experiments on lineup procedures (Wells et al., 1998; Wells & Olson, 2003). Experiments often involve showing participants a video of a mock crime and then having them identify the suspect. Within this basic model, researchers can control all sorts of relevant variables, such as randomly assigning the participants to identify suspects from a simultaneous photo spread versus a sequential spread. Importantly, the experiments include conditions in which the true perpetrator's photo is not included in either lineup to test for false-positive identifications.

Wells and colleagues have repeatedly shown that in simultaneous lineups, false identifications are significantly more likely than when individual suspects are viewed in a sequence, one at a time. A likely explanation is that simultaneous lineups encourage the *relative judgment principle:* The witness assumes the suspect is included and selects the person who looks most like the suspect relative to the others in the lineup (Wells, 1984). Once this decision is made, the witness's memory incorporates that judgment through misinformation and imagery. In contrast, the sequential procedure allows the witness to base her judgment on an absolute criterion: The suspect in each photo either is or is not the perpetrator, and so the witness is much less likely to falsely identify someone. They can always assume the next photo might be the suspect.

There are many other influences on eyewitnesses' memories. For example, if an investigator responds to an eyewitness's identification with "Good job! You identified our key suspect," the witness is likely to become much more confident in the memory even if it is inaccurate (Smalarz & Wells, 2014). When multiple variables influence eyewitness testimony, the effects can add up to produce confidence in a false memory. How can the science of memory improve this process? Here are the six main suggestions for reforming procedures:

1. *Employ double-blind procedures.* In Module 2.1 we described how double-blind procedures, in which critical details about a study are kept from both the experimenter and subject, help reduce bias. Similarly, a double-blind lineup can prevent an investigator from biasing an eyewitness, either intentionally or accidentally.

2. *Use appropriate instructions.* For example, the investigator should include the statement, "The suspect might

not be present in the lineup." Eyewitnesses often assume the guilty person is in the lineup, so they are likely to choose a close match. This risk can be greatly reduced by instructing the eyewitness that the correct answer may be "none of the above."

3. *Compose the lineup carefully*. The lineup should include individuals who match the eyewitness's description of the perpetrator, not the investigator's beliefs about the suspect.

4. *Use sequential lineups*. When an entire lineup is shown simultaneously, the witness may assume one of the people is guilty and settle on the best candidate. If the people in the lineup are presented one at a time, witnesses are less likely to pick out an incorrect suspect because they are willing to consider the next person in the sequence.

5. *Require confidence statements*. Eyewitness confidence can change as a result of an investigator's response, or simply by seeing the same suspect in multiple lineups, neither of which make the testimony any more accurate. Therefore, confidence statements, where the witness reports her level of confidence (e.g., not confident at all, moderately confident, highly confident), should be taken after an identifications is made.

6. *Record the procedures*. Eyewitness researchers have identified at least a dozen specific things that can go wrong during identification procedures. By recording these procedures, expert witnesses can evaluate the reliability of testimony during hearings.

Can we critically evaluate research on eyewitness testimony?

Psychological research on proper ways of gathering eyewitness testimony has uncovered some important variables, and it is difficult to argue with the outcomes of so many experiments. The main criticism of this research is that it is so far removed from the context that it may not tell us much about actual crimes. Experiments tend to involve undergraduate student participants witnessing staged crimes in relative comfort whereas real crime situations are stressful and the consequences of misidentification are much more profound. The only way to address these concerns is to apply them in actual criminal investigations. Recent research has attempted to address this question. Results suggest that although the sequential method is beneficial, the advantage over the simultaneous lineup is much less pronounced than when studied in the laboratory (Wells, Steblay, & Dysart, 2014).

How is this relevant to the legal system?

In the United States, more than 220 individuals convicted of crimes have been exonerated based on DNA evidence; more than 75% of the original convictions were the result of mistaken eyewitness testimony (Innocence Project,

2010; Wells & Quinlivan, 2009). Considering that many cases do not have DNA evidence available (it has been lost or destroyed, or the quality of DNA samples has deteriorated), there are likely to be many more wrongful convictions in this country that we will never know about. Given the constructive nature of memory, it should come as no surprise to hear that an eyewitness gets it wrong from time to time. The consequences of this kind of wrongful conviction are dire: An innocent person goes to jail while a potentially dangerous person stays free (Figure 7.17). In this video, Police Lineup, Dr. Margaret Bull Kovera of John Jay College of Criminal Justice explains factors that could affect the accuracy of eyewitness testimony.

Watch POLICE LINEUP

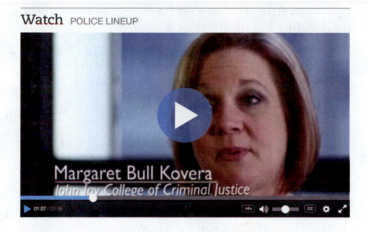

Margaret Bull Kovera
John Jay College of Criminal Justice

Figure 7.17 The Role of Eyewitness Errors in Wrongful Convictions

Eyewitness testimony is absolutely crucial to the operation of our legal system, but how reliable is it? Figure 7.17 summarizes more than 200 cases of exonerations (convictions that have been overturned due to new evidence after the trial) made possible since 1989, thanks to the help of The Innocence Project. Do eyewitness mistakes seem to play a major role in these reversals? If so, what does this relationship suggest about research on eyewitness testimony?

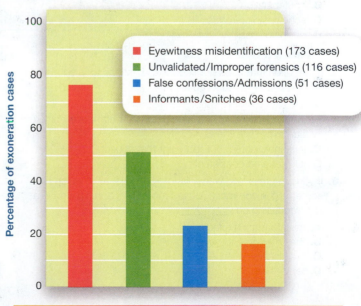

Module 7.3 Summary

7.3a   Know ... the key terminology used in discussing how memories are organized and constructed:

constructive memory
DRM procedure
false memory
imagination inflation
misinformation effect
recovered memory
recovered memory controversy
schema

7.3b   Understand ... how schemas serve as frameworks for encoding and constructing memories.

Schemas guide our attention, telling us what to expect in certain circumstances. They organize long-term memories and provide us with cues when it comes time to retrieve those memories.

7.3c   Understand ... how psychologists can produce false memories in the laboratory.

Psychologists have found that a number of factors contribute to the construction of false memories, including misinformation, imagination inflation, and the semantic similarities used in the DRM procedure.

7.3d   Apply ... what you have learned to judge the reliability of eyewitness testimony.

If you examined the data in Figure 7.17, then you should have some sense of the reliability of eyewitness testimony. Of the 225 exonerations, 77% of the cases included erroneous eyewitness testimony, which was more than any other contributing factor. Given this high correlation, we believe research on eyewitness testimony should continue to find ways of reducing errors. The results research on memory and how to reduce errors should be applied to investigative techniques used by law enforcement officers.

Meanwhile, psychology students have the potential to become trial attorneys, investigators, or jurors; therefore they should be prepared to apply their knowledge when the need arises.

7.3e   Analyze ... the arguments in the "recovered memory" debate.

You should first understand the premise behind the idea of recovered memories: Some people believe that if a memory is too painful, it might be blocked from conscious recollection, only to be recovered later through therapeutic techniques. Others argue that it is difficult to prove that a "recovered" memory is actually recovered. Given how easy it is to create false memories, they argue, any memory believed to be recovered should be viewed with skepticism.

Module 7.3 Quiz

Know . . .

1. The act of remembering through recalling a framework and then adding specific details is known as _____.
   A. constructive memory
   B. confabulation
   C. schematic interpretation
   D. distinctiveness

Understand . . .

2. Information that does not fit our expectations for a specific context is likely to be forgotten if:
   A. it is extremely unusual.
   B. it only fits our expectations for another completely different context.
   C. it is unexpected, but really not that unusual.
   D. it is schema consistent.

3. If you are presented with a list of 15 words, all of which have something in common, you are most likely participating in a study focusing on _____.
   A. misinformation effects
   B. the DRM procedure
   C. imagination inflation
   D. repression

Apply . . .

4. Jonathan is choosing a perpetrator from a lineup in a robbery that he witnessed. You can be most confident in his selection if:
   A. the authorities smiled after Jonathan's response so that he would feel comfortable during the lineup procedure.
   B. the authorities had the lineup presented all at the same time so Jonathan could compare the individuals.
   C. the lineup included individuals of different races and ethnicities.
   D. Jonathan was given the option to not choose any of the people from the lineup if no one fit his memory.

Analyze . . .

5. Psychologists who study false memories have engaged in a debate over the validity of recovered memories. Why are they skeptical about claims of recovered memories?
   A. They have never experienced recovered memories themselves.
   B. Many of the techniques used to create false memories in research bear a striking similarity to the techniques used to recover memories in therapy.
   C. Brain scans can easily distinguish between true and false memories.
   D. Scientists have proved that it is impossible to remember something that you have once forgotten.

Module 7.4 Scientific Literacy Challenge: Can You Build a Better Memory?

It is not uncommon to hear people complain about their memory: "I'm terrible with names," and "I can never remember jokes" and "I thought I knew it but then got to the test and I just blanked."

With these and other complaints being so common, it is not surprising that there is now a variety of software packages and online services that claim to improve memory ability through cognitive exercises. Is "brain training" something that would appeal to you? Take a moment to write out some thoughts on brain training before continuing to the activity.

JOURNAL PROMPT

Are there any aspects of your memory that you would like to improve? Do you believe there is potential for cognitive exercises to improve memory ability for you or someone else?

What do we know about brain-training programs?

Imagine that you have just finished a conversation about how so many people have difficulty remembering names. Then, you come across this advertisement for a brain training website. As you study the ad, see if you can recognize some of the key terms and concepts from Chapter 7.

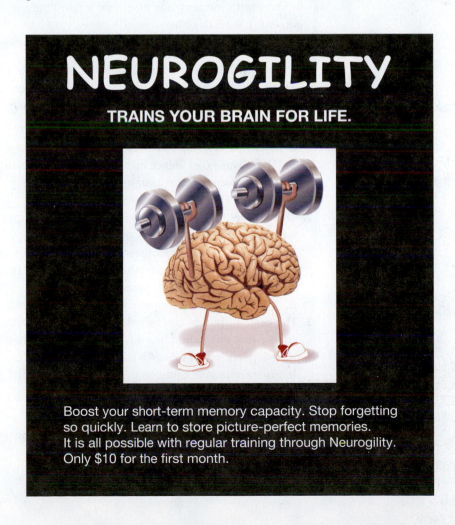

NEUROGILITY
TRAINS YOUR BRAIN FOR LIFE.

Boost your short-term memory capacity. Stop forgetting so quickly. Learn to store picture-perfect memories. It is all possible with regular training through Neurogility. Only $10 for the first month.

This program makes some pretty big claims, but there are plenty of people who would love to get the results it promises. Read on to find out if Neurogility is likely to be effective.

How do scientists study brain-training programs?

If you conduct a quick web search for "brain-training evidence" you will find it yields quite a few results. Some of these are from recognizable scientific publications or organizations, and others from quality journalism outlets. Here is an excerpt from a magazine article describing a brain-training study. As you read, pay attention to the highlighted concepts that address scientific research.

In the first study of this brain-training program, a group of volunteers participated in a free 30-day trial offered by the company in exchange for agreeing to have their data released anonymously to an independent group of researchers. As Neurogility claimed, there was a noticeable gain in scores on several of the tasks. However, skeptics pointed out that those improvements were only found for the specific games in which participants practiced and not on other tests of the same basic skills. Nearly two dozen studies have been published since then and in a recent meta-analysis (a statistical analysis that combines the results of many smaller studies), the same pattern emerged. Thus, most experts are beginning to believe that brain training is not really effective. However, there is still hope for the brain-training companies. There is one very recent experiment in which older adults who completed a specially designed driving game showed improvements in short-term memory and attention. Interestingly, in this case, the results did seem to generalize to other skills.

This is a quick review of a number of studies, but several important concepts were described. Were you able to identify qualities of good science in these examples? Test yourself with these questions:

1. Why were researchers skeptical of the first study?
   a. It did not use objective measurements.
   b. There was no evidence that it would generalize to other activities.
   c. The measurement was unreliable.
   d. It did not include a sample.
2. The authors of the meta-analysis were able to find nearly two dozen studies on the same topic. Why is this?
   a. Scientists can increase the support for a hypothesis through replication.
   b. Researchers hoped to establish ecological validity.
   c. In order to identify a convenience sample.
   d. It is the most effective way to establish a dependent variable.
3. The first study was conducted in cooperation with the company. In order to reduce the chance that this would bias anyone, researchers should _____.
   a. ask participants to sign a waiver
   b. use random assignment
   c. administer more than one cognitive test
   d. use a double-blind procedure

Now that we have seen some of the evidence, let's engage in critical thinking.

How do we think critically about brain-training programs?

Brain-training programs have been scrutinized by scientists who specialize in memory and cognition. Particular attention has been placed on claims such as those made by Neurogility. Check your critical thinking skills by matching the tenets of critical thinking listed here with the four statements related to the research you read.

1. Examine the nature and source of the evidence.
2. Examine assumptions and biases—both yours and those of your information sources.
3. Consider alternative viewpoints.
4. Be curious and ask questions.

a. If practice makes people better at those specific tasks, I wonder if the program might be able to generalize more if it included a wider variety of tasks?

b. The evidence for the conclusions drawn comes from over 20 experimental studies conducted by different groups of researchers and they replicated the same basic findings.

c. The researchers who published those studies are at universities, not at for-profit corporations who may be competing for market share of brain-training programs.

d. Perhaps we should examine it from another angle and see whether brain training might be effective in helping people whose skills in certain areas may have declined, such as elderly people.

Answers: 1. b 2. c 3. d 4. a

This represents a good start on applying critical thinking to Neurogility. Now, read on to see how this evidence might be applied.

How is brain training relevant?

Research on brain-training programs involving young to middle-aged adults has not been very promising, and yet the study with older adults suggests that there might be some beneficial application of these programs after all. If the finding that older adults benefit from memory training can be replicated and it generalizes to other abilities, resources such as Neurogility may prove valid and useful.

Consider the following question and share any newly formed thoughts you may have about brain training.

SHARED WRITING

What are a couple of ways in which brain training would be useful for older adults? It may be useful to think about specific memory complaints people have and describe how a brain-training program might be designed to address them.

Chapter 7 Quiz

1. Which type of memory can hold information for only a few seconds?
   A. Semantic memory
   B. Short-term memory
   C. Sensory memory
   D. Long-term memory

2. "About seven" is a famous estimate for:
   A. the number of memory stores in the human brain.
   B. the capacity of long-term memory.
   C. the number of minutes information can stay in short-term memory without rehearsal.
   D. the capacity of short-term memory.

3. Latasha remembers visiting Gettysburg on a cloudy day when she was a child. She recalls being bored at the time, but now wishes she had paid more attention. Latasha's memory is an example of a(n) _____ memory.
   A. episodic
   B. semantic
   C. sensory
   D. nondeclarative

4. Long-term potentiation refers to the ability of neurons to:
   A. increase their size.
   B. decrease their size.
   C. strengthen their signaling with other neurons.
   D. weaken their signaling with other neurons.

5. Damage to the hippocampus is most likely to lead to the loss of:
   A. recent memories that have been consolidated.
   B. sensory memory.
   C. recent memories that have not yet been consolidated.
   D. procedural memories.

6. According to the LOP framework, how well we encode long-term information is most directly related to:
   A. how often we encounter the information.
   B. how deeply we process the information.
   C. how long we are exposed to the information.
   D. how motivated we are to learn the information.

7. Which of the following statements is true about flashbulb memories?
   A. They are far more accurate than standard memories.
   B. They are typically no more accurate than standard memories.
   C. They last for a much shorter period than standard memories.
   D. They contain fewer details than standard memories.

8. Early research into forgetting by Hermann Ebbinghaus found that forgetting occurs:
   A. slowly over a long period of time.
   B. mostly between 12 and 24 hours after the learning event.
   C. slowly at first, but the rate of forgetting increases over time.
   D. quickly at first, but the rate of forgetting slows over time.

9. What role are schemas believed to play in memory?
   A. Schemas store complete memories of events that can be "played back" at will.
   B. Schemas ensure that memories are highly accurate.
   C. Schemas organize information so that memories are easier to encode, store, and recall.
   D. Schemas act as buffers while memories are being consolidated.

10. Terri participated in an experiment where she watched a video of a staged robbery. The research assistant told her a police officer had arrested a man wearing a red baseball cap who was found in the area. Although Terri's video did not include anyone with a red hat, she now recalls seeing it when she describes what she saw. This is an example of the:
    A. levels of processing effect.
    B. imagination inflation effect.
    C. DRM effect.
    D. misinformation effect.

11. Which of the following systems coordinates attention and the exchange of information among memory storage components?
    A. Episodic buffer
    B. Central executive
    C. Phonological loop
    D. Visuospatial sketchpad

12. If you are learning vocabulary for a psychology exam, you are better off using a(n) _____ technique.
    A. maintenance rehearsal
    B. elaborative rehearsal
    C. serial processing
    D. consolidation

13. Which of the following systems maintains information in memory by repeating words and sounds?
    A. Episodic buffer
    B. Central executive
    C. Phonological loop
    D. Visuospatial sketchpad

14. Memories that can be verbalized, whether they are about your own experiences or your knowledge about the world, are called _____.
    A. nondeclarative memories
    B. procedural memories
    C. conditioned memories
    D. declarative memories

15. Dual coding seems to help memory by:
    A. allowing for maintenance rehearsal.
    B. ensuring that the information is encoded in multiple ways.
    C. ensuring that the information is encoded on two separate occasions.
    D. duplicating the rehearsal effect.

Chapter 8
Thought and Language

Module 8.1 The Organization of Knowledge

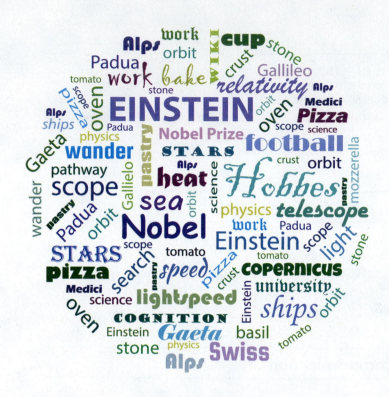

⌄ Learning Objectives

8.1a Know . . . the key terminology associated with concepts and categories.

8.1b Understand . . . theories of how people organize their knowledge about the world.

8.1c Understand . . . how experience and culture can shape the way we organize our knowledge.

8.1d Apply . . . your knowledge to identify prototypical examples.

8.1e Analyze . . . the claim that the language we speak determines how we think.

Have you ever become lost on the web? It happens to most of us at some point. Imagine going to a site like Wikipedia to answer a homework question about Albert Einstein, then you see he won the Nobel Prize and click that link to see exactly what that entails, and next thing you know a half hour has passed and you are reading that the first known usage of the word "pizza" was over a millennium ago in the coastal Italian town of Gaeta. You know you have become lost because you cannot retrace the steps you took to get

Gaeta from Einstein's Nobel Prize. What makes those steps possible is that there are no facts existing in isolation; all information is interconnected. This holds true whether you are following links on the Internet or searching your own memory for some bit of trivia. One of the fundamental puzzles of cognitive psychology is to understand what links together all the facts that comprise knowledge of the world, and to learn how those links are formed and activated when we learn and think.

Imagine trying to record everything you ever learned about the world—how many books could you fill? For psychologists, understanding how much we know is less interesting than understanding how we keep track of all that we know. In this module, we explore these tracking processes and examine closely the way these processes work.

Concepts and Categories

Concepts and categories are used for memory, decision making, language, and so on; in other words, cognition would not be possible without them. A **concept** *is the mental representation of an object, event, or idea.* As it happens, there are no completely independent concepts. You do not have just one concept for *chair*, for instance, or one for *table*, and one for *sofa*. Instead, each of these concepts can be divided into smaller groups with more precise labels, such as *armchair* or *coffee table*. Similarly, all of these items can be lumped together under the single label, *furniture*. Psychologists use the term **categories** *to refer to clusters of interrelated concepts.* We tend to take everyday categories like *furniture* for granted because they come to our minds so automatically. Others require a bit of work, for example: Should a district attorney prosecute a suspect's actions as homicide or manslaughter? Should the staff at a video-streaming website list a new release as either a *comedy* or *drama* if the film has elements of both? Psychology attempts to explain not what makes up a category, but how people go about categorizing the objects and ideas they encounter.

CLASSICAL CATEGORIES: DEFINITIONS AND RULES
Rule-based categorization (sometimes referred to as **classical categorization**) *is the process of identifying category members according to a set of rules or a set of defining features*—something similar to applying a dictionary definition (Stanton & Nosofsky, 2013). For example, you may or may not know that the geometric term *balbis* is a shape with two defining features: It is a straight line segment and each end stops where that end meets another straight line at a right angle. Using this definition, and going one step at a time, try to identify the balbis within one (and only one) of these letters: S P H.

As you attempt this exercise, it is important to keep in mind that it takes a few seconds to apply the rules consciously, especially if you are encountering the definition of a balbis for the first time. You might think to yourself, S has no straight lines, P has a straight line, but it does not end at another straight line, and H has three straight lines. Furthermore, the horizontal line meets perpendicular straight lines and both ends. The middle line in the H is technically a balbis!

Generally, rule-based theories of categorization can happen so fast that you are not even aware that you are applying them. For instance, consider how easily you can understand sentences written in your native language; without realizing it, you are applying some pretty complex grammar to understand those sentences.

As straightforward as this seems, rule-based categorization does not tell the full story of how we link concepts together. For starters, people categorize things all the time without having a full list of rules to apply to the task. In addition, researchers must address the problem of **graded membership**—*the observation that some concepts appear to make better category members than others.* For example, see if the definition in Table 8.1 fits your definition of *bird* and then categorize the items in the table accordingly.

Ideally, you said no to the apple, and yes to the sparrow and penguin. But, did you notice any difference in how you responded to the sparrow and penguin? Psychologists have researched classical categorization using a behavioral measure known as the *sentence-verification technique,* where volunteers wait for a sentence to appear in front of them on a computer screen and respond as fast as they can with a yes or no answer to statements such as *A sparrow is a bird* or *A penguin is a bird.* The choice the subject makes, as well as his reaction time to respond, are measured by the researcher. Sentence-verification shows us that some members of a category are recognized faster than others (Olson et al., 2004; Rosch & Mervis, 1975). In other words, subjects almost always answer "yes" faster to sparrow than to penguin. This seems to go against a classical, rule-based categorization system because both sparrows and penguins are equally good fits for the definition, but sparrows are somehow more bird-like than penguins. Thus, a modern

---

Table 8.1 Categorizing Objects According to the Definition of *Bird*

Definition: Any of the class Aves of warm-blooded, egg-laying, feathered vertebrates with forelimbs modified to form wings.

Now, categorize a set of items by answering *yes* or *no* regarding the truth of the following sentences:
1. A sparrow is a bird.
2. An apple is a bird.
3. A penguin is a bird.

SOURCE: American Heritage Dictionary, 2007

Figure 8.1 A Prototypical Bird

A prototypical bird might look something like this one on the right.

It combines features of actual birds, such as those below.

approach to categorization must explain how "best examples" influence how we categorize items.

CATEGORIZATION BY COMPARISON: PROTOTYPES AND EXEMPLARS Prototypes offer an alternative explanation for graded membership. When you hear the word *bird*, what mental image comes to mind? Does it resemble a penguin? Or is your image closer to a robin or sparrow? The most frequent image that comes to mind is what psychologists call a prototype (see Figure 8.1). **Prototypes** *are mental representations of an average category member* (Rosch, 1973). If you took an average of the three or four most familiar types of birds, you would get a prototypical bird.

Prototypes allow for classification by resemblance rather than rules. When you encounter a little creature you have never seen before, its basic shape—maybe just its silhouette—is compared to your prototype of a bird. If it is a close match, you can classify the creature as a bird. No rules or definitions are involved, just a set of similarities in overall shape and function (this overall similarity is referred to as a *family resemblance*). See Table 8.2 to apply prototype categorization. Comparisons can also be made

by **exemplar**, a *specific category member that serves as a reference point for the entire category*. While exemplars also allow for classification by family resemblance, they differ from prototypes in that they are specific cases rather than generalized, average category members. For example, what comes to mind when you think of the general category of dog? If your own dog comes to mind, you have an exemplar. If you do not think of a specific dog, but instead have the image of a dog somewhere between a golden retriever, chocolate lab, and German shepherd, then you would be using a prototype.

Prototypes and exemplars help explain graded membership—why some category members make better examples than others. In addition, prototypes and exemplars allow for quick, perceptual judgments in situations where there is not likely to be much confusion, and these judgments are generally good enough (Rouder & Ratcliffe, 2006). For example, if you know you want to enter a building you have never visited before, you can probably identify the door at first glance and without much thought, even if the door is one with a doorknob or one that revolves. Either way, you would not need to consult a dictionary to make sure it has all the right features.

Table 8.2 Applying Prototype Categorization

Apply prototype categorization to the following questions. Compare your answers with those provided under objective 8.1d on page 255.

1. What is the best example for the category of fish: a hammerhead shark, a trout, or an eel?
2. What do you consider to be a prototypical sport? Why?
3. Some categories are created spontaneously, yet still have prototypes. For example, what might be a prototypical object for the category "What to save if your house is on fire"?

Figure 8.2 A Semantic Network Diagram for the Category "Animal"

The nodes include the basic-level categories, *Birds* and *Fish*. Another node represents the broader category of *Animals*, while the lowest three nodes represent the more specific categories of *Robins*, *Emus*, and *Trout*.

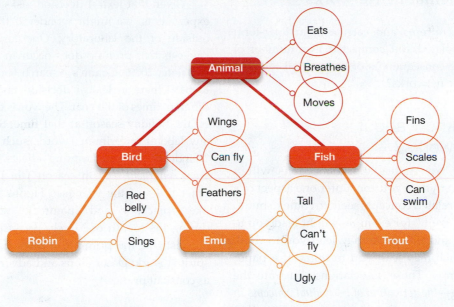

To review, there are two approaches that explain how we make categorizations: rules and resemblance. Which approach is correct? According to research, we can follow either approach depending on how complicated the specific example might be. If there are a few major distinctions between items, we use resemblance; if there are complications, we switch to rules (Feldman, 2003; Rouder & Ratcliff, 2004, 2006). You might even categorize the same thing two different ways. For example, in the case of seeing a bat dart by, your first impression might be "bird" because it resembles a bird. But when you have a moment to think about it, you might recall that a bat fits the definition of a mammal; in other words, it has hair, is reproduced through live birth rather than eggs, and so on.

NETWORKS AND HIERARCHIES Concepts do not just float freely in your memory. Instead, they have many connections among them that can be represented in a network diagram. A **semantic network** *is an interconnected set of nodes (or concepts) and the links that join them to form a category* (see Figure 8.2). *Nodes* are circles that represent concepts, and *links* connect them together to represent the structure of a category as well as the relationships among different categories (Collins & Loftus, 1975).

Something you may notice about Figure 8.2 is that it is arranged in a *hierarchy*—that is, it consists of a structure moving from general to very specific. This organization helps us understand how categories work in daily thought and language by identifying the *basic level category*, which is located in the middle row of the diagram (where birds and fish are) (Johnson & Mervis, 1997; Rosch et al., 1976). A number of qualities make the basic level category unique:

- Basic level categories are the terms used most often in conversation.
- They are the easiest to pronounce.
- They are the level at which prototypes exist.
- They are the level at which most thinking occurs.

Here is an easy test generated by the animal network in Figure 8.2. If you were asked to react to dozens of sentences, and the following two sentences were included among them, which do you think you would mark as "true" the fastest?

- *A robin is a bird.*
- *A robin is an animal.*

As you can see in the network diagram, *robin* and *bird* are closer together; in fact, to connect *robin* to *animal*, you must first go through *bird*. Sure enough, people regard the sentence "A robin is a bird" as a true statement faster than "A robin is an animal."

Now consider another set of examples. Which trait do you think you would verify faster?

- *A robin has wings.*
- *A robin eats.*

Using the connecting lines as we did before, we can predict that it would be the first statement about wings. As research shows, our guess would be correct.

Working the Scientific Literacy Model

Priming and Semantic Networks

The thousands of concepts and categories in long-term memory are not isolated, but connected in a number of ways. What are the consequences of forming all the connections in semantic networks?

What do we know about semantic networks?

In your daily life, you notice the connections within semantic networks anytime you encounter one aspect of a category and other related concepts seem to come to mind. Hearing the word "fruit," for example, might lead you to think of an apple, and the apple may lead you to think of a computer, which may lead you to think of a paper that is due tomorrow. These associations illustrate the concept of **priming**—*the activation of individual concepts in long-term memory*. Interestingly, research has shown that priming can also occur without your awareness; "fruit" may not have brought the image of a watermelon to mind, but the concept of a watermelon may have been primed nonetheless.

How can science explain priming effects?

Psychologists can test for priming through reaction time measurements, such as those in the sentence verification tasks discussed earlier or through a method called the *lexical decision task*. With the lexical decision method, a volunteer sits at a computer and stares at a focal point. Next, a string of letters flashes on the screen. The volunteer responds yes or no as quickly as possible to indicate whether the letters spell a word (see Figure 8.3). Using this method, a volunteer should respond faster that "apple" is a word if it follows the word "fruit" than if it follows the word "bus."

Given that lexical decision tasks are highly controlled experiments, we might wonder if they have any impact outside of the laboratory. One test by Jennifer Coane suggests that priming does occur in everyday life (Coane & Balota, 2009). Coane's research team invited volunteers to participate in lexical decision tasks about holidays at different times of the year. The words they chose were based on the holiday season at that time. Sure enough, without any laboratory priming, words such as "nutcracker" and "reindeer" showed priming effects at times when they were *congruent* (or "in season") in December, relative to other times of the year (see Figure 8.4). Similarly, words like "leprechaun" and "shamrock" showed a priming effect during the month of March. Because the researchers did not instigate the priming, it must have been the holiday spirit at work: Decorations and advertisements must serve as constant primes.

Can we critically evaluate this information?

Priming influences thought and behavior, but is certainly not all-powerful and, in fact, it can be very weak at times. Because the strength of priming can vary a great deal,

---

Figure 8.3 A Lexical Decision Task

In a lexical decision task, an individual watches a computer screen as strings of letters are flashed on the screen. The subject must respond as quickly as possible to indicate whether the letters spell a word.

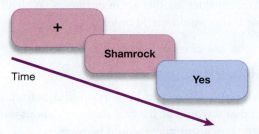

Figure 8.4 Priming Affects the Speed of Respones on a Lexical Decision Task

Average response times were faster when the holiday-themed words were *congruent* (in season), as represented by the blue bars. This finding is consistent for both the first half and second half of the list of words.

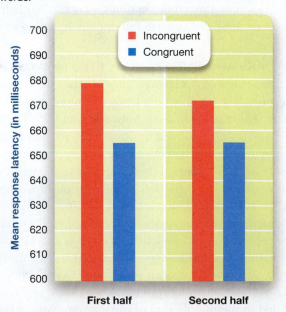

some published experiments have been very difficult to replicate—and in important criterion of quality research (see Module 2.1). So, while most psychologists agree that priming is an important area of research, there have been very open debates at academic conferences and in peer-reviewed journals about the best way to conduct the research and how to interpret the results (Cesario, 2014; Klatzky & Creswell, 2014).

Why is this relevant?

Advertisers know all too well that priming is more than just a curiosity; it can be used in a controlled way to promote specific behaviors. For example, cigarette advertising is not allowed on US television stations, but large tobacco companies can sponsor anti-smoking ads. Why would a company advertise against its product? Researchers brought a group of smokers into the lab to complete a study on television programming and subtly included a specific type of advertisement between segments (they did not reveal the true purpose of the study until after it was completed). Their participants were four times as likely to light up after watching a tobacco-company anti-smoking ad than if they saw the control group ad about supporting a youth sports league (Harris et al., 2013). It would appear that while the verbal message is "don't smoke," the images actually prime the behavior. Fortunately, more healthful behaviors have been promoted through priming; for example, carefully designed primes have been shown to reduce mindless snacking (Papies & Hamstra, 2010) and binge-drinking in college students (Goode et al., 2014).

JOURNAL PROMPT

The Lexical Decision Task: Summarize in your own words how the lexical decision task works, and explain why it is relevant to the phenomenon of priming.

Culture and Categories

As a species, human beings share a common biology—the same basic nervous system, the same physiological needs, the same cognitive capacities. On the other hand, human beings do not all share a common culture: They may speak different languages, live in different social structures, and practice different religions. These differences have raised a question about *categorical thinking*—whether the categories by which human beings classify ideas or thoughts are perfect representations of the natural world, or whether they are representations of a specific culture's way of understanding the world. Researchers have explored this question through numerous cross-cultural studies. In one case, researchers in

psychology and anthropology asked individuals from the Itza' Maya people of Guatemala to identify varieties of plants and animals in and around their villages. The researchers knew these plants and animals to be extremely relevant to various aspects of the families' culture, including diet, medicine, and safety; in addition, the people of these villages did not have exposure to scientific taxonomy, which has been designed to represent the natural world as accurately as possible. Surprisingly, the Itza' identified and named (that is, *categorized*) plants and animals similar to what other groups around the world would have chosen, and these closely resembled the scientific taxonomy used at the researchers' universities in the United States. On the other hand, the basic level categories among the Itza' was more specific for these plants and animals than among US college students from predominately urban or suburban environments, where food and medicine come from a store (Medin & Atran, 2004; Berlin, 1974). From this study, we can conclude that categories are remarkably similar across many cultures, but that *experience*, as opposed to culture per se, can vary the way people speak and think about them. In other words, the Itza' have more experience in the physical environment in which these plants and animals are naturally found, and will, therefore, identify and speak them at a more specific level.

Experiential differences do not preclude the significance of cultural differences, however. Cultural differences often lead to questions of **linguistic relativity** (or the **Whorfian hypothesis**, named for Benjamin Whorf)—*the proposal that the language we use determines how we perceive the world.* To support the Whorfian hypothesis, evidence would have to show that people from different cultures not only speak differently about the same categories, but also think, remember, and behave differently about them. In one study conducted to test this hypothesis, researchers explored how different cultures categorize color. The English language, for example, uses distinct names for blue and green. By comparison, the Dani people of New Guinea have one word for blue-green, but no words to distinguish what English speakers consider prototypically blue or prototypically green. Are these language differences reflected in the way people categorize and remember colors? The research yielded mixed results.

When asked to categorize color samples, English speakers set aside a stack of cards for samples that seemed bluer and another stack for those that seemed greener. The Dani, however, created just one stack that combined these cards into a single blue-green category (Roberson et al., 2000). Subsequent research, however, has attempted to clarify whether this effect occurred because the language

Figure 8.5 Your Culture and Your Point of View

(a) Which of these two pictures do you think a North American would be more likely to take?
(b) Which two go together?

(a)   (b)

differences led the subjects to actually perceive color differently (true linguistic relativity) or if they were just using language as a means to complete the sorting task. For example, when individuals were asked to use a verbal distracter (producing irrelevant speech), it prevented them from thinking about the color samples by name during the sorting task. In that case, there are no differences between cultures (Roberson & Davidoff, 2000). In summary, linguistic relativity may be true wherein specific languages influence categorization, but the brain's color perception system continues to work in the same way.

Psychologists have also discovered that cultural factors influence not just how we categorize individual objects, but also how objects in our world relate to one another. Animals, relatives, household appliances, colors, and other entities all fall into categories. However, people from different cultures might differ in how they categorize such objects. In North America, cows are sometimes referred to as "livestock" or "farm animals," whereas in India, where cows are regarded as sacred, neither category would apply.

In addition, how objects are *related* to each other differs considerably across cultures. Which of the two photos in Figure 8.5a do you think a student from the United States would take? Researchers asked both American and Japanese university students to take a picture of someone, from whatever angle or degree of focus they chose. American students were more likely to take close-up pictures, whereas Japanese students typically included surrounding objects (Nisbett & Masuda, 2003). When asked which two objects go together in Figure 8.5b, American college students tend to group cows with chickens—because both are animals. In contrast, Japanese students coupled cows with grass, because grass is what cows eat (Gutchess et al., 2010; Nisbett & Masuda, 2003). These examples

demonstrate cross-cultural differences in perceiving how objects are related to their environments. People raised in the United States tend to focus on a single characteristic, whereas Japanese people tend to view objects in relation to their environment.

Researchers have even found differences in brain function when people of different cultural backgrounds view and categorize objects (Park & Huang, 2010). Figure 8.6 reveals differences in brain activity when Westerners and East Asians view photos of objects, such as an animal, against a background of grass and trees. Areas of the brain devoted to processing both objects and background become activated when Westerners view these photos, whereas only areas devoted to background processes become activated in East Asians (Goh et al., 2007).

Figure 8.6 Brain Activity Varies by Culture

Brain regions that are involved in object recognition and processing are activated differently in people from Western and Eastern cultures. Brain regions that are involved in processing individual objects are more highly activated when Westerners view focal objects against background scenery, whereas people from East Asian countries appear to attend to background scenery more closely than focal objects.

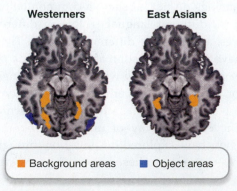

Westerners   **East Asians**

■ Background areas   ■ Object areas

Myths in Mind

How Many Words for Snow?

From time to time, people repeat a bit of "wisdom" about how language relates to thinking. One often-cited example is about the Inuit Eskimos, who are thought to have many words for snow, each with a different meaning. For example, *aput* means snow that is on the ground, and *gana* means falling snow. This observation, which was made in the early 19th century by anthropologist Franz Boas, was often repeated and embellished with claims that Inuit people had dozens of words for different types of snow. With so many words for snow, it was thought that perhaps the Inuit people perceive snow differently than someone who does not live with it year-round. Scholars used the example to argue that language determines how people categorize the world.

Research tells us that we must be careful in overgeneralizing the influence of language on categorization. The reality is that Inuits seem to categorize snow the same way a person from the United States does. Someone from Nebraska can tell the difference between falling snow, blowing snow, sticky snow, drifting snow, and so on, just as well as an Inuit who lives with snow year-round (Martin, 1986). Therefore, we see that the linguistic relativity hypothesis is incorrect in this case: The difference in vocabulary for snow does not lead to differences in perception.

Module 8.1 Summary

8.1a   Know . . . the key terminology associated with concepts and categories:

categories
concept
exemplar
graded membership
linguistic relativity (Whorfian hypothesis)
priming
prototypes
rule-based categorization
semantic network

8.1b   Understand . . . theories of how people organize their knowledge about the world.

First, certain objects and events are more likely to be associated in clusters. The priming effect demonstrates this phenomenon; for example, hearing the word "fruit" makes it more likely that you will think of "apple" than, say, "table." More specifically, we organize our knowledge about the world through semantic networks, which arrange categories from general to specific levels. Usually we think in terms of basic-level categories, but under some circumstances we can be either more or less specific.

8.1c   Understand . . . how experience and culture can shape the way we organize our knowledge.

One of many possible examples of this influence is the difference in how people from North America and Eastern Asia look at objects and scenes. People from North America (and Westerners in general) tend to focus on individual, focal objects in a scene, whereas people from Japan tend to focus on how objects are interrelated.

8.1d   Apply . . . your knowledge to identify prototypical examples.

Prototype and exemplar-based categorization allow us to be extremely efficient in recognizing members of a category. You might test yourself as you go about your day. Perhaps if you find yourself looking over a lunch menu this week, you could ask yourself, "What is a prototypical sandwich, and what is not prototypical?" If you answered the club sandwich and the grilled brie and pear sandwich, respectively, most people would agree. Table 8.2 offered an exercise in identifying prototypes, so you may wish to review it. We came up with the following responses:

1. For most people, a trout would be a better example for a fish. Hammerheads and eels have unique shapes, but trout are very "fish-like"—they are better prototypes for this category.
2. For many Americans, prototypical sports might include baseball, football, and basketball. For much of the rest of the world, the prototypical sport is probably soccer. Sports that are not considered prototypical by many would include competitive cheerleading, windsurfing, and even curling.
3. When people respond to this category, they usually settle on prototypical items that are difficult or impossible to replace—for example, photo albums and other memorabilia, prized possessions, and heirlooms.

8.1e   Analyze . . . the claim that the language we speak determines how we think.

Researchers have shown that language can influence the way we think, but it cannot entirely shape how we perceive the world. For example, people can categorize colors even if they do not have specific words for them.

Module **8.1** Quiz

Know . . .

1. _____ refer to mental representations of objects, events, or ideas.
   - **A.** Categories
   - **B.** Concepts
   - **C.** Primes
   - **D.** Networks

Understand . . .

2. _____ categorization approaches assume that all members of a category share a number of defining features.
   - **A.** Basic-level
   - **B.** Prototypical
   - **C.** Priming
   - **D.** Rule-based

3. What did researchers find when they compared plant and animal naming of rural villagers in Central America to urban dwellers in the United States?
   - **A.** People who rely on the plants and animals for daily needs often named them at a more specific level.
   - **B.** People from both communities relied on the same basic-level category names.
   - **C.** The Itza' Maya and the urban dwellers had such different ways of categorizing nature that direct comparisons were impossible.
   - **D.** Vast differences in plant and animal life in the two locations made it impossible to make any direct comparisons.

Apply . . .

4. When a professor asked the class to name the first fruit that came to mind, over 80% of the students said either apple, orange, or banana. This illustrates that _____.
   - **A.** students are generally conformists
   - **B.** most people are limited by relying on rule-based categorization
   - **C.** these are very prototypical fruits
   - **D.** any single concept can be placed into only one category

Analyze . . .

5. Research on linguistic relativity suggests that:
   - **A.** language has a complete control over how people categorize the world.
   - **B.** language can have some effects on categorization, but the effects are limited.
   - **C.** language has no effect on categorization.
   - **D.** researchers have not addressed this question.

Module 8.2   Problem Solving, Judgment, and Decision Making

Learning Objectives

8.2a Know . . . the key terminology of problem solving and decision making.

8.2b Understand . . . the characteristics that problems have in common.

8.2c Understand . . . how obstacles to problem solving are often self-imposed.

8.2d Apply . . . your knowledge to determine if you tend to be a maximizer or a satisficer.

8.2e Analyze . . . whether human thought is primarily logical or intuitive.

Roommates Kurt and Antoine just started college and decided to spend their fall break on a camping trip. Coming from Germany, Kurt was not able to bring much to school with him, and he wound up spending two weeks visiting nearly a dozen outdoors stores and online retailers, and read product reviews until late in the night. He wound up spending an astonishing amount of money on a sleeping bag and tent—more than many students will spend on recreation all year. Antoine also needed gear, but he simply went to a sporting goods store and picked up something affordable off the shelf. That first night at the campsite, Kurt mocked Antoine's plain, amateurish equipment. However, by the end of the trip, it was clear that despite unequal equipment, they had equal amounts of fun. If anything, Antoine seemed happier with his purchases, as Kurt was expecting so much more.

It would seem that one of the greatest benefits of living in a highly technological, consumer-based society is the luxury of choice. However, psychological science has shown that for some people and in some situations, the luxury of choice might actually be better described as a burden. Barry Schwartz and his colleagues have found in the laboratory what Antoine noticed at the campsite: Individuals who regularly strive for perfection in their decisions—maximizers, as they are called—are often less satisfied than people who simply try to find what is good enough to suit their purposes.

Problems and decisions are everywhere. Some decisions are as simple as figuring out which pair of socks to wear, whereas others can be life-defining experiences, such as deciding which career to pursue and whether to make a commitment to a life partner. Psychologists are interested in how all of these decisions are made, and study both the careful, rational approaches to problems and decisions as well as the more intuitive aspects of thought.

Defining and Solving Problems

In psychological terminology, **problem solving** *means accomplishing a goal when the solution or the path to the solution is not clear* (Leighton & Sternberg, 2003; Robertson, 2001). Despite how different individual problems may seem, they all share some key components, and we attempt to solve them in predictable ways.

THE PARTS OF A PROBLEM To scientifically study the infinite range of problems people face, psychologists break them down into three elements: The *initial state* describes what the condition is at the outset of a problem, and the *goal state* describes what you need or desire as an outcome. Sometimes getting to the goal state is easy, but at other times it can require you to overcome *obstacles*—that is, something that slows or prevents progress toward the goal state. With those three features in place, it is up to you, the problem-solver, to figure out how to overcome the obstacles to reach the goal. The techniques we use to reach the goal state are called *operators*.

When considering a problem, it is important to keep in mind how well it is *defined*. In Table 8.3, the **ill-defined problem** *lacks definition in one or more ways and does not have a definite goal state*—unlike the **well-defined problem**, *which has a specific goal state or states*. A well-defined problem, as the table shows, is more easily solved.

PROBLEM-SOLVING STRATEGIES AND TECHNIQUES Many theories of problem solving and decision making describe two general types of thought: One is more objective, logical, slower, and requires more effort and working memory whereas the other is more subjective, intuitive, and quicker, and, therefore, less demanding (Evans, 2006; Holyoak & Morrison, 2005). Many people identify with one type or the other; do you think of yourself as calm and logical, or are you more intuitive, tending to trust your gut instincts? The truth is that all of us engage in both types

Figure 8.7 Problem-Solving in Hangman

In a game of hangman, your job is to guess the letters in the word represented by the four blanks to the left. If you get a letter right, your opponent will put it in the correct blank. If you guess an incorrect letter, your opponent will draw a body part on the stick figure. The goal is to guess the word before the entire body is drawn.

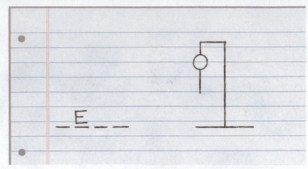

of thinking and, in all likelihood, even the most logical people probably operate intuitively most of the time.

When we think logically, we rely on **algorithms**, *which are problem-solving strategies based on a series of clearly defined steps or rules.* Computers are very good at using algorithms because they can follow a preprogrammed set of steps and perform thousands of operations every second. People, however, are not always so careful. We humans tend to rely on intuition to find operators and solutions that "just seem right." These are called **heuristics**: *problem-solving strategies that stem from prior experiences and provide an educated guess as to what is the most likely solution.*

To further compare algorithms and heuristics, let us examine a low-risk problem with relatively simple strategies—the children's word-game known as hangman (Figure 8.7). Here, the goal state is to spell a word. In the initial state, you have none of the letters or other clues to guide you, and your obstacles are to overcome blanks without guessing the wrong letters. How would you go about selecting operators?

On one hand, an algorithm might go like this: Guess the letter *A*, then *B*, then *C*, and so on through the alphabet until you lose or until the word is spelled. However, this would not be a very successful approach. An alternative algorithm would be to find out how frequently each letter occurs in the alphabet and then guess the letters in that order until the game ends with you winning or losing. (According to the *Oxford English Dictionary*, *E* is most

Table 8.3 Well-Defined and Ill-Defined Problems

Problem Definition	Initial State	Operator	Goal State
Well-defined	I'm cold.	Put on a sweater.	I'm comfortable.
Ill-defined	I need to think of a topic for my term paper.	Flip through your favorite chapter in the textbook to find what interests you.	I'm going to write about culture and language.

frequent, *A* is second most frequent, then *R, I*, and so on [OED, 2011].) On the other hand, a heuristic might be useful. For example, if you discover the last letter is *G*, you might guess that the next-to-last letter is *N*, because you know that many words end with *-ing*.

As you can see, some problems (such as the hangman game) can be approached with either algorithms or heuristics. In other words, most people start out a game like hangman with an algorithm: Guess the most frequent letters until a recognizable pattern emerges, such as *-ing*, or the letters *-oug* (which are often followed by *h*, as in *tough* or *cough*) appear. At that point, you might switch to heuristics and guess which words would be most likely to fit in the spaces.

COGNITIVE OBSTACLES Imagine that you are running late while getting dressed for an interview. Your only suit is wrinkled, but the iron is not working. What could you do? There are a number of obstacles to this problem, mainly the lack of the obvious tool and limited time to shop or borrow a replacement. The only way to solve this problem is to dream up a new way to iron clothes, and that will require creative thinking. This is a type of cognitive obstacle, one that is based on how you understand a problem, or how innovative you can be in finding a solution. As long as you believe that the only solution is an iron, you will be stuck with a wrinkled suit. Conversely, if you entertain other possibilities, you can overcome mental obstacles to problem solving. The Internet teems with examples of easy solutions to problems like these called "life hacks." Perhaps you can figure out a way to hack the broken-iron problem?

Cognitive obstacles are often frustrating because they are self-imposed; you know there is a solution but cannot figure out what it is. Researchers have used a variety of problems in the lab to study this tendency, with one of the most popular being the nine-dot problem (Figure 8.8; Maier, 1930). The goal is to connect all nine dots using only

Figure 8.8 The Nine-Dot Problem

On a piece of paper, connect all nine dots using only four straight lines and without lifting your pen or pencil (Maier, 1930). The solution to the problem can be seen in Figure 8.9.

Figure 8.9 The Five Daughter Problem

Maria's father has five daughters: Lala, Lela, Lila, and Lola. What is the fifth daughter's name?

four straight lines and without lifting your pen or pencil off the paper. Try solving the nine-dot problem before you read further.

Here is something to think about when solving this problem: Most people impose limitations on where the lines can go, even though those limits are not a part of the rules. An explanation of the self-imposed limitation can be found with the solution to the nine-dot problem (see Figure 8.10).

Having a routine solution available for a problem can be great. Sometimes, however, routines may impose cognitive barriers that impede solving a problem if circumstances change such that the routine solution no longer works. A **mental set** *is a cognitive obstacle that occurs when an individual attempts to apply a routine solution to what is actually a new type of problem.* A mental set can also occur when an individual applies a routine solution when a much easier solution is possible.

Figure 8.9 presents a problem that often elicits a mental set. The answer appears in the summary for objective 8.2c on page 265, but make your guess before you check it. Did you get it right? If not, then you probably succumbed to mental set. If you got the solution right this first time, congratulations! It might be interesting to try this problem on a friend to see if she gets caught off guard.

In some situations, a person experiences **functional fixedness**, *which occurs when an individual encounters a potential operator, but can think of only its most obvious function.* For example, irons use steam to loosen up the wrinkles in clothing. Functional fixedness might prevent an individual from considering hanging wrinkled slacks in the bathroom during a hot shower. Afterwards, you can warm a skillet on the stove and then use that as a makeshift iron to flatten out any remaining creases. Life hacking simply involves breaking out of that state of fixedness in which a frying pan is just a pan.

Problem solving shows up in every aspect of life, but as you can see, there are basic cognitive processes that

Figure 8.10 One Solution to the Nine-Dot Problem

In this case, the tendency is to see the outer edge of dots as a boundary, and to assume that one cannot go past that boundary. However, if you are willing to extend some of the lines beyond the dots, it is actually quite a simple puzzle to complete.

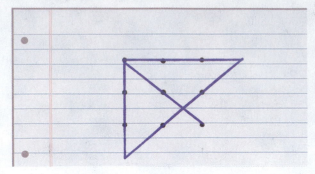

Figure 8.11 The Conjunction Fallacy

There are more bank tellers in the world than there are bank tellers who are feminists, so there is a greater chance that Linda comes from either (A) or (B) than just (B) alone.

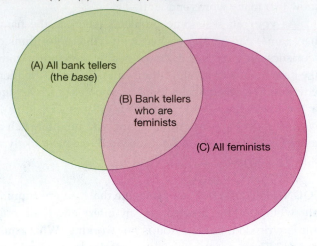

appear no matter what the context. We identify initial and goal states, try to determine the best operators, and hope that we do not get caught by unexpected obstacles—self-created ones, especially.

Judgment and Decision Making

Like problem solving, judgments and decisions can be based on logical algorithms, intuitive heuristics, or a combination of the two types of thought (Gilovich & Griffin, 2002; Holyoak & Morrison, 2005). We tend to use heuristics more often than we realize, even those of us who consider ourselves to be logical thinkers. Here we look more closely at specific types of heuristics and consider how they influence our process of making judgments and decisions.

REPRESENTATIVENESS AND AVAILABILITY One way to illustrate the two types of thought is to examine how individuals make judgments about probabilities and frequencies. For an example, try this problem before reading any further:

> Linda is 31 years old, single, outspoken, and very bright. She majored in philosophy. As a student, she was deeply concerned with issues of discrimination and social justice, and also participated in antinuclear demonstrations. Which is more likely?
>
> **A.** Linda is a bank teller.
> **B.** Linda is a bank teller and is active in the feminist movement.

So which one did you choose? Researchers who presented this problem to participants in a classic study reported that (B) was chosen more than 80% of the time. If you chose (B), then you probably do not see anything wrong with the choice, although (A) is actually more likely and would be the correct choice (Tversky & Kahneman, 1982). But how? Logic tells us that the world has a certain number of (A) bank tellers; this number would be considered the *base rate*, or the rate at which

you would find a bank teller at random in the world's population. Among the base group, there will be a certain number of people in the *conjunction* of two categories. These are the (B) bank tellers who are feminists, as shown in Figure 8.11. In other words, there are many more bank tellers in general than bank tellers who are also feminists. Instead of logic, however, most of us apply the **representativeness heuristic**—*making judgments of likelihood based on how well an example represents a specific category.* While we cannot identify any traits in Linda that seem like a typical bank teller, we can identify traits that make Linda seem like a feminist—her past social activism *represents* feminism; thus, we come up with an answer based on representativeness.

The question about Linda illustrates a particular use of representativeness called the *conjunction fallacy* in which the conjunction appears more likely than the base rate. You can find examples of this fallacy in all aspects of life; it is a perfectly normal type of reasoning. However, some of the more interesting examples involve superstitious beliefs, paranormal explanations, and conspiracy theories, all of which stem from the assumption that unusual events require unusual explanations. In fact, individuals who score higher on tests of paranormal beliefs are more likely to commit conjunction errors in general, and this is found among people who are intrigued by conspiracy theories as well (Brotherton & French, 2013). Consider this version of the same basic problem you read earlier:

> Leanne arrives home late one evening after visiting her sister, who lives six miles away, and goes to bed. Leanne rarely has nightmares, but this night she is awakened by a particularly frightening dream. Which of the following events is most likely to have occurred? Which is least likely?

A. *Leanne dreams that a house is on fire.*

B. *A fire breaks out in Leanne's sister's house.*

C. *Leanne dreams that a house is on fire, and a fire breaks out in Leanne's sister's house.*

You should be able to recognize that A and B are broader events, which each have their own base rate. Again, some people will apply the representitiveness heuristic and choose (C), the conjunction of the two other events, which is actually the least likely. However, not everyone will make that mistake. In this case, you are only likely to choose (C) if it appears to represent something you already believe in—perhaps the symbolic power of dreams. If you are a skeptic, you are far less likely to be tempted by the conjunction fallacy (Brotherton & French, 2013).

A related decision-making tendency is the **availability heuristic**—*estimating the frequency of an event based on how easily examples of it come to mind.* In other words, we assume that if examples are readily *available*, then they must be very frequent. For example, researchers asked volunteers which was more frequent in the English language:

A. Words that begin with the letter *K*

B. Words that have *K* as the third letter

Most subjects chose (A) even though it is not the correct choice. The same thing happened with the consonants *L, N, R, and V*, all of which appear as the third letter in a word more often than they appear as the first letter (Tversky & Kahneman, 1973). This outcome reflects the application of the availability heuristic: People base judgments on the information most readily available.

Of course, heuristics often do produce correct answers. Subjects in the same study were asked which was more common in English:

A. Words that begin with the letter *K*

B. Words that begin with the letter *T*

In this case, more subjects found that words beginning with T were readily available to memory, and they were correct. The heuristic helped provide a quick intuitive answer.

There are numerous real-world examples of the availability heuristic. Most of us can think of examples of police brutality, kidnapping, and terrorist attacks—these are events that easily come to mind. However, we are also likely to overestimate the risks of each of these events, in part because it is easier to think of *examples* of these events than it is to think of times when they do *not* occur.

JOURNAL PROMPT

The Availability Heuristic: The availability heuristic is highly relevant to people's assessment of risk (e.g., likelihood of being struck by lightning). Identify an event not mentioned in the text that you think people tend to overestimate in terms of its likelihood. Why do you think this happens?

ANCHORING EFFECTS Some heuristics are based on how problems are presented. Issues such as wording, the variety of multiple-choice options, and frames of reference can have a profound impact on judgments. One such effect—known as the **anchoring effect**—*occurs when an individual attempts to solve a problem involving numbers and uses previous knowledge to keep (i.e.,* anchor*) the response within a limited range.* For example, individuals in one study were asked to think aloud when answering questions such as: *When was George Washington elected president?* Participants would reply with thoughts such as "The United States declared independence from England in 1776, and it probably took a few years to elect a president, so Washington was elected in…1789" (Epley & Gilovich, 2001, p. 392). Thus the signing of the Declaration of Independence in 1776 serves as the *anchor* for Washington's election.

Anchors are more effective when they are generated by the individual making the judgments, but they can also have effects when introduced by the experimenter (Epley & Gilovich, 2006; Kahneman & Miller, 1986). For example, consider what happened when researchers asked the same question to two different groups, using a different anchor each time:

A. What percentage of African nations belongs to the United Nations? Is it greater than or less than 10%? What do you think the exact percentage is?

B. What percentage of African nations belongs to the United Nations? Is it greater than or less than 65%? What do you think the exact percentage is?

The individuals in group (A), who received the 10% anchor, estimated the number to be approximately 25%. Individuals in the group (B), who received the 65% anchor, estimated the percentage at approximately 45%. In this case, the anchor obviously had a significant effect on the estimates.

THE BENEFITS OF HEURISTIC THINKING As you have seen in this section, the heuristics used in making judgments and decisions can lead us astray from time to time. Nevertheless, the point of studying these errors is not to show how naive people can be. Actually, this line of research helps psychologists understand why heuristics are so often beneficial—they help us make decisions as efficiently as possible. It is not difficult to imagine situations in which this might be helpful, such as when avoiding threat. If you encounter an animal with dirty fur, baring its teeth, and growling at you, the representativeness heuristic will help you identify that it represents a potential threat. It is probably better to decide quickly and leave rather than pause to consider the logic of the situation. So, while it would be a mistake to think that all human cognition is logical, it would be equally mistaken to take an overly

Table 8.4 Contradictory and Exculpatory Statements for Democratic and Republican Presidential Candidates

Sample statement set: George W. Bush
Initial: "First of all, Ken Lay is a supporter of mine. I love the man. I got to know Ken Lay years ago, and he has given generously to my campaign. When I'm president, I plan to run the government like a CEO runs a country. Ken Lay and Enron are a model of how I'll do that." —Candidate George Bush, 2000
Contradictory: Mr. Bush now avoids any mention of Ken Lay and is critical of Enron when asked.
Exculpatory: People who know the president report that he feels betrayed by Ken Lay and was genuinely shocked to find that Enron's leadership had been corrupt.

Sample statement set: John Kerry
Initial: During the 1996 campaign, Kerry told a *Boston Globe* reporter that the Social Security system should be overhauled. He said Congress should consider raising the retirement age and means-testing benefits. "I know it's going to be unpopular," he said. "But we have a generational responsibility to fix this problem."
Contradictory: This year [2004], on *Meet the Press*, Kerry pledged that he will never tax or cut benefits to seniors or raise the age for eligibility for Social Security.
Exculpatory: Economic experts now suggest that, in fact, the Social Security system will not run out of money until 2049, not 2020, as they had thought in 1996.

SOURCE: Drew Western, Pavel S. Blagov, Keith Harenski, Clint Kilts, and Stephan Hamann, 'Neural Bases of Motivated Reasoning: An fMRI Study of Emotional Constraints on Partisan Political Judgment in the 2004 U.S. Presidential Election', Journal of Cognitive Neuroscience, 18:11 (November, 2006), pp. 1947–1958. © 2006 by the Massachusetts Institute of Technology. Reprinted with permission.

pessimistic view of human thought (Gilovich & Griffin, 2002). Knowing that people are susceptible to errors can help us to be better critical thinkers, allowing us to spend time evaluating our solutions, judgments, and decisions.

BELIEF PERSEVERANCE AND CONFIRMATION BIAS Whenever we solve a problem or make a decision, we have an opportunity to evaluate the outcome to make sure we got it right and to judge how satisfied we are with the decision. However, that does not always happen in such a clear-cut manner.

Imagine you and several friends sit down for a poker match with an old deck of cards. The dealer removes the cards from the box and counts to make sure they are all present. At first, he comes up with 51 cards—one short. The second try, he gets 52 cards—the correct amount. Now that he has reached the expected number, he goes on to deal the first round. What is wrong with his reasoning in this case?

Belief perseverance *occurs when an individual believes he has the solution to the problem or the correct answer for a question* (e.g., How many cards are in this deck?), *and accepts only evidence that will confirm those beliefs.* Our dealer knew the correct number of cards would be 52. He exhibited the belief perseverance by ignoring the count that gave him 51 as some sort of mistake; meanwhile, the count that confirmed his idea that there should be 52 cards was considered to be correct.

Along the same general lines, the **confirmation bias** *occurs when an individual searches for only evidence that will confirm his or her beliefs instead of evidence that might disconfirm them.* This differs from belief perseverance in that the confirmation bias is the search for a particular type of evidence, not a way of evaluating evidence that already exists. In the case of our dealer, he could have laid out all 13 cards from each suite to ensure that he had a full deck—that would have been a logical way to identify if any cards were missing. Instead, he exhibited the confirmation bias by seeking out only confirmatory evidence.

Confirmation bias and belief perseverance together can dramatically influence a person's beliefs, especially in relation to complex, emotionally charged areas such as religion and politics. In fact, much of the research on these biases shows that people treat evidence in ways that minimize negative or uncomfortable feelings while maximizing positive feelings (Westen et al., 2006). For example, one study examined the brain regions and self-reported feelings involved in interpreting information about presidential candidates during the campaigns. The participants were all deeply committed to either the Republican or Democratic candidate, and they all encountered information that was threatening toward each candidate, as shown in Table 8.4. As you can see from the results in Figure 8.12, participants had strong emotional reactions to threatening (self-contradictory) information about their own candidate, but not to the alternative candidate, or a relatively neutral person, such as a retired network news anchor. Analyses of the brain scans demonstrated that very different neural processes were at work in each condition. When the threat was directed at the participant's own candidate, brain areas associated with ignoring or suppressing information were more active, whereas few of the regions associated with logical thinking were activated (Westen et al., 2006).

Working the Scientific Literacy Model

Maximizing and Satisficing in Complex Decisions

One privilege of living in a technologically advanced, democratic society is that we get to make so many decisions for ourselves. However, for each decision there can be more choices than we can possibly consider. As a result, two types of consumers have emerged in our society. *Satisficers* are individuals who seek to make decisions that

Figure 8.12 Ratings of Perceived Contradictions in Political Statements

Democrats and Republicans reached very different conclusions about candidates' contradictory statements. Democrats readily identified the opponent's contradictions but were less likely to do so for their own candidate; the same was true for Republican responders.

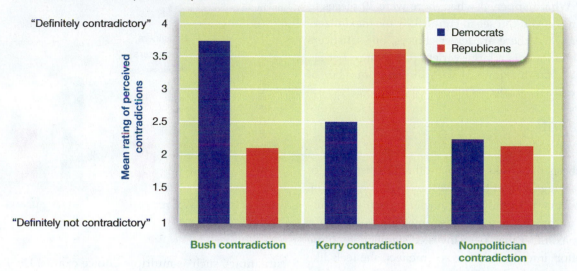

are, simply put, "good enough." In contrast, *maximizers* are individuals who attempt to evaluate every option for every choice until they find the perfect fit. Most people exhibit some of both behaviors, satisficing at times and maximizing at other times. However, if you consider all the people you know, you can probably identify at least one person who is an extreme maximizer—he will always be comparing products, jobs, classes, and so on, to find out who has made the best decisions. At the same time, you can probably identify an extreme satisficer—the person who will be satisfied with his or her choices as long as they are good enough.

What do we know about maximizing and satisficing?

If one person settles for the good-enough option, while another searches until he finds the best possible option, which individual do you think will be happier with the decision in the end? Most people believe the maximizer will be happier, but this is not always the case. In fact, researchers such as Barry Schwartz have no shortage of data about the *paradox of choice*: the observation that more choices can lead to less satisfaction. In one study, the researchers asked participants to recollect both large (more than $100) and small (less than $10) purchases and report the number of options they considered, the time spent shopping and making the decision, and the overall satisfaction with the purchase. Sure enough, those who ranked high on a test of maximization invested more time and effort, but were actually less pleased with the outcome (Schwartz et al., 2002; Polman, 2010).

In another study, researchers questioned recent college graduates about their job search process. Believe it or

not, maximizers averaged 20% higher salaries, but were less happy about their jobs than satisficers (Iyengar et al., 2006). This outcome occurred despite the fact that the opposite would seem to be true—*if* humans were perfectly logical decision makers.

So now we know that just the presence of alternative choices can drive down satisfaction—but how can that be?

How can science explain maximizing and satisficing?

To answer this question, researchers asked participants to read vignettes that included a trade-off between number of choices and effort (Dar-Nimrod et al., 2009). Try this example for yourself:

Your cleaning supplies (e.g., laundry detergent, rags, carpet cleaner, dish soap, toilet paper, glass cleaner) are running low. You have the option of going to the nearest grocery store (5 minutes away), which offers four alternatives for each of the items you need, or you can drive to the grand cleaning superstore (25 minutes away), which offers 25 different alternatives for each of the items (for approximately the same price). Which store would you go to?

In the actual study, maximizers were much more likely to spend the extra time and effort to have more choices. Thus, if you decided to go to the store with more options, you are probably a maximizer. What this scenario does not tell us is whether having more or fewer choices was pleasurable for either maximizers or satisficers.

See how well you understand the nature of maximizers and satisficers by predicting the results of the next study: Participants completed a taste test of one piece of chocolate, but they could choose one piece of chocolate from an array of 6 pieces or an array of 30 pieces. When there were 6 pieces, who was happier—maximizers or satisficers? What happened when there were 30 pieces to choose from? As you can see in Figure 8.13, the maximizers are happier when there are fewer choices, but satisficers win out when there is a large variety (Dar-Nimrod et al., 2009). In fact, the maximizers with the large number of choices were least satisfied of all participants!

Can we critically evaluate this information?

One hypothesis that seeks to explain the dissatisfaction of maximizers suggests that they invest more in the decision, so they expect more from the outcome. Imagine that a satisficer and a maximizer purchase the same digital camera for $175. The maximizer may have invested significantly more time and effort into the decision so, in effect, she feels like she paid considerably more for the camera. At the end of the day, however, the two consumers have the same product.

Regardless of the explanation, we should keep in mind that maximizers and satisficers are preexisting categories. People cannot be randomly assigned to be in one category or another, so these findings represent the outcomes of correlational research. We cannot be sure that the act of maximizing leads to dissatisfaction based on these data. Perhaps maximizers are the people who are generally less satisfied, which in turn leads to maximizing behavior.

Why is this relevant?

Although we described maximizing and satisficing in terms of purchasing decisions, you might also notice that these styles of decision making can be applied to other

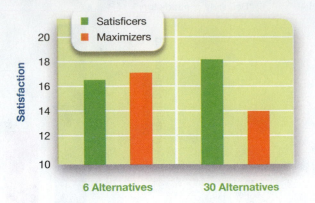

Figure 8.13 Satisfaction of Maximizers and Satisficers
The relative satisfaction of maximizers and satisficers depends on how many choices are available. Maximizers are happier when there are fewer alternatives, whereas satisficers are happier when there are more options.

situations, such as multiple-choice exams. Do you select the first response that sounds reasonable (satisficing), or do you carefully review each of the responses and compare them to one another before marking your choice (maximizing)? Once you make your choice, do you stick with it, believing it is good enough (satisficing), or are you willing to change your answer to make the best possible choice (maximizing)? Despite the popular wisdom that you should never change your first response, there may be an advantage to maximizing on exams. Research focusing on more than 1,500 individual examinations showed that when people change their answers, they improve their score 51% of the time and hurt their score only 25% of the time (Kruger et al., 2005). Rate your own tendencies to maximize or satisfice with the activity in Table 8.5.

Table 8.5 Self Assessment: Maximizer or Satisficer?

Rate the following items on a scale from 1 (completely disagree) to 7 (completely agree), with 4 being a neutral response.

1. Whenever I'm faced with a choice, I try to imagine what all the other possibilities are, even ones that aren't present at the moment.
2. No matter how satisfied I am with my job, it's only right for me to be on the lookout for better opportunities.
3. When I am in the car listening to the radio, I often check other stations to see whether something better is playing, even if I am relatively satisfied with what I'm listening to.
4. When I watch TV, I channel surf, often scanning through the available options even while attempting to watch one program.
5. I treat relationships like clothing: I expect to try a lot on before finding the perfect fit.
6. I often find it difficult to shop for a gift for a friend.
7. When shopping, I have a difficult time finding clothing that I really love.
8. No matter what I do, I have the highest standards for myself.
9. I find that writing is very difficult, even if it's just writing to a friend, because it's so difficult to word things just right. I often do several drafts of even simple things.
10. I never settle for second best.

When you are finished, average your ratings together to find your overall score. Scores greater than 4 indicate a tendency to maximize. Scores; less than 4 indicate a tendency to satisfice. Approximately one-third of the population scores below 3.25 and approximately one-third scores above 4.75. Where does your score place you?

Module 8.2 Summary

8.2a   Know . . . the key terminology of problem solving and decision making:

algorithms
anchoring effect
availability heuristic
belief perseverance
confirmation bias
functional fixedness
heuristics
ill-defined problem
mental set
problem solving
representativeness heuristic
well-defined problem

8.2b   Understand . . . the characteristics that problems have in common.

All problems have initial states and goal states with obstacles in between. We use operators to overcome the obstacles and achieve goals states. Also, many problems include subgoals. Problems can range from well-defined to ill-defined.

8.2c   Understand . . . how obstacles to problem solving are often self-imposed.

Many obstacles arise from the individual's mental set, which occurs when a person focuses on only one known solution and does not consider alternatives. Similarly, functional fixedness can arise when an individual does not consider alternative uses for familiar objects. This type of obstacle can be seen in Figure 8.10 where many assume that the fifth daughter's name is Lulu—that would fit the pattern established by the older daughter's name. However, the question clearly states that her name is Maria.

8.2d   Apply . . . your knowledge to determine if you tend to be a maximizer or a satisficer.

People who are consistently one or the other tend to know it. Like any other trait, people also fall somewhere in the middle of the maximizer–satisficer continuum. This may be because on matters and decisions that are most important or meaningful people will maximize, but otherwise are comfortable being satisficers. Where do you fall on that continuum? If you are not sure yet, complete the scale in Table 8.5 to find out how you compare to others.

8.2e   Analyze . . . whether human thought is primarily logical or intuitive.

This module provides ample evidence that humans are not always logical. Heuristics are helpful decision-making and problem-solving tools, but they do not follow logical principles. Even so, the abundance of heuristics does not mean that humans are never logical; instead, they simply point to the limits of our rationality.

Module 8.2 Quiz

Defining and Solving Problems

Know . . .

1. _____ are problem-solving strategies that provide a reasonable guess for the solution.
   - **A.** Algorithms
   - **B.** Heuristics
   - **C.** Operators
   - **D.** Subgoals

Understand . . .

2. When a writer or artist sits down to begin a new piece of work, the creator does not know what it will look like when it is finished. This is a(n) _____.
   - **A.** ill-defined problem
   - **B.** well-defined problem
   - **C.** algorithm
   - **D.** operator state

3. Louis needs a screwdriver to fix his remote-controlled car but he doesn't have one on hand. It does not occur to him that the dime in his pocket could serve as a makeshift substitute. This is because he is experiencing _____.
   - **A.** mental set
   - **B.** prototyping
   - **C.** functional fixedness
   - **D.** an ill-defined problem

Apply . . .

4. If you usually spend twice as long as your dinner companions poring over the menu, considering every choice and fretting over which one would be best, then you are almost certainly _____.
   - **A.** experiencing mental set
   - **B.** a satisficer
   - **C.** facing an operator
   - **D.** a maximizer

Analyze . . .

5. Why do psychologists assert that heuristics are beneficial for problem solving?
   - **A.** Heuristics increase the amount of time we spend arriving at good solutions to problems.
   - **B.** Heuristics decrease our chances of errors dramatically.
   - **C.** Heuristics help us make decisions efficiently.
   - **D.** Heuristics are considered the most logical thought pattern for problem solving.

Module 8.3   Language and Communication

Learning Objectives

8.3a   Know . . . the key terminology from the study of language.

8.3b   Understand . . . how language is structured.

8.3c   Understand . . . how genes and the brain are involved in language use.

8.3d   Apply . . . your knowledge to distinguish between units of language such as phonemes and morphemes.

8.3e   Analyze . . . whether species other than humans are able to use language.

Dog owners are known for attributing a lot of intelligence, emotion, and "humanness" to their canine pals. Sometimes they may appear to go overboard—such as Rico's owners, who claimed their border collie understood 200 words, most of which refer to different toys and objects he likes to play with. According to their story, they could show Rico a toy, repeat its name a few times, and toss the toy into a pile of other objects; Rico would then retrieve the object upon verbal command. Rico's ability appeared to go well beyond the usual "sit," "stay," "heel," and perhaps a few other words that dog owners expect their companions to understand.

Claims about Rico's language talents soon drew the attention of scientists, who skeptically questioned whether the dog was just responding to cues by the owners, such as their possible looks or gestures toward the object they asked their pet to retrieve. The scientists set up a carefully controlled experiment in which no one present in the room knew the location of the object that was requested. Rico correctly retrieved 37 out of 40 objects. The experimenters then tested the owners' claim that Rico could learn object names in just one trial. Rico again confirmed his owners' claims, and the researchers concluded that his ability to understand new words was comparable to that of a 3-year-old child (Kaminski et al., 2004). Work with Rico seems to have instigated a bit of competition to determine who has the smartest dog. Another border collie named Chaser learned a whopping 1,022 nouns over a 3-year period (Pilley & Reid, 2011).

These researchers answered some interesting questions about language in a nonhuman species, but many still remain.

Communication happens just about anywhere you can find life. Dogs bark, cats meow, monkeys chatter, and mice can emit sounds undetectable to the human ear when communicating. Honeybees perform an elaborate dance to communicate the direction, distance, and quality of food sources (vonFrisch, 1967). Animals even communicate by marking their territories with their distinct scent. Language is among the many ways that humans communicate. It is quite unlike the examples of animal communication mentioned previously. So what differentiates language from these other forms of communication?

JOURNAL PROMPT

Defining Language: Before you proceed, define what the term "language" means to you. Does your definition exclude the possibility that nonhuman animals use this form of communication too?

What Is Language?

Language, like many other cognitive abilities, flows so automatically that we often overlook how complicated it really is. It is not until we try to learn a new language in adulthood or try to communicate with someone who does not speak our native language that its true complexity becomes clear. **Language** *is a form of communication that involves the use of spoken, written, or gestural symbols that are combined in a rule-based form.* As we explore different forms of communication, the line between what is and is not language becomes blurred, but a few basic features can help make distinctions (Harley, 2001).

One characteristic of language is that we use it to communicate about objects and events that are not in the present time and place. We use language to imagine things that are happening on another planet, or things that are happening inside of atoms. A college student can say, "We're going to order pizza tonight," without her roommate thinking the pizza is already there. But if you tell your dog, "I'll give you a treat later tonight," your dog will probably only hear "Treat" with meaningless sounds before and after it. Naturally, that means your dog will expect the treat right away.

Languages can produce entirely new meanings. At worst, this facility allows people to tell tall tales, such as those found in supermarket tabloids: *Bat Boy Found in Cave!* This particular tabloid story concerned a creature that was part bat and part boy. It is bizarre, and we may not believe it, but we can understand it in a number of ways depending on how we decide to put the two words "bat" and "boy" together. In contrast, the signals animals themselves use stand alone and pairing them together does not produce new meanings. Thus, although dogs may appear to understand many different words, they do not appear to understand their relationships to other words when put into sentences.

Language also differs from other types of communication in that it is passed down from parents to children. No matter how well your dog responds to commands such as "sit," "stay," or "roll over," an animal will not be able to sit her puppies down and explain the meaning to them.

PHONEMES AND MORPHEMES: THE BASIC INGREDIENTS OF LANGUAGE Languages contain discrete units that exist at differing levels of complexity the most basic of which are individual sounds. When people speak, they assemble these units into larger and more complex units such as suffixes, prefixes, and entire words and sentences.

Phonemes *are the most basic of units of speech sounds.* You can identify phonemes rather easily; the phoneme associated with the letter *t* (which is written as /t/, where the two forward slashes indicate a phoneme) is found at the end of the word *pot* or near the beginning of the word *stop*. If you pay close attention to the way you use your tongue, lips, and vocal cords, you will notice *coarticulation*: phonemes have slight variations depending on the other letters around them. Pay attention to how you pronounce the /t/ phoneme in *stop*, *stash*, *stink*, and *stoke*. Your mouth will move in slightly different ways each time, and there will be very slight variations in sound, but you are likely to hear it as the same basic phoneme. Individual phonemes typically do not have any meaning by themselves; if you want someone to stop doing something, asking him to /t/ will not suffice.

Morphemes *are the smallest meaningful units of a language.* Some morphemes are simple words, whereas others may be suffixes or prefixes. For example, the word *pig* is a morpheme—it cannot be broken down into smaller units of meaning. You can combine morphemes, however, if you follow the rules of the language. If you want to pluralize *pig*, you can add the morpheme /-s/, which will give you *pigs*. If you want to describe a person as a pig, you can add the morpheme /-ish/ to get *piggish*. In fact, you can add all kinds of morphemes to a word as long as you follow the rules. You could even say *piggable* (able to be pigged) or *piggify* (to turn into a pig). These words do not make much literal sense, but they combine morphemes according to the rules; thus we can make a reasonable guess as to the speaker's intended meaning (see Table 8.6 to make sure you can distinguish phonemes from morphemes).

Table 8.6 Morpheme or Phoneme?

Which of these represent a single phoneme and which represent a morpheme? Do any of them represent both? Answers are provided in the module summary, objective 8.3d, on page 274.

1. /dis/
2. /s/
3. /k/

Figure 8.14 Syntax Allows Us to Understand Language by the Organization of the Words

The rules of syntax help us divide a sentence into noun phrases, verb phrases, and other parts of speech (Pinker, 1994).

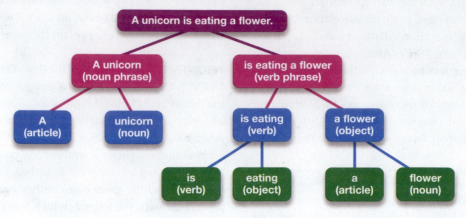

Our ability to combine morphemes into words is one distinguishing feature of language that sets it apart from other forms of communication. In essence, language gives us *productivity*—the ability to combine units of sound into an infinite number of meanings.

Finally, there are the words that make up a language. **Semantics** *is the study of how people come to understand meaning from words*. Humans have a knack for this kind of interpretation, and each of us has an extensive mental dictionary to prove it. Not only do normal speakers know tens of thousands of words, but they can often understand new words they have never heard before based on their understanding of morphemes.

As you can see, languages derive their complexity from several elements, including phonemes, morphemes, and semantics. But this is just the shopping list—we still need to figure out how to mix these ingredients together.

SYNTAX   Perhaps the most remarkable aspect of language is **syntax**, *the rules for combining words and morphemes into meaningful phrases and sentences*. But despite mastering their native language's rules in childhood, most speakers cannot tell you what the rules are; syntax just seems to come naturally. We can begin to understand what syntax is by looking at its most basic units: noun phrases and verb phrases. To show how syntax helps us derive meaning from language, we may consider an example of an unfortunate newspaper headline that is ambiguous, meaning the same words can be interpreted differently depending on the syntax you apply to it. Start with the basic headline: *Debate over school lunches heating up*. The meaning you derive depends on what you consider to be the noun phrase. Most likely, the editors wanted you to arrive at a solution in which the noun phrase includes *Debates over school lunches* and the verb phrase is *heating up*. After all, the story was about increasingly divisive political arguments in a school district over the costs and benefits of minimum fresh fruit and vegetable requirements.

However, because it is a headline, you might also view the entire thing as a noun phrase that simply serves as a label. Without a verb phrase, the debate must be about the temperature of the kids' lunches. Thus, the syntax goes beyond simple word meanings to help you arrive at your understanding of a sentence (see Figure 8.14).

PRAGMATICS   Unlike the abstract processes of syntax, **pragmatics** *involves the nonlinguistic elements of language use* such as the speaker's behaviors and intentions, and the social situation in which the language is used (Carston, 2002). One way to conceptualize these elements is to assume that speakers are guided by the *cooperative principle*, which states that pragmatic rules apply to conversation, so entering into a conversation is essentially agreeing to cooperate. For example, you may have witnessed a situation over a meal when someone asked, "Can you pass the salt?" Given that the speaker's intention is to eat and that the salt is out of reach, it would be reasonable to assume that the sentence is a polite request, not a question about your ability to handle condiments.

Pragmatics reminds us that sometimes *what* is said is not as important as *how* it is said. For example, a student who says, "I ate a 50 pound cheeseburger," is most likely stretching the truth, but you probably would not call him a liar. Pragmatics helps us understand what he implied. The voracious student was actually *flouting*—or blatantly disobeying—a rule of language in a way that is obvious (Grice, 1975; Horn & Ward, 2004). There are all sorts of ways in which flouting the rules can lead to implied, not literal meanings; a sample of those are shown in Table 8.7.

Language Development, Evolution, and the Brain

Numerous processes are involved in the development and support of human language. These processes require genes, brain regions, and complex interactions of these

Table 8.7 Pragmatic Rules Guiding Language Use

The Rule	Flouting the Rule	The Implication
Say what you believe is true.	My roommate is a *giraffe*.	He does not *really* live with a giraffe. Maybe his roommate is very tall?
Say only what is relevant.	Is my blind date good-looking? *He's got a great personality*.	She didn't answer my question. He's probably not very attractive.
Say only as much as you need to.	I like my lab partner, but he's no *Einstein*.	Of course he's not Einstein. Why is she bothering to tell me this? She probably means that her partner is not very smart.

components that begin during early development. Also, evidence for an evolutionary basis of language comes from work comparing nonhuman species with those of human children. Each of these topics is explored in this section.

LANGUAGE IN THE BRAIN   Language involves numerous regions distributed throughout the brain, especially the cerebral cortex. Reading requires visual areas, listening involves auditory areas, and the memories that provide ideas and the words to talk about them are distributed throughout the cortex. The most unique and specialized aspects of language, however, are based in the left hemisphere (for the vast majority of the human population), in regions known as Wernicke's area and Broca's area, which are named in recognition of the researchers who developed the modern views of their function (Buckingham, 2006; introduced in Module 3.3). The roles of these regions can be illuminated through brain imaging technology, but we can also examine what happens when they malfunction due to injury or disease. **Aphasias** *are language disorders caused by damage to the brain structures that support using and understanding language.* As you will soon see, a number of distinct abilities can be affected by such conditions.

Figure 8.15 Two Language Centers of the Brain

Broca's and Wernicke's areas of the cerebral cortex are critical to language function.

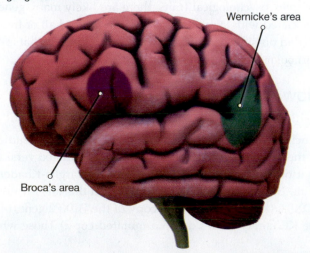

Wernicke's area

Broca's area

Located toward the middle, back portion of the temporal lobe, you will find **Wernicke's area**, *the area of the brain most associated with finding the meaning of words* (Figure 8.15). Damage to this area results in *Wernicke's aphasia*, a language disorder in which a person has difficulty understanding the words he hears. We know this problem is associated with semantics rather than syntax, because an individual's speech sounds normal at first—the syntax, intonation, accent, and demeanor are normal, but the word choices do not make sense (Akmajian et al., 2001; Caspari, 2005). For example, one individual with Wernicke's aphasia engaged in this conversation:

Examiner: Do you like it here in Kansas City?

Person with aphasia: Yes, I am.

Examiner: I'd like to have you tell me something about your problem.

Person with aphasia: Yes, I, ugh, cannot hill all of my way. I cannot talk all of the things I do, and part of the part I can go alright, but I cannot tell from the other people. I usually most of my things. I know what can I talk and know what they are, but I cannot always come back even though I know they should be in, and I know should something eely I should know what I'm doing …

Because of the confusing nature of the speech, a severe case of Wernicke's aphasia could be mistaken for a type of schizophrenia (see Module 13.4 for a description of schizophrenia). Nevertheless, aphasia is a disorder of language, not of other cognitive abilities. Individuals who are fortunate enough to recover some of their language abilities report that, during the worst part of the disorder, they knew when someone was speaking, but they could not understand it—they could not understand even their own speech.

Broca's area *is a frontal lobe structure involved in articulating speech sounds that comprise words* (Figure 8.15). As shown in Figure 8.15 Broca's area appears adjacent to a strip of the brain known as the motor cortex that helps us control body movements. Given its proximity to the motor cortex, Broca's area has long been associated with the production of speech (Buckingham, 2006). However, its work entails much more than just signaling the muscles to move; it is also involved in adding grammatical flourishes to words that have already been selected and combining them into syntactically appropriate phrases. Broca's area functions in other ways, too. For example, it is active when processing musical notes (Maess et al., 2001).

A person with damage to this area will most likely be diagnosed with *Broca's aphasia* (Akmajian et al., 2001; Dick et al., 2001). Although most of these individuals can still speak, doing so is obviously very difficult for them. As a result, their speech is limited to a series of single words intertwined with filled pauses (uh, er, ...); even gesturing with speech can be affected (Skipper et al., 2007). The individual words are often produced without normal grammatical flair: no articles, suffixes, or prefixes. Here is a sample of speech collected during a study of Broca's aphasia:

> Examiner: Tell me, what did you do before you retired?
> Person with aphasia: Uh, uh, uh, pub, par, partender, no.
> Examiner: Carpenter?
> Person with aphasia: (Nodding to signal yes) Carpenter, tuh, tuh, twenty year.

Notice that the individual has no trouble understanding the question or coming up with the answer. His difficulty is in getting the word *carpenter* into an appropriate phrase and pronouncing it. Did you also notice the missing morpheme /-s/ from *twenty year*?

Broca's aphasia can include some difficulties in comprehending language as well. In general, the more complex the syntax, the more difficult it will be to understand. Compare these two sentences:

> The girl played the piano.
> The piano was played by the girl.

These are two grammatically correct sentences (although the second is somewhat awkward) that have the same meaning but different syntax. An individual with Broca's aphasia is likely to understand the first, more direct method, but much less likely to understand the second sentence, which is more complex. Given the difficulty with producing syntax, we might expect these sentences to be understood as follows:

> Girl ... play ... piano
> Piano ... ? ... play ... girl

How does the brain pull all of the language components together to produce coherent speech? Thus far we have focused on two areas of the cerebral cortex—Broca's and Wernicke's areas—but other brain structures contribute as well. Wernicke's area requires inputs from the cerebellum, basal ganglia, and hippocampus, to work correctly. The cerebellum, known for its role in balance and coordination, also plays a role in coordinating and organizing speech. The basal ganglia help control voluntary movement, including learning and making speech sounds. The circuitry of the basal ganglia supports our ability to articulate grammatically correct sentences. For example, the basal ganglia helps us articulate "I went to the store," rather than "I wented to the store." Perhaps not surprisingly, people with Parkinson's disease—a condition that adversely affects the basal ganglia—have difficulty using irregular verbs (Ullman et al., 1997). As you can see, our amazing faculty of language relies on numerous brain regions.

Working the Scientific Literacy Model

Genes and Language

The unique brain specializations underlying human language are likely supported by specific genes. Given that language is a universal trait of the human species, it likely has a genetic substrate that awaits interaction with the environment. How could we possibly find specific genes for this complex ability?

What do we know about genes and language?

Many scientists believe there is overwhelming evidence that language is a unique feature of the human species, and that language evolved to solve problems related to survival and reproductive fitness. Language adds greater efficiency to thought, allows us to transmit information without requiring us to have direct experience with potentially dangerous situations, and, ultimately, facilitates communicating social needs and desires. Claims that language promotes survival and reproductive success are difficult to test directly with scientific experimentation, but there is a soundness to the logic of the speculation. We can also move beyond speculation and actually examine how genes play a role in human language. As with all complex psychological traits, there are likely many genes associated with language. Nevertheless, amid all of these myriad possibilities, one gene has been identified that is of particular importance.

How can science explain a genetic basis of language?

Much of what we know about this gene comes from studies of the KE family, many of whom carry a mutated version of it on chromosome 7 (see Figure 8.16; Vargha-Khadem et al., 2005). Each gene has a name—and this one is called FOXP2. (All humans carry a copy of the FOXP2 gene, but the KE family passes down a mutated copy.) Those who

Figure 8.16 Inheritance Pattern for the Mutated FOXP2 Gene in the KE Family

Family members who are "affected" have inherited a mutated form of the FOXP2 gene, which results in difficulty with articulating words. As you can see from the center of the figure, the mutated gene is traced to a female family member, and has been passed on to the individuals of the next two generations.

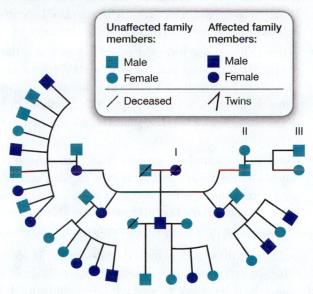

inherit the mutated copy have great difficulty putting thoughts into words (Tomblin et al., 2009). Thus, it appears that the physical and chemical processes that FOXP2 codes for are related to language function.

What evidence indicates that this gene is specifically involved in language? If you were to ask the members of the family who inherited the mutant form of the gene to speak about how to change the batteries in a flashlight, they would be at a loss. A rather jumbled mixture of sounds and words might come out, but nothing that could be easily understood. However, these same individuals have no problem actually performing the task. Their challenges with using language are primarily restricted to the use of words, not with their ability to *think*.

Scientists have used brain-imaging methods to further test whether the FOXP2 mutation affects language. One group of researchers compared brain activity of family members who inherited the mutation at FOXP2 with those who did not (Liégeois et al., 2003). During the brain scans, the participants were asked to generate words themselves, and also to repeat words back to the experimenters. As you can see from the interactive brain scans, the members of the family who were unaffected by the mutation showed normal brain activity: Broca's area of the left hemisphere became activated, just as expected. In contrast, Broca's area in the affected family members was silent, and the brain activity that did occur was unusual for this type of task (Figure 8.17).

Can we critically evaluate this evidence?

As you have now read, language has multiple components. Being able to articulate words is just one of many aspects of using and understanding language. The research on FOXP2 is very important, but reveals only how a single gene relates to one aspect of language use. Also, as many scientists have argued, language is a unique product of human evolution and, therefore, has a genetic basis. The studies of FOXP2 actually may not lend much support to this argument of human uniqueness. This gene is found in both mice and birds as well as in humans, and the human version shares a very similar molecular structure to the versions observed in these species. Interestingly, the molecular structure and activity of the FOXP2 gene in songbirds (unlike non-songbirds) is similar to that in humans (Vargha-Khadem et al., 2005). As we will also see later, some other interesting similarities between human and nonhuman language have been identified.

Why is this relevant?

This work illuminates at least part of the complex relationship between genes and language. Other individual genes that have direct links to language function will likely be discovered someday as well. Also, it is possible that this information could be used to help us further understand the genetic basis of language disorders.

Figure 8.17 Brain Scans of KE Family

The unaffected group shows a normal pattern of activity in Broca's area, while the affected group shows an unusual pattern.

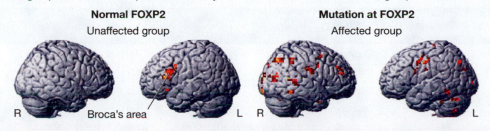

AGE OF ACQUISITION: THE SENSITIVE PERIOD FOR LEARNING A LANGUAGE Learning a new language presents unique challenges. Adults, even if they take courses to learn a new language, may still find it difficult to master due to trouble with pronunciation and grammar, limited opportunity to practice it, or a tendency to speak only their primary language at home. Children, however, are more likely to pick up a new language without so much effort, especially if they are immersed in it and exposed to it on a daily basis—such as in school. Eventually, they develop language skills equivalent to those of their peers. They will have roughly the same vocabulary, the same accents, and even the same slang. Research on this phenomenon has led psychologists to identify what they describe as a *sensitive period* for language—a time during childhood in which children's brains are primed to develop language skills (see also Module 10.1; Hakuta et al., 2003; Hernandez & Li, 2007). Similar results are found when deaf children receive cochlear implants (devices designed to restore hearing; described in Module 4.3). For the first years of life, they cannot hear language, so their development is delayed. Children who receive the implants by age two, however, develop better speech than children who receive them after age four (Nicholas & Geers, 2007).

PATTERNS OF LANGUAGE ACQUISITION Early psychologists focused only on behavioral approaches to language learning. They believed that language was learned through imitating sounds and being reinforced for pronouncing and using words correctly (Skinner, 1985). Although it is certainly true that imitation and reinforcement are involved in this process, they are only one part of the complex process of learning language (Messer, 2000). Because of this, psychologists use the term *language acquisition* when referring to children instead of *language learning*. Here are a few examples that illustrate how learning through imitation and reinforcement is just one component of language development:

- Children often produce phrases that include incorrect grammar or word forms. Because adults do not use these phrases, it is highly unlikely that such phrases are imitations.

- Children learn irregular verbs and pluralizations on a word-by-word basis. At first, they will use "ran" and "geese" correctly. However, when children begin to use grammar on their own, they overgeneralize the rules. A child who learns the /-ed/ morpheme for past tense will start saying *runned* instead of *ran*. When she learns that /-s/ means more than one, she will begin to say *gooses* instead of *geese*. It is also unlikely that children would produce these forms by imitating.

- When children use incorrect grammar, or when they overgeneralize their rules, parents may try to correct them. Although children will acknowledge their parents' attempts at instruction, this method does not seem to work. Instead, children go right back to overgeneralizing.

- Children's vocabulary growth does not appear to require reinforcement and occurs too rapidly to attributed to conditioning. Psychologists describe the acquisition of vocabulary **fast mapping**—*the ability to map words onto concepts or objects after only a single exposure.*

In light of these and many other examples, it seems clear that an exclusive behavioral approach falls short in explaining how language is learned, particularly in children. After all, if reinforcement and imitation were the primary means by which language was acquired, then adults should be able to learn just as well as children. And, regardless of the language, children seem to acquire language in stages, as shown in Table 8.8.

CAN ANIMALS USE LANGUAGE? In the mid-1950s, before language acquisition was understood very well, psychologists became interested in testing whether behavioral techniques could get animals to use language. One group of researchers attempted to teach spoken English to a chimpanzee named Viki (Hayes & Hayes, 1951). Viki was **cross-fostered**, *meaning that she was raised as a member of a family that was not of the same species.* The psychologists learned a lot from Viki about how smart chimpanzees can be, but she managed to whisper only about four words, even after many years of effort. A later group of researchers suggested that Viki's difficulty to use language might have been with speaking, and not with language

Table 8.8 Milestones in Language Acquisition

Average Time of Onset (Months)	Milestone	Example
1–2	Cooing	Ahhh, ai-ai-ai
4–10	Babbling (consonants start)	Ab-ah-da-ba
8–16	Single-word stage	Up, mama, papa
24	Two-word stage	Go potty
24+	Complete, meaningful phrases strung together	I want to talk to Grandpa.

itself. To test this hypothesis, psychologists immersed a baby chimpanzee named Washoe in American Sign Language (ASL), the same way human infants are immersed in their own native language. Eventually, she learned approximately 200 signs. She was able to generalize signs from one context to another and to use a sign to represent entire categories of objects, not just specific items. For example, while Washoe learned the sign for the word "open" on a limited number of doors and cupboards, she subsequently signed "open" for many different doors, cupboards, and even bottled beverages. The findings with Washoe were later replicated with other chimps (Gardner et al., 1989).

Instead of using sign language, some researchers have developed a completely artificial language to teach to apes. This language consists of symbols called *lexigrams*—small keys on a computerized board that represent words and, therefore, can be combined to form complex ideas and phrases. One subject of the research using this language is a bonobo named Kanzi (bonobos are another species of chimpanzee). Kanzi has learned approximately 350 symbols through training, but he learned his first symbols simply by watching as

Kanzi is a bonobo chimpanzee that has learned to use an artificial language consisting of graphical symbols that correspond to words. Kanzi can type out responses by pushing buttons with these symbols, shown in this photo. Researchers are also interested in Kanzi's ability to understand spoken English (which is transmitted to the headphones by an experimenter who is not in the room).

researchers attempted to teach his mother how to use the language. In addition to the lexigrams he produces, Kanzi seems to recognize about 3,000 spoken words. His trainers claim that Kanzi's skills constitute language (Savage-Rumbaugh & Lewin, 1994). They argue that he can understand symbols and at least some syntax; that he acquired symbols simply by being around others who used them; and that he produced symbols without specific training or reinforcement. Those who work with Kanzi conclude that his communication skills are quite similar to those of a young human, in terms of both the elements of language (semantics and syntax) and the acquisition of language (natural and without effortful training).

Despite their ability to communicate in complex ways, the debate continues about whether these animals are using something comparable to human language (Gillespie-Lynch et al., 2014). Many researchers who have worked closely with language-trained apes observed too many critical differences between humans and chimps to conclude that language extends beyond our species (Anderson, 2006; Seidenberg & Pettito, 1979). For example:

Washoe was the first chimpanzee taught to use some of the signs of American Sign Language. Washoe died in 2007 at age 42 and throughout her life challenged many to examine their beliefs about human uniqueness.

- One argument is that apes communicate only with symbols, not with syntax, as humans do. The majority of apes produce single signs, a couple of signs strung together, or apparently random sequences.

- There is little reputable experimental evidence showing that apes pass their language skills to other apes.

- Productivity—creating new words (gestures) and using existing gestures to name new objects or events—is rare, if it occurs at all.

- Some of the researchers become very engaged in the lives of these animals and talk about them as friends and family members (Fouts, 1997; Savage-Rumbaugh & Lewin, 1994). This tendency has left critics to wonder the extent to which personal attachments to the animals might interfere with the objectivity of the data.

Finally, we should point out that animal language studies use *human* language as their frame of reference.

In an alternate universe where dolphins attempt to teach humans their own system of communication, it is likely they would end up publishing skeptical critiques about the miniscule skills their human subjects acquired. Humans have evolved a remarkably complex capacity to use language for communication, while nonhumans have systems serving unique and adaptive functions of their own.

Module 8.3 Summary

8.3a Know . . . the key terminology from the study of language:

aphasias
Broca's area
cross-foster
fast mapping
language
morpheme
phoneme
pragmatics
semantics
syntax
Wernicke's area

8.3b Understand . . . how language is structured.

Sentences are broken down into words that are arranged according to grammatical rules (syntax). The relationship between words and their meaning is referred to as semantics. Words can be broken down into morphemes, the smallest meaningful units of speech, and phonemes, the smallest sound units that make up speech.

8.3c Understand . . . how genes and the brain are involved in language use.

Studies of the KE family show that the FOXP2 gene is involved in our ability to speak. However, mutation to this gene does not necessarily impair people's ability to think. Thus the FOXP2 gene seems to be important for just one of

many aspects of human language. Multiple brain areas are involved in language—two particularly important ones are Broca's and Wernicke's areas.

8.3d Apply . . . your knowledge to distinguish between units of language such as phonemes and morphemes.

Table 8.6 on page 267 helped you to practice with the following:

1. /dis/
2. /s/
3. /k/

The first one is a morpheme only, because each letter contributes phonemes. Together, they represent a single unit of meaning, which implies being *separate or apart from* (as in *dis*belief). The next is a phoneme that makes a single sound without any specific meaning. The last could be both. For example, it adds a sound to the end of a noun along with the notion of plurality.

8.3e Analyze . . . whether species other than humans are able to use language.

Nonhuman species certainly seem capable of acquiring certain aspects of human language. Studies with apes have shown that they can learn and use some sign language or, in the case of Kanzi, an artificial language system involving arbitrary symbols. Critics have pointed out that many differences between human and nonhuman language use remain.

Module 8.3 Quiz

Know . . .

1. What are the rules that govern how words are strung together into meaningful sentences?
   - **A.** Semantics
   - **B.** Pragmatics
   - **C.** Morphemics
   - **D.** Syntax

Understand . . .

2. The smallest units of language that convey meaning are known as:
   - **A.** semantics.
   - **B.** morphemes.
   - **C.** phonemes.
   - **D.** syntaxes.

Understand . . .

3. Besides being based in a different region of the brain, a major distinction between Broca's aphasia and Wernicke's aphasia is that:
   - **A.** words from people with Broca's aphasia are strung together fluently, but often make little sense.
   - **B.** Broca's aphasia is due to a FOXP2 mutation.
   - **C.** Wernicke's aphasia results in extreme stuttering.
   - **D.** words from people with Wernicke's aphasia are strung together fluently, but often make little sense.

Apply . . .

4. Newton has been studying English for about a month and keeps getting tripped up by irregular verbs, often saying runned instead of ran. Although technically incorrect, this shows that Newton has learned that the _____ *–ed* is a suffix that indicates past tense.

   A. morpheme
   B. phoneme
   C. pragmatic
   D. syntax

Analyze . . .

5. What is the most accurate conclusion from research conducted on primate language abilities?

   A. Primates can learn some aspects of human language, though many differences remain.
   B. Primates can learn human language in full.
   C. Primates cannot learn human language in any way.
   D. There are not enough research data to reach reliable conclusions on this topic.

Module 8.4   Scientific Literacy Challenge: Second-Language Learning

In many parts of the world, children are raised in homes and neighborhoods where more than one language is spoken. This is far less common in the United States, despite the many languages spoken among the immigrating families, visiting workers and students, and tourists. Wouldn't it be helpful to ensure that children in the United States learn a second language from a young age?

Before you start this activity, take a minute to write your thoughts about giving children the opportunity to learn a second language.

JOURNAL PROMPT

What are some pros and cons of providing language-learning opportunities to all school-aged children in the United States? How have your views been shaped by your own language experiences?

What do we know about second-language learning?

Read the following excerpts from a letter-to-the-editor, sent to a local newspaper from a community's school superintendent. As you read, note the boldfaced key terms from Chapter 8.

Give our students a second language

By Irene Jordan, Ed.D.

I am the superintendent in a school district where more than 40 languages are spoken. The community has been wonderful in supporting the diverse needs of students and families, many of which are displaced refugees. In addition to basic needs, our community provides lessons in spoken and written English. Although I am proud of our community for that, I am disappointed that we have been unable to work in the opposite direction; that is, we cannot garner support for programs to teach non-English languages to our native students. It is true that Spanish and French are offered at the high school, but I believe once students reach high school it is too late to truly master a language. There is a **sensitive period** in language development where children are able to acquire everything from basic **phonemes** to complex **syntax** in a way that adults cannot. I laid out the evidence for this in my last letter to this newspaper. This week, I am going to argue that the benefits of learning a second language are not just social in nature—children reap cognitive benefits as well.

Clearly Dr. Jordan understands that children acquire language more readily than adults. Let's look at how she applies scientific research to argue that there are cognitive benefits that go along with language learning.

How do scientists study second-language learners?

Here, the argument the superintendent provides is not so much about the cultural importance of speaking a second language but about how it benefits overall cognition. Try to identify the elements of scientific research behind these statements, especially for the statements that have been highlighted.

Here are some of the ways in which the cognitive benefits of second-language education have helped elementary school-aged children.

- One study of 13,000 children in Louisiana's public schools showed significantly higher achievement test scores in all subjects among those who had second-language education in their curriculum. This is regardless of a child's race or socioeconomic status.
- Another report found students earned significantly higher language arts and math scores on a standard test after one semester of weekly, 90-minute foreign language study sessions.
- Kansas City opened foreign language magnet schools in the late 1980s. The first class of kindergarten students in that program was scoring well above average in all subjects on the state's standardized tests by the end of fifth grade. Interestingly, the biggest improvement was not in language, it was in mathematics.
- In multiple studies, the children who get the biggest benefit from second-language education comes from demographic groups that, on average, have lower test scores and poorer school performance.
- One study showed that students who completed three or more years of second-language study had significantly higher rates of college admissions and college completion.

Were you able to identify important elements of research in the author's examples? Test yourself with the quiz below.

1. In the study from Louisiana, the dependent variable was
   a. whether the children received second-language instruction.
   b. the race or socioeconomic status of the children.
   c. achievement test scores in all subjects.
   d. the state the children lived in.
2. The study from Louisiana focused only on public schools, so we do not know if the same results would be found among students who attend private schools or are home-schooled. This is a problem of
   a. the Hawthorne effect.
   b. generalizability.
   c. a dependent variable.
   d. peer review.
3. None of these studies are true experiments because
   a. they do not involve random assignment to one of two or more conditions.
   b. they lack independent variables.
   c. the children are from too many different grade levels.
   d. math tests are unrelated to language skills.

Answers: 1. c 2. b 3. a

Dr. Jordan was able to cite several studies that supported her position. Now, let's read how Dr. Jordan critically evaluates the research.

How should we think critically about second-language education?

Remember that critical thinking involves curiosity and reasonable levels of skepticism. As you read the next paragraph, search for the signs of critical thinking.

> This is just a small handful of studies, but they represent every student in the schools that were studied. They all confirm my point: Second-language education is correlated with a child's cognitive abilities in many areas, not just in verbal skills. I assure you that this selection of examples is not biased; I did not only report examples that supported my views while ignoring the others. In fact, I did not have a strong opinion until after I read about the abundance of research on the topic. Moreover, each of these studies was conducted by state governments or testing agencies who have expertise in these areas, but no financial or other stake in whether languages are taught.

The statements below will help you identify several aspects of critical thinking. Match the following critical thinking statements to the highlighted passages that illustrate them, and identify which statement is not addressed in the letter.

1. The author is careful not to confuse correlational evidence with cause-and-effect relationships.
2. The author examined whether her biases might influence the results.
3. The author is making an appeal to common sense.
4. The author considers the credibility of her sources.

1. Green 2. Blue 3. Does not appear in article 4. Yellow

How is second-language education relevant?

Now that she has provided evidence for her views, Dr. Jordan will need to explain what this means for her district. Read her conclusion and then explore any newly formed thoughts you may have about second-language learning.

> In summary, I think the data provide convincing evidence in favor of language education. Generally, the pushback we have received has been patriotic ("We speak English in America"), financial ("Would we have to hire new teachers?"), or academic ("It would have to replace more important subjects"). I believe the research outweighs those and any other arguments I have heard so far. That is why the adoption of second-language education is a key item on my strategic plan, and on the agenda for next Monday's open School Board meeting. Thank you,
>
> *Irene Jordan*

SHARED WRITING

After reading this letter, are you more or less favorable toward second-language education? Explain why, and incorporate information about how your own language experience may influence your reasoning.

Chapter 8 Quiz

1. According to rule-based categorization, people use _____ to decide if an object belongs to a specific category.
   A. prototypes
   B. semantic networks
   C. a set of specific features
   D. categorization by comparison

2. The linguist relativity hypothesis suggests that:
   A. the way we think about categories affects the language we use.
   B. there are many different ways to describe the same category.
   C. words are organized mentally based on their relationship to each other.
   D. the language that we use affects how we think about the world.

3. A _____ is a mental representation of an average member of a category.
   A. basic-level category
   B. prototype
   C. similarity principle
   D. network

4. When Kwan's computer stopped working, he called the company's technical support line. The technician followed a predetermined set of steps from a manual to diagnosis and help Kwan fix his computer over the phone. The steps that the technician followed are an example of what type of problem-solving strategy?
   A. Algorithmic
   B. Anchoring
   C. Functional fixedness
   D. Heuristic

5. People often overestimate the danger of shark attacks because it is fairly easy to think of news stories and reports of shark attacks. This is an example of how the _____ can sometimes lead to poor judgments.
   A. availability heuristic
   B. anchoring effect
   C. functional fixedness effect
   D. representativeness heuristic

6. Han and Nalini both bought the same new cell phone. Han spent several weeks reviewing the dozens of different phones and reading reviews online, trying to find the best phone possible for his needs. Nalini simply bought the first phone that met her needs. Given the research on maximizers and satisficers, which is most likely to be the outcome?
   A. Han and Nalini will end up equally satisfied about their purchases.
   B. Han will be more satisfied with his purchase than Nalini.
   C. Nalini will be more satisfied with her purchase than Han.
   D. Han will spend less time researching his purchase next time.

7. Steps taken toward reaching the solution of a problem are called _____.
   A. goal states
   B. initial states
   C. operators
   D. algorithms

8. Seth tells his friend that he got two tickets to a big concert next week, to which his friend replies, "Get out of town!" Because of the context, Seth knows his friend is expressing excitement and doesn't really want him to leave town. This is an example of:
   A. pragmatics.
   B. linguistic relativity.
   C. semantics.
   D. syntax.

9. The _____ occurs when an individual searches for only evidence that will confirm his or her beliefs.
   A. availability heuristic
   B. confirmation bias
   C. belief perseverance
   D. satisficing

10. Studies where researchers have attempted to teach language to nonhuman animals have generally found that:
    A. chimpanzees and gorillas are the only animal species that can fully learn language.
    B. some animals are capable of learning elements of human language, but they have not convincingly demonstrated human-like language use.
    C. animals are incapable of learning even the most basic elements of human language.
    D. dolphins are the only animal species that can fully learn language.

11. Why do psychologists assert that heuristics are beneficial for problem solving?
    A. Heuristics increase the amount of time we spend arriving at good solutions to problems.
    B. Heuristics decrease our chances of errors dramatically.
    C. Heuristics help us make decisions efficiently.
    D. Heuristics are considered the most logical thought pattern for problem solving.

12. The fact that humans so often rely on heuristics is evidence that:
    A. humans are not always rational thinkers.
    B. it is impossible for humans to think logically.
    C. it is impossible for humans to use algorithms.
    D. humans will always succumb to the confirmation bias.

13. What is fast mapping?

   A. The rapid rate at which chimpanzees learn sign language.

   B. The ability of children to map concepts to words with only a single example.

   C. The very short period of time that language input can be useful for language development.

   D. A major difficulty that people face when affected by Broca's aphasia.

14. The study of how people extract meaning from words is called _____.

   A. syntax

   B. pragmatics

   C. semantics

   D. flouting

15. Studies of the KE family and the FOXP2 gene indicate that:

   A. language is controlled entirely by a single gene found on chromosome 7.

   B. language is still fluent despite a mutation to this gene.

   C. this particular gene is related to one specific aspect of language.

   D. mutations affecting this gene lead to highly expressive language skills.

Chapter 9
Intelligence, Aptitude, and Cognitive Abilities

Module 9.1 Measuring Aptitude and Intelligence

Learning Objectives

9.1a Know . . . the key terminology associated with intelligence and intelligence testing.

9.1b Understand . . . the purpose of standardization and norms in intelligence testing.

9.1c Understand . . . the relationship between reliability and validity in testing.

9.1d Apply . . . the concepts of test standardization and norms to make judgments about specific test scores.

9.1e Analyze . . . the use of brain size as an estimate of mental ability.

9.1f Analyze . . . whether intelligence and aptitude tests make useful predictions about performance.

Every spring, football fans in the United States turn their attention to "the draft," where professional teams in the National Football League (NFL) take turns selecting the best amateur players to join their teams. Pride, potential championships, and a lot of money are at stake, so teams use all the information they can get to inform their decisions. As a part of the run-up to the draft, the candidates attend workouts, demonstrating their physical aptitude through tests of speed, strength, coordination, and agility. But what about the cognitive aspects of the game? Like chess masters, football

players need to thoroughly understand the strategic aspects of their game. Each player must memorize his responsibilities for each possible play and make quick judgments once the action begins. To assess their intelligence, candidates participating in the NFL draft must complete the Wonderlic, a 50-question test that is administered by organizations nationwide to gauge the aptitude of prospective employees; it is completed in less than 12 minutes.

Despite decades of use, journalists question whether it can reliably predict success in professional football. NFL teams do not share test scores, but some scores have leaked out and blog-gers and fans are often more amused than impressed by them. For example, two of the best quarterbacks in the NFL Hall of Fame—Dan Marino and Terry Bradshaw—scored around 15 out of 50 (the average in the overall population is 20). On the other hand, two future Hall-of-Famers—Peyton Manning and Tom Brady—scored around 30. Without the actual scores for a large sample of players, we cannot discern whether the Wonderlic actually predicts success in the NFL. However, the scores can be used to counter the caricature of the "dim-witted jock"— the average score of NFL players is actually a point or two higher than the average score of the overall population.

Each of us differs in how we look, act, and feel. Similarly, intelligence appears to differentiate each individual. Intelligent people are described as "brainy," "bright," "wise," or "sharp," whereas those deemed less intelligent are described unflatteringly as "dim," "slow," or "dense." Typically, these descriptors are used in reference to how much a person knows, as well as how successful the individual is at solving problems. We can improve on our everyday notions of intelligence by applying a psychological definition to this concept. **Intelligence** *is the ability to think, understand, reason, and cognitively adapt to and overcome obstacles* (based on Neisser et al., 1996). Thus, intelligence reflects not just how much you know, but how you recognize and solve problems. The history of psychology has seen dozens of methods for measuring this complex idea. We will begin this chapter by examining attempts at measuring intelligence, and then reviewing how these methods have shaped modern views of intelligence.

Achievement and Aptitude

Tests of mental ability come in many different forms to serve various purposes. **Achievement tests** *measure knowledge and thinking skills that an individual has acquired.* On a small scale, the quizzes and tests you take in your college courses are achievement tests. On a much larger scale, statewide and nationwide achievement tests are designed to measure whether students are performing up to standards established by school districts or Departments of Education, such as the Common Core standards that have been so heavily debated in recent years.

In contrast to achievement tests, **aptitude tests** *are designed to measure an individual's potential to perform well on a specific range of tasks.* College entrance exams such as the SAT claim to measure the test taker's potential as a college student, whereas other aptitude tests are designed to test for specific jobs. The Armed Services Vocational Aptitude Battery (ASVAB) measures aptitude for the entire range of military jobs, from languages and communications to tank and helicopter mechanics. In short, achievement tests measure current abilities, and aptitude tests predict future performance.

CONSTRUCTING AND EVALUATING TESTS The task of constructing questionnaires and tests falls under a branch of psychology known as **psychometrics**, *which is the measurement of psychological traits and abilities*—including personality, attitudes, and intelligence. Using psychometric theory and methods, psychologists carefully construct and then evaluate test items to ensure they effectively measure the abilities or traits they are intended to measure.

Two important concepts in psychometrics and research methods in general are reliability and validity. As defined in Module 2.1, validity is the degree to which an instrument or procedure actually measures what it claims to measure. There are several ways of demonstrating the validity of a test. For example, a psychologist might look for *predictive validity*—the degree to which a test predicts future performance. Studies conducted by testing companies and independent university researchers have provided some support for the SAT in this way, showing a positive correlation between

Achievement tests measure knowledge in a certain area. Students may take such tests to evaluate knowledge prior to advancing a grade.

Aptitude tests measure a person's potential to perform a range of specific tasks.

SAT scores and first-year grade-point averages (Coyle & Pillow, 2008; Sackett et al., 2011). However, others argue that the correlation is quite modest and that alternative approaches may be more valid predictors of GPA. In fact, personality traits such as conscientiousness and curiosity may be three or four times better than intelligence at predicting success in college (Poropat, 2014).

We should also examine whether tests are reliable. Module 2.1 defined *reliability* as the measurement of the degree to which a test provides consistent and stable answers across multiple observations and points in time. One method of evaluating reliability is through a construct known as *test–retest reliability*. In the same way that you depend on a reliable car to always start, a psychologist should be able to depend on a reliable test to produce consistent scores. Research has shown that students who take the SAT a second time generally increase their score by a small amount, and this increase in scores is not due to changes in intelligence. Therefore, the SAT is not a perfectly reliable test (the retest scores differ from those obtained on the original test). Because these changes are not large, however, the SAT does demonstrate some degree of reliability (Coyle, 2006).

STANDARDIZATION AND NORMS A **standardized test** *is a test that has a set of questions or problems that are administered and scored in a uniform way across large numbers of individuals.* Standardization allows psychologists to establish **norms**, *statistics that allow individuals to be evaluated relative to a typical or standard score,* by administering the same test to hundreds, if not thousands, of individuals. For example, some of the most widely used intelligence tests have a norm or average score of 100. Another statistic called the *standard deviation* (defined in Module 2.4) measures how individual scores spread out above or below a mean; the standard deviation may be thought of as the average distance away from the average. As shown in Figure 9.1, a specific intelligence test might have a standard deviation set to 15 points. Thus, not only do we know what is above or below average, but we also know whether a score is far above average or only slightly below average. Another way to assess this variation is by examining **percentile rank**—*the percentage of scores below a certain point.* For example, a score of 100 has a percentile rank of 0.50, meaning that 50% of the population scores below this level. A score of 85 has a percentile rank of approximately 0.16, indicating that 16% of the population scores below it (See Table 9.1). Of course, a test that is "normed" with one set of people may not be representative of another group, so you may find that a specific test actually has multiple sets of norms—perhaps separate norms for boys and girls or for those who are not native English speakers.

Approaches to Intelligence Testing

So far our examples have described the style of testing that is probably most familiar to you—the kind that involves a series of standardized, multiple-choice questions that you can respond to on a bubble sheet or through testing software. Certainly, some aptitude tests are of this variety, but attempts to measure intelligence itself usually include diverse measures ranging from assessment of brain size to recording how fast a person reacts to stimuli; there are

Figure 9.1 The Normal Distribution of Scores for a Standardized Intelligence Test

This distribution of intelligence test scores in the population is standardized to have a mean of 100, so half of the population scores higher than 100, and half score lower than 100. The standard deviation (roughly, the average number of points away from the average) is approximately 15. Note the percentages in the curve. Nearly 68% of the population's scores fall within one standard deviation from the mean (between 85 and 115) and approximately 95% of scores fall within two standard deviations of the mean (between 70 and 130).

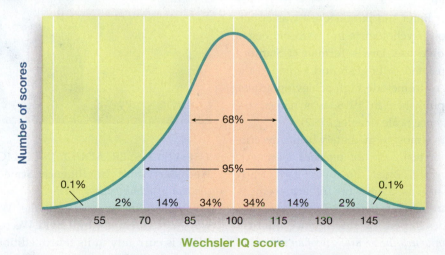

Table 9.1 Understanding Testing Norms

On a standardized test with a mean of 500 and a standard deviation of 100, which of the following are typical scores, high scores, or low scores?

> Student A scored a 550.
> Student B scored a 425.
> Student C scored a 375.
> Student D scored a 700.

Answers: Student A = typical; Student B = typical; Student C = low; Student D = high

even purely behavioral measures that assess intelligence in other species. In this section, we examine several ways that intelligence has been measured.

THE STANFORD-BINET TEST In 1904, the French government created the Commission on the Education of Retarded Children. As part of this commission, Alfred Binet and Theodore Simon developed a method of assessing children's academic achievement at school (Siegler, 1992). The problem was easy to see: A new law required all children to attend school, and many of the students who showed up were woefully unprepared. Could there be a standardized way of assessing which students would need assistance to catch up, and which students were ahead of the rest?

Binet and Simon's work resulted in an achievement test—a measure of how well a child performed at various cognitive tasks relative to other children of his age. Because the focus was on performance at certain age levels, Binet preferred to say that the test measured **mental age**, *the average or typical test score for a specific chronological age*, rather than intelligence. Under this system, a 7-year-old child with a mental age of 7 would be considered average because her mental age matched her chronological age. In contrast, a 10-year-old student who was behind at school might have a mental age of 8, meaning his score was the same as the average 8-year-old child's score. With this information in hand, teachers could determine that the student would need extra help to bring his mental age up to his chronological age.

The practicality of Binet and Simon's test was apparent to others, and soon psychologists in California began to adapt it for their own use. Lewis Terman at Stanford University had it translated to English and extended the test beyond school ages to include high-achieving adults. This modified test, published in 1916, was named the Stanford-Binet Intelligence Scale (Siegler, 1992).

Terman and others almost immediately began describing the **Stanford-Binet test** *as a test intended to measure innate (genetic) intelligence*. Binet, however, had clearly viewed his original test as a measure of achievement, not as a measure of an innate capacity. Nonetheless, soon after, William Stern developed the **intelligence quotient (IQ)**—*a measurement in which the mental age of an individual*

is divided by the person's chronological age and then multiplied by 100. For example, a 10-year-old child with a mental age of 7 would have an IQ of $7/10 \times 100 = 70$. The IQ score replaced the idea of a mental age—something that reflects progress in school—with a number purporting to measure a person's ability.

It might seem as if stating a mental age is no different from calculating an IQ ratio, but it certainly can be. Consider whether one of these two statements sounds more optimistic than the other:

- He has a mental age of 7, so he is 3 years behind.
- He has an IQ of 70, so he is 30 points below average.

To many, mental age leaves the door open to catching up because the student is described as behind—after two more years of school his mental age and chronological age could both be 12. The IQ, however, sounds almost like the diagnosis of a permanent condition. If that is the case, then no amount of help or education will affect the student; his IQ will seemingly be the same throughout his life. Psychologist Amy Marin explains the history of Terman, Binet, and the birth of the IQ in the following video, The History of Intelligence Testing: Binet and Terman.

Watch THE HISTORY OF INTELLIGENCE TESTING: BINET AND TERMAN

Amy Marin
Phoenix College

THE WECHSLER ADULT INTELLIGENCE SCALE The **Wechsler Adult Intelligence Scale (WAIS)** *is the most commonly administered intelligence test used on adolescents and adults*. Its predecessor, the Wechsler-Bellvue test, was first developed by David Wechsler in 1939, and the WAIS is currently in its fourth edition. (In an ironic twist,

Figure 9.2 Subscales of the Wechsler Adult Intelligence Scale

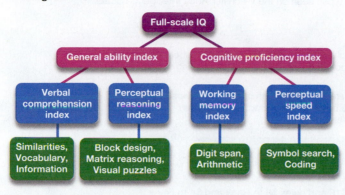

Wechsler himself was classified as having mild intellectual disabilities—"feeble minded" was the term used at the time—as a 9-year-old child when his family immigrated to the United States from Romania.)

The WAIS provides a single IQ score for each test taker—the Full-scale IQ—but also breaks intelligence into a General Ability Index (GAI) and a Cognitive Proficiency Index (CPI), as shown in Figure 9.2.

The GAI is computed from scores on the Verbal Comprehension and Perceptual Reasoning indices. These measures tap into an individual's intellectual abilities without placing so much emphasis on how fast he can solve problems and make decisions. The CPI, in contrast, is based on the Working Memory and Processing Speed subtests. It is included in the Full-scale IQ category because greater working memory capacity and processing speed allow more cognitive resources to be devoted to reasoning and solving problems. Figure 9.3 shows some sample test items from the WAIS.

RAVEN'S PROGRESSIVE MATRICES Many of the original standardized tests required knowledge of the test developer's culture and language and as a result, individuals from different cultures and social classes were at an immediate disadvantage when taking these tests. However, a number of psychologists reasoned that intelligence is more about the processes of acquiring and using information, which means it would be independent of culture and language. A person should not be penalized on an intelligence test if he did not have an English vocabulary or never had the opportunity to learn something about a culture. If a test could find some way to circumvent culture and language, then psychologists would have a fairer, more valid, "culture-free" test.

In the 1930s, John Raven developed **Raven's Progressive Matrices** (often shortened to just Raven's Matrices), *an intelligence test that emphasizes problems that are intended not to be bound to a particular language or culture.* The main set of tasks found in Raven's Matrices

measure the extent to which test takers can see patterns in the shapes and colors within a matrix and then determine which shape or color would complete the pattern (see Figure 9.4). Note how this type of problem does not require knowledge of a specific language, culture, or human-made object or custom.

If you give the problem in Figure 9.4 a try, you will probably notice that it requires some thought; but how does it gauge intelligence? According to Raven, two abilities are vital to intelligent behavior: identifying and extracting important information (*deductive reasoning*) and then applying it to new situations (*reproductive reasoning*). Performance on Raven's Matrices corresponds to performance on other intelligence measures, particularly the proficiency index of the WAIS.

The types of problems you see on the WAIS and Raven's Matrices likely fit your general understanding of how intelligence is tested. In addition, some measures attempt to tap into other aspects of cognitive performance, such as perception and memory. In fact, these measures have a long history in intelligence testing.

JOURNAL PROMPT

Cultural Influences on Testing: Explain why it is important to devise intelligence tests that are not bound to the knowledge and skills valued by a single culture.

MEASURING PERCEPTION AND MEMORY In the mid-1800s, before Binet and Simon began their work, Sir Francis Galton set out to explain why intelligence and success appeared to run in families. Galton explained this trend by good breeding—he believed individuals from these families were genetically gifted (see also Module 1.2; Fancher, 2009). With this hypothesis, Galton became one of the first to try to scientifically measure intelligence through a program of research he called **anthropometrics** (*literally, "the measurement of people"*), *a historical term referring to the method of measuring physical and mental variation in humans.* He presented a series of perceptual tests to hundreds of people but was unable to support his hypothesis. Although his motivation and methods were quite different from Binet and Simon's, he shares with them an influence that is still seen in modern intelligence research. Contemporary approaches to measuring intelligence have moved away from the use of perceptual tests and toward assessment of working memory (described in Module 7.1). Psychologists pursuing this line of research have found high correlations between working memory capacity and standardized intelligence tests (Ackerman et al., 2005; Chuderski, 2013). This should not be surprising because working memory tests measure how well one can hold instructions and information in memory while completing problem-solving tasks (Unsworth et al., 2014).

Figure 9.3 Types of Problems Used to Measure Intelligence

These hypothetical problems are consistent with the types seen on the Wechsler Adult Intelligence Scale.

Processing Speed Index

Symbol search	View groupings of symbols for specific numbers of each symbol, and fill in a blank with a missing symbol.
Coding	Match different symbols with specific numbers, and fill in a blank with a correct symbol given a certain number.

Working Memory Index

Arithmetic	Jack has $16 and owes $8 to Hank and $4 to Frank. What percentage of the original $16 will Jack still have after he pays Hank and Frank?
Digit span	Recall the order of number strings in both forward and reverse directions.

Perceptual Reasoning Index

Matrix reasoning	View the pattern in the top two rows and fill in the blank of the third row.

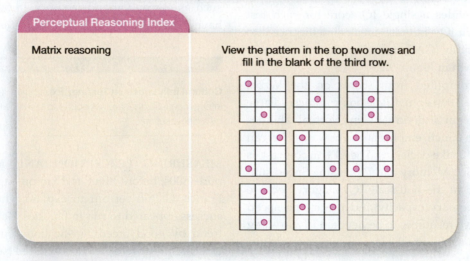

Block Design

Which three pieces are needed to make this puzzle?

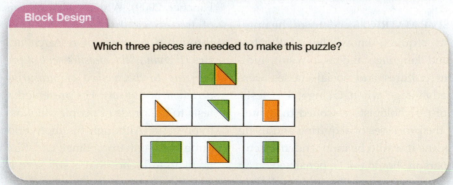

Verbal Comprehension Index

Vocabulary	What does *profligate* mean?
Similarities	In what way are a bicycle and a car alike?
Information	On which continent is Japan located?

Figure 9.4 Sample Problem from Raven's Progressive Matrices

Which possible pattern (1–8) should go in the blank space?

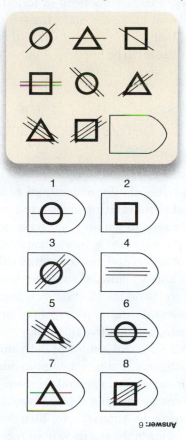

Answer: 6

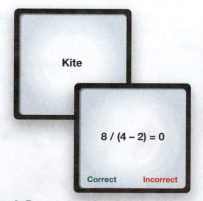

Sir Francis Galton believed that intelligence was something people inherit. Thus, he believed that an individual's relatives were a better predictor of intelligence than practice and effort.

Perhaps after examining the operation span measure in Figure 9.5 it is clearer to you why working memory is related to intelligence. However, despite a great deal of overlap in working memory scores and other measures of intelligence, debate persists about exactly how strong this relationship is and why it exists (Harrison et al., 2014; Dang et al., 2014). It is possible that working memory capacity contributes to intelligence because it allows more information and more complex reasoning strategies during problem solving. Working memory processes also help us ignore irrelevant and distracting information (Unsworth et al., 2014). At the very least, working memory tasks seem to tap into abilities that allow us to solve problems and express our mental abilities.

Figure 9.5 A Memory Task for Intelligence Testing

In the operation span task, a series of target words are shown one at a time, interspersed with equations that must be judged for accuracy. Once all of the words have been shown—typically between two and five of them—subjects are asked to pick the words out of a list of containing both target and distracter words.

House	$(7 - 3) \times 2 = 8$ Correct Incorrect	Kite		House Pencil Nose Kite
1. Study this word	2. Judge whether the math problem is correct or incorrect			4. Identify which words were and were not previously studied

$8 / (4 - 2) = 0$

Correct   Incorrect

3. Repeat steps 1 and 2 with different words and problems multiple times

Working the Scientific Literacy Model

Brain Size and Intelligence

In the days before modern brain imaging was possible, researchers typically obtained skulls from deceased subjects, filled them with fine-grained matter such metal pellets, and then transferred the pellets to a flask to measure the volume. However, without a way to measure the intelligence of a deceased person directly, the researchers generally compared average skull sizes among racial or ethnic groups based on the assumption that they already knew who was more or less intelligent. These efforts taught us little about any relationship between intelligence and brain or skull size. Many studies were highly flawed and inevitably led to conclusions that White males (and therefore the White male scientists who conducted these experiments) had the largest brains and, therefore, were the smartest of the human race (Gould, 1981). Modern approaches to studying the brain and intelligence are far more sophisticated, thanks to newer techniques and a more enlightened knowledge of the brain's form and functions.

What do we know about brain size and intelligence?

Brain-based approaches to measuring intelligence rest on a commonsense assumption: Thinking occurs in the brain, so a larger brain should be related to greater intelligence. But does scientific evidence support this commonsense notion? One approach to the question is to look across species with different brain sizes and problem-solving skills. One recent study to adopt this approach found that across 36 species, there was a clear correlation between a larger brain and better performance on the task (MacLean et al., 2013). This might be troubling to humans, however, because an elephant's 11-pound brain or the sperm whale's

18 pound brain dwarf our own 2½- to 3-pound brains. Does that mean they are superior at abstract reasoning? Not necessarily. Among mammals in particular, researchers find that the encephalization quotient—a formula calculating brain size relative to overall body size—is often a better indicator of intelligence (Cairo, 2011). So, across species, brain size does seem to be important. But what if we compare brain sizes among humans?

How can science explain the relationship between brain size and intelligence?

The most straightforward approach to this question requires two pieces of information from a large sample of individuals: a brain and an intelligence test score. Although it is relatively easy to get an intelligence test score, getting someone's brain size is more complicated. Nonetheless, Sandra Witelson and her colleagues (2006) managed to collect 100 brains following autopsies from individuals with known scores on the WAIS. When researchers made detailed anatomical measurements of the entire brain and regions that support cognitive skills, they found that brain size accounted for about a third of individual differences in verbal intelligence. Brain imaging provides less drastic means of estimating brain size, and dozens of studies using magnetic resonance imaging (MRI) have reported similar size-intelligence correlations (Cairo, 2011; Bouchard, 2014).

The size of the brain and its various regions is just one way of looking at intelligence. One of the most obvious features of the human brain is its convoluted surface. This gray surface varies in thickness from person to person, and the thickness of the cortex is highly associated with general intelligence (Menary et al., 2013). These convolutions (called *gyri*; pronounced "ji-rye") comprise the outer part of the cerebral cortex (see Figure 9.6). The number and size of these cerebral gyri is greater in species that have complex cognitive and social lives, such as elephants,

---

Figure 9.6 Does Intelligence Increase with Brain Size?

While the size of the brain may have a modest relationship to intelligence, the convolutions or "gyri" along the surface of the cortex are another important factor: Increased convolutions are associated with higher intelligence test scores.

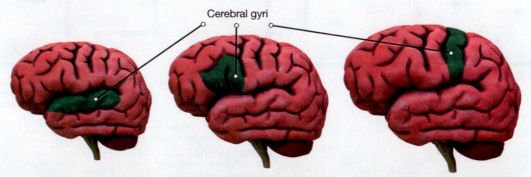

Cerebral gyri

Albert Einstein's intellect was remarkable, but the size of his brain was no greater than average. However, researchers discovered some peculiar features within his parietal lobe—an area known to be involved in processing mathematical and spatial information.

dolphins, and primates (Marino, 2002; Rogers et al., 2010). In humans, the degree of convolutions is highly associated with WAIS scores (Luders et al., 2008).

Can we critically evaluate this issue?

We must keep in mind that the correlations described only reveal tendencies, and having a smaller brain does not mean an individual cannot be a genius. In fact, one of the most famous brains of the 20th century—that of Albert Einstein—was rather below average in size (Falk et al., 2013). This single exception does not invalidate all of the work on brain size and intelligence, but it reminds us that other factors may account for individual differences in intelligence and achievement.

Why is this relevant?

The relationship between brain size and intelligence can be used to better understand clinical conditions. For example, individuals who go through prolonged periods of alcohol abuse appear to lose brain mass along with certain cognitive skills (Luhar et al., 2013). Neurodegenerative disorders such as Alzheimer's are also marked by loss of brain volume. Even in healthy adults, brain volume gradually declines with age; however, this effect is less pronounced among those who remain the healthiest in old age (Wolf et al., 2014). Understanding the biochemical processes that lead to brain loss may lead to preventative treatments that slow or even stop the declines.

Module 9.1 Summary

9.1a Know . . . the key terminology associated with intelligence and intelligence testing:

achievement tests
anthropometrics
aptitude tests
intelligence
intelligence quotient (IQ)
mental age
norms
percentile rank
psychometrics
Raven's Progressive Matrices
standardized test
Stanford-Binet test
Wechsler Adult Intelligence Scale (WAIS)

9.1b Understand . . . the purpose of standardization and norms in intelligence testing.

Standardization of testing content as well as the conditions in which tests are administered is critical because comparisons among scores between individuals cannot be made unless tests are standardized. Establishing norms provides numbers with which individual scores can be compared.

9.1c Understand . . . the relationship between reliability and validity in testing.

A test that gives similar scores for an individual from one time to the next is reliable. A valid test is one that measures what it is supposed to measure. For a test to be valid, it must be reliable. However, a test can be reliable but not valid.

9.1d Apply . . . the concepts of test standardization and norms to make judgments about specific test scores.

Standardized tests have consistent sets of questions that are administered in a consistent way for all test takers. Standardization allows test makers to develop norms, the statistics that identify what scores are typical (such as the mean) versus scores that are higher or lower than normal (and how much). Table 9.1 provided a chance to apply the concept of test norming to some examples. It is important to understand that tests are "normed" with a mean as the center point and standard deviation as a measure of variation for test takers. Knowing these two statistics allows us to determine with precision how individual scores fall within the normal distribution of a test.

9.1e   Analyze . . . the use of brain size as an estimate of mental ability.

The correlation between brain size and intelligence is modest. Brain size is a general measurement; it may be that specific regions of the cerebral cortex, as shown by convolutions of the cortical surface, account for some of the variations across intelligence test scores.

9.1f   Analyze . . . whether intelligence and aptitude tests make useful predictions about performance.

When intelligence and aptitude tests are developed, their creators conduct studies to assess the validity of the instrument. In some cases, they look for predictive validity, which is the ability of a test to predict performance in a specific area. For example, the SAT predicts college GPA to some degree and intelligence tests such as the Wonderlic can predict job success. Conversely, we do not know how well the Wonderlic can predict success in the NFL.

Module 9.1 Quiz

Know . . .

1. A test designed to measure the degree to which knowledge has been learned would be referred to as a(n) _____ test.

    A. matrices
    B. achievement
    C. aptitude
    D. normative

Understand . . .

2. Because of norms in intelligence testing, psychologists are able to:

    A. evaluate an intelligence test to determine if it is reliable.
    B. evaluate an intelligence test to determine if it is valid.
    C. understand why there are learning disabilities.
    D. evaluate individuals relative to a typical or standard score on an intelligence test.

3. Jan has developed a software package to measure intelligence through images rather than verbal skills. Initial testing shows that when the same volunteers took the test multiple times, their scores would vary by up to 40%. It is difficult to know which score to believe. Therefore, Jan knew he had to work on improving the tests _____.

    A. standardization
    B. norms
    C. reliability
    D. mental age

Apply . . .

4. Yuri received a score of 115 on his IQ test and as a result is a part of the 84th percentile. In terms of his score compared to the population, this result means that:

    A. 84% of the population's scores are lower than Yuri's score.
    B. 84% of the population's scores are higher than Yuri's score.
    C. 16% of the population's scores are equivalent to Yuri's score.
    D. 84% of the population's scores are equivalent to Yuri's score.

Analyze . . .

5. Which of the following statements best summarizes the relationship between brain size and intelligence?

    A. Brain size is a great predictor of intelligence—the larger the brain, the greater the intelligence.
    B. There is no relationship between brain size and intelligence whatsoever.
    C. Brain size and intelligence are related only in Caucasian people.
    D. There are modest correlations between brain size, convolutions of the cortex, and intelligence.

Module **9.2**   Understanding Intelligence

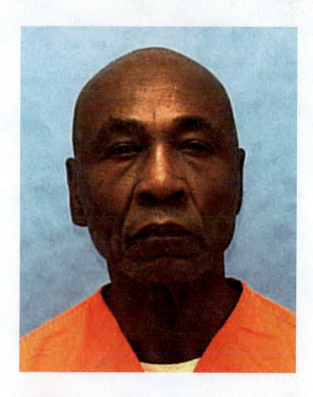

⌄ Learning Objectives

9.2a Know . . . the key terminology related to understanding intelligence.

9.2b Understand . . . why intelligence is divided into fluid and crystallized types.

9.2c Understand . . . the puzzling "Flynn effect"—a generational rise in IQ scores.

9.2d Apply . . . your knowledge to identify examples from the theory of successful intelligence.

9.2e Analyze . . . whether teachers should spend time tailoring lessons to each individual student's learning style.

In May 2014, the U.S. Supreme Court issued a ruling that saved Freddie Lee Hall from execution—at least for the time being. The court did not argue about the severity of the punishment itself; the 1978 sexual assault and murder for which Hall was convicted clearly fit the criteria for the death penalty in Florida, the state in which he was tried. Instead, the court reinterpreted a 2002 decision that protects individuals with mental retardation from execution. There is no question among those involved that Hall has intellectual challenges. Records indicate that Hall has been tested a number of times

with IQ scores generally being in the low 70s. However, Florida and several other states have set an IQ score of 70 as the cutoff point for retardation, and so to many—including four of the nine Supreme Court justices—Hall's sentence should be carried out. Despite this, the defense successfully convinced the majority of justices that intelligence cannot be summarized as a single score. As Justice Kennedy wrote, "Intellectual disability is a condition, not a number" and therefore, the intellectual ability of an individual should be determined in multiple ways, not just with a single test score.

As you will read in this module, this case brought before the Supreme Court is a legal version of a question that psychologists have wrestled with for more than a century: Exactly what is intelligence?

Recall that the definition of intelligence incorporates the ability to think, understand, reason, and cognitively adapt to and overcome obstacles. How do all of these concepts fit under the category of intelligence? Is it a single cognitive ability that produces all of these activities? Or is each concept distinct? As you will learn in this module, a full picture of intelligence involves various perspectives on how many different abilities fall under the term *intelligence.*

Intelligence as a Single, General Ability

Scientific arguments and evidence for general intelligence date back to early 20th-century work by Charles Spearman. Spearman (1923) began by developing techniques to calculate correlations among multiple measures of mental abilities. One of these techniques, known as **factor analysis**, *is a statistical technique that reveals similarities among a wide variety of items.* For example, individuals' scores from different measures of vocabulary, reading comprehension, and verbal reasoning might correlate enough to reveal an underlying "language ability" factor. Similarly, if an individual does well in algebra, she is likely to do well in geometry and calculus. Perhaps that is not surprising, given that these subjects are all mathematical in nature, but Spearman's factor analysis techniques allowed researcher to measure the degree to which multiple tests overlap.

The correlations among different mental abilities led Spearman to hypothesize the existence of a **general intelligence (g)**—*a concept that intelligence is a basic cognitive trait comprising the ability to learn, reason, and solve problems regardless of their nature.* Spearman's concept of *g* is relevant today and can be assessed with wide range of intelligence tests administered by psychologists (Bouchard, 2014). There is even evidence that *g* exists in other species, including the humble laboratory mouse (Matzel et al., 2013). It is a useful construct because is related to a number of positive outcomes such as higher educational achievement, better health, and longer lives while having the opposite relationship with several undesirable outcomes as shown in Figure 9.7 (Coyle et al., 2014; Deary et al., 2010; Nisbett et al., 2012). The fact that *g* can predict so many things is compelling evidence, and yet there are some interesting reasons to consider the alternative that intelligence is actually more than one ability.

Figure 9.7 General Intelligence Is Related to Various Outcomes

General intelligence (*g*) does more than just describe intellectual ability; it also predicts psychological well-being, income, and successful long-term relationships.

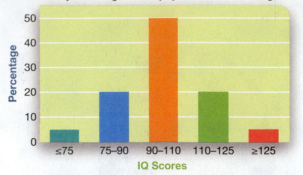

Total percentage of the population in this range:

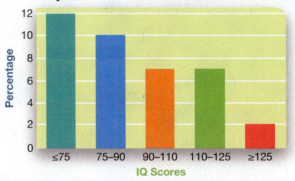

Individuals in this range who divorced within five years:

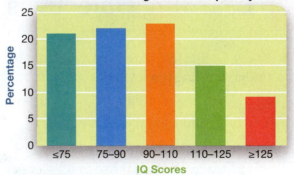

Individuals in this range who live in poverty:

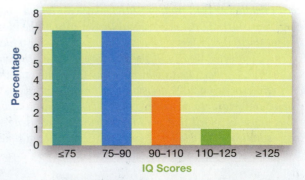

Individuals in this range who have been incarcerated:

Working the Scientific Literacy Model

Testing for Fluid and Crystallized Intelligence

Most of us recognize that our friends, family, and colleagues express their intelligence differently. Thus, we should be able to use scientific methodology to determine whether these different expressions of intelligence reflect actual distinct mental abilities.

What do we know about different types of intelligence?

Intelligence appears to be divisible into at least two categories. Some types of problem solving and thinking fall into the category of **fluid intelligence (Gf)**, *a type of intelligence that is used to adapt to new situations and solve new problems without relying on previous knowledge*. Tests of Gf involve problems that do not require prior experience with the task or any specialized knowledge and may include tasks such as pattern recognition and solving geometric puzzles, such as Raven's Matrices (described in Module 9.1). **Crystallized intelligence (Gc)**, like an actual crystal, *is a form of intelligence that relies on extensive experience and knowledge and, therefore, tends to be relatively stable and robust* (Figure 9.8; Cattell, 1971). Intelligence tests measure Gc with vocabulary, similarity/difference, and reading comprehension problems, because all of these tasks require prior knowledge (Figure 9.9). The idea underlying Gf and Gc probably makes sense, but does scientific evidence support the division of intelligence into these two categories?

Figure 9.8 Fluid and Crystallized Intelligence

Fluid intelligence is dynamic and changing and may eventually become crystallized into a more permanent form.

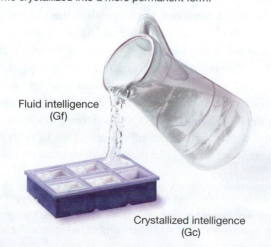

Fluid intelligence
(Gf)

Crystallized intelligence
(Gc)

Figure 9.9 Measuring Fluid and Crystalized Intelligence

(a) The Tower of London test requires a test taker to plan and keep track of rules. The test taker is given the towers with colored beads arranged in an initial position, and must rearrange them so that they match a given goal position. The rules make it challenging by allowing only one bead to be removed from the towers at a time.

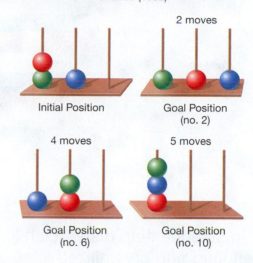

Tower of London Test
Shallice (1982)

2 moves

Initial Position   Goal Position
(no. 2)

4 moves   5 moves

Goal Position   Goal Position
(no. 6)   (no. 10)

(b) Vocabulary and informational knowledge, represented by the questions below, are thought to be components of crystallized intelligence.

Do *irony* and *coincidence* mean the same thing?
What does *abstruse* mean?

Which South American countries are these?

PACIFIC OCEAN

ATLANTIC OCEAN

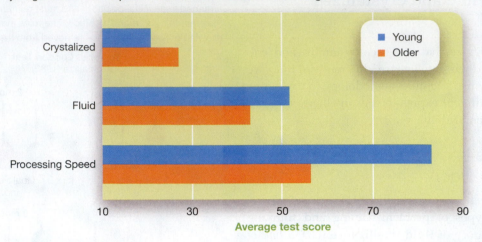

Figure 9.10 Age Differences in Crystalized and Fluid Intelligence

Older adults tend to score higher than younger adults on tests of crystalized intelligence, while younger adults tend to perform better on measures of fluid intelligence and processing speed.

How can science help distinguish between fluid and crystallized intelligence?

The hypothesis that we have both Gf and Gc intelligence has been tested by examining how each type changes over the life span (Cattell, 1971; Horn & Cattell, 1967). In one study, a group of young adults (average age of 22) was compared to a group of older adults (average age of 74) on cognitive tests such as Raven's Matrices, which measures fluid intelligence, and the Mill Hill test, which measures crystallized intelligence (Manard et al., 2014). Figure 9.10 reveals a noticeable difference: Younger adults fare better on the fluid intelligence test and a related test of processing speed.

Gc, by comparison, involves accumulated knowledge. Thus, as long as an individual keeps learning new information, Gc is likely to increase. As you can see in the figure, older adults have the advantage in this domain. Healthy, older adults generally do not show much decline, if any at all, in these skills (Bergman & Almkvist, 2013). Observations of decreased fluid and conserved Gc memory abilities in older adults are also supported by neurological studies. The functioning of brain regions associated with Gf intelligence tasks declines sooner than the functioning of those regions supporting Gc intelligence tasks (Burgaleta et al., 2014; Geake & Hansen, 2010).

Can we critically evaluate evidence for distinguishing Gc and Gf?

There is certainly a lot of strong evidence that fluid and crystallized intelligence are distinct from each other. The tasks that measure each type of intelligence are different from each other, and age affects how well people do on them. Nevertheless, we should be careful not to overgeneralize these findings. Older people may be slower and somewhat less successful at tasks measuring reaction time and problem-solving skills, but they also excel in certain domains. Consider social conflicts and dilemmas, which can be highly complex, nuanced, and difficult to resolve (and therefore require fluid intelligence). Research has shown that older adults are better at reasoning about social conflicts and predicting their outcomes than are younger adults (Grossman et al., 2010).

Why is this relevant?

Recognizing the distinctness of Gf and Gc can help to reduce stereotypes and expectations about intelligence in older age. Rather than constantly reminding older adults that the brain and cognitive abilities decline with age, we should emphasize their strengths. Furthermore, in the United States there is a tendency to marginalize the elderly, and, along with them, untapped wisdom. Also, the theory that more than one type of intelligence exists may help explain individual differences in performance on intelligence tests found at any age. The notion of general intelligence may not fully capture the complex and individualized ways that people express their cognitive skills. Strong evidence supports the contention that intelligence comes in both fluid and crystallized forms—but could there be even more?

Intelligence as Multiple, Specific Abilities

Imagine a fellow student claims to have done great on his history final while bombing his calculus exam, attributing it to the fact that he is just not a "math person." Then, another student celebrates an A on her French exam. No one is surprised given that she has the highest grade in your physics class—she is obviously a genius. If you spend time around students, you will hear these ideas in conversation and may not think twice about them. But if you examine them, you will see that the first student assumes there are very distinct types of intelligence: He has the type related to humanities but not the type related to math. The second student is described with the opposite view: If you have the scientific and mathematical intelligence to do well in physics, you must have the intelligence to do well with languages too. Which view is correct?

So far, we have discussed the view that intelligence is a single, general ability. However, even in Spearman's time, researchers argued that *g* might be oversimplifying intelligence. L. L. Thurstone, for example, examined scores of general intelligence tests with modifications to the factor analysis procedure. This produced seven different clusters of what he termed *primary mental abilities*, including familiar topics such as reading comprehension, spatial reasoning, numerical ability, and memory span. Modern proponents of multiple intelligence types cite other evidence as well (Gardner, 1983):

- An individual may experience a head injury or stroke and lose one ability (such as language production) without any loss in other aspects of intelligence. For example, an individual might lose the ability to understand sentences that use the passive voice (e.g., "The ball was chased by the dog"), yet still understand sentences that use the active voice (e.g., "The dog chased the ball").

- **Savants** *are individuals with low mental capacity in most domains but extraordinary abilities in other specific areas such as music, mathematics, or art.* If intelligence was a single ability, then we would not expect such brilliance in one area and impaired functioning in others.

- When psychologists look beyond traditional ways of viewing intelligence (i.e., language, math, and problem-solving ability), they find people vary a great deal in terms of physical, social, and artistic skills that are not well explained by *g*.

Several contemporary psychologists have formulated multifaceted models of intelligence. For example, Robert Sternberg and colleagues (2014) have offered an alternative known as *successful intelligence*, which defines

Stephen Wiltshire is a savant who has autism. Although he has mental impairments in many areas, his artistic skills are amazing. Wiltshire is capable of viewing extremely complex landscapes and drawing them from memory with great accuracy and clarity.

intelligence more in terms of being successful at achieving goals and adapting to the environment. In being successful, an individual will demonstrate three types of intelligence:

Analytical intelligence is the verbal, mathematical problem-solving type of intelligence that probably comes to mind when we speak of intelligence. It is close to the concept of academic achievement and the notion of intelligence as measured by *g*.

Practical intelligence is the ability to address real-world problems that are encountered in daily life, especially those that occur in an individual's specific work context and family life.

Creative intelligence is the ability to create new ideas to solve problems. Obviously, artists must have some level of creative intelligence, but the same is true for any kind of designer. It also takes creative intelligence to be a scientist because creative thinking is often required to conceive of good scientific hypotheses and develop ways of testing them.

In addition, Sterberg's research team often includes a fourth element, *wisdom*, which is the ability to make sure that learning and ability is put to use in a responsible and effective way (Sternberg et al., 2012; see Table 9.2). This theory is largely an attempt to reframe intelligence as a more practical concept than the highly abstract *g*. In fact, researchers have been able to make modest improvements for some students when it comes to academic goals such

Table 9.2 Applying the Concept of Successful Intelligence

Classify whether the individual in the following scenario scores low or high in each of the four aspects of intelligence (creative, practical, analytical, and wisdom).

Katrina is an excellent chemist. She has always performed well in school, so it is no surprise that she earned her doctorate from a prestigious institution. She has made many contributions and discoveries related to chemistry. She has used her knowledge to come up with creative ways to improve people's lives. However, she seems to fall short in some domains. For example, Katrina does not know how to cook her own meals and if anything breaks at her house, she has to rely on someone else to fix it.

Answers: creative, analytical, wisdom = high, practical = low. This person has academic success in a challenging scientific discipline, suggesting a high level of creative and analytic skill. Applying this knowledge to public good reflects wisdom. Lacking everyday skills suggests lower practical intelligence.

as gaining admission to college and being successful in academics and campus life. In contrast, the theory has shown virtually no benefit when serving as the basis for designing grade school curricula (Sternberg et al., 2014).

Howard Gardner (1999) proposed the concept of **multiple intelligences**, *a model claiming that eight different forms of intelligence exist, each independent from the others*. Gardner argued that the eight forms of intelligence listed in Table 9.3 are all unique ways of expressing intellectual abilities. His theory makes intuitive sense: People can be great with language but clumsy and uncoordinated; we know people who have amazing strength, agility, and stamina, but who cannot hum a simple tune or add double-digit numbers without a calculator. But are these abilities really forms of intelligence? For example, does being able to control body movement and balance constitute intelligence, or is this better described as a talent or skill?

These questions are relevant to a number of educational practices that have used the notion of multiple intelligences to promote the idea of **learning styles**, *the hypothesis that individuals are fundamentally different in how they best acquire information*. The most common sets of learning styles include divisions such as visual, auditory, reading/writing, and kinesthetic/tactile (moving and touching)—you probably see the connection with the theory of multiple intelligences. Many educators claim that students tend to learn best using their own personal style. These claims require further critical and scientific scrutiny to test their validity.

EVALUATING THEORIES OF SINGLE AND MULTIPLE INTELLIGENCES So is intelligence one ability or many? Decades of scientific inquiry suggest the answer is "It depends." Researchers have found that scores among various types of cognitive tests are positively correlated,

Myths in Mind

Learning Styles

We all know there are differences in how people choose to study; some read, some talk, some may watch. This has lured many to believe in the nonscientific concept of learning styles, the proposal that each individual will learn best in the mode that fits his or her style. For example, if a person is classified as a visual learner, he should score better on tests for information he learned visually than on tests for the same type of information learned through physical interaction. A kinesthetic learner should retain more information she learned through physical interaction than information she learned through listening. To validate the concept, a researcher would need to conduct a simple experiment: Individuals with a specific learning style could be randomly assigned to learn in one of two conditions: a matching condition (such as visual learners studying visually) or a mismatched condition (visual learners studying auditorily). When comparing the two groups, the individuals in the matched condition should score much higher on a test of the material.

Although this is truly a simple experiment, the largest review of learning styles research to date shows that this experiment does not produce the predicted effects (Pashler et al., 2009). Dozens of studies have failed to show any benefit for studying according to an individual's learning style; in fact, some studies completely contradict what the learning styles hypothesis would predict. This result probably occurs because regardless of how you encounter something—reading, watching, listening, or physically interacting—you still need to store the meaning of the information to retain it over the long term (Willingham, 2004). As a result, it does not make sense for teachers to tailor their instructional methods to fit individual learning styles; in fact, doing so might actually take away from methods that are far more important, such as aligning their teaching and learning methods to fit the material. In other words, a visual presentation is not especially useful to a self-described visual learner as compared to an auditory learner, but visual presentations are extraordinarily important for teaching visual information, such as how to identify a style of painting or classify species of plants by the shape of their leaves.

Table 9.3 Gardener's Proposed Forms of Intelligence

Verbal/linguistic intelligence	The ability to read, write, and speak effectively
Logical/mathematical intelligence	The ability to think with numbers and use abstract thought; the ability to use logic or mathematical operations to solve problems
Visuospatial intelligence	The ability to create mental pictures, manipulate them in the imagination, and use them to solve problems
Bodily/kinesthetic intelligence	The ability to control body movements, to balance, and to sense how one's body is situated
Musical/rhythmical intelligence	The ability to produce and comprehend tonal and rhythmic patterns
Interpersonal intelligence	The ability to detect another person's emotional states, motives, and thoughts
Self/intrapersonal intelligence	Self-awareness; the ability to accurately judge one's own abilities, and identify one's own emotions and motives
Naturalist intelligence	The ability to recognize and identify processes in the natural world—plants, animals, and so on
Existential intelligence	The tendency and ability to ask questions about purpose in life and the meaning of human existence

supporting the one-ability hypothesis (Johnson et al., 2008; Johnson et al., 2004; Nisbett et al., 2012). However, correlations occur in the population, not in any one individual. Therefore, some individuals may have unusual differences in ability, such as low mathematical intelligence, but high language intelligence. In addition, scores on different types of mathematical tests have higher correlations with one another than they do with verbal tests, and vice versa. Thus, mathematical and verbal abilities are distinct, but they probably share at least some common source.

Psychologists took these factors into account and developed the hierarchical model shown in Figure 9.11. Diagrams A and B summarize historical views you are now familiar with. Diagram C sums up the modern, general consensus that intelligence can be traced to a single common construct called *g*, and within it we can separate out verbal and mathematical intelligence. Interestingly, the animal-based research that has identified *g* is also consistent with this hierarchical approach (Matzel et al., 2013). For example, animals that perform well on working memory tasks also tend to score higher on tests that assess cognitive abilities related to intelligence.

It may be easier to understand the advantage of this type of model by using an analogy. Chimps and gorillas are clearly two different types of animals, but both are primates, which also means they are mammals. Thus, they are distinct at some levels, but similar at others. That is exactly what research has shown about intelligence. The abilities to comprehend written text and to produce written text may, in fact, be different intelligences, but they are both forms of verbal intelligence, so both contribute to general intelligence.

Figure 9.11 Differing Perspectives on Intelligence

Spearman proposed a single, general intelligence that could affect scores on *all* varieties of tasks, as shown in (a). Later, Thurstone and others argued for separate, unrelated primary mental abilities as shown in (b). The dominant view today incorporates the evidence in favor of both, as shown in (c). It appears that individuals can have large differences in verbal and mathematical skills (separate abilities), although in the general population, they produce high correlations that support the concept of *g* (Willingham, 2004).

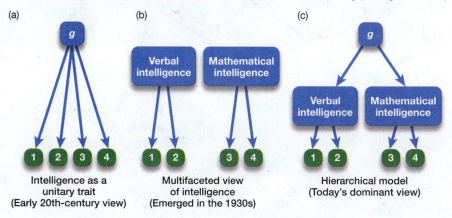

(a) Intelligence as a unitary trait (Early 20th-century view)

(b) Multifaceted view of intelligence (Emerged in the 1930s)

(c) Hierarchical model (Today's dominant view)

Notes:
• "*g*" stands for general, a single factor underlying all intelligent behavior.
• Numbered boxes represent multiple tests of different intellectual abilities.

The Flynn Effect: Is Everyone Getting Smarter?

For reasons that are not yet clearly understood, performance on standardized intelligence tests has been improving at a steady pace for decades. James Flynn initially found evidence of a gradual rise in IQ test performance by examining the changing norms on standardized tests. One frequently used test was normed to have an average of 100 in 1953. When a new version of the test was developed 25 years later, psychologists set it up to have a norm of 100 as well. In theory, an adult who scored the average of 100 on the 1947 version of the test should have the same score on the 1978 version; it is the same individual taking basically the same test, after all. However, when researchers actually tried having the same adults take both versions of the test, the participants' average was about 8 points higher on the old test (Flynn, 1984). After reviewing many similar studies that were reported since 1932, James Flynn and other researchers have estimated that the averages increase about 1 point every 3 years (Flynn, 2007; Trahan, 2014). This phenomenon is now known as the **Flynn effect**, and it refers to the steady population level increases in intelligence test scores over time (Figure 9.12).

The Flynn effect leads us to ask, are today's kids really smarter than previous generations (Flynn, 2013)?

A number of psychologists offered this hypothesis based on factors such as improved nutrition, health care, and early childhood programs. This is supported by the observation that the lowest scores have not been nearly so far below average in recent decades. This suggests test scores are rising simply because people now have more experience taking tests (Pietschnig et al., 2013; te Nijenhuis et al., 2014). One proposal known as the rule-dependence model draws from the fact that technology has crept into every facet of life throughout much of the world; perhaps the increased exposure to television, computers, and video games enhances individuals' processing speed and visualization abilities that are particularly important to tests of fluid intelligence (Armstrong & Woodley, 2014). With this variety of competing views, the best conclusion we can draw is that intelligence researchers have significant work for the foreseeable future.

Whatever led to these increases in IQ scores over time, the most recent data suggest that the Flynn effect might be coming to an end—or may even be reversing—in wealthy countries that have a long history of testing. Not only have intelligence test scores leveled off, but in some cases they have even declined (Dutton & Lynn, 2013; Sundet, 2004; Teasdale & Owen, 2005). In contrast, developing countries may just be at the beginning of their own run of experiencing the Flynn effect (Daley et al., 2003).

Figure 9.12 The Flynn Effect

For decades, there has been a general trend toward increasing IQ scores. This trend, called the Flynn effect, has been occurring since standardized IQ tests were first administered.

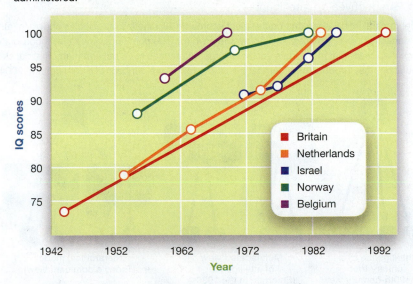

Module **9.2** Summary

9.2a   Know . . . the key terminology related to understanding intelligence:

crystallized intelligence (Gc)
factor analysis
fluid intelligence (Gf)
Flynn effect
general intelligence (*g*)
learning styles
multiple intelligences
savants

9.2b   Understand . . . why intelligence is divided into fluid and crystallized types.

Mental abilities encompass both the amount of knowledge accumulated and the ability to solve new problems. This understanding is consistent not only with our common views of intelligence but also with the results of decades of intelligence testing. Also, the observation that fluid intelligence can decline over the life span, even as crystallized intelligence remains constant, lends further support to the contention that they are different abilities.

9.2c   Understand . . . the puzzling "Flynn effect"—a generational rise in IQ scores.

Why the Flynn effect occurs is unclear, but it shows remarkable consistency across different populations and intelligence tests. The rise in IQ scores has been too rapid to be accounted for by hereditary factors. Changes in education, nutrition, increased familiarity with testing procedures, and other environmental factors may be related, but do not alone account for it. Increased experience with a technological environment may have something to do with the Flynn effect.

9.2d   Apply . . . your knowledge to identify examples from the theory of successful intelligence.

Table 9.2 provided a scenario in which you could apply the components of successful intelligence: creative, analytical, practical, and wisdom. This theory departs from the concept of fluid and crystallized intelligence and considers how intelligence is expressed in a variety of ways and contexts.

9.2e   Analyze . . . whether teachers should spend time tailoring lessons to each individual student's learning style.

Certainly, no one would want to discourage teachers from being attentive to the unique characteristics that each student brings to the classroom. However, large-scale reviews of research suggest that there is little basis for individualized teaching based on learning styles (e.g., auditory, visual, kinesthetic).

Module **9.2** Quiz

Know . . .

1. What is factor analysis?
   A. A method of ranking individuals by their intelligence
   B. A statistical procedure that is used to identify which sets of psychological measures are highly correlated with each other
   C. The technique of choice for testing fluid intelligence
   D. The technique of choice for testing crystallized intelligence

Understand . . .

2. Which of the following is a reason for classifying intelligence into both fluid and crystallized forms?
   A. The two types of intelligence change differently over the life span
   B. To account for both verbal abilities and physical abilities
   C. Intelligence tests are difficult to score if problems are not divided into categories
   D. Each individual has their own specialized way of learning

3. Which of the following is a more likely explanation of the Flynn effect?
   A. Better testing technology
   B. Practice effects of taking intelligence tests
   C. Improvements in the gene pool
   D. Exposure to technology

Apply . . .

4. Hussein is a small business owner. He was a C– student in school and does not generally think of himself as very "smart." Nonetheless, Hussein does an excellent job of running his business and dealing intelligently with real-world problems when they arise. According to the theory of successful intelligence, which type of intelligence is Hussein demonstrating?
   A. Creative
   B. Analytical
   C. Crystallized
   D. Practical

Analyze . . .

5. What is the best way to explain the scientific knowledge about learning styles?
   A. If teachers match instruction to each student's learning style, the individual students will be able to acquire more knowledge and skills than otherwise possible.
   B. Not only do proposed learning styles have no effect on learning, they actually take time away from teachers' use of highly effective strategies.
   C. Auditory learners almost always benefit from auditory instruction, even if the material is inherently visual (e.g., based on shape or color).
   D. There are at least six dominant learning styles that define how individuals learn best.

Module 9.3 Heredity, Environment, and Intelligence

 ## Learning Objectives

9.3a Know . . . the key terminology related to heredity, environment, and intelligence.

9.3b Understand . . . different approaches to studying the genetic basis of intelligence.

9.3c Apply . . . your knowledge of entity and incremental theories to understand your own beliefs about intelligence.

9.3d Analyze . . . claims that infant intelligence is increased by viewing educational television programming.

9.3e Analyze . . . the meaning of group-level differences in intelligence scores.

The fact that you are enrolled in a college course shows that you have strong intellectual abilities and can achieve academically. However, here are a few kids that might challenge you: Peter finished his mathematics A Levels (a high school completion exam in England) when he was just 7 years old. Paula completed an advanced mathematics course at Cambridge—one of the world's greatest universities—at age 9. Anna-Marie, who speaks six languages, finished A Levels in computing at 11, and completed her master's in mathematics at Oxford University—another of the world's greatest universities at 19. Christiana is the youngest student to ever enroll in a British university (at age 11) and Samantha, who happens to be gold-medal winning sprinter, completed high school math at age 6. In addition to sharing amazing educational credentials, these kids all share the same last name. The Imafidon siblings—along with their parents—are often referred to as Britain's smartest family. Although they all grew up together and were supported by the same nurturing parents, this much talent in one family leads many to wonder what is in their genes. In this module, we will examine how science might explain the environmental and genetic influences for intelligence.

JOURNAL PROMPT

Entity vs. Incremental Beliefs: Before diving into this topic, describe your beliefs about the nature of intelligence. Specifically, is it something we can change or something that remains the same throughout the life span? Explain.

It is easy to make intuitive judgments about sources of intelligence, especially for people who perform at high levels. Perhaps you see someone graduating at the top of her high school class and say, "Not surprising—her older brother was valedictorian." Maybe it is not that surprising, but what does this pattern imply about where the high intelligence came from? Perhaps the valedictorians inherited a good set of genes, grew up in a family that fostered intellectual development, or received special attention from teachers who provided challenges and opportunities beyond the standard curriculum. As we will see in this module, there are multiple contributors to intelligence—each of which plays a small but significant role.

Intelligence and Heredity

Scientists have been looking for evidence of hereditary influences on intelligence ever since the first attempts to measure it—long before genes had ever been identified. In the 1860s, Sir Francis Galton used heredity in his efforts to prove that certain families were intellectually superior (Module 9.1). In the 1930s, the anthropologist Samuel Morton measured skull sizes in an attempt to show racial and ethnic differences in cognitive ability and assumed that skull size—and therefore intelligence—were almost entirely genetically determined. Interest in

the topic has not subsided over the years. If anything, new genetic research techniques have only stimulated more research. Thanks to the Human Genome Project (discussed in Module 3.1) and modern brain imaging techniques, scientists can now view the genetics of intelligence in ways Galton and Morton could not have imagined. As the researcher Robert Plomin put it, psychologists can study genetics, genes, and the genome (Plomin & Spinath, 2004). Plomin and Spinath (2004) describe behavioral genetics as a three-layered approach, with each layer asking different, yet related questions:

- Genetics: To what degree is intelligence an inherited trait?
- Genes: If intelligence does have a genetic component, which genes are involved?
- Genome: If we can identify which genes contribute to intelligence, then how exactly do they contribute to brain development and function?

TWIN AND ADOPTION STUDIES Decades of research on families, adopted children, and twins has shown that genetic similarity contributes to intelligence test scores. Several important findings from this line of work are summarized in Figure 9.13 (Plomin & Spinath, 2004). The most obvious trend in the figure shows that as the degree of

Figure 9.13 Intelligence and Genetic Relatedness

Several types of comparisons reveal genetic contributions to intelligence (Plomin & Spinath, 2004). Generally, the closer the biological relationship between people, the more similar their intelligence scores.

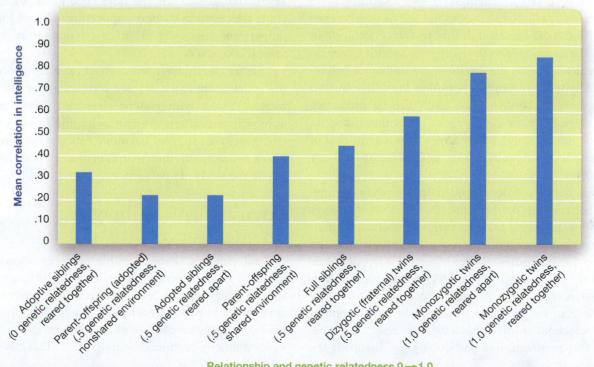

genetic relatedness increases, similarity in IQ scores also increases. Intelligence scores between parents and their children and between siblings are statistically related, with correlations between 0.40 and 0.50. Also, identical twins are more alike in intelligence than are fraternal twins. Nevertheless, we cannot jump to the conclusion that genes are more important than environmental factors when it comes to intelligence. If you look more closely at Figure 9.13, you will notice that the environment is important, too. Offspring are more similar to the parents with whom they grow up. This can be seen by comparing parents and offspring who share an environment with those who do not, as is the case with adopted children and their biological parents.

The last two bars on the right of Figure 9.13 present perhaps the strongest evidence for a genetic basis for intelligence. Identical twins share 100% of their genes, and their intelligence scores have a correlation of approximately 0.85 when they are raised together. This is a higher figure than for fraternal twins—which is quite compelling evidence for a strong genetic component to intelligence. Of course, the twin pairs are growing up in a similar environment, which could also account for the strong correlation. Yet even when identical twins are adopted and raised apart, their intelligence scores are still correlated at approximately 0.80—a very strong relationship. In fact, this is about the same number that researchers find when the same individuals take the same intelligence test twice—now *that* is identical.

BEHAVIORAL GENOMICS AND INTELLIGENCE Twin and adoption studies show that some of the individual differences observed in intelligence scores can be attributed to genetic factors, but it does not tell us which genes account for the differences. For this, researchers engage in behavioral genomics—the study of how specific genes, in their interactions with the environment, influence behavior (see Module 3.1). Studies scanning the entire human genome show that intelligence levels can be predicted, to some degree, by the collection of genes that individuals inherit, but no single genes account for a great deal of intelligence independently (Craig & Plomin, 2006; Deary et al., 2009).

Researchers have developed mouse models of intelligence because, unlike humans, there are ethical ways of randomly assigning mice to various genetic and environmental conditions and conducting experiments. **Gene knockout (KO) studies** *involve removing a specific gene thought to be involved in a trait (such as intelligence) and testing the effects of removing the gene by comparing behavior of animals without the gene with those that have it.* In one of the first knockout studies of intelligence, researchers discovered that removing one particular gene disrupted the

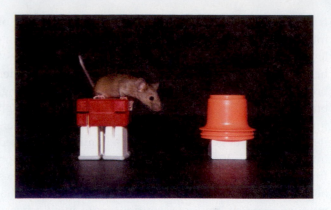

The Princeton University lab mouse, Doogie (named for the fictional whiz kid, Doogie Howser, from a 1980s television program), is able to learn faster than other mice thanks to a bit of genetic engineering. Researchers inserted a gene known as NR2B that helps create new synapses and, apparently, leads to quicker learning.

ability of mice to learn spatial layouts (Silva et al., 1992). Since this investigation was completed, numerous studies using gene knockout methods have shown that specific genes are related to performance on tasks that have been adapted to study learning and cognitive abilities in animals (Robinson et al., 2011).

Scientists can also take the opposite approach to knocking genes out; they can insert genetic material into mouse chromosomes to study the changes associated with the new gene. The animal that receives this so-called gene transplant is referred to as a transgenic animal. This approach may sound like science fiction. In fact, researchers have been able to engineer transgenic mice that are better than average learners (Cao et al., 2007; Tang et al., 1999). Transgenic mice that have been given a gene regulating the chemical changes supporting memory formation outperform nontransgenic mice on numerous cognitive tasks (Nakajima & Tang, 2005).

Genes clearly have some effect on intelligence. From the genetics approach, we see correlations of intelligence increase along with genetic similarity. From the gene approach, researchers are narrowing their search for specific genes that support cognitive functioning. How these genes interact with the environment is another key question in the study of intelligence.

Environmental Influences on Intelligence

Beyond genetics, there is ample evidence showing that multiple environmental factors directly influence intelligence. There are also indirect effects in that environment is related to how well genetics can predict intelligence. For example, the genetic influence on intelligence is more significant among high-income individuals that have access to high-quality education. Among lower-income individuals, the environment varies so widely that it masks some of the genetic contributions (Brant et al., 2013; Tucker-Drob, Briley, & Harden, 2013).

HEALTH AND NUTRITION Numerous studies correlate health, schooling, and intelligence. These correlations should not be too surprising when comparing people living in the extremes—children living in poverty and those in affluent households, for example. But according to a Spanish study, a statistically significant relationship between nutrition and intelligence exists even among high-socioeconomic grade-school children. This relationship holds even after removing influences of gender and income from the analysis (Arija et al., 2006). Some evidence even shows that nutritional supplements can help overcome this factor among children who may not consume balanced diets (Benton, 2001). It is tempting to assume that nutrition leads to better brain functioning, but this link is not fully understood at this time. An alternative would be simply that children who eat well are more prepared to learn during the school day (Kleinman et al., 2002).

Income   There are good reasons to believe that income is a relevant environmental contributor to intelligence (Turkheimer et al., 2003). High-socioeconomic-status students are more likely to enjoy the advantages of better schools and teachers, and they experience more interactions with highly educated adults (Duncan & Murnane, 2011). Low-income households face higher stress levels on a day-to-day basis, and this stress can distract children from school; in addition, the stress responses can negatively impact brain development (Evans & Schamberg, 2009). Interestingly the effects are not necessarily permanent: Children raised in impoverished orphanages show a remarkable recovery in intelligence after being placed in foster care as compared to those who remain behind (Nelson et al., 2007).

Education   Health, nutrition, and environmental stimulation are critical and they exert much of their influence on IQ through education. Healthy, well-nourished children are better able to engage in the enriching school environment. In doing so, children not only accumulate factual knowledge and learn academic skills, but they also become more intelligent as a result. A review of the research on education and schooling shows that children's IQ scores are significantly lower if they are not attending school (Ceci & Williams, 1997; Nisbett, 2009). This relationship has been observed in numerous contexts, such as in occupied Europe during World War II, in remote villages where teachers have not been available, and over long summer breaks from school.

Birth Order   Being the oldest sibling has its advantages. Psychologists have found that the IQ of first-born children is, on average, 3 points higher than that of second-born siblings and 4 points higher than that of third-borns (Kristensen & Bjerkedal, 2007). It is unlikely that this effect is the result of genetic factors. One hypothesis is that the

Socioeconomic status is related to intelligence. People from low-socioeconomic backgrounds typically have far fewer opportunities to access educational and other important resources that contribute to intellectual growth.

Figure 9.14 Birth Order and Intelligence

A study examining records of over 200,000 men enlisted in the Norwegian military revealed that older siblings tend to score slightly higher on intelligence than younger siblings.

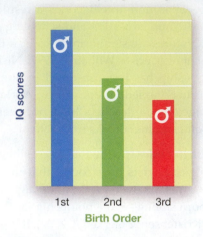

First-born men had slightly higher IQs than their respective younger siblings.

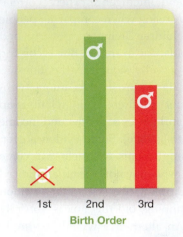

Even if the first-born sibling died at a young age, this relationship still holds.

first born plays the role of tutor for the younger siblings; teaching may benefit the intellectual development of the older sibling whereas the younger children do not have as many opportunities to do the same (see Figure 9.14; Sulloway, 2007).

Parents are often particularly concerned about these factors, given that they have some degree of control over them. For many parents, efforts to increase their child's intelligence begin as soon as they realize a baby is on the way and intensify the moment the baby arrives. This concern has led to some claims by makers of products designed for infants that intelligence can be accelerated and enhanced by certain types of television programming and DVDs.

Myths in Mind

Can Media Make Babies Smarter?

Watching television at a very young age may slow the processes of cognitive and intellectual development.

In the United States, nearly two-thirds of children age 2 years and younger watch television every day, and the daily average viewing time is about 80 minutes (Rideout & Hamel, 2006). Yet, the American Academy of Pediatrics recommends that children younger than 2 years old not watch television at all. What if, however, the time spent in front of the TV is devoted to watching educational programs? There are plenty of options to choose from—programs like the Baby Einstein series are marketed specifically for cognitive enrichment. Yet the research shows that, despite the intentions of such programs, infants who spend more time viewing educational television score lower in verbal comprehension and performance tests when assessed at age 6 or 7 years (Christakis, 2009; Zimmerman & Christakis, 2005). Programs based mostly on pantomime or simplified sing-alongs (rather than narrative) have also been negatively correlated with vocabulary development for children between 6 months and 2½ years of age (Linebarger & Walker, 2005). These studies point out the drawbacks of the "electronic babysitter." Even so, baby videos might not be all bad. Their effects may be neutral or even positive after age 3 or so, when children can understand more complex programs. Also, regardless of age, it is probably a good idea for a parent to maintain an ongoing conversation with the child about the shows they watch (Barr et al., 2008).

Group Similarities and Differences in Test Scores

Although psychological tests are designed to be taken by individuals, many people have speculated about the meaning of test results on a much broader scale—between males and females, among various ethnicities, in criminals versus law-abiding citizens, and among other segments of society. Many psychologists who study group differences believe it is important to do so because public policies and laws are often based on assumptions about group equalities or inequalities. Therefore, it is important that society be well informed on the pertinent issues (Hunt & Carlson, 2007).

DO MALES AND FEMALES HAVE UNIQUE COGNITIVE SKILLS? On average, males and females score about the same on most intelligence tests (see Figure 9.15; Halpern & LaMay, 2000; Hyde, 2005). However, there appears to be greater variability among males (Deary et al., 2007; Dykiert et al., 2009). Thus, among the top 1% of scores on general intelligence tests, there will be more males, but the same is true of the lowest 1% of all test scores as well (Ceci et al., 2009).

If you are looking for reliable differences in test scores between the sexes, you must examine specific abilities. For example, average scores on tasks of verbal fluency often tip in the favor of females. Conversely, average scores on tests of visual-spatial manipulation ability tend to favor males (see Figure 9.16; Halpern & LaMay, 2000; Lewin et al., 2001; Weiss et al., 2003).

These differences are not always present; boys and girls are born with roughly equal spatial abilities (Spelke, 2005), so any differences that emerge in childhood and beyond could be the result of socialization, other experiences, or genetically controlled maturational process. Psychologists find ample evidence that stereotypes lead to differential treatment of

boys and girls at a young age (Robinson-Cimpian et al., 2014). Therefore, when it comes to spatial tasks, it may be that socialization could improve boys' performance, it could hinder girls' growth in this skill, or some combination of the two; similar processes might contribute to girls' advantage in verbal tasks. On the other hand, the difference in test scores might not represent differences in abilities at all. As you will read in a moment, scores are affected by differences in how males and females experience the test-taking situation.

What makes the study of sex differences and similarities important? If sex differences are the result of socialization and stereotypes, then educational institutions and public policymakers may develop strategies to challenge these

Figure 9.15 Intelligence Distributions for Males and Females

There is very little difference in average IQ scores for males and females; in fact, there is much more overlap than difference. The major sex-related difference is the fact that males usually produce wider variability in test scores than females. Males are more likely to be found in the upper and lower extremes.

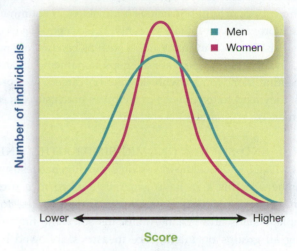

Figure 9.16 Mental Rotation and Verbal Fluency Tasks

Some research indicates that, on average, males outperform females on mental rotation tasks (a), while females outperform males on verbal fluency (b).

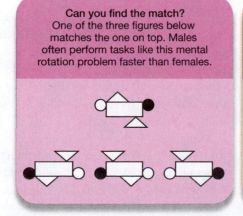

(a)　(b)

Figure (a): Can you find the match? One of the three figures below matches the one on top. Males often perform tasks like this mental rotation problem faster than females.

Figure (b): Conversely, women tend to outperform men on verbal fluency tasks like this one. In 60 seconds, name as many words that start with the letter "G" that you can think of. OR In 60 seconds, name as many different kinds of animals you can think of.

stereotypes. This is currently happening in science, technology, engineering, and mathematics (STEM) fields where women have long been underrepresented. Stereotypes about women's abilities in those fields are largely to blame, rather than any innate difference in abilities. We know this because various programs sponsored by educational institutions and scientific organizations have provided more mentoring and enrichment opportunities, such as internships and summer research programs for female students. These actions leveled gender distributions in many fields such as behavioral and life sciences, although there are still gaps in mathematics and engineering. For women who do take on careers in those fields, they tend to experience every bit as much success as their male counterparts (Ceci et al., 2009).

RACIAL AND SOCIOECONOMIC SIMILARITIES AND DIFFERENCES Since the inception of intelligence testing, researchers in this area have generally ranked measures by large geographical groups. In the United States, for example, Asians and Asian Americans score the highest among all groups on intelligence measures, followed by people of European, Latin American, and African heritage (Nisbett et al., 2012; Rushton & Jensen, 2005). Intelligence test scores also differ among the various social classes in the United States, with a strong correlation between measures of wealth or social status and IQ.

As is the case with comparing males and females, a statistical difference between two groups reflects only averages, not the individuals within those groups. The average differences between European Americans and Asian Americans is negligible—about the same 2- to 5-point range that some researchers find between the sexes and with greatly overlapping distributions. By comparison, the difference between African Americans and Asian Americans is quite large—approximately 15 points (one standard deviation). If the small differences between males and females have implications for education and public policy, then certainly the large differences among races deserve attention.

When researchers interpret racial and ethnic differences as mostly genetic, many will conclude that the differences substantial and resistant to change (Rushton & Jensen, 2005). If that is the case, they argue, then why should the public spend time and resources trying to compensate for the differences with minority scholarships, Head Start programs, and other interventions?

As it turns out, there are some good reasons to disagree with this argument. For one, differences in social class, rather than genetic heritage, may actually be responsible for the disparity in intelligence scores. As we have learned, the environment influences cognitive abilities in numerous ways. A cycle of poverty, low income, and low opportunity leads to lower scores on intelligence tests. Studies of children who have been adopted, however, suggest that there is a strong environmental influence: It

is unlikely that predominately high-IQ individuals are putting more children up for adoption. It is more plausible that adoptive parents (who are carefully screened, trained, and supervised) are themselves more affluent, more intelligent, and more enriching than the average parent. This relationship seems likely because the rise in test scores and school performance occurs in both same-race and mixed-race adoptions (van IJzendoorn & Juffer, 2005).

SUMMARY OF GROUP-DIFFERENCES RESEARCH Identifying sex, racial, and ethnic differences were the primary inspiration driving the work of the first intelligence researchers—Francis Galton, Samuel Morton, and others—and, as you can see, the debate is still going strong (Hunt & Carlson, 2007; Jensen, 2002). How is it that more than a century of work has not been able to resolve these questions? A part of the problem is that these are political as much as psychological issues; they involve moral conflicts about the inherent equality or inequality of people. Whenever individuals have this level of emotion, it can be difficult to resolve differences in opinion.

In addition, the research is almost entirely correlational—it is just not possible to conduct randomized experiments (e.g., randomly assigning someone to a certain socioeconomic class, for example). Nonetheless, correlations are often interpreted in ways that support assumptions and wishful thinking, reflecting both the confirmation bias and belief perseverance (described in Module 8.2): If you believe something is true, then you are likely to look for and interpret correlations in a way that supports your conviction. To see how this plays out with actual research, consider this finding: Brain-imaging studies show that women have greater cerebral blood flow (Halpern & LaMay, 2000). This fact could be used by proponents of opposite sides of an argument: Perhaps women have greater blood flow because they are less intelligent and, therefore, their brains have to work harder. Conversely, perhaps women are more intelligent than men, and the rich blood supply is simply more evidence in their favor.

Beyond the Test: Personal Beliefs Affect IQ Scores

If you were to ask individuals about their own intelligence, do you think they would give you an honest response, or perhaps try to appear modest? Would they give you an accurate estimate or believe themselves to be smarter than they really are? Trends in this line of research show only a modest amount of accuracy across the population—there is a relatively low correlation between what people estimate their intelligence to be and their actual test scores, ranging from 0.10 to 0.30 in most studies (e.g., Furnham & Chamorro-Premuzic, 2004). Even so, our beliefs about intelligence can have a strong effect on our personal performance, as well as the expectations we have of others.

Beliefs About Intelligence

Test scores are not necessarily pure measures of a person's knowledge or intelligence. Social context and personal experiences and beliefs about mental abilities may be contributing factors to such scores.

What do we know about how beliefs affect test scores?

Educators and parents have long been perplexed by students who consistently achieve below what their ability would predict. This is an especially important issue for students because children's self-perceptions of their mental abilities have a strong influence on their academic performance (Greven et al., 2009). For some students, it is simply a matter of apathy, but for others, it can be a frustrating experience.

Thus it was truly a serious matter when psychologist Carol Dweck (2002) responded to a colleague's inquiry about "Why smart people can be so stupid." Her research has found some interesting conclusions in that there seem to be two influential beliefs about the nature of intelligence. First is **entity theory**: *the belief that intelligence is a fixed characteristic and relatively difficult (or impossible) to change.* Second is **incremental theory**: *the belief that intelligence can be shaped by experiences, practice, and effort.* According to Dweck and colleagues, beliefs based on entity theory and incremental theory have different effects on academic performance.

How can science help explain the effects of beliefs on performance?

According to Dweck's research, the differences between the two theories are not nearly as important as the differences in behavior that result. In experiments by Dweck and her colleagues, students were identified as holding either entity theories or incremental theories. The students had the chance to answer 476 general knowledge questions dealing with topics such as history, literature, math, and geography. They received immediate feedback on whether their answers were correct or incorrect. Those who held entity theories were more likely to give up in the face of highly challenging problems, and they were likely to withdraw from situations that resulted in failure. These individuals believe that successful people were born that way, so why keep punishing yourself if you simply do not have the ability to succeed? By comparison, people with incremental views of intelligence were more resilient (Mangels et al., 2006). If they are motivated to succeed at a task, then they will work through failures and challenges—if intelligence and ability can change, then it makes sense to keep pursuing goals.

Resilience is a desirable trait, so Dweck and her colleagues tested a group of junior high students to see whether incremental views could be taught (Blackwell et al., 2007). In a randomized, controlled experiment, they taught one group of seventh graders incremental theory—that they could control and change their ability. This group's grades increased over the school year, whereas the control group's grades actually declined (Figure 9.17). Thus, if you are skeptical about your own abilities, it might pay to look into Dweck's research more closely.

Can we critically evaluate this research?

The work by Dweck and others you will read about later in this module shows how beliefs affect cognitive performance. Their findings encourage a liberal approach to learning—anytime a belief about intelligence can be changed for the better, then that change should probably be made. However, as you have learned in this chapter, psychologists have identified different types of intelligence, including fluid,

Figure 9.17 Personal Beliefs Influence Grades

Students who hold incremental views of intelligence (i.e., the belief that intelligence can change with effort) show improved grades in math compared to children who believe that intelligence is an unchanging entity (Blackwell et al., 2007).

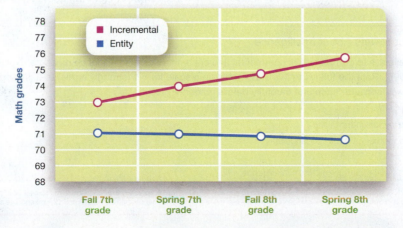

crystallized, analytical, practical, and others (see Module 9.2). Each of us differs in our relative strengths and limitations for each. Someone who is amazingly analytical may struggle with tasks requiring practical intelligence—even if that person is told that she can change.

Why are beliefs about intelligence relevant?

As you have learned in this module, intelligence is greatly modified by numerous environmental factors. Awareness of these factors and adoption of an incremental view of intelligence increases students' potential to boost their academic performance. This relationship certainly has important implications for both occupational and classroom work. Actually, Carol Dweck and colleague Lisa Sorich Blackwell have developed a program called *Brainology* that is designed to help elementary school, middle school, and high school students achieve higher levels of confidence and motivation by teaching them that the brain can be strengthened through experience. Furthermore, this type of knowledge can help people overcome the negative effects that stereotypes seem to have on cognitive performance. See Table 9.4 to examine your own beliefs about intelligence.

STEREOTYPES UNDERMINE TEST PERFORMANCE Psychologists have found that Asian Americans score higher on standardized intelligence tests than African Americans—an outcome that meshes with commonly held cultural stereotypes. Psychologists have found that even subtle reminders of stereotypes can negatively impact affect how one performs on tests of aptitude and achievement. This linkage is the basis of **stereotype threat**: *When people are aware of stereotypes about their social group, they may fear being reduced to that stereotype* (Steele, 1997). Such a fear can have both short- and long-term effects. In a math classroom, a female student might experience a subtle reminder of gender stereotypes (perhaps just having a male teacher, or overhearing comments from peers), and the effect would be a distraction and a test score that underestimates her true ability. Over the long term, such experiences may become incorporated into one's self-concept, a process called *disidentification* (Steele, 1997). Disidentification can be seen in

Black students who, early in school, have similar test scores to White students, but over time become separated from their White counterparts by an achievement gap. For many Black students, lower scores and grades have resulted from stereotype threat and other social influences rather than reflecting an innate lack of skill. Psychologist and social cognition researcher Keith Maddox explains just how powerful stereotype threat can be in the following video, Intelligence Tests and Stereotypes.

Watch INTELLIGENCE TESTS AND STEREOTYPES

Keith Maddox
Tufts University

Psychologists have also strengthened the evidence base for stereotype threat by showing how stereotypes take their toll. Dozens of studies have identified at least three influences, many of which create large effects (Nguyen & Ryan, 2008; Schmader et al., 2008). First, stereotype threat leads to physiological anxiety, resulting in more than just physical discomfort during tests. In brain imaging experiments, women who experienced stereotype cues before solving math problems showed less activity in the frontal lobes than members of a control group, and more activity in emotional circuitry. As predicted, these women also solved fewer problems (Krendl et al., 2008). Second, stereotype threat causes individuals to focus more on how they are performing than on the test itself. Third, individuals also try to ignore negative thoughts about their performance. Both of these activities place a high demand on working memory, leaving fewer cognitive resources available to solve the problems (Beilock et al., 2007; Rydell et al., 2009).

Table 9.4 Evaluating Your Beliefs About Intelligence

One way to assess your own beliefs is to complete the incremental and entity theories of intelligence measure developed by Carol Dweck and her colleagues (Dweck et al., 1995). Rate the following five statements on a scale from 1 (strongly agree) to 6 (strongly disagree). Although the items may sound repetitive, please consider each one carefully before responding to it.

1. I have a certain amount of intelligence and I really can't do much to change it.

2. There are not enough intelligent people in the world.

3. My intelligence is something about me that I can't change very much.

4. I believe I am an intelligent person.

5. I can learn new things but I can't really change my basic intelligence.

Now, add up your responses to statements 1, 3, and 5. If you scored 9 or less, you tend to endorse the *entity theory* approach to intelligence; if you scored 12 or more, you tend to endorse the *incremental* approach. In Dweck's research, approximately 15% of respondents fell in between the two camps, so if you scored between 9 and 12, you endorse some aspects of each type of theory.

Module **9.3** Summary

9.3a Know . . . the key terminology related to heredity, environment, and intelligence:

entity theory
gene knockout (KO) studies
incremental theory
stereotype threat

9.3b Understand . . . different approaches to studying the genetic basis of intelligence.

Behavioral genetics typically involves conducting twin or adoption studies. Behavioral genomics involves looking at gene–behavior relationships at the molecular level. This approach often involves using animal models, including knockout and transgenic models.

9.3c Apply . . . your knowledge of entity and incremental theories to understand your own beliefs about intelligence.

Do you believe that intelligence is fixed or is it something you can improve with time and effort? Researchers show that these beliefs—known as entity and incremental theories, respectively—are good predictors of behavior. Because they are more likely to endorse the belief that intelligence is fixed, entity theorists may give up more readily when

challenged with a cognitive task. Incremental theorists are more likely to persevere and overcome obstacles, which would seem to be a positive trait. Table 9.4 gave you an opportunity to explore your own beliefs about intelligence.

9.3d Analyze . . . claims that infant intelligence is increased by viewing educational television programming.

As you read in the Myths in Mind feature, television viewing appears to have no benefits for cognitive development, and in some cases, inhibits it. This relationship is especially strong in children younger than 3 years old.

9.3e Analyze . . . the meaning of group-level differences in intelligence scores.

In some cases, average intelligence scores differ between groups, such as between males and females. It is possible that this variation is the result of genetic or brain-based differences. However, there are abundant, plausible explanations based on situational and experiential factors. In the case of male and female comparisons, perhaps there are more males at both ends of the spectrum (with very low and very high IQs), which may account for why a higher proportion of males are represented in fields that rely on mathematical and engineering skill.

Module **9.3** Quiz

Know . . .

1. When scientists insert genetic material into an animal's genome, the result is called a _____.
   - **A.** genomic animal
   - **B.** transgenic animal
   - **C.** chromosomal transplant
   - **D.** fraternal twin

Understand . . .

2. How do gene knockout studies help to identify the contribution of specific genes to intelligence?
   - **A.** After removing or suppressing a portion of genetic material, scientists can look for changes in intelligence.
   - **B.** After inserting genetic material, scientists can see how intelligence has changed.
   - **C.** Scientists can rank animals in terms of intelligence, and then see how the most intelligent animals differ genetically from the least intelligent.
   - **D.** They allow scientists to compare identical and fraternal twins.

Apply . . .

3. If you believe that intelligence is relatively fixed, then you advocate a(n) _____ theory of intelligence.
   - **A.** incremental
   - **B.** entity
   - **C.** sexist
   - **D.** hereditary

Analyze . . .

4. Research on television viewing by children under the age of 2 shows that:
   - **A.** TV is especially detrimental to children aged 3 years or older.
   - **B.** there is never any benefit from television, not even from educational programs.
   - **C.** infants who watch educational shows are, on average, better learners when they reach school age.
   - **D.** even educational programming shows little to no benefit.

5. Which of the following is the most accurate summary of the research on gender and intelligence?
   - **A.** On average, males and females score about the same on tests of general intelligence.
   - **B.** There are more women in the top 1% of all test takers, whereas the lowest 1% includes more men.
   - **C.** Boys are more successful on tests of spatial reasoning as early as 1 week of age.
   - **D.** Researchers have not been able to identify any differences in test scores between males and females.

Module 9.4 Scientific Literacy Challenge: Admissions Tests

We assume that like most college students, you have taken standardized tests — probably some tests in school and, quite likely, a test for college admission. Think back to those tests and your reactions to the scores you earned. Do you believe standardized tests have accurately assessed your achievement or aptitude levels? Before you read on, write about your thoughts on those experiences.

JOURNAL PROMPT

What do you think influenced your past standardized test scores more: your ability, your educational experiences, or perhaps the way you studied and prepared for the test? Do you believe those scores have been reasonably good predictors of your performance in college? Why or why not?

What do we know about college admissions tests?

Read the following article written by a higher education newspaper columnist and see what you can gather from his views on college admissions tests. Although you are probably familiar with standardized testing, remember to pay attention to the boldfaced key terms and concepts from Chapter 9.

Time to Rethink College Admissions Tests

By Rajneesh Shekhar

For decades, college-bound high school students have faced the dreaded rites of passage known as the SAT and ACT. Recently, however, colleges have begun to consider personality tests as a supplement to—sometimes even a replacement for—traditional **aptitude tests**. After all, a conscientious student who takes his work seriously should be able to perform quite well. However, to understand this move, it is important to understand why **standardized tests** ever became so widely used in the first place.

Tests like the ACT and SAT are **normed**, meaning admissions officers can compare an individual's scores to all other test-takers in terms of **percentile ranks**. This is important because other criteria, such as high school GPA, reflect all sorts of uncontrolled variables. It is often impossible to tell from a transcript whether a student's school had a typical curriculum or was rather unconventional, or whether grading standards were really tough or relaxed. Standardized tests allow admissions board members to make direct comparisons among students, independent of any influence uncontrolled variables may have.

The problem with trying to level the playing field this way, however, is that colleges *want* people from diverse backgrounds which, if you think about it, is exactly what standardized tests were designed to ignore. To complicate matters, college aptitude tests vary a great deal among different social groups: In the United States, White and Asian students perform better, on average, than Black and Latino students on the SAT and ACT. Students from higher income families with better-educated parents also do better on standardized tests. Is that really helping colleges build the student body they aspire to?

This is where personality tests may show their value. They offer the benefits of standardization—they can be measured and evaluated quickly, and the resulting scores compared across a large number of students. And, unlike aptitude tests, they do not present some of the barriers to success experienced by members of different demographic groups. The one question that remains is, how *well* does personality predict academic performance?

Shekhar's article suggests that personality measures could replace aptitude tests for college admissions decisions. Before we accept or reject the idea, we should question why one would prefer measures of personality to predict what is essentially "college aptitude" when there are already tests that claim to measure it. Is there evidence supporting personality tests as a viable alternative to current standards?

How do scientists study college admissions tests?

Here, Shekhar presents evidence from a peer-reviewed article that supports his view. Pay close attention to the type of design, the variables, and other important elements of the research.

College deans are not interested in just any old personality trait—they are not looking for talkative students, students who are thrill-seekers, or students who tend to get along with everyone just to have fun people around. Instead, they have in mind a number of traits that are connected to academic performance. One such trait is self-discipline—the ability to focus on a task, resist distractions, and maintain a level of motivation that allows for success.

Angela Duckworth and Martin Seligman of the University of Pennsylvania actually tested whether self-discipline predicts academic success among middle school students. In a 2005 paper published in *Psychological Science*, they reported a study in which more than 100 eighth graders completed a short self-report measure called the Brief Self-Control Scale. In case students were more interested in appearing smart than being accurate, Duckworth and Seligman also had students rated by parents and teachers. The psychologists also collected achievement test and IQ scores along with grades and other measures of academic success. The results are impressive: The self-discipline scores were much better predictors of academic success than either IQ or achievement tests. To build confidence in their results, Duckworth and Seligman replicated the study with another group of middle school students and found similar results. Their interpretation is simple and clear: A student's self-discipline is a better predictor of academic success.

Let's see how well you can identify scientific concepts embedded in Shekhar's article excerpt with this brief quiz.

1. The writer addressed the study's operational definitions when he…
   a. summarized the results of both studies with "self-discipline matters more than IQ."
   b. explains that the study focused on academic success at school rather than how well the parents believed the students were doing.
   c. tells us that some students are thrill-seekers.
   d. explains that the specific personality trait studied in this research was self-discipline, and that it was measured with a specific self-report measure.

2. The researchers knew that participants might exaggerate or overstate their positive personality traits to seem like better students. Therefore, the researchers also collected parents' personality ratings for each student. This is meant to address
   a. social desirability.   c. sampling.
   b. replication.   d. ecological validity.
3. The fact that researchers used the actual academic data from real students at a real school during a regular academic year suggests that the predictions have
   a. replicability.   c. generalizability.
   b. ecological validity.   d. anecdotal evidence.

The study was definitely thought-provoking, so let's move on to think critically about the results and whether they support the claim that personality tests should supplement or replace standardized scholastic tests.

How do we think critically about college admissions tests?

Remember that critical thinking involves curiosity and reasonable levels of skepticism. Critical thinkers continue to ask questions while evaluating the quality of the answers they find. As you read the next paragraph of the article, actively search for specific statements relevant to critical thinking.

> I found the study of self-discipline in 8th graders interesting, so I contacted a testing company executive (who asked to remain nameless) to seek his opinion. He was unimpressed, and pointed out that it is a lot easier to fake a certain personality trait than intelligence or knowledge. Although he obviously has a stake in maintaining the status quo—his job depends on it—that is a point worth considering. Perhaps the better, more intelligent students catch on to the fact that self-discipline is a desirable trait and therefore try to make themselves seem as disciplined as possible. Of course, the researchers considered that as well, and that is why they also used self-discipline scores from teachers and parents.
>
> My own question is whether this study would turn out the same if conducted with college students. There are significant personal changes in the traditional five-year span between 8th grade and college, even more so for students who return to higher education later in life. Imagine heading back to college for a nursing degree after a 10-year hiatus. You could be one of the most self-disciplined people on earth, but you forget a lot in 10 years. The individual would likely rank among the top applicants in measures of personality strength and character, but relatively low on a standardized test. It will be very important for colleges and universities to study whether self-discipline is as important (or perhaps more important) in college students.

Is the author applying critical thinking? Decide if the following statements are true or false and select which color sentence supports your decision. Note that not all of these items are included in the article.

1. The author demonstrated skepticism and curiosity by raising questions.
2. The writer identified potential sources of bias.
3. There is information to support the credibility of all the sources.
4. He considered the generalizability of the study.

Now that we have considered the evidence, let's think about how this information is relevant.

How is this research on college admissions tests relevant?

Gaining acceptance to a chosen college is an important step toward career and lifetime success. Thus, decisions about admissions testing are important.

Read about some of the pros and cons of putting these ideas into practice and then share any newly formed thoughts you may have about admissions tests in the writing activity that follows.

Some colleges and universities are looking into creative alternatives to standardized tests. For example, some have already gone "test-optional," meaning that they will accept something beyond the normal application in place of standardized test scores. This may be a series of essays that describe how a student has handled adversity and persevered through difficult situations. Although some people fear that this will lead to underprepared students at their schools, a recent study of over 30 test-optional institutions showed that there is no meaningful difference in the achievement levels of those who took standardized tests versus those admitted via alternative measures of aptitude.

SHARED WRITING

Do you agree that colleges should consider alternatives to standardized testing for admissions criteria? If colleges rely on personality rather than aptitude tests, is there any reason to believe the quality of students will change?

Chapter 9 Quiz

1. Which of the following is the best psychological definition of intelligence?
   A. How much a person knows
   B. The ability to think, understand, reason, and cognitively adapt to and overcome obstacles
   C. The score on an intelligence test
   D. The ability to quickly learn new material

2. Jonah receives the results of his intelligence test, which describes his score as having a percentile rank of 0.70 (or 70%). What does this information indicate about Jonah's intelligence score?
   A. He has an IQ of 70.
   B. He has an IQ of 30.
   C. His score is greater than the score of 70% of the population.
   D. His score is less than the score of 70% of the population.

3. Using the original formula for the intelligence quotient, an 8-year-old child with a mental age of 10 would have an IQ that:
   A. is exactly 100.
   B. is greater than 100.
   C. is less than 100.
   D. could be greater or less than 100, depending on which specific intelligence test was administered.

4. Which of the following statements is true about the relationship between brain size and some aspects of intelligence?
   A. Brain size is moderately related to intelligence.
   B. There is no relationship between brain size and intelligence.
   C. Brain size is an almost perfect predictor of intelligence.
   D. The number and size of cerebral gyri, but not overall brain size, are related to intelligence.

5. Identical twins reared together and apart tend to score similarly on standardized measures of intelligence. Which of the following statements does this finding support?
   A. Intelligence levels are based on environmental factors for both twins reared together and twins reared apart.
   B. Environmental factors are stronger influences on twins raised together compared to twins reared apart.
   C. The "intelligence gene" is identical in both twins reared together and reared apart.
   D. Genes are an important source of individual variations in intelligence test scores.

6. What does the Flynn effect refer to?
   A. The increase in average IQ test scores over decades
   B. The decrease in average IQ test scores over decades
   C. The higher IQ test average scores for Asian Americans compared to European Americans
   D. The lower IQ test average scores for African Americans compared to European Americans

7. Which of the following statements supports the theory that intelligence is determined in part by genes?
   A. The correlation between IQ scores is stronger for fraternal twins than it is for identical twins.
   B. Diet and lifestyle factors influence intelligence.
   C. Offspring are more similar to their parents when they grow up with them as opposed to when children are raised apart from their parents.
   D. Identical twins separated by adoption still have highly correlated IQ scores.

8. What do scientists know about gender differences on tests of visual-spatial abilities?
   A. There are none.
   B. Boys generally start out with an advantage but girls are the same by middle school.
   C. Boys and girls are born with roughly equal abilities.
   D. Girls start out with an advantage but by adolescence, boys tend to score better.

9. Carlos, who is Hispanic, is asked to take an IQ test by a job placement company. As he sits down to take the test, Carlos begins to think about how minorities in the United States, including Hispanics, are often viewed as less intelligent than others. These thoughts cause Carlos to experience discomfort and anxiety during the test, which then have a negative impact on his test result. Carlos's dilemma is an example of what psychologists call _____:
   A. the Flynn effect
   B. covert discrimination
   C. stereotype threat
   D. confirmation bias

10. Raven's Matrices were developed to improve on which issue with intelligence tests?
   A. Cross-cultural barriers
   B. Inconsistency of scores with retesting
   C. The time needed to complete a test
   D. Comparisons of old versus young people

11. A psychologist wishes to use achievement test scores to identify students for a gifted and talented program. Which percentile rank would be the most useful to her?
   A. 10th and above
   B. 20th and below
   C. 90th and above
   D. 80th and below

12. Which of the following statements is an argument for multiple intelligences?
   A. Statistical analyses show that all varieties of intelligence tests are highly correlated with one another.
   B. Most individuals who score high on verbal tests also score high on quantitative and performance tests.
   C. Some individuals score high on verbal tests but very low on quantitative tests, and vice versa.
   D. Some people would rather listen to a lecture than view a film because they are "auditory" learners.

13. _____ refers to the steady population level increases in intelligence test scores over time.
   A. Fluid intelligence
   B. The Flynn effect
   C. Predictive validity
   D. The reliability effect

14. Which of the following is not part of the theory of successful intelligence?
   A. Practical
   B. Analytical
   C. Kinesthetic
   D. Creative

15. As a major exam approaches, a teacher who is hoping to reduce stereotype threat and promote an incremental theory of intelligence would most likely:
   A. remind test takers that males tend to do poorly on the problems.
   B. remind students that they inherited their IQ from their parents.
   C. cite research of a recent study showing that a particular gene is linked to IQ.
   D. let students know that hard work is the best way to prepare for the exam.

Chapter 10
Life Span Development

Module 10.1 Methods, Concepts, and Prenatal Development

Learning Objectives

10.1a Know . . . the key terminology relating to concepts in developmental psychology and prenatal development.

10.1b Understand . . . how development proceeds in both stage-like and continuous fashion over the life span.

10.1c Apply . . . your understanding to identify research designs.

10.1d Analyze . . . the effects of preterm birth.

10.1e Analyze . . . the pros and cons of cross-sectional and longitudinal designs.

If you listen long enough, you can probably discriminate spoken French from German, even if you do not know either language. But what about crying? Psychologists have discovered that babies actually cry with an accent. Researchers analyzed the crying of 60 babies born to either French or German parents and discovered that their sounds had characteristics of their native tongue. French babies cry with a rising melody contour, meaning that they gradually rise toward a peak of intensity at the end of their cries. In contrast, German babies cry with a falling contour, meaning that they start at high intensity and then trail off. This difference is apparent at only a few days of age and reflects the same sound patterns characteristic of their respective languages (Mampe et al., 2009). Apparently, language development is well under way before birth, and infants are preparing to interact with their worlds before they fully enter them. Since psychological development is happening before people are even born, how developed is the brain before birth, and what kinds of experiences can newborns have? Developmental psychology focuses on these and many other questions related to how we grow and adapt to the world.

Developmental psychology *is the study of change and stability of human physical, cognitive, social, and behavioral characteristics across the life span.* Take just about anything you have encountered so far in this book, and you will probably find psychologists approaching it from a developmental perspective. Neuroscientists examine changes in the nervous system that occur even before birth, and track them all the way through old age. Psychologists study how social behavior originates in the context of parent–offspring bonds and flourishes and expands to include extended family, close friends, enemies, romantic relationships, and broader social and cultural groups. This subfield of psychology is absolutely essential because much of what occurs through early development influences behavior throughout the life span.

In this module, we begin by reviewing the methods for studying development and then explore the beginnings of life, starting with prenatal development.

Measuring Developmental Trends: Methods and Patterns

Studying development requires some special methods for tracking and measuring change. Also, modeling how development occurs involves some key terms and concepts that we explore in this section.

METHODS OF MEASURING DEVELOPMENT Developmental psychologists generally rely on a few different designs for measuring how psychological traits and abilities change over time. One approach, called a **cross-sectional design**, *is used to measure and compare samples of people at different ages at a given point in time.* Imagine you are designing a study examining the effects of premature birth on learning and thinking abilities from infancy through adulthood. How would you recruit volunteers? One way would be to compare people of different age groups—say, groups of 1-, 5-, 10-, and 20-year-olds who were born prematurely. In contrast, a **longitudinal design** *follows the development of the same set of individuals through time.* With this type of study, you might identify a set of 50 infants and measure their cognitive development annually over the course of 20 years (see Figure 10.1).

A longitudinal study of one group can be costly and time consuming. This research design is also hampered by the issue of *attrition*, which occurs when participants drop out, become ineligible, pass away, or can no longer participate in a study for other reasons. Even so, some of the longest-duration studies of this nature have lasted for decades and have been passed from one generation of researchers to the next as the original psychologists retire and new scientists take over. In contrast, the cross-sectional design has the advantage of convenience—it is

Figure 10.1 Cross-Sectional and Longitudinal Methods

In cross-sectional studies different groups of people—typically of different ages—are compared at a single point in time. In longitudinal studies, the same group of subjects is tracked over multiple points in time.

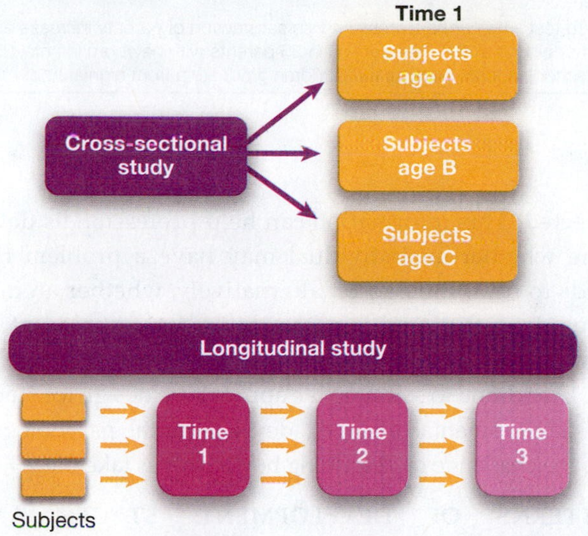

more time- and cost-efficient to compare people of different ages at once, rather than to follow the same individual for, say, 20 years.

One major issue to consider in cross-sectional designs is the potential for **cohort effects**, *which are consequences of being born in a particular year or narrow range of years.* ("Cohort" and "generation" refer to similar things in this context.) Differences across age cohorts can be due to numerous factors, including societal, nutritional, medical, and many other influences on physical and behavioral development. If you studied the effects of premature birth on cognitive development using a cross-sectional design, for example, you would likely note cohort effects. Some possible effects might include differences in medical care for infants who are born prematurely—infants generally get better care now than their counterparts did 20 years ago, and this improvement is reflected in much higher survival rates (Saigal & Doyle, 2008). It is possible that the 1-year-old cohort might develop differently than the 20-year-old cohort because of differences in infant health care. Longitudinal designs, unlike cross-sectional studies, avoid problems associated with cohort effects (see Table 10.1 to practice applying research design terminology).

Developmental studies yield important data. Information about developmental trends can help researchers and clinicians identify what is "normal" for a given age, such as the normal age range for the onset of language or the typical age at which memory decline might be

Table 10.1 Applying Developmental Research Designs

Read the following scenarios and decide whether the research design was cross-sectional or longitudinal.

1. Forty infants were selected at birth to participate in a study focusing on the development of facial expressions. Researchers used a standard set of stimuli for eliciting smiling and frowning to test each infant's response at 1 week, 1 month, 6 months, and 12 months of age. They compared how the expressions occurred for each infant at each point in time.

2. To test whether happiness and life satisfaction of parents increase as their children grow older, researchers recruited 100 volunteers. They compared happiness and life satisfaction in 25 parents with newborn infants, 25 parents with children starting kindergarten, 25 parents with children in grade school, and 25 parents with children graduating from high school.

Answers: 1. longitudinal, 2. cross sectional

expected. This information can help professionals determine whether an individual may have a problem that needs to be addressed or, alternatively, whether an individual is exceptional in some ability for a person of his or her age.

In addition to selecting the appropriate design for studying developmental changes, developmental psychologists face the challenge of describing how changes take place.

PATTERNS OF DEVELOPMENT: STAGES AND CONTINUITY Parents are all too aware of how fast their children seem to grow up; if they blink, they may miss something important in their child's development. A parent away on a business trip might miss her child's first steps or words. A child away at summer camp might return home after undergoing a remarkable growth spurt. These rapid changes model development as a progression of abrupt transitions in physical or mental skills, followed by slower, more gradual change. Psychologists describe this pattern of change as a series of *stages*. The transition from stage to stage is very much like a growth spurt, except marked by rapid shifts in thinking and behaving rather than size. In addition, stages are more than increases in size, speed, or amount; they also represent a fundamental shift in the *type* of abilities. This understanding can be seen in developmental milestones of motor development (crawling, standing, and walking; see Module 10.2).

Of course, an adult returning from a business trip likely will not observe a similarly drastic change in the behavior of her spouse. Adults tend to change at a slower, steadier pace—what developmental psychologists would call continuous change. It is not unusual for adults to complain about putting on a few extra pounds or taking longer to recover from a workout. Cognitively, adults continue learning new words, facts, and skills, but these are gradual, continuous changes. Although distinct changes such as menopause occur during adulthood, generally speaking there are few fundamental changes that occur naturally and abruptly in normal adult development.

What accounts for the rapid physical and behavioral transitions that occur during early development? Complex interactions between genetics and the childrearing environment are constantly determining developmental processes. Also, for change to take place so rapidly during early development, it helps if the individual is particularly sensitive and attentive to the stimulation that facilitates behavioral and cognitive growth.

THE IMPORTANCE OF SENSITIVE PERIODS During infancy and childhood, exposure to specific types of environmental stimulation is critical to healthy development. For example, to become fluent in their native language, infants need to be exposed to speech during their first few years of life. As you have already read, infants even seem to pick up accents before they are born. A **sensitive period** is *a window of time during which exposure to a specific type of environmental stimulation is needed for normal development of a specific ability*. Long-term deficits can emerge if the needed stimulation, such as language input, is missing during a sensitive period.

Sensitive periods have been found in humans and other species for abilities such as depth perception, balance, and recognition of parents as well as future potential mates. A sensitive period for adopting and identifying with a culture may be uniquely human. Among immigrants of all ages, it is the younger individuals (0 to 20 years) who are quicker to identify more strongly with their new culture (Cheung et al., 2011). The phenomenon of sensitive periods reminds us that the environment and the developing brain are linked in complex and adaptive ways.

Brain and Early Behavior

We begin our exploration of developmental psychology from a very early point in time. As previously noted, we can start to explore psychological development before birth even happens. In this section we learn how the prenatal and early postnatal environment affects psychological development. Table 10.2 shows how genetics and environment begin to shape an individual throughout pregnancy, or what is called *gestation*.

Table 10.2 Phases of Prenatal Development

A summary of the stages of human prenatal development and some of the major events at each.

Germinal: 0 To 2 Weeks

Major Events

Migration of the blastocyst from the fallopian tubes and its implantation in the uterus. Cellular divisions take place that eventually lead to multiple organ, nervous system, and skin tissues.

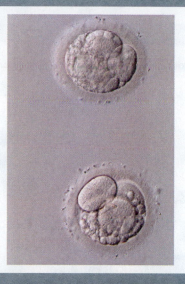

Embryonic: 2 To 8 Weeks

Major Events

Stage in which basic cell layers become differentiated. Major structures such as the head, heart, limbs, hands, and feet emerge. The embryo attaches to the placenta, the structure that allows for the exchange of oxygen and nutrients and the removal of wastes.

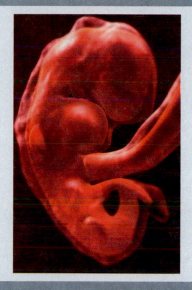

Fetal Stage: 8 Weeks To Birth

Major Events

Brain development progresses as distinct regions take form. The circulatory, respiratory, digestive, and other bodily systems develop. Sex organs appear at around the third month of gestation.

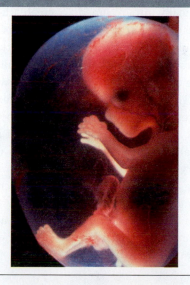

Figure 10.2 Prenatal Brain Development

The origins of the major regions of the brain are already detectable at four weeks' gestation. Their differentiation progresses rapidly, with the major forebrain, midbrain, and hindbrain regions becoming increasingly specialized.

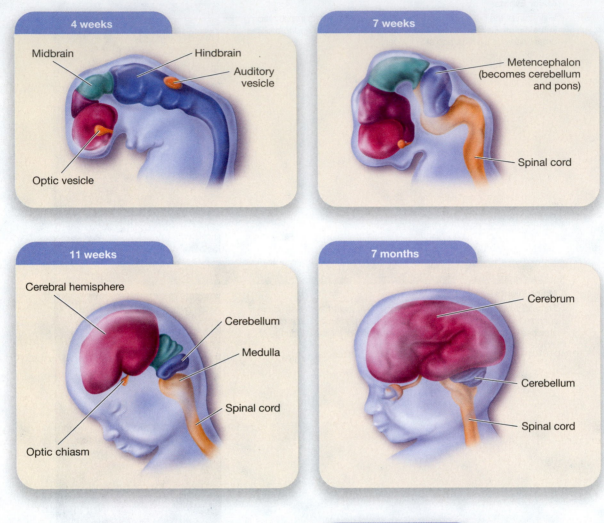

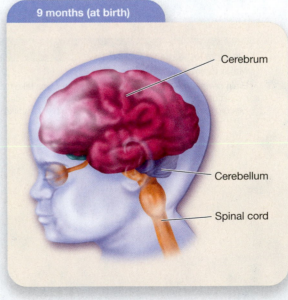

FETAL BRAIN DEVELOPMENT The beginnings of the human brain can be seen during the *embryonic stage*, between the second and third weeks of gestation. Cells that are genetically programmed to create the nervous system migrate to their appropriate sites and begin to differentiate into nerve cells. The first sign of the major divisions of the brain—the forebrain, the midbrain, and the hindbrain—are apparent beginning at only 4 weeks' gestation. By the 11th week of gestation, the differentiations between the cerebral hemispheres, the cerebellum, and the brain stem are apparent. During the final months of pregnancy, a fatty tissue called myelin builds up around developing nerve cells, a process called *myelination*. Myelin insulates nerve cells, enabling them to conduct messages more rapidly and efficiently (see Module 3.2). At birth, the newborn has an estimated 100 billion neurons and a brain that is approximately 25% the size and weight of an adult brain (see Figure 10.2).

The Long-Term Effects of Premature Birth

The prenatal environment is perfectly suited for the developing fetus. It provides ideal conditions for the delicate brain and body to prepare for life outside the womb. Therefore, premature birth can leave a newborn extremely vulnerable.

What do we know about premature birth?

Typically, humans are born at a gestational age of around 37 weeks (9 months). **Preterm infants** *are born at 36 weeks or earlier*. Depending on their gestational age, they can be extremely underweight compared to full-term infants, and vital regions of the brain and body may be underdeveloped. Even with modern medical care, a preterm infant born at around 25 weeks has only a 50% chance of surviving (Janjour, 2014). Fetal development happens very quickly, so survival rates reach 95% at around 30 weeks of gestation, which is still well short of full-term gestation (Jones et al., 2005).

Surviving preterm birth is only the first in a series of challenges faced by these vulnerable infants. An underdeveloped nervous system may have both short- and long-term negative effects on psychological and cognitive functioning. Thus a well-established procedure for nurturing preterm infants is needed.

How can science be used to help preterm infants?

The Newborn Individualized Developmental Care and Assessment Program (NIDCAP) is a behaviorally based intervention in which preterm infants are given intensive care during early development. One important component is keeping the brain healthy and protected against potentially harmful experiences (Als et al., 2012). Lights, stress, physical pain, and other factors can interfere by over-stimulating an underdeveloped brain. NIDCAP minimizes these to promote healthy brain development in preterm infants.

Controlled studies suggest that this program works. Researchers randomly assigned 117 infants born at gestational age 29 weeks or less to receive either NIDCAP or standard care in a prenatal intensive care unit. The infants were periodically tested for neurological and behavioral maturity. Within 9 months of birth, the infants who received NIDCAP showed significantly improved motor skills, attention, and other infant behavioral measures. In addition, compared with the preterm infants who had standard care, infants in the NIDCAP arm of the study showed improved brain development (including more advanced development of neural pathways between major brain regions; McAnulty et al., 2009).

These are promising results, but is this intervention beneficial over the long term? In follow-up studies, eight-year-olds who were born preterm and were given NIDCAP treatment scored higher on some (but not all) measures of thinking and problem solving, and also showed better frontal lobe functioning, compared to same-aged school children who were born preterm but did not have NIDCAP treatment (McAnulty et al., 2010; see also Ohlsson & Jacobs, 2013; Als, 2013).

Can we critically evaluate this research?

Premature birth in no way guarantees that an individual will experience developmental problems. People born preterm do experience slightly higher rates of cognitive impairment as teenagers, but more than half have no cognitive problems associated with premature birth at all (Gray et al., 2007). In fact, the majority of children who survive a preterm birth before 29 weeks' gestational age show typical sensory, emotional, and physical development in adolescence. The research on NIDCAP suggests that some effects may linger through age 8, especially if specialized treatment is not provided to the premature newborn. One important consideration is that the research we have discussed here involved infants and children who generally have reliable access to health care and a supportive environment.

Why is this relevant?

Across 184 nations, between 5 and 18% of babes are born prematurely (World Health Organization, 2014). For these children, medical advances have increased the likelihood of survival, and behaviorally based interventions, such as NIDCAP, can reduce the chances of long-term negative effects of preterm birth. One application of behaviorally based interventions concerns developing countries where health care services may be minimal, if they even exist. Researchers have found that the risks for physical and cognitive deficits in preterm infants can be reduced with some surprisingly simple interventions. For example, massaging preterm infants for 15 minutes per day can result in a 50% greater daily weight gain compared with preterm infants who are not massaged (Field et al, 2006). Massage therapy also reduces stress-related behavior and increases parasympathetic nervous system responses in preterm infants (Hernandez-Reif et al., 2007; Diego, Field, Hernandez-Reif, 2014). A method called *kangaroo care* focuses on constant, ongoing physical contact between infants and their mothers, as well as breastfeeding. Kangaroo care methods in developing countries, as well as in the United States, have also been shown to improve the physical and psychological health of preterm infants (Conde-Agudelo et al., 2011).

JOURNAL PROMPT

Preterm Births: Summarize what can be done to reduce health and cognitive risks associated with preterm birth.

NUTRITION, TERATOGENS, AND FETAL DEVELOPMENT Nutrition is critical for normal fetal development. Pregnant women typically require an almost 20% increase in energy intake during pregnancy, including foods high in protein and calcium. Malnutrition, illness, and some drugs can result in mild to very severe physical and psychological effects on the developing fetus. A **teratogen** *is a substance, such as a drug, that is capable of producing physical defects.* These defects typically appear at birth or shortly after. Because of this risk, expectant mothers who take certain medications, such as those used to treat epilepsy, are typically advised to stop taking the medication at some point during pregnancy. Discontinuing a medication, of course, has to be balanced with the need to ensure that the expectant mother is in good health.

Alcohol and tobacco can be teratogens if they are consumed at the wrong times and in large amounts during pregnancy. Drinking too much alcohol can cause **fetal alcohol syndrome**, *a condition that involves abnormalities in mental functioning, growth, and facial development in the offspring of women who use alcohol during pregnancy* (Jones & Smith, 1973; O'Leary, 2010). Smoking during pregnancy increases the likelihood of low birth weight; additionally, mothers who smoke have a 30% chance of premature birth. Both drinking and smoking increase the newborn's risk of illness or death (Centers for Disease Control and Prevention [CDC], 2009; Rogers, 2009). Children born to mothers who smoked during pregnancy are also at greater risk for having problems with some aspects of emotional development and impulse control (Brion et al., 2010; see Figure 10.3).

Figure 10.3 Teratogens and Prenatal Development

Numerous substances, including drugs and alcohol, can interfere with normal prenatal development.

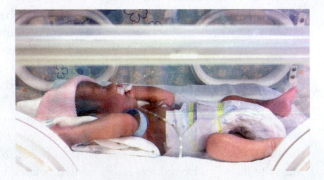

Smoking decreases blood oxygen and raises uterine concentrations of poisonous nicotine and carbon monoxide, increasing the risk of miscarriage, premature birth, or death during infancy. Babies exposed to smoke are also as much as three times more likely to die from the mysterious and tragic phenomenon of sudden infant death syndrome—an unexpected and not directly explainable death of a child younger than age one.

Alcohol, like many other substances, readily passes through the placental membranes, leaving the developing fetus vulnerable to its effects. This individual has fetal alcohol syndrome.

Myths in Mind

Vaccinations and Autism

In the late 1990s, a team of researchers claimed that the combined vaccination for measles, mumps, and rubella (MMR) was linked to the development of autism (Wakefield et al., 1998). The MMR vaccination is given to millions of children around their first birthday; a second dose is administered at approximately the time they start school. Of course, scientific evidence that such a widespread treatment could lead directly to autism alarmed many parents, many of whom refused to have the vaccine given to their young children.

The hypothesis that the MMR vaccine causes autism unraveled when other groups of scientists could not replicate the original findings. The knockout blow to the MMR–autism hypothesis came when it was discovered that Andrew Wakefield, the doctor who published the original study in 1998, was found to have financial interests in linking the disease with the vaccine. His research was funded by lawyers who sued makers of vaccines for damages. In 2010, the original 1998 paper was retracted by *The Lancet,* the medical journal that published it. Also, a thorough investigation revealed numerous counts of misconduct by Wakefield, and the UK revoked his medical license.

Fortunately, such cases of fraud are rare in science. There is no scientific evidence that the MMR vaccine causes autism. Unfortunately, this instance of scientific fraud has had far-reaching effects—leading to a general distrust of vaccines among a large segment of the population. The consequences of the anti-vaccination movement is apparent in recent disease outbreaks, including one in which dozens of children were infected with measles while visiting Disneyland in 2015.

Drugs, alcohol, and other prenatal teratogens are of major concern to parents and doctors alike. The health of newborn infants can also be compromised by exposure to other harmful pathogens such as bacteria and viruses. Within their first year after birth, infants are given vaccinations to protect them against conditions such as measles, mumps, and rubella (MMR). A small but vocal group have claimed that the MMR vaccine causes autism, a psychological disorder characterized by impaired social functioning and, typically, mental disabilities; this supposition has been debunked in recent years, however.

SENSORY AND MOTOR ABILITIES OF NEWBORNS Anyone who interacts with infants is probably curious about what their world is like. What can they see, hear, or smell, and what may still be a work in progress? At the beginning of this module, we revealed that the tone of infants' crying has an accent resembling the signature melodies of their native language. Thus sensory experiences, and learning, occur before birth. By month four of prenatal development, the brain starts receiving signals from the eyes and ears. Psychologists have determined that infants can see objects up to only 12 to 15 inches away at birth (approximately the same distance between the mother's face and a breastfeeding infant) and that they reach the normal 20/20 visual capacity between 6 and 12 months of age. Color vision also appears to take some time to develop, but by at least 2 months infants begin discriminating different colors. By 8 months, infants can usually perceive basic shapes and objects as well as adults do (Csibra et al., 2000; Fantz, 1961).

Generally speaking, newborns prefer sweet and savory flavors, and tend to avoid bitter and sour. However, even in utero experiences with different flavors impact infant food preferences. The flavors of foods that mothers consume are detectable in amniotic fluid and in breast milk, which in turn are preferred shortly after birth and at weaning (Beauchamp & Mennella, 2011). In the last months of gestation and the first months of life, the muscles and nervous system become developed enough to demonstrate basic **reflexes**—*involuntary muscular reactions to specific types of stimulation* (Table 10.3). These reflexes provide newborns and infants with a basic set of responses for feeding and interacting with their caregivers. Just a few days after birth, newborns show complex responses to social cues—such as imitating facial expressions of their caregivers (Meltzoff & Moore, 1977).

Table 10.3 Infant Reflexes

The Rooting Reflex	
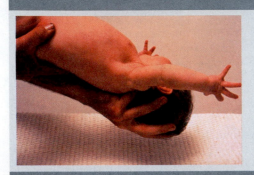	The *rooting reflex* is elicited by stimulation to the corners of the mouth, which causes infants to orient themselves toward the stimulation and make sucking motions. The rooting reflex helps the infant begin feeding immediately after birth.
The Moro Reflex	
	The *Moro reflex*, also known as the "startle" reflex, occurs when infants lose support of their head. Infants grimace and reach their arms outward and then inward in a hugging motion. This may be a protective reflex that allows the infant to hold on to the mother when support is suddenly lost.
The Grasping Reflex	
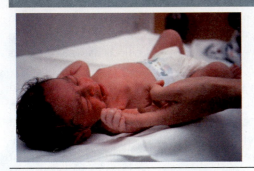	The *grasping reflex* is elicited by stimulating the infant's palm. The infant's grasp is remarkably strong and facilitates safely holding on to one's caregiver.

Module **10.1** Summary

10.1a Know . . . the key terminology relating to concepts in developmental psychology and prenatal development:

cohort effect
cross-sectional design
developmental psychology
fetal alcohol syndrome
longitudinal design
preterm infant
reflexes
sensitive period
teratogen

10.1b Understand . . . how development proceeds in both stage-like and continuous fashion over the life span.

Physical and behavioral development in the early years tends to fit a stage model of development. Change can also be gradual and continuous. Adulthood typically does not involve changes as drastic as those observed during infancy and childhood, although adults must still face major challenges and life phases.

10.1c Apply ... your understanding to identify research designs.

Studying development can be very challenging because researchers aim to describe how behavior changes over time. The two general methods used are longitudinal and cohort designs—each of which has advantages over the other. Critically evaluating a developmental study requires understanding which method was used in conducting it. If you have not already, practice by completing the activity Applying Developmental Research Designs in Table 10.1.

10.1d Analyze ... the effects of preterm birth.

Health risks increase considerably with premature births (e.g., especially those occurring at just 25 weeks' gestation rather than the normal 37 weeks). Use of proper caregiving procedures, especially personalized care that emphasizes parent infant contact, breastfeeding, and minimal sensory stimulation for the underdeveloped brain, increases the chances that preterm infants will remain healthy. Long-term studies indicate that with proper care children who were born preterm will not be disadvantaged relative to peers born at normal term.

10.1e Analyze ... the pros and cons of cross-sectional and longitudinal designs.

Cross-sectional data can be gathered at a single point in time, making a study adhering to this design less time consuming to complete than a study with a longitudinal design. Cross-sectional designs are also less likely to be affected by attrition (subjects dropping out). However, cross-sectional designs are vulnerable to cohort effects—that is, age differences may be due to historical factors rather than developmental differences. Longitudinal designs are less significantly affected by cohort effects because the same individuals are followed through the duration of the study.

Module 10.1 Quiz

Know ...

1. Which of the following would not qualify as a teratogen?
   A. Cigarette smoke
   B. Alcohol
   C. Prescription drug
   D. All of the above are possible teratogens.

Understand ...

2. A developmental psychologist's research suggests that coordination improves gradually over time rather than in short bursts of rapid change. These results reflect a _____ view of developmental change.
   A. stage
   B. psychosocial
   C. continuous
   D. cohort

Apply ...

3. A researcher has only one year to complete a study on a topic that spans the entire range of childhood. To complete the study she should use a _____ design.
   A. cohort
   B. longitudinal
   C. correlational
   D. cross-sectional

Analyze ...

4. Which of the following statements best summarizes the effects of preterm birth?
   A. Preterm births are typically fatal.
   B. The worrisome effects of preterm birth are exaggerated. There is little to worry about.
   C. Some physical and cognitive problems may be present during early development, but eventually are reduced or eliminated with proper care and treatment.
   D. Cohort effects make it impossible to answer this question.

5. _____ effects are a potential confounding variable in cross-sectional developmental studies, though an advantage is that they _____.
   A. preterm; take less time to conduct than longitudinal studies
   B. cohort; take less time to conduct than longitudinal studies
   C. cohort; take more time to conduct than longitudinal studies
   D. prenatal; do not require control groups

Module **10.2** Infancy and Childhood

 ## Learning Objectives

10.2a Know . . . the terminology associated with infancy and childhood.

10.2b Understand . . . the cognitive changes that occur during infancy and childhood and the ways in which sociocultural influences can shape development.

10.2c Understand . . . the concept of attachment and the different styles of attachment.

10.2d Apply . . . the stages of cognitive development to examples.

10.2e Analyze . . . evidence that some cognitive abilities are present at birth.

Infants, toddlers, and young children, cute as they may be, are often regarded as "egocentric" (or, less charitably, "selfish"). These are terms that could be used to describe all people who insist on getting their own way and fail to consider how their actions affect others—yet, we expect children to act this way (to a point). Both parents and psychologists agree that socializing children to behave in an "appropriate" way is important. However, a number of psychologists have noted that some toddlers between 15 and 24 months of age have already demonstrated an ability to share, show empathy, and display a sense of fairness toward others. To test this observation, researchers staged a situation in which an adult divided milk and crackers between two other adults while the toddlers watched. In some cases the snack was evenly divided, and in others it was unequally divided. The observant toddlers stared longer at the adults facing off with an unequally sized snack than when the milk and crackers were equally divided (Schmidt & Sommerville, 2011). It was as though the violation of fairness drew their attention—perhaps to see what might ensue as a result. Relatedly, by the time they have the motor skills to do so, infants without any prompting, will help others who have dropped something and will share their toys—even their favorite ones (Dunfield & Kuhlmeier, 2010). These are by no means examples of egocentric or selfish behavior. Although parents have their work cut out for them in terms of social-izing their children, the cognitive machinery required for suc-cessful socialization comes partially assembled. In this module we explore these and other cognitive abilities that unfold dur-ing infancy and childhood.

Although human infants are relatively helpless for an extended period of time, the complexity of the human brain and behavior begins to unfold immediately after birth. The physical, cognitive, and social transitions that occur between infancy and childhood are remarkably ordered, yet are also influenced by individual genetic and sociocultural factors. In this module, we integrate some important stage perspectives to explain psychologi-cal development through childhood.

Physical Changes in Infancy and Childhood

Infant motor development proceeds in stages—from crawling, to standing, to walking—over the course of the first 12 to 18 months of life (Figure 10.4).

The major structures of the brain are all present at birth, but their development is ongoing through early adulthood. During childhood, the cerebral cortex thickens, first in the sensory and motor areas, and then in regions involved in perception and eventually higher-order think-ing and planning (Gogtay et al., 2004; Marsh et al., 2009). These changes in brain development directly correspond with the development of cognitive abilities through late childhood.

Changes at the level of individual cells include myelination, which begins prenatally (see Module 10.1), accelerates through infancy and childhood, and then con-tinues gradually for several decades. In addition, two events are occurring at the level of synapses—that is, in the junctions between connecting nerve cells (Module 3.2). The formation of billions of new synapses, a process called *synaptogenesis*, occurs at blinding speed through infancy and childhood, and continues through the life span. Along with synaptogenesis, the process of **synaptic pruning**, *the loss of weak nerve cell connections, accelerates during brain development through infancy and childhood* (Figure 10.5). Both synaptogenesis and synaptic pruning serve to increase brain functionality by strengthening needed connections between nerve cells and weeding out unnecessary ones.

Figure 10.4 Motor Skills Develop in Stages

This series shows infants in different stages of development: (a) raising the head, (b) rolling over, (c) propping up, (d) sitting up, (e) crawling, and (f) walking.

(a)   (b)

(c)   (d)   (e)   (f)

Figure 10.5 The Processes of Synaptic Pruning

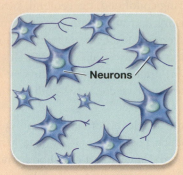

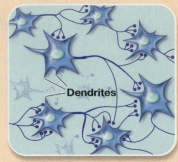

1. At birth, the infant's brain has a complete set of neurons but far fewer synaptic connections than an adult's brain.

2. During the first year, the axons grow longer, the dendrites increase in number, and a surplus of new connections is formed.

3. Over the next few years, active connections are strengthened, while unused connections disintegrate.

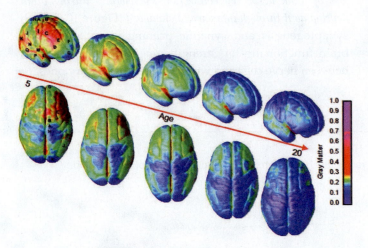

Brain development through early adulthood. Gray matter of the cerebral cortex continues to thicken from childhood all the way through young adulthood (Gogtay et al., 2004).

Cognitive Changes: Piaget's Cognitive Development Theory

Jean Piaget (1896–1980) is often credited with initiating the modern science of **cognitive development**—*the study of changes in memory, thought, and reasoning processes that occur throughout the life span*. In his own work, Piaget focused on cognitive development spanning infancy through early adolescence. Here we review his theory and offer insight into modern work that builds upon it.

Piaget was interested in explaining how different ways of thinking and reasoning develop. According to Piaget, knowledge accumulates and is modified by two processes—assimilation and accommodation. In the case of *assimilation*, children add new information, but interpret it based on what they already know. A young child who is familiar with only the family's pet Chihuahua might develop a concept that all dogs are furry creatures that stand less than a foot tall. Because this is not true, her concept of dogs will eventually be modified through a different process. *Accommodation* occurs when children modify their belief structures based on experience. When the child encounters a Great Dane, she might first refer to it as horse, but will eventually correctly accommodate the Great Dane into her concept of what a dog is. The processes of assimilation and accommodation continue throughout the progressive steps of cognitive development.

Piaget's observations led him to theorize that cognition develops in four distinct stages from birth through early adolescence: the sensorimotor stage, the preoperational stage, the concrete operational stage, and the formal operational stage. *Developmental milestones* are an important feature of Piaget's theory. As infants and children progress from one stage to the next, they obtain mastery of some important concept or skill (see Table 10.4).

THE SENSORIMOTOR STAGE: OBJECTS AND THE PHYSICAL WORLD Adults are capable of abstract thinking; they can imagine the continued existence of their cars, homes, and loved ones, even if those things are not physically present. Four-month-old infants, however, seem incapable of such abstract thinking or imagination, which is a type of abstraction—what exists in the mind is a representation of the objects and people in the physical environment. Unlike adults, infants' thinking and exploration of the world are based on immediate *sensory* (e.g., seeing, touching) and *motor* (e.g., grasping, mouthing) experiences. Piaget identified these experiences as part of the earliest period of cognitive development, which he named the **sensorimotor stage**. *Spanning birth to two years, this stage*

Table 10.4 Piaget's Stages of Cognitive Development

Stage	Description
Sensorimotor (0–2 years)	Cognitive experience is based on direct, sensory experience with the world as well as motor movements that allow infants to interact with it. Object permanence is the significant developmental milestone of this stage.
Preoperational (2–7 years)	Thinking moves beyond the immediate appearance of objects. Child understands physical conservation and that symbols, language, and drawings can be used to represent ideas.
Concrete operational (7–11 years)	The ability to perform mental transformations for objects that are physically present emerges. Thinking becomes logical and organized.
Formal operational (11 years–adulthood)	The capacity for abstract and hypothetical thinking develops. Scientific reasoning and thinking becomes possible.

refers to the period in which infants' thinking and understanding about the world is based on sensory experiences and physical actions they perform on objects.

If Piaget is right and infants think in terms of sensorimotor experience, then what happens when an object is out of sight and out of reach? Very young infants may not understand that the object continues to exist. Notice that this is not a problem for a two-year-old child. He can be very aware that his favorite dinosaur toy awaits him in another room while he has to sit at the dinner table; in fact, he might not be able to get the toy out of his mind. **Object permanence** *is the ability to understand that objects exist even when they cannot be seen or touched,* and Piaget proposed that it is a major milestone of cognitive development.

THE PREOPERATIONAL STAGE: QUANTITY AND NUMBERS According to Piaget, once children have mastered sensorimotor tasks, they have progressed to the next stage of development. The **preoperational stage**, *which spans ages two through seven years, is characterized by an understanding of symbols, pretend play, and mastery of the concept of conservation.* During this stage, children can look at and think about physical objects, although they

have not quite attained abstract thinking abilities. They may count objects and use numbers in their language, yet they remain limited in their use of mental operations (hence the name *pre*operational). One way to illustrate this quality is through the cognitive ability of **conservation**, *the knowledge that the quantity or amount of an object is not related to the physical arrangement and appearance of that object* (Figure 10.6).

Although abstract thinking abilities are a work in progress for young children, they do begin to understand some basic principles. The children in Figure 10.7 are committing *scale errors* in the sense that they appear to interact with a doll-sized slide and a toy car as if they were the real thing, rather than miniatures (DeLoache et al., 2004). By 2 to 2½ years, scale errors decline as children begin to understand properties of objects and how they are related. At around 3 years children begin to understand symbolic relationships. For example, 3-year-olds understand that a scale model of a room can symbolize an actual room (Figure 10.7). Children who view an experimenter placing a miniature toy within the scale model will quickly locate the actual toy when allowed to enter the room symbolized by the scale model (DeLoache, 1995). Abilities such as this are precursors to more advanced abilities of mental abstraction.

Object permanence is tested by examining reactions that infants have to objects when they cannot be seen. Children who have object permanence will attempt to reach around the barrier or will continue looking in the direction of the desired object.

Figure 10.6 Testing Conservation

A child views two equal amounts of fluid, one of which is then poured into a taller container. Children who do not yet understand conservation believe that there is more fluid in the tall, narrow container compared to the shorter one. A similar version of this task can be done using equal arrays of separate objects.

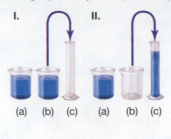

Row A
Row B

Which has more, row A or row B, or do they both have the same?

Row A
Row B

Now which has more, row A or row B, or do they both have the same?

THE CONCRETE OPERATIONAL STAGE: USING LOGICAL THOUGHT Conservation is one of the main skills marking the transition from the preoperational stage to what Piaget called the **concrete operational stage** *(roughly spanning ages 7 to 11 years), when children develop skills in using and manipulating numbers as well as logical thinking*. Children in the concrete operational stage are able to classify objects according to properties such as size, value, shape, or some other physical characteristic. Thinking becomes increasingly logical and organized. For example, a child in the concrete operational stage recognizes that if X is more than Y, and Y is more than Z, then X is more than Z (a property called transitivity). This ability to think logically about physical objects transitions into more abstract realms in Piaget's fourth and final stage of cognitive development.

THE FORMAL OPERATIONAL STAGE: ABSTRACT AND HYPOTHETICAL THOUGHT The **formal operational stage** *(spanning from approximately 11 years of age and into adulthood) involves the development of advanced cognitive processes such as abstract reasoning and hypothetical thinking*. Scientific thinking, such as gathering evidence and systematically testing possibilities, is characteristic of this stage. Thinking can exist entirely in hypothetical realms. Additional details on cognitive development at this age can be found in the next two modules where we will discuss adolescent and adult cognitive abilities. Practice applying Piaget's stages of cognitive development in Table 10.5.

Figure 10.7 Scale Errors and Testing for Scale Model Comprehension

The children in photos (a) and (b) are making scale errors. One child is attempting to slide down a toy slide and another is attempting to enter a toy car. Three-year-olds understand that a scale model represents an actual room (c). The adult pictured is using a scale model to indicate the location of a hidden object in an actual room of this type. At around 3-years, children understand that the scale model symbolizes an actual room and will go directly to the hidden object after viewing the scale model.

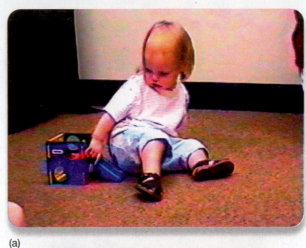

(a)

(b)

(c)

Table 10.5 Applying Piaget's Theory

Each of the following scenarios describes behavior and thinking of different children. Read these cases and identify where each child is in terms of cognitive development.

1. Bridgette's understanding of her world is largely based on her direct interactions with objects, which includes mouthing, grasping, and handling them. Which stage of Piaget's cognitive development is she most likely in? What is a major cognitive milestone that occurs during this stage?

2. Jared is able to add and subtract as long as he is able to use actual objects in computing the problems. According to Piaget, Jared is probably in which stage of cognitive development?

3. Ranjit and his brother receive $1 for allowance. One week, his father mysteriously gave 100 pennies to his brother, but "only" 10 dimes to Ranjit. Ranjit's frustration with this situation is likely due to his being in which stage of cognitive development? (Hint: Ranjit knows that money has value, but lacks the ability to understand conservation.)

4. A teacher wants to ask her students to describe what the United States would be like if the country were still run by England. According to Piaget, which stage of cognitive development would the students need to have reached to offer thoughtful answers to this scenario?

Answers: 1. Sensorimotor; object permanence. 2. Concrete Operational. 3. Preoperational. 4. Formal Operational

---

Evaluating Piaget

Piaget was immensely successful at opening our eyes to the cognitive development of infants and children. Nevertheless, new methods for testing cognitive development suggest that he may have underestimated some aspects of infant cognitive abilities. For example, infants appear to understand some basic principles of the physical and social worlds very shortly after birth.

What do we know about cognitive abilities in infants?

The **core knowledge hypothesis** *is a view on development proposing that infants have inborn abilities for understanding some key aspects of their environment* (Spelke & Kinzler, 2007). It is a bold claim to say that babies know something about the world before they have even experienced it, so we should closely examine the evidence for this hypothesis.

First, how can we know what infants know or what they perceive? One frequently used method for answering this question relies on the habituation–dishabituation response. **Habituation** *refers to a decrease in responding with repeated exposure to an event*, something infants are well known for doing. For example, if an infant views the same stimulus over and over, she will stop looking at it. Conversely, infants are quite responsive to novelty or changes in their environment. Thus, if the stimulus suddenly changes, the infant will display **dishabituation**, *an increase in responsiveness with the presentation of a new stimulus. In other words, the infant will return her gaze to the location that was once boring.*

How can science help explain infant cognitive abilities?

Habituation and dishabituation have been used to measure whether infants understand many different concepts, including abstract numbers—an ability that most people imagine appears much later in development. Elizabeth Spelke and colleagues have conducted numerous experiments on this topic. In one study, 16 infants just two days of age were shown arrays on a video screen of either 4 or 12 identical small shapes (e.g., yellow triangles, purple circles). The researchers also sounded a tone 4 or 12 times (tu-tu-tu-tu or ra-ra-ra-ra-ra-ra-ra-ra-ra-ra-ra-ra) at the same time they showed the shapes (see Figure 10.8). Sometimes the number of shapes the infants saw matched the number of tones they heard (4 yellow triangles and 4 ra-ra-ra-ra tones); at other times the number of shapes and tones were mismatched (12 ra's and 4 purple circles). Whether

A popular method for testing infant cognitive abilities is to measure the amount of time infants look at events. Researchers measure habituation and dishabituation to infer what infants understand.

Figure 10.8 Testing Infant's Understanding of Quantity

In this study, infants listened to tones that were repeated either 4 or 12 times while they looked at objects that had either 4 or 12 components. Infants spend more time looking at visual arrays when the number of items they see matches the number of tones they hear.

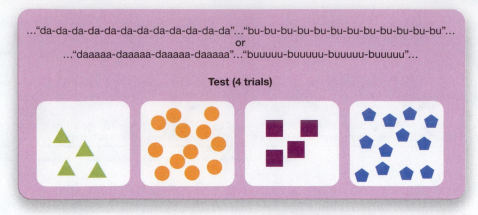

the stimuli were circles or triangles and the tones were "ra" or "tu" did not matter: The infants were attentive when what they saw and heard matched. In other words, they looked longer at the shapes when the tone that accompanied them matched in number, compared to when they did not match. The researchers believe that this and similar findings provide evidence that even very young infants have a rudimentary appreciation for abstract numbers (Hevia et al., 2014; Izard et al., 2009). By using the habituation and dishabituation responses, researchers are seeking to better understand infant cognitive abilities. Watch the following video, Habituation, to see an example.

Watch HABITUATION

Can we critically evaluate alternative explanations?

Many of the studies of early cognitive development discussed in this module used the "looking time" procedure,

although not all psychologists agree that it is an ideal way of determining what infants understand or perceive (Aslin, 2007; Rivera et al., 1999). We cannot know exactly what infants are thinking, and perhaps they look longer at events and stimuli simply because these are more interesting, rather than because they understand anything in particular about them. Also, just like with studies of adults, we cannot necessarily generalize findings from infants, even though they have accumulated only a mere 48 hours of knowledge. In the study of abstract numbers (shapes and tones) just described, only 16 infants managed to complete the study. Forty-five others were too fussy or sleepy to successfully finish the task.

Why is this relevant?

Until relatively recently both professionals and parents believed that infants had very limited cognitive activity and were only motivated for physical contact, warmth, and nutrition. Research showing that infants perceive the world in such a rich way suggests otherwise. Granted, meeting infants' primary needs should be a focal point of parenting, but an appreciation for the subtle but complex world of the infant is important as well. Understanding the cognitive capacities of young people of any age is an important part of childrearing and teaching.

COMPLEMENTARY APPROACHES TO PIAGET Piaget's theories have had a lasting impact on modern developmental psychology. Even so, some details of his theories have generated controversy in the decades since they were proposed. In particular, Piaget generally underestimated the abilities of infants and their rates of development, and his emphasis on cognitive tasks overlooked sociocultural and biological elements of cognitive growth.

The dynamics that occur between children and their parents, teachers, and peers form the sociocultural context in which cognitive development occurs. Children who try to master a skill alone may find themselves up against obstacles that are difficult to overcome, whereas children who are not allowed to work through problems lack opportunities to exercise and improve their abilities. Therefore, it seems that optimal development may occur somewhere in between these two scenarios, an area that psychologist Lev Vygotsky (1978) named the **zone of proximal development**—*development is ideal when a child attempts skills and activities that are just beyond what he or she can do alone, but the child has guidance from adults who are attentive to his or her progress* (Singer & Goldin-Meadow, 2005). This interactive approach to teaching and learning is an important facilitator of cognitive development in children. **Scaffolding** *is the approach to teaching in which the teacher matches guidance to the learner or student's needs,* and can thus be seen as a strategy for promoting development within the zone of proximal development. Toddlers, for example, naturally begin using language in fairly simple ways. For example, while reading a book with a parent, a toddler may point to and name objects on the pages. This is to be expected, and in the early phases of language development scaffolding can be extensive with parents repeating the same words back several times. As language progresses, lessening the amount of scaffolding and asking toddlers to elaborate on what they see and think while reading (rather than telling them or "controlling" the conversation) is associated with increased vocabulary development (Murase, 2014). Scaffolding is an approach that can be applied to cognitive abilities and motor skills and requires close engagement with the child, controlling any frustration that arises, and being mindful of when he is ready to take the next step.

JOURNAL PROMPT

Scaffolding: How are Piaget's theory and the concepts of scaffolding and the zone of proximal development relevant to primary school education?

Social Development: Forming Attachments and Understanding Others

We know that humans are social creatures; teens and adults are keenly aware of their social status and need for companionship, and they work to form and maintain relationships. But what about newborns—what are their social needs and interests?

TYPES OF ATTACHMENT An **attachment** *is an enduring emotional bond formed between individuals.* More than that, attachment is a motivation to seek others for close physical and emotional comfort, especially during stressful situations. In evolutionary terms, safety and survival underlie the motivation to form attachments (Bowlby, 1951). Isolation from others—namely, those who play nurturing and caring roles—can be as disastrous as nutritional starvation.

In the 1950s, psychologist Harry Harlow began conducting experiments to determine just how strong the need for attachment was in monkeys in comparison to other motivators such as food. He showed that monkeys deprived of maternal care would cling compulsively to

Caregivers who are attentive to the learning and abilities of a developing child provide scaffolding for cognitive development.

An infant rhesus monkey clings to a "surrogate" mother that is covered with a cloth, rather than to an object that provides food.

a piece of terrycloth wrapped around a cylinder of wire mesh that loosely resembled the body shape of an adult monkey. Infant monkeys spent less time with an identical wire object that lacked the terrycloth, even though the infant's food was attached to it.

Further research suggested that infant bonds shaped social interactions later in life. Primates denied social contact during infancy displayed abnormal social and sexual behaviors in adulthood as well (Harlow et al., 1965). However, these behavioral problems are not necessarily permanent. Given regular social contact, their behavior returned to relatively normal levels (Suomi & Harlow, 1972).

Harlow's work on attachment may appear to be inhumane. However, his conclusions contrasted with a predominant view held by Behaviorists at the time emphasizing the drive to eat as the primary motivating factor binding child to mother (Harlow, 1958). Harlow's work implied otherwise, showing that the social bond was just as critical, if not more so, for attachment. His experiments might make us feel uneasy, but in a historical context his work can also be interpreted as a positive change for how psychologists viewed parent–child bonding.

For ethical reasons, Harlow's studies with monkeys cannot be replicated with human infants. Instead, psychologists have developed methods of studying attachment that are only mildly stressful and mimic natural situations, such as the stranger anxiety that typically develops around 8 months of age. Some laboratory experiments have used the *strange situation* protocol in which the primary caregiver brings an infant into a room that has some toys on the floor and a stranger nearby (Figure 10.9; Ainsworth, 1978). The mother leaves the room for a few moments and returns; meanwhile, the experimenter monitors the infant.

Attachment styles are categorized by the reactions the infants exhibit when the mother leaves and returns. Using this procedure, researchers have identified two general categories of attachment: secure and insecure (Ainsworth, 1978).

1. *Secure attachment.* The caregiver is a base that the child uses as he or she explores. In the strange situation, the child plays comfortably while the mother is in the room. The child may or may not cry when the mother leaves, and seeks contact with her upon returning.

2. *Insecure attachment* (which has three subtypes):

   - Disorganized. The child does not have a consistent pattern of behavior either when the mother leaves or when she returns. The child might freeze for a moment, seemingly unsure of what to do next.
   - Resistant. The child is upset when the mother leaves, but is angry when she returns.
   - Avoidant. The child is not upset when the mother leaves, and does not seek contact when she returns.

Figure 10.9 Measuring Attachment Styles: The Strange Situation Experiment

Studies of attachment by Mary Ainsworth involved a mother leaving her infant with a stranger. Ainsworth believed that the infant's attachment styles could be categorized according to his or her behavioral and emotional responses to the mother leaving and returning.

Mother   Stranger

After identifying the main attachment styles, psychologists began to ask how infants develop the styles that are characteristic to them. Certainly the social environment that parents create plays a role. When emotional and communicative responses between parent and infant are closely coordinated, secure attachment styles form (Hane et al., 2003). By comparison, if parents respond inconsistently and slowly to their infants, then insecure attachments are more likely.

While the environment that parents provide influences an infant's course of attachment development, an infant's predisposition toward a particular style of attachment also has an impact. For example, infants differ in **temperament**, or *general emotional reactivity—the root from which several aspects of adult personality grow.* Two types of temperament are high-reactive and low-reactive. *High-reactive* infants tend to respond with vigorous activity of their limbs; they arch their backs and cry when confronted with unfamiliar stimuli. *Low-reactive* infants show less motor activity and less distress when exposed to unfamiliar stimuli. As high-reactive infants mature, they become timid and react negatively to unfamiliar people, whereas low-reactive infants are more likely to show willingness to approach unfamiliar people and situations (Kagan et al., 1998). Thus, emotional reactivity to the strange situation, or any other situation that elicits emotions, also depends on inherited predispositions of infants.

The intense anxiety that infants and toddlers experience when their primary caregiver is absent, or whose absence is pending, reaches a peak between 10- and 18-months of age and then begins to decline. The first attachments form during infancy, but they remain essential to well-being throughout the life span and continue to form in a variety contexts, such as in romantic relationships. Interestingly, patterns of attachment in romantic relationships reflect back on styles of attachment formed during infancy (Hofer, 2006). A longitudinal study spanning more than 20 years showed that people who were securely attached as infants were better able to recover from interpersonal conflict with their romantic partners (Salvatore et al., 2011).

SOCIAL COGNITION   During infancy and into childhood, the basic need for contact comfort expands as developing children become more aware of the complexity of their social environment. At approximately 24 months of age, toddlers and young children show evidence of **self-awareness**, *the ability to recognize one's individuality*. The presence of self-awareness is typically tested by observing infants' reactions to their reflection in a mirror or on video (Bahrick & Watson, 1985; Bard et al., 2006). Self-awareness becomes increasingly sophisticated over the course of development, progressing from early recognition of oneself in a mirror or on video, to having the ability to reflect on one's own feelings, decisions, and appearance.

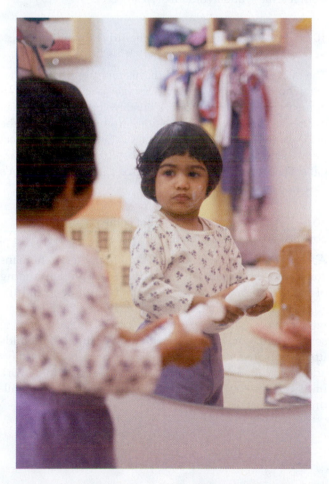

Between 18 and 24 months of age toddlers show that they can recognize themselves in a mirror.

Figure 10.10 Piaget's Test for Egocentric Perspectives on Children

Piaget used the three-mountain task to test whether children can take someone else's perspective. The child would view the object from one perspective while another person viewed it from a different point of view. According to Piaget, children are no longer exclusively egocentric if they understand that the other person sees the object differently.

By the time children reach their fifth birthday, they become self-reflective, show concern for others, and are intensely interested in the causes of other people's behavior.

What about awareness of others? Young children are sometimes described as **egocentric**, *meaning that they perceive and interpret the world in terms of the self* (Piaget & Inhelder, 1956). This does not imply that children are selfish or inconsiderate. For example, a two-year-old may attempt to hide by simply covering her own eyes. From her perspective, she is hidden. Piaget tested for egocentrism by sitting a child in front of an object, and then presenting pictures of that object from four angles. While sitting opposite the child, Piaget would ask her to identify which image represented the object from Piaget's perspective, but many children would select the image corresponding to their own perspective (Figure 10.10). Piaget concluded that children were egocentric through the preoperational phase (ending around age seven).

Modern research indicates that children take the perspective of others long before the preoperational phase is complete. Perspective taking in young children has been demonstrated in studies of **theory of mind**—*the ability to recognize the thoughts, beliefs, and expectations of others, and to understand that these can be different from one's own*. Adults may have difficulty putting themselves in another person's shoes from time to time, but young children may find it next to impossible. Consider the following scenario:

An experimenter offers three-year-old Andrea a box of chocolates. Upon opening the box, Andrea discovers not candy, but rather pencils. Joseph enters the room and she watches as Joseph is offered the same box. The researcher asks Andrea, "What does Joseph expect to find in the box?"

This is called the *false-belief task*. On the one hand, if Andrea answers "pencils," then she does not understand that Joseph is being misled; more importantly, she believes that Joseph knows the same thing she does. On the other hand, Andrea might tell the experimenter that Joseph expects to see chocolates. If so, she must understand that Joseph holds a false belief about the contents of the box and, therefore, Andrea is taking the mental perspective of another person. This task is commonly used to study the development of theory of mind (Lillard, 1998; Wimmer & Perner, 1983). Children typically pass this test at ages four to five years, although younger children may pass if they are told that Joseph is about to be tricked. The shift away from egocentric thought does not occur overnight. Older children may still have difficulty taking the perspective of others. The presence of theory of mind in young children suggests that they move away from egocentric thought at an earlier age than once believed, however.

Module 10.2 Summary

10.2a   Know . . . the key terminology associated with infancy and childhood:

attachment
cognitive development
concrete operational stage
conservation
core knowledge hypothesis
dishabituation
egocentric
formal operational stage
habituation
object permanence
preoperational stage
scaffolding
self-awareness
sensorimotor stage
synaptic pruning
temperament
theory of mind
zone of proximal development

10.2b   Understand . . . the cognitive changes that occur during infancy and childhood and the ways in which sociocultural influences can shape cognitive development.

According to Piaget's theory of cognitive development, infants mature through childhood via orderly transitions across the sensorimotor, preoperational, concrete operational, and formal operational stages. According to Vygotsky, cognitive development unfolds in a social context between caregivers/teachers and children. Specifically, children's skills are nurtured by adults who are sensitive to the cognitive capacities that individual children have attained.

10.2c   Understand . . . the concept of attachment and the different styles of attachment.

In developmental psychology, attachment refers to the enduring social bond between child and caregiver. Work on nonhuman primates by Harry Harlow demonstrated the strength of attachment motivation. Research involving the "strange situation" reveals the various styles of attachment that may form between children and their caregivers. Children are either securely or insecurely attached, and insecure attachments can be further divided into disorganized, resistant, and avoidant styles.

10.2d   Apply . . . the stages of cognitive development to examples.

The major theorist discussed in this module was Jean Piaget, who described four general stages of cognitive development. Each stage comprises the development of distinct cognitive abilities, and transitions from one stage to the next are marked by significant milestones such as object permanence and conservation. Table 10.5 "Applying Piaget's Theory" offered some practice at applying Piaget's four stages to examples.

10.2e   Analyze . . . evidence that some cognitive abilities are present at birth.

According to the core-knowledge hypothesis, humans come into the world with a rudimentary understanding of various cognitive domains, such as arithmetic and the ways in which physical objects are related. Experiments with newborns and very young infants suggest that, to some extent, our adult understanding of the world builds upon capacities that can be detected from our first days after birth. These studies suggest that Piaget's framework underestimates the cognitive abilities of infants and children at each stage of development.

Module 10.2 Quiz

Know . . .

1. Recognizing that the quantity of an object does not change despite changes in physical arrangement or appearance is referred to as: _____.

   A. object permanence
   B. scale comprehension
   C. conservation
   D. number sense

Understand . . .

2. The development of infant motor skills is best described as:

   A. a genetic process with no environmental influence.
   B. completely due to the effects of encouragement.
   C. a mixture of biological/physical maturation and learning.
   D. progressing in continuous, rather than stage, fashion.

3. Infants who are insecurely attached may do which of the following when a parent leaves and then returns during the strange situation procedure?

   A. Show anger when mom leaves, but happiness when she returns.
   B. Show anger when mom leaves, and is indifferent to her when she returns.
   C. Refuses to engage with the stranger in the room.
   D. Is happy when mom leaves and angry when she returns.

Apply . . .

4. A teacher plans to assign her students the task of imagining and describing what the world would be like if all water disappeared completely for 24 hours. Piaget would probably predict that only children in the _____ stage of development would be capable of even entertaining this scenario.

   A. formal operational
   B. preoperational
   C. sensorimotor
   D. concrete operational

Analyze . . .

5. Research on newborns indicates that they have a sense of number and quantity. What does this finding suggest about Piaget's theory of cognitive development?

   A. It confirms what Piaget claimed about infants in the sensorimotor phase.
   B. Some infants are born with superior intelligence.
   C. Culture determines what infants are capable of doing.
   D. Piaget may have underestimated some cognitive abilities of infants and children.

Module **10.3** Adolescence and Adulthood

Learning Objectives

10.3a Know . . . the key terminology concerning adolescence, adulthood, and aging.

10.3b Understand . . . the different ways in which identity and social status develop.

10.3c Apply . . . your understanding of the categories of moral development and identity statuses.

10.3d Analyze . . . the relationship between brain development and adolescent judgment and risk taking.

10.3e Analyze . . . the stereotype that middle and old age are associated with unhappiness.

Fifty years ago, CBS ran a major hit show called I Love Lucy, which starred Lucille Ball and Desi Arnaz. Before the show first premiered, the Philip Morris cigarette company, which sponsored the CBS network, rejected Arnaz's being on the show because they did not think his thick accent and Cuban heritage should be combined with Lucille Ball's American persona (despite the fact that they were married in real life). Ball insisted on casting Arnaz and the show, which was a huge hit, was ahead of its time in featuring an ethnically mixed couple. Today, portrayals of diverse family dynamics have become commonplace in entertainment. The show

Modern Family includes a gay couple and one of mixed ethnicity. Both the universal everydayness of marriage as well as the unique cultural challenges that interracial couples experience are featured. Parents and children of interracial families face unique challenges. A biracial couple may have a very different set of expectations and beliefs about parenting, for example. And children of interracial couples and adopted children living in interracial households can have diverse cultural and linguistic experiences. Television offers one perspective into this type of family environment. Psychologists have studied how a diverse upbringing affects both children and the challenges that parents face. In this module, we explore the unfolding cognitive and social worlds experienced by adolescents, and, conversely, parenting, marriage, and other aspects of adulthood.

Puberty *marks the biological transition into adolescence*, which begins at around 11 years of age for girls and 13 years for boys. It spans through young adulthood, but unlike with puberty, no unique biological event marks the transition into young adulthood—which, as we will see, is culturally determined. In Module 10.2 we discussed cognitive development during infancy and childhood. Here we continue with concerns unique to adolescence. Adolescents are an interesting group; they are cognitively and socially more sophisticated than children, yet they behave in sometimes very impulsive ways. Their behavior often goes to extremes in terms of energy, curiosity, imagination, and emotion. Individuals during this stage of development also demonstrate rapid and obvious changes in physical growth. In this section, we begin by exploring these physical changes and then move on to discuss the personal and social changes that adolescents face.

Cognitive Development: Thinking and Moral Reasoning in Adolescence

Between the onset of adolescence and young adulthood, some key cognitive abilities approach their peak. Beginning at approximately 12 years of age, adolescents show significant improvements in their abilities to use logic and reasoning (what Piaget referred to as *formal operational thinking*; see Module 10.2). Youths of this age begin thinking abstractly about things that are not present and about events or scenarios that are entirely impossible or hypothetical (Klaczynski, 1993). This ability is a major advance beyond the concrete thinking that characterizes late childhood. During this time, adolescents also develop the ability and capacity to think scientifically and view problems from multiple perspectives.

Working the Scientific Literacy Model

Adolescent Risk and Decision Making

Adolescents have the ability to think critically, but this does not mean that they always do. People of any age may take risks or make poor decisions, but adolescents are particularly prone to them, and adolescents' reasoning and decision making do not always lead to the best outcomes (Steinberg, 2007). Unplanned pregnancies, drug and alcohol abuse, vehicular accidents, and violence are more common during adolescence than during any other stage of life. Adolescents have greater difficulty inhibiting their

Figure 10.11 Extended Brain Development
The prefrontal cortex (darker section) continues to develop through adolescence and even into young adulthood.

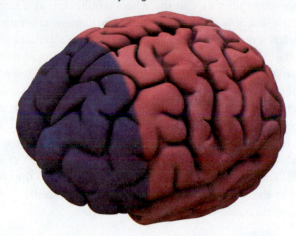

impulses than do adults, and they can also be less inclined to plan and envision future consequences of their behavior.

What do we know about adolescence and decision making?

Although adolescents begin to show the cognitive and social sophistication of adults, hormonal and neurological changes are still under way, which helps to explain some of the struggles that youth of this age experience. In recent years, psychologists and neuroscientists have implicated ongoing changes in the *prefrontal cortex* as the basis of some of the behavioral issues that are especially likely to occur during adolescence (Figure 10.11). The prefrontal cortex is involved in impulse control, regulates mood, and facilitates planning, organizing, and reasoning. To the naked eye, an adolescent brain looks like an adult brain. However, as discussed in Modules 10.1 and 10.2, the processes of myelination (growth of brain white matter) and synaptic pruning (loss of unused connections between brain cells) continue through adolescence (Giorgio et al., 2010). Thus, the adolescent brain is still developing in critical areas, particularly those involved in decision making and impulse control.

How can science explain brain development and decision making in adolescents?

In addition to looking at changes in brain anatomy over time, we should ask how actual brain activity is affected in adolescents who make risky decisions.

One study sought to address this issue by scanning the brains of adolescents while they played a *Wheel of Fortune* game. Named after the television game show, this task asked participants to view a screen that presented them with two choices. One option—the riskier choice—was to place a $6 bet that a spinning wheel would stop at a target that it had only a 25% chance of hitting. A less risky choice was to bet $1 that the wheel would stop at a target that it had a 50% chance of hitting. The game was set up to simulate a real-life decision between a high-risk choice that has the potential to bring a larger monetary reward and a low-risk choice that offers only a small reward. As the participants played the game, their brains were scanned using functional magnetic resonance imaging. The researchers discovered that adolescents who selected the riskier choice had less brain activity in their prefrontal cortex compared to adolescents who avoided the risky choice (Shad et al., 2011). This is just one of many studies pointing to the conclusion that risky decision making by adolescents has a basis in their still-developing frontal cortex.

Can we critically evaluate this research?

Brain research offers a plausible scientific explanation for why adolescents are prone to risk taking and poor decision making. However, a less than fully developed prefrontal cortex does not completely rob adolescents of the capacity for making good decisions and avoiding risk, nor does it relieve them of assuming responsibility for their actions. Adolescents can also be risk averse and make excellent, well-considered decisions, just as they can accept blame and take credit when due. In addition, risk taking and decision making are related to temperament and personality characteristics, which vary from one individual to the next, no matter what their age. The study using the *Wheel of Fortune* task showed that some of the adolescents who participated in the study—namely, those who showed higher activity in their prefrontal cortex—chose to avoid risky bets.

Situational factors also influence whether adolescents take risks. Psychologists have found that in some situations, adolescents are no more likely to engage in risky behavior than adults. When adolescents are with other adolescents, however, this propensity changes (see Figure 10.12). This finding and others like it indicate that strategies for reducing adolescent risk taking and impulsivity should appreciate the important role that situational and social factors play in adolescents' decision making.

It should be noted, too, that risk taking and impulsivity extend into early adulthood (e.g., among college students), and can certainly continue in other ways throughout adulthood (e.g., gambling, infidelity, etc.; Willoughby et al., 2013). These observations as well as the finding that adolescents differ greatly as individuals in terms of risky behavior suggest that the still-developing brain argument, while interesting and compelling, does not tell the whole story about adolescent behavior.

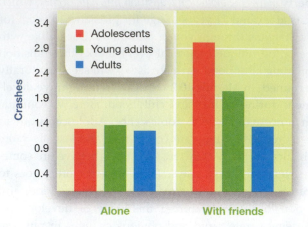

Figure 10.12 What Drives Teenagers to Take Risks? One key factor in risk taking is simply other teenagers. When teens play a driving video game with other teens, they crash more than when playing the same game when alone, and more than adults playing the game (from Steinberg, 2007).

Why is this relevant?

Scholars, parents, and insurance companies, to name a few concerned parties, regard adolescent risk-taking behavior to be a major public health problem (Steinberg, 2008). Risky behavior and poor decision making lead to both self- and other-inflicted harm and injury. Workers in mental and public health professions have spent countless hours and devoted vast expenditures of public funds to implementing programs—some successful, some not—that seek to steer adolescents toward making better decisions, such as avoiding unprotected sex, smoking, alcohol, and drug use (Reyna & Farley, 2006).

MORAL DEVELOPMENT: LEARNING RIGHT FROM WRONG Early beliefs about right and wrong form during childhood, particularly as very young children learn which behaviors are punished or rewarded. It is during adolescence that beliefs about right and wrong become increasingly complex and sophisticated. Right and wrong remain important endpoints, but adolescents come to understand that there can be a lot of space between these two alternatives. Psychologists are interested in how moral reasoning develops and how people apply moral beliefs to the various situations they encounter. Traditionally, studies of moral development pose dilemmas to people of different ages and examine the details of their responses. For example, imagine the following scenario, unlikely as it may be:

A trolley is hurtling down the tracks toward a group of five unsuspecting people. You are standing next to a lever that, if pulled, would direct the trolley onto another track, thereby saving the five individuals. However, on the second track stands a single, unsuspecting person, who would be struck by the diverted trolley.

Table 10.6 Kolberg's Stages of Moral Reasoning

Stage of Moral Development	Description	Application to Trolley Dilemma
Preconventional morality	*Characterized by self-interest in seeking reward or avoiding punishment.* Preconventional morality is considered a very basic and egocentric form of moral reasoning.	"I would not flip the trolley track switch because I would get in trouble."
Conventional morality	*Regards social conventions and rules as guides for appropriate moral behavior.* Directives from parents, teachers, and the law are used as guidelines for moral behavior.	"I would not flip the switch. It is illegal to kill, and if I willfully intervened, I would have probably violated the law."
Postconventional morality	*Considers rules and laws as relative.* Right and wrong are determined by more abstract principles of justice and rights.	"I would flip the switch. The value of five lives exceeds that of one, and saving them is for the greater good of society."

What would you choose to do? Would you pull the lever, allowing five to live but causing one to die? Would you do nothing? Moral dilemmas provide interesting tests of development because they place an individual's values in conflict with each other. Obviously, five lives are more than one—yet most of us recognize that it is not up to us to make such decisions. Unfortunately, this hypothetical dilemma does not include a bullhorn that you could use to warn the unsuspecting people. The only alternative is to pull the switch or do nothing. Saying you would or would not pull the lever is only the starting point to understanding your moral development. Two people could come up with the same answer for very different reasons. It is how and why you made your choice that is of greater interest to psychologists studying moral development. Based on work using similar hypothetical dilemmas, Lawrence Kohlberg (1984) described three stages of moral reasoning that he regarded as universal to all humans (see Table 10.6).

It must be noted that Kohlberg focused on how *males* reason about moral dilemmas. Clearly, a theory about human behavior cannot be universal if it is based on research involving members of only one gender. Based on later work done by other psychologists interested in moral reasoning, it appears that girls reason *differently* about moral dilemmas than boys (Gilligan, 1982). Females appear to base moral decisions more on caring relationships and less on justice and abstract principles that Kohlberg emphasized (Jaffee & Hyde, 2000). Also, *knowing* that something is right or wrong is very different from *feeling* that it is right or wrong. Early studies of moral development have been criticized because moral reasoning was viewed as a cognitive and problem-solving process. To some extent it is, but in our everyday lives our moral decisions are largely based on emotional reactions. According to the *social intuitionist model* of morality, our moral judgments are not guided solely by reason, but also by our emotional, intuitive reactions to a moral dilemma. For example, imagine the following scenario (adapted from Haidt, 2001).

Julie and Steven are brother and sister. They are traveling together in France on summer vacation from college. One night they are staying alone in a cabin near the beach. They decide that it would be interesting and fun if they shared a romantic kiss. At the very least it would be a new experience for each of them. They both enjoy the experience but they decide not to do it again. They keep that night as a special secret, which makes them feel even closer to each other.

How do you react to this scenario? Was what took place between the two siblings acceptable? In deciding on your answer, it is likely that you did not think through the pros and cons of the situation, weighing each carefully and questioning the reasoning behind your arguments, until you reached a decision. The first time people hear a scenario like this, their emotional intuition typically guides them to their initial decision as to whether the act was moral. What generally follows a snap decision (another way of saying "intuitive judgment") is thoughtful and reflective reasoning, which often amounts to an after-the-fact attempt to put into words how one feels about a sexual act between siblings. You might think, "I don't know—it just isn't right because they are brother and sister!" The intuitionist approach to moral decision making complements the more cognitive-based approach that emphasizes logic and reasoning. Moral thinking can be just as much an emotional process as it is a rational one.

Emotion is a major component of moral thinking and decision making.

Social Development: Identity and Relationships in Adolescence

Two major changes occur during adolescence: the recognition of what makes an individual unique and the formation of close social relationships that include romantic and sexual partners. Here we cover both of these critical experiences.

WHO AM I? IDENTITY FORMATION DURING ADOLESCENCE An important part of adolescence is the development of an **identity**, *a self-image and a perception of one's unique and individual characteristics*. This includes trying to figure out one's desired career, and religious and political orientations. As identity develops, adolescents tend to describe themselves in terms of personal qualities ("I am a good listener"), social qualities ("My family and I are Hindu"), and future goals ("I am going to be an artist") (Harter & Monsour, 1992). They engage in a greater variety of activities and become independent from their parents. The sense of self that develops can be such a conglomeration of many different ideas that perhaps we should replace the term "self" with "selves." Thus, before they reach young adulthood, adolescents may experience numerous identity crises. An *identity crisis* involves curiosity, questioning, and exploration of different selves. One month a teenage boy might be interested in playing varsity football and lifting weights, and the next month he might ponder abandoning sports to pursue music. All the while, he may be wondering where he would best fit in, be most successful, or make more friends.

Identity formation is also a time for deciding whether to make personal commitments to a set of values and goals. Although parents may influence these decisions, adolescents tend to strive for greater autonomy in this regard. A girl may decide she no longer wants to attend church with her parents; alternatively, she may embrace this practice and seek additional service opportunities. **Identity statuses** *are the processes and outcomes of identity development that include elements of both crisis and personal commitment.*

As an individual questions and tries out different identities and commitments, he or she might also experience any one of four possible identity statuses (Marcia, 1980):

- *Identity achievement*: Consideration of different identities, followed by commitment to a particular one.
- *Identity diffusion*: A reluctance or refusal to commit to an identity and respond to identity crises.
- *Identity foreclosure*: A situation in which adolescents do not experience identity crises and commit to the roles and values that are handed down by their parents.
- *Identity moratorium*: Prolonged experimentation with different identities. This can involve delaying commitment to a single identity and frequent identity crises.

To practice applying these statuses to examples, see Table 10.7.

Developmental psychologist James Marcia categorized these identity statuses in the 1980s. More recent studies have confirmed that these identity statuses remain relevant and applicable to adolescents today (Meeus, 2011). Do any of these identity statuses sound familiar to you? In studying them, you may have noticed that one particular status sums up your own experiences. Researchers have found that adolescents tend to be relatively consistent in the type of identity status they show throughout this period of their life (Meeus, et al., 2012). Ultimately, the search for identity, no matter how uncomfortable it might be, is a necessary task for adolescents.

Identity formation is also influenced by sociocultural factors such as gender and ethnicity. As introduced at the beginning of this module, growing up in a multiracial/multicultural household can pose unique challenges for children and adolescents. While such diversity can be rewarding and offer unique preparation for facing diversity-related challenges outside of the home, it can create confusion about identity development as well. Some scholars have suggested that mixed ethnic identification results in decreased self-esteem and strained peer relationships. However, such conclusions have only been drawn

Table 10.7 Applying Identity Statuses

Read the following scenarios and identify which identity status applies to each.

1. Gabrielle's family live in a rural region and subsist primarily from foods that they grow at home. She is home-schooled and spends most of her time with her parents and siblings. As she reached adulthood, Gabrielle remained at home and took over the task of overseeing the schooling and farm work done by younger members of the family.

2. Isaiah reached adulthood having joined many different social groups and dabbling in just about any activity he could. He experienced discomfort with this and envied people who were able to focus their interests, though he continued "shopping around" for a prolonged period of his life.

3. Julie avoids committing to choosing a major and finishing college, does not have a stable group of friends to whom she can relate, and avoids any kind of extracurricular pursuits. Which of Marcia's four identity statuses best applies to Julie?

4. Mateo moved among different social groups and explored different interests, played several sports in high school, and was involved in different academic activities. Toward the end of high school he committed to a group of students who shared common interests and pursued scholarships to enter a business school and play baseball.

Answers: 1. Identity Foreclosure, 2. Identity Moratorium, 3. Identity Diffusion, 4. Identity Achievement

from samples of people who have actively sought mental health services for problems associated with their family environment. Studies from the general population of people with multiracial backgrounds show that identity development is comparable to that of people with single race backgrounds (Shih & Sanchez, 2005).

PEER GROUPS AND STATUS As adolescents become more interested in social status and romantic relationships, their peer relationships become increasingly important and layered with different emotional experiences (Brown & Klute, 2006). Friendships, which are a priority, grow closer and involve mutual trust and intimacy; yet, they also have the potential for causing great pain and sadness. Friendships develop within a broader social context of small groups or *cliques*, and the membership and intensity of friendships within these cliques are constantly changing (Cairns & Cairns, 1994). Adolescent *crowds*—often referred to with labels such as "jocks," "bros," "Goths," "normals," "loners," and "stoners"—are larger than cliques and are characterized by common social and behavioral conventions.

As interest in social status grows, so does the importance of popularity. Popular individuals are those who have high social status within their group. Compared to the effects of low social status, the effects of popularity have been less studied. Psychologists who study popularity categorize individuals into two groups (Cillessen & Rose, 2005):

- *Sociometric popularity*: Individuals who are well known and respected, and who display low levels of aggression. These adolescents may participate in high-status activities such as athletics or cheerleading, but their participation does not translate into aggression or hostility toward lower-status individuals.

- *Perceived popularity*: Adolescents who are perceived as popular and may be more well known than sociometrically popular people, but are not necessarily well liked and are more prone to engage in verbally and physically aggressive ways.

The individuals falling into these categories use different methods of maintaining their high status. Adolescents who are sociometrically popular are more likely to engage in cooperative and prosocial behaviors to resolve conflict, whereas perceived popular individuals may default to aggression or coercion. During adolescence, aggression typically becomes less physical and more "relational"—meaning that hostility is expressed not through force, but rather through strategies such as exclusion or spreading rumors (Rose et al., 2004; Rose & Swenson, 2009).

Because social status becomes such a central issue for adolescents, the experience of peer rejection and of being of low social status becomes especially troubling. Both psychologists and the media have given low-status adolescents a great deal of attention because of the widespread belief that these individuals are at the highest risk for engaging in antisocial behaviors, particularly those of a violent nature. Incidents of violence, including school shootings, by adolescents who are low in social rank reinforce this ongoing concern. Homicide rates increase dramatically during adolescence and reach their peak by 24 years of age (CDC, 2010).

While some low-status adolescents opt to operate with relatively few social connections, others turn to virtual social networks for online friendships. In fact, the majority of adolescents in the United States spend many hours a day engaged in digital media—namely social media and other forms of online communication. Recent studies indicate that spending time online

For decades, television shows and movies have offered glimpses into life within adolescent cliques and crowds. The portrayals may be exaggerated, but they are often successful because viewers can closely identify with the characters' experiences.

actually makes adolescents feel more socially connected (Valkenburg & Peter, 2009)—this is contrary to earlier studies that suggested otherwise (Kraut et al., 1998). A probable reason for this shift is that a decade ago being online meant spending time in public chat rooms and playing multiuser games that mostly involved interacting with strangers. In contrast, adolescents today spend most of their online hours social networking and communicating with real friends (Valkenburg & Peter, 2009). Thus, their social connectedness may actually be increasing. Yet, the question as to whether the quality of online interactions is inferior to face-to-face interactions remains. Psychologists have found that communicating online promotes even greater self-disclosure, which in turn leads to improved quality of relationships and sense of well-being (Kraut et al., 2002; Valkenburg & Peter, 2009). Of course, increased self-disclosure can also be excessive and inappropriate, not to mention permanent in the online world, potentially leading to public embarrassment.

The issue of whether online interaction is detrimental to adolescent mental health is multifaceted. Certainly, there are some negative aspects, such as "cyberbullying" and other forms of abuse. Online bullying can be just as hostile and problematic as face-to-face encounters. And, because it can be done anonymously—with neither name nor face—the problem is growing. Cyberbullying can bring out aggression in people who might not otherwise behave in this fashion. Those who do engage in cyberbullying tend to have difficulties with emotions, attention, and other behavioral problems (Sourander et al., 2010).

Although problems associated with bullying, popularity, and status are common experiences for many adolescents, the development of peer relationships marks a

What happened to Amanda Todd epitomized the devastating effects of cyberbullying. She took her own life after experiencing months of sexual and emotional harrassment both online and in person.

significant change in their social development, as does the increase in sexual activity and the development of intimate partnerships.

JOURNAL PROMPT

Popularity: Do you think that the categories of sociometric and perceived popularity fit with your own experiences in high school? In other words, do you think people who were regarded as popular tended to fall into these two categories? Explain. Is there another category of popularity that you think is not accounted for by either of the two terms? If so, describe it.

ADOLESCENT SEXUALITY Seeking distance from parents in favor of peers and romantic partners is a defining motive of adolescence. However, our culture often goes to great lengths to curb sexual behavior among teenagers—they either promote abstinence-only programs or send the message that premarital sex is psychologically harmful and physically risky. While sex and reproduction are normal outcomes of adolescence from an evolutionary perspective, a predominant view in the United States is that adolescent sexual behavior is risky and deviant. But is there evidence to justify this view?

Let us first examine the notion that adolescent sexual behavior is deviant: An estimated 70% of people in the United States have had sexual intercourse by 19 years of age (Martinez, Copen, & Abma, 2011). This high percentage suggests that adolescent sexual behavior is actually normal, not deviant. Furthermore, adolescent sexual activity is not statistically related to deviant activities such as substance abuse or criminal convictions (Donahue et al., 2013).

Now let us analyze the claims that adolescent sexual behavior is risky and leads to negative consequences. As discussed earlier in this module, adolescence is a time during which young people tend toward poor decision making and may struggle with impulse control. In the case of sex, this might result in the contraction of a sexually transmitted infection (STI), an unwanted pregnancy, or a dangerous and harmful encounter. According to recent evidence, over 50% of reported STIs occurred among adolescents and young adults, 82% of teen pregnancies were unwanted, and around 10% of sexual encounters were described as "unwanted" by women who had sex prior to age 20 (Guttmacher Institute, 2013). These are alarming numbers that certainly require our attention and concern, but it is worth noting that contraceptive use among US adolescents is constantly trending upward—despite the problematic rates of STI incidence and unwanted pregnancies. In fact, adolescents actually use contraception more frequently than do unmarried, sexually active adults (Reece et al., 2010). This suggests that many adolescents are mindful of risks and take necessary precautions to avoid STIs and unwanted pregnancies.

In addition to the notion that adolescent sexual activity is risky and deviant, another widespread belief is that sexually active adolescents are prone to developing depression and other psychological problems. This claim oversimplifies how adolescents (or people of any age) engage in sex. Whether there are any negative outcomes of sexual activity depends on many things, including the context of the relationship. Sex without commitment ("hooking up") can increase the chances of a negative psychological reaction. Testing this hypothesis is challenging, however, because it requires that we disentangle whether risk for depression makes sex more likely, or, alternatively, whether sex at a young age leads to depression. Adolescent females in particular are more likely to report negative feelings about having sex outside of a dating relationship. One reason is that our culture, despite its enlightenment on many issues, tends to engage in "slut shaming"—imposing guilt and judgment upon (usually) females for engaging in sexual behavior that violates societal expectations (Vrangalova, Bukberg, & Rieger, 2014). In contrast to hooking up, sex in committed relationships is much less likely to be associated with negative psychological effects.

Rather than focus on negative consequences of sexual activity, it may be more beneficial for adolescents to focus on *sexual well-being*. This shift in approach would foster an individual's worth as a sexual being, promote comfort in asserting interests and preferences (including remaining abstinent), and entitle an individual to feelings of physical pleasure and satisfaction. This approach does not preclude taking precautions to avoid pregnancy and transmission of STIs (Harden, 2013). It is also important to note that the concept of sexual well-being is not intended to endorse or encourage sexual activity, but, rather, to promote healthy sexual behavior and decision making (including abstinence) and to reverse negative attitudes about sex in general. In a study of predominantly African American adolescents, it was found that both abstinent and sexually active females reported similarly high levels of sexual well-being (Hensel & Fortenberry, 2013).

Part of promoting sexual well-being is recognizing and accepting that not all sexual relationships are heterosexual. Sexual and emotional interest in members of the same sex generally appears during early adolescence, regardless of whether an individual identifies himself or herself as homosexual at adulthood (Savin-Williams & Cohen, 2004). Sexual orientation typically becomes fully recognized during high school or somewhat later (e.g., during college).

How homosexual adolescents navigate their developing sexual orientation depends on many factors, including how their family and peers perceive them, as well as how they perceive themselves. Adolescents who are homosexual or **gender nonconforming**, that is, *they engage in interests and mannerisms that are stereotypical of the opposite sex*, have the added challenge of coping with negative treatment from others. Research suggests that gay, lesbian, and bisexual people are at increased risk for mental disorders (e.g., depression), suicidal thoughts, and substance misuse (King et al., 2008). However, it is also possible that negative psychological well-being is not very strongly associated with sexual orientation per se, but rather gender nonconformity. Males and females who are homosexual but conform to expectations about their respective gender expectations do not experience the same degree of negative psychological well-being as do gender nonconforming people (Rieger & Savin-Williams, 2012). This is not to say homosexual males and females who are gender conforming do not experience unique and significant challenges to which heterosexual people are immune. Rather, they are relatively buffered from the negative treatment experienced by homosexual people who are also gender nonconforming.

Adulthood and Aging

Puberty signals the transition from childhood to adolescence. In contrast, there is no well-defined biological event that marks the transition from adolescence to adulthood. In the United States, turning 18 is a somewhat arbitrary threshold to adulthood, but most 18-year-olds in North America do not take on full adult responsibilities.

Not that long ago, when traditional college students moved to campus each year, parents would help them transport their belongings from the car to the dorm room, say goodbye, and go their separate ways. More recently, however, college staff members have noticed a big change—the parents cannot seem to leave, and their close ties with their children do not just end at the dormitory doorstep. One student's parents even attended the first day of class with their daughter, and then marched her up to the registrar's office to drop the class when they were not satisfied. Psychologist Jeffrey Arnett says this occurrence could be evidence of *emerging adulthood*, a new stage in social development. According to Arnett (2004, 2010), the process of forming an identity occurs during emerging adulthood and can span well into the 20s. Delaying career, family and other major endeavors (not to mention the increasingly common practice of moving back to live with one's parents) are characteristic of emerging adulthood.

To put it simply, adulthood is largely determined by sociocultural norms and expectations about establishing a long-term relationship, perhaps having children, buying a house, retiring, and so on. Because there is no true biological or psychological marker that signals adulthood, psychologists who study the entire life span divide adulthood based on age brackets: Young adulthood spans 18 to 40 years, middle adulthood from 40 to 65 years, and older adulthood from 65 years onward. However, as the phenomenon of emerging adulthood shows (as well as increases in longevity among many groups of people), these brackets do not capture the full complexity of post-childhood development.

In this chapter you have read about stage theories of development, particularly Piaget's theory of cognitive development. Of historical importance is Erik Erikson, who in contrast to Piaget and others focusing on a relatively short portion of the life span (e.g., infancy through childhood), described different challenges faced by people of all ages. For example, developing a basic sense of trust is central to infancy, and forming an identity is major part of adolescence. Erikson, in his extension beyond early development, considered the formation of lasting, committed adult relationships, finding a sense of purpose and making meaningful contributions to society, and having a sense of accomplishment in older age to be major stages that adults go through (Erikson, 1963). In this module we will consider some modern extensions of Erikson's work.

COGNITION AND THE BRAIN Some gradual changes in thinking, memory, and other cognitive skills are to be expected as people age. However, with healthy aging these changes have relatively little impact on daily life. While it may be easy for a person in their 50s to prematurely chalk up forgetting to the occasional "senior moment," it is also quite likely that lapses in memory can be ascribed to having a life full of major responsibilities. Physical changes do occur within the brain, such as a reduction in volume of the cerebral cortex and blood flow, which can coincide with some decreases in mental performance (Allen et al., 2005). As discussed in Chapter 9, intelligence comes in different forms, such as fluid and crystallized intelligence. While the speed and flexibility of fluid intelligence tends to decline in middle and old age, the wisdom and sophistication of crystallized intelligence remains steady for those who age well. Cognitive functioning, however, is multifaceted and includes far more than fluid and crystalized components. We can look even more specifically at whether and how abilities change across the life span (Hartshorne & Germine, 2015). On average, people reach peak levels of performance in vocabulary, factual knowledge, and understanding of common concepts (e.g., how home loans work) during their 50s. People in their teens and early 20s tend to be well behind older adults when it comes to these tasks,

but they enjoy their peak abilities for short-term memory (e.g., for words and stories) and reasoning tasks.

Adults who experience good physical health through older age can maintain remarkably solid cognitive abilities. However, there are some distinctly age-related problems that afflict elderly people.

With age comes increased risk for developing serious *neurodegenerative conditions* involving significant loss of nerve cells and nervous system functioning. These problems become increasingly common as people reach their late 60s. **Dementia** *refers to a set of symptoms including mild to severe disruption of mental functioning, memory loss, disorientation, poor judgment, and decision making.* Approximately 14% of people older than 71 years of age have dementia. Nearly 10% of these cases involved a type of dementia called **Alzheimer's disease**—a *degenerative and terminal condition resulting in severe damage of the entire brain* (see Figure 10.13). Alzheimer's disease rarely appears before age 60, and it usually lasts 7 to 10 years from onset to death (although some individuals may live for 20 years with it).

Early symptoms include forgetfulness for recent events, poor judgment, and some mood and personality changes. As the disease progresses, people struggle to recognize family members, have frequent memory loss, and experience confusion. In the most advanced stages of Alzheimer's disease, affected individuals may fail to recognize themselves and develop difficulty with basic bodily processes such as swallowing and bowel and bladder control.

What accounts for such extensive deterioration of cognitive abilities and memory? Alzheimer's disease is

Figure 10.13 Alzheimer's Disease Risk

The chances of developing Alzheimer's disease increase with age. Researchers are testing several genetic and physiological reasons why the disease is more prevalent in women.

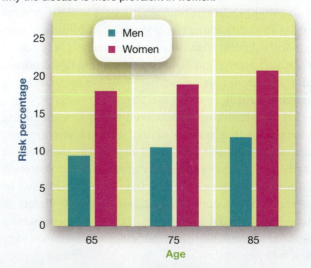

Figure 10.14 How Alzheimer's Affects the Brain

Advanced Alzheimer's disease is marked by significant loss of both gray and white matter throughout the brain. The brain of a person with Alzheimer's disease typically has a large buildup of plaques of a protein called amyloid beta, which kills nerve cells. Also, tau proteins maintain the structure of nerve cells in the normal brain; these proteins are often found to be defective in the Alzheimer's brain, resulting in neurofibrillary tangles.

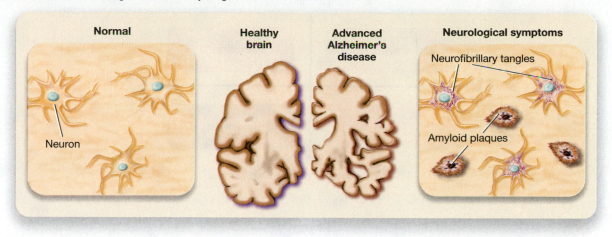

probably due to a buildup of proteins that clump together in the spaces between neurons, interrupting their normal activity. In addition, another type of protein builds up and forms tangles within nerve cells, which severely disrupts their structural integrity and functioning (Figure 10.14). Many different research groups are currently searching for specific genes that are associated with Alzheimer's disease. The genetic risk (i.e., the heritability of the disease) is very high for people who develop an early-onset form (age 30–60) of Alzheimer's disease. In particular, people who inherit three high-risk genes have a 50% chance of developing early-onset Alzheimer's (Bertram et al., 2010). In those individuals with later-onset (age 60+) disease, the genetic link is not as consistent. However, one study of 56,000 participants discovered five different genes that together may be responsible for the cellular processes that lead to the death of brain cells (Naj et al., 2011).

SOCIAL DEVELOPMENT: INTIMACY, COMMITMENT, AND PARENTING As adolescents transition into adulthood, the nature of their social relationships begins to change as, for many, finding a potential lifelong partner and having a family become focal interests. At some point, young adults begin to separate from their parents, and move toward cultivating caring, compassionate, and intimate relationships.

Adults may pair up in the form of marriage, civil unions, or cohabitation (living together as unmarried partners). Overall, marriage appears to benefit physical and mental health. Married couples monitor their medical care more effectively, report greater sexual satisfaction and frequency, and are more financially secure than are unmarried people (Waite & Gallagher, 2000). The most tempting, and perhaps easiest, conclusion is that marriage causes greater physical and mental health, but it is also plausible that people who are healthier are more likely to marry. Also, marital dissatisfaction is a major stressor that can have a negative impact on health (Matthews & Gallo, 2003).

According to numerous longitudinal studies of married couples conducted over the past few decades (Gottman & Levenson, 1992, 2002), the emotional expressions couples direct toward each other during arguments are key predictors as to whether they will stay together. For example, couples who show contempt for each other during arguments are the most likely to have long-term marital problems. In addition to contempt, criticism, defensiveness, and stonewalling (becoming unresponsive to the other person) have also been identified as the most disastrous ways of communicating with one's partner. Conversely, key predictors of a successful marriage include whether *both* partners are willing and able to give up some level of control, to focus on solving problems that are solvable, and to nurture fondness and admiration toward the other.

After marriage or partnership, parenting is another major experience that defines many people's young and middle adult years. This all-consuming activity involves caring for the physical, cognitive, social, and emotional needs of children. You have probably noticed that there are many different ways of addressing these needs. In high school, you may have compared notes with friends about how your parents and their parents interacted with you, set expectations for schoolwork and behavior, and enforced rules. If you are not yet a parent, you may be

Figure 10.15 Parenting Styles

Psychologists believe that parenting styles can be classified into four categories that vary along the dimensions of warmth versus detachment, and low versus high expectations.

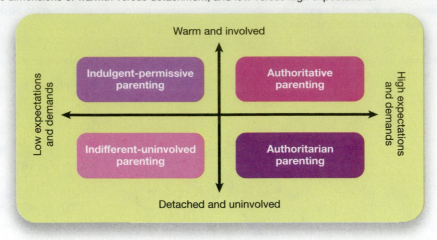

surprised to find out that parents also compare notes—they want to know the best ways to carry out their responsibilities. So what does the research say about parenting practices?

Psychologists have identified multiple parenting styles—that is, different patterns in discipline, guidance, and involvement (see Figure 10.15; Baumrind, 1971; Maccoby & Martin, 1983):

- **Authoritative parenting** *is characterized by the expression of warmth and responsiveness to the needs of children, but also by exercising control over certain actions and decisions made by children.*

- **Authoritarian parenting** *emphasizes excessive control over children and less expression of warmth.*

- **Indulgent-permissive parenting** *emphasizes warm but indifferent parenting, with little attempt to control children, even in positive and helpful ways.*

- **Indifferent-uninvolved parenting** *is characterized by neither warmth nor control toward children.*

Identifying these categories of parenting might give the impression that we could accurately label parents as one type or another. In reality, parents may switch between different parenting styles depending on the circumstances. For example, authoritative parents might become authoritarian if they feel their sense of power over a child is compromised, or might become more permissive as an adolescent ages and shows that he or she can make good decisions on his or her own. Practice applying the different parenting styles to the activity in Table 10.8.

Psychologists—and parents, of course—are interested in how a specific style of parenting might influence a child's behavior and well-being. Researchers have found that children of authoritative parents tend to be more socially aware, assertive, friendly, and independent than are children consistently exposed to the other three styles (Baumrind, 1991). These findings are not based on experimental research, however, so we cannot be sure the degree to which the parenting is shaping the behavior. Parenting styles that are harsh and lacking in support, as well as

Table 10.8 Understanding Parenting Styles

Read each scenario and identify which style of parenting best applies.

Seventeen-year-old Chloe rarely gets into any serious trouble. Even so, her parents mandate that she return straight home from school, punish her if she does not follow strict house rules, and provide little emotional or interpersonal affection. Which style of parenting do Chloe's parents employ?

Stephanie's mother frequently asks how she is doing in school and with friends, and spends as much time as she can with her daughter. However, her mother does not set a time for Stephanie to come home at night, and she is unconcerned if Stephanie fails some classes and quits attending school club meetings. Stephanie's mother seems to display which type of parenting?

Sung's parents enforce some fairly strict rules around the house, and they establish consequences for doing poorly in school and for misbehavior. They keep to these rules consistently and ensure that Sung understands them. His parents also express love and warmth toward their son. Which style of parenting best describes Sung's parents?

Xavier's parents allow him to pursue his interests but rarely ask about whether he enjoys them or how he is progressing. When he returns from school each day, neither parent asks what he did in school or whether he needs any help with schoolwork.

Answers: 1. Authoritarian parenting, 2. Indulgent parenting, 3. Authoritative parenting, 4. Indifferent parenting

warm and nurturing parenting styles, do tend to be transmitted from one generation to the next (Belsky, 2007).

Parenting can bring overwhelming joy, but it can also reduce personal and marital happiness. On the one hand, children tend to stabilize marriages, as they become the objects of mutual, cooperative focus for the parents. On the other hand, parents report a decline in marital satisfaction within the first two years of having children (Belsky & Rovine, 1990). Marital satisfaction is usually highest before the birth of the first child and declines until children have left home, after which satisfaction tends to rise again (Glenn, 1990). Marital difficulties can increase between parents who may be struggling with adolescent children who are seeking their autonomy (Steinberg, 1987).

You may have heard of the **empty nest syndrome**, *a phenomenon in which parents experience a sense of sadness and loss when their children have left home.* Parents who see their children off to college or other pursuits away from home experience a dramatic change in their own roles—from that of mother and father back to wife and husband. Some parents in this situation realize that they no longer have the same things in common; divorce may be the result of this experience. However, the general trend is quite the opposite—marital satisfaction for both husbands and wives increases after children leave home. In fact, married older adults are just as likely to report being very satisfied with marriage as are newlyweds (Rollins, 1989; Gorchoff, John, & Helson, 2008).

JOURNAL PROMPT

Parenting Styles: Do you think that the different parenting styles identified in this module adequately capture the complexities of parenting? In your experience would you categorize one or both of your parents as consistently falling into one of the four categories, or do your parent(s) show more than one style?

Although parents may experience sadness or even divorce when their children move out, the general trend is toward an increase in marital satisfaction.

EMOTIONAL CHANGES   Late adulthood can be a phase of life characterized by considerable change and adjustment. Many older people experience the death of a spouse, the loss of close friends, some loss of personal freedoms such as driving or living without assistance, and one or more physical conditions that require regular medical monitoring and treatment. Older adults also realize and contemplate the reality of dying. It is no wonder why younger people often sympathize with the elderly and often make assumptions that life experiences during the twilight years are to be feared. Depression in older adults often accompanies other physical illnesses, just as it does in young people. Even so, healthy older adults are actually no more likely to become depressed than are younger people. The reality is that as long as basic emotional and social needs are met, old age can be a joyful time (Charles & Carstensen, 2009).

Older people are more likely than their younger counterparts to see the glass as half full; in other words, they are generally more optimistic than young adults and adolescents. This perspective is reflected in how they deal with adversity as well as in how they deal with negative emotional experiences from the past. Personality factors also contribute to aging well: Low levels of anxiety and hostility and high levels of optimism are associated with better physical health (Smith & Spiro, 2002). However, optimism in older age may not be universal to people of all cultures. Although older people in the United States tend to be more optimistic than younger adults, older adults in China tend to be less optimistic than younger adults (You et al., 2009).

To get a good sense of what it is like to grow older, it is important to consider emotional experience. Researchers who have examined emotions throughout the life span tend to find that negative emotions decline with age while positive emotions increase in frequency (Figure 10.16).

Emotional well-being *is the subjective experience of both positive and negative emotions, and is measured by life satisfaction, happiness, and the balance between negative and positive emotional experiences* (Charles & Carstensen, 2009). Emotional well-being tends to increase as people get older. Why might this be? Perhaps this trend runs counter to what we expect as time winds down. One explanation is that with wisdom and experience come the ability to avoid situations that may elicit negative emotions. Older people simply become better at putting themselves in situations that will elicit positive emotions. Also, the goals that older people set differ from those set by younger people. Younger people are planning for a long-term and uncertain future. In contrast, older people are more likely to set goals that emphasize positive emotional and meaningful experiences (Carstensen et al., 1999).

Figure 10.16 Emotion, Memory, and Aging

Younger people have superior memory for whether they have seen positive, negative, or neutral pictures compared with older people. However, notice that younger people remember positive and negative pictures equally, whereas older people are more likely to remember positive pictures (Charles et al., 2003).

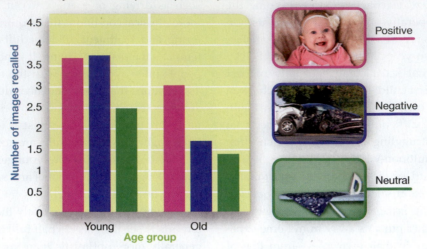

Module 10.3 Summary

10.3a Know . . . the key terminology concerning adolescence, adulthood, and aging:

Alzheimer's disease
authoritarian parenting
authoritative parenting
conventional morality
dementia
emotional well-being
empty nest syndrome
gender nonconforming
identity
identity statuses
indifferent-uninvolved parenting
indulgent-permissive parenting
postconventional morality
preconventional morality
puberty

10.3b Understand . . . the different ways in which identity and social status develop.

Identity formation is the central issue of adolescence. Different outcomes of identity development were described by Marcia, including identity achievement, identity diffusion, identity foreclosure, and identity moratorium. Status achievement is also a major issue of adolescence. Its effects can be seen in those who struggle to gain popularity in its different forms (sociometric and perceived). Failure to achieve status and form friendships may lead to isolation and the problematic behaviors discussed in this module.

10.3c Apply . . . your understanding of the categories of moral development and identity statuses.

As you know by now, developmental psychology has a long tradition of describing the growth of different characteristics in terms of stages and categories; in this case moral development and identity. Remembering and understanding the categories and underlying concepts require some practice. If you are unsure of your understanding of how moral development and identity statuses are categorized, review "Kohlberg's Stages of Moral Reasoning," and complete the activity in Table 10.7 Applying Identity Statuses.

10.3d Analyze . . . the relationship between brain development and adolescent judgment and risk taking.

Problems with judgment involve a region of the brain called the prefrontal cortex, which is involved in planning, reasoning, and emotion and impulse control. This region of the brain continues to change, via myelination and synaptic pruning, during adolescence. The underdeveloped state of prefrontal cortex may account for the problems with decision making and impulse control observed during adolescence. Nevertheless, this factor alone does not explain problematic adolescent behavior, as adolescents who tend to avoid risks and make prudent decisions also have still-developing frontal lobes.

10.3e Analyze . . . the stereotype that middle or old age is associated with unhappiness.

Research shows that older adults do face issues that might lead to unhappiness—changes in health, family structure, and activities that generally accompany aging. At the same time, the research shows that such challenges do not necessarily condemn a person to unhappiness. In fact, healthy older adults tend to have a very positive outlook on life. Optimism and life satisfaction tend to increase, and older adults have the wisdom to put themselves in situations that will be favorable to their well-being.

Module 10.3 Quiz

Know . . .

1. Which of the following is not a symptom of Alzheimer's disease?

   A. Memory problems
   B. Disorientation
   C. Obsessive behaviors
   D. Personality changes

Understand . . .

2. A primary difference between someone who has "sociometric" popularity versus someone with "perceived" popularity is that:

   A. someone who is sociometrically popular is likely to engage in prosocial behaviors.
   B. someone who is sociometrically popular is likely to be wealthy and snobbish.
   C. people with perceived popularity tend to show more prosocial behaviors.
   D. people with perceived popularity are more likely to be wealthy and snobbish.

Apply . . .

3. Evan takes on the roles and values of his parents. Marcia and other psychologists might categorize him as experiencing: _____.

   A. identity achievement   **C.** identity foreclosure
   B. identity diffusion   **D.** identity moratorium

Analyze . . .

4. Which of the following may help explain why adolescent decision making is sometimes problematic?

   A. Adolescents are still in the concrete operational stage of development.
   B. Adolescents are limited to inductive and deductive reasoning.
   C. Adolescents' decisions are overly based on emotions.
   D. The adolescent prefrontal cortex, which controls decision-making processes, is still developing.

5. Which statement best summarizes emotion and life satisfaction at old age?

   A. Older adults are more likely to focus on positive experiences than younger people.
   B. Older adulthood is primarily characterized by despair and anxiety about aging.
   C. Older adults are typically diagnosed with depression.
   D. Older adults are no different from younger adults in terms of depression and life satisfaction.

Module 10.4 Scientific Literacy Challenge: Free-Range Parenting

Childhood is a time of learning, growing, and developing skills and independence. Thus, children would seem to thrive if they are able to get out and explore their world. However, childhood is also a time of vulnerability, and so parents are vigilant and constantly work to ensure their children's safety. These opposing motives can be a challenge for parents. Before you read the article on "free-range parenting" from a parenting blog, take a moment to think about your childhood and how the adults in your life tried to find balance between controlling you and letting you learn to make your own decisions.

JOURNAL PROMPT

Thinking back to your elementary school years, can you recall a time when your parents or caregivers were more lenient with you than your friends' parents were with them? Did that have a positive or negative effect on you?

What do we know about the free-range parenting style?

Read the following blog post about the concept of free-range parenting and free-range children, paying close attention to the bolded key terms and concepts covered in Chapter 10.

The Argument for Free-Range Children

By May Rios, staff writer

In December 2014, police stopped two children, Rafi and Dvora Meitiv, who were found walking alone in Silver Springs, Maryland. Police alerted Child Protective Services and, in the ensuing investigation, the parents were found guilty of "unsubstantiated child neglect." Certainly the 6- and 10 year-old siblings need supervision, but these were not what psychologists call **indifferent-uninvolved parents**, meaning parents who show little attachment or control with their children. They were simply letting the kids walk home from a park. Now, the parents are asking, when did encouraging independence and exercise become a crime?

Authoritative parenting has long been associated with the most positive social and emotional outcomes. It includes warmth and reflects strong attachment, but moderate levels of control. However, **parenting styles** evolve over time, reflecting legitimate concerns about violent crime, drugs, and accidental injuries. In response to these concerns, trends have been shifting toward parents exerting increased control over children's free time by scheduled sanctioned, organized activities (such as sports or music lessons) and placing greater restrictions on how far they can roam. As a result, today's **cohort** of children spends far more free time at home—90% according to a recent UCLA report—than any previous generation that has been studied. To many, this is stifling childhood growth and leading to problems with obesity, a lack of self-sufficiency, and a sense of entitlement. If that is the case, then perhaps we should foster a culture of free-ranging children: Kids should be empowered to wander off on their own for extended periods of time, make their own choices, and solve their own problems.

Now that we know a little about the concept of a free-range parenting style and why people are debating it, read on to find out what types of evidence Rios provided to support the movement.

How do scientists study free-range parenting?

There is no shortage of opinions about how to raise children. As a psychology student, you should anticipate that some parenting advice can be supported by substantial evidence, some advice has a little evidence to support it, and a lot of it is just bad advice. When you read this section of Rios's blog post, pay attention to the types of evidence she offers and how strong they are.

While undoubtedly horrific, statistics show that stranger abduction accounts for less than .001% of missing children: child abduction is far more common when there are custodial disputes between estranged parents. In fact, all cases of missing children have dropped by a third in the past 20 years. In the past 10 years, physical assaults against children are down by a third, and sexual assaults—including foiled attempts—are down by nearly half. Note that these figures correlate with the increasing prevalence of cell phones. Equipping children with both technology and decision-making skills promotes their safety.

There are numerous disadvantages to an over-controlled, highly programmed childhood. For example, self-report studies show that over-protective parenting is correlated with lower implicit and explicit self-esteem and higher levels of anxiety. Surveys of college students have shown that ==those children who have 'helicopter parents' (parents who seem to hover over them, controlling or giving advice and feedback on their every move) have higher levels of depression and report lower quality of life.==

Did you recognize any specific research concepts? Try answering the following questions to see what you can identify correctly.

1. The blog implies that the more controlling parents are, the lower the quality of life a child experiences. This indicates a _____ research design.
    a. correlational
    b. experimental
    c. random assignment
    d. double-blind
2. The blogger mentions implicit and explicit self-esteem, but most readers are not going to know exactly what those terms mean. This would be cleared up if the blogger addressed
    a. the independent variable.
    b. whether this is experimental or quasi-experimental.
    c. the operational definitions for these terms.
    d. ecological validity.
3. Stranger abductions are extraordinarily rare compared to abductions by family members. In this comparison, the number of abductions in each group would be a(n)
    a. dependent variable.
    b. confounding variable
    c. generalizing variable
    d. anecdote.

Answers: 1. *a* 2. *c* 3. *a*

How do we think critically about free-range parenting?

Remember that critical thinking involves curiosity and reasonable levels of skepticism. Critical thinkers continue to ask questions while evaluating the quality of the answers they find. As you read the next paragraph of the blog post, search for evidence that Rios is applying critical thinking skills.

This is just a glimpse of the data free-range parents can use to support their cause, but not everyone agrees whole-heartedly. The fact that assaults and abductions are rare does not make them any less terrible. Providing some control and supervision is merited and, to many parents, asking a child to stay on the same block is as simple and harmless as asking them to buckle their seatbelts. ==Another observation is that the drop in crime rates does not just correlate with cell phones, it also correlates with more restrictive parenting. This means that more restrictive parenting is every bit as likely to reduce the crime rate as cell phones, at least from a statistical perspective.== The same reasoning applies to the psychological data. It is clear that there are correlations between over-controlling parenting and negative emotions. ==If you are predisposed to agree with the free-range parents, you might be quick to interpret the parenting as a causal influence.== However, an unbiased critique would suggest that children with negative emotions might actually elicit increased attempts by parents to control their activities. ==Also, it could be that the negative affect some students experienced lead them to remember their childhood differently, or evaluate their parents differently than students with more positive emotions.==

The statements below will help you identify several aspects of critical thinking. Match the following critical thinking statements to the highlighted passages that illustrate them.

1. The author shows that critical thinking involves considering alternative explanations.
2. The author tries to identify sources of bias that might influence how people interpret results.
3. The author identifies a confounding variable in a correlational example.

1. Blue 2. Green 3. Yellow

Rios has demonstrated cautious skepticism and a good deal of critical thinking. Read on to find out how free-range advocates wish to apply the evidence.

How is the idea of free-range parenting relevant?

The evidence shows that criminal activity that affects children is down and that overly controlled parenting is associated with several negative effects. How is this relevant to the parents of the Meitiv children, and to any other adults who care for children? Read the rest of the article and then share any newly formed thoughts you may have about free-range parenting in the writing activity that follows.

> How much autonomy should children have? Almost everyone will have to face this problem at some point, either as a parent or a caretaker. But the issue is not limited to those who directly care for a child— those officers in Silver Springs had to make that decision when they saw the Meitiv children. As for the parents, they told ABC News that they were, "shocked and outraged that we have been deemed negligent for granting our children the simple freedom to play outdoors. We fully intend to appeal.... We also have no intention of changing our parenting approach."

SHARED WRITING

After reading this article, do you think the police went too far in stopping the Meitiv children and reporting their parents to Child Protection Services?

Chapter 10 Quiz

1. To study the effect of daycare programs on academic performance, a researcher follows the same 30 children who did or did not attend daycare programs as they go through kindergarten to sixth grade. Which type of design is the researcher using?
   A. Cross-sectional
   B. Cohort
   C. Latitudinal
   D. Longitudinal

2. Which of the following is true about the connection between the MMR vaccine and autism?
   A. There is no scientific evidence that the MMR vaccine causes autism.
   B. The connection between MMR and autism remains unclear.
   C. There is strong scientific evidence that the MMR vaccine causes autism.
   D. The MMR vaccine causes autism if administered more than once.

3. Harry Harlow's research with infant monkeys demonstrated the importance of:
   A. good nutrition for cognitive development.
   B. physical contact and the bond infants form with their mothers.
   C. punishment in shaping behavior.
   D. self-esteem in socialization.

4. A healthy adult with no signs of dementia in his or her 80s is likely to have the most difficulty doing which of the following tasks?
   A. Remembering how many feet are in a mile
   B. Recalling the definition of the word "antepenultimate"
   C. Knowing the names of his or her grandchildren
   D. Solving an abstract logic problem

5. The effects of language deprivation during infancy and childhood can be irreversible. This fact is best explained by which concept?
   A. Cohort effects
   B. Sensorimotor functioning
   C. Sensitive period
   D. Stage theories

6. Which of the following is not a likely factor that would create a *cohort effect* for a study on lifetime cognitive development in healthy people?
   A. Differences in genes between individuals
   B. Differences in educational practices over time
   C. Changes in the nutritional availability
   D. Changes in prescription drug use

7. Which of the following has not been recommended for helping preterm infants survive and thrive?
   A. Reduce stimulation
   B. Massage
   C. Engage in ongoing physical contact
   D. Increase stimulation

8. Parents who attend to their children's psychological abilities and guide them through the learning process are using: _____.
   A. scaffolding
   B. tutoring
   C. core knowledge
   D. the zone of proximal development

9. A child in the sensorimotor stage may quit looking at or reaching for a toy if you move it out of sight. This behavior reflects the fact that the child has not developed _____.
   A. core knowledge
   B. object permanence
   C. conservation
   D. preoperations

10. Temperament refers to:
    A. whether a child is likely to get angry.
    B. body temperature at birth.
    C. a child's ability to recognize himself or herself in a mirror.
    D. general emotional reactivity.

11. Two-year-old Irina talks to her brother, who is wearing headphones and looking away, and becomes frustrated that he is (or seems to be) ignoring her. Irina's misunderstanding is likely due to the fact that she has yet to develop: _____.
    A. theory of mind
    B. self-awareness
    C. egocentrism
    D. stranger anxiety

12. An enduring emotional bond characterized by a strong motivation for physical and psychological comfort is referred to as: _____.
    A. empathy
    B. attachment
    C. object permanence
    D. theory of mind

13. Rachel believes that it is wrong to steal only because doing so could land her in jail. Which level of Kohlberg's moral development scheme is Rachel applying in this scenario?
    A. postconventional
    B. preconventional
    C. preoperational
    D. conventional

14. You remember that your parents were warm and responsive but set reasonable rules and expectations for your behavior. They would most likely be characterized as having an _____ parenting style.
    A. authoritative
    B. authoritarian
    C. indulgent-permissive
    D. indifferent-uninvolved

15. Marital satisfaction in couples with children tends to increase:
    A. when the child reaches two years of age.
    B. after children have left the nest.
    C. when the child reaches adolescence.
    D. when the child has reached the formal operational stage of development.

Chapter 11
Motivation and Emotion

Module 11.1 Hunger and Eating

Learning Objectives

11.1a Know . . . the key terminology of motivation and hunger.

11.1b Understand . . . the biological, cognitive, and social processes that shape eating patterns.

11.1c Understand . . . the major eating and weight-control problems people face.

11.1d Apply . . . your knowledge of hunger regulation to better understand and evaluate your own eating patterns.

11.1e Analyze . . . the roles of texture and taste in satiation.

It may be true that "you are what you eat," but recent research has suggested a new twist on this old saying; it may be that "you are how you eat." Do you prefer to eat on the run, following the US tradition of fast food? Or do you prefer the French approach of having a leisurely dinner over the course of an evening? It may be that your preference for either mode of eating affects not only what you ingest, but also how you think and behave in other ways. Psychologists have recently discovered that when individuals are exposed to images and thoughts of fast food, they do not just eat fast—they do everything fast (Zhong & DeVoe, 2010).

One study had volunteers look at fast-food logos and describe their favorite items from those restaurants. Afterward, the participants read faster, showed preferences for time-saving products, and even chose to receive small payments immediately rather than waiting a week for larger sums. Think about your own experiences—are you more likely to see a person multitasking, perhaps holding a book in one hand and food in the other, at a fast-food place or a fine dining establishment? It appears that the fast-food environment is not just about getting a quick meal, but speeds up other aspects of our thinking and behaving as well (DeVoe et al., 2013).

The study of **motivation** *concerns the physiological and psychological processes underlying the initiation of behaviors that direct organisms toward specific goals.* These initiating factors, or motives, include the thoughts, feelings, sensations, and bodily process that lead to goal-directed behavior. Motivation is essential to an individual's survival because at its most basic level it contributes to **homeostasis**, *the body's physiological processes that allow it to maintain consistent internal states in response to the outer environment.* These states include physiological needs such as appropriate body temperature as well as indicators of hunger and thirst. Take thirst, for example. When bodily water levels fall below normal, cells release chemical compounds that maintain the structure and fluid levels of cells. Receptors in the body respond to the increased concentrations of these compounds, as well as to the lower water volume, and send messages to the brain. These messages trigger thirst signals in the brain, which in turn motivates us to seek water or other fluids, thereby maintaining homeostasis (Figure 11.1).

In addition to satisfying our basic physiological needs, motivation is social in nature. Humans, like many other species of animals, are highly motivated to form social bonds. Motivation addresses some uniquely human goals as well, such as achieving success at school or work. Across the domains of physiological, social, and achievement motivation, psychologists view motives as consisting of two main parts. First, our motivated behavior involves **drives**—*the physiological triggers that tell us we may be deprived of something and cause us to seek out what is needed, such as food.* We also respond to **incentives** *(or goals), which are the stimuli we seek to reduce drives such as social approval and companionship, food, water, and other needs* (Figure 11.2). These concepts also apply to material covered in the other modules in this chapter. Here we will focus on the motivation to eat.

Physiological Aspects of Hunger

As children, most of us learned to equate hunger—the motivation to eat—with a growling stomach. It is tempting to conclude that stomach contractions cause hunger; indeed,

Figure 11.1 Maintaining Physiological Balance

Homeostasis is the process of maintaining relatively stable internal states. For example, this diagram illustrates how homeostasis regulates thirst and the body's fluid levels.

Figure 11.2 Drives and Incentives

Our motivation to reduce a drive, or in response to an incentive, can lead to the same behavior.

this belief has been around for a long time (Cannon & Washburn, 1921). In reality, a growling stomach is only one of many physical processes associated with hunger. At the opposite end of the spectrum, a full stomach is only one cue for **satiation**—*the point in a meal when we are no longer motivated to eat*. Thus, homeostasis of food intake is balanced between hunger motives and satiation.

The on and off switches involved in hunger can be found in a few regions of the hypothalamus (see Module 3.2). Researchers have found that stimulating the *lateral hypothalamus* causes rats to begin to eat; thus this structure may serve as an "on" switch (Delgado & Anand, 1952). In contrast, the *ventromedial* region of the hypothalamus appears to serve as the "off" switch; damage to this area leads to obesity in lab animals. A related area, the *paraventricular* nucleus of the hypothalamus, also signals that it is time to stop eating by inhibiting the lateral hypothalamus.

The hypothalamus, like any other brain region, does not work alone. It is generally more accurate to think of the hypothalamus as a busy hub of activity that sends and receives signals throughout the body. When it comes to eating and hunger, this area receives information about tastes, textures, and smells through nerves coming from the mouth and nose, and it exchanges this information with the frontal cortex.

The hypothalamus also takes on the job of monitoring blood chemistry for levels of sugars and hormones involved in energy regulation. For example, the hypothalamus detects changes in the level of **glucose**, *a sugar that serves as a primary energy source for the brain and the rest of the body*. Highly specialized neurons called *glucostats* detect glucose levels in the fluid outside of the cell. When glucose levels drop, glucostats signal the hypothalamus that energy supplies are low, and hunger increases (Langhans, 1996a, 1996b). After food reaches the stomach and intestines, sugars are absorbed into the bloodstream and transported throughout the body. *Insulin*, a hormone secreted by the pancreas, helps cells store this circulating glucose for future use. As insulin levels rise in response to consumption of a meal, hunger decreases—but so do glucose levels, which eventually leads to hunger again a few hours later. Glucose, glucostats, and insulin are merely pieces of the hunger puzzle, however. In fact, a psychologist can better predict how much a person will eat by simply asking, "How hungry are you?" than by measuring blood glucose levels (Pittas et al., 2005).

Other hunger-related hormones include *ghrelin*, a hormone secreted in the stomach that stimulates stomach contractions and appetite (Cummings, 2006). Ghrelin is also released by the hypothalamus, where—in contrast to what it does in the stomach—it functions to decrease appetite. Another key chemical in regulating hunger is *cholecystokinin* (CCK) (Badman & Flier, 2005). As the intestines expand, neurons release CCK, which communicates to the hypothalamus that it is time to stop eating. These hormones and other biological processes interact with equally complex psychological factors to determine when and how much we eat.

Psychological Aspects of Hunger

People will go to great lengths to get their favorite treats and will avoid other items that taste bad unless they are extremely hungry. As a reinforcer, food can equal or even exceed the power of highly addictive drugs, and, both stimulate the same type of dopamine receptors in the brain (Christensen et al., 2008; Koerber et al., 2013). Some people even report cravings for a "sugar fix"—a term that seems to imply that addiction to candy bars is comparable to an addiction to a drug such as heroin. The phrase *sugar fix* may seem an exaggeration, but is it possible that sugar actually does act like a drug? Sugar and some addictive drugs share a few interesting similarities. Ordinary sucrose—plain white granulated sugar—can stimulate release of dopamine in the *nucleus accumbens*, a brain region associated with the reinforcement and reward (Rada et al., 2005). Taste is another powerful force behind our motivation to eat. Thus, eating is more than just maintaining homeostasis. In addition to the body's efforts to monitor energy needs, eating is motivated by psychological factors that include physical qualities of food such as its flavor and texture, as well as the availability of food, the social setting, and cravings.

The rat on the left has swollen to enormous proportions after researchers created lesions to its ventromedial hypothalamus. Compare it to the more typical rat on the right.

TASTES, TEXTURES, AND EATING   If the only factors underlying our motivation to eat were calories and essential nutrients, a few simple foods consumed every day for our entire lives would suffice. However, for those fortunate enough to have plentiful food available, taste and variety motivate decisions about what to eat. One unfortunate consequence of this relationship is that, generally speaking, the most popular foods are the ones that contain the most dietary fat and sugar. Let's look more specifically at fat.

Why Dietary Fat Can Be So Tempting

Some of the most popular foods in the United States are loaded with fat, including red meat, cheese, ice cream, and anything deep fried. Psychologists and neuroscientists are discovering why people can be so driven to consume these and other fattening foods.

What do we know about consuming fatty foods?

As we learned in Module 4.4, taste is based on patterns of stimulation of receptors on the tongue and mouth. These receptors have evolved to help us decide whether to consume or reject food. Dietary fat presents an interesting paradox: Humans have a strong preference for fat, raising the possibility that it is (or was) a dietary necessity. Nevertheless, long-term consumption of foods that are high in fat and cholesterol is associated with cardiovascular disease and other health problems. So why are people motivated to consume dietary fat?

How can science explain the common craving for fattening foods?

In modern times, fat receptors on the tongue can seem like an enemy, but they were likely advantageous in an evolutionary sense because they facilitated consuming high-calorie foods. Research on animal subjects shows that when fat receptors on the tongue are stimulated, the brain releases endorphins and dopamine—both of which are responsible for the subjective sense of pleasure and reward (Mizushige et al., 2007). It is possible that finding pleasure in consuming fat aided ancestral humans in procuring calorie-rich foods during times of lean food availability.

The animal work involved the use of recording techniques that cannot be employed with humans. To conduct similar experiments with humans, scientists have used brain imaging technology (Grabenhorst & Rolls, 2014). In one study, participants had their brains scanned while they tasted various substances. At different times the participants tasted either a fatty solution (vegetable oil), sucrose (a sweet taste), or a tasteless control substance. Brain activity was recorded while these different taste stimuli were delivered to participants through a plastic tube. The participants were also asked to rate the pleasantness of each stimulus. Overall, the participants rated the fatty substance favorably, and the brain scans showed activation in regions of the brain associated with pleasure sensations when fat was delivered (de Araujo & Rolls, 2004).

Can we critically evaluate this research?

A magnetic resonance imaging (MRI) machine hardly approximates the cozy atmosphere of the home dining room or a quaint restaurant. Despite general preferences for fatty foods, few of us sip on vegetable oil. However, if the research results described previously generalize to other experiences, then we can better understand how cravings for fatty foods come about—that is, they directly stimulate pleasure-sensing areas of the brain. Furthermore, although the research described may be sound, the explanation for why fat receptors evolved requires speculation that may not be directly testable in an MRI machine or psychology laboratory.

Why is this relevant?

Scientific studies have long confirmed the health risks brought on by high-fat diets. What is less understood is how and why we crave these foods, as opposed to lettuce or carrot sticks. Understanding how fat is sensed in our taste system and its links to the reward centers of the brain may help with treatments for avoiding or reducing excessive consumption of unhealthy foods.

Figure 11.3 The Pleasure of Taste

When fat receptors of the tongue are stimulated, the cingulate cortex—a region of the brain involved in emotional processing—is activated. The orbitofrontal cortex is involved in linking food taste and texture with reward.

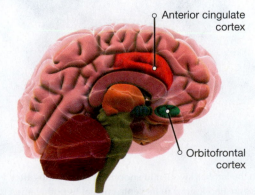

Anterior cingulate cortex

Orbitofrontal cortex

Although chemical receptors in the mouth and nose are detecting the tastes and smells of food, touch receptors in the mouth are detecting the textures of the food and relaying this information to the *orbitofrontal cortex*, which in turn contributes information to the overall sensation of eating (Figure 11.3; de Araujo & Rolls, 2004). These cells help us distinguish a runny spaghetti sauce from a thick one or crunchy peanut butter from the creamy variety. Other cells distinguish between fatty and lean meats or even between spicy and bland foods (Rolls et al., 2003). Texture, as you have likely found, is an important part of the eating experience.

What if we could get all the nutrition we needed by swallowing one small tablet each day? Would we still be motivated to eat so as to enjoy the taste and texture of food? It appears that even if we took such a pill we would still want to eat. Researchers demonstrated this with *tube feeding*, a technique used with patients in the hospital who cannot chew or swallow. Tube feeding satisfies the body's nutritional needs by delivering nutrients directly to the stomach. People who are tube fed, and therefore not calorie deprived, report being equally hungry as people who are on placebos and are hooked up to a tube-feeding apparatus but are not actually fed anything (Stratton et al., 2003). It appears that the pleasure of eating is motivation enough, even if we do not actually need the nutrients.

FOOD VARIETY AND EATING To what extent does food availability affect how much we eat? The question is more difficult to answer than you might think. Imagine sitting down to a bottomless supply of your favorite meal. Watching each helping disappear would probably serve as a reminder that it is approaching time to stop. But what

American astronauts in the 1960s may not have been thrilled about their meals. Even though the tubes contained actual foods the astronauts enjoyed on Earth, such as beef with vegetables, they lost most of their appeal when pureed and served in a tube.

if someone interfered with your ability to keep track of how much you had eaten? This scenario is not what we would expect in normal situations, but it would allow for an ideal test of how food availability affects how much you will eat.

Psychologists created this situation in the laboratory through a technique known as the *bottomless bowl* of soup. Volunteers were asked to eat soup until they had enough. In the experimental condition, a tube continued to fill the soup bowl from the bottom so that it could not be detected by the volunteers. These individuals stopped eating after consuming, on average, 70% more than those participants who knowingly refilled their bowls. Even more interesting is what happened—or did not happen—in terms of feelings and thoughts: The individuals eating from bottomless bowls did not feel any more satiated, nor did they believe they had eaten any more than the individuals in the control group. It turns out we are not so good at putting on the brakes when we cannot keep track of how much we have consumed (Wansink et al., 2005).

The results of the bottomless soup bowl study can be explained by **unit bias**, *the tendency to assume that the unit of sale or portioning is an appropriate amount to consume*. In some cases, this assumption works well. A single banana comes individually wrapped and makes for a healthy portion; it is an ideal unit (Geier et al., 2006). In contrast, packaged and preportioned foods often come in far-larger-than-healthy sizes. A normal bottle of soda today is likely to be 20 ounces, but a few decades ago the same product came in a 6-ounce bottle. Despite the huge difference in volume, each is seen as constituting one unit of soda. As a consequence, individuals are now likely to consume more than three times as much soda in one sitting as their elders would have.

Cells in the orbitofrontal cortex respond to perceptual qualities of food texture, such as the difference between a runny spaghetti sauce and a thick one.

Compare a modern soft drink serving (top) to the historical serving size (bottom). Despite the massive increase in volume, modern consumers still consider the unit of packaging as a normal-sized serving.

EATING AND THE SOCIAL CONTEXT Eating is more than just a physical drive—there are at least three main social motives influencing our eating as well (Herman et al., 2003):

1. *Social facilitation: Eating more.* Dinner hosts may encourage guests to take second and even third helpings, and individuals with a reputation for big appetites will be prodded to eat the most. Perhaps the strongest element of social facilitation is simply the amount of time spent at the table: The longer a person sits socializing, the more likely he or she is to continue nibbling (Berry et al., 1985).

2. *Impression management: Eating less.* Sometimes people self-consciously control their behavior so that others will see them in a certain way—a phenomenon known as *impression management.* For example, you probably know that it is polite to chew with your mouth closed. Similarly, the *minimal eating norm* suggests that another aspect of good manners—at least in some social and cultural settings—is to eat small amounts to avoid seeming rude (Herman et al., 2003).

3. *Modeling: Eating whatever they eat.* At first exposure to a situation, such as a business dinner, a new employee may notice that no one eats much and everyone takes their time. The newcomer will see the others as models, and so he too will restrain his eating. Later, he may be introduced to his friend's family reunion where everyone is having a second or third helping. In this case, he will be likely to eat more, even if he is already feeling full (Herman et al., 2003).

Clearly, eating is not just a matter of maintaining homeostasis. It is best described as a behavior motivated by biological, social, and individual psychological factors. Awareness of how social factors influence eating, and regulating food intake accordingly, can help address growing health concerns about dietary habits (Herman & Polivy, 2011).

Disorders of Eating

Our dietary habits are influenced by biological dispositions, our beliefs and perceptions about eating and our bodies, and sociocultural factors. Unfortunately, these motivational systems do not always lead us to good health.

OBESITY Obesity *is a disorder of positive energy balance, in which energy intake exceeds energy expenditure.* Some refer to this phenomenon as an epidemic in the United States, and it has spread across the world as well. In 2013, all 50 US states had at least a 20% prevalence rate of obesity (Figure 11.4; Centers for Disease Control and Prevention [CDC], 2013). One of the major problems in controlling obesity is the difficulty in ensuring long-term maintenance of weight loss. The weight-loss options we encounter on an almost daily basis are numerous—but some are good, whereas others are simply gimmicks. The gimmicks often claim to be proven, easy solutions for weight loss. For example, advertisements tell people that they can lose weight without exercising, just by taking a pill. People are also told that combining healthy dietary habits and exercise is the only way to lose weight. Even when following this advice, many people find shedding pounds to be an arduous, if impossible, task.

Why can weight management be so difficult? One problem is that both the drive to eat and the incentive

Figure 11.4 Obesity Map of US

Obesity rates in the US are extremely high. This map shows the prevalence of obesity (having a body mass index of 30 or higher) among adults in each US state and territory. As of 2013 no state has an obesity rate lower than 20%.

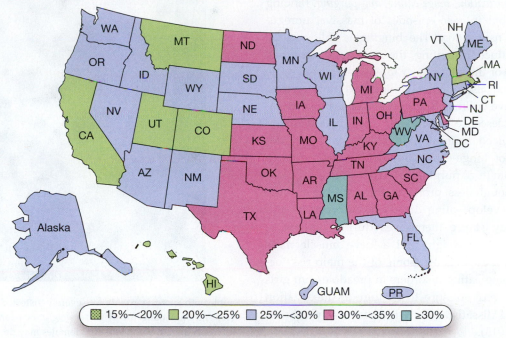

value of food increase with deprivation (Raynor & Epstein, 2003). This trend makes patterns of overeating notoriously difficult to change. Several studies have shown that girls and adolescents who diet are heavier at adulthood (Field et al., 2003; Stice et al., 2005). The restraint involved in dieting—especially avoiding certain highly reinforcing foods—may actually make the foods even more reinforcing in the long run. When it comes to food, absence makes the heart grow fonder.

It is normal to be sensitive to the reinforcing, pleasurable aspects of food, but some individuals are more prone to overeating than others. Research suggests that people who are obese have an increased sensitivity to food and food-related cues. For instance, when children who are obese are allowed to smell or eat just a small sample of candy bars, cakes, and savory nuts, they eat more of these items when given the opportunity than do normal-weight children (Jansen et al., 2003). Also, people who are obese have significantly higher

metabolic activity in those regions of the brain that respond to sensations of the mouth, lips, and tongue (Wang et al., 2002). These findings suggest that people with obesity have more intense, rewarding sensory experiences when it comes to food. But note that the relationship is correlational: It does not tell us whether increased sensitivity to food cues causes obesity, or vice versa.

ANOREXIA AND BULIMIA   Disorders of eating also take the form of dangerous attempts to lose weight, as with **anorexia nervosa**, *an eating disorder that involves (1) self-starvation, (2) intense fear of weight gain and a distorted perception of body image, and (3) a denial of the serious consequences of severely low weight.* Other problems associated with anorexia include consecutive loss of menstrual periods (amenorrhea) and a loss of sexual motivation. The disorder usually occurs during mid to late adolescence and has been on the rise during the 20th century (see Table 11.1

Table 11.1 Statistical Characteristics of Eating Disorders

Lifetime prevalence of anorexia	Women: 0.9%	Men: 0.3%
Lifetime prevalence of bulimia	Women: 1.5%	Men: 0.5%
	Women and Men combined	
Percentage of people with anorexia who are receiving treatment	34%	
Percentage of people with bulimia who are receiving treatment	43%	
Average duration of anorexia	1.7 years	
Average duration of bulimia	8 years	

SOURCE: Hudson, J., Hiripi, E., Pope, H., & Kessler, R. (2007). The prevalence and correlates of eating disorders in the National Comorbidity Survey replication. *Biological Psychiatry*, 61 (3), 348–358.

for some statistical information about eating disorders; Hudson et al., 2007).

Bulimia nervosa *is an eating disorder characterized by periods of food deprivation, binge-eating, and purging.* Binging involves short but intense episodes of massive, unregulated calorie consumption. The binging is followed by purging (self-induced vomiting, the most common type), fasting, laxative or diuretic use, or intense exercise. People with anorexia may also purge, but this is less common than in those who have bulimia. Bulimia nervosa is most prevalent in late adolescence and young adulthood (Hudson et al., 2007). A related disorder, *binge-eating disorder*, includes major periods of binge-eating, but without attempts to avoid weight gain (e.g., purging).

Males, although less prone to these problems than females, also develop eating disorders. Adolescents and young men may starve themselves during periods of high exercise to lose weight and achieve muscle mass (Ricciardelli & McCabe, 2004). Some of the main risk factors for developing eating disorders in preadolescent girls include a perceived pressure to be thin, an idealization of thinness, and dissatisfaction with one's body (Rhode, Stice, & Marti, 2015).

People with anorexia experience severely distorted views of their body. Although dangerously underweight they continue to both fear and feel being fat. Both males and females may develop anorexia.

Module 11.1 Summary

11.1a Know . . . the key terminology of motivation and hunger:

anorexia nervosa
bulimia nervosa
drives
glucose
homeostasis
incentives
motivation
obesity
satiation
unit bias

11.1b Understand . . . the biological, cognitive, and social processes that shape eating patterns.

Ghrelin and CCK are released into the bloodstream from the stomach; ghrelin signals hunger, whereas CCK signals fullness (satiety). Energy is delivered through the bloodstream in the form of glucose, and the hormone insulin helps the cells throughout the body store this fuel. These substances are monitored by the hypothalamus, which signals hunger when not enough glucose is available to the cells. You should also have an understanding of the effects of psychological cues, such as the unit bias and the variety of available foods, as well as social cues, such as the minimal eating norm.

11.1c Understand . . . the major eating and weight-control problems people face.

This module discussed issues related to obesity and the difficulties that individuals face when trying to change their body weight (and image of their body). For example, restricting food intake may actually increase the reward value of food. Other problems include anorexia and bulimia, both of which involve periods of self-starvation and a fear of gaining weight. Bulimia also includes purging, such as through vomiting or the use of laxatives.

11.1d Apply . . . your knowledge of hunger regulation to better understand and evaluate your own eating patterns.

Do you finish an entire package of a food item, as the minimal eating norm would suggest? Or do you check to ensure you are getting an appropriate serving size? Try this activity to find out exactly how you eat. Starting first thing tomorrow, keep a food diary for the next 3 days. In other words, keep a record of everything you eat over this period, recording when you ate, what you ate, and what made you feel like eating. It is important to be honest with yourself and to be reflective: Did you eat because your stomach rumbled, because you were craving something, or perhaps because the food was just there? It is okay to list more than one reason for each entry in your food diary.

At the end of the 3-day period, tally how often each reason for eating appeared in your diary. Make note of what proportion of the time you ate for each reason. Ask yourself: Are the results surprising? Do they make you want to think more about the reasons you eat? (Note: You can also try to work from memory and re-create a food diary from the past 3 or 4 days, but the results might not be as accurate).

11.1e   Analyze . . . the roles of texture and taste in satiation.

A number of innovative studies have demonstrated that tastes and textures play a role in signaling the end of a meal. For example, we know that people can receive the necessary nutrition through tube feeding, yet they still choose to eat so as to experience the sensations associated with food.

Module 11.1 Quiz

Know . . .

1. The _____ region of the hypothalamus is associated with the onset of eating, whereas the _____ region is associated with the offset.
   A. lateral; ventromedial
   B. ventromedial; lateral
   C. anterior; posterior
   D. anterior; ventromedial

Understand . . .

2. Sometimes being around others can:
   A. lead you to eat more than you normally would.
   B. lead you to eat less than you normally would.
   C. either a or b, depending on what others were doing.
   D. neither a nor b; others do not influence our eating.

3. What is one reason psychologists believe obese people respond differently to food reinforcement compared to people of normal weight?
   A. Obese people typically have less exposure to diverse food groups.
   B. Brain imaging studies show less activity in obese individuals' brains in response to food compared to the brains of people of normal weight.
   C. Brain imaging studies show greater activity in obese individuals' brains in response to food compared to the brains people of normal weight.
   D. Obese people do not respond differently to food reinforcement than people of normal weight.

Apply . . .

4. In Europe, the typical container of fruit and yogurt is roughly 6 ounces. In the United States, the same food item is usually packaged in 8-ounce containers. The unit bias predicts that:
   A. a French person in the United States would be likely to eat the entire container, even though it contains 25% more than the typical French serving.
   B. an American visiting Paris would almost certainly miss the extra 2 ounces of yogurt.
   C. a French person visiting the United States would carefully evaluate the differences in packaging to ensure that he or she does not consume more than usual.
   D. all people would be unsatisfied with the 6-ounce serving in France.

Analyze . . .

5. How does research using tube feeding show that tastes and textures are an important part of satiation?
   A. Tube feeding has been shown to increase taste sensations.
   B. Even though the tube-fed volunteers received all the nutrition they needed, they were still motivated to eat.
   C. The texture of food delivered via tube can be seen by volunteers, which decreases their appetite.
   D. Tube-fed volunteers stop eating because their nutrition needs have been met.

Module 11.2   Sexual Motivation

 Learning Objectives

11.2a   Know . . . the key terminology associated with sexual motivation.

11.2b   Understand . . . similarities and differences in sexual responses in men and women.

11.2c   Apply . . . information from surveys to understand your own views of sexuality.

11.2d   Analyze . . . different explanations for what determines sexual orientation.

Why do humans have sex? Psychologists Cindy Meston and David Buss have asked just this question in their research on human sexual motivation. Specifically, they asked college students why they have sex and tabulated the many different responses offered by both males and females (Meston & Buss, 2007). There are so many possible answers to this open-ended question. Certainly more than if we asked the same about why birds, bees, or meerkats have sex. Here are some of the reasons the students came up with:

- *"I wanted to get back at my partner for cheating on me."*
- *"Because of a bet."*
- *"I wanted to end the relationship."*
- *"It feels good."*
- *"I wanted to show my affection toward the other person."*
- *"I wanted to feel closer to God."*

Although we will never know for sure, birds, bees, and meerkats likely have sex to reproduce (a reason that was far down the list for college students). Naturally the motivation to have sex has its complex, underlying physiology. As we will see in this module, however, human sexual motivation is expressed and experienced in diverse ways—at least 237 different ways, according to Meston and Buss's research.

There is a long and continuously updated history of erroneous beliefs about sex and reproduction. Physicians once believed that women who are menstruating can spoil a ham by touching it, and masturbation was thought to cause blindness or insanity (or so adults told their children). We have come a long way toward a modern and scientific understanding of human sexual motivation and behavior. Human sexuality is certainly complex. A notable observation is that, in humans, sex frequently occurs without an end goal of reproduction. For our species, sex serves many purposes that differ from its primary biological function. But sex is not unique in this regard; people eat when they are not hungry and drink when they are not thirsty. However, sex for purposes other than reproduction appears to be rare in nonhuman species. Interestingly, masturbation occurs in some primate species, and the bonobo chimpanzee engages in frequent genital contact, touching, and other sexual behaviors without actually copulating (de Waal & Lanting, 1997; Starin, 2004). Researchers have made significant progress toward understanding the roles played by biological, personal, and sociocultural influences on the complex topic of human sexuality.

Human Sexual Behavior: Psychological and Biological Influences

Each individual differs in their **libido**—*the motivation for sexual activity and pleasure*. What accounts for these individual differences in sex drive? This is not an easy question to answer because differences can be explained by a combination of biological and sociocultural factors. A useful starting point to this question is to ask about gender differences in sexuality, including sexual thoughts, activities, and preferences. Evolutionary psychology predicts that males in general will have a greater interest in sex than do females, including frequency of sexual fantasy, and desire for more sex and a greater number of sexual partners. Theories from social and cultural perspectives predict that females learn to inhibit their sexuality, and conversely, males are encouraged to express it. Self-report surveys of sexual activity are a primary method used for gathering data to test hypotheses such as these.

For the following answer *male, female*, or *no difference*:

- Which gender reports masturbating most frequently?
- Which gender is more likely to report having had casual sex?
- Which gender reports engaging in oral sex more frequently?

According to a meta-analysis, males are more likely than females to masturbate and report casual sex, and there is no difference between males and females in frequency of oral sex (Petersen & Hyde, 2010). The general trend is that when we examine data about gender and sexuality, some differences between males and females appear, but the genders tend to be far more similar in their patterns of sexual activity than common stereotypes might suggest. Both evolutionary and cultural influences impact the expression of sexual motivation and behavior in males and females, and among people of varying sexual orientations.

Obviously, sex is an important and relevant topic for psychology, but it is also one of the most challenging to study. Sex generally happens in private, and many people prefer to keep it that way. Nonetheless, psychologists use a variety of methods to understand the complexities of human sexual behavior, including interviews, questionnaires, physiological measures, and even direct observations of behavior. Interviews and questionnaires are the least intrusive techniques and, therefore, are the most commonly used.

PSYCHOLOGICAL MEASURES OF SEXUAL MOTIVATION One of the first scientists to tackle the topic of human sexual behavior was Alfred Kinsey, a zoology professor who studied wasps before turning his attention to human sexuality. Between 1938 and 1952, Kinsey and his colleagues at Indiana University interviewed thousands of people and published their results in a pair of books known as the Kinsey Reports (1948, 1953). At the time, Kinsey's work was particularly shocking to many people because he openly reported and discussed homosexuality and how frequently it occurred (even among people who identify as heterosexual). This led Kinsey to believe that sexual orientation varied by degree and therefore could not be categorized with an either–or distinction (see Table 11.2). By modern standards, Kinsey's methods were quite flawed and rather controversial. Kinsey tended to make sweeping generalizations about his findings that were based on limited samples. Despite these practices, Kinsey's work on sexuality continues to influence discussion on sexual behavior and motivation.

The questionnaire method of studying human sexual motivation has continued since Kinsey's time. At the

Table 11.2 A Continuum of Sexual Orientation

Kinsey and his associates defied the convention of identifying people as either heterosexual or homosexual by measuring sexual interests on a continuous scale.

0	1	2	3	4	5	6
Exclusively heterosexual	Predominantly heterosexual; only incidentally homosexual	Predominantly heterosexual; more than incidentally homosexual	Equally heterosexual and homosexual	Predominantly homosexual; more than incidentally heterosexual	Predominantly homosexual; only incidentally heterosexual	Exclusively homosexual

SOURCE: Kinsey Institute for Research in Sex, Gender, and Reproduction, Inc.

beginning of this module, we introduced a study conducted by psychologists Meston and Buss, who used anonymous questionnaires to ask more than 1,500 college students to identify their reasons for having sex. We listed a few reasons provided by the students—some conventional (to express affection) and others perhaps more surprising (to feel closer to God). We return to this study to discuss some general themes that emerged—notably, the four shown in Figure 11.5.

As you can see in Figure 11.5, physical, personal, and social factors underlie sexual motivation. For the respondents in Meston and Buss's study, physical reasons were related to sensations and pleasures of sex. Many respondents used sex for what might be described as instrumental reasons; sex was a means of accomplishing a goal such as financial or personal gain, or revenge. College students were also motivated by emotional reasons and because of feelings of insecurity. Reproduction ranked far down the list, which might seem surprising for a study whose results were published under the title "Why Humans Have Sex" (Meston & Buss, 2007). Also note that this study surveyed college students, who represent a relatively small slice of humanity. Other survey-based studies of sexual motivation have found additional factors that motivate sexual behavior, such as expressing value and nurturance toward one's partner, experiencing stress relief, enhancing one's perception of personal power and, of course, having children (Hill & Preston, 1996). Sexual motivation is also tied to relationship context. For example, women are more motivated by physical reasons for short-term sexual relationships and emotional reasons for long-term ones, regardless of whether the individual engages in heterosexual or same-sex relationships (Armstrong & Reissing, 2015). You can evaluate your own attitudes about sex and compare with others by completing the activity in Table 11.3.

BIOLOGICAL MEASURES OF SEX Several decades of work have revealed that sexual motivation is controlled by a distinct set of biological processes. Starting in the 1950s, researchers William Masters and Virginia Johnson described the human sexual response cycle based on their observations of 27 male and 118 female prostitutes who agreed to masturbate or have intercourse while under observation (Masters & Johnson, 1966). Participants were monitored with heart rate and blood pressure equipment, as well as with more peculiar devices such as the penile plethysmograph or vaginal photoplethysmograph, which are designed to measure blood flow to the genitalia. Masters and Johnson's initial study allowed them to develop their methods and work with participants who, according to the researchers, were less likely to be sexually inhibited than non-prostitutes. Masters and Johnson followed up this study with observations of hundreds of men and women to characterize the physiological changes that occur during sex. Figure 11.6 summarizes their observations of human sexual responding in males and females. The **sexual response cycle** *describes the phases of physiological change during sexual activity, which comprises four primary stages: excitement, plateau, orgasm, and resolution.* Dividing the sexual response cycle into phases allowed the researchers to describe the cascade of physiological changes that occur during sexual behavior. The cycle applies to both male and female sexual responses,

---

Figure 11.5 Why Have Sex?

Self-reported reasons for having sex by college undergraduates (Meston & Buss, 2007).

1. For physical reasons.

"The person's physical appearance turned me on."

"I want to achieve an orgasm."

2. To help attain a goal.

"I wanted to get a raise."

"I wanted to hurt an enemy."

3. For emotional reasons.

"I realized I was in love."

"I wanted to intensify my relationship."

4. Because of insecurity.

"I felt obligated to."

"I wanted to be nice."

Table 11.3 Attitudes Toward Sex Survey

How do you feel about sexuality? You can apply what we have learned from research to understand if you take a generally permissive attitude (people have the right to do what they want) or a more conservative one. Respond to each of the items below by assigning a score on a scale from 1 (strongly agree) to 5 (strongly disagree). Note that it is not necessary to be sexually active to complete this scale—simply respond to the general principle of each item.

1. I do not need to be committed to a person to have sex with him or her.
2. Casual sex is acceptable.
3. I would like to have sex with many partners.
4. One-night stands are sometimes enjoyable.
5. It is okay to have ongoing sexual relationships with more than one person at a time.
6. Sex as a simple exchange of favors is okay if both people agree to it.
7. The best sex is with no strings attached.
8. Life would have fewer problems if people could have sex more freely.
9. It is possible to enjoy sex with a person and not like that person very much.
10. It is okay for sex to be just a good physical release.

Once you have assigned a number to each item, average your responses to get your overall score. In one study of more than 200 college students, men averaged a score of 3.63 and women averaged a score of 4.47 on this scale (Hendrick et al., 2006). How do you compare? Given what you have learned about the biological and cultural factors that influence sexuality, are you surprised by the gender difference? Which other factors might influence the norms?

although there are differences between sexes in how these stages are experienced and their duration. The work of Masters and Johnson and those who have followed in their footsteps reveal a complex picture of male and female sexual responses.

One topic of particular interest is how males and females differ in their patterns of orgasm. Roughly 25% of women surveyed reported that they did not experience orgasm during masturbation or sexual intercourse (Dunn et al., 2005), whereas only 2% of men did not experience orgasm. Men usually experience a single orgasm

followed by a **refractory period**, *a time during which erection and orgasm are not physically possible.* In contrast, some women experience multiple orgasms without a refractory period.

What about the subjective experience of orgasm? Do women and men feel differently during orgasm? This challenging question was taken up by a group of researchers who asked college students to write detailed descriptions of their orgasm experiences. Researchers removed clues to the sex of each writer by changing terms such as *penis* or *vagina* to *genitals*. Then, male and

Figure 11.6 Sexual Response Cycles

(a) Masters and Johnson's studies showed that males typically experience a single orgasm followed by a refractory period—a time during which orgasm cannot be physically achieved again. Then they experience resolution, unless they continue sexual activity.
(b) Women typically have a more varied sexual response profile than men. Here are a few examples. Line A indicates a woman who has multiple orgasms, Line B a woman who does not experience orgasm, and Line C a woman who has a single orgasm.

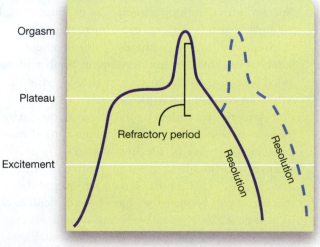

(a) The male sexual response cycle

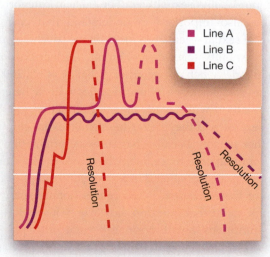

(b) The female sexual response cycle

female physicians, psychologists, and medical students judged whether each description came from a male or female. The judges were no better than chance at guessing the gender of the authors, and neither female nor male judges were any better than the other at guessing (Vance & Wagner, 1976). This outcome suggests that, to some degree, males and females have similar subjective experiences during orgasm.

Although sexual activity involves the whole body, researchers have also focused on brain activity in women who experienced orgasm while being monitored by functional magnetic resonance imaging (fMRI) (Komisaruk et al., 2006). Stimulation of the breasts, nipples, and vaginal areas causes sensory nerves to send signals to the hypothalamus. The hypothalamus, in turn, stimulates the pituitary gland to release a hormone called *oxytocin*, which plays a role in orgasm and postorgasm physiology. Oxytocin release is associated with, among other things, feelings of physical pleasure and social bonding. Blood levels of oxytocin surge just after orgasm and may remain elevated for at least five minutes, with females releasing higher levels than males (Carmichael et al., 1994; Huynh et al., 2013). In addition, the dopamine-rich reward centers of the brain become highly active during orgasm (Holstege et al., 2003).

The survey and interview methods discussed to this point have provided a rich set of data about human sexuality. Other researchers have approached this topic from a biological standpoint by looking at the physiological and brain basis of sexual motivation and behavior.

Variations in Sexual Orientation

Sexual orientation *is a consistent preference for sexual relations with members of the opposite sex (heterosexuality), same sex (homosexuality), or either sex (bisexuality).* As Kinsey pointed out decades ago, sexual orientation is probably best described as a continuum between pure homosexuality and pure heterosexuality rather than in categorical terms. It is also important to understand that current definitions of sexual orientation focus on the psychological aspects of sexuality (e.g., desire, emotion, identification) rather than strictly behavioral criteria (Bailey et al., 2000). This means that someone who identifies with a heterosexual orientation will have feelings of attraction for the opposite sex, even if they never have any sexual contact with another person. Because heterosexual orientation is the most common preference, many have asked why some people prefer emotional and sexual relationships with members of the same sex. What causes homosexuality? If you think about that question, however, you might see where assumptions about normality come into play— people rarely ask, "What causes heterosexuality?" Perhaps we should ask what causes individuals to experience a

Sexual orientation is not exclusively determined by patterns of sexual behavior. It also includes aspects of identity and emotional connection. Scientists are discovering that sexual orientation is an outcome of complex gene and environmental interactions.

sexual orientation in the first place. We can confidently conclude that variations in sexual orientation do not arise from conscious choices, but there still remain questions how the interplay between biology and environment influences sexual orientation.

SEXUAL ORIENTATION AND THE BRAIN Scientists have taken several approaches to examining the brain basis of sexual orientation, usually by comparing brains of people who self-identify as homosexual or heterosexual (Savic et al., 2010). First, they have used imaging technology to see if structures of the human brain, especially those involved in sexual behavior such as the hypothalamus, differ between homosexual and heterosexual people. Scientists have also used functional brain imaging to see whether actual brain activity differs. Like heterosexual behavior, homosexual behavior is found in nonhuman species, providing opportunities to examine actual brain tissue and also to perform experimental manipulations on hormones during early phases of development to test the effects they have on the developing brain and behavior once sexual maturity is reached (Roselli et al., 2011). So what has come of this work?

An early and widely touted study conducted by Simon LeVay showed that, on average, homosexual men had a smaller subregion of the hypothalamus, a brain region known to be involved in sexual motivation (LeVay, 1991; see Figure 11.7). Scientists have been skeptical of LeVay's results, in part because they have been difficult to replicate (Lasco et al., 2002) and also because of the overlap in size of the hypothalamus between heterosexual and homosexual men also evident in Figure 11.7. In addition, it is not

Figure 11.7 Sexual Orientation and the Brain

An early study of the brain basis of sexual orientation found that homosexual males had a smaller subregion (INAH3) of the hypothalamus within the medial preoptic area (LeVay, 1991).

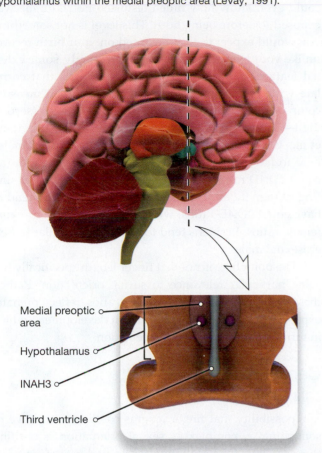

Medial preoptic area

Hypothalamus

INAH3

Third ventricle

clear why minor variations in hypothalamus size would relate to sexual orientation. Finally, some of the homosexual men whom LeVay studied died of complications associated with HIV, which was not true for the heterosexual men. Thus, the HIV, and not sexual orientation per se, could have accounted for the differences in their brains. Although Levay's results were not definitive, his original conclusions about the hypothalamus have received support from more modern work, and his study stimulated considerable scientific curiosity and debate about links between the brain and sexual orientation. Subsequent research has shown that differences in sexual orientation are associated with the size of the amygdalae (structures related to emotional responses; Savic & Lindström, 2008) and the thickness of several major regions of the cortex (Abé et al., 2014). As we will see, it may be that early hormonal influences on the developing brain, going all the way back to the prenatal environment, play a role in these differences.

In addition to differences in brain structure, the brain's functioning can differ according to one's sexual orientation. Brain imaging studies have shown that sexual stimuli elicit different patterns of brain activity in homosexual and heterosexual people. In one study, homosexual men and heterosexual women showed greater activation of the medial preoptic area of the hypothalamus while smelling a male derivative of testosterone found in sweat. This brain region, which is involved in sexual behavior

There is a popular misconception that homosexual behavior is "unnatural" and that it is only a human behavior. However, homosexual behavior has been reported in many different nonhuman species, such as bonobo chimpanzees, koala bears, bottlenose dolphins, and sheep. In fact, researchers have found that 8% to 10% of rams show preferences for mounting other rams, and the most obvious difference researchers have found between male-preferring and female-preferring rams is a smaller region of the hypothalamus in the former (Roselli et al., 2004).

in many different species, including humans, did not become activated when heterosexual men smelled male sweat (Savic et al, 2005). Homosexual males and heterosexual females show greater activity in the brain's reward centers when viewing pictures of genitalia of sexually aroused males. The same pattern of brain activity is found in homosexual women and heterosexual men viewing pictures of female genitalia (Ponseti et al., 2006). These findings may not provide the final answer about the brain basis of sexual orientation, but they do indicate that differences in sexual motivation are based on differences in specific patterns of brain activity. To understand the source of those differences, we should examine how the brain develops.

Working the Scientific Literacy Model

Hormones and Sexual Orientation

Starting in the prenatal environment, hormones impact the development of the brain. It may be that variations in sexual orientation are related to hormonal influences on the brain at this early stage. Scientists have tested this hypothesis in both animal subjects and humans.

What do we know about hormones and sexual orientation?

Testosterone *is a steroid hormone present in both males and females,* albeit typically at higher levels in males, and is known to influence sexual behavior in two main ways. First, surges in testosterone are associated with elevated sexual arousal in both sexes, and second, testosterone has long-term effects on sexual development.

Researchers have long noted that prenatal hormone levels influence sex-specific behavior and sexual preferences in nonhuman species (Morris et al., 2004). During human development—and in particular during the second and fifth months of pregnancy, when the fetal brain is developing rapidly—the amount of testosterone the fetus encounters influences behavior later in life. An excess amount of testosterone results in boys who are more masculine; if the fetus is female, high testosterone exposure is associated with an increased chance of showing male typical behavior, and sometimes homosexual orientation. Low circulating levels of testosterone during prenatal development results in behaviors that are seen as more typically female, whether the fetus is genetically female or male. Males exposed to low prenatal testosterone levels are more likely to identify with feminine pursuits and show homosexual preferences (Rahman, 2005).

How can scientists study hormones and sexual orientation?

One detail you may be wondering about is how anyone could even know how much testosterone he or she was exposed to before being born. This level is not something you would expect to find recorded on your birth record, unlike your length and weight. Interestingly, some external features can be measured in adulthood that correlate with prenatal testosterone exposure. One measure compares the relative length of the index finger (second digit—2D) and ring finger (fourth digit—4D) (Manning et al., 1998; Grimbos et al., 2010). Heterosexual females tend to have index and ring fingers of equal length (an equal 2D:4D ratio). Heterosexual males have longer ring fingers than index fingers. On average, gay males tend to have equal 2D:4D ratios, which aligns with heterosexual female ratios. Lesbians tend to have ratios similar to heterosexual males.

The point here is not that finger length specifically has some particular relevance to sexual orientation. Rather, these differences in finger length ratios reflect prenatal exposure to testosterone during brain development, which in turn may influence sexual orientation.

Can we critically evaluate this finding?

The possibility that finger lengths could be indicative of something as complex as sexual orientation is exciting to researchers who are interested in understanding what leads people toward different sexual preferences. Sexual orientation is a complex aspect of human (and nonhuman) behavior. Nonetheless, most researchers of 2D:4D ratios use a categorical (either–or) approach by identifying participants as either heterosexual or homosexual. Remember, as described in Table 11.2, psychologists since Kinsey's time have viewed sexual orientation as ranging on a continuum, rather than an absolute either–or category. Different results might emerge from sexual orientation research if a continuous—rather than categorical—measure of sexual orientation is used (Kraemer et al., 2006). Also, as discussed in Module 2.1, being able to replicate research results is a critical component of the scientific process. Not all research on finger length ratios suggests that heterosexual and homosexual people differ in this measure (Grimbos et al., 2010).

Why is this relevant?

Many common beliefs remain about why people are homosexual, and many of these beliefs are entirely erroneous, if not potentially harmful. An example is the belief that homosexuality is a choice and, therefore, can be changed. In reality, there are no valid scientific data to back this claim. Biologically informed ideas about how homosexuality arises provide a more complete, accurate picture, and give society the necessary perspective for better understand sexual minorities.

GENETICS AND SEXUAL ORIENTATION Sexual orientation may be associated with a unique combination of genes. There is a higher genetic correlation for homosexuality between identical twins compared with fraternal twin pairs. Correlations ranging between 0.30 and 0.60 for homosexuality have been reported for both men and women, suggesting that approximately half of the individual differences found in sexual orientation are the result of genetic factors (Figure 11.8; Bailey & Pillard, 1995; Bailey et al., 1993; Kirk et al., 2000). This result tends to hold true for gay men across multiple studies. In contrast, the research is inconsistent when it comes to females; studies have also failed to find a heritable component to homosexuality in women (Bailey et al., 2000; Långström et al., 2010). As we have learned, genetic correlational studies do not tell us which specific genes are associated with a trait. Attempts to identify the actual genes related to homosexuality have yielded mixed results, but scientists have identified a particular region comprising several genes on the eighth and the sex-linked X chromosome that *may* be a genetic marker for homosexuality in men (Sanders et al., 2015; see also Rice et al., 1999).

In summary, genes appear to play at least some role in sexual orientation, but particularly for men. However, this statement does not mean that sexual orientation is *determined* by genetics. The nervous and endocrine systems are remarkably sensitive to the environment, and they interact with a variety of sociocultural factors (Meston & Ahrold, 2010). In Module 3.1 we introduced the term *epigenetics*, which involves environmental triggering of on and off switches that guide the expression of genes. In the case of sexual orientation, it may be that epigenetic processes involving the interplay between prenatal hormones and developing brain anatomy account for where people find themselves on the continuum of sexual orientation (Ngun & Vilain, 2014).

From a scientific perspective it is relatively safe to say that cultural influences have a meager effect, at best,

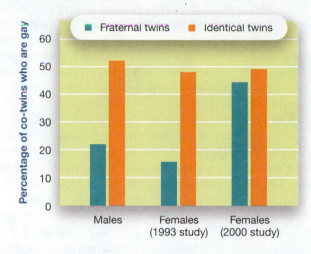

Figure 11.8 Genetics and Sexual Orientation
Twin studies tend to show consistently higher genetic correlations for sexual orientation between male identical twins compared to fraternal twins. This finding indicates that male homosexuality has a genetic basis. Results of studies comparing female identical and fraternal twins are not as consistent.

on sexual orientation. There are more homosexual people in urban areas than in rural regions, probably because homosexual people are more likely to settle in urban areas. Students who attend same-sex schools are more likely to have homosexual experiences than students in mixed-sex schools, but this does not increase the likelihood of a homosexual orientation when students from same-sex schools reach adulthood (Wellings et al., 1994). Moreover, young males of the Sambia tribe in New Guinea are required to engage in sexual acts with adult males, but this practice does not appear to be associated with increases in either homosexual or heterosexual orientation in adulthood (Bailey, 2003). In all likelihood, complex gene–environment interactions determine sexual orientation, and purely environmental or cultural explanations are insufficient explanations for its development.

JOURNAL PROMPT

Understanding Sexuality: Why do you think researchers seek to understand biological factors underlying homosexuality? How is what you read relevant to questions about nature and nurture?

Myths in Mind

Sex After 60?

Living in a culture that emphasizes youth can make it difficult to talk about—or even think about—the sexual lives of older people. Sex often seems like something that only younger people care about, starting with the surge of hormones in adolescence and lasting until parenthood. Recent years, however, have brought us a wave of advertisements showing older couples discussing sexual intimacy. Because sexuality is such an important part of life, it is worth asking what happens to sex and sexuality as people age.

In one survey (Lindau et al., 2007), almost three-fourths of the 57- to 64-year-old respondents reported sexual contact with a partner in the past year, as did half of the 64- to 75-year-olds and one-fourth of the respondents between ages 75 and 85. Sexuality does not always require a partner: Almost half of the men and one-fourth of the women in the survey reported masturbating within the past year.

Does sexuality decline in the senior years? It seems that for many people, it does. Nevertheless, these data clearly show that many seniors remain sexually active into their 80s. This sexuality is not without problems; approximately 40% of women in the survey cited lack of desire as a problem, and almost the same percentage of men reported erectile problems.

Research confirms that many senior adults remain sexually active.

Module 11.2 Summary

11.2a   Know . . . the key terminology associated with sexual motivation:

libido
refractory period
sexual orientation
sexual response cycle
testosterone

11.2b   Understand . . . similarities and differences in sexual responses in men and women.

The similarities in sexual response cycles found in men and women can be explained by a common reproductive physiology in both sexes. However, males experience a distinct phase called the *refractory period*, during which erection or orgasm are not physiologically possible. The hormone oxytocin is released following orgasm, with higher levels occurring in women.

11.2c   Apply . . . information from surveys to understand your own views of sexuality.

Learning about the psychological, social, and biological basis of sexual motivation can be eye opening. Typically, the topic either remains private, or when sex becomes rel-

evant to our lives we may tend not to think of it in scientific terms. Each individual has their own beliefs and attitudes about sex—you had an opportunity to measure and compare your own thoughts in the Attitudes Toward Sex Survey (Table 11.3). Perhaps reading this module influenced how you answered, or will answer if you have not yet taken the survey.

11.2d   Analyze . . . different explanations for what determines sexual orientation.

Several lines of evidence point to biological factors contributing to homosexuality. For example, small differences in brain anatomy are observed between homosexual and heterosexual males. Exposure to testosterone in the prenatal environment may contribute to homosexual orientation as well; homosexuality has been attributed to low testosterone levels during prenatal development in males and exposure to higher than normal levels of testosterone for homosexual females. Also, twin studies indicate that homosexuality has a significant genetic component, particularly in males. These findings point to biological factors interacting with environmental ones.

Module 11.2 Quiz

Know . . .

1. _____ refers to one's motivation for sexual behavior and pleasure.
   - **A.** Libido
   - **B.** Excitement
   - **C.** Orgasm
   - **D.** Cybersex

2. In what order do the phases of the sexual response cycle occur?
   - **A.** plateau, orgasm, resolution, excitement
   - **B.** excitement, plateau, orgasm, and resolution
   - **C.** orgasm, resolution, excitement, plateau
   - **D.** excitement, orgasm, resolution, plateau

Understand . . .

3. The male sexual response cycle includes a(n) _____ during which erection and orgasm are not physically possible, whereas the female sexual response cycle most often does not.
   - **A.** plateau
   - **B.** refractory period
   - **C.** oxytocin release
   - **D.** sensitive period

Apply . . .

4. Based on results from surveys about people's motivation for sex, it can be concluded that:
   - **A.** there is not much of a relationship between the biological and psychological basis for having sex.
   - **B.** people only have sex for one or two reasons.
   - **C.** sexual activity ends at old age.
   - **D.** reasons why people report having sex are highly varied.

Analyze . . .

5. Brain differences between homosexual and heterosexual adults should be interpreted as:
   - **A.** a result of both genetic and environmental factors.
   - **B.** due solely to inherited, genetic differences.
   - **C.** proof that the brain structure between homosexual men and heterosexual women is identical.
   - **D.** due solely to environmental factors.

Module 11.3 Social and Achievement Motivation

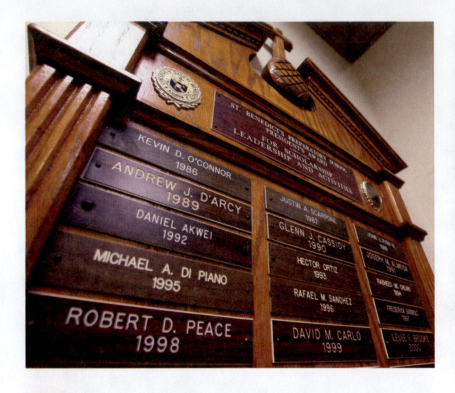

Learning Objectives

11.3a Know . . . the key terminology of social and achievement motivation.

11.3b Understand . . . how thoughts about mortality can motivate people.

11.3c Apply . . . theories of motivation to understand your personal motivation to achieve in school or your career.

11.3d Analyze . . . claims that a sense of belonging is something people need versus something they want.

The need for interpersonal relationships and the motivation to achieve can be both powerful and, at times, very much at odds with each other. Just how strong and how conflicted these motives can be is especially evident in the life story of Robert Peace, who grew up among poverty and drugs in New Jersey. His father was imprisoned for double murder during his childhood and his mother worked multiple jobs to keep Robert fed and enrolled at the private school she moved him to so that his remarkable and unique mind could be nurtured. Peace earned straight As and academic honors at St. Benedict's academy and was admitted to Yale University, where he earned a degree in molecular biology and biophysics. He might sound like the

bookish type who preferred to be in the laboratory or alone reading and studying in his room. However, all through his childhood and college years he developed and nurtured close friendships and he was actively involved in sports. His motivation to achieve and to belong is what drew so many people to him. Tragically, both during, and especially after, his time at Yale, Peace gravitated toward the life his mother and teachers had worked so hard to get him out of. His need to be around others and to belong did not waver, but he had no inclination to continue achieving academically. He took a job with a major airline shuttling luggage and guiding airplanes; not a typical career path for a Yale graduate. It was later discovered that

Peace had been using this job to distribute and deal drugs to different regions. His downward turn toward heavy drug use and dealing, and away from a bright future in the career of his choice, ended tragically when he was gunned down one day while walking out of a friend's house (pictured on previous page). Where did Robert go wrong? The answer may lie in the conflict between his motivation to belong and his motivation to achieve, two topics we'll explore next.

The Need to Belong

Everyone acknowledges that humans require satisfaction of at least a few basic needs for survival, such as adequate food, water, clothing, and shelter. The basic needs that keep the body functioning are fundamental for all species. Other necessities also exist, beginning with the need to have meaningful social relationships and continuing with uniquely human needs for self-esteem and self-actualization (discovering and achieving purpose in life).

Figure 11.9 shows how psychologist Abraham Maslow (1943) conceived of this increasing complexity of motivational needs. At the base of the "hierarchy of needs" are physiological motives that must be satisfied before all others are considered. After these needs are addressed, an individual may turn to higher-level needs such as the need for love and belonging, self-esteem, and achievement. Researchers have explored how and why we are motivated to become affiliated with others, but it was not until recently that psychologists have begun to treat this issue as a "fundamental need to belong"—a need as basic as nourishment and protection (Baumeister & Leary, 1995).

The **need to belong** *(sometimes known as affiliation motivation) is the motivation to maintain relationships that involve pleasant feelings such as warmth, affection, appreciation, and mutual concern for each person's well-being.* In addition, an individual must have the sense that these feelings are part of a permanent relationship, such as a friendship, kinship, or shared group membership (Baumeister & Leary, 1995). A strong sense of belonging brings more than warmth and happiness; it appears to be fundamental in the same way that food and shelter are needs—all are things that humans cannot survive without.

Although we all probably want to have pleasant interactions, it is the second part of the definition—a sense of permanence—that emphasizes the type of needs we have. Specifically, an individual who has many positive social interactions with a series of different individuals does not enjoy the same satisfaction and other benefits as an individual who interacts with only a few people, but regularly and for a long period of time. For example, an executive

Figure 11.9 Maslow's Hierarchy

According to Abraham Maslow, human needs are organized as a hierarchy, with basic needs at the bottom, and personal fulfillment and other uniquely human characteristics at the top.

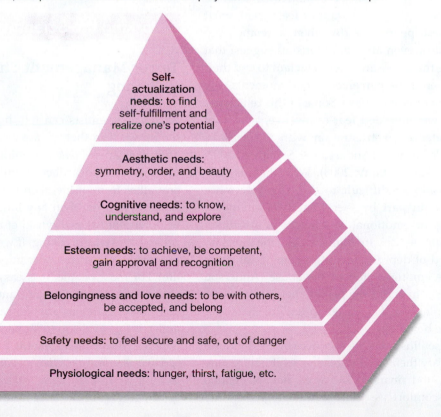

who flies all over the continent may have fascinating conversations with fellow passengers every week, yet feel extremely lonely. Meanwhile, imagine a couple living on a rural farm who see only a few neighbors during the week and participate in church on weekends. The permanence of their family, community, and church is significant, and they will probably be much more satisfied with their sense of belongingness over the long run.

Psychologists have found that social connectedness is a good predictor of overall health, whereas loneliness is a risk factor for illnesses such as heart disease and cancer (Cacioppo et al., 2003). Loneliness elevates a person's risk for having hypertension, a weaker immune system, and high levels of stress hormones. This relationship holds true even when lonely and nonlonely individuals have the same amount of social interaction; it is the sense of belonging that counts (Hawkley et al., 2003). Even simple indicators such as living alone or an individual's rating of the statement "I feel lonely" predict chances of survival after heart attacks and bypass surgeries (Herlitz et al., 1998; Rozanski et al., 1999). Most people now accept that cigarette smoking has severe direct effects on health, but few recognize that loneliness is equally good at predicting one's life expectancy (House, et al., 1988).

The need to belong is evident from the great lengths to which people go to form and maintain relationships. Generally, friendships and romantic relationships have their foundations in warm feelings and mutual attraction, so we might be tempted to say that people maintain relationships because they are positive experiences. But consider this point: If humans are motivated to form bonds because belonging is pleasant or feels good, what should we expect people to do when a relationship turns unpleasant or even abusive? Statistics suggest that people receiving the abuse are often reluctant to end their relationships, even if the perceived "good moments" are interspersed with ongoing abuse. Some of this reluctance is explained by well-founded fear of revenge, a sense of financial dependence, or frustration with the services that are available to help (Anderson & Saunders, 2003; Grauwiler, 2008; Kim & Gray, 2008). Why, then, is ending the relationship so difficult to do? This reluctance can be explained in part by the strength of emotional bonds. Breaking an emotional attachment is a difficult and painful thing to do. In many cases, the breakup involves a period of depression and psychological stress that exceeds the emotional toll of the abuse (Anderson & Saunders, 2003). In short, the need to belong can be so strong that people find it is easier to endure the abuse than to break the bond.

Parenting also illustrates the sacrifices that individuals will make to satisfy their need to belong. Children require personal, social, and financial sacrifices, not to mention the physical discomfort associated with pregnancy and

The stresses of parenting can actually lead an individual to report lower levels of happiness. However, having children remains one of the most celebrated aspects of adult life.

delivery. Parenthood does not provide the health benefits of other types of relationships, and it can be associated with higher levels of emotional distress and depression and lower levels of marital satisfaction, at least while children are young (e.g., Evenson & Simon, 2005; Umberson et al., 2010). Despite these inconveniences and the associated emotions, having children is one of the most celebrated aspects of adult life in many cultures—thanks in large part to the need to belong.

The power of our need to belong is also evident when our survival and well-being are threatened—or even when just reminded that they *could* be threatened.

Working the Scientific Literacy Model

Terror Management Theory and the Need to Belong

As far as scientists can tell, humans are unique among life on earth in that we are aware of our own mortality. This realization creates a uniquely human problem that one researcher described bluntly: If humans are just like any other form of life, then we "may be no more significant or enduring than any individual potato, pineapple, or porcupine" (Pyszczynski et al., 2004, p. 436). This is a provocative way of asking, If we all must die, what makes humans think we are more important than other forms of life? For most people, it is easy to answer this question: Our personal identities, our family and friends, a sense of spiritual or religious purpose, and a sense of nationalism and patriotism distinguish us from pineapples and porcupines. **Terror management theory** *is a psychological perspective asserting that the human fear of mortality motivates behavior, particularly those that preserve self-esteem and sense of belonging.*

What do we know about terror management theory?

Life-threatening experiences certainly are terrifying and emotional. However, we can maintain a sense of calm in our lives because we use *anxiety buffers*—concepts and beliefs that prevent death-related anxiety. These elements include a worldview, such as religious and political beliefs, and a sense of self-esteem. Thus, the thought of death is a motivation to belong to something more enduring and much larger than oneself. We can rely on spiritual or religious purpose, the future generations of family, or the continuation of our native culture or way of life to bolster our sense of self-worth (Maxfield et al., 2014; Pyszczynski et al., 2004).

How can scientists study terror management?

To measure the motivational power of terror management, researchers induce *mortality salience*—an increased awareness of death—with simple reminders. For example, volunteers may write a paragraph or two about what happens when people die, whereas a control group writes about something unpleasant that does not make mortality more apparent (salient), such as the discomfort of a dental root canal. In experiments, simply writing about death is enough to motivate individuals to increasingly defend their own worldview (their spiritual and political beliefs; Weise et al., 2008).

The fact that mortality salience increases defensiveness is one thing, but perhaps even more interesting are the tactics that psychologists have used to reduce the impact of mortality salience. For example, when psychologists followed the mortality salience stimulus by asking participants to think positive thoughts about their parents, the effects of the mortality salience disappeared (Cox et al., 2008). This and other related experimental procedures suggest that belonging to something more permanent—a family, a community, or a religion—really does help manage death-related anxiety.

Can we critically evaluate this evidence?

When mortality salience research began two decades ago, many critics questioned whether it was really thoughts of death that created these experimental effects, or whether the effects simply represented a reaction to the unpleasantness of the study materials. Terror management theorists quickly responded by pointing out that the same effects do not arise among members of control groups who have been exposed to unpleasant stimuli ranging from dental pain to the anxiety of public speaking. Perhaps just as convincing is the fact that a recent meta-analysis of 277 studies confirmed that responses to mortality salience can be reliably produced in the laboratory (Burke et al., 2010).

Why is this relevant?

Mortality salience is not a temporary effect occurring only in the context of laboratory experiments. For example, US voters receiving mortality salience treatments were more likely than others to support President George W. Bush's invasion of Iraq during his 2004 bid for reelection (Cohen et al., 2005), and more willing to accept civilian casualties in ongoing wars (Pyszczynski et al., 2006). Mortality salience also influences major life decisions such as financial planning. People are more likely to choose to save money for the future than spend it when confronted with their own mortality (Zaleskiewicz et al., 2013).

JOURNAL PROMPT

Mortality Salience: Now that you have learned about mortality salience, describe an example from your own experience that seems to support terror management theory. Before answering, think about how your experience might have influenced how you view your priorities, loved ones, or whether there was a change in how you think and behave.

Achievement Motivation

Achievement motivation *is the drive to perform at high levels and to accomplish significant goals.* It often involves the need to compete with and outperform other individuals. It can be seen in the desire to master a task, with or without other incentives or rewards. Achievement motivation can be observed in a student's approach to school, an entrepreneur's desire to build a business, or an athlete's hopes of winning a gold medal (McClelland, 1985).

If you consider your own experiences, you can probably identify situations in which you feel highly motivated and others that fail to get you going. This is a normal part of motivation, and we see wide variation in the amount and type of motivation people experience. For example, **mastery motives** *are motives that reflect a desire to understand or overcome a challenge* (e.g., a genuine desire to master

This person is clearly procrastinating—there is a good chance that his work is a performance-avoidance goal.

Table 11.4 Motivation to Achieve

An individual's motivation to achieve is a combination of two factors: the desire to master something (versus simply performing) and the desire to gain (approach) or avoid something.

	Mastery: "I want to learn this ... "	Performance: "I just want a good grade"
Approach	... because it's so interesting.	... so they will know how smart I am.
Avoidance	... because I would hate to feel uninformed.	... so I don't look dumb.

a task), whereas **performance motives** *are generally those motives that are geared toward gaining rewards or public recognition.* Another way to contrast motives is to compare approach and avoidance goals. **Approach goals** *are enjoyable and pleasant incentives that we are drawn toward, such as praise or financial reward.* **Avoidance goals** *are unpleasant outcomes such as shame, embarrassment, or emotional pain, which we try to avoid.* If you combine these two perspectives, you will see why some psychologists refer to motivation as a 2 × 2 framework (see Table 11.4; Elliot & McGregor, 2001).

Have you ever found yourself starting a paper the day before it was due? Or studying for a test into the early morning hours rather than starting your preparation a few days earlier? Procrastination relates to the goals in the 2 × 2 achievement framework. Researchers have found that students are most likely to procrastinate when they are working on avoidance goals. Apparently, it is difficult to write a term paper if your only motivation is to avoid failing or appearing unintelligent; these motives are different from actually wanting to write a paper. Procrastination is least likely when mastery and approach goals are combined. When students are genuinely interested in learning about a topic and expect to gain something by completing the project, it is much easier for them to get started right away (Howell & Watson, 2007).

As a student, you have probably experienced all of these motivations, finding some subjects so interesting you

want to learn more (approach, mastery) and others seem so dull that you would never study them if they were not required for a degree (approach, performance). It might be tempting to assume that you can experience only one form of motivation at a time, but that does not seem to be the case (Elliott & Murayama, 2008). There is no reason why you cannot be motivated to learn and simultaneously experience a motivation to finish your degree. To further examine your own motivation to achieve and, if interested, compare with others, complete the activity on Table 11.5.

Cultural upbringing influences the motivation to achieve. Psychologists recruited US-born and East Asian college students who identified themselves as having a low interest in mathematics to participate in a study on achievement motivation. The students read materials about how to use a unique method for computing multiplication problems. Within the instructional materials for the math problems were passages that explained the utility of the technique, including its importance for improving memory and succeeding in graduate school and employment. Half of the participants from each culture participated in this condition, and the second half were assigned to a control group who learned the math technique but did not have the utility of doing so explained to them. All students computed sample problems using the method introduced in the instructional materials and rated whether they found the technique to be useful. The researchers

Table 11.5 Applying Concepts of Achievement Motivation

Thinking about your Psychology course, respond to each statement by assigning a score on a scale of 1 ("Not at all true of me") to 7 ("Very true of me"). Then find your average response for each set of three questions. Compare your scores to the averages for each score.

	Mastery	Performance
Approach	1. I want to learn as much as possible from this class. 2. It is important for me to understand the content of this course as thoroughly as possible. 3. I desire to completely master the material presented in this class. Average score: 5.52	1. It is important for me to do better than other students. 2. It is important for me to do well compared to others in this class. 3. My goal in this class is to get a better grade than most of the other students. Average score: 4.82
Avoidance	1. I worry that I may not learn all that I possibly could in this class. 2. Sometimes I'm afraid that I may not understand the content of this class as thoroughly as possible. 3. I am often concerned that I may not learn all that there is to learn in this class. Average score: 3.89	1. I just want to avoid doing poorly in this class. 2. My goal in this class is to avoid performing poorly. 3. My fear of performing poorly in this class is often what motivates me. Average score: 4.49

SOURCE: Elliot, A. J. & McGregor, H. A. (2001). A 2 × 2 achievement goal framework. *Journal of Personality and Social Psychology, 80,* 501–519.

found that in comparison to US students, East Asian students with little interest in math reported greater interest in learning the task, and they tried harder when told it would be useful for future schooling and employment prospects (Shechter et al., 2011). This is not to imply that Westerners do not value skills that will help them succeed. In fact, this same group of researchers found that US students found the math technique to be more valuable if it helped with more immediate demands, such as managing finances and measuring ingredients.

Module **11.3** Summary

11.3a   Know . . . the key terminology of social and achievement motivation:

achievement motivation
approach goals
avoidance goals
mastery motives
need to belong
performance motives
terror management theory

11.3b   Understand . . . how thoughts about mortality can motivate people.

Terror management theory explains that the threat of death can motivate people to become more religious and patriotic and to bolster their self-esteem. This effect can be seen in a number of studies showing that participants have a more favorable disposition toward their own groups and a more negative attitude toward outsiders.

11.3c   Apply . . . theories of motivation to understand your personal motivation to achieve in school or your career.

The activity Applying Concepts of Achievement Motivation asked you to evaluate what motivates your academic work (Table 11.5). However, you hopefully appreciate that the 2 × 2 framework encompassing mastery-performance and approach-avoidance dimensions applies to any endeavor that taps into your motivation to achieve.

11.3d   Analyze . . . claims that a sense of belonging is something people need versus something they want.

Although belonging may not be the most basic need on Maslow's hierarchy—those positions are usually assigned to food, water, and shelter—it is a significant need nonetheless. Research has shown that doing without has some drastic consequences. Not only is loneliness related to depression, but it is also associated with a reduced life span. The fact that belonging is essential to good health and longevity provides strong support for classifying it as a need, not just something people want.

Module **11.3** Quiz

Know ...

1. If a student is a pre-med major because she is curious about how the body works and how it recovers from disease, psychologists would say that she has _____ motives. If the student is studying pre-med because she thinks this major will impress people, then psychologists would say that she has _____ motives.

    A. mastery; performance   **C.** performance; avoidance
    B. performance; mastery   **D.** avoidance; mastery

2. According to _____ theory, motivation to connect with others can stem from reminders that life will not go on forever.

    A. achievement   **C.** approach-avoidance
    B. affiliation   **D.** terror management

Understand ...

3. What happens when researchers induce mortality salience using essay writing procedures?

    A. Participants motivation states are not changed.
    B. Participants are increasingly motivated to defend their own worldview.
    C. Participants decrease their sense of attachment to their families.
    D. Participants are motivated to change their perceptions of death.

Apply ...

4. If you are studying math problems because you really want to win an award, psychologists would say you have _____ goals; if you are just hoping that you do not get the lowest score in the class, you are exhibiting _____ goals.

    A. avoidance; approach
    B. approach; mastery
    C. approach; avoidance
    D. approach; mastery

Analyze ...

5. What point did Maslow intend to communicate when he placed love and belonging in the middle of his hierarchy of needs?

    A. Individuals generally must take care of physiological needs first, but must satisfy love and belonging needs before developing healthy self-esteem.
    B. Love and belonging are not essential human needs.
    C. Individuals generally must first have a healthy self-esteem before they can satisfy love and belonging needs.
    D. Love and belonging are more important than physiological needs.

Module 11.4 Emotion

Learning Objectives

11.4a Know . . . the key terminology associated with emotion.

11.4b Understand . . . different theories of emotion.

11.4c Apply . . . your knowledge of theories of emotion.

11.4d Analyze . . . evidence for and against the use of lie detector tests.

One day, 18-year-old John Sharon and his girlfriend went on a drinking binge and wound up in the Arizona desert. There, Sharon experienced a series of violent seizures. He finally managed to call home for help, but by the time his father arrived, something had changed; Sharon was beginning to think he was God. No, he was not mentally ill, despite what was presumably a period of delusional thinking. Instead, physicians diagnosed him with temporal lobe epilepsy (TLE).

As neuroscientist V. S. Ramachandran describes it, TLE is a disorder that involves massive neural misfiring within the temporal lobe. This condition often affects the brain's limbic system, which is known to contribute to the experience of emotions. In essence, Ramachandran believes that Sharon's epileptic episode jolted a portion of his brain that

allows him to experience intense joy. Apparently, the jolt is stronger than a typical brain would ever create, so Sharon interprets his emotional experiences as beautiful, intense, and deeply spiritual. Just talking about the feelings can actually bring tears to his eyes. Also, rather than perceiving TLE as a disabling condition, Sharon feels sorry for people who cannot share his experiences.

It turns out that John Sharon is not alone. Many people have experienced this profound emotional response following TLE seizures and, curiously, they tend to describe them in religious or spiritual terms. These experiences offer insight into the workings of the emotional brain and reveal that our emotional experiences are influenced by how we interpret external events and the internal physiological reactions they elicit.

Like many well-known psychological terms, emotion is challenging to define scientifically. We will follow common convention in psychology and define **emotion** *as a psychological experience involving three components: (1) subjective thoughts and experiences with (2) accompanying patterns of physical arousal and (3) characteristic behavioral expressions.* For example, anger may involve thoughts and feelings of frustration, aggravation, and possibly ill will. Anger is accompanied by increased heart rate and is expressed with clenched teeth and fists, or tightly pursed lips and a pinched brow. Each of our different emotions is accompanied by characteristic experiences, expressions, and physiological reactions. In this module we explore biological, psychological, and sociocultural influences on our emotional experiences and expressions.

Children who are born both deaf and blind show the same facial expressions and emotions as people who see and hear. This is one of many pieces of evidence that our emotions have a strong, biological basis.

Many of our emotional experiences come from hard-wired responses, and some basic ones such as anger and happiness appear across the human spectrum. See if you can make a prediction: If facial expressions are universal to all humans, which kinds of expressions would you expect to see on the faces of people who have been blind and deaf since birth or very early in life? Would they have the same basic expressions as everyone else, despite the fact that they have never seen a smile or frown, and never heard laughter or crying? As you can see from the photo, it appears that they do. Because these individuals have not seen or heard these expressions before, it is likely that at least basic expressions for emotions such as happiness, sadness, anger, surprise, fear, and disgust are biologically hard-wired, rather than something learned from watching others.

Biology of Emotion

Our emotions involve a complex interplay of physiological processes. Many of our emotional reactions involve the autonomic nervous system (ANS; see Module 3.3), which

conveys information between the spinal cord and the blood vessels, glands, and smooth muscles of the body. The ANS maintains processes such as heart rate, respiration, and digestion, which, as you have almost certainly experienced, are also affected by emotional events. Both the ANS and specialized regions of the brain are interconnected in complex ways, giving rise to our *experience* of emotion.

THE AUTONOMIC RESPONSE: FIGHT OR FLIGHT? Let's examine two situations that might provoke fear. First, imagine you are taking a peaceful walk and suddenly encounter a charging, snarling dog. The physiological aspect of this emotional experience would involve a division of the ANS called the *sympathetic nervous system,* which generally increases your energy and alertness to enable you to handle frightening or dangerous situations— that is, it activates the fight-or-flight response. This sudden burst of energy involves increased heart rate, respiration, sweat, and alertness. To fuel this response, the sympathetic nervous system draws energy away from bodily functions that can wait until the end of an emergency, such as immune responses and sexual arousal (see Figure 11.10).

Now imagine a giant auditorium where you are about to give a speech. You may feel anxiety building as audience members trickle in. This situation bears no resemblance to facing down a charging dog, yet your sympathetic nervous system produces many of the same effects. These two scenarios illustrate that similar physiological responses apply to life-threatening situations as well as those that are merely perceived as threatening, such as public speaking.

Once you finish the speech, or when you realize that the dog is tethered to a tree out of reach, you will most likely feel the calming effects regulated by another division of the ANS called the *parasympathetic nervous system.* The parasympathetic nervous system typically uses energy more sparingly, bringing your heart rate and respiration back to resting rates and focusing on nonemergency tasks, such as digestion (Figure 11.10). See the fight-or-flight response in action in the following animation, The Visual Brain: Stress and Health.

Watch THE VISUAL BRAIN: STRESS AND HEALTH

Figure 11.10 The Autonomic Nervous System and Emotional Responding

The ANS is involved in emotional responding. The sympathetic division prepares the body to respond to stress, and the parasympathetic division restores the body to normal conditions.

Parasympathetic		Sympathetic
Pupils constricted	Eyes	Pupils dilated
Salivating	Mouth	Dry
No goose bumps	Skin	Goose bumps
Dry	Palms	Sweaty
Constricted passages	Lungs	Dilated passages
Decreased rate	Heart	Increased rate
Directed toward internal organs and muscles	Blood	Directed to muscles
Decreased activity	Adrenal glands	Increased activity
Stimulated	Digestion	Inhibited

The physiological responses we have described thus far mostly apply to what occurs below the neck. This certainly does not diminish their psychological importance; activity in the ANS has actually been regarded as sufficient evidence to determine whether someone is being truthful or is lying. In other words, these responses serve as a primary measure used in the polygraph.

The polygraph measures physiological arousal during a series of questions, some of which are worded specifically to detect whether the subject is lying. But are these devices reliable means of lie detection?

EMOTION AND DECEPTION The polygraph measures respiration, blood pressure, and palm sweat, which are responses of the ANS. It is also called a "lie detector" when referring to one application of it because these responses are thought to increase when someone lies. Most US courts do not accept polygraph results as valid evidence. Regardless, the system is used in some situations, such as when evaluating statements made by convicted sex offenders, in divorce cases, and occasionally in employee screening and evaluation. Although many support its use, controlled studies of polygraph recordings suggest that they provide evidence of arousal (that is what they are designed to do), but they are not valid indicators of lying (Iacono, 2001; Saxe, 1994).

Some researchers are turning to brain imaging in their search for a more reliable lie detection method (Simpson, 2008). Activity in regions of the frontal and parietal lobes increase when subjects are being deceptive, compared to when they tell the truth. In some studies, patterns of brain activity have been used to discriminate false from true statements 78% of the time (Langleben et al., 2005). That level is not perfect, of course, but it suggests this technology is potentially more reliable than the polygraph.

A comparatively inexpensive method of detecting deception is to examine facial expressions and other non-verbal cues. Paul Ekman and his colleagues found that federal officers and judges, sheriffs, and psychologists are able to detect deception at greater-than-chance levels, and with interest and experience, some individuals seem to be better at spotting lies (Ekman, et al., 1999). In fact, Ekman has shown that people can be trained to detect the subtle nonverbal "microexpressions" indicative of lying. A guilty person might betray herself with a brief and very subtle furrowing of the brow, a microexpressive sign of distress, the moment the lie is told.

The meaning behind facial expressions changes with subtle modifications. For example, one version of smiling is genuine, while another is reserved for social graces. Can you tell which is which from this photo? Psychologist Paul Ekman (pictured) has discovered many nuances in our facial "microexpressions."

THE EMOTIONAL BRAIN: PERCEPTION AND ACTION
Along with responses governed by the ANS, our emotional experiences involve several brain areas, some of which were mentioned in the story that opened this module. For example, the limbic system is critical to emotional processing. It includes the hippocampus, hypothalamus, amygdala, and various cortical regions (also described in Module 3.3).

The *amygdala* is of particular interest to scientists who study emotion. It is involved in assessing and interpreting situations to determine which types of emotions are appropriate. Also, it seems to connect the perception or interpretation of these situations to brain regions that stimulate the physiological responses required for action (Feldman Barrett & Wager, 2006; Sergerie et al., 2008). For example, the amygdala is active when we view threatening stimuli or situations, such as an angry or fearful facial expression. Once a threat is detected, the amygdala stimulates the body into action by sending messages to the sympathetic branch of the ANS, causing increased pulse, respiration, and sweat, as well as by sending messages to motor centers controlling startle or freezing reactions.

Neuroscientists believe that emotional responses such as fear can follow two separate pathways. Sensory information first goes through the thalamus, and then may go directly to the amygdala, which immediately stimulates hormonal and autonomic responses. This route is sometimes called the *fast pathway* because the body is readied for action before the stimulus is even fully perceived and interpreted. Second, the thalamus relays information to the sensory areas of the brain, such as those devoted to vision, which then stimulate the amygdala and physiological responses. This *slow pathway* involves conscious recognition of the stimulus and situation (Figure 11.11). Although it plays a critical role in emotion processing, the amygdala is not the only brain region responsible for our emotions because patients with amygdala damage continue to have emotional reactions (Anderson & Phelps, 2000).

As you know from John Sharon's story at the beginning of the module, emotions other than fear can arise

Figure 11.11 Emotional Pathways in the Brain
The amygdala is a key brain structure in the processing of emotion. Neuroscientist Joseph LeDoux has described both "slow" and "fast" pathways of emotional processing. Fast pathways are routed from sensory areas of the brain through the amygdala and directly to the autonomic nervous system for quick action. The slow pathway is routed through the cortex where the situation is processed at a higher level of awareness.

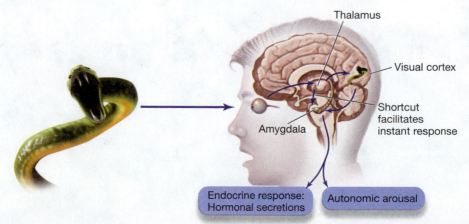

from electrical activity in the brain. The full range of our emotional experiences involves different areas of the cerebral cortex. Generally speaking, people who are prone to depression and more negative emotion tend to have more activity in the right frontal lobe, whereas people who are prone to happiness and positive emotion tend to have more activity in the left frontal lobe (Urry et al., 2004). Each of our complex, primary emotions, such as fear, anger, happiness, and surprise, seems to involve a component of the limbic system. Even so, it is difficult to distinguish each emotion just by looking at brain images of a person experiencing that emotion. Brain imaging studies have shown that our emotions involve regions distributed all over the brain (Barrett & Wager, 2006). Given these details, you probably would not be surprised to find that different forms of epilepsy, other brain diseases, and even brain injuries can lead to changes in emotional processing.

The Psychological Experience of Emotions: Competing Theories

One challenge for psychologists has been to determine the relationship between bodily arousal and the psychological experience of emotion. Imagine you are home alone late at night, and a faint sound comes from the back of the house. Your heart starts to race as you leap from the couch and try to determine whether the noise was just the cat knocking something over, a breeze blowing through an open window, or an intruder breaking into your home. Why did you have this surge of fear and panic? Did the possibility of an intruder cause your heart to race? Or did your racing heart cause you to consider that it could be an intruder? The James-Lange and Cannon-Bard theories of emotion represented early attempts to answer these questions, and both remain relevant to modern-day explanations of our emotions.

THE JAMES-LANGE AND CANNON-BARD THEORIES OF EMOTION According to the **James-Lange theory of emotion**, *our physiological reactions to stimuli (the racing heart) precede and give rise to the emotional experience (the fear)*. Notice that the subjective experience of fear follows the physiological response. The James-Lange theory goes one step further, claiming that your sense of fear is determined by how your body responds. This idea may contradict your own common-sense experiences of emotion. It may seem to make more sense that your subjective sense of fear comes first—your heart races because you feel frightened. Psychologists Walter Cannon and Philip Bard disagreed with the James-Lange theory on the principle that a physiological reaction cannot give rise to an emotion. Our hearts can race in a variety of situations, even when running up a flight of stairs, so this response alone is not enough to create emotions such as surprise, anger, or fear.

An alternative to the James-Lange theory is the **Cannon-Bard theory of emotion**, *which states that emotions such as fear or happiness occur simultaneously with their physiological components* (Figure 11.12). This may sound like common sense to you. Based on your own emotional experiences, it may seem impossible that a physiological reaction could precede awareness of feeling afraid, happy, surprise, or angry. It might seem like common sense that our physiological reactions and awareness of emotional experience occur together. In fact, common sense does not always win out; not all evidence supports the Cannon-Bard theory, either.

Figure 11.12 Competing Theories of Emotion

What is the correct order of events when it comes to emotional experiences? The James-Lange and Cannon-Bard theories differ in their predictions.

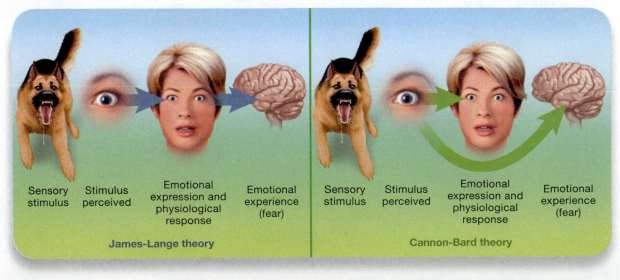

Sensory stimulus — Stimulus perceived — Emotional expression and physiological response — Emotional experience (fear)

James-Lange theory

Sensory stimulus — Stimulus perceived — Emotional expression and physiological response — Emotional experience (fear)

Cannon-Bard theory

The James-Lange theory—that our mental, subjective experiences are influenced by bodily responses that precede them—is consistent with the **facial feedback hypothesis**: *If emotional expressions influence subjective emotional experiences, then the act of forming a facial expression should elicit the specific, corresponding emotion.* In other words, if you are smiling, then you should find things more pleasant. Give this exercise a try: Hold a pencil in your mouth sideways without letting your lips touch it—just your teeth. Research participants who held a pencil in their mouths in this way were essentially smiling whether they meant to or not. As the facial feedback hypothesis predicted, they reported elevated levels of happiness (Strack et al., 1988).

You might argue that the positive emotional experience came from the silliness of holding a pencil in this way. However, psychologists tested a control condition to rule out this hypothesis: They asked participants to hold the pencil in their mouth using only their lips, not letting their teeth come into contact with the pencil. This method naturally produced a sad face and, sure enough, it led to decreased mood (Larsen et al, 1992).

Based on these results, it appears that facial feedback affects some of our emotional responses. Not all emotions are affected by facial feedback, however. Take surprise, for example. Sometimes when you are surprised, your eyes widen, your brows rise, and your jaw drops. But surprise can also be experienced with little facial expression, and researchers have shown that the facial feedback hypothesis is not as applicable to surprise as it is to happiness and sadness (Reisenzein & Studtman, 2007). These findings are inconsistent with the James-Lange theory, which predicts that the facial expression would happen before the emotion is actually felt. Furthermore, people with spinal cord damage may lack the physiological accompaniments of emotions, but they still report feeling emotions as intensely as they did before their injuries (Cobos et al., 2002).

SCHACHTER'S TWO-FACTOR THEORY   To this point, we have considered only subjective and physiological experiences that accompany emotions. In reality, our emotions also involve thoughts, memories, beliefs, and interpretations of experiences. According to Stanley Schachter, these cognitive aspects of emotional experiences are critical. Schachter agreed with James and Lange that our physical reactions give rise to our emotional experiences. However, many different emotions can elicit physical arousal, so our interpretation of why we are aroused is what creates the emotional experience. Schachter's **two-factor theory of emotion** *holds that patterns of physical arousal and the cognitive labels we attach to them form the basis of our emotional experiences* (Figure 11.13). Physical arousal is the first factor to come into play (as James and Lange predict), and along with this state comes a cognitive label

Figure 11.13 Two-Factor Theory

According to Schachter and Singer, emotions are experiences composed of physiological responses and the cognitive labels we give them.

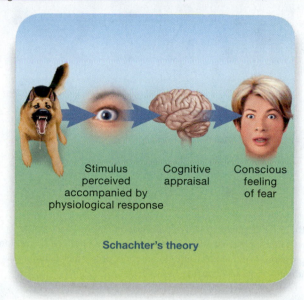

Stimulus perceived accompanied by physiological response

Cognitive appraisal

Conscious feeling of fear

Schachter's theory

for the experience, such as "I am afraid." Combining the two factors, the physical and cognitive, gives rise to the emotional experience of fear.

Schachter's theory gives us a more complete account of emotional experience. John Sharon's case from the beginning of the module illustrates this theory in action: He had a bodily experience (intense brain activity caused by the temporal lobe seizure) that resulted in a euphoric, deeply spiritual experience. Looking around the Arizona desert, he saw no clear reason to feel such bliss, so perhaps he concluded that it must be God. This scenario demonstrates that the label we put on emotional experiences frames how we perceive and interpret the experiences. To illustrate with a more familiar experience, we have all probably appeared stressed, harried, or distracted and had a friend stop to ask "how are you?": After a moment's pause for cognitive appraisal, we attach a label that best describes the emotional state we are in.

The Role of Culture in Emotions

Have you ever traveled to a region where you could not speak the language? If so, you probably found yourself relying on facial expressions and other nonverbal cues to decide whether a local was trustworthy or friendly. Facial expressions probably help a foreign traveler determine who to ask for directions or which vendor to approach or avoid in a market. Cultural psychologists, and almost any world traveler for that matter, have long known that humans show many similar emotional expressions regardless of their language and background. Researchers have ventured

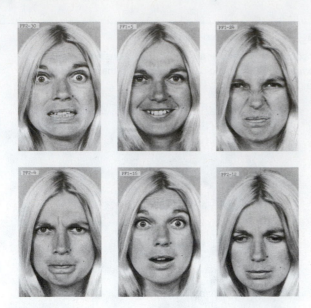

Although this photo spread depicts just one individual, people across many different cultures can accurately identify each emotional expression. Another basic emotion is contempt, which is not as easy to identify from facial expressions.

out into some of the most remote regions of the world and confirmed that humans all recognize basic emotions such as fear, anger, happiness, sadness, surprise, and disgust (Ekman et al., 1987; Elfenbein & Ambady, 2003; Izard, 1994).

Humans have basic, universal ways of expressing some core emotions. Nevertheless, people raised within a specific culture show characteristics that are specific to their region (Elfenbein & Ambady, 2003). Put simply, cultural groups have unique **emotional dialects**—*which are variations across cultures in how common emotions are expressed.* For example, people from North America and from Gabon (a country in West Africa) both experience contempt. However, North Americans are more likely to

Even in the most formal occasions, and even among royalty, it can be impossible to stifle emotions. Web surfers were thrilled to catch England's Prince Harry succumbing to a fit of laughter during this formal state ceremony. What could have been so funny?

lower their brow, and Gabonese people are more likely to raise their upper lip when expressing this emotion.

The situation or context is a major factor in determining when members of different cultures express certain emotions. **Display rules** *refer to the unwritten expectations we have regarding when it is appropriate to show a certain emotion.* Imagine biting into what looks like a delicious chocolate chip cookie that actually turns out to be disgusting. Your expression of disgust would be easily recognized around the world. Now, imagine this event happening in a situation where you are trying to make a good impression—perhaps you are in your instructor's office appealing a grade and he offers you a homemade treat. If it turned out to taste awful, you would likely attempt to inhibit your feeling of disgust. Culture-specific display rules can be found the world over. The British norm of "keeping a stiff upper lip" and the adage "never let them see you sweat" are examples (Elfenbein et al., 2007).

Working the Scientific Literacy Model

Cultural Variations in Emotion Interpretation

Even through cultural and language barriers, people recognize a smile or a frown with relative ease. However, interpreting why someone is smiling or frowning involves the additional step of interpretation, which can differ among cultures.

What do we know about cultural influences on the interpretation of emotions?

Interpreting emotional expressions can be subtle and complex. Certainly each individual person can differ in how they interpret emotions—and differences at the cultural level occur as well. Some cultures may value public expression of emotion, whereas others believe emotions should be expressed privately. Integrating gestures and using emphasis in voice tone may be the norm for some cultures but not others. Furthermore, the function of emotional expressions is to communicate information to someone else. Differences in display rules, emotional dialects, and cultural values can thus lead to differences in the interpretation of emotion.

How can science explain cultural variations in emotion interpretation?

To answer this question, psychologists asked students from both Western and Asian universities to judge the emotion of the central figure in the scenes depicted in

Figure 11.14 Interpreting Social and Emotional Context
How is the man in the middle of these pictures feeling?

Figure 11.14. Western students tended to focus on the facial expression of the central figure. Thus, if the individual was smiling, they would report he was happy, and they did not interpret his happiness with respect to how the surrounding people appeared to feel. In contrast, Asian students interpreted the central figure's emotion in reference to what people in the background might be feeling (Masuda et al., 2008).

The tendency for Asian students to focus on people in the background was further confirmed in two different ways. First, the participants were later asked whether they recognized the background figures, and Asian students were more accurate than Western students in remembering whether they saw specific individuals in the background. Also, using a device that tracks the actual eye movements of the participants, the researchers discovered that Asian students spent more time actually looking at the entire picture, rather than just the central character (Figure 11.15; Masuda et al., 2008).

Figure 11.15 East–West Differences in Interpreting Emotion

In comparison to Asian people, Westerners spend more time looking at the focal individual in a scene and interpret his or her emotions without reference to surrounding individuals (Masuda et al., 2008).

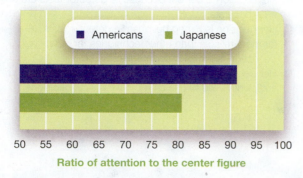

Ratio of attention to the center figure

Legend: ■ Americans ■ Japanese

X-axis: 50 55 60 65 70 75 80 85 90 95 100

Can we critically evaluate these findings?

Our emotional expressions include many components that we attend to, including context, facial expressions, body posture, and tone of voice. Given these additional elements, it would seem reasonable to ask whether findings from looking at a picture in a laboratory experiment actually apply to more complex situations that include movement and sounds and other events that are missing from the still pictures. In fact, some evidence indicates that similar results would be found when listening to voices. For instance, Japanese people have been observed not only to attend to facial expressions when interpreting emotion, but also to pay particularly close attention to tone of voice (Tanaka et al., 2010).

Why is this relevant?

Reading and understanding cultural display rules is a vital part of our social existence. Although cross-cultural research demonstrates that all people share some common core emotions, the existence of emotional dialects and display rules can complicate the interpretation of emotions in people who may be unfamiliar. Indeed, people's accuracy in interpreting the emotional expressions of people from different cultures can be much lower in comparison to their interpretation of the expressions of members of their own culture (Elfenbein & Ambady, 2002). Thus, culturally based display rules and emotional dialects can also lead to misunderstandings during encounters between people of different cultures. Awareness of this possibility should be elevated when traveling to an unfamiliar place or when hosting guests from afar.

JOURNAL PROMPT

Emotional Dialects: Why is it important to recognize emotional dialects and display rules? Do these terms only apply to situations in which people of different countries and ethnic backgrounds are being compared? Why or why not?

Module 11.4 Summary

11.4a Know . . . the key terminology associated with emotion:

Cannon-Bard theory of emotion
display rules
emotion
emotional dialects
facial feedback hypothesis
James-Lange theory of emotion
two-factor theory of emotion

11.4b Understand . . . different theories of emotion.

For decades, scientists have sought a solid theory of human emotion. By now you should be able to explain three primary attempts to explain emotion. The James-Lange theory predicts that physiological responses such as a racing heart will precede the emotional experience, such as fear. In contrast, the Cannon-Bard theory predicts that both physiology and the emotional experiences will occur together. Two-factor theory incorporates a cognitive component of appraisal. First, we have a physiological reaction to a stimulus or situation, next we appraise it by determining which emotion is appropriate, and then comes the conscious experience of the emotion we label as fear, anger, happiness, or whatever it may be.

11.4c Apply . . . your knowledge of theories of emotion.

To explain emotion, you need to consider the physiological responses that occur and the behaviors used to express the emotion (facial expressions, postures). In addition, it is important that there is cognitive appraisal relating the physiological responses to the actual context or situation that elicited them. Sympathetic arousal can occur in a wide variety of emotional circumstances, so an appraisal or interpretation of an event is critical. In analyzing emotion, each of these components—the physical and cognitive components—need to be applied.

11.4d Analyze . . . evidence for and against the use of lie detector tests.

For decades, the polygraph has been used as a lie detection method. Scientists have scrutinized the test to evaluate its validity as a reliable detector of truthfulness and deception. The modern consensus is that the polygraph reliably measures physiological arousal but does not achieve a universally acceptable level of accuracy in detecting lies.

Module 11.4 Quiz

Know ...

1. The _____ is a set of brain regions involved in emotional processing.
   - **A.** cortex
   - **B.** hindbrain
   - **C.** limbic system
   - **D.** parietal lobe

2. After narrowly avoiding a car accident, your arousal returns to a baseline state because of activity in the _____.
   - **A.** sympathetic nervous system
   - **B.** parasympathetic nervous system
   - **C.** hypothalamus
   - **D.** amygdala

Understand ...

3. Which of the following is a weakness of the James-Lange theory of emotion?
   - **A.** Cognitive appraisal of the situation is not a key component.
   - **B.** The theory does not address the subjective feeling of emotion.
   - **C.** The theory ignores the role of physiological reactions.
   - **D.** Awareness always precedes physiological reactions during emotions.

Apply ...

4. Joseph's mother tells him to smile more if he wants to feel better. She is applying the _____ theory of emotion.
   - **A.** Cannon-Bard
   - **B.** two-factor
   - **C.** James-Lange
   - **D.** slow/fast path

Analyze ...

5. A judge is dismissing evidence based on a lie detector test. What can you conclude about her decision?
   - **A.** Her decision is wrong because lie detector tests are valid.
   - **B.** Her decision is correct because lie detector tests are only 99% accurate.
   - **C.** Her decision is wrong because lie detector tests are far more reliable than other techniques for detecting deception, such as brain imaging.
   - **D.** Her decision is correct because lie detector tests are not sufficiently valid to use as a basis for legal decisions.

Module 11.5   Scientific Literacy Challenge: Airport Behavioral Screening

Air travelers are well aware that security-screening lines can be very long and slow moving. It turns out that the Transportation Safety Administration (TSA, the agency in charge of airport security) attempts to use that time to their advantage—as people are standing in line or loading their shoes and carry-ons onto the conveyer belt, specially trained TSA officers are scrutinizing the crowd for suspicious behavior. But do you believe their effort is worth the expense and effort required to train TSA agents? Take a moment to write your thoughts about behavioral security screenings.

Are you optimistic that TSA agents can identify dangerous passengers based on their behavior in the security line? Do you think simply observing people is more effective than choosing them at random to physically search? Explain.

What do we know about behavioral screening?

Read the following article written by a business editor at a popular business journal. As you read her opinions on the effectiveness of behavioral screening, pay close attention to the key terms and concepts covered in Chapter 11.

Civil liberties group joins taxpayer watchdogs to question airport screening techniques

By Minh Ngoc, business editor, *Quarterly Review of Business Ethics*

This week, the American Civil Liberties Union (ACLU) filed a lawsuit against the US federal government over behavioral screening practices in the nation's airports. The government program drawing fire is known as the Screening of Passengers by Observation Techniques (SPOT), a system devised to use physical and behavioral cues to identify potentially dangerous passengers. The ACLU's accusation against SPOT is really quite serious because it portrays behavioral screening methods as a sanctioned form of racial profiling. In bringing this suit, the ACLU is forming unlikely allies among fiscal conservatives who equally opposed the SPOT program because of its high costs to taxpayers. Further, both groups argue that there is no evidence that SPOT is effective in the first place. Could they be right? And where did SPOT come from?

SPOT originated in the wake of the 9-11 attacks and the justifiably heightened anxiety about airport security that ensued. The government officials and consultants who developed SPOT won support for it by claiming it was based on the science of **emotion**. While most of us think of emotion as subjective—our feelings of happiness or sadness, for example—scientists remind us that it includes internal, physical changes as well as changes in behavior, such as facial expressions and other nonverbal behaviors. The SPOT program is firmly rooted in the notion that emotional expressions associated with concealing criminal intent (e.g., terrorist activity) will appear in telltale "**microexpressions**" of potential perpetrators. If this idea sounds familiar, it's because it is a similar to the **polygraph** (aka lie detector). While the polygraph is designed to measure deception through the responses of the **autonomic nervous system**, SPOT is designed to detect deception in how a person stands, fidgets, and glances around.

Now that you know more about what behavioral screening involves, we should look for evidence that it works. Read on to find out what the writer has learned so far.

How do scientists study airport behavioral screening?

The evidence that could support or refute the validity of the SPOT program comes from a number of sources, including laboratory research and data collected at airports. Look for specific scientific concepts while you learn about the evidence.

> SPOT has come under these types of attacks before, but its defenders remain steadfast; in part because they have found supporting evidence for the program. For example, one of the main companies that provides SPOT training to TSA officers has been tracking the number of flags (selecting an individual for advanced screening) and the rates of arrests that result. Significantly, a greater number of passengers who were stopped using SPOT methods were subsequently arrested and convicted compared to the number of people caught with the use of random screenings. This finding would seem to support the validity of the SPOT methods.
>
> Others are less than impressed, and a report from the Government Accounting Office (GOA) provided several reasons why. For one, the GOA cited four recent analyses of several hundred peer-reviewed scientific articles that report no convincing evidence that individuals using behavioral screening methods could detect deception at any better-than-chance levels. But the articles were predominately based on laboratory studies, many of which involved reading microexpressions, which may not apply to the full set of behaviors that actual security screeners watch for.
>
> The GAO report concedes that data from actual airport screening stations lend support to SPOT, meaning that the methods they seem to have chosen help them catch potentially dangerous people. However, the GAO also points out that the data do not result from controlled experiments. For example, the SPOT officers themselves admit that the criteria are based on subjective interpretation rather than objective markers, and therefore security personnel often disagree with each other over whether a specific individual should be flagged.

Hopefully you identified some opportunities to evaluate the quality of evidence presented. Complete the short quiz below to identify some of the scientific concepts that pertain to the article.

1. Which of the following might lead critics to doubt the *reliability* of behavioral screening as a security measure?
   a. Laboratory studies may not relate to real-life events.
   b. There is often a lack of agreement among TSA security officers about which passengers to flag.
   c. All of the research was based on anecdotal observations, rather than systematic studies.
   d. The fact that the review was conducted by the GAO
2. Data collected from airports could have been accomplished by _____, meaning the research team watched the screeners on duty (when and where they were doing their job).
   a. naturalistic observation
   b. surveying
   c. experimentation
   d. validation

3. Which part of the article supports the suggestion that behavioral screening has *ecological validity*, meaning that the criteria for flagging and searching a traveler often results in a dangerous individual not boarding a plane?

    a. The screeners often do not agree on who to flag.

    b. Data from airports show that sometimes screeners correctly identify possible criminals, whereas laboratory research tends to show that people cannot consistently detect subtle emotional microexpressions.

    c. The airport studies fail to achieve the ideals of controlled experimentation.

    d. The research has not been published in peer-reviewed journals.

Answers: 1. b 2. a 3. b

Now that you have read about the evidence, you should have a sense for the types of data provided by each side of the debate. As you read on, apply principles of critical thinking to the issue.

How can we think critically about airport behavioral screening?

As you read the next paragraph of the article, actively search for specific statements relevant to critical thinking.

> So who are we to believe? Back in 2003, the experts who established the program and provided the initial SPOT training could claim long, distinguished academic careers. They seem to think their reputation should make them immune to criticism. That was probably true at a time when the policy makers and much of the public was in a "security at any cost" mindset. With a little hindsight and a great deal less anxiety, there is much more skepticism now. In fact, those who side with the ACLU are quick to point out that the same individuals whose reputation and wealth rest on continued funding for SPOT are nearly the only ones producing evidence for the program. On the other side of the issue, we have the GAO. My regular readers know that I trust very little of what comes out of Washington, but in this case, I cannot see what the GAO could possibly stand to gain from spinning the data gathered on the SPOT program one way or the other. They certainly do not have as much at stake as those who provide the SPOT training.

The statements below will help you identify several aspects of critical thinking. Match the following critical thinking statements to the highlighted passages that illustrate them.

1. The writer pointed out the danger of appealing to authority.

2. There is clear reason to suspect bias in one or more individuals or groups mentioned in this article.

3. There have been signs of overly emotional thinking.

1. Blue 2. Yellow 3. Green

In her conclusions, the writer discusses why this story is relevant to the readers.

How is airport behavioral screening relevant?

As you read the conclusion of the article, think about the original point of the issue, which is to keep the public safe. After doing so, explore any newly formed thoughts you may have about airport behavioral screening.

I chose to write about this topic because of the ACLU's actions this week. They are joining a small group of other organizations who base their anti-SPOT arguments on moral and financial grounds. However, at the heart of both of these issues is really the complaint that the techniques do not work to begin with. If it was wildly effective, it would be worth the money. If, on top of that, only guilty people were flagged, then there might be fewer complaints of demographic profiling. The facts are that behavioral screening has never been shown to catch people who would not have been caught during the electronic screening procedures. To me, that is a crucial piece of evidence, thus I believe it is time to put behavioral screening to rest.

SHARED WRITING

If you were to fly on a commercial airline, would you feel safer knowing that there were specially trained agents looking for suspicious microexpressions? What do you consider to be the pros and cons of the SPOT program?

Chapter 11 Quiz

1. In general, what effect does the presence of other people have on the amount of food an individual eats?
   A. The presence of others makes people eat less.
   B. The presence of others makes people eat more.
   C. The presence of others has no effect on the amount people typically eat.
   D. The presence of others can make people eat more or less than usual, depending on the situation.

2. Alfred Kinsey is famous for being one of the first scientists to study _____.
   A. human sexuality
   B. obesity in children
   C. peer pressure
   D. facial expressions

3. Which of the following factors increases an individual's risk for illness, heart disease, and even cancer?
   A. Mortality salience
   B. Loneliness
   C. Performance motives
   D. Avoidance goals

4. Louis practices shooting baskets after school because he doesn't want his friends to make fun of him for being bad at basketball. Louis's motivation to practice is most accurately described as driven by a(n) _____ goal.
   A. shame
   B. mastery
   C. avoidance
   D. approach

5. Some people who have temporal lobe epilepsy describe sensations of _____ when seizures occur.
   A. extra-sensory perception
   B. "raw fear"
   C. out-of-body experience
   D. religious experience

6. Controlled studies of polygraph recordings indicate that they should be most accurately described as detecting _____.
   A. parasympathetic activity
   B. lies
   C. arousal
   D. negative emotions

7. Gillian drinks a lot of coffee while studying all night. The caffeine in the coffee causes Gillian's heart to start racing and her hands to begin shaking. Suddenly, Gillian begins to feel fear and anxiety for no apparent reason. Gillian's experience is best explained by which theory of emotions?
   A. Maslow's hierarchy of needs
   B. James-Lange theory of emotion
   C. Facial feedback
   D. Cannon-Bard theory

8. Which of the following statements is true about how humans display emotions?
   A. While some basic emotions are universally recognized, different cultures have unique ways of displaying some emotions.
   B. All emotional displays are understood across all cultures.
   C. There are no emotional displays that are universally understood across all cultures.
   D. Emotional displays are determined by context, but not by culture.

9. Affiliation motivation is:
   A. the drive to have as many friends as possible.
   B. the desire to be around other people as often as possible.
   C. the need to have at least a few permanent meaningful relationships.
   D. the desire to be isolated from others.

10. People are least likely to procrastinate when they are genuinely interested in the task and believe they can gain something from it. This is known as a(n) _____ goal.
    A. mastery-avoidance
    B. mastery-approach
    C. performance-avoidance
    D. avoidance-mastery

11. Steven is paralyzed from the neck down and does not experience the autonomic responses that usually accompany fear. Despite this injury, he continues to experience fear. Which theory of emotion is contradicted by this observation?
    A. Cannon-Bard
    B. Two-factor theory
    C. James-Lange theory
    D. Physiological theory

12. A(n) _____ refers to when it is appropriate to show a specific emotion.
    A. emotional dialect
    B. display rule
    C. context rule
    D. display dialect

13. Which of the following is an example of an emotional dialect?
    A. Experiencing anger
    B. Avoiding laughter in church
    C. Raising one's chin to express contempt
    D. Smiling as a sign of happiness

14. Which of the following is an example of a display rule?
    A. Biting one's lip in embarrassment
    B. Dropping one's jaw in surprise
    C. Suppressing anger during a debate
    D. Expressing happiness to a loved one

15. The on-off switches for hunger sensations are located in the _____.
    A. sympathetic nervous system
    B. amygdala
    C. parasympathetic nervous system
    D. hypothalamus

Chapter 12
Personality

Module 12.1 Contemporary Approaches to Personality

 ## Learning Objectives

12.1a Know . . . the key terminology associated with contemporary approaches to personality.

12.1b Understand . . . the behaviorist and social-cognitive views of personality.

12.1c Apply . . . the Big Five personality traits to understand your own personality.

12.1d Analyze . . . claims that criminal profiling can help solve crimes.

What does your living space say about you? That alphabetized bookshelf and bathroom full of grooming products suggest conscientiousness. The modern art prints and concert posters of avant-garde musicians reveal an openness to experiencing new and exciting things. The three pet cats and extensive DVD collection? Possibly signs of an introverted homebody.

It might sound like we are just making assumptions here, but scientific research backs up the notion that personality can be measured by examining the details of the places we inhabit—whether real or virtual. Psychologist Sam Gosling and his colleagues have, with permission, closely scrutinized people's offices, bedrooms, and even social media profiles for clues about their personalities (Back et al., 2010; Gosling, 2008; Gosling et al., 2002). In one study, teams of seven or eight observers entered people's bedrooms and offices and rated the personality types of the occupants with a standardized personality scale. Not only did the observers frequently agree with each other in their ratings, but their ratings also matched up with how the occupants rated their own personality. You may be looking around at your own room now—and one thing that might come to mind is that some belongings have been there a very long time and symbolize the core of who you are. Other clues, such as the clothing strewn all over the floor, may simply reflect that you lead a busy life at the moment and not that you are a slob by nature. Either way, your personal surroundings reveal important information about you.

Personality *is a characteristic pattern of thinking, interacting, and reacting that is unique to each individual, and remains relatively consistent over time and situations. Psychologists* have long searched for a theory of personality that would describe and explain how people develop these behavioral patterns, but the search has proven to be very challenging. The first two modules in this chapter focus on contemporary, scientific research on personality. In Module 12.3, we will offer some historical perspectives that lack scientific rigor, but provide a sense of how far the field of personality psychology has come.

Some psychologists study personality by using an **idiographic approach**, *meaning that they focus on creating detailed descriptions of individuals and their unique personality characteristics.* An idiographic approach might involve focusing on one person, and then providing a rich description of what makes that person unique and identifying factors that may have led to the development of that personality (Carlson et al., 2010). Other psychologists are interested in describing personality in terminology that can apply to any member of the population. The concept of *shyness*, for example, can be used to describe anyone if used correctly (e.g. *he is very shy or she is not shy at all*). This reflects a **nomothetic approach**, *which examines personality in large groups of people, with the aim of making generalizations about personality structure.*

The difference between the idiographic and nomothetic approaches is sometimes unclear, because they share some similarities and often use similar terms (Grice et al., 2006). Even so, psychologists—especially those who want to know general characteristics about personality—find the distinction useful. In this module, we focus on the nomothetic approach to personality and examine how labels like *shy* or *outgoing* can be used scientifically to identify individuals' patterns of behavior.

The Trait Perspective

Several decades ago, some very patient and determined psychologists tallied nearly 18,000 English words that could be used to describe an individual's **personality traits**, *labels applied to specific attributes of personality, such as "reserved," "cheerful," "outgoing," and "adventurous"* (Allport & Odbert, 1936). This is the origin of the trait perspective, which describes personality based on how well each of these traits describes a specific person. To accomplish this labeling, trait researchers have devised a variety of personality scales. Some scales present a list of trait labels and ask an individual to rate how well the trait describes him or her. Other rating scales present specific behaviors to represent traits, such as "I like to meet new people" to assess how outgoing you are (see Table 12.1). The advantage of measuring traits through personality scales is that individuals can be described as scoring high or low on a specific trait. As a consequence, we can compare and contrast individual personalities: Whereas one student might be considered neat and orderly, his roommate might be considered quite messy and disorganized.

Of course, we cannot expect to understand personality if we have to evaluate each individual in terms of all 18,000 attributes. To help reduce the complexity introduced by using so many terms, personality psychologists use **factor analysis**, *a statistical technique that reveals statistical similarities among a wide variety of items* (also applied to intelligence tests in Module 9.1). For instance, when applied to personality descriptors, the three terms *friendly, warm,* and *kind* have some underlying similarities; *distant, cold,* and

---

Table 12.1 Measuring Extraversion

Please indicate the degree to which you disagree or agree with each statement as it applies to you by circling the number in the corresponding column. Notice that the statements range left to right from Strongly Disagree to Strongly Agree regardless of the numbers within the column.

	Strongly Disagree	Disagree	Neutral	Agree	Strongly Agree
I feel comfortable around people.	1	2	3	4	5
I have little to say.	5	4	3	2	1
I make friends easily.	1	2	3	4	5
I keep in the background.	5	4	3	2	1
I am skilled in handling social situations.	1	2	3	4	5
I would describe my experiences as somewhat dull.	5	4	3	2	1
I am the life of the party.	1	2	3	4	5
I don't like to draw attention to myself.	5	4	3	2	1
I know how to captivate people.	1	2	3	4	5
I don't talk a lot.	5	4	3	2	1

Now, sum the ten numbers that you circled. That is your total extraversion score.
You may get a sense of how introverted or extraverted you are by where your score falls between the lowest possible (5, an extreme introvert) and highest possible (50, an extreme extravert).
You can get an even better idea by comparing your score to the norm established with a sample of more than one hundred 18- to 24-year-old college students.

    5–23 Definitely introverted
    24–29 Sometimes introverted
    30–34 Sometimes extraverted
    35–45 Definitely extraverted

Source: International Personality Item Pool. http://ipip.ori.org/newNEOKey.htm#Extraversion

aloof are very similar to each other, but have nearly opposite meanings to the other three. Factor analysis would reduce all six terms to one trait (referred to as a *factor in statistical terms*) that could be labelled as *friendliness*. Depending on how people rate themselves, they could score very high in friendliness if they indicate that they are warm and kind, or, in contrast, they could score very low in friendliness if they describe themselves as cold and aloof.

THE FIVE FACTOR MODEL A trend in modern personality psychology is to reduce personality to its core components. Using factor analysis, psychologist Raymond Cattell (1946) identified 16 key personality traits, thereby simplifying and standardizing the number of dimensions psychologists needed to describe the composition of personality. But even 16 factors might be more than we need to describe personality. McCrae and Costa (1987), creators of the *NEO Personality Inventory*, found that personality could be reduced to five major dimensions called the **Five Factor Model** (or just the Big Five personality factors), *which is a trait-based approach to personality measurement that includes extraversion, emotional stability (also referred to by the opposite quality, neuroticism), conscientiousness, agreeableness, and openness* (see Figure 12.1).

Figure 12.1 The Big Five Personality Dimensions

The NEO-PI-R is a widely used measure of personality. To complete this scale, people rate the degree to which a variety of statements describe their typical behavior. Altogether, these statements measure the traits of openness, conscientiousness, extraversion, agreeableness, and neuroticism. (To help you remember the Big Five, note that the first letters of the traits spell out OCEAN.)

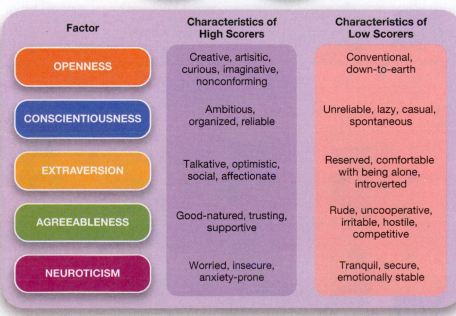

Factor	Characteristics of High Scorers	Characteristics of Low Scorers
OPENNESS	Creative, artisitic, curious, imaginative, nonconforming	Conventional, down-to-earth
CONSCIENTIOUSNESS	Ambitious, organized, reliable	Unreliable, lazy, casual, spontaneous
EXTRAVERSION	Talkative, optimistic, social, affectionate	Reserved, comfortable with being alone, introverted
AGREEABLENESS	Good-natured, trusting, supportive	Rude, uncooperative, irritable, hostile, competitive
NEUROTICISM	Worried, insecure, anxiety-prone	Tranquil, secure, emotionally stable

The Five Factor Model is probably the most widely used of the trait-based approaches, and it can predict many real-world behaviors. For example, extraverted people tend to report happier moods than do introverts (Lischetzke & Eid, 2006), and extraverted college students are likely to achieve high status in student groups such as fraternities and sororities (Anderson et al., 2001). On the downside, extraverts are more prone to risk taking and substance abuse problems (Martsh & Miller, 1997). Conscientious individuals are likely to have positive health-related behaviors, longevity, and higher levels of achievement (Chamorro-Premuzic & Furnham, 2003; Roberts et al., 2005). Thus, the Big Five are not just important for describing individuals but are also useful for understanding people's behavior, thoughts, and emotions. It is encouraging that what people report about their personalities generally corresponds to their actual behavior. Still, we should accept this approach without critical thinking; we should ask whether people accurately portray their personalities when completing self-reports.

Working the Scientific Literacy Model

How Accurate Are Self-Ratings?

Ratings of personality traits can predict a variety of behaviors and outcomes, ranging from career choices to overall health. But for these predictions to be meaningful, the ratings must be accurate. Imagine a researcher would like to measure personality traits for around 50 volunteers. Who should he trust to provide the best information: The volunteers themselves? Close friends or relatives?

What about a computer? This is the challenge, and there are a few things to consider when deciding the best approach.

What do we know about how people assess personality?

We know that people are not always completely honest about themselves. For example, a recent graduate completing a personality profile for a job interview might bend the truth to appear more serious, responsible, and motivated. Even if he is honest about his personality, there is a chance that he does not see himself as others do. His father may see him as irresponsible and immature. If that is the case, then whose opinion is correct? A significant amount of personality research has been dedicated to figuring out how to get the most accurate assessments possible.

How can science determine the accuracy of personality ratings?

For the past few decades, personality researchers have investigated the accuracy of personality ratings by comparing how people rate their own personality traits with how others, such as a family member or roommate, rate them (Connelly & Ones, 2010; Funder & West, 1993). This is a way of testing whether others see us as we see ourselves. Also, do different relations, such as mom, sister, and best friend from high school share a similar view of the same individual? These studies tend to show that the degree to which people agree on their assessment of other people's personality is connected to familiarity: Spouses and other family members tend to agree with each other and with how individuals rate themselves, as shown by relatively strong correlations among these relations (Figure 12.2).

Figure 12.2 Self and Other Personality Ratings

If you were to complete a self-rated personality inventory, and then have family members and other loved ones rate your personality using the same scales, how well would your answers match? Here we see that there is a relatively strong correlational relationship between how people rate their own levels of extraversion with ratings completed by family members, spouses, parents, and siblings. Similar results have been reported for emotional stability, openness, agreeableness, and conscientiousness.

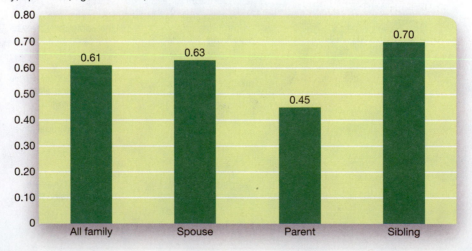

Figure 12.3 Who Knows You Best?

Friends, family, and other close relations tend to agree on their ratings of others on the Big Five personality dimensions. There are relatively strong correlations between how people rate themselves and how they are rated by relatives, friends, and loved ones. Despite the fact that people tend to spend a great deal of their time with coworkers, coworkers were not as accurate in their ratings. Interestingly, computer-based judgments of personality, which relied exclusively on people's Facebook "likes," were just as accurate as friends and family ratings (Youyou, Kosinski, & Stillwell, 2015).

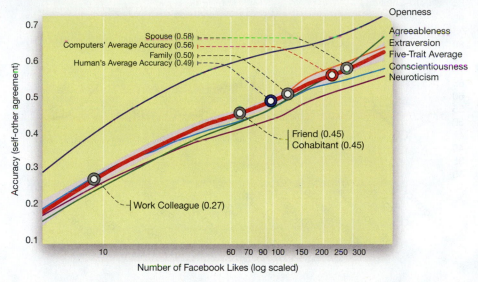

Friends and roommates are not too far behind, but even complete strangers have some degree of agreement.

These are results you would expect if people are willing and able to provide accurate self-assessments. Therefore, it would seem that we can trust most individuals to rate themselves. What is perhaps most interesting, however, is that a computer program was able to outperform all other relations except spouses by using peoples' Facebook likes as a source of personal information (Figure 12.3; Youyou et al., 2015)!

Can we critically evaluate this research?

If accuracy is going to be measured by correlation statistics, it is important to understand what the correlation coefficient means. If you had a sample of 1,000 twins, you would find a perfect 1.0 correlation between the ages of each pair. If you know one twin's age, then you can be quite sure of the other's. The weakest possible correlation is 0.0; this is what you would find if you and a friend flipped coins at the same time. If your coin landed on heads, what would that tell you about your friend's coin? Nothing. If you did this hundreds of times, you would find that there is zero correlation between the two events because each flip has zero influence on the other. With that in mind, consider that the correlation of family members and self-ratings are around .5, which is halfway between a nonexistent correlation and a perfect one. Researchers have seen enough correlations in their time to know that .5 is typically very meaningful and significant,

but this still leaves what remains between .5 and 1.0 to be explained by other factors.

Why is this relevant?

Accurate ratings are essential to research because we rely on them to understand other variables. Personality can predict health, well-being, and success at work and at school. Without accurate personality measures, we would be missing out on a lot of important knowledge. Also, the finding that computers can be programmed to make accurate personality judgments is something we should pause to consider. On the one hand, this has enormous potential for marketing (it is already happening) and could streamline the process of measuring personality in both research and clinical settings. However, it also raises questions about privacy and related issues introduced by technology. As you may have noticed, posting information about yourself online elicits advertisements with an uncanny familiarity of your "likes."

NORMAL AND ABNORMAL PERSONALITY: THE MMPI-2 Researchers often measure the Big Five traits to explore general, everyday behavior: how people behave at work, engage in personal relationships, choose hobbies, and so on. Personality psychologists are also interested in traits that may predispose people to experience psychological problems. These traits can be identified and studied with tests such as the **Minnesota Multiphasic Personality Inventory (MMPI-2)**, *a multiple-question personality inventory that is used to characterize both normal personality dimensions and profiles that fit various psychological*

Figure 12.4 The MMPI Personality Inventory

The purple shaded area between points 50 and 65 represent the normal range. Scores above or below these points indicate an abnormal personality (relative to the population norm) for a given dimension. The person represented here scored high on measures of depression and other possible mental disorders.

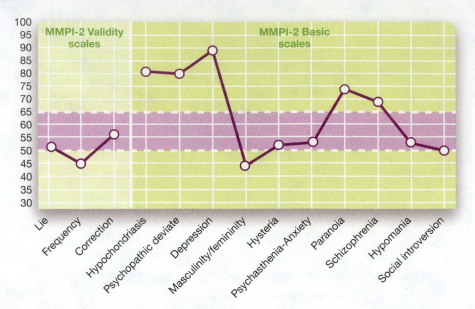

disorders (something we will cover in greater detail in Chapters 13 and 14). The MMPI-2 provides a multidimensional profile of each individual who completes it. As you can see in Figure 12.4, profiles such as *schizophrenia* and *psychopathic deviancy* are included in the MMPI-2.

The main purpose of the MMPI-2 is to discriminate between "normal" and "abnormal" characteristics. While tests of the Big Five have been constructed with specific traits in mind, the developers of the MMPI took a very different approach; specifically, they did not construct the items on the MMPI to resemble specific traits in any obvious way. Instead, the researchers identified a set of individuals who had been diagnosed with a variety of psychological disorders and asked them to respond to hundreds of true/false items on a personality inventory. Then they asked people in a sample taken from the general population to do the same. Researchers identified a number of response patterns among individuals with disorders that did not occur in the general sample. These personality profiles are now used to identify individuals with a variety of psychological problems.

The MMPI-2 is widely used for psychological evaluation, where the intent is to treat individuals who may potentially have psychological problems. However, it has created some controversy when used for other purposes. In at least two court cases (*Karraker v. Rent-A-Center, Inc.* and *Miller v. City of Springfield*), employers that used the MMPI-2 for promotion or hiring decisions have been found guilty of violating the Americans with Disabilities Act (ADA). The ADA prohibits the use of medical information in making employment decisions. In each of these cases, the plaintiffs accused a company (Rent-A-Center) and a police department (City of Springfield) of refusing to hire them based on the results of the MMPI-2, which contained medical information. In the *Miller* case, the plaintiff scored high on the depression scale and argued that the refusal to hire her was based on this score. In both cases, judges sided with the plaintiffs.

PERSONALITY TRAITS OVER THE LIFE SPAN Do our personality traits remain fixed, or do they change significantly over the life span? To address this question, we should consider personality from its beginnings. Newborn infants typically are not described with the same range of adjectives that we use for adults; adults may be thought of as talkative, ambitious, greedy, and arrogant, whereas infants probably are not. However, within their first few months of life, infants do show the beginnings of personality characteristics. As described in Module 10.2, *temperament* refers to personality-like attributes that appear to be present at birth, and includes such characteristics as activity level, mood, attention span, and distractibility (Rothbart & Bates, 2006). Some infants are generally active and happy, whereas others are more tranquil and still others are easily upset. If traits are stable, long-term characteristics, then we would expect to find that temperament is a good predictor of adult personality. To some extent, this is the case: Infant temperament predicts the adult personality traits of neuroticism, extraversion, and conscientiousness (Evans & Rothbart, 2007). The temperament styles found in infancy seem to represent an innate, biological basis upon which personality is built.

Figure 12.5 Personality Over the Life Span

Average scores of emotional stability, conscientiousness, agreeableness, and social dominance (an aspect of extraversion) all increase through adulthood. Openness to experience generally rises through early adulthood and remains steady through the life span (Roberts et al., 2006).

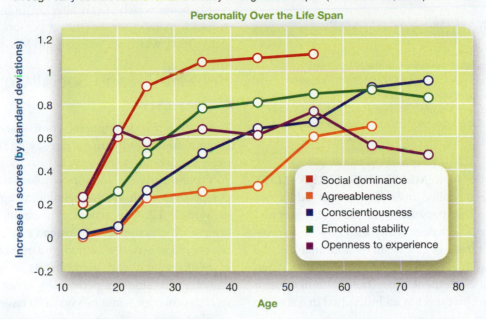

Just because there is consistency between temperament and personality does not mean that personality cannot change. Young adults tend to experience fewer negative emotions than do adolescents, reflecting decreases in neuroticism (Donnellan et al., 2007). In addition, emotional stability, conscientiousness, agreeableness, and social dominance (an aspect of extraversion) all increase in early adulthood (Roberts et al., 2006; see Figure 12.5). Later in life, self-ratings of personality traits remain remarkably consistent. In one meta-analysis (an analysis of multiple already-published studies), researchers compiled data from 152 studies involving more than 50,000 participants who were tracked for at least one year (Roberts & Del Vecchio, 2000). Children in this study were found to be less stable in their personality traits, but by middle age people showed relatively little change in their personality traits over time (see also Briley & Tucker-Drob, 2014).

PERSONALITY TRAITS AND STATES Trait labels may go a long way toward describing what people are like. However, many psychologists are quick to point out that no matter how useful traits may seem, people's behavior is also determined by situational factors and context. You may know someone whom you would describe as very calm and tranquil, yet when a baseball umpire makes a bad call, he protests so loudly that he is barely recognizable. Definitions of personality typically include an element of consistency, but this does not mean that people are always consistent in the ways they behave. In contrast to a personality trait, a **state** *is a temporary physical or psychological engagement that influences behavior.* Perhaps your

normally calm friend lashed out at the umpire because it was in the last inning of a very close game. In this case, the situation motivates his behavior more than his usual calm demeanor—something that is not unusual. Even people who seem so consistent in how they express their neuroticism, agreeableness, or extraversion will not behave in the same way across all situations, and this observation has led to some strong criticisms of trait theories of personality (Mischel, 1968; Mischel & Shoda, 1998).

How states and situational factors influence our behavior is a challenging topic because there are so many situations or states we can find ourselves in during any particular day. You can be awake or asleep, confident or unsure, you may have money or no money, and you may be in a crisis situation or completely relaxed. The list could go on forever and as you might have guessed, psychologists have tried to see just how long it goes. In one study, 77 college students were asked to describe as many situations they might encounter at any given time. Their total reached more than 7,000. Perhaps you can now see why many psychologists would rather focus on a smaller number of dimensions. Fortunately, Saucier and colleagues (2007) took these 7,000 situations and reduced them to 4 general aspects of situations that are most likely to influence our behavior:

1. Locations (e.g., being at work, school, or home)
2. Associations (e.g., being with friends, alone, or with family)
3. Activities (e.g., awake, rushed, studying)
4. Subjective states (e.g., mad, sick, happy)

These situations influence how and when our personality traits are expressed. Identifying these situations is important because they contribute to our psychological states, and they interact with personality traits to determine our behavior.

JOURNAL PROMPT

Your Big 5: Table 12.1 provides a chance to measure your extraversion score and compare it to the norm. If you completed similar measures for the rest of the Big 5 (openness, conscientiousness, extraversion, agreeableness, and neuroticism), how do you think you would score? For each trait, identify whether you think you would score high, moderate, or low and describe an example of your behavior that illustrates your answer.

OTHER METHODS FOR MEASURING PERSONALITY

In addition to personality inventories, two additional methods for measuring personality include *interviews* and *behavioral assessments*. In a personality interview, a psychologist asks a structured set of questions and analyzes the responses to create an individual personality profile. When using a behavioral assessment, a psychologist will create a personality profile by observing an individual in a specific context or situation. Behavioral assessments are often used for the purposes of employee hiring and job placement, as well as for observing younger children who may not be suited to taking a self-report personality inventory. These methods are valuable in that they involve careful and close observation, which can allow for a rich and detailed understanding of the individual. However, a drawback to both is that responding directly to an interviewer or knowing that one is being watched can alter an individual's behavior. A fourth method for measuring personality includes projective tests, which we will cover in Module 12.3.

Behaviorist and Social-Cognitive Perspectives

Traits allow for descriptions, comparisons, and even predictions among individuals. But saying that someone is an extrovert does not tell us why or how they became that way. To explain behavior, some psychologists have taken other perspectives such as the behavioral approach described in Module 1.2. This school of thought shuns terms that are purely descriptive and instead emphasizes observable relationships between stimuli and responses and the role of reinforcement and punishments in shaping behavior. Although the study of personality is not central to behavioral psychology, some behaviorists have argued that personality consists of various response tendencies that are linked to specific situations. For example, in a small social gathering, which would be the stimulus, you could respond in any number of ways: dominating a conversation, asking

Myths in Mind
Does Criminal Profiling Solve Crimes?

Thanks to imaginative novelists and screenwriters, almost everyone in the United States has heard of *criminal profiling*, the use of behavioral evidence to predict and profile traits of suspects and offenders as a means for solving crimes. It is often portrayed with extraordinarily smart, tough investigators who see their work as part science, part intuition. As with any other type of fiction, it is important to make distinctions about what is real versus what is simply entertaining.

It is also important to distinguish profiling from the science of criminology. *Criminology* is an academic discipline that might involve having trait inventories completed by convicted criminals or professionals who work with them; scores on these inventories are then correlated with various types of crime and criminal methods. This approach yields useful evidence about who has committed specific crimes in the past, but criminal profiling involves far more than this.

Profilers argue that clues from a crime scene can also reveal something about personality. For example, some perpetrators are classified as *organized*, indicating that the crime appears to have been planned. The criminal has erased any clues that would allow them to be easily caught, and perhaps left false clues that might steer investigators toward another suspect.

Organized criminals tend to be intelligent and have strong verbal skills, even if they only use those skills to further their narcissistic goals (Schlessigner, 2009). Combining knowledge of criminology research and the scene that is under investigation results in a profile: A combination of personality traits and demographic characteristics believed to describe the guilty person and intended to help search for and interrogate the suspect.

Unfortunately for investigators, there is little evidence that profiles can help solve crimes (Snook et al., 2008). The correlations between most personality traits and criminal behavior tend to be quite weak. In essence, this means that not everyone who commits a certain type of crime has the same set of traits, and not everybody with that set of traits has committed any crimes. Even when combinations of traits (like narcissism, a lack of empathy, and sadism) do correlate more strongly to crime, they tend to apply to such a large number of people that questioning everyone who matched would be nearly impossible and would not guarantee results. This is true for demographic characteristics as well: Knowing that most serial killers are male is very helpful and allows us to understand the nature of the crime, but nobody would argue that we should detain and question every boy or man whenever a serial killing is suspected.

Figure 12.6 Behavioral and Social-Cognitive Approaches to Personality

(a) Behaviorist Account of Personality. Behaviorists thought that what psychologists call personality was an expression of relationships between behavior, rewards, and punishment. Behaviorists avoided referring to personality traits and dispositions, but rather focused on how past experiences predict future behaviors. For example, whether someone tends to be pessimistic might be based on past experiences in which their behaviors failed to produce any desirable consequences. **(b) Reciprocal Determinism and the Social-Cognitive Approach.** According to Albert Bandura and colleagues, personality is a product of dynamic interactions between behavior and reinforcement, and, importantly, the beliefs, expectancies, and dispositions of the individual.

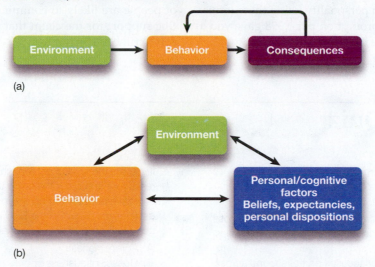

(a)

(b)

a lot of questions, or remaining silent. If you have a history of being reinforced for asking questions, you will likely repeat the behavior each time you are in this situation. Over time, it becomes a standard pattern of behavior. A behaviorist would note that using the personality dimension of "extraversion" is an unnecessary addition—it is just a label that does not help us understand the simple relationship between stimulus and response. Thus, the behaviorist perspective emphasizes the importance of the situation, rather than a relatively stable personality trait, in determining behavior (Figure 12.6).

Building on the behaviorist approach, Albert Bandura formulated a social-cognitive theory of personality based on the idea that people do not simply respond to cues in the environment, but rather actively engage with it.

Individuals can choose which environments to enter, they can manipulate and modify their environments, and even learn from watching others' behavior in those situations (Bandura, 2001). For example, a person who experiences anxiety about how to behave at a party might *choose* to turn down the next invitation and opt for an evening at home with a book. If so, this person will probably remain quiet and introverted. However, if the person chooses to take a risk and go to the party, they may find confidence if they had a good time and eventually become quite confident at future parties. This reflects Bandura's theory of **reciprocal determinism**—*the idea that behavior, internal (personal) factors, and external factors interact to determine one another, and that our personalities are based on interactions among these three aspects* (see Figure 12.6).

Module **12.1** Summary

12.1a Know . . . the key terminology associated with contemporary approaches to personality:

factor analysis
Five Factor Model (Big Five personality factors)
idiographic approach
Minnesota Multiphasic Personality Inventory (MMPI-2)
nomothetic approach
personality
personality traits
reciprocal determinism
state

12.1b Understand . . . the behaviorist and social-cognitive views of personality.

A strict behavioral account of personality identifies the stimuli and situational factors that control the various responses that can be elicited. When this perspective is adopted, there is little use of trait terminology, such as neuroticism or conscientiousness, and no reference to cognitive factors such as beliefs or thoughts. The social-cognitive approach to personality also accounts for situational factors and behavior, but adds a cognitive element that interacts with the environment in such a way that situations, behavior, and thoughts are determined in reciprocal fashion.

12.1c Apply . . . the Big Five personality traits to understand your own personality.

The Five Factor model is a very popular approach to characterizing personality. Psychologists use self- and other ratings to describe individual differences in openness, conscientiousness, agreeableness, extraversion, and neuroticism. As you read this module, you may have attempted to informally rate your own personality using these terms. Table 12.1 and the journal prompt on page 398 gave you a chance to apply the Big Five to your own personality.

12.1d Analyze . . . claims that criminal profiling can help solve crimes.

Criminology is an important field of study that incorporates various aspects of psychological science, including the study of personalities. Criminal profiling draws from that research and also data that is collected at crime scenes. Although criminology has taught us a lot about what types of people are likely to commit crimes, there is little scientific support for the claim that criminal profiling can help solve crimes.

Module 12.1 Quiz

Know . . .

1. Which of the following statements best describes the difference between the nomothetic and idiographic approaches to personality?

   A. The nomothetic approach focuses on traits found across large groups, whereas the idiographic approach focuses on individuals.

   B. The idiographic approach focuses on traits found across large groups, whereas the nomothetic approach focuses on individuals.

   C. The idiographic approach relies on measures such as the Big Five, whereas the Big Five is of no use to a nomothetic approach.

   D. The idiographic approach allows psychologists to ask questions about the genetic and cultural basis of personality traits.

2. Which of the following concepts developed by Bandura refers to interactions that occur among behavior, internal, and external factors as an explanation for personality?

   A. Reciprocal determinism
   B. Positive psychology
   C. Intersubjectivity
   D. Egocentrism

Understand . . .

3. Kaitlin describes herself as unmotivated. She has not felt rewarded by her attempts to succeed at school or work and, therefore, has given up trying. How might a psychologist who adopts a strict behaviorist approach account for Kaitlin's behavior?

   A. Kaitlin believes that she cannot succeed and, therefore, avoids putting herself in situations where she might fail.

   B. Kaitlin has a history of not being reinforced for trying to succeed and, therefore, has stopped trying.

   C. Kaitlin focuses too much on negatives and does not have a positive outlook on life.

   D. Kaitlin has low levels of the trait known as extraversion.

Apply . . .

4. If you are the type of person who tends to go to the same restaurant and order the same thing, stick to your daily routine, and have possibly turned down opportunities to travel to new destinations, which of the Big Five factors would account for this description of your personality?

   A. Agreeableness
   B. Conscientiousness
   C. Openness
   D. Neuroticism

Analyze . . .

5. Criminal profiling is a hugely popular concept that captures the interest of television viewers. What is the reality about the validity of criminal profiling?

   A. There is little evidence that it allows investigators to zero in on specific suspects.

   B. It works, but the MMPI-2 is needed in order to accurately profile suspects.

   C. It works if a picture of a suspect's dwelling is made available for personality analysis.

   D. It is equally good as physical evidence, DNA, and related measures.

Module **12.2** Cultural and Biological Approaches to Personality

⌄ Learning Objectives

12.2a Know . . . key terminology associated with cultural and biological approaches to personality.

12.2b Understand . . . how evolution has influenced personality.

12.2c Apply . . . your knowledge to understand personality differences (and similarities) among cultures.

12.2d Analyze . . . claims that personality traits can be traced to a single gene or brain circuit.

Some psychologists have claimed that the United States is rather WEIRD in comparison to most of the world's population (Henrich et al., 2010). You may or may not agree with that claim right away, but in this case, **WEIRD** *is an acronym for "Western, Educated, Industrialized, Rich, and Democratic." Armed with that understanding, you might now be more inclined to agree that the United States is rather WEIRD.*

The concept of WEIRD places is crucial for understanding personality. Many psychological studies of personality are conducted on WEIRD undergraduates at WEIRD universities. Papers summarizing these studies are published and the data inform psychologists' conceptions of human personality. What does this work show? For one, WEIRD people look favorably upon projecting a positive image of the self, and showing others how good they are. Meanwhile,

researchers in other parts of the world often come up with different findings: People of East Asia tend to focus on acknowledging ways that they can improve (Heine & Buchtel, 2009). This cultural difference has been found to persist across multiple studies, and this raises the age-old question about whether these differences are influenced more by genes or the environment in which people are raised.

One goal among personality psychologists is to characterize what human beings are like—to boil the essence of what it is to be human down to a set of core attributes along people's varying dimensions. To fully understand human personality, studies must include people of all ages from many different cultures and geographic regions (Church, 2010; McAdams & Pals, 2006).

Culture and Personality

A textbook on international business advises a simple handshake, calm voices, and reserved posture and gestures when conducting business in Japan, but regular physical contact and emotional expression if the meeting is in Brazil. These recommendations are based on cultural customs, but our tendency to stereotype might lead us to believe that Japanese people are introverts while Brazilians are extroverts. Psychologists must address issues of cultural norms when studying individuals: To what extent does a specific behavior represent personality instead of culture? Before we dig deeper into this topic, answer the following question in true/false form:

True or False?

1. Canadians are much more agreeable than people from the United States.
2. Men and women have vastly different personalities.
3. People from the United States are pushy.
4. People from England are reserved.
5. Swiss people are conventional and closed off to new experiences.
6. Women are more warm and compassionate than men.
7. Chinese people value group cohesiveness.

We will provide answers in the module summary. Analyzing cultural differences and similarities in personality is much more complicated than gathering firsthand impressions or stereotypes. As you can see from reviewing the answers to the questions above, sometimes the differences hold true, at least to some degree, and sometimes not. Also, one major challenge to doing cross-cultural work is finding a standardized measure of personality that can be translated and administered in languages other than English. The first module in this chapter introduced the Big Five personality dimensions, which include neuroticism, extraversion, openness, agreeableness, and conscientiousness (see Figure 12.1). These factors were discovered by researchers working in WEIRD places—the United States, Canada, and Europe. Psychologists also realize that just because a factor such as conscientiousness appears in data from the United States, it does not necessarily mean that the same factor would appear everywhere in the world. To find out whether the Big Five traits are truly universal, a large team of psychologists measured traits of more than 17,000 people speaking 28 different languages and inhabiting 56 countries on 6 continents (they did not visit Antarctica). As it turns out, translations of the Big Five personality were validated across cultures (Schmitt et al., 2007; see also McCrae et al., 2005). This does not mean that individuals are all alike, only that when it comes to the basic composition of personality, the same five traits apply anywhere you go.

Another question addressed in this large-scale study was whether trait averages differ among cultures. The researchers found numerous cross-cultural differences in average personality ratings. People from Serbia and Croatia tended to be the most extraverted of the nations sampled, whereas the most introverted people came from Bangladesh and France. People from Chile and Belgium were the most open to experience, while respondents from Japan and Hong Kong rated low on the openness scale. Looking at a more worldwide distribution, people from East Asia were the least extraverted. People from Africa were the most agreeable and conscientious of all regions (see Figure 12.7; Schmitt et al., 2007). Many of the findings in these large-scale cross-cultural studies defy cultural stereotypes (Terracciano et al., 2005). For example, we might be inclined to think that cultures consisting of people who score high on conscientiousness would have the strongest economies, but no such relationship was found. In fact, nations that scored highest on conscientiousness had a relatively poor global economic standing.

Although the five-factor structure has been found in other cultures, we must remember that they are called Big Five because they provide clear, statistically based distinctions between the ways people can behave not because they are the *only* five traits. There are personality traits that are unique to specific parts of the world, and they provide interesting and meaningful descriptions of individuals even if they are not as "big" in the statistical sense. For example, researchers in China have identified a factor labeled *interpersonal relatedness*—a combination of harmony, tradition, and relationships with others—as well as a dependability factor (Cheung et al., 1996).

Overall, research using Big Five measures does show cross-cultural consistency, and as discussed in Module 12.1, personality traits tend to become increasingly consistent and stable as people age. But also recall that there can be some change in personality. Perhaps you or someone you know has parents who migrated from a different country. Children born to first-generation immigrant families are likely to behave in ways that are consistent with their culture of origin, but they also change in ways that are consistent with new cultural norms. Does this suggest that personality traits have actually changed? Cross-cultural research using the Big Five shows that personality changes do occur in people who actively participate in their new cultural surroundings (Güngör et al., 2013). The presence of both consistency and change in personality leads to further questions, such as how genes interact with the environment to shape personality.

Finally, we would not want to overstate or reinforce the idea that people from WEIRD populations are all alike. Perhaps you moved far away from home to attend college and are discovering what you can only describe as culture shock because the people seem to act "differently." Even if your travel in the United States has been limited, you

Figure 12.7 Cultural Differences in Levels of Conscientiousness

This graph shows how average self-reported levels of conscientiousness differ among thousands of people studied across numerous cultures and nations (from Schmitt et al., 2007).

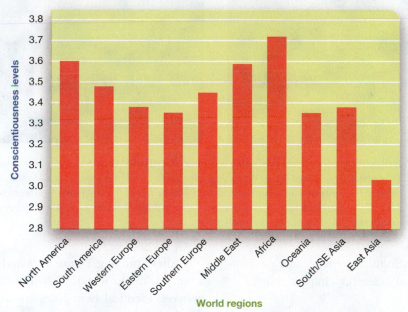

can likely appreciate that there are regional differences, although they are often exaggerated when expressed as stereotypes or caricatures. Figure 12.8 captures some of these regional differences. Perhaps they confirm your own experiences or expectations. Not all WEIRD people are the same after all.

Genes, Evolution, and Personality

As in many other areas of psychology, people regularly speculate about the nature and nurture of personality. If you have your mother's sense of humor, is it in the genes, or have you just learned to enjoy life by her example? Psychologists conduct twin studies and employ other

Figure 12.8 Personality Differences in the United States

Large scale studies including hundreds of thousands of individuals reveal geographical differences in personality. These maps present the three main personality profiles that emerged in this research along with associated regions in the U.S.

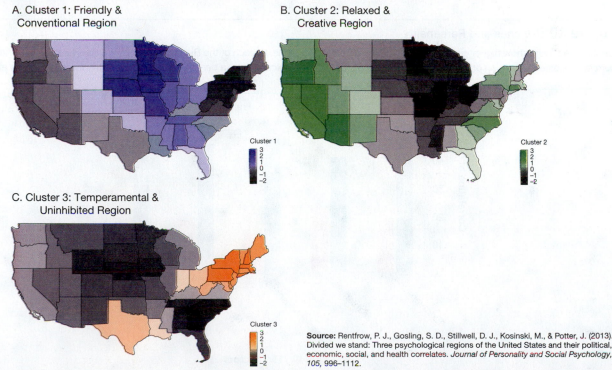

A. Cluster 1: Friendly & Conventional Region

B. Cluster 2: Relaxed & Creative Region

C. Cluster 3: Temperamental & Uninhibited Region

Source: Rentfrow, P. J., Gosling, S. D., Stillwell, D. J., Kosinski, M., & Potter, J. (2013). Divided we stand: Three psychological regions of the United States and their political, economic, social, and health correlates. *Journal of Personality and Social Psychology, 105*, 996–1112.

Highly detailed and specific similarities between identical twins who were reared apart tend to draw a great deal of interest. Gerald Levey and Mark Newman are identical twins who were reared apart. When they eventually met, it turns out they had many similarities. For example, both chose the same profession. In contrast, Paula Bernstein and Elyse Schein are identical twins who were separated at birth, and upon uniting at age 35 discovered they were very different from each other. Despite the compelling example of Levey and Newman, we must remember that the environment has substantial influence on personality.

research techniques to distinguish genetic and environmental sources of individual differences in personality.

TWIN STUDIES Twin studies using the Big Five have shown that identical (monozygotic) twins have a stronger correlation for each personality trait than do fraternal (dizygotic) twins. As you can see from Figure 12.9, the genetic correlations for identical twin pairs are approximately .50 for all five factors, significantly higher than the correlations for fraternal twin pairs (who average approximately .20). Although the environment contributes to variation in personality, research on its genetic basis indicates that genes are responsible for many of the differences we see among individuals (Tellegen et al., 1988).

After studying Figure 12.9 and thinking about twins a bit, you might wonder whether the stronger similarities between identical twin pairs are due to something other than genes. Identical twins are often treated in very similar ways, especially during their younger and formative years. Non-twin siblings or fraternal twins reared together share a very similar environment, but perhaps the environments shared by identical twins reared together is even more similar by comparison. If this is true, then the strong correlations seen in Figure 12.9 between identical twin pairs might be environmentally based. It turns out that twin studies conducted on identical twins who were reared apart yield the same basic findings as studies of twins who were reared together—they are more alike than fraternal

Figure 12.9 Genes and Personality

Identical twin pairs show higher genetic correlations than do fraternal twins for each of the Big Five personality traits. Numerical estimates of genetic correlations differ depending on the populations sampled, but studies typically show a genetic basis for each of the five factors (Bae et al., 2013).

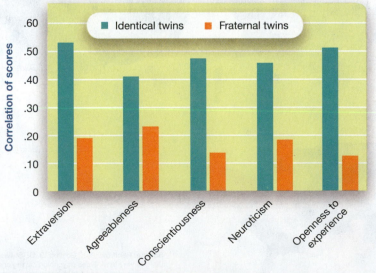

twins or non-twin siblings (Tellegen et al., 1988). The genetic correlations range from .39 to .58, indicating that despite growing up in different environments the identical twins converged toward having similar personalities.

Although the results of twin studies reveal that heredity plays an important role in personality development, parenting and other environmental influences certainly matter. As discussed in Modules 10.2 and 10.3, the environments that parents provide and their style of parenting certainly do influence the ways their children behave. Another point to consider is that twin studies do not tell us which specific genes may account for individual differences. Newer molecular methods are used to answer this type of question.

Working the Scientific Literacy Model

From Molecules to Personality

Scientists have identified groups of genes contributing to physical characteristics and susceptibility to diseases, and have increasingly been applying the same methods to learn about personality.

What do we know about specific genes and personality?

To think about how genes relate to personality, we should start with familiar brain chemicals with known functions. Serotonin, among other things, regulates mood and emotion. One of the genes that codes for serotonin activity has been found on human chromosome 17. Specifically, this **serotonin transporter gene** *codes for proteins that transport serotonin molecules within the tiny spaces (synapses) between nerve cells.* Many of our genes are polymorphic (*poly* = "multiple"; *morph* = "form"), meaning that there are different versions of the same gene that lead to different physical or behavioral characteristics. Two possible variations of the serotonin transporter gene have been identified: a short copy and a long copy. People who inherit short copies from one or both parents are predisposed to anxiety, shyness, and negative emotional reactions in interpersonal situations (Battaglia et al., 2005; Lesch et al., 1996). This gene codes for proteins that reside in the synapses between nerve cells and are responsible for moving serotonin back into cell membranes of recently fired nerve cells for reuse.

How do scientists study genes and personality?

One method for studying genes and personality is to compare responses on self-report questionnaires of personality in people who have inherited different copies of the serotonin transporter gene. People who inherit short copies of the gene tend to report greater levels of anxiety

and neuroticism compared to people who inherit two long copies. However, these differences depend on which of the many different varieties of self-report questionnaires are used (Schinka et al., 2004).

Experimental methods can also help us answer questions about genes and personality. In one study, participants provided a hair sample so researchers could extract DNA to determine which combination of serotonin transporter genes they had inherited. The participants completed a task that monitored their attentional focus to pictures of positive (e.g., a piece of chocolate), negative (a black widow spider), or neutral (a kitchen table) stimuli. (To avoid contaminating the experiment, the participants were not informed of the DNA test results.) Previous research has shown that people who have problems with anxiety focus their attention on threatening stimuli more than nonanxious people (Bar-Haim et al., 2007). It turns out that participants who had inherited two short versions of the serotonin transporter gene did not avoid looking at the negative images, whereas those who inherited two long copies looked more at positive images (Figure 12.10). Not only are short copies of this gene related to self-reported levels of anxiety, but they are also relevant to immediate reactions to stimuli that may be perceived as threatening (Fox et al., 2009, 2011).

Can we critically evaluate this genetic evidence?

An advantage of molecularly based genetic work over the twin studies described earlier is that this research holds the possibility of revealing cause-and-effect links between genes and personality. To date, however, this linkage still only remains a possibility. At this point the general consensus is that a vast number of genes, each of which has only a very small effect, account for individual differences in personality (Bae et al., 2013). The fact that genes are correlated to personality may lead you to wonder whether your personality is *caused* by the specific genes you inherit for, say, serotonin activity. It is important to remember that genes *interact* with the environment to produce behavior.

Why is this relevant?

Knowledge about how genes and personality are related can help psychologists identify risk factors for developing mental disorders. As we will see in Module 13.3, genetic studies of personality help us better understand the biological basis of psychological disorders such as anxiety and depression. This work raises some interesting possibilities, such as the potential to screen individuals to assess their risk of developing a disorder. In turn, at-risk individuals might be better helped with early detection and treatment. Also, links between DNA and personality may lead some psychologists to speculate and test hypotheses about how our personalities have evolved.

Figure 12.10 Genes, Serotonin, and Personality

People who inherit two copies of the long version of the serotonin transporter gene frequently shift their attention toward positive images and avoid looking at negative images. People who inherit the short version of this gene do not show this bias. This association may reveal a connection between genes and personality traits such as neuroticism.

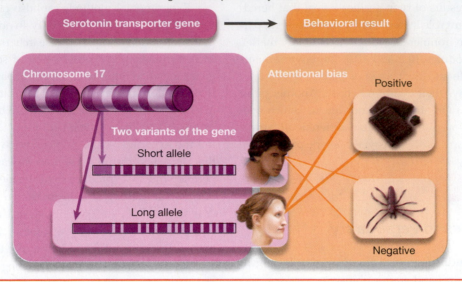

ANIMAL BEHAVIOR: THE EVOLUTIONARY ROOTS OF PERSONALITY One compelling argument for the evolution of personality is the presence of personality traits in numerous nonhuman species (Sih et al., 2015). For example, scientists have studied one particular species of bird (*Parus major*) that lives in Europe and Asia. These birds display two different types of behavior when they encounter new environments. One personality type is bold in its exploration of new environments and less responsive to external stimuli. The other type is more timid, less exploratory, and more reactive to external stimulation. These two personality types are known to have a strong genetic basis. Which of the two personality types is adaptive depends on what kind of year the birds are having. If there are limited resources, aggressive birds have greater reproductive success. In years where resources are plentiful, timid birds have greater success, possibly because the aggressive birds succumb to the downsides of being less responsive and wary of external stimulation, such as predators (Dingemanse et al., 2004).

Psychologists are finding that aspects of human personality are applicable to diverse species such as hyenas, octopuses, and chimpanzees, among many others.

The Big Five personality traits have been very useful in describing human behavior. Interestingly, they have been found in a rich diversity of other species, such as hedgehogs, ants, rhinos, and primates (Gosling, 2001). Clearly these animals cannot fill out the paper-and-pencil or computerized versions of a personality inventory such as the NEO-PI-R. Instead, people who are familiar with the animals rate their behaviors according to the five factors. Typically, observers strongly agree on their ratings of extraversion and neuroticism in the animals studied (Gosling, 2001).

Our closest primate cousins are a good place to look for personality characteristics in nonhumans. In one study, a list of adjectives was taken from a standardized measure of the Big Five and people who were familiar with the chimpanzee subjects rated how well the adjectives applied to each chimp on a 1- to 7-scale. Of the Big Five traits, extraversion, conscientiousness, and agreeableness were reliably found in the chimps (Weiss et al., 2007). Some researchers even argue you do not need a backbone to have a personality. Octopuses, for example, show stable individual differences in measures of activity, reactivity, and avoidance (Mather & Anderson, 1993).

EVOLUTION AND INDIVIDUAL DIFFERENCES IN PERSONALITY TRAITS Each person differs in personality, and as we have learned, genes contribute to these differences. Evolution involves changes in traits occurring within reproducing populations over many generations; it occurs at the level of populations. Individual differences have traditionally been regarded as evolutionary "noise," meaning that differences in personality are randomly distributed among individuals (Buss, 2009; Tooby & Cosmides, 1990). Genetically speaking, one individual within an entire breeding population cannot have much of an effect on how a trait evolves—unless this individual alone somehow breeds with most, if not all, receptive members. But this is not how mating tends to happen, and people do not tend to pair up, mate, and procreate at random. Personality characteristics may play an important role in determining how people pair up, which pairings produce children, and in the success of lasting relationships.

For example, when it comes to your surroundings, do you think your current environment is a matter of accident and external circumstance? Consider these questions:

- Did you do a random search of colleges and universities to decide where you would go?

- In high school and college, did you randomly point at students to decide who would be your casual acquaintances, lifelong friends, and romantic partners?

- Did you randomly select from a list of clubs or sports to determine which one you would spend hours of your free time?

If you made completely random choices, you might describe feeling like a fish out of water. We assume you answered "no" to these obvious questions, but this exercise illustrates that we *choose* particular environments, and typically there are reasons for making those choices: Our personalities influence decisions about with whom we associate, where we choose to go to school, and whether we spend hours every afternoon engaged in mastering chess, football drills, or dance routines. The extravert and the introvert, the neurotic and the tranquil, and the conscientious and the careless gravitate toward the respective niches they best fill.

This pattern has been confirmed in studies that monitored the language and social interactions of college students in their natural environments. Psychologists using special recording devices that monitor language and social interactions every 12 minutes found that over a four-week period, college students were remarkably consistent in the social environments they chose (Mehl & Pennebaker, 2003). They—and the rest of us—select environments that suit their personality characteristics and actively avoid those that might lead to discomfort. To the extent that fish make choices, few would opt for giving life on land a shot.

The importance of personality to social bonding is not trivial. Compatible personalities are the basis of successful friendships, professional relationships, and especially romantic relationships. You have likely heard the phrase "Opposites attract." The few examples you may be thinking of notwithstanding, for the most part we pair up with those who are most like us. Psychologists have found that across various cultures, spouses tend to be similar in some personality dimensions (McCrae et al., 2008; Bailey et al., 2013). In the human and animal kingdom, we call this phenomenon **assortative mating**—*choosing sexual partners who are similar to the individual doing the searching.* Assortative mating is among several evolutionary processes that account for the evolution of personality traits (Bailey et al., 2013). Personality traits can evolve among populations when (1) they have a heritable genetic basis, (2) individual members of the species pair up and mate in nonrandom, assortative fashion, and (3) the personality traits are influenced by natural selection (e.g., there is a survival and reproductive advantage to expressing extraversion).

The consistent appearance of core personality traits, such as the Big Five, across cultures and species indicates that these traits have been important to survival. At the same time, personality is flexible. Thus, evolution appears to also have favored variation in personality that allows us to fill diverse social and environmental niches.

JOURNAL PROMPT

Your Culture and You: Think about your own personality. Do you think that your upbringing and culture have played a central role in shaping it, or do you think that genetic inheritance has played a greater role? In your answer perhaps select one of the Big Five traits and use it to explain your answer and include examples.

The Brain and Personality

Ancient medicine (circa 400 B.C.) was guided by the theory of humorism. According to this theory, the body consisted of four humors—including blood, phlegm, black bile, and yellow bile. Physical illness and disorders of personality were attributed to imbalances among the four humors. For example, persistent sadness—including what we now call depression—was believed to result from too much black bile (which is the literal translation of the modern word "melancholy").

Science took a positive step forward when physicians, and those who would eventually become psychologists, decided that the skull and its contents were a better place to look to understand personality. In the late 1700s, a German doctor, Franz Gall, developed *phrenology*—the theory that personality characteristics corresponded to individual differences in brain structure that could be assessed by measuring the shape and contours of the skull surface (see Module 1.2). Phrenology held sway well into the 1800s. Its practitioners were correct in postulating that different psychological functions were localized in specific regions of the brain, but it turns out that the shape of the skull has little, if anything, to do with personality.

As knowledge about the brain has grown, psychologists have been better able to link personality characteristics with specific brain regions. Hans Eysenck, a pioneer in this area, proposed that arousal states of the brain are the basis of extraversion and that the reactivity of the limbic system (the emotional circuits, including the amygdala), reticular activating system, and cortex are correlated with extraversion (Figure 12.11; Eysenck, 1967). People who have decreased reactivity in these brain regions are basically "underaroused." In other words, they may be less sensitive to naturally occurring rewards. As a consequence, they seek out novel social and emotional stimulation. Introverts, by comparison, have higher reactivity within these brain regions and, therefore, seek less stimulation than do extraverts.

Modern-day researchers use imaging technology to examine the brain basis of personality. Neuroscientists have sought to determine how each of the Big Five traits maps onto brain anatomy. In one study using magnetic resonance imaging (MRI), researchers took detailed measures of brain volume in more than 100 participants who also rated themselves on the Big Five inventory. The scientists discovered that ratings on four of the Big Five traits—neuroticism, extraversion, agreeableness, and conscientiousness—corresponded to the size of predicted brain regions (DeYoung et al., 2010). People who rated themselves as high on conscientiousness had a correspondingly large region called the middle frontal gyrus, which is known to be involved in self-regulation and engaging in planned actions. Well-developed abilities to self-regulate (e.g., ensuring one's needs are met but with appropriate regard for others) and planning are associated with conscientiousness. A region of the brain called the medial orbitofrontal cortex, which is involved in reward processing, was larger in people who scored high on extraversion (see Figure 12.12).

The complexity of personality and of the brain makes it unreasonable to suppose we could ever point at a single region and declare it to be the center of any single personality trait. That said, we have come a long way from the days when personality was described in terms of the four humors of blood, phlegm, and black and yellow bile.

Figure 12.11 Extraversion, Introversion, and the Brain

Early work on the brain basis of personality linked reactivity of cortical areas, the limbic system, and the reticular activating system with extraversion and introversion.

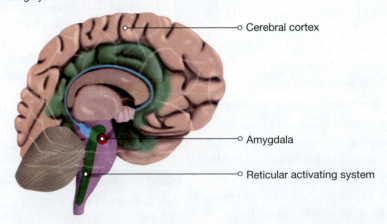

Cerebral cortex

Amygdala

Reticular activating system

Figure 12.12 Measuring Personality and Brain Anatomy

People's self-ratings of the Big Five traits correspond to their brain volume in specific regions. Here we see two (among several) regions of the brain where size is positively correlated with ratings of extraversion and conscientiousness (DeYoung et al., 2010).

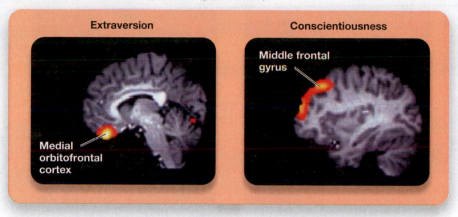

Module 12.2 Summary

12.2a   Know . . . key terminology associated with cultural and biological approaches to personality:

assortative mating
serotonin transporter gene
WEIRD

12.2b   Understand . . . how evolution has influenced personality.

Evolutionary psychologists speculate that traits such as neuroticism and extraversion evolved because they solved environmental and social problems encountered by our distant ancestors. Although this hypothesis is difficult to test directly, different sources of evidence lend support to it. The widespread occurrence of these personality traits among different species indicates that they are adaptive. Also, modern-day humans use individual differences in personality structure to decide on mating and possibly long-term partner choices.

12.2c   Apply . . . your knowledge to understand personality differences among cultures.

Major theories and inventories of personality attempt to capture the basic, core elements of personality. When it comes to cultural variation, people of different nationalities may, on average, be more or less open to experience, anxious, or extraverted. However, it remains possible that members of a different culture or nationality may have a unique personality trait that is not accounted for in the Big Five. It is important to avoid stereotyping or overestimating cultural differences in personality. If you responded to the true-or-false questions on page 408, you have probably now considered these words of caution.

The answers to those questions are as follows:

1. False. They rate about the same on this trait.
2. False. Although there are some differences, they are generally very small.
3. False. Americans are no more so than members of cultures who do not have this stereotype.
4. False. See "People from the United States are pushy."
5. False. Interestingly, Swiss people actually tend to hold this belief about themselves, but data suggest they are no more or less closed off to new experiences than members of countries who do not hold this stereotype.
6. True. This is generally the case, although the difference between genders is probably small.
7. True. As you read in this module people in China tend to embrace collectivism.

As you can see from this activity, there are some very general personality differences that occur between members of large groups. However, the consensus is that our stereotypes of people from entire countries tend to be inaccurate or at best exaggerated (Terracciano et al., 2005).

12.2d Analyze . . . claims that personality traits can be traced to a single gene or brain circuit.

Biologically based research on personality has demonstrated that there is a significant heritable (genetic) basis for individual differences in personality. This has even been demonstrated at the level of individual genes, as shown in research on the serotonin transporter gene. Also, size variation in brain anatomy is correlated with some specific aspects of some personality traits. For example, a brain region that plays a role in self-regulation is positively correlated with high scores on the personality dimension of conscientiousness (a large middle frontal gyrus is correlated with high conscientiousness). All of this is very informative, but it must be remembered that individual and cultural experience interacts with these biological processes. Furthermore, personality traits, such as those comprising the Big Five, entail complex behavioral, cognitive, and emotional processes that are not likely attributable to the activity of a single gene or brain circuit.

Module 12.2 Quiz

Know . . .

1. What does the WEIRD acronym refer to?
   A. Psychologists' preoccupation with abnormal personalities
   B. A single, specific group on which major perspectives and theories of personality are based
   C. A database that compiles personality profiles from people of all walks of life
   D. The application of personality to the various cultures from East Asia

Understand . . .

2. When it comes to personality, the phrase "opposites attract" seems to be the exception rather than the rule. People typically match up pretty closely when it comes to choices of romantic partners. Which evolutionary principle has been used to explain this phenomenon?
   A. Natural selection
   B. Assortative mating
   C. Adaptation
   D. Survival of the fittest

3. Even when identical twins are reared apart, they still tend to be very similar in personality. How is this strong evidence that genes contribute to personality?
   A. The similarities remain, even though there were probably significant differences in how the siblings were raised.
   B. Identical twins who were reared apart were most likely treated in very similar ways.
   C. There are fewer similarities when twins are reared together.
   D. Actually, identical twins who are raised apart show very little similarity.

Apply . . .

4. Results from applying the Big Five personality traits in other countries reveal that:
   A. people all over the world are identical in the patterns of their personality traits.
   B. people all over the word are radically different in the patterns of their personality traits.
   C. there are some cross-cultural differences as well as many similarities in the patterns of people's personality traits.
   D. the Big Five was not understood in other parts of the world because of language translation problems.

Analyze . . .

5. Which of the following statements best describes what psychologists know about the genetic basis of personality?
   A. Twin studies are the only source of information available about the genetics of personality.
   B. Technology is not sophisticated enough to link genes and personality characteristics.
   C. Genes do not contribute to personality characteristics.
   D. Some genes have been identified that underlie specific behaviors that relate to personality traits.

Module 12.3 Psychodynamic and Humanistic Approaches to Personality

Learning Objectives

12.3a Know . . . the key terminology related to the psychodynamic and humanistic approaches to personality.

12.3b Understand . . . how people use defense mechanisms to cope with conflicting thoughts and feelings.

12.3c Apply . . . both psychodynamic and humanistic perspectives to explain personality.

12.3d Analyze . . . the strengths and weaknesses of psychodynamic perspectives.

In the spring of 2010, wikileaks.org posted a graphic video recording from a US military helicopter. The video involved images in which the helicopter gunned down a group of men on the ground and voice recordings of the crew gaining permission to fire and coordinating the attack. These scenes alone would be disturbing to many individuals, but what drew the most attention—and public criticism—was the tone of the helicopter crew's dialogue. The pilot and gunner could be clearly heard joking about the fate of the men on the ground, daring them to run or raise a weapon, and then chuckling as they surveyed dead bodies on the ground.

The sharp contrast of the gruesome images with the light banter of the crew led many to question the psychological makeup of the soldiers involved. How can someone joke about the violent deaths of others, even if they are enemies? One argument suggests that these specific soldiers must be sadistic killers with no respect for human life. Others defend the soldiers by saying that they are typical individuals, that killing is psychologically troubling for all of us, and that the responses heard on the video are a means of coping with the stress of combat. If so, then, almost anyone in the same position would do the same thing.

Either interpretation of the soldiers' behavior is relevant to personality psychology. As you have learned in the previous two modules, personality represents a rigid or "fixed" way of being, but situational influences can also defy expectations about how individuals behave. Another view might suggest that conscious and unconscious mental processes interact to influence personality development, and also account for individual, unique ways of responding to a complex social world. **Psychodynamic theories of personality** *focus on how personality arises through complex interactions involving conscious and unconscious processes that occur from early development on through adulthood.* Personality is one of many psychological topics that the psychodynamic approach addresses. Psychodynamic psychologists also address mental health and therapies, a topic we will explore further in this Chapter 14.

The Psychodynamic Perspective

The psychodynamic approach to personality began with Sigmund Freud in the late 1800s. Freud was an Austrian physician who examined a patient's personality, just as a cardiologist would examine a patient's heart. Freud was interested in how personality is structured, how it functions, and how disorders arise. Because he came from a medical perspective, Freud's studies of personality were largely based on individual cases of people who sought his help for psychological difficulties they were experiencing.

Theories introduced by Freud have evolved considerably through time. Some have been abandoned, while remnants of others can be found in modern psychology. The psychodynamic perspective on personality does not consist of a single theory, but rather has evolved into a family of different theories that, despite their differences, are based on a few key observations (see Westen, 1998):

1. *Unconscious thoughts, memories, and emotions operate simultaneously and are major influences on our behavior.* Although we spend most of our time with the feeling that we are in control of our actions, closer examination suggests that unconscious thoughts and emotions can motivate our behavior. For example, a person might behave aggressively toward someone he feels threatened by, even though no actual threat has ever been directed toward him. Perhaps at an unconscious level he is afraid and therefore reacts defensively even though such a response is unwarranted.
2. *Personality takes shape in early childhood and children learn to regulate their emotions during this period of development.* Psychodynamic theorists place a great deal of importance on early childhood experiences. Although adults may change their behavior with effort, personality is thought to be formed well before adulthood. An important part of childhood is learning appropriate and acceptable ways of experiencing and expressing thoughts and emotions.
3. *Mental representations of the self and others shape how the individual acts.* The nature of key social relationships, particularly with the parents, determines personality development. During childhood, individuals learn about relationships from interacting with family or other caregivers, and they learn about themselves from the way they are treated.

Although these observations are not unique to psychodynamic psychology, they represent some of the core beliefs that shaped psychodynamic thinking. Keep them in mind as you read about personality theories, starting with Freud's approach.

THE STRUCTURE OF PERSONALITY Like many other psychodynamic theorists, Freud hypothesized that the human psyche consists of multiple, sometimes conflicting, processes. He theorized that three hypothetical, interacting parts exist: the *id*, the *ego*, and the *superego* (Figure 12.13). Each part has its own unique principle guiding it, and each contributes unique factors to an individual's personality.

The **id** *represents a collection of basic biological drives, including those directed toward sex and aggression.* Freud believed the id was fueled by an energy called *libido*. Although this term is more commonly used in reference to sexual energy, the libido also controls other biological urges such as hunger. The id motivates people to seek out experiences that bring pleasure, with little regard for the appropriateness or consequences of their realization. As a consequence, the id is said to operate according to the *pleasure principle*. The search for instant gratification motivated by the id may not always be appropriate from a social perspective, however—and that is where the ego comes into play.

The **ego** *is the component of personality that keeps the impulses of the id in check*—to delay the gratification sought by the id until it is socially appropriate. The ego represents the ability to understand that an individual cannot eat, engage in sexual activity, or otherwise give in to the id all the time. Therefore, it is said to operate according to the *reality principle*.

The third component of the human psyche, the **superego**, *was thought to develop during our upbringing; it serves as an inner voice we hear when we shame ourselves for acting inappropriately or lavish praise on ourselves for doing something good.* The moral composition of the superego is primarily learned from the authority of one's parents or guardians.

Interestingly, Freud emphasized that the influence of the id is present at birth, whereas the superego must develop with experience. This concept would seem to suggest that people are born to be bad—thus some have argued that Freud had a rather grim view of human personality. Once the three components are in place, the id, ego, and superego operate simultaneously, at times in harmony and at others in conflict. In fact, this *intrapsychic conflict* is one of the hallmarks of Freud's theory. Consider the soldiers described at the beginning of the module: From Freud's perspective, everyone has an id that provides

Figure 12.13 The Freudian Structure of Personality

A popular depiction of how Freud viewed personality features an iceberg, with the unconscious mind residing below the surface and conscious awareness at only the tip of the iceberg. The id is completely submerged, whereas the ego and the superego operate at both unconscious and conscious levels. One shortcoming of this analogy, however, is that it does not represent the *dynamics* of psychodynamic theory. Specifically, intrapsychic conflict involves the three aspects of personality shifting and applying pressure on each other constantly.

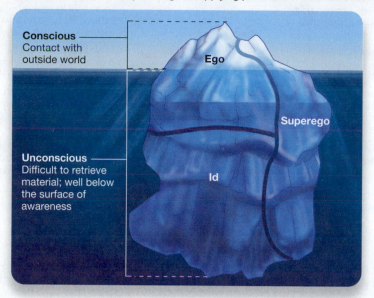

Conscious
Contact with outside world

Unconscious
Difficult to retrieve material; well below the surface of awareness

Ego

Superego

Id

the aggressive drives to act as a soldier, even though the superego might nag that "killing is wrong," and the ego may simply concentrate on the reality of the current situation. Understanding intrapsychic conflict in this manner can help a psychoanalyst (i.e., someone who approaches therapy from a psychodynamic perspective) understand an individual's personality. What is especially important is uncovering conflicts that are unresolved, which might result in guilt if the superego wins out, or in hostility if the id is victorious.

UNCONSCIOUS PROCESSES AND PSYCHODYNAMICS

How can psychodynamics claim the id is a driving force if we are not aware of it? Freud's answer was that our behavior is controlled by both unconscious and conscious processes. The *unconscious* mind includes impulses and drives that we are not directly aware of, whereas *conscious* thoughts are those for which you are aware.

Consider an example of how conscious and unconscious processes operate simultaneously. A person who was raised to believe in gender and ethnic equality is aware of his beliefs about women, men, and members of other ethnicities. He is riled when he overhears a degrading sexist or ethnic remark. This person's conscious awareness of his thoughts and emotions suggests that he fully believes in equality. A psychodynamic psychologist might say his attitude toward others is based on a well-developed superego. However, when this same person hears a story about a doctor, he might assume the doctor is male if this was not directly specified in the story. In addition, he may consistently choose to sit away from members of other ethnicities

when he rides the subway. These responses would suggest that the individual's conscious belief in equality may not similarly reside in his unconscious mind.

Recent laboratory experiments have revealed rather significant discrepancies between conscious and unconscious attitudes, thoughts, and emotions (Banaji & Heiphetz, 2010). The conflicts that arise because of these discrepancies are dealt with in a variety of ways—in particular, through the use of what have been termed defense mechanisms.

Defense Mechanisms   Because Freud was a physician interested in mental problems, he focused a great deal of attention on the conflicts and experiences that invoke anxiety. He was particularly interested in the idea that so many conflicts occurred unconsciously. To explain this phenomenon, he and his daughter Anna (also a key figure in early psychodynamic psychology) identified a number of **defense mechanisms**, *which are unconscious strategies the ego uses to reduce or avoid anxiety, guilt, and other unpleasant feelings* (Freud, 1936). Table 12.2 lists several of these mechanisms, some of which appear to have scientific support. Groups of defense mechanisms tend to share some similarities, such as rationalization and denial, which both allow anxiety-provoking thoughts to enter consciousness, but then change the way they are understood. The person who avoids sitting next to someone of a different ethnicity while on the subway may try to *rationalize* his actions by convincing himself that his choice was based on seating space rather than prejudice. Another person may have a series of embarrassing binge-drinking episodes that damage important relationships, and yet deny she has a drinking problem by

Table 12.2 Defense Mechanisms

According to psychodynamic views of personality, the ego uses defense mechanisms to reduce anxiety caused by urges or impulses originating from the id.

Defense Mechanism	Definition	Freudian Application	Modern Example*
Repression/suppression	Actively drowning out thoughts, memories, or wishes.	Feelings of anger toward the same-sexed parent are rejected.	Using fMRI technology, researchers have observed distinct patterns of brain activity when subjects were asked to forget information (Anderson et al., 2004).
Denial	Resistance to perceiving what actually occurs.	Feelings of aggression toward the same-sexed parent are avoided.	People tend to believe they are less vulnerable than the "average person" to misfortunes such as losing a job or getting a debilitating illness (Perloff & Fetzer, 1986).
Isolation	Creating a mental gap between a threatening thought and other feelings or thoughts.	Anxiety associated with toilet training and disapproval from parents is avoided by dismissing parental wishes.	People who are given little time to process evaluations from others are more likely to dismiss negative feedback than people given a lot of time to process their evaluations (Hixon & Swann, 1993).
Reaction formation	Altering an unacceptable impulse into its opposite.	Anxiety that accompanies hostility toward one's same-sexed parent is reduced by expressing affection.	Men who report negative attitudes toward homosexuality show greater physical arousal in response to images of men engaged in homosexual activity than do nonhomophobic men (Adams et al., 1996).

*Some of these examples, such as repression, are the source of ongoing debate among psychologists.

SOURCE: Based on Freudian Defense Mechanisms and empirical findings in modern social psychology: Reaction formation, projection, displacement, undoing, isolation, sublimation and denial" by R.F. Baumeister, K. Dale, and K. L. Sommer, (1998), *Journal of Personality, 66,* 1081–1124.

convincing herself that she can stop any time she chooses. Other defense mechanisms tackle anxiety by simply trying to keep it out of consciousness altogether.

Working the Scientific Literacy Model

Suppression as a Defense Mechanism

Defense mechanisms can work in many ways, from changing the way we think about events (rationalization), to changing the way we experience them (sublimation). If the purpose of a defense mechanism is to prevent anxiety, there may be no better way than to keep the thoughts out of mind altogether, processes known as repression and suppression.

What do we know about suppression?

Defense mechanisms may occur in response to *thought intrusions*—the tendency for traumatic events to keep popping into mind, often in ways that interfere with daily functioning. *Repression* is the unconscious act of keeping troubling ideas out of awareness. Because it is hypothesized to be an unconscious process, it cannot be observed directly and is only inferred from situations in which it appears to have occurred. As a result, many psychologists who do not adopt a psychodynamic approach are skeptical of it (see also Module 7.3). In contrast, **suppression** is *the conscious attempt to block out or ignore troubling thoughts*. Because it is based on a conscious decision, it is possible to study suppression in experiments. Suppression and repression may be helpful if they free up cognitive resources and reduce the continuing distress.

How can scientists study suppression?

Experiments on suppression often begin by having participants view emotional images, such as grisly pictures of injuries and death, each of which is paired with a neutral retrieval cue that may later serve as a reminder of the emotionally charged image. Next, experimenters may provide instructions for *direct suppression*, which asks participants to intentionally banish all thoughts of the upsetting image, or they may instruct the participants to engage in *thought substitution*, such as thinking about the retrieval cue paired with a different, non-emotional event. Both techniques produce suppression effects; participants who use these techniques have fewer thought intrusions and, when cued to recall the suppressed thoughts, remember fewer details than members of control conditions. Additionally, brain scans indicate that both techniques involve signals from the frontal lobes, which interfere with memory formation in the hippocampus (Benoit & Anderson, 2012; Kupper et al., 2014). Other research suggests that suppression may be beneficial; individuals who are better at suppressing negative thoughts have lower levels of neuroticism and spend less time ruminating over their troubles (Ryckman & Lambert, 2015) and suppression may decrease the duration of physiological responses to stress (Lemaire et al., 2014).

Can we critically evaluate the research on suppression?

The research described suggests that people can suppress unpleasant information and may even benefit from it. However, the experimental research takes place in a laboratory with images of trauma experienced by others. Does suppression work the same way outside the lab when people experience real trauma, such as violent crime or severe car accidents? The fact that so many individuals experience thought intrusions suggests that there is a limit to the power of this mechanism. In addition, the research on long-term benefits of suppression is purely correlational, and much of it self-reported. Therefore, we should consider the alternative explanation that people who are less neurotic simply believe that they suppress often and effectively. These points aside, the concept of suppression offers a level of scientific rigor and support not often achieved in psychodynamic research on personality.

Why is suppression relevant?

With a greater understanding of suppression, psychotherapists can develop techniques to encourage appropriate and effective use of suppression. Doing so might help individuals function more effectively and experience lower levels of emotional distress. Along with that, further laboratory and therapy-based research should shed light on when suppression might do more harm than good, perhaps by ignoring a very real problem that should be directly addressed.

JOURNAL PROMPT

Suppression: Suppression was studied in the laboratory experiment you just read about. Do you think that it happens in normal everyday life too? If not, why? And if so, describe a personally relevant example that comes to mind.

PSYCHOSEXUAL DEVELOPMENT   We do not come into the world knowing how to manage daily life, nor do we know right from wrong. To Freud, the infant is a bundle of impulses; it is only through experience that the ego and superego can emerge. Freud explained that these aspects of personality develop through a series of stages that occur mostly in the first five years of life (as summarized in Table 12.3). In each stage, pleasurable sensory experiences are focused in different parts of the body, and the id is driven to experience as much as possible.

Freud described the first part of life as the oral stage: A phase in which infant attention focuses on sensations of the mouth. This is a biological impulse that ensures the infant is motivated to get nourishment. Imagine what it must be like for an infant in the oral stage: For the first year, everything is great—you cry and you get fed—and you spend the rest of your time putting your hands and all sorts of other objects in your mouth. Then one day, weaning suddenly begins and your mother tells you that you have to wait to eat. You have never been told "no" before! This is a normal part of development in which the child learns to delay gratification; this represents the development of the ego, which serves to adapt to social realities. For some individuals, this process is more difficult and may result in a **fixation**, *in which an individual becomes preoccupied with obtaining the pleasure associated with a particular stage.* Freud might explain that habits such as biting your fingernails or excessive gum chewing stem from unresolved conflict during the oral stage. In the anal stage, the main conflict arises from developing basic self-control including toilet-training. Fixation in this stage results in being excessively neat and organized (*anal-retentive*) or, on the opposite end of the spectrum, a person who becomes sloppy and messy. He would attribute these habits to very early life experiences that remain in the unconscious mind, labeling them as oral or anal fixations.

Modern psychodynamic psychologists generally do not agree that Freud's stages of psychosexual development are directly applicable to personality development. Clinical psychologists, however, attest to observing patterns that are consistent with Freud's observations of each stage of psychosexual development (Westen, 1998). For example, one study reported that children are more likely to show affection to the same-sexed parent and aggression toward the opposite-sexed parent (Watson & Getz, 1990). This is reminiscent of the Oedipal complex occurring during the phallic stage (see Table 12.3), although you should notice there is no reference to sexual attraction toward the opposite-sexed parent.

EXPLORING THE UNCONSCIOUS WITH PROJECTIVE TESTS   How can a psychoanalyst become aware of something that is, by definition, unavailable to consciousness? Freud employed techniques such as *dream*

Table 12.3 Stages of Psychosexual Development According to Freud

Stage	Pleasure Focus	Fixation Results
Oral (0–18 months)	Actions of the mouth—sucking, chewing, swallowing	Excessive pleasure derived from eating, drinking, smoking, and other oral activities
Anal (18–36 months)	Bowel elimination, control	Excessive cleanliness or sloppiness
Phallic (3–6 years)	Genitals	Castration anxiety (males), or penis envy (females)
Latency (6 years until puberty)	Sexual interests in period of dormancy	None
Genital (puberty and after)	Sexual experiences with other people	None

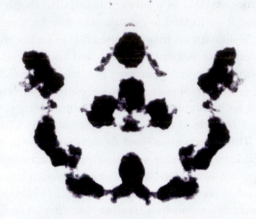

Some psychologists attempt to measure personality characteristics by analyzing the verbal responses clients use to describe what they see in a Rorschach inkblot such as this.

In the Thematic Apperception Test, the individual is asked to tell a story about what is happening in different images. Responses are thought by some to reveal something important about personality.

Figure drawing is another projective technique used by some psychologists. The content of the drawings is analyzed and interpreted by the therapist. It turns out that these drawings are somewhat related to artistic ability and intelligence, but not personality (Lilienfeld et al., 2000). This is a problem of validity. The figure drawing technique does not appear to measure what it claims to measure: personality.

analysis; that is, he viewed dreams as direct links to the unconscious mind. According to Freud, because the id does not use language, the conscious mind can make sense of dreams only by interpreting what they symbolize. Freud also noticed clues to the unconscious in the little things people do, a gesture, a slip of the tongue, or even a joke. To Freud, all of these behaviors are clues to what is going on in the unconscious mind.

Since Freud's time, some have attempted to develop more standardized techniques for probing the unconscious. These **projective tests** *are personality tests in which ambiguous images are presented to an individual to elicit responses that reflect unconscious desires or conflicts.* They are called "projective" because the image itself might not represent anything in particular, but rather how an individual describes the stimulus is thought to be a projection of her own thoughts and personality. Most psychologists are very skeptical of these tests, however, and they are only used by a small minority of psychologists (Hojnoski et al., 2006; Lilienfeld et al., 2000). This is largely because projective tests have low *interrater reliability*, meaning that two people giving the same test to the same person often come up with different interpretations. If different testers regularly come up with different answers, then it would appear that the tests are more of a source of interpretation rather than a tool to access specific information.

ALTERNATIVE PSYCHODYNAMIC APPROACHES Freud attracted many followers, but some of his contemporaries took psychodynamic psychology in different directions. They recognized that sex and aggression are not the only motives relevant to personality development; indeed, other motivational forces, such as the need for belonging and the need for achievement are important aspects of personality. Like Freud, however, these theorists emphasized the existence of multiple, unconscious processes and the importance of development.

Swiss psychologist Carl Jung (1875–1961) originally worked with Freud, but had strong, bitter disagreements and parted ways. In doing so, Jung (the Ju in his name is pronounced like "you") founded **analytical psychology**, *a branch of psychology that describes personality as it relates to unconscious archetypes.* These *archetypes* are images and symbols that are thought to have universal meaning among all humans, such as archetypes for a mother or father, and a notion of a God. Jung believed that in addition to a personal unconscious, humans also possess a *collective unconscious* filled with memories that can be traced to our ancestral past. Because these archetypes are generally unconscious, they were thought to organize human thoughts and behavior, and therefore personality.

Others who followed in Freud's footsteps included Alfred Adler (1870–1937) and Karen Horney (pronounced HORN-eye; 1885–1952), both of whom placed far less emphasis on sexual conflict and personality development than did Freud. Adler viewed the social environment as critical to personality development. He believed that people develop an *inferiority complex*, an abnormal personality that results from struggling with feelings of inferiority in one's social environment. Horney, like Adler, saw social dynamics as critical to personality. Instead of sexual conflicts, Horney viewed interpersonal conflict between children and their parents as important to personality development.

Freud's theories are widely criticized as sexist and overly focused on the darks sides of humanity; this is related to another fault which is that he drew his ideas almost entirely from individuals experiencing psychological problems. Perhaps most important is that these are largely pseudoscientific ideas, meaning that they do not generate hypotheses that can be confirmed or disconfirmed. For instance, if we were to tell you that, while growing up, you were sexually attracted to your opposite-sexed parent, you could say one of two things: You could either confirm that this was the case, or you could deny it. In the latter case, a Freudian psychoanalyst could simply say you were employing a defense mechanism and *repressing* the memories. Thus, this idea cannot be falsified.

These are just a few critiques of Freud's theory, but they signal serious problems with his ideas. Thus it is not surprising that other psychologists took psychodynamic theory in different directions. Contemporary psychodynamic psychologists primarily work in the field of clinical psychology, where recent research shows that modern psychodynamic approaches can be an effective treatment for certain disorders (Shedler, 2010). We will encounter psychodynamics again in Module 14.2.

Humanistic Approaches to Personality

Other psychologists keen on understanding human personality took the idiographic approach and focused on what contributes to each individual's happiness and fulfillment. Abraham Maslow (1908–1970) believed that all humans seek to fulfill a hierarchy of needs, which begins with satisfying basic motivations for food and physical safety, and progresses toward more psychologically complex experiences such as feeling a sense of security

and love for others and by others. When basic needs for love are met, human beings seek to achieve self-esteem. The most advanced stage of personality development is reached with **self-actualization**, *which involves reaching our fullest potential* (Maslow, 1968; see also Module 11.3). During the mid-20th century, Maslow and others created a movement called **humanistic psychology** *that emphasized the unique and positive qualities of human experience and potential.* This perspective was viewed as an alternative to psychodynamic theory as well as to behaviorism, both of which did not acknowledge an important role for free will in human behavior.

Like Maslow, Carl Rogers (1902–1987) held a more optimistic view of humanity. According to his **person-centered perspective**, *people are basically good, and given the right environment, their personality will develop fully and normally.* Humans, he said, have the motivation and potential to expand their horizons, mature, and fulfill each of their capacities. During his career Rogers became increasingly focused on a particular aspect of personality, the **self-concept**—*that is, the collection of feelings and beliefs we have about who we are.* Those persons with a positive self-concept are aware of their qualities, including both their limitations and their abilities. Those individuals with a negative self-concept focus on what they want to be (their "ideal self"), rather than on what they actually are. For example, a person with limited ability to play music may insist on joining a band, but may develop a negative self-concept because he is focusing on an ideal version of himself, rather than on his real self.

In conclusion, humanistic ideas offer an alternative approach to personality that stands in stark contrast to psychodynamic theory. One advantage to Rogers's work is that his theories were tested empirically, which was not the case with Freud's work. Many who prefer the humanistic approach do so not for scientific reasons, however, but because they value the more optimistic view of human nature and the potential for free will that are lacking in the psychodynamic approach. To test your knowledge about distinctions between psychodynamic and humanistic views, complete the activity in Table 12.4.

Table 12.4 Applying Psychodynamic and Humanistic Views of Personality

Consider the following possible quotes made by psychologists who take either a psychodynamic or humanistic in their approach to personality. For each quote, identify which approach would apply to the claim or point being made.

1. "Interactions between our primal drives and our attempts to control them are judged by an inner voice resembling that of our parents"
2. "One barrier to developing a complete and mature personality is a negative self-concept. A belief that we cannot change or improve"
3. "People are inherently good, and are not controlled by deviant or instinctive urges"
4. "Failure to resolve intrapsychic conflicts during early development will have lingering negative effects on adult personality"

Answers: 1. Psychodynamic, 2. Humanistic, 3. Humanistic, 4. Psychodynamic

Module 12.3 Summary

12.3a   Know . . . the key terminology related to the psychodynamic and humanistic approaches to personality:

analytical psychology
defense mechanisms
ego
fixation
humanistic psychology
id
person-centered perspective
projective tests
psychodynamic theories of personality
self-actualization
self-concept
superego
suppression

12.3b   Understand . . . how people use defense mechanisms to cope with conflicting thoughts and feelings.

According to the psychodynamic perspective, defense mechanisms activate whenever our unconscious drives come into conflict with the ego or the superego. These mechanisms may involve repressing urges, displacing them, or even finding subtle, more acceptable ways of expressing them.

12.3c   Apply . . . both psychodynamic and humanistic perspectives to explain personality.

Each school of thought offers a very different perspective on personality. One key difference to consider is that the psychodynamic perspective emphasizes internal conflict and unconscious processes, while humanistic perspectives emphasize free will and the inherent good of people. The activity in Table 12.4 will help you distinguish the two views.

12.3d   Analyze . . . the strengths and weaknesses of psychodynamic perspectives.

Psychodynamic theories can provide some compelling explanations for human motivation. For example, it is easy to understand how social and moral conflicts arise when couched in terms of a struggle between the id and the ego. At the same time, this approach does not have a lot of scientific support. It is not possible to objectively identify the structure of an individual's personality from this perspective; instead, psychodynamic theorists must rely on subjective interpretations. Attempts to add rigor to the process by developing and using projective tests have been largely unsuccessful.

Module 12.3 Quiz

Know . . .

1. According to Freud, the _____ is the personality component that is responsible for seeking to satisfy basic biological needs.
   A. id
   B. ego
   C. superego
   D. libido

2. In contrast to psychodynamic theory, humanistic theory emphasizes:
   A. how defense mechanisms affect behavior.
   B. how personalities are determined by biology.
   C. how personality is determined by the environment.
   D. free will.

Understand . . .

3. A defense mechanism would be employed:
   A. by the id to create conflict.
   B. by the superego to reduce or avoid conflict.
   C. by the ego to reduce or avoid conflict.
   D. by the superego to create conflict.

Apply . . .

4. Steven lied to about his brother to avoid getting in trouble with his parents, but now he is experiencing extreme guilt. According to Freud, this guilt would arise due to the activity of the _____.
   A. Oedipal complex
   B. ego
   C. superego
   D. libido

Analyze . . .

5. Why have psychologists questioned the practice of using projective tests to measure personality?
   A. Evaluators very often agree on how to interpret an individual test.
   B. Evaluators often do not agree on how to interpret an individual test.
   C. Because using trait inventories is preferred for insurance purposes.
   D. These tests often provide disturbing details about a person's unconscious.

Module 12.4 Scientific Literacy Challenge: Online Matchmaking

Online matchmaking services are a big business, garnering multimillion dollar profits each year. Members of these services join because they find it difficult to meet other singles in person, and that first dates can bring too many disappointing discoveries of mismatched personalities and interests. The businesses claim to offer a scientific solution based on the psychology of personality and relationships. However, these businesses want to protect their secrets, so they do not reveal their data or their methods of determining which members will make a good match. Without access to that information, we must look to outside sources of evidence to evaluate their level of success. Before you start this activity, take a minute to write your thoughts about matchmaking sites.

JOURNAL PROMPT

Perhaps you are a current or past member of a matchmaking site. If not, imagine you just created an account with the largest company in the business. If you were honest in completing your personality tests and interest inventories, do you believe they could accurately predict what type of person you would be most compatible with?

What do we know about online matchmaking sites?

The advertisement promises to help people find compatible romantic partners based on their personality and lifestyle. Read on to find out if this approach is likely to be effective.

Personal Introductions

"We will introduce you to that perfect someone."

At Personal Introductions, you will receive a full profile of interests, values, and **personality traits** for every match we identify. Using scientifically developed surveys and the **Big 5 model** of individual personalities, we are able to take the guesswork out of finding you that perfect someone.

- Create profile. FREE
- Search millions of partners. FREE
- Cancel any time

I am :
From :
Birthday :
Username :
Password :
Email :   Click here

FREE TRIAL

How do scientists study online matchmaking?

Online matchmaking companies appear in the news, on talk shows, and in other popular media, thanks to their popularity and the impressive profits they bring in. In a straightforward web search, we found a number of recent articles posted by reputable news sources, many with links to scientific journals. Here is an example of one popular news magazine's report; make sure you pay attention to the scientific concepts, particularly those in the highlighted sections.

There is no shortage of data on matchmaking, but the results are not always clear. One of the positives is that people can definitely make the first connection. This particular website's user satisfaction surveys indicate that it is much easier to introduce yourself online and, in many cases, it is more comfortable than in-person introductions. The sites also have success in that, on average, the surveys show that about 20% of respondents are currently in a relationship with someone they met online. However, the outcomes are not always great. A recent longitudinal study followed members of one matchmaking site, as well as couples who met for the first time in person, and found that couples who met online were more likely to break up, whether they got married or not. Researchers interpreted this to mean that the algorithms—mathematical formulas used to find compatible mates—are really not as effective as the companies claim. However, another interpretation is that the algorithms are fine, but members are trying to make such a good impression that they aren't that honest or accurate when they create their profiles.

Several important concepts were described in this brief overview of matchmaking sites. Were you able to identify qualities of good science? Test yourself with the following quiz, and note that the highlighted areas in the article are highly relevant to the questions.

1. What is the research design described in the longitudinal study described?
   a. Correlational
   b. Experimental
   c. Natural observation
   d. Quasi-experimental
2. The user satisfaction survey and the longitudinal studies were conducted with the clientele of a single company. If you applied the findings to understand all matchmaking services and their customers, you would be venturing a conclusion about the _____.
   a. generalizability of the studies
   b. sample
   c. ecological validity of the study
   d. reliability of the measurements
3. The paragraph ends by questioning whether members of online matchmaking sites are prone to _____.
   a. random sampling
   b. socially desirable responding
   c. the Hawthorne effect
   d. validating

Answers: 1. d 2. a 3. b

Now that we have seen some of the evidence, let's engage in critical thinking.

How do we think critically about online matchmaking services?

Below are four tenets of critical thinking. Match each tenet to one of the four statements that follow, considering how the tenet applies to the statement about matchmaking services.

1. Do not rely on anecdotal evidence.
2. Tolerate ambiguity.
3. Examine assumptions and biases—both yours and those of your information sources.
4. Consider alternative viewpoints.

a. The survey showing user satisfaction was conducted by one of the matchmaking companies—which is hardly an impartial perspective.

b. Site members seem to like that it is much easier to meet the right kind of people, and yet the research also says that couples who meet online are more likely to break up. I guess I'd like to learn more before I can decide whether I would use one of these services.

c. My brother always tries to get me to use the site because he got married to someone he met online and he swears this matchmaking method works. However, his is just one example. The surveys described in this article suggest that his relationship is probably not typical.

d. Although based on the research the reporter questioned the quality of matchmaking computer algorithms, I do think it is important to ask how honest people are being with what they present in their profiles, or whether some other unexplored variable explains differences between online and in-person relationship success.

Answers: 1. *c* 2. *b* 3. *a* 4. *d*

This represents a good start on addressing online dating with critical thinking. Now, read on to see how this evidence might be applied.

How are online matchmaking services relevant?

People invest so much time and emotional energy trying to find the right person. Consumers of online matchmaking services are no exception—don't be fooled by the convenience this avenue might offer. Read about the relevance of these services and share your thoughts about online matchmaking services.

There is no sign that web-based matchmaking is going away, so it is important that its users keep realistic expectations. It seems clear that these sites do make the introductions significantly easier and more comfortable for many. Although some data suggest that relationships formed online are less successful than those formed in person, we also know that couples who have met through these services have lived happily ever after. Improving online matchmaking experiences and outcomes may be a matter of gathering more basic research on successful couples. These could lead to more effective computer algorithms to match profiles. On the other hand, it could be a matter of finding the right type of people to join: Maybe introverts would benefit from the easier introductions whereas extroverts benefit more from meeting in person.

SHARED WRITING

Why do you think couples who form via online avenues may be more likely to break up than are those who meet in person? Try to incorporate personality concepts into your answer.

Chapter 12 Quiz

1. Some psychologists use a(n) _____ approach to studying personality, which is a person-centered method in which researchers focus on individual people and their unique personalities.
   A. nomothetic
   B. factor-analysis
   C. idiographic
   D. reciprocal

2. Unlike the strict behaviorists' view, Bandura's theory of reciprocal determinism:
   A. emphasizes the importance of learning.
   B. acknowledges that people shape and determine their environments.
   C. emphasizes the importance of traits.
   D. assumes that traits are not stable over time.

3. What do twin studies indicate about the role of genes in personality?
   A. Heredity plays an important role in personality.
   B. Dizygotic twins are more likely than monozygotic twins to share personality traits.
   C. Personality is almost entirely determined by parenting and other environmental factors.
   D. Personality appears to be related to two different copies of a serotonin transporter gene.

4. Research into animal personalities suggests that:
   A. unlike human personality traits, animal personality traits have no genetic basis.
   B. humans are the only animals who have true emotions.
   C. the Big Five personality traits can be observed only in primates.
   D. the Big Five personality traits occur in many different types of animals.

5. Daniel's psychiatrist shows him a series of cards with abstract inkblots on them and asks Daniel to describe what he sees. When Daniel asks about the test, his psychologists refers to it as a(n) _____.
   A. projective test
   B. trait inventory
   C. Big Five questionnaire
   D. psychoanalytic personality report

6. As a response to both behaviorism and psychodynamic theory, Abraham Maslow (among others) initiated a movement called _____, which emphasized the unique and positive qualities of human experience and potential.
   A. phrenology
   B. humanistic psychology
   C. analytical psychology
   D. self-actualization

7. A major difference between the Big Five and the MMPI-2 is:
   A. the Big Five is ideally suited for measuring abnormal personality traits.
   B. the Big Five is an idiographic approach, whereas the MMPI-2 takes a nomothetic approach to measuring personality.
   C. the MMPI-2 accounts for states and situational factors, whereas the Big Five does not.
   D. the MMPI-2 can be used to measure abnormal personality traits and functioning.

8. Your friend, who is *normally* introverted, curses in outrage at the taxi driver who is trying to overcharge you. This event is most likely due to his _____.
   A. temperament
   B. subjective/situational state
   C. idealized self
   D. Big Five personality traits

9. Alternative approaches to personality such as the behavioral and cognitive approaches complement trait theories of personality because:
   A. behavior and personal experience, which influence personality, are major parts of the alternative approaches.
   B. trait theories focus on the negatives of personality.
   C. it is easier to observe behavior than to ask someone to fill out a personality inventory.
   D. trait theories focus only on the positive aspects of personality.

10. An outdated approach claiming that behavior and personality were based on the sizes of various regions of the skull surface was called:
    A. magnetic resonance imaging.
    B. alchemy.
    C. phrenology.
    D. humorism.

11. Hans Eysenck proposed that arousal states of the brain are the basis of extraversion, citing the importance of all but which of the following systems?
    A. Limbic system
    B. Parasympathetic nervous system
    C. Reticular activating system
    D. Cortex

12. Which of the following is *not* a point of emphasis for psychodynamic theories of personality?
    A. The role of unconscious motives
    B. The importance of early social relationships
    C. Learning how to cope with and regulate emotion
    D. Using trait descriptions to describe personality

13. According to Freud, which of the following is the order in which the stages of psychosexual development occur?
    A. Oral, anal, phallic, latency, genital
    B. Oral, anal, genital, phallic, latency
    C. Anal, oral, phallic, latency, genital
    D. Latency, oral, anal, genital, phallic

14. The aspect of consciousness proposed by Carl Jung that is a store of archetypes representing symbols and experiences common to all cultures is called the _____.
    A. preconscious
    B. subconscious
    C. analytical conscious
    D. collective unconscious

15. Alexandra's older sister is praised for being good at math, but Alexandra struggles with the subject. What would the resulting feelings of being "not good enough" be called?
    A. Negative reinforcement
    B. Negative archetype
    C. Inferiority complex
    D. Oedipal complex

Chapter 13
Psychological Disorders

Module 13.1 Defining and Classifying Psychological Disorders

Learning Objectives

13.1a Know . . . the key terminology associated with defining and classifying psychological disorders.

13.1b Understand . . . how disorders are viewed as either dimensional or categorical.

13.1c Understand . . . the differences between the concepts of psychological disorders and insanity.

13.1d Apply . . . your knowledge to reduce stigma and misunderstandings about psychological disorders you might encounter.

13.1e Analyze . . . whether the benefits of labeling psychological disorders outweigh the disadvantages.

Scientific knowledge about mental illness and its treatment changed at a blinding speed throughout the 20th century. In 1900, for individuals with serious disorders that we would now call psychosis, there was little hope for improvement and they were often thought of as an embarrassment by their families. Therefore, many were locked away in asylums where the public did not have to see them or speak of them. By 2000, there were effective treatments for many disorders that allow individuals who would have once been locked in an "insane asylum" to live in less restrictive settings, often at home. But as the scientific advances allowed people to live more *healthy lives, the social changes—the sense of embarrassment people feel about disorders—had not matched that pace. Mental health advocates asked: What good are treatments if people are afraid to seek them out? How are people to adapt to more healthy lives if they constantly cope with stereotypes about their condition? Based on these concerns, mental health advocates have shifted much more attention to fighting stigmatization—a sense of shame or disgrace—about mental health and have made amazing strides. Even 15 years ago, you would not expect openness at a formal, high-profile society event, but at the 2015 Academy Award ceremony, one award winner spoke about his suicide attempt as a teen and another spoke of losing her son to suicide. In 2000, it would have been shocking to have a professional football player speak openly about his experience with mental illness. Yet in 2014, Brandon Marshall of the Chicago Bears did just that, publicizing his personal struggle with borderline personality disorder as part of his efforts to fight stigma. In this module, we will discuss how psychologists understand psychological disorders, and encourage you to think about how friends, relatives, physicians, jurors, and society as a whole understand mental health.*

We routinely encounter information about psychological disorders such as depression or autism from many sources, including news, talk shows, and advertisements for prescription drugs. The amount of information floating around about these disorders is vast, and it can be challenging to sift through and critically analyze this enormous volume. To understand psychological disorders, we will apply two complementary models.

First is the **medical model**, which means *using our understanding of medical conditions to understand psychological conditions*. Just as diabetes has a set of symptoms, probable causes, and likely outcomes, so do psychological disorders. There are also preventive measures, interventions, and treatments targeted toward psychological disorders, just as there are for conditions such as diabetes or cancer. Today it might seem natural to talk about psychological problems in these terms, but in fact, the medical model has not always been the norm. Throughout history and in various cultures, other explanations have been proposed for what we now call psychological disorders. For example, hallucinations may be symptomatic of a psychological disorder in the United States. However, in another place or time, that same individual might be viewed as possessed by evil spirits, the victim of a curse, or even a prophet.

The second model we adopt includes the multiple perspectives of the *biopsychosocial model* (Table 13.1), first introduced in Module 1.1. For example, one biological factor contributing to depression involves disrupted activity of neurotransmitters such as serotonin. Psychological factors include persistent negative beliefs about the self (e.g., *nothing I do makes any difference in the world*) and feelings of hopelessness. Social factors such as impoverished

neighborhoods and stressful family problems contribute to the development of depression as well. As is the case with many physical disorders such as diabetes, psychological disorders can rarely be traced to a single cause, so the biopsychosocial approach helps us develop a comprehensive understanding of psychological disorders.

This chapter focuses on psychological disorders, which, generally speaking, comprise abnormal behavioral and cognitive functioning. Before we go any further, however, we need to identify what is meant by *abnormal* when it comes to human behavior and experience.

JOURNAL PROMPT

Culture and Mental Illness: Do you think that the term *abnormal* is relative from one individual to the next, or one cultural group to the next? Explain.

Defining and Diagnosing Abnormal Behavior

Abnormal psychology *is the psychological study of mental illness*, but the term *abnormal* needs some clarification. A person who deliberately cuts or burns himself is behaving abnormally because few people inflict such damage on themselves. Earning a medical degree before the age of 20 is even less typical, statistically speaking, but is not a symptom of mental illness. The difference between these two non-normal activities is that self-injury is a **maladaptive behavior**, *or behavior that hinders a person's ability to function in work, school, relationships, or society*. To distinguish between the abnormal and the unusual, mental health professionals consider three main criteria:

- The behavior causes distress to self or others.
- The behavior impairs the ability to function in day-to-day activities.
- The behavior increases the risk of injury, death, legal problems, or punishment for breaking rules or other detrimental consequences.

At first glance, these criteria may seem to suggest that mental illness is devastating and debilitating to the point where it would be obvious to anyone. However, signs of mental illness can—and often do—go unnoticed by others.

Table 13.1 Biological, Psychological, and Sociocultural Factors Influence Both Physical and Mental Disorders

	Diabetes	Major Depression
Biological	Genetic influences on pancreatic function; excessive refined sugars	Genetic influences on neurotransmitter production and function; sleep disruption; lack of positive emotional arousal
Psychological	Poor food choices; sedentary lifestyle; alcohol abuse	Negative self-concept; pessimism; negative life experiences
Sociocultural	Familial and cultural foods and traditions; limited budget for groceries; lack of physical and nutritional education in the schools; lack of role models	Lack of social support; social withdrawal; lack of psychological services; stigma regarding psychological treatments

It is not uncommon for individuals to keep distressing thoughts and feelings to themselves, or for the signs of mental illness to be more prominent in some contexts than others. To make matters more complicated, some individuals have been wildly successful in a few areas of life while the debilitating aspects of the illness are overlooked. Thus, many individuals who experience mental illness can get by without help, but their quality of life and functioning are impaired nonetheless.

A final point to consider is that psychological disorders can be *dimensional* in nature; they consist of typical experiences, except that they are more severe and longer lasting than usual, and they may occur in inappropriate contexts. We know that everyone experiences sadness, changes in appetite, or a night of sleeplessness, so the challenge of a diagnosis is determining when those characteristics are severe enough to be considered depression. Despite the dimensional nature of most disorders, diagnostic labels such as bipolar disorder or posttraumatic stress disorder (PTSD) can imply that conditions are more clear cut. This *categorical* view is appropriate for a disorder such as Down syndrome because it involves an unusual genetic condition: An individual either has the extra 21st chromosome linked to Down syndrome or does not.

When attempting to diagnose mental illness, psychologists and psychiatrists rely on the *Diagnostic and Statistical Manual for Mental Disorders* (**DSM-5**) (the 5 reflects the fact that it is currently in its fifth edition). Published by the American Psychiatric Association, the DSM-5 *offers guidelines for diagnosing the presence and*

severity of all varieties of mental disorder. For each disorder listed in the *DSM-5*, the guidelines convey several important pieces of information: a set of symptoms that define the condition, how to distinguish it from other disorders that share some of the same symptoms, and the *prognosis*, or how these symptoms will persist or change over time, with or without professional treatment.

The *DSM-5* includes many improvements over the previous edition in that it represents what professionals have learned from latest scientific research and is meant to make diagnosis less complicated. Despite these advantages, the *DSM-5* still has some limitations. Although its guidelines allow for reliable diagnosis of some disorders—multiple professionals will arrive at the same diagnosis for one person—other individuals' cases prove difficult to classify (Regier et al., 2013). Thus, a growing number of psychologists and psychiatrists argue that research should attempt to identify more objective markers of mental disorders such as brain abnormalities (Insel, 2014) or carefully structured interview procedures (Aboraya et al., 2014).

Mental Health in the Public Sphere

Psychological disorders represent a significant health concern. Nearly 20% of adults will experience a disorder within a typical year with about a fifth of those cases classified as severe (National Institutes of Mental Health [NIMH], 2015). Also, serious mental illnesses cut across numerous demographics such as age, gender, and ethnicity (Figure 13.1). Even if you are one of those fortunate individuals who has not personally experienced a psychological

Figure 13.1 Prevalence of Serious Mental Illness Among US, Adults (2012)

The numbers indicate the estimated percentage of the US population diagnosed with a serious mental illness. As you can see, mental illness affects people of all walks of life.

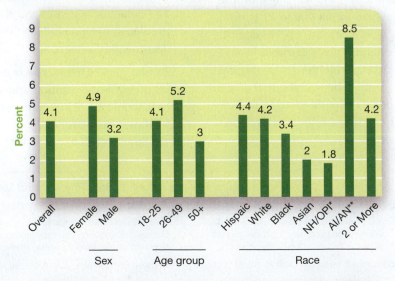

Data courtesy of SAMHSA.   NH/OPI* = Native Hawaiian/Other Pacific Islander
AI/AN** = American Indian/Alaska native

Source: http://www.nimh.nih.gov/health/statistics/prevalence/serious-mental-illness-smi-among-us-adults.shtml

disorder, you will benefit from being able to read about and understand mental health issues; if you consider that one in five adults experience a disorder in a given year, it is hard to imagine that you would not live or work with individuals who would benefit from your understanding.

Two major issues about mental health in the public sphere include (1) unjustified stigma about psychological disorders and (2) how the insanity defense factors into criminal cases. We will address both issues in this section.

Labeling, Stigma, and Psychological Disorders

The *DSM-5* provides names or *labels* for psychological disorders, which, in turn, indicate a set of symptoms, probable causes, and potential treatments. However, these diagnostic labels can also have their drawbacks, the worst of which is stigmatization.

What do we know about the stigma of mental disorders?

Stigmas include negative stereotypes about what it means to have a psychological disorder, and stigmatization may lead to discrimination, unjustified fears, and alienation. Attaching such labels can also lead people to misinterpret normal behavior as symptoms of a disorder. Even mental health professionals can be influenced by this practice, as shown by David Rosenhan's classic study from the 1970s. In his investigation, eight normal, healthy individuals volunteered to go to psychiatric hospitals with complaints about auditory hallucinations. All eight were admitted to the hospitals for either schizophrenia or manic depression (bipolar disorder). After their admission, these so-called patients behaved normally, complaining of no psychiatric symptoms whatsoever. Nonetheless, they remained hospitalized for an average of 19 days (Rosenhan, 1973). Apparently, the initial diagnosis led the hospital staff to misinterpret even normal behavior as symptoms of an illness.

How can science explain the personal effects of stigmatization?

Contemporary research is examining the stigma of mental illness from multiple perspectives using self-reports such as surveys and interviews. Perhaps the most important perspective comes from individuals who have been diagnosed. Many people find themselves sensing the stigma in their social interactions; this can lead to feelings of ostracism and isolation. You can imagine how this can compound the experience of depression, a disorder already characterized by feelings of hopelessness and loneliness (Switaj et al., 2014). From another perspective, even family members of people with mental illness report stigma by association. They often report feeling ostracized and judged as well, almost as if they have caused their loved one to experience the disorder (van der Sanden et al., 2014). More recently, researchers have examined *internalized stigma*—how individuals might come to view themselves more negatively because of their experience with mental illness. Internalized stigma is associated with lower self-esteem and, along with the perceptions of general stigma, a tendency to avoid treatments (Corrigan et al., 2014; Lannin et al., 2015).

Can we critically evaluate this information?

Few people would doubt that stigma can be real and harmful, but some have asked to what degree a diagnostic label itself might be the main source of the problem. If labels can lead professionals to view psychiatric patients differently, as in Rosenhan's study, they may produce the same effect—or an even stronger one—in the general public. However, we should also consider that the "patients" in this study were eventually released with "in remission" status, which also tells us that the psychiatrists and staff caring for them correctly interpreted their behavior after a sufficient period of time observing them. It would be far more shocking if the hospital workers made no attempt to help people who entered their facility.

Not all evidence suggests that psychiatric labels lead to negative views of individuals among the general public. It may be that, rather than a label, the symptoms themselves can be a source of stigma. Schizophrenia is a label for people who might experience delusions and hallucinations, mood disorders provide labels for

Stigma often leads to feelings of isolation. These feelings can, in turn, worsen the negative emotions associated with so many disorders.

persistent sadness social withdrawal, and personality disorders include emotional and sometimes aggressive or abrasive behaviors. These symptoms are likely to cause more interpersonal difficulty than a label. Therefore, we would argue that the public, like professionals, should be educated as to the nature of disorders along with the harm that stigma can cause.

Why is this relevant?

Researchers have identified a number of techniques that work in reducing stigmatization, at least for the short term (Stubbs, 2014). For example, research shows that personal contact and knowledge of biopsychosocial explanations of mental illness are associated with lower stigma (Boyd et al., 2010). Student groups at the high school and college levels have had success in reducing the stigma associated with mental illness at their campuses (McKinney, 2009; Murman et al., 2014). Finally, there are also politically oriented groups working to erase stigma through changes in public policy (Carter et al., 2014). Keep these findings in mind as you read the rest of this chapter; as an informed student you will be less likely to judge others and more likely to seek help yourself, or recommend it to others, if it is ever needed (See Table 13.2).

Highly publicized cases involving mental illness often get played out in courtroom proceedings, which can further lead to distorted views of people who are mentally ill. This brings us to the issue of the insanity defense.

THE INSANITY DEFENSE The **insanity defense** *is the legal strategy of claiming that a defendant was unable to differentiate between right and wrong when the criminal act was committed.* Although the insanity defense is always based on testimony from a psychiatrist (and often psychologists), it is important to note that insanity is a legal concept and not a specific disorder or an entry in the *DSM-5*. In fact, it is possible to plead temporary insanity without ever receiving a formal psychological diagnosis or, conversely, to have a psychological disorder—even a rather severe one—without being judged insane.

When successful, this insanity defense can greatly reduce the charges an individual must face, or reduce the duration or severity of a sentence. This was the case for Ebony Wilkerson, who drove her minivan with her three children inside into the Atlantic Ocean at Daytona Beach, Florida. The state's psychiatrist determined that she was legally insane, which resulted in lowering the charges from attempted second-degree murder to felony child endangerment; charges for which she was eventually found not guilty. Although this verdict prevented jail time, she was ordered to be treated in a secure, residential mental health center until the professionals there believed she was no longer a threat.

Court decisions like these can bring out strong emotions because some see it as an easy excuse for criminals to escape punishment. In reality, a successful insanity defense is a rare occurrence. Judicial systems do not keep a running count of insanity pleas, so estimating its use is a time-consuming process that few are willing to undertake. In the past 25 years, the best samples of court records and surveys of prosecuting or defense attorneys indicate that the plea is advanced in less than 1% of federal cases. Even then, it has a rather poor success rate—it is successful less than 20% of the time (Melton et al., 2007; Valdes, 2005).

Table 13.2 Attitudes Toward Mental Illness

Complete the following scale to measure your attitude toward mental illness. For each of the items, circle the number that best describes how much you agree or disagree with the statement.

Item	Completely Disagree				Completely Agree
If I had a mentally ill relative, I wouldn't want anyone to know.	1	2	3	4	5
Most of my friends would see me as being weak if they thought that I had a mental illness.	1	2	3	4	5
I would be very embarrassed if I were diagnosed as having a mental illness.	1	2	3	4	5
Mentally ill people scare me.	1	2	3	4	5
I would cross the street if I saw a mentally ill person coming to avoid passing him or her.	1	2	3	4	5
I think that mentally ill people are strange and weird.	1	2	3	4	5
Find your total score by adding up the numbers you circled and dividing by 6.					

Interpretation: This scale measures stigma toward individuals who have a mental illness. Compare your score to a large sample of high school students. Their average on this same scale was 2.13, with higher scores indicating greater levels of stigma. For those with a family member diagnosed with a mental disorder, the mean dropped to 2.05.

Source: Watson, A. C., Miller, F. E., & Lyons, J. S. (2005). Adolescent Attitudes Toward Serious Mental Illness. *Journal of Nervous and Mental Disease, 193,* 769–772.

Module 13.1 Summary

13.1a   Know . . . the key terminology associated with defining and classifying psychological disorders:

abnormal psychology
Diagnostic and Statistical Manual for Mental Disorders (DSM-5)
insanity defense
maladaptive behavior
medical model

13.1b   Understand . . . how disorders are viewed as either dimensional or categorical.

Disorders are defined and identified according to patterns of symptoms. Some symptoms and disorders are categorical because an individual clearly has the symptoms or does not. However, many, if not most, psychological disorders are dimensional in nature; they vary by degree of severity.

13.1c   Understand . . . the differences between the concepts of psychological disorders and insanity.

Many people get their information about psychological disorders from fiction or sensationalized events in the news, so it is important to make distinctions between the psychological concept of a disorder and the legal concept of insanity. Most people with psychological disorders are not considered insane; in fact, only a small minority of people ever could be. Within the legal system, individuals may be declared insane if they were unable to tell right from wrong when they committed an offense. This designation in no way provides a diagnosis of any specific type of mental disorder.

13.1d   Apply . . . your knowledge to reduce stigma and misunderstandings about psychological disorders you might encounter.

We all have misunderstandings about psychological disorders, but we reduce the tendency to stigmatize in at least two ways: Learning the material in this chapter should help, but also examine your own personal thoughts to distinguish what your assumptions are versus what science can tell. The activity in Table 13.2 "Attitudes toward mental illness" is a way to assess your own views on stigma and mental illness.

13.1e   Analyze . . . whether the benefits of labeling psychological disorders outweigh the disadvantages.

To evaluate the importance of the *DSM-5*'s labels, it would be helpful to consider their functions. They organize large amounts of information about symptoms, causes, and outcomes into terminology that mental health professionals can work with. From a practical point of view, this system meets the requirements of the insurance companies that pay for psychological services. One downside to this process is that once the label is applied, people may misinterpret behaviors that are perfectly normal.

Module 13.1 Quiz

Know . . .

1. The _____ uses an understanding of physical conditions to think about psychological conditions.
   - **A.** biopsychosocial model
   - **B.** dimensional view
   - **C.** categorical view
   - **D.** medical model

Understand . . .

2. Viewing a psychological disorder as an extreme case of otherwise normal behavior reflects the _____.
   - **A.** dimensional view
   - **B.** medical model
   - **C.** categorical view
   - **D.** biopsychosocial model

3. As described in this section, insanity:
   - **A.** is itself a psychological disorder.
   - **B.** describes a person with *any* psychological disorder.
   - **C.** is not recognized by the legal profession or judicial system.
   - **D.** is a legal term meaning that an individual could not distinguish between right and wrong when he or she broke a law.

Apply . . .

4. Which of the following has been demonstrated an effective way to reduce stigma?
   - **A.** Learning about biopsychosocial explanations for disorders
   - **B.** Understanding that all disorders can be treated as categorical conditions
   - **C.** Avoiding contact with individuals who might exhibit abnormal behaviors
   - **D.** Role-playing by asking to be admitted to a psychiatric hospital

Analyze . . .

5. Which statement best describes the effects of labeling someone with a mental disorder?
   - **A.** Labeling always leads to negative perceptions of the individual with the disorder.
   - **B.** Labeling can have either positive or negative effects, depending on factors such as context and expectations.
   - **C.** Knowing that someone has a mental disorder always leads to caring and compassionate responses.
   - **D.** Labeling does not work because the *DSM-5* categories are not adequate.

Module **13.2** Personality and Dissociative Disorders

Learning Objectives

13.2a Know . . . the key terminology associated with personality and dissociative disorders.

13.2b Understand . . . the phenomenon of dissociation and how a dissociative disorder might occur.

13.2c Apply . . . the biopsychosocial model to understand the causes of personality disorders.

13.2d Analyze . . . the status of dissociative identity disorder as a legitimate diagnosis.

Psychopath is one of the most evocative psychological terms out there and it often conjures up images of a ruthless serial killer. Psychologists are more likely to use the term psychopathy *when describing a collection of traits including self-centeredness, superficial charm, little or no empathy, dominance, and dishonesty. They could be referring to a serial killer, but then again they could also be talking about the men who have served as President of the United States. Psychologists have actually found correlations among psychopathic qualities and presidential performance. Presidents with higher levels of dominance, for example, are more likely to be viewed as world leaders, to*

start new programs, and demonstrate other measures of success (Lilienfeld et al., 2012). Psychopath will not be appearing on any campaign slogans during the next election cycle. Still, this illustrates that personality traits like dominance or empathy can be thought of as dimensions. Some of us regularly show empathy, some rarely, and some do not. As you move down the scale, you will eventually find psychopathy. A combined lack of empathy and ruthlessness can reflect a personality disturbed enough to be classified as a psychological disorder. Psychopathy is associated with antisocial personality disorder, one of several disorders of personality functioning.

In this module, we will begin by examining what happens when individuals experience problems during personality development and the effects it can have on their lives—and on others' lives as well. This discussion will be followed by examination of a different type of disorder known as *dissociative disorders*. Despite their differences, these two categories of disorders are similar in that they are among the most intriguing and challenging to understand.

Defining and Classifying Personality Disorders

Personality disorders *are particularly unusual patterns of behavior for one's culture that are maladaptive, distressing to oneself or others, and resistant to change.* Patterns of behavior in people with a personality disorder might involve an excessive desire to gain attention and approval from others, a dysfunctional style of relating to others, or a lack of empathy and regard for others. Note that these descriptions are dimensional in nature; they could apply to *anyone* at some point, so it is important to remember that the actual disorders represent extreme and persistent cases.

As Table 13.3 shows, the *DSM-5* identifies clusters of personality disorders involving (1) odd or eccentric behavior; (2) dramatic, emotional, and erratic behavior; and (3) anxious, fearful, and inhibited behavior. In this module, we will focus on the disorders that comprise the second category.

BORDERLINE PERSONALITY At the core of personality disorders is emotional dysfunction, and one of the clearest examples of this is borderline personality disorder. **Borderline personality disorder** *is characterized by intense extremes between positive and negative emotions, an unstable sense of self, impulsivity, and difficult social relationships.* Borderline personality disorder is estimated to affect almost 3% of the population in the United States and is highly correlated with anxiety, substance abuse, and mood disorders such as depression (Tomko et al., 2014).

Each of the characteristics of borderline personality disorder seems connected to all-or-none thinking. For example, a person with it may fall in love quickly, professing deep commitment and affection, but just as quickly become disgusted by his partner's perceived imperfections. Friends, family, colleagues, and even public figures can also be idealized and despised in the same way. Thus, the all-or-none thinking associated with borderline personality disorder prevents an individual from rationally dealing with the fact that, in even the best relationship, some expectations are not met and there are bound to be periods of conflict.

As a part of their troubled relationships, people with borderline personality disorder can become paranoid, suspecting that everyone else has similarly unpredictable feelings. Their fear of abandonment is typically intense, and it may drive them to go to extremes to prevent the loss of a relationship. It may also lead to risky sexual behavior as the individual desperately tries to secure relationships. One of the most distinguishing features of borderline

Table 13.3 Varieties of Personality Disorders with Brief Descriptions of Each

Cluster	Description
• Odd, eccentric	• **Paranoid Personality Disorder** distrust and suspiciousness such that others' motives are interpreted as malevolent. • **Schizoid Personality Disorder** detachment from social relationships and a restricted range of emotional expression. • **Schizotypal Personality Disorder** acute discomfort in close relationships, cognitive or perceptual distortions, and eccentricities of behavior.
• Dramatic, emotional, erratic	• **Antisocial Personality Disorder** disregard for, and violation of, the rights of others. • **Borderline Personality Disorder** instability in interpersonal relationships, self-image, and affects, and marked impulsivity. • **Histrionic Personality Disorder** excessive emotionality and attention seeking. • **Narcissistic Personality Disorder** grandiosity, need for admiration, and lack of empathy.
• Anxious, fearful, inhibited	• **Avoidant Personality Disorder** social inhibition, feelings of inadequacy, and hypersensitivity to negative evaluation. • **Dependent Personality Disorder** submissive and clinging behavior related to an excessive need to be taken care of. • **Obsessive-Compulsive Personality Disorder** preoccupation with orderliness, perfectionism, and control.
• **Personality Disorder Not Otherwise Specified** is a category provided for two situations: 1) the individual's personality pattern meets the general criteria for a Personality Disorder and traits of several different Personality Disorders are present, but the criteria for any specific Personality Disorder are not met; or 2) the individual's personality pattern meets the general criteria for a Personality Disorder, but the individual is considered to have a Personality Disorder that is not included in the classification (e.g., passive-aggressive personality disorder).	

Source: American Psychiatric Association. (2000). *Diagnostic and statistical manual of mental disorders* (4th ed., text revision). Washington, DC: Author.

personality disorder is the tendency toward *self-injury*, which may involve cutting or burning oneself. Suicide attempts are also quite common among people with this disorder.

HISTRIONIC PERSONALITY Emotional dysfunction can also be seen in **histrionic personality disorder**, *which is characterized by excessive attention seeking and dramatic behavior.* "Histrionic" comes from a Latin word meaning "like an actor or like a theatrical performance"—an apt label for this disorder. People who have histrionic personality disorder are typically successful at drawing people in with flirtatiousness, provocative sexuality, and flattery, but they are simply playing the roles they believe are necessary to be the center of attention. Thus, people with histrionic personality disorder are characterized by extreme shallowness and emotional immaturity.

NARCISSISTIC PERSONALITY **Narcissistic personality disorder** *is characterized by an inflated sense of self-importance and an intense need for attention and admiration, as well as intense self-doubt and fear of abandonment.* These narcissistic feelings leave little room for empathy. In fact, people with narcissistic personality disorder are known to manipulate and arrange their relationships to make sure their own needs are met, no matter the toll it takes on others. Because of these tendencies, you can see evidence of the

According to Greek mythology, Narcissus discovered his image reflecting from the surface of a pool of water. Unable to tear himself away from the beauty of his own face, Narcissus wasted away and died at the water's edge. In modern times, narcissism describes a person who has an inflated sense of self-importance.

disorder in all aspects of behavior. For example, evidence of narcissistic personality disorder may even be found in your classroom: Students with narcissistic tendencies are more likely to engage in academic dishonesty than others, and do so without guilt or remorse (Brunell et al., 2011). Relatedly, another disorder characterized by a lack of guilt or remorse, called *antisocial personality disorder*, has long captured the attention of psychologists, criminologists, and the general public.

Working the Scientific Literacy Model

Antisocial Personality Disorder

Antisocial personality disorder (APD) *refers to a condition marked by a habitual pattern of willingly violating others' personal rights, with little sign of empathy or remorse.* It is a difficult condition to deal with because the actions of people with APD are often distressful and alarming, and the individuals themselves are rarely motivated to change.

What do we know about antisocial personality disorder?

Numerous problematic behaviors characterize APD: People with APD tend to be physically and verbally abusive, destructive, and frequently find themselves in trouble with the law. Symptoms of the disorder typically appear during childhood and adolescence—most often with boys—as patterns of harming or torturing people or animals, destroying property, stealing, and being deceitful (Lynam & Gudonis, 2005). Behind the behaviors, you will usually find the traits of psychopathy that were described in the opening of this module. If you associate *psychopath* with serial killers, you would be equally correct in making that association with APD. However, keep in mind that serial killers represent only a small subset of people with APD or psychopathy. In fact, people who have either antisocial tendencies or full-blown manifestations of APD can be found throughout society. Given their high potential for inflicting physical and psychological harm on others, scientists have sought to understand what is unique about people with APD, and whether this information can be used help treat people who have been diagnosed with it.

How can science explain antisocial personality disorder?

You may have heard stories of people who have snapped under stress and committed horrific acts; this type of situation is different from what would be expected from someone with APD. In contrast, people with APD are *under*-reactive to stress. A flash of light, a loud sound, or the sudden appearance of an angry face will startle most, but individuals with APD show weak startle responses—such as blinking—when exposed to unpleasant stimuli. In one study, researchers recorded the electrical signals of the muscles that control eye blinking while presenting disturbing images to a group of people with APD and a control group without APD. You can see the results in Figure 13.2, in which the strength of the startle response is indicated by the height of the bars. The group of people with APD (the bars on the right side) have much weaker responses than the group without APD (on the left; Levenston et al., 2000).

Figure 13.2 Emotional Responses of Individuals with Antisocial Personality Disorder

This graph shows the strength of autonomic response to three types of pictures: mutilations, assault, and threat. Responses are much greater among control subjects (those who do not have APD; the three bars on the left) than among the individuals with antisocial personality disorder (the three bars on the right).

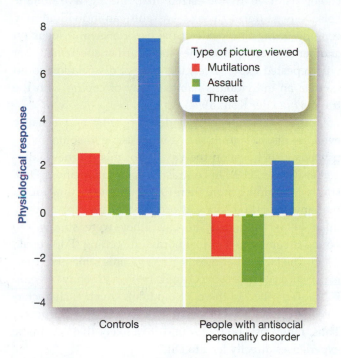

Can we critically evaluate this information?

We must be careful not to assume that all people with APD or psychopathy are violent criminals. Psychopathy can be found in white-collar criminals who cheat and lie for profit. For example, Wall Street power broker Bernard Madoff admitted to stealing billions of dollars from investors who trusted him with their money. Madoff has shown little remorse for ruining the fortunes of many individuals and institutions—including charities. Some have suggested

that, although he committed no violent crime, the level of deceit, maliciousness, and egocentrism he exhibited is psychopathic in nature.

Why is this relevant?

Identifying how physiology and brain function differ in people with APD and psychopathy is certainly helpful for psychologists who are trying to treat these disturbing behavioral patterns. People with APD tend to be highly resistant to psychological therapies, so drug treatments that can alter the physiological processes underlying the disorder may be needed. Also, antisocial patterns are often detectable during childhood and adolescence, which are critical periods of brain development. Perhaps therapies will be more highly beneficial if started at an early age, rather than in adulthood.

THE DEVELOPMENT OF PERSONALITY DISORDERS Discovering the origins of personality disorders has been challenging, largely because multiple causes are likely at play; they clearly require the biopsychosocial model. The case of APD serves a good example of how researchers understand the development of a personality disorder. The *DSM-5* criteria for APD includes the minimum age of 18 years, but this is not to suggest that traits suddenly appear in early adulthood. Instead, children may be diagnosed with *conduct disorder* when they exhibit severe aggression toward people and often animals, persistent lying or stealing, destructiveness, and a pervasive disregard for rules and authority. Many children with conduct disorder are eventually diagnosed as psychopathic or APD.

During early childhood, most people begin to adapt to social expectations and norms in part by delaying gratification—putting off an immediate reward to later receive a bigger reward or to conform to rules and manners. The biopsychosocial model helps explain why children with conduct disorder fail to adapt to these social expectations. From a social perspective, living in unstable households and neighborhoods is a risk factor (Vaughn et al., 2010). Some children raised in unstable settings might find it adaptive to take advantage of opportunities immediately before they vanish, rather than delay gratification (this can certainly happen in even the most prosperous neighborhoods as well). Interestingly, difficulty in delaying gratification is associated with frontal lobe activity, and brain studies have shown lower levels of frontal lobe function in conduct disorder and APD (Haney-Caron et al., 2014). Also, in these contexts children are often mistreated. Although most children have a reasonably good understanding of how breaking rules might have negative consequences, children with conduct disorder often learn that they will receive negative consequences regardless, and so they develop a disregard for authority figures and simply behave as they wish. Not all children who experience maltreatment develop conduct disorder. In fact, some respond by becoming depressed, and researchers have found specific genetic markers that indicate which trajectory is more likely (Beach et al., 2015). Thus, the research on APD illustrates that psychological, biological, and social factors interact as personality disorders develop (see Table 13.4).

Of course, not all personality disorders are the same, and researchers have been able to uncover clues to the development of their distinctive characteristics. For example, borderline personality disorder (BPD) may stem from profound *invalidation* during childhood, meaning that a child's caregivers did not respond to his or her emotions as if they were real or important (Crowell et al., 2009). As a result, adults with BPD never master the ability to identify and control emotions and tend to react more strongly to everyday life stressors (Glaser et al., 2008).

A final consideration is the high levels of comorbidity among personality disorders. **Comorbidity** *is the presence of two disorders simultaneously or the presence of a second disorder that affects the one being treated.* For example, substance abuse is often comorbid with personality disorders (Goldstein et al., 2007; Gudonis et al., 2009). Their intertwining may actually influence the ongoing development of a personality disorder: It is possible that the personality disorder leads to substance abuse, which, in turn, strengthens the personality problems in a vicious cycle.

Dissociative Identity Disorder

Have you ever been so engaged in driving, reading a book, or playing a game that you were totally unaware of what was going on around you? Psychologists refer to this as a *dissociative experience* because of the separation—or dissociation—between you and your surroundings. Dissociative experiences may arise while you are intensely focused on one activity, or when you drift off while not doing anything in particular, such as daydreaming during a long lecture. People differ in their tendencies to dissociate, but such experiences seem completely normal.

In a few cases, some people have such extreme experiences that they may be diagnosed with a **dissociative disorder**, *a category of mental disorder characterized by a split between conscious awareness from feeling, cognition, memory, and identity* (Kihlstrom, 2005). Probably the most familiar member of this category is **dissociative identity disorder (DID)** (sometimes referred to as *multiple personality disorder* in popular media), *in which a person claims that his or her identity has split into one or more distinct alter personalities, or alters.* Alters may differ in gender, sexual orientation, personality, memory, and autobiographical sense of self. The dissociation of alter identities can be so strong that one alter may have no memory of events experienced by other alters.

In most cases, dissociative disorders such as DID are thought to be brought on by extreme stress. Some psychologists have hypothesized that, during a traumatic episode (e.g., during a sexual assault), an individual may cope by trying to block out the experience and focus on another time and place. They have further speculated that with repeated experiences, this type of dissociation could become an individual's habitual way of coping with the trauma (van der Kolk, 1994).

Because so few people develop DID, and because even the disorder itself seems implausible to some, many psychologists question the validity of this diagnosis altogether (Gillig, 2009). In contrast to speculation about DID, studies examining more than 10,000 trauma victims found that any forgetting that did occur could be explained by infantile or childhood amnesia (they were simply too young to remember) or just normal forgetting (Pope et al., 2000). The fact is that most trauma victims remember their experiences (Cahill & McGaugh, 1998), and many develop PTSD (described in the next module), which is characterized by the lack of an ability to forget or ignore trauma. Thus, many psychologists find it unlikely that traumatic experiences directly lead to DID.

Table 13.4 Applying the Biopsychosocial Model to Antisocial Personality Disorder

For antisocial personality disorder and psychopathy:

1. Name one or two biological influences associated with APD and psychopathy.

2. What is at least one psychological factor that distinguishes people with these personality disorders from normal people? (e.g., How does their thinking or emotional processing differ?)

3. What are at least two social or cultural factors associated with APD and psychopathy?

Answers:
1. People with psychopathy show reduced startle reflex and reduced activity in the frontal lobes.
2. Individuals with psychopathy have difficulty learning and following rules. They also lack empathy and show dampened negative emotion to negative events.
3. People who develop psychopathy or APD are more likely to grow up in distressed home environments or neighborhoods where prosocial rules are not easily learned. A history of childhood sexual, physical, or emotional abuse is also associated with APD and psychopathy.

Although there is little doubt that people regularly have dissociative experiences, a serious condition like DID is difficult to test for given that the symptoms are subjective experiences. However, there are alternative approaches that might be able to detect DID. For example, in one study patients viewed words and pictures and were tested for recall of the stimuli either when they were experiencing the same alter as when they learned, or when they were experiencing a different alter. The results suggested that some types of learning do not transfer between alter identities, thus supporting the diagnosis (Eich et al., 1997). Skeptics, however, might point out that similar results can be produced in the general population simply by instructing volunteers (who do not claim to have DID) to imagine themselves in different contexts (Sahakyan & Kelley, 2002). Moreover, a similar study examining brain recordings (known as event-related potentials) found that the brain activity during recall was similar whether the information was learned in the same state or in another alter (Allen & Movius, 2000). This would suggest that there is no neurological difference between personalities.

Some other observations offer compelling reasons to be skeptical about diagnosing DID. First, 80% of patients diagnosed with DID were unaware of having the disorder before starting therapy (Putnam, 1989). These observations suggest that DID may have its origins in the context of therapy, rather than being a response to trauma. Second, in 1970, there were 79 documented cases of DID (then referred to as multiple personality disorder). In 1986, there were around 6,000; by 1998, the number had risen to more than 40,000 (Lilienfeld & Lynn, 2003). The numbers continue to rise, although compared to other major disorders the prevalence of DID in the population is low. Why did the rate of DID skyrocket from 79 cases to more than 40,000 cases per year in less than three decades? This increased prevalence could simply be a product of awareness: After professionals learned how to identify the disorder, they could begin to diagnose it more effectively. However, it is also possible that the drastic increase seen from 1970 through the 1980s in particular resulted from social and cultural effects, such as the popularization of a film called *Sybil*, which purported to tell the true story of a woman with DID. Diagnoses of DID rose shortly after this film was released. Similarly, the disorder was nonexistent in Japan in 1990 (Takahashi, 1990), but Japanese psychologists began diagnosing patients with DID when the disorder was described by North Americans (An et al., 1998). To many psychologists, these observations point to a predominantly sociocultural phenomenon in which cultural beliefs and therapists determine how the symptoms are manifested (Lilienfeld et al., 1999).

Module 13.2 Summary

13.2a   Know . . . the key terminology associated with personality and dissociative disorders:

antisocial personality disorder (APD)
borderline personality disorder
comorbidity
dissociative disorder
dissociative identity disorder (DID)
histrionic personality disorder
narcissistic personality disorder
personality disorders

13.2b   Understand . . . the phenomenon of dissociation and how a dissociative disorder might occur.

Dissociation can be explained in everyday phenomena such as daydreaming. However, a dissociative disorder may occur when perceptions of mind, body, and surroundings are severely and chronically separated, such as in purported cases of dissociative identity disorder.

13.2c   Apply . . . the biopsychosocial model to understand the causes of personality disorders.

Take antisocial personality disorder and psychopathy for example: Researchers have been able to study how it develops over the life span, which provides insight into the range of biopsychosocial influences. If you have not done so already, relate your knowledge of the biopsychosocial model to the activity in Table 13.4.

13.2d   Analyze . . . the status of dissociative identity disorder as a legitimate diagnosis.

The lack of a physical basis for the disorder and its unusual rate and patterns of diagnosis rightly bring about skepticism. For example, diagnoses of DID increased dramatically after a film depicted a purported case of DID. Ensure that your evaluation (of any condition, not just DID) is not biased by fictional or sensationalized accounts you have seen or read. However, it is also important to remember that many of the mental disorders for which we have a greater understanding were at one time considered mysterious and controversial.

Module 13.2 Quiz

Know . . .

1. _____ refers to a condition marked by a habitual pattern of willingly violating others' personal rights, with very little sign of empathy or remorse.
   A. Borderline personality disorder
   B. Narcissistic personality disorder
   C. Histrionic personality disorder
   D. Antisocial personality disorder

2. Which of the following individuals demonstrates the definition of comorbidity?
   A. A person who has both borderline personality disorder and a substance abuse disorder
   B. A person who is histrionic who both seeks excessive attention and is emotionally hyper-reactive
   C. A person with borderline personality disorder who is impulsive and tends to be in unstable relationships
   D. A person who experiences a personality disorder that turns out to be fatal

Understand . . .

3. What is a defining characteristic of dissociative identity disorder (DID)?
   A. Believe they no longer exist or are real
   B. Lose the sensation of an appendage with no physical or neurological evidence
   C. Emotional distance and callousness
   D. A claim that multiple personalities inhabit one body

Apply . . .

4. Which of the following biopsychosocial factors is least likely to be related to personality disorders?
   A. Stress reactivity
   B. History of abuse
   C. Decreased activity of the frontal lobes
   D. Enjoyment of pain

Analyze . . .

5. Skeptics have argued against the validity of DID in a number of different cases. What is their reasoning?
   A. The disorder appears to be based on cultural expectations.
   B. Most people who experience trauma do not dissociate.
   C. The vast majority of cases come from a very small number of therapists.
   D. Skeptics have cited all of these arguments.

Module **13.3**   Anxiety and Mood Disorders

Learning Objectives

13.3a Know . . . the key terminology related to anxiety and mood disorders.

13.3b Understand . . . the different types of mood and anxiety disorders.

13.3c Understand . . . how anxiety or mood disorders can be self-perpetuating.

13.3d Apply . . . your knowledge of anxiety and mood disorders to be alert to people in need.

13.3e Analyze . . . whether maladaptive aspects of psychological disorders might arise from perfectly normal, healthy behaviors.

Waking up with a headache, fever, or sore throat, unpleasant as it is, is not at all unusual. But what about waking up to obsessive–compulsive disorder (OCD)? When it comes to mental disorders, people typically think of signs that something is "not quite right" about a person's behavior, and what follows may be a gradual unfolding of more noticeable personality, behavioral, or emotional problems. Although this is how mental disorders typically develop, sudden onset of OCD—a serious anxiety disorder—has been documented in cases in which young children were infected by bacterial streptococci. Shortly after exposure to the infection, some children rapidly developed symptoms of OCD, including extremely repetitive

behaviors and having irrational fears and obsessions (Snider & Swedo, 2004). But why might a relatively common infection result in such rapid behavioral and emotional changes in some children? The answer seems to be that when the immune system mounts its reaction to the bacterial infection, it also damages cells in the caudate, a part of the brain related to impulse control, as well as related structures in the same vicinity. As we will see in this module, one theory about OCD is that compulsive, repetitive behaviors (such as hand washing) are ways of dealing with the lost sense of impulse control—a loss that occurs when the caudate is damaged (Huyser et al., 2009). If this theory is correct, then, at least in this case, a psychological disorder can be acquired virtually overnight. This is an exceptional example to two categories of disorder—those involving problems with mood and anxiety—that are among the most prevalent in the world.

Anxiety and mood disorders are among the most common types of psychological disorders. If you have any personal experience with mental illness—maybe you or someone close to you has experienced it—then there is a good chance you will come across a description of the disorder in this module.

Anxiety Disorders

Intense, persistent anxiety can be painful and maladaptive, no matter the source or how it is expressed in an individual's thoughts and behaviors. The *DSM-5* describes three main categories of disorders for which anxiety is a key symptom: Anxiety Disorders, Obsessive–Compulsive Disorders, and Trauma and Stressor-Related Disorders. These are among the most frequently diagnosed disorders, affecting more than 20% of the adult population in the United States (NIMH, 2015).

We all experience anxiety to some degree; it is based on a normal physiological and psychological response to stressful events known as the *fight-or-flight response* (Nesse

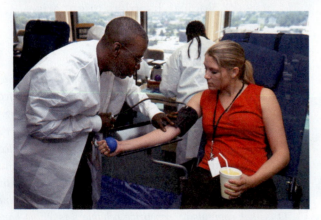

Fight or flight…freeze or faint? In addition to fight-or-flight responses, mammals can also react by freezing—as in the "deer in the headlights" response—or by fainting, as some will do at the sight of blood (Bracha et al., 2004).

& Ellsworth, 2009). We experience this response as a racing, pounding heart, increased respiration, knots in the stomach, and sweaty or clammy hands. These physical changes reflect a shift in energy away from nonemergency tasks like digestion and toward fighting or fleeing. The fight-or-flight response seems to be common to all mammals, and it is an adaptive response to threats.

If the physiological reactions involved in anxiety are adaptive, then our challenge is to identify symptoms that go beyond typical psychological responses and become maladaptive. As discussed in Module 13.1, the distinction between a typical psychological state and a disorder combines extremes in duration and severity, and a disordered state may be a disproportionate response to real-life events, or it may occur without any precipitating event whatsoever. Anxiety disorders take on a variety of different forms, with bouts of anxiety elicited by highly specific situations or objects, or without any clear reason.

GENERALIZED ANXIETY DISORDER Generalized anxiety disorder (GAD) *involves frequently elevated levels of anxiety that are not a response to any particular situation*—the anxiety is *generalized* to just about anything. Additionally, people with GAD often feel irritable and have difficulty sleeping and concentrating, which are not unusual experiences for people with any type of anxiety problem. What makes GAD distinct from other anxiety disorders is that people who have it often struggle to identify the specific reasons for why they are anxious. Moreover, the anxiety that people with GAD experience does not seem to go away, even if a particular problem or issue is resolved. Rather, the anxiety becomes redirected toward some other concern. The onset of GAD can be attributed to a variety of factors, not all of which are clear, but major life changes commonly precede its onset (Newman & Llera, 2011).

PANIC DISORDER AND AGORAPHOBIA Panic disorder *is an anxiety disorder marked by repeated episodes of sudden, intense fear.* This condition is distinct from GAD because the anxiety occurs in short segments lasting up to 10 minutes, but can be much more severe. The key feature of this disorder is *panic attacks*—moments of extreme anxiety that include a rush of physical activity paired with frightening thoughts. A panic attack escalates when the sudden, intense fear causes increased physical arousal, and the increased physical symptoms feed the frightening thoughts.

For some, a sense of intense fear or a panic response becomes associated with more than one situation. When this fear becomes serious, it may be diagnosed as the distinct, but clearly related disorder **agoraphobia**, *an intense fear of visiting open, public places out of fear of having a panic attack.* As a result of this fear, the individual may begin to avoid public settings so as to avoid the embarrassment and trauma of a panic attack. In its most extreme forms, agoraphobia leads an individual to stay inside his or her home almost permanently.

Working the Scientific Literacy Model

Specific Phobias

In contrast to GAD, where an individual's anxiety occurs in response to many situations, a **phobia** *is a severe, irrational fear of an object or specific situation.* Some of the most common phobias are listed in Table 13.5. The best-known form of phobia is probably **specific phobia**, *which involves an intense fear of an object, activity, or organism.* These include fears of things such as specific animals, heights, thunder, blood, and injections or other medical procedures. (Social phobias, which are very common, are a different category of phobias that are discussed later.)

What do we know about specific phobias?

Phobias develop through unpleasant or frightening experiences—for example, a person who is bitten by a dog might develop a dog phobia. But negative experiences tell only part of the story—not all dog bite victims develop phobias. The overwhelming majority of the triggers for phobias are objects or situations we may *need* to fear, or at least be cautious about. This linkage leads psychologists to believe there is a genetic component to a fear of heights, snakes, and other potential dangers from our evolutionary history (Öhman & Mineka, 2001); in other words, we may be *biologically predisposed* to fear some objects (see Module 6.1).

How can science explain specific phobias?

If organisms really are biologically prepared to fear certain things, then scientists should be able to find a genetic basis for this tendency. One approach to studying how genes influence fear and anxiety comes from selective breeding techniques. To use this approach, one group of researchers tested a strain of mice for fear conditioning and ranked the mice from least to most easily conditioned. Specifically, they used a classical conditioning technique in which the mice heard a tone followed by an electric shock. Fear was measured by the length of time the mice held still in fear in response to the tone—mice typically show fear by freezing in place (Ponder et al., 2007).

The most fearful mice were then allowed to breed with each other across four generations. The least fearful animals were also paired up and allowed to breed. As Figure 13.3 shows, across these four generations, fear responses became more and more distinct, with the third and fourth generations being very different from each other; the mice bred from the most fearful families became even more easily conditioned than their great grandparents. Thus, the researchers showed that the disposition to learn certain types of fears can be genetically influenced.

Can we critically evaluate this research?

Fear learning in mice may not *seem* applicable to fear experienced by humans. Although this research informs us that the genes of mice can be selectively bred to increase susceptibility to acquire fear responses, humans are a different species. Though valuable, this particular study does not specify how anxiety and fear are coded in the human genome. Therefore, it is reasonable to look for evidence related specifically to humans. Further, this research might lead you to believe that humans have developed biological tendencies to fear dangerous things in general, but that does not seem to be the case. As described in Module 6.1, the objects and events people tend to fear have been a part of human experience for thousands of years—long enough to influence our genetic makeup. This would explain why so many people rapidly develop phobias of snakes or spiders—the threats our ancestors faced—whereas relatively few people develop intense phobias about more modern potential dangers, such as guns.

Why is this relevant?

It is important for mental health professionals to understand that phobias have a genetic component. This relationship suggests that not all fears should be treated equally, nor should all individuals with phobias be treated the same way. By isolating genetic tendencies and determining how they affect the nervous system, researchers will be able to develop more specialized forms of treatment for phobias, and potentially for other anxiety disorders as well.

Table 13.5 What Are We Afraid of?

	Currently Experiencing the Phobia	Have Experienced the Phobia at One Time
Animals (snakes, birds, or other animals)	4.7%	50.3%
Natural environment (e.g., heights, storms, water)	5.9%	62.7%
Blood or bodily injury (including injections)	4.0%	42.5%
Situations (e.g., dentists, hospitals, crowded places)	5.2%	55.6%
Other specific objects	1.0%	10.6%

Source: "What are We So Afraid Of?" from "The Epidemiology of DSM-IV specific phobia in the USA: Results from the National Epidemiologic Survey on Alcohol and Related Conditions" Adaptation of Table 3 from "The Epidemiology of DSM-IV Specific Phobia in the USA: Results from the National Epidemiologic Survey on Alcohol and Related Conditions" by F. S. Stinson, et al. (2007) *Psychological Medicine, 37,* 1047–1059.

Figure 13.3 Anxiety Levels are Inherited in an Animal Model

Over the course of just a few generations, mice from the highly fearful genetic strain show increasingly strong fear responses as indicated by the height of the red bars.

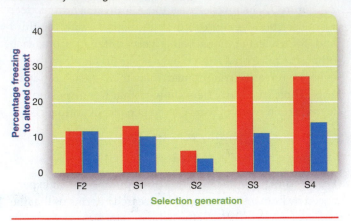

SOCIAL PHOBIAS **Social anxiety disorder** *is an irrational fear of being observed, evaluated, or embarrassed in public.* Although each of these are real fears for anyone, someone with social anxiety disorder experiences them to an excessive and unreasonable degree, which leads to avoidance of actual or merely potential social interactions. Consider the day of a college student who has social anxiety:

- This student always shows up to class right as it begins so he does not have to risk awkward conversation with classmates he does not know. Even worse, what if everyone else is having conversations and he has to sit alone without talking to anyone?

- Despite being hungry, the student will not go into the cafeteria because his roommate is not around. He cannot face the prospect of sitting with strangers, especially without his roommate. He finds a quiet spot near the library and gets lunch from a vending machine.

- Walking across a quiet part of campus, he sees his professor approaching. Not knowing if the professor would recognize him, he wonders if he should say hello. Thinking about this issue makes him so tense, he pretends to stop and read a text message to avoid eye contact.

As you can see, the day is a series of unpleasant, tense moments in situations that most people would find completely ordinary. The distress the student feels and the degree to which he shapes his life around his social phobia suggest that he has social anxiety disorder. To make a formal diagnosis of this disorder, a psychologist would need to evaluate the student's full set of symptoms and their duration.

JOURNAL PROMPT

Fear or Phobia? The distinction between a phobia and a normal, healthy fear is an important one. What makes the two different and why do psychologists distinguish them?

OBSESSIVE-COMPULSIVE DISORDER The disorder you read about in the introduction to this module is known as **obsessive-compulsive disorder (OCD)**, *which is a disorder characterized by unwanted, inappropriate, and persistent thoughts (obsessions); repetitive stereotyped behaviors (compulsions); or a combination of the two* (see Figure 13.4).

Figure 13.4 Prevalence of Symptoms in People Diagnosed with Obserssive-Compulsive Disorder

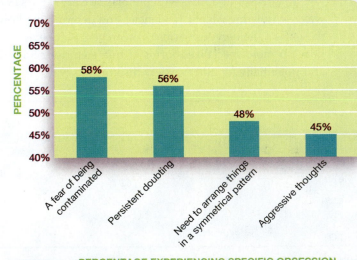

PERCENTAGE EXPERIENCING SPECIFIC OBSESSION

PERCENTAGE EXPERIENCING SPECIFIC COMPULSION

We introduced this disorder at the outset by describing how it can occur suddenly in children; however, OCD typically does not set in until young adulthood. In addition, it is a dimensional disorder in which normal precautions, such as practicing good hygiene, can develop into extreme, irrational thoughts and behaviors that cannot be ignored. Most of us have had unwanted thoughts such as an annoying song that was stuck in our head, but a person with obsessions about cleanliness might be so worried about picking up germs from everything he touches that he can barely bring himself to do anything at all. As a result of these obsessions, the individual may seek to reduce the anxiety, sometimes in problematic ways such as washing his hands until they become so dried out that he bleeds.

TRAUMA AND STRESS-RELATED DISORDERS The *DSM-5* includes a category of disorders that arise from trauma or severe stressors. Within this category, Posttraumatic stress disorder (PTSD) is perhaps the most widely known. As described in Module 13.1, PTSD arises from exposure to trauma, which might involve direct experience, witnessing an event, or simply getting prolonged and detailed information about trauma that is excessively graphic or strikes too close to home.

Characteristic symptoms of PTSD include:

- Re-experiencing the event in the form of flashbacks, nightmares, and other vivid, anxiety-provoking thoughts.

- Avoidance occurs when the individual avoids contexts similar to when the trauma or stressor was experienced. Sights, sounds, and smells can all lead to painful re-experiencing symptoms.

- Negative emotions and thoughts repeatedly intrude upon the individual. This may include sadness, anger, guilt, helplessness, or other negative emotions that relate back to the original experience.

- Altered arousal and activity might involve increases in anger, substance abuse, and high-risk behavior. Individuals with PTSD often report that they are always on the lookout for repeated stressors and they are easily startled, even by familiar stimuli.

Although PTSD is probably the best-known disorder from this category, there are other disorders that are quite common, but not always recognized. One example is *adjustment disorder*, which arises from the stress of having to adjust to new situations. Children go through serious stress as parents get divorced, and adults may experience this after being laid off from work. Adjustment disorders do not necessarily arise from a specific traumatic event, but they can have lingering consequences similar to PTSD, including avoidance, negative emotions, and altered arousal and activity.

Figure 13.5 Vicious Cycle of Panic Attacks

THE VICIOUS CYCLE OF ANXIETY One of the most difficult aspects of anxiety is that it tends to be self-perpetuating (Figure 13.5). In a sense, having an anxiety disorder today sets you up to have an anxiety disorder next week as well (Hofmann, 2007). For example, think about a young girl who tries to pet a neighbor's cat, but the cat scratches her. The incident did not leave a lasting physical scar, but years later the girl still feels nervous around cats. She is reluctant to even enter a house if the owners have a cat, but if she does, she remains nervous until the cat is taken away to another room or let outside. How might this behavior contribute to a vicious cycle? The sight of a cat triggers an anxiety response. When the cat is removed from the situation, or when the girl avoids the situation altogether, the anxiety fades. This process of reducing the fear, in turn, can actually reinforce the phobia.

Mood Disorders

Mood disorders affect roughly 9.5% of adults in the United States—nearly 21 million people (NIMH, 2015). As a result of a combination of biological, cognitive, and sociocultural differences, rates of depression are twice as high among

Many people have experienced problems with a mood disorder. Those with depression may endure extended periods of sadness and hopelessness that have no apparent cause.

women as among men, and three times as high among people living in poverty (Hyde et al., 2008). There is also a genetic susceptibility to mood disorders. In this section we discuss the two major types of mood disorders—major depression and bipolar disorder.

MAJOR DEPRESSION AND BIPOLAR DISORDER

Feelings of sadness and depression are normal aspects of human experience. By comparison, **major depression** *is a disorder marked by prolonged periods of sadness, feelings of worthlessness and hopelessness, social withdrawal, and cognitive and physical sluggishness*. With this definition, it should be clear that depression involves more than just feeling sad for a long period of time—cognition becomes depressed as well. Affected individuals have difficulty concentrating and making decisions. Attention and memory shift toward unpleasant and unhappy events. Physiologically, people with major depression may be lethargic and sleepy, yet experience insomnia. They may experience a change in appetite and the onset of digestive problems such as constipation. People who are feeling sad do not necessarily experience all of these cognitive and biological symptoms, so major depression is clearly a distinct psychological disorder.

Bipolar disorder (formerly referred to as manic depression) *is characterized by extreme highs and lows in mood, motivation, and energy*. It shares many symptoms with major depression—some distinguish the two by referring to major depression as *unipolar*—but it occurs only a third as often as depression (NIMH, 2015). Mania is the polar opposite—a highly energized state that is accompanied by inflated self-confidence and recklessness. Some

individuals in this phase talk so fast that their thoughts cannot keep up, others run up credit card bills of thousands of dollars with the idea that somehow they can afford it, and others engage in risky, thrill-seeking behavior with a sense of invincibility. The specific symptoms will vary from person to person as well as the timing. Some people with bipolar disorder experience only a few manic episodes in their lives, whereas others go through mania several times each year. Still others, known as "rapid cyclers," experience abrupt mood swings, sometimes within hours.

BIOPSYCHOSOCIAL ASPECTS OF DEPRESSION

Although many mysteries remain, much is known about the biological basis of depression. Twin studies suggest an underlying genetic risk for developing major depression (Figure 13.6). Also, there have been many molecular genetic studies to identify specific strands of DNA associated with physiological factors in depression (Klengel & Binder, 2013). Brain imaging research has identified two primary regions of interest related to depression: (1) the *limbic system*, which is active in emotional responses and processing, and (2) the dorsal (back) of the frontal cortex, which generally plays a role in controlling thoughts and concentrating. As is the case with panic disorder, a vicious cycle appears to occur with depression. The overactive limbic system responds strongly to emotions and sends signals that overwhelm frontal lobe processes (see Figure 13.7), and the decrease in frontal lobe functioning reduces the ability to concentrate and control what one thinks about (Gotlib & Hamilton, 2008). Depression is also linked to impaired

Figure 13.6 Genetic Relatedness and Major Depression

Identical (monozygotic) twins have a greater chance of both developing major depression compared to fraternal (dizygotic) twins. Notice that the genetic correlation is highest for female monozygotic twins.

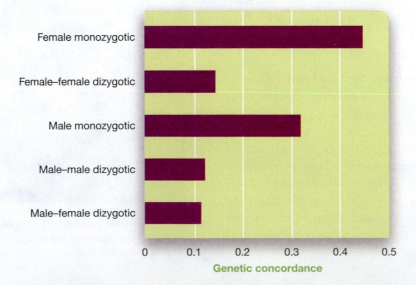

Genetic concordance

Figure 13.7 Depression and the Brain

Brain imaging research has shown higher than normal levels of activity in the limbic system of people with depression while responding to negative emotional information. This response slows activity in the dorsal frontal cortex, making it more difficult for the individual to control thoughts—especially thoughts that might break the vicious cycle.

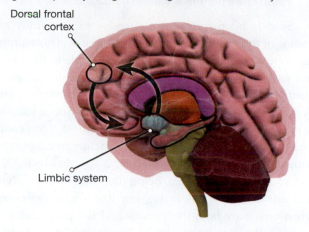

Dorsal frontal cortex

Limbic system

neurogenesis (the development of new nerve cells) in the hippocampus (Rothenichner et al., 2014).

Abnormally reduced activity of various neurotransmitters of the brain—especially serotonin, dopamine, and norepinephrine—are thought to be associated with depression. The abnormal activity of these neurotransmitters is linked to other physiological systems. The negative emotions of depression co-occur with bodily stress reactions involving the endocrine and immune systems (Fagundes et al., 2013). The result is increased risk for viral illnesses, heart disease, and higher mortality rates in people who are chronically and severely depressed.

Depression is also a disorder of cognition. The cognitive characteristics of depression include rumination (prolonged dwelling over negative thoughts) and a difficulty shifting attention away from negative emotions (Joorman & Vanderlind, 2014). Interestingly, people with depression also report much less detail in autobiographical memories (Sumner et al., 2014). For example, if you ask most people what personal memory comes to mind when they hear "sadness," they will give a specific experience such as when a close friend moved to another city. In contrast, people with depression are more likely to provide a general type of event—such as when they feel ostracized—which is consistent with the fact that sadness is much more pervasive for them. Finally, a characteristic *depressive explanatory style* emerges, in which a depressed individual explains life with three qualities: internal, stable, and global (Ledrich & Gana, 2013). Imagine an individual with depression does something as minor as losing his keys, and refer to Figure 13.8 to see the depressive explanatory style at work.

Biological and cognitive components of depression interact with socioeconomic and environmental factors. As Figure 13.9 shows, just living in a specific neighborhood can be a risk factor for three main reasons (Cutrona et al., 2006; Kessler et al., 2014). First, poor neighborhoods are associated with higher daily stress levels because of substandard housing and facilities, increased crime rates, and lack of desirable businesses (e.g., high numbers of adult bookstores and bars, combined with low numbers of revenue-generating family establishments). Second, people living in these neighborhoods are more vulnerable to stressors such as unemployment because they often lack connections, mentors, and job opportunities that professionals have access to in better neighborhoods. Third, disrupted social ties are more prevalent in poor neighborhoods. Low rates of home ownership combined with difficulty making rent can lead to high turnover; people may not know their neighbors well and, therefore, take less interest in one another's well-being.

Figure 13.8 Three Elements of the Depressive Explanatory Style

The three elements of the depressive explanatory style are internalizing, stabilizing, and globalizing.

I'm so stupid! I always lose my keys when I'm in a hurry. This ruins everything.

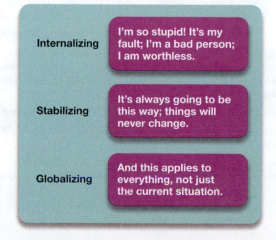

Internalizing
I'm so stupid! It's my fault; I'm a bad person; I am worthless.

Stabilizing
It's always going to be this way; things will never change.

Globalizing
And this applies to everything, not just the current situation.

Figure 13.9 Social Influences on Depression

Stress and living conditions are linked with increased incidences of depression.

SUICIDE   It is difficult to imagine a worse outcome from a mood disorder than suicide. For many people, it is equally difficult to imagine how anyone could reach such a low point. Nonetheless, suicide remains a serious public health concern. Recent statistics from the US Centers for Disease Control indicate just how serious a problem it is:

- Suicide is the 11th most-frequent cause of death in the United States.

- It is the third-leading cause of death among teens.

- Males are four times more likely than females to die by suicide.

- Native American and non-Hispanic White Americans are more than twice as likely to die by suicide than other racial and ethnic groups.

- Despite the most commonly held beliefs, the annual suicide rates among adults 65 years of age and older is typically 70% to 100% higher than the rate for teens.

- Fortunately, research, treatment, and public awareness have significantly reduced the suicide rate among youth since the 1980s (Gould et al., 2003).

Suicide often comes as a surprise to the family and friends of the victim, although in some cases clear warning signs are evident (Table 13.6). Among people in their teens and early 20s, the most significant risk factors are mood disorders, recent and extremely stressful life events, a family history of mood disorders (with or without suicide), easy access to a lethal means of suicide (most significantly, firearms), and the presence of these factors in conjunction with substance abuse (Gould et al., 2003; Moscicki, 2001). For younger individuals, being the victim of bullying and ostracism is a risk factor, but it is a greater concern when youth are both the victims and the perpetrators of bullying (Klomek et al., 2007). Family and friends have reported that in the weeks before a suicide, individuals have behaved in ways that are now recognized as warning signs. For example, an individual may verbally express despair and hopelessness (*I just want to give up; Nothing matters anymore; They'll be sorry when I'm gone*), give away personal possessions, suddenly withdraw from work or school, have crying spells, or obtain a means of committing the act. Table 13.6 offers information about resources to help people who are experiencing suicidal thoughts.

Table 13.6 Warning Signs of Suicide and Helpful Resources

Learn how to recognize the danger signals. Be concerned if someone you know:

- Talks about committing suicide
- Has trouble eating or sleeping
- Exhibits drastic changes in behavior
- Withdraws from friends or social activities
- Loses interest in school, work, or hobbies
- Prepares for death by writing a will and making final arrangements
- Gives away prized possessions

- Has attempted suicide before
- Takes unnecessary risks
- Has recently experienced serious losses
- Seems preoccupied with death and dying
- Loses interest in his or her personal appearance
- Increases alcohol or drug use

Source: American Psychological Association. (2011). Retrieved from http://www.apa.org/topics/suicide/signs.aspx

Thousands of people contact suicide telephone helplines every day. Evidence suggests that the most successful calls provide more than just empathy; they involve problem-solving, referrals, education about treatment, and follow-up calls (Mishara et al., 2007; Mishara & Daigle, 1997). Make sure you can identify sources for help in case you encounter someone who may need it.

In case of an immediate crisis, call 1-800-273-8255. And also consult: http://www.suicidepreventionlifeline.org/

For information about local services or providers, call the National Alliance on Mental Illness (https://www.nami.org/) at 1-800-950-6264.

In addition to NAMI's services, students taking courses on a campus should check to see if there is a counseling service available. Many universities and colleges provide free access to students.

Module **13.3** Summary

13.3a **Know . . . the key terminology related to anxiety and mood disorders:**

agoraphobia
bipolar disorder
generalized anxiety disorder (GAD)
major depression
obsessive-compulsive disorder (OCD)
panic disorder
phobia
social anxiety disorder
specific phobias

13.3b **Understand . . . the different types of mood and anxiety disorders.**

Although anxiety disorders share many similarities in symptoms, they differ in terms of what brings about the symptoms and the intensity of the symptoms. The cues that trigger anxiety range widely: In generalized anxiety disorder, just about anything may cause anxiety; in specific phobias, an individual fears only certain objects. Likewise, the intensity can range from near-constant worrying to the brief periods of highly intense anxiety in phobias and panic disorder. There are fewer mood disorders discussed in this module, so it may be simpler to distinguish the two: Although depression and bipolar disorder both involve depressive symptoms (periods of negative mood, social withdrawal, difficulty concentration, and so on), only bipolar includes the elements of mania (periods of high energy, racing thoughts, and excitability).

13.3c **Understand . . . how anxiety or mood disorders can be self-perpetuating.**

Both depression and anxiety are characterized by a vicious cycle: With anxiety, anxious or fearful thoughts can lead to physiological arousal; physiological arousal can lead to escape and avoidance to get rid of the immediate fear, which in turn reinforces the anxious thoughts. In depression, a similar pattern can occur with depressed thoughts, self-blame, and social withdrawal.

13.3d **Apply . . . your knowledge of anxiety and mood disorders to be alert to people in need.**

It takes years of formal training to diagnose mental disorders. However, you now know some of the most noticeable signs of mood and anxiety disorders, and that there are different ways the disorders manifest. Suicide risk is elevated for people with mental illness. Table 13.6 provided a list of warning signs and resources for helping people at risk for committing suicide. In addition to reviewing this table, take a moment to identify how to contact your college's counseling center (most physical campuses have one). If you are a distance learner or if your school does not provide access to a counseling center, the National Alliance on Mental Illness helps individuals find treatment professionals in their local communities.

13.3e **Analyze . . . whether maladaptive aspects of psychological disorders might arise from perfectly normal, healthy behaviors.**

To analyze this issue, we need to examine the specific symptoms that occur in someone who has a phobia and is showing an adaptive response (fear, anxiety) but to an inappropriate stimulus or situation. It is perfectly reasonable and healthy to be cautious about heights, for example, in the sense that falls can be dangerous, even life-threatening. This reaction is maladaptive only when the fear response is so intense or out of context that it interferes with daily life. Imagine a house painter who cannot climb a ladder or scaffold; unless she overcomes her fear, she will have to make major adjustments to accommodate her fear.

Module 13.3 Quiz

Know . . .

1. _____ is characterized by periods of intense depression as well as periods with elevated mood and energy levels.

   A. Major depression
   B. Unipolar depression
   C. Bipolar disorder
   D. Generalized anxiety disorder

Understand . . .

2. The difference between obsessions and compulsions is that:

   A. obsessions are repetitive behaviors, whereas compulsions are fears about specific events.
   B. obsessions are repetitive, unwanted thoughts, whereas compulsions are repetitive behaviors.
   C. obsessions are temporary, whereas compulsions are practically permanent.
   D. obsessions and compulsions are the same thing.

3. The idea that anxiety disorders can be self-perpetuating means that:

   A. anxiety in one situation always causes anxiety in another situation, regardless of what is happening in those situations.
   B. the emotions associated with anxiety lead to physiological responses, which in turn lead to more anxious emotions, creating a vicious cycle.
   C. you choose when and what to be anxious about.
   D. anxiety is always limited to one situation or place.

Apply . . .

4. Sharon feels she is constantly nagged by a strong feeling of tension and worry, no matter what the situation may be. No specific trigger brings these feelings on. This has gone on for months and is so bad that it is hurting her productivity at work and the quality of her home and family life. If you could encourage her to seek treatment, what would a psychologist most likely tell her?

   A. She needs help overcoming her specific phobia.
   B. Panic attacks can be successful treated.
   C. She may have generalized anxiety disorder.
   D. Everyone feels anxiousness, stress, and tension sometimes and so it is not really a sign of a disorder.

Analyze . . .

5. If anxiety leads to the onset of so many different disorders, how can it be a beneficial, adaptive process?

   A. It cannot be an adaptive process.
   B. The physiological response underlying anxiety prepares us to fight or flee.
   C. Anxiety is a good way to gain sympathy.
   D. The anxiety response evolved to help attract mates.

Module 13.4   Schizophrenia

 ## Learning Objectives

13.4a Know . . . the key terminology associated with schizophrenia.

13.4b Understand . . . how different neurotransmitters affect individuals with schizophrenia.

13.4c Understand . . . the genetic and environmental contributions to schizophrenia.

13.4d Apply . . . your knowledge to identify symptoms of schizophrenia.

13.4e Analyze . . . claims that schizophrenia is related to genius or violent behavior.

After reading about numerous mental disorders you would not be faulted for thinking the brain is a fragile structure. It certainly can be. However, consider a brain that comprehends unfathomably complex mathematics and creatively disentangles and models natural patterns. Yet, this same brain often struggles to distinguish reality from fiction and spins itself into an entirely confused and chaotic state. Such was the brain of John Nash, a mathematician and Nobel laureate in economics. To academics, Nash was known first for his intellectual ideas. To the general public, he was best recognized as a genius who had schizophrenia. Both are true. By his middle and late twenties Nash was

an established giant in the fields of mathematics and economics (he completed his doctorate at 22 years of age). Around this time he also started showing telltale symptoms of schizophrenia, including paranoia and delusional thinking. Among his many unusual experiences, Nash heard voices that were not there and believed there were government conspiracies against him. Despite his mental illness (and, contrary to popular belief, not because of it), Nash was one of the greatest scholars of our time.

Schizophrenia is among the most debilitating of psychological conditions, and it has affected people for at least as long as written history. Writings from early history describe people who seem to have lost touch with reality, who hear voices from within, and who produce bizarre speech and behaviors. These symptoms of schizophrenia can give rise to false beliefs that individuals are possessed by demons or spirits. As we will see, recent scientific findings are providing a different explanation.

Symptoms and Characteristics of Schizophrenia

Schizophrenia *is a mental disorder characterized by chronic and significant breaks from reality, a lack of integration of thoughts and emotions, and serious problems with attention and memory.* One obvious sign of breaking from reality is the experience of **hallucinations**, *which are false perceptions of reality such as hearing internal voices.* Patients may also experience **delusions**, *which are false beliefs about reality.* For example, a person with schizophrenia may have a *delusion of grandeur*, believing that he is Jesus, the Pope, or the president. Consider the following personal account of a man named Kurt Snyder, who wrote a book about his experiences with schizophrenia during college:

> *I thought about fractals and infinity for many years. I always told myself I was on the verge of discovery, but I simply had to think a little bit harder about it. I just wasn't thinking hard enough. The reality is that the problems I was trying to solve were far beyond my mental abilities, but I didn't recognize this fact. Even though I had no evidence to substantiate my self-image, I knew in my heart that I was just like Einstein, and that someday I would get a flash of inspiration. I didn't recognize the truth—that I am not a genius. I kept most of my mathematical ideas to myself and spoke to very few people about them. I was paranoid that someone else would solve the riddle first if I provided the right clues. (Snyder, 2006, p. 209)*

Kurt's experiences, and those of many other individuals diagnosed with schizophrenia, attest to the mind-altering experiences that characterize this disorder.

Schizophrenia occurs throughout the world, and affects an estimated 0.4% to 0.7% of its population (Bhugra, 2005). Men are more likely to have the disorder (7:5 ratio) and tend to develop it earlier in life than women (Aleman et al., 2003). The onset of schizophrenia, in the form of an acute psychotic episode, typically occurs during late adolescence or young adulthood (DeLisi, 1992). More subtle signs, as discussed later in this module, can also appear early—even among toddlers.

Mental health professionals classify symptoms into positive and negative categories. **Positive symptoms** *refer to the presence of unusual behavioral patterns, such as confused and paranoid thinking, and inappropriate emotional reactions.* Positive symptoms involve the presence of maladaptive behavior. In contrast, **negative symptoms** *involve the absence of more typical and adaptive behaviors, such as dampened emotional reactions*

Kurt Snyder began experiencing schizophrenia in college. *Me, Myself, and Them* is his personal account of living with schizophrenia.

and lack of speech and motivation. The *DSM*-5 recognizes that no individual is likely to show every possible symptom of schizophrenia, and notes that any one or combination of the following may warrant a diagnosis:

- Hallucinations or delusions
- Disorganized speech, which consists of sequences of unrelated, incoherent ideas
- Disorganized or catatonic behavior, consisting of behavior and emotional expressions that are poorly integrated and incoherent, and possibly unpredictable. **Catatonia** *is a state of prolonged periods of immobility and muteness.* Repetitive and purposeless movements may also occur.
- Negative symptoms

People who experience bouts of catatonia will remain immobile, even if in a bizarre position, for extended periods of time.

Table 13.7 Applying Symptoms of Schizophrenia to Examples

1. Rosalita was helped to a chair and she has sat there, virtually motionless, for about 2 hours.	a. This is not schizophrenia b. Delusion
2. Eyanna refuses to go to the dentist. "Last time I went," she said, "they put a transmitter in my teeth so that the agents can control my thoughts."	c. Catatonia d. Hallucination
3. Jeff has begun experiencing extreme fear of dogs. He tells himself that few dogs are dangerous, and yet his body seems to tell him otherwise.	
4. Jinhai hears voices conversing about the pending end of the world, yet he is alone and nobody is nearby.	

Answers: 1c, 2b, 3a, 4d

Individuals with schizophrenia experience several problems with cognitive functioning. These range from basic startle responses, such as eye blinking (Perry et al., 2002), to the skills involved in standardized achievement tests—test scores tend to drop during adolescence as symptoms of the disorder accelerate (Fuller et al., 2002). Many complex cognitive abilities involve the prefrontal cortex, a brain region showing significant neurological decline in individuals with schizophrenia (Wright et al., 2000). One such ability is working memory, the memory system that allows us to keep track of a train of thought, organize the sequence of a conversation, and handle multiple memory tasks for a short period of time. Therefore, working memory deficits may partially explain the disorganized thoughts and speech characteristic of schizophrenia (Park et al., 1999).

Social interaction is also difficult for people with schizophrenia. They typically have difficulty reasoning about social situations and show relatively poor social adjustment (Done et al., 1994). In addition, people with schizophrenia may maintain a neutral masklike expression on their faces, and show little response to smiles or other expressions from people around them. (Penn & Combs,

2000). Practice applying the different symptom labels to behavioral examples in the activity on Table 13.7.

Biological Factors of Schizophrenia

Several techniques have been employed to discover the causes and correlates of schizophrenia. As is the case with other types of disorders, no single definitive explanation has emerged, but it seems clear that a complete answer will draw from each facet of the biopsychosocial model.

SCHIZOPHRENIA AND THE NERVOUS SYSTEM One noticeable neurological characteristic of people with schizophrenia is apparent in the size of the brain ventricles, the fluid-filled spaces occurring within the core of the brain. People with schizophrenia have ventricular spaces that are 20% to 30% larger than the corresponding spaces in people without schizophrenia (see Figure 13.10) (Gottesman & Gould, 2003). The larger ventricular spaces correspond to a loss of brain matter. In fact, the volume of the entire brain is reduced by approximately 2% in individuals with schizophrenia—a small but significant difference. In particular, the reduced volume can be found in structures such as the amygdala, hippocampus, and

Myths In Mind

Schizophrenia Is Not a Sign of Violence or Genius

Schizophrenia is a widely recognized term, but it is often misunderstood to mean "split personality." It is an entirely different disorder than multiple personality disorder (now called dissociative identity disorder; see Module 13.2). Other misconceptions are more difficult to dispel, such as the belief that "madness" goes along with genius, or that schizophrenia makes a person dangerous. These myths persist because of high-profile cases such as those involving Ted Kaczynski and John Nash. Kaczynski, a bright mathematician, became famous as the "Unabomber" after sending mail bombs to prominent researchers at various universities. Nash, who was introduced at the beginning of this module, was another math genius but lived a peaceful, productive life as a researcher at Princeton University; the film *A Beautiful Mind* is based on the story of his life.

Few individuals with schizophrenia commit offenses even approaching the degree of violence brought about by Kaczynski. Moreover, when violence does occur, substance abuse and other factors tend to play a role (Douglas et al., 2009; Fazel et al., 2009). What may be most surprising is that people with mental illness are actually more likely to be *victims* of crime—up to 11 times more likely than nonmentally ill people (Teplin et al., 2005). Perhaps people with schizophrenia should be concerned about the rest of the population.

Also, despite the two well-publicized cases of Kaczynski and Nash, people with schizophrenia typically score slightly below average on IQ tests (Woodberry et al., 2008).

Figure 13.10 Schizophrenia and the Brain

The brains of two genetically identical individuals, one affected with schizophrenia and the other unaffected, are shown here. The arrows point to the spaces created by the ventricles of the brain. Note the significant loss of brain matter in the affected individual.

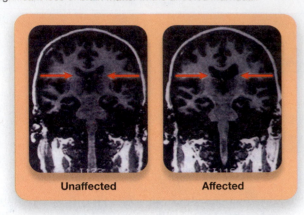

Unaffected   Affected

cerebral cortex (Wright et al., 2000; Roalf et al., 2015). It is important to remember that the anatomical changes associated with schizophrenia may not *cause* the disorder; rather, they might just tend to occur in people who have it.

The brains of people with schizophrenia are not just different in size; they also function differently. Individuals with schizophrenia have been shown to have a lower level of activity in their frontal lobes than those without schizophrenia. In particular, people who have a long history with the disorder show lower levels of activity in their frontal lobes either when they are at a resting state or when their frontal lobes are activated by a cognitive task (Hill et al., 2004). As you just read, these individuals tend to have smaller amygdala and hippocampal regions. These

Psychologists have long noted that individuals who are being treated with antipsychotic drugs that block dopamine tend to be heavy smokers. One possible reason is that both the rewarding experiences and the impaired concentration associated with dopamine are reduced by the medication. Heavy nicotine use stimulates the reward and cognitive centers of the brain, thereby helping compensate for the dampening effects the medication has on dopamine (Winterer, 2010).

differences also correspond to reduced activity of these structures during cognitive tasks (Hempel et al., 2003).

Imbalances in chemicals coursing through the brain seem to lead to the disordered thinking and emotions associated with schizophrenia. Specifically, individuals with schizophrenia have overactive receptors for the neurotransmitter dopamine (Heinz & Schlagenhauf, 2010). The excess dopamine activity may be involved in producing the outward symptoms of schizophrenia, such as hallucinations and delusions, but not the negative symptoms such as flattened emotion and lack of speech (Andreasen et al., 1995).

Another neurotransmitter, called *glutamate*, appears to be *underactive* in brain regions, including the hippocampus and the frontal cortex, of individuals with schizophrenia. Coincidently, glutamate receptor activity is also inhibited by the drug PCP (angel dust), which in high doses can cause disordered behavior and thinking mirroring that of schizophrenia.

GENETICS Studies using twin, adoption, and family history methods have shown that as genetic relatedness increases, the chance that a relative of a person with schizophrenia will also develop the disorder increases (Modinos et al., 2013; see Figure 13.11). For example, if one identical twin has schizophrenia, the other twin has a 25% to 50% chance of developing it. This rate is significantly higher than the 10% to 17% rate found in dizygotic (fraternal) twin pairs (Gottesman, 1991).

For decades, behavioral genetic studies have shown that genes contribute to schizophrenia, but they cannot

Figure 13.11 Genetic Influences for Schizophrenia

The more genetic similarity an individual has to a person with schizophrenia, the more likely that he or she will also develop the disorder.

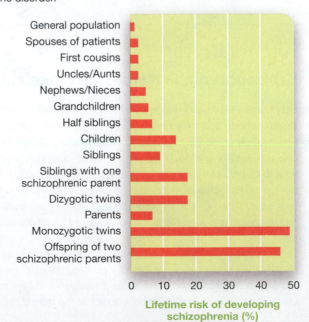

Lifetime risk of developing schizophrenia (%)

identify the specific genes that contribute to the disorder. However, with the benefit of technological advances in molecular genetics several candidate genes associated with schizophrenia have been discovered. For example, scientists have discovered a distinct pattern of genetic irregularities that is found in 15% of individuals with schizophrenia, compared with only 5% of healthy controls (Walsh et al., 2008). On the one hand, this relationship suggests a possible genetic contribution to schizophrenia. On the other hand, the genetic abnormality was not found in 85% of the individuals. Thus, like most psychological disorders, schizophrenia cannot be diagnosed by examining a single gene. Whether an individual develops schizophrenia is probably determined by multiple genetic and molecular switches that are turned on or off in a particular pattern. Critically, the pattern is determined by interactions with the environment (Modinos et al., 2013; EU-GEI, 2014).

JOURNAL PROMPT

Biology of Schizophrenia: Reading about biological factors and mental disorders, such as schizophrenia, can lead one to believe that they are the culprits leading to mental illness. Does a biological influence on a mental disorder mean that one is destined to have it eventually, or have it permanently once diagnosed? Why or why not?

Environmental and Cultural Influences on Schizophrenia

Research on the neuroscience of schizophrenia has made inroads toward discovering its causes. But remember a few observations: First, many people who *do not* have mutant versions of the genes involved in schizophrenia may still develop the disorder and, second, an identical twin has roughly a 50% chance of developing schizophrenia if her twin has it. Finally, although approximately 1% of the world population may have the disorder, as much as 10% of the population is at a *genetic risk* for developing schizophrenia (Meehl, 1990). These observations indicate that schizophrenia is not strictly a genetic disorder, and they suggest that we should consider some environmental factors that influence brain development and functioning.

ENVIRONMENTAL AND PRENATAL FACTORS When we think about environmental influences, we have to stretch back as far as possible—even before birth. For example, people with schizophrenia are statistically more likely to have been born during winter months (Tochigi et al., 2004). One plausible explanation for this link is that the brain develops a great deal during the second trimester, which would coincide with the onset of flu season for wintertime births. Furthermore, extreme stress such as loss of a spouse and even exposure to war during pregnancy may increase the chances that the infant will subsequently develop schizophrenia. From examples like these, scientists speculate that exposure to viruses or stress hormones may put a person at risk for schizophrenia (Brown & Derkits, 2010; King et al., 2010).

There are a variety of risk factors occurring during childhood and adolescence can increase the chance that schizophrenia will develop. One factor is heavy cannabis use. A small proportion of cannabis users develop psychotic symptoms, possibly because the drug interacts with the genes involved in schizophrenia (Caspi et al., 2005; Radhakrishnan, Wilkinson, & D'Souza, 2014). Head injuries occurring before age 10 also put people who are genetically vulnerable to schizophrenia at greater risk for developing the disorder (AbdelMalik et al., 2003). *Psychosocial stress* is a broad term covering poverty, unemployment, discrimination, divorce, and traumatic events. Being raised in an urban environment, where psychosocial stressors are more abundant, puts individuals who are genetically vulnerable at an even greater risk for developing schizophrenia (van Os et al., 2004; Holtzman et al., 2013).

CULTURAL FACTORS In Module 13.1, we introduced the topic of cultural perceptions of mental illness. Differing cultural perspectives are evident when it comes to schizophrenia and even influences the types of experiences that individuals report having. In the United States, people with European ancestry tend to focus on the mental experiences of the disorder, such as disorganized thinking and emotions. This is associated with the view that schizophrenia is a mental disorder quite distinct from other types of illness. In contrast, people from Latin America often focus more on how schizophrenia affects the body, such as by producing tension or tiredness. They conceive of the disorder as any other form of illness, rather a unique or distinct type (Weisman et al., 2000).

Another cultural variation is known as *running amok*, which is sometimes used in the United States to describe unusual, energetic, and out-of-control behavior. The term "amok" is actually Indonesian in origin. Psychiatrist Emil Kraepelin concluded that amok is similar to what we call psychosis, albeit with some notable differences. For example, auditory hallucinations—seem to be virtually absent among Indonesian people with schizophrenia. Kraepelin attributed this difference to the low use of speech in this culture (Jilek, 1995).

Beliefs about mental illness are linked to varying cultural views of the world (McGruder, 2004). Many people throughout the world, such as the Swahili of Tanzania, believe that what we call schizophrenia is a sign that spirits have invaded the body. In some cultures, the self is perceived as not wholly separate from an individual, but rather "permeable" to other entities or beings. Spirits, which are thought to overpower humans, can therefore invade the body. When you compare those views with the scientific approach found in the United States, you should see how essential culture is in understanding disorders.

Working the Scientific Literacy Model

The Neurodevelopmental Hypothesis of Schizophrenia

Schizophrenia is obviously a complex disorder, and no one explanation has been able to account for all the variations in symptoms, severity, and duration. A combination of biopsychosocial variables, and the timing in which they occur, may account for the development of the disorder.

Some of the first indicators of schizophrenia are found during infancy and childhood. Children with unusual and unnecessary motor movements, particularly on the left side of the body, may be more likely to develop the disorder.

What do we know about the neurodevelopmental hypothesis?

Factors related to the onset of schizophrenia influence behavior even before birth. The **neurodevelopmental hypothesis (of schizophrenia)** *states that irregular biological and environmental factors interact during prenatal, infant, and child development to produce symptoms of schizophrenia* (Walker et al., 2010). It is important to distinguish this approach from other possibilities, such as a *neurodegenerative hypothesis* proposing that the brain deteriorates to produce schizophrenia. As its name implies, the neurodevelopmental hypothesis posits that the brain grows into a schizophrenic state rather than degenerating into one.

How can science test the neurodevelopmental hypothesis?

The neurodevelopmental hypothesis draws from research on genetics and prenatal events. In addition, the developmental emphasis of the hypothesis gains strength from behavioral evidence collected during childhood and adolescence. For example, when psychologists viewed home movies of infants and children who subsequently developed schizophrenia, they noted that these children showed some unusual motor patterns, primarily on the left side of the body, such as jerky, repeated, and unnecessary arm movements (Walker et al., 1994). Siblings who did not have schizophrenia did not show these same motor patterns. Similar observations were made in a study of 11- to 13-year-old boys who were considered at risk for schizophrenia. The boys were videotaped eating lunch and observers noted any unusual social behavior and neuromotor (movement) functioning. Kids who showed a combination of these symptoms were more likely to be diagnosed with schizophrenia as adults compared to kids who did not show these behaviors (Schiffman et al., 2004).

In adolescence, psychologists can detect the schizophrenia *prodrome,* a collection of characteristics that resemble mild forms of schizophrenia symptoms. For example, a teenager might become increasingly socially withdrawn and have some difficulty with depression and anxiety. But the most telling—and most perplexing—problems include experiences that resemble hallucinations and delusions, with the exception that the affected individual does not fully believe them. For example, a teen might say, "I seem to keep hearing my mother calling my name before I fall asleep, even when I know she isn't home. It is strange … " (Walker et al., 2010, p. 206).

Can we critically evaluate this information?

Unusual body movements certainly do not mean a child will develop schizophrenia in early adulthood. Nevertheless, it is at least one irregular developmental pattern that might reflect neurological abnormalities. Its emergence would be consistent with that predicted by the neurodevelopmental hypothesis, which rests on the idea that vulnerability to schizophrenia is present at birth (Walker et al., 2010). Similarly, at some point in adolescence, while most individuals will report at least one of these collections of symptoms, those who report all of them are at increased risk for schizophrenia.

Why is this relevant?

By identifying developmental patterns and catching them early, it may be possible to alter the progression of the disorder, thereby preventing the onset of schizophrenia, or at least controlling its severity. In recent years, a number of attempts to prevent schizophrenia from developing in high-risk populations have been made, but have not proved effective (McGlashan et al., 2006; McGorry et al., 2002). To accomplish this goal, researchers will have to rely on all aspects of the biopsychosocial model: genetics, the function and structure of the brain, neurotransmitters, prenatal influences, and psychosocial factors.

Module **13.4** Summary

13.4a Know . . . the key terminology associated with schizophrenia:

catatonia
delusions
hallucinations
negative symptoms
neurodevelopmental hypothesis (of schizophrenia)
positive symptoms
schizophrenia

13.4b Understand . . . how different neurotransmitters affect individuals with schizophrenia.

Abnormal levels of dopamine (too much) and glutamate (too little) are associated with symptoms of schizophrenia.

13.4c Understand . . . the genetic and environmental contributions to schizophrenia.

The neurodevelopmental hypothesis claims that at least some neurological abnormalities are present at birth, although it does not state to what degree these abnormalities are genetic or environmental. Nevertheless, some research suggests that prenatal exposure to the flu or to significant amounts of stress hormones are all risk factors for schizophrenia. Genetics

seem to play a role, as twin studies show that if one identical twin has schizophrenia, the other has up to a 50% chance of developing the disorder—a substantial increase over the 1% occurrence rate in the general population.

13.4d Apply . . . your knowledge to identify symptoms of schizophrenia.

There are diverse symptoms associated with schizophrenia that include positive and negative varieties. The activity in Table 13.7 provided an opportunity to practice matching symptoms with terminology.

13.4e Analyze . . . claims that schizophrenia is related to genius or violent behavior.

As you have read, some high-profile cases highlight people with schizophrenia who are intellectually brilliant. In reality, however, research tells us that the average intelligence of people with schizophrenia is not much different from those of the general population; in fact, it is a little bit lower than the norm. Similarly, the belief that schizophrenia leads to violence derives from a small group of high-profile examples. In truth, there does not seem to be increased risk of violence associated with schizophrenia alone.

Module **13.4** Quiz

Know . . .

1. A person with schizophrenia who has become convinced that she is royalty is experiencing a(n) _____.
   - **A.** delusion
   - **B.** negative symptom
   - **C.** catatonic state
   - **D.** manic state

Understand . . .

2. Which of the following statements is most accurate concerning the biochemical basis of schizophrenia?
   - **A.** The neurotransmitter dopamine is overly active.
   - **B.** Dopamine is underactive.
   - **C.** Serotonin levels are too low.
   - **D.** There is too much glutamate activity.

3. The underlying genetic basis for schizophrenia can be described as follows:
   - **A.** A single gene puts people at risk for it, especially if the environment switches it on.
   - **B.** Evidence suggests a minimal role for genetics, with environmental factors playing the strongest role.
   - **C.** If a combination of about 10 genes are inherited, the disorder occurs regardless of environmental triggers.
   - **D.** Multiple genes have been identified as risk factors, and environmental events, especially ones occurring prenatally, further increase the risk of developing the disorder.

Apply . . .

4. A patient who is nonresponsive and remains still in odd postures is showing what type of symptom of schizophrenia?
   - **A.** Disorganized
   - **B.** Positive
   - **C.** Catatonic
   - **D.** Hallucinogenic

Analyze . . .

5. Which of the following statements best summarizes the relationship between schizophrenia and violence?
   - **A.** Generally, people with schizophrenia are no more likely to become violent than nonmentally ill people, and if violence occurs, other factors, such as substance abuse, are likely to contribute to its cause.
   - **B.** People with schizophrenia are twice as likely to be violent as nonmentally ill people.
   - **C.** People with schizophrenia are far more peaceful than non-mentally ill people.
   - **D.** People with schizophrenia cannot differentiate right from wrong, and therefore are prone to violence.

Module 13.5 Scientific Literacy Challenge: Bereavement

The editors of the *DSM-5* were challenged by the dimensional nature of many psychological disorders, such as depression. One tough question they struggled with was, at what point does sadness and a lack of energy or motivation become depression? This lack of certainty was particularly difficult when a debate erupted over bereavement. Specifically, mental health professionals argued whether sadness and mourning following the death of a loved one constitutes a diagnosable form of depression. Eventually it was decided that people going through bereavement could be diagnosed with major depressive disorder. The *DSM-5* now recommends a formal diagnosis of depression, even if the loss of a loved one is what triggers the change in mood and emotional functioning. Before you continue on to an article that presents some strong opinions on the matter, consider your own thoughts about the relationship between bereavement and depression.

JOURNAL PROMPT

This chapter described what constitutes a psychological disorder. With the concepts of mental illness in mind, do you think it seems appropriate or inappropriate to diagnose an individual who is bereaving with major depression? Please explain.

What do we know about bereavement?

In the following column, the president of a regional psychological association argues that the *DSM-5* did the right thing by modifying the requirements for a diagnosis of major depressive episode. As you read the beginning paragraph of his column, make sure you recognize and understand the boldfaced key terms from Chapter 13.

Bereavement belongs in the *DSM-5*

By Alberto Herrera, President, Tri-State Association for Mental Health

One of the public's key misunderstandings about psychology is what constitutes a psychological disorder. Part of the problem is the difficulty of using **categorical** labels to describe things that are fundamentally **dimensional** in nature. That is definitely the case with bereavement. Prior to the publication of the *DSM-5*, the diagnosis of **Major Depression** included a "bereavement exclusion," indicating that the sadness associated with losing a loved one was somehow different from the sadness associated with traditional depression. In effect, prior to the 2013 publication of the *DSM-5* people could not be diagnosed with major depression if they had recently lost a loved one. Now, individuals who have recently lost a loved one can be diagnosed with major depression, even if they had never experienced depression before. Diagnosing someone with major depression during what seems like a very normal time to feel sad has caused some people to feel uneasy. It is seen as a move to turn a normal process into a pathology. This very type of issue is what makes some members of the public question our discipline's methods. It has been a contentious move in mental health fields as well. However, I argue in favor of this change, and once you look at the evidence, I think you will agree.

Now that we know what the controversy is, read on to find out what kind of evidence Dr. Herrera gathered to support his position.

How do scientists study bereavement?

Bereavement by itself is not the same thing as major depression, but as you will read here, research shows that it *can* be, and sometimes is. Make sure you pay attention to the scientific terms and concepts, especially in the highlighted sections, and then test yourself with the quiz that follows.

Recently, the journal *Depression and Anxiety* published a review of nine studies that altogether compared over 1,000 individuals experiencing a major depressive episode (MDE) without bereavement to individuals who were diagnosed with a major depressive episode in an extended bereavement period (MDB). The findings are compelling:

- MDE and MDB involve the same frequency and severity of symptoms, as measured by standardized tests for depression.
- MDE and MDB are not different in terms of how long episodes last and how likely they are to reoccur.
- MDE and MDB have similar levels of genetic influence.
- MDE and MDB are equally likely to respond to treatments, and respond to the same type of treatments.

In summary, the most significant difference between MDE and MDB is that one of them follows the loss of a loved one. With the behaviors, treatments, and response to treatments being nearly identical, why should the diagnosis be any different?

Dr. Herrera provided a quick review of the research, but you should be able to spot some important concepts here. Take the quiz below to see which concepts you identified.

1. The review compares two groups of people in multiple studies, but none of them are experiments because
   a. there is no random assignment.
   b. they use convenience sampling.
   c. they do not have a dependent variable.
   d. they do not have reliability.
2. The writer refers to depression scales that were used in the studies, which means that he addressed _____.
   a. the independent variable
   b. whether this is experimental or quasi-experimental
   c. the operational definitions of depression
   d. sample size
3. The scores on the depression scales would constitute a(n) _____.
   a. dependent variable.
   b. confounding variable
   c. generalizing variable
   d. demand characteristics

1.a 2.c 3.a

How do we think critically about bereavement?

Remember that critical thinking involves curiosity and reasonable levels of skepticism. As you read the next paragraph of the editorial, actively search for specific statements relevant to critical thinking.

I have long been convinced that this change to the *DSM* was needed. I don't have anything personal to gain from this and it might not even affect my practice. However, I do think the change will help in the long run. Those who argued to keep the bereavement exclusion predicted that the numbers of Major Depression diagnoses would skyrocket, but that just hasn't happened, according to the article in *Depression and Anxiety*. That is because the mental health profession has been differentiating between MDE and milder forms depression or sadness for years; nothing has changed in that regard.

Did Dr. Herrera apply critical thinking? The statements below will help you identify several aspects of critical thinking. Match the following critical thinking statements to the highlighted passages that illustrate them.

1. The author shows that critical thinking involves considering alternative viewpoints.
2. The author tries to identify sources of bias that might influence how people interpret results.
3. The author adds credibility to the evidence by indicating a reputable source of information.

1. Blue 2. Yellow 3. Green

Dr. Herrera seems to have demonstrated cautious skepticism and a good deal of critical thinking. Next let's see how Dr. Herrera's point of view applies to clinical psychology.

How is diagnosing bereavement relevant?

In closing, Dr. Herrera explains how he thinks removing the bereavement exclusion will help clinical psychologists. Read the following excerpt, then explore any newly formed thoughts you may have about bereavement in the writing activity that follows.

Dropping the bereavement exclusion does nothing to change how people experience the symptoms of depression. What it does change is very important, however. Identifying depression helps the individual understand that what they are experiencing is a known condition, that they are not alone in those feelings, and that there is a high probability of a successful treatment. These same ideas are communicated to clinicians as well. Therefore, I anticipate the change will shape the way the next generation of professionals thinks about treating people in bereavement.

SHARED WRITING

Do you accept or reject Dr. Herrera's conclusion that people who are bereaving should, if circumstances warrant, be diagnosed with depression and receive treatment for it? How, if at all, did his evidence and critique shape your opinion?

Chapter 13 Quiz

1. Psychologists and psychiatrists use the criteria laid out in the most recent edition of the _____ to diagnose psychological disorders.
   A. *Dimensional and Categorical Atlas of Mental Health*
   B. *International Diagnostic Guidelines*
   C. *Guide to Psychopathology and Abnormal Behavior*
   D. *Diagnostic and Statistical Manual for Mental Disorders*

2. Which of the following is not a psychiatric criterion for mental illness?
   A. Expression of behavior that causes distress to self or others
   B. The condition must be categorical.
   C. Impairment of functioning
   D. Increased risk of lost freedom, pain, or death

3. Aaliyah's few friends complain that she is often melodramatic and emotionally immature. Aaliyah loves attention (especially from men) and is constantly flirting, often inappropriately. If Aaliyah was diagnosed with a psychological disorder, which of the following would be the most likely candidate?
   A. Narcissistic personality disorder
   B. Borderline personality disorder
   C. Histrionic personality disorder
   D. Antisocial personality disorder

4. Which of the following disorders do psychologists believe is *not* a valid diagnosis?
   A. Dissociative identity disorder
   B. Schizophrenia
   C. Histrionic personality disorder
   D. Posttraumatic stress disorder

5. In addition to suffering from panic attacks, people with panic disorder often develop an intense fear of:
   A. having a panic attack when they are alone.
   B. public places.
   C. germs.
   D. leaving the stove on.

6. Huynh washes his hands 100 or more times each day. The constant washing causes the skin on his hands to dry and crack, yet he continues to engage in this behavior. Huynh's behavior is an example of _____.
   A. an obsession
   B. agoraphobia
   C. a compulsion
   D. a negative symptom

7. Allison has an intense fear of flying, so much so that she cannot even bear to close her eyes and imagine that she is on a plane. From this brief description, Allison may be experiencing:
   A. a specific phobia.
   B. a social phobia.
   C. a generalized phobia.
   D. normal levels of anxiety.

8. _____ are false beliefs about reality, whereas _____ are false perceptions of reality such as hearing internal voices.
   A. Positive symptoms; negative symptoms
   B. Negative symptoms; positive symptoms
   C. Hallucinations; delusions
   D. Delusions; hallucinations

9. Suppose a friend described schizophrenia as having a "split personality." How would you respond?
   A. "This is a common misconception caused by people confusing schizophrenia with dissociative identity disorder."
   B. "Only disorganized schizophrenia is characterized by a splitting of personalities."
   C. "That point is controversial; psychologists cannot agree on whether schizophrenia involves a splitting of personality."
   D. "That is an accurate description of schizophrenia."

10. Which of the following statements is true about the average brain of individuals with schizophrenia when they are compared to the brains of individuals who do not have the disorder?
    A. There are no known anatomical differences.
    B. The overall size of the brain is actually larger than normal in people with schizophrenia.
    C. Dopamine activity is lower than normal in people with schizophrenia.
    D. The fluid-filled spaces at the core of the brain are larger in people with schizophrenia.

11. Which of the following is *not* a characteristic of personality disorders?
    A. Traits that are inflexible and maladaptive
    B. Significant functional impairment or subjective distress
    C. Marked deviation from cultural expectations
    D. Typically diagnosed with medical tests

12. _____ involves intense extremes between positive and negative emotions, an unstable sense of self, impulsivity, and difficult social relationships.
   A. Borderline personality disorder
   B. Narcissistic personality disorder
   C. Histrionic personality disorder
   D. Antisocial personality disorder

13. There have been several famous cases of people with superior intellectual abilities as well as schizophrenia. Does this mean that schizophrenia is the cause or the result of genius?
   A. No; in fact, the average IQ of people with schizophrenia may be slightly lower than average.
   B. Yes; in fact, the average IQ of people with schizophrenia is approximately 15% higher than average.
   C. Yes, because people who are that smart are likely to develop schizophrenia simply because they know too much.
   D. No, because schizophrenia is associated with very low IQs.

14. Depression is associated with lower activity in the frontal lobe, which may result in:
   A. lack of appetite.
   B. difficulty concentrating and thinking.
   C. periods of elevated mood and energy.
   D. constipation.

15. Which of the following is not classified as an anxiety disorder?
   A. Panic attack
   B. GAD
   C. Bipolar disorder
   D. Social phobia

Chapter 14
Therapies

Module 14.1 Treating Psychological Disorders

Learning Objectives

14.1a Know . . . the key terminology associated with mental health treatment.

14.1b Understand . . . the major barriers to seeking help for psychological disorders.

14.1c Understand . . . the importance of empirically supported treatments.

14.1d Apply . . . your knowledge to understand your own attitudes toward help-seeking.

14.1e Analyze . . . whether technology can deliver useful options for therapy.

Medical doctors are required to follow the Hippocratic Oath—an agreement binding them to do no harm and to use the safest and most effective methods for treating patients. Like physicians, psychologists must be aware of the possibility that a specific type of treatment could worsen a condition and, therefore, should be avoided. For example, Scared Straight was a program developed in the 1970s that involved exposing at-risk youth to prisons and prisoners. The interventions were based on the premise that shocking or scaring the youths with the harsh realities of prison life would deter criminal activity. These scare tactics involved blunt descriptions of prison violence, along with verbal aggression

directed at adolescents attending the sessions. The program may have succeeded in scaring and shocking adolescents, but they did not necessarily proceed down a straight path. Many were later convicted of crimes and incarcerated. According to some analyses, participation in the program was actually associated with an increased chance that adolescents would commit crimes (Petrosino et al., 2013). Scared Straight and other methods for helping people can, in fact, do more harm than good (Lilienfeld, 2007). Although a rare case, this example reminds us how important it is that all approaches to treating both mental and physical health need to be carefully tested prior to use.

In Chapter 13 we described some of the major psychological disorders. Here we address **psychotherapy**—*the processes and techniques for resolving personal, emotional, behavioral, and social problems so as to improve well-being.* We will address who uses psychotherapy, who provides it, and how it is evaluated.

An ever-growing number of people seek help for psychological problems. This includes individuals who are being treated for serious psychiatric conditions, as well as people seeking help for common issues such as stress, marital and relationship problems, loneliness, dissatisfaction at work, problems with impulsiveness, or persistent anxiety. Not all groups of people are equally likely to seek treatment. In general, women participate in psychotherapy more often than men, and people aged 35 through 55 seek treatment more often than younger adults and the elderly (Addis & Mahalik, 2003; Olfson & Marcus, 2010). Researchers within the United States have found that Caucasians are more likely to seek psychotherapy than are African American and Hispanic individuals (see Figure 14.1; Olfson & Marcus, 2010; Olfson et al., 2002). Finally, people from the United States and Canada are generally more likely to seek therapy than people from many other regions, as demonstrated in research on college students from countries as diverse as Israel, Hungary, Japan, and Korea (Cohen et al., 1998; Masuda et al., 2005; Yoo & Skovholt, 2001).

Figure 14.1 Who Seeks Treatment?

Whether someone seeks outpatient psychological therapy services depends on numerous factors, including ethnicity, sex, education level, and age.

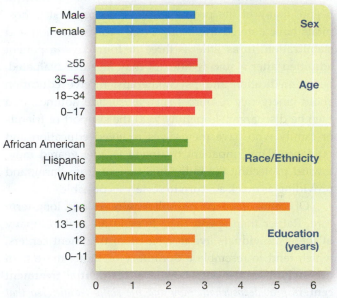

Percentage of individuals in the population seeking outpatient mental health services

Figure 14.2 Types of Treatment People Use

Prescription drugs are the most prevalent mental health option followed by outpatient visits with a therapist, and then inpatient care (numbers are for adults aged 18 and older in the United States who sought mental health treatment).

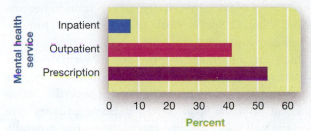

Mental Health Providers and Settings

Many treatment settings are available for people in need of mental health care. The type of treatment people receive depends on several factors, including their age, the type and severity of the disorder, and the existence of any legal issues and concerns that coincide with the need for treatment. Professional mental health services include psychotherapy and prescription drugs, and are delivered through inpatient care and outpatient office visits (see Figure 14.2 and also Module 14.3). Care may be received from many different types of mental health professionals with varying backgrounds.

MENTAL HEALTH PROVIDERS   In popular culture, the terms "psychologist" and "psychiatrist" are often (and erroneously) used as if they mean the same thing. In fact, some major distinctions separate the two and, even among psychologists, there are a variety of specialized providers.

Perhaps the best known are **clinical psychologists** and **counseling psychologists**; *both labels describe mental health professionals with doctoral degrees who diagnose and treat mental health problems ranging from the everyday to the chronic and severe.* The distinction between the two fields is mostly historical and academic, meaning that you could receive treatment from a psychologist and not be able to ascertain whether their degree is in clinical or counseling psychology. Both types of psychologists may earn the familiar PhD, but some graduate training programs offer a PsyD (Doctor of Psychology). Practitioners of clinical and counseling psychology work in many capacities and settings. They may provide individual or group therapy in an office or institution such as a hospital, and some are now experimenting with online treatment. They may conduct psychological evaluations, or conduct research at universities and medical schools. The professional label "psychologist" is generally reserved for those who have completed doctoral training, whereas someone with a master's degree in psychology can provide psychotherapy with a job title such as Licensed Mental Health Counselor (it may vary depending by the state in which they practice). Similarly, professionals with a Master of Social Work degree can train to become Licensed Clinical Social Workers (LCSW) and provide psychotherapy as well.

There are also medical providers. **Psychiatrists** *are physicians who specialize in mental health, and who diagnose and treat mental disorders primarily through prescribing medications that influence brain chemistry.* Some primary care physicians will also prescribe medications, but generally limit themselves to mild or moderate anxiety or depression while referring more severe problems to psychiatrists. Like psychologists, physicians may see patients on an outpatient or inpatient basis; the difference is in training and the emphasis on drugs versus psychotherapy. Currently in the United States, clinical psychologists can only prescribe medications if they are licensed and practice in New Mexico, Louisiana, Illinois, or Guam. Even in those locations, the PhD is not sufficient; prescription privileges are only awarded to those who have completed a specialized certification program.

INPATIENT TREATMENT AND DEINSTITUTIONALIZA-TION Throughout much of human history, people experiencing severe disorders—now known by names such as bipolar disorder, schizophrenia, or Alzheimer's disease—were often separated from society. They may have been physically removed from the city or, in the 1800s and 1900s, locked in an asylum. These actions hardly qualify as treatments because there was no hope that the individuals would get better. Instead, the goals were to "protect" the public and to provide basic care for individuals whose families could not do so (Wright, 1997).

Sadly, history tells us that many mental institutions were not the most caring places; in fact, they appeared rather stark and depressing. Patients were mostly warehoused without receiving much in the way of treatment, education, or recreation. This lack of physical and mental stimulation seems to have sealed the fate of the patients, putting them in a position where they would never recover. To make matters worse, some institutions relied on restraints such as chains and straightjackets, and the employee profile fit the modern idea of a jailhouse guard rather than a nurse or therapist.

By the 1950s, a grassroots campaign had formed in response to the obvious shortfalls of this treatment. Known as **deinstitutionalization**, *this movement pushed for returning people to their communities and families and enabling them to receive treatment on an outpatient basis.* The results were largely successful, and the movement convinced several sectors of society—namely, government, the public,

Today, some people with severe mental disorders reside in an institution or hospital that specializes in mental health care. These settings are dramatically different than they were just a few decades ago, when they were called "insane asylums" and other unfortunate names.

and social scientists—that asylums were causing more problems than they solved.

Deinstitutionalization has not done away with the need for inpatient care, but modern science has provided many ways to improve the experience from warehousing to actual treatment. In the decades since this movement began, many of the people admitted to psychiatric hospitals have entered the facilities only for evaluation and stabilization. In as little as three or four days, a patient admitted after a suicide attempt may be fully evaluated, begin medication and psychotherapy, receive education about emergency resources such as suicide hotlines, and then be discharged, hopefully with the support of friends or family who have themselves received education and guidance. Thus, inpatient treatment is now geared more toward protecting the individual patient from harm, and providing as quick a return to society as possible.

Of course, some people still require serious, long-term care. Rather than spend their lives in an asylum, many of these individuals live in residential treatment centers, which tend to resemble a dormitory or motel more than the asylums of the past. Low-level **residential treatment centers** *provide psychotherapy and life skills training so that the residents can become integrated into society to the greatest extent possible.* Medium- to high-level centers place increasing restrictions on individuals, so they may have the appearance of a hospital equipped like a medium-security prison. These facilities are intended for individuals with a more dangerous history—perhaps people who have committed physical or sexual assault—and so they are far less common than any other treatment location.

OUTPATIENT TREATMENT AND PREVENTION Outpatient therapy and inpatient housing simultaneously grew in popularity through the early 20th century. Their emergence paved the way for deinstitutionalization, which was essentially a call to move people with mental illness to the community where they could receive outpatient treatment. After deinstitutionalization began, however, homelessness and substance abuse became major problems for people with severe mental illness. People with less intense problems sometimes found themselves facing financial barriers and stigma when they sought help.

To meet these needs, some psychologists moved away from doing individual, one-on-one therapy to see what they could do for the community. From this new orientation arose **community psychology,** *an area of psychology that focuses on identifying how individuals' mental health is influenced by the neighborhood, economics, social groups, and other community-based variables.* By operating at this level, community psychologists can emphasize prevention and screening. They may initiate public awareness campaigns,

develop group therapies and other resources, advocate for jobs and education, and offer free or low-cost group counseling in neighborhoods where private mental health services are not available. For example, to prevent depression, community psychologists may conduct research into the environmental and neighborhood factors that contribute to stress, anxiety, and depression, and then work with community groups to resolve these problems. In addition, they may develop programs to counter negative cognitive patterns and bolster positive thinking in schools and community centers.

Barriers to Psychological Treatment

There is clear evidence that treatments improve quality of life for people with mental illness, but a nationwide survey shows that only around 40% of all US adults with a serious mental illness had received professional care (NIMH, 2011; USDHHS, 2011; see Figure 14.3). If you include less-serious psychological conditions, that percentage has been estimated to be as high as 50% to 70% in the United States and western Europe (Alonso et al., 2004; Thornicroft, 2008; Wittchen & Jacobi, 2011). People frequently minimalize psychological problems they experience, which in turns reduces that chance that they will seek help. It may be that people are not aware that their symptoms can be

Figure 14.3 Barriers to Treatment

Reasons for not seeking mental health in adults 18 and over and in need of services

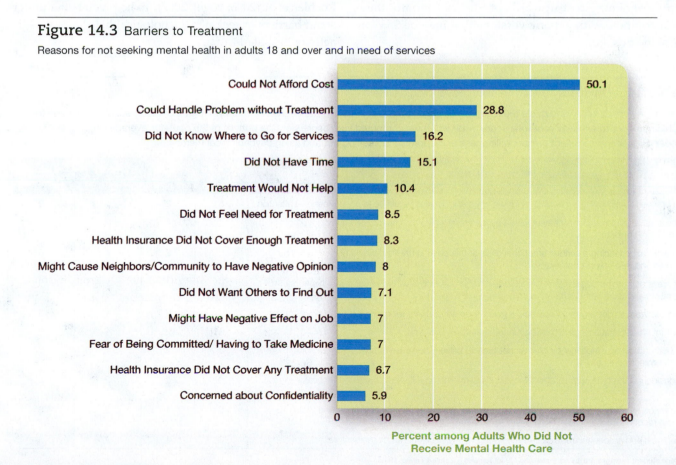

Percent among Adults Who Did Not Receive Mental Health Care

successfully treated by therapy or medication, or that their distress is severe enough to seek it (Mansfield et al., 2005; Vanheusdan et al., 2008). Researchers have also begun to focus on barriers to treatment—financial, cultural, and other factors that prevent individuals from receiving therapy.

EXPENSE AND OPPORTUNITY Survey research indicates that the cost of treatment is probably the most significant barrier (Colonna-Pydyn et al., 2007; USDHHS, 2011). Psychotherapy often costs more than $100 per hour, and prescription drugs can be expensive; brand-name drugs used to treat schizophrenia may cost as much as $400 per month. Indirect costs include time away from work, transportation, and child care. All of these factors can be especially burdensome to lower-income families who have less control over work schedules, fewer mental health facilities in their neighborhoods, and more frequently rely on public transportation. This explains why members of some socioeconomic groups are more likely than others to initiate treatment at a hospital emergency room rather than scheduling an appointment with a psychologist or other provider (Snowden, Catalano, & Shumway, 2009). To overcome these barriers, some community organizations provide offices in lower-income areas and charge fees on a sliding scale, which means the cost of a one-hour session is greatly reduced based on an individual's income. Finally, while brand-name antidepressants may cost upwards of $185 per month, they must compete with generic versions that may be $33 for the same dosage.

STIGMA AND SELF-CONSCIOUSNESS Even among individuals who believe they need treatment, many resist seeking help because of *stigma*—a collection of negative stereotypes associated with psychological disorders (introduced in Module 13.1; Vogel et al., 2009). Imagine an executive taking time off for cancer treatment—people would likely be very supportive. The same level of understanding is rarely true for conditions such as depression or anxiety. For related reasons, many adults also refuse treatment for their children (Hinshaw, 2005; Vogel et al., 2007). Sadly, stigma against people with mental disorders can result in job and housing discrimination, and ostracism by family, peers, and coworkers.

Stigma becomes a barrier largely by making an individual concerned about what others might think. This self-consciousness can also arise from the discomfort of sharing problems with anyone, including professionals (USDHHS, 2011). Masculinity emphasizes independence, so even if a problem is acknowledged, men often believe they should just "get over it" rather than appear weak (Berger et al., 2005; Mahalik et al., 2003).

The good news about stigma is that it is on the decline. Mental health advocates have demonstrated that when the public is informed and educated about mental illness, stereotyping and stigma are reduced. More importantly, evidence indicates that these and similar campaigns succeed in getting people in need to find help (Bell et al., 2010; Rochlen et al., 2006; Vogel, 2007). To help you better understand barriers to seeking psychological help, complete the activity in Table 14.1.

Table 14.1 Attitudes Toward Seeking Psychological Help

Read each item carefully and circle the response in the column that indicates the degree to which you agree or disagree. Next, average the circled numbers to arrive at your total score. After you have computed your score view the bottom of the page for averages separated by gender. Higher scores reflect greater willingness and approval of seeking out and using psychological therapy.

Item	Agree	Partly Agree	Partly Disagree	Disagree
If I believed I was having a mental breakdown, my first inclination would be to get professional attention.	3	2	1	0
The idea of talking about problems with a psychologist strikes me as a poor way to get rid of emotional conflicts.	0	1	2	3
If I were experiencing a serious emotional crisis at this point in my life, I would be confident that I could find relief in psychotherapy.	3	2	1	0
There is something admirable in the attitude of a person who is willing to cope with his or her conflicts and fears without resorting to professional help.	0	1	2	3
I would want to get psychological help if I were worried or upset for a long period of time.	3	2	1	0
I might want to have psychological counseling in the future.	3	2	1	0
A person with an emotional problem is not likely to solve it alone; he or she is likely to solve it with professional help.	3	2	1	0
Considering the time and expense involved in psychotherapy, it would have doubtful value for a person like me.	0	1	2	3
A person should work out his or her own problems; getting psychological counseling would be a last resort.	0	1	2	3
Personal and emotional troubles, like many things, tend to work out by themselves.	0	1	2	3

College student averages are 1.6 for males and 1.9 for females (Fischer & Farina, 1995).

INVOLUNTARY AND COURT-ORDERED TREATMENT
Although many individuals voluntarily seek mental health care, a substantial number have been required to contact mental health services by the courts or employers. The majority of these cases stem from erratic or disturbing behavior resulting in legal trouble, such as driving while intoxicated or engaging in domestic violence. In the United States, more than 40 states have laws that allow court-ordered outpatient treatments for people with severe disorders (Applebaum, 2005).

Obviously, forcing someone into treatment brings up serious ethical and legal questions. Nonetheless, the evidence shows that a significant number of people benefit from mandated treatment, as indicated by their adherence to treatment and reduced encounters with law enforcement (Hough & O'Brien, 2005; Pollack et al., 2005; Swartz & Swanson, 2004).

Working the Scientific Literacy Model

Technology and Mental Health Treatment

Technology may offer solutions for overcoming some of the major barriers to treatment. Psychologists are developing communications and mobile applications that are designed to alleviate symptoms associated with psychological problems, such as anxiety, without requiring anyone to set foot in their offices.

What do we know about technology and mental health treatment?

Holding therapy sessions via video chat is becoming increasingly common. This method is particularly useful in helping people who have trouble accessing a therapist's office because of geographical distance or limited access to transportation. It may also address some of the self-consciousness some people experience when thinking about disclosing personal experiences face-to-face.

There are many ways technology can deliver treatment, and here we will focus on one: a mobile app game designed to reduce anxiety. People who are chronically anxious tend to direct their attention toward negative stimuli and events and are also hypersensitive to threats, even ones that are only perceived. For example, if given the choice between looking at a smiling face, an angry one, or opting to look away, their attention is biased toward the angry face (Browning, Holmes, & Harmer, 2010). Focusing on an angry face will in turn sustain the anxiety. The good news is that a technique called *attention-bias modification training* helps reduce the tendency to focus on threatening stimuli, but can this training be delivered effectively through mobile technology?

How can science help us learn more about technology and mental health treatment?

A digital game app figures into a rather unique approach to alleviating anxiety associated with an attentional bias toward negative stimuli. Researchers designed a game in which players tracked the movements of animated characters that appeared briefly on a screen, and then "hid" inside of a burrow of a grassy area. The player could earn points by matching the rustling of the grass with the location in which one of two characters presented at each trial hid (Dennis & O'Toole, 2014).

In the study utilizing this game, a group of college students who scored high on an anxiety scale were divided into an attention modification group and a placebo control group. For the attention modification group the game was set so that the rustling grass, and thus the players' attention, was always directed toward the animated character with a positive facial expression, and for the control group the rustling grass was set to occur equally near a character with either a negative or neutral expression. Students sat in a laboratory room and played several rounds of this game for up to 45 minutes. Following the gaming session, all participants were tested for their attentional bias toward neutral or angry human faces, and their self-reported anxiety levels were measured (Figure 14.4). Students who played the version of the mobile app that rewarded attending to the positive animated character for a 45-minute gaming period were less likely to look at angry human faces and reported feeling less anxiety than the students in the control group (Dennis & O'Toole, 2014).

Can we critically evaluate this evidence?

Although experiments show the app is effective in the short term, we do not yet know whether it provides long-term benefits of anxiety reduction. Also, the game focuses on attentional bias to negative stimuli, which is just one aspect of anxiety and therefore it alone would not be a sufficient treatment for helping someone with an anxiety disorder. On the other hand, when packaged as a mobile app, an individual would be able to get an additional dose of the game's treatment whenever she needed it. Finally, aside from the effectiveness of the game, individuals need to be aware of privacy issues when seeking therapy from online sources. Before submitting personal information to an online therapist who may use this type of technology, it would be very important to ensure the security of the technology and that the providers adhere to established ethical guidelines of psychological practice.

Figure 14.4 Treating Anxiety with Digital Technology

After playing a computer game that manipulated attention to positive, negative, or neutral emotional stimuli, both groups completed a task in which their attention to negative or neutral facial expressions was recorded.

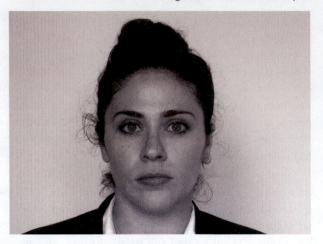 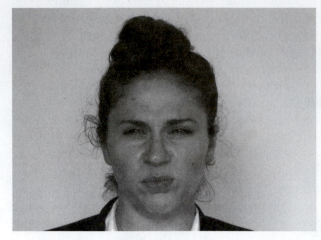

Why is this relevant?

Recall that the game was developed in part to help people overcome barriers to receiving treatment. Problems with cost and accessibility to mental health care cannot, and should not, be solved with an app alone. Major societal, governmental, and corporate efforts are required to make lasting change. That said, digital technology offers creative and accessible ways of helping people manage their mental health.

JOURNAL PROMPT

Technology and Mental Health: What are some pros and cons that you can think of with regard to using digital technology to improve mental health?

Evaluating Treatments

The US Food and Drug Administration (FDA) requires that manufacturers demonstrate the safety and usefulness of many over-the-counter drugs and all drugs that require prescriptions. To provide this evidence, drug makers must pay to have studies conducted by their staff or researchers at major universities, medical centers, and private laboratories. These randomized, double-blind, controlled experiments help determine whether a drug has its intended effects and the side effects that might result. It may be somewhat surprising to learn that there is comparatively little oversight over something as important as psychological therapy. How important is it to know whether a certain psychological intervention will produce results, cause damage, or be a waste of money? This question is one that psychologists have spent decades tackling. In the mid-1990s, the American Psychological Association set up task forces to evaluate different therapy practices; as of 2005, these task forces

had made their findings and recommendations available online (APA, 2009). To answer the question as to whether therapy works, psychologists need to conduct sound, controlled research.

EMPIRICALLY SUPPORTED TREATMENTS **Empirically supported treatments** *(also called evidence-based practices) are treatments that have been tested and evaluated using sound research designs* (Chambless & Ollendick, 2001; De Los Reyes & Kazdin, 2008). The most rigorous way of testing whether a certain therapy works is through an experiment in which volunteers are randomly assigned to a treatment group (e.g., a type of therapy) and to a control group (Figure 14.5). Experiments should be double-blind, meaning that neither the patient nor the individual evaluating the patient is aware of which treatment the patient receives. These procedures are relatively easy to implement in a drug study, but can be challenging to employ when studying psychological therapies. A therapist, of course, knows which type of treatment she administers. Also, every patient and every therapist is unique. Part of the effectiveness of therapy comes from the *therapeutic alliance*—the relationship that emerges in therapy. Therefore, even though a therapist may implement the same steps and procedures in therapy, each session is likely to be different. Due to these and other factors, few studies meet the rigorous criteria required for evidence-based therapy (DeRubeis & Crits-Cristoph, 1998).

Some psychologists believe that modeling the evaluation of psychotherapy after drug testing ignores some of the nuances and complexity that exist in the process of therapy (Westen & Bradley, 2005). Techniques for conducting therapy are developed through psychologists engaging in actual clinical practice, not in controlled laboratory settings as done in drug testing. Also, a type of

Figure 14.5 Testing Whether Therapy Has Empirical Support

Procedures for testing whether a therapy has empirical support, and therefore is a viable option to offer to clients, requires rigorous procedures and scrutiny as diagrammed below. Critical to this process is random assignment of each participant to the treatment or placebo groups, double-blind procedures, and statistical comparisons to determine whether the new proposed therapy is superior to no treatment, and also, if possible, to a standard therapy that already has established empirical support.

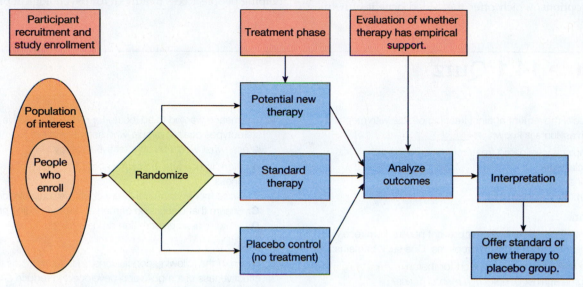

therapy may *appear* no better than a control condition not because it is flawed, but because of the highly variable quality of therapists who use it, which range from counselors with minimal training to experienced clinicians with medical and doctoral degrees. By analogy, if a drug was created in many different laboratories by chemists of widely varying skill, we would be unsurprised if the drug did not appear to work. The drug could be abandoned despite the hidden potential that would remain because a variable was not properly controlled (the training and skill of the chemists). Therefore, in addition to evaluating treatments, practices and procedures for training therapists need to be evaluated and held to high standards (Shoham et al., 2014).

Module 14.1 Summary

14.1a Know . . . the key terminology associated with mental health treatment:

clinical psychologist
community psychology
counseling psychologist
deinstitutionalization
empirically supported treatments
psychiatrist
psychotherapy
residential treatment center

14.1b Understand . . . the major barriers to seeking help for psychological disorders.

Some of the most common barriers include expense, availability, ethnicity, gender, and attitudes toward therapy. For example, males are more likely to view help-seeking as a sign of weakness and, in the United States, African American and Latino individuals are less likely to receive treatment than Caucasian Americans.

14.1c Understand . . . the importance of empirically supported treatments.

Psychotherapies need to be tested for their effectiveness using appropriate and rigorous experimental designs. Empirically supported treatments demonstrate that the technique being evaluated works better than doing nothing at all, and that it works better than existing treatments that are suspected to be less effective.

14.1d Apply . . . your knowledge to understand your own attitudes toward help-seeking.

In this module you learned about several barriers toward seeking treatment, such as avoiding negative stereotypes and stigma against those who seek it. Yet, only about half of the people who could benefit from treatment actually receive it. How do your own attitudes toward seeking treatment relate to these observations? Completing the Attitudes Toward Seeking Psychological Help survey (Table 14.1) might help you better answer this question.

14.1e **Analyze . . . whether technology can deliver useful options for therapy.**

Technological approaches such as online video sessions with a therapist, web-based programs, and mobile apps are becoming widely available. Studies reveal much potential for these options, which offer the added benefit of helping people overcome barriers to receiving treatment (e.g., cost and availability). However, there are limitations to what these approaches offer and they do not actually remove barriers to receiving adequate mental health care. This would require continued progress in governmental and societal support for helping people access treatment for psychological problems.

Module 14.1 Quiz

Know . . .

1. The social movement against keeping people with mental illness in asylums is known as _____.
   A. empirically validated treatments
   B. social work
   C. deinstitutionalization
   D. community psychology

Understand . . .

2. There are several barriers that prevent people from receiving treatment for mental health problems. One such barrier is:
   A. the lack of empirical support for therapy.
   B. stigma against people with mental illness.
   C. the best therapies are only accessible through digital technologies.
   D. most of the population must receive a court-ordered mandate for therapy, which rarely happens.

3. What does it mean to say that a therapy has "empirical support"?
   A. Insurance companies prefer it.
   B. Therapists prefer to use it.
   C. Research studies confirm that it is effective compared to no treatment and possibly compared to other alternatives.
   D. Research studies demonstrate that it can do a better job than drugs.

Apply . . .

4. If someone wanted to advocate for reducing negative stereotypes against people who seek treatment for mental illness, what would be an effective strategy?
   A. Work to educate the public about the nature of mental illness
   B. Raise money so that therapy could be available for all
   C. Ensure that discussion of mental illness remains private
   D. Make generic prescription drugs available to all

Analyze . . .

5. Which of the following conclusions best summarizes the effectiveness of a mobile app developed to reduce anxiety?
   A. It has no benefit whatsoever.
   B. It provides long-term relief from anxiety.
   C. It replaces anxiety with gaming addiction.
   D. Using the app reduces attention directed toward negative stimuli.

Module 14.2   Psychological Therapies

Learning Objectives

14.2a Know . . . the key terminology related to psychological therapies.

14.2b Understand . . . the general approaches to conducting major types of psychotherapy.

14.2c Apply . . . your knowledge to identify major therapeutic techniques.

14.2d Analyze . . . the pros and cons of the major types of psychotherapy.

Almost any bartender or hairstylist will tell you that a portion of their role, whether they like it or not, is to hear about people's problems and concerns. Relatedly, as professors we hear many of our students explain how they have always been "a good listener," and very often they are the person in their peer group that everyone turns to for advice. This is what attracted them to the psychology major. These are admirable qualities and certainly make for great friendships—some of us are never asked for our opinions. But does being a good therapist mean the same thing as being a good bartender, stylist, or friend? Is treatment more than just listening and offering advice? In this module, you will find that the answer to each question is probably yes and no; successful therapy involves good listening and mutual respect, but it is based on much more than that.

Module 14.1 introduced psychotherapy as the processes for resolving personal, emotional, behavioral, and social problems to improve well-being. Psychotherapy is a broad term, as mental health providers practicing psychotherapy can choose from many different approaches to help people. What unifies them under the category of psychotherapy—rather than biological or medical therapy—is the fact that they all address problems through communication between client and therapist. The first style of therapies we will consider, insight therapies, include the earliest forms of psychotherapy.

Insight Therapies

Psychologists have long believed that self-knowledge and understanding can lead to positive changes in behavior. This is certainly the case for **insight therapies**, *which is a general term referring to psychotherapy that involves dialogue between client and therapist for the purposes of gaining awareness and understanding of psychological problems and conflicts.* We begin our look at insight therapies with **psychodynamic therapies**, *forms of insight therapy that emphasize the need to discover and resolve unconscious conflicts.*

PSYCHOANALYSIS: EXPLORING THE UNCONSCIOUS
Psychoanalysis *is an insight therapy developed by Sigmund Freud that became the precursor to modern psychodynamic therapies.* If you read Module 12.3, then you are familiar with some of the core concepts of Freud's approach, such as unconscious motivation. Freud hypothesized that certain fundamental urges, such as sexuality, appetites, and aggression, are constantly influencing how we think and behave, even when we are not aware of them. He proposed that many unconscious motivations are so unacceptable that people develop ways of keeping them out of conscious awareness. Moreover, because people are already repressing sexual and aggressive impulses, any distasteful experiences can be suppressed as well, such as frightening, intimidating, or humiliating moments (Freud, 1896/1954). Needless to say, Freud believed that each individual's unconscious mind could be an ominous place.

As an insight therapy, the primary goal of psychoanalysis is to help the client understand past experiences, relationships, and personal conflicts, and then apply that understanding to improve mental and emotional functioning. Freud and his followers based their practice on some core ideas summarized in Table 14.2.

These core ideas may sound straightforward, except for one crucial point: Accessing the unconscious mind is tricky business. The client cannot tell you much about it because, by definition, unconscious means that he is not aware of it. Freud and his associates came up with several methods and concepts they believed would help them access the unconscious realm so as to cure unhealthy minds. For example, the therapeutic method of **free association** *instructs the client to reveal any thoughts that arise, no matter how odd or meaningless they may seem.* This exercise is meant to allow the individual a chance to avoid self-censorship and offer something revealing about herself. This has likely happened to you in conversation—when you suddenly find yourself talking about a totally different topic than the one that started it, yet you have no idea how you changed subjects. Free association allows the same sort of phenomenon to occur, but with just the client speaking. On the surface, the transitions from topic to topic may not seem important, but if the therapist analyzes the content and the connections of free association, it is thought that important ideas will be revealed.

[D]reams are not a somatic (bodily), but a mental, phenomenon. (Freud, 1920, p. 90)

If Freud is correct, dreams can be a useful source of information about unconscious conflicts. However, the unconscious mind cannot describe past conflicts because it lacks a language to do so. Instead, Freud proposed, emotions take on symbolic qualities, which is why dreams so often feature bizarre imagery and very loose storylines. To make sense of this jumble, a trained psychoanalyst might conduct **dream analysis**, *a method of understanding unconscious thought by interpreting the manifest content (what happens in the dream) to get a sense of the latent content (the unconscious elements that motivated the dream;)* (see Module 5.2, Figure 14.6).

The process of discovering unconscious conflict through psychoanalysis can create considerable discomfort. If you have managed to keep painful memories unconscious, why would you want to bring them back up again? According to Freud, patients of psychoanalysis engage in what he called **resistance**—*a tendency to avoid directly answering crucial questions posed by the therapist.* Patients may get angry at the analyst, or even become cynical about the whole process. Others may edit their own thoughts before speaking, or may try to joke around to change the subject. This leads to an interesting dynamic between patient and psychoanalyst called **transference**—*a psychoanalytic process that involves patients directing the emotional experiences that they are reliving toward the therapist.* A patient who discusses ongoing feelings of anger toward his father may begin directing these feelings toward the analyst during therapy sessions. The analyst uses transference to move the therapy forward by pointing out parallels between the client's anger toward herself and the father, and discussing ways of understanding and coping with the feelings.

Table 14.2 Core Ideas Forming the Basis of Psychoanalysis

Adults' psychological conflicts have their origins in early experiences.
These conflicts affect the thoughts and emotions of the individual, and their source often remains outside of conscious awareness.
The unconscious conflicts and their effects are called *neuroses* (anxieties).
By accessing the unconscious mind, the analyst and patient can gain a better understanding of the early conflicts that lead to neuroses.
Once the conflicts are brought to the surface, the analyst and the patient can work through them together.

Figure 14.6 Dream Analysis

We can illustrate what Freud hoped to discover with one particular dream analysis he wrote about: A patient dreamed he was riding his bicycle down a street when suddenly a dog ran him down and bit his ankle as he attempted to pedal away. Meanwhile, two elderly ladies sat by and laughed at the incident. This is the manifest content, but what might the dream mean—what is the latent content? Freud pointed out that in his waking life the patient had repeatedly seen a woman walking a dog and, although he was very attracted to her, he felt great anxiety about approaching her. The man had consciously devised a plan to use the dog as an excuse to strike up a conversation with the woman. Unfortunately, the anxiety caused by fear of rejection manifested itself in an unpleasant dream about being attacked by a dog, accompanied by the humiliation of being laughed at (Freud, 1920, pp. 165–166).

MODERN PSYCHODYNAMIC THERAPIES Today, Freudian-based psychoanalysis is a highly specialized approach requiring extensive training and is practiced by a relatively small proportion of therapists. Nevertheless, Freud's ideas have remained influential and some newer therapies have evolved from traditional psychoanalysis. One example is **object relations therapy**, *a variation of psychodynamic therapy that focuses on how early childhood experiences and emotional attachments influence later psychological functioning*. In contrast to psychoanalysis, object relations therapy does not center on repressed sexual and aggressive conflicts. Instead, the focus is on objects, which include real

or imagined people in a child's life, events that occurred with these people, as well as the child's understanding of himself. The early interactions between the child and close relations, such as parents, results in the development of a mental model for the child; as a consequence, he will form and maintain relationships as an adult based on his representations of childhood relationships. Thus, if a child has positive relationships with his mother but negative ones with his father, this will then serve as a model for how females and males who resemble his mother and father will behave during adulthood. The object relations therapist's job is to help the client understand the underlying patterns in relationships, which often involve issues of trust, fear of abandonment, or dependence on others. Once therapy produces insight, then the client and the therapist can work through any problems they may have identified.

Both object relations therapy and psychoanalysis share the goal of helping individuals gain insight into how and why their current functioning was affected by early events. In addition to these approaches, other variations on the process of therapy have been developed.

HUMANISTIC THERAPY One particularly significant alternative to psychoanalysis comes from humanistic psychology. In the 1950s, humanistic psychologists broke from psychoanalytic approaches, creating a new discipline based on at least five fundamental differences (listed in Table 14.3). Perhaps the biggest difference is the shifted focus from long-lasting, unconscious conflicts to the individual's strengths and potential for growth. This shift was thought to empower individuals with the ability to overcome their problems. Also, rather than interpreting the hidden meanings of dreams and free associations, the humanistic therapist's role is to listen and understand.

American psychologist Carl Rogers (1902–1987) developed a version of humanistic therapy called **person/client-centered therapy**, *which focuses on developing each individual's ability to solve problems and reach her full potential with the encouragement of the therapist*. As a humanist, Rogers believed that all individuals could reach their full potential. However, people experience psychological

---

Table 14.3 Contrasting Psychoanalytic and Humanistic Views of Major Psychological Issues and Debates

Issue	Psychoanalysis	Humanistic Therapy
Conscious versus unconscious	Focuses on unconscious drives	Focuses on conscious experience
Determinism versus free will	Behavior is determined by repressed sexual and aggressive instincts	Behavior is chosen freely
Weaknesses versus strengths	Everyone has neuroses	Everyone has strengths
Responsibility for change	The analyst interprets and explains to the patient what is wrong	The therapist asks the client what is wrong and attempts to help clarify issues
Mechanism of change	Insight into unconscious conflicts allows problems to be worked through	Unconditional positive regard allows a person to develop and heal

problems when others impose *conditions of worth*, meaning that they appear to judge or lose affection for a person who does not live up to expectations. Such an individual might be a father who is never satisfied with his child's report card or a wife who gets angry at her spouse over failing to keep his promises. If loved ones give the impression that they no longer respect the person or that they love the person less because of the individual's actions, then they have imposed conditions of worth.

Conditions of worth can produce long-term consequences to psychological health because the individual is then likely to change his behavior in an attempt to regain affection. If this happens frequently, then the individual is no longer living his own life, but merely living out the expectations of others. That, to Carl Rogers, is a key aspect of any psychological dysfunction.

The critical aspect of client-centered therapy lies within the dialogue that unfolds between therapist and client. The therapist must show *unconditional positive regard* through genuine, empathetic, and nonjudgmental attention. If the therapist can remove all conditions of worth, clients may begin to express themselves without fear and begin to develop inner strength. Finally, with self-confidence and strength, clients can accept disagreement with others and focus on living their lives to the fullest. Hear an overview of how humanistic therapy works in the video Humanistic Therapy.

Watch HUMANISTIC THERAPY

EVALUATING INSIGHT THERAPIES As discussed in Module 14.1, therapies should be used only if there is empirical support that they actually work. Psychodynamic therapies meet some of the rigorous criteria for empirically supported therapies, though surprisingly few studies in this area have been conducted with proper research design and control conditions. Ultimately, the effectiveness of insight therapies depends on the condition being treated. Studies that have used rigorous research designs have shown that psychodynamic therapy has low to moderate positive outcomes for treating depression, anxiety,

dependence on opiate drugs (e.g., heroin), personality disorders, and general psychological complaints that do not have a formal diagnostic category (Abbass et al., 2014; Gibbons et al., 2008). Insight therapies can help people gain understanding and awareness of the nature of their psychological problems, but as you will soon read, many people with mild to severe psychological problems improve without in-depth exploration of past issues and internal conflicts.

Behavioral, Cognitive, and Group Therapies

Behavioral therapies *address problematic behaviors and responses, and the environmental factors that trigger them, as directly as possible.* A core belief underlying the behavioral approach to therapy is that maladaptive patterns of behavior result from conditioning and learning, and therefore can be modified by applying principles of learning. For example, part of addiction treatment may involve breaking the cycle of reinforcement associated with drug taking. Helping the individual find reinforcement in healthy activities, and also reducing the reward value of drugs, are important steps to treatment. View the video Behavior Therapy to hear a synopsis of how this approach works.

Watch BEHAVIOR THERAPY

EXPOSURE AND SYSTEMATIC DESENSITIZATION Public speaking strikes fear in many, and so makes for a good place to think about how behavioral therapy can be applied. Most individuals experience at least some anxiety about public speaking, but for some people this anxiety increases to the point that merely thinking about delivering a speech can induce intense stress, worry, and even panic attacks. External cues, such as the professor who assigns a speech, fellow students, the ticking clock, and the dreaded podium at the front of the class, may all elicit anxiety. In addition, internal stimuli such a racing heart, sweaty palms, and shakiness can make anxiety spin out of control—perhaps to the point of triggering a full-blown panic attack.

We can use classical conditioning, described in Module 6.1, to help us understand how anxiety is acquired as well as how it can be reduced. The anxiety-provoking internal and external stimuli become *conditioned stimuli* (see Figure 14.7). The more intense these stimuli, the more likely it is that a panic attack will occur. Using behavioral therapy, the psychologist might help the individual focus on the conditioned stimuli that precede the panic attacks, and work to control responses to them prior to an upcoming public speaking engagement. Often, a client in treatment with a behavioral therapist undergoes **exposure therapy**—*a set of procedures in which exposure to the feared situation is done repeatedly and gradually under controlled conditions* (Foa, Gillihan, & Bryant, 2013). Examples include guidance by the therapist to use mental imagery, as well as exposure to actual pictures, models, or recordings of the feared stimulus. When conducted appropriately, exposure therapy mimics the process of extinction in classical conditioning, in which the feared event (the conditioned stimulus) is no longer paired with the aversive event (the unconditioned stimulus). Such extinction treatments can result in a loss of persistent and intrusive fear responses (Norrholm et al., 2008).

Exposure treatments can create stress for the client, even if the therapist begins with a very low-level cue. For this reason, therapists using exposure therapy can incorporate relaxation techniques into their treatment. **Systematic desensitization** *is a classic technique in which gradual exposure to a feared stimulus or situation is blended with relaxation training* (Wolpe, 1990). The gradual exposure allows for an individual to practice relaxing under conditions that elicit mild anxiety, and then slowly progress to greater levels of anxiety-provoking stimuli. If the individual can eventually relax during moderately high levels of exposure to the feared stimulus or situation, then the anxiety response can be extinguished. Behavioral therapists and their clients

Figure 14.7 Classical Conditioning and Systematic Desensitization

Classical conditioning can contribute to fears that we acquire, such as driving after having a car accident. Systematic desensitization is designed to reduce or eliminate these conditioned responses.

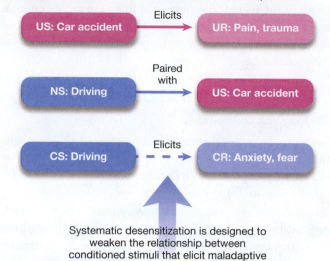

Systematic desensitization is designed to weaken the relationship between conditioned stimuli that elicit maladaptive responses such as extensive fear or anxiety.

follow three main steps in conducting systematic desensitization, which are outlined in Table 14.4 in an example applied to public speaking.

Working the Scientific Literacy Model

Virtual Reality Therapies

A challenge to applying exposure therapy is that people intentionally avoid contact with feared stimuli and situations—so even taking the first step toward a therapist's office can be challenging. This is one reason why people

Table 14.4 Applying Steps of Systematic Desensitization to Fear of Public Speaking

1. *Build an anxiety hierarchy.* This involves the therapist assisting the client in creating a list of stimuli that arouse fear responses, starting with the stimulus or situation that evokes the least amount of anxiety and ending with the stimulus that elicits the most anxiety.

   Think about and visualize:
   1. Doing library research for a presentation
   2. Preparing slides and note cards
   3. Practicing the presentation alone
   4. Practicing the presentation with a small group of friends
   5. Leaving for campus on the day of the presentation
   6. Class starting
   7. Being called up to give the presentation
   8. Setting up and looking out at the audience
   9. Beginning to speak
   10. Delivering the presentation

2. *Relaxation training.* During this phase, the client learns to respond to relaxation suggestions from the therapist as they work through the hierarchy. This is typically done using mental imagery while the client is visiting the therapist's office.

3. *Work through the hierarchy.* Steps 1 and 2 are combined here as the therapist works through the hierarchy with the client while engaging in relaxation techniques.

who may have posttraumatic stress disorder (PTSD) never seek treatment, even though exposure therapies are particularly effective for treating it (Kessler, 2000; Eftekhari et al., 2013). One approach to conducting exposure therapy is to have the client use mental imagery—simply imagining being in the feared situation—but this may not be enough to help them in the *actual* anxiety-provoking situation in real life. Virtual reality technology can be used to address these challenges.

What do we know about virtual reality exposure?

Recently, behavioral therapists have tested whether virtual technologies can help people overcome PTSD. **Virtual reality exposure (VRE)** *is a treatment that uses graphical displays and audio to simulate an actual environment, typically involving one that includes multiple emotional triggers such as a war zone.* The reality it creates helps address two problems associated with traditional systematic desensitization methods described previously. First, people who use mental imagery alone can easily become avoidant and fail to comply with the therapist's suggestions. Second, and most importantly, VRE exposure can provide a realistic and user-controlled approximation to the feared situation.

How can scientists study virtual reality exposure?

Psychologists at Emory University in Atlanta have been experimenting with a simulator called Virtual Iraq, which was developed to deliver two possible scenarios—being in a Middle Eastern city or driving a Humvee through a desert road in simulated war conditions (Figure 14.8). The weather, time of day, background noise, civilians, aerial craft, and ground vehicles can be programmed by the therapist to change as desired during the exposure sessions. There is also the option to provide simulated gunfire and bomb explosions. Smell cues are available using an air compressor that pumps in odors of burning rubber, garbage, diesel fuel, and gunpowder (Cukor et al., 2009). Using this technology, psychologists have conducted multiple VRE sessions with combat veterans. The therapist carefully controls the amount of exposure that the client receives. By repeated, gradual, and controlled exposure to the fear-eliciting stimuli the client's fear is (if the therapy works) extinguished, much like learned responses can be extinguished through classical conditioning (see Module 6.1). In addition to exposure treatments, the therapist provides other means of therapy and support to help the client reprocess the traumatic event(s).

In one set of trials, 20 active-duty soldiers who were diagnosed with PTSD following combat activity underwent

Figure 14.8 Virtual Reality Exposure Therapy

Combat veterans diagnosed with PTSD have participated in virtual reality therapies involving simulated exposure to traumatic events. Therapists work with clients to help them process and cope with their fears.

VRE therapy. Their PTSD symptoms were measured before and after therapists guided them through VRE treatment in the Virtual Iraq simulator. At the conclusion of their therapy, the soldiers' PTSD symptoms declined by 50%, with 16 of the soldiers no longer meeting the criteria for the disorder (Rizzo et al., 2010). The soldiers reported fewer disturbing thoughts about stressful events that occurred during military service; fewer disturbing dreams; reduced physical reactions such as heart pounding, sweating, and trouble breathing; and less avoidance of activities that trigger memories of military service. VRE using the Virtual Iraq simulator appeared to work, and may be as effective as traditional exposure therapy (Gonçalves et al., 2013).

Can we critically evaluate this evidence?

From an experimental standpoint, this study should have used a control group that received no treatment, or a comparison group that received some other treatment method, such as insight therapy. Without a control group, we are left to wonder how other variables might have influenced the improvement in PTSD symptoms, such as the mere passage of time or the simple fact that people were expressing interest and concern for the veterans. Of course, the researchers know this as well, so we should expect further studies to include improved experimental methods. Until those results become available, we can remain cautiously optimistic.

Why is this relevant?

Psychologists are now applying VRE to a broad range of situations, including common fears such as air travel and heights. A major advantage is that VRE also allows clients and therapists to have close control over the systematic exposure to the feared situation, and it allows the therapist to tailor the situation to the client's needs (Hodges et al., 2001). A final important point to make is that it is essential that only highly qualified and experienced therapists conduct exposure therapy with clients, as symptoms could potentially worsen as exposure can potentially increase, rather than extinguish, stress and anxiety.

JOURNAL PROMPT

Exposure Therapy: Exposing people to situations that elicit fear might seem like a risky proposition. Why do you think exposure therapies tend to be quite effective when implemented correctly?

COGNITIVE-BEHAVIORAL THERAPIES Behavioral therapies are very effective ways of changing or eliminating maladaptive behaviors, but they do not directly address problematic thoughts. Clinical psychologists also emphasize

the role that cognitive processes play in psychological disorders such as depression and substance abuse, and work to improve mental health by disrupting and reversing negative thought patterns (Onken, 2015). This perspective can be traced back to Albert Ellis (1962) and Aaron Beck (1963), who observed that the overwhelmingly negative thought patterns of people with depression could be reduced by replacing negative thinking with more realistic and rational thought patterns. Over time, they formalized procedures for conducting what is now called cognitive-behavioral therapy.

Cognitive-behavioral therapy *is a form of therapy that consists of procedures such as exposure, cognitive restructuring, and stress inoculation training.* Exposure—the behavioral technique described earlier in this module—is an important component to the process. This is particularly true in situations where specific events or contexts create problems, such as surviving a traumatic experience. Exposure allows the client and the therapist to process and work through the feelings associated with the event, whereas avoidance leaves the stressor in place, perhaps allowing the problem to worsen.

Next, *cognitive restructuring* occurs as the client's beliefs and interpretations about events are modified such that they can be viewed with greater objectivity and clarity. For example, someone who develops depression after losing her job might believe the layoff was deserved. She can work with the therapist to clarify whether this is a rational explanation for the situation. From these discussions, the therapist and client may put a restructuring plan in place. When thoughts of unnecessary self-blame occur, the client might stop and say to herself, "It was actually poor management; I could not have stopped it." Alternatively, if she is partially responsible, she must learn to think about how she can make amends, prevent future mistakes, and not beat herself up over past failures. In either case, the restructuring involves moving from thoughts like "I am a bad person"; "I deserve this"; "Nobody can help me," to a more productive and rational set of thoughts. Experimental studies affirm the value of cognitive restructuring. By exercising activity of the frontal lobes and the executive control processes they control, depressed people spend less time thinking about negative emotional events (Cohen, Mor, & Henik, 2015).

Finally, people who experience stress and anxiety may benefit from relaxation techniques, as they allow the client to regain emotional control and perspective on the negative experiences. This phase of treatment, sometimes called *stress inoculation training*, helps the client put traumatic memories into perspective in a way that promotes the individual's well-being.

One thing you may not have noticed about cognitive-behavioral therapy: These techniques all require the client—not just the therapist—to do serious work. The therapist can help by teaching a client ways to identify problematic thoughts and some techniques for restructuring the problem. Ultimately, however, the client must manage all the work once he leaves the psychologist's office. Thus, cognitive-behavioral therapy may actually involve homework, reading, and studying. Review the basics of cognitive-behavioral therapy in the video Cognitive-Behavioral Therapy (CBT).

Watch COGNITIVE-BEHAVIORAL THERAPY (CBT)

GROUP AND FAMILY THERAPIES   In some situations, clients may benefit greatly by participating in *group therapy* sessions. One advantage of group therapy is that it is typically more affordable than individual sessions. Also, groups may be organized in many different ways to suit different purposes. Members may share a particular problem, such as interpersonal conflicts, substance use, or adjustment problems.

Psychologists who conduct *family therapy* help people cope with numerous types of problems, such as dynamics involving each individual family member or for assistance in dealing with one particular individual, such as an abusive parent or a troubled adolescent. Clearly, family therapy is different from individual psychotherapy. The problems that an individual brings into psychotherapy sessions are typically not isolated in a social sense. Problems with anger, depression, or anxiety often stem from a broader social context—in particular, that of the family. Family therapists take a **systems approach**, *an orientation toward family therapy that involves identifying and understanding what each individual family member contributes to the entire family dynamic.*

As an example, think of a family with a male child being treated for schizophrenia. He may have spent many months in individual psychotherapy sessions. How family members react to him when he experiences acute episodes of schizophrenia alters his behavior, for better or for worse. Also, how he is treated after he has received treatment and the schizophrenia is in remission can have a significant impact on his well-being. Remission rates among people with schizophrenia who are given emotional support at home are quite high (Hooley, 2007). In this situation, then, the family therapist's job is to help the entire family make adjustments to the disorder, whether the symptoms are present or are in remission.

As you can see, there are many different forms of therapy. Practice applying your knowledge of them by completing the activity in Table 14.5.

EVALUATING COGNITIVE, BEHAVIORAL, AND GROUP THERAPIES   Behavioral therapies have been shown to be particularly effective at treating symptoms associated with anxiety disorders, such as obsessive–compulsive disorder and specific phobias (Chambless & Ollendick, 2001). They have also proved useful for increasing or decreasing specific problematic behaviors.

Cognitive-behavioral therapy has been particularly effective in treating depression, which is reassuring since this method of therapy was specifically developed to treat it (Hollon et al., 2002). A randomized controlled study of cognitive-behavioral therapy and interpersonal therapy (a specialized type of insight therapy) showed that both approaches were equally effective at reducing depressive symptoms (Lemmens et al., 2015). Thus, therapists trained to use both styles can consult with clients to determine their preference. Cognitive-behavioral therapies are also effective in treating anxiety, obesity, and eating disorders. A specific strength of cognitive-behavioral therapy is that it focuses on definable and concrete relationships between events and the emotions and reactions experienced by clients. This provides a solid basis from which to work in

---

Table 14.5 Applying Therapy Styles

Imagine you are helping someone with a phobia find a therapist for treatment, and you speak with three professionals about the approach they would take. Match their response with the corresponding school of thought. Note: Not all the schools of therapy will be used.

1. I would ask the individual to describe his train of thought when he encounters the feared object. Then I would ask him to explain why it is irrational to think that way, and we would try to replace his irrational thoughts with more reasonable, less anxiety-provoking beliefs.	a. Humanistic therapy b. Cognitive-behavioral therapy c. Psychodynamic therapy d. Family therapy e. Behavioral therapy
2. I would ask the patient to think about his earliest childhood experiences with the object, and then to speak freely about those memories at length. We would try to discover the significance of that object in his early development.	
3. We would take an active approach. One important step is to teach the client how to be calm and relaxed while gradually introducing the feared stimulus.	

Answers: 1. Cognitive-behavioral therapy, 2. Psychodynamic therapy, 3. Behavioral therapy

therapy sessions. Also, cognitive-behavioral therapy yields quicker results than does traditional psychoanalysis.

Nevertheless, cognitive and behavioral therapies alone may not alter the numerous problem behaviors associated with a major disorder. For example, behavioral therapy may be used to help individuals with schizophrenia cope with auditory hallucinations, but it does not eliminate them (Thomas et al., 2010).

CLIENT AND THERAPIST FACTORS As you have read, different approaches to therapy have different success rates, depending on the nature of the problem (see Table 14.6 for a summary). But some professionals have questioned how the very different types of therapy described in this chapter can all be effective. Perhaps it is not the specific style

of therapy that works, but factors inherent to therapists and clients. The *common factors* approach to research has produced evidence that all effective psychotherapies share common factors such as trust, bonding, and collaboration between therapist and client (Laska et al., 2014). These are critical to achieving positive outcomes in therapy regardless of the therapist's theoretical approach. Why is this? One reason is that if the client does not trust the therapist, or simply does not like her, then the client is unlikely to return for a second session. In fact, most attempts to begin psychotherapy end after the first session (Gibbons et al., 2011). Similarly, when the client and therapist agree on goals and a plan for the therapy, and a personal bond forms in the treatment process, the outcome is more likely to be positive (Hoffart et al., 2013).

Table 14.6 Pros and Cons of the Major Types of Therapies

	Pros	Cons
Insight therapies	• Can provide deep understanding of the self	• Long term and often very expensive • Can have limited application to people with serious disorders
Behavioral and cognitive therapies	• Relatively time- and cost-efficient • Addresses immediate thoughts and behavioral problems • Addresses both mild and severe problems	• Does not necessarily offer deeper understanding of psychological problems
Group/family therapies	• Allows individuals to empathize and relate to others with similar problems • Gives family members insight into how each individual contributes to both positive and negative aspects of family life	• Does not fully address individual issues (although group and family therapies are often used in combination with individualized therapy)

Module 14.2 Summary

14.2a   Know . . . the key terminology related to psychological therapies:

behavioral therapy
cognitive-behavioral therapy
dream analysis
exposure therapy
free association
insight therapy
object relations therapy
person/client-centered therapy
psychoanalysis
psychodynamic therapy
resistance
systematic desensitization
systems approach
transference
virtual reality exposure (VRE)

14.2b   Understand . . . the general approaches to conducting major types of psychotherapy.

Each therapy seems to be different. Psychoanalysis, for example, works by uncovering hidden conflicts, whereas humanistic therapy focuses on removing barriers to a person's growth and sense of worth. Behavioral and cognitive therapies focus on how physical and social environments affect behaviors and thought patterns, and seek to alter one or both to make positive changes. Therapies also take place with groups and families.

14.2c   Apply . . . your knowledge to identify major therapeutic techniques.

There are numerous approaches reviewed in this module. The nature of the psychological problem that is being treated, as well as the theoretical orientation of the psychologist offering the therapy, accounts for the diversity of treatment options. Completing the Applying Therapy Styles activity will help you distinguish some different ways that therapy is conducted (Table 14.5).

14.2d Analyze . . . the pros and cons of the major types of psychotherapy.

Each therapy has its strengths and limitations, and which therapy is ideal will depend on factors such as the nature of the problem and preferences and characteristics of the client. A rich and extensive dialogue with a therapist is

characteristic of the insight therapies reviewed in this module, but this can also mean that they will involve time commitment and possible expense that exceeds that of other approaches. Behavioral and cognitive therapies tend to focus on specific problems but might not result in deeper insight into the nature of the problem, which could be viewed as a limitation to this approach. Group and family therapies can help people confront interpersonal problems and gain understanding about both the self and others who share similar concerns. However, without also doing individual therapy, a client in family or group therapy may not be able to fully address his or her own needs.

Module 14.2 Quiz

Know . . .

1. _____ consists of key procedures including exposure, cognitive restructuring, and stress inoculation training.
   A. Cognitive-behavioral therapy
   B. Family therapy
   C. Virtual reality exposure therapy
   D. Exposure therapy

Understand . . .

2. _____ refers to a phenomenon of psychoanalysis in which the client begins directing emotional responses toward the therapist.
   A. Resistance
   B. Befriending
   C. Objectifying
   D. Transference

3. A major strength of cognitive-behavioral therapy is that:
   A. concrete and definable problems are identified and directly addressed.
   B. it prevents resistance from occurring.
   C. it is not affected by the quality of the client–therapist relationship.
   D. it develops transference between client and therapist.

Apply . . .

4. Neil is facing difficulties with anger and depression, and his parents are having trouble managing his behaviors and responding appropriately. To address all of these concerns, the most beneficial treatment in this situation would be _____.
   A. cognitive-behavioral therapy
   B. family therapy
   C. virtual reality exposure therapy
   D. exposure therapy

Analyze . . .

5. What has research concluded in regard to the effectiveness of insight therapies?
   A. Insight therapies are always very effective.
   B. Insight therapies are never effective.
   C. Insight therapies do not help people gain awareness of the nature of their psychological problems, so they tend to not be effective.
   D. The effectiveness of insight therapies depends on the conditions that are being treated.

Module 14.3   Biomedical Therapies

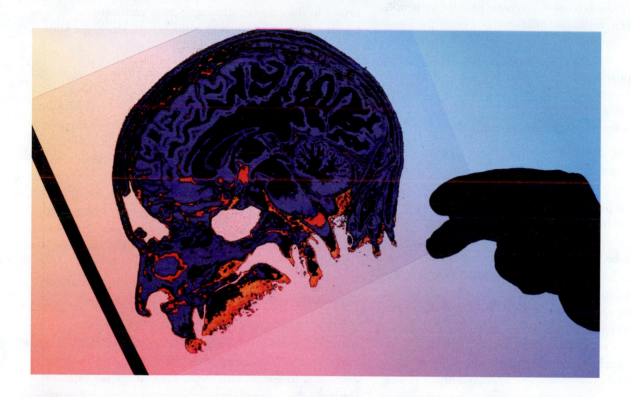

 ## Learning Objectives

14.3a Know . . . the key terminology associated with biological treatments.

14.3b Understand . . . how the drugs described in this module affect brain functioning.

14.3c Understand . . . how various medical therapies that do not involve drugs work.

14.3d Apply . . . your knowledge of drug therapies to different psychological conditions.

14.3e Analyze . . . whether alternative biologically based treatments to prescription drugs work.

Eating, talking on the phone, and driving are normal activities for the awake. However, doing them while asleep ranges from harmless to fatal. Some people who take the sleep drug Ambien (zolpidem) have found themselves doing these and other bizarre activities in their sleep. Tragically, for the first 20 years that Ambien was available, a disproportionately high number of women experienced such side effects, and many overdosed on the drug even though they took the prescribed amount. The Food and Drug Administration now requires doctors to reduce previously standard Ambien dosages for women by 50%. Why these problems with Ambien happened in the first place is something you might be wondering about. It may be surprising, if not upsetting, to know that drug testing procedures, beginning in the early phases of testing on animals through initial trials on people, have traditionally only been conducted on males. We will explore this issue further in this module. Drugs that affect brain functioning, such as sleep medications and antidepressants, have become commonplace. Knowledge of how they work, their limitations, and other concerns is critical information for a scientifically informed public.

Drug Treatments

Psychotropic drugs *are medications designed to alter psychological functioning.* The original drug treatments for psychological problems were initiated in institutional and clinical settings, primarily targeting very severe cases. Since then, drug treatments have become mainstream practice for people experiencing even relatively mild psychological problems and symptoms. The result is that psychotropic drugs, such as those used to treat depression, are among the most prescribed forms of medicine in the United States (Olfson & Marcus, 2009). As with all medication, however, psychotropic drugs can have side effects that should be discussed in consultation with a professional healthcare provider.

ANTIPSYCHOTIC DRUGS   Antipsychotic drugs *are used to treat disorders such as schizophrenia, and are sometimes prescribed to people with severe mood disorders.*

As discussed in Module 13.4, symptoms of schizophrenia are related to increased activity of dopamine, possibly because of the presence of an overabundance of dopamine receptors in the brain. The first antipsychotic medications (e.g., *Thorazine, Halodol*) were designed to block dopamine receptors. These drugs are not without side effects, however: Dopamine is also associated with movement, so blocking its transmission can result in **tardive dyskinesia**, *a neurological condition marked by involuntary movements and facial tics.*

The newer generation of medications is referred to as *atypical antipsychotics* or second-generation antipsychotics. The various atypical antipsychotics on the market vary in their exact effects, but generally speaking they primarily seem to reduce dopamine and serotonin activity. Atypical antipsychotics work for almost half of the individuals who take them, reducing the severity of symptoms but not necessarily eliminating them altogether (Leucht et al., 2009). Unfortunately, studies show that their effects weaken over time, such that symptoms can return.

Second-generation antipsychotics have the advantage of carrying a low risk for tardive dyskinesia. Nevertheless, they are not without risk. For example, the atypical antipsychotic drug *Zyprexa* was hailed as a major breakthrough for individuals with schizophrenia, but this drug, like many of this type, causes drastic weight gain and thus has been linked to the onset of diabetes. Other medications such as Clozapine, the first atypical antipsychotic drug, are known to compromise the body's white blood cells.

ANTIANXIETY DRUGS   Antianxiety drugs *are prescribed to alleviate nervousness and tension, and to prevent and reduce panic attacks.* Widely prescribed examples include *Xanax* (alprazolam), *Valium* (diazepam), and *Ativan* (lorazepam). These drugs affect the activity of gamma-aminobutyric acid (GABA), an inhibitory neurotransmitter that reduces neural activity (see Module 3.2). They appear to temporarily alter the structure of GABA receptors, allowing more GABA molecules to inhibit the firing of nerve cells. The effects of antianxiety drugs such as *Xanax* are relatively short-lived. They take effect within minutes of ingestion and may last for only a few hours. Also, perhaps because many of the symptoms between anxiety and depression overlap, antidepressant drugs may be prescribed to treat anxiety.

ANTIDEPRESSANTS AND MOOD STABILIZERS   As the name suggests, **antidepressant drugs** (or antidepressants) *are prescribed to reduce negative mood and other symptoms of depression.* In general, antidepressant drugs target areas of the brain that, when functioning normally, are rich in *monoamine neurotransmitters*—serotonin, norepinephrine, and dopamine. With multiple neurotransmitters involved, antidepressants come in several varieties, each with a unique way of altering brain chemistry (Figure 14.9). Two early versions of antidepressant drugs include *monoamine oxidase inhibitors (MAOIs)* and *tricyclic antidepressants.* Monoamine oxidase inhibitors (MAOIs) block the activity of an enzyme

Figure 14.9 Antidepressant Effects at the Synapse

The major antidepressant drugs have different ways of increasing the transmission of neurotransmitters such as serotonin, dopamine, and norepinephrine at the synapses.

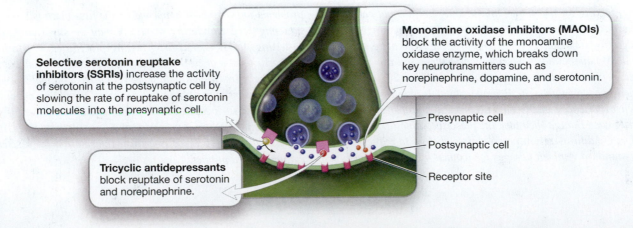

called monoamine oxidase, which breaks down serotonin, dopamine, and norepinephrine at the synaptic clefts of nerve cells. If monoamine oxidase activity is inhibited, fewer dopamine, serotonin, and norepinephrine neurotransmitters are metabolized, leaving more of them available at the synapses. *Tricyclic antidepressants* block the reuptake of serotonin and norepinephrine (Figure 14.9).

Newer generation antidepressant drugs have been developed that may work better and have fewer side effects than MAOI and tricyclic antidepressants. As the name implies, *selective serotonin reuptake inhibitors (SSRIs)* block the reuptake of the neurotransmitter serotonin (Figure 14.9). You likely recognize the name *Prozac* (fluoxetine), which is an SSRI that appeared on the market in 1987 and since has been among the most commonly used. Other SSRIs include *Zoloft* (sertraline) and *Paxil* (paroxetine). Drugs similar to SSRIs, called selective serotonin-norepinephrine reuptake inhibitors (SNRIs), have also been developed to inhibit the reuptake of both serotonin and norepinephrine.

It is important to note that inhibiting neurotransmitter reuptake is a *hypothesis* about how SSRIs work. SSRIs may do more than just block the reuptake of serotonin. They are also linked to increased *neurogenesis*—the growth of new neurons—in the hippocampus. Impaired functioning of the hippocampus is one neurological symptom of depression. Researchers have hypothesized that once neurogenesis kicks in—a process that may take weeks— cognition and emotional functioning improve (Jacobs, 2004; Tanti & Belzung, 2013). This may help explain why any benefits of taking antidepressants are not evident until a few weeks after beginning them.

Mood stabilizers *prevent or reduce the manic phases of bipolar disorder. Lithium* was one of the first mood stabilizers to be prescribed regularly in psychiatry. From the 1950s to the 1980s, it was the standard drug treatment for depression and bipolar disorder. Lithium, a salt compound, can be quite effective, but it can also be toxic to the kidneys and endocrine system. Today, doctors generally prefer to prescribe alternative drugs because they seem to be more effective and safer than lithium (Thase & Denko, 2008). For example, people with bipolar disorder now take anticonvulsant medications such as valproate (marketed under the brand name *Depakote*), and antipsychotic medications may also be prescribed for bipolar disorder.

Work the Scientific Literacy Model

Ketamine: A Different Kind of Antidepressant

The major available antidepressant drugs increase the activity of the monoamine neurotransmitters serotonin, dopamine, and norepinephrine. For decades, different variations of these drugs have been tested and developed, but what about other neurotransmitter systems that we discussed in Module 3.2? Chemists and pharmacologists have been turning their attention to glutamate, which is a primary excitatory neurotransmitter, and the drug *ketamine*, which affects the transmission of glutamate (see also Module 5.3).

What do we know about ketamine?

Ketamine is primarily used as a general anesthetic in human and veterinary medical procedures, but has shown promise for treating conditions such as chronic pain, and, increasingly, some mental disorders. Ketamine affects the transmission of glutamate within a highly complex molecular circuit (Sleigh et al., 2014). Although at high doses, ketamine blocks glutamate, and therefore has an anesthetic effect, at lower doses it actually heightens glutamate activity. A carefully controlled increase in glutamate activity can be very helpful for depression: It supports the formation of new synapses within the prefrontal cortex, making up for the abnormally sparse synapses in this region of the depressed brain (Duman et al., 2012).

How can scientists study ketamine effects on depression?

By now you likely appreciate that the ideal test of whether a drug works is to conduct an experiment that includes double-blind procedures, a placebo control group, and random assignment to treatment groups. Several studies on ketamine that satisfy these criteria have been conducted on patients who had not responded well to traditional antidepressant drugs. In one study, 72 people completed a standardized self-report measure of depression and then were randomly assigned to receive either intravenous ketamine or a placebo. Depressive symptoms in the patients who received ketamine were significantly lower than those receiving a placebo 24-hours after drug administration (Murrough et al., 2013).

Can we critically evaluate this evidence?

Although 24-hours of relief from depression is a step in the right direction, it is not enough for patients who are debilitated by depression for weeks and months at a time. Additional studies using ketamine have shown that repeated administration can prolong its effects, though more work will be needed before ketamine could become a standard treatment for depression (DeWilde et al., 2015). While that research is being carried out, there are a few other factors preventing it from being widely

Table 14.7 Categorizing Psychotropic Drugs

Identify the most likely drug to be prescribed for each of the conditions listed.

Drug	Condition
1. Selective serotonin reuptake inhibitor	a) Anxiety
2. Antipsychotics (e.g., Clozapine)	b) Bipolar disorder
3. Lithium	c) Depression
4. Xanax	d) Schizophrenia

Answers: 1=c, 2=d, 3=b, 4=a

distributed. First, ketamine is only available through intravenous injection, which means it is more difficult to routinely and quickly administer in comparison to a pill. (However, an intranasal inhalant version does show promise.) In addition, it is a highly potent and potentially lethal substance that could easily lead to accidental overdose or even be used in suicide attempts. Therefore, in its current form, it should only be administered by medical professionals.

Why is this relevant?

For decades, the drug industry has focused on developing antidepressant drugs that affect monoamine neurotransmitters. Results of their effectiveness have been mixed, as we will soon explore further. Depression is a complex disorder that likely affects many chemical processes of the brain, so exploring glutamate transmission between nerve cells may help uncover new options for patients. Also, the tragedy of suicide is all too common for severely depressed people, so having fast-acting options like ketamine to use in conjunction with intensive therapy can help save lives.

Practice matching drug categories to psychological conditions they are typically prescribed for in Table. 14.7.

EVALUATING DRUG THERAPIES It may be tempting to think that since drugs target the chemical bases of psychological disorders, they should be more effective than psychotherapy. This general conclusion is not warranted, although in some cases drugs offer quicker and more effective effects on symptoms than do psychotherapies. Research generally shows that drugs are more effective when combined with other types of therapy. For example, psychotherapy alone may not be sufficient for treating severe disorders such as schizophrenia. Therapists have found that people with schizophrenia tend to have difficulty imagining themselves in past and future situations—abilities that would otherwise enable them to engage in self-reflection and understanding (D'Argembeau et al., 2008). Drugs may help reduce these symptoms and facilitate the process of talking therapy.

Taking antidepressant medication in no way ensures that the symptoms of depression will subside. Approximately 50% to 60% of people who take antidepressants improve within a few months—but 30% of people improve to similar levels by taking a placebo (Hollon et al., 2002). It may be that those who benefit the most from antidepressants are primarily people who have problems with major depression, and much less so, if at all, for people with milder forms of it (Undurraga & Baldessarini, 2012). Similar to the outcomes found in drug studies, 50% to 60% of people benefit from psychotherapy in treating depression. Thus, we cannot conclude that drugs are either more effective or should replace traditional psychotherapy. Combining the two types of treatment is often the best course of action for treating depression. Notably, the combination of psychotherapy and antidepressants is more effective in treating major depression than medication alone (Cuijpers et al., 2014; Hollon et al., 2014). Even though many individuals may benefit from taking psychotropic medications, they typically remain cautious about using them.

Although modern antidepressants have been around for more than 20 years, and antipsychotic medications have been available for more than 50 years, many people remain skeptical about the safety of psychotropic drugs (Dijkstra et al., 2008). Attitudes have been changing, however, as increasing numbers of people have come to believe that biology is a primary cause of disorders such as major depression (Blumner & Marcus, 2009). Even so, consumer caution is certainly warranted. As previously mentioned, the antipsychotic drug Zyprexa can have serious side effects. Examination of internal documents from Eli Lilly, the company that patented and sold the drug, indicated that these effects were willfully withheld from the public. The high-stakes financial interests of drug companies can be in conflict with the interests of people who need the drugs. These conflicting needs lead to the type of problem encountered with Zyprexa, and can also lead to exaggerated claims about the effectiveness of some medications, as well as risky off-label use (prescribing the drug for a non-approved use). This set of problems will be difficult to overcome because the work of the researchers who evaluate the drugs is often funded by the drug companies themselves.

Myths in Mind

Antidepressant Drugs Are Happiness Pills

A common belief is that antidepressants are "happiness pills"—that their chemical magic not only causes depression to disappear, but also brings on optimism and a rush of positive emotion. In reality, antidepressant drugs can alleviate depression (when they work), but it is inaccurate to conclude that they alone increase happiness.

The happiness pill misconception about antidepressants has led many to believe that taking a high dose of antidepressants will induce a euphoric high, much like cocaine or heroin. This is also a myth. Although some people have attempted to abuse antidepressants by taking high doses (even crushing and snorting them for quicker delivery to the brain), there is no evidence that an intense rush of happiness results. Remember that SSRIs typically take a couple of weeks to work. Taking a high dose, or snorting crushed-up pills, neither magnifies their effect nor reduces the two-week waiting period before any effects become evident.

Antidepressants support the neurochemistry that allows for normal brain functioning, which includes the possibility of experiencing happiness. In short, individuals without depression should not expect to feel greater happiness if they take the drugs.

View the video Biomedical Therapies to learn about various circumstances in which this approach is used.

Watch BIOMEDICAL THERAPIES

ALTERNATIVES TO DRUG THERAPIES Researchers are finding some beneficial alternatives to drugs, especially for individuals who have mild to moderate mental health problems. Numerous studies have shown that exercise is more effective than placebo at relieving depressive symptoms, and it can be as effective as standard SSRI medications (Brené et al., 2007). There are at least two reasons to believe exercise might trump medication for some people. First, the obvious health benefits of exercise (e.g., cardiovascular fitness, muscle tone) provide for a higher quality of life in general. Second, the change in lifestyle that comes with a regular exercise program actually prevents relapse of depressive symptoms better than medication (Babyak et al., 2000).

So what is it about exercise that alleviates depressive symptoms? Several mechanisms are probably at work. In the short term, exercise is associated with the release of endorphins, which reduce pain sensation and increase mood. However, the beneficial effects of endorphins are relatively short term. Over time, active individuals typically increase their energy levels and participate in enjoyable activities, both of which can act against the social withdrawal and negative cognitive style associated with depression. Finally, neuroscience research indicates that exercise actually increases activity within the brain's reward circuitry and facilitates neurogenesis in the hippocampus (Brené et al., 2007; Tanti & Belzung, 2013).

Over-the-counter herbal remedies are an option that many people have sought to address their mental health problems. St. John's wort is among the most well-known herbal substances that people take in the hope of alleviating depressive symptoms. St. John's wort became so popular that a major long-term study was conducted to evaluate the strong claims that were made about its benefits. In this study, St. John's wort was compared with a common prescription SSRI antidepressant and a placebo control over a six-week period in 332 mild to moderately depressed people who were randomly assigned to one of the three conditions. The SSRI was only moderately effective compared with the placebo, which is not an uncommon finding even in carefully controlled studies. St. John's wort was no more effective than the placebo (Hypericum Depression Trial Study Group, 2002).

Dietary factors have been linked to depression. Population level epidemiological studies indicate that reduced consumption of fish and plant material, and increased consumption of saturated fat, is related to elevated rates of depression. Omega-3 fatty acids from fish and other marine sources include compounds that facilitate healthy functioning and physical integrity of nerve cells. Omega-3 fatty acids also reduce inflammatory responses that are known to inhibit regular nerve cell activity. Of course, other variables may explain the correlational relationship between depression and low consumption of omega-3 fatty acids. People who consume food that lacks in nutritional value may have other unhealthy habits that increase their risk of depression. However, experimental studies using randomized placebo-controlled methods show that depressive symptoms are reduced when omega-3 fatty acids are consumed (reviewed in Rechenberg, 2015).

DIVERSITY AND DRUG TREATMENTS The one-size-fits-all approach to medicine is changing. This is reflected in the 2015 Obama administration's Precision Medicine Initiative, which aims to provide financial and technological resources allowing doctors to use genetic information about their patients to better determine which treatment works best for each individual, rather than an "average" person. The initiative will affect mental health care. As an example of how precision medicine would work, consider monoamine oxidase inhibitors (MAOIs) used to treat depression. Based on genetic inheritance, each individual differs in natural levels of the enzyme monoamine oxidase. Someone who inherits a version of the gene that is associated with high levels of the enzyme will break down high levels of naturally occurring dopamine and serotonin. An MAOI medication would be much less likely to work for people with high levels of this enzyme—perhaps there is not a safe dosage that could overcome the genetic predisposition toward having high levels of MAO enzymes. An individual's genetic profile can tell a doctor that experimenting with an MAO inhibitor drug would not likely work, and to instead save the patient time and money and consider other options.

Just as each individual differs in genetic makeup, so too do populations. Therefore, racial background can be an important factor for healthcare providers to consider when prescribing psychotropic medications. Doctors in Japan, for example, use dosage tables specifically calibrated to maximize effectiveness of antipsychotic, antidepressant, and other psychotropic medications taken by Japanese patients (Inada & Inagaki, 2015). Dosage adjustments are made because of genetically mediated physiological responses that Japanese patients have to the drugs. Relatedly, small but detectable genetic differences between African American and Caucasian people influence responses to antidepressants. For example, genetic factors are among the reasons why African American people showed less benefit from Celexa, an SSRI, compared with Caucasians (Murphy et al., 2013).

At the beginning of this module we saw the consequences of prescribing the sleep-aide Ambien using a one-size-fits-all approach. Males and females respond differently to the drug, with males eliminating it from their bodies more rapidly than females. Thus, Ambien stays within females for a longer period of time, and can lead to continued impairment into the morning hours. This increases the likelihood of accidents and other adverse events related to taking too large of a dose. The National Institute of Health now requires that all drug testing include both males and females—even beginning in the earliest phases of drug development in which drugs are tested on animals.

JOURNAL PROMPT

Medications: People tend to have different reactions and hold different beliefs about drugs such as statins, which are used to lower blood cholesterol, and psychotropic drugs for treating conditions such as anxiety and depression. Why do you think people react this way?

Surgery and Brain Stimulation

People who do not experience sufficient assistance from therapy or drugs may opt for technological and surgical methods, most of which are used for severe symptoms and disorders. Today, these procedures are generally safe and carefully tested and scrutinized, though that has not always been the case.

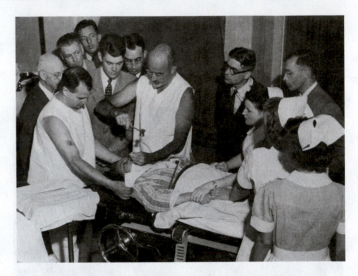

Walter Freeman performing a frontal lobotomy surgery

SURGERY You have likely heard chilling stories about the *frontal lobotomy* procedure. A small but significant minority of neurologists of the 1800s and 1900s experimented with surgically removing regions of the cortex in the hope of "curing" psychological problems. Portuguese surgeon Antonio Moniz believed that the prefrontal cortex was the source of many psychological problems, and reasoned that destroying it would cure them. Moniz used either chemicals or a wire loop to destroy the frontal lobe. The procedure was imported to the United States by Walter Freeman, a surgeon who modified Moniz's technique in a way he considered simpler but equally effective. Freeman used a device resembling an ice pick to pierce the orbit of the eye, lodge it within the brain, and move it around until the frontal lobes were detached from the rest of the brain. This manipulation was done without anesthesia and on an outpatient basis. Freeman believed the procedure to be miraculously successful (despite the high percentage of patients who died from internal bleeding and other complications). Freeman and the few others who were willing to perform lobotomies used the procedure on some 4,000 people despite resistance from the medical community and the public.

By the 1970s, the prefrontal lobotomy was discontinued in the United States. Although the procedure has given an unfortunate reputation to just about any psychologically based medical intervention, there are several available techniques that are safe and often quite effective.

A **lesion** *is a damaged area of tissue, such as a group of nerve cells.* Brain lesions are never created on human subjects for basic research purposes. However, in some cases, when all other treatments have not worked to satisfaction, a surgeon may create small brain lesions in patients. Some people with depression, obsessive–compulsive disorder, and other anxiety disorders have undergone lesion surgery directed at a cluster of cells located in the anterior cingulate cortex (Cosgrove & Rauch, 2003; Fitzgerald et al., 2005; Steele et al., 2008). This procedure, called an *anterior cingulotomy*, has no more risks or side effects than do many of the drugs used to treat these disorders. Also, the use of brain imaging technology allows surgeons to carry out the procedure with great precision.

BRAIN STIMULATION Several procedures have been developed that involve stimulating brain regions that are known to be affected by mental disorders. **Electroconvulsive therapy (ECT)** *is a procedure in which a temporary seizure is induced via an electrical current.* Introduced in the 1930s, ECT has been viewed negatively for much of its history, in part because in its early days it was quite risky. Over the years, procedures for delivering ECT have improved dramatically. Patients are now given sedatives and muscle relaxers to reduce the discomfort they may experience and to prevent injury related to convulsions. Thus, ECT has gone from being viewed as a torturous "shock treatment" to a relatively normal and safe procedure, although it is still reserved for the most severe cases of disorders such as depression and schizophrenia. The side effects are relatively mild, typically consisting of some amnesia, but only for events occurring around the time of the treatment.

Why does ECT work? Which changes in the nervous system does ECT stimulate? Scientists are not sure why inducing what is basically a controlled seizure can have positive outcomes for many individuals. One likely possibility is that ECT facilitates the expression of genes that code for neurotransmitter systems affecting mood (deJong et al., 2014).

Transcranial magnetic stimulation (TMS) *is a therapeutic technique in which a focal area of the brain is exposed to a powerful but safe magnetic field.* TMS does not involve anesthesia or inducing a seizure. Clinical researchers have discovered that repeated stimulation to parts of the frontal lobes of the cortex reduces depressive symptoms (Chistyakov et al., 2005; Gaynes et al., 2014). The FDA has approved the use of this technique for treating major depression in people who have not improved with drugs or ECT. This technique holds considerable promise, and it may turn out to be of value in reducing symptoms of other mental disorders, such as schizophrenia (Slotema et al., 2010). **Deep-brain stimulation (DBS)** *involves electrically*

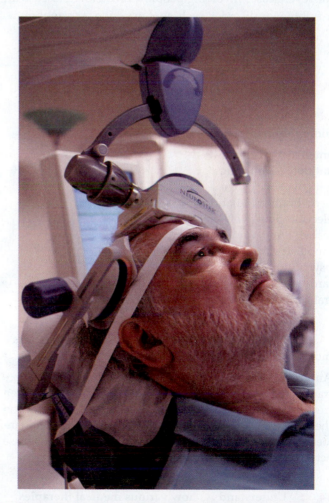

Delivering brief pulses of a strong magnetic field to the cerebral cortex has been shown to help alleviate symptoms of severe depression, and possibly other disorders. This individual is undergoing transcranial magnetic stimulation.

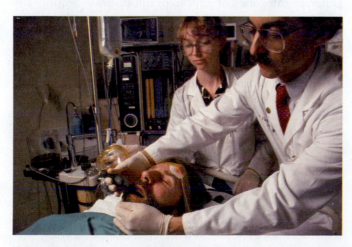

People with depression or bipolar disorder may elect to undergo electroconvulsive therapy if other treatments have not been successful.

stimulating highly specific regions of the brain. A device serving as a brain pacemaker is implanted and connected to electrode-tipped wires that are routed to under-stimulated brain regions. Deep-brain stimulation produces quick results, though there are some troublesome side effects to consider. In particular, some patients have experienced internal bleeding and infection. Also, even though the wires and electrodes are placed with the utmost precision, it is possible that behavioral side effects can occur, such as depression, aggression, penile erection, and laughter (Kringelbach et al., 2007).

Scientists are not sure exactly how DBS works. It has primarily been applied to people who have movement disorders such as Parkinson's disease. More recently, it has been used to help treat depression and obsessive–compulsive disorder. Deep-brain stimulation holds the promise of alleviating the need to perform a lesion surgery, such as the anterior cingulotomy (Kringelbach & Aziz, 2009).

EVALUATING SURGERY AND BRAIN STIMULATION
Technological and surgical methods are typically reserved for severe cases involving people who are diagnosed with a full-blown disorder such as depression, schizophrenia,

or obsessive–compulsive disorder. Some of these methods continue to be controversial because an outdated procedure like the frontal lobotomy immediately comes to mind. Surgeries that involve destroying brain tissue are still used in extreme cases, but less invasive methods such as DBS and TMS are also becoming more widely available. A common belief is that ECT causes lasting cognitive impairments, but the evidence for this is contradicted by the majority of research on people who have been treated with it (Rose et al., 2003).

Combining the treatments covered in this chapter is common, such as seeing a therapist and taking prescribed antidepressants, or combining drugs with ECT. Why do people need more than one form of treatment? In some cases, there is an urgent need to take action—for example, if the individual is suicidal. Also, for more serious cases, a single treatment may provide very little benefit. For example, the drug lithium has such a long history of use because it works so well, with relapse rates at around 20% (Keller & Baker, 1991). In contrast, half of people who undergo ECT end up relapsing back into depression, although combining antidepressants with ECT can help improve long-term outcomes (Haghighi et al., 2013).

Module 14.3 Summary

14.3a Know . . . the key terminology associated with biological treatments:

antianxiety drugs
antidepressant drugs
antipsychotic drugs
deep-brain stimulation (DBS)
electroconvulsive therapy (ECT)
lesion
mood stabilizers
psychotropic drugs
tardive dyskinesia
transcranial magnetic stimulation (TMS)

14.3b Understand . . . how the drugs described in this module affect brain functioning.

Antidepressant drugs typically target monoamine neurotransmitter activity, with differing mechanisms of action (review Figure 14.9). Many of the antipsychotic drugs on the market reduce dopamine activity in the brain. Antianxiety drugs tend to target GABA receptors and increase activity of this inhibitory neurotransmitter.

14.3c Understand . . . how various medical therapies that do not involve drugs work.

Other procedures available for treating mental illness include electroconvulsive therapy, transcranial magnetic stimulation,

deep-brain stimulation, and focal lesions. In some cases, such as with ECT, researchers are still unsure about which aspect of the treatment produces the therapeutic results. Stimulation techniques increase the brain activity in targeted areas, whereas lesions prevent brain activity. By targeting the areas responsible for specific behaviors, thoughts, or emotions, treatments can have dramatic effects on behavior.

14.3d Apply . . . your knowledge of drug therapies to different psychological conditions.

Different categories of psychological disorder require different treatments, and this includes the drugs that might be prescribed for each. The activity "Categorizing Psychotropic Drugs" in Table 14.7 provided an opportunity to test your ability to match up common drug names with the conditions they are often prescribed to treat. (Do keep in mind that a single drug might be used to treat symptoms of different disorders. For example, drugs developed to treat schizophrenia may reduce symptoms of bipolar disorder.)

14.3e Analyze . . . whether alternative biologically based treatments to prescription drugs work.

There are many other options and they have varying rates of success. Data do not support the conclusion that herbal remedies such as St. John's wort reduce depression any better than do placebos. On the other hand, intake of omega-3 fatty acids seems to reduce depressive symptoms, as does exercise for people with mild cases. An important consideration regarding whether alternatives work concerns the severity of mental illness. Treatments that involve surgery or technologies such as transcranial magnetic stimulation, deep-brain stimulation, or electroconvulsive therapy are used in cases of severe illness, and only after medication options have been exhausted. Also, ketamine, which is a drug treatment but not available in prescription form, shows promise for rapidly reducing symptoms of depression and possibly other mental disorders.

Module 14.3 Quiz

Know . . .

1. The category of drugs used to treat symptoms of bipolar disorder are called:
    A. ketamine.
    B. antipsychotics.
    C. mood stabilizers.
    D. antidepressants.

Understand . . .

2. _____ affect the nervous system by blocking reuptake of serotonin in neurons.
    A. Lesions
    B. Antianxiety medications
    C. Mood stabilizers
    D. SSRIs

3. If a doctor wanted to activate a very specific brain region in the hope of alleviating symptoms of a mental disorder, she would most likely use which of the following procedures?
    A. Focal lesion
    B. Lithium
    C. Electroconvulsive therapy
    D. Deep-brain stimulation

Apply . . .

4. Procedures such as electroconvulsive therapy, transcranial magnetic stimulation, or administering ketamine would most likely occur in which of the following scenarios?
    A. Mild anxiety
    B. Extreme, treatment resistant depression
    C. Mild to moderate depression
    D. Hallucinations associated with schizophrenia

Analyze . . .

5. A new age "guru" openly criticizes medical procedures for treating psychological problems, citing the frontal lobotomy as his only evidence. Which statement best contradicts his critique?
    A. The frontal lobotomy is no longer used and has been replaced with scientifically supported treatments.
    B. Frontal lobotomies are now relatively safe to perform.
    C. Frontal lobotomies actually work very well for schizophrenia, but not for bipolar disorder.
    D. The argument is irrelevant, as medical procedures are being phased out in favor of new age treatments.

Module 14.4   Scientific Literacy Challenge: Bibliotherapy

There are more self-help books available than anyone would care to count, much less read. Many of these books are based on anecdotes, personal experiences, or ideas that sell easily despite a lack of supporting evidence. However, within the extensive self-help genre there are books that offer readers *bibliotherapy*—the use of books and other printed materials to address specific, and relatively mild psychological problems. For more serious concerns, such as major depression, bibliotherapy might be used in conjunction with more involved treatment such as psychotherapy and prescription drugs. In either situation, the best of these books deliver scientifically validated therapeutic suggestions and techniques.

JOURNAL PROMPT

If you had a friend or family member who began to show signs of mild depression, would you feel confident in suggesting bibliotherapy to them? Explain.

What do we know about bibliotherapy?

Take a look at the back cover of this book. As you read, make sure you understand Chapter 14's key terms and concepts that are printed in boldface.

Being Well Being You, now in its fourth edition, has helped thousands gain **insight** into their feelings while coping with depression. This is not just a self-help book; it is a therapist in written form. It guides the reader through several activities and exercises practiced in **cognitive-behavioral** and **humanistic** therapies. Although readers can use it for independent bibliotherapy, it has also been a popular supplement to traditional **psychotherapy** and **antidepressant medication**.

The claims made on the book jacket sound good, but that does not mean it can deliver the same level of treatment as a trained professional can. Read on to find out if bibliotherapy is likely to be helpful.

How do scientists study bibliotherapy?

Self-help books make a lot of promises and offer hope to those who are searching for relief from their troubles. But how well do self-help books really work? Here is what we found in our research:

> One study followed 170 older adults who were experiencing depression. The patients were evenly divided into two groups: one received a copy of a biblioptherapy manual titled *Coping with Depression* and another that received antidepressant medication. After three months, the group who read the book and completed the exercises provided showed no signs of reduced depression compared to the medication group. However, a second study tracked the symptoms in a group of patients whose primary care physicians had been trained on how to properly instruct them to use bibliotherapy. In this experiment, patients who read a book titled *Feeling Good* showed as much improvement as those who had been randomly assigned to use standard treatment with antidepressants. Finally, there was a third study: a meta-analysis combining results of numerous studies testing whether bibliotherapy works. This particular meta-analysis combined multiple studies, each of which evaluated the same book, and the results were positive: over four weeks, those who read the book had reduced depression compared to those who did not. Based on these studies, it appears that bibliotherapy brings mixed results, and, if it is to work, proper procedures for administering it need to be followed.

Several important concepts were described in the above studies. Were you able to identify qualities of good science in these examples? Test yourself with these questions:

1. The first and second studies described found different results. This may be due to the use of different books. The specific book used in the study would be part of the _____.
   a. dependent variable
   b. operational definition of procedures used
   c. sample
   d. quasi-experiment
2. The authors of the meta-analysis found multiple studies on the same topic. Why is there more than one published study on what appears to be the same topic?
   a. Scientists can increase the support for a hypothesis through replication.
   b. Researchers hoped to establish ecological validity.
   c. Researchers hoped to identify a convenience sample.
   d. It is the most effective way to measure a dependent variable.
3. The second study described randomly assigned primary care patients to one of two conditions. This suggests that the study was based on a _____ design.
   a. quasi-experimental
   b. correlational
   c. natural observation
   d. experimental

Answers: 1. *b* 2. *a* 3. *d*

Now that we have seen some of the evidence, let's engage in critical thinking.

How do we think critically about bibliotherapy?

The statements below will help you identify several aspects of critical thinking. Match the following critical thinking elements to the statements that illustrate them.

1. Be curious and ask questions.
2. Tolerate ambiguity.
3. Consider alternative explanations.
4. Examine the nature and source of the evidence

a. I wonder if books are more useful for long-term depression or for people who have only been experiencing symptoms for a short time?
b. Not all research gives us the same answer, so we know that bibliotherapy probably can help, but we still need to learn more about why or when it is successful.
c. A friend suggested that it might not be the book itself that is helpful. Maybe people willing to use the book correctly are less depressed to start with.
d. The meta-analysis, which is a peer-reviewed research article, showed that numerous independent studies confirmed that reading and following advice from a specific book reduces symptoms of depression.

Answers: 1. a 2. b 3. c 4. d

This represents a good start on addressing bibliotherapy with critical thinking. Now, read on to see how this evidence might be applied.

How is bibliotherapy relevant?

Sometimes it is easy to determine whether a self-help technique is worthwhile or if it is ineffective or even counterproductive. Read these suggestions for how bibliotherapy might be applied and then share any newly formed thoughts you may have about bibliotherapy in the writing activity that follows.

> The evidence is not all in favor in the use of bibliotherapy, but it does seem to suggest that the right book used for long enough can be helpful. Major advantages of using self-help options include low cost, convenience, and the anonymity they offer for those who want it. Self-help options are easy to find. In fact, many people consult online resources to get help for depression, anxiety, substance abuse problems, and sexual health. If you do turn to self-help resources for your psychological problems, remember to choose wisely and stay committed to the program. Research has shown that not all treatments are successful, and that compliance and follow-through with some forms of self-help are probably quite a bit lower than in face-to-face therapy sessions. Thus the ideal course of treatment is probably to speak with a professional at least once—especially if symptoms are severe—to find out whether self-help is appropriate for your situation.

SHARED WRITING

Based on your knowledge of scientific procedures and critical thinking skills, what specifically would you look for in a self-help book? Alternatively, what would you actively avoid in a book?

Chapter 14 Quiz

1. Rita is a mental health professional who has a master's degree. She generally works with people who are having difficulty dealing with mild depression or anxiety, or are generally having trouble with stress or coping; she does not work with individuals who have more severe mental disorders such as schizophrenia or major depression. Rita is most likely a _____.
   A. counseling psychologist
   B. psychiatrist
   C. clinical psychologist
   D. forensic psychologist

2. The rigorous testing of specific psychotherapies is difficult, in part because:
   A. clients do not want to receive experimental treatments.
   B. most people prefer self-help treatments.
   C. therapists cannot be blind to the type of therapy they are administering.
   D. few therapists are willing to participate in such studies.

3. Carl Rogers developed a type of therapy called _____, which focuses on individuals' abilities to solve their own problems and reach their full potential with the encouragement of the therapist.
   A. object relations therapy
   B. psychoanalysis
   C. insight therapy
   D. person/client-centered therapy

4. Family therapists take a _____ approach, an orientation toward family therapy that involves identifying and understanding what each individual family member contributes to the entire family dynamic.
   A. client-centered
   B. psychoanalytic
   C. systems
   D. systematic desensitization

5. In general, antidepressant drugs are believed to work by:
   A. decreasing monoamine activity in the brain.
   B. increasing monoamine activity in the brain.
   C. increasing GABA activity in the brain.
   D. decreasing GABA activity in the brain.

6. Research into the effectiveness of antidepressants indicates that the most effective treatment for many people is:
   A. taking antidepressant drugs alone.
   B. psychotherapy without any pharmaceutical therapy.
   C. taking antidepressants combined with antipsychotic drugs.
   D. combining antidepressant drugs with psychotherapy.

7. In the middle of the 20th century, Walter Freeman and others infamously treated thousands of patients with a procedure known as _____.
   A. shock therapy
   B. the frontal lobotomy
   C. deep-brain stimulation
   D. anterior cingulotomy

8. Which of the following statements is true about electroconvulsive therapy (ECT)?
   A. ECT can be an effective treatment for severe cases of depression.
   B. ECT is no longer considered a valid or ethical form of treatment.
   C. ECT is still performed in the same way it was delivered in the 1930s and 1940s.
   D. ECT triggers a controlled stroke.

9. The processes for resolving personal, emotional, behavioral, and social problems so as to improve well-being are known as _____.
   A. psychotherapy
   B. barriers to help-seeking
   C. minimalizing
   D. compensation

10. Which type of provider is permitted to prescribe medications in all 50 states?
    A. Psychiatrist
    B. Clinical psychologist
    C. Clinical social worker
    D. Medical psychologist

11. _____ is the relationship that emerges in therapy and is an important aspect of effectiveness.
    A. Client insight
    B. Altruism
    C. Therapeutic alliance
    D. Friendship

12. A kindergarten teacher (unintentionally) places conditions of worth on her students. What does this mean?
    A. She always lets her students know how much she values them.
    B. She regularly tries to draw compliments out of her students.
    C. She acts as if a student no longer matters to her or the school if he misbehaves.
    D. She provides monetary rewards for good behavior.

13. _____ involves a process in which the client faces feared situations gradually and under controlled conditions.
    A. Client-centered therapy
    B. Family therapy
    C. Insight therapy
    D. Exposure therapy

14. Tardive dyskinesia is:
    A. a side effect of some antipsychotic drugs that involves motion control problems.
    B. an antidepressant that breaks down enzymes in the synapse.
    C. the growth of new neurons in the adult brain.
    D. a side effect of antidepressant drugs.

15. Imagine that a friend asks you what you have heard about St. John's wort because he is considering using it to alleviate his depression. Which of the following is probably the safest conclusion you can draw?
    A. Many people have reported improvements with St. John's wort, but the effects are typically mild and improvements may depend on the quality of the brand.
    B. St. John's wort is superior to prescription antidepressant medications.
    C. Your friend may as well take a placebo: Scientific evidence does not support the conclusion that St. John's wort reduces symptoms of depression.
    D. St. John's wort is superior to cognitive-behavioral therapies.

Chapter 15
Social Psychology

Learning Objectives

15.1a Know . . . the key terminology associated with social influence.

15.1b Understand . . . why individuals conform to others' behaviors and thoughts.

15.1c Understand . . . how individuals and groups can influence attitudes and behaviors.

15.1d Apply . . . your knowledge of cognitive dissonance to see how well your beliefs match your behaviors.

15.1e Analyze . . . whether social influence can lead people to behave in ways they believe are wrong.

Style is one of the most apparent forms of social influence. A fashion-conscious individual learns from paying attention to what others are wearing and makes his decisions based on what their styles communicate about their personalities. In contrast, some people seem to be immune to social influence in this area; they throw on whatever is handy—just baggy fleece sweatpants and an oversized shirt will do. They may not make a strong first impression, but they save a lot of money and are arguably more comfortable. Fashion is just one example of social influence, and being fashionable is a way of embracing and perhaps even enjoying that influence. Recently, an interesting phenomenon called normcore *has emerged as a new fashion trend in some areas. Normcore is a hybrid style in which the baggy sweatpants and oversized shirt worn by the least fashionable among us have been adopted by the most fashion-oriented and image-conscious people, including the A-list fashion model pictured here. As a result, you could see two people dressed in the exact same clothing for entirely different reasons: one because she cares so little about social trends, and the other because she cares so much.*

Fashion is only one of countless ways an individual's behavior can be shaped by others. **Social psychology** *examines how social influences can operate in any context*. This takes us from the mundane behaviors such as such as sitting in a waiting room full of strangers to making political decisions that can ultimately make the difference between war and peace.

We tend to feel as if we are in charge of our own behavior—that we are free to determine what we do and do not do, and that we act for good reasons, not just to go along with the crowd. Social psychology challenges these ideas with strong evidence that much of our behavior depends more on *where* we are than on *who* we are.

Norms, Roles, and Conformity

No matter their culture humans are remarkably sensitive to whether behavior is socially acceptable. When you walk down the street, is it appropriate to make eye contact with strangers? In some situations, doing so would make you vulnerable to hostility or could insult passers-by. When you step into an elevator, do you stand with your back to the door and announce the floors to fellow passengers? You might get some odd looks if you did. Here, we investigate how our behavior is influenced by what is deemed acceptable and expected.

NORMS AND ROLES   **Social norms** *are the (usually unwritten) guidelines for how to behave in social contexts*. Norms include everything from the manners we use in polite company, to the topics that are suitable for conversation and the types of clothing deemed appropriate. Although norms are general rules that apply to members of a group, **social roles** *are guidelines that apply to specific positions within the group*. Because roles are so specific, we often have labels for them such as professor, student, coach, parent, and even prison guard, which happens to be one of the most famous roles in psychology. The Stanford Prison Experiment of the early 1970s has become a memorable and controversial narrative of how quickly people might adapt to assigned roles. Researchers at Stanford University recruited a group of young men and randomly assigned them to play the part of prisoner or guard in a makeshift jail in the basement of the psychology building. The lead investigator,

Volunteers were randomly assigned to play guards or prisoners in the Stanford Prison Study in 1971. Each group took their roles so seriously that the researchers called off the experiment before it was even halfway completed.

Phillip Zimbardo, coached the guards on how to play the role, even relying on consultation from a former prisoner on how to best mimic actual prison guard behaviors he experienced while incarcerated. Not surprisingly, some guards became quite hostile and abusive, and in response many of the "prisoners" became helpless and submissive (Haney et al., 1973). The study was terminated before the planned 2-week period. The reason offered by Zimbardo at the time was that the situation had gotten out of hand and was taking its toll on the prisoners' physical and psychological health. This study has long been recognized as a striking demonstration of "the power of the situation"; how social roles and situational factors determine our behavior.

Classic studies such as this are an essential part of learning about psychology, and social psychology in particular leans heavily on them to illustrate foundational concepts. It is also important to separate interesting story and narrative from scientific reality. Recall the concept of *demand characteristics* covered in Module 2.1: Experiments are contaminated and confounded if researchers provide inadvertent (or in Zimbardo's case purposeful) information about how they expect a research study to play out. Because the guards received coaching on how to play their role, we cannot infer that it was the role itself that led to the change in behavior; it is more likely they were playing the role of research participant and following the instructions they were given (see Banuazizi & Movahedi, 1975). Interestingly, in the early 2000s a similar study, the British Prison Study, controlled for demand characteristics and found that the guards were reluctant to engage in abusive behavior, and the prisoners eventually coalesced to agree on strategies with how to deal with being locked up together, and thereby improved their well-being over the course of the study (Haslam & Richer, 2012). Thus, the power of the situation can bring people together to play the role of "survivor."

Prison studies aside, the importance of norms can be illustrated with the problem of alcohol abuse on college campuses, which, among other negative outcomes, is associated with more than 1,800 student deaths and 97,000 sexual assaults per year (National Institute on Alcohol and Addiction [NIAA], 2015). All students have perceptions about drinking norms including how much the typical student drinks and how students judge others' drinking behavior. Statistics from the National Institute on Alcohol and Addiction give us *actual* norms for how 18- to 22-year-olds are drinking:

- More than 60% of college students reported drinking alcohol, compared to 51% of non-students in that age range
- 40% reported binge-drinking (five or more drinks on one occasion for men, four or more for women) compared to 35% of non-students
- 14% report heavy drinking (binging at least five times in a month) compared to 10% of non-students

Students who perceive norms to be high tend to overestimate rates of drinking and are much more likely to be binge-drinkers and heavy drinkers themselves (Foster et al., 2015; Wardell & Read, 2013). We should keep in mind that this is correlational research, so we cannot establish whether the norms lead to more drinking or vice versa, but research suggests that interventions aimed at correcting misperceptions of the norm can lead to decreased alcohol abuse (LaBrie et al., 2013; Ridout & Campbell, 2014). We should also keep in mind that alcohol use is just one example of the power of norms. In fact, our perceptions of what is normal are likely to influence everything we do.

MIMICRY AND CONFORMITY **Mimicry** *occurs when one person copies another's behavior*. It can be a useful skill at times, such as in a foreign country where you do not know the language and no one is around to help you translate. How will you get by? If you want to ride public transportation, just watch what the other passengers are doing. Do they buy tickets before boarding, or do they pay a driver once they board? Following another's lead is often the best way to go, even if you are just walking into a new restaurant in your neighborhood.

But mimicry is not always a conscious choice. We also mimic subtle movements—especially emotional expressions—without even knowing it. This seems to be an important part of forming and maintaining social relationships: Mimicry is more likely when interacting with acquaintances rather than strangers, with positive emotions than negative, with people we find attractive rather than plain or unattractive, and with people we like rather than dislike (Farley, 2014; Hess & Fischer, 2014).

The study of mimicry focuses on how we are influenced by a single individual, but being part of a group can affect our behaviors as well. **Conformity** *refers to a change in behavior to fit in with a group, whether it is intentional or not*. In the 1950s Solomon Asch developed a creative way to study conformity in the lab and conducted a series of studies that are nearly as famous as the Stanford Prison Experiment. In this method, a research participant would join a study that involved very simple and obvious perceptual judgments that anyone should get right (see Figure 15.1). However, Asch would have each participant in a room with research confederates who were instructed at times to give the wrong answer. Despite the simplicity of the task, the participants would often conform to the rest of the group and give an incorrect answer (Asch, 1951, 1955, 1956). By repeating this same basic procedure and making subtle changes each time, Asch was clearly able to demonstrate that people conform and he identified a number of personal and situational factors that lead to conformity.

Why we sometimes conform so readily is an important psychological question. There are two clear reasons and they lead to different types of conformity. First, *public*

Figure 15.1 Perceptual Judgment Task Used in Asch's Conformity Studies

Which of the comparison lines is the same length as the standard line? The correct answer is line B, and most people find that to be obvious. However, in Asch's experiments, many people conformed with the confederates and gave the wrong answer. For some participants, including the man in this photo, the experience must have been baffling.

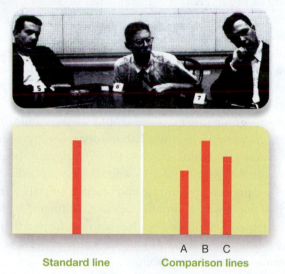

Standard line   A B C
                  Comparison lines

compliance occurs when an individual modifies what they say or do without internalizing their conformity (Cialdini & Goldstein, 2004). This generally means that the person sacrifices a little honesty about their own beliefs to avoid criticism or rejection from the group. Second, *private acceptance* occurs when individuals actually change their internalized beliefs and opinions as well as their public behavior. In this situation, the conforming individual is likely to see other group members as being better informed, having more skill, or perhaps better taste, thus they are a good source of information. One study illustrated how this may work: A group of young heterosexual men participated in a study of facial attractiveness by rating photographs of females on a scale from 1 to 10. Then they received randomly assigned feedback indicating that the average rating for that same face was higher, lower, or the same. In subsequent trials, many of the participants changed their ratings to conform to the perceived group norm even though nobody was directly observing their

behavior. It would appear that this represents private compliance—perhaps perceptions of attractiveness really are influenced by what others think (Huang et al., 2014). In summary, whether and when we conform is influenced by a variety of personal and situational factors (Table 15.1).

Group Influence and Authority

Whether you know it or not, there is a really good chance that your performance at work or play is to some extent determined by others in your group. Groups can improve your performance, or they may lead you to slack off. Some groups unite their members—even if their ideas are foolhardy—while other situations are divisive. Similar patterns of social influence have been seen among corporations, in presidential cabinet meetings, and believe it or not, among all sorts of species in the animal kingdom—even the lowly cockroach! Because groups are an important part of education, work, and play, it is important to understand the social influences on individual performance.

SOCIAL LOAFING AND SOCIAL FACILITATION You probably have had at least one teacher or professor who saw value in assigning group projects. However, every class charged with completing a group project involves at least one student who feels she has done the entire project herself and at least one student who spent group meeting time texting or playing on his phone. Sound familiar? The importance of group activity in all aspects of life has led psychologists to ask whether groups help or hurt individual performance. Oddly enough, the answer is both, and so psychologists need to explain which personal and situational factors lead to one or the other.

Social loafing *occurs when an individual working as part of a group or team reduces his or her effort.* The individual may or may not be aware that he is loafing, but the behavior affects the group process nonetheless. Two of the most remarkable findings about social loafing are that it can appear in all sorts of tasks, including physical activities (swimming, rope-pulling), cognitive activities (problem solving, perceptual tests), and creativity (songwriting) and that it seems to occur equally across all types of groups, regardless of age, gender, and nationality (Karau & Williams, 2001; Latane et al., 2006).

Table 15.1 Personal and Situational Factors Contribute to Conformity

People Tend to Be Less Likely to Conform When . . .	People Tend to Be More Likely to Conform When . . .
Only one other person is in the vicinity	There is a larger group in the vicinity
There are only male group members	There is a high proportion of female group members
There are only strangers in the room	There are friends, family, or acquaintances in the vicinity
There are extremely clear and simple tasks	The task is unclear or ambiguous
There is one other nonconformist in the room	Others conform first
Responses are made anonymously	Responses are made publicly

Given the universal nature of social loafing, researchers have been able to identify a number of situational influences with the potential to turn just about anyone into a loafer:

- *My effort will not help my performance.* Loafing may occur if an individual believes she is not capable of doing well.

- *My performance will not make a difference to the group's performance.* Loafing tends to occur when an individual believes he could do well but the group as a whole would do poorly, or perhaps that the group would do fine without him.

- *The group may get rewarded but it won't matter to me.* The group might get paid, but each individual's share is perceived as too small. Or perhaps conflict between group members can lead to loafing. Either way, the loafing members just want to get the group effort over with.

- *No one else is trying hard.* Social loafing can be contagious. If one group member loafs, others may loaf as well (Karau & Williams, 2001).

If you think about the reverse of these situational influences, you should be able to predict what prevents social loafing: If an individual believes her contribution will help the group succeed and get rewarded, and if she values the rewards, then she is likely to put forth her best effort (Goren et al., 2003).

Not all groups have problems with social loafing; in fact, in some groups the reverse happens. **Social facilitation** *occurs when an individual's performance is better in the presence of others than when alone.* For example, a runner who completes a mile in a little more than 5 minutes by himself might finally break the 5-minute mark when running with his track teammates. Notice in this example that the runner is among peers, which is quite different from being around others who are only observing. Does having an audience help people do their best, or does it only lead to stage fright? The answer depends on ability and confidence to a large extent—when individuals have already mastered a task, the audience can help, whereas for novices, having an audience can hurt performance (Bell & Yee, 1989; MacCracken & Stadulis, 1985).

GROUPTHINK Despite the old proverb, two heads are not always better than one, and six can be downright harmful. Probably the best example of this case is the phenomenon of **groupthink**, *a decision-making problem in which group members avoid arguments and strive for agreement.* At first, this might sound like a good thing. Conflicts can be unpleasant for some people and they can certainly get in the way of group decision making. But groupthink does not always promote good decision making. This is because when everyone avoids argument, three main problems occur. First, the group often becomes overconfident and gains a sense of excitement about its progress. Second, group members may minimize or ignore potential problems and risks. Third, they may apply social pressure to members who are not fully in support of the idea in an effort to get them to conform (Ahlfinger & Esser, 2001; Janis, 1972).

Some groups are more susceptible to groupthink than others, as Table 15.2 shows. Laboratory research revealed that when groupthink occurs, there is almost always a strong or "directive" leader—specifically, an individual who suppresses dissenters and encourages the group to consider fewer alternative ideas (Ahlfinger & Esser, 2001). Experimental research has also confirmed that the more the group members have in common—especially in terms of shared sociopolitical perspectives—the more likely they are to fall into the patterns of groupthink (e.g., Schulz-Hardt et al., 2000).

Despite the similarities among the groups that have succumbed to groupthink, plenty of cases can be cited where groups with strong leaders and a shared background did not fall into groupthink patterns. Also, one should realize that groupthink does not always lead to bad decisions (Kerr & Tindale, 2004). In some cases of groupthink, the group might have stumbled on the best solution early in the decision process, so any alternatives that were introduced really would not be needed.

OBEDIENCE TO AUTHORITY One of the most powerful forms of social influence is authority, and social psychologists are particularly interested in what leads an individual to **obedience**—*complying with instructions or orders from an individual who is in a position of authority.* Authority comes from a combination of social roles and contexts. Individuals are likely to obey parents, teachers, bosses, and law enforcement officials because they generally agree that those titles indicate authority. However, authority can be situational. For example, if you walk into an examination room for a physical and

Table 15.2 Risk Factors for Groupthink

- The group is highly cohesive; group members come from similar backgrounds and approach the problems from the same general perspective.
- There is a strong leader in the group, someone who can control the conversation and can keep the focus on his or her idea, whether it is the appointed leader or a strong personality.
- The group ignores outside experts and dismisses expert opinions that do not agree with the group. They only seek information that will support their ideas.

SOURCE: "Some of the risk factors for groupthink" from "The nature of social influence in groupthink: Compliance and Internalization" From McCauley, C. (1987). The nature of social influence in groupthink: Compliance and internalization. *Journal of Personality and Social Psychology*, 57, 250–260.

The "shock generator" that the teacher operated to punish the learner.

The "learner" gets set up to participate in the experiment. He is being hooked up to the device that the teacher believes will deliver a shock.

The experimenter explains to the "teacher" what the experimental procedure entails and how to use the shock generator.

Although most subjects were highly obedient, some, such as this person, refused to continue complying with the experimenter's orders.

the physician asks you to undress, you most likely will comply. Your reaction is likely to be much different if your physician asks this of you upon running into you at the supermarket.

Not everyone is equally fond of or influenced by authority. Just as individuals can be described as introverted or extroverted, people differ in their level of *authoritarianism* (Ludeke & Krueger, 2013). Individuals who score high on personality tests of this trait tend to prefer strong authorities across almost all domains of life whether they serve as a leader or as a follower. In contrast, those at the lower end of the scale may have an "authority problem" and regularly clash with those in charge.

Differences in authoritarianism can be seen in many parts of life. In politics, for example, authoritarianism is correlated with conservative viewpoints such as calling for stronger military or asking for stricter punishments in the judicial system. The strongest conservatives even chastise liberals for a lack of respect and discipline, particularly in times of protest (Frimer et al., 2014; Haidt, 2012). It is not that people with liberal political views completely eschew authority, however. Experiments indicate that liberals are every bit as much in favor of obedience to authority when a specific issue is aligned with their cause, such as using the authority and power of the federal government to enforce civil rights or freedom of expression (Frimer et al., 2014).

Just how much influence can an authority figure have over an individual's behavior? It is one thing for an employee to complete a report for her supervisor. It is quite another thing for her to engage in behaviors that conflict with her values—perhaps inflicting pain on another—just because her boss requested it. To explore just how far people will go to obey authority figures, psychologist Stanley Milgram conducted a series of classic studies in the 1960s. This innovative procedure involved bringing a volunteer into a laboratory under the premise of a study on learning. The participant was to be a "teacher," and another participant (who was actually a confederate) was the "learner." Obedience came into play

when the teacher was asked to deliver what seemed to be increasingly painful electrical shocks each time the learner made a mistake. The teachers experienced a great deal of distress from the pain they seemed to be causing, and yet most continued to deliver the increasingly powerful shocks simply because the authority figure—the researcher in a white lab coat—instructed them to. To confirm that authority was the key factor, Milgram tested different variations of this experiment by having the experimenter wear street clothes instead of a lab coat or by having a second authority figure express concern for the learner. Whenever the figure of authority was weakened, the rates of obedience were significantly lower (Milgram, 1963, 1974; Miller, 1986).

The Milgram obedience studies, much like Zimbardo's Stanford Prison Experiment, are widely recognized, discussed, and also questioned because of the ethical issues it raises about improper treatment of research participants. And, like the Prison study, scholars question many critical experimental details that could result in a different, less-sensational interpretation of results (Reicher, Haslam, & Miller, 2014). Nonetheless, Milgram's research clearly provided a thought-provoking experimental setting to explore obedience. In the 50 years since, his method has been replicated across a number of cultural situations on different continents and although obedience rates vary a great deal, there usually is at least some level of conformity (Blass, 2012).

JOURNAL PROMPT

Research Ethics: Do you think that any discomfort experienced by research subjects in Milgram's studies of obedience is justified by the knowledge obtained from the work? Why or why not?

Attitudes and Actions

Phrases such as "everyone is entitled to his or her own opinion" reflect the generally accepted belief that people form their own attitudes. Most of us like to think that we develop our own opinions and are largely free from bias. In reality, it is likely that we have a *bias blind spot*; in other words, we tend to be blind to social influences on our beliefs (Pronin et al., 2002). Social psychologists have demonstrated that our beliefs and opinions are formed under the influence of the social groups in which we live. Think about the roles that political party affiliation has on attitudes. Do you consider yourself liberal or conservative? Have you joined a political movement because you identify with all the beliefs of the group? Or, is it the other way around: Does your membership in a political party shape your beliefs?

CONFORMING TO GROUP ATTITUDES To answer these questions, researchers have tested attitude changes on fictional political issues, such as a proposed law to pay generous unemployment benefits. When told the law was backed by Democrats, political conservatives denounced the proposal as too expensive, whereas the liberals supported it. When the experimenters presented the same proposal to participants as a Republican initiative, the conservatives were more approving, but liberals said that it did not pay enough. Thus, we can see that individuals were responding not only to the actual proposal (to pay an $800 monthly benefit) but also to the political party that proposed it (Cohen, 2003).

These trends are also at work in nonfictional politics, of course, provided two conditions are met. First, the issue at hand needs to be highly identified with the group. It is not likely that the opinions of either liberals or conservatives would be affected if they were told a proposal was supported by their university's badminton club; welfare programs and badminton have little, if any, connection to each other in most people's minds. However, there are clear differences in how the two political parties treat social programs. Second, there must be some ambiguity in the issue. If the proposal is clear—such as a complete ban on abortion or capital punishment—then the party label will have little influence. In fact, those issues are what lead many individuals to their party choice. By comparison, issues such as the exact amount of welfare payments are beyond what most voters concern themselves with, so they turn to the party for guidance.

GROUP POLARIZATION Sometimes groups affect attitudes through direct means, such as informing their members what the official party line is on issues such as abortion or the environment. At other times, dynamic effects of group membership intensify members' attitudes, thereby increasing the differences between groups. **Group polarization** *occurs when members of a group discuss characteristic attitudes of their group and, as a result, their views become stronger.* When this happens in two competing groups, their opinions become polarized, meaning that the two groups become further apart in their opinions (see Figure 15.2).

Why do groups become polarized? Several forces appear to be at work within a group, beginning with the simple fact that in group discussions, individuals hear the group's position articulated over and over again (Brauer et al., 1995). In the process, individuals are likely to hear more and more of the arguments for their

Figure 15.2 Group Polarization

Imagine a formal debate on a topic such as the legalization of marijuana for medical purposes. Over the course of the debate, members of the two sides are likely to become more distinct or polarized in their opinions—a process known as *group polarization*.

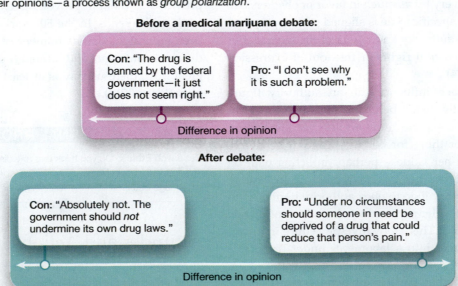

Before a medical marijuana debate:

Con: "The drug is banned by the federal government—it just does not seem right."

Pro: "I don't see why it is such a problem."

Difference in opinion

After debate:

Con: "Absolutely not. The government should *not* undermine its own drug laws."

Pro: "Under no circumstances should someone in need be deprived of a drug that could reduce that person's pain."

Difference in opinion

Figure 15.3 The Circle of Attitudes and Actions
We all know that attitudes can affect our behaviors, but did you know that your behavior can change your attitude?

position, but will probably encounter no support and certainly arguments against the other position. In a few cases, polarization may occur because the individuals want to identify closely with their group, almost as if it were a competition to be the most "group-like" individual in the discussion (Krizan & Baron, 2007).

COGNITIVE DISSONANCE Our actions, beliefs, and attitudes are not independent of each other. Sometimes a state of tension can exist between two thoughts or beliefs. For the woman who spent years pursuing admission into a prestigious law school, only to be rejected, she will experience distress because of the difference between her goals and the reality of the situation. To cope with the emotions, she might minimize the importance of attending that school claiming that the nearby state university, although not prestigious, is actually a better fit for her. This is an example of **cognitive dissonance**, *which occurs when an individual has two thoughts (cognitions) that are inconsistent with each other (dissonance) and, as a result, experiences motivation to reduce the discrepancy.* Although the tension caused by dissonance can range from devastating to mildly distressing, and some people will be less comfortable with it than others, the key point is that it provides

motivation for an individual to either change a behavior, a belief, or an attitude.

Consider another example to see how cognitive dissonance might work: A boy in a convenience store wants a pack of gum but has no money to purchase it. He notices the clerk is busy with other customers, so he decides to slip the gum into his pocket. Tension rises from cognitive dissonance; he knows his actions are in conflict with his belief that stealing is wrong. What can the boy do? One way to reduce the dissonance is to change the behavior and return the gum. However, what often happens is that the attitude changes. In this case, the boy might change his thoughts about stealing by thinking, "It is only a few cents so it won't affect this big company" or "Other kids in my neighborhood steal candy from here all the time." This transformation explains why cognitive dissonance is so important to the study of attitudes. The boy's attitude toward stealing loses some of its negativity ("It is not that bad") and the behavior stays the same (Gosling et al., 2006; McKimmie et al., 2009). Thus, it is not always the attitude that affects the behavior; sometimes the behavior can affect the attitude (see Figure 15.3). Before you read on, we recommend completing the Attitudes Scale in Table 15.3 for an additional look at the relationship between attitudes and behavior.

Table 15.3 Attitudes Scale

Rate the following items on a scale from 1 (strongly disagree) to 5 (strongly agree).

A1. World hunger is a serious problem that needs attention.	1 2 3 4 5
A2. Our country needs to address the growing number of homeless.	1 2 3 4 5
A3. The right to vote is one of the most valuable rights of American citizens.	1 2 3 4 5
A4. Our government should pay more attention to how its citizens want their taxes to be spent.	1 2 3 4 5
Total points for A1 to A4:	

Next rate whether you perform the following behavior on a regular basis using a scale of 1 (never) to 5 (on a regular and frequent basis).

B1. Do you personally do anything to lessen world hunger (e.g., donate food or money, volunteer time, write your representative)?	1 2 3 4 5
B2. Do you personally do anything to help the homeless?	1 2 3 4 5
B3. Did you vote in the most recent elections for which you were eligible to do so, including city and county elections?	1 2 3 4 5
B4. Do you personally convey your feelings to the government (e.g., write your representatives or participate in protests)?	1 2 3 4 5
Total points for B1 to B4:	

Now subtract your B score from your A score. Approximately 99% of people have a positive score, which indicates that their behavior does not exactly match their ideals. If you are like most people, you may feel some cognitive dissonance; the larger the number, the more dissonance you should feel. Thus, you should feel compelled to explain why the numbers are so different. You probably have some good reasons, starting with the fact that you only have so much time and limited resources to help. These explanations should help you reduce the cognitive dissonance.

SOURCE: "Attitudes Scale" adapted from "Bringing cognitive dissonance to the classroom" Adapted from "Bringing cognitive dissonance to the classroom" by D. M. Carkenord & J. Bullington (1993) *Teaching of Psychology, 20*(1), 41–43. Copyright © 1993 by Sage Publications. Reprinted by permission of Sage Publications.

Figure 15.4 Central and Peripheral Routes to Persuasion

There are two routes for persuasion. The central route provides information, while the peripheral route uses social psychological techniques such as the foot-in-the-door method to influence attitudes and behavior.

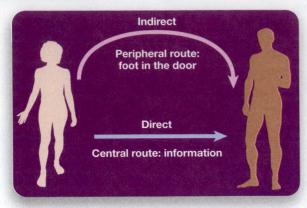

PERSUASION A clever person could introduce cognitive dissonance to persuade you to behave in a certain way. Imagine a representative from a charity who tries to increase donations by first getting people to express how important it is to fight hunger. Then, she can ask for a donation. If you just agreed that fighting hunger is important and realize that you have not done so, you will experience dissonance. This may work in favor of the charity if you decide to reduce the dissonance with a donation. On the other hand, you might reduce the dissonance by telling yourself you support other charities, you only have limited resources and have to take care of yourself first.

Whatever happened to persuading people by explaining the facts? Researchers have asked that question and, in the process, they have discovered that there are two paths to persuasion (Cacioppo et al., 1986; Petty et al., 1997). As Figure 15.4 shows, you can take the **central route (to persuasion)** *in which individuals take time, evaluate evidence, and use valid logic and arguments.* We like to think that most of our attitudes and beliefs are arrived at through the central route. In reality, though, we arrive at many of our beliefs through the persuasion techniques described. These make up the **peripheral route (to persuasion)**, *in which quick judgments are made based on limited evidence, and emotions and vague impressions are used more than logic.*

How do you know which path to take? Generally, when people believe a topic is important and when they have time to make decisions, the central route is more persuasive. Because this route involves more reasoning, it appeals to those with high intelligence and those who like to think about and solve problems. When topics that are less important to an individual and decisions are likely to be made quickly, the peripheral route may be more persuasive.

Two-Step Persuasion Techniques

The study of social influence clearly shows that our behaviors are flexible and can change to fit the social environment. It follows that these processes can in turn be used as tools for persuasion.

What do we know about persuasion?

The simplest way to demonstrate persuasion through social influence is through an old salesperson's trick called the **foot-in-the-door technique**, *which involves making a simple request followed by a more substantial request.* To the traveling salesmen of a few decades ago, literally getting one's foot in the door meant that a homeowner could not shut you out. In social psychology, it may involve any request for something simple—which is the metaphorical foot in the door—followed by a more substantial request (Burger, 1999; Cialdini, 2000).

To see this technique in action, refer to Figure 15.5. If we asked individuals to commit to an hour at a fundraising booth, we might be frustrated with the results. But if we ask someone for a small commitment—perhaps just signing a petition—it likely will be easier to convince that person to come back for a full hour later.

Taking an opposite approach to persuasion, the **door-in-the-face technique** *begins with a large request that is likely to be turned down, followed by a smaller request that is likely to be accepted.* Rather than asking someone to volunteer an hour of her time, ask her for a huge commitment—perhaps volunteering 4 days every week. The individual is likely to say no, but when given the chance to sign up for a more reasonable amount of time, she may feel relieved and jump at the chance.

How can science explain persuasion?

These techniques belong to a family of methods that involve a two-step sequence of requests. They may sound simple, but they clearly work when applied correctly (Dillard et al., 1984; Pascual & Guéguen, 2005). But the question remains: Why do they work?

Psychologist Robert Cialdini argues that these techniques work best when the individual is operating mindlessly. It generally requires willpower—some would call it *self-control*—to resist persuasion (Cialdini & Goldstein, 2004). However, willpower can only last so long. Imagine that the power of self-control is a finite form of energy: The first step in the request might deplete an individual's

Figure 15.5 The Two-Step Persuasion Technique to Encourage Community Service

The foot-in-the-door technique (top) starts with a small request and then moves on to a larger request. The door-in-the-face technique (bottom) does the reverse. It begins with a highly demanding request and then appears to settle for a much smaller one.

"Would you you sign a petition for this cause?"   "Sure!"

"Could you also give an hour of your time to volunteer for the cause?"

"Would you be willing to volunteer four days each week to help our cause?"

"Well, how about just spending an hour with us this Saturday afternoon?"

ability to willfully control their behavior, making it harder to resist requests. The second request comes before you have had time to "refuel" your self-control supply, making it more likely that you will comply.

This has been illustrated in experiments with the foot-in-the-door technique in which participants were randomly assigned to either an experimental condition where they completed a questionnaire about dietary habits, or to a control group that did not. Both groups were then asked to complete a universally challenging task for college students: Come up with arguments for why tuition should be increased. The members of the group that had completed the questionnaire about dietary habits apparently had depleted their self-regulatory energy; they produced significantly fewer arguments against the tuition increase

than did the control group. Sure enough, they were also more likely to comply with an additional request to keep a food diary for 2 weeks (Fennis, et al., 2009).

Can we critically evaluate this evidence?

The research shows that two-step compliance techniques really work, but what are their limitations? You probably would not be able to go out this afternoon and convince someone to contradict their deeply held values. Although as the classic studies in the module show us, social influence can lead people to behave in ways they object to and even experience distress over. Also, these techniques probably have limited effects when other paths of influence are in place. In other words, a boss might be able to lure a new employee to work overtime through a combination of authority and persuasion, but the employee may not be able to get a paid vacation from the boss.

Why is this relevant?

These two-step techniques can be applied to a number of situations. Cialdini and his colleagues showed that the foot-in-the-door technique could be used to recruit volunteers to work with juvenile delinquents (Cialdini et al., 1975), whereas other researchers were able to bolster support for a canned food drive (Burger & Caldwell, 2003) and a center for disabled children (Davis & Knowles, 1999) by making sequential requests. Those who work in marketing, advertising, political campaigning, and public

relations are constantly developing and implementing persuasion strategies. A first step is to identify the degree to which the message should be central or peripheral. In many cases, individuals who have little evidence to support their claim can encourage others to use peripheral processing by increasing emotional appeals and urging quick judgments. Anyone with a television is sure to have encountered the "act now" technique, which encourages individuals to act quickly without further deliberation. Although it does not affect everyone it reaches, this method is effective in swaying those who are close to purchasing a product to follow through. Similarly, messages that play on fear can overpower messages that are based solely on rational evidence, provided that the warnings seem like real threats (Nabi, 2002).

Module 15.1 Summary

15.1a Know . . . the key terminology associated with social influence:

central route (to persuasion)
cognitive dissonance
conformity
door-in-the-face technique
foot-in-the-door technique
group polarization
groupthink
mimicry
obedience
peripheral route (to persuasion)
social facilitation
social loafing
social norms
social psychology
social roles

15.1b Understand . . . why individuals conform to others' behaviors and thoughts.

At its most basic level, conforming begins with mimicry, in which people simply imitate others' behaviors. Mimicry seems to help form social bonds and encourages prosocial behavior. Conformity usually describes the way an individual's more complex beliefs and behaviors evolve to become like the group's. This change often happens unconsciously; in fact, we are said to have a bias blind spot that prevents us from seeing how our beliefs are shaped by group membership.

15.1c Understand . . . how individuals and groups can influence attitudes and behaviors.

In addition to conformity, attitudes and behaviors can be changed through persuasion techniques. The two-step

procedures of the foot-in-the-door and door-in-the-face techniques are applied by an individual who is intending to persuade or convince another person. In addition, unintentional phenomena exist. For example, in groupthink, the excitement of a group's progress leads individuals to think alike and to be overconfident in their group's decisions.

15.1d Apply . . . your knowledge of cognitive dissonance to see how well your beliefs match your behaviors.

The attitudes scale in Table 15.3 was designed to illustrate how cognitive dissonance arises along with the cognitive reactions that seem to reduce the dissonance, but it was only one example. Next time you find yourself facing a decision about your actions pay attention to how dissonance might be at work. It may be a conflict between deciding to eat healthier and then finding yourself staring at cartons of ice cream at the grocery store. What would you do to reduce the dissonance: Change your behavior by walking away from the temptation? Or help yourself to a pint and change your thoughts—you can start eating healthy tomorrow.

15.1e Analyze . . . whether social influence can lead people to behave in ways they believe are wrong.

This module described a number of ways that individuals change their behaviors, whether to fit a role, to comply with what the rest of the group is doing, or to follow instructions from authority figures. Examples from the Stanford Prison Experiment and Milgram's obedience studies demonstrate how all of these social influences can lead a person to behave much differently—even more cruelly—than the individual ever believed he could.

Module 15.1 Quiz

Know . . .

1. Social roles differ from norms in that:
   A. they are expectations for a specific individual in a situation.
   B. they are expectations for how nearly everyone should behave in a situation.
   C. they cannot be enforced.
   D. they are created by the individuals instead of being taught by society.

Understand . . .

2. When making a difficult decision, group members sometimes strive for agreement so as to avoid arguments, a phenomenon known as _____.
   A. social loafing
   B. obedience
   C. social facilitation
   D. groupthink

3. Sequential persuasion techniques like the foot-in-the-door technique may work because they:
   A. rely on authority figures.
   B. wear down one's sense of self-control.
   C. rely on deception.
   D. offer no alternatives.

Apply . . .

4. Kyle is an independent filmmaker who has always believed that big Hollywood movies are garbage. Recently, however, he agreed to work on a big-budget Hollywood movie because the pay was good. Now he tells his friends, "Not all Hollywood movies are that bad." Kyle's change in attitude is likely the result of _____.
   A. cognitive dissonance
   B. conformity
   C. groupthink
   D. group polarization

Analyze . . .

5. Which of the following is not a key contributor to social loafing?
   A. A group member believes that her effort will not help the group performance.
   B. A teammate believes that success might be rewarding to others in the group, but not to himself.
   C. An individual actively sabotages the group's performance out of spite.
   D. One person sees that the others are not putting forth much effort.

Module 15.2   Social Cognition

Learning Objectives

15.2a   Know . . . the key terminology associated with social cognition.

15.2b   Understand . . . how we form first impressions and how these impressions influence us.

15.2c   Apply . . . your understanding of the different ways we explain our own behavior versus the behavior of others.

15.2d   Analyze . . . the common belief that stereotypes can only be derogatory.

In 2014, the news seemed to be filled with one specific type of tragic event and its aftermath—police shooting of unarmed men. The individual stories unfolded differently, but in many cases it involved a male of a racial or ethnic minority group and a police officer who feared the man was reaching for a weapon. The public discourse becomes heated with accusations of racism among police pitted against the need for police officers to defend themselves in dangerous situations. For this module on social psychology, we will assume that the overwhelming majority of the population would prefer peaceful resolutions where no one is harmed. Yet we also assume that the majority believes law enforcement is necessary in our society and believes that police officers are not inherently bad people. How then might social psychology work towards preventing these tragic events?

Several processes relevant to social psychology can help explain their occurrence: first impressions, the difference between quick intuitive thoughts versus deliberate judgments, and attitudes and beliefs about race. A better understanding of these factors has led to changes in training and police procedures. However, recent history tells us there is still more to learn.

Social psychologists have increasingly focused on *social cognition*, which is the study of cognitions (perceptions, thoughts, and beliefs) an individual may have about social contexts (other people, groups, or situations). There is an underlying theme in social-cognitive research that there are two varieties of thought. **Intuitive thought** *is quick,* *effortless, automatic thinking (in fact, it requires great effort when you try to control it).* Intuitions tend to be based on associations; an individual encounters a person or situation and some things just "pop" into mind. In contrast, **deliberative thought** *is a more careful, effortful, and rational process.* In contrast with intuitive thought, it is slower, and usually takes place one step at a time (Chaiken & Trope, 1999; Kahneman, 2003; Todorov et al., 2005).

Intuitive thinking precedes deliberation. Consider a situation in which a person is trying to control his temper at work because he feels he is the only person doing his job. What happens when this man discovers a coworker got promoted before him? His intuitive thought—that automatic impulse—might be that he is justified in yelling at the boss and insulting the coworker. His intuitive thought may very well be correct that he should be angry, but then deliberative thought begins. This type of thought reminds him that what he says and does will eventually mean keeping or losing his job. If he goes overboard, he might just get fired.

The distinction between intuitive and deliberative thought is apparent in the ways we form impressions and beliefs about other people.

Person Perception

Person perception *refers to the processes by which individuals form judgments and categorize other people* (Kenny, 2004). It begins immediately in our social encounters and is guided by our past experiences with others. The power of first impressions can be explained by the automatic side of social cognition. Upon first encountering someone, we have very little information on which to evaluate him or her. As a consequence, we rely on **schemas**—*clusters of knowledge and expectations about individuals and groups* (schemas were also covered in Module 7.3). A person's gender, race, and style of dress all activate schemas, and these schemas automatically bring certain traits to mind.

THIN SLICES OF BEHAVIOR Two remarkable aspects of first impressions are how fast they are formed and how accurate they can be. Imagine this scenario: You walk into a classroom for a review session for the final exam. After 30 seconds, you realize that you are early, and the previous class has not yet been dismissed. Nonetheless, in the 30 seconds that elapsed you have already had time to size up the professor; she has made her first impression on you. As she leaves the classroom, a student assistant announces that he will be distributing course evaluation forms. As the forms are passed down the aisle, you take one. Of course, you will not fill it out—that would be dishonest. But what if you did?

The immediate act of forming first impressions has been researched through a technique called **thin slices**—*basing judgments of others on very limited information.* In studies of this process a researcher might present short video clips or even a still photo of an individual—these are the "thin slices" of behavior that participants use to make judgments of personal qualities. These judgments can be compared to the judgments made by others who have much more information—either because they saw more of the video or, in our example, because they attended the course for an entire semester.

Using the thin-slices method, researchers found that participants who watched 30 seconds of a college lecture (without sound) gave instructor ratings that were remarkably similar to the end-of-semester ratings of that same class (Ambady & Rosenthal, 1993; Tom et al., 2010). Additional research has shown even higher levels of

Based on these photos, would you expect these instructors to be interesting or boring? Easy or challenging? Well-prepared or off-the-cuff? Thin-slices research tells us that it takes less than 30 seconds of video to decide—and to be reasonably accurate.

agreement when rating high school teachers and using even thinner slices—even as short as 6 seconds (Ambady & Rosenthal, 1993)! You may find it surprising that, outside of the classroom, research participants were able to make reasonably accurate judgments of trustworthiness, competence, likeability, and aggressiveness in as little as half a second of exposure to a photograph (Willis & Todorov, 2006). Further exposure to a face does not change ratings much, although it does have the tendency to increase the judges' confidence in their ratings. In other words, the impression is more or less the same, but the judges feel they have more reason to believe it.

Taken together, thin-slice research demonstrates just how quickly impressions are formed. The process of person perception on first encountering someone often yields accurate information about what he is like—but, of course, first impressions are not always the most reliable. Furthermore, relying too much on information from first impressions can negatively affect how relationships develop.

SELF-FULFILLING PROPHECIES AND OTHER EFFECTS OF FIRST IMPRESSIONS First impressions certainly produce quick and long-lasting effects on how we perceive others. Simple cues, such as facial appearance, have been shown to influence everything from how a jury treats a defendant to how people will vote. For example, one study asked participants to act as jurors and evaluate evidence against a defendant. These participants were less likely to find a defendant guilty when shown a photograph of a person who simply appeared more trustworthy (Porter et al., 2010). Participants in another study made judgments about the competence of congressional candidates just by looking at their faces, and those judgments predicted a surprisingly high 70% of the election outcomes (Todorov et al., 2005).

An individual's impression of others can also lead to a **self-fulfilling prophecy**, *which occurs when a first impression affects the observer's behavior and, as a result, the first impression comes true*. In fact, this phenomenon has been under scientific investigation for a long time in the context of teacher–student interactions. When teachers have high expectations of a student, they behave differently toward that student: Teachers will tend to spend less time addressing behavior (especially for boys), present more challenging work, and give more reinforcement and constructive criticism than they will for a student whom they perceive to have less promise (Jussim, 1986). This finding holds true whether the teachers form their own expectations about a student or researchers give teachers randomly assigned high or low achievement test scores for the students (Brophy & Good, 1970; Rosenthal & Jacobson, 1968). The self-fulfilling prophecy is complete when students with low expectations placed on them receive lower grades from their teachers and lower scores on standardized tests because of this differential treatment. Interestingly, self-fulfilling prophecies are not always the product of incorrect first impressions; they might even occur years into a relationship. This possibility was illustrated in a survey that asked adolescents and their parents about the teen's marijuana use (Lamb & Crano, 2014). The sample included a large number of teens who had never tried it; in some cases, the parents correctly believed this, but in other cases, the parents did not. In a follow-up survey a year later, the adolescents in this second group were significantly more likely to have tried marijuana at least once.

Thin Slices: Describe an example in which the social psychological concept of thin slices was confirmed in your experience, and an experience in which a thin-slice impression proved to be false.

ATTRIBUTIONS In some sense, all people are armchair psychologists, describing and explaining behavior in an intuitive and unscientific way. *Attributions* are the explanations we make about the causes of behavior. They tend to start out as automatic, intuitive explanations. Think about what might happen in a close call while driving: As you drive along, a car suddenly swerves in front of you, requiring you to slam on the brakes and turn the wheel sharply. Quick—what is the first thing that comes to mind about the other driver? That is how quickly most attributions are initially formed.

To shed light on how attributions work, psychologists distinguish two main types. First, with an **internal attribution** *(also known as a dispositional attribution), the observer explains the actor's behavior as a result of some intrinsic quality of the actor*: He is lazy, she wants attention, and so on (see Figure 15.6). Second, with an **external attribution** *(also known as a situational attribution), the observer explains the actor's behavior as the result of the social or environmental context* (Heider, 1958).

Truthfully, most behaviors are a complex blend of disposition and situation; nonetheless, we have clear biases in the type of attribution we use when we explain why others behave as they do. Specifically, we often commit the **fundamental attribution error**—*a tendency to make internal attributions for others' behaviors while ignoring external influences* (Ross, 1977). Think about that driver swerving in traffic. Which kind of personal qualities would correspond to bad driving? He must be self-centered, hostile, and an all-around terrible driver. These are all internal, dispositional qualities and they might be true, but they might not. But did you even consider external causes—perhaps a blown-out tire? Most often we will not, unless we actually take the time to make a more thoughtful attribution.

When explaining our own behavior, our attributions are much more generous. For example, if we swerve into

Figure 15.6 Internal and External Attributions

Internal attributions are based on qualities or actions of the individual, whereas external attributions focus on the context in which the individual is situated.

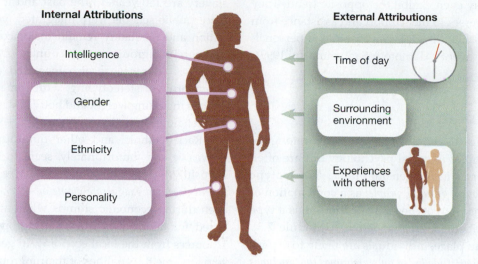

Internal Attributions

- Intelligence
- Gender
- Ethnicity
- Personality

External Attributions

- Time of day
- Surrounding environment
- Experiences with others

the adjacent lane while driving, we are likely to blame an object in the road or someone else recklessly trying to merge onto the highway. These kinds of external attributions prevent us from putting the blame on ourselves, a phenomenon known as the **self-serving bias**: *We will use internal attributions for ourselves when we do something well, but external attributions when we fail or commit errors.* If we successfully avoid an accident, we are likely to credit it to our alertness and driving skill—both internal, dispositional attributions that led to a successful outcome. This

bias may seem a little selfish, but there is reason to believe it contributes to well-being. For example, people with severe forms of depression and anxiety appear much less susceptible to the self-serving bias—by perhaps as much as 50% (Mezulis et al., 2004). Thus, the self-serving bias might actually reduce our chances for psychological distress. Apply the process of attribution by completing the activity in Table 15.4.

Finally, we should point out that fundamental attribution error is largely a cultural phenomenon. Although it

Table 15.4 Description of Self and Others

First, consider your own personality and behaviors. For each of these 10 rows, put an *X* by the one personality trait that best describes your behavior. If you cannot pick one, put the *X* beside "Depends on the situation."

Next, think about a classmate. For each row, put an *O* by the one personality trait that best describes your classmate, or put the *O* beside "Depends on the situation."

1. Serious	Joyful	Depends on the situation
2. High-energy	Low-key	Depends on the situation
3. Plans for the future	Lives for the present	Depends on the situation
4. Reserved	Emotionally expressive	Depends on the situation
5. Dignified and formal	Casual and relaxed	Depends on the situation
6. Skeptical of others	Trusting	Depends on the situation
7. Cautious	Bold and daring	Depends on the situation
8. Conscientious and orderly	Carefree and spontaneous	Depends on the situation
9. Argumentative	Agreeable	Depends on the situation
10. Realistic	Idealistic	Depends on the situation
Add up the *X*s in these two columns here: _____		Add up the *X*s in this column _____
Add up the *O*s in these two columns here: _____		Add up the *O*s in this column _____

Finally, compare the number of *X*s and *O*s on the left side of the table. Did you have more *O*s than *X*s? According to research, most people from the United States will have more *O*s on the left side because they tend to attribute others' behavior to personality traits. The same individuals should have more *X*s than *O*s on the right side of the table because of a tendency to see one's own behavior as situational. Compare your scores with others in your class—especially with those of classmates from cultures other than your own.

SOURCE: "Description of Self and Others" from "Behavior as seen by the actor and as seen by the observer" Adapted from Nisbett, R. E., Caputo, C., Leganta, P., & Marecek, J. (1973). Behavior as seen by an actor and as seen by the observer. *Journal of Personality and Social Psychology, 27*(2), 154–164.

is easy to find examples in the United States, people from East Asia are much more likely to consider the situation when making attributions (Choi et al., 1999). In fact, people from Japan may even exhibit the opposite trend: They may attribute successes to the support and assistance from family and peers while downplaying the role of personality, intelligence, or talent (Akimoto & Sanbonmatsu, 1999).

Stereotypes, Prejudice, and Discrimination

Stereotypes, prejudice, and discrimination are among the most important topics in social psychology but are often misunderstood terms in the general public. A **stereotype** *is a set of beliefs about a group of people*; as a combination of ideas and opinions, stereotypes may be viewed as a type of schema (described in greater detail in Module 7.3). With stereotypes in place, individuals are likely to experience **prejudice**, *an attitude based on stereotypes that includes emotions and value judgments as well*. Finally, **discrimination** *is a behavior based on prejudice*.

There are some connections between stereotypes and attributions. Think about a rival high school or college sports team. The other team would be considered the **outgroup**—*a collection of people who are perceived as different*. The outgroup does not have to be disliked or in competition with your own group; just the perception of difference is enough to make the distinction between groups. Your own classmates, who make up your ingroup, are perceived as having more positive qualities. Thus, there is a similarity between the self-serving bias and what we call the **ingroup bias**, *which occurs when we attribute positive qualities to the social group we belong to*.

Given the pervasive nature of prejudice and the profound consequences it can have, it is important to have a thorough understanding of ways to identify and measure prejudice and its social and cognitive origins.

SOCIAL TRENDS IN STEREOTYPES AND PREJUDICE
Everyone is familiar with the legacy of racial prejudice in the United States. Arguments over the legitimacy of slavery are 150 years in the past and it has been decades since public schools were integrated, yet racial discrimination and inequality remain major concerns among all demographic groups in this country (Doherty, 2013). The emphasis on race has also increased our awareness of other forms of stereotyping, with some of the major categories including weight and body size, sexual orientation, and religious affiliation.

Racial, ethnic, and other outgroup stereotypes are pervasive and, unfortunately, seem to thrive in times of hardship. **Scapegoating** *occurs when people use stereotypes to misplace and exaggerate blame on others*. This is regularly seen during economic slumps when an outgroup is targeted for taking jobs from the ingroup or for draining resources from the local economy. In general, people tend to overvalue the qualities of their ingroup and undervalue the qualities of other groups (Cialdini & Richardson, 1980).

White people in the United States are increasingly concerned about whether they appear prejudiced (Plant et al., 2010) and are more likely than ever to say that racism is a problem (Jones, 2008). Today young African Americans and Latinos are more likely to obtain diplomas and higher education degrees than even a generation ago. They are also expected to live longer than the preceding generations and are more likely to achieve middle-class socioeconomic status, including a comfortable income and home ownership. Despite the positive message that these trends send, racial and ethnic differences persist in the United States. For example, Africans and African Americans experience more physical and aggressive treatment from police (Gabrielson et al., 2014).

Even among those who publicly denounce prejudice and discrimination, there are some who may be trying to disguise their true feelings and still others who are

---

Myths in Mind

All Stereotypes Are Based on Negative Characteristics

The stereotypes that people are concerned most about are usually based on negative characteristics. However, a hidden danger of stereotypes is found in benevolent (well-intentioned) stereotyping that emphasizes desirable attributes, such as being good at math. Benevolent stereotypes have been studied a great deal with regard to sexism. For example, researchers have distinguished between *hostile sexism*, or stereotypes that have negative views of one or both sexes, and *benevolent sexism*, which includes positive views of one or both sexes (Glick & Fiske, 1996, 2001). To examine this concept in the social context, consider the somewhat dated saying that women are "the fairer sex." A person using this phrase may mean it as a compliment, implying that women are virtuous and empathetic. As a number of psychologists have pointed out, even well-intended stereotypes can place restrictions on an individual's behavior. By considering them to be "virtuous," women may be held to different standards than men in a variety of ways ranging from leadership ability to sexuality. As a result, they may be passed over for promotions at work (particularly when the type of job requires assertiveness) and be seen as dependent on men for money or protection (Glick & Fiske, 1996, 2001). Thus, negative effects of stereotyping can occur even when the intentions of an individual may have been complimentary.

unaware of their own subtle prejudices. For example, researchers have found subtle but reliable differences in facial expressions and brain activity when both Black and White participants were shown pictures of both Black and White faces, even among those who express little or no prejudice (Cunningham et al., 2004; Eberhardt, 2005; Vanman et al., 2004). Consistent with research on thin slices, in another study, Black participants could identify which White actors in a silent videotape were more prejudiced than others—after only 20 seconds of viewing (Richeson & Shelton, 2005)!

Records of police encounters over the past 30 years confirm what many in the United States have long claimed: Police use more aggressive techniques on minority suspects than White suspects (Inn, Wheeler, & Sparling, 1977; Smith, 2004; Weitzer & Tuch, 2004). In fact, between 2010 and 2012, Black males were 21 times more likely to die in police confrontations than White suspects (Gabrielson et al., 2014).

The lesson should be a powerful one: Even if one abhors prejudice, she may implicitly hold the stereotypes that lead to prejudice and discrimination. As research with police shooting shows, it is important to acknowledge implicit stereotypes and automatic judgments, because otherwise the results may be tragic.

Working the Scientific Literacy Model

Explicit Versus Implicit Measures of Prejudice

Research has left us with a contradiction: Public opinion says that prejudice is unpopular, yet social scientists and psychologists have produced data demonstrating it occurs quite frequently. How could this be?

What do we know about measuring prejudice?

One explanation is that members of the public have simply learned to conceal their prejudice to be polite or politically correct. Another intriguing possibility is that some people are deceiving themselves; perhaps they harbor prejudice but do not realize it. Is that even possible? To address this question, psychologists have distinguished between measures of explicit and implicit prejudice. **Explicit prejudice** *occurs when individuals confess to or openly demonstrate their stereotypes.* **Implicit prejudice** *includes forms of stereotyping and prejudice that are kept silent, either intentionally or because individuals are unaware of their own prejudices* (Greenwald & Banaji, 1995; Nosek, 2007). The methods of measuring implicit prejudice are trickier, yet psychologists can infer that it exists based on the research cited earlier.

How can science study implicit prejudice?

One means of measuring implicit prejudice is the Implicit Associations Test (IAT; Greenwald et al., 1998). The IAT measures how fast people can respond to images or words flashed on a computer screen. To complete the test, a person uses two fingers and two computer buttons. As Figure 15.7 shows, one button represents two ideas—that is where the associations come into play. In round 1, if the computer presents a White face, the subject should press the button on the right. If the subject sees a positive word, such as "peace," he should press the same button. In other words, White features and pleasant words are paired on one button. The other button pairs Black individuals with negative words. With these associations, it takes an average of 800 milliseconds (four-fifths of a second) to press the correct button.

Round 2 rearranges the associations. If the participant sees a White person, he is still supposed to press the right button, but this time he also uses that button for negative words, such as "pain" or "war." If the computer presents a Black person or a positive word, such as "peace," the subject is to press the left button. In this situation, subjects took 1,015 milliseconds to press the correct button, or more than one-fifth of a second longer than in round 1.

Why does it take longer to respond when there is a Black/positive button than when there is a Black/negative button? The researchers reasoned that our racial schemas associate more negativity with Blacks than with Whites. Thus, even if those associations are implicit—in other words, the individual is not aware of those associations—they still affect the participants' responses.

Can we critically evaluate this evidence?

One of the first questions we should ask is whether the second round takes longer because participants are already used to the first round. The creators of the IAT have controlled for this by placing practice rounds before the actual tests. In addition, they have randomized the order in which the two key rounds have been presented and found that the order does not matter: The averages for each set of associations is the same whether they come first or second. The IAT produces reliable results, but some psychologists have questioned its validity: Is the IAT really a measure of prejudice? Racial stereotypes are familiar to virtually all members of a culture, so perhaps the IAT is actually measuring what an individual knows about stereotypes rather than her beliefs about them. In response, the developers of the IAT point to evidence from dozens of studies showing that the IAT predicts discriminatory behavior better than self-reported prejudice (Greenwald et al., 2015).

Figure 15.7 The IAT Procedure

There are two main conditions in the IAT. To complete the first (a), participants must use one button to identify Black faces and negative words and another button to identify White faces and positive words. In the other main condition (b), the positive and negative words are switched to be paired with the other race (Black/positive and White/negative). Average response times are faster when Black is paired with negative words and White is paired with positive words (c). Is this a sign of hidden prejudice?

(a)

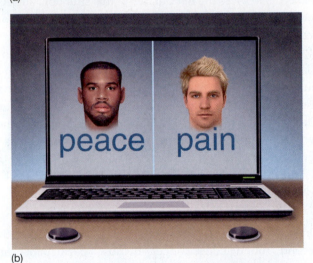

(b)

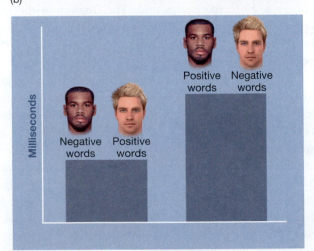

(c)

The split-second differences in the IAT may be related to officers' increased use of deadly force with Black suspects, including cases where the suspect is unarmed. Here, a police officer undergoes virtual reality training designed to reduce shooting errors.

Why is this relevant?

The consequences of a laboratory computer task pale in comparison to a tragedy such as the shooting of an unarmed person. However, there is a connection between the two: Both situations involve a split-second decision in which race is known to have an effect. Since the introduction of the IAT, psychologists have developed other quick-decision methods to study how officers make decisions to use deadly force, often focusing on the role of race (James et al., 2014). These tasks have become increasingly realistic over time, such as one recent study that attempted the following:

- Rather than using pictures, they used interactive videos in which characters appeared and reach into pockets for either a weapon or something harmless like a phone.
- Rather than presenting an isolated image on a computer screen, the videos are presented in high-crime or low-crime neighborhoods
- Instead of measuring reactions by the press of a keyboard button, researchers measured responses with an electronic gun similar to a video game controller (Cox et al., 2014).

These types of advances not only allow for better understanding of how the decisions are made, but they also provide practical guidance for law enforcement. For example, many police departments require cadets to complete dozens of hours of training related to shoot/don't shoot decisions in simulation settings and sometimes even with actors armed with foam pellet guns. Most important, the data show that extensive training works for police officers; even student volunteers in the lab can be trained to reduce shooting errors through such means (Correl et al., 2007; Biggs et al., 2015).

Module 15.2 Summary

15.2a Know . . . the key terminology associated with social cognition:

deliberative thought
discrimination
explicit prejudice
external (situational) attribution
fundamental attribution error
implicit prejudice
ingroup bias
internal (dispositional) attribution
intuitive thought
outgroup
person perception
prejudice
scapegoating
schemas
self-fulfilling prophecy
self-serving bias
stereotype
thin slices

15.2b Understand . . . how we form first impressions and how these impressions influence us.

We quickly form impressions, even when only thin slices of behavior are available to us. These impressions can be surprisingly accurate, but in some cases they may lead to self-fulfilling prophecies.

15.2c Apply . . . your understanding of the different ways we explain our own behavior versus the behavior of others.

It is probably not possible for us to just watch someone behave without quickly thinking of an explanation for his or her actions. That does not mean we are correct, of course. The fundamental attribution error reflects a bias to attribute others' behavior to external sources whereas the self-serving bias allows us to take credit for the good things we experience and avoid responsibility for the bad. If you have not done so already, try the activity in Table 15.4 to see these processes in action.

15.2d Analyze . . . the common belief that stereotypes can only be derogatory.

Stereotypes can stem from good intentions—even an attempt to compliment can be based on an assumption about group membership. However, referring to women as the "fairer sex" or assuming that someone is intelligent or athletic can be insulting and produce other negative effects.

Module 15.2 Quiz

Know . . .

1. _____ occurs when individuals misplace or exaggerate blame on members of another group.
   A. Implicit prejudice
   B. The fundamental attribution error
   C. Thin slice
   D. Scapegoating

Understand . . .

2. Which of the following statements about thin slices is most accurate?
   A. Thin slices lead to inaccurate impressions of others.
   B. In many instances, lasting and often accurate impressions of others form in just a few moments.
   C. Thin-slice impressions are 100% accurate.
   D. Thin slices work only when rating the attractiveness of others.

3. Unconscious forms of prejudice are thought to be measured with the implicit associations test. This test is based on:
   A. the types of words people typically make up when they see a person of a specific race.
   B. how long it takes people to respond to positive or negative words along with Black or White faces.
   C. changes in heart rate that accompany photos of people from different racial backgrounds.
   D. increased activity in the emotional centers of the brain that are associated with specific races.

Apply . . .

4. Donald, once poor, inherited $5 million and decided to donate $1,000 to a local charity. Donald believes he took this step because he is a kind and generous man. Donald might be demonstrating _____.
   A. the fundamental attribution error
   B. hindsight bias
   C. self-serving bias
   D. cognitive dissonance

Analyze . . .

5. Which of the following statements about stereotypes and prejudice is false?
   A. Stereotypes can be expressed outwardly and very explicitly.
   B. All stereotypes are of negative characteristics.
   C. Stereotypes are often experienced implicitly.
   D. Prejudice has become increasingly unpopular in the United States.

Module 15.3   Helping and Harming Others

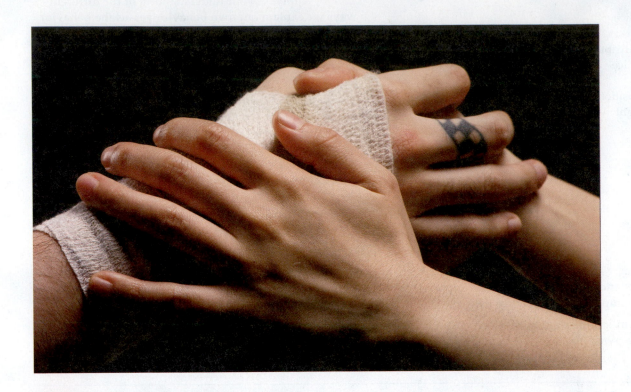

 ## Learning Objectives

15.3a Know . . . the key terminology in the study of helping and aggression.

15.3b Understand . . . cognitive and biological theories of helping.

15.3c Understand . . . biopsychosocial influences on aggression.

15.3d Apply . . . your knowledge to assess your own levels of altruism.

15.3e Analyze . . . the role of biological factors and testosterone in aggressive behavior.

If you have ever witnessed someone getting a severe injury—even a fictional character on a screen—you may have winced, gritted your teeth, or even moaned with sympathy pain. It is a reaction that seems to be hard-wired into the human nervous system. However, if you had never actually felt pain before, do you think you could possibly be sensitive to pain in others? It seems plausible that, without having personal experience of being jabbed with a needle or stubbing a toe, it would be impossible to recognize pain in others.

As it happens, there is a rare group of people who we can ask. These individuals have a condition called congenital insensitivity to pain (CIP)—a genetic condition that disables

components of the nervous system specialized to sense and perceive pain. For most of us, a broken bone or severe burn would be sheer agony, but these injuries would barely register for someone who has CIP, and it would be a sense of pressure rather than pain. Remarkably, even people with CIP actually share in others' pain that they could not possibly feel. As long as they can see and hear emotional cues that someone is suffering, they have the same kind of "sympathy pain" that everyone else does (Danziger et al., 2009). That fact that the lack of pain perception in CIP does not affect sympathy pain suggests that sympathy is an innate part of the human nervous system. Sympathy is one of many capacities we have to help survive in complex, social groups.

Group membership is so fundamental to human experience that it is difficult to imagine life without family, friends, coworkers, or a community. But for any of these groups to function effectively, the members have to figure out how to get along. Prosocial behaviors are those that promote social functioning, group cohesion, or the well-being of individual members. Sometimes these behaviors are easy and enjoyable, at other times they are responses to emergencies, and sometimes serious challenges must be overcome to demonstrate prosocial behaviors. In contrast, antisocial behaviors may serve one individual or a small group at the expense of the greater community. In this module, we examine the personal and group qualities that make coexistence peaceful or tumultuous, as well as the extent to which people will go to help or hurt one another.

Empathy, Altruism, and Helping

Humans are motivated to behave in prosocial ways for a number of reasons: We have **empathy**, *the ability to take others' perspective and imagine what thoughts and feelings must arise from their situations*. These lead to feelings of compassion or distress; we often want to ease others' suffering as we would our own. We live in communities where empathic feelings become the established norms: Those who do not show empathy and concern are seen as troubled and antisocial (Batson, 2007; Jensen et al., 2014). Various psychological processes, shown in Figure 15.8, lead to empathic regard for others.

SOCIAL-COGNITIVE APPROACHES TO HELPING   The capacity for empathy would seem to be a prerequisite for helping others; the more empathy an individual reports, the more likely the person is to help. This is true even if helping requires little effort (Davis & Knowles, 1999). At the individual level, the willingness to help depends on the situation—some situations seem more urgent than others—and it can depend on the individual—some individuals regularly feel more empathy than others. As you

might expect, research shows that our empathy extends more toward those in our own groups (Hewstone et al., 2002). Even so, this finding does not mean that we always refuse to help people outside of our groups. When strangers or members of other groups are in need, people are more likely to help when they can find similarities or likeable qualities. Also, individuals who feel they have a strong, secure bond with family and friends seem to be more likely to help others regardless of their group membership (Mikulincer & Shaver, 2005; Sturmer et al., 2005).

Much of our helping behavior can be explained by **social-exchange theory**, *which states that an individual will consider the costs and benefits of helping another before she acts*. This approach treats helping much like a financial arrangement between individuals and society. The currency in these arrangements is not necessarily monetary, however—benefits may include positive feelings and social approval for one's deeds. Also, the cost and benefit ratios of these arrangements can be highly variable. Simple acts of charity, such as dropping coins in the Salvation Army collection pot, bring the benefit of feeling good about oneself at little cost. By comparison, a decision to donate a kidney to a loved one involves weighing considerable physical and emotional costs and risks against the great benefits of increasing someone's longevity and easing that person's suffering.

Helping behavior can also take the form of **altruism**—*helping others in need without receiving or expecting reward for doing so*. From a social-exchange perspective, altruism is a bad deal; you risk or give more than

Wesley Autrey leapt in front of a New York subway train to save a complete stranger, Cameron Hollopeter, who had fallen on the tracks after having a seizure. Autrey literally covered Hollopeter and held him still between the tracks as the train cars rolled just inches above his body. His heroism received coverage from the network television news and the major newspapers, and he was invited to appear on several talk shows. Autrey's act was an amazing example of altruism, as he could not have possibly considered any benefit to himself at the moment of his brave act.

Figure 15.8 Factors Contributing to Empathy

According to Batson and colleagues (2007), empathy stems from our capacity to perceive that another person is in need and to value that individual's welfare. Empathy can be expressed with or without the ability to actually adopt the perspective of another person.

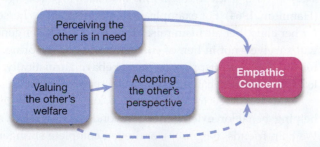

Table 15.5 A Self-Report Altruism Scale

Rate each item in the far left column on a scale ranging from 1 (Never) to 5 (Very Often). Then add up the points to calculate your total score.

	Never	Once	More than once	Often	Very often
1. I have given directions to a stranger.	1	2	3	4	5
2. I have given money to a charity.	1	2	3	4	5
3. I have given money to a stranger who needed it (or asked me for it).	1	2	3	4	5
4. I have donated goods or clothes to a charity.	1	2	3	4	5
5. I have done volunteer work for a charity.	1	2	3	4	5
6. I have donated blood.	1	2	3	4	5
7. I have helped carry a stranger's belongings (books, parcels, etc.).	1	2	3	4	5
8. I have delayed an elevator and held the door open for a stranger.	1	2	3	4	5
9. I have allowed someone to go ahead of me in a lineup (at photocopy machine, in the supermarket).	1	2	3	4	5
10. I have let a neighbor whom I didn't know too well borrow an item of some value to me (e.g., a dish, tools, etc.)	1	2	3	4	5
11. I have helped a classmate who I did not know that well with a homework assignment when my knowledge was greater than his or hers.	1	2	3	4	5
12. I have helped an acquaintance to move households.	1	2	3	4	4

SOURCE: "The Self-Report Altruism Scale" (slightly adapted) From "The altruistic personality and the Self-Report Altruism Scale" by J. Rushton, R. D. Chrisjohn, & G. Fekken. (1981) *Personality and Individual Differences, 2*(4), 293–302.

The average score from a sample of twelve 24-year-old college students was 39. How did you match up?

you can expect to personally gain. To some degree, we can explain altruism using the **social responsibility norm**: *Society teaches us that the value of helping goes beyond the benefits an individual might receive, and that individuals who cannot help themselves require special help.* With this norm in place, people feel compelled to help children, the elderly, and those with medical crises (See Table 15.5).

BIOLOGICAL APPROACHES TO HELPING Empathy is evident from various physiological processes (Decety, 2010). A specialized type of nerve cell called a *mirror neuron* may play a supporting role in empathic behavior. **Mirror neurons** *respond to the actions and expressions of others and are correlated with the ability to understand another's intentions and emotions* (Kaplan & Iacoboni, 2006). A review of brain imaging studies show that the mirror neuron system is activated during the experience of empathy, and damage to this system is correlated with decreased empathy (Baird et al., 2011). Similarly, the neurons involved in pain perception are active when an individual sees another in pain, or even when he just imagines the pain (Minio-Paluello et al., 2006). Mirror neurons are interesting in their own right, but much remains to be learned about whether and how essential they are to empathy and other complex social behaviors (Hickok, 2014).

Although we have described empathy as a human behavior, we should point out that many other species can share others' emotions, at least to some extent. Few would argue that laboratory mice write inspired poetry to share their emotional states with their litter mates, but there is clear evidence that when one member of the group experiences pain, the others can learn from and become distressed by it (Panksepp & Panksepp, 2013). This *emotional contagion*—the spreading of an emotion from one member of a group to the others—is likely to be one of the evolutionary roots behind humans' ability to empathize. Empathy is one thing, but what about the evolutionary roots of altruism? If an organism sacrifices itself for another, it will not be able to pass on the genes that influence altruistic behavior. Survival and reproduction are keys to evolutionary success, so behaviors that put individuals at risk must ultimately serve these purposes.

The concept of *costly signaling* explains acts of altruism as signals to others that the helper would be a valuable mate (McAndrew, 2002). Helping others can be risky, but it can also be a way to assert that the individual doing the helping is healthy, capable, and dependable. These are all good qualities for a mate, and so altruism might ultimately increase the chances of passing on one's genes. Evolutionary processes can also boost altruism through **kin selection**, *which predicts that altruistic behavior is most likely to occur when it benefits the individual's genetic legacy* (Hamilton, 1964). For example, if a mother sacrifices herself for her child, her altruism raises the chances that her genes will survive—not in her, of course, but in her offspring. It follows that her offspring will also behave altruistically, at least to the extent that altruistic behavior is inherited.

One challenge to the process of kin selection is that helping behavior extends well beyond genetic relatives. We help friends, neighbors, and even complete strangers.

Reciprocal altruism can be found among vampire bats. When adult bats return to the cave after gathering blood from their hosts, locating their hungry offspring can be challenging. Bats will feed unrelated offspring if they cannot find their own brood—an example of reciprocal altruism.

Reciprocal altruism *refers to helping behavior extended to nongenetic relatives, with the possibility that the favor may be later returned* (Trivers, 1971). The phenomenon of reciprocal altruism may sound like something uniquely human, but it also occurs in nonhuman species.

FAILING TO HELP: THE BYSTANDER EFFECT If you saw someone who was at risk for assault, would you intervene and try to prevent it? We all like to think that we would, but all too often people do not. This is the **bystander effect** (also known as *bystander apathy*), *the observation that an individual is less likely to help when they perceive that others are not helping*. In the following video Under the Influence of Others, we learn about the bystander effect as explained by psychologist Sam Sommers. We also learn about the concept of merging individual identity with group identity from psychologist William Swan, and what his research tells us about behavior in groups.

Watch UNDER THE INFLUENCE OF OTHERS

In one of the first studies of bystander apathy, an individual volunteer was ushered into a small room while one to three other research participants (who were actually research confederates) were said to be waiting in similar rooms to have a conversation over intercoms. As they waited, one confederate reported being prone to seizures and subsequently asked for help as a seizure apparently began. Researchers found that the more confederates there were, the longer it took the true participant to react to the calls for help (Latane & Darley, 1968).

Several factors contribute to the bystander effect. When one person sees another in need of help, he or she may ask, *What happens if I try to intervene and wind up embarrassing myself? What if the others know something I don't? Am I blowing this out of proportion* (Karakashian et al., 2006; Prentice & Miller, 1996)? These are natural questions and fortunately, they do not always result in the bystander effect. This is especially true for bystanders with specific training, such as CPR (Huston et al., 1981), or those with a social connection to the person in need (Levine & Crowther, 2008).

To put this topic into context, let us return to the situation where someone is at risk of being assaulted. This is all too common on college campuses where one in five women report being victim of a sexual assault (Anderson & Clement, 2015). A substantial number of these crimes begin to arise at parties and clubs where the victims and perpetrators are presumably surrounded by peers. What if those peers intervened when they noticed one of their friends was behaving aggressively with a woman? Or took a friend home when her judgment had been affected by alcohol so much that she was unaware of a threat? In fact, there are a number of programs designed to reduce the incidence of these types of assaults by educating students and encouraging them to get involved. For example, over 25 years, one US university sponsored seminars to teach students how to spot risks, effective ways to respond, and foster a climate where intervening is expected. During this period, surveys show that unwanted sexual experiences have been cut by more than 50% (University of New Hampshire, 2012).

Aggression

At its most basic level, **aggression** *is any behavior intended to hurt or harm an individual* (Anderson & Bushman, 2002). Aggression toward others comes in a variety of forms. People can be either physically or verbally aggressive. Aggression can occur in socially sanctioned contexts, such as sporting events, or in contexts that violate the rights of others, as in assault. Aggression can involve provoking others, or it can be reactive, as when responding to insults or threats. Like altruism, aggression is influenced by both the person and the situation. Because research shows some interesting and important links between biological factors and aggression, we will start our exploration there.

Biological Influences on Aggression

People have long speculated that aggressive tendencies can be inherited, even before scientists uncovered modern concepts of genes and evolution. Many also believe that hormones are the reason why young males are the most aggressive demographic group. But how much credit should we give to biological explanations of aggression?

What do we know about the biology of aggression?

Families seem to differ in their aggressive tendencies, and at an individual level some people react with especially high levels of defensiveness and aggression when threatened. The heritability of aggressive behaviors among humans is estimated to be approximately 0.50, suggesting a significant role for genes (Rhee & Waldman, 2002). Scientists have identified specific brain regions, chemicals, and genes that interact with environmental triggers to aggressive responses. A key to understanding the biological basis of aggression is to identify how the environment triggers these biological factors.

How can science explain the biology of aggression?

Aggressive behavior is related to functioning of the amygdala, which is part of the brain's limbic system. Men who are prone to violence show abnormal activity in the limbic regions of the brain (Pardini & Phillips, 2010). Furthermore, amygdala responding appears to be related to testosterone levels. The amygdala has receptors for testosterone, and testosterone levels affect the activation of the amygdala in response to threatening situations (Derntl et al., 2009).

Correlational research has found that more aggressive males tend to have unusually high testosterone levels and are also prone to crime, drug use, and impulsiveness (Dabbs et al., 2001). Numerous potential candidate genes are thought to play a role in this relationship (Craig & Halton, 2009). One gene is known to code for the receptors that androgens bind to. This gene varies in length between individuals, with some people inheriting "short" versions and others inheriting "long" versions of it. (The

length of the gene is the result of the number of repeat molecular sequences that comprise the DNA molecule; long versions have more repeats.)

Researchers suspected that this gene might be implicated in human aggressive tendencies—notably male aggression. In one study, investigators examined the androgen receptor gene of 645 men, 374 of whom had been convicted of murder or rape, and compared it to the androgen receptor gene of the 271 controls who had no violent history. The males with histories of criminal violence were statistically more likely to have inherited the short version of the androgen receptor gene. Additionally, the men who were especially violent offenders (e.g., who committed rape and then murder) had the shortest copies of this gene (Rajender et al., 2008).

Can we critically evaluate this evidence?

Testosterone has gained the reputation as the hormone driving male aggression but it is also found in women, in whom it serves most of the same functions as in men. This function seems to be reactive because an individual's baseline ("resting") level of testosterone may not be a good predictor of aggression. However, competitive or aggressive contexts elicit increases in testosterone (not the other way around) and people who have particularly strong fluctuation in testosterone levels during competition may behave more aggressively. In addition, aggression is just one of many behaviors associated with testosterone; this hormone is also involved in psychological processes that have nothing to do with aggression. For example, testosterone and its receptors are abundant in many regions of the brain involved in thinking and memory, so the hormone plays a role in those functions.

Although research indicates that people who are aggressive have unusual activity in the areas of the brain associated with emotion, it is important not to simplify the issue. Research certainly does show that amygdala responding is related to aggression, and that abnormal conditions of this brain structure can result in emotional and behavioral problems. This line of thinking can be taken too far, however. Just four decades ago, clinical researchers at a juvenile mental hospital in Australia surgically removed the amygdalae from youths who were prone to aggression-related problems. It was not until 2007 when this type of surgery was formally banned (White & Williams, 2009).

Why is this relevant?

The costs of violent aggression are high. An estimated 2.2 million people require medical treatment for violence-related incidents each year in the United States, at an estimated cost of $37 billion in health care and lost work

Testosterone is related to aggression, but mostly in response to competitive and aggressive contexts.

productivity (Corso et al., 2007). The additional costs of incarceration and legal proceedings make the investigation of aggression and its causes a critical area of study. Fortunately, biological factors do not destine boys to grow up violent. Psychologists have shown that at-risk children who learn and use strategies to cope with negative emotions elicited by competition and conflict show reduced testosterone levels and aggression relative to controls. Furthermore, the benefits extend into adulthood: Those who learned coping skills showed less reactive aggression when provoked (Carre et al., 2014).

JOURNAL PROMPT

Biology of Aggression: From an evolutionary perspective, why is aggression important? Specifically, describe three or more contexts in which aggressive behavior would promote survival and reproductive success.

PERSONALITY AND AGGRESSION People vary in their tolerance and even preference for violence. Some individuals enjoy the unmitigated violence of ultimate fighting or the over-the-top theatrics of professional wrestling, and at the other end of the spectrum are individuals who cannot bring themselves to honk their car horn when it is clearly justified.

Dozens of studies have examined how different personality traits are related to aggression, and their results reveal two distinct patterns. First, some individuals seem to be naturally prone to aggression in just about any situation, whether they are provoked or not. Psychologists refer to this tendency as *trait aggression*, because the hostility seems to be as much as a trait for these individuals as shyness or politeness is for others. Other people can still be aggressive, but only when they feel threatened or provoked. These *reactive-aggressive* individuals tend to be more competitive,

self-centered, impulsive, and quick to anger than the rest of the population (Bettencourt et al., 2006).

THE SITUATIONAL CAUSES OF AGGRESSION Even for those individuals who are low in trait aggression, situational factors can greatly impact their aggressive behaviors. It is probably not surprising that the biggest cause is interpersonal provocation such as insults or physical attack (Berkowitz, 2003). For children, aggressive behavior may be a response to bullying. For adults, it may be a response to grown-up forms of bullying in the workplace, or any other form of perceived maltreatment from one's supervisors or peers (Baron, 1999; LeBlanc & Barling, 2004).

The **frustration-aggression hypothesis** *describes another major contributor to aggression, which occurs when an individual is prevented from achieving a goal—especially if the goal should be within reach—and experiences frustration as a result.* Prolonged frustration or meaningless frustration is especially likely to trigger aggressive responses. Even when there is a perfectly reasonable explanation for the frustration, aggression is still likely to occur (Dill & Anderson, 1995). One of the most familiar forms of frustration-related aggression is road rage. When drivers are stuck in traffic and when they feel threatened by careless, slow, or aggressive drivers, they are more likely to become aggressive themselves (Dukes et al., 2001; Galovski et al., 2006).

CULTURAL INFLUENCES ON AGGRESSION Culture relates to aggression in at least three ways: It involves beliefs about what are normal or acceptable ways to handle or resolve conflict, institutions or other formal procedures for addressing conflict, and the various elements of that culture that can lead to conflict. These can be seen in **cultures of honor**: *social groups that expect individuals to protect themselves and their property by whatever means necessary, including violence* (Cohen et al., 1996; Nisbett

The frustration-aggression hypothesis states that aggression arises from frustration—the inability to reach a goal when it should be relatively easy to do. This is especially clear in road rage caused by traffic jams and slow drivers.

& Cohen, 1996). This perspective stands in contrast to a culture of law, which relies on institutions and formal procedures (the courts, penal codes, and law enforcement officers) to manage conflict; the cultures and actually punish aggression rather than endorse it. In cultures of honor, individuals, especially males, are expected to fiercely protect their home and property, and to react strongly to even mild insults toward themselves and their families. Failure to do so will come at a high social cost, so it is essential not to be seen as a pushover in front of the community.

Before addressing the relevant research, read the beginning of this scenario and try to imagine how it would end:

> *Shortly after arriving at the party, Jill pulled her husband Steve aside, obviously bothered by something. Jill told Steve that Larry had already made two passes at her that evening. Steve kept an eye on Larry and within 5 minutes Larry tried to kiss Jill again (adapted from Nisbett & Cohen, 1996).*

How would you complete this story? Would Steve privately confront Larry and point out that his behavior is inappropriate? Or would Steve react violently and threaten or attack him?

In a study at the University of Michigan, two factors influenced how college men finished the story: (1) whether they had been offended before reading it, and (2) their geographic region of upbringing in the United States. In this experiment, the offense occurred when, an actor (who was a part of the study) bumped into the volunteer and mumbled an obscenity. This provocation led Southern males to complete the stories like the preceding one with more violent themes compared to Northern males. In addition, the researchers collected saliva samples and analyzed testosterone levels following the incident; Southerners had higher testosterone levels than did Northerners (Figure 15.9). Thus, they claimed that the Southern men were raised in a culture of honor that made them more aggressive. This

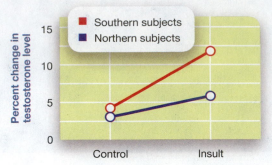

Figure 15.9 Men from a Culture of Honor React More Strongly to Perceived Insults

Compared to Northerners, the testosterone levels of Southern research participants increased greatly after they were bumped before an experiment.

interpretation has been questions, however; perhaps the culture of honor allowed them to have normal levels of aggression, whereas the men from Michigan and other northern states had lost theirs.

What leads to the geographical differences in aggression? Cultures of honor are often found far away from urban centers, where law enforcement is weakest or cannot respond quickly. The location goes along with the fact that cultures often start out as agrarian, which means individuals are prepared to respond quickly to threats to livestock including predators and thieves. Even as fewer and fewer people in the United States live in rural areas, cultural changes often come gradually, and some regions have maintained the traditional culture of honor. In the Southeast for example, the rate for murders based on honor and interpersonal conflict (i.e., not murders associated with other felonies, such as armed robbery) far exceeds the rates for the rest of the country, and people are far more accepting of individuals who have committed violence in the name of honor and self-defense (Nisbett & Cohen, 1996).

Module 15.3 Summary

15.3a   Know . . . the key terminology in the study of helping and aggression:

aggression
altruism
bystander effect
cultures of honor
empathy
frustration-aggression hypothesis
kin selection
mirror neurons
reciprocal altruism
social-exchange theory
social responsibility norm

15.3b   Understand . . . cognitive and biological theories of helping.

According to social-exchange theory, people weigh the financial and personal costs of helping and altruism. Evolutionary accounts explain altruism as a result of kin selection, in which helping relatives ultimately benefits reproductive fitness. Reciprocal altruism occurs in cases where helping is directed toward nonrelatives, with the expectation that favors will eventually be returned.

15.3c   Understand . . . biopsychosocial influences on aggression.

Recall the example from Nisbett and Cohen (1996), who found that young adults with ties to rural areas of the southeastern United States tend to be more aggressive than Northerners. These psychologists explain this difference in terms of a culture of honor.

15.3d   Apply . . . your knowledge to assess your own levels of altruism.

If you have not done so already, complete a brief version of the Self-Report Altruism Scale in Table 15.5. The average score from a sample of 50 college students was 39. Do you think the score accurately reflects how you relate to others?

15.3e   Analyze . . . the role of biological factors and testosterone in aggressive behavior.

The limbic system (e.g., amygdala) and testosterone levels are correlated with aggression. Testosterone levels peak in competitive situations and during aggressive encounters. Genetic links between testosterone levels and violence have also been identified. However, not all violent people have high testosterone levels, and testosterone has more functions than just playing a role in aggression. Receptors for testosterone are also found in the brain regions responsible for thinking and memory.

Module 15.3 Quiz

Know . . .

1. Behavior that places the helper at significant risk or certain harm for the benefit of another is referred to as _____.
   A. altruism
   B. empathy
   C. costly signaling
   D. social responsibility norm

Understand . . .

2. Aggressive behavior has its brain basis in the _____.
   A. adrenal glands
   B. brain stem
   C. mirror neurons
   D. limbic system

3. Which of the following is the most plausible explanation for the bystander effect?
   A. There are more people who simply do not care enough to help others than originally thought.
   B. People fear embarrassment that could come from helping another.
   C. The person in need is likely to be unrelated, and nonrelatives are not worth helping.
   D. Bystanders refuse help because of their own experiences. When they were in need, nobody helped them.

Apply . . .

4. If you witnessed a severe accident, what would have the most influence on your decision to help those who were injured?
   A. Your job involves first aid, so you shouldn't be expected to do it for free.
   B. The individuals who were injured are violating the social responsibility norm.
   C. The individuals who were injured are engaged in costly signaling.
   D. You have a set of friends and family members you feel very close to.

Analyze . . .

5. Which conclusion has been drawn concerning the research on testosterone and aggression?
   A. Individuals who have high baseline levels of testosterone tend to be more aggressive than average.
   B. Testosterone only increases in response to aggression.
   C. Testosterone is not involved in aggression among females.
   D. There is little psychologists can do to prevent aggression in high-testosterone individuals.

Module 15.4 Scientific Literacy Challenge: Gender and Scientific Careers

Over the past 50 years, women have been acquiring jobs and finding success in many different STEM fields (Science, Technology, Engineering, and Mathematics), particularly in the biological and medical sciences. However, there are a few STEM fields where women are far outnumbered by men, mostly within the fields of computer science and engineering. Is the deficit of women in these fields a problem that society should address?

Before you start this activity, write a paragraph or two about what you think might be holding women back in computer science and engineering.

JOURNAL PROMPT

What societal factors do you think contribute to there being fewer women in STEM fields?

What do we know about gender and scientific careers?

Read excerpts of this letter to the editor written by Marcella Grant, a high school physical science teacher. Does Ms. Grant have a good understanding of why we need to increase girls' interest in technology-related fields? As you read, make sure you understand the boldfaced key terms from Chapter 15.

Helping girls stay excited about science and technology

By Marcella Grant,
Physical Science teacher, River Bend High School

I am happy to announce the start of a new program for our middle and high school girls called *Advancing Physics, Engineering, and Computer Science for Girls* (APECS for Girls), and I am asking for volunteer help from interested members of the community. Did you know that through middle and high school, girls take courses in math, computer, and physical sciences as often as boys do? By the end of college, however, women account for less than 20% of all degrees in those areas represented by APECS for Girls.

APECS for Girls is an evidence-based program that can increase girls' interest in technology related fields. The activities in the program challenge commonly held **stereotypes** about girls' abilities along with the **social norms** about the types of jobs we expect women to hold. Although girls probably do not face as much **explicit prejudice** or outright **discrimination** as they did 50 years ago, societal influences remain a barrier to women pursuing and succeeding in APECS-related careers. However, the peer and mentoring networks formed in APECS provide social support to face those challenges head on.

Ms. Grant began by laying the groundwork for the program. Read on to learn about the details of the program and evidence that it may work.

How do scientists study gender and scientific careers?

Here, the writer tells us about how contexts, relationships, and classroom activities encourage girls to participate in more technology and engineering related activities. As you read, be sure make note of the scientific concepts that are highlighted.

APECS provides mentoring opportunities to female students from professional women and women from area universities with majors in the targeted disciplines. Assessment surveys show that the quality of mentoring relationships were associated with self-reported interest and self-confidence in the girls' abilities to succeed in APECS-related careers.

During APECS programs, girls tackle projects that encourage personal interaction, collaboration, and creativity. Surveys of school-aged girls indicate that these are elements of STEM activities that are particularly important to their involvement. For example, one activity involves providing students with an engineering problem that requires teamwork in identifying the best solution, and dividing into subgroups to develop the required mechanisms to solve it.

Mentoring and project-based activities appear to be a successful combination for encouraging interest in STEM among girls. In one large evaluation study, APECS was implemented in multiple Girl Scout groups, with a total of 1,200 participants. For a comparison, girls of the same age and from the same schools who did not participate in APECS for Girls were also tracked. At the end of the program that year, the APECS for Girls participants, in comparison with control participants, reported significantly greater confidence in their knowledge about science, what scientists do at work, liking science, feeling confident about engaging in science, and intending to choose a career in science.

Were you able to identify important elements of research in these examples? Test yourself with the quiz below.

1. How was the success of the APECS program measured?
    a. natural observation
    b. self-report
    c. inferential statistics
    d. hypothesis testing
2. We should assume the Girl Scouts' APECS data come from a quasi-experimental design because
    a. it lacked an independent variable.
    b. the girls were probably not randomly assigned to join Girl Scouts or to be in the comparison group.
    c. it did not mention a double-blind technique.
    d. the data were not collected in a laboratory.
3. Finding promising results in a sample of Girl Scouts does not necessarily mean that the program will be effective for all girls. In other words, it may not _____.
    a. generalize to other girls of the same age
    b. adequately account for demand characteristics
    c. be double-blind
    d. adequately reduce gender bias

Answers: 1. *b* 2. *b* 3. *a*

Ms. Grant was able to cite several studies that supported her position. Now, let's critically evaluate the research.

How should we think critically about gender and scientific careers?

Remember that critical thinking involves curiosity and reasonable levels of skepticism. As you read through the passage below, search for specific statements relevant to critical thinking.

> We are excited to bring APECS to the River Bend area because we think it shows a lot of promise. At the same time, we realize that the data do not show an increase in women *choosing* APECS careers, only that girls are more engaged in science and feel better about it. Another issue to consider is that the direct evidence for APECS comes from the Girl Scout study. What if the greater scientific interest and self-confidence is due to the type of child who joins Girl Scouts? They may not represent girls from diverse demographic groups. Finally, only a portion of the data provided in these studies have been published in peer review journals. Other survey data comes from APECS itself. It is clearly a reputable organization, but there is the potential for unintended bias.

The statements below will help you identify several aspects of critical thinking. Match the following critical thinking statements to the highlighted passages that illustrate them. Note that not all statements are represented in the text.

1. The author interprets non-experimental evidence correctly.
2. The author reminds us not to rely on appeals to authority, even if she is an authority herself.
3. The author identifies and tolerates ambiguity in the data.
4. The author examined whether bias might influence the results.

1. Green 2. Not addressed 3. Yellow 4. Blue

Now that you have completed the critical thinking exercise, read to find out how this research may be applied.

How is this gender and STEM research relevant?

Read how Ms. Grant concludes her proposal, and then in the writing activity that follows, consider any newly formed thoughts you may have about keeping girls interested in STEM fields.

> All in all, we believe that APECS for Girls can make a difference to our students. Empowering our girls to pursue education and careers in technology and engineering will provide them with opportunities for stimulating and lucrative careers. It is important for our community, as technological and engineering jobs are among the fastest growing sectors of business, and we are increasingly filling positions with employees from other parts of the world, and with a continuing discrepancy in gender equity. But to make this program the best it can be, we will need help from the community. If you are a female professional or student in an APECS related area and would like to mentor, please let me know. Other ways to encourage our girls is to host a visit to your technology-related workplace, provide materials for technological activities, or simply be a source of encouragement and support.
>
> Thank you,
> Marcella Grant

SHARED WRITING

Are you persuaded that a program like APECS might increase the likelihood that girls will pursue STEM-related careers? What changes could be made in our educational system to address the lack of female representation in many STEM fields?

Chapter 15 Quiz

1. Which of the following does not explain why social loafing may occur?
   - A. The individual believes that even if the group succeeds, there will be very little reward in it for each individual group member.
   - B. The individual believes that the group will fail no matter what her contribution is.
   - C. The individual believes that she has little to contribute to a group.
   - D. The other group members refuse to work with the individual.

2. We tend to think of our beliefs as being our own, and as being immune to group influences. This phenomenon is known as _____.
   - A. groupthink
   - B. the bias blind spot
   - C. social facilitation
   - D. self determinism

3. _____ is complying with instructions from an individual who has authority.
   - A. Obedience
   - B. Groupthink
   - C. Conformity
   - D. Mimicry

4. What makes the central route to persuasion distinct from the peripheral route?
   - A. The central route relies on information and evaluation of options, whereas the peripheral route is based on intuition and quick decisions.
   - B. The central route is based on reinforcement, whereas the peripheral route is based on punishment.
   - C. The central route takes longer than the peripheral route.
   - D. The central route is based on intuition and quick decisions, whereas the peripheral route relies on information and evaluation of options.

5. The fundamental attribution error is the tendency to attribute the actions of others to _____.
   - A. ingroup factors
   - B. outgroup factors
   - C. their disposition
   - D. the situation

6. _____ occurs when an individual has two thoughts that are inconsistent with each other, creating a motivation to reduce the discrepancy.
   - A. Groupthink
   - B. Social facilitation
   - C. Cognitive dissonance
   - D. Obedience

7. Which of the following is a criticism of the Implicit Associations Test (IAT)?
   - A. The IAT may measure only familiarity with a stereotype, not actual prejudice.
   - B. The IAT actually measures explicit prejudice, not implicit prejudice.
   - C. The IAT is not reliable when subjects are retested.
   - D. Subjects can change their responses to make themselves appear less prejudiced.

8. Some researchers believe that humans' capacity for empathy is based on the nerve cells called _____.
   - A. sympathy neurons
   - B. mirror neurons
   - C. empathy cells
   - D. altruism neurons

9. The concept of _____ explains why parents would risk their own lives to rescue one of their children.
   - A. self-serving bias
   - B. a culture of honor
   - C. reciprocal altruism
   - D. kin selection

10. Society teaches that the value of helping goes beyond the benefits an individual might receive, and that individuals who cannot help themselves require special help. Based on _____, people feel compelled to help individuals who cannot help themselves, such as the elderly and people with medical crises.
    - A. altruism
    - B. empathy
    - C. costly signaling
    - D. the social responsibility norm

11. Which of the following is an example of the phenomenon of costly signaling in action?
    - A. Making a private donation to a hospital
    - B. Failing to help because others are around
    - C. Showing off one's wealth
    - D. Chasing down a thief who has stolen a stranger's purse

12. Which scenario is best explained by the frustration-aggression hypothesis?
    - A. You are stuck in heavy traffic and you start to threaten other motorists.
    - B. You threaten another person who is behaving inappropriately toward a family member.
    - C. You have excessively high levels of testosterone so you seek out aggressive situations.
    - D. All of these situations can be explained using the frustration-aggression hypothesis.

13. Greg asked you to sign a petition for his student fundraising group. After he gets your signature, he asks you for a small donation. Which technique does Greg seem to be using?
    - A. Foot-in-the-door
    - B. Central route
    - C. Door-in-the-face
    - D. None of the above

14. While working on a group project in class, Dustin tries extra hard and volunteers to take on more work than the rest of the group. Based on this, fellow group members decide to slack off a little. Dustin's group is demonstrating _____.
    - A. social facilitation
    - B. cognitive dissonance
    - C. social loafing
    - D. disobedience

15. If you were raised in a culture of honor, you are most likely to _____.
    - A. avoid aggressive acts at all costs.
    - B. rely solely on the legal system to provide justice.
    - C. insult or attack others without provocation.
    - D. be accepting of situations in which someone took revenge on another person.

Chapter 16
Health, Stress, and Coping

16.1 Behavior and Health

- Smoking
  Working the Scientific Literacy Model: Media Exposure and Smoking
- Obesity
- Psychosocial Influences on Health
- Module 16.1 Summary
- Module 16.1 Quiz

16.2 Stress and Illness

- Physiology of Stress
- Stress, Immunity, and Illness
  Working the Scientific Literacy Model: Relationships and Health
- Stress, Personality, and Illness
- Module 16.2 Summary
- Module 16.2 Quiz

16.3 Coping and Well-Being

- Coping
- Perceived Control
  Working the Scientific Literacy Model: Compensatory Control and Health
- Nutrition and Exercise
- Module 16.3 Summary
- Module 16.3 Quiz

16.4 Scientific Literacy Challenge: Forgiveness

Chapter 16 Quiz

Module 16.1 Behavior and Health

 ## Learning Objectives

16.1a Know . . . the key terminology related to health psychology.

16.1b Understand . . . how genetic and environmental factors influence obesity.

16.1c Apply . . . your knowledge to exert more control over your own health.

16.1d Analyze . . . whether associating with people who smoke leads to smoking in adolescents.

Should body weight be a basis for how much tax people pay? Some politicians, hospital administrators, and other members of society advocate a "fat tax"—taxing individuals for any excess weight, or for nonessential food items that contribute to being overweight. Sugary soft drinks contribute hundreds of calories to our daily diet without providing any nutrition, and do little to leave a person feeling full and satisfied. So, like cigarettes, should additional taxes be attached to these products for the same reasons that cigarettes are so heavily taxed? Some healthcare providers are pursuing such a plan. State employees in Alabama who were obese had once been directed to lose weight by year's end or face increased monthly health insurance costs. On one hand, this may sound like blatant discrimination and focusing on just one of many economic burdens associated *with obesity. On the otherhand, there is a parallel precedent for fat tax plans—namely, the massive taxes on cigarettes that serve to discourage smoking and help cover the costs of treating smoking-related illnesses. In this module, we examine different factors that affect our mental and physical well-being, and also consider the extent to which physical health is based on psychological processes such as choosing and deciding.*

To what degree do you believe your behavior affects your health? Each day we make choices that shape our physical and mental health. We decide what to eat and what to avoid eating, whether to exercise or be inactive. The choices people make about their career paths

Table 16.1 Estimated Annual Deaths in the United States Due to Behavior-Related Risk Factors

This table presents the estimated number of deaths annually in the United States due to specific behavior-related risk factors such as diet, exercise, and tobacco and alcohol use. To put this in context, there are between 2.4 million and 2.5 million deaths in the United States each year (CDC, 2009a; USDHHS, 2014). The 330,800 male deaths related to tobacco use represent over 13% of all deaths in the United States each year.

Risk Factor	Male	Female	Total
Tobacco use[1]	330,800	225,000	555,800
High blood pressure	164,000	231,000	395,000
Overweight and obesity	114,000	102,000	216,000
High blood sugar	102,000	89,000	190,000
High LDL cholesterol	60,000	53,000	113,000
Alcohol use	45,000	20,000	64,000

SOURCE: Based on Danaei, G., Ding, E. L., Mozafarian, D., Taylor B, & Rehm J. (2009). The preventable causes of death in the United States: Comparative risk assessment of dietary, lifestyle, and metabolic risk factors. *PLoS Med, 6*(4), e1000058. doi: 10.1371/journal. pmed.1000058

[1]USDHHS, 2014

similarly influence health. Workplace stress levels for air traffic controllers are quite different from those experienced by librarians. The numerous and complex connections between behavior and health certainly have created an important niche for *health psychologists*, who study both positive and negative impacts that our behavior and decisions have on health, survival, and well-being.

The need for health psychologists has increased considerably over the 20th century, as most premature deaths today are attributable to lifestyle factors (see Table 16.1). A century ago, people in the United States were likely to die from influenza, pneumonia, tuberculosis, measles, and other contagious diseases. Advances in medicine have served to keep these conditions under much better control. Instead, people are now much more likely to die from tobacco use, alcohol use, obesity, and inactivity. In fact, the Center for Disease Control (CDC) estimates that the top five causes of death in the United States each year (accounting for about two-thirds of all deaths—around 900,000) are from diseases or accidents related to behavior. Further, estimates indicate that lifestyle changes could have prevented 20% to 40% of those (CDC, 2014; Yoon et al., 2014).

Smoking

Smoking cigarettes causes life-shortening health problems including lung, mouth, and throat cancer; heart disease; and pulmonary diseases such as emphysema. The life expectancy of the average smoker is at least 10 years shorter than that of a nonsmoker. The costs in lives and money attributable to smoking are massive, as shown in Table 16.2. Despite the starkly ominous figures, an estimated 22% (69 million) of US adults smoke cigarettes (USDHHS, 2014).

Working the Scientific Literacy Model

Media Exposure and Smoking

If smoking is so dangerous, why do people do it? This is a perplexing question not only for psychologists, but also for many smokers. One reason may be the exposure young people have to other people who smoke: parents, friends, and even characters on television and in the movies.

What do we know about media influences on smoking?

Many different factors influence whether someone becomes a smoker, including family and local culture, personality characteristics, and socioeconomic status. Thus, people may smoke because they associate it with valued traits or societal roles, such as attractiveness, rebelliousness, and individualism. Each day, approximately

Table 16.2 Health Costs of Tobacco Use

- Tobacco use causes an estimated 5 million deaths worldwide each year.
- Cigarette smoking is the leading preventable cause of death in the United States.
- One in five US deaths is due to cigarette smoking.
- Smoking does not just harm adults—and estimated 1,000 infants die in the United States annually due to smoking-related prenatal conditions and sudden infant death syndrome.
- Cigarette smoking is costly: The United States loses an estimated $150 billion in lost work productivity and $132 billion in adults healthcare expenses each year.

SOURCE: Based on Centers for Disease Control and Prevention (CDC). (2009b). Retrieved June 20, 2011, from http://www.cdc.gov/tobacco/data_statistics/fact_sheets/fast_facts/index.htm; USDHHS, 2014

2,000 adolescents in the United States try their first ciga-rette, and many become full-time smokers (Heatherton & Sargent, 2009). An important question that health psychol-ogists grapple with concerns the societal factors that lead young people to smoke. Here we will focus on a single influence: exposure to smoking in movies and entertain-ment. Although smoking in films has declined over the past couple of decades, there are still numerous widely popular movies in which characters smoke (Sargent & Heatherton, 2009).

How can science help us analyze the effects of smoking in movies?

To what extent does smoking in movies contribute to ado-lescent smoking? To find out, researchers conducted a random-digit-dialing survey of 6,522 US adolescents from all major geographic regions and socioeconomic groups. The adolescents reported their age and indicated whether they smoked, and identified whether they had seen specific popular movies that featured smoking. The more exposure the adolescents had to movies that featured smoking, the more likely they were to have tried it (see Figure 16.1). This relationship persisted even after the researchers con-trolled for socioeconomic status, personality, and parental and peer influences on smoking (Heatherton & Sargent, 2009). Although this study showed a clear correlation link-ing smoking in movies and adolescent smoking, it did not explain why this correlation exists.

It appears that how people identify with smokers may influence their decision to smoke. An experimental study showed that adolescents who had positive responses to a protagonist who smoked were much more likely to

associate smoking with their own identities. This relation-ship was observed in both adolescents who already smoked and even those who did not smoke (Dal Cin et al., 2007).

Can we critically evaluate this evidence?

It is hard to establish that watching movie stars smoke cigarettes causes adolescents to smoke, even though the studies reviewed here suggest that it does. When research-ers tracked the amount of smoking featured in popular movies from 1990 to 2007, they found that as the incidence of smoking in movies rose, smoking among adolescents increased after a short period of time. Likewise, when smoking in movies decreased, a decline in adolescent smoking followed (Sargent & Heatherton, 2009). However, the problem with these correlations is that multiple expla-nations could be put forth for why they exist. Perhaps the truth is the other way around: People who are already willing to smoke might be more attracted to movies that feature smoking.

Why is this relevant?

Tobacco-related illness imposes a major societal burden in terms of lost work productivity and rising healthcare costs. As the research shows, cigarette smoking in movies is just one of many influences on smoking behavior. Of course, it may be one influence that could be easier to control than, say, peer pressure. With scientific research in hand, advo-cacy groups such as Smoke Free Movies and the National Association of Attorneys General have a sound basis for arguing against smoking in movies—especially those that adolescents are likely to watch.

Figure 16.1 Smoking and the Movies

The more 10- to 14-year-olds view smoking in movies, the more likely they are to smoke (Heatherton & Sargent, 2009).

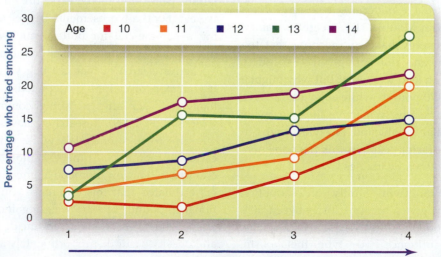

There is some good news related to smoking rates. The prevalence of smoking in the United States declined steadily since the 1990s (CDC, 2010d). State and local laws are reducing the risks posed by secondhand smoke exposure by banning smoking in many public places—especially restaurants and public buildings. As mentioned at the beginning of the module, steep taxes applied to unhealthy products such as tobacco also act as a deterrent against their use. Not only does such a policy tend to reduce the number of smokers (a 10% increase in cigarette price reduces cigarette consumption by an estimated 3% to 5%; USDHSS, 2012), but it also raises funds for healthcare and anti-smoking campaigns. A related issue to consider concerns the rise of e-cigarettes and potential health risks associated with their use (Lerner et al., 2015).

Obesity

You have likely heard of the "freshman 15"—the supposed number of pounds traditional-aged college students can expect to gain during their first year of school. This is often attributed to increased food intake, decreased physical activity, and, for many students, increased levels of alcohol consumption. In reality, the 15-pound estimate is actually inflated, but there is an element of truth to the saying: Those male and female students who gain weight during their early college career put on an average of 6 pounds (Gropper et al., 2009).

Six pounds is not a lot of weight—but habits formed during any period of time, freshman year or otherwise, can be difficult to break. If the habits persist, the student will almost certainly be overweight (if not obese) by graduation. Obesity is defined by **body mass index (BMI)**, *a statistic commonly used for estimating a healthy body weight that factors in an individual's height:* Overweight is a BMI over 25 and obese is a BMI of 30 or more. Obesity is associated with numerous detrimental health consequences, such as cardiovascular disease, diabetes, osteoarthritis (degeneration of bone and cartilage material), and some forms of cancer. As discussed in Module 11.1, weight is gained because of a positive energy balance, meaning that too many calories come in and not enough are expended. Obviously, overeating can lead to obesity. But why might a 6-foot-tall male weigh 170 pounds while enjoying massive amounts of food and a relatively inactive lifestyle, while another person of similar height and lifestyle weighs in at 200 pounds? Several factors explain this phenomenon, including biological and social variables.

BIOLOGICAL FACTORS Twin, family, and adoption studies all suggest that genes account for between 50% and 90% of the variation in body weight (Maes et al., 1997). Genetic factors influence body type, metabolism, and other physiological processes that contribute to body weight and size. At the molecular level, the gene LEP (for "leptin") is associated with obesity. **Leptin** *is a hormone released by fat cells and inhibits hunger by binding to receptors located on organs, tissues, and also the hypothalamus, which is involved in regulating hunger* (see Module 11.1). If leptin receptors, which are coded by the LEP gene, are not sufficiently sensitive to the hormone, then the individual may fail to recognize that food intake is no longer necessary. The result is overeating and obesity.

One hypothesis about obesity begins with the idea that genes contribute to a physiological **set point**, *a mechanism that maintains body weight around a physiologically programmed level.* The set point is not an exact number of pounds, but rather a relatively small range encompassing 10% to 20% of one's weight. Your initial set point is controlled by genetic mechanisms, but your actual weight can be modified by environmental factors—namely, what and how much you eat. According to set point theory, if someone gains 10% of his body weight (e.g., increasing from 150 to 165 pounds) his set point would make a corresponding shift upward—the body acts as though its normal weight is now 165 pounds. Metabolism slows correspondingly, such that additional energy expenditure is now required to take the weight off. This may explain why people who gain extra weight may shed a few pounds with relative ease, but find it overwhelmingly difficult to continue losing or even maintaining their weight once they reach an initial goal.

In addition to set point, another relevant influence on weight loss is simply individual differences in physical activity. Specifically, people who gain weight expend less energy in their normal day-to-day activities (Weinsier et al., 2002). Thus, the difficulty with losing the weight may be related to lower activity levels. Both changes in set point and reduced activity levels make it increasingly difficult to shed pounds.

SOCIAL FACTORS Sociocultural influences, including family, peers, and media exposure greatly influence what we eat. Food advertisements trigger eating—after watching a commercial for buttery microwave popcorn, you have probably found yourself rummaging around in the kitchen in search of that last bag you hope is still there. If your popcorn supply is depleted, you are still far more likely to snack after watching commercials about food (Harris et al., 2009). Researchers have found that children who see food commercials while watching a 30-minute cartoon program consume 45% more snack food than do children who view nonfood commercials. The researchers estimated that this difference could lead to an additional 10 pounds of extra weight gained each year (Harris et al., 2009). Also, increased incidences of overweight and obesity occur disproportionately among children who grow up in poverty (Lipling et al, 2012), where low-cost, high-fat diets are commonplace. An attempt to ban fast-food restaurants in South Los Angeles had no impact on obesity (Sturm & Hattori, 2015).

The cost of health care rises with body mass index. Questions over who is responsible for paying these costs have generated heated debates. Should a person who is overweight or obese be obligated to pay more tax toward health care to offset the higher cost of his or her care? Before answering, consider the fact that healthcare costs also rise because of diseases that have little to do with lifestyle. Also, research on employment statistics indicates that workers who are overweight or obese are paid less than thin colleagues with similar qualifications—a finding that has led economists to suggest that the disparity in wage earnings is about equal to the size of the difference in medical costs incurred by thin versus overweight and obese people (Bhattacharya & Bundorf, 2005).

THE SEDENTARY LIFESTYLE Modern conveniences have reduced the amount of physical activity required of most people. Many jobs involve very little physical activity, and home entertainment has evolved into activities that typically require nothing more than sitting and, often, snacking. Such pleasurable activities can easily replace exercise. Many children and adolescents are indoctrinated into this lifestyle from their early years. In turn, childhood obesity rates have risen drastically, accompanied by the availability of an even greater variety of sedentary activities, such as video games. Researchers have found that the amount of time that children spend playing sedentary video games or watching TV is positively correlated with levels of obesity, but recent evidence suggests active video games—such as those that involve dancing—might actually be a good way to break sedentary habits (Ferrar & Golley, 2015; Mitre et al., 2011).

Now that you have read about numerous variables that influence health, you may be wondering about which ones you can control versus those that you cannot. Complete the activity in Table 16.3 to evaluate your own beliefs about health.

Psychosocial Influences on Health

The environments where we work, live, and play and the people with whom we interact influence both our physical and mental health. College dormitories are a prime example, especially in the fall of each academic year. Frequently, dormitory space is overbooked, leaving some students without an established living space, and forcing people

Table 16.3 The Health Locus of Control Scale

Each of the following items is a belief statement about your health with which you may agree or disagree. Beside each statement is a scale that ranges from strongly disagree (1) to strongly agree (6). For each item, circle the number that represents the extent to which you agree or disagree with that statement. Please make sure that you answer every item and that you circle only one number per item. This is a measure of your personal beliefs; obviously, there are no right or wrong answers.

Item	Strongly Disagree			Strongly Agree		
1. If I get sick, it is my own behavior that determines how soon I get well again.	1	2	3	4	5	6
2. No matter what I do, if I am going to get sick, I will get sick.	1	2	3	4	5	6
3. I am in control of my health.	1	2	3	4	5	6
4. Most things that affect my health happen to me by accident.	1	2	3	4	5	6
5. When I get sick, I am to blame.	1	2	3	4	5	6
6. Luck plays a big part in determining how soon I will recover from an illness.	1	2	3	4	5	6
7. The main thing that affects my health is what I myself do.	1	2	3	4	5	6
8. My good health is largely a matter of good fortune.	1	2	3	4	5	6
9. If I take care of myself, I can avoid illness.	1	2	3	4	5	6
10. No matter what I do, I'm likely to get sick.	1	2	3	4	5	6
11. If I take the right actions, I can stay healthy.	1	2	3	4	5	6
12. If it's meant to be, I will stay healthy.	1	2	3	4	5	6

First, add up the total of your circled responses for the odd-numbered items only: _____

Now add up the total of your circled responses for the even-numbered items only: _____

Here is how you should interpret your scores: The first scale based on odd-numbered items measures the degree to which you believe you have control over your own health. The average of this scale in the original study was 24.1, with higher values indicating a greater sense of control over one's health. The second scale based on even-numbered items measures the degree to which you believe chance is involved in your health. Again, higher scores indicate a greater sense that luck is involved, and the average in the original study was 15.1.

SOURCE: Adapted from "Development of the Multidimensional Health Locus of Control (MHLC) Scales" by K. A. Wallston, B. S. Wallston, & R. DeVellis (1978), *Health Education & Behavior*, 6(1), 160–170.

to live in cramped conditions. Single rooms may be converted into doubles, and "suites" may appear where there had been none. Perhaps not surprisingly, these conditions lend themselves to the increased spread of influenza and other viruses amid a fairly stressed group of individuals. In addition, these conditions affect the way that individuals interact with one another.

Years ago, psychologists compared students who lived in well-designed dormitory arrangements versus those living in improvised and poorly designed conditions. The crowded, poorly designed accommodations caused students to lose their sense of control over whom they could interact with or avoid. The researchers found that students living in the stressful environment were less socially interactive with strangers, had difficulty with working in small groups, and gave up more easily in a competitive game (Baum & Valins, 1977). The students living in the less than ideal conditions seemed to feel helpless, which in turn affected how they interacted with others. For most students, better accommodations await them at home, and larger spaces open up at the end of the semester. However, for many living with very low incomes, the stresses of poor housing may be permanent.

POVERTY AND DISCRIMINATION Health and wealth increase together. People who live in affluent communities not only enjoy better access to health care, but also have a greater sense of control over their environments and have the resources needed to maintain a desired lifestyle. People who experience poverty, discrimination, and other social stressors have higher incidences of depression, anxiety, and other mental health problems (Tracy et al., 2008). The lack of control associated with life in poverty continues a negative cycle compromising human health and well-being.

Furthermore, health problems are magnified by stress. Heart disease is prevalent in socioeconomically disadvantaged populations, and children who experience adverse socioeconomic circumstances are at greater risk for developing heart disease in adulthood (Fiscella et al., 2009; Saban et al., 2014). This relationship likely reflects the compound effects of stress; and a poorer diet is often found among individuals residing in communities of low socioeconomic status.

Discrimination is another stressor that can compromise physical and mental health, and is particularly problematic because it is often uncontrollable and unpredictable. Being a target of prejudice and discrimination is linked to increased blood pressure, heart rate, and secretions of stress hormones, which when experienced over long periods of time compromise physical health. For example, when people perceive that they are the targets of racism, their blood pressure remains elevated throughout the day, and it recovers poorly during sleep (Brondolo

People who are of low socioeconomic status are at increased risk for poor health. Numerous factors, including limited access to health care, stress, poor nutrition, and discrimination, collectively place children growing up in these communities at greater risk for developing health problems.

et al., 2008; Steffen et al., 2003). Discrimination also puts people at greater risk for engaging in unhealthy behaviors such as smoking and substance abuse (Bennett et al., 2005; Landrine & Klonoff, 1996). Finally, discrimination, or even the perception of discrimination, can put the body on sustained alert against threats. The stress response that this state elicits can have negative, long-term effects on physical health, as you will read in Module 16.2.

FAMILY AND SOCIAL ENVIRONMENT Our close, interpersonal relationships impact our health. Isolation not only brings about great subjective discomfort, but also has negative influences on physical health (Cacioppo & Cacioppo, 2014). It is even estimated that chronic loneliness is as great a risk to premature death as obesity (Holt-Lunstad, Smith, & Layton, 2010). **Social resilience**, *the ability to keep positive relationships and endure and recover from social isolation and life stressors*, can protect individuals from negative health consequences of loneliness (Cacioppo, Reis, & Zautra, 2011).

Married people and couples in long-term partnerships are less likely to feel isolated (though it is incorrect to assume married people do not experience loneliness). There are long-term health benefits to the committed. Individuals in heterosexual marriages tend to live longer and have better mental and physical health than do unmarried adults. Married couples enjoy the benefits of social support, combined resources, and they tend to have better health habits (Kiecolt-Glaser & Newton, 2001; Stessman et al., 2014). Of course, marriage can also be a considerable source of stress. Married couples who are experiencing ongoing problems with their relationship tend to experience more health problems, especially among women and older adults (Liu & Waite, 2014). On the whole, it appears that marriage might be healthy for heterosexual adults, but less is known about same-sex marriages because of the limited time since the first states began to recognize them. However, some researchers expect to see similar health benefits in both direct and indirect ways. For example, research has already shown improvements in mental health (Hatzenbuehler et al., 2012; Wright et al., 2013). Indirectly, same-sex benefits from employers means more people are covered by health insurance and can take advantage of medically related tax benefits (Gonzales, 2014).

SOCIAL CONTAGION You have almost surely found yourself eating food simply because others around you were doing so, even if you were not actually hungry. The simple presence of other people is a puzzling social influence on our behavior—easy to observe, but challenging to explain. Social scientists have discovered an even more puzzling pattern of behaviors spreading among individuals. Body weight seems to spread socially, and not just the pound or so gained from packing in extra food at a birthday party just because others around you were also eating. Body weight changes can spread widely among individuals within social groups. Fluctuations can go in either direction—weight may increase or decrease. The same even appears to happen with smoking—either starting or quitting. It may be that many of our health and lifestyle choices are influenced by what others around us are doing.

These phenomena are examples of **social contagion**, *the often subtle, unintentional spreading of a behavior as a result of social interactions.* Social contagion of body weight, smoking, and other health-related behaviors have been documented in the Framingham Heart Study. The National Heart Institute began this ongoing study in 1948 to track 15,000 residents of Framingham, Massachusetts. Participants made regular visits to their doctors, who recorded important health statistics such as heart rate, body weight, and other standard physical measures. Scientists working with the Framingham data noticed that over time, clusters of people from this study group became increasingly similar in certain characteristics—such as body weight increases or decreases, starting or quitting smoking, and even levels of happiness (Christakis

Social contagion in the dorms. Your college roommate may influence your GPA more than you know—for better or for worse. At Dartmouth College, students are randomly assigned to their dorm rooms rather than matched on various characteristics, as is customary at many schools. This practice makes Dartmouth's roommate pairs a diverse mixture. Professor Bruce Sacerdote (2001) found that GPA levels are influenced by one's roommate. Students with high GPAs elevate the GPAs of their lower-scoring roommates, and vice versa.

& Fowler, 2007, 2008; Fowler & Christakis, 2008). Upon closer inspection, researchers found that these clusters were not just similar in terms of health, they included groups of friends and acquaintances. It was as though the behaviors spread in the same way a virus would. Although genetic factors certainly do influence our health, this work seems to show just how powerful social factors can be.

Social networking sites like Facebook greatly extend the reach of social contagion beyond that of our immediate neighbors and peers. One innovative study found that people who posted glum messages about rainy weather (likely with pictures to prove it) in turn elicited negative emotional status updates from Facebook friends who were actually having sunny days (Coviello et al., 2014).

JOURNAL PROMPT

Social Contagion: Have you experienced social contagion in action? Describe an example or two of social contagion that you have experienced. Try to think of one example in which a healthy behavior spread in contagious fashion, and one example of an unhealthy behavior.

Module **16.1** Summary

16.1a   Know . . . the key terminology related to health psychology:

body mass index (BMI)
leptin
set point
social contagion
social resilience

16.1b   Understand . . . how genetic and environmental factors influence obesity.

Twin and adoption studies indicate that inheritance plays a strong role as a risk factor for obesity (or, for that matter, as a predictor of healthy body weight). Furthermore, environmental influences on weight gain are abundant. Cultural, family, and socioeconomic factors influence activity levels and diet, even in very subtle ways, such as through social contagion.

16.1c Apply . . . your knowledge to exert more control over your own health.

As you learned in this module, health is influenced by multiple factors. Some of these might be beyond our control, while others we have some measure of control over. The experience of discrimination, for example, is not something that one individual can expect to control because the injustice is perpetrated by someone else. For those factors that we have greater measure of control over, having a sense of control over our health can lead to improved outcomes. The

activity Locus of Control and Health in Table 16.3 provided an opportunity to measure the degree to which you feel that your own behaviors affect mental and physical health.

16.1d Evaluate . . . whether associating with people who smoke leads to smoking in adolescents.

Correlational trends certainly show that smoking in popular movies is positively related to smoking among adolescents (e.g., increased exposure is related to increased incidence of smoking). Controlled laboratory studies suggest a cause-and-effect relationship exists between identification with story protagonists who smoke and smoking behavior by young viewers.

Module 16.1 Quiz

Know . . .

1. _____ is a hypothesized mechanism that serves to maintain body weight around a physiologically programmed level.
   A. BMI
   B. Set point
   C. Obesity
   D. A sedentary lifestyle

2. Which psychological term refers to the often subtle, unintentional spreading of a behavior as a result of social interactions?
   A. Health psychology
   B. Social contagion
   C. Discrimination
   D. Observational learning

Understand . . .

3. Which of the following factors is not related to a person's weight?
   A. Exposure to food advertisements
   B. Sedentary lifestyle
   C. Genetics and set point
   D. All of these are related to weight.

Apply . . .

4. To avoid gaining weight during the freshman year of college, a person should do all of the following except:
   A. increase physical activity.
   B. decrease caloric intake.
   C. increase alcohol intake.
   D. be aware of the new stressors the individual will face.

Analyze . . .

5. Which of the following statements is the best evidence that viewing smoking in movies plays a causal (rather than correlational) role in influencing people's perception of smoking and willingness to try smoking?
   A. Long-term trends show that increased or decreased incidence of smoking by adolescents follows increases or decreases in rates of smoking in movies.
   B. The more adolescents smoke, the more smoking occurs in movies.
   C. Advertisements for smoking occur more frequently, along with smoking by film actors.
   D. Adolescent smoking occurs at roughly the same rate regardless of how smoking is depicted in films.

Module 16.2 Stress and Illness

Learning Objectives

16.2a Know . . . the key terminology associated with stress and illness.

16.2b Understand . . . the physiological reactions that occur under stress.

16.2c Understand . . . how the immune system is connected to stress responses.

16.2d Apply . . . a measure of stressful events to your own experiences.

16.2e Analyze . . . the claim that ulcers are caused by stress.

The frustration and embarrassment of choking under pressure is undeniable. Whether the stakes are a championship title or gaining admission to a preferred college, a sudden, inexplicable shift to subpar performance can be devastating. According to psychologist Sian Beilock, the culprit in such cases may be the negative effects that stress has on working memory—the short-term capacity to hold and manipulate information. Calculating a 15% tip for a bill of $43.84 at a restaurant, or while the pizza delivery person waits, requires working memory processes. The pressure of your date or the

pizza delivery person looking on impatiently may result in your appearing either foolishly generous or cheap.

Beilock has conducted experiments on how stress affects the cognitive resources needed for problem solving. For example, in one study, research volunteers were asked to solve math problems. Some were told that if they solved the problems correctly, they would earn money for themselves as well as for a partner they were paired with; if they did not perform well, both the volunteer and the partner would lose money. Beilock and her colleagues have found that this type of pressure draws resources away from the working memory processes needed for success (Beilock, 2010; Maloney et al., 2014). Stressful thoughts readily occupy working memory space and cause the unfortunate experience of choking under pressure. Stress, both good and bad, is a part of everyday life for most people, and here we look at how it affects the brain and rest of the body, and how individuals cope with stress.

On any given day, we are likely to experience frustration, conflict, pressure, and change. All of these experiences, and others as well, involve stress. **Stress** *is a psychological and physiological reaction that occurs when perceived demands exceed existing resources to meet those demands.*

Stress refers to both events (stressors) and experiences in response to these events (the stress response). Stressors can take a wide variety of forms, such as single events (giving a speech, getting into a minor car accident) and chronic events (illness, marital problems, ongoing job-related challenges).

We can probably all agree that events such as car accidents and relationship troubles are stressful. However, psychologists have discovered that any two individuals may react very differently even if they have experienced the same stressful event. To explain why and how people differ, psychologists Richard Lazarus and Susan Folkman developed a cognitive appraisal theory of stress (Lazarus & Folkman, 1984). Here, the term *appraisal* refers to the cognitive act of assessing and evaluating the potential threat and demands of an event, and these appraisals occur in two steps. First, the individual perceives a potential threat and initiates a *primary appraisal* by asking herself, "Is this a threat?" If the answer is no, then she will not experience any stress; but if the answer is yes, she will experience a physiological stress reaction (perhaps a racing heart and sweaty palms) as well as an emotional reaction (perhaps anxiety and fear). As these events unfold, the *secondary appraisal* begins—she must determine how to cope with the threat. During secondary appraisal, she may determine that she knows how to cope with the stressor or that the stressor goes beyond her ability to cope.

Life changes are a major source of stress, whether they bring about positive or negative emotions. Also, whether something is stressful varies by degree. Psychologists have actually ranked stressful events according to their magnitude, as can be seen in the Social Readjustment Rating Scale in Table 16.4 (Holmes & Rahe, 1968). The highest-stress events include death of a spouse and divorce, while holidays and traffic tickets occupy the lower end of the spectrum. According to the psychologists who developed this scale, as the points in the left column of Table 16.4 accumulate, a person's risk for becoming ill increases. For example, 300 or more points put people at significant risk for developing heart problems and

An event like this involves a primary appraisal phase in which the individual assesses the level of stress caused by the accident. Even though it was a minor collision; his stomach may feel like it is in a knot and he may begin to worry about the consequences. As the stress sets in, his secondary appraisal may help him cope if he remembers that he has insurance to cover the damage, he considers that nobody was injured, and remembers how his parents have always been supportive and understanding.

infections. As we will see, our stress responses are closely linked to numerous physiological systems, such as cardiovascular and immune system functioning.

Life-stress experiences for adults will not necessarily generalize across all age groups. Recognizing this fact, some psychologists have focused specifically on what is stressful to college students. The right-hand column of Table 16.4 ranks stressful events reported by college students.

Some level of stress can actually be helpful—without it, motivation to perform can decline. Conversely, as Sian Beilock and many other psychologists have shown, too much stress taxes cognitive resources, resulting in poorer performance. Task complexity is an important factor to consider when it comes to describing the relationship between stress and performance. Generally speaking, higher levels of arousal facilitate solving relatively simple problems, while complex tasks are better performed

Table 16.4 Life Stress Inventories for the General Adult Population and for College Students

Original Social Readjustement Rating Scale (Holmes & Rahe, 1967)		A Life Stress Inventory Applicable to College Students (Renner & Mackin, 1998)	
Rating	Item	Rating	Item
100	Death of a spouse	100	Being raped
73	Divorce	100	Finding out that you are HIV-positive
65	Marital separation	98	Being accused of rape
63	Jail term	97	Death of a close friend
63	Death of a close family member	96	Death of a close family member
53	Personal injury or illness	94	Contracting a sexually transmitted disease (other than AIDS)
50	Marriage	91	Concerns about being pregnant
47	Fired at work	90	Finals week
45	Marital reconciliation	90	Concerns about your partner being pregnant
45	Retirement	89	Oversleeping for an exam
44	Change in health of family member	89	Flunking a class
40	Pregnancy	85	Having a boyfriend or girlfriend cheat on you
39	Sex difficulties	85	Ending a steady dating relationship
39	Gain of new family member	85	Serious illness in a close friend or family member
39	Business readjustment	84	Financial difficulties
38	Change in financial state	83	Writing a major term paper
37	Death of close friend	83	Being caught cheating on a test
36	Change to different line of work	82	Drunk driving
35	Change in number of arguments with spouse	82	Sense of overload in school or work
31	*Mortgage exceeding $10,000	80	Two exams in one day
30	Foreclosure of mortgage or loan	77	Cheating on your boyfriend or girlfriend
29	Change in responsibilities at work	76	Getting married
29	Son or daughter leaving home	75	Negative consequences of drinking or drug use
29	Trouble with in-laws	73	Depression or crisis in your best friend
28	Outstanding personal achievement	73	Difficulties with parents
26	**Wife begins or stops work	72	Talking in front of a class
26	Begin or end school	69	Lack of sleep
25	Change in living conditions	69	Change in housing situation (hassles, moves)
24	Revision of personal habits	69	Competing or performing in public
23	Trouble with boss	68	Getting in a physical fight
20	Change in work hours or conditions	66	Difficulties with a roommate
20	Change in residence	65	Job changes (applying, new job, work hassles)
20	Change in schools	65	Declaring a major or concerns about future plans
19	Change in recreation	62	A class you hate
19	Change in church activities	61	Drinking or use of drugs
18	Change in social activities	60	Confrontations with professors
17	Mortgage or loan less than $10,000*	58	Starting a new semester
16	Change in sleeping habits	57	Going on a first date
15	Change in number of family get-togethers	55	Registration
15	Change in eating habits	55	Maintaining a steady dating relationship
13	Vacation	54	Commuting to campus or work, or both
12	Christmas	53	Peer pressures
11	Minor violations of the law	53	Being away from home for the first time
	Total	52	Getting sick
		52	Concerns about your appearance
		51	Getting straight A's
		48	A difficult class that you love
		47	Making new friends, getting along with friends
		47	Fraternity or sorority rush
		40	Falling asleep in class
		20	Attending an athletic event (e.g., football games)
			Total

*today, of course, this figure would be much higher

**modern-day inventories such as this would indicate "spouse or partner," rather than "wife"

Figure 16.2 Arousal and Performance

Performance is related to at least two critical factors—the difficulty of the task and the level of arousal/stress while they are being performed. For easy tasks, moderately high arousal helps; for difficult tasks, lower levels of arousal are optimal.

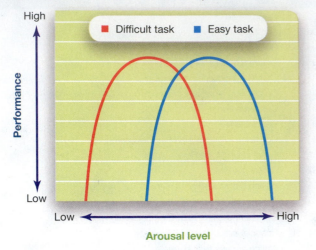

Watch BASICS: STRESS AND HEALTH

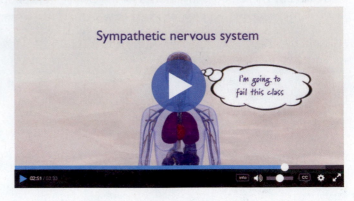

under lower levels of arousal (see Figure 16.2). Evaluate your own stress experiences by completing the activity in Table 16.5.

To reiterate the definition of this term, stress occurs when perceived demands exceed the resources we believe we have to cope with the demands. In either case, our bodies have evolved important physiological and neural mechanisms to regulate our responses to stress.

Physiology of Stress

Stress involves distinct feelings and sensations when they are relatively brief, such as giving an oral presentation in class, as well as when they are chronic such as the cumulative effect of a challenging school year. Walter Cannon, an early researcher of stress, noted that the physical responses to stressors were somewhat general, despite the fact that stress can come from a variety of sources that may be biological, cognitive, or social in nature. Cannon described this general reaction as a *fight-or-flight response*, a set of physiological changes that occur in response to psychological or physical threats. In this video, Basics: Stress and Health, you will learn about current stress research and see what happens in the body during the fight-or-flight response.

Hans Selye (1956) looked beyond the immediate fight-or-flight response and saw the unfolding of a larger pattern of responding to stress. He named this pattern the **general adaptation syndrome (GAS)**—*a theory of stress responses involving stages of alarm, resistance, and exhaustion*. As GAS illustrates, a stressful event, such as a mild shock if you see a rat, or a pop quiz if you are a college student, first elicits an *alarm* reaction. Alarm consists of your recognition of the threat and the physiological reactions that accompany it. As the stressful event continues, the second part of this adaptive response, known as *resistance*, is characterized by coping with the event (freezing for the rat, and for you gathering your thoughts and mentally preparing for the quiz). The third and final stage is *exhaustion*—the experience depletes your physical resources and your physiological stress response declines.

Since the work of Cannon and Selye, psychologists have further uncovered the highly complex physiological interactions that occur during and after stress. In their search, two key pathways have been identified: the autonomic pathway and the HPA axis, which we discuss next.

THE STRESS PATHWAYS You can likely attest to the fact that stress involves your whole body. During stressful times the heart races, palms get sweaty, and the stomach feels like it is tied in a knot. These sensations are the result of activity in the *autonomic pathway*, which originates in the brain and extends to the body where stress can be felt in the form of tension, nervousness, and arousal. Recall from Module 3.3 that the nervous system consists of the central nervous system (brain and spinal cord) and the peripheral nervous system, which includes the autonomic nervous system. In

---

Table 16.5 How Stressed Are You? Apply the life stress inventory to your own experiences and compare overall scores with others.

To complete this activity, refer to the values next to each stressful event listed in the right column of Table 16.4. Add up the numbers that apply to your experiences to compute your total stress score. After you have done so, see below to compare your computed averages from a college student sample.

Renner and Mackin (1998) gathered data on a sample of 257 undergraduate college students using the same instrument (range: 17–45 years; mean: 19.75 years). They reported an average stress score of 1,247 (standard deviation: 441), with scores ranging from 182 to 2,571. How did you compare with their sample?

Figure 16.3 Stress Pathways of the Body

The stress pathways of the body include the autonomic nervous system and the HPA axis. Both systems converge on the adrenal glands. The autonomic response involves stimulation of the adrenal medulla of the sympathetic nervous system, resulting in the release of epinephrine and norepinephrine—chemicals that stimulate the fight-or-flight response. Activity of the HPA axis results in stimulation of the adrenal cortex, which releases cortisol into the bloodstream.

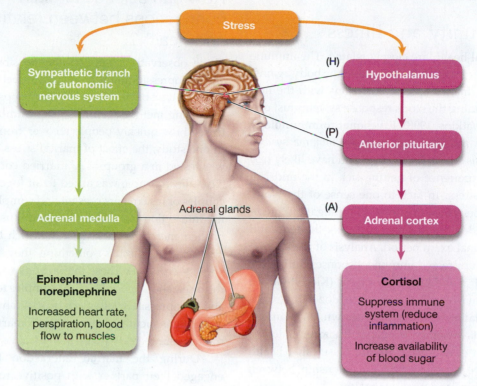

response to stress, the hypothalamus stimulates a group of sympathetic nervous system cells called the *adrenal medulla* (located within the adrenal glands) to release epinephrine and norepinephrine, which then trigger bodily changes associated with the fight-or-flight response (see Figure 16.3).

Another physiological system involved in the stress response is the **hypothalamic–pituitary–adrenal (HPA) axis**, *a neural and endocrine circuit that provides communication between the nervous system (the hypothalamus) and the endocrine system (pituitary and adrenal glands)*. Think of the HPA axis as a series of steps supporting the body's stress response. When you perceive that you are in a stressful situation, the hypothalamus releases a substance called corticotrophin-releasing factor, which stimulates the pituitary gland to release adrenocorticotrophic hormone. This hormone in turn stimulates the release of **cortisol**, *a hormone secreted by the adrenal cortex that prepares the body to respond to stressful circumstances*. For example, cortisol may stimulate increased access to energy stores or lead to decreased inflammation (immune system activity). In summary, both the sympathetic nervous system (through the release of epinephrine and norepinephrine) and the HPA axis (through the release of cortisol) function to prepare us to respond to stress. Watch the following video The HPA Axis to see how this system works.

Watch THE HPA AXIS

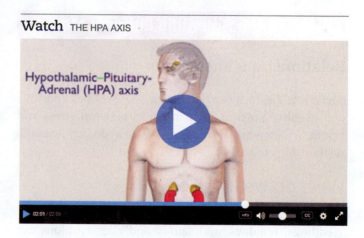

OXYTOCIN: TO TEND AND BEFRIEND Not all stress responses are about fighting or fleeing; in fact, some have the opposite effect. Stress sometimes leads people to seek close contact and social support, a phenomenon known as the *tend and befriend response* (Taylor, 2002; von Dawans et al., 2012). This reaction may be promoted by the release of **oxytocin**, *a stress-sensitive hormone that is typically associated with maternal bonding and social relationships*. Oxytocin influences social bonding in both males and females, but women seem to rely more on this particular physiological adaptation to cope with stress (Taylor, 2006). This unique stress response for females is thought to have evolutionary significance. For females of many species, the responsibility to avoid harm and protect offspring under stressful circumstances has likely survival advantages over fighting or running away.

Stress, Immunity, and Illness

Stress and physical health are closely related. The immune system, which is responsible for protecting the body against infectious disease, has complex connections with the nervous system, including the stress response systems just discussed (Maier & Watkins, 1998). **Psychoneuroimmunology** *is the study of the relationships among the immune system, behavior, and nervous system functioning.* You have likely had the unfortunate experience of getting sick in the midst of a period of high stress. In fact, in one sense of the word, final exams may be unhealthy. In one investigation, medical students provided blood samples during the term and again during the final exam period. Analysis of these blood samples showed suppressed immune responses during the high-stress period at the end of the term (Kiecolt-Glaser, 1984). This is not an isolated phenomenon; dozens of experimental and correlational studies have shown, for example, that stress predicts whether people will succumb to the cold virus (Cohen et al., 1998). Another issue that health psychologists have explored is the relationship between intimate relationships and physical health.

Working the Scientific Literacy Model

Relationships and Health

Social relationships can be a major source of both positive and negative stress. Given the links between stress and health, it seems reasonable to ask: How do our personal relationships relate to health?

What do we know about relationships and health?

Weddings, holidays, and family and class reunions can bring great joy and closeness, yet can be very stressful. Friendships and romantic relationships can involve negative stress when there is conflict or disagreement, or when individuals feel misunderstood or disregarded. Periods of social distress can distract someone from work, school, and other daily activities. In addition, this type of stress can even affect how the body responds to illness or injury.

Oxytocin, and another hormone called *vasopressin*, are involved in social behavior and bonding. We previously discussed the role of oxytocin in moderating stress responses, primarily in females. People with high vasopressin levels also tend to report better relationship quality

with their spouses (Walum et al., 2008). Interestingly, both of these hormones also interact with the immune system, specifically to reduce inflammation.

How can science explain connections between relationships and health?

These observations suggest the possibility that oxytocin and vasopressin might be related to better physical health in the context of close social relationships. A common, if not surprising method for measuring immunity and health is to see how quickly people recover from a minor wound. In one study, the effect of marital stress on wound healing was tested in a group of 37 married couples (Gouin et al., 2010). Each couple was asked to sit together with no other couples or researchers present and complete a series of marital interaction tasks, including a discussion of the history of their marriage and a task in which both spouses were instructed to discuss something they wished to change about themselves. These interactions were videotaped and the researchers also took blood samples to measure oxytocin and vasopressin levels. Each participant also consented to receiving a suction blister on the forearm, which is a very minor wound created with a medical vacuum pump.

During the marital interaction tasks, those who engaged their partner with positive responses including acceptance, support, and self-disclosure had higher levels of oxytocin and vasopressin. Those who responded with hostility, withdrawal, and distress had lower levels (Figure 16.4). In addition, the suction blister wounds healed more quickly over an 8-day period in individuals with high oxytocin and vasopressin levels. (Suction wounds heal to 100% within 12 days.)

The health-promoting effects of oxytocin are also evident from placebo-controlled studies. In another experiment, married couples were given either an intranasal solution of oxytocin or a placebo. The couples then engaged in discussion about conflict within their marriage. Those who received a boost of oxytocin showed more positive, constructive behavior during their discussion compared to couples in the placebo group. The researchers also measured cortisol levels from saliva samples obtained from each individual. Those in the oxytocin group had lower cortisol levels compared to couples in the placebo group (Ditzen et al., 2009).

Can we critically evaluate this evidence?

It might be tempting to conclude that a boost of oxytocin or vasopressin could be the key to marital happiness, stress reduction, and physical health. Although the studies you just read about are related to these important

Figure 16.4 Relationship Quality Is Related to Physiological Responses

Higher oxytocin and vasopressin levels are associated with positive social interactions between married couples.

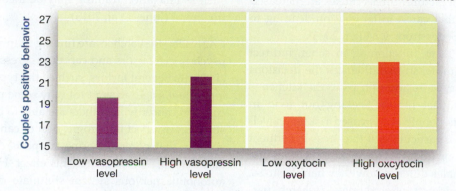

qualities, it is important to avoid oversimplifying what their results mean. Claims that supplemental oxytocin can make anyone happier and better at love, marriage, sex, and even "mind reading" should be looked at with skepticism. Advertisements for such products are not hard to find. However, scientists are still in the relatively early stages of learning how oxytocin and vasopressin affect social behavior in humans, and how they are related to immune system function (Gouin et al., 2010; Macdonald & Macdonald, 2010).

Why is this relevant?

Although these studies were conducted with married couples, the physiological and physical healing benefits of close, positive social relationships extend to romantic relationships, friendships, and family. Procedures for healing physical injury currently focus on repair to damaged areas and preventing infection from setting in. In addition to these critical steps, it appears that managing psychological stress is also important for facilitating recovery from wounds (Gouin & Kiecolt-Glaser, 2011).

JOURNAL PROMPT

Oxytocin: Oxytocin levels are elevated in couples who show positive responses to each other while dealing with a stressful event. Levels are lower in couples who show negative behavior toward one another. One might conclude that high oxytocin levels *cause* couples to behave more lovingly toward each other. Explain how this relationship could be correlational, rather than causally related.

CORONARY HEART DISEASE High stress levels increase risk of **coronary heart disease**—*a condition in which plaques form in the blood vessels that supply the heart with blood and oxygen, resulting in restricted blood flow.* A nine-year study of 12,000 healthy males found that those experiencing chronic stress with their families or at work were 30% more likely to die from coronary heart disease than were men who were not chronically stressed

(Matthews & Gump, 2002). Coronary heart disease begins when injury and infection damage the arteries of the heart. This damage triggers the inflammatory response by the immune system—white blood cells travel to affected areas in an attempt to repair the damaged tissue. These cells

Does someone need a hug? Psychologists have conducted controlled experimental studies confirming that social support, including receiving hugs, reduces susceptibility to the common cold (Cohen et al., 2015).

gather cholesterol and form dangerous plaques, which can rupture, break off, and block blood flow. So how does stress fit into this picture? Stress causes an increased release of molecules that cause inflammation, leading to heart complications (Segerstrom & Miller, 2004).

Stress influences heart functioning in other, indirect ways as well. For example, stress influences the decisions we make at the grocery store and in trips to the kitchen—decisions that can impact health. Seeking out food in response to stress puts people at increased risk for developing health problems, particularly if the stress is frequent and the food is of poor quality. However, as we learned earlier, males and females differ in how they handle stress. In one study, psychologists offered male research participants snacking options of healthy foods (peanuts and grapes) or unhealthy options (M&Ms and potato chips) while they were given an unsolvable anagram puzzle (stressful) or a solvable anagram (non-stressful). Perhaps counter to what you might predict, men in the no-stress condition ate more junk food than did the men who were stressed by the unsolvable anagram (Zellner et al., 2007). This finding contrasts with the tendencies of female participants—in a similar experiment, women ate more junk food when stressed (Zellner et al., 2006).

An unsolvable anagram is an acute stressor that is easy to leave behind. By comparison, job, family, and other potential sources of stress are much more challenging to manage. So how do real-life chronic stressors affect eating? Chronic stress leads to greater consumption of calorie-rich, less-healthy foods—which likely fits with your own experiences. Why do we turn to tasty, calorie-rich foods when stressed? The answer may seem obvious—it's called "comfort food" for a reason. Stress actually alters the physiological pathways that lead us to food. Evolution has equipped us with a tendency to increase food intake under times of stress. Recall that when the HPA axis is stimulated under stressful circumstances it releases cortisol. Researchers now think that this stress response leads us to regard calorie-rich food as more rewarding than when we are not stressed (Adam & Epel, 2007; Pool et al., 2014).

AIDS Acquired immune deficiency syndrome (AIDS) is a disease caused by infection with the human immunodeficiency virus (HIV). This disease saps the immune system's ability to fight off infections, to such an extent that even conditions that are relatively harmless to most of the population can be devastating to an individual with AIDS. Patients in industrialized countries with more medical options have a better prognosis than those living in impoverished areas. Retroviral therapies have greatly increased the longevity, health, and overall quality of life of patients. However, living with HIV can bring many forms of stress, and the release of cortisol can even

further dampen the ability to fend off infection. Therefore, researchers are exploring how psychological interventions such as relaxation training may be incorporated into HIV treatment (Jones et al, 2013)

CANCER Researchers are finding numerous links between psychosocial factors and cancer progression (Lutgendorf et al., 2013). Several factors, such as the type of cancer and an individual's age, account for why some people rapidly succumb to cancer while others are able to beat it. In addition, stress levels affect the progression of cancer. Why is this? It appears that norepinephrine supports cancer cell growth, and that cortisol magnifies this effect. Hormones from the autonomic nervous system stimulate cells that reside in tumors, which ultimately results in growth and proliferation of these masses (Antoni, 2013). Thus, when someone experiences stress, the autonomic nervous system and HPA axis naturally respond, but their reactions compromise how well the individual can fight the disease.

For many people, stress levels can be changed and the course of a disease such as cancer can be slowed. For example, individuals who have undergone assertiveness training and learn anger management techniques show reduced autonomic responses and hormonal activity associated with the HPA axis (Antoni et al., 2007). Also, those who are optimistic and cope by using humor and keeping a positive outlook (and thus experience less stress) show physiological benefits such as greater immune response (Lutgendorf et al., 2007).

Psychologists are finding that the stress–illness relationship is a very complex one, involving numerous physiological systems. Also, the effects of mental stress on physical functioning are diverse. Recall that stress can come in a variety of forms—at the very least, we can divide it into acute and chronic variations. It appears that stress also has dual influences on immunity. Acute stressors tend to activate the immune system, whereas chronic exposure to stress generally causes suppression of the immune system (Segerstrom & Miller, 2004).

Stress, Personality, and Illness

How people handle and cope with stress often depends on their personality. First consider your own responses to a common stressful event. Imagine you have a one-hour break between classes, during which you need to get lunch and also visit one of your professors across campus. When you arrive at your professor's office, you see a line of other students awaiting their turn, and the current occupant is blathering on and on about something completely unrelated to schoolwork. How would you tend to react in this situation? Would you become agitated, angry, resentful, and fidgety? Or would you be more inclined to strike up a conversation with others in line to help pass the time? Your answer will likely depend on various factors—but each of us tends to have a common style of responding to stressful events.

Personality characteristics and stress coping skills are also related to long-term health, as well as recovery from illness. **Type A personality** *describes people who tend to be impatient and worry about time, and are easily angered, competitive and, highly motivated*. In contrast, **Type B personality** *describes people who are more laid back and characterized by a patient, easygoing, and relaxed disposition* (Friedman & Rosenman, 1974). The concept of Types A and B did not originate in psychology. Rather, cardiologists suspected that people who were prone to stress had poorer physical health. They identified these individuals as Type A, and their studies revealed that people who fall in the Type A category are far more likely to have heart attacks than are Type B people. This initial finding has been replicated many times, though the correlation between levels of Type A characteristics and coronary heart disease is only moderate. Other factors, not just how a person copes with stress, may further elevate the risk of coronary heart disease. People who have a Type A personality also engage in behaviors that compromise physical health, such as drinking large quantities of alcohol, smoking, and sleeping less than people with a Type B personality. Thus, numerous correlated factors may explain the relationship between Type A personality and risk of coronary heart disease.

The distinction between Types A and B personalities has not satisfied all behavioral scientists and physicians. Being quick to anger is a characteristic of Type A individuals, but so is being hyper-motivated to succeed at work. Perhaps there is something more specific about personality that increases one's risk for developing heart disease. More recent research has shown that people who are prone to hostility and anger are at greater risk for developing coronary heart disease (Razzini et al., 2008). Other personality characteristics linked to coronary heart disease include anxiety and depression.

Outlook on life seems to influence physical health as well. People who are optimistic tend to have a positive outlook on life and have a constructive way of explaining the causes of everyday events. Pessimists have a more negative perception of life and tend to see the glass as half-empty. Optimism is correlated with better physical health than pessimism. For example, optimists have lower incidence of cardiovascular problems such as congestive heart failure and stroke (Kim et al., 2014; Kim et al., 2011). Pessimism can even compromise health when it comes to viral responses. Women who tend toward pessimism and test positive for the HPV virus (a papilloma virus known to cause cervical cancer) have lower counts of white blood cells that fight disease than do optimistic women with the HPV virus. If stressed, pessimistic women run a greater risk of developing cervical cancer (Antoni et al., 2006).

Myths in Mind
Stress and Ulcers

People typically associate ulcers—open sores in the lining of the esophagus, stomach, and small intestine—with people working in high-stress jobs, such as police officers or air traffic controllers. The belief that stress causes people to develop ulcers is widespread. In actuality, most ulcers are caused by a bacterium, *Helicobacter pylori*, which can cause inflammation of the lining of various regions of the digestive tract. This bacterium is surprisingly common, and approximately 10% to 15% of people who are exposed to it will develop an ulcer resulting from inflammation. Thus, stress does not cause ulcers, although it can worsen their symptoms. Also, smoking, alcohol, pain relievers, and a poor diet—anything that can irritate the digestive system—increases problems associated with ulcers.

Contrary to popular belief, chronic stress, like that experienced by air traffic controllers, will not cause a stomach ulcer.

Module 16.2 Summary

16.2a Know ... the key terminology associated with stress and illness:

coronary heart disease
cortisol
general adaptation syndrome (GAS)
hypothalamic–pituitary–adrenal (HPA) axis
oxytocin
psychoneuroimmunology
stress
Type A personality
Type B personality

16.2b Understand ... the physiological reactions that occur under stress.

When a person encounters a stressor, the hypothalamus stimulates the sympathetic nervous system to act, triggering the release of epinephrine and norepinephrine from the adrenal medulla. This reaction is often referred to as the fight-or-flight response. Another part of the stress response system is the HPA axis, in which the hypothalamus stimulates the pituitary gland to release hormones that in turn stimulate the adrenal cortex to release cortisol, which prepares the body to deal with stressful situations.

16.2c Understand ... how the immune system is connected to stress responses.

Cortisol suppresses the immune system, leaving people more vulnerable to illness and slowing recovery time from illness and injury.

16. 2d Apply ... a measure of stressful events to your own experiences.

An important take home message from this module is that stress has a cumulative effect, and, depending on the amount and the nature of the stressors, as well as personality characteristics, stress can negatively affect both short- and long-term health. Taking an inventory of what is causing stress can help you sort out the different stressors, and also evaluate those that you can and cannot control. This is an important step to stress management. The activity How Stressed Are You? (Table 16.5) offers one way to look at your own stressors.

16. 2e Analyze ... the claim that ulcers are caused by stress.

Ulcers are damaged areas of the digestive tract often caused by infection with the bacterium *Helicobacter pylori*. Stress and other factors, such as diet and alcohol consumption, can worsen the condition of ulcers, but stress alone does not cause them.

Module 16.2 Quiz

Know ...

1. Which of the following is not a component of Selye's general adaptation syndrome?
   A. Resistance
   B. Alarm
   C. Flight
   D. Exhaustion

Understand ...

2. A major difference between the tend and befriend stress response and the responses mediated by the autonomic pathway and the HPA axis is that:
   A. the tend and befriend response involves cortisol activity.
   B. men are more likely to express the tend and befriend response.
   C. the tend and befriend response facilitates care for offspring and others in a social group.
   D. the tend and befriend response is a negative stress reaction, whereas the autonomic pathway and HPA axis responses are positive reactions.

3. How are the stress response and immune systems related?
   A. Illness is a cause a stress, but not the other way around.
   B. The two systems are physiologically separate, but by coincidence are sometimes activated at the same time.
   C. They are both controlled by the same brain regions.
   D. Increased stress levels directly impact the functioning of the immune system.

Apply ...

4. What is a sound recommendation for managing stress among hospital patients?
   A. Reduce stress, and therefore cortisol release, as much as possible.
   B. Introduce a mild amount of stress so that the HPA-axis can prime the immune system.
   C. Offer oxytocin inhalers to induce relaxation in patients.
   D. Allow people to attain their preferred level of stress (equal to what they would experience outside of the hospital).

Analyze ...

5. Researchers have concluded that the actual cause of ulcers is _____.
   A. stress
   B. bacterial infection
   C. genetics
   D. poor diet

Module 16.3 Coping and Well-Being

⌄ Learning Objectives

16.3a Know . . . the key terminology associated with coping and well-being.

16.3b Understand . . . how control over the environment influences coping and outlook.

16.3c Understand . . . positive and negative styles of coping.

16.3d Apply . . . your knowledge to better understand your own tendencies when dealing with stressful situations.

16.3e Analyze . . . whether activities such as relaxation techniques, meditation, and biofeedback actually help people cope with stress and problems.

What is the best way to cope with a personal disaster, such as losing your job? Writing about how the event makes you feel may not seem like a priority, but according to psychologist James Pennebaker, it may be one of the best strategies for coping and regaining the emotional resources needed to move on. Pennebaker, a leading researcher on the psychological benefits of writing, decided to intervene when a local computing and electronics firm laid off 60 workers. All he asked the workers to do was to write. But their instructions on how to write were different: Half the volunteers were randomly assigned to write about their "deepest thoughts and feelings surrounding the job loss, and how their lives,

both personal and professional, had been affected" (Spera et al., 1994, p. 725). In contrast, the control group members were told to write about their plans for the day and how they planned to find another job, which is much less personal and emotional. After a month of weekly 20-minute writing sessions, the group members who were writing about their emotions were getting hired much more frequently than the control group members. This was a double-blind, randomized study, so the differences between the groups can be traced to the writing. Similar methods have been used in Pennebaker's studies of first-year college students, people grieving the loss of a loved one, and other groups experiencing stressful transitions. The result was the same each time—group members who wrote meaningful narratives of their emotions and thoughts came out ahead, not just in terms of mental health, but also physically and in terms of their performance at work or school.

In this module, we will present some widely used solutions for coping with stress and behavioral methods that can help improve mental and physical health. We will also discuss some topics that might be less familiar, but may prove useful in how you cope with stress and negative events. Finally, we will discuss how stress and successful coping are closely related to our sense of control.

Coping

Equally important to understanding how stress works is learning how to cope with it. **Coping** *refers to the processes used to manage demands, stress, and conflict.* Some of us approach a problem or stressor, such as large monetary debt or a setback at work, by taking a problem-solving approach. In other words, we cope by defining the problem and working toward a solution. However, not all stressors are brought about by problems that have identifiable solutions. For example, emotional coping is probably better suited to dealing with an issue such as the loss of a loved one. Neither style of coping is superior to the other—the two are often combined and their suitability depends on the nature of the problem (Folkman & Lazarus, 1980).

Not all coping techniques actually help; some may simply replace one problem with another. For example, some people turn to alcohol or drugs to temporarily avoid feelings of stress, and some turn to food. Ice cream, chocolate, and salty snacks are popular—but probably unhealthy—methods of coping. In this section, we will examine the major ways of coping by focusing first on the positive approaches, and then on some of the negative ways that people cope.

POSITIVE COPING STRATEGIES Psychology has a bit of a reputation for focusing on the negative, including how damaging stress can be. But psychologists also study what makes people thrive, even in the face of extreme stress. This area of study, known as **positive psychology**, *uses scientific methods to study human strengths and potential.* Research in this area has identified numerous adaptive and constructive ways in which people cope with problems; these strategies produce meaningful solutions to stressful problems or, at the very least, healthy ways of living with them.

Optimism *is the tendency to have a favorable, constructive view on situations and to expect positive outcomes.* The effectiveness of optimism for coping with stress is particularly evident in studies of freshmen adjusting to their first semester of college. Students who were optimistic by nature experienced relatively low levels of stress and depression and were also proactive in seeking out peers for support and companionship. Overall, their adjustment to college was better than the adjustment of those students who were pessimistic in nature (Brissette et al., 2002). People who are optimistic in the face of adversity are better able to approach problems from various angles and come up with constructive solutions. Some evidence also indicates that they are more physiologically equipped to deal with stress than are pessimists. Optimists are better protected against cardiovascular illnesses than pessimists (Kim et al., 2011; Kim et al., 2014), and optimism is associated with quicker recovery following acute coronary problems such as heart attacks (Ronaldson et al., 2015).

Coping is also influenced by **resilience**, *the ability to effectively recover from illness or adversity.* Individuals differ in their ability to bounce back from events such as disaster, disease, or major loss. Resilient people tend to have one or more factors stacked in their favor. Financial and social resources, opportunities for rest and relaxation, and other positive life circumstances contribute to resiliency. Even so, amazing stories of resiliency can be found among individuals living with unimaginable stress. Thus, personality and emotional characteristics are also important contributors to resiliency in the face of adversity. One amazing example is that of Victor Frankl, an early- and mid-20th-century Austrian psychiatrist. Frankl was already an influential physician and therapist when he, his wife, and family were forced into concentration camps during World War II. Frankl found himself in the role of helping people adjust to life in the concentration camp. He encouraged others to tap into whatever psychological resources they had left to cope with very bleak circumstances. Frankl not only helped others find resiliency, but also became more aware of his own resiliency as he had to find meaning in his own circumstances. Eventually Frankl's wife and parents were deported to different concentration camps, where they were murdered. Despite his own enormous losses, Frankl continued helping others to cope and find solace under the worst of circumstances (Frankl, 1959).

Psychologists have long focused on the negative outcomes of stress, but stories such as Frankl's demonstrate that stress and trauma can also lead people to recognize and use positive qualities. In fact, psychologists describe the phenomenon of **posttraumatic growth**, *the capacity to grow and experience long-term positive effects in response to negative events* (Calhoun & Tedeschi, 2013). It happens in response to events such as automobile accidents, sexual and physical assault, combat, and severe and chronic illnesses. Individuals who experience posttraumatic growth often report feeling a greater sense of vulnerability, yet over time develop an increased inner strength. They also report finding greater meaning and depth in their relationships, a greater sense of appreciation for what they have, and an increased sense of spirituality.

Posttraumatic growth is not an alternative reaction to posttraumatic stress. Rather, the two conditions occur together. Clinicians recognize that the growth occurs during the process of coping with stress, not because of the event itself. Clinical psychologists trained in working with trauma victims help facilitate the growth process, and assist individuals in finding the interpersonal and social resources needed for healing.

BIOFEEDBACK, RELAXATION, AND MEDITATION As you have been reading this chapter, your circulatory system has been pumping blood and maintaining blood pressure, your lungs have been breathing in air, and your digestive system may have been working on a recent meal, all without the tiniest bit of conscious effort. Certainly you can hold your breath for a moment using conscious effort, but can you hold your heartbeat? Change your blood pressure? If you are like most of us, you cannot control all of these autonomic functions, but that does not mean it is impossible.

Biofeedback *is a therapeutic technique involving the use of physiological recording instruments to provide feedback that increases awareness of bodily responses.* The psychologists who developed this technique believed that by seeing or hearing a machine's representation of bodily processes, people could gain awareness of stress responses and bring them under voluntary control. For example, a patient with chronic stress could use feedback on his blood pressure, heart rate, and tension of his facial muscles to monitor and, possibly, control his stress responses. As you can imagine, this ability would have very useful applications to clinical psychology. However, after some promising findings, the excitement over biofeedback has subsided,

Meditation is practiced in many cultures, often for the purposes of promoting psychological well-being, health, and stress reduction.

in part because it was found that simple relaxation techniques were just as useful.

Many people find great benefit in using *relaxation* and *meditation* techniques to cope with stress and life's difficult periods. Relaxation and meditation techniques are designed to calm emotional responses as well as physiological reactions to stress. People frequently regard meditation as either a religious or new-age ritual—something that takes years of practice from which only "experts" can benefit. This is hardly an accurate summary of meditation. There are different types of meditation, two of which are (1) *mindfulness*, which involves attending to all thoughts, sensations, and feelings without attempting to judge or control them, and (2) *concentrative*, in which the individual focuses on breathing and a specific thought or sensation, such as an image or a repeated sound (Cahn & Polich, 2006). Meditation is most successful when performed in a quiet environment, when the person assumes a relaxed position (but not sufficient to support napping), and when he or she remains passive except for mindfulness activity or focusing attention.

Brain imaging work may take us a step closer to actually visualizing the connections between mind and body. A complex form of meditation called *integrated mind–body training* was developed from traditional Chinese medicine; it involves a combination of mindfulness with traditional meditative practices. This probably sounds mystical and beyond scientific scrutiny. However, Chinese scientists conducted brain scans on students who practiced integrated mind–body training. Over the course of the training, the students' brains appeared to develop an increased ability to control bodily physiology. A region of the midfrontal cortex called the *anterior cingulate* was particularly relevant; this area is involved in various aspects of processing reward and emotion. In this study, activity within the anterior cingulate was associated with the

Biofeedback involves the use of physiological monitoring, which allows the patient to see and sometimes hear the output of his or her physiological reactions.

participants' increased control over parasympathetic nervous system responses. The increased parasympathetic activity accounted for the heightened sense of relaxation experienced while meditating. This result was not found in students who engaged in a simpler relaxation technique that did not involve integrating mind–body interactions (Tang et al., 2009). Thus, scientific studies of meditation appear to confirm its health benefits, and are also bringing us closer to understanding precisely how the nervous system is linked with other bodily processes, such as the immune system (Morgan et al., 2014).

RELIGION AND SPIRITUALITY   Many people use religion and spiritual inspiration as their primary coping mechanism during stressful situations, both large and small. They may use any combination of religious practices, depending on the specific nature of the faith: prayer, meditation, religious counseling, and social support from family and congregations. All of these efforts can provide strength and comfort during difficult times, but they may also be associated with greater overall happiness. Psychologists have become increasingly curious about the possible health benefits associated with religion and spirituality. Numerous studies indicate that people who are religious and are actively engaged with religious practices do, in fact, live a bit longer than do people who are less religious or nonreligious (McCullough et al., 2000).

A hasty interpretation of these results might lead one to conclude that religion causes people to live longer—that the experiences of prayer and church going lead to the greater longevity. However, the studies in this area actually produce correlational, not experimental, data—psychologists cannot randomly assign people to be religious or not. Consequently, we must consider alternative explanations. For example, lifestyle factors are also at play. People of Muslim, Jewish, or Christian faith are more likely to engage in healthy behaviors, including wearing seatbelts, visiting the dentist, and avoiding consumption of alcohol and cigarette smoking (reviewed in McCullough & Willoughby, 2009). Religions also tend to have negative views of criminal activity, drug abuse, and risky sexual behavior. Thus the increased longevity is probably related to the greater self-control and self-regulation that are characteristic of many religious belief systems.

Generally, people who are religious show greater well-being and lower levels of depression (Smith et al., 2003). The determination of whether religion protects people from depression depends on the point of view taken, however. People who cope with problems using positive aspects of religion (e.g., viewing stressors with kindness or collaborating with others in solving problems) are less prone to depression than religious people

who adopt negative appraisals of their problems and concerns, such as viewing problems as a result of God's punishment (Ano & Vasconcelles, 2005; McCullough & Willoughby, 2009).

NEGATIVITY AND PESSIMISM   Adversity elicits a wide range of emotions and reactions. **Negative affectivity** *refers to the tendency to respond to problems with a pattern of anxiety, hostility, anger, guilt, or nervousness.* We occasionally might hear of someone who deals with a difficult breakup by socially withdrawing from others, becoming angry and resentful, and oftentimes growing hostile enough to threaten and harass the other person with phone calls, repeated texting, or spreading of rumors. Although the anger and upset feelings are perfectly normal reactions, clearly these hostile behaviors are a negative and destructive way of coping. However, for some individuals, this manner of dealing with adversity is consistent, and occurs across a broad number of situations, even ones that are trivial by comparison to a breakup.

Related to negative affectivity is what psychologists refer to as **pessimistic explanatory style**, *which is the tendency to interpret and explain negative events as internally based and as a constant, stable quality* (Burns & Seligman, 1989). The pessimism even bubbles to the surface when events occur beyond one's personal control, such as a natural disaster or war. It is certainly evident in common events as well—for example, a laid-off employee who struggles to find a job may attribute the problem to his perceived inability to network properly or because he is simply doomed to failure. In addition, individuals with a pessimistic explanatory style are at risk for health problems due to stress and increased inflammation (Bennett et al., 2012; Roy et al., 2010). Notably, pessimism appears to have long-term consequences on health. Researchers at the Mayo Clinic administered personality tests assessing optimism and pessimism to patients who came into the clinic for general medical issues during the 1960s. Thirty years later, the data on optimism and pessimism were compared to patient survival, and the researchers found a 19% increase in mortality risk in people who were consistently pessimistic (Maruta et al., 2000). Perhaps a good attitude does more than help individuals cope emotionally with illness; perhaps it actually helps them overcome it. To get a sense of how you cope with stress, see the activity in Table 16.6.

Perceived Control

As Dr. Pennebaker's story from the beginning of this module illustrates, the most stressful of circumstances are the ones that people have little or no control over. For example, children who reside in abusive homes have no control

Table 16.6 How Do You Cope with Stress? Complete the scale below, which was designed to measure optimistic versus pessimistic coping styles.

	Strongly Disagree		Neutral		Strongly Agree
1. In uncertain times, I usually expect the best.	0	1	2	3	4
2. If something can go wrong for me, it will.	4	3	2	1	0
3. I always look on the bright side of things.	0	1	2	3	4
4. I'm always optimistic about my future.	0	1	2	3	4
5. I hardly ever expect things to go my way.	4	3	2	1	0
6. Things never work out the way I want them to.	4	3	2	1	0
7. I'm a believer in the idea that "every cloud has a silver lining."	0	1	2	3	4
8. I rarely count on good things happening to me.	4	3	2	1	0

Now add up the total of the numbers you circled: _____

SOURCE: Scheier, M. F., & Carver, C. S. (1985). Optimism, coping, and health: Assessment and implications of generalized outcome expectancies. *Health Psychology, 4*(3), 219–247. doi:10.1037/0278-6133.4.3.219

over their circumstances, nor do the victims of natural disasters. Each situation can result in people acquiring a sense that their behavior has little effect on external events.

Laboratory experiments have demonstrated the negative impact that a lack of control has on health and behavior. A classic example comes from work on avoidance learning in dogs conducted in the 1960s by Martin Seligman and his colleagues (Seligman & Maier, 1967; see Figure 16.5). In this study, dogs were exposed to an avoidance learning procedure in which they were placed in a chamber with an electric grid on the floor of one side, where the shock was delivered, and a panel that the dogs could jump over to reach a "safe" zone where there was no shock. Some dogs learned that if a dimming light preceded the shock, they could quickly jump to the safe zone, avoiding the shock altogether. Another group of dogs was first conditioned to the light stimulus paired with an inescapable shock. These dogs were then placed in the avoidance chamber, but did not attempt to avoid the shock when the light dimmed. Rather, they would lie down, whine, and appear resigned to receive the shock. This finding was described as **learned helplessness**—*an acquired suppression of avoidance or escape behavior in response to unpleasant, uncontrollable circumstances.*

Learned helplessness has been offered as an explanation for how people with depression tend to view the world. People with depression are prone to hold beliefs that their actions have no influence on external events, and that their environment and circumstances dictate outcomes. To some extent these beliefs may be true, but when generalized to just about any situation, they can negatively affect mental and physical well-being. The parallels to Seligman's work are rather clear. In some circumstances, humans and some nonhuman species will simply endure pain rather than initiate ways to avoid or escape it.

Figure 16.5 The Learned Helplessness Procedure

In Seligman and Maier's study, dogs that could avoid a painful shock would quickly learn to do so. Conversely, dogs that initially learned they could not avoid a shock remained passive when the opportunity to do so was given. The acquired failure to avoid or escape unpleasant circumstances that are perceived as uncontrollable is referred to as learned helplessness.

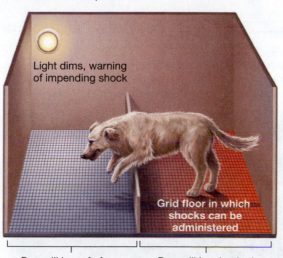

Light dims, warning of impending shock

Grid floor in which shocks can be administered

Dog will be safe from shock on this side

Dog will be shocked on this side

Working the Scientific Literacy Model

Compensatory Control and Health

The idea of a random world and a lack of personal control can be discomforting. For example, hurricanes and tornados are often referred to as "acts of God," rather than the result of an unfortunate meeting between extreme meteorological activity and populated areas. But does having a sense of control lead to better health?

What do we know about how people cope with seemingly random events?

Some people feel as if they are the victims of random events, while others believe themselves to be the beneficiaries of the whims of life. However, the idea that randomness dictates worldly events can create anxiety in people. Even if a person believes randomness is the rule, he or she can become highly motivated to find meaning in the world and, through this search, a sense that the course of events is determined by the will of individuals or God (Kay et al., 2009). In this way, many people cope with stressful life events through **compensatory control**— *psychological strategies used to preserve a sense of nonrandom order when personal control is compromised* (Kay et al., 2009). For example, people who are skeptical of any divine purpose in the world may change their view in the wake of personal or societal tragedy. Loss of a family member or being the unwitting victim of an economic depression, for example, are types of events known to draw people toward religion. These observations are primarily correlational, but researchers have conducted experiments to determine causal relationships between sense of control and beliefs about randomness versus orderliness.

How can science explain compensatory control?

To study compensatory control, researchers have developed a laboratory task that manipulates people's sense of personal control over a situation (Whitson & Galinsky, 2008). In one study, participants completed a concept identification task in which two symbols were presented on a computer screen, and the participant had to guess which symbol correctly represented the concept that the computer had chosen (e.g., the color of the symbol, its shape). The computer provided feedback on whether the participants chose the correct or incorrect symbol after each trial. Half of the participants received accurate feedback, while the other half received completely random feedback—sometimes their correct answers were recorded as incorrect, and vice versa. Participants receiving random feedback reported feeling a lower sense of control on a self-report measure.

Following the concept identification task, the participants then viewed multiple pictures, such as those shown in Figure 16.6. If you look closely, you will see that one of the pictures has a horse-like figure in it, whereas the other image has no discernible pattern. Participants in both conditions reported seeing faintly drawn figures, such as the horse. However, participants who had a diminished sense of control induced by the random feedback they received on the computer task were more likely to report seeing patterns within completely random images (Whitson & Galinsky, 2008).

It appears that when people feel their sense of control is undermined, they compensate by heightening their search for structure in the world, to the point of calling upon their imagination. This is evident in other domains as well, not just detecting patterns in random, snowy images. People also gain a greater need for structure and become increasingly willing to believe in superstitious rituals and to endorse conspiracy theories when their sense of control is diminished (Figure 16.7; Kay et al., 2009; Whitson & Galinksy, 2008).

Can we critically evaluate this evidence?

A major advantage of the study described here is that the researchers were able to experimentally induce a perceived lack of control in the participants who received random feedback on their performance on the computerized

---

Figure 16.6 Seeing Images Where There Are None

Do you see a figure in the image on the left? You may see a figure resembling a horse. What about on the right? There is no discernible image intended for this image. Psychologists have found that individuals who feel as though they lack control are more likely to detect patterns in the image at right than are people who feel a greater sense of control (Whitson & Galinsky, 2008).

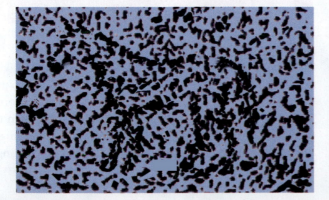
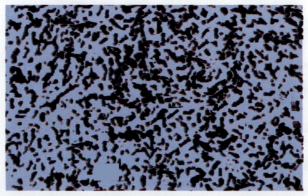

Figure 16.7 Exercising Compensatory Control

When people feel as though they lack control over the world, their need for structure, perceptual order, and beliefs in superstition and conspiracies increases. The orange bars show that participants who perceive that they are in control of events were unlikely to see images in snowy pictures and did not hold superstitious beliefs or endorse conspiracy theories. As the green bars indicate, when the same people perceive that they have lost a sense of control during the experimental procedure, the pattern is completely reversed. The participants report a greater need for structure, perceive images in random arrays, become more superstitious, and endorse conspiracy theories (Kay et al., 2009).

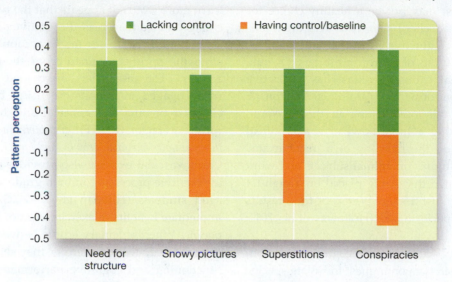

task. The observation that these participants then perceived images within randomness and showed a heightened belief in superstition and conspiracies may help to explain how people respond to lost control outside of the laboratory. Of course, one limitation is that a real-world lack of control, such as that which occurs in the face of natural disaster or loss of a job, has far greater consequences. Thus, as with any laboratory experiment, there is a limit to the degree to which the results generalize. Also, earlier we commented that belief in a divine force such as God can buffer people from the discomfort produced by the notion that natural and societal events are largely, if not completely, outside of their control. It is important to add that this is not a statement on the existence of God, but rather a description of how perception of events can influence what people believe.

Why is this relevant?

Having a sense of control greatly affects how we think about and interpret the world. In addition, it affects our health. Individuals who believe they can predict and influence present and future events tend to have improved physical and mental well-being compared to people who believe the opposite. For example, patients who are scheduled to undergo medical procedures, such as a colonoscopy, have reduced anxiety for the procedure if they are given clear, informative tutorials about the procedure before it occurs (Luck et al., 1999).

People may also compensate for their lack of control by performing superstitious rituals, which can provide a sense of at least partial control over outcomes. This can be seen in everyday examples, such as among athletes who follow the same steps when preparing for a game, as well as in extreme, maladaptive forms, such as in obsessive–compulsive disorder (covered in Module 13.3). Doing nothing is one response, as Seligman and Maier discovered in their studies of learned helplessness. With lost control, people are also more likely to develop beliefs that the world is not random and is controlled and orderly. This perception manifests through beliefs of an intervening God, as well as greater likelihood of defending social and political institutions that offer control of world events (Kay et al., 2009).

Nutrition and Exercise

"You are what you eat" is a well-worn phrase that was probably around long before scientists confirmed that it holds true. However, we now know that what we eat influences brain physiology and functioning. This being the case, psychologists have begun to investigate how diet affects intellectual ability and performance at work and school.

NUTRITION AND COGNITIVE FUNCTION Long-term consumption of fattening and sugary foods can have a negative impact on cognitive functioning. But what about the short-term effects? You have probably heard of the importance of a good breakfast more times than you care to recall. However, breakfast is the most often skipped meal, especially among children and adolescents (Rampersaud et al., 2005). Many people report not having time to eat (or not making time) and a lack of appetite for breakfast foods.

Skipping breakfast may not be a healthy choice for people heading off to school or work. The brain utilizes large amounts of glucose and other nutrients for energy and in the synthesis of neurotransmitters. Overall, research indicates that eating breakfast has a positive effect on academic performance (Adolphus, Lawton, & Dye, 2013). But does this mean eating anything? Would you be better off eating a huge bowl of sugary cereal than eating nothing on the morning of a major exam? Carefully controlled studies on animal subjects and work with humans has shown that being placed on a high-fat nonnutritious diet for just a short period of time results in reduced cognitive performance (Holloway et al., 2011; Murray et al., 2009).

The relationship between diet and cognitive functioning has led some researchers on a quest to isolate specific compounds that are best suited to improving cognition. Certain chemicals found in various plants, called flavanols, appear to improve, or at least help sustain, cognitive functioning (Brickman et al., 2014). It appears that these chemicals protect nerve cells (Reznichenko et al., 2005). Other dietary supplements, such as the omega-3 fatty acids found in fish, can improve brain functioning when combined with exercise (van Praag et al., 2007; Wu et al., 2008).

EXERCISE Exercise has considerable physical and psychological benefits, as people ranging from weekend warriors to long-term exercisers can attest. Barring injury, we typically do not hear a committed exerciser express regret about her active lifestyle. So which specific aspects of exercise account for all of its benefits? Obviously, exercise benefits the cardiovascular, muscular, and other physiological systems. How does the nervous system factor in?

Exercise has short-term benefits on mental functioning. For example, researchers in Germany asked college student participants to do all-out sprints, to jog, or to do nothing. The students who sprinted were able to learn 20% more items on a vocabulary list than the students who jogged or were inactive (Winter et al., 2007). Why did this occur? Perhaps the sprinters were more motivated than the others. This explanation sounds plausible, but the researchers randomly assigned healthy participants to the three groups—so there should not be anything inherent to the sprinter group that would lead them to learn more words. It appears that the type of exercise they engaged in led to increased cognitive performance. Which physiological processes might account for the cognitive edge the sprinters gained from their intense physical activity? The researchers discovered that the students who engaged in intense exercising had increased levels of dopamine, epinephrine, and **brain-derived neurotrophic factor (BDNF)**—*a protein in the nervous system that promotes survival, growth, and formation of new synapses*. Cardiovascular exercise also provides immediate benefits in cognitive processing in both grade-school and college-aged students (Hillman et al., 2003, 2014). But these immediate benefits of exercise are not limited to younger people. When sedentary adults between 60 and 85 years of age take up weekly exercise, they show improved brain functioning and cognitive performance (Hillman et al., 2008; Stothart et al., 2014).

One important issue to address is whether these short-term effects translate into lifelong cognitive benefits from exercise. Results from long-term studies indicate that a lifestyle that includes regular exercise helps preserve cognitive function and the brain systems that support it (van Praag, 2009). Researchers have found that older people who are at genetic risk for developing Alzheimer's disease and who show cognitive impairments can slow the rate of memory decline by exercising (Lautenschlager et al., 2008). It appears that levels of brain chemicals such as BDNF are boosted by exercise, which helps explain the changes in the brain that account for the cognitive benefits. Furthermore, exercise supports the development of new nerve cells in the hippocampus, a critical area for memory and cognitive activity (van Praag, 2008).

JOURNAL PROMPT

Coping with Stress: Now that you have read about many different coping styles, use terminology from the module to describe how you tend to cope with stress. What positive ways of coping that you learned about (or others you can think of) would you like to use more often?

Module **16.3** Summary

16.3a Know . . . the key terminology associated with coping and well-being:

biofeedback
brain-derived neurotrophic factor (BDNF)
compensatory control
coping
learned helplessness
negative affectivity
optimism
pessimistic explanatory style
positive psychology
posttraumatic growth
resilience

16.3b Understand . . . how control over the environment influences coping and outlook.

Psychologists have discovered that people (and dogs) become more willing to allow unpleasant events to occur if they learn that their behavior brings no change. Having at least some degree of control helps people with coping and improves their outlook on challenging circumstances. When control is threatened, people use compensatory responses, such as detecting order within random images.

16.3c Understand . . . positive and negative styles of coping.

Whether someone copes using a positive or negative style is related to personality (e.g., optimism versus pessimism).

Positive coping includes the concept of resilience—the ability to recover from adversity, and even benefit from the experience, as is the case with posttraumatic growth. Coping via negative affectivity and pessimism can have both psychological and physiological disadvantages.

16.3d Apply . . . your knowledge to better understand your own tendencies when dealing with stressful situations.

We all fall somewhere on the optimism–pessimism continuum. Completing the How Do You Cope With Stress activity in Table 16.6 provides a sense of where you might fall on it with regard to how you respond to stress. As you read in this module, there are diverse ways of coping with stress, and the strategies we use affect our mental and physical health.

16.3e Analyze . . . whether activities such as relaxation techniques, meditation, and biofeedback actually help people cope with stress and problems.

Meditation and other relaxation methods have been found to be quite effective in reducing stress. While some training and practice may be necessary, these techniques are by no means inaccessible to those who are motivated to pursue them.

Module **16.3** Quiz

Know . . .

1. _____ is the tendency to respond to problems with a pattern of anxiety, hostility, anger, guilt, or nervousness.
   A. A coping style
   B. Negative affectivity
   C. Pessimism
   D. An aggression complex

Understand . . .

2. A mentally healthy person who is prone to claiming that patterns exist where there are none:
   A. is showing negative affectivity.
   B. is showing signs of posttraumatic growth.
   C. probably feels a lost sense of control over a problem or situation.
   D. has a pessimistic explanatory style.

3. _____ is a positive coping strategy, while _____ is a negative style of coping.
   A. Meditation; resilience
   B. Pessimistic explanatory style; negative affectivity
   C. Meditation; alcohol
   D. Posttraumatic growth; resilience

Apply . . .

4. If someone experiences a major setback in their physical health, what would be a good step toward helping them cope and possibly recover?
   A. Take care of all of their needs and avoid letting them stress about details of the illness.
   B. Remind them of previous times they experienced luck and that it could happen again.
   C. Load up on alternative, nonmedical options.
   D. Find ways that they can gain a sense of control over their health and ways to overcome the illness.

Analyze . . .

5. What is the most accurate conclusion regarding the effects of meditation on stress and well-being?
   A. Mediation helps the individual control his or her physiological responses, thereby decreasing stress and preventing health problems such as cardiovascular disease.
   B. Advanced training in mediation will decrease stress in a manner similar to simple relaxation techniques.
   C. Mediation is the absolute best way to combat stress and protect your body from disease.
   D. Mediation is not a commonly used way of managing stress.

Module 16.4 Scientific Literacy Challenge: Forgiveness

Imagine a 50-year-old man with coronary heart disease visits with his physician. After receiving his prescription, he is reminded to eat a healthy diet, exercise, and manage his stress. But what if forgiveness was added to the list? Could this possibly be of any health benefit?

Before you start this activity, take a minute to write your thoughts on forgiveness.

JOURNAL PROMPT

Write about some ways you think that forgiving someone could have mental and physical health benefits.

What do we know about forgiveness?

Most people know at least *something* about how to live a healthy lifestyle, but forgiveness might not be an obvious choice on the list. In the commentary below, Steve Hanserd, a registered nurse, writes about how his staff is preparing to start a forgiveness intervention for their patients. As you read, remember that it is important to know the boldface key terms and concepts that are covered in Chapter 16.

Forgiveness Leads to a Change of Heart

By Steve Hanserd, RN, President, Association of Cardiac Care Professionals

We have an exciting new project in the works at the CCP medical center: A forgiveness intervention against **heart disease**. Forgiveness has been added to our list of the lifestyle changes we strongly recommend for patients with heart disease. Forgiveness rebuilds relationships and promotes **social resilience**. Social resilience is an important part of psychological health, and research indicates that it may improve physical health as well.

People who choose *not* to forgive, and instead hold onto resentment and anger, suffer numerous health consequences. Anger stimulates the **hypothalamic-pituitary-adrenal (HPA) axis**, our primary stress response system. Sustained activity of the HPA axis leads to negative physical effects, including compromised immune function. The goal of our intervention is to teach, encourage, and facilitate forgiveness. This is not just any forgiveness, but *unconditional* forgiveness. This is the conscious choice to let a transgression go without any conditions or demands; it means the individual is not waiting for an apology or retribution for a wrong that he has suffered.

Mr. Hanserd has stated his position and explained it well. Let's see how well he supported his position with scientific evidence below.

How do scientists study forgiveness?

In this section, the author introduces what he has learned about the science of forgiveness. As you read it, try to identify where the article addresses key elements of quality research and then complete the short quiz that follows.

The research supporting the benefits of forgiveness seems pretty clear. Studies published in the *Journal of Behavioral Medicine* showed that people who rarely forgive experience more episodes of anger than others. Anger, in turn, is associated with significantly worse cardiovascular conditions and related risk factors, such as sleep. Of those who do forgive, there are further differences: Individuals who forgive *conditionally* are likely to die earlier than those who forgive unconditionally.

We also know something about how forgiveness works. By decreasing the stress associated with resentment and anger, forgiving can decrease blood pressure, according to research published in the *Journal of Positive Psychology*. Experiments also found that individuals trained with forgiveness techniques showed healthier immune systems, including more disease fighting cells and reduced inflammation responses, which lead to better health.

Finally, the research also shows that forgiveness can be learned and practiced. There is a tendency for some people to be more consistent with forgiveness than others; it is a personality trait of sorts. But there have been several controlled experiments in which adults assigned to a forgiveness-training program improved their ability to consciously let go of an offense better than did controls, which is good evidence that an intervention might be successful.

Hopefully you spotted the references to the important scientific concepts. Test yourself by completing this short quiz, referring back to the article to find the answers.

1. One study showed that people who regularly forgive show lower levels of anger, and that people who experience less anger have better cardiovascular health. From this, we can confidently say that
    a. anger causes cardiovascular problems.
    b. cardiovascular problems cause people to become angry.
    c. forgiveness prevents heart disease.
    d. these variables are correlated with each other.
2. In the research on immunity reported in the *Journal of Positive Psychology*, which of the following was a dependent variable described in the paragraph?
    a. occupation of the participants
    b. presence of a heart condition
    c. inflammation levels
    d. anger
3. What can a scientifically literate individual assume about a study published in a scientific journal (such as the *Journal of Behavioral Medicine*)?
    a. The study was reviewed and published by a credible source.
    b. All the research in it consists exclusively of randomized, placebo-controlled designs.
    c. The editor of the journal hired some psychologists to write about their research.
    d. Claims of health benefits of forgiveness represent psychologists' personal opinions.

Answers: 1. *d* 2. *c* 3. *a*

Next, let's read about how Mr. Hanserd thinks about this program.

How should we think critically about forgiveness?

Remember that critical thinking involves curiosity and reasonable levels of skepticism. Critical thinkers continue to ask questions while evaluating the quality of the answers they find. As you read through the passage below, search for specific statements relevant to critical thinking.

This is probably the most exciting project I have had the privilege to work on, but I have to remain focused. There is a lot of work left for us to get the program started, which also involves accepting that some research we come across will not necessarily support what we are doing. I continue to remind myself that we don't know yet how helpful our program will be and we will have to collect a substantial amount of data to have strong evidence. Much of the research is correlational in nature so we are not yet 100% sure that forgiveness is what is driving the health benefits we see. I have every reason to be optimistic, however, because there is a growing number of experiments connecting forgiveness to health.

The statements below will help you identify several aspects of critical thinking. Match the following critical thinking statements to the highlighted passages that illustrate them. Note that at least one of these statements is not addressed in Mr. Hanserd's commentary.

1. The author addressed overly emotional thinking.
2. The author addressed the problems of anecdotal evidence.
3. The author appears to tolerate the ambiguity rather than insist on certainty.
4. The author examined the nature and quality of the evidence.

1. Yellow 2. Not addressed 3. Green 4. Blue

Now that you have completed this critical thinking exercise, continue to the next page to think about how this information can be applied.

How is forgiveness relevant?

Mr. Hansard suggests that forgiveness can be studied and applied in a scientific manner to promote physical and mental health. Read how he makes the connection between the research and application in his article, and then consider any newly formed thoughts you may have about the topic in the writing activity that follows.

Forgiveness is not a cure-all, of course. It is never going to be a substitute for the appropriate medication and healthy lifestyle choices related to diet, exercise, and smoking. However, it is very important to realize that forgiveness can have significant impact on health. Therefore, a combination of education, instruction, and practice should help our patients, especially for those who are inclined to carry a grudge rather than to forgive.

SHARED WRITING

Do *you* think forgiving might be a useful intervention for cardiovascular patients? If possible, share an instance in your life in which forgiveness seemed to help your overall health.

Chapter 16 Quiz

1. What effect does watching food commercials have on the eating habits of viewers?
   A. Food commercials generally have little to no effect on eating habits.
   B. People are more likely to eat the specific product being advertised in the commercial, but not other unrelated foods.
   C. Snacking in general is more likely after viewers watch a food commercial.
   D. The eating habits of adults are influenced more by food commercials than are the eating habits of children.

2. The HPA axis involves which three structures?
   A. Hippocampus, pituitary gland, adrenal glands
   B. Hypothalamus, pineal gland, adenoids
   C. Hippocampus, pineal gland, adrenal glands
   D. Hypothalamus, pituitary gland, adrenal glands

3. A hormone that is associated with enhanced immune responses and social bonding is called _____.
   A. HPA
   B. cortisol
   C. oxytocin
   D. *Helicobacter pylori*

4. Which aspect of Type A personality is most closely correlated with increased risk for heart disease?
   A. Competitiveness
   B. Anger and hostility
   C. Patience
   D. Worrying about time

5. Biofeedback is a therapeutic technique involving:
   A. focusing on a specific thought or sensation, such as an image or a repeated sound.
   B. attending to all thoughts, sensations, and feelings without attempting to judge or control them.
   C. the use of physiological recording instruments to provide feedback that increases awareness of bodily responses.
   D. bodily interaction with thinking and emotion.

6. Gretta is in an abusive relationship with her boyfriend. Although leaving her boyfriend is an obvious way to end the abuse, Gretta has been in this situation for so long that she no longer feels she has any control over it. Gretta's situation illustrates the concept of _____.
   A. compensatory control
   B. posttraumatic growth
   C. resilience
   D. learned helplessness

7. Which of the following statements about how discrimination influences health is most accurate?
   A. Discrimination is unrelated to poor health.
   B. People who experience discrimination are likely to compensate for it by making positive health-related choices.
   C. An immediate increase in heart rate is the biggest problem associated with experiencing discrimination.
   D. Experiencing discrimination stimulates the stress response, which can bring about long-term health problems.

8. In modern times, the leading causes of death in industrialized nations such as the United States are _____.
   A. viral infections
   B. bacterial infections
   C. lifestyle factors
   D. Each of these are equal contributors.

9. What is psychoneuroimmunology?
   A. The study of the relationship between immune system and nervous system functioning
   B. The study of both the positive and negative effects that our behavior and decisions have on health, survival, and well-being
   C. A condition in which plaques form in the blood vessels that supply the heart with blood and oxygen, resulting in restricted blood flow
   D. A hormone secreted by the adrenal gland

10. How does stress affect cancer?
    A. Stress decreases the number of white blood cells in the body, which results in cancer progression.
    B. Hormones from the autonomic nervous system stimulate cells that reside in tumors, which can in turn stimulate growth and proliferation of the tumors.
    C. Stress decreases the growth of cancer cells.
    D. Stress does not affect cancer.

11. People with _____ personality type are patient and easygoing, and have relaxed disposition, whereas _____ personality individuals tend to be impatient and are easily angered, competitive, and highly motivated.
    A. Type A; Type B
    B. stressed; relaxed
    C. Type B; Type A
    D. relaxed; stressed

12. The health risk most likely to be associated with Type A personality is _____.
    A. AIDS
    B. cancer
    C. the cold virus
    D. coronary heart disease

13. What does it mean to say someone is resilient?
    A. The person has the ability to effectively recover from illness or adversity.
    B. The person tends to be calm when challenged or stressed.
    C. The person shows the tendency to have a favorable, constructive view on situations and to expect positive outcomes.
    D. The person uses only positive processes to manage demands, stress, and conflict.

14. _____ is an acquired suppression of avoidance or escape behavior in response to unpleasant, uncontrollable circumstances.
    A. Compensatory control
    B. Learned helplessness
    C. Coping
    D. Resilience

15. People often turn to religion to explain natural disasters. This behavior demonstrates the concept of _____.
    A. compensatory control
    B. learned helplessness
    C. coping
    D. resilience

Chapter 17
Industrial and Organizational Psychology

Module 17.1 Personnel Psychology: Hiring and Maintaining an Effective Workforce

 ## Learning Objectives

17.1a Know . . . the key terminology of personnel psychology.

17.1b Understand . . . interviews, testing, and assessment center methods of personnel selection.

17.1c Understand . . . methods used in employee performance appraisals.

17.1d Apply . . . your knowledge of personnel psychology to identify likely KSAOs for a given job.

17.1e Analyze . . . the relative value of structured versus unstructured interview selection techniques.

The first and arguably most important step in hiring employees is to create a clear, comprehensive description of the job. Given that the job of President of the United States is the most important job in the country, it should follow that there must be a thorough, well-written job description somewhere in Washington, D.C. If there is not, then how would we know who to hire? Interestingly, there is no single job description. The Constitution does identify a few specific responsibilities in general terms: command the armed forces; make treaties; appoint ambassadors, judges, and heads of departments; commission military officers; and enforce the laws of the nation. In addition, he (or someday soon, she), should let Congress know how things are going and meet with political figures from other countries. Finally, the president has the freedom to grant pardons and consult with heads of the departments. (These are in Article II, sections 2 and 3 if you are interested.) If you think about these descriptors, none of them give much detail—no specifics on how to accomplish those tasks and no benchmarks to assess performance. No wonder there are such heated debates every 4 years when the job comes open again.

In this chapter, we will apply psychology to the setting in which most adults spend the majority of their waking hours: the workplace. As defined in Module 1.3, I/O psychology is the study of behavior and thought in work settings. According to the Society of Industrial-Organizational Psychology (SIOP), the field serves three main goals: (1) to help employers deal with employees fairly; (2) to help make jobs more interesting and satisfying; and (3) to help workers be more productive.

The first hints of I/O psychology emerged in the late 1800s from a desire to develop management practices that would have the same degree of precision as engineering. In fact, much of the first scientific research on employee behavior was published in the major academic journal for mechanical engineers (van de Water, 1997). The merging of engineering and psychology into *industrial psychology* made sense at the time because the US economy was based on manufacturing—mining raw materials and turning them into useful products. Industrial psychologists did the same thing with human labor—finding the raw strength and talent and turning it into a productive workforce. From this moment came a new type of profession: *personnel psychology*. Although the term "personnel psychology" is used less frequently today, this field has become one of the major components of I/O psychology. Psychologists working in this area focus on hiring people with potential, ensuring they are adequately trained, managing and motivating employees, and evaluating performance. If this sounds like the job of the human resources (HR) department to you, you are largely correct because HR professionals engage in many of the same activities. There are a few noticeable differences, however. I/O psychologists are more likely have a scientific focus and draw on recent peer-reviewed research. They are more likely to serve as consultants and to work on fixing problems or improving performance. In contrast, HR professionals are more likely to be involved in day-to-day operations and running the programs that are already in place. Finally, there are areas such as managing employee benefits that are part of every HR department, but rarely if ever involve psychologists.

Since the 1960s, psychologists have found more opportunities as the US economic structure has shifted from manufacturing to service industries (Katzell & Austin, 1992). More jobs have moved into offices; a growing number of work teams began brainstorming and communicating together to solve problems rather than spreading out to individual stations along an assembly line. In addition, successful employees have become mobile, able to move from job to job based on the strength of their accomplishments. Thus, psychology in the workplace now includes more *organizational psychology*, focusing on the culture and organizational qualities of work.

Job Analysis: Understanding the Requirements for the Job

One of the main contributions of I/O psychology has been the development of methods for **job analysis**, *the process of writing a detailed description of a position to support hiring, training, performance evaluation, and organization* (Sanchez & Levine, 2012). As part of the job analysis, psychologists identify tasks of the job along with the **KSAOs**—*the knowledge, skills, abilities, and other traits required to do it well.* Psychologists turn to a variety of sources for this task, such as incumbents (people who already hold the job), their supervisors, and subject-matter experts (people who have technical expertise related to the job). Interviewing multiple incumbents, supervisors, and subject-matter experts provides diverse perspectives on a specific job as well as how that individual contributes to the KSAOs on a department or organization-wide level (Crook et al., 2011).

Job analysis might seem simple at first because it is relatively easy to find a collection of tasks and assign them to an individual. This might be the case for jobs that follow a set routine and include a fixed number of tasks—such as a custodial employee who vacuums and removes trash on a daily basis. However, the more complex and varied the task, the more difficult it is to pin down a job description (Dierdorff & Morgeson, 2007). Jobs also tend to change based on technology, the economy, and popular trends (this is especially true of the presidency), so job analyses should be updated regularly, especially in high-tech positions (Bobko et al., 2008). Finally, incumbents often engage in a process called **job crafting**, *which means taking on or creating additional roles and tasks for a position over time* (Demerouti, 2014). These changes are often initiated by individual employees to better fit their unique KSAOs, and that can lead to great job satisfaction and engagement. On the other hand, they may distract newcomers from what the essential tasks of the job really are. Therefore, researchers are currently exploring how to optimize the job crafting process to benefit the individual employee and the organization (Demerouti et al., 2015).

There are thousands of different occupations, and no individual psychologist could analyze them all. Fortunately, a substantial number of these jobs have already been thoroughly studied and the corresponding job analyses published on the Internet as part of a US government project. This project is available to anyone in the general public—you just need to search for the Occupational Information Network or O*NET (http://online.onetcenter.org/). O*NET is a collection of databases that describe jobs from six domains (see Figure 17.1). If you are interested in becoming a clinical psychologist, just go to O*NET, type in this job title, and start searching. There you will find the six categories of descriptors that will help you learn more about the job; if you are an employer, you will find which type of person you may want to hire.

Figure 17.1 The O*NET Concept Chart

O*NET provides information about types of jobs and the requirements for workers that may fill them.

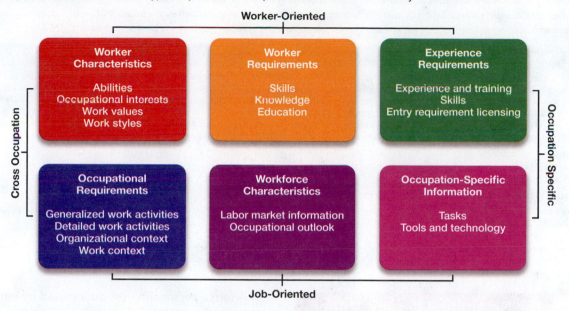

Selection: Hiring the Right People

When the job analysis is complete, employers should have a list of KSAOs in hand and can turn their attention to hiring the best possible workers. The ideal worker would be someone whose KSAOs match those required for the job (see Table 17.1 for an example).

INTERVIEWING Certainly the most familiar and most widely used employee selection method is the job interview. In the basic interviewing technique known as an **unstructured interview**, *an employer discusses a variety of job- and personality-related topics with a candidate with relatively few prepared questions to guide the conversation*. From this dialogue, the employer can draw reasonably accurate conclusions about the applicant's personality (Blackman, 2002). However, the unstructured nature allows the interview to get off track, which raises several problems. For example, different candidates will experience different interviews, making comparisons less reliable.

Structured interviews *present the same set of questions to each job candidate with planned (rather than unstructured) follow-up questions* (see Table 17.2). This structure removes some of the uncertainty associated with unstructured interviews. In addition, the interviewer is trained to follow the same procedures in each interview and uses a standardized form to ensure each interview session is consistent as possible (Levashina et al., 2014).

Structured interviews typically include questions about qualifications and interests—the basics of KSAOs. In addition, they allow an opportunity to ask *behavioral interview questions* that explore how a candidate has exhibited desirable (or undesirable) behaviors in the past. *Situational interview questions*—questions about how the candidate would respond to a situation that is relevant to the job—also provide structure to an interview (Klehe & Latham, 2006). These questions can actually be drawn from real situations that incumbents have faced in the past. When developing these questions, psychologists might ask low-quality and high-quality employees how they have responded to that situation in the past. By comparing a candidate's response to the incumbents' responses, psychologists can get a sense of how well a candidate will perform on the job.

JOURNAL PROMPT

Your Dream Job: What are the KSAOs for your dream job?

Table 17.1 KSAOs for a Job Analysis of Social Work

Knowledge	Psychology, sociology, therapy and counseling, basic law
Skills	Listening, social perceptiveness, critical thinking, service orientation, judgment
Abilities	Oral communication, written communication, problem sensitivity (ability to anticipate problems)
Other traits	Concern for others, ability to control stress, persistence, integrity, dependability

Table 17.2 Sample Questions for a Structured Interview

Notice that these questions are two ways assessing the same underlying traits. The behavioral question asks about specific examples of past behaviors, whereas the situational question presents a hypothetical situation that may happen in the future. With either question, interviewers can apply the same scoring system (bottom row) that reflects the actions the company believes is best suited for the job.

Behavioral Interview Question	Situational Interview Question
Tell me about a time when someone took over the leadership of a group project and ignored contributions that were not in accordance with his or her own opinion. What were the circumstances? What exactly did you do? What was the outcome?	Your group is working on an important project with a very tight deadline. All of you want the best results possible because there is a substantial bonus at stake. One member of your group was especially successful in this area the last quarter. Supported by two other group members, she takes the lead on your group project. She keeps the minutes and controls the flow of information during the discussion. However, you have the strong impression that she only records ideas supportive of her position and makes decisions on issues without consulting with others. What would you do?

Scoring Guide:

5 Involve the other group members; ask them their opinions on the topic of discussion; ask everyone to take notes; ask the leader to send her notes for correction and supplementation by the others.

3 Ask someone to take the minutes and send them to the group for comment.

Or: confront the current leader only if I am not satisfied with the direction the project is taking. Do nothing if I think that the solution achieved so far is actually good for the project.

1 Do nothing.

Working the Scientific Literacy Model

Personality Selection Tests

Anyone who has interviewed for a job experiences concern over whether he or she is qualified or the "right" person for the position. Of course, employers are looking for just the right person, too, and many are turning to personality tests to help them in their search.

What do we know about personality selection measures?

One of the most significant aspects of job analysis is the identification of a list of KSAOs that can help employers make decisions about which type of person would be the best fit for a job. Therefore, one of the primary aspects of personnel selection is determining whether a person has the right knowledge, abilities, and personality traits. One of the most popular means of assessing an individual's qualifications for a job is with a test, including testing of personality traits and cognition.

Before a personality test can be used by employers to select employees, I/O psychologists must first determine which personality traits are associated with success or failure in a specific position. This area of research is called **validation studies** *in which researchers administer tests to a large sample of incumbents and evaluate their performance to find correlations between job performance and personality traits or cognitive abilities* (Ryan & Ployhart, 2014).

How can scientists study personality-based selection tests?

Personality-based selection tests draw heavily from trait theories (described in Module 12.1). In fact, many of the self-report tests used in personality research are also used for personnel selection. Meta-analyses (which combine the results of many earlier studies) as far back as 1991 have supported their use for this purpose (Barrick & Mount, 2005; Salgado, 1997; Tett et al., 1991). One of the more popular personality models is the Big Five (also known as the Five Factor Model; see Table 17.3), and the most popular self-report measure of the Big Five personality traits has been the NEO-PI.

Table 17.3 The Big Five Personality Traits as Measured by the NEO-PI

Each of these traits represents a dimension. For example, someone who scores high on a test of conscientiousness fits the description in this table. Someone with a very low score on the same test is likely to be late to appointments and make careless mistakes.

Neuroticism (versus emotional stability)	Experiencing negative affect (anger, hostility, nervousness) and being emotionally unsettled
Extraversion	Being sociable, affectionate, fun-loving
Openness	Showing imagination, seeking novelty and variety
Agreeableness	Being trusting, having the tendency to get along with others and to avoid conflict
Conscientiousness	Paying attention to procedures and details; following rules; being neat, organized, and timely

Figure 17.2 Conscientiousness Can Predict Job Performance

The red line shows that high conscientiousness is associated with better job performance than low conscientiousness scores (the green line) among pharmaceutical sales representatives. Performance was measured by the number of prescriptions written for a specific medication by physicians in his or her territory. Data were collected for each quarter during the first year the drug was available (Thoresen et al., 2004).

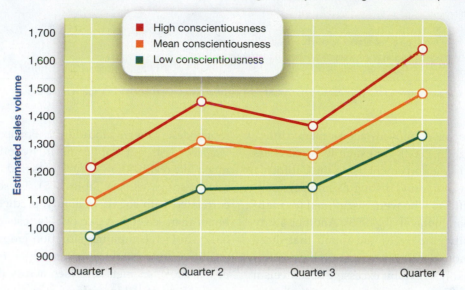

For example, Figure 17.2 shows how conscientiousness predicts success among sales representatives for pharmaceutical companies (Thoresen et al., 2004). In each quarter of the year shown in the figure, those sales representatives who rate high in conscientiousness outperformed their peers with low levels of conscientiousness. Meanwhile, traits of agreeableness and openness did not predict success. Therefore, if we were consulting for a major drug company, we could recommend hiring applicants who score high in conscientiousness.

Can we critically evaluate this evidence?

One of the key issues in personality selection is *impression management*—our tendency to try to put forth a specific image. This happens when applicants see discrepancies between their own personality and the traits that would make an ideal candidate. As a result, they may present misleading information about their own personality. There are methods that can improve measurement by detecting false responses; including focusing on observable behaviors, using multiple ratings, or using statistical techniques to identify candidates whose profiles are so ideal that they are just too good to be true (Levashina et al., 2014; Speer et al., 2014; van Hooft & Born, 2012) In addition, personality-based selection is also limited in that it assumes personality is a relatively stable trait, but perhaps it is possible to create work environments that encourage specific traitlike behaviors. In other words, the right training program or incentives might help a person who is usually low in conscientious to be more conscientious while at work.

Why is this relevant?

Personality inventories measuring the Big Five can be useful across many different lines of work, as shown in Table 17.4. Not only can personality tests be used to select specific individuals, but they can also be used to rule out individuals whose profiles suggest that they would be low

Table 17.4 The Big Five Can Predict Performance in a Variety of Jobs

Type of Work	Traits Associated with High Performance	Citation
Pharmaceutical sales	Conscientiousness	Thoresen et al. (2004)
Fitness center managers and employees	A combination of extraversion and emotional stability	Judge & Erez (2007)
Factory production line workers	Emotional stability	Buttigieg (2006)
Entrepreneurs	Openness, emotional stability, and agreeableness	Zhao & Seibert (2006)
Camp counselors	Extraversion, agreeableness, conscientiousness	Loveland et al. (2005)

Table 17.5 A Sample Situational Judgment Test Item

A man on a very urgent mission during a battle finds he must cross a stream about 40 feet wide. A blizzard has been blowing and the stream has frozen over. However, because of the snow, he does not know how thick the ice is. He sees two planks about 10 feet long near the point where he wishes to cross. He also knows where there is a bridge about 2 miles downstream. Under the circumstances he should:

A. Walk to the bridge and cross it.
B. Run rapidly across on the ice.
C. Break a hole in the ice near the edge of the stream to see how deep the stream is.
D. Cross with the aid of the planks, pushing one ahead of the other and walking on them.
E. Creep slowly across the ice.

SOURCE: From "The Psychometric History of Selected Ability Constructs" by L. C. Northrop (1998). U. S. Department of Personnel Management, Washington, DC. P.190.

performers or disruptive employees across many different types of jobs (Salgado, 2002). For example, researchers studied a division of law enforcement using the California Personality Inventory and found distinguishing personality profiles among officers who were disciplined for inappropriate conduct (Sarchione et al., 1998). Another study investigated university employees and found that those who scored low on conscientiousness but high on extraversion were more likely to exhibit excessive absenteeism (Judge et al., 1997). I/O psychologists can apply similar methods to almost any imaginable career.

One issue you may have considered is that personality is not the only determining factor when selecting employees. Employers are also likely to want to know more about the various cognitive skills that applicants may bring.

COGNITION-BASED SELECTION TESTS As an alternative or supplement to personality tests, some psychologists use cognitive selection tests, which are based on topics described in Module 9.1. For example, *situational judgment tests* put applicants in hypothetical situations, much like reality-show contestants find themselves in job-related scenarios (see Table 17.5). These tests, which are correlated with cognitive ability, predict job performance better than self-report personality tests (Scherbaum et al., 2012). In fact, combining situation judgments with direct cognitive tests produces even better results (Clevenger et al., 2001). In meta-analyses across dozens of studies in a variety of fields, tests of cognitive ability have usually been shown to do a better job at predicting performance compared to personality tests (Salgado et al., 2003; Schmidt & Hunter, 1998; see Table 17.6).

Just like personality tests, cognitive tests must go through validation studies that serve to identify who should be selected and who should be turned away. Cognitive tests are far more difficult to fake than personality tests, but a new set of problems can arise from their use. Such instruments may be based on culturally specific skills or knowledge. As a result two individuals with

Table 17.6 Cognition Predicts Training Success and Performance

Workers in a variety of careers completed tests of mental abilities and, for many careers, these scores correlated with performance during and after training.

Type of Work	Correlation with Training	Correlation with Performance
Apprentice	—	0.26
Chemist	—	0.28
Driver	0.22	0.26
Electrician	0.28	0.35
Information clerk	0.31	0.46
Engineer	0.23	0.28
Manager	0.25	—
Mechanics	—	0.21
Police	0.12	0.13
Sales	0.34	—
Skilled worker	0.28	0.17
Typing	0.23	0.31

SOURCE: From "A meta-analytic study of general mental ability validity for different occupations in the European community" by J. Salgado, N. Anderson, S. Moscoso, C. Bertua, F. de Fruyt, & J. Rolland (2003). *Journal of Applied Psychology, 88*(6), 1068–1081. American Psychological Association.

different gender, ethnic, or cultural backgrounds may score differently on the same test, despite having equal performance measures on the job (Gardner & Deadrick, 2012; Kirnan et al., 2009). This possibility presents an ethical problem in that cognitive tests may discriminate based on ethnicity, gender, or culture rather than on candidates' actual potential.

THE ASSESSMENT CENTER Personnel selection can be approached from a number of directions, as you can see, and it would seem that the best methods would involve a combination of techniques. **Assessment centers** *capitalize on multiple approaches to personnel selection by combining a variety of assessments, such as personality, cognitive, interpersonal skills, and sometimes physical ability tests* (Meriac et al., 2014). Although this term suggests a physical location—perhaps an office complex where people come for day-long appointments—an assessment center actually refers to the process, not the location where it takes place.

Some of the unique aspects of assessment centers are the reliance on multiple raters, and the use of raters who have special training in assessment as well as the job that is being filled. This increases the validity of the process considerably (Roch et al., 2012). Assessment centers regularly put candidates through **job simulations**—*role-playing activities that are similar to situations encountered in the actual job.* This also gives assessment centers slightly higher validity than either situational judgment tests or cognitive instruments (Hermelin et al., 2007; Krause et al., 2006). Nevertheless, assessment centers are not without drawbacks. Given the number of tests and the complexity of the simulations involved, assessment centers can be time-consuming (they can last multiple days) and expensive (as much as $1,000 per day for a single candidate) to operate.

In summary, there may never be a perfect means of predicting which candidate will be the best possible person for the job. There are more techniques than we have described here, and even more are bound to be used in the future as new technologies and social trends emerge. For example, some companies have asked for an applicant's Facebook or Twitter passwords to get a more candid look at personality and behavior. Not surprisingly, this has been met with great resistance (Schneider et al., 2015). Despite the inevitable change in methods, several elements underlying those methods appear to be here to stay: Personnel selection tools will continue to match individuals with positions based on KSAOs, and the methods used to do so will be tested for validity. It is also likely that these methods will involve some combination of interviewing; tests of personality, cognitive ability, or physical ability; and some form of situational decision making.

Performance Appraisal

Personnel selection may come first, but **performance appraisal**—*the evaluation of current employees*—is every bit as important (Kline & Sulsky, 2009). Evaluation ensures that employees are doing their jobs correctly; if not, then they may need additional training or incentives to bring their performance up to the desired level. When employees do their work well, they need to be recognized with awards, bonuses, or raises and, in some cases, they may be given more challenging tasks or additional responsibilities to keep them engaged. Unfortunately, when employees do not respond to feedback, evaluations can also result in termination. In short, without proper evaluation techniques, productivity suffers. Thus, even though employees often dread the scrutiny of an evaluation, the benefits to the company are typically well worth it.

WHAT NEEDS TO BE EVALUATED? A good deal of employee evaluation is based on a supervisor's overall rating of an employee. An overall rating is often sufficient for evaluating work performance (Viswesvaran et al., 2005); however, employers often want to evaluate some more specific aspects of work performance (Rotundo & Sackett, 2002):

- *Task performance* describes how well an employee performs the assigned duties for his or her position in the organization.
- *Organizational citizenship behavior* (*OCB*) is the degree to which an employee contributes beyond what is expected (e.g., exceptional teamwork, leadership).
- *Counterproductive behavior* includes actions that interfere with one's own (and sometimes others') productivity, such as absenteeism, lateness, dishonesty, and inappropriate interpersonal behaviors.

Although overall ratings are often sufficient, collecting information from each of these three areas promotes balanced assessments that look at all the contributions an employee makes as well as anything that reduces productivity.

WHO CONDUCTS THE EVALUATION? The traditional approach to employee evaluation is for the immediate supervisor to review the employee's work over a period of time and provide one-on-one feedback. This makes sense because the supervisor knows which tasks have been assigned and how they were performed. However, a supervisor has only one perspective, and his evaluation may be biased for or against an employee based on the quality of their relationship. A clever employee may be substandard in many aspects of the job, yet have the ability to present a positive image to the boss. Therefore, it is essential to include other points of view in the evaluation process.

Figure 17.3 Employee Evaluation

The 360-degree feedback method provides evaluation information from all directions.

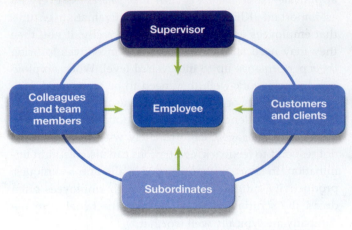

Multisource assessment or **360-degree feedback** *provides evaluation information from many different perspectives within and beyond an organizatio*n. The 360-degree analogy reminds us that the employee receives feedback from all angles (see Figure 17.3). In addition to the traditional supervisory evaluation, multisource assessments include information from an employee's coworkers, anyone whom he or she may supervise, and perhaps customers or clientele that he or she might serve. In many cases, the employee will even rate himself or herself.

In theory, 360-degree feedback is a great method of employee evaluation because it covers all aspects of the job: The supervisor can look over workload and productivity, the peers and supervised employees can report on teamwork and leadership, and customers can report on professionalism and service. Indeed, research on 360-degree feedback generally has shown positive results with the approach, but poorly designed evaluations can backfire (Nowack & Mashihi, 2012). For example, power structures in an organization might appear to

be threatened. Specifically, managers appear to remember feedback from other management more so than feedback from subordinates, and some managers react cynically to subordinate feedback, especially if they believe that the procedure may be unfair (McCarthy & Garavan, 2007; Smither et al., 2005).

PREVENTING BIAS IN EVALUATION If proper controls are lacking, a number of biases and errors have the potential to make the evaluation process more difficult. One such error is the **halo effect**, *in which a rater thinks highly about one aspect of an employee's job or personality and this leads him or her to provide similar ratings for other aspects of the employee's work.* Another error, called the **contrast effect**, *occurs when a rater evaluates one employee who is strong in a number of dimensions such that, by comparison, the next employee is likely to appear weak, even if he is an average worker by other measures.* Think about these effects in the context of a sales office. One worker may be particularly good at making contacts with new clients, but only has moderate success actually completing the sale. We could see evidence of the halo effect if her manager rated her highly for both making contacts and completing sales. Now consider a moderately successful sales representative who is evaluated after the star performer. Despite his consistency, the contrast effect between him and the star salesperson may leave him with a lower rating than he deserves—unless an appropriate rating system is in place.

This module has merely scratched the surface of performance appraisals, but there are some clear messages to take home. First, appraisals are absolutely essential to successful businesses because they promote positive behaviors and create opportunities to correct negative behaviors. Because assessments occur infrequently, however, managers must rely on their memories to evaluate employees, which leaves a large opening for errors. Thus, systematic methods should be used along with multiple points of view. With these in place, assessment should be a valuable tool for any employer.

Module **17.1** Summary

17.1a Know . . . the key terminology of personnel psychology:

360-degree feedback
assessment center
contrast effect
halo effect
job analysis
job crafting
job simulations
KSAOs
performance appraisal

structured interview
unstructured interview
validation studies

17.1b Understand . . . interviews, testing, and assessment center methods of personnel selection.

The two major types of interviews are structured and unstructured. Job candidates also may be tested to assess their personality type and cognitive ability. These results are used to determine whether a candidate is suited to a particular company and, if so, for which specific job he or she is most suited. Assessment centers often combine both personality and cognitive testing with simulations of actual work situations.

17.1c Understand . . . methods used in employee performance appraisals.

The 360-degree feedback (also known as multisource assessments) provide the most detailed information on employee performance. It typically involves evaluating task performance, organizational citizenship behavior, and counterproductive behavior.

17.1d Apply . . . your knowledge of personnel psychology to identify likely KSAOs for a given job.

The journal prompt on page 567 invited you to identify KSAOs for a job you desire or one you currently or previously held. This process hopefully helped you apply an

important aspect of job analysis. You can compare your answers by going to www.onetonline.org and searching for the job title you wrote about.

17.1e Analyze . . . the relative value of structured versus unstructured interview selection techniques.

In an unstructured interview, an employer discusses a variety of job- and personality-related topics with a candidate, and asks a few prepared questions to guide the conversation. However, comparisons among employees can be difficult to make with this method, and potential sources of bias can creep into the interview. Structured interviews present the same set of questions drawn directly from the job analysis to ensure their relevance to the position. They provide for consistency across candidates and focus on job-related information rather than shared interests. Requiring interviewers to follow a specific set of questions reduces opportunities for bias.

Module **17.1** Quiz

Know . . .

1. Sometimes an employee expands her job to include new tasks and responsibilities over time. This departure from the original job description is known as:
   - **A.** job crafting.
   - **B.** workplace expansion.
   - **C.** employee drifting.
   - **D.** job analysis.

Understand . . .

2. If a psychologist conducts a performance appraisal using feedback from supervisors, subordinates, peers, and clients, he is most likely using the _____ approach.
   - **A.** telescoping
   - **B.** compass
   - **C.** 360-degree feedback
   - **D.** task performance

3. What is one of the unique aspects of assessment centers?
   - **A.** Reliance on multiple assessment methods
   - **B.** The size of the building
   - **C.** Their physical location
   - **D.** The reliance on a single type of assessment test

Apply . . .

4. If you are interested in finding out what is required for any given job, you should refer to _____ for important and accurate information.
   - **A.** job net
   - **B.** job crafting
   - **C.** O*NET
   - **D.** the occupational index

Analyze . . .

5. One advantage of structured interviews is that they:
   - **A.** present the same questions to each candidate to ensure each interview is consistent.
   - **B.** allow the conversation to drift from topic to topic depending on what is interesting.
   - **C.** provide valid assessments of cognitive ability.
   - **D.** remove any possibility of cultural bias and stereotype threat.

Module 17.2   Affect, Attitudes, and Behavior at Work

Learning Objectives

17.2a Know . . . the key terminology of employee affect and attitudes.

17.2b Understand . . . job satisfaction, burnout, and the attitudes and affect that go along with them.

17.2c Understand . . . the risk factors for, and varieties of, workplace aggression.

17.2d Apply . . . your knowledge of satisfaction and burnout to ensure you maintain high motivation for college courses and your career.

17.2e Analyze . . . various methods for preventing burnout and encouraging job satisfaction.

Did you know that almost half of new teachers leave the profession within 5 years (Lambert, 2006)? This means more than half of all teachers spent about the same amount or more time in college than they did in their teaching careers. For Craig, a former teacher, the job seemed perfect because he liked reading and history, he interacted well with teens at the high school level, and he believed he could make positive changes in boys' lives on the wrestling and track teams. He knew that the pay would not be great, but

he was so excited that he finished his education degree in 4 years and charged headlong into his first teaching job.

Craig does not know how it happened, but one day 3 years later, he looked around at the piles of papers and began to wonder if he should stay up all night grading or call in sick the next day. He would have finished the paperwork during his planning period earlier that day, except that he had to deal with overprotective parents who had no idea—and refused to believe—how poorly their son behaved at school. The apathy of many of his students began to sink in: If they could not bother to try harder on the assignments, then perhaps Craig should not put so much effort into planning classes and giving feedback on rough drafts. He began to feel emotionally and physically exhausted after each day's work, and felt resentment toward the principal who always sided with the parents and the superintendent. Faced with so many obstacles, he felt as if nothing he could do would matter in the long run. After his fourth year, Craig left teaching for good and took a job in sales.

This is an all-too-familiar scenario for educational professionals. What is interesting about this case is how motivated Craig was at the beginning of his career—he worked hard for a modest salary and even volunteered to do more than the typical teacher. But then frustration set in, and along with it came a range of negative physiological, psychological, and social effects.

Psychologists have found that employees who show positive affect perform better at work than employees with negative affect.

Productivity and success at work are largely the result of the behavior of the members who make up the workforce. This aspect of the workplace environment goes beyond the simple question of whether workers are doing their job or not. Indeed, the attitudes and emotional energy that people bring to work ultimately affect their overall productivity and job satisfaction. In this module, we will explore how emotions and behaviors in the workplace can affect a company and its workers. Review some of the factors that influence success and achievement in the video Intelligence Tests and Success.

Watch INTELLIGENCE TESTS AND SUCCESS

Employee Affect, Attitudes, and Job Satisfaction

I/O psychologists have become increasingly interested in researching affect—individuals' emotional responses—regarding their jobs and work in general (Thoresen et al., 2003). The work in this vein includes research on both **positive affect (PA)**, *the tendency to experience positive emotions such as happiness, satisfaction, and enthusiasm,* and **negative affect (NA)**, *the tendency to experience negative emotions,*

including frustration, anger, and distress. Even if you have held only one job, chances are you have experienced both varieties of affect. However, some individuals tend to experience more of one type than another, a quality known as *trait affectivity*.

There are at least two important reasons for I/O psychologists' interest in affect, the first of which may be called the happier is smarter hypothesis: Employees who have PA traits seem to make better decisions and may also be more creative (Côté, 1999). (Incidentally, the happier is smarter hypothesis has been found among college students as well—so remember to think positive about your psychology course.) In addition, a variety of research shows that PA is associated with teamwork, organizational citizenship, improved negotiating techniques, and general performance (Alessandri et al., 2012).

I/O psychologists also study affect because when positive or negative affect becomes so consistent that it is as reliable as personality traits, this attitude can influence employees who are satisfied with their jobs (Connolly & Viswesvaran, 2000; Watson & Slack, 1993). Along these lines, PA employees are less likely to quit and, in general, show more organizational commitment (Côté, 1999).

JOB SATISFACTION VERSUS BURNOUT   The balance between positive and negative emotions reflects how satisfied people are with their jobs. Positive or negative thoughts about work are expressed as job attitudes, a combination of affect and thoughts an employee holds about his or her job (Brief & Weiss, 2002). **Job satisfaction** *refers to the degree to which an employee is content with his or her work,* and is most likely to be achieved by people with positive job attitudes (see Figure 17.4). For many people, starting a new job can produce a sense of intense satisfaction, also known as a *honeymoon period* (Boswell et al., 2009). Job satisfaction typically rises and

Figure 17.4 Sources of Job Satisfaction

Job satisfaction stems from multiple factors, including personal qualities and the work environment.

Personality
Coworkers
Nature of the job
Job expectations
Organizational fit
Fair and ethical treatment
→ **Job satisfaction**

falls throughout a career, however. The lower periods may include the experience of burnout, a combination of persistent emotional and physical exhaustion, cynical attitudes about the job, and a sense that one's work has little meaning (Table 17.7; Maslach, 2003).

Professions such as teaching, law, and medicine require a conscious commitment and years of education, just as skilled labor and crafts (electricians, plumbers, artisans) require training, practice, and often an apprenticeship. It should not come as a surprise, then, that many people who make this type of commitment enter the workforce with a sense of satisfaction and engagement. But what keeps some people feeling satisfied? And what about those who experience job satisfaction despite taking a job they thought they would eventually dread?

The commonsense notion that enjoyable jobs, coworkers, and supervisors all contribute to job satisfaction does seem to be correct (Mossholder et al., 2005), but job satisfaction goes beyond these factors. For example, a teacher may be highly satisfied with the effect he could have on students, but only marginally satisfied with the income. Satisfaction also depends on the situation you find yourself in—you may be perfectly suited to design computer software but just because you have a job in this field does not guarantee satisfaction.

Satisfaction also reflects whether the job is what the employee expected, and whether they believe their KSAOs really fit the job (Gabriel et al., 2014). Moreover, achieving job satisfaction and avoiding burnout depend on how employees are treated, promoted, and challenged. Research shows that it is actually good to challenge workers, particularly those high in cognitive ability, as long as the organization supports their extra efforts (Wallace et al., 2009). In fact, among teachers, more complex teaching

strategies are equated with lower levels of burnout, even though they require more effort (Ben-Ari et al., 2003).

Individual differences in affective qualities lead to burnout for some people and job satisfaction for others, regardless of the job. For example, people who are extraverted and emotionally stable (the opposite of neuroticism) tend to be more satisfied with their job (Judge et al., 2002). Also, whether someone is satisfied or experiences burnout depends on self-appraisals—his or her beliefs about ability, worth, and level of control (Judge & Bono, 2001). Thus, job satisfaction is related to the following factors:

- *Self esteem*, which includes beliefs about one's value and worth as a human being.
- *Self-efficacy*, which involves beliefs about one's ability to accomplish certain goals or complete specific tasks.
- *Locus of control*, which is a set of beliefs about one's ability to control one's work environment and success.

As you can see, a certain degree of job satisfaction seems to be based on an individual's disposition, and this tends to make job satisfaction relatively stable as long as an individual holds a job (Dormann & Zapf, 2001).

The likelihood of experiencing job satisfaction versus burnout is also related to the interaction between the individual and his or her environment (Best et al., 2005; Maslach, 2003). When our skills, energy level, and aspirations match our job, then we are likely to be engaged. A mismatch—such as a teacher who is highly engaged and enthusiastic but works with students who are unmotivated and at a school with low administrative support—can be enough to lead an individual to change jobs (Staw et al., 1986).

Some people may become dissatisfied with a job simply because there is a lack of opportunity to express positive affectivity or because they are not suited for the job in the first place. Our language is filled with phrases that illustrate this mismatch: another day, another dollar; it's a living; TGIF (thank God it's Friday). All of these phrases bring to mind a person who works out of necessity but does not find much fulfillment in the workplace. In contrast to these kinds of employed-but-uninspired workers, other people experience factors that actively drive satisfaction down; instead of boredom, they feel distress, dread, and perhaps even anger about their work.

Table 17.7 Job Satisfaction Versus Burnout

Job Satisfaction		Burnout
Energy	←*Physical and emotional experience*→	Exhaustion
Optimism	←*Attitudes about job*→	Cynicism
Accomplishment	←*Beliefs about self*→	Lack of accomplishment

Burnout *is the overarching term describing feelings of low job satisfaction.* It is characterized by three qualities: physical and emotional exhaustion; a cynical, pessimistic attitude about the organization; and a feeling that nothing of significance has been accomplished. The work environment can accelerate burnout through the nature of the tasks, insufficient resources, and unpleasant social situations (Spector, 2002). And if one employee gets burned out, beware: Burnout has even been shown to be contagious (Bakker et al., 2005).

Exhaustion comes from the nature of the work: Dull, repetitive work can create stress by challenging a worker to maintain her attention despite severe boredom (Maslach, 2003). Similarly, piling on too much work can be stressful, even if the work would be interesting at a slower pace. Cynicism derives from a negative or ineffective interpersonal environment; it can be agonizing to walk into the office each morning if you are aware that you will have to face a boss who is out of touch and work on projects that seem to be pointless. Finally, feelings of ineffectiveness may arise from any situation in which the employee cannot access the necessary information or resources for the job (Park et al., 2014). This can be a stressful situation because the employee must constantly invent new ways to do his or her job or simply accept that he or she will not be able to perform up to his or her standards.

Are you experiencing student burnout? The scale in Table 17.8 might help.

Burnout is characterized by physical and emotion exhaustion, cynicism, and a sense that the work has little importance.

Answer this question. And could these same factors apply to our teacher's story from the beginning of the module? Certainly Craig felt the work piling up, and he believed that he lacked the resources to do his job well. Interpersonally, he felt the administrators did not support his work, and neither the students nor their parents offered much encouragement.

ABSENTEEISM AND TURNOVER As dissatisfaction and burnout increase, a number of undesirable behaviors may begin to surface. One of the first to appear is **absenteeism**—*regularly missing work for either legitimate or questionable reasons.* According to major surveys, 1.5% to

Table 17.8 The Student Burnout Inventory

To complete the Student Burnout Inventory, circle the number that best describes you on the following scale. Simply add up the circled numbers in each section to find your scores. To find out how you compare to others, see the summary for Objective 17.2d on page 582.

	Never		Sometimes			Always	
I feel emotionally drained by my studies.	0	1	2	3	4	5	6
I feel used up at the end of a day at the university.	0	1	2	3	4	5	6
I feel tired when I get up in the morning and I have to face another day at the university.	0	1	2	3	4	5	6
Studying or attending a class is really a strain for me.	0	1	2	3	4	5	6
I feel burned out from my studies.	0	1	2	3	4	5	6
Total Exhaustion Score =							
I have become less interested in my studies since my enrollment at the university.	0	1	2	3	4	5	6
I have become less enthusiastic about my studies.	0	1	2	3	4	5	6
I have become more cynical about the potential usefulness of my studies.	0	1	2	3	4	5	6
I doubt the significance of my studies.	0	1	2	3	4	5	6
Total Cynicism Score =							
I can effectively solve the problems that arise in my studies.	6	5	4	3	2	1	0
I believe that I make an effective contribution to the classes that I attend.	6	5	4	3	2	1	0
In my opinion, I am a good student.	6	5	4	3	2	1	0
I feel stimulated when I achieve my study goals.	6	5	4	3	2	1	0
I have learned many interesting things during the course of my studies.	6	5	4	3	2	1	0
During class I feel confident that I am effective in getting things done.	6	5	4	3	2	1	0
Total Professional Efficacy Score =							

SOURCE: Schaufeli, W. B., Martínez, I. M., Marques Pinto, A., Salanova, M., & Bakker, A. B. (2002). Burnout and engagement in university students: A cross-national study. *Journal of Cross-Cultural Psychology, 33*(5), 464–481.

Figure 17.5 Vacation Temporarily Relieves Burnout

Burnout is measured here on a self report scale ranging from 1 to 7, with 7 indicating the most burnout. As shown by the decline in the center of the graph, a week or more of vacation can greatly reduce burnout. However, burnout returns to nearly the same level in a matter of 3 weeks.

2.5% of the US workforce is absent on any given workday (Commerce Clearing House, 2006). Although absence as a result of a major illness or crisis is completely excusable, burnout can lead people to lower their standards for what constitutes an emergency. In other words, a happy worker may miss 1 day with the flu, whereas a burned-out worker might take 3 days off (Schaufeli et al., 2009; Ybema et al., 2010).

Many consider absenteeism to be the first step driving the problem of **turnover**, *the rate at which existing employees leave the organization* (Griffeth et al., 2000). Turnover is more than just a nuisance for managers who must hire and train new workers; it is also a major expense for organizations. The real cost of turnover includes searching for and hiring a new employee, training that employee, and the loss of productivity until the new worker becomes proficient.

Of course, having disgruntled workers on the job may not be any better than having them skip work. Dissatisfied employees are likely to engage in counterproductive behaviors that may reduce productivity for the rest of the organization (Berry et al., 2007). If the stress is social in nature, the disgruntled workers may engage in social forms of disruption aimed at other people. Examples include loud and incessant complaining, starting rumors, and even harassment. In other situations, workers who feel they have been treated unfairly may attempt to reward themselves through theft, or perhaps they may attack the company through vandalism.

REDUCING THE EFFECTS OF BURNOUT Given the major problems that burnout presents to both employers and employees, researchers have examined various ways to prevent or reduce burnout and its ill effects. Some key advice is that burnout interventions should occur at the organizational level, because qualities of the job, social environment, and availability of resources have the largest impact on burnout.

For example, physical exercise and cognitive-behavioral stress management skills may help employees manage their reactions to stress more effectively (Richardson & Rothstein, 2008). In addition, employers can offer raises in hopes of making the job more rewarding, although problems with the workload and social environment will not go away just because the paycheck is a little larger. As the phrase TGIF suggests, time away from work is beneficial, as long as the worker enjoys the vacation, but, as shown in Figure 17.5, the relief from burnout does not last much longer than the holiday itself (Fritz & Sonnentang, 2006; Kühnel & Sonnentang, 2011). After all, the employee who returns from vacation has to walk right back into the situation that led to burnout.

The real solution to employee dissatisfaction seems to be proactive—addressing the source of the problem before it gets out of control. A significant but limited amount of dissatisfaction seems to be related to personality, so a company can start by hiring people whose KSAOs fit the job and the organization—a selection process described in Module 17.1. Once workers are hired, effective training is essential and mentoring can help make the transitions go smoothly (Payne & Huffman, 2005).

Workplace Aggression

On occasion, a frightening work-related story will dominate the news for a few days—a recently dismissed employee returns to his former workplace seeking violent revenge. The extreme nature of these nationally reported incidents tends to overshadow the vast majority of cases that present a real threat to workers and their businesses. In its more common forms, workplace aggression may involve verbal hostility, obstructionism (making someone's job more difficult), and overt aggression, such as assaults or vandalism (Baron et al., 1999). The victims of workplace aggression are likely to have lower satisfaction and may even quit their jobs, so psychologists have been trying to understand the causes of this undesirable behavior and its long-term effects on individuals and the organizations they work for (Lapierre et al., 2005).

Hostility in the Workplace

Common sense suggests that, to be productive and satisfied workers, people need to feel safe around their coworkers. However, not all workplaces meet this description. What leads some workers to create a hostile work environment?

What do we know about hostility in the workplace?

Hostility can take on many forms. In its less dangerous forms, it is often referred to as workplace bullying; surveys suggest that at least half of all employees in the United States experience at least one incidence per week. This results in negative emotional reactions, and of course, that is the primary reason to consider it. But surveys of employees indicate that almost all have reduced productivity as a result, either through time spent worrying or just deciding they do not care as much anymore (Porath & Pearson, 2011).

An obvious response to this problem is to look for screening instruments that might be able to predict who is likely to become aggressive, and particularly those people who might become violent. Achieving this goal can be challenging, however. After all, potential employees probably do not intend to express aggressiveness when they begin their jobs and, even if they did, they would probably not disclose their planned aggression in an interview.

How can scientists study hostility in the workplace?

A number of factors slightly increase a person's risk for being aggressive at work, such as fitting a highly competitive, achievement-oriented personality profile and having a history of aggressive behavior (LeBlanc & Barling, 2004). Research also suggests that males are more prone to aggression than females (Rutter & Hine, 2005). One particularly telling trait for aggression is alcohol abuse. Interestingly, alcohol use by itself does not predict aggression, though the combination of heavy alcohol use and

Figure 17.6 Qualities Leading to Workplace Violence
Each of these qualities is associated with increased risk of committing aggressive acts in the workplace. Traits with arrows are significantly more likely to contribute to one target than the other.

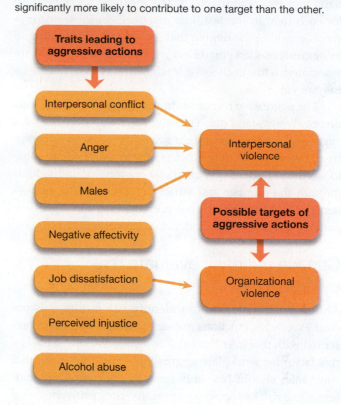

perceived injustice or maltreatment is an ominous pairing (Greenburg & Barling, 1999; Jockin et al., 2001). Some research has shown that organizational variables are better predictors of workplace aggression than personal traits (see Figure 17.6). One such study looked at both personal and situational variables and found that when organizational policies treated employees unfairly, or when supervisors were strict and abusive, the risk for aggression increased significantly (Inness et al., 2005).

In the past decade, psychologists have turned to a new method of detecting aggressive tendencies: the conditional reasoning test. This method presents current or prospective employees with a series of word problems similar to the standardized reading comprehension tests you have probably completed in school (see Table 17.9;

Table 17.9 Illustrative Conditional Reasoning Problems

1. Electronics retailers are now pushing extended service plans that extend product warranties for an additional term, such as six months or a year. If you purchase one of these plans along with a new stereo or appliance, for example, they will repair or replace the item at no extra cost for the duration of the plan. What is the most likely reason these extended service plans have become so popular with retailers?

   a. They provide consumers with confidence and peace of mind when they make an expensive purchase.

   b. If that level of protection was included in the price of a product, everyone would be paying more. Therefore, these plans allow those who are not concerned to purchase the product at a lower price.

   c. Electronics are only built to last so long. If the stores know the product usually lasts for 13 months, they can sell a lot of 12-month warranties without having to provide any services in return.

   d. Stores are offering repair services more than in the past. This is simply a way of paying for those services in advance, which is often cheaper in the long run.

SOURCE: Based on "A conditional reasoning measure for aggression" by L. R. James et al. (2005). *Organizational Research Methods, 8*(1), 69–99.

James et al., 2005; James & LeBreton, 2010). The word problems do not explicitly talk about aggression, yet this measure seems to be able to accurately identify potentially aggressive individuals. It appears to work because for each item in the test, one response choice seems reasonable only to the degree that an individual is willing to be aggressive. Can you detect which items in the table are associated with aggressive tendencies? It may not be as easy as you think.

The aggressive responses in conditional reasoning tests do not always stand out. Therefore, anyone—even the least aggressive among us—might select the aggressive choice from time to time. Nonetheless, these measures are able to accurately identify potentially aggressive individuals through the number and variety of situations. If enough items are on the test, it does not take long for aggressive patterns to emerge in an individual's responses.

Can we critically evaluate this evidence?

Although psychologists can identify risk factors, it is not clear exactly what actions managers should take when presented with this information. For example, being male is a risk factor for workplace aggression—does that mean that companies should hire only females? To complicate matters, some risk factors for aggression—competitiveness and achievement motivation, for example—are also desirable qualities for certain positions.

Why is this relevant?

Despite these challenges, psychologists hope that a thorough understanding of workplace aggression will lead to methods of decreasing violence. In terms of selection, a predictive tool such as the conditional reasoning method may be able to distinguish between nonviolent workers and those who present a threat. Once these individuals are on the job, psychologists may eventually be able to monitor the work environment to identify situations that might interact with personalities to produce hostile situations. Thus, preventive measures could be put in place before any overt acts of aggression occur.

JOURNAL PROMPT

Workplace Bullies: How would you cope with a workplace bully?

SEXUAL HARASSMENT Sexual harassment is a well-known term in industrialized societies, so it might surprise you to learn that the term did not come into use until the 1970s. Despite its familiarity, the concept of sexual harassment can be difficult to define because sexuality is such a multifaceted aspect of human behavior. The best way to distinguish harassment from other behavior is to emphasize the fact that harassment is unwelcomed sexual attention. In the United States, this understanding is clearly stated in the official legal definition of sexual harassment developed by the Equal Employment Opportunity Commission (EEOC, 2011): **sexual harassment** includes *"unwelcome sexual advances, requests for sexual favors, and other verbal or physical harassment of a sexual nature."* Such harassment may come in various forms, such as quid pro quo harassment in which a supervisor promises raises or other benefits in return for sexual favors. A hostile work environment is a situation in which a worker feels threatened or demeaned by sexual advances, insults, or other comments of a sexual nature.

The EEOC—the government agency that oversees formal charges of sexual harassment in the United States—summarized their statistics for the first decade of the 2000s. Data indicate that the agency received 12,000 to 15,000 complaints each year, with the vast majority (85% to 90%) being filed by women (EEOC, 2011). However, the number of complaints by males has been slowly increasing. Despite the large numbers, these incidents include only the legal complaints; many more cases likely go unreported because individuals are embarrassed or afraid to file complaints, they believe their case is not severe enough, or they do not have confidence in the formal procedures.

Aside from the sex differences in harassment, few demographic characteristics can be used to identify those individuals who are most likely to harass their fellow workers. Harassment seems to be equally likely to occur in all types of jobs and organizations, but is slightly more likely to occur when the harasser has higher educational levels and status in the organization (Pina et al., 2009). Personality researchers have found that the Big Five personality traits, which are so important to other I/O issues, have little or no relationship to sexual harassment. However, a few more specific traits are related to harassment, such as honesty-humility, which is negatively correlated with harassment (Lee et al., 2004), whereas authoritarianism (the tendency to favor strong authority and strict enforcement of rules) is positively associated with harassment (Begany & Milburn, 2002).

Because of the gender differences and power issues inherent in the problem of sexual harassment, many psychologists have turned to the sociocultural perspective to explain why it occurs. Many social stereotypes depict men as the predominant breadwinners in the family and as leaders of organizations. For some men, the power ascribed to them by these stereotypes crosses over from home life and organizational roles into the realm of their sexual interests.

Other psychologists adopt a biological perspective, explaining that males and females have evolved differing motives for sex: Men seek quantity and diversity in sexual partners, whereas women look for partners with resources. If this is true, then it might explain both the tendency for

Myths in Mind

The Many Misunderstandings About Sexual Harassment

Psychologists investigating sexual aggression, including sexual harassment, have documented a number of pervasive myths. These myths are not just incorrect but are actually dangerous. People who accept these myths are more likely to commit sexual harassment and other forms of sexual aggression. For the rest of the population, endorsing the myths makes it less likely that victims will receive the support they need. Here are some of the most widely held myths about sexual harassment:

Myth: Modern work settings include more women and more protections, so harassment has not been a significant problem in recent years.

Reality: Sexual harassment is still a significant problem. Nearly half of all women report harassment at some point, and the EEOC receives as many as 15,000 complaints each year.

Myth: Sexual harassment must be sexual in nature.

Reality: Sexual harassment includes discrimination based on a person's sex, even if no sexual contact is suggested.

Myth: Sexual harassment requires the instigator to have bad intentions.

Reality: Sexual harassment is determined by its consequences, not the aggressor's intentions. If sexual advances are unwelcome but persist anyway, then they constitute harassment. This is true even if the instigator does not consciously mean any harm.

Myth: A person has to physically touch another person for the act to be considered harassment.

Reality: Sexual harassment is any unwanted sexual advance, including phone calls, e-mails, and notes.

Myth: Women secretly enjoy the sexual attention. Playing hard to get is just part of the game.

Reality: Sexual harassment by definition is unwelcomed and unwanted. Harassment is different from consensual flirting and dating.

Myth: An individual could avoid being sexually harassed if he or she really wanted.

Reality: Some people suffer harassment quietly for fear of retaliation. The instigator may be physically intimidating or have control over raises and promotions at work.

---

males to be the perpetrators of sexual harassment and the frequent power imbalances between males and females that exist in organizations (i.e., predominantly male supervisors) (Pina et al., 2009).

Both the sociocultural and biological views help explain why some men sexually harass, but they are not as successful in explaining why most men do not. Further, they do little to account for the cases in which women are the instigators.

Perhaps the most important aspect of sexual harassment is understanding exactly why it is such a serious problem. First and foremost is the obvious disrespect for an individual that harassment and other forms of aggression exhibit. Research also shows decreases in job satisfaction and commitment to the organization, as well as increases in physical and emotional illness, following sexual harassment (Willness et al., 2007).

Module 17.2 Summary

17.1a   Know . . . the key terminology of employee affect and attitudes:

absenteeism
burnout
job satisfaction
negative affect (NA)
positive affect (PA)
sexual harassment
turnover

17.2b   Understand . . . job satisfaction, burnout, and the attitudes and affect that go along with them.

Job satisfaction seems to come from a combination of energy, optimism, and a sense of accomplishment, whereas burnout seems to derive from the opposite effects—exhaustion,

cynicism, and feeling a lack of accomplishment. To maintain job satisfaction, it helps to have a challenging job with support from management. People with positive affectivity (PA) also tend to feel more satisfied.

17.2c   Understand . . . the risk factors for, and varieties of, workplace aggression.

Aggression can take the form of physical acts, but also includes verbal aggression and some types of obstructionism. Many risk factors may potentially contribute to workplace aggression, such as having a competitive, achievement-oriented personality or a history of aggression. In addition, substance abuse (e.g., alcohol), an abusive supervisor, and a sense that the individual has been treated unfairly increase the risk of workplace aggression.

17.2d   Apply . . . your knowledge of satisfaction and burnout to ensure you maintain high motivation for college courses and your career.

Psychologists have applied the concept of burnout to college students, who are prone to experiencing exhaustion, cynicism, and decreased efficacy, just as employees are. We hope you completed the college student version of the Maslach Burnout Inventory in Table 17.8 on page 577 (Schaufeli et al., 2002) to see how you compare to others. In one study of 191 University of Georgia students, average scores for the three facets of burnout were 17.95 for exhaustion, 11.1 for cynicism, and 26.0 for personal effectiveness (Pisarek, 2009). If you score higher than that, you are at risk for being burned out!

17.2e   Analyze . . . various methods for preventing burnout and encouraging job satisfaction.

The best techniques are probably preventive measures: Hiring people with the right skills and personality for the job reduces the chance for burnout while increasing chances for satisfaction. Stress management skills and time off from work are both helpful for existing employees. Although pay raises may seem like a good idea for boosting job satisfaction, they probably do little to address the actual causes of burnout.

Module 17.2 Quiz

Know . . .

1. _____ is the rate at which existing employees leave the organization.
   - A. Burnout
   - B. Negative affect
   - C. Turnover
   - D. Job satisfaction

Understand . . .

2. Absenteeism refers to:
   - A. when an employee regularly misses work for illegitimate reasons.
   - B. when an employee regularly misses work for any reason.
   - C. the rate at which employees leave the company.
   - D. the policy of allowing workers to accumulate sick leave and vacation time.

3. Which of the following is an accurate statement concerning sexual harassment?
   - A. An individual could avoid being sexually harassed if he or she really wanted.
   - B. Modern work settings include more women and more protections, so harassment has become much less of a problem in recent years.
   - C. Sexual harassment is determined by its consequences, not by the aggressor's intentions.
   - D. A person has to physically touch another person for the act to be considered harassment.

Apply . . .

4. How do exercise and stress management skills work to reduce or prevent burnout?
   - A. They provide a distraction from work.
   - B. They make the job more rewarding.
   - C. They help the employee reduce reactions to stress.
   - D. Actually, they do very little to reduce or prevent burnout.

Analyze . . .

5. You are a capable employee who feels very positive about your work skills. However, layoffs are a constant threat and you play no part in deciding who stays and who goes at your company. Your job satisfaction may suffer because:
   - A. you have low self-efficacy.
   - B. you probably have low self-esteem about your job.
   - C. you lack a sense of control over your work.
   - D. the managers are verbally abusive.

Module **17.3**   Leadership and Teamwork

Learning Objectives

17.3a   Know . . . the key terminology associated with leadership and teamwork.

17.3b   Understand . . . which skills and personal qualities predict good leadership.

17.3c   Understand . . . why certain input and process qualities lead to more effective teams.

17.3d   Apply . . . your knowledge to identify types of leaders with whom you work or study.

17.3e   Analyze . . . whether leaders should focus more on inspiring good work or should stick to rewarding it.

Leadership is essential to organizations in all walks of life, although we often associate it with politics, the military, or coaching. Leadership in the more traditional workplace is every bit as important, and many employees strive for the salary, influence, and status that comes with a management title. That is probably the main reason that the master's in business administration (MBA) degree is the most awarded graduate degree in the United States (nearly 200,000 are awarded each year). However, if you look at a list of billionaires over the past 15 years, you might be surprised at what you find. That list would include Richard Branson who started Virgin in London

and built it into an empire that includes a record label and an airline among its many businesses. Here in the United States, "Auntie" Anne Beiler amassed a fortune selling pretzels in shopping malls. Wang Yung-Ching made his billions in plastics and died the wealthiest man in Taiwan in 2008. Mukash Tagiani founded Landmark, a retail giant based in Dubai, and Spain's Amancio Ortega Gaono became a billionaire in the same line of work. None of these billionaires had MBAs. In fact, none of them completed college. Given that they led their business so effectively, psychologists are curious about the personal qualities that make some appear to be natural-born leaders.

It is difficult to imagine a work environment that does not benefit from high-quality leadership. Consider some of the benefits good leadership provides to an organization:

- A common set of objectives and goals
- A means of identifying, recognizing, and rewarding quality work
- Ethics and acceptable practices for working toward those goals
- Guidelines for acceptable behavior at work, including how to treat colleagues and clients

Even a self-employed professional who works alone benefits from a clear understanding of these four areas. So if leadership is key, how can companies acquire good leadership? Do they simply need to find someone with all the right qualities? Or could anyone be a leader with the right training?

Finding and Producing Effective Leaders

Leadership emergence *is the degree to which individuals are viewed as leaders by others* (Judge et al., 2002). Leaders generally share a set of personal qualities that distinguish them from the rest of the workforce. When the opportunity arises, the individual who possesses these characteristics will naturally emerge from the group and the situation as a leader. In terms of personality, this means that researchers should be able to administer personality tests to members of a number of organizations and pick out the leaders simply by looking at the patterns in the test results (Foti & Hauenstein, 2007). In reality, identifying leaders is not so clear-cut, although relatively stable personality and cognitive traits do significantly predict who becomes a leader. From the Big Five personality dimensions (Table 17.3; also discussed in Module 12.1), high emotional stability, extraversion, openness, and conscientious are associated with leader emergence (Judge et al., 2002).

In addition to predicting leader emergence, it is important to predict which leaders will be most effective. The Big Five model has a fairly good track record of predicting who will be an effective leader, along with self-monitoring—the tendency to reflect on and regulate one's own behavior in response to social cues (Day & Schleicher, 2006). Individuals who score high on self-monitoring measures are likely to think about what makes an effective leader, and then monitor their own behavior to ensure they are exhibiting those traits. In doing so, a shy individual who knows that extraverts do well as leaders may try to develop habits to overcome his appearance of shyness. In contrast, a low self-monitoring individual is unlikely to notice that his introverted personality is preventing his emergence or effectiveness as a leader.

Although we can certainly point to many impressive female leaders, a commonly held stereotype says that men make better leaders than women. Surveys suggest that in the United States and Europe, employees prefer to work for male bosses and often believe that males have more of the traits necessary for leadership (Cuadrado et al., 2015; Eagly, 2007). Surprisingly, one European sample showed that the stereotype that males were better leaders was even more prevalent among female employees (Cuadrado et al., 2015). However, this stereotype does not stand up to investigation. On average, women show more desirable leadership styles and traits than men (Eagly, 2007) and, although males tend to rate their own leadership as more effective, females get higher ratings of effectiveness than others (Paustian-Underdahl et al., 2014).

Perhaps the survey research really indicates that people expect leaders to be assertive—a characteristic that tends to be associated with masculinity. **Assertiveness** *is the degree to which an individual will work to achieve or protect one's interests.* Television and films are filled with stereotypes of bosses ranging from meek pushovers to power-wielding bullies, and neither makes for good management in fiction or in real life. As Figure 17.7 shows, leaders with the "right touch" can be assertive when it is called for, but not all the time (Ames, 2008).

To pull together the various traits and capabilities that produce effective leadership, researchers Hogan and Warrenfeltz (2003) developed the comprehensive model of leadership skills that is summarized in Table 17.10. As you read through the list of these skills, think about how they may apply to the people you know in leadership positions. Do these qualities capture what good leaders do? And are poor leaders lacking in one or more of these areas? Research confirms that this is the case, at least to a certain extent. Meta-analyses have found strong correlations between these four domains and performance (Ones et al., 1993; Vinchur et al., 1998).

Figure 17.7 Assertiveness Predicts Leadership Effectiveness

The most effective leaders are neither the least assertive nor the most assertive—they have just the "right touch," as indicated by the peak in the middle of the graph (Ames, 2008).

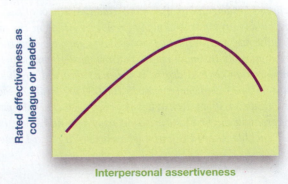

Table 17.10 Skills and Abilities of Successful Leaders

Domain	What It Represents	Sample Capabilities
Intrapersonal	High standards of performance for oneself	Is able to control emotions Is willing to take a stand Has career ambition and perseverance Shows integrity, ethics Shows self-confidence
Interpersonal	Social skills and role-playing ability	Has talent for building relationships Is sensitive to office politics Exhibits listening and negotiating skills Shows good communication
Business	Abilities and technical knowledge needed to plan and coordinate efforts	Has intelligence and technical skill Shows experience and understanding how the organization functions Has decision-making ability Sets priorities and goals
Leadership	Influence and team-building skills	Supports and motivates workers Sets standards for others' behaviors Develops and communicates a vision for the organization Motivates others

SOURCE: Based on From "Educating the modern manager" by R. Hogan & R. Warrenfeltz (2003), *Academy of Management Learning & Education, 2*(1), 74–84.

LEADERSHIP STYLES There are many ways to lead successfully, and psychologists have identified several different styles of leader (Bass, 1997). Typically, the most desirable style is **transformational leadership**, which is *a combination of charisma, intellectualization, and a focus on individuals within an organization*. Charisma blends together charm, attractiveness, and communication ability, which collectively produce an extremely influential personality. Charismatic leaders energize the organization by making a job seem to be extremely important and meaningful, thereby inspiring others through positive emotions (Shamir et al., 1993).

Transformational leadership also involves intellectual stimulation, which encourages deliberate thought regarding work tasks and the job in general. Through intellectualization, the worker does not mindlessly perform tasks, but asks what the function of the task might be, and considers alternative and creative approaches to the task.

The transformational style is linked to a number of positive outcomes. For example, intellectualization and individual focus helps workers understand their tasks and roles more fully, which in turn leads to a greater sense of psychological well-being (Nielsen et al., 2008). In this environment, workers feel a heightened sense of commitment to their jobs and to others in the workplace. Ultimately, the transformational style leads to better productivity, thanks to the collective effects of motivated, thoughtful employees (Bass et al., 2003; Jung & Sosik, 2002). As such, it is often considered to be a preferred type of management.

Whereas transformational leadership involves inspiration and vision, transactional leadership treats social exchanges like business transactions. Specifically,

transactional leadership *encourages employee or team member behaviors through rewards and punishments*. An active approach to transactional leadership would involve a leader closely watching workers, rewarding those who follow instructions and meet expectations. Alternatively, transactional leaders can be passive, practicing management by exception. With this approach, leaders let workers go about their tasks and intervene only when an exception—some sort of problem—arises. Compared to transformation, transactions are much less inspiring; nevertheless, this style can be effective in certain situations, such as short-term crises that require quick responses. If a sales group is below their quota near the end of the month, a manager might try to get results by increasing the amount of bonus cash available to the most successful employees, while threatening to fire the least successful. This might get the sales force moving for a week, but it would be an exhausting place to work for a year.

The final leadership approach is barely leadership at all. Translated from French, laissez-faire is roughly equivalent to the English phrase "leave it alone." Thus, **laissez-faire leadership** *describes the style of someone who has been appointed to a position of leadership, but who does not engage any either transformational or transactional behaviors*—he or she simply leaves the workers alone.

In the end, both the transformational and transactional styles of leadership can be effective, and a great many managers use both. The important results to remember are the correlations with each leadership style: Transformational leadership has a strong association with satisfied, motivated employees or team members (Kovjanic et al., 2013), whereas a laissez-faire style does not (Skogsta et al., 2014).

Working the Scientific Literacy Model

Character and Leadership

Employees look to leaders to learn how to be productive and which tasks to take on. But leaders are also role models for what is acceptable and what is unacceptable. Because that is the case, should we look for leaders with character?

What do we know about character and leadership?

In the early 2000s, a number of highly publicized scandals erupted surrounding corporate executives, including events at major corporations such as Enron and Tyco. A few years later, the financial crisis in the United States began with the failure of many of the country's largest financial institutions. To many people, it appeared that we were experiencing a crisis in leadership (Riggio et al., 2010). This problem was not as a result of the inability to lead—in fact, many of the affected companies had very strong leaders—but rather to the moral and ethical qualities of the choices those leaders made. The response of many psychologists was to search for the virtues that we expect from our leaders. Another approach was to investigate character in leadership, with definitions of character centered on those individual qualities that guide a leader to make moral and ethical decisions (Thompson & Riggio, 2010).

How can scientists study character and leadership?

One approach to studying character in leadership is to consider the traits or virtues that separate a truly ethical leader from a person who simply leads. Ronald Riggio and his colleagues identified four primary virtues from philosophical and psychological works on leadership: prudence, fortitude, temperance, and justice. Prudence is a practical type of wisdom that involves the ability to "make the appropriate decision that minimizes harm and maximizes good" (Riggio et al., 2010, p. 237). Fortitude is the courage to make difficult—even prudent—decisions. Virtuous leaders also display temperance in that they can exercise control over their emotional reactions and make reasonable decisions. Finally, the virtue of justice means that a leader should be able to follow rules but also make decisions based on principles of fairness. The researchers administered a questionnaire to thousands of employees who rated various types of leaders on these virtues, and statistical analyses confirmed that these traits correspond with ethical leadership. Perhaps more importantly, these

virtues correlate positively with desirable outcomes, such as a sense of empowerment among employees, and identification with the organization as a whole.

Can we critically evaluate this evidence?

We should be cautious in accepting the virtues of prudence, fortitude, temperance, and justice as the only ones that comprise character in leadership. The research techniques employed suggest that they are important, but other qualities may also play a role in ethical leadership. For example, some researchers have included personal integrity and forgiveness as important qualities (Grahek et al., 2010). In addition, researchers have asked about the nature and nurture of character. To what extent can these qualities be taught?

Why is this relevant?

One obvious application of this information is that leadership virtues can be applied to the study of leadership emergence, and it follows that psychological measures such as the Leadership Virtues Questionnaire might be used for screening potential leaders. Imagine you are in charge of hiring new managers for your organization: Would you like to know who possesses high levels of these four traits? Another application would be in the training of managers. Most definitions of character in leadership emphasize the idea that character comes from experience; therefore, it might be possible to train individuals who are strong in other aspects of leadership to also practice these virtues.

JOURNAL PROMPT

Leadership Styles: Think about your current or most recent work supervisor. (If you have not been employed, you could pick an instructor from another course.) Which leadership style most closely describes that person? In your writing, describe how specific behaviors exemplify the elements of that person's leadership style.

Working in Teams

Modern organizations almost always make use of teams—groups of individuals with shared goals and responsibilities. Most likely you are currently a member of several teams—perhaps a sports team, a group project for class, a drama or dance company, or naturally, a team of coworkers. The past two decades have seen the rapid growth of **virtual teams**, *production or project teams that are physically separated but operate largely (or completely) by electronic communications*. New software tools facilitate collaboration and conferences over the Internet, so companies are able to save the time and expense of traveling while gaining greater access to experts around the world.

To understand how teams function, psychologists often divide teamwork into three parts: input, process, and output. These areas seem to apply to all teams, so what distinguishes a sports team from a software development project team is simply the specific types of inputs, processes, and outputs.

INPUTS Team inputs include qualities such as the nature of the organization, management, the type of work the team is assigned, and the individuals who make up the team—basically, anything that is present before the process gets under way. For example, when members know that the team will be provided with motivation and rewards as a group, the outputs are usually more successful, and it is the responsibility of the organization's management to determine how rewards are allocated (Pritchard, 1995). Naturally, teams need members who have strong skills related to the assigned tasks, but did you know that teamwork itself is a skill? Research shows that intelligence, conflict resolution ability, and communication skills are all correlated with successful teams (Stevens & Campion, 1999). Not surprisingly, extraversion, agreeableness, and conscientiousness have also been associated with positive team outcomes (Barrick et al., 1998; Morgeson, Reider, & Campion, 2005).

PROCESS: WHAT THE TEAM DOES Team processes are essential to successful group performance (LePine et al., 2008). Obviously, communication will play an important role anytime multiple people are involved. Equally important, but perhaps less obvious, is the issue of planning and coordination, meaning that individuals' tasks fit their roles and skills, and that individual contributions fit together in a timely and orderly fashion (Fisher, 2014). Imagine a poorly coordinated assembly line where one group takes longer to complete its task than the next group down the line. Such a breakdown in coordination will leave one group idle and unproductive throughout portions of the shift.

Other social processes that can impede team effectiveness involve concepts you read about in Module 15.1. Social loafing is particularly detrimental to group success: It occurs when some group members produce less effort on a team than they do alone. When social loafing occurs, the team does not realize the full benefit from its working members (Latané et al., 1979).

From a more cognitive perspective, group decision making can also be either an asset or a liability. In cases of groupthink (see Module 15.1), individuals within the team develop strong convictions about an idea. As groupthink builds, all members begin to agree, and proposed actions tend to become riskier and maybe even too far-fetched to be feasible. Because the group seems to be approaching a unanimous decision, individuals become more and more certain about the correctness of their decision, and they maintain this belief until it is finalized. In some cases, this kind of agreement is helpful, but there are consequences when groupthink runs out of control: The decision can be wrong. One of the best-known examples led to the explosion of the space shuttle *Challenger* (Morehead et al., 1991). In this case, a small group of engineers had warned other workers about fuel tank seals freezing in cold weather. However, the team in charge of the launch convinced themselves that launching was a good idea, despite the risks linked to the seals. The *Challenger* launched, only to explode before it had been airborne for 2 minutes. Had team members employed correct team decision making, perhaps the disaster could have been avoided. Such an effort might have involved appointing a specific team member to question individual decisions, looking for outsiders to weigh in on the debate, or even breaking into smaller groups for discussions so that the social pressure would not be so great (Priem et al., 1995).

OUTPUT Perhaps the main reason to develop work teams is to increase efficiency. Certainly production teams are more efficient, as are well-coordinated project teams. When the goal is to innovate, teams—especially teams with diverse members—tend to outperform individuals (Axtell et al., 2006). Conversely, individuals are not subject to groupthink, so in many cases well-qualified people can make better decisions alone than with a group (Gigone & Hastie, 1997).

Outputs comprise more than just the products and services that result from teams; they also include benefits to the individual and the organization as a whole. Individuals may find increased job satisfaction thanks to positive experiences interacting with colleagues, a feeling of shared purpose, and the sense that they have achieved something bigger than they could have done by themselves (Henttonen et al., 2014; Meneghel et al., 2014).

Module 17.3 Summary

17.3a   Know . . . the key terminology associated with leadership and teamwork:

assertiveness
laissez-faire leadership
leadership emergence
transactional leadership
transformational leadership
virtual teams

17.3b   Understand . . . which skills and personal qualities predict good leadership.

From a personality perspective, leaders tend to be emotionally stable, extraverted, open, and conscientious. Good leaders are able to monitor their own behavior. Transformational leaders—those who are charismatic and intellectual, and who focus on the individuals within an organization—are usually preferable.

17.3c   Understand . . . why certain input and process qualities lead to more effective teams.

Teams are usually most successful when the members share motivation and rewards. When individual members are intelligent, good communicators, and good problem solvers, the team will perform well.

17.3d   Apply . . . your knowledge to identify types of leaders with whom you work or study.

Did you respond to the journal prompt on page 586 asking about a leader at work or school? If so, you have already practiced applying leadership styles. As you get to know these leadership styles better, it is interesting to apply them to leaders in various contexts at work and elsewhere—politicians, coaches, and so on. Think about the leaders you appreciate and admire the most. What style best describes them?

17.3e   Analyze . . . whether leaders should focus more on inspiring good work or should stick to rewarding it.

Research shows that leadership styles have their place. Transformational leadership—the more inspirational form—is probably better at fostering creativity, whereas transactional leadership may be better in situations that call for attention to detail.

Module 17.3 Quiz

Know . . .

1. Assertiveness is best characterized by:
   A. how strict a person is.
   B. the degree to which a person protects his or her interests.
   C. how closely a leader monitors others.
   D. adherence to written policies.

Understand . . .

2. Leaders with character exhibit which of the following traits?
   A. Frugality
   B. Fortitude
   C. Politeness
   D. Good looks

3. Which of the following is most important for a successful work team?
   A. The team is well coordinated and efforts are well planned.
   B. Team members all receive the same based pay to avoid conflict.
   C. Team members are based mostly on individual performance.
   D. A team leader spends little time offering direction or feedback on performance.

Apply . . .

4. Lauren, your boss, encourages you to work hard by paying you extra when you succeed. What is her style of leadership?
   A. Transactional
   B. Transformational
   C. Instinctive
   D. Laissez-faire

Analyze . . .

5. Transactional leadership styles are most effective when:
   A. the leader is assertive.
   B. the leader manages by exception.
   C. the task requires close attention to detail.
   D. the employees are already highly motivated.

Module 17.4   Scientific Literacy Challenge: Money as a Motivator

Imagine you are an executive with a medium-sized furniture company that has suffered from lagging employee performance across all divisions: The designers have been providing really dull style samples; at the factory, the quality of the product has been slipping; and at the stores, the sales teams are experiencing high absenteeism. Obviously, you and your management team need to come up with something to reenergize your employees, but what should you do? Using the following writing activity, spend a few minutes thinking about ways of increasing motivation and performance in the company.

JOURNAL PROMPT

Describe in detail a strategy for increasing motivation and performance and explain why you believe it could work.

What do we know about employee motivation?

Read this blog entry from Yvette James, a business consultant. Think about what she is suggesting, and decide whether her argument is convincing to you. Be sure to pay attention to the bold-faced key terms and concepts covered in Chapter 17.

Money can't buy happiness, but can it buy happy workers?

By Yvette James

Here is a fact that is so obvious that it is rarely, if ever, mentioned in business schools: If you want to hire employees, you have to pay them. Getting employees is one thing, but getting the most out of them is another. So if you want *motivated* employees, do you have to pay them more?

Before you answer this question, imagine you are a consultant for a company where employees report high levels of **burnout**, and managers struggle with constant **turnover**. In that type of situation, many supervisors have taken the **transactional** style, relying primarily on financial rewards for increased performance (of course, it may also involve threats of layoffs or demotions). Unfortunately for them, their strategy may not buy motivated employees. In fact, they may wind up with the opposite. After all, when you visit a workplace where employees report high **job satisfaction**, you will hear about pride, creativity, and a sense of ownership; few people say they love their work simply because it pays well. Clearly, job performance and satisfaction are related to more than the size of the paycheck.

Now that Ms. James has stated her opinion, she needs to provide some evidence to justify it. Let's see what kind of research she found on workplace motivation.

How do scientists study pay as a motivator?

Motivation is applicable in every area of psychology. Here, we see Ms. James is emphasizing evidence from the fields of I/O psychology and developmental psychology, among others.

To illustrate how little influence money has, Tim Judge and colleagues conducted a review of the data from over 90 studies that included around 15,000 employees. After sifting through all of that information, they discovered a rather meager 0.14 correlation between job satisfaction and pay. This suggests that the overwhelming majority of job satisfaction has to do with variables other than pay, such as the nature of the job and the work environment. Interestingly, this holds true even when workers evaluate their satisfaction only with their paycheck: the actual amount they earn has far less to do with pay satisfaction than other aspects of the job (the correlation is around 0.22).

Job satisfaction is not the same as motivation, although the two concepts are certainly connected. In order to examine the evidence on motivation, we can turn to Steven Deci of the University of Rochester. Deci and his colleagues combined the results of over 120 experimental studies that compared the effects of "extrinsic" motivators—rewards ranging from marshmallows for children to money for adults—to "intrinsic" motivators such as feelings of enjoyment or accomplishment. Deci's team produced overwhelming evidence that the extrinsic motivators actually *decrease* performance on the laboratory tasks, often by 20% or more.

What did you notice about the research this blogger cited? Take the following brief quiz to test yourself, paying attention to the highlighted passages above for clues to the answers.

1. Deci's research focused on comparing the effects of intrinsic and extrinsic motivators on laboratory task performance. In this work, the independent variable is:
   a. the feelings of enjoyment or accomplishment.
   b. performance on laboratory tasks.
   c. whether intrinsic or extrinsic motivators were used.
   d. correlation.
2. Which finding that Ms. James described in the blog is *least* likely to generalize to workplace populations?
   a. How children respond when marshmallows are used as motivators.
   b. How adults respond when money is a motivator.
   c. The fact that Judge combined 90 studies and responses from over 15,000 people
   d. That extrinsic motivators can decrease performance.
3. What can we conclude from Judge's review of job satisfaction?
   a. The same basic findings have been replicated in many studies.
   b. Pay is the only variable that predicts employee satisfaction.
   c. Strict supervisors lead to better work performance.
   d. It is not possible to do experiments with employees.

Answers: 1. c 2. a 3. a

Now that we have seen some of the evidence, let's move on to engage in critical thinking.

How do we think critically about using money as a motivator?

The statements below will help you identify several aspects of critical thinking. Match the following critical thinking statements to the highlighted passages that illustrate them.

Obviously, these findings do not mean you should cut employee pay; if you recommended that, yours would be a very short career as a consultant. Case studies in specific sectors bear this out. For example, one study showed that Costco pays its store employees an average of 72% more than its competitor, Sam's Club (with benefits, the difference is even higher). The turnover rates of the two stores are 17% and 44% respectively. Considering that replacing a full-time employee costs about 1.5 times that individual's salary, Costco might actually be making the smarter financial choice. However, people work at either Sam's or Costco for many different reasons, so the turnover rate could be due to something else, such as work preparedness or management practices.

It is worthwhile to note, however, that businesses can have very different cultures and attitudes about money, and work can change over time. Moreover, some research has been restricted to the laboratory, where, oftentimes, college freshman are working for extra credit rather than a mortgage and their kids' orthodontics. The freshman may not behave in the same ways, or have comparable motives to work and earn in comparison to non-college students.

Is this blogger applying critical thinking? Evaluate the important elements of critical thinking below and apply them to what you read above. Can you match each element to one of the highlighted sections of the blog post?

1. Consider that the evidence might lack ecological validity.
2. Be cautious not to assume causality from quasi-experimental comparisons.
3. Question whether the results would generalize to other samples.

1. Blue 2. Yellow 3. Green

Understanding variables that affect job satisfaction are certainly important for the well-being of our workforce and for economic productivity. Here, the author further explores the implications of this work.

How is this relevant to business?

Ms. James questions whether money really is the best way to motivate workers and she backs up her claim with some evidence. Read how she suggests managers apply the information, and then consider any newly formed thoughts you may have about the topic in the writing activity that follows.

In summary, money probably buys neither happiness nor happy employees. Instead, managers and consultants alike should focus on what factors lead to successful outcomes like increasing job satisfaction and helping employees avoid burnout. As I wrote in my previous post, we should make sure employees have the resources they need, and a supportive environment in which to work—bullies, gossips, and crude joke-tellers make it difficult to perform at a high level. Employees thrive when they have clear job expectations and the freedom to find creative ways of getting the job done.

SHARED WRITING

After reading about the research, do you believe money can be a successful motivator? In what workplace situations would you recommend it to a friend or relative who is a manager?

Chapter **17** Quiz

1. During job analysis, psychologists will identify the essential KSAOs. Which one of the following qualities is not a KSAO?
   A. Knowledge
   B. Skills
   C. Abilities
   D. Organization

2. An assessment center is:
   A. an office or meeting room that is used for structured interviews.
   B. a process of screening potential employees using a variety of tests and simulations.
   C. a method of evaluating how well a current employee is performing.
   D. a personality test.

3. Which of the following statements is true regarding the use of personality-based selection tests for hiring?
   A. Some personality traits can be useful predictors of performance at various jobs.
   B. Personality traits can be useful predictors of which candidates will do poorly at a job, but do not predict which candidates are likely to succeed.
   C. Conscientiousness is the only personality trait that correlates with performance across a wide range of jobs.
   D. Personality-based selection tests are not a useful tool for predicting job performance.

4. An employee who always goes above and beyond what his or her employer asks is demonstrating good _____.
   A. task performance
   B. organizational citizenship behavior
   C. situational judgment
   D. counterproductive behavior

5. Steve's supervisor is always impressed at his ability to come up with creative solutions to problems at work. Because of this talent, the supervisor has a good opinion of Steve as an overall employee, despite the fact that he is frequently late to work and sometimes has poor productivity. The supervisor's overall good opinion of Steve is likely the result of _____.
   A. the contrast effect
   B. the halo effect
   C. the 360-degree bias
   D. the mixed-performance bias

6. If a psychologist completes a performance appraisal for a superstar employee, then the next employee may seem weak in comparison. This can lead to _____.
   A. the contrast effect
   B. the halo effect
   C. the downsizing effect
   D. stereotype threat

7. "Locus of control" refers to:
   A. whether an individual feels more in control at home or at work.
   B. a set of beliefs about the person's ability to control his or her work environment and success.
   C. a person's beliefs about his or her value and worth as a human being.
   D. the skills that a person can use to affect his or her work environment.

8. The "Conditional Reasoning Test" could theoretically be used by employers to detect _____ in employees.
   A. mental illness
   B. success potential
   C. aggressive tendencies
   D. high intelligence levels

9. Which of the following statements is true regarding male versus female leadership?
   A. On average, women show more desirable leadership styles and traits than men.
   B. On average, men show more desirable leadership styles and traits than women.
   C. In the United States, employees prefer to work for female bosses.
   D. Men are more effective leaders than women.

10. In general, the _____ style of leadership is considered the most desirable.
    A. transactional
    B. laissez-faire
    C. passive
    D. transformational

11. An employee is often shows up late, gossips frequently about colleagues, and occasionally exaggerates his performance on weekly reports is engaged in _____.
    A. anti-organizational citizenship
    B. counterproductive behavior
    C. negative affectivity
    D. transactionality

12. Which of the following best describes the laissez-faire approach to leadership?
    A. A team leader anticipates errors that people might potentially make and works to avoid them.
    B. A team leader controls worker behavior through rewards and punishments.
    C. A team leader strives to make rewards for good work equitable across all team members.
    D. A team leader spends little time offering direction or feedback on performance.

13. The concept of burnout does not include _____.

   A. exhaustion

   B. a cynical, pessimistic attitude about the organization

   C. the belief that nothing of significance is ever accomplished

   D. awareness that supervisors give undeserved special treatment to other employees.

14. Ben is especially good at one of his job duties called "case closing." He actually enjoys it too, so he and his supervisor have rewritten his job description to include closing cases for everyone in the department. Ben and his supervisor are engaged in _____.

   A. job crafting

   B. job analysis

   C. reallocation

   D. transformation

15. Which of the following would be an example of a virtual team?

   A. A group of workers around the globe who coordinate their efforts through teleconferencing and e-mail

   B. A computer simulation of how employees might interact

   C. A group of employees who have similar jobs, but who do not actually interact with one another

   D. A group of employees in which one member does the majority of the work that is claimed by the team

Glossary

360-degree feedback   A technique that provides evaluation information for an employee from various perspectives within and beyond an organization; also known as multisource assessment.

abnormal psychology   The psychological study of mental illness.

absenteeism   Regularly missing work, whether for legitimate or questionable reasons.

absolute threshold   The minimum amount of energy or quantity of a stimulus required for it to be reliably detected at least 50% of the time it is presented.

acetylcholine   A neurotransmitter found at junctions between skeletal muscles and nerves, as well as in the brain, where it is involved in the processes of arousal and attention.

achievement motivation   The drive to perform at high levels and to accomplish significant goals.

achievement tests   Tests that measure knowledge and thinking skills that an individual has acquired.

acquisition   The initial phase of learning in which a response is established.

acronym   A pronounceable word that can be broken up so that each letter represents the first letter in a phrase or set of items.

action potential   A wave of electrical activity that originates at the base of the axon and rapidly travels down its length; the firing of a nerve cell.

activation–synthesis hypothesis   Prediction that dreams arise from brain activity originating from bursts of excitatory messages arising from the brain stem.

adrenal glands   A pair of endocrine glands located adjacent to the kidneys that release stress hormones, such as cortisol and epinephrine.

aggression   Any behavior that is intended to hurt or harm an individual.

agonists   Drugs that enhance or mimic the effects of neurotransmission.

agoraphobia   An intense fear of having a panic attack or lower-level panic symptoms in public.

algorithms   Problem-solving strategies that are based on a series of rules.

all-or-none principle   The observation that individual nerve cells fire at the same strength every time an action potential occurs.

altruism   Behavior that places the helper at significant risk or certain harm for the benefit of another.

Alzheimer's disease   A degenerative and terminal condition resulting in severe damage of the entire brain.

amnesia   A profound loss of at least one form of memory.

amygdala   A structure in the forebrain that facilitates memory formation for emotional events, mediates fear responses, and appears to play a role in recognizing and interpreting emotional stimuli, including facial expressions.

analytical psychology   A branch of psychology that describes personality as the result of unconscious archetypes.

anchoring effect   An effect that occurs when an individual attempts to solve a problem involving numbers and uses pervious knowledge to keep (i.e., anchor) the response within a limited range.

anecdotal evidence   An individual's story or testimony about an observation or event that is used to make a claim as evidence.

anorexia nervosa   An eating disorder that involves (1) self-starvation, (2) intense fear of weight gain and a distorted perception of body image, and (3) a denial of the serious consequences of severely low weight.

antagonists   Drugs that inhibit neurotransmissions by blocking the receptors for or synthesis of the neurotransmitter.

anterograde amnesia   The inability to form new memories for events occurring after a brain injury.

anthropometrics   A historical term referring to the method of measuring physical and mental variations in humans.

antianxiety drugs   Drugs prescribed to alleviate nervousness and tension, and to prevent and reduce panic attacks.

antidepressant drugs   Drugs prescribed to elevate mood and reduce other symptoms of depression.

antipsychotic drugs   Drugs used treat disorders such as schizophrenia, and sometimes patients with severe mood disorders.

antisocial personality disorder (APD)   A personality disorder marked by a habitual pattern of willingly violating others' personal rights, with little sign of empathy or remorse.

aphasias   Language disorders caused by damage to the brain structures that support the use and understanding of language.

appeal to authority   A claim that is based on belief in an expert's testimony, even when no supporting data or scientific evidence is present.

appeal to common sense   A claim that appears to be sound, but lacks supporting scientific evidence.

applied psychology   A branch of psychology that uses psychological knowledge to address problems and issues across various settings and professions, including law, education, clinical psychology, and business organization and management.

approach goals   Enjoyable and pleasant incentives that we are drawn toward, such as praise or financial reward.

aptitude tests   Tests designed to measure an individual's potential to perform well in a specific range of tasks.

assertiveness   The degree to which an individual will work to achieve or protect one's interests.

assessment centers   A method of personnel selection that capitalizes on multiple approaches to selection by combining personality, cognitive, and sometimes physical ability tests.

assortative mating   Choosing sexual partners who are similar to the individual doing the searching.

attachment   An enduring emotional bond formed between individuals.

authoritarian parenting   A parenting style in which parents exercise excessive control over children and are less likely to express warmth toward them.

authoritative parenting   A parenting style characterized by the expression of warmth and responsiveness to the needs of children, but exercising control over certain actions and decisions made by children.

autonomic nervous system   The portion of the peripheral nervous system that is responsible for controlling involuntary activity of the organs and glands.

availability heuristic   A strategy for estimating the frequency of an event based on how easily examples of it come to mind.

avoidance goals   Unpleasant outcomes that we try to avoid, such as shame, embarrassment, or emotional pain.

avoidance learning   A specific type of negative reinforcement that removes the possibility of an aversive stimulus occurring.

axon   The projection of a neuron that transports information from the neuron to neighboring neurons in the form of an electrochemical reaction.

basal ganglia   A set of forebrain structures involved in facilitating planned movements, skill learning, and are also integrated with the brain's reward system.

behavioral genetics   The study of how genes and environment influence behavior.

behavioral genomics   The study of how specific genes, in their interactions with the environment, influence behavior.

behavioral therapy   A form of therapy that addresses problem behaviors and thoughts, and the environmental factors that trigger them, as directly as possible.

behaviorism   The dominant approach to psychology in the United States starting in the first half of the 20th century, which had a singular focus on studying only observable behavior, with little to no reference to mental events or instincts as possible causes of behavior.

belief perseverance   A cognitive bias that occurs when an individual believes he or she has the solution to the problem or the correct answer for a question, and accepts only evidence that will confirm those beliefs.

binocular depth cues   Distance cues that are based on the differing perspectives of both eyes.

biofeedback   A therapeutic technique involving the use of physiological recording instruments to provide feedback that increases ones awareness of bodily responses.

biopsychosocial model   An approach to explaining behavior as a product of biological, psychological, and sociocultural factors.

bipolar disorder   A type of mood disorder characterized by extreme highs and lows in mood, motivation, and energy; sometimes referred to as manic depression.

body mass index (BMI)   A statistic commonly used for estimating a healthy body weight that factors in an individual's height.

borderline personality disorder (BPD)   A psychological disorder involving intense extremes between positive and negative emotions, an unstable sense of self, impulsivity, and difficult social relationships.

bottom-up processing   A perceptual process in which a whole stimulus or concept is constructed from bits of raw sensory information.

brain-derived neurotrophic factor (BDNF)   A protein in the nervous system that promotes survival, growth, and formation of new synapses.

brain stem   A portion of the hindbrain on top of the spinal cord that comprises the medulla, pons, reticular formation, and cerebellum.

Broca's area   A frontal lobe structure that controls humans' ability to articulate the speech sounds that make up words.

bulimia nervosa   An eating disorder characterized by periods of food deprivation, binge-eating, and purging.

burnout   A combination of persistent emotional and physical exhaustion, cynical attitudes about the job, and a sense that one's work has little meaning.

bystander effect   The situation in which, as an individual looks around at other bystanders and notices that no one else is helping, the bystander freezes.

Cannon-Bard theory of emotion   The theory that emotions such as fear or happiness occur simultaneously with their physiological components.

case study   An in-depth report about the details of a specific case.

catatonia   A state of prolonged periods of immobility and muteness.

categories   Groups of interrelated concepts.

cell body   The part of a neuron that contains the nucleus and the genetic information of the cell; also known as the *soma*.

central executive   The control center of working memory; it coordinates attention and the exchange of information among the three storage components.

central nervous system (CNS)   The division of the nervous system consisting of the brain and the spinal cord.

central route (to persuasion)   A path to persuasion in which individuals take time, evaluate evidence, and use valid logic and arguments to arrive at attitudes or beliefs.

central tendency   A measure of the central point of a distribution of numbers.

cerebellum   A portion of the hindbrain involved in the coordination, timing, and learning of movements as well as maintaining balance.

cerebral cortex   The convoluted, wrinkled outer layer of the brain that is involved in multiple higher functions, such as thought, language, and personality.

chromosomes   Structures in the cellular nucleus that are lined with all of the genes an individual inherits.

chunking   The process of organizing smaller units of information into larger, more meaningful units.

circadian rhythms   Internally driven daily cycles of approximately 24 hours that affect physiological and behavioral processes.

classical conditioning   Learning that occurs when a neutral stimulus begins to elicit a response that was originally caused by another stimulus.

clinical psychologist   A mental health professional with a doctoral degree who diagnoses and treats mental health problems ranging from the everyday to the chronic and severe.

clinical psychology   The field of psychology concerned with diagnosing and treating mental and behavioral disorders.

cochlea   A fluid-filled membrane in the ear that is coiled in a snail-like shape and contains the structures that convert sound into neural impulses.

cognitive-behavioral therapy   A form of therapy that consists of procedures such as exposure, cognitive restructuring, and stress inoculation training.

cognitive development   The changing abilities and processes of memory, thought, and reasoning that occur throughout the life span.

cognitive dissonance   The situation in which an individual has two thoughts (cognitions) that are inconsistent with each other (dissonance) and, as a result, experiences motivation to reduce the discrepancy.

cohort effects   Consequences of being born in a particular year or narrow range of years.

coma   A state marked by complete loss of consciousness and suppressed brain stem reflexes.

community psychology   An area of psychology that focuses on identifying how individuals' mental health is influenced by the neighborhood, economics, social groups, and other community based variables.

comorbidity   The presence of two disorders simultaneously, or the presence of a second disorder that affects the one being treated.

compensatory control   The psychological strategies people use to preserve a sense of nonrandom order when personal control is compromised.

concept   The mental representation of an object, event, or idea.

concrete operational stage   The third stage of cognitive development, spanning ages 7 to 11 years, when children develop skills in using and manipulating numbers as well as logical thinking.

conditioned response (CR)   A learned response that occurs to the conditioned stimulus.

conditioned stimulus (CS)   A once neutral stimulus that elicits a conditioned response because it has a history of being paired with an unconditioned stimulus.

conditioned taste aversion   The acquired dislike of or disgust for a food or drink because that food or drink was paired with illness.

conduction hearing loss   Hearing loss resulting from damage to any of the physical structures that conduct sound waves to the cochlea.

cones   Photoreceptors in the eye that are sensitive to the different wavelengths of light that we perceive as color.

confirmation bias   A cognitive bias that occurs when an individual searches for only evidence that will confirm his or her beliefs instead of evidence that might disconfirm them.

conformity   The situation in which an individual's behavior changes to fit with the behavior of a group.

confounding variables   Factors outside of the researcher's control that might affect the results of a study.

consciousness   Our subjective thoughts, perceptions, experiences of the world, and self-awareness.

conservation   Knowledge that the quantity or amount of an object is not related to the physical arrangement and appearance of that object.

consolidation   The process of converting short-term memories into long-term memories in the brain.

constructive memory   A process by which we first recall a generalized schema and then add in specific details.

continuous reinforcement   A schedule in which every response made results in reinforcement.

contrast effect   A type of error in the evaluation process in which a rater evaluates one employee who is very strong in a number of dimensions such that, by comparison, the next employee is likely to appear weaker, even though he or she may be an average worker by other measures.

control group   A group in an experiment that does not receive the treatment and, therefore, serves as a comparison to an experimental group.

control processes   Elements of memory systems that shift information from one memory store to another.

convenience samples   A sample consisting of those individuals who are the most readily available.

conventional morality   A type of moral thinking that regards social conventions and rules as guides for appropriate moral behavior, and emphasizes taking directives from parents, teachers, and the law.

convergence   A depth cue that occurs when the eye muscles contract so that both eyes focus on a single object.

coping   Processes used to manage demands, stress, and conflict.

core knowledge hypothesis   A view on development that proposes infants have inborn abilities for understanding some key aspects of their environment.

cornea   A clear layer that covers the front portion of the eye and contributes to our ability to focus our vision on an object.

coronary heart disease   A condition in which plaques form in the blood vessels that supply the heart with blood and oxygen, resulting in restricted blood flow.

corpus callosum   The area of the brain connecting the two cerebral hemispheres.

correlational research   A technique for measuring the degree of association between two or more variables.

cortisol   A hormone secreted by the adrenal cortex that prepares the body to respond to stressful circumstances.

counseling psychologist   A mental health professional who typically works with people needing help with common problems such as stress, coping, and mild forms of anxiety and depression, rather than severe mental disorders.

critical thinking   Exercising curiosity and skepticism when evaluating the claims of others, and with our own assumptions and beliefs.

cross-foster   The act of raising an animal as member of a family that is not of the same species.

cross-sectional design   A research design used to measure and compare samples of people from different age groups at one point in time.

crystallized intelligence (Gc)   A form of intelligence that relies on extensive experience and knowledge and, therefore, tends to be relatively stable and robust.

cultures of honor   Social groups that expect individuals to protect themselves and their property by whatever means necessary, including violence.

debriefing   An ethical procedure in which researchers explain the true nature of a study, and especially the nature of and reason for any deception after it has been completed.

deception   Misleading or only partially informing participants in a research study about the true topic or hypothesis under investigation.

declarative memory   Memories we are consciously aware of and can that be verbalized, including facts about the world and one's own personal experiences.

deep-brain stimulation (DBS)   A technique that involves electrically stimulating highly specific regions of the brain.

defense mechanisms   Unconscious strategies that the ego uses to reduce or avoid anxiety, guilt, and other unpleasant feelings.

deinstitutionalization   A grass-roots movement that pushed for returning people from mental institutions to their communities and families and enabling individuals to receive treatment on an outpatient basis.

déjà vu   A distinct feeling of having seen or experienced a situation that is impossible or unlikely to have previously occurred.

deliberative thought   An intentional and effortful form of thinking.

delusions   False beliefs about reality.

demand characteristics   Inadvertent cues given off by the experimenter or the experimental context that provide information about how participants are expected to behave in a research study.

dementia   A set of symptoms including mild to severe disruption of mental functioning, memory loss, disorientation, poor judgment, and decision making.

dendrites   The small branches radiating from the cell body of a neuron that receive messages from other cells and transmit the message toward the cell body.

dependence   A need to take a drug to ward off unpleasant physical withdrawal symptoms; often referred to as addiction.

dependent variable   The observation or measurement that is recorded during the experiment and subsequently compared across all groups in a research study.

descriptive statistics   A set of techniques used to organize, summarize, and interpret data.

determinism   The belief that all events are governed by lawful, cause-and-effect relationships.

developmental psychology   The study of change and stability of human physical, cognitive, social, and behavioral characteristics across the life span.

Diagnostic and Statistical Manual for Mental Disorders **(DSM-V)** The manual that establishes criteria for the diagnosis of mental disorders.

difference threshold The smallest detectable difference between stimuli.

discrimination (in learning) A process in which an organism learns to respond to one original stimulus but not to new stimuli that may be similar to the original stimulus.

discrimination Any behavior based on prejudice.

discriminative stimulus A cue or event indicating that a response, if made, will be reinforced.

dishabituation An increase in responsiveness following a change in a stimulus or event.

display rules The unwritten expectations people have regarding when it is appropriate to show a certain emotion.

dissociation theory (of hypnosis) An explanation of hypnosis as a unique state in which consciousness is divided into an observer and a hidden observer.

dissociative disorder A category of mental disorders characterized by a split between conscious awareness from feeling, cognition, memory, and identity.

dissociative identity disorder (DID) A condition in which people claim that their identity has split into one or more distinct alter personalities, or alters; sometimes referred to as multiple personality disorder.

divided attention Attending to several stimuli or tasks at once.

dizygotic twins Twins who were conceived by two different eggs and two different sperm, but still shared the same womb; also known as *fraternal twins.*

DNA (deoxyribonucleic acid) Molecules formed in a double-helix shape that contain four amino acids: adenine, cytosine, guanine, and thymine.

door-in-the-face technique A technique that begins with a large request that is likely to be turned down, followed by a smaller request that is likely to be accepted.

dopamine A monoamine neurotransmitter involved in movement, mood, and processing of rewarding experiences.

double-blind study An experimental procedure in which neither the participant nor the experimenter knows the exact treatment received by any individual.

dream analysis A method of understanding unconscious thought by interpreting the manifest content (what happens in the dream) to get a sense of the latent content (the unconscious elements that motivated the dream).

drive A physiological trigger that tells us we may be deprived of something and causes us to seek out what is needed, such as food.

DRM (Deese-Roediger-McDermott) procedure A research technique in which participants study a list of highly related words called semantic associates.

dual coding The phenomenon that occurs when information is stored in more than one form— such as a verbal description and a visual image, or a description and a sound.

ecological validity The degree to which the results of a laboratory study can be applied to or repeated in the natural environment.

ecstasy (MDMA) An illegal club/rave drug known to heighten sensory experiences, intensify social bonding, and have hallucinogenic effects.

ego A component of personality that mediates the id through the reality principle.

egocentric Perceiving and interpreting the world in terms of the self.

elaborative rehearsal Prolonging exposure to information by thinking about its meaning.

electroconvulsive therapy (ECT) A psychiatric treatment in which an electrical current is passed through the brain to induce a temporary seizure.

electroencephalogram (EEG) A measure of brain activity that uses electrodes attached to the scalp to measure patterns of brain activity.

emotion A psychological experience involving three components: (1) subjective thoughts and experiences, (2) accompanying patterns of physical arousal, and (3) characteristic behavioral expressions.

emotional dialects Variations across cultures in how core emotions are expressed.

emotional well-being The subjective experience of both positive and negative emotions, which are typically measured by life satisfaction, happiness, and the balance between negative and positive emotional experiences.

empathy The emotional concern that one individual has for another's well-being.

empirically supported treatments Also called evidence based therapies; treatments that have been tested and evaluated using sound research designs.

empiricism A philosophical tenet that knowledge comes through experience.

empty nest syndrome A phenomenon in which parents experience a sense of sadness and loss when their children have left home.

encoding The process of storing information in a long-term memory system.

encoding specificity principle The concept that retrieval is most effective when it occurs in the same context as encoding.

endorphin A chemical produced by the pituitary gland and the hypothalamus that functions to reduce pain and induce feelings of pleasure.

entity theory The belief that intelligence is a fixed characteristic and relatively difficult (or impossible) to change.

epigenetics Study of how gene expression (switching genes off and on) is influenced by interactions with the environment.

episodic buffer A storage component of working memory that combines the images and sounds from the other two components (the phonological loop and visuospatial sketchpad) into coherent, story-like episodes.

episodic memory A type of declarative memory for personal experiences that seems to be organized around episodes and is recalled from a first-person perspective.

escape learning A process in which an organization learns that a response removes an unpleasant or undesirable stimulus that is already present.

evolution The change in the frequency of genes occurring in an interbreeding population over generations.

exemplar A specific category member that serves as a reference point for the entire category.

experimental group The group in an experiment that is exposed to the independent variable.

explicit prejudice The situation in which an individual confesses to or openly demonstrates his or her stereotypes.

exposure therapy A set of procedures in which exposure to a feared situation is done repeatedly and gradually under controlled conditions.

external (situational) attribution The situation in which the observer explains the actor's behavior as a result of the social context.

extinction (in classical conditioning) The loss or weakening of a conditioned response when a conditioned stimulus and an unconditioned stimulus no longer occur together.

extinction (in operant conditioning) The weakening of an operant response when reinforcement is no longer available.

facial feedback hypothesis A prediction that if emotional expressions influence subjective emotional experiences, then the act of forming a facial expression should elicit the specific corresponding emotion.

factor analysis A statistical technique used by psychologists to reveal statistical similarities underlying a wide variety of items.

false memory Remembering events that did not occur, or incorrectly recalling details of an event.

fast-mapping The ability to map words onto concepts or objects after only a single exposure.

fetal alcohol syndrome A condition resulting in abnormalities in mental functioning, growth, and facial development in the offspring of women who use alcohol during pregnancy.

first letter technique A mnemonic technique that uses the first letters of a set of items to spell out words that form a sentence.

Five Factor Model (Big Five personality factors) A trait-based approach to personality measurement that includes extraversion, emotional stability (also referred to by the opposite quality, neuroticism), conscientiousness, agreeableness, and openness.

fixation A preoccupation with obtaining pleasure during psychosexual development, resulting in failure to progress as expected.

fixed-interval schedule A schedule that reinforces the first response occurring after a set amount of time passes.

fixed-ratio schedule A schedule in which reinforcement is delivered after a specific number of responses have been completed.

flashbulb memory An extremely vivid and detailed memory about an event and the conditions surrounding how one learned about the event.

fluid intelligence (Gf) A type of intelligence that is used to adapt to new situations and solve new problems without relying on previous knowledge.

Flynn effect The finding of steady population-level increases in intelligence test scores over time.

foot-in-the-door technique A persuasion technique that involves a request for something simple, followed by a more substantial request.

forebrain The most visibly obvious region of the whole brain; it consists of multiple interconnected structures that are critical to such complex processes as emotion, memory, thinking, and reasoning.

forensic psychology The branch of psychology that encompasses work in the criminal justice system, including interactions with the legal system and its professionals.

formal operational stage The fourth stage of cognitive development, beginning at approximately 11 years of age and continuing into adulthood, that involves advanced cognitive processes such as abstract reasoning and hypothetical thinking.

fovea The central region of the retina, which contains the highest concentration of cones. The fovea ensures that objects we center our vision upon are the clearest and most colorful relative to objects in the periphery.

free association A therapeutic method that instructs the patient to reveal any thoughts that arise, no matter how odd or meaningless they may seem.

frequency The number of observations that fall within a certain category or range of scores.

frequency theory (of hearing) A theory of hearing stating that the perception of pitch is related to the frequency at which the basilar membrane vibrates.

frontal lobe Region of the cortex that is involved in higher cognitive functions, such as planning, regulating impulses and emotion, language production, and voluntary movement.

frustration-aggression hypothesis A prediction that aggression will occur when an individual is prevented from achieving a goal and experiences frustration as a result.

functional fixedness A problem-solving obstacle that occurs when an individual identifies a potential operator, but can think of only its most obvious function.

functional MRI (fMRI) Technology that measures changes in blood flow, which is correlated with neural activity, throughout the brain.

functionalism The study of the purpose and function of behavior and conscious experience.

fundamental attribution error The tendency to make internal attributions for others while ignoring external attributions.

gamma-amino butyric acid (GABA) A primary inhibitory neurotransmitter of the nervous system, which prevents neurons from generating action potentials.

gate-control theory A theory that explains our experience of pain as an interaction between nerves that transmit pain messages and those that inhibit these messages.

gender nonconforming Pattern of having interests and mannerisms that are stereotypical of the opposite sex.

gene The basic unit of heredity that is responsible for guiding the process of creating the proteins that make up the body's physical structures, and regulating development and physiological processes throughout the life span.

gene knockout (KO) studies A method of removing a specific gene thought to be involved in a trait (such as intelligence) and testing the effects of removing the gene by comparing behavior of animals without the gene with those that have it.

general adaptation syndrome (GAS) An early theory of stress responses involving stages of alarm, resistance, and exhaustion.

general intelligence (g) The concept that intelligence is a basic cognitive trait comprising the ability to learn, reason, and solve problems regardless of their nature.

generalizability The degree to which one set of results can be applied to other situations, individuals, or events.

generalization A process in which a response that originally occurs to a specific stimulus also occurs to different, though similar stimuli.

generalized anxiety disorder (GAD) A type of anxiety disorder involving frequently elevated levels of anxiety that are not directed at or limited to any particular situation.

genotype The genetic makeup of an organism.

Gestalt psychology An approach emphasizing that psychologists need to focus on the whole of perception and experience, rather than its parts.

glial cells Specialized cells of the nervous system that are involved in manufacturing myelin, mounting immune responses in the brain, removing wastes, and synchronizing activity of the billions of neurons that constitute the nervous system.

glucose A sugar that serves as a primary energy source of the brain and the rest of the body.

glutamate An excitatory neurotransmitter in the nervous system that plays a critical role in the processes of learning and memory.

graded membership The observation that some concepts appear to make better category members than other concepts.

group polarization The situation in which members of a group discuss characteristic attitudes and the individuals experience an increase in those attitudes as a result.

groupthink A decision-making problem in which group members avoid argument and strive for agreement.

gustatory system System involved in the sensation and perception of taste.

habituation A decrease in responding with repeated exposure to an event.

hallucinations False perceptions of reality, such as hearing internal voices.

hallucinogenic drugs A category of drugs that bring about visual, auditory, and sometimes tactile distortions, and alter how people perceive their own thinking.

halo effect A type of error in the appraisal process in which a rater thinks highly of an aspect of an employee's job or personality, which in turn leads him or her to unintentionally overrate other aspects of the employee's performance.

haptics The active, exploratory aspect of touch sensation and perception.

Hawthorne effect Situations in which behavior changes as a result of being observed.

health psychology The study of how individual, biological, and environmental factors affect physical health.

heritability A statistic, expressed as a number between zero and one, that represents the degree to which genetic differences between individuals contribute to individual differences in a behavior or trait found in a population.

heuristics Problem-solving strategies that stem from previous experiences and provide an educated guess as to what is the most likely solution.

hindbrain Brain structures that are critical to controlling basic, life-sustaining processes.

hippocampus A structure in the brain located below the amygdala in the limbic system; it is responsible for learning and memory.

histrionic personality disorder (HPD) A category of personality disorder characterized by excessive attention seeking and dramatic behavior.

homeostasis The body's physiological processes that allow it to maintain consistent internal states in response to the outer environment.

hormones Chemicals produced by the endocrine system that regulate bodily functions and behavior.

humanistic psychology A perspective of psychology that focuses on the unique aspects of each individual human, their freedom to act, their rationale thought, and the belief that humans are fundamentally different from other animals.

hypnosis A procedure of inducing a heightened state of suggestibility.

hypothalamic–pituitary–adrenal (HPA) axis A neural and endocrine circuit that involves communication between the nervous system (the hypothalamus) and the endocrine system (pituitary and adrenal glands).

hypothalamus A brain structure that regulates basic biological needs and motivational systems.

hypothesis A testable prediction about processes that can be observed and measured.

hypothesis test A statistical test for the difference between the means of the two groups relative to the variability one would expect due to chance in the means.

id A component of personality underlying basic biological drives, including those related to sex and aggression.

identity A person's self-image and perception of his or her unique and individual characteristics.

identity statuses The processes and outcomes of identity development that include elements of both crisis and personal commitment.

idiographic approach (to personality) An approach to the study of personality that uses detailed descriptions of individuals and their unique personality characteristics.

ill-defined problem A problem with either an ambiguous initial state or an ambiguous goal state.

imagination inflation The increased confidence in a false memory following repeated imagination of the event.

imitation Recreation of a motor behavior or expression, often to accomplish a specific goal.

implicit prejudice Forms of stereotyping and prejudice that are kept silent either intentionally or because the individual is unaware of their own prejudice.

inattentional blindness A failure to notice clearly visible events or objects because attention is directed elsewhere.

incentives (goals) The stimuli we seek to reduce the drives such as those related to social approval and companionship, food, water, and other needs.

incremental theory The belief that intelligence can be shaped by experiences, practice, and effort.

independent variable The variable in an experiment that the experimenter manipulates to distinguish between groups participating in the study.

indifferent-uninvolved parenting A parenting style in which the parents show neither warmth toward nor control over their children.

indulgent-permissive parenting A parenting style in which the parents show warmth toward their children, but do not attempt to control their children, even in positive and helpful ways.

industrial and organizational (I/O) psychology A branch of applied psychology in which psychologists work for businesses and other organizations to improve employee productivity and the organizational structure of the company or business.

informed consent A research procedure in which a potential volunteer must be informed (know the purpose, tasks, and risks involved in the study) and give consent (agree to participate based on the information provided) without pressure.

ingroup bias Attribution of positive qualities to the social groups we belong to (i.e., our in-group).

insanity defense A legal strategy of claiming that a defendant was unable to differentiate between right and wrong when the criminal act was committed.

insight therapies A general term referring to psychotherapy that involves dialogues between client and therapist for the purposes of gaining awareness and understanding of psychological problems and conflicts.

insomnia A condition marked by a severe lack of sleep.

institutional review board (IRB) A committee of researchers and officials at an institution charged with the protection of human research participants.

intelligence The ability to think, understand, reason, and cognitively adapt to and overcome obstacles.

intelligence quotient (IQ) A measurement in which the mental age of an individual is divided by the person's chronological age and then multiplied by 100.

internal (dispositional) attribution The observer's explanation of the actor's behavior as some intrinsic quality of the individual.

intuitive thought Quick, effortless, automatic thinking.

iris The round muscle that adjusts the size of the pupil and gives the eyes their characteristic color.

James-Lange theory of emotion The theory that our physiological reactions to stimuli (e.g., a racing heart) precede and give rise to an emotional experience (e.g., fear).

job analysis The process of writing a detailed description of a position in terms of its required knowledge, skills, abilities, and other traits, as well as evaluating the value of the position for the overall organization.

job crafting The processes of taking on or creating additional roles and tasks for a position over time.

job satisfaction The degree to which an employee is content with his or her work.

job simulations Role-playing activities that are very similar to situations encountered on the actual job.

kin selection The explanation that altruistic behavior is most likely to occur when it confers a genetic benefit to the individual.

kinesthesis Our sense of bodily motion and position.

KSAOs The knowledge, skills, abilities, and other traits required for a specific job.

laissez-faire leadership A leadership style describing someone who has been appointed to a position of leadership, but who does not engage in many (if any) leadership processes.

language A form of communication that involves the use of spoken, written, or gestural symbols that are combined in a rule-based form.

latent content In psychoanalytic terms, the underlying meaning of a dream, which is believed by some to be behind the images and symbols in dreams.

latent learning Learning that is not immediately expressed in terms of a response until the organism is reinforced for doing so.

leadership emergence The degree to which individuals are viewed as leaders by others.

learned helplessness An acquired suppression of avoidance or escape behavior in response to unpleasant, uncontrollable circumstances.

learning A process by which behavior or knowledge changes as a result of experience.

learning styles The hypothesis that individuals are fundamentally different in how they best acquire information.

lens The structure that focuses light onto the back of the eye.

leptin A hormone released by fat cells that inhibits hunger by binding to receptors located on organs, tissues, and also the hypothalamus, which is involved in regulating hunger.

lesion A damaged area of tissue, such as a group of nerve cells.

lesioning A technique in which researchers intentionally damage an area in the brain.

libido The motivation for sexual activity and pleasure.

limbic system A region in the forebrain including several networked structures involved in emotion and memory.

linguistic relativity (Whorfian hypothesis) The theory that the language we encounter and use determines how we understand the world; also known as the Whorfian hypothesis.

longitudinal design A research design that follows the development of the same set of individuals through time.

long-term memory (LTM) A memory store that holds information for extended periods of time, if not permanently.

long-term potentiation (LTP) An enduring increase in connectivity and transmission of neural signals between nerve cells that fire together.

magnetic resonance imaging (MRI) Technology designed to acquire highly detailed images of brain anatomy via exposure to a strong (and harmless) magnetic field.

magnetoencephalography (MEG) Technology that measures the magnetic fields created by the electrical activity of nerve cells in the brain.

maintenance rehearsal Prolonging exposure to information by repeating it.

major depression A disorder marked by prolonged and unjustified periods of sadness, feelings of hopelessness and worthlessness, social withdrawal, and cognitive and physical sluggishness.

maladaptive behavior Behavior that hinders a person's ability to function in work, school, relationships, or society.

manifest content In psychoanalytic terms, the imagery and storylines that make up a dream.

marijuana A drug derived from the *Cannabis* plant that produces a combination of hallucinogenic, stimulant, and relaxing (narcotic) effects.

mastery motives Motives that reflect a desire to understand or overcome a challenge (e. g., a genuine desire to master a task).

materialism The belief that humans, and other living beings, are composed exclusively of physical matter.

mean The arithmetic average of a set of numbers.

median A measure of central tendency based on the 50th percentile—the point on the horizontal axis at which 50% of all observations are lower, and 50% of all observations are higher.

medical model (of psychological disorders) Using one's understanding of medical conditions to think about psychological conditions.

meditation Any procedure that involves a shift in consciousness to a state in which an individual is highly focused, aware, and in control of mental processes.

mental age The average or typical test score for a specific chronological age.

mental set A cognitive obstacle that occurs when an individual attempts to apply a routine solution to what is actually a new type of problem.

method of loci A mnemonic method that connects words to be remembered to locations along a familiar path.

midbrain A region of the brain residing just above the hindbrain that primarily functions as a relay station between sensory and motor areas.

mimicry Copying another person's behavior.

minimally conscious state (MCS) A disordered state of consciousness marked by the ability to make small intentional movements and respond to very basic instructions.

Minnesota Multiphasic Personality Inventory (MMPI-2) Multiple-question personality inventory used to measure both normal and abnormal personality functioning across several profiles.

mirror neurons Specialized brain cells that respond to the actions and expressions of others and are correlated with the ability to understand another's intentions and emotions.

misinformation effect An effect that occurs when information occurring after an event becomes part of the memory for that event.

mnemonics Techniques that are intended to improve memory for specific information.

mode A measure of central tendency represented by the category with the highest frequency (the category with the most observations).

monocular cues Depth cues that we can perceive with only one eye.

monozygotic twins Genetically identical twins conceived from the same egg.

mood stabilizers Drugs that are used to prevent or reduce the manic side of bipolar disorder.

morpheme The smallest meaningful units of language.

motivation Physiological and psychological processes underlying the initiation of behaviors that direct organisms toward specific goals.

multiple intelligences A model claiming there are eight different forms of intelligence, each independent from the others.

myelin A fatty sheath that insulates axons from one another, resulting in increased speed and efficiency of neural communication.

narcissistic personality disorder (NPD) A condition marked by a tendency to have an inflated sense of self-importance and an intense need for attention and admiration, as well as intense self-doubt and fear of abandonment.

narcolepsy A disorder in which a person experiences extreme daytime sleepiness and even sleep attacks.

naturalistic observation An unobtrusive observation and recording of behavior as it occurs in the subject's natural environment.

natural selection A primary mechanism for evolutionary change; the process by which favorable traits become increasingly common in a population of interbreeding individuals, while traits that are unfavorable become less common.

nature and nurture relationships The inquiry into how heredity (nature) and environment (nurture) influence behavior and mental processes.

need to belong The motivation to maintain relationships that involve pleasant feelings such as warmth, affection, appreciation, and mutual concern for each person's well-being; sometimes called affiliation motivation.

negative affect (NA) The tendency to experience negative emotions including frustration, anger, and distress.

negative affectivity The tendency to respond to problems with a pattern of anxiety, hostility, anger, guilt, or nervousness.

negatively skewed distribution A type of distribution in which the curve has an extended tail to the left of the cluster.

negative punishment A decrease in a behavior because it removes or diminishes a particular stimulus.

negative reinforcement The strengthening of a behavior because it removes or diminishes a stimulus.

negative symptoms (of schizophrenia) Symptoms of schizophrenia involving the absence of adaptive behavior.

neurocognitive hypothesis of dreaming Hypothesis that dreaming is not a completely random by-product of brain stem activity but rather reflects waking preoccupations and emotional experiences.

neurodevelopmental hypothesis A hypothesis that states irregular biological and environmental factors interact during child development to produce symptoms of schizophrenia.

neuron One of the major types of cells found in the nervous system, which is responsible for sending and receiving messages throughout the body.

neuroplasticity The capacity for the brain to change over the course of the life span as the result of individual experiences.

neurotransmitters Chemicals that function as messengers within the body, thereby allowing neurons to communicate with one another.

nightmares Particularly vivid and disturbing dreams that occur during REM sleep.

night terrors Intense bouts of panic and arousal that awaken an individual from sleep, typically in a heightened emotional state.

nociception Activity of nerve pathways that respond to uncomfortable stimulation.

nomothetic approach (to personality) An approach to the study of personality that examines personality in large groups of people, with the aim of making generalizations about personality structure.

nondeclarative memory A form of memory including actions or behaviors that you can remember and perform without awareness.

norepinephrine A neurotransmitter involved in regulating stress responses, including increasing arousal, attention, and heart rate.

normal distribution Sometimes called the bell curve; a symmetrical distribution with values clustered around a central, mean value.

norms Statistics that allow individuals to be evaluated relative to a typical or standard score.

obedience Complying with instructions or orders from an individual who is in a position of authority.

obesity A disorder of positive energy balance, in which energy intake exceeds energy expenditure.

objective measurements The measure of an entity or behavior that, within an allowed margin of error, is consistent across instruments and observers.

object permanence The ability to understand that objects exist even when they cannot be seen or touched.

object relations therapy A variation of psychodynamic therapy that focuses on how early childhood experiences and emotional attachments influence later psychological functioning.

observational learning A type of learning in which changes in behavior and knowledge result from watching others.

obsessive–compulsive disorder (OCD) A type of anxiety disorder characterized by unwanted, inappropriate, and persistent thoughts (obsessions); repetitive, stereotyped behaviors (compulsions); or a combination of the two.

occipital lobes The areas of the cerebral cortex where visual information is processed.

olfactory epithelium A thin layer of cells that are lined by sensory receptors called cilia (involved in perception of smell).

olfactory system The sense of smell; the detection of airborne particles with specialized receptors located in the nose.

operant conditioning A type of learning in which behavior is determined by consequences.

operational definitions Statements that describe the procedures (or operations) and/or specific measures that are used to record observations in a research study.

opiates Drugs such as heroin and morphine that reduce pain and induce extremely intense feelings of euphoria; also called narcotics.

opponent-process theory (of color vision) The theory that we perceive color in terms of opposite ends of the spectrum—red to green, yellow to blue, and white to black.

optic nerve A collection of neurons that gather sensory information, exit at the back of the eye, and connect with the brain.

optimism The tendency to have a favorable, constructive view on situations and to expect positive outcomes.

outgroup Social groups to which we do not belong.

oxytocin A stress-sensitive hormone associated with maternal bonding and social relationships.

panic disorder An anxiety disorder marked by repeated episodes of sudden, very intense fear.

parasympathetic nervous system A division of the autonomic nervous system that is responsible for maintaining homeostasis (balance) by returning the body to a baseline, nonemergency state.

parietal lobes A region of the cortex located behind the frontal lobes that is responsible for the sense of touch and bodily awareness.

partial (intermittent) reinforcement A schedule in which only a certain number of responses are rewarded, or a certain amount of time must pass before reinforcement is available.

partial reinforcement effect The observation that organisms conditioned under partial reinforcement resist extinction longer than those conditioned under continuous reinforcement.

peer review A process in which papers submitted for publication in scholarly journals are read and critiqued by experts in the specific field of study.

percentile rank The percentage of scores below a certain point.

perception Attending to, organizing, and interpreting stimuli that we sense.

perceptual constancy The ability to perceive objects as having constant shape, size, and color despite changes in perspective.

performance appraisal The evaluation of current employees.

performance motives Motives that are geared toward gaining rewards or public recognition.

peripheral nervous system (PNS) A major division of the nervous system that transmits signals between the brain and the rest of the body; it is divided into two subcomponents, the somatic system and the autonomic system.

peripheral route (to persuasion) A path to persuasion in which quick judgments are made based on limited evidence and use emotions and vague impressions more than logic.

persistent vegetative state (PVS) A state of minimal to no consciousness, in which the patient's eyes may be open, and the individual develops sleep–wake cycles without clear signs of consciousness.

personality A characteristic pattern of thinking, interacting, and reacting that is unique to each individual, and that remains consistent over time and situations.

personality disorder A category of mental disorders that include particularly unusual patterns of behavior for one's culture that are maladaptive, distressing to oneself or others, and resistant to change.

personality traits Labels applied to specific attributes of personality such as "shy," "cheerful," "outgoing," and "adventurous."

person-centered perspective Humanistic perspective emphasizing that people are basically good and that, given the right environment, they will develop fully and normally.

person/client-centered therapy A humanistic therapy method that focuses on individuals' ability to solve their own problems and reach their full potential with the encouragement of the therapist.

person perception The processes by which individuals form judgments and categorize other people.

pessimistic explanatory style The tendency to interpret and explain negative events as internally based and as a constant, stable quality.

phenotype The observable characteristics of an organism, including physical structures and behaviors.

phobia A type of anxiety marked by severe, irrational fear of a particular object or situation.

phoneme The most basic unit of a speech sound.

phonological loop A storage component of working memory that relies on rehearsal and stores information as sounds (i.e., as an auditory code).

pitch The perceptual experience of sound wave frequencies.

pituitary gland The master gland of the endocrine system that produces hormones and sends commands about hormone production to the other glands of the endocrine system.

placebo effect A measurable and experienced improvement in health or behavior that cannot be attributable to a medication.

place theory of hearing A theory stating that how we perceive pitch is based on the location (place) along the basilar membrane that sound stimulates.

polysomnography A set of objective measurements used to examine physiological variables during sleep.

population In a research context, the group that researchers want to generalize about.

positive affect (PA) The tendency to experience positive emotions such as happiness, satisfaction, and enthusiasm.

positively skewed distribution A type of distribution in which the long tail is on the right of the cluster.

positive psychology The use of scientific methods to study human strengths and potential.

positive punishment A process in which a behavior decreases because it adds to or increases a particular stimulus.

positive reinforcement The strengthening of behavior after potential reinforcers such as praise, money, or nourishment follow that behavior.

positive sleep state misperception A condition in which an individual substantially overestimates the amount of sleep the person is getting.

positive symptoms (of schizophrenia) Symptoms of schizophrenia characterized by behaviors that should not occur, such as confused and paranoid thinking, and inappropriate emotional reactions.

positron emission tomography (PET) scans Technology in which a low level of radioactive glucose is injected into the blood, and its movement to regions of the brain engaged in a particular task is measured (active nerve cells use up the glucose at a faster rate than do resting cells).

postconventional morality A type of moral reasoning that considers rules and laws as relative while right and wrong are determined by more abstract principles of justice and rights.

posttraumatic growth The capacity to grow and experience long-term positive effects in response to negative events.

pragmatics The study of nonlinguistic elements of language use.

preconventional morality A very basic, egocentric form of moral reasoning characterized by self-interest in seeking reward or avoiding punishment.

prejudice An attitude that relies on the beliefs found in stereotypes, including emotions and value judgments.

preoperational stage The second stage of cognitive development, spanning ages two through seven years, that is characterized by understanding of symbols, pretend play, and mastery of the concept of conservation.

preparedness The biological predisposition to rapidly learn a response to a particular class of stimuli.

preterm infants Infants born at 36 weeks' gestation or earlier.

primary auditory cortex A major perceptual center of the brain involved in perceiving what we hear.

primary reinforcers Stimuli that satisfy basic motivational needs.

priming The activation of individual concepts in long-term memory.

proactive interference   A type of interference that occurs when the first information learned (e.g., in a list of words) occupies memory, leaving fewer resources left to remember the newer information.

problem solving   Accomplishing a goal when the solution or the path to the solution is not clear.

procedural memories   A form of nondeclarative memory that involves patterns of muscle movements (motor memory).

projective tests   Personality tests in which ambiguous images are presented to an individual to elicit responses that reflect unconscious desires or conflicts.

prototype   A mental representation of an average category member.

pseudoscience   Ideas that are presented as science but actually do not utilize basic principles of scientific thinking or procedure.

psychiatrist   A physician who specializes in mental health, and who diagnoses and treats mental disorders primarily through prescribing medications that influence brain chemistry.

psychiatry   A branch of medicine concerned with the treatment of mental and behavioral disorders.

psychoactive drugs   Drugs that affect thinking, behavior, perception, and emotion.

psychoanalysis   An approach developed by Sigmund Freud and his associates that attempts to explain how behavior and personality are influenced by unconscious processes.

psychodynamic theory (of personality)   Early theory of personality that focused on how personality arises through complex interactions involving motivational conscious and unconscious processes that occur from early development on through adulthood.

psychodynamic therapies   Forms of insight therapy that emphasize the need to discover and resolve unconscious conflicts.

psychology   The scientific study of behavior, thought, and experience.

psychometrics   The measurement of psychological traits and abilities—including personality, attitudes, and intelligence.

psychoneuroimmunology   The study of the relationship between immune system and nervous system functioning.

psychophysics   The study of how physical energy such as light and sound and their intensity relate to psychological experience.

psychotherapy   Processes for resolving personal, emotional, behavioral, and social problems so as to improve well-being.

psychotropic drugs   Medications designed to alter psychological functioning.

puberty   The physical transition from childhood to adolescence, culminating in reproductive maturity.

punisher   A reinforcing stimulus whose delivery is contingent upon a response, with the result being a decrease in behavior.

punishment   A process that decreases the future probability of a response.

pupil   The part of the eye that regulates the amount of light allowed to enter by changing its size; it dilates to allow more light to enter and constricts to allow less light in.

quasi-experimental research   A research technique in which the two or more groups that are compared are selected based on predetermined characteristics, not random assignment.

random assignment   A technique for dividing samples into two or more groups.

random sample   A method of obtaining participants for research in which every individual in a population has an equal chance of being included.

Raven's Progressive Matrices   An intelligence test emphasizing problems that are intended not to be bound to a particular language or culture.

reciprocal altruism   Helping behavior that is extended to nongenetic relatives, with the possibility that the favor may be later returned.

reciprocal determinism   A social cognitive perspective on personality that focuses on how behavior, internal (personal) factors, and external factors interact to determine one another, and that posits our personalities are based on interactions among these three aspects.

recovered memory   A memory of a traumatic event that is suddenly recovered after the memory of that event has been unconsciously for a long period of time.

recovered memory controversy   A heated debate among psychologists about the validity of recovered memories.

reflex   An involuntary muscle reaction to a specific type of stimulation.

refractory period (of a neuron)   A brief period of time (approximately 2 milliseconds) during which a neuron cannot fire following an action potential.

refractory period (of the sexual response cycle)   Time period during which erection and orgasm are not physically possible.

rehearsal   Repeating information until you do not need to remember it anymore.

reinforcement   A process in which an event or reward that follows a response increases the likelihood of that response occurring again.

reinforcer   A stimulus that is contingent upon a response, and increases the probability of that response occurring again.

reliability   A characteristic of a measure that provides consistent and stable answers across multiple observations and points in time.

REM sleep   A stage of sleep characterized by quickening brain waves, deep relaxation, inhibited body movement, and rapid eye movements (REM).

REM sleep behavior disorder   A condition in which people do not show the typical restriction of movement during REM sleep; in fact, they appear to be acting out the content of their dreams.

replication   A process of repeating a study and finding a similar outcome each time.

representativeness heuristic   A strategy of making judgments of likelihood based on how well an example represents a specific category.

residential treatment centers   Facilities that provide psychotherapy and life skills training so that the residents can become integrated into society as best as possible.

resilience   The ability to effectively recover from illness or adversity.

resistance   A tendency of psychoanalysis patients to avoid directly answering crucial questions posed by the therapist.

resting potential   The stable, inactive state of a neuron that is not transmitting or receiving messages.

restless legs syndrome   A persistent feeling of discomfort in the legs, accompanied by the urge to continuously shift the legs into different positions.

retina   The inner surface of the eye consisting of specialized receptors that absorb light and send signals about properties of light to the brain.

retinal disparity   The difference in relative position of an object as seen by both eyes, which provides information to the brain about depth; also called binocular disparity.

retrieval   Bringing information from long-term memory back into short-term memory.

retroactive interference   Interference that occurs when the most recently learned information overshadows some other information that has not made it into long-term memory.

retrograde amnesia   A condition in which memory for the past is lost.

reuptake A process whereby neurotransmitter molecules that have been released into the synapse are reabsorbed into the axon terminals of the presynaptic neuron.

rods Photoreceptors that occupy peripheral regions of the retina, and are highly sensitive under low light levels.

rule-based categorization (classical categorization) The process of identifying category members according to a set of rules or a set of defining features.

sample A select group of population members.

satiation A point in a meal when a person is no longer motivated to eat.

savants Individuals with low mental capacity in most domains but extraordinary abilities in other specific areas such as music, mathematics, or art.

scaffolding An approach to teaching in which the teacher matches guidance to the learner or student's needs.

scapegoating The tendency to misplace and exaggerate blame based on stereotypes.

schedules of reinforcement Rules that determine when reinforcement is available.

schema A cluster of knowledge that constitutes one's knowledge about events, objects, and ideas.

schizophrenia A collection of mental disorders characterized by chronic and significant breaks from reality, a lack of integration of thoughts and emotions, and serious problems with attention and memory.

school psychology A branch of psychology that involves work with students with special needs, such as emotional, social, or academic problems.

scientific literacy The ability to understand, analyze, and apply scientific information.

scientific method A way of learning about the world through collecting observations, proposing explanations for the observations, developing theories to explain them, and using the theories to make predictions about future events.

sclera The white, outer surface of the eye.

secondary reinforcers Reinforcing stimuli that acquire their value through learning.

sedative drug A drug that depresses the activity of the central nervous system; also called "downers."

selective attention The style of attention that involves focusing on one particular event or task while ignoring other stimuli.

self-actualization Reaching one's fullest potential by meeting needs ranging from basic (satisfying hunger) to complex (engaging in loving relationships).

self-awareness The ability to recognize one's individuality.

self-concept A collection of feelings and beliefs a person has about who he or she is.

self-fulfilling prophecy The situation in which a first impression affects the observer's behavior, and as a result, the first impression comes true.

self-reporting A research method in which responses are provided directly by the people who are being studied, typically through face-to-face interviews, phone surveys, paper-and-pencil tests, and web-based questionnaires.

self-serving bias Using internal attributions to take credit for success, while using external attributions to avoid responsibility for failures or mistakes.

semantic memory A type of declarative memory that includes facts about the world.

semantic network An interconnected set of nodes (concepts) and the links that join them to form a category.

semantics The study of how people come to understand meaning from words.

sensation The process of detecting external events by sense organs and turning those events into neural signals.

sensitive period A window of time in which exposure to a specific type of environmental stimulation is needed for normal development of a specific ability.

sensorimotor stage The first stage of cognitive development, spanning birth to age two years, when infants' thinking and understanding about the world is based on sensory experiences and physical actions they perform on objects.

sensorineural hearing loss Hearing loss that results from damage to the cochlear hair cells (sensory) and the neurons comprising the auditory nerve (neural).

sensory adaptation The reduction of activity in sensory receptors with repeated exposure to a stimulus.

sensory memory A memory store that accurately holds perceptual information for a very brief amount of time.

serial position effect The tendency to recall the first few items form a list and the last few items, but only an item or two from the middle of the list.

serotonin A monoamine neurotransmitter involved in regulating sleep, appetite, and mood.

serotonin transporter gene A gene that codes for proteins that transport serotonin molecules within the synapses between nerve cells.

set point A hypothesized mechanism that serves to maintain body weight around a physiologically programmed level.

sexual harassment Unwelcome sexual advances and other conduct of a sexual nature that implicitly or explicitly affects an individual's employment.

sexual orientation Consistent preference for sexual relations with members of the opposite sex (heterosexuality), same sex (homosexuality), or either sex (bisexuality).

sexual response cycle The phases of physiological change during sexual activity, which consists of four primary stages: excitement, plateau, orgasm, and resolution.

shaping A procedure in which a specific operant response is created by reinforcing successive approximations of that response.

short-term memory (STM) A memory store with limited capacity and duration (less than a minute).

signal detection theory A theory stating that whether a stimulus is perceived depends on both sensory experience and judgments made by the subject.

single-blind study An experimental procedure in which the participants do not know the true purpose of the study, or else they do not know which type of treatment they are receiving (for example, a placebo or a drug).

sleep apnea A disorder characterized by the temporary inability to breathe during sleep.

sleep state misperception (SSM) A condition in which a person substantially underestimates the amount of sleep she gets.

social anxiety disorder An irrational fear of being observed, evaluated, or embarrassed in public.

social contagion The often subtle, unintentional spreading of a behavior as a result of social interactions.

social-cognitive theory (of hypnosis) The concept that hypnosis arises from beliefs and expectations about the effects of hypnosis.

social desirability (socially desirable responding) An occurrence in which participants in a research study respond in ways that increase the chances that they will be viewed favorably.

social-exchange theory An approach that treats helping much like a financial arrangement between individuals and society; before an individual acts, she will consider the costs and benefits of helping.

social facilitation The situation in which an individual's performance is better in the presence of others than when alone.

social loafing The situation in which an individual working as part of a group or team reduces his or her effort.

social norms Unwritten guidelines for how to behave in social contexts.

social psychology A broad discipline that examines individual behavior in social contexts, including the people, locations, and social expectations that have the potential to change our behavior.

social resilience The ability to keep positive relationships and endure and recover from social isolation and life stressors.

social responsibility norm The idea that the value of helping goes beyond the benefits an individual might receive, and that individuals who cannot help themselves require special help.

social roles Specific sets of behaviors that are assigned to an individual within a given social context.

somatic nervous system A component of the peripheral nervous system that includes the nerves that receive sensory input from the body and that control skeletal muscles; it is responsible for voluntary and reflexive movement.

somnambulism A disorder that involves wandering and other activities while asleep; also known as sleepwalking.

sound localization The process of identifying where sound comes from.

specific phobias Disorders involving an intense fear of an object, activity, or organism.

spontaneous recovery The reoccurrence of a previously extinguished conditioned response, typically after some time has passed since extinction.

standard deviation A measure of variability around the mean.

standardized test Any test that includes a set of questions or problems that are administered and scored in a uniform (in other words, standardized) way across large numbers of individuals.

Stanford-Binet test A test intended to measure innate (genetic) intelligence.

state A temporary physical or psychological engagement that influences behavior.

statistical significance A situation in which means of groups under comparison are farther apart than one would expect them to be by random chance alone.

stereotype A set of beliefs about a group of people.

stereotype threat The situation in which people become aware of stereotypes about their social group, resulting in fear of being reduced to that stereotype.

stimulants A category of drugs that speed up the nervous system, and typically enhance wakefulness and alertness.

storage The time and manner in which information is retained between encoding and retrieval.

stores Elements of memory systems that retain information in memory without using it for any specific purpose.

stress Psychological and physiological reactions that occur when perceived demands exceed existing resources to meet those demands.

structuralism An attempt to analyze conscious experience by breaking it down into basic elements, and to understand how these elements work together.

structured interview An interview procedure in which an employer presents the same set of questions to each job candidate with planned (rather than unstructured) follow-up questions.

substance P A neurotransmitter involved in pain perception.

superego A component of personality that directs moral behavior and decisions; it is thought to develop during a child's upbringing, and serves as an inner voice we hear when we shame ourselves for acting inappropriately or lavish praise on ourselves for doing something good.

suppression A conscious attempt to block out or ignore troubling thoughts.

sympathetic nervous system A division of the autonomic nervous system that is responsible for the fight-or-flight response of an increased heart rate, dilated pupils, and decreased salivary flow—responses that prepare the body for action.

synapse A microscopically small space that separates individual nerve cells.

synaptic cleft A minute space between the terminal button and the dendrite where neurotransmitters cross between presynpatic and postsynaptic cells.

synaptic pruning A process in which weak and unused nerve cell connections are lost.

syntax The rules for combining words and morphemes into meaningful phrases and sentences.

systematic desensitization A technique in which gradual exposure to a feared stimulus or situation is blended with relaxation training.

systems approach An orientation toward family therapy that involves identifying and understanding what each individual family member contributes to the entire family dynamic.

tardive dyskinesia A neurological condition marked by involuntary movements and facialtics.

temperament A general emotional reactivity typically found in infants that serves as a basis for the development of the adult personality.

temporal lobes A region of the cerebral cortex that is responsible for the processing of sound, including language and music. The temporal lobes are also involved in recognizing faces and objects.

teratogen A substance, such as a drug, that is capable of producing physical defects in a fetus.

terror management theory Psychological perspective asserting that the human fear of mortality motivates behavior, particularly those behaviors that preserve self-esteem and sense of belonging.

testing effect The finding that completing practice tests can improve exam performance, even without additional studying.

testosterone A hormone that is involved in the development of sex characteristics and the motivation of sexual behavior.

thalamus A brain structure involved in relaying sensory information. What we see and hear is routed through the thalamus and then proceeds to more specialized regions of the brain for further processing.

theory An explanation for a broad range of observations that also generates new hypotheses and integrates numerous findings into a coherent whole.

theory of mind The ability to recognize the thoughts, beliefs, and expectations of others.

thin slices A research technique in which a researcher presents a very short video tape or still photo of an individual, which participants then use to make judgments of personal qualities.

tolerance A process in which repeated drug use results in a need for a higher dose to get the intended effect.

top-down processing Form of perceptual processing in which prior knowledge and expectations guide what is perceived.

transactional leadership A leadership style that encourages employee or team member behaviors through rewards and punishments.

transcranial magnetic stimulation (TMS) A procedure in which researchers send an electromagnetic pulse to a targeted region of the brain, which can either stimulate or temporarily disable it.

transduction The process in which physical or chemical stimulation is converted into a nerve impulse that is relayed to the brain.

transference A psychoanalytic process in which patients direct the emotional experiences that they are reliving toward the therapist.

transformational leadership A leadership style that combines charisma, intellectualization, and a focus on individuals within an organization.

trichromatic theory (Young-Helmholtz theory) A theory that maintains color vision is determined by three different cone types that are sensitive to short, medium, and long wavelengths of light.

turnover The rate at which existing employees leave an organization.

two-factor theory of emotion A prediction that patterns of physical arousal and the cognitive labels we attach to them form the basis of our emotional experiences.

Type A personality A term describing people who tend to be impatient and worry about time, and who are easily angered, competitive, and highly motivated.

Type B personality A term describing people who are more laid back and characterized by a patient, easygoing, and relaxed disposition.

unconditioned response (UR) A reflexive, unlearned reaction to an unconditioned stimulus.

unconditioned stimulus (US) A stimulus that elicits a reflexive response without learning.

unconditioned stimulus (US) A stimulus that elicits a reflexive response without learning.

unit bias The tendency to assume that the unit of sale or portioning is an appropriate amount to consume.

validation studies Studies in which researchers administer tests to a large sample of incumbents along with an evaluation of their performance to find correlations between job performance and personality traits or cognitive abilities.

validity The degree to which an instrument or procedure actually measures what it claims to measure.

variability The degree to which scores are dispersed in a distribution.

variable The object, concept, or event being measured.

variable-interval schedule A schedule of reinforcement in which the first response is reinforced following a variable amount of time.

variable-ratio schedule A schedule of reinforcement in which the number of responses required to receive reinforcement varies according to an average.

virtual reality exposure (VRE) A therapeutic technique that uses real-time computer graphical displays that create a sense that the client is immersed in an actual environment.

virtual teams Production or project teams that are physically separated but operate largely (or completely) by electronic communication.

visuospatial sketchpad A component of working memory that maintains visual images and spatial layouts in a visuospatial code.

Wechsler Adult Intelligence Scale (WAIS) The most commonly used intelligence tested used on adolescents and adults.

WEIRD An acronym for "Western, Educated, Industrialized, Rich, and Democratic."

well-defined problem A problem that has both a clear initial state and a clear goal state.

Wernicke's area The area of the brain most closely associated with finding the meaning of words.

Whorfian hypothesis See *linguistic relativity*.

working memory A model of short-term remembering that includes a combination of memory components that can temporarily store small amounts of information for a short period of time. It is composed of the phonological loop, the visuospatial sketchpad, and the episodic buffer.

zeitgeist A general set of beliefs of a particular culture at a specific time in history.

zone of proximal development A concept proposed by Lev Vygotsky explaining that development is ideal when children attempt skills and activities that are just beyond what they can do alone, but they have adults who are attentive to their progress and can provide guidance.

References

Abbass, A. A., Kisely, S. R., Town, J. M., Leichsenring, F., Driessen, E., De Maat, S., … & Crowe, E. (2014). Short-term psychodynamic psychotherapies for common mental disorders (review). *Cochrane Database Systematic Reviews, 7*, 1–85.

AbdelMalik, P., Husted, J., Chow, E. W., & Bassett, A. S. (2003). Childhood head injury and expression of schizophrenia and multiply affected families. *Archives of General Psychiatry, 60*, 231–236.

Abé, C., Johansson, E., Allzén, E., & Savic, I. (2014). Sexual orientation related differences in cortical thickness in male individuals. *PLoS ONE, 9*(12), e114721.

Aboraya, A., El-Missiry, A., Barlowe, J., John, C., Ebrahimian, A., Muvvala, S., … & Price, E. (2014). The reliability of the Standard for Clinicians' Interview in Psychiatry (SCIP): A clinician-administered tool with categorical, dimensional and numeric output. *Schizophrenia Research, 156*(2–3), 174–183. doi:10.1016/j.schres.2014.04.025

Ackerman, P. L., Beier, M. E., & Boyle, M. O. (2005). Working memory and intelligence: The same or different constructs? *Psychological Bulletin, 131*, 30–60.

Adair, G. (1984). The Hawthorne effect: A reconsideration of the methodological artifact. *Journal of Applied Psychology, 69*, 334–345.

Adam, T. C., & Epel, E. S. (2007). Stress, eating, and the reward system. *Physiology and Behavior, 91*(4), 449–458.

Addis, M. E., & Mahalik, J. R. (2003). Men, masculinity, and the contexts of help seeking. *American Psychologist, 58*, 5–14.

Adolphus, K., Lawton, C., & Dye, L. (2013). The effects of breakfast on behavior and academic performance in children and adolescents. *Frontiers in Human Neuroscience, 7*(425). doi:10.3389/fnhum.2013.00425

Aeschleman, S. R., Rosen, C. C., & Williams, M. R. (2003). The effect of non-contingent negative and positive reinforcement operations on the acquisition of superstitious behaviors. *Behavioral Processes, 61*, 37–45.

Aggarwal, R., & Saeed, S. R. (2005). The genetics of hearing loss. *Hospital Medicine, 66*, 32–36.

Ahlfinger, N. R., & Esser, J. K. (2001). Testing the groupthink model: Effects of promotional leadership and conformity predisposition. *Social Behavior and Personality, 29*, 31–41.

Ainsworth, M. D. S. (1978). The development of infant–mother attachment. In B. M. Caldwell & H. N. Ricciuti (Eds.), *Review of child development research* (Vol. 3, pp. 1–94). Chicago: University of Chicago Press.

Akimoto, S. A., & Sanbonmatsu, D. M. (1999). Differences in self-effacing behavior between European and Japanese Americans: Effect on competence evaluations. *Journal of Cross-Cultural Psychology, 30*(2), 159–177.

Akmajian, A., Demers, R. A., Farmer, A. K., & Harnish, R. M. (2001). *Linguistics: An introduction to language and communication.* Cambridge, MA: MIT Press.

Aleman, A., Kahn, R. S., & Selten, J. P. (2003). Sex differences in the risk of schizophrenia. *Archives of General Psychiatry, 60*, 565–571.

Alessandri, G., Vecchione, M., Tisak, J., Deiana, G., Caria, S., & Caprara, G. V. (2012). The utility of positive orientation in predicting job performance and organisational citizenship behaviors. *Applied Psychology: An International Review, 61*(4), 669–698. doi:10.1111/j.1464-0597.2012.00511.x

Alladin, A., & Alibhai, A. (2007). Cognitive hypnotherapy for depression: An empirical investigation. *International Journal of Clinical and Experimental Hypnosis, 55*(2), 147–166.

Allen, J. S., Bruss, J., Brown, C. K., & Damasio, H. (2005). Normal neuroanatomical variation due to age: The major lobes and a parcellation of the temporal region. *Neurobiology of Aging, 26*(9), 1245–1260.

Allen, J. B., & Movius, H. I. (2000). The objective assessment of amnesia in dissociative identity disorder using event-related potentials. *International Journal Of Psychophysiology, 38*(1), 21–41. doi:10.1016/S0167-8760(00)00128-8

Allen, C. T., & Shimp, T. A. (1990). On using classical conditioning methods for researching the impact of ad-evoked feelings. In S. J. Agres, J. A. Edell, & T. M. Dubitsky (Eds.), *Emotion in advertising: Theoretical and practical explorations* (pp. 19–34). Westport, CT: Quorum Books.

Allport, G., & Odbert, H. W. (1936). Trait names: A psycholexical study. *Psychological Monographs, 47*, 211.

Alonso, J., Angermeyer, M. C., Bernert, S., Bruffaerts, R., Brugha, T. S., & Bryson, H. (2004). Use of mental health services in Europe: Results from the European Study of the Epidemiology of Mental Disorders (ESEMeD) project. *Acta Psychiatrica Scandinavica, 420*, 47–54.

Als, H. (2013). Re: Ohlsson and Jacobs, NIDCAP: A systematic review and meta-analyses. *Pediatrics, 132*(2), e552–e553.

Als, H., Duffy, F., Mcanulty, G., Butler, S., Lightbody, L., Kosta, S., … & Warfield, S. (2012). NIDCAP improves brain function and structure in preterm infants with severe intrauterine growth restriction. *Journal of Perinatology, 32*(10), 797–803.

Ambady, N., & Rosenthal, R. (1993). Half a minute: Predicting teacher evaluations from thin slices of nonverbal behavior and physical attractiveness. *Journal of Personality and Social Psychology, 64*, 431–441.

American Academy of Sleep Medicine. (2005). *ICSD-2: International classification of sleep disorders* (2nd ed.): *Diagnostic and coding manual.*

American Heart Association. (2015). The American Heart Association's Diet and Lifestyle Recommendations. Retrieved March 19, 2015, from http://www.heart.org/HEARTORG/GettingHealthy/NutritionCenter/HealthyEating/The-American-Heart-Associations-Diet-and-Lifestyle-Recommendations_UCM_305855_Article.jsp

American Psychiatric Association. (2000). *Diagnostic and statistical manual of mental disorders* (4th ed., text revision). Washington, DC: Author.

American Psychological Association. (2004, September). Getting a good night's sleep with the help of psychology. Retrieved June 10, 2011, from http://www.apa.org/research/action/sleep.aspx

American Psychological Association. (2009). Task force on evidence-based practice. Retrieved from http://www.apa.org/practice/resources/evidence/evidence-based-report.pdf

American Psychological Association. (2011). Suicide warning signs. Retrieved from http://www.apa.org/topics/suicide/signs.aspx

Ames, D. (2008). In search of the right touch: Interpersonal assertiveness in organizational life. *Current Directions in Psychological Science, 17*(6), 381–385.

An, K., Kobayashi, S., Tanaka, K., Kaneda, H., Su-gibayashi, M., & Okazaki, J. (1998). Dissociative identity disorder and childhood trauma in Japan. *Psychiatry and Clinical Neurosciences, 52*, 111–114.

Anderson, A. K., & Phelps, E. A. (2000). Expression without recognition: Contributions of the human amygdala to emotional expression. *Psychological Science, 11*, 106–111.

Anderson, C., John, O., Keltner, D., & Kring, A. (2001). Who attains social status? Effects of personality and physical attractiveness in social groups. *Journal of Personality and Social Psychology, 81*(1), 116–132.

Anderson, C. A., Berkowitz, L., Donnerstein, E., Huesmann, L. R., Johnson, J. D., Linz, D., Mala-muth, N. M., & Wartella, E. (2003). The influence of media violence on youth. *Psychological Science in the Public Interest, 4*, 81–110.

Anderson, C. A., & Bushman, B. J. (2002). Human aggression. *Annual Review of Psychology, 53*, 27–51.

Anderson, D., & Saunders, D. (2003). Leaving an abusive partner: An empirical review of predictors, the process of leaving, and psychological well-being. *Trauma, Violence, & Abuse, 4*(2), 163–191.

Anderson, J. E., & Dunning, D. (2014). Behavioral norms: Variants and their identification. *Social and Personality Psychology Compass, 8*(12), 721–738. doi:10.1111/spc3.12146

Anderson, M. C., Ochsner, K. N., Kuhl, B., et al. (2004). Neural systems underlying the suppression of unwanted memories. *Science, 303*, 232–235.

Anderson, N. & Clement, S. (2015, June 12). College Sexual Assault. *The Washington Post.* Retrieved from http://www.washingtonpost.com/sf/local/2015/06/12/1-in-5-women-say-they-were-violated/

Anderson, S.R. (2006). *Dr. Doolittle's delusion: Animals and the uniqueness of human language.* New Haven, CT: Yale University Press.

Andreasen, N. C., Arndt, S., Alliger, R., Miller, D., & Flaum, M. (1995). Symptoms of schizophrenia: Methods, meaning, and mechanisms. *Archives of General Psychiatry, 52*, 341–351.

Andrews, P. W., Gangestad, S. W., & Matthews D. (2002). Adaptationism—how to carry out an exaptationist program. *Behavioral and Brain Sciences, 25*(4), 489–553.

Ano, G. G., & Vasconcelles, E. B. (2005). Religious coping and psychological adjustment to stress: A meta-analysis. *Journal of Clinical Psychology, 61*, 461–480.

Antoni, M. H. (2013). Psychosocial intervention effects on adaptation, disease course and biobehavioral processes in cancer. *Brain, Behavior, and Immunity, 30*(suppl.), S88–S98. doi:10.1016/j.bbi.2012.05.009

Antoni, M., Schneiderman, N., & Penedo, F. (2007). Behavioral interventions and psychoneuroimmunology. In R. Ader, R. Glaser, N. Cohen, & M. Irwin (Eds.), *Psychoneuroimmunology* (4th ed., pp. 615–703). New York: Academic Press.

Applebaum, P. (2005). Assessing Kendra's Law: Five years of outpatient commitment in New York. *Psychiatric Services, 56*, 791–792.

Araujo, I. E., & Rolls, E. T. (2004). Representation in the human brain of food texture and oral fat. *Journal of Neuroscience, 24*, 3086–3093.

Arija, V., Esparó, G., Fernández-Ballart, J., Murphy, M., Biarnés, E., & Canals, J. (2006). Nutritional status and performance in test of verbal and non-verbal intelligence in 6 year old children. *Intelligence, 34*(2), 141–149.

Armstrong, E. L., & Woodley, M. A. (2014). The rule-dependence model explains the commonalities between the Flynn effect and IQ gains via retesting. *Learning And Individual Differences, 29*, 41–49. doi:10.1016/j.lindif.2013.10.009

Armstrong, H. L., & Reissing, E. D. (2015). Women's motivations to have sex in casual and committed relationships with male and female partners. *Archives of Sexual Behavior.* doi:10.1007/s10508-014-0462-4

Arnett, J. J. (2004). *Emerging adulthood: The winding road from the late teens through the twenties.* New York: Oxford University Press.

Arnett, J. J. (2010). Oh, grow up! Generational grumbling and the new life stage of emerging adulthood: Commentary on Trzesniewski & Donnellan (2010). *Perspectives on Psychological Science, 5*, 89–92.

Arnold, K. M., & McDermott, K. B. (2013). Free recall enhances subsequent learning. *Psychonomic Bulletin & Review, 20*(3), 507–513. doi:10.3758/s13423-012-0370-3

Arrango, M. T., Kivity, S., & Shoenfeld, Y. (2015). Is narcolepsy a classical autoimmune disease? *Pharmacological Research, 92C*, 6–12.

Asch, S. E. (1951). Effects of group pressure upon the modification and distortion of judgments. In H. Guetzkow (Ed.), *Groups, leadership and men: Research in human relations* (pp. 177–190). Oxford, UK: Carnegie Press.

Asch, S. E. (1955). Opinions and social pressure. *Scientific American, 193*(5), 31–35.

Asch, S. E. (1956). Studies of independence and conformity: A minority of one against a unanimous majority. *Psychological Monographs, 70*(9, No. 416).

Ashtari, M., Avants, B., Cyckowski, L., Cervellione, K. L., Roofeh, D., Cook, P., Gee, J., Sevy, S., & Kumra, S. (2011). Medial temporal structures and memory functions in adolescents with heavy cannabis use. *Journal of Psychiatric Research, 45*, 1055–1066.

Aslin, R. N. (2007). What's in a look? *Developmental Science, 10*, 48–53.

Atkinson, R. C., & Shiffrin, R. M. (1968). Human memory: A proposed system and its control processes. In K. W. Spence & J. T. Spence (Eds.), *The psychology of learning and motivation: Advances in research and theory* (Vol. 2, pp. 89–195). New York: Academic Press.

Avena, N. M., Rada, P., & Hoebel, B. G. (2008). Evidence for sugar addiction: Behavioral and neurochemical effects of intermittent, excessive sugar intake. *Neuroscience and Biobehavioral Reviews, 32*, 20–39.

Avidan, G., & Behrmann, M. (2008). Implicit familiarity processing in congenital prosopagnosia. *Journal of Neuropsychology, 2*(1), 141–164.

Awh, E., Barton, B., & Vogel, E. K. (2007). Visual working memory represents a fixed number of items, regardless of complexity. *Psychological Science, 18*, 622–628.

Axtell, C., Holman, D., & Wall, T. (2006). Promoting innovation: A change study. *Journal of Occupational and Organizational Psychology, 79*(3), 509–516.

Babyak, M., Blumenthal, J. A., Herman, S., Khatri P., Doraiswamy M., Moore K., Craighead W. E., Baldewicz T. T., & Krishnan K. R. (2000). Exercise treatment for major depression: Maintenance of therapeutic benefit at 10 months. *Psychosomatic Medicine, 62*, 633–638.

Back, M. D., Stopfer, J. M., Vazire, S., Gaddis, S., Schmukle, S. C., Egloff, B., & Gosling, S. (2010). Facebook profiles reflect actual personality, not self-idealization. *Psychological Science, 21*, 372–374.

Baddeley, A. (2001). Is working memory still working? *American Psychologist, 56*, 851–864.

Baddeley, A. (2012). Working memory: Theories, models, and controversies. *Annual Review Of Psychology, 63*, 1–29. doi:10.1146/annurev-psych-120710-100422

Baddeley, A. D., Thomson, N., Buchanan, M. (1975). Word length and the structure of short-term memory. *Journal of Verbal Learning & Verbal Behavior, 14*(6), 575–589.

Badman, M. K., & Flier, J. S. (2005). The gut and energy balance: Visceral allies in the obesity wars. *Science, 307*, 1909–1914.

Bae, H. T., Sebastiani, P., Sun, J. X., Andersen, S. L., Daw, E. W., Terracciano, A., Ferrucci, L, & Perls, T. T. (2013). Genome-wide association study of personality traits in the long life family study. *Frontiers in Genetics, 8*(4), 64. doi:10.3389/fgene.2013.00065

Bahrick, H. (1984). Semantic memory content in permastore: Fifty years of memory for Spanish learned in school. *Journal of Experimental Psychology: General, 113*, 1–29.

Bahrick, L. E., & Watson, J. S. (1985). Detection of intermodal proprioceptive–visual contingency as a potential basis of self-perception in infancy. *Developmental Psychology, 21*, 963–973.

Bailey, J. M. (2003). *The man who would be queen.* Washington, DC: Joseph Henry Press.

Bailey, J. M., Dunne, M. P., & Martin, N. G. (2000). Genetic and environmental influences on sexual orientation and its correlates in an Australian twin sample. *Journal of Personality and Social Psychology, 78*, 524–536.

Bailey, J. M., & Pillard, R. C. (1995). Genetics of human sexual orientation. *Annual Review of Sex Research, 6*, 126–150.

Bailey, J. M., Pillard, R. C., Neale, M. C., & Agyei, Y. (1993). Heritable factors influence sexual orientation in women. *Archives of General Psychiatry, 50*, 217–223.

Bailey, D. H., Walker, R. S., Blomquist, G. E., Hill, K. R., Hurtado, A. M., & Geary, D. C. (2013). Heritability and fitness correlates of personality in the Ache, a natural-fertility population in Paraguay. *PLoS One, 8*(3), e59325.

Baird, A. D., Scheffer, I. E., & Wilson, S. J. (2011). Mirror neuron system involvement in empathy: A critical look at the evidence. *Social Neuroscience, 6*(4), 327–335. doi:10.1080/17470919.2010.547085

Bakker, A. B., Le Blanc, P. M., & Schaufeli, W. B. (2005). Burnout contagion among intensive care nurses. *Journal of Advanced Nursing, 51*(3), 276–287. doi:10.1111/j.1365-2648.2005.03494.x

Balch, W., Myers, D., & Papotto, C. (1999). Dimensions of mood in mood-dependent memory. *Journal of Experimental Psychology: Learning, Memory, and Cognition, 25*, 70–83.

Banaji, M. R., & Heiphetz, L. (2010). Attitudes. In S. T. Fiske, D. T. Gilbert, & G. Lindzey (Eds.), *Handbook of social psychology* (pp. 348–388). New York: John Wiley & Sons.

Bandura, A. (2001). Social cognitive theory: An agentic perspective. *Annual Review of Psychology, 52,* 1–26.

Bandura, A., Ross, D., & Ross, S. A. (1961). Transmission of aggression through imitation of aggressive models. *Journal of Abnormal and Social Psychology, 63,* 575–582.

Bandura, A., Ross, D., & Ross, S. A. (1963). Imitation of film-mediated aggressive models. *Journal of Abnormal and Social Psychology, 66,* 3–11.

Banuazizi, A., & Movahedi, S. (1975). Interpersonal dynamics in a simulated prison: A methodological analysis. *American Psychologist, 30,* 152–160.

Barbanoj, M. J., Riba, J., Clos, S., Giménez S., Grasa E., & Romero S. (2008). Daytime Ayahuasca administration modulates REM and slow-wave sleep in healthy volunteers. *Psychopharmacology (Berl.), 196,* 315–326.

Bard, K. A., Todd, B., Bernier, C., Love, J., & Leavens, D. A. (2006). Self-awareness in human and chimpanzee infants: What is measured and what is meant by the mirror-and-mark test? *Infancy, 9,* 185–213.

Bar-Haim, Y., Lamy, D., Pergamin, L., Bakermans-Kranenburg, M. J., & van Ijzendoorn, M. H. (2007). Threat-related attentional bias in anxious and nonanxious individuals: a metaanalytic study. *Psychological Bulletin, 133,* 1–24.

Barnes, J., Dong, C. Y., McRobbie, H., Walker, N., Mehta, M., & Stead, L. F. (2010). Hypnotherapy for smoking cessation. *Cochrane Database of Systematic Reviews, 6*(10), CD001008. doi:10.1002/14651858. CD001008.pub2

Baron, R. A. (1999). Social and personal determinants of workplace aggression: Evidence for the impact of perceived injustice and the Type A behavior pattern. *Aggressive Behavior, 25,* 281–296.

Baron, R. A., Neuman, J. H., & Geddes, D. (1999). Social and personal determinants of workplace aggression: Evidence for the impact of perceived injustice and the Type A behavior pattern. *Aggressive Behavior, 25,* 281–296.

Barr, R., Zack, E., Garcia, A., & Muentener, P. (2008). Infants' attention and responsiveness to television increases with repetition and parental interaction. *Infancy, 13,* 30–56.

Barrick, M. R., & Mount, M. K. (2005). Yes, personality matters: Moving on to more important matters. *Human Performance, 18,* 359–372.

Barrick, M. R., Stewart, G. L., Neubert, M. J., & Mount, M. K. (1998). Relating member ability and personality to work-team processes and team effectiveness. *Journal of Applied Psychology, 83*(3), 377–391.

Bartlett, F. C. (1932). *Remembering: A study in experimental and social psychology.* Cambridge, UK: Cambridge University Press.

Barton, G. J., De Asha, A. R., van Loon, E. C. P., Geijtenbeek, T., Robinson, M. A. (2014). Manipulation of visual biofeedback during gait with a time delayed adaptive Virtual Mirror Box. *Journal of Neuroengineering and Rehabilitation, 11,* 101.

Bass, B. (1997). Does the transactional–transformational leadership paradigm transcend organizational and national boundaries? *American Psychologist, 52*(2), 130–139.

Bass, B. M., Avolio, B. J., Jung, D. I., & Berson, Y. (2003). Predicting unit performance by assessing transformational and transactional leadership. *Journal of Applied Psychology, 88,* 207–218.

Batson, C., Eklund, J., Chermok, V. L., Hoyt, J. L., & Ortiz, B. G. (2007). An additional antecedent of empathic concern: Valuing the welfare of the person in need. *Journal of Personality and Social Psychology, 93*(1), 65–74.

Battaglia, M., Ogliari, A., Zanoni, A., Citterio, A., Pozzoli, U., Giorda, R., Maffei, C., & Marino, C. (2005). Influence of the serotonin transporter promoter gene and shyness on children's cerebral responses to facial expressions. *Archives of General Psychiatry, 62,* 85–94.

Batalla, A., Bhattacharyya, S., Yücel, M., Fusar-Poli, P., Crippa, J. A., Nogué, S., Torrens, M., Pujol, J., Farré, M., & Martin-Santos, R. (2013). Structural and functional imaging studies in chronic cannabis users: A systematic review of adolescent and adult findings. *PLoS ONE, 8,* e55821.

Baum, A., & Valins, S. (1977). *Architecture of social behavior: Psychological studies of social density.* Hillsdale, NJ: Erlbaum.

Baumeister, R. F., Dale, K., & Sommer, K. L. (1998). Freudian defense mechanisms and empirical findings in modern social psychology: Reaction formation, projection, displacement, undoing, isolation, sublimation and denial. *Journal of Personality, 66,* 1081–1124.

Baumeister, R. F., & Leary, M. R. (1995). The need to belong: Desire for interpersonal attachments as a fundamental human motivation. *Psychological Bulletin, 117,* 497–529.

Baumrind, D. (1971). Current patterns of parental authority. *Developmental Psychology Monographs, 4*(1, Pt 2).

Baumrind, D. (1991). Parenting styles and adolescent development. In J. Brooks-Gunn, R. Lerner, & A. C. Petersen (Eds.), *The encyclopedia on adolescence* (pp. 746–758). New York: Garland.

Baym, C., Corbett, B., Wright, S., & Bunge, S. (2008). Neural correlates of tic severity and cognitive control in children with Tourette syndrome. *Brain: A Journal of Neurology, 131*(1), 165–179.

Beach, S. H., Brody, G. H., Gunter, T. D., Packer, H., Wernett, P., & Philibert, R. A. (2010). Child maltreatment moderates the association of MAOA with symptoms of depression and antisocial personality disorder. *Journal of Family Psychology, 24*(1), 12–20. doi:10.1037/a0018074

Beauchamp, G., & Mennella, J. (2011). Flavor perception in human infants: Development and functional significance. *Digestion, 83*(suppl 1), 1–6.

Beck, A. T. (1963). Thinking and depression: I. Idiosyncratic content and cognitive distortions. *Archives of General Psychiatry, 9,* 324–333.

Beck, D. M., & Kastner, S. (2009). Top-down and bottom-up mechanisms in biasing competition in the human brain. *Vision Research, 49,* 1154–1165.

Begany, J. J., & Milburn, M. A. (2002). Psychological predictors of sexual harassment: Authoritarianism, hostile sexism, and rape myths. *Psychology of Men & Masculinity, 3,* 119–126.

Beilock, S. L. (2010). *Choke: What the secrets of the brain reveal about getting it right when you have to.* New York: Free Press.

Beilock, S., Rydell, R., & McConnell, A. (2007). Stereotype threat and working memory: Mechanisms, alleviation, and spillover. *Journal of Experimental Psychology: General, 136*(2), 256–276.

Bekinschtein, T. A., Cardozo, J., & Manes, F. F. (2008). Strategies of Buenos Aires waiters to enhance memory capacity in a real-life setting. *Behavioral Neurology, 20,* 65–70.

Bell, P. A., & Yee, L. A. (1989). Skill level and audience effects on performance of a karate drill. *Journal of Social Psychology, 129*(2), 191–200.

Bell, R. A., Paterniti, D. A., Azari, R., Duberstein, P. R., & Epstein, R. M. (2010). Encouraging patients with depressive symptoms to seek care: A mixed methods approach to message development. *Patient Education and Counseling, 78*(2), 198–205.

Belsky, J. (2007). Childhood experiences and reproductive strategies. In R. I. M. Dunbar & L. Barrett (Eds.), *Oxford handbook of evolutionary psychology* (pp. 237–253). New York: Oxford University Press.

Belsky, J., & Rovine, M. (1990). Patterns of marital change across the transition to parenthood. *Journal of Marriage and the Family, 52,* 109–123.

Ben-Ari, R., Krole, R., & Har-Even, D. (2003). Differential effects of simple frontal versus complex teaching strategy on teachers' stress, burnout, and satisfaction. *International Journal of Stress Management, 10*(2), 173–195.

Bennett, G. G., Wolin, K. Y., Robinson, E. L., Fowler, S., & Edwards, C. L. (2005). Racial/ethnic harassment and tobacco use among African American young adults. *American Journal of Public Health, 95,* 238–240.

Bennett, K. K., Adams, A. D., & Ricks, J. M. (2012). Pessimistic attributional style and cardiac symptom experiences: Self-efficacy as a mediator. *North American Journal of Psychology, 14*(2), 293–306.

Benoit, R. G., & Anderson, M. C. (2012). Opposing mechanisms support the voluntary forgetting of unwanted memories. *Neuron, 76*(2), 450–460. doi:10.1016/j.neuron.2012.07.025

Benton, D. (2001). Micro-nutrient supplementation and the intelligence of children. *Neuroscience & Biobehavioral Reviews, 25*(4), 297–309.

Berger, J. M., Levant, R., McMillan, K. K., Kelleher, W., & Sellers, A. (2005). Impact of gender role conflict, traditional masculinity ideology, alexithymia, and age on men's attitudes towards psychological help seeking. *Psychology of Men & Masculinity, 6,* 73–78.

Berger, R., & Phillips, N. (1995). Energy conservation and sleep. *Behavioural Brain Research, 69*(1), 65–73.

Bergman, I., & Almkvist, O. (2013). The effect of age on fluid intelligence is fully mediated by physical health. *Archives of Gerontology and Geriatrics, 57*(1), 100–109. doi:10.1016/j.archger.2013.02.010

Berkowitz, L. (2003). Affect, aggression and antisocial behavior. In R. J. Davidson, K. Scherer, & H. H. Goldsmith (Eds.), *Handbook of affective sciences* (pp. 804–823). New York/Oxford, UK: Oxford University Press.

Berlin, B. (1974). *Principles of Tzeltal plant classification*. New York: Academic Press.

Berridge, K. C., Robinson, T. E., & Aldridge, J. W. (2009). Dissecting components of reward: 'liking', 'wanting', and learning. *Current Opinion in Pharmacology, 9*(1), 65–73. doi:10.1016/j.coph.2008.12.014

Berry, C., Ones, D., & Sackett, P. (2007). Interpersonal deviance, organizational deviance, and their common correlates: A review and meta-analysis. *Journal of Applied Psychology, 92*(2), 410–424.

Berry, S. L., Beatty, W. W., & Klesges, R. C. (1985). Sensory and social influences on ice-cream consumption by males and females in a laboratory setting. *Appetite, 6*, 41–45.

Bersaglieri, T., Sabeti, P. C., Patterson, N., Vanderploeg, T., Schaffner, S. F., Drake, J. A., Rhodes, M., Reich, D. E., & Hirschhorn, J. N. (June 2004). Genetic signatures of strong recent positive selection at the lactase gene. *The American Journal of Human Genetics, 74*(6), 1111–1120. doi:10.1086/421051

Bertram, L., Lill, C. M., & Tanzi, R. E. (2010). The genetics of Alzheimer's disease: Back to the future. *Neuron, 68*, 270–281.

Best, D. (2009). Secondhand and prenatal tobacco smoke exposure. *Pediatrics, 123*, e1017–e1044.

Best, R., Stapleton, L., & Downey, R. (2005). Core self-evaluations and job burnout: The test of alternative models. *Journal of Occupational Health Psychology, 10*, 441–451.

Bettencourt, B. A., Talley, A., Benjamin, A. J., & Valentine, J. (2006). Personality and aggressive behavior under provoking and neutral conditions: A meta-analytic review. *Psychological Bulletin, 132*, 751–777.

Bhatara, A., Tirovolas, A., Duan, L. M., Levy, B., & Levitin, D. J. (2011). Perception of emotional expression in musical performance. *Journal of Experimental Psychology: Human Perception and Performance, 37*, 921–934.

Bhattacharya, J., & Bundorf, M. K. (2005). *The incidence of healthcare costs of obesity*. Working Paper #11303. National Bureau of Economic Research.

Bhugra, D. (2005). The global prevalence of schizophrenia. *Plos Medicine, 2*, 372–373.

Biggs, A. T., Cain, M. S., & Mitroff, S. R. (2015). Cognitive training can reduce civilian casualties in a simulated shooting environment. *Psychological Science, 26*(8), 1164–1176. doi:10.1177/0956797615579274

Birbaumer, N., Veit, R., Lotze, M., Erb, M., Hermann, C., Grodd, W., Flor, H. (2005). Deficient fear conditioning in psychopathy: A functional magnetic resonance imaging study. *Archives of General Psychiatry, 62*(7), 799–805.

Bjork, E., & Bjork, R. (2011). Making things hard on yourself, but in a good way: Creating desirable difficulties to enhance learning. In M. Gernsbacher, R. Pew, L. Hough, & J. Pomerantz (Eds.), *Psychology and the Real World* (pp. 55–64). New York: Worth.

Bjork, R., Dunlosky, J., & Kornell, N. (2012). Self-regulated learning: Beliefs, techniques, and illusions. *Annual Review of Psychology, 64*, 417–444.

Blackman, M. (2002). Personality judgment and the utility of the unstructured employment interview. *Basic and Applied Social Psychology, 24*, 241–250.

Blackwell, L., Trzesniewski, K., & Dweck, C. (2007). Implicit theories of intelligence predict achievement across an adolescent transition: A longitudinal study and an intervention. *Child Development, 78*(1), 246–263.

Blake, R., Palmeri, T. J., Marois, R., & Kim, C-Y. (2005). On the perceptual reality of synesthetic color. In L. C. Robertson & N. Sagiv (Eds.), *Synesthesia* (pp. 47–73). Oxford, UK: Oxford University Press.

Blandin, Y., & Proteau, L. (2000). On the cognitive basis of observational learning: Development of mechanisms for the detection and correction of errors. *Quarterly Journal of Experimental Psychology: Human Experimental Psychology, 53*, 846–867.

Blass, T. (2012). A cross-cultural comparison of studies of obedience using the Milgram paradigm: A review. *Social and Personality Psychology Compass, 6*(2), 196–205. doi:10.1111/j.1751-9004.2011.00417.x

Blum, K., Oscar-Berman, M., Demetrovics, Z., Barh, D., & Gold, M. (2014). Genetic Addiction Risk Score (GARS): Molecular neurogenetic evidence for predisposition to Reward Deficiency Syndrome (RDS). *Molecular Neurobiology, 50*(3), 765–796.

Blumner, K., & Marcus, S. (2009). Changing perceptions of depression: Ten-year trends from the General Social Survey. *Psychiatric Services, 60*, 306–312.

Bobko, P., Roth, P., & Buster, M. (2008). A systematic approach for assessing the currency ("up-to-dateness") of job-analytic information. *Public Personnel Management, 37*, 261–277.

Boesch, C. (1991). Teaching among wild chimpanzees. *Animal Behaviour, 41*, 530–532.

Bollinger, T., Bollinger, A., Oster, H., & Solbach, W. (2010). Sleep, immunity, and circadian clocks: A mechanistic model. *Gerontology, 56*(6), 574–580.

Boomsma, D. I., Van Beijsterveldt, C. E. M., & Hudziak, J. J. (2005). Genetic and environmental influences on anxious/depression during childhood: A study from the Netherlands Twin Register. *Genes, Brain, and Behavior, 4*, 466–481.

Borgelt, L., Franson, K., Nussbaum, A., & Wang, G. (2013). The pharmacologic and clinical effects of medical cannabis. *Pharmacotherapy: The Journal of Human Pharmacology and Drug Therapy, 33*(2), 195–209.

Boswell, W., Shipp, A., Payne, S., & Culbertson, S. (2009). Changes in newcomer job satisfaction over time: Examining the pattern of honeymoons and hang-overs. *Journal of Applied Psychology, 94*(4), 844–858.

Bouchard, T. J. (2014). Genes, evolution and intelligence. *Behavior Genetics, 44*(6), 549–577. doi:10.1007/s10519-014-9646-x

Bouton, M. E. (2010). The multiple forms of "context" in associative learning theory. In B. Mesquita, L. Feldman Barrett, & E. Smith (Eds.), *The Mind in Context* (pp. 233–258). New York: The Guilford Press.

Bowlby, J. (1951). Maternal care and mental health. *World Health Organization Monograph*, Serial No. 2.

Boyd, J. E., Katz, E. P., Link, B. G., & Phelan, J. C. (2010). The relationship of multiple aspects of stigma and personal contact with someone hospitalized for mental illness, in a nationally representative sample. *Social Psychiatry and Psychiatric Epidemiology, 45*(11), 1063–1070.

Bracha, H., Ralston, T., Matsukawa, J., Williams, A., & Bracha, A. (2004, October). Does "fight or flight" need updating? *Psychosomatics: Journal of Consultation Liaison Psychiatry, 45*(5), 448–449.

Brand, A., Smith, E. S., & Lewin, G. R. (2010). Functional neurokinin and NMDA receptor activity in an animal naturally lacking substance P: the naked mole-rat. *PLoS One, 21*(5)12. doi:10.1371/journal.pone.0015162.

Brant, A. M., Munakata, Y., Boomsma, D. I., DeFries, J. C., Haworth, C. A., Keller, M. C., & … Hewitt, J. K. (2013). The nature and nurture of high IQ: An extended sensitive period for intellectual development. *Psychological Science, 24*(8), 1487–1495.

Bransford, J. D., & Johnson, M. K. (1973). Considerations of some problems of comprehension. In W. Chase (Ed.), *Visual information processing* (pp. 383–438). Oxford, UK: Academic.

Brauer, M., Judd, C. M., & Gliner, M. D. (1995). The effects of repeated expressions on attitude polarization during group discussions. *Journal of Personality and Social Psychology, 68*(6), 1014–1029.

Braun, S. M. G., & Jessberger, S. (2014). Adult neurogenesis: Mechanisms and functional significance. *Development, 141*, 1983–1986. doi:10.1242/dev.104596

Braz, J., Solorzano, C., Wang, X., Basbaum, A. I. (2014). Transmitting pain and itch messages: A contemporary view of the spinal cord circuits that generate gate control. *Neuron Review, 82*, 522–536.

Brené, S., Bjørnebekk, A., Aberg, E., Mathé, A. A., Olson, L., & Werme, M. (2007). Running is rewarding and antidepressive. *Physiology and Behavior, 92*, 136–140.

Brickman, A. M., Khan, U. A., Provenzano, F. A., Yeung, L. K., Suzuki, W., Schroeter, H., ... Small, S. A. (2014). Enhancing dentate gyrus function with dietary flavanols improves cognition in older adults. *Nature Neuroscience, 17*(12), 1798–1803. doi:10.1038/nn.3850

Brief, A., & Weiss, H. (2002). Organizational behavior: Affect in the workplace. *Annual Review of Psychology, 53*(1), 279–307.

Briley, D. A., & Tucker-Drob, E. M. (2014). Genetic and environmental continuity in personality development: A meta-analysis. *Psychological Bulletin, 140*(5), 1303–1331. doi:10.1037/a0037091

Brion, M. J., Victora, C., Matijasevich, A., Horta, B., Anselmi, L., Steer, C., Menezes, A. M., Lawlor, D. A., Davey Smith, G. (2010). Maternal smoking and child psychological problems: Disentangling causal and noncausal effects. *Pediatrics, 126*, e57–e65.

Brissette, I., Scheier, M. F., & Carver, C. S. (2002). The role of optimism and social network development, coping, and psychological adjustment during a life transition. *Journal of Personality and Social Psychology, 82*, 102–111.

Brondolo, E., Libby, D. J., Denton, E., Thompson, S., Beatty, D. L., Schwartz, J. (2008). Racism and ambulatory blood pressure in a community sample. *Psychosomatic Medicine, 70*, 49–56.

Brophy, J. E., & Good, T. L. (1970). Teachers' communication of differential expectations for children's classroom performance. *Journal of Educational Psychology, 61*, 365–374.

Brotherton, R., & French, C. C. (2014). Belief in conspiracy theories and susceptibility to the conjunction fallacy. *Applied Cognitive Psychology, 28*(2), 238–248. doi:10.1002/acp.2995

Brown, A. S. (2003). A review of the déjà vu experience. *Psychological Bulletin, 129*, 394–413.

Brown, A. S., & Derkits, E. J. (2010). Prenatal infection and schizophrenia: A review of epidemiologic and translational studies. *American Journal of Psychiatry, 167*, 261–280.

Brown, B. B., & Klute, C. (2006). Friendships, cliques, and crowds. In G. R. Adams & M. D. Berzonsky (Eds.), *Blackwell handbook of adolescence* (pp. 330–348). Malden, MA: Blackwell.

Brown, J. (1958). Some tests of the decay theory of immediate memory. *Quarterly Journal of Experimental Psychology, 10*, 12–21.

Brown, R., & Kulik, J. (1977). Flashbulb memories. *Cognition, 5*, 73–99.

Brown, W. M., Lee Cronk, L., Grochow, K., Jacobson, A., Liu, C. K., Popović, Z., & Trivers, R. (2005). Dance reveals symmetry especially in young men. *Nature, 438*, 1148–1150.

Browning, M., Holmes, E. A., Charles, M., Cowen, P. J., & Harmer, C. J. (2012). Using attentional bias modification as a cognitive vaccine against depression. *Biological Psychiatry, 72*, 572–579.

Brunell, A. B., Staats, S., Barden, J., & Hupp, J. M. (2011). Narcissism and academic dishonesty: The exhibitionism dimension and the lack of guilt. *Personality and Individual Differences, 50*(3), 323–328.

Bubic, A., Susac, A., & Palmovic, M. (2014). Keeping our eyes on the eyes: The case of Arcimboldo. *Perception, 43*, 465–468.

Buck, L. B., & Axel, R. (1991). A novel multigene family may encode odorant receptors: A molecular basis for odor recognition. *Cell, 65*, 175–187.

Buckingham, H. (2006). A pre-history of the problem of Broca's aphasia. *Aphasiology, 20*, 792–810.

Burgaleta, M., MacDonald, P. A., Martínez, K., Román, F. J., Álvarez-Linera, J., González, A. R., & ... Colom, R. (2014). Subcortical regional morphology correlates with fluid and spatial intelligence. *Human Brain Mapping, 35*(5), 1957–1968. doi:10.1002/hbm.22305

Burger, J. M. (1999). The foot-in-the-door compliance procedure: A multiple-process analysis and review. *Personality and Social Psychology Review, 3*(4), 303–325.

Burger, J. M., & Caldwell, D. F. (2003). The effects of monetary incentives and labeling on the foot-in-the-door effect: Evidence for a self-perception process. *Basic and Applied Social Psychology, 25*(3), 235–241.

Burke, B. L., Martens, A., & Faucher, E. H. (2010). Two decades of terror management theory: A meta-analysis of mortality salience research. *Personality and Social Psychology Review, 14*(2), 155–195.

Burns, M., & Seligman, M. (1989). Explanatory style across the life span: Evidence for stability over 52 years. *Journal of Personality and Social Psychology, 56*(3), 471–477.

Bushman, B. J., & Anderson, C. A. (2007). Measuring the strength of the effect of violent media on aggression. *American Psychologist, 62*, 253–254.

Bushman, B. J., & Anderson, C. A. (2009). Comfortably numb: Desensitizing effects of violent media on helping others. *Psychological Science, 20*, 273–277.

Buss, A. H., & Perry, M. (1992). The Aggression Questionnaire. *Journal of Personality and Social Psychology, 63*(3), 452–459.

Buss, D. M. (1989). Sex differences in human mating preferences: Evolutionary hypotheses tested in 37 different cultures. *Behavioral and Brain Sciences, 12*, 1–49.

Buss, D. M. (2009). How can evolutionary psychology successfully explain personality and individual differences? *Perspectives on Psychological Science, 4*, 359–366.

Buston, P. M., & Emlen, S. T. (2003). Cognitive processes underlying human mate choice: The relationship between self-perception and mate preference in Western society. *Proceedings of the National Academy of Sciences, 100*, 8805–8810.

Buttigieg, S. (2006). Relationship of a biodata instrument and a Big 5 personality measure with the job performance of entry-level production workers. *Applied H.R.M. Research, 11*(1), 65–68.

Cacioppo, J. T., Reis, H. T., & Zautra, A. J. (2011). Social resilience. *American Psychologist, 66*, 43–51.

Cacioppo, J. T., & Cacioppo, S. (2014). Social relationships and health: The toxic effects of perceived social isolation. *Social and Personality Psychology Compass, 8*, 58–72.

Cacioppo, J. T., Hawkley, L. C., & Bernston, G. G. (2003). The anatomy of loneliness. *Current Directions in Psychological Science, 12*, 71–74.

Cacioppo, J. T., Petty, R. E., Kao, C., & Rodriguez, R. (1986). Central and peripheral routes to persuasion: An individual difference perspective. *Journal of Personality and Social Psychology, 51*(5), 1032–1043.

Cahill, L., & McGaugh, J. L. (1998). Mechanisms of emotional arousal and lasting declarative memory. *Trends in Neuroscience, 21*, 294–299.

Cahn, B. R., & Polich, J. (2006). Meditation states and traits: EEG, ERP and neuroimaging studies. *Psychological Bulletin, 132*, 180–211.

Cairns, R., & Cairns, B. (1994). *Lifelines and risks: Pathways of youth in our time.* New York: Cambridge University Press.

Cairó, O. (2011). External measures of cognition. *Frontiers in Human Neuroscience, 5*, 108.

Calderwood, C., Ackerman, P. L., & Conklin, E. L. (2014). What else do college students "do" while studying? A investigation of multitasking. *Computers and Education, 75*, 19–29.

Calhoun, L. G., & Tedeschi, R. G. (2013) *Posttraumatic growth in clinical practice.* New York: Brunner Routledge.

Cannon, W. B., & Washburn, A. L. (1921). An explanation of hunger. *American Journal of Physiology, 29*, 441–454.

Cao, X., Cui, Z., Feng, R., Tang, Y., Qin, Z., & Mei, B. (2007). Maintenance of superior learning and memory function in NR2B transgenic mice during ageing. *European Journal of Neuroscience, 25*(6), 1815–1822.

Capafons, A., Mendoza, M., Espejo, B., Green, J., Lopes-Pires, C., Selma, M., et al. (2008). Attitudes and beliefs about hypnosis: A multicultural study. *Contemporary Hypnosis, 25*(3), 141–155.

Carkenord, D. M., & Bullington, J. (1993). Bringing cognitive dissonance to the classroom. *Teaching of Psychology, 20*(1), 41–43.

Carlson, E. N., Furr, R. M., & Vazire, S. (2010). Do we know the first impressions we make? Evidence for idiographic meta-accuracy and calibration of first impressions. *Social Psychological and Personality Science, 1*, 94–98.

Carlson, M. L., Breen, J. T., Gifford, R. H., Driscoll, C. L., Neff, B. A., Beatty, C. W., Peterson, A. M., & Olund, A. P. (2010). Cochlear implantation in the octogenarian and nonagenarian. *Otology and Neurotology, 31*, 1343–1349.

Carmichael, M. S., Warburton, V. L., Dixen, & Davidson, J. M. (1994). Relationships among cardiovascular, muscular, and oxytocin responses during human sexual activity. *Archives of Sexual Behavior, 23*, 59–79.

Carmody, T. P., Duncan, C., Simon, J. A., Solkowitz, S., Huggins, J., Lee, S., & Delucchi, K. (2008). Hypnosis for smoking cessation: A randomized trial. *Nicotine & Tobacco Research, 10*(5), 811–818.

Carstensen, L. L., Isaacowitz, D., & Charles, S. T. (1999). Taking time seriously: A theory of socioemotional selectivity. *American Psychologist, 54,* 165–181.

Carston, R. (2002). *Thoughts and utterances: The pragmatics of explicit conversation.* New York: Blackwell.

Carter, A. C., Brandon, K., & Goldman, M. S. (2010). The college and noncollege experience: A review of the factors that influence drinking behavior in young adulthood. *Journal of Studies on Alcohol and Drugs, 71*(5), 742–750.

Carter, R., Shimkets, R. P., & Bornemann, T. H. (2014). Creating and changing public policy to reduce the stigma of mental illness. *Psychological Science in the Public Interest, 15*(2), 35–36. doi:10.1177/1529100614546119

Cartwright, R., Agargun, M., Kirkby, J., & Friedman, J. K. (2006). Relation of dreams to waking concerns. *Psychiatry Research, 141,* 261–270.

Caruso, E. M., Waytz, A., & Epley, N. (2010). The intentional mind and the hot hand: Perceiving intentions makes streaks seem likely to continue. *Cognition, 116*(1), 149–153.

Caspari, I. (2005). Wernicke's aphasia. In L. LaPointe (Ed.), *Aphasia and related neurogenic language disorders* (3rd ed., pp. 142–154). New York: Thieme.

Caspi, A., Hariri, A. R., Holmes, A., Uher, R., & Moffitt, T. E. (2010). Genetic sensitivity to the environment: The case of the serotonin transporter gene and its implications for studying complex diseases and traits. *American Journal of Psychiatry, 167,* 509–527.

Caspi, A., Moffitt, T. E., Cannon, M., Taylor, A., Craig, I. W., Harrington, H., McClay, J., Mill, J., Martin, J. Braithwaite, A. & Poulton, R. (2005). Moderation of the effect of adolescent-onset cannabis use on adult psychosis by a functional polymorphism in the catechol-O-methyltransferase gene: Longitudinal evidence of a gene X environment interaction. *Biological Psychiatry, 57,* 1117–1127.

Cattell, R. B. (1946). *The description and measurement of personality.* New York: Harcourt, Brace & World.

Cattell, R. B. (1971). *Abilities: Their structure, growth, and action.* New York: Houghton Mifflin.

Cavallera, G., & Giudici, S. (2008). Morningness and eveningness personality: A survey in literature from 1995 up till 2006. *Personality and Individual Differences, 44*(1), 3–21.

Cave, E., & Holm, S. (2003). Milgram and Tuskegee: Paradigm research projects in bioethics. *Health Care Analysis, 11,* 27–40.

Ceci, S., & Williams, W. (1997). Schooling, intelligence, and income. *American Psychologist, 52*(10), 1051–1058.

Ceci, S., Williams, W., &. Barnett, S. (2009). Women's underrepresentation in science: Sociocultural and biological considerations. *Psychological Bulletin, 135*(2), 218–261.

Centers for Disease Control and Prevention (CDC). (2009). Tobacco use and pregnancy. Retrieved August 1, 2010, from http://www.cdc.gov/reproductivehealth/tobaccousepregnancy/index.htm

Centers for Disease Control and Prevention (CDC). (2009a, April 17). *National Vital Statistics Reports, 57*(14).

Centers for Disease Control and Prevention (CDC). (2009b). Smoking & tobacco use. Retrieved June 20, 2011, from http://www.cdc.gov/tobacco/data_statistics/fact_sheets/fast_facts/index.htm

Centers for Disease Control and Prevention (CDC). (2010). NCHS vital statistics system for numbers and deaths. Retrieved June 15, 2011, from http://www.cdc.gov/NCHS/data/nvsr/nvsr58/nvsr58_19.pdf

Centers for Disease Control and Prevention (CDC). (2010a, April 5). Compared with whites, Blacks had 51% higher and Hispanics had 21% higher obesity rates. Retrieved from http://www.cdc.gov/Features/dsObesityAdults/

Centers for Disease Control and Prevention (CDC). (2010b). Obesity and socioeconomic status in adults: United States, 2005–2008. *NCHS Data Brief, 50.* Retrieved January 13, 2011, from http://www.cdc.gov/nchs/data/databriefs/db50.htm

Centers for Disease Control and Prevention (CDC). (2010c). Obesity and socioeconomic status in children and adolescents: United States, 2005–2008. *NCHS Data Brief, 51.* Retrieved January 13, 2011, from http://www.cdc.gov/nchs/data/databriefs/db51.htm

Centers for Disease Control and Prevention (CDC). (2010d, September 10). Vital signs: Current cigarette smoking among adults aged ≥ 18 years—United States, 2009. Retrieved July 9, 2011, from http://www.cdc.gov/mmwr/preview/mmwrhtml/mm5935a3.htm

Centers for Disease Control (2013). Obesity prevalence maps. Retrieved September 20, 2015, from http://www.cdc.gov/obesity/data/prevalence-maps.html

Cepeda, N. N., Pashler, H., Vul, E., et al. (2006). Distributed practice in verbal recall tasks: A review and quantitative synthesis. *Psychological Bulletin, 132,* 354–380.

Cepeda, N., Vul, E., Rohrer, D., Wixted, J., & Pashler, H. (2008). Spacing effects in learning: A temporal ridgeline of optimal retention. *Psychological Science, 19*(11), 1095–1102.

Cesario, J. (2014). Priming, replication, and the hardest science. *Perspectives On Psychological Science, 9*(1), 40–48. doi:10.1177/1745691613513470

Chabris, C. F., Weinberger, A., Fontaine, M., & Simons, D. J. (2011). You do not talk about Fight Club if you do not notice Fight Club: Inattentional blindness for a simulated real-world assault. *I-Perception, 2*(2), doi:10.1068/i0436

Chaiken, S., & Trope, Y. (1999). *Dual-process theories in social psychology.* New York: Guilford Press.

Chambless, D., & Ollendick, T. (2001). Empirically supported psychological interventions: Controversies and evidence. *Annual Review of Psychology, 52,* 685–716.

Chamorro-Premuzic, T., & Furnham, A. (2003). Personality traits and academic exam performance. *European Journal of Personality, 17,* 237–250.

Chan, B. L., et al. (2007). Mirror therapy and phantom limb pain. *New England Journal of Medicine, 357,* 2206–2207.

Charles, S. T., & Carstensen, L. L. (2009). Social and emotional aging. *Annual Review of Psychology, 61,* 383–409.

Charles, S. T., Mather, M., & Carstensen, L. L. (2003). Focusing on the positive: Age differences in memory for positive, negative, and neutral stimuli. *Journal of Experimental Psychology, 85,* 163–178.

Charron, S., & Koechlin, E. (2010). Divided representation of concurrent goals in the human frontal lobes. *Science, 328,* 360–363.

Chaudhari, N., Landin, A. M., & Roper, S. D. (2000). A metabotropic glutamate receptor variant functions as a taste receptor. *Nature Neuroscience, 3,* 113–119.

Chentsova-Dutton, Y. E., & Tsai, J. L. (2007). Cultural factors influence the expression of psychopathology. In S. O. Lilienfeld, & W. T. O'Donohue (Eds.), *The great ideas of clinical science: 17 principles that every mental health professional should understand* (pp. 375–396). New York: Routledge/Taylor & Francis Group.

Cheung, B. Y., Chudek, M., & Heine, S. J. (2011). Evidence for a sensitive period for acculturation: Younger immigrants report acculturating at a faster rate. *Psychological Science, 22,* 147–152.

Cheung, F. M., Leung, K., Fan, R. M., Song W., Zhang J-X., & Zhang J-P. (1996). Development of the Chinese Personality Assessment Inventory. *Journal of Cross-Cultural Psychology, 27,* 181–199.

Chiesa, A., & Serretti, A. (2010). Mindfulness based cognitive therapy for psychiatric disorders: A systematic review and meta-analysis [Electronic publication ahead of print]. *Psychiatry Research.*

Chistyakov, A.V., Kaplan, B., Rubicheck, O., Kreinin, I., Koren, D., Feinsod, M., & Klein, E. (2005). Antidepressant effects of different schedules of repetitive transcranial magnetic stimulation vs. clomipramine in patients with major depressions: Relationship to changes in cortical excitability. *International Journal of Neuropsychopharmacology, 8,* 223–233.

Choi, I., Nisbett, R. E., & Norenzayan, A. (1999). Causal attribution across cultures: Variation and universality. *Psychological Bulletin, 125*(1), 47–63.

Christakis, D. A. (2009). The effects of media usage: What do we know and what should we learn? *Acta Paediatrica, 98,* 8–16.

Christakis, N. A., & Fowler, J. H. (2007). The spread of obesity in a large social network over 32 years. *New England Journal of Medicine, 357,* 370–379.

Christakis, N. A., & Fowler, J. H. (2008). The collective dynamics of smoking in a large social network. *New England Journal of Medicine, 358,* 2249–2258.

Christensen, C., Silberberg, A., Hursh, S., Huntsberry, M., & Riley, A. (2008). Essential value of cocaine and food in rats: Tests of the exponential model of demand. *Psychopharmacology, 198,* 221–229.

Chuderski, A. (2013). When are fluid intelligence and working memory isomorphic and when are they not? *Intelligence, 41*(4), 244–262. doi:10.1016/j.intell.2013.04.003

Church, A. T. (2010). Current perspectives in the study of personality across cultures. *Perspectives on Psychological Science, 5,* 441–449.

Cialdini, R. B. (2000). *Persuasion: Influence and practice* (4th ed.). New York: Allyn & Bacon.

Cialdini, R. B., & Goldstein, N. J. (2004). Social influence: Compliance and conformity. *Annual Review of Psychology, 55,* 591–621.

Cialdini, R. B., & Richardson, K. D. (1980). Two indirect tactics of image management: Basking and blasting. *Journal of Personality and Social Psychology, 39,* 406–415.

Cialdini, R. B., Vincent, J. E., Lewis, S. K., Catalan, J., Wheeler, D., & Darby, B. (1975). Reciprocal concessions procedure for inducing compliance: The door-in-the-face technique. *Journal of Personality and Social Psychology, 31*(2), 206–215.

Cillessen, A. H. N., & Rose, A. J. (2005). Understanding popularity in the peer system. *Current Directions in Psychological Science, 14,* 102–105.

Clancy, S. A. (2005). *Abducted: How people come to believe they were kidnapped by aliens.* Cambridge, MA: Harvard University Press.

Cleary, A. (2008). Recognition memory, familiarity, and déjà vu experiences. *Current Directions in Psychological Science, 17*(5), 353–357.

Cleary, A. M., Ryals, A. J., & Nomi, J. S. (2009). Can déjà vu result from similarity to a prior experience? Support for the similarity hypothesis of déjà vu. *Psychonomic Bulletin and Review, 16,* 1082–1088.

Clement, S., Schauman, O., Graham, T., Maggioni, F., Evans-Lacko, S., Bezborodovs, N., … & Thornicroft, G. (2015). What is the impact of mental health-related stigma on help-seeking? A systematic review of quantitative and qualitative studies. *Psychological Medicine, 45*(1), 11–27. doi:10.1017/S0033291714000129

Clevenger, J., Pereira, G., Wiechmann, D., Schmitt, N., & Harvey, V. (2001). Incremental validity of situational judgment tests. *Journal of Applied Psychology, 86*(3), 410–417.

Coane, J. H., & Balota, D. A. (2009). Priming the holiday spirit: Persistent activation due to extraexperimental experiences. *Psychonomic Bulletin & Review, 16*(6), 1124–1128.

Cobos, P., Sánchez, M., García, C., Nieves, V. M., & Vila, J. (2002). Revisiting the James versus Cannon debate on emotion: Startle and autonomic modulation in patients with spinal cord injuries. *Biological Psychology, 61,* 251–269.

Cohen, B., Guttmann, D., & Lazar, A. (1998). The willingness to seek help: A cross-national comparison. *Cross-Cultural Research: The Journal of Comparative Social Science, 32,* 342–357.

Cohen, N., Mor, N., & Henik, A. (2015). Linking executive control and emotional response: A training procedure to reduce rumination. *Clinical Psychological Science, 3*(1), 15–25.

Cohen, D., Nisbett, R. E., Bowdle, B. F., & Schwarz, N. (1996). Insult, aggression, and the Southern culture of honor: An "experimental ethnography." *Interpersonal Relations and Group Processes, 70,* 945–960.

Cohen, F., Ogilvie, D. M., Solomon, S., Greenberg, J., & Pyszczynski, T. (2005). American roulette: The effect of reminders of death on support for George W. Bush in the 2004 presidential election. *Analyses of Social Issues and Public Policy (ASAP), 5,* 177–187.

Cohen, G. L. (2003). Party over policy: The dominating impact of group influence on political beliefs. *Journal of Personality and Social Psychology, 85*(5), 808–822.

Cohen, S., Frank, E., Doyle, B. J., Skoner, D. P., Rabin, B. S. & Gwaltney, J. M. (1998). Types of stressors that increase susceptibility to the common cold. *Health Psychology, 17,* 214–223.

Cohen, S., Janicki-Deverts, D., Turner, R. B., & Doyle, W. J. (2015). Does hugging provide stress-buffering social support? A study of susceptibility to upper respiratory infection and illness. *Psychological Science, 26*(2), 135–147. doi:10.1177/0956797614559284

Collins, A. M., & Loftus, E. F. (1975). A spreading-activation theory of semantic processing. *Psychological Review, 82,* 407–428.

Colonna-Pydyn, C., Gjesfjeld, C., & Greeno, C. (2007). The factor structure of the Barriers to Treatment Participation Scale (BTPS): Implications for future barriers scale development. *Administration and Policy in Mental Health and Mental Health Services Research, 34,* 563–569.

Conde-Agudelo, A., Belizan, J. M., & Diaz-Rossello, J. (2011). Kangaroo mother care to reduce morbidity and mortality in low birthweight infants. *Cochrane Database Systematic Reviews, 3.* doi:10.1002/14651858.CD002771.pub2

Connolly, J. J., & Viswesvaran, C. (2000). The role of affectivity in job satisfaction: A meta-analysis. *Personality and Individual Differences, 29,* 265–281.

Connelly, B. S., & Ones, D. S. (2010). An other perspective on personality: Meta-analytic integration of observers' accuracy and predictive validity. *Psychological Bulletin, 136*(6), 1092–1122. doi:10.1037/a0021212

Conway, J. M., Lombardo, K., & Sanders, K. C. (2001). A meta-analysis of incremental validity and nomological networks for subordinate and peer rating. *Human Performance, 14*(4), 267–303.

Corballis, M. C. (1993). *The lopsided ape.* Oxford, UK: Oxford University Press.

Correll, J., Park, B., Judd, C. M., & Wittenbrink, B. (2007). The influence of stereotypes on decisions to shoot. *European Journal of Social Psychology, 37*(6), 1102–1117.

Corrigan, P. W., Druss, B. G., & Perlick, D. A. (2014). The impact of mental illness stigma on seeking and participating in mental health care. *Psychological Science in the Public Interest, 15*(2), 37–70. doi:10.1177/1529100614531398

Corso, P. S., Mercy, J. A., Simon, T. R., et al. (2007). Medical costs and productivity losses due to interpersonal and self-directed violence in the United States. *American Journal of Preventative Medicine, 32,* 474–482.

Cosgrove, G. R., & Rauch, S. L. (2003). Stereotactic cingulotomy. *Neurosurgery Clinics of North America, 13,* 225–235.

Cosmides, L., & Tooby, J. (2013). Evolutionary psychology: New perspectives on cognition and motivation. *Annual Review of Psychology, 64,* 201–229. doi:10.1146/annurev.psych.121208.13162

Côté, S. (1999). Affect and performance in organizational settings. *Current Directions in Psychological Science, 8*(2), 65–68.

Coviello, L., Sohn, Y., Kramer, A. D. I., Marlow, C., Franceschetti, M., Christakis, N. A., & Fowler, J. A. (2014). Detecting emotional contagion in massive social networks. *PLoS ONE, 9*(3), e90315. doi:10.1371/journal.pone.0090315

Cowan, N., Lichty, W., & Grove, T. R. (1990). Properties of memory for unattended spoken syllables. *Journal of Experimental Psychology: Learning, Memory, and Cognition, 16*(2), 258–269.

Cox, C., Arndt, J., Pyszczynski, T., Greenberg, J., Abdollahi, A., & Solomon, S. (2008). Terror management and adults' attachment to their parents: The safe haven remains. *Journal of Personality and Social Psychology, 94*(4), 696–717.

Cox, W. L., Devine, P. G., Plant, E. A., & Schwartz, L. L. (2014). Toward a comprehensive understanding of officers' shooting decisions: No simple answers to this complex problem. *Basic and Applied Social Psychology, 36*(4), 356–364. doi:10.1080/01973533.2014.923312

Coyle, T. (2006). Test–retest changes on scholastic aptitude tests are not related to g. *Intelligence, 34*(1), 15–27.

Coyle, T., & Pillow, D. (2008). SAT and ACT predict college GPA after removing g. *Intelligence, 36*(6), 719–729.

Coyle, T. R., Purcell, J. M., Snyder, A. C., & Richmond, M. C. (2014). Ability tilt on the SAT and ACT predicts specific abilities and college majors. *Intelligence, 46*(1), 18–24. doi:10.1016/j.intell.2014.04.008

Craig, I., & Plomin, R. (2006). Quantitative trait loci for IQ and other complex traits: Single-nucleotide polymorphism genotyping using pooled DNA and microarrays. *Genes, Brain and Behavior, 5*(suppl 1), 32–37.

Craig, I. W., & Halton, K. E. (2009). Genetics of human aggressive behavior. *Human Genetics, 126,* 101–113.

Craik, F., & Lockhart, R. (1972). Levels of processing: A framework for memory research. *Journal of Verbal Learning & Verbal Behavior, 11,* 671–684.

Craik, F. M., & Rose, N. S. (2012). Memory encoding and aging: A neurocognitive perspective. *Neuroscience and Biobehavioral Reviews, 36(7),* 1729–1739. doi:10.1016/j.neubiorev.2011.11.007

Craik, F., & Tulving, E. (1975). Depth of processing and the retention of words in episodic memory. *Journal of Experimental Psychology: General, 104,* 268–294.

Craik, F., & Watkins, M. (1973).The role of rehearsal in short-term memory. *Journal of Verbal Learning & Verbal Behavior, 12,* 599–607.

Crane, N., Schuster, R., Fusar-Poli, P., & Gonzalez, R. (2013). Effects of cannabis on neurocognitive functioning: Recent advances, neurodevelopmental influences, and sex differences. *Neuropsychology Review, 23(2),* 117–137.

Creswell, J. D., Pacilio, L. E., Lindsay, E. K., & Brown, K. W. (2014). Brief mindfulness meditation training alters psychological and neuroendocrine responses to social evaluative stress. *Psychoneuroendocrinology, 44,* 1–12. doi:10.1016/j.psyneuen .2014.02.007

Critchley, H., Daly, E., Phillips, M., Brammer, M., Bullmore, E., Williams, S., Van Amelsvoort, T., Robertson, D., David, A., & Murphy, D. (2000). Explicit and implicit neural mechanisms for processing of social information from facial expressions: A functional magnetic resonance imaging study. *Human Brain Mapping, 9,* 93–105.

Crook, T. R., Todd, S. Y., Combs, J. G., Woehr, D. J., Ketchen, D. J. Jr. (2011). Does human capital matter? A meta-analysis of the relationship between human capital and firm performance. *Journal of Applied Psychology, 96(3):*443–56.

Crowell, S. E., Beauchaine, T. P., & Linehan, M. M. (2009). A biosocial developmental model of borderline personality: Elaborating and extending linehan's theory. *Psychological Bulletin, 135(3),* 495–510. doi:10.1037/a0015616

Csibra, G., Davis, G., Spratling, M. W., & Johnson, M. H. (2000). Gamma oscillations and object processing in the infant brain. *Science, 290,* 1582–1585.

Cuadrado, I., García-Ael, C., & Molero, F. (2015). Gender-typing of leadership: Evaluations of real and ideal managers. *Scandinavian Journal of Psychology, 56(2),* 236–244. doi:10.1111/sjop.12187

Cuijpers, P., Sijbrandij, M., Koole, S. L., Anderson, G., Beekman, A. T., & Reynolds, C. F. (2014). Adding psychotherapy to antidepressant medication in depression and anxiety disorders: A meta-analysis. *World Psychiatry, 13(1),* 56–67.

Cukor, J., Spitalnick, J., Difede, J., Rizzo, A., & Rothbaum, B. O. (2009). Emerging treatments for PTSD. *Clinical Psychology Review, 29,* 715–726.

Cummings, D. (2006). Ghrelin and the short- and long-term regulation of appetite and body weight. *Physiology & Behavior, 89(1),* 71–84.

Cunningham, W. A., Johnson, M. K., Raye, C. L., Gatenby, J. C., Gore, J. C., & Banaji, M. R. (2004). Separable neural components in the processing of Black and White faces. *Psychological Science, 15,* 806–813.

Cutrona, C., Wallace, G., & Wesner, K. (2006). Neighborhood characteristics and depression: An examination of stress processes. *Current Directions in Psychological Science, 15(4),* 188–192.

D'Argembeau, A., Raffard, S., & Van der Linden, M. (2008). Remembering the past and imagining the future in schizophrenia. *Journal of Abnormal Psychology, 117,* 247–251.

Dabbs, J. M., Riad, J. K., & Chance, S. E. (2001). Testosterone and ruthless homicide. *Personality and Individual Differences, 31,* 599–603.

Dal Cin, S., Gibson, B., Zanna, M. P., Shumate, R., & Fong, G. T. (2007). Smoking in movies, implicit associations of smoking with the self, and intentions to smoke. *Psychological Science, 18,* 559–563.

Daley, T. C., Whaley, S. E., Sigman, M. D., Espinosa, M. P., & Neumann C. (2003). IQ on the rise: The Flynn effect in rural Kenyan children. *Psychological Science, 14(3),* 215–219.

Damisch, L., Stoberock, B., & Mussweiler, T. (2010). Keep your fingers crossed! How superstition improves performance. *Psychological Science, 21,* 1014–1020.

Danaei, G., Ding, E. L., Mozaffarian, D., Taylor B, & Rehm J. (2009). The preventable causes of death in the United States: Comparative risk assessment of dietary, lifestyle, and metabolic risk factors. *PLoS Med, 6(4),* e1000058. doi:10.1371/journal.pmed.1000058

Dang, C., Braeken, J., Colom, R., Ferrer, E., & Liu, C. (2014). Why is working memory related to intelligence? Different contributions from storage and processing. *Memory, 22(4),* 426–441. doi:10.1080/09658211.2013.797471

Danziger, N., Faillenot, I., & Peyron, R. (2009). Can we share a pain we never felt? Neural correlations of empathy in patients with congenial insensitivity to pain. *Neuron, 61,* 203–212.

Darley, J. M., & Latane, B. (1968). Bystander intervention in emergencies: Diffusion of responsibility. *Journal of Personality and Social Psychology, 8,* 377–383.

Dar-Nimrod, I., & Heine, S. J. (2006). Exposure to scientific theories affects women's math performance. *Science, 314(5798),* 435. doi:10.1126/science.1131100

Dar-Nimrod, I., Rawn, C. D., Lehman, D. R., & Schwartz, B. (2009). The maximization paradox: The costs of seeking alternatives. *Personality and Individual Differences, 46(5–6),* 631–635.

Darwin, C. (1872). *The expression of emotion in man and animals.* London: John Murray.

Dastoor, S. F., Misch, C. E., & Wang, H. L. (2007). Botulinum toxin (Botox) to enhance facial macroesthetics: A literature review. *Journal of Oral Implantology, 33(3),* 164–171.

Davidson, T. L., Sample, C. H., & Swithers, S. E. (2014). An application of Pavlovian principles to the problems of obesity and cognitive decline. *Neurobiology of Learning and Memory, 108,* 172–184.

Davis, B., & Knowles, E. S. (1999). A disrupt-then-reframe technique of social influence. *Journal of Personality and Social Psychology, 76(2),* 192–199.

Day, D., & Schleicher, D. (2006). Self-monitoring at work: A motive-based perspective. *Journal of Personality, 74(3),* 685–713.

DeGutis, J. M., Chiu, C., Grosso, M. E., & Cohan, S. (2014). Face processing improvements in prosopagnosia: successes and failures over the last 50 years. *Frontiers in Human Neuroscience, 8,* 561.

de Jong, J. O., Arts, B., Boks, M. P., Sienaert, P., van den Hove, D. L., Kenis, G., … & Rutten, B. P. Epigenetic effects of electroconvulsive seizures. *Journal of Electroconvulsive Therapy, 30(2),* 152–159.

De Los Reyes, A., & Kazdin, A. (2008). When the evidence says, "yes, no, and maybe so": Attending to and interpreting inconsistent findings among evidence-based interventions. *Current Directions in Psychological Science, 17,* 47–51.

de Waal, F. B. M., & Lanting, F. (1997) *Bonobo: The forgotten ape.* Berkeley and Los Angeles, CA: University of California Press.

Deary, I. R, Irwing, P., Der, G., & Bates, T. C. (2007). Brother–sister differences in the g factor in intelligence: Analysis of full, opposite-sex siblings from the NLSY1979. *Intelligence, 35(5),* 451–456.

Deary, I. J., Johnson, W., & Houlihan, L. M. (2009). Genetic foundations of human intelligence. *Human Genetics, 126,* 215–232.

Deary, I. J., Penke, L., & Johnson, W. (2010). The neuroscience of human intelligence differences. *Nature Reviews Neuroscience, 11,* 201–211.

Deary, I. J., Weiss, A. & Batty, G.D. (2010). Intelligence and personality as predictors of illness and death. *Psychological Science in the Public Interest, 11,* 53–79.

Decety, J. (2010). To what extent is the experience of empathy mediated by shared neural circuits? *Emotion Review, 2(3),* 204–207.

Delgado, J. M. R., & Anand, B. K. (1952). Increase of food intake induced by electrical stimulation of the lateral hypothalamus. *American Journal of Physiology, 172,* 162–168.

DeLisi, L. E. (1992). The significance of age of onset for schizophrenia. *Schizophrenia Bulletin, 18,* 209–215.

DeLoache, J. S. (1995). Early understanding and use of symbols: The model model. *Current Directions in Psychological Science, 4,* 109–113.

DeLoache, J. S., Uttal, D. H., & Rosengren, K. S. (2004). Scale errors offer evidence for a perception–action dissociation early in life. *Science, 304,* 1027–1029.

Demerouti, E. (2014). Design your own job through job crafting. *European Psychologist, 19(4),* 237–247. doi:10.1027/1016-9040/a000188

Demerouti, E., Bakker, A. B., & Halbesleben, J. B. (2015). Productive and counterproductive job crafting: A daily diary study. *Journal of Occupational Health Psychology* [Epub ahead of print] doi:10.1037/a0039002

Dennis, T. A., & O'Toole, L. J. (2014). Mental health on the go: Effects of a gamified attention-bias modification mobile application in trait-anxious adults. *Clinical Psychological Science, 2,* 576–590.

Department of Justice. (2001). Policing and homicide, 1976–98: Justifiable homicide by police, police officers murdered by felons (NCJ180987). Washington, DC: Bureau of Justice Statistics.

Derntl, B., Windischberger, C., Robinson, S., Kryspin-Exner, I., Gur, R. C., Moser, E., & Habel, U. (2009). Amygdala activity to fear and anger in healthy young males is associated with testosterone. *Psychoneuroendocrinology, 34*(5), 687–693.

DeRubeis, R., & Crits-Christoph, P. (1998). Empirically supported individual and group psychological treatments for adult mental disorders. *Journal of Consulting and Clinical Psychology, 66,* 37–52.

DeVoe, S. E., House, J., & Zhong, C-B. (2013). Fast food and impatience: A socioecological approach. *Journal of Personality and Social Psychology, 105,* 476–494.

DeWilde, K. E., Levitch, C. F., Murrough, J. W., Mathew, S. J., & V. Iosifescu, D. (2015). The promise of ketamine for treatment-resistant depression: Current evidence and future directions. *Annals of the New York Academy of Science, 1345,* 47–58.

DeYoung, C. G., Hirsh, J. B., Shane, M. S., Papademetris, X., Rajeevan, N., & Gray, J. R. (2010). Testing predictions from personality neuroscience: Brain structure and the Big Five. *Psychological Science, 21,* 820–828.

Díaz-Morales, J. F. (2007). Morning and evening-types: Exploring their personality styles. *Personality and Individual Differences, 43*(4), 769–778.

Dick, D. M. (2007). Identification of genes influencing a spectrum of externalizing psychopathology. *Current Directions in Psychological Science, 16,* 331–335.

Dick, F., Bates, E., Wulfeck, B., Utman, J. A., Dronkers, N., & Gernsbacher, M. A. (2001). Language deficits, localization, and grammar: Evidence for a distributive model of language breakdown in aphasic patients and neurologically intact individuals. *Psychological Review, 108,* 759–788.

Diego, M., Field, T., & Hernandez-Reif, M. (2014). Preterm infant weight gain is increased by massage therapy and exercise via different underlying mechanisms. *Early Human Development, 90*(3), 137–140.

Diehl, M., Chui, H., Hay, E. L., Lumley, M. A., Grühn, D., & Labouvie-Vief, G. (2014). Change in coping and defense mechanisms across adulthood: Longitudinal findings in a European American sample. *Developmental Psychology, 50*(2), 634–648. doi:10.1037/a0033619

Dierdorff, E., & Morgeson, F. (2007). Consensus in work role requirements: The influence of discrete occupational context on role expectations. *Journal of Applied Psychology, 92*(5), 1228–1241.

Dijkstra, A., Jaspers, M., & van Zwieten, M. (2008). Psychiatric and psychological factors in patient decision making concerning antidepressant use. *Journal of Consulting and Clinical Psychology, 76,* 149–157.

Dill, J., & Anderson, C. A. (1995). Effects of justified and unjustified frustration on aggression. *Aggressive Behavior, 21,* 359–369.

Dillard, J. P., Hunter, J. E., & Burgoon, M. (1984). Sequential-request persuasive strategies: Meta-analysis of foot-in-the-door and door-in-the-face. *Human Communication Research, 10*(4), 461–488.

Dingemanse, N. J., Both, C., Drent, P. J., & Tinbergen, J. M. (2004). Fitness consequences in a fluctuating environment. *Proceedings of the Royal Society of London, Series B, 271,* 847–852.

Ditzen, B., Schaer, M., Gabriel, B., Bodenmann, G., Ehlert, U., & Heinrichs, M. (2009). Intranasal oxytocin increases positive communication and reduces cortisol levels during couple conflict. *Biological Psychiatry, 65,* 728–731.

Doherty, C. D. (2013) For African Americans, discrimination is not dead. Retrieved from http://www.pewresearch.org/fact-tank/2013/06/28/for-african-americans-discrimination-is-not-dead

Domhoff, G. W. (2001). A new neurocognitive theory of dreams. *Dreaming, 11,* 13–33.

Domjan, M., Cusato, B., & Krause, M. A. (2004). Learning with arbitrary versus ecological conditioned stimuli: Evidence from sexual conditioning. *Psychonomic Bulletin and Review, 11,* 232–246.

Donahue, K. L., Lichtenstein, P., Långström, N., & D'Onofrio, B. M. (2013). Why does early sexual intercourse predict subsequent maladjustment? Exploring potential familial confounds. *Health Psychology, 32,* 180–189.

Done, D. J., Crow, T. J., Johnstone, E. C., & Sacker, A. (1994). Childhood antecedents of schizophrenia and affective illness: Social adjustment at ages 7 and 11. *British Medical Journal, 309,* 699–703.

Donnellan, M. B., Conger, R. D., & Burzette, R. G. (2007). Personality development from late adolescence to young adulthood: Differential stability, normative maturity, and evidence for the maturity-stability hypothesis. *Journal of Personality 75*(2), 237–264.

Dormann, C., & Zapf, D. (2001). Job satisfaction: A meta-analysis of stabilities. *Journal of Organizational Behavior, 22,* 483–504.

Douglas, K. S., Guy, L. S., & Hart, S. D. (2009). Psychosis as a risk factor for violence to others: A meta-analysis. *Psychological Bulletin, 135,* 679–706.

Drew, T., Vo, M., & Wolfe, J. (2013). The invisible gorilla strikes again: Sustained inattentional blindness in expert observers. *Psychological Science, 24*(9), 1848–1853.

Dukes, R. L., Clayton, S. L., Jenkins, L. T., Miller, T. L., & Rodgers, S. E. (2001). Effects of aggressive driving and driver characteristics on road rage. *Social Science Journal, 38,* 323–331.

Duman, R. S., Li, N., Liu, R. J., Duric, V., & Aghajanian, G. (2012). Signaling pathways underlying the rapid antidepressant actions of ketamine. *Neuropharmacology, 62*(1), 35–41.

Duncan, G. J., & Murnane, R. J. (Eds.). (2011). Whither opportunity? Rising inequality, schools, and children's life chances. New York, NY: Russell Sage.

Dunfield, K., & Kuhlmeier, V. (2010). Intention-mediated selective helping in infancy. *Psychological Science, 24*(4), 523–527.

Dunn, K. M., Cherkas, L. F., & Spector, T. D. (2005). Genetic influences on variation in female orgasmic function: a twin study. *Biology Letters, 1,* 260–263.

Dunst, B., Benedek, M., Bergner, S., Athenstaedt, U, & Neubauer, A. C. (2013). Sex differences in neural efficiency: Are they due to stereotype threat effect? *Personality and Individual Differences, 55*(7), 744–749. doi:10.1016/j.paid.2013.06.007

Durgin, F. H., Baird, J. A., Greenburg, M., Russell, R., Shaughnessy, K., & Waymouth, S. (2009). Who is being deceived? The experimental demands of wearing a backpack. *Psychonomic Bulletin and Review, 16,* 964–969.

Dutton, E., & Lynn, R. (2013). A negative Flynn effect in Finland, 1997–2009. *Intelligence, 41*(6), 817–820. doi:10.1016/j.intell.2013.05.008

Dweck, C. (2002). Beliefs that make smart people dumb. In R. J. Sternberg (Ed.), *Why smart people can be so stupid* (pp. 24–41). New Haven, CT: Yale University Press.

Dweck, C., Chiu, C., & Hong, Y-y. (1995). Implicit theories and their role in judgments and reactions: A world from two perspectives. *Psychological Inquiry, 6,* 267–285.

Dykiert, D., Gale, C., & Deary, I. (2009). Are apparent sex differences in mean IQ scores created in part by sample restriction and increased male variance? *Intelligence, 37*(1), 42–47.

Eagly, A. (2007). Female leadership advantage and disadvantage: Resolving the contradictions. *Psychology of Women Quarterly, 31*(1), 1–12.

Eagly, A., Karau, S., & Makhijani, M. (1995). Gender and the effectiveness of leaders: A meta-analysis. *Psychological Bulletin, 117*(1), 125–145.

Eberhardt, J. L. (2005). Imaging race. *American Psychologist, 60,* 181–190.

Edwards, J. G., Gibson, H. E., Jensen, T., Nugent, F., Walther, C., Blickenstaff, J., & Kauer, J. A. (2010). A novel non-CB1/TRPV1 endocannabinoid-mediated mechanism depresses excitatory synapses on hippocampal CA1 interneurons. *Hippocampus, 22*(2), 209–221.

Eftekhari, A., Ruzek, J., Crowley, J., Rosen, C., Greenbaum, M., & Karlin, B. (2013). Effectiveness of national implementation of prolonged exposure therapy in veterans affairs care. *JAMA Psychiatry, 20*(9), 949–955.

Eich, E., Macaulay, D., Lowenstein, R. J., & Dihle, P. H. (1997). Memory, amnesia, and dissociative identity disorder. *Psychological Science, 8,* 417–422.

Eimer, M., Gosling, A., & Duchaine, B. (2012). Electrophysiological markers of covert face recognition in developmental prosopagnosia. *Brain, 135,* 542–554.

Ekman, P., Friesen, W., O'Sullivan, M., Chan, A., Diacoyanni-Tarlatzis, I., Heider, K., et al. (1987, October). Universals and cultural differences in the judgments of facial expressions of emotion. *Journal of Personality and Social Psychology, 53*(4), 712–717.

Ekman, P., O'Sullivan, M., & Frank, M. G. (1999). A few can catch a liar. *Psychological Science, 10,* 263–266.

Elfenbein, H. A., & Ambady, N. (2002). On the universality and cultural specificity of emotion recognition: A meta-analysis. *Psychological Bulletin, 128,* 203–235.

Elfenbein, H. A., & Ambady, N. (2003). Universals and cultural differences in recognizing emotions. *Current Directions in Psychological Science, 12,* 159–164.

Elfenbein, H. A., Beaupré, M., Lévesque, M., & Hess, U. (2007). Toward a dialect theory: Cultural differences in the expression and recognition of posed facial expressions. *Emotion, 7,* 131–146.

Elkins, S. R., & Moore, T. M. (2011). A time-series study of the treatment of panic disorder. *Clinical Case Studies, 10*(1), 3–22.

Elliot, A. J., & McGregor, H. A. (2001). A 2 × 2 achievement goal framework. *Journal of Personality and Social Psychology, 80,* 501–519.

Elliot, A. J., & Murayama, K. (2008). On the measurement of achievement goals: Critique, illustration, application. *Journal of Educational Psychology, 100,* 613–628.

Ellis, A. (1962). *Reason and emotion in psychotherapy.* New York: Lyle Stuart.

Ellis, B. J., & Garber, J. (2000). Psychosocial antecedents of variation in girls' pubertal timing: Maternal depression, stepfather presence, and marital and family stress. *Child Development, 71,* 485–501.

Ellis, L., & Ames, M. (1987). Neurohormonal functioning and sexual orientation: A theory of homosexuality–heterosexuality. *Psychological Bulletin, 101,* 233–258.

Epley, N., & Gilovich, T. (2001). Putting adjustment back into the anchoring and adjustment heuristic: Differential processing of self-generated and experimenter-provided anchors. *Psychological Science, 12,* 391–396.

Epley, N., & Gilovich, T. (2006). The anchoring-and-adjustment heuristic: Why the adjustments are insufficient. *Psychological Science, 17,* 311–318.

Equal Employment Opportunity Commission (EEOC) (2011). Sexual harassment. Retrieved July 14, 2011, from http://www.eeoc.gov/eeoc/statistics/enforcement/sexual_harassment.cfm

Erikson, E. (1963). *Childhood and society.* New York: Norton.

Estraneo, A., Moretta, P., Cardinale, P., De Tanti, A., Gatta, G., Giacino, J. T., & Trojano, L. (2015). A multicentre study of intentional behavioural responses measured using the Coma Recovery Scale-Revised in patients with minimally conscious state. *Clinical Rehabilitation, 29*(8), 803–808. doi:10.1177/0269215514556002.

European Network of National Networks studying Gene-Environment Interactions in Schizophrenia (EU-GEI), van Os, J., Rutten, B. P., Myin-Germeys, I., Delespaul, P., Viechtbauer, W., van Zelst, C., … & Mirjanic, J. (2014). Identifying gene-environment interactions in schizophrenia: contemporary challenges for integrated, large-scale investigations. *Schizophrenia Bulletin, 40*(4), 729–736. doi:10.1093/schbul/sbu069

Evans, D., & Rothbart, M. K. (2007). Developing a model for adult temperament. *Journal of Research in Personality, 41,* 868–888.

Evans, G., & Schamberg, M. (2009). Childhood poverty, chronic stress, and adult working memory. *Proceedings of the National Academy of Sciences, 106,* 6545–6549.

Evans, J. St. B. T. (2006). The heuristic-analytic theory of reasoning: Extension and evaluation. *Psychonomic Bulletin & Review, 13,* 378–395.

Evenson, R., & Simon, R. (2005). Clarifying the relationship between parenthood and depression. *Journal of Health and Social Behavior, 46,* 341–358.

Eysenck, H. J. (1967). *The biological basis of personality.* Springfield, IL: Charles C. Thomas.

Facts and Statistics. (n.d.). Retrieved April 8, 2015, from http://www.distraction.gov/content/get-the-facts/facts-and-statistics.html

Fagundes, C. P., Glaser, R., Hwang, B. S., Malarkey, W. B., & Kiecolt-Glaser, J. K. (2013). Depressive symptoms enhance stress-induced inflammatory responses. *Brain, Behavior, and Immunity, 31,* 172–176. doi:10.1016/j.bbi.2012.05.006

Falk, D., Lepore, F. E., & Noe, A. (2013). The cerebral cortex of Albert Einstein: A description and preliminary analysis of unpublished photographs. *Brain: A Journal of Neurology, 136*(4), 1304–1327.

Fancher, R. (2009). Scientific cousins: The relationship between Charles Darwin and Francis Galton. *American Psychologist, 64,* 84–92.

Fantz, R. L. (1961). The origin of form perception. *Scientific American, 47,* 627–638.

Farajnia, S., Deboer, T., Rohling, J., Meijer, J., & Michel, S. (2014). Aging of the suprachiasmatic clock. *The Neuroscientist, 20*(1), 44–55.

Farley, S. D. (2014). Nonverbal reactions to an attractive stranger: The role of mimicry in communicating preferred social distance. *Journal of Nonverbal Behavior, 38*(2), 195–208. doi:10.1007/s10919-014-0174-4

Fazel, S., Långström, N., Hjern, A., Grann, M., & Lichtenstein, P. (2009). Schizophrenia, substance abuse, and violent crime. *Journal of the American Medical Association, 301,* 2016–2023.

Feldman Barrett, L., & Wager, T. D. (2006). The structure of emotion: Evidence from neuroimaging studies. *Current Directions in Psychological Science, 15,* 79–83.

Feldman, J. (2003). The simplicity principle in human concept learning. *Current Directions in Psychological Science, 12,* 227–232.

Fennis, B. M., Janssen, L., & Vohs, K. D. (2009). Acts of benevolence: A limited-resource account of compliance with charitable requests. *Journal of Consumer Research, 35*(6), 906–924.

Ferguson, C. J. (2013). Violent video games and the Supreme Court: Lessons for the scientific community in the wake of Brown v. Entertainment Merchants Association. *American Psychologist, 68*(2), 57–74. doi:10.1037/a0030597

Ferguson, C. (2013). Spanking, corporal punishment and negative long-term outcomes: A meta-analytic review of longitudinal studies. *Clinical Psychology Review, 33*(1), 196–208.

Ferguson, C. J., & Kilburn, J. (2009). The public health risks of media violence: A meta-analytic review. *Journal of Pediatrics, 154,* 759–763.

Ferrar, K. & Golley, R. (2015). Adolescent diet and time use clusters and associations with overweight and obesity and socioeconomic position Health Education and Behavior, 5(5), 361-369. doi: 10.14336/AD.2014.0500346.

Ferster, C. B., & Skinner, B. F. (1957). *Schedules of reinforcement.* Englewood Cliffs, NJ: Prentice Hall.

Field, A. E., Austin, S. B., Taylor, C. B., Malspeis, S., Rosner, B, Rockett, H. R., Gillman. W., & Colditz, G. A. (2003). Relation between dieting and weight change among preadolescents and adolescents. *Pediatrics, 112,* 900–906.

Field, T., Diego, M. A., Hernandez-Reif, M., Deeds, O., & Figuereido, B. (2006). Moderate versus light pressure massage therapy leads to greater weight gain in preterm infants. *Infant Behavior and Development, 29,* 574–578.

Finley, J., Benjamin, A., & McCarley, J. (2014). Metacognition of multitasking: How well do we predict the costs of divided attention. *Journal of Experimental Psychology: Applied, 20*(2), 158–165.

Fiscella, K., Tancredi, D., & Franks, P. (2009). Adding socioeconomic status to Framingham scoring to reduce disparities in coronary risk assessment. *American Heart Journal, 157*(6), 988–994.

Fischer, E. H., & Farina, A. (1995). Attitudes toward seeking professional psychological help: A shortened form and considerations for research. *Journal of College Student Development, 36,* 368–373.

Fisher, D. M. (2014). Distinguishing between taskwork and teamwork planning in teams: Relations with coordination and interpersonal processes. *Journal of Applied Psychology, 99*(3), 423–436. doi:10.1037/a0034625

Fitzgerald, K. D., Welsh, R. C., Gehring, W. J., Abelson, J. L., Himle, J. A., Liberzon, I., & Taylor, S. F. (2005). Error-related hyperactivity of the anterior cingulate cortex in obsessive–compulsive disorder. *Biological Psychiatry, 57*, 287–294.

Fluke, S. M., Webster, R. J., & Saucier, D. A. (2014). Methodological and theoretical improvements in the study of superstitious beliefs and behaviour. *British Journal of Psychology, 105*, 102–126.

Flynn, J. R. (1984). The mean IQ of Americans: Massive gains 1932 to 1978. *Psychological Bulletin, 95*, 29–51.

Flynn, J. R. (2007). American IQ gains from 1932 to 2002: The WISC subtests and educational progress. *International Journal of Testing, 7*, 209–224.

Flynn, J. R. (2013). The "Flynn Effect" and Flynn's paradox. *Intelligence, 41*(6), 851–857. doi:10.1016/j.intell.2013.06.014

Foa, E. B., Gillihan, S. J., & Bryant, R. A. (2013). Challenges and successes in dissemination of evidence-based treatments for posttraumatic stress: Lessons learned from prolonged exposure therapy for PTSD. *Psychological Science in the Public Interest, 14*, 65–111.

Foell, J., Bekrater-Bodmann, R., Diers, M., & Flor, H. (2014). Mirror therapy for phantom limb pain: Brain changes and the role of body representation. *European Journal of Pain, 18*, 729–732.

Folkman, S., & Lazarus, R. S. (1980). An analysis of coping in a middle-aged community sample. *Journal of Health and Social Behavior, 21*, 219–239.

Fontanilla, D., Johannessen, M., Hajipour, A. R., Cozzi, N. V., Meyer, B. J., & Ruoho, A. E. (2009). The hallucinogen N, N-dimethyltryptamine (DMT) is an endogenous sigma-1 receptor regulator. *Science, 323*(5916), 934–937.

Forbes, C. E. & Leitner, J. B. (2014). Stereotype threat engenders neural attentional bias toward negative feedback to undermine performance. *Biological Psychology, 102*, 98–107. doi:10.1016/j.biopsycho.2014.07.007. [Epub 2014 Jul 23]

Foroud, T., Edenberg, H. J., & Crabbe, J. C. (2010). Genetic research: Who is at risk for alcoholism? *Alcohol Research & Health, 33*(1–2), 64–75.

Foster, D. W., Neighbors, C., & Krieger, H. (2015). Alcohol evaluations and acceptability: Examining descriptive and injunctive norms among heavy drinkers. *Addictive Behaviors, 42*, 101–107. doi:10.1016/j.addbeh.2014.11.008

Foti, R., & Hauenstein, N. (2007). Pattern and variable approaches in leadership emergence and effectiveness. *Journal of Applied Psychology, 92*(2), 347–355.

Fournier, A. K., Ehrhart, I. J., Glindemann, K. E., & Geller, E. (2004). Intervening to decrease alcohol abuse at university parties: Differential reinforcement of intoxication level. *Behavior Modification, 28*(2), 167–181.

Fouts, R. S. (1997). *Next of kin: What chimpanzees tell us about who we are.* New York: Avon Books.

Fowler, J. H., & Christakis, N. A. (2008). Dynamic spread of happiness in a large social network: Longitudinal analysis over 20 years in the Framingham Heart Study. *British Medical Journal, 337*, a2338.

Fox, E., Ridgewell, A., & Ashwin, C. (2009). Looking on the bright side: Biased attention and the human serotonin transporter gene. *Proceedings of the Royal Society, B., 276*, 1747–1751.

Fox, E., Zougkou, K., Ridgewell, A., & Garner, K. (2011). The serotonin transporter gene alters sensitivity to attention bias modification: Evidence for a plasticity gene. *Biological Psychiatry, 70*(11), 1049–1054. doi:10.1016/j.biopsych.2011.07.004

Frank, M. G., & Cantera, R. (2014). Sleep, clocks, and synaptic plasticity. *Trends in Neurosciences, 37*(9), 491–501. doi:10.1016/j.tins.2014.06.005

Frankl, V. (1959). *Man's search for meaning.* New York: Washington Square Press.

Franks, N., & Richardson, T. (2006). Teaching in tandem-running ants. *Nature, 439*, 153.

Freire, A., Lee, K., & Symons, L. (2000). The face-inversion effect as a deficit in the encoding of configural information: Direct evidence. *Perception, 29*, 159–170.

Freud, A. (1936). *The ego and the mechanisms of defense.* London: Hogarth Press & Institute of Psycho-Analysis.

Freud, S. (1896/1954). *The origins of psychoanalysis: Letters to Wilhelm Fliess.* London: Imago.

Freud, S. (1920). *A general introduction to psychoanalysis.* New York: Liveright Publishing.

Friedman, M., & Rosenman, R. H. (1974). *Type A behavior and your heart.* New York: Knopf.

Frimer, J. A., Gaucher, D., & Schaefer, N. K. (2014). Political conservatives' affinity for obedience to authority is loyal, not blind. *Personality And Social Psychology Bulletin, 40*(9), 1205–1214. doi:10.1177/0146167214538672

Fritz, C., & Sonnentag, S. (2006). Recovery, well-being, and performance-related outcomes: The role of workload and vacation experiences. *Journal of Applied Psychology, 91*, 936–945.

Fuller, R., Nopoulos, P., Arndt, S., O'Leary, D., Ho, B. C., & Andreasen, N. C. (2002). Longitudinal assessment of premorbid cognitive functioning in patients with schizophrenia through examination of standardized scholastic test performance. *American Journal of Psychiatry, 159*, 1183–1189.

Funder, D. C., & West, S. G. (1993). Consensus, self-other agreement, and accuracy in personality judgment: An introduction. *Journal of Personality, 61*(4), 457–476. doi:10.1111/j.1467-6494.1993.tb00778.x

Furnham, A., & Chamorro-Premuzic, T. (2004). Estimating one's own personality and intelligence scores. *British Journal of Psychology, 95*(2), 149–160.

Gaboriau, L., Victorri-Vigneau, C., Gerardin, M., Allain-Veyrac, G., Jolliet-Evin, P., & Grall-Bronnec, M. (2014). Aripiprazole: A new risk factor for pathological gambling? A report of 8 case reports. *Addictive Behaviors, 39*, 562–565.

Gabriel, A. S., Diefendorff, J. M., Chandler, M. M., Moran, C. M., & Greguras, G. J. (2014). The dynamic relationships of work affect and job satisfaction with perceptions of fit. *Personnel Psychology, 67*(2), 389–420. doi:10.1111/peps.12042

Gabrieli, J. E., Corkin, S., Mickel, S. F., & Growdon, J. H. (1993). Intact acquisition and long-term retention of mirror-tracing skill in Alzheimer's disease and in global amnesia. *Behavioral Neuroscience, 107*(6), 899–910. doi:10.1037/0735-7044.107.6.899

Gabrielson, R., Jones, R. G., & Sagara, E. (2014, October 10). Deadly Force, in Black and White. Retrieved from http://www.propublica.org/article/deadly-force-in-black-and-white.

Gage, F. H. (2000). Mammalian stem cells. *Science, 287*, 1433–1438.

Galanter, E. (1962). Contemporary psychophysics. In R. Brown, E. Galanter, E. H. Hess, & G. Mandler (Eds.), *New directions in psychology* (p. 231). New York: Holt, Rinehart, & Winston.

Gallo, D., Roberts, M., & Seamon, J. (1997). Remembering words not presented in lists: Can we avoid creating false memories? *Psychonomic Bulletin & Review, 4*, 271–276.

Galovski, T. E., Malta, L. S., & Blanchard, E. B. (2006). Theories of aggressive driving. In T. E. Galovski, L. S. Malta, & E. B. Blanchard (Eds.), *Road rage: Assessment and treatment of the angry, aggressive driver* (pp. 27–44). Washington, DC: American Psychological Association.

Ganek, H., Robbins, A., & Niparko, J. (2012). Language Outcomes After Cochlear Implantation. *Otolaryngologic Clinics of North America, 45*(1), 173–185.

Gangestad, S. W., Thornhill, R., & Yeo, R. A. (1994). Facial attractiveness, developmental stability, and fluctuating asymmetry. *Ethology and Sociobiology, 15*, 73–85.

Gardner, D. G., & Deadrick, D. L. (2012). Moderation of selection procedure validity by employee race. *Journal of Managerial Psychology, 27*(4), 365–382. doi:10.1108/02683941211220180

Garcia, J., Ervin, F. R., & Koelling, R. A. (1966). Learning with prolonged delay of reinforcement. *Psychonomic Science, 5*, 121–122.

Gardner, H. (1983). *Frames of mind: The theory of multiple intelligences.* New York: Basic Books.

Gardner, H. (1999). *Intelligence reframed: Multiple intelligences for the 21st century.* New York: Basic Books.

Gardner, R. A., Gardner, B. T., & VanCantfort, T. E. (1989). *Teaching sign language to chimpanzees.* Albany, NY: State University of New York Press.

Gariepy, J., Watson, K., Du, E., Xie, D., Erb, J., Amasino, D., & Platt, M. (2014). Social learning in humans and other animals. *Frontiers in Neuroscience, 8*(58).

Garry, M., & Polaschek, D. (2000). Imagination and memory. *Current Directions in Psychological Science, 9,* 6–10.

Garry, M., Manning, C., Loftus, E., & Sherman, S. (1996). Imagination inflation: Imagining a childhood event inflates confidence that it occurred. *Psychonomic Bulletin & Review, 3*(2), 208–214.

Gaser, C., & Schlaug, G. (2003). Brain structures differ between musicians and non-musicians. *Journal of Neuroscience, 23,* 9240–9245.

Gaynes, B. N., Lloyd, S. W., Lux, L., Gartlehner, G., Hansen, R. A., Brode, S., Jonas, D. E., Swinson-Evans, T., Viswanathan, M., Lohr, K. N. (2014). Repetitive transcranial magnetic stimulation for treatment-resistant depression: a systematic review and meta-analysis. *Journal of Clinical Psychiatry, 75*(5), 477–489. doi:10.4088/JCP.13r08815

Gazzaniga, M. S. (1967). The split-brain in man. *Scientific American, 217,* 24–29.

Gazzaniga, M. S. (2000). Cerebral specialization and interhemispheric communication. *Brain, 123,* 1293–1326.

Geake, J. G., & Hansen, P. C. (2010). Functional neural correlates of fluid and crystallized intelligence. *Neuroimage, 49,* 3489–3497.

Geier, A., Rozin, P., & Doros, G. (2006). Unit bias: A new heuristic that helps explain the effect of portion size on food intake. *Psychological Science, 17*(6), 521–525.

Gentile, D. A., Li, D., Khoo, A., Prot, S., & Anderson, C. A. (2014). Mediators and moderators of long-term effects of violent video games on aggressive behavior: Practice, thinking, and action. *JAMA Pediatrics, 168*(5), 450–457.

Gershoff, E. T. (2002). Parental corporal punishment and associated child behaviors and experiences: A meta-analytic and theoretical review. *Psychological Bulletin, 128,* 539–579.

Gershoff, E. T., & Bitensky, S. H. (2007). The case against corporal punishment of children: Converging evidence from social science research and international human rights law and implications for U.S. public policy. *Psychology, Public Policy, and the Law, 13,* 231–272.

Gershoff, E. T., Lansford, J. E., Sexton, H. R., Davis-Kean, P., & Sameroff, A. J. (2012). Longitudinal links between spanking and children's externalizing behaviors in a national sample of White, Black, Hispanic, and Asian American families. *Child Development, 83*(3), 838–843.

Giacino, J., Ashwal, S., Childs, N., Cranford, R., Jennett, B., Katz, D., et al. (2002). The minimally conscious state: Definition and diagnostic criteria. *Neurology, 58*(3), 349–353.

Gibbons, M., Crits-Christoph, P., & Hearon, B. (2008). The empirical status of psychodynamic therapies. *Annual Review of Clinical Psychology, 4,* 93–108.

Gibbons, M. C., Rothbard, A., Farris, K. D., Wiltsey Stirman, S., Thompson, S. M., Scott, K., … & Crits-Christoph, P. (2011). Changes in psychotherapy utilization among consumers of services for major depressive disorder in the community mental health system. *Administration and Policy in Mental Health and Mental Health Services Research, 38*(6), 495–503. doi:10.1007/s10488-011-0336-1

Gigone, D., & Hastie, R. (1997). Proper analysis of the accuracy of group judgments. *Psychological Bulletin, 121*(1), 149–167.

Gillespie-Lynch, K., Greenfield, P. M., Lyn, H., Savage-Rumbaugh, S. (2011). The role of dialogue in the ontogeny and phylogeny of early symbal combinations: A cross-species comparison of bonobo, chimpanzee, and human learners. *First Language, 31*(4), 442–460. doi:10.1177/0142723711406882

Gillig, P. M. (2009). Dissociative identity disorder: A controversial diagnosis. *Psychiatry, 6*(3), 24–29.

Gilligan, C. (1982). In a different voice: Psychological theory and women's development. Cambridge, MA: Harvard University Press.

Gilovich, T., Griffin, D., & Kahneman, D. (2002). *Heuristics and biases: The psychology of intuitive judgment.* New York, NY: Cambridge University Press.

Gilovich, T., Vallone, R., & Tversky, A. (1985). The hot hand in basketball: On the misperception of random sequences. *Cognitive Psychology, 17,* 295–314.

Giorgio, A., Watkins, K. E., Chadwick, M., James, S., Winmill, L., Douaud, G., De Stefano N., Matthews, P. M., Smith, S. M., Johansen-Berg, H., James, A. C., et al. (2010). Longitudinal changes in grey and white matter during adolescence. *Neuroimage, 49,* 94–103.

Glaser, J. P., Os, J. V., Mengelers, R., & Myin-Germeys, I. (2008). A momentary assessment study of the reputed emotional phenotype associated with borderline personality disorder. *Psychological Medicine, 30,* 1–9.

Glenn, N. D. (1990). Quantitative research on marital quality in the 1980s: A critical review. *Journal of Marriage and the Family, 52,* 818–831.

Glick, P., & Fiske, S. T. (1996). The ambivalent sexism inventory: Differentiating hostile and benevolent sexism. *Journal of Personality and Social Psychology, 70,* 491–512.

Glick, P., & Fiske, S. T. (2001). An ambivalent alliance: Hostile and benevolent sexism as complementary justifications for gender inequality. *American Psychologist, 56,* 109–118.

Glindemann, K. E., Ehrhart, I. J., Drake, E. A., & Geller, E. S., (2007). Reducing excessive alcohol consumption at university fraternity parties: A cost-effective incentive/reward intervention. *Addictive Behaviors, 32*(1), 39–48.

Glindemann, K. E., Wiegand, D. M., & Geller, E. S. (2007). Celebratory drinking and intoxication: A contextual influence on alcohol consumption. *Environment and Behavior, 39*(3), 352–366.

Godden, D., & Baddeley, A. (1975). Context-dependent memory in two natural environments: On land and underwater. *British Journal of Psychology, 66,* 325–331.

Godlee, F., Smith, J., & Marcovitch, H. (2011). Wakefield's article linking MMR vaccine and autism was fraudulent. *British Medical Journal, 342,* c7452. doi:10.1136/bmj.c7452

Gogtay, N., Giedd, J. N., Lusk, L., Hayashi, K. M., Greenstein, D., Vaituzis, C., et al. (2004). Dynamic mapping of human cortical development during childhood through early adulthood. *Proceedings of the National Academy of Sciences, 101,* 8174–8179.

Goh, J. O., Chee, M. W., Tan, J. C., Venkatraman, V., Hebrank, A., Leshikar, E. D., et al. (2007). Age and culture modulate object processing and object-scene binding in the ventral visual area. *Cognitive, Affective, & Behavioral Neuroscience, 7,* 44–52.

Goldin, P. R., & Gross, J. J. (2010). Effects of mindfulness-based stress reduction (MBSR) on emotion regulation in social anxiety disorder. *Emotion, 10,* 83–91.

Goldin, P., Ziv, M., Jazaieri, H., Hahn, K., & Gross, J. J. (2013). MBSR vs aerobic exercise in social anxiety: fMRI of emotion regulation of negative self-beliefs. *Social Cognition and Affective Neuroscience, 8,* 65–72.

Goldman-Rakic, P. S. (1996). The prefrontal landscape: Implications of functional architecture for understanding human mentation and the central executive. *Philosophical Transactions of the Royal Society of London (B Biological Sciences), 351*(1346), 1445–1453.

Goldstein, R. B., Compton, W. M., Pulay, A. J., Ruan, W. J., Pickering, R. P., Stinson, F. S., & Brant, B. F. (2007). Antisocial behavioral syndromes and DSM-IV drug use disorders in the United States: Results from the National Epidemiologic Survey on Alcohol Related Conditions. *Drug and Alcohol Dependence, 90,* 145–158.

Gopnik, A. (2010). *The philosophical baby.* New York: Farrar, Straus, & Giroux

Gonçalves, R., Pedrozo, A., Coutinho, E., Figueira, I., Ventura, P., & Slater, M. (2012). Efficacy of virtual reality exposure therapy in the treatment of PTSD: A systematic review. *PLoS ONE, 7*(12), E48469–E48469.

Gonzales, G. (2014). Same-sex marriage: A prescription for better health. *New England Journal of Medicine, 370,* 1373–1376. doi: 10.1056/NEJMp1400254

Goodall, J. (1999) *Reason for hope: A spiritual journey.* New York: Warner Books.

Goode, C., Balzarini, R. H., & Smith, H. J. (2014). Positive peer pressure: Priming member prototypicality can decrease undergraduate drinking. *Journal of Applied Social Psychology, 44*(8), 567–578. doi:10.1111/jasp.12248

Gorchoff, S., John, O., & Helson, R. (2008). Contextualizing change in marital satisfaction during middle age: An 18-year longitudinal study. *Psychological Science, 19*(11), 1194–1200.

Goren, H., Kurzban, R., & Rapoport, A. (2003). Social loafing vs. social enhancement: Public goods provisioning in real-time with irrevocable commitments. *Organizational Behavior and Human Decision Processes, 90*, 277–290.

Gosling, P., Denizeau, M., & Oberlé, D. (2006). Denial of responsibility: A new mode of dissonance reduction. *Journal of Personality and Social Psychology, 90*, 722–733.

Gosling, S. D. (2001). From mice to men: What can we learn about personality from animal research? *Psychological Bulletin, 127*, 45–86.

Gosling, S. D. (2008). *Snoop: What your stuff says about you.* New York: Basic Books.

Gosling, S. D., Ko, S. J., Mannarelli, T., & Morris, M. E. (2002). A room with a cue: Personality judgments based on offices and bedrooms. *Personality Processes and Individual Differences, 82*, 379–398.

Gotlib, I., & Hamilton, J. (2008). Neuroimaging and depression: Current status and unresolved issues. *Current Directions in Psychological Science, 17*, 159–163.

Gottesman, I. (1991). *Schizophrenia genesis.* New York: W. H. Freeman.

Gottesman, I., & Gould, T. D. (2003). The endophenotype concept in psychiatry: Etymology and strategic intentions. *American Journal of Psychiatry, 160*, 636–645.

Gottman, J. M., & Levenson, R. W., (1992). Marital processes predictive of later dissolution: Behavior, physiology and health. *Journal of Personality and Social Psychology, 63*, 221–233.

Gottman, J., & Levenson, R. W. (2002). A two-factor model for predicting when a couple will divorce: Exploratory analyses using 14-year longitudinal data. *Family Process, 41*(1), 83–96.

Gouin, J. P., & Kiecolt-Glaser, J. K. (2011). The impact of psychological stress on wound healing: Methods and mechanisms. *Immunology and Allergy Clinics of North America, 31*, 81–93.

Gouin, J-P., Carter, C. S., Pournajafi-Nazarloo, H., Glaser, R., Malarkey, W. B., Loving, T. J., Stowell, J., & Kiecolt-Glaser, J. K. (2010). Marital behavior, oxytocin, vasopressin, and wound healing. *Psychoneuroendocrinology, 35*, 1082–1090.

Gould, M. S., Greenberg, T., Velting, D. M., & Shaffer, D. (2003). Youth suicide risk and preventive interventions: A review of the past 10 years. *Journal of the American Academy of Child and Adolescent Psychiatry, 42*, 386–405.

Gould, S. J. (1981). *The mismeasure of man.* New York: W. W. Norton.

Gould, S. J., & Lewontin, R. C. (1979). The spandrels of San Marco and the panglossian paradigm: A critique of the adaptationist approach. *Proceedings of the Royal Society of London, 205*, 581–598.

Gouzoulis-Mayfrank, E., & Daumann, J. (2006). The confounding problem of polydrug use in recreational ecstasy/MDMA users: A brief overview. *Journal of Psychopharmacology, 20*, 188–193.

Grabenhorst, F., & Rolls, E. (2014). The representation of oral fat texture in the human somatosensory cortex. *Human Brain Mapping, 35*, 2521–2530.

Graham, K., & Wells, S. (2004). Aggression among young adults in the social context of the bar. *Addiction Research and Theory, 9*, 193–219.

Grahek, M. S., Thompson, A., & Toliver, A. (2010). The character to lead: A closer look at character in leadership. *Consulting Psychology Journal: Practice and Research, 62*(4), 270–290.

Granpeesheh, D., Tarbox, J., & Dixon, D. R. (2009). Applied behavior analytic interventions for children with autism: A description and review of treatment research. *Annals of Clinical Psychiatry, 21*, 162–173.

Grant, J. (2014). Meditative analgesia: The current state of the field. *Annals of the New York Academy of Sciences, 1307*, 55–63.

Grant, J. A., & Rainville, P. (2009). Pain sensitivity and analgesic effects of mindful states in Zen meditators: A cross-sectional study. *Psychosomatic Medicine, 71*, 106–114.

Grauwiler, P. (2008). Voices of women: Perspectives on decision-making and the management of partner violence. *Children and Youth Services Review, 30*(3), 311–322.

Gray, R., Petrou, S., Hockley, C., & Gardner, F. (2007). Self-reported health status and health-related quality of life of teenagers who were born before 29 weeks' gestational age. *Pediatrics, 120*, e86–e93.

Greenwald, A. G., & Banaji, M. R. (1995). Implicit social cognition: Attitudes, self-esteem, and stereotypes. *Psychological Review, 102*(1), 4–27.

Greenwald, A. G., McGhee, D. E., & Schwartz, J. L. K. (1998). Measuring individual differences in implicit cognition: The implicit association test. *Journal of Personality and Social Psychology, 74*, 1464–1480.

Greven, C. U., Harlaar, N., Kovas, Y., Chamorro-Premuzic, T., & Plomin, R. (2009). More than just IQ: School achievement is predicted by self-perceived abilities—but for genetic rather than environmental reasons. *Psychological Science, 20*, 753–762.

Grice, J. W., Jackson, B. J., & McDaniel, B. L. (2006). Bridging the idiographic–nomothetic divide: A follow-up study. *Journal of Personality, 74*, 1191–1218.

Grice, P. (1975). Logic and conversation. In P. Cole & J. Morgan (Eds.), *Syntax and semantics* (p. 3). New York: Academic Press.

Griffeth, R., Hom, P., & Gaertner, S. (2000). A meta-analysis of antecedents and correlates of employee turnover: Update, moderator tests, and research implications for the next millennium. *Journal of Management, 26*(3), 463–488.

Griffiths, R. R., Richards, W. A., Johnson, M. W., McCann, U. D., & Jesse, R. (2008). Mystical-type experiences occasioned by psilocybin mediate the attribution of personal meaning and spiritual significance 14 months later. *Journal of Psychopharmacology, 22*, 621–632.

Grimbos, T., Dawood, K., Burriss, R. P., Zucker, K. J., & Puts, D. A. (2010). Sexual orientation and the second to fourth finger length ratio: A meta-analysis in men and women. *Behavioral Neuroscience, 124*, 278–287.

Gropper, S. S., Simmons, K. P., Gaines, A., Drawdy, K., Saunders, D., Ulrich, P., & Connell, L. J. (2009). The freshman 15: A closer look. *Journal of American College Health, 58*, 223–231.

Grossman, I., Na, J., Varnum, M. E., Park, D. C., Kitayama, S., & Nisbett, R. E. (2010). Reasoning about social conflicts improves into old age. *Proceedings of the National Academy of Sciences, 107*, 7246–7250.

Groves, C. L., Anderson, C. A., & DeLisi, M. (2014). A response to Ferguson: More red herring. *PsycCRITIQUES, 59*(10) article 9. doi:10.1037/a0036266

Gudonis, L. C., Derefinko, K., & Giancola, P. R. (2009). The treatment of substance misuse in psychopathic individuals: Why heterogeneity matters. *Substance Use & Misuse, 44*(9–10), 1415–1433.

Guedj, E., Aubert, S., McGonigal, A., Mundler, O., & Bartolomei, F. (2010). Déjà-vu in temporal lobe epilepsy: Metabolic pattern of cortical involvement in patients with normal brain MRI. *Neuropsychologia, 48*(7), 2174–2181.

Güngör, D., Bornstein, M. H., De Leersnyder, J., Cote, L., Ceulemans, E., & Mesquita, B. (2013). Acculturation of personality: A three-culture study of Japanese, Japanese Americans, and European Americans. *Journal of Cross-Cultural Psychology, 44*(5), 701–718. doi:10.1177/0022022112470749

Gutchess, A. H., Hedden, T., Ketay, S., Aron, A., & Gabrieli, J. D. (2010). Neural differences in the processing of semantic relationships across cultures. *Social Cognitive and Affective Neuroscience, 5*, 254–263.

Guttmacher Institute. (2014). *American teens' sexual and reproductive health: Fact sheet.* New York, NY: Author.

Haber, J., & Jacob, T. (2007). Alcoholism risk moderation by a socio-religious dimension. *Journal of Studies on Alcohol and Drugs, 68*(6), 912–922.

Haghighi, M., Salehi, I., Erfani, P., Jahangard, L., Bajoghli, H., Holsboer-Trachsler, E., & Brand, S. (2013). Additional ECT increases BDNF-levels in patients suffering from major depressive disorders compared to patients treated with citalopram only. *Journal of Psychiatric Research, 47*(7), 908–915.

Haidt, J. (2001). The emotional dog and its rational tail: A social intuitionist approach to moral judgment. *Psychological Review, 108*, 814–834.

Haidt, J. (2012). *The righteous mind: Why good people are divided by politics and religion.* New York, NY: Pantheon/Random House.

Hakuta, K., Bialystok, E., & Wiley, E. (2003). Critical evidence: A test of the critical-period hypothesis for second-language acquisition. *Psychological Science, 14*, 31–38.

Hollon, S., Thase, M., & Markowitz, J. (2002). Treatment and prevention of depression. *Psychological Science in the Public Interest, 3*, 39–77.

Halpern, D. F. (1996). *Thought and knowledge: An introduction to critical thinking.* Mahwah, NJ: Lawrence Erlbaum.

Halpern, D., & LaMay, M. (2000). The smarter sex: A critical review of sex differences in intelligence. *Educational Psychology Review, 12*(2), 229–246.

Hamilton, W. D. (1964). The genetical evolution of social behavior. I. *Journal of Theoretical Biology, 7*, 1–16.

Hane, A. A., Feldstein, S., & Dernetz, V. H. (2003). The relation between coordinated interpersonal timing and maternal sensitivity in four-month-old infants. *Journal of Psycholinguistic Research, 32*, 525–539.

Haney, C., Banks, C., & Zimbardo, P. (1973). Interpersonal dynamics in a simulated prison. *International Journal of Criminology & Penology, 1*, 69–97.

Haney-Caron, E., Caprihan, A., & Stevens, M. C. (2014). DTI-measured white matter abnormalities in adolescents with Conduct Disorder. *Journal of Psychiatric Research, 48*(1), 111–120. doi:10.1016/j.jpsychires.2013.09.015

Harley, T. A. (2001). *The psychology of language: From data to theory.* New York: Psychology Press.

Harlow, H. F. (1958). The nature of love. *American Psychologist, 13*, 673–685.

Harlow, H. F., Dodsworth, R. O., & Harlow, M. K. (1965). Total social isolation in monkeys. *Proceedings of the National Academy of Sciences, 54*, 90–97.

Harris, J. L., Bargh, J. A., & Brownell, K. D. (2009). Priming effects of television food advertising on eating behavior. *Health Psychology, 28*(4), 404–413.

Harris, J. L., Pierce, M., & Bargh, J. A. (2013). Priming effect of antismoking PSAs on smoking behavior: A pilot study. *Tobacco Control, 23*(4), 285–290. doi:10.1136/tobaccocontrol-2012-050670. [Epub 2013 Jan 15].

Harrison, T. L., Shipstead, Z., & Engle, R. W. (2015). Why is working memory capacity related to matrix reasoning tasks? *Memory & Cognition, 43*(3), 389–396. doi:10.3758/s13421-014-0473-3

Harter, S., & Monsour, A. (1992). Developmental analysis of conflict caused by opposing attributes in the adolescent self-portrait. *Developmental Psychology, 28*, 251–260.

Hartshorne, J., & Germine, L. (2015). When does cognitive functioning peak? The asynchronous rise and fall of different cognitive abilities across the lifespan. *Psychological Science, 26*(4), 433–443. doi:10.1177/0956797614567339. [Epub 2015 Mar 13].

Harvey, A. G. (2011). Sleep and circadian functioning: critical mechanisms in the mood disorders? *Annual Review of Clinical Psychology, 7*, 297–319.

Haslam, S., & Reicher, S. (2012). When prisoners take over the prison: A social psychology of resistance. *Personality and Social Psychology Review, 16*(2), 154–179. doi:10.1177/1088868311419864

Hatsopoulos, N. G., & Donoghue, J. P. (2009). The science of neural interface systems. *Annual Review of Neuroscience, 32*, 249–266.

Hatzenbuehler, M. L., O'Cleirigh, C., Grasso, C., Mayer, K., Safren, S., & Bradford, J. (2012). Effect of same-sex marriage laws on health care use and expenditures in sexual minority men: A quasi-natural experiment. *American Journal of Public Health, 102*, 285–291.

Hawkley, L. C., Burleson, M. H., & Berntson, G. G. (2003). Loneliness in everyday life: Cardiovascular activity, psychosocial context, and health behaviors. *Journal of Personality and Social Psychology, 85*, 105–120.

Hayes, K. J., & Hayes, C. (1951). The intellectual development of a home-raised chimpanzee. *Proceedings of the American Philosophical Society, 95*, 105–109.

Heatherton, T. F., & Sargent, J. D. (2009). Does watching smoking in movies promote teenage smoking? *Current Directions in Psychological Science, 18*, 63–67.

Hebb, D. O. (1947). The effects of early experience on problem solving at maturity. *American Psychologist, 2*, 306–307.

Heider, F. (1958). *The psychology of interpersonal relations.* New York: Wiley.

Heine, S. J., & Buchtel, E. E. (2009). Personality: The universal and the culturally specific. *Annual Review of Psychology, 60*, 369–394.

Heinz, A., & Schlagenhauf, F. (2010). Dopaminergic dysfunction in schizophrenia: Salience attribution revisited. *Schizophrenia Bulletin, 36*, 472–485.

Hempel, A., Hempel, E., Schönknecht, P., Stippich, C., & Schröder, J. (2003). Impairment in basal limbic function in schizophrenia during affect cognition. *Psychiatry Research, 122*, 115–124.

Hendrick, C., Hendrick, S. S., & Reich, D. A. (2006). The brief sexual attitudes scale. *Journal of Sex Research, 43*, 76–86.

Henrich, J., Heine, S. J., & Norenzayan, A. (2010) The weirdest people in the world? *Behavioral and Brain Sciences, 33*, 61–135.

Hensel, D. J., & Fortenberry, J. D. (2013). A multidimensional model of sexual health and sexual and prevention behavior among adolescent women. *Journal of Adolescent Health, 52*, 219–227.

Henttonen, K., Johanson, J., & Janhonen, M. (2014). Work-team bonding and bridging social networks, team identity and performance effectiveness. *Personnel Review, 43*(3), 330–349. doi:10.1108/PR-12-2011-0187

Herlitz, J., Wiklund, I., Caidahl, K., Hartford, M., Haglid, M., & Karlsson, B. W. (1998). The feeling of loneliness prior to coronary artery bypass grafting might be a predictor of short- and long-term postoperative mortality. *European Journal of Vascular and Endovascular Surgery, 16*, 120–125.

Herman, C., & Polivy, J. (2011). Self-regulation and the obesity epidemic. *Social Issues and Policy Review, 5*(1), 37–69. doi:10.1111/j.1751-2409.2011.01025.x

Herman, C. P., Roth, D. A., & Polivy, J. (2003). Effects of the presence of others on food intake: A normative interpretation. *Psychological Bulletin, 129*, 873–886.

Hermelin, E., Lievens, F., & Robertson, I. T. (2007). The validity of assessment centres for the prediction of supervisory performance ratings: A meta-analysis. *International Journal of Selection and Assessment, 15*(4), 405–411. doi:10.1111/j.1468-2389.2007.00399.x

Hernandez, A. E., & Li, P. (2007). Age of acquisition: Its neural and computational mechanisms. *Psychological Bulletin, 133*, 638–650.

Hernandez-Reif, M., Diego, M., & Field, T. (2007). Preterm infants show reduced stress behaviors and activity after 5 days of massage therapy. *Infant Behavior and Development, 30*, 557–561.

Hess, U., & Fischer, A. (2014). Emotional mimicry: Why and when we mimic emotions. *Social and Personality Psychology Compass, 8*(2), 45–57. doi:10.1111/spc3.12083

Hevia, M., Izard, V., Coubart, A., Spelke, E., & Streri, A. (2014). Representations of space, time, and number in neonates. *Proceedings of the National Academy of Sciences, 111*(13), 4809–4813.

Hewstone, M., Rubin, M., & Willis, H. (2002). Intergroup bias. *Annual Review of Psychology, 53*, 575–604.

Heyes, C. M., & Galef, B. G. Jr. (Eds.). (1996). *Social learning in animals: The roots of culture.* San Diego: Academic Press.

Hickok, G. (2014). *The myth of mirror neurons: The real neuroscience of communication and cognition.* New York: W.W. Norton.

Hilgard, E. (1994). Neodissociation theory. In S. J. Lynn & J. W. Rhue (Eds.), *Dissociation: Clinical and theoretical perspectives* (pp. 32–51). New York: Guilford Press.

Hill, C. A., & Preston, L. K. (1996). Individual differences in the experience of sexual motivation: Theory and measurement of dispositional sexual motives. *Journal of Sex Research, 33*, 27–45.

Hill, K. E., Mann, L., Laws, K. R., Stippich, C., & Schröder, J. (2004). Hypofrontality in schizophrenia: A meta-analysis of functional imaging studies. *Acta Psychiatrica Scandinavica, 110*, 243–256.

Hillman, C., Pontifex, M., Castelli, D., Khan, N., Raine, L., Scudder, M., … & Kamijo, K. (2014). Effects of the FITKids randomized controlled trial on executive control and brain function. *Pediatrics, 134*(4), E1063–E1071.

Hillman, C. H., Snook, E. M., & Jerome, G. J. (2003). Acute cardiovascular exercise and executive control function. *International Journal of Psychophysiology, 48*(3), 307–314.

Hingson, R. W., Zha, W., & Weitzman, E. R. (2009). Magnitude of and trends in alcohol-related mortality and morbidity among U.S. college students ages 18–24, 1998–2005. *Journal of Studies on Alcohol and Drugs, 16*(suppl), 12–20.

Hinshaw, S. (2005). The stigmatization of mental illness in children and parents: Developmental issues, family concerns, and research needs. *Journal of Child Psychology and Psychiatry, 46*(7), 714–734.

Hirschberg, R., & Giacino, J. (2011). The vegetative and minimally conscious states: Diagnosis, prognosis and treatment. *Neurologic Clinics, 29*(4), 773–786.

Hirst, W., Phelps, E., Buckner, R., Budson, A., Cuc, A., Gabrieli, J., et al. (2009). Long-term memory for the terrorist attack of September 11: Flashbulb memories, event memories, and the factors that influence their retention. *Journal of Experimental Psychology: General, 138*(2), 161–176.

Hobson, J. (2005). In bed with Mark Solms? What a nightmare! A reply to Domhoff (2005). *Dreaming, 15*(1), 21–29.

Hobson, J., Pace-Schott, E., & Stickgold, R. (2000). Dreaming and the brain: Toward a cognitive neuroscience of conscious states. *Behavioral and Brain Sciences, 23*(6), 793–842.

Hodges, L. F., Anderson, P., Burdea, G. C., Hoffman, H. G., & Rothbaum, B. O. (2001). VR as a tool in the treatment of psychological and physical disorders. *IEEE Computer Graphics and Applications, 21*(6), 25–33.

Hofer, M. A. (2006). Psychobiological roots of early attachment. Current Directions in *Psychological Science, 15,* 84–88.

Hoffart, A., Øktedalen, T., Langkaas, T. F., & Wampold, B. E. (2013). Alliance and outcome in varying imagery procedures for PTSD: A study of within-person processes. *Journal of Counseling Psychology, 60*(4), 471–482. doi:10.1037/a0033604

Hofman, M. A. (2014). Evolution of the brain: When bigger is better. *Frontiers in Neuroanatomy, 8*(15), 1–12. doi:10.3389/fnana.2014.00015

Hofmann, S. (2007). Cognitive factors that maintain social anxiety disorder: A comprehensive model and its treatment implications. *Cognitive Behaviour Therapy, 36,* 193–209.

Hogan, R., & Warrenfeltz, R. (2003). Educating the modern manager. *Academy of Management Learning & Education, 2*(1), 74–84.

Hojnoski, R. L., Morrison, R., Brown, M., & Matthews, W. J. (2006). Projective test use among school psychologists: A survey and critique. *Journal of Psychoeducational Assessment, 24*(2), 145–159.

Holland, P. (2008). Cognitive versus stimulus-response theories of learning. *Learning & Behavior, 36*(3), 227–241.

Holleran, S. E., Mehl, M. R., & Levitt, S. (2009). Eavesdropping on social life: The accuracy of stranger ratings of daily behavior from thin slices of natural conversations. *Journal of Research in Personality, 43,* 660–672.

Hollon, S.D., DeRubeis, R.J., Fawcett, J., Amsterdam, J.D., Shelton, R.C., Zajecka, J., Young, P.R., & Gallop, R. (2014). Effects of cognitive therapy with antidepressant medications vs antidepressants alone on the rate of recovery in major depressive disorder. *JAMA Psychiatry, 71,* 1157–1164.

Holloway, C., Cochlin, L., Emmanuel, Y., Murray, A., Codreanu, I., Edwards, L., … Clarke, K. (2011). A high-fat diet impairs cardiac high-energy phosphate metabolism and cognitive function in healthy human subjects. *American Journal of Clinical Nutrition, 93,* 748–755.

Holmes, T. H., & Rahe, R. H. (1967). The Social Readjustment Rating Scale. *Journal of Psychosomatic Research, 11,* 213–218.

Holstege, G., Georgiadis, J. R., Paans, A. M. J., Meiners, L.C., van der Graaf, F. H. C. E., &, Reinders, A. A. T. (2003). Brain activation during human male ejaculation. *Journal of Neuroscience, 23,* 9185–9193.

Holt-Lunstad, J., Smith, T., Layton, J., & Brayne, C. (2010). Social relationships and mortality risk: A meta-analytic review. *PLoS Medicine, 7*(7), e1000316. doi:10.1371/journal.pmed.1000316

Holtzman, C., Trotman, H., Goulding, S., Ryan, A., Macdonald, A., Shapiro, D., … & Walker, E. (2013). Stress and neurodevelopmental processes in the emergence of psychosis. *Neuroscience, 249,* 172–191. doi:10.1016/j.neuroscience.2012.12.017

Holyoak, K. J., & Morrison R. G. (2005). Thinking and reasoning: A reader's guide. In K. J. Holyoak & R. G. Morrison (Eds.), *The Cambridge handbook of thinking and reasoning* (pp. 1–9). New York: Cambridge University Press.

Hooley, J. (2007). Expressed emotion and relapse of psychopathology. *Annual Review of Clinical Psychology, 3,* 329–352.

Hoover, A. E., Démonet, J. F., & Steeves, J. K. (2010). Superior voice recognition in a patient with acquired prosopagnosia and object agnosia. *Neuropsychologia, 48,* 3725–3732.

Horn, J. L., & Cattell, R. B. (1967). Age differences in fluid and crystallized intelligence. *Acta Psychologica, 26,* 107–129.

Horn, L. R., & Ward, G. (2004). *The handbook of pragmatics.* Malden, MA: Blackwell.

Horner, V., & Whiten, A. (2005). Causal knowledge and imitation/emulation switching in chimpanzees (Pan troglodytes) and children (Homo sapiens). *Animal Cognition, 8,* 164–181.

Hough, W., & O'Brien, K. (2005). The effect of community treatment orders on offending rates. *Psychiatry, Psychology and Law, 12,*(2), 411–423.

House, J., DeVoe, S. E., & Zhong, C. B. (2014). Too impatient to smell the roses: Exposure to fast food impedes happiness. *Social Psychological and Personality Science, 5*(5), 534–541. doi:10.1177/1948550613511498

House, J. S., Landis, K. R., & Umberson, D. (1998). Social relationships and health. *Science, 241,* 540–545.

Howell, A. J., & Watson, D. C. (2007). Procrastination: Associations with achievement goal orientation and learning strategies. *Personality and Individual Differences, 43*(1), 167–178.

Huang, Y., Kendrick, K. M., & Yu, R. (2014). Conformity to the opinions of other people lasts for no more than 3 days. *Psychological Science, 25*(7), 1388–1393. doi:10.1177/0956797614532104

Hubel, D. H., & Wiesel, T. N. (1962). Receptive fields, binocular interaction and functional architecture in the cat's visual cortex. *Journal of Physiology, 160,* 106–154.

Hudson, J., Hiripi, E., Pope, H., & Kessler, R. (2007). The prevalence and correlates of eating disorders in the National Comorbidity Survey replication. *Biological Psychiatry, 61*(3), 348–358.

Huffman, M. A. (1996). Acquisition of innovative cultural behaviors in nonhuman primates: A case study of stone handling, a socially transmitted behavior in Japanese macaques. In C. M. Heyes & B. Galef (Eds.), *Social learning in animals: The roots of culture* (pp. 267–289). San Diego: Academic Press.

Hunt, E., & Carlson, J. (2007). Considerations relating to the study of group differences in intelligence. *Perspectives on Psychological Science, 2*(2), 194–213.

Huston, T. L., Ruggiero, M., Conner, R., & Geis, G. (1981). Bystander intervention into crime: A study based on naturally-occurring episodes. *Social Psychology Quarterly, 44,* 14–23.

Huynh, H., Willemsen, A., & Holstege, G. (2013). Female orgasm but not male ejaculation activates the pituitary. A PET-neuro-imaging study. *NeuroImage, 76,* 178–182. doi:10.1016/j.neuroimage.2013.03.012

Huyser, C., Veltman, D. J., de Haan, E., & Boer, F. (2009). Paediatric obsessive– compulsive disorder, a neurodevelopmental disorder? Evidence from neuroimaging. *Neuroscience and Biobehavioral Reviews, 33,* 818–830.

Hyde, J. (2005). The gender similarities hypothesis. *American Psychologist, 60*(6), 581–592.

Hyde, J., Mezulis, A., & Abramson, L. (2008). The ABCs of depression: Integrating affective, biological, and cognitive models to explain the emergence of the gender difference in depression. *Psychological Review, 115,* 291–313.

Hypericum Depression Trial Study Group. (2002). Effect of Hypericum perforatum (St. John's wort) in major depressive disorder: A randomized controlled trial. *Journal of the American Medical Association, 287,* 1807–1814.

Iacono, W. G. (2001). Forensic "lie detection": Procedures without scientific basis. Journal of Forensic Psychology Practice, 1, 75–85.

Inada, T. & Inagaki, A. (2015). Psychotropic dose equivalence in Japan. *Psychiatry and Clinical Neurosciences, 69*(8), 440–447. doi:10.1111/pcn.12275

Inn, A., Wheeler, A. C., & Sparling, C. L. (1977). The effects of suspect race and situation hazard on police officer shooting behavior. *Journal of Applied Social Psychology, 7*, 27–37.

Inness, M., Barling, J., & Turner, N. (2005). Understanding supervisor-targeted aggression: A within-person, between-jobs design. *Journal of Applied Psychology, 90*, 731–739.

Innocence Project. (2010, November). Retrieved November 14, 2012 from http://www.innocenceproject.org/Content/Eyewitness_Identification_Reform.php

Insel, T. R. (2014). The NIHM Research Domain Criteria (RDoC) Project: Precision medicine for psychiatry. *The American Journal of Psychiatry, 171*(4), 395–397. doi:10.1176/appi.ajp.2014.14020138

Itan, Y., Powell, A., Beaumont, M. A., Burger, J., & Thomas, M. G. (2009). The origins of lactase persistence in Europe (M. Tanaka, Ed.). *PLoS Computational Biology 5*(8): e1000491. doi:10.1371/journal.pcbi.1000491.

Iudicello, J. E., Woods, S. P., Vigil, O., Scott J. C., Cherner M., Heaton R. K., Atkinson J. H., Grant I. & HIV Neurobehavioral Research Center (HNRC) Group. (2010). Longer term improvement in neurocognitive functioning and affective distress among methamphetamine users who achieve stable abstinence. *Journal of Clinical and Experimental Neuropsychology, 32*, 704–718.

Iyengar, S. S., Wells, R. E., & Schwartz, B. (2006). Doing better but feeling worse: Looking for the "best" job undermines satisfaction. *Psychological Science, 17*(2), 143–150.

Izard, C. E. (1994). Innate and universal facial expressions: Evidence from developmental and cross-cultural research. *Psychological Bulletin, 115*, 288–299.

Izard, V., Sann, C., Spelke, E. S., & Streri, A. (2009). Newborn infants perceive abstract numbers. *Proceedings of the National Academy of Sciences, 106*, 10382–10385.

Jacobs, B. (2004). Depression: The brain finally gets into the act. *Current Directions in Psychological Science, 13*, 103–106.

Jaffee, S., & Hyde, J. S. (2000). Gender differences in moral orientation: A meta-analysis. *Psychological Bulletin, 126*, 703–726.

Jarjour, I.T. (2015). Neurodevelopmental outcome after extreme prematurity: A review of the literature. *Pediatric Neurology, 52*(2), 143–152. doi:10.1016/j.pediatrneurol.2014.10.027. [Epub 2014 Nov 4].

James, L., Klinger, D., & Vila, B. (2014). Racial and ethnic bias in decisions to shoot seen through a stronger lens: Experimental results from high-fidelity laboratory simulations. *Journal of Experimental Criminology, 10*(3), 323–340. doi:10.1007/s11292-014-9204-9

James, L. R., & LeBreton, J. M. (2010). Assessing aggression using conditional reasoning. *Current Directions in Psychological Science, 19*(1), 30–35.

James, L. R., McIntyre, M. D., Glisson, C. A., Green, P. D., Patton, T. W., LeBreton, J. M., Frost, B. C., Russell, S. M., Sablynski, C. J., Mitchell, T. R., & Williams, L. J. (2005). A conditional reasoning measure for aggression. *Organizational Research Methods, 8*(1), 69–99.

Janis, I. L. (1972). *Victims of groupthink: A psychological study of foreign policy decisions and fiascoes.* Boston: Houghton Mifflin.

Janowsky, J. (2006). Thinking with your gonads: Testosterone and cognition. *Trends in Cognitive Sciences, 10*(2), 77–82.

Jansen, A., Theunissen, N., Slechten, K., Nederkoorn, C., Boon, B., Mulkens, S., (2003). Overweight children overeat after exposure to food cues. *Eating Behaviors, 4*, 197–209.

Jensen, A. R. (2002). Galton's legacy to research on intelligence. *Journal of Biosocial Science, 34*, 145–172.

Jensen, M. P. & Patterson, D. R. (2014). Hypnotic approaches for chronic pain management. *American Psychologist, 69*(2), 167–177.

Jilek, W. G. (1995). Emil Kraepelin and comparative sociocultural psychiatry. *European Archives of Psychiatry and Clinical Neuroscience, 245*, 231–238.

Jockin, V., Arvey, R. D., & McGue, M. (2001). Perceived victimization moderates self-reports of workplace aggression and conflict. *Journal of Applied Psychology, 86*, 1262–1269.

Joel, D. (2011). Male or female? Brains are intersex. *Frontiers in Integrative Neuroscience, 5*(57), 1–5.

Johns, M. W. (1991). A new method for measuring daytime sleepiness: The Epworth sleepiness scale. *Sleep, 14*(6), 540–545.

Johns, M., Schmader, T., & Martens, A. (2005). Knowing is half the battle: Teaching stereotype threat as a means of improving women's math performance. *Psychological Science, 16*, 175–179.

Johnson, K. E., & Mervis, C. B. (1997). Effects of varying levels of expertise on the basic level of categorization. *Journal of Experimental Psychology: General, 126*, 248–277.

Johnson, M. P. & Patterson, D. R. (2014). Hypnotic approaches for chronic pain management: Clinical implications of recent research findings. *American Psychologist, 69*(2), 167–177.

Johnson, W., Bouchard, T. J., Krueger, R. F., McGue, M., & Gottesman, I. I. (2004). Just one g: Consis-tent results from three test batteries. *Intelligence, 32*, 95–107.

Johnson, W., te Nijenhuis, J., & Bouchard, T. (2008). Still just 1 g: Consistent results from five test batteries. *Intelligence, 36*, 81–95.

Johnson, W., Turkheimer, E., Gottesman, I. I., & Bouchard, T. J., Jr. (2009). Beyond heritability: Twin studies in behavioral research. *Current Directions in Psychological Science, 18*(4), 217–220.

Jones, D., Owens, M., Kumar, M., Cook, R., Weiss, S.M. (2013). The effect of relaxation interventions on cortisol levels in HIV-sero-positive women. *Journal of the International Association of Providers of AIDS Care, 13*(4). doi:10.1177/2325957413488186

Jones, H. B. & George, S. (2011). 'You never told me I would turn into a gambler': A first person account of dopamine agonist-induced gambling addiction in a patient with restless leg syndrome. *British Medical Journal Case Reports, 2011*, PMC3171036. doi:10.1136/bcr.07.2011.4459

Jones, H. P., Karuri, S., Cronin, C. M., Ohlsson, A., Peliowski, A., Synnes, A., & Lee, S. K. (2005) Actuarial survival of a large Canadian cohort of preterm infants. *BMC Pediatrics, 5*(40), 1–13.

Jones, J. (2008). Majority of Americans say racism against Blacks is widespread. Retrieved from http://www.gallup.com/poll/109258/majority-americans-say-racism-against-blacks-widespread.aspx

Jones, K. L., & Smith, D. W. (1973). Recognition of the fetal alcohol syndrome in early infancy. *Lancet, 2*, 999–1001.

Jonides, J., Lacey, S., & Nee, D. (2005). Processes of working memory in mind and brain. *Current Directions in Psychological Science, 14*, 2–5.

Joormann, J., & Vanderlind, W. M. (2014). Emotion regulation in depression: The role of biased cognition and reduced cognitive control. *Clinical Psychological Science, 2*(4), 402–421. doi:10.1177/2167702614536163

Judge, T. A., & Bono, J. E. (2001). Relationship of core self-evaluations traits—self esteem, generalized self efficacy, locus of control, and emotional stability—with job satisfaction and job performance: A meta-analysis. *Journal of Applied Psychology, 86*, 80–92.

Judge, T. A., Bono, J. E., Ilies, R., & Gerhardt, M. W. (2002). Personality and leadership: A qualitative and quantitative review. *Journal of Applied Psychology, 87*(4), 765–780.

Judge, T. A., Heller, D., & Mount, M. K. (2002). Five-factor model of personality and job satisfaction: A meta-analysis. *Journal of Applied Psychology, 87*, 530–541.

Judge, T., & Erez, A. (2007). Interaction and intersection: The constellation of emotional stability and extraversion in predicting performance. *Personnel Psychology, 60*, 573–556.

Judge, T., Martocchio, J., & Thoresen, C. (1997). Five-factor model of personality and employee absence. *Journal of Applied Psychology, 82*, 745–755.

Julius, D., & Basbaum, A. I. (2001). Molecular mechanisms of nociception. *Nature, 413*, 203–210.

Jung, D. I., & Sosik, J. J. (2002). Transformational leadership in groups: The role of empowerment, cohesiveness, and collective effectiveness. *Small Group Research, 33*, 313–336.

Jussim, L. (1986). Self-fulfilling prophecies: A theoretical and integrative review. *Psychological Review, 93*, 429–445.

Jussim, L., & Harber, K. D. (2005). Teacher expectations and self-fulfilling prophecies: Knowns and unknowns, resolved and unresolved controversies. *Personality and Social Psychology Review, 9*(2), 131–155.

Kagan, J., Snidman, N., & Arcus, D. (1998). Childhood derivatives of high and low reactivity in infancy. *Child Development, 69*, 1483–1493.

Kahneman, D. (2003). A perspective on judgment and choice: Mapping bounded rationality. *American Psychologist, 58,* 697–720.

Kahneman, D., & Miller, D. T. (1986). Norm theory: Comparing reality to its alternatives. *Psychological Review, 93,* 136–153.

Kaminski, J., Call, J., & Fischer, J. (2004). Word learning in a domestic dog: Evidence for "fast mapping." *Science, 304*(5677), 1682–1683.

Kaplan, J. T., & Iacoboni, M. (2006). Getting a grip on other minds: Mirror neurons, intention understanding, and cognitive empathy. *Social Neuroscience, 1*(3–4), 175–183.

Karakashian, L. M., Walter, M. I., & Christopher, A. N. (2006). Fear of negative evaluation affects helping behavior: The bystander effect revisited. *North American Journal of Psychology, 8,* 13–32.

Karau, S. J., & Williams, K. D. (2001). Understanding individual motivation in groups: The collective effort model. In M. E. Turner (Ed.), *Groups at work: Theory and research* (pp. 113–141). Mahwah, NJ: Lawrence Erlbaum Associates.

Karch, C., & Goate, A. (2014). Alzheimer's disease risk genes and mechanisms of disease pathogenesis. *Biological Psychiatry, 77*(1), 43–51. doi: 10.1016/j.biopsych.2014.05.006

Katzell, R. A., & Austin, J. T. (1992). From then to now: The development of industrial-organizational psychology in the United States. *Journal of Applied Psychology, 77*(6), 803–835.

Kawai, M. (1965). Newly acquired pre-cultural behavior of a natural troop of Japanese monkeys on Koshima Island. *Primates, 6,* 1–30.

Kay, A. C., Whitson, J. A., Gaucher, D., & Galinsky, A. D. (2009). Compensatory control: Achieving order through the mind, our institutions, and the heavens. *Current Directions in Psychological Science, 18,* 264–268.

Kazdin, A. E., & Benjet, C. (2003). Spanking children: Evidence and issues. *Current Directions in Psychological Science, 12,* 99–103.

Keller, M. B., & Baker, L. A. (1991) Bipolar disorder: Epidemiology, course, diagnosis, and treatment. *Bulletin of the Menninger Clinic, 55,* 172–181.

Kellis, M., Wold, B., Snyder, M. P., Bernstein, B. E., Kundaje, A., Marinov, G. K., Ward, L. D., Birney, E., Crawford, G. E., Dekker, J., Dunham, I., Elnitski, L. L., Farnham, P. J., Feingold, E. A., Gerstein, M., Giddings, M. C., Gilbert, D. M., Gingeras, T. R., Green, E. D., Guigo, R., Hubbard, T., Kent, J., Lieb, J. D., Myers, R. M., Pazin, M. J., Ren, B., Stamatoyannopoulos, J. A., Weng, Z., White, K. P., & Hardison, R. C. (2014). Defining functional DNA elements in the human genome. *Proceedings of the National Academy of Sciences USA, 111*(17):6131–6138. doi:10.1073/pnas.1318948111.

Kendler, K. S., Eaves, L. J., Loken, E. K., Pedersen, N. L., Middeldorp, C. M., Reynolds, C., Boomsma, D., Lichtenstein, P., Silberg, J., Gardner, C. O. (2011). The impact of environmental experiences on symptoms of anxiety and depression across the life span. *Psychological Science, 22*(10):1343–1352. doi:10.1177/0956797611417255.

Kenny, D. A. (2004). PERSON: A general model of interpersonal perception. *Personality and Social Psychology Review, 8,* 265–280.

Kerr, N. L., & Tindale, R. S. (2004). Group performance and decision making. *Annual Review of Psychology, 55,* 623–655.

Kessler, R. C. (2000). Posttraumatic stress disorder: The burden to the individual and to society. *Journal of Clinical Psychiatry, 61*(suppl 5), 4–12.

Kessler, R. C., Duncan, G. J., Gennetian, L. A., Katz, L. F., Kling, J. R., Sampson, N. A., … & Ludwig, J. (2014). Associations of housing mobility interventions for children in high-poverty neighborhoods with subsequent mental disorders during adolescence. *JAMA: Journal of the American Medical Association, 311*(9), 937–947. doi:10.1001/jama.2014.607

Kiecolt-Glaser, J. (1984). Psychosocial modifiers of immunocompetence in medical students. *Psychosomatic Medicine, 46*(1), 7–14.

Kiecolt-Glaser, J. K., & Newton, T. L. (2001). Marriage and health: His and hers. *Psychological Bulletin, 127,* 472–503.

Kihlstrom, J. F. (1997). Hypnosis, memory and amnesia. *Philosophical Transactions of the Royal Society of London B: Biological Sciences, 352,* 1727–1732.

Kihlstrom, J. F. (2005). Dissociative disorders. *Annual Review of Clinical Psychology, 1,* 227–253.

Kihlstrom, J. (2013). Neuro-hypnotism: Prospects for hypnosis and neuroscience. *Cortex, 94*(10), 1891–1898.

Kim, E. S., Park, N., Peterson, C (2011). Dispositional optimism protects older adults from stroke: The Health and Retirement Study. *Stroke, 42*(10), 2855–2859. doi:10.1161/STROKEAHA.111.613448

Kim, E. S., Smith, J., Kubzansky, L. D. (2014). Prospective study of the association between dispositional optimism and incident heart failure. *Circulation: Heart Failure, 7*(3), 394–400. doi:10.1161/CIRCHEARTFAILURE.113.000644.

Kim, J., & Gray, K. A. (2008). Leave or stay? Battered women's decision after intimate partner violence. *Journal of Interpersonal Violence, 23,* 1465–1482.

King, M., Semlyen, J., Tai, S., Killaspy, H., Osborn, D., Popelyuk, D., & Nazareth, I. (2008). A systematic review of mental disorder, suicide, and deliberate self-harm in lesbian, gay and bisexual people. *BMC Psychiatry, 8,* 70–70.

King, S., St. Hilaire, A., & Heidkamp, D. (2010). Prenatal factors in schizophrenia. *Current Directions in Psychological Science, 19,* 209–213.

Kinsey, A, Pomeroy, W., & Martin, C. (1948). *Sexual behavior in the human male.* Bloomington, IN: Indiana University Press.

Kirk, K. M., Bailey, J. M., Dunne, M. P., & Martin, N. G. (2000). Measurement models for sexual orientation in a community twin sample. *Behavioral Genetics, 30,* 345–356.

Kirnan, J., Alfieri, J., Bragger, J., & Harris, R. (2009). An investigation of stereotype threat in employment tests. *Journal of Applied Social Psychology, 39*(2), 359–388.

Kirsch, I., & Lynn, S. (1998). Dissociation theories of hypnosis. *Psychological Bulletin, 123*(1), 100–115.

Kirsch, I., Lynn, S. J., Vigorito, M., & Miller, R. R. (2004). The role of cognition in classical and operant conditioning. *Journal of Clinical Psychology, 60*(4), 369–392.

Kirsch, I., Montgomery, G., & Sapirstein, G. (1995). Hypnosis as an adjunct to cognitive-behavioral psychotherapy: A meta-analysis. *Journal of Consulting and Clinical Psychology, 63*(2), 214–220.

Klaczynski, P. A. (1993). Reasoning schema effects on adolescent rule acquisition and transfer. *Journal of Educational Psychology, 85,* 679–692.

Klatzky, R. L., & Creswell, J. D. (2014). An intersensory interaction account of priming effects—And their absence. *Perspectives on Psychological Science, 9*(1), 49–58. doi:10.1177/1745691613513468

Klatzky, R., & Lederman, S. (2011). Haptic object perception: Spatial dimensionality and relation to vision. *Philosophical Transactions of the Royal Society B: Biological Sciences, 366*(1581), 3097–3105.

Klehe, U., & Latham, G. (2006). What would you do—really or ideally? Constructs underlying the behavior description interview and the situational interview in predicting typical versus maximum performance. *Human Performance, 19*(4), 357–382. doi:10.1207/s15327043hup1904_3

Kleider, H., Pezdek, K., Goldinger, S., & Kirk, A. (2008). Schema-driven source misattribution errors: Remembering the expected from a witnessed event. *Applied Cognitive Psychology, 22*(1), 1–20.

Kleinman, R. E., Hall, H., Green, H., Korzec-Ramirez, D., Patton, K., Pagano, M. E. (2002). Diet, breakfast, and academic performance in children. *Annals of Nutrition and Metabolism, 46*(suppl 1), 24–30.

Klengel, T., & Binder, E. B. (2013). Gene-environment interactions in major depressive disorder. *The Canadian Journal of Psychiatry/La Revue Canadienne de Psychiatrie, 58*(2), 76–83.

Klimstra, T. A., Bleidorn, W., Asendorpf, J. B., van Aken, M. G., & Denissen, J. A. (2013). Correlated change of Big Five personality traits across the lifespan: A search for determinants. *Journal of Research in Personality, 47*(6), 768–777. doi:10.1016/j.jrp.2013.08.004

Kline, T., & Sulsky, L. (2009). Measurement and assessment issues in performance appraisal. *Canadian Psychology/Psychologie Canadienne, 50*(3), 161–171.

Klomek, A., Marrocco, F., Kleinman, M., Schonfeld, I., & Gould, M. (2007). Bullying, depression, and suicidality in adolescents. *Journal of the American Academy of Child & Adolescent Psychiatry, 46,* 40–49.

Koelsch, S., Skouras, S., Fritz, T., Herrera, P., Bonhage, C., Küssner, M., & Jacobs, A. (2013). The roles of superficial amygdala and auditory cortex in music-evoked fear and joy. *NeuroImage, 81,* 49–60.

Koerber, J., Goodman, D., Barnes, J., & Grimm, J. (2013). The dopamine D2 antagonist eticlopride accelerates extinction and delays reacquisition of food self-administration in rats. *Behavioural Pharmacology, 24*(8), 633–639. doi:10.1097/FBP.0000000000000002

Kohlberg, I. (1984). *The psychology of moral development: Essays on moral development* (Vol. II). San Francisco: Harper & Row.

Kohno, M., Morales, A. M., Gharemani, D. G., Hellemann, G., & London, E. D. (2014). Risky decision making, prefrontal cortex, and mesocorticolimbic functional connectivity in methamphetamine dependence. *Journal of the American Medical Association, 71*(7), 812–820.

Kolb, B., Mychasiuk, R., Muhammed, A., & Gibb, R. (2013). Brain plasticity in the developing brain. *Progress in Brain Research, 207*, 35–64. doi:10.1016/B978-0-444-63327-9.00005-9

Komisaruk, B. R., Beyer-Flores, C., & Whipple, B. (2006). *The science of orgasm.* Baltimore, MD: Johns Hopkins University Press.

Koppel, B. S., Brust, J. C., Bronstein, J. C., Youssof, S., Gronseth, G., & Gloss, D. (2014). Systematic review: Efficacy and safety of medical marijuana in selected neurologic disorders: Report of the Guideline Development Subcommittee of the American Academy of Neurology. *Neurology, 82*(17), 1556–1563.

Kornell, N. (2009). Optimising learning using flashcards: Spacing is more effective than cramming. *Applied Cognitive Psychology, 23*, 1297–1317.

Kornell, N., & Bjork, R. A. (2007). The promise and perils of self-regulated study. *Psychonomic Bulletin & Review, 14*(2), 219–224.

Kostic, B., & Cleary, A. M. (2009). Song recognition without identification: When people cannot "name that tune" but can recognize it as familiar. *Journal of Experimental Psychology: General, 138*, 146–159.

Kotchoubey, B., Kaiser, J., Bostanov, V., Lutzenberger, W., & Birbaumer, N. (2009). Recognition of affective prosody in brain-damaged patients and healthy controls: A neurophysiological study using EEG and whole-head MEG. *Cognitive, Affective, & Behavioral Neuroscience, 9*, 153–167.

Kouprina, N., Pavlicek, A., Mochida, G. H., Solomon, G., Gersch, W., Yoon, Y. H., et al. (2002). Accelerated evolution of the ASPM gene controlling brain size begins prior to human brain expansion. *PloS Biology, 2*, 0653–0663.

Kovjanic, S., Schuh, S. C., & Jonas, K. (2013). Transformational leadership and performance: An experimental investigation of the mediating effects of basic needs satisfaction and work engagement. *Journal of Occupational and Organizational Psychology, 86*(4), 543–555.

Kraemer, B., Noll, T., Delsignore, A., Milos, G., Schnyder, U., & Hepp, U. (2006). Finger length ratio (2D:4D) and dimensions of sexual orientation. *Neuropsychobiology, 53*, 210–214.

Krause, D., Kersting, M., Heggestad, E., & Thornton, G. (2006). Incremental validity of assessment center ratings over cognitive ability tests: A study at the executive management level. *International Journal of Selection and Assessment, 14*, 360–371.

Kraut, R., Kiesler, S., Boneva, B., Cummings, J., Helgeson, V., & Crawford, A. (2002). Internet paradox revisited. *Journal of Social Issues, 58*, 49–74.

Kraut, R., Patterson, M., Lundmark, V., Kiesler, S., Mukopadhyay, T., & Scherlis, W. (1998). Internet paradox: A social technology that reduces social involvement and psychological well-being? *American Psychologist, 53*, 1017–1031.

Krendl, A. C., Richeson, J. A., Kelley, W. M., & Heatherton, T. F. (2008). The negative consequences of threat: A functional magnetic resonance imaging investigation of the neural mechanisms underlying women's underperformance in math. *Psychological Science, 19*, 168–175.

Kringelbach, M. L., & Aziz, T. Z. (2009). Deep brain stimulation: Avoiding errors of psychosurgery. *Journal of the American Medical Association, 301*, 1705–1707.

Kringelbach, M. L., Jenkinson, N., Owen, S. L. F., & Aziz, T. Z. (2007). Translational principles of deep brain stimulation. *Nature Reviews Neuroscience, 8*, 623–635.

Kristensen, P., & Bjerkedal, T. (2007). Explaining the relation between birth order and intelligence. *Science, 316*, 1717–1718.

Krizan, Z., & Baron, R. S. (2007). Group polarization and choice-dilemmas: How important is self-categorization? *European Journal of Social Psychology, 37*(1), 191–201.

Kruger, J., Wirtz, D., & Miller, D. (2005). Counterfactual thinking and the first instinct fallacy. *Journal of Personality and Social Psychology, 88*(5), 725–735.

Krystal, A. (2009). A compendium of placebo-controlled trials of the risks/benefits of pharmacological treatments for insomnia: The empirical basis for U.S. clinical practice. *Sleep Medicine Reviews, 13*(4), 265–274.

Kühnel, J., & Sonnentag, S. (2011). How long do you benefit from vacation? A closer look at the fade-out of vacation effects. *Journal of Organizational Behavior, 32*(1), 125–143.

Kundu, P., & Cummins, D. D. (2013). Morality and conformity: The Asch paradigm applied to moral decisions. Social Influence, 8(4), 268-279. doi:10.1080/15534510.2012.727767

Küpper, C. S., Benoit, R. G., Dalgleish, T., & Anderson, M. C. (2014). Direct suppression as a mechanism for controlling unpleasant memories in daily life. *Journal of Experimental Psychology: General, 143*(4), 1443–1449. doi:10.1037/a0036518

LeBlanc, M. M., & Barling, J. (2004). Workplace aggression. *Current Directions In Psychological Science, 13*(1), 9–12. doi:10.1111/j.0963-7214.2004.01301003.x

LaBrie, J. W., Lewis, M. A., Atkins, D. C., Neighbors, C., Zheng, C., Kenney, S. R., … & Larimer, M. E. (2013). RCT of web-based personalized normative feedback for college drinking prevention: Are typical student norms good enough? *Journal of Consulting and Clinical Psychology, 81*(6), 1074–1086. doi:10.1037/a0034087

Lamb, C. S., & Crano, W. D. (2014). Parents' beliefs and children's marijuana use: Evidence for a self-fulfilling prophecy effect. *Addictive Behaviors, 39*(1), 127–132. doi:10.1016/j.addbeh .2013.09.009

Lambert, L. (2006). Half of teachers quit in 5 years. *The Washington Post.* Retrieved from http://www.washingtonpost.com/wp-dyn/content/article/2006/05/08/AR2006050801344.html

Laming, D. (2010). Serial position curves in free recall. *Psychological Review, 117*(1), 93–133.

Lang, A., Craske, M., Brown, M., & Ghaneian, A. (2001). Fear-related state dependent memory. *Cognition & Emotion, 15*, 695–703.

Lang, E. V., Benotsch, E. G., Fick, L. J., Lutgendorf, S., Berbaum, M. L., Berbaum, K. S., Logan, H., & Spiegel, D. (2000). Adjunctive nonpharmacological analgesia for invasive medical procedures: A randomised trial. *Lancet, 355*, 1486–1490.

Langhans, W. (1996a). Metabolic and glucostatic control of feeding. *Proceedings of the Nutritional Society, 55*, 497–515.

Langhans, W. (1996b). Role of the liver in the metabolic control of eating: What we know—and what we do not know. *Neuroscience and Biobehavioral Review, 20*, 145–153.

Langleben, D. D., Loughead, J. W., Bilker, W. B., Ruparel, K., Childress, A. R., Busch, S. I., & Gur, R.C. (2005). Telling truth from lie in individual subjects with fast event–related fMRI. *Human Brain Mapping, 26*, 262–272.

Långström, N., Rahman, Q., Carlström, E., & Lichtenstein, P. (2010). Genetic and environmental effects on same-sex sexual behavior: A population study of twins in Sweden. *Archives of Sexual Behavior, 39*, 75–80.

Lannin, D. G., Vogel, D. L., Brenner, R. E., & Tucker, J. R. (2015). Predicting self-esteem and intentions to seek counseling: The internalized stigma model. *The Counseling Psychologist, 43*(1), 64–93. doi:10.1177/0011000014541550

Lapierre, L. M., Spector, P. E., & Leck, J. D. (2005). Sexual versus nonsexual workplace aggression and victims' overall job satisfaction: A meta-analysis. *Journal of Occupational Health Psychology, 10*(2), 155–169.

Larsen, R., Kasimatis, M., & Frey, K. (1992). Facilitating the furrowed brow: An unobtrusive test of the facial feedback hypothesis applied to unpleasant affect. *Cognition & Emotion, 6*(5), 321–338.

Lasco, M. S., Jordan, T. J., Edgar, M. A., Petito, C. K., Byne, W., et al. (2002). A lack of dimorphism of sex or sexual orientation in the human anterior commissure. *Brain Research, 936*, 95–98.

Laska, K. M., Gurman, A. S., & Wampold, B. E. (2014). Expanding the lens of evidence-based practice in psychotherapy: A common factors perspective. *Psychotherapy, 51*(4), 467–481. doi:10.1037/a0034332

Lasselin, J., Rehman, J. U., Akerstedt, T., Lekander, M., & Axelsson, J. (2014). Effect of long-term sleep restriction and subsequent recovery sleep on the diurnal rhythms of white blood cell subpopulations. *Brain, Behavior, and Immunity*, pii: S0889-1591(14)00479-6. doi: 10.1016/j.bbi.2014.10.004

Latane, B., & Darley, J. M. (1968). Group inhibition of bystander intervention in emergencies. *Journal of Personality and Social Psychology, 10*(3), 215–221.

Latané, B., Williams, K., & Harkins, S. (1979). Many hands make light the work: The causes and consequences of social loafing. *Journal of Personality and Social Psychology, 37*(6), 822–832.

Latane, B., Williams, K., & Harkins, S. (2006). Many hands make the light work: The causes and consequences of social loafing. In J. M. Levine & R. L. Moreland (Eds.), *Small groups* (pp. 297–308). New York: Psychology Press.

Lautenschlager, N. T., Cox, K. L., Flicker, L., Foster, J., van Bockxmeer, F. M., Xiao, J., Greenop, K., & Almeida, O. P. (2008). Effect of physical activity on cognitive function in older adults at risk for Alzheimer disease: A randomized trial. *Journal of the American Medical Association, 300*, 1027–1037.

Lavie, P. (2001). Sleep–wake as a biological rhythm. *Annual Review of Psychology, 5*, 277–303.

Lawrence, G., Callow, N., & Roberts, R. (2013). Watch me if you can: Imagery ability moderates observational learning effectiveness. *Frontiers in Human Neuroscience, 7*, 522. [Epub date 2013 Sep 5].

LeDoux, J. E. (2012). Evolution of human emotion: A view through fear. *Progress in Brain Research, 195*, 431–442.

Ledrich, J., & Gana, K. (2013). Relationship between attributional style, perceived control, self-esteem, and depressive mood in a nonclinical sample: A structural equation-modelling approach. *Psychology and Psychotherapy: Theory, Research and Practice, 86*(4), 413–430. doi:10.1111/j.2044-8341.2012.02067.x

Lee, K, Gizzarone, M., & Ashton, M. (2004). Personality and the likelihood to sexually harass. *Sex Roles, 49*, 59–69.

Leighton, J. P., & Sternberg, R. J. (2003). Reasoning and problem solving. In A. F. Healy & R. W. Proctor (Eds.), *Handbook of psychology: Experimental psychology* (Vol. 4, pp. 623–648). Hoboken, NJ: John Wiley & Sons.

Lemaire, M., El-Hage, W., & Frangou, S. (2014). Reappraising suppression: Subjective and physiological correlates of experiential suppression in healthy adults. *Frontiers In Psychology, 5*. http://dx.doi.org/10.3389/fpsyg.2014.00571

Lemmens, L. H., Arntz, A., Peeters, F., Hollon, S. D., Roefs, A., & Huibers, M. J. (2015). Clinical effectiveness of cognitive therapy v. interpersonal psychotherapy for depression: Results of a randomized controlled trial. *Psychological Medicine, 2*, 1–16. [Epub ahead of print].

LePine, J. A., Piccolo, R. F., Jackson, C. L., Mathieu, J. E., & Saul, J. R. (2008). A meta-analysis of teamwork processes: Tests of a multidimensional model and relationships with team effectiveness criteria. *Personnel Psychology, 61*(2), 273–307.

Lerner, C. A., Sundar, I. K., Watson, R. M., Elder, A., Jones, R., Done, D., … & Rahman, I. (2015). Environmental health hazards of e-cigarettes and their components: Oxidants and copper in e-cigarette aerosols. *Environmental Pollution, 198*, 100–107. doi:10.1016/j.envpol.2014.12.033

Lesch, K-P., Bengel, D., Heils, A., et al. (1996). Association of anxiety-related traits with a polymorphism in the serotonin transporter gene regulatory region. *Science, 273*, 1527–1531.

Leucht, S., Arbter, D., Engel, R., Dienel, A., & Kieser, M. (2009). How effective are second-generation antipsychotic drugs? A meta-analysis of placebo-controlled trials. *Molecular Psychiatry, 14*(4), 429–447.

Levashina, J., Hartwell, C. J., Morgeson, F. P., & Campion, M. A. (2014). The structured employment interview: Narrative and quantitative review of the research literature. *Personnel Psychology, 67*(1), 241–293. doi:10.1111/peps.12052

Levashina, J., Weekley, J. A., Roulin, N., & Hauck, E. (2014). Using blatant extreme responding for detecting faking in high-stakes selection: Construct validity, relationship with general mental ability, and subgroup differences. *International Journal of Selection and Assessment, 22*(4), 371–383. doi:10.1111/ijsa.12084

LeVay, S. (1991). A difference in hypothalamic structure between heterosexual and homosexual men. *Science, 253*, 1034–1037.

Levenston, G. K., Patrick, C. J., Bradley, M. M., & Lang, P. J. (2000). The psychopath as observer: Emotion and attention in picture processing. *Journal of Abnormal Psychology, 109*(3), 373–385.

Levin, R. (1994). Sleep and dreaming characteristics of frequent nightmare subjects in a university population. *Dreaming, 4*, 127–137.

Levine, M., & Crowther, S. (2008). The responsive bystander: How social group membership and group size can encourage as well as inhibit bystander intervention. *Journal of Personality and Social Psychology, 95*(6), 1429–1439.

Levitin, D. J. (2008). *The world in six songs: How the musical brain created human nature.* New York: Dutton.

Levy, B., Pilver, C., Chung, P., & Slade, M. (2014). Subliminal strengthening improving older individuals' physical function over time with an implicit-age-stereotype intervention. *Psychological Science, 25*(12), 2127–2135.

Lewin, C., Wolgers, G., & Herlitz, A. (2001). Sex differences favoring women in verbal but not in visuospatial episodic memory. *Neuropsychology, 15*(2), 165–173.

Lewis, R. L., & Gutmann, L. (2004). Snake venoms and the neuromuscular junction. *Seminars in Neurology, 24*, 175–179.

Li, C. (2010). Primacy effect or recency effect? A long-term memory test of Super Bowl commercials. *Journal of Consumer Behaviour, 9*(1), 32–44.

Lie, H., Rhodes, G., & Simmons, L. (2008). Genetic diversity revealed in human faces. *Evolution, 62*(10), 2473–2486. doi:10.1111/j.1558-5646.2008.00478.x

Liégeois, F., Badeweg, T., Connelly, A., Gadian, D. G., Mishkin, M., & Vargha-Khadem, F. (2003). Language fMRI abnormalities associated with FOXP2 gene mutation. *Nature Neuroscience, 6*, 1230–1237.

Lilienfeld, S. (2007). Psychological treatments that cause harm. *Perspectives on Psychological Science, 2*, 53–70.

Lilienfeld, S. O., & Arkowitz, H. (2009, February). Lunacy and the full moon. *Scientific American, 20*, 64–65.

Lilienfeld, S. O., & Lynn, S. J. (2003). Dissociative identity disorder: Multiple personality, multiple controversies. In S. O. Lilienfeld, J. M. Lohr, & S. J. Lynn (Eds.), *Science and pseudoscience in clinical psychology* (pp. 109–142). New York: Guilford Press.

Lilienfeld, S. O., Lynn, S. J., Kirsch, I., Chaves, J. F., Sarbin, T. R., Ganaway, G. K., & Powell, R. A. (1999). Dissociative identity disorder and the sociocognitive model: Recalling the lessons of the past. *Psychological Bulletin, 125*, 507–523.

Lilienfeld, S. O., Waldman, I. D., Landfield, K., Watts, A. L., Rubenzer, S., & Faschingbauer, T. R. (2012). Fearless dominance and the U.S. presidency: Implications of psychopathic personality traits for successful and unsuccessful political leadership. *Journal of Personality and Social Psychology, 103*(3), 489–505. doi:10.1037/a0029392

Lilienfeld, S. O., Wood, J. M., & Garb, H. N. (2000). The scientific status of projective techniques. *Psychological Science in the Public Interest, 1*, 27–66.

Lillard, A. (1998). Ethnopsychologies: Cultural variations in theories of mind. *Psychological Bulletin, 123*, 3–32.

Lin, C., Davidson, T., & Ancoli-Israel, S. (2008). Gender differences in obstructive sleep apnea and treatment implications. *Sleep Medicine Reviews, 12*(6), 481–496.

Lindau, S. T., Schumm, L. P., Laumann, E. O., Levinson, W., O'Muircheartaigh, C. A., & Waite, L. J. (2007). A study of sexuality and health among older adults in the United States. *New England Journal of Medicine, 357*(8), 762–774.

Linebarger, D., & Walker, D. (2005). Infants' and toddlers' television viewing and language outcomes. *American Behavioral Scientist, 48*(5), 624–645.

Lischetze, T., & Eid, M. (2006). Why extraverts are happier than introverts: The role of mood regulation. *Journal of Personality, 74*, 1127–1161.

Little, A., Jones, B., & Debruine, L. (2011). Facial attractiveness: Evolutionary based research. *Philosophical Transactions of the Royal Society B: Biological Sciences, 366*(1571), 1638–1659. doi:10.1098/rstb.2010.0404

Little, A., & Jones, B. (2012). Variation in facial masculinity and symmetry preferences across the menstrual cycle is moderated by relationship context. *Psychoneuroendocrinology, 37*(7), 999–1008. doi:10.1016/j.psyneuen.2011.11.007.

Liu, H., Waite, L. (2014). Bad marriage, broken heart? Age and gender differences in the link between marital quality and cardiovascular risks among older adults. *Journal of Health and Social Behavior, 55*(4), 403–423. doi:10.1177/0022146514556893.

Liu, J. H., & Latané, B. (1998). Extremitization of attitudes: Does thought- and discussion-induced polarization cumulate? *Basic and Applied Social Psychology, 20*(2), 103–110.

LoBue, V. (2014). Deconstructing the snake: The relative roles of perception, cognition, and emotion on threat detection. *Emotion, 14*(4), 701–711. doi:10.1037/a0035898

Loftus, E. (1975). Leading questions and the eyewitness report. *Cognitive Psychology, 7*, 560–572.

Loftus, E. (1997, August 17). Creating false memories, *Scientific American. 277*(3), 70-75.

Loftus, E. F., & Davis, D. (2006). Recovered memories. *Annual Review of Clinical Psychology, 2*, 469–498.

Loveland, J., Gibson, L., Lounsbury, J., & Huffstetler, B. (2005). Broad and narrow personality traits in relation to the job performance of camp counselors. *Child & Youth Care Forum, 34*, 241–255.

Lovibond, P. F., Calagiuri, B. (2013). Facilitation of voluntary goal-directed action by reward cues. *Psychological Science, 24*(10), 2030–2037.

Luck, A., Pearson, S., Maddern, G., & Hewett, P. (1999). Effects of video information on precolonoscopy anxiety and knowledge: A randomised trial. *Lancet, 354*, 2032–2035.

Ludeke, S. G., & Krueger, R. F. (2013). Authoritarianism as a personality trait: Evidence from a longitudinal behavior genetic study. *Personality and Individual Differences, 55*(5), 480–484. doi:10.1016/j.paid.2013.04.015

Luders, E., Narr, K., Bilder, R., Szeszko, P., Gurbani, M., Hamilton, L., Toga, A. W., & Gaser, C. (2008). Mapping the relationship between cortical convolution and intelligence: Effects of gender. *Cerebral Cortex, 18*(9), 2019–2026.

Luhar, R. B., Sawyer, K. S., Gravitz, Z., Ruiz, S. M., & Oscar-Berman, M. (2013). Brain volumes and neuropsychological performance are related to current smoking and alcoholism history. *Neuropsychiatric Disease and Treatment, 9*, 1767–1784.

Luo, Y., Hawkley, L. C., Waite, L., & Cacioppo, J. T. (2012). Loneliness, health, and mortality in old age: A national longitudinal study. *Social Science & Medicine, 74*, 907–914.

Lutgendorf, S. K., Costanzo, E., & Siegel, S. (2007). Psychosocial influences in oncology: An expanded model of biobehavioral mechanisms. In R. Ader, R. Glaser, N. Cohen, & M. Irwin (Eds.), *Psychoneuroimmunology* (4th ed., pp. 869–895). New York: Academic Press.

Lutgendorf, S., Slavich, G., Degeest, K., Goodheart, M., Bender, D., Thaker, P., ... & Sood, A. (2013). Non-cancer life stressors contribute to impaired quality of life in ovarian cancer patients. *Gynecologic Oncology, 131*(3), 667–673. doi:10.1016/j.ygyno.2013.09.025

Lynam, D. R., & Gudonis, L. (2005). The development of psychopathology. *Annual Review of Clinical Psychology, 1*, 381–407.

Lynn, S. J., & Kirsch, I. (1996). False memories, hypnosis, and fantasy-proneness. *Psychological Inquiry, 7*, 151–155.

Lynn, S., Nash, M., Rhue, J., Frauman, D., & Sweeney, C. (1984). Nonvolition, expectancies, and hypnotic rapport. *Journal of Abnormal Psychology, 93*, 295–303.

Maccoby, E. E., & Martin, J. A. (1983). Socialization in the context of the family: Parent–child interaction. In P. H. Mussen & E. M. Hetherington, *Handbook of child psychology: Vol. 4. Socialization, personality, and social development* (4th ed., pp. 1–101). New York: Wiley.

MacCracken, M. J., & Stadulis, R. E. (1985). Social facilitation of young children's dynamic balance performance. *Journal of Sport Psychology, 7*, 150–165.

Macdonald, K., & Macdonald, T. M. (2010). The peptide that binds: A systematic review of oxytocin and its prosocial effects in humans. *Harvard Review of Psychiatry, 18*, 1–21.

Mack, A. (2003). Inattentional blindness: Looking without seeing. *Current Directions in Psychological Science, 12*, 180–184.

MacLean, E. L., Hare, B., Nunn, C. C., Addessi, E., Amici, F., Anderson, R. C., ... & Zhao, Y. (2013). The evolution of self-control. PNAS, 111(20), E2140–E2148. doi:10.1073/pnas.1323533111

Maes, H. H., Neale, M. C., & Eaves, L. J. (1997). Genetic and environmental factors in relative body weight and human adiposity. *Behavioral Genetics, 27*, 325–351.

Maess, B., Koelsch, S., Gunter, T. C., & Friederici, A. D. (2001). Musical syntax is processed in Broca's area: An MEG study. *Nature Neuroscience, 4*, 540–545.

Magaletta, P. R., Mulvey, T. A., & Grus, C. L. (2010). What can I do with a degree in psychology? Retrieved from http://www.apa.org/workforce/presentations/2010-psychology-degree.pdf

Maguire, E. A., Gadian, D. G., Johnsrude, I. S., Good, C. D., Ashburner, J., Frackowiak, R. S., & Frith, C. D. (2000). Navigation-related structural changes in the hippocampus of taxi drivers. *Proceedings of the National Academy of Sciences, 97*, 4398–4403.

Mahalik, J., Good, G., & Englar-Carlson, M. (2003). Masculinity scripts, presenting concerns, and help seeking: Implications for practice and training. *Professional Psychology: Research and Practice, 34*, 123–131.

Maier, N. F. (1930). Reasoning in humans. I. On direction. *Journal of Comparative Psychology, 10*(2), 115–143.

Maier, N. F. (1931). Reasoning in humans. II. The solution of a problem and its appearance in consciousness. *Journal of Comparative Psychology, 12*(2), 181–194.

Maier, S. F., & Watkins, L. R. (1998). Cytokines for psychologists: Implications of bidirectional immune-to-brain communication for understanding behavior, mood, and cognition. *Psychological Review, 105*, 83–107.

Maloney, E. A., Sattizahn, J. R., & Beilock, S. L. (2014). Anxiety and cognition. *WIREs Cognitive Science, 5*, 403–411. doi:10.1002/wcs.1299

Mampe, B., Friederici, A. D., Christophe, A., & Wermke, K. (2009). Newborns' cry melody is shaped by their native language. *Current Biology, 19*, 1994–1997.

Manard, M., Carabin, D., Jaspar, M., & Collette, F. (2014). Age-related decline in cognitive control: The role of fluid intelligence and processing speed. *BMC Neuroscience, 15*. doi:10.1186/1471-2202-15-7

Mangels, J. A., Butterfield, B., Lamb, J., Good, C., & Dweck, C. S. (2006). Why do beliefs about intelligence influence learning success? A social cognitive neuroscience model. *Social Cognitive and Affective Neuroscience, 1*, 75–86.

Mannes, S. M., & Kinstch, W. (1987). Knowledge organization and text organization. *Cognition and Instruction, 4*, 91–115.

Manning, J. T., Scutt, D., Wilson, J., & Lewis-Jones, D. I. (1998). The ratio of the 2nd to 4th digit length: A predictor of sperm numbers and levels of testosterone, LH and oestrogen. *Human Reproduction, 13*, 3000–3004.

Mansfield, A. K., Addis, M. E., & Courtenay, W. (2005). Measurement of men's help seeking: Development and evaluation of the barriers to help seeking scale. *Psychology of Men & Masculinity, 6*, 95–108.

Marcia, J. E. (1980). Identity in adolescence. In J. Adelson (Ed.), *Handbook of adolescent psychology* (pp. 159–187). New York: Wiley.

Marino, L. (2002). Convergence of complex cognitive abilities in cetaceans and primates. *Brain, Behavior, and Evolution, 59*, 21–32.

Marsh, R., Gerber, A. J., & Peterson, B. S. (2009). Neuroimaging studies of normal brain development and their relevance for understanding childhood neuropsychiatric disorders. *Journal of the American Academy of Child and Adolescent Psychiatry, 47*, 1233–1251.

Martin, L. (1986). "Eskimo words for snow": A case study in the genesis and decay of an anthropological example. *American Anthropologist, 88*, 418–423.

Martin, R. A. (2004). "Sense of humor and physical health: Theoretical issues, recent findings, and future directions." *Humor: International Journal of Humor Research, 17*, 1–19.

Martsh, C. T., & Miller, W. R. (1997). Extraversion predicts heavy drinking in college students. *Personality and Individual Differences, 23*, 153–155.

Maruta, T., Colligan, R. C., Malinchoc, M., & Offord, K. P. (2000). Optimists vs pessimists: Survival rate among medical patients over a 30-year period. *Mayo Clinic Proceedings, 75*, 140–143.

Maslach, C. (2003). Job burnout: New directions in research and intervention. *Current Directions in Psychological Science, 12*, 189–192.

Maslach, C., Jackson, S. E., & Leiter, M. P. (1996). *Maslach burnout inventory* (3rd ed.). Palo Alto, CA: Consulting Psychologists Press.

Maslow, A. (1943). A theory of human motivation. *Psychological Review, 50*, 370–396.

Maslow, A. (1968). *Toward a psychology of being* (2nd ed.). New York: Van Nostrand.

Masters, W., & Johnson, V. (1966). *Human sexual response*. Boston: Little, Brown.

Masters, W. H., & Johnson, V. E. (1966). *Human Sexual Response*. Boston: Little, Brown.

Masuda, A., Suzumura, K., Beauchamp, K. L., Howells, G. N., & Clay, C. (2005). United States and Japanese college students' attitudes towards seeking professional psychological help. *International Journal of Psychology, 40*, 303–313.

Masuda, T., Ellsworth, P. C., Mesquita, B., Leu, J., Tanida, S., & van de Veerdonk, E. (2008). Placing the face in context: Cultural differences in the perception of facial emotion. *Journal of Personality and Social Psychology, 94*, 365–381.

Mather, J. A., & Anderson, R. C. (1993). Personalities of octopuses (Octopus rubescens). *Journal of Comparative Psychology, 107*(3), 336–340.

Matthews, K., & Gump, B. B. (2002). Chronic work stress and marital dissolution increase risk of posttrial mortality in men from the Multiple Risk Factor Intervention Trial. *Archives of Internal Medicine, 162*, 309–315.

Matute, H. & Blanco, F. (2014). Reducing the illusion of control when an action is followed by an undesired outcome. *Psychonomic Bulletin and Review, 21*, 1087-1093.

Matzel, L. D., Sauce, B., & Wass, C. (2013). The architecture of intelligence: Converging evidence from studies of humans and animals. *Current Directions In Psychological Science, 22*(5), 342–348. doi:10.1177/0963721413491764

Maxfield, M., Greenberg, J., Pyszczynski, T., Weise, D. R., Kosloff, S., Soenke, M., Abeyta, A. A., & Blatter, J. (2014). Increases in generative concern among older adults following reminders of mortality. *International Journal of Aging and Human Development, 79*(1), 1–21.

Mazzoni, G., & Memon, A. (2003). Imagination can create false autobiographical memories. *Psychological Science, 14*, 186–188.

McAdams, D. P., & Pals, J. L. (2006). A new Big Five: Fundamental principles for an integrative science of personality. *American Psychologist, 61*, 204–217.

McAndrew, F. T. (2002). New evolutionary perspectives on altruism: Multilevel-selection and costly-signaling theories. *Current Directions in Psychological Science, 11*(2), 79–82.

McAnulty, G., Duffy, F. H., Butler, S., Bernstein, J. H., Zurakowski, D., & Als, H. (2010). Effects of newborn individualized developmental care and assessment program (NIDCAP) at age 8 years: Preliminary data. *Clinical Pediatrics (Philadelphia), 49*, 258–270.

McAnulty, G., Duffy, F. H., Butler, S., Parad, R., Ringer, S., Zurakowski, D., & Als, H. (2009). Individualized developmental care for a large sample of very preterm infants: Health, neurobehaviour and neurophysiology. *Acta Paediatrica, 98*, 1920–1926.

McCarthy, A., & Garavan, T. (2007). Understanding acceptance of multisource feedback for management development. *Personnel Review, 36*, 903–917.

McCauley, C. (1987). The nature of social influence in groupthink: Compliance and internatalization. *Journal of Personality and Social Psychology, 57*, 250–260.

McClelland, D. C. (1985). How motives, skills, and values determine what people do. *American Psychologist, 40*, 812–825.

McCrae, R. R., Martin, T. A., Hrebickova, M., Urbanek, T., Boomsma, D. I., Willemsen, G., & Costa, P. T., Jr. (2008). Personality trait similarity between spouses in four cultures. *Journal of Personality, 76*, 1137–1164.

McCrae, R. R., & Costa, P. (1987). Validation of the Five-Factor Model of personality across instruments and observers. *Journal of Personality and Social Psychology, 52*(1), 81–90.

McCrae, R. R., Terracciano, A., et al. (2005). Personality profiles of cultures: Aggregate personality traits. *Journal of Personality and Social Psychology, 89*, 407–425.

McCullough, M. E., Hoyt, W. T., Larson, D. B., Koenig, H. G., & Thoresen, C. E. (2000). Religious involvement and mortality: A meta-analytic review. *Health Psychology, 19*, 211–222.

McCullough, M. E., & Willoughby, B. L. (2009). Religion, self-regulation, and self-control: Associations, explanations, and implications. *Psychological Bulletin, 135*, 69–93.

McDaid, C., Duree, K. H., Griffin, S. C., Weatherly, H. L. A., Stradling, J. R., Davies, J. O, Sculpher, M. J., & Westwood, M. E. (2009). A systematic review of continuous positive airway pressure for obstructive sleep apnoea–hypopnoea syndrome. *Sleep Science Reviews, 13*, 427–436.

McGlashan, T. H., Zipursky, R. B., Perkins, D., Addington, J., Miller, T., & Woods, S. W. (2006). Randomized double-blind clinical trial of olanzapine versus placebo in patients prodromally symptomatic for psychosis. *American Journal of Psychiatry, 163*, 790–799.

McGorry, P. D., Yung, A. R., Phillips, L. J., Yuen, H. P., Francey, S., & Cosgrave, E. M. (2002). Randomized controlled trial of interventions designed to reduce the risk of progression to first-episode psychosis in a clinical sample with subthreshold symptoms. *Archives of General Psychiatry, 59*, 921–928.

McGruder, J. (2004). Disease models of mental illness and aftercare patient education: Critical observations from meta-analyses, cross-cultural practice and anthropological study. *British Journal of Occupational Therapy, 67*, 310–318.

McKimmie, B. M., Terry, D. J., & Hogg, M. A. (2009). Dissonance reduction in the context of group membership: The role of metaconsistency. *Group Dynamics: Theory, Research, and Practice, 13*(2), 103–119.

McKinney, K. G. (2009). Initial evaluation of Active Minds: A student organization dedicated to reducing the stigma of mental illness. *Journal of College Student Psychotherapy, 23*(4), 281–301.

McNally, R. J., Lasko, N. B., Clancy, S. A., Macklin, M. L., Pitman, R. K., & Orr, S. P. (2004). Psychophysiological responding during script-driven imagery in people reporting abduction by space aliens. *Psychological Science, 15*, 493–497.

Medin, D. L., & Atran, S. (2004). The Native Mind: Biological Categorization and Reasoning in Development and Across Cultures. *Psychological Review, 111*(4), 960–983. doi:10.1037/0033-295X.111.4.960

Mednick, S. C., Cai, D. J., Shuman, T., Anagnostaras, S., & Wixted, J. T. (2011). An opportunistic theory of cellular and systems consolidation. *Trends In Neurosciences, 34*(10), 504–514. doi:10.1016/j.tins.2011.06.003

Meehl, P. (1990). Toward an integrated theory of schizotaxia, schizotypy, and schizophrenia. *Journal of Personality Disorders, 4*, 1–99.

Meeus, W. (2011). The study of adolescent identity formation 2000–2010: A review of longitudinal research. *Journal of Research on Adolescence, 21*, 75–94.

Meeus, W., van de Schoot, R., Keijsers, L., & Branje, S. (2012). Identity statuses as developmental trajectories: A five-wave longitudinal study in early-to-middle and middle-to-late adolescents. *Journal of Youth and Adolescence, 41*, 1008–1021.

Mehl, M. R., & Pennebaker, J. W. (2003). The sounds of social life: A psychometric analysis of students' daily social environments and natural conversations. *Journal of Personality and Social Psychology, 84*, 857–870.

Melton, G. B., Petrila, J., Poythress, N. G., & Slobogin, C. (2007). *Psychological evaluations for the courts: A handbook for mental health professionals and lawyers* (3rd ed.). New York: Guilford Press.

Meltzoff, A. N., & Moore, M. K. (1977). Imitation of facial and manual gestures by human neonates. *Science, 198*, 75–78.

Melzack, R., & Wall, P. D. (1965). Pain mechanisms: A new theory. *Science, 150*, 971–979.

Melzack, R., & Wall, P. D. (1982). *The challenge of pain*. New York: Basic Books.

Menary, K., Collins, P. F., Porter, J. N., Muetzel, R., Olson, E. A., Kumar, V., … & Luciana, M. (2013). Associations between cortical thickness and general intelligence in children, adolescents and young adults. *Intelligence, 41*(5), 597–606. doi:10.1016/j.intell.2013.07.010

Meneghel, I., Salanova, M., & Martínez, I. M. (2014). Feeling good makes us stronger: How team resilience mediates the effect of positive emotions on team performance. *Journal of Happiness Studies.* doi:10.1007/s10902-014-9592-6

Meriac, J. P., Hoffman, B. J., & Woehr, D. J. (2014). A conceptual and empirical review of thestructure of assessment center dimensions. *Journal of Management, 40*(5), 1269–1296. doi:10.1177/0149206314522299

Messer, D. (2000). State of the art: Language acquisition. *The Psychologist, 13*, 138–143.

Meston, C. M., & Ahrold, T. (2010). Ethnic, gender, and acculturation influences on sexual behaviors. *Archives of Sexual Behavior, 39*, 179–189.

Meston, C. M., & Buss, D. M. (2007). Why humans have sex. *Archives of Sexual Behavior, 36*, 477–507.

Meston, C. M., Levin, R. J., Sipski, M. L., Hull, E. M., & Heiman, J. R. (2004). Women's orgasm. *Annual Review of Sex Research, 15*, 173–257.

Mezulis, A. H., Abramson, A. Y., Hyde, J. S., & Hankin, B. L. (2004). Is there a universal positivity bias in attributions? A meta-analytic review of individual, developmental, and cultural differences in the self-serving attributional bias. *Psychological Bulletin, 130*, 711–747.

Mikulincer, M., & Shaver, P. R. (2005). Attachment security, compassion, and altruism. *Current Directions in Psychological Science, 14*, 34–38.

Milgram, S. (1963). Behavioral study of obedience. *Journal of Abnormal and Social Psychology, 67*, 371–378.

Milgram, S. (1974). *Obedience to authority: An experimental view.* New York: Harpercollins.

Miller, A. G. (1986). *The obedience experiments: A case study of controversy in social science.* New York: Praeger.

Miller, G. (1956). The magical number seven, plus or minus two: Some limits on our capacity for processing information. *Psychological Review, 63*(2), 81–97.

Miller, I. J., Jr., & Reedy, F. E. (1990). Variations in human taste bud density and intensity perception. *Physiology and Behavior, 47*, 1213–1219.

Milling, L. (2009). Response expectancies: A psychological mechanism of suggested and placebo analgesia. *Contemporary Hypnosis, 26*(2), 93–110.

Minio-Paluello, I., Avenanti, A., & Aglioti, S. (2006). Left hemisphere dominance in reading the sensory qualities of others' pain? *Social Neuroscience, 1*, 320–333.

Mischel, W. (1968). *Personality and assessment.* New York: Wiley.

Mischel, W., & Shoda, Y. (1998). Reconciling processing dynamics and personality dispositions. *Annual Review of Psychology, 49*, 229–258.

Mishara, B. L., Chagnon, F., Daigle, M., Balan, B., Raymond, S., Marcoux, I., Bardon, C., Campbell, J. K., & Berman, A. (2007). Which helper behaviors and intervention styles are related to better short-term outcomes in telephone crisis intervention? Results from a silent monitoring study of calls to the U.S. 1-800-SUICIDE Network. *Suicide and Life Threatening Behavior, 37*, 308–321.

Mishara, B. L., & Daigle, M. S. (1997). Effects of different telephone intervention styles with suicidal callers at two suicide prevention centers: An empirical investigation. *American Journal of Community Psychology, 5*, 861–885.

Mitre, N., Foster, R. C., Lanningham-Foster, L., & Levine, J. A. (2011). The energy expenditure of an activity-promoting video game compared to sedentary video games and TV watching. *Journal of Pediatric Endocrinology and Metabolism, 24*(9–10), 689–695.

Mizushige, T., Inoue, K., & Fushiki, T. (2007). Why is fat so tasty? Chemical reception of fatty acid on the tongue. *Journal of Nutritional Science and Vitaminology, 53*(1), 1–4.

Modinos, G., Iyegbe, C., Prata, D., Rivera, M., Kempton, M., Valmaggia, L., ... & Mcguire, P. (2013). Molecular genetic gene–environment studies using candidate genes in schizophrenia: A systematic review. *Schizophrenia Research, 15*(2–3), 356–365.

Molina, J., & Mendoza, M. (2006). Change of attitudes towards hypnosis after a training course. *Australian Journal of Clinical & Experimental Hypnosis, 34*(2), 146–161.

Montgomery, G. H., DuHamel, K. N., & Redd, W. H. (2000). A metaanalysis of hypnotically induced analgesia: How effective is hypnosis? *International Journal of Clinical and Experimental Hypnosis, 48*(2), 138–153.

Montgomery, G. H., Hallquist, M. N., Schnur, J. B., David, D., Silverstein, J. H., & Bovbjerg, D. H. (2010). Mediators of a brief hypnosis intervention to control side effects in breast surgery patients: Response expectancies and emotional distress. *Journal of Consulting and Clinical Psychology, 78*(1), 80–88.

Moore, D. W. (2005). Three in four Americans believe in paranormal. Princeton, NJ; Gallup News Service. Retrieved June 4, 2010, from www.gallup.com/poll/ 16915/three-four-americans-believeparanormal.aspx

Morehead, G., Ference, R., & Neck, C. P. (1991). Group decision fiascoes continue: Space Shuttle Challenger and a revised groupthink framework. *Human Relations, 44*, 539–550.

Morgan, N., Irwin, M.R., Chung, M., & Wang, C. (2014). The effects of mind-body therapies on the immune system: Meta-analysis. *PLoS One, 9*, e100903.

Morgan, H. L., Turner, D.C., Corlett, P.R. et al. (2010). Exploring the impact of ketamine on the experience of illusory body ownership. *Biological Psychiatry, 69*, 35–41.

Morgeson, F. P., Reider, M. H., & Campion, M. A. (2005). Selecting individuals in team settings: The importance of social skills, personality characteristics, and teamwork knowledge. *Personnel Psychology, 58*(3), 583–611.

Morin, C., Bootzin, R., Buysse, D., Edinger, J., Espie, C., & Lichstein, K. (2006). Psychological and behavioral treatment of insomnia: Update of the recent evidence (1998–2004). *Sleep: Journal of Sleep and Sleep Disorders Research, 29*(11), 1398–1414.

Morris, J., Jordan, C., & Breedlove, S. (2004, October). Sexual differentiation of the vertebrate nervous system. *Nature Neuroscience, 7*(10), 1034–1039.

Moscicki, E. K. (2001). Epidemiology of completed and attempted suicide: Toward a framework for prevention. *Clinical Neuroscience Research, 1*, 310–323.

Murase, T. (2014). Japanese mothers' utterances about agents and actions during joint picture-book reading. *Frontiers in Psychology, 5*(357).

Murman, N. M., Buckingham, K. E., Fontilea, P., Villanueva, R., Leventhal, B., & Hinshaw, S. P. (2014). Let's Erase the Stigma (LETS): A quasi-experimental evaluation of adolescent-led school groups intended to reduce mental illness stigma. *Child & Youth Care Forum, 43*(5), 621–637. doi:10.1007/s10566-014-9257-y

Murphy, E., Hou, L., Maher, B., Woldehawariat, G., Kassem, L., Akula, N., ... & Mcmahon, F. (2013). Race, genetic ancestry and response to antidepressant treatment for major depression. *Neuropsychopharmacology, 38*, 2598–2606.

Murray, A. J., Knight, N. S., Cochlin, L. W., McAleese, S., Deacon, R. M. J., Rawlins, N. P., & Clarke, K. (2009). Deterioration of physical performance and cognitive function in rats with short-term high-fat feeding. *FASEB Journal, 23*, 4353–4360.

Murrough, J., Iosifescu, D., Chang, L., Jurdi, R., Green, C., Perez, A., ... & Mathew, S. (2013). Antidepressant efficacy of ketamine in treatment-resistant major depression: A two-site randomized controlled trial. *American Journal of Psychiatry, 170*(10), 1134–1142.

Murtagh, D. R., & Greenwood, K. M. (1995). Identifying effective psychological treatments for insomnia: A meta-analysis. *Journal of Consulting and Clinical Psychology, 63*, 79–89.

Nabi, R. L. (2002). Anger, fear, uncertainty, and attitudes: A test of the cognitive-functional model. *Communication Monographs, 69*(3), 204–216.

Nahamis, E., Shepard, J., & Reuter, S. (2014). It's OK if 'my brain made me do it:' People's intuitions about free will and neuroscientific prediction. *Cognition, 133*(2): 502–516.

Nairne, J. S. (1996). Short-term/working memory. In E. L. Bjork & R. A. Bjork (Eds.), *Memory* (pp. 101–126). San Diego, CA: Academic Press.

Naj, A. C., Jun, G., Beecham, G.W., Wang, L-S., Var-darajan, B.N., Buros, J., et al. (2011). Common variants of MS4A4/MS4A6E, CD2AP, CD33 and EPHA 1 are associated with late-onset Alzheimer's disease. *Nature Genetics, 43,* 436–441.

Nakajima, A., & Tang, Y-P. (2005). Genetic approaches to the molecular/neuronal mechanisms underlying learning and memory in the mouse. *Journal of Pharmacological Sciences, 99,* 1–5.

Nakamura, M., Kanbayashi, T., Sugiura, T., & Inoue, Y. (2011). Relationship between clinical characteristics of narcolepsy and CSF orexin-A levels. *Journal of Sleep Research, 20*(1, Pt1), 45–49.

Nash, R., Wade, K., & Lindsay, D. (2009). Digitally manipulating memory: Effects of doctored videos and imagination in distorting beliefs and memories. *Memory & Cognition, 37*(4), 414–424.

National Association for College Admission Counseling (NACAC). (2008). Report of the Commission on the Use of Standardized Tests in Undergraduate Admission. Retrieved from http://www.nacacnet.org/research/PublicationsResources/Marketplace/research/Pages/TestingCommissionReport.aspx

National Institute on Alcohol and Addiction (2015). College Drinking. Retrieved from http://www.niaaa.nih.gov/alcohol-health/special-populations-co-occurring-disorders/college-drinking.

National Institutes of Health. (2009, July). Taste disorders. NIH Publication No. 09-3231A. Retrieved June 8, 2011, from http://www.nidcd.nih.gov/health/smelltaste/taste.html

National Institutes of Health (NIH). (2009). Statistics related to overweight and obesity. Retrieved February 15, 2010, from http://win.niddk.nih.gov/statistics/#preval

National Institutes of Mental Health (2015). Serious Mental Illness (SMI) Among U.S. Adults. Retrieved from http://www.nimh.nih.gov/health/statistics/prevalence/serious-mental-illness-smi-among-us-adults.shtml

National Institute of Mental Health (NIMH). (2011). Retrieved from http://www.nimh.nih.gov/statistics/3USE_MT_ADULT.shtml

National Highway and Traffic Safety Administration (2010). Traffic Safety Facts: Research Note. Retrieved from http://www-nrd.nhtsa.dot.gov/Pubs/811650.pdf

National Science Foundation. (2010). National science indicators. Retrieved from http://www.nsf.gov/statistics/seind10/c7/c7s2.htm

Neisser, U. (1979). The control of information pickup in selective looking. In A.D. Pick (Ed.), *Perception and its development: A tribute to Eleanor Gibson* (pp. 201–219). Hillsdale, NJ: Erlbaum.

Neisser, U. (2000). Snapshots or benchmarks? In U. Neisser & I. Hyman (Eds.), *Memory observed: Remembering in natural contexts* (2nd ed., pp. 68–74). New York: Worth Publishing.

Neisser, U., Boodoo, G., Bouchard, T. J., Boykin, A. W., Brody, N., Ceci, S. J., Halpern, D. F., Loehlin, J. C., Perloff, R., Sternberg, R. J., & Urbina, S. (1996). Intelligence: Knowns and unknowns. *American Psychologist, 51,* 77–101.

Neisser, U., & Harsch, N. (1992). Phantom flashbulbs: False recollections of hearing the news about Challenger. In E. Winograd & U. Neisser (Eds.), *Affect and accuracy in recall: Studies in flashbulb memories* (pp. 9–31). Cambridge, UK: Cambridge University Press.

Nelson, C. A., Zeanah, C. H., Fox, N. A., Marshall, P. J., Smyke, A. T., & Guthrie, D. (2007). Cognitive recovery in socially deprived young children: The Bucharest early intervention project. *Science, 318,* 1937–1940.

Nesse, R., & Ellsworth, P. (2009). Evolution, emotions, and emotional disorders. *American Psychologist, 64,* 129–139.

Newell, B., & Shanks, D. (2014). Unconscious influences on decision making: A critical review. *Behavioral and Brain Sciences, 37,* 1–19.

Newman, M. G., & Llera, S. J. (2011). A novel theory of experiential avoidance in generalized anxiety disorder: A review and synthesis of research supporting a contrast avoidance model of worry. *Clinical Psychology Review, 31,* 371–382.

Ngun, T. C. & Vilain, E. (2014). The biological basis of human sexual orientation: Is there a role for epigenetics? *Advanced Genetics, 86,* 167–184. doi:10.1016/B978-0-12-800222-3.00008-5. PMID: 25172350

Nguyen, H., & Ryan, A. (2008). Does stereotype threat affect test performance of minorities and women? A meta-analysis of experimental evidence. *Journal of Applied Psychology, 93*(6), 1314–1334.

Nicholas, J. G., & Geers, A. E. (2007). Will they catch up? The role of age at cochlear implantation in the spoken language development of children with severe to profound hearing loss. *Journal of Speech, Language, and Hearing Research, 50,* 1048–1062.

Nielsen, K., Randall, R., Yarker, J., & Brenner, S. (2008). The effects of transformational leadership on followers' perceived work characteristics and psychological well-being: A longitudinal study. *Work & Stress, 22*(1), 16–32.

Nielsen, M., & Tomaselli, K. (2010).Overimitation in Kalahari Bushman children and the origins of human cultural cognition. *Psychological Science, 21,* 729–736.

Nielson, K., Yee, D., & Erickson, K. (2005). Memory enhancement by a semantically unrelated emotional arousal source induced after learning. *Neurobiology of Learning and Memory, 84,* 49–56.

Nijenhuis, J., Jongeneel-Grimen, B., & Kirkegaard, E. O. (2014). Are Headstart gains on the g factor? A meta-analysis. *Intelligence, 46,* 209–215. doi:10.1016/j.intell.2014.07.001

Niparko, J. K., Tobey, E. A., Thal, D. J., Eisenberg, L. S., Wang, N. Y., Quittner, A. L., Fink, N. E. (2010). Spoken language development in children following cochlear implantation. *Journal of the American Medical Association, 303,* 1498–1506.

Nisbett, R. (2009). *Intelligence and how to get it: Why schools and cultures count.* New York: W. W. Norton.

Nisbett, R. E., Aronson, J., Blair, C., Dickens, W., Flynn, J., Halpern, D. F., & Turkheimer, E. (2012). Intelligence: New findings and theoretical developments. *American Psychologist, 67*(2), 130–159. doi:10.1037/a0026699

Nisbett, R. E., Caputo, C., Legant, P., & Marecek, J. (1973). Behavior as seen by the actor and as seen by the observer. *Journal of Personality and Social Psychology, 27*(2), 154–164.

Nisbett, R. E., & Cohen, D. (1996). *Culture of honor: The psychology of violence in the South.* Boulder, CO: Westview Press.

Nisbett, R. E., & Masuda, T. (2003). Culture and point of view. *Proceedings of the National Academy of Sciences, 100,* 11163–11170.

Norrholm, S. D., Vervliet, B., Jovanovic, T., Boshoven, W., Myers, K. M., Davis, M., Rothbaum, B., & Duncan, E. (2008). Timing of extinction relative to acquisition: A parametric analysis of fear extinction in humans. *Behavioral Neuroscience, 122,* 1016–1030.

Norton, A., Zipse, L., Marchina, S., & Schlaug, G. (2009). Melodic intonation therapy: Shared insights on how it is done and why it might help. *Annals of the New York Academy of Sciences, 1169,* 431–436.

Nosek, B. A. (2007). Implicit–explicit relations. *Current Directions in Psychological Science, 16,* 65–69.

Nowack, K. M., & Mashihi, S. (2012). Evidence-based answers to 15 questions about leveraging 360-degree feedback. *Consulting Psychology Journal: Practice And Research, 64*(3), 157–182. doi:10.1037/a0030011

Nyi, P. P., Lai, E. P., Lee, D. Y., Biglete, S. A., Torrecer, G. I., & Anderson, I. B. (2010). Influence of age on Salvia divinorum use: Results of an Internet survey. *Journal of Psychoactive Drugs, 42,* 385–392.

O'Connor, A. R., & Moulin, C. J. (2006). Normal patterns of déjà experience in a healthy, blind male: Challenging optical pathway delay theory. *Brain and Cognition, 62,* 246–249.

O'Connor, A., & Moulin, C. (2008). The persistence of erroneous familiarity in an epileptic male: Challenging perceptual theories of déjà vu activation. *Brain and Cognition, 68*(2), 144–147.

O'Connor, A. R., & Moulin, C. J. (2010). Recognition without identification, erroneous familiarity, and déjà vu. *Current Psychiatry Reports, 12,* 165–173.

O'Leary, C. M., Nassar, N., Kurinczuk, J. J., de Klerk, N., Geelhoed, E., Elliot, E. J., & Bower, C. (2010). Prenatal alcohol exposure and risk of birth defects. *Pediatrics, 126,* e843–e850.

Ohlsson, A., & Jacobs, S. (2013). NIDCAP: A systematic review and meta-analyses of randomized controlled trials. *Pediatrics, 131*(3), e881–e893.

Öhman, A., & Mineka, S. (2001). Fears, phobias, and preparedness: Toward an evolved module of fear and fear learning. *Psychological Review, 108,* 483– 522.

O'kane, G., Kensinger, E. A., & Corkin, S. (2004). Evidence for semantic learning in profound amnesia: An investigation with patient H.M. *Hippocampus, 14*(4), 417–425. doi:10.1002/hipo.20005

Olds, J., & Milner, P. (1954). Positive reinforcement produced by electrical stimulation of the septal area and other regions of the rat brain. *Journal of Comparative and Physiological Psychology, 47*, 419–428.

Olfson, M., & Marcus, S. C. (2009). National patterns in antidepressant medication treatment. *Archives of General Psychiatry, 66*, 848–856.

Olfson, M, & Marcus, S. C. (2010). National trends in outpatient psychotherapy. *American Journal of Psychiatry, 167*, 1456–1463.

Olfson, M., Marcus, S. C., Druss, B., & Pincus, H. A. (2002). National trends in the use of outpatient therapy. *American Journal of Psychiatry, 159*, 1914–1920.

Olivo, E., Dodson-Lavelle, B., Wren, A., Fang, Y., & Oz, M. (2009). Feasibility and effectiveness of a brief meditation-based stress management intervention for patients diagnosed with or at risk for coronary heart disease: A pilot study. *Psychology, Health & Medicine, 14*(5), 513–523.

Olson, M. A., & Fazio, R. H. (2001). Implicit attitude formation through classical conditioning. *Psychological Science, 12*, 413–417.

Olson, K. R., Lambert, A. J., & Zacks, J. M. (2004). Graded structure and the speed of category verification: On the moderating effects of anticipatory control for social vs. non-social categories. *Journal of Experimental Social Psychology, 40*(2), 239–246.

Ones, D., Viswesvaran, C., & Schmidt, F. (1993). Comprehensive meta-analysis of integrity test validities: Findings and implications for personnel selection and theories of job performance. *Journal of Applied Psychology, 78*(4), 679–703.

Onken, L. S. (2015). Cognitive training: Targeting cognitive processes in the development of behavioral interventions. *Clinical Psychological Science, 3*(1), 39–44.

Ophir, E., Nass, C., & Wagner, A. D. (2009). Cognitive control in media multitaskers. *Proceedings of the National Academy of Sciences, 106*, 15583–15587.

Orne, M. T. (1962). On the social psychology of the psychological experiment: With particular reference to demand characteristics and their implications. *American Psychologist, 17*, 776–783.

Owen, A. M., & Coleman, M. R. (2008). Functional neuroimaging of the vegetative state. *Nature Reviews Neuroscience, 9*, 235–243.

Owen, A. M., Coleman, M. R., Boly, M., et al. (2006). Detecting awareness in the vegetative state. *Science, 313*, 1402.

Oxford English dictionary. (2011). Retrieved June 16, 2011, from http://dictionary.oed.com/entrance.dtl

Paivio, A. (1991). Dual coding theory: Retrospect and current status. *Canadian Journal of Psychology, 45*, 255–287.

Paller, K. (2004). Electrical signals of memory and of the awareness of remembering. *Current Directions in Psychological Science, 13*, 49–55.

Pallesen, S., Hilde, I., Havik, O., & Nielsen, G. (2001). Clinical assessment and treatment of insomnia. *Professional Psychology: Research and Practice, 32*(2), 115–124.

Pan, L., Blanck, H., Sherry, B., Dalenius, K., & Grummer-Strawn, L. (2012). Trends in the prevalence of extreme obesity among US preschool-aged children living in low-income families, 1998-2010. *JAMA, 308*(24), 2563–2565. doi:10.1001/jama.2012.108099

Panksepp, J., & Panksepp, J. B. (2013). Toward a cross-species understanding of empathy. *Trends in Neurosciences, 36*(8), 489–496. doi:10.1016/j.tins.2013.04.009

Papies, E. K., & Hamstra, P. (2010). Goal priming and eating behavior: Enhancing self-regulation by environmental cues. *Health Psychology, 29*(4), 384–388. doi:10.1037/a0019877

Pardini, D. A., & Phillips, M. (2010). Neural responses to emotional and neutral facial expressions in chronically violent men. *Journal of Psychiatry and Neuroscience, 35*, 390–398.

Park, D. C., & Huang, C-M. (2010). Culture wires the brain: A cognitive neuroscience perspective. *Perspectives on Psychological Science, 5*, 391–400.

Park, H. I., Jacob, A. C., Wagner, S. H., & Baiden, M. (2014). Job control and burnout: A meta-analytic test of the Conservation of Resources model. *Applied Psychology: An International Review, 63*(4), 607–642. doi:10.1111/apps.12008

Park, S., Püschel, J., Sauter, B. H., Rentsch, M., & Hell, D. (1999). Spatial working memory deficits and clinical symptoms of schizophrenia: A 4-month follow-up study. *Biological Psychiatry, 46*, 392–400.

Park, T. J., Lu, Y., Jüttner, R., Smith, E. S., Hu, J., Band, A., et al. (2008). Selective inflammatory pain insensitivity in the African naked mole-rat (Heterocephalus glaber). *PLoS Biology, 6*, e13.

Parrot, A. C. (2014). The potential dangers of using MDMA for psychotherapy. *Journal of Psychoactive Drugs, 46*(1), 37–43.

Parsons, H. M. (1974). What happened at Hawthorne?: New evidence suggests the Hawthorne effect resulted from reinforcement contingencies. *Science, 183*, 922–932.

Pascual, A., & Guéguen, N. (2005). Foot-in-the-door and door-in-the-face: A comparative meta-analytic study. *Psychological Reports, 96*(1), 122–128.

Pashler, H. (1994). Dual-task interference in simple tasks: Data and theory. *Psychological Bulletin, 116*(2), 220–244.

Pashler, H., McDaniel, M., Rohrer, D., & Bjork, R. (2008). Learning styles: Concepts and evidence. *Psychological Science in the Public Interest,9*(3), 105–119.

Patihis, L., Ho, L. Y., Tingen, I. W., Lilienfeld, S. O., & Loftus, E. F. (2014). Are the 'memory wars' over? A scientist-practitioner gap in beliefs about repressed memory. *Psychological Science, 25*(2), 519–530. doi:10.1177/0956797613510718

Paulesu, E., Frith, C., & Frackowiak, R. (1993). The neural correlates of the verbal component of working memory. *Nature, 362*, 342–345.

Paustian-Underdahl, S. C., Walker, L. S., & Woehr, D. J. (2014). Gender and perceptions of leadership effectiveness: A meta-analysis of contextual moderators. *Journal of Applied Psychology, 99*(6), 1129–1145. doi:10.1037/a0036751

Payne, J. D., & Kensinger, E. A. (2010). Sleep's role in the consolidation of emotional episodic memories. *Current Directions in Psychological Science, 19*, 290–295.

Payne, S. C., & Huffman, A. H. (2005). A longitudinal examination of the influence of mentoring on organizational commitment and turnover. *Academy of Management Journal, 48*(1), 158–168.

Peeters, M., & Giuliano, F. (2007). Central neurophysiology and dopaminergic control of ejaculation. *Neuroscience and Biobehavioral Reviews, 32*, 438–453.

Penn, D. L., & Combs, D. (2000). Modification of affect perception deficits in schizophrenia. *Schizophrenia Research, 46*, 217–229.

Perlman, D., Salomons, T., Davidson, R., & Lutz, A. (2010). Differential effects on pain intensity and unpleasantness of two meditation practices. *Emotion, 10*(1), 65–71.

Perloff, L. S., & Fetzer, B. K. (1986). Self-other judgments and perceived vulnerability to victimization. *Journal of Personality and Social Psychology, 50*, 502–510.

Perry, W., Feifel, D., Minassian, A., Bhattacharjie, B. S., & Braff, D. L. (2002). Information processing deficits in acutely psychotic schizophrenia patients medicated and unmedicated at the time of admission. *American Journal of Psychiatry, 159*, 1375–1381.

Petersen, J., & Hyde, J. (2010). A meta-analytic review of research on gender differences in sexuality, 1993–2007. *Psychological Bulletin, 136*(1), 21–38. doi:10.1037/a0017504

Peterson, L., & Peterson, M. (1959). Short-term retention of individual verbal items. *Journal of Experimental Psychology, 58*, 193–198.

Petrosino, A., Turpin-Petrosino, C., Hollis-Peel, M.E., & Lavenberg, J.G. (2013). 'Scared Straight' and other juvenile awareness programs for preventing juvenile delinquency. *Cochrane Database Systematic Reviews 30*, 4, CD002796.

Petty, R. E., Wegener, D. T., & Fabrigar, L. R. (1997). Attitudes and attitude change. *Annual Review of Psychology, 48*, 609–647.

Pew Research Center. (2013). Public's Views on Human Evolution. Retrieved March 19, 2015, from http://www.pewforum.org/2013/12/30/publics-views-on-human-evolution/

Piaget, J., & Inhelder, B. (1956). *The child's conception of space.* Boston: Routledge & Kegan Paul.

Pietschnig, J., Tran, U. S., & Voracek, M. (2013). Item-response theory modeling of IQ gains (the Flynn effect) on crystallized intelligence: Rodgers' hypothesis yes, Brand's hypothesis perhaps. *Intelligence, 41*(6), 791–801. doi:10.1016/j.intell.2013.06.005

Pilley, J., & Reid, A. (2011). Border collie comprehends object names as verbal referents. *Behavioural Processes, 86*(2), 184–195. doi:10.1016/j.beproc.2010.11.007

Pina, A., Gannon, T., & Saunders, B. (2009). An overview of the literature on sexual harassment: Perpetrator, theory, and treatment issues. *Aggression and Violent Behavior, 14*(2), 126–138.

Pinker, S. (1994). *The language instinct.* New York: William Morrow.

Pisarik, C. T. (2009). Motivational orientation and burnout among undergraduate college students. *College Student Journal, 43*(4, Pt B), 1238–1252.

Pittas, A. G., Hariharan, R., Stark, P. C., Hajduk, C. L., Greenberg, A. S., & Roberts, S. B. (2005). Interstitial glucose level is a significant predictor of energy intake in free-living women with healthy body weight. *Journal of Nutrition, 135,* 1070–1074.

Plant, E., Devine, P. G., & Peruche, M. B. (2010). Routes to positive interracial interactions: Approaching egalitarianism or avoiding prejudice. *Personality and Social Psychology Bulletin, 36*(9), 1135–1147.

Plomin, R., Corley, R., DeFries, J. C., & Fulker, D. W. (1997). Nature, nurture, and cognitive development from 1 to 16 years: A parent–offspring adoption study. *Psychological Science, 8,* 442–447.

Plomin, R., & Crabbe, J. (2000). DNA. *Psychological Bulletin, 126*(6), 806–828.

Plomin, R., & Deary, I. (2014). Genetics and intelligence differences: Five special findings. *Molecular Psychiatry, 20*(1), 98–108. doi:10.1038/mp.2014.105

Plomin, R., & Spinath, F. M. (2004). Intelligence: Genetics, genes, and genomics. *Journal of Personality and Social Psychology, 86*(1),112–129.

Pollack, D., McFarland, B., Mahler, J., & Kovas, A. (2005). Outcomes of patients in a low-intensity, short-duration involuntary outpatient commitment program. *Psychiatric Services, 56,* 863–866.

Polman, E. (2010). Why are maximizers less happy than satisfiers? Because they maximize positive and negative outcomes. *Journal of Behavioral Decision Making, 23*(2), 179–190. doi:10.1002/bdm.647

Ponder, C. A., Kliethermes, C. L., Drew, M. R., Mul-ler, J. J., Das, K. K., Risbrough, V. B., Crabbe, J. C., Gilliam, T.C., & Palmer, A. A. (2007). Selection for contextual fear conditioning affects anxiety-like behaviors and gene expression. *Genes, Brain & Behavior, 6*(8), 736–749.

Ponseti, J., Bosinski, H. A., Wolff, S., Peller, M., Jansen, O., Mehdorn, H. M., Büchel, C., & Siebner, H. R. (2006). A functional endophenotype for sexual orientation in humans. *NeuroImage, 33,* 825–833.

Pool, E., Brosch, T., Delplanque, S., & Sander, D. (2015). Stress increases cue-triggered "wanting" for sweet reward in humans. *Journal of Experimental Psychology: Animal Learning and Cognition, 41*(2), 128–136. doi: 10.1037/xan0000052

Pope, H. G., Jr., Oliva, P. S., & Hudson, J. I. (2000). Repressed memories: B. Scientific status. In D. L. Faigman, D. H. Kay, M. J. Saks, & J. Sanders (Eds.), *Modern scientific evidence: The law and science of expert testimony* (pp. 154–195). St. Paul, MN: West.

Porath, C. L., & Pearson, C. M. (2011). Emotional and behavioral responses to workplace incivility and the impact of hierarchical status. *Journal of Applied Social Psychology, 42*(S1), E326–E357.

Poropat, A. E. (2014). Other-rated personality and academic performance: Evidence and implications. *Learning and Individual Differences, 34,* 24–32.

Porter, S., ten Brinke, L., & Gustaw, C. (2010). Dangerous decisions: The impact of first impressions of trustworthiness on the evaluation of legal evidence and defendant culpability. *Psychology, Crime & Law, 16*(6), 477–491. doi:10.1080/10683160902926141

Prentice, D. A., & Miller, D. T. (1996). Pluralistic ignorance and the perpetuation of social norms by unwitting actors. In M. P. Zanna (Ed.), *Advances in experimental social psychology* (Vol. 29, pp. 161–209). San Diego, CA: Academic Press.

Priem, R. L., Harrison, D. A., & Muir, N. (1995). Structured conflict and consensus outcomes in group decision making. *Journal of Management, 21*(4), 691–710.

Prince, T. M., & Abel, T. (2013). The impact of sleep loss on hippocampal function. *Learning & Memory, 20*(10), 558–569.

Pritchard, R. (Ed.). (1995). *Productivity measurement and improvement: Organizational: case studies.* Westport, CT: Praeger/Greenwood.

Pronin, E., Lin, D. Y., & Ross, L. (2002). The bias blind spot: Perceptions of bias in self versus others. *Personality and Social Psychology Bulletin, 28*(3), 369–381.

Propper, R. E., Stickgold, R., Keeley, R., & Christman, S. D. (2007). Is television traumatic? Dreams, stress and media exposure in the aftermath of September 11, 2001. *Psychological Science, 18,* 334–340.

Putnam, F.W. (1989). *Diagnosis and treatment of multiple personality disorder.* New York: Guilford Press.

Pyszczynski, T., Abdollahi, A., Solomon, S., Greenberg, J., Cohen, F., & Weise, D. (2006). Mortality salience, martyrdom, and military might: The Great Satan versus the Axis of Evil. *Personality and Social Psychology Bulletin, 32*(4), 525–537.

Pyszczynski, T., Greenberg, J., Solomon, S., Arndt, J., & Schimel, J. (2004). Why do people need self-esteem? A theoretical and empirical review. *Psychological Bulletin, 130*(3), 435–468.

Rada, P., Avena, N. M., & Hoebel, B. G. (2005). Daily bingeing on sugar repeatedly releases dopamine in the accumbens shell. *Neuroscience, 134*(7), 737–744.

Radhakrishnan, R., Wilkinson, S. T., & D'Souza, D. C. (2014). Gone to pot—A review of the association between cannabis and psychosis. *Frontiers In Psychiatry, 5.*

Rahman, Q. (2005). The neurodevelopment of human sexual orientation. *Neuroscience and Biobehavioral Reviews, 29,* 1057–1066.

Rajender, S., Pandu, G., Sharma, J. D., Gandhi, K. P. C., Singh, L., Thangaraj, K., et al. (2008). Reduced CAG repeats length in androgen receptor gene is associated with violent criminal behavior. *International Journal of Legal Medicine, 122,* 367–372.

Ramachandran, V. S., & Altschuler, E. L. (2009). The use of visual feedback, in particular mirror visual feedback, in restoring brain function. *Brain, 132,* 1693–1710.

Ramchand, R., Schell, T. L., Karney, B. R., Osilla, K. C., Burns, R. M., & Caldarone, L. B. (2010). Disparate prevalence estimates of PTSD among service members who served in Iraq and Afghanistan: Possible explanations. *Journal of Trauma and Stress, 23,* 59–68.

Rampersaud, G. C., Pereira, M. A., Girard, B. L., Adams, J., & Metzl, J. (2005). Breakfast habits, nutritional status, body weight, and academic performance in children and adolescents. *Journal of the American Diet Association, 105*(5), 743–760.

Ranganathan, M., & D'Souza, D. C. (2006). The acute effects of cannabinoids on memory in humans: A review. *Psychopharmacology, 188,* 425–444.

Rasmussen, E. B., & Newland, M. C. (2008). Asymmetry of reinforcement and punishment in human choice. *Journal of the Experimental Analysis of Behavior, 89,* 157–167.

Raynor, H. A., & Epstein, L. (2003). The relative-reinforcing value of food under differing levels of food deprivation and restriction. *Appetite, 40,* 15–24.

Razzini, C., Bianchi, F., Leo, R., Fortuna, E., Siracusano, A., & Romeo, F. (2008). Correlations between personality factors and coronary artery disease: From type A behaviour pattern to type D personality. *Journal of Cardiovascular Medicine, 9*(8), 761–768.

Rechenberg, K. (2015). Nutritional interventions in clinical depression. *Clinical Psychological Science.* doi:10.1177/2167702614566815

Reece, M., Herbenick, D., Schick, V., Sanders, S. A., Dodge, B., & Fortenberry, J. D. (2010). Condom use rates in a national probability sample of males and females ages 14 to 94 in the United States. *The Journal of Sexual Medicine, 7,* 266–276.

Regehr, C., Glancy, D., Pitts, A., & LeBlanc, V. R. (2014). Interventions to reduce the consequences of stress in physicians: A review and meta-analysis. *The Journal of Nervous and Mental Disease, 202*(5), 353–359.

Regier, D. A., Narrow, W. E., Clarke, D. E., Kraemer, H. C., Kuramoto, S. J., Kuhl, E. A., & Kupfer, D. J. (2013). DSM-5 field trials in the United States and Canada, part II: Test-retest reliability of selected categorical diagnoses. *The American Journal of Psychiatry, 170*(1), 59–70. doi:10.1176/appi.ajp.2012.12070999

Reicher, S. D., Haslam, S. A., & Miller, A. G. (2014). What makes a person a perpetrator? The intellectual, moral, and methodological arguments for revisiting Milgram's research on the influence of authority. *Journal of Social Issues, 70*(3), 393–408. doi:10.1111/josi.12067

Reisenzein, R., & Studtmann, M. (2007). On the expression and experience of surprise: No evidence for facial feedback, but evidence for a reverse self-inference effect. *Emotion, 7,* 612–627.

Rendell, L., & Whitehead, H. (2001). Culture in whales and dolphins. *Behavioral and Brain Sciences, 24*, 309–382.

Renner, M., & Mackin, R. (1998). A life stress instrument for classroom use. *Teaching of Psychology, 25*(1), 46–48.

Rentfrow, P. J., Goldberg, L. R., Stillwell, D. J., Kosinski, M., Gosling, S. D., & Levitin, D. J. (2012). The song remains the same: A replication and extension of the music model. *Music Perception, 30*(2), 161–185. doi:10.1525/mp.2012.30.2.161

Rescorla, R. A. (1968). Probability of shock in the presence and absence of CS in fear conditioning. *Journal of Comparative and Physiological Conditioning, 66*(1), 1–5.

Rescorla, R. A. (1988). Pavlovian conditioning: It's not what you think it is. *American Psychologist, 43*(3), 151–160.

Rescorla, R.A. (1991) Associative relations in Instrumental learning: The eighteenth Bartlet Memorial Lecture. *Quarterly Journal of Experimental Psychology, 43B*, 1–23.

Rescorla, R. A., & Wagner, A. R. (1972). A theory of Pavlovian conditioning: Variations in the effectiveness of reinforcement and nonreinforcement. In A. H. Black & W. F. Prokasy (Eds.), *Classical conditioning II: Current research and theory* (pp. 64–99). New York: Appleton-Century-Crofts.

Reyna, V. F., & Farley, F. (2006). Risk and rationality in adolescent decision making: Implications for theory, practice, and public policy. *Psychological Science in the Public Interest, 7*, 1–44.

Reznichenko. L., Amit, T., Youdim, M.B., & Mandel, S. (2005). Green tea polyphenol (–)-epigallocatechin-3-gallate induces neurorescue of long-term serum-deprived PC12 cells and promotes neurite outgrowth. *Journal of Neurochemistry, 93*, 1157–1167.

Rhee, S., & Waldman, I. D. (2002). Genetic and environmental influences on antisocial behavior: A meta-analysis of twin and adoption studies. *Psychological Bulletin, 128*(3), 490–529.

Rhodes, G., Louw, K., & Evangelista, E. (2009). Perceptual adaptation to facial symmetries. *Psychonomic Bulletin and Review, 16*, 503–508.

Ricard, M., Lutz, A., & Davidson, R. J. (November, 2014). Mind of the meditator. *Scientific American, 311*(5), 39–45.

Ricciardelli, L. A., & McCabe, M. P. (2004). A biopsychosocial model of disordered eating and the pursuit of muscularity in adolescent boys. *Psychological Bulletin, 130*, 179–205.

Rice, G., Anderson, C., Risch, N., & Ebers, G. (1999). Male homosexuality: Absence of linkage to microsatellite markers at Xq28. *Science, 284*(5414), 665–667.

Rice, T. R., & Hoffman, L. (2014). Defense mechanisms and implicit emotion regulation: A comparison of a psychodynamic construct with one from contemporary neuroscience. *Journal of the American Psychoanalytic Association, 62*(4), 693–708. doi:10.1177/0003065114546746

Rich, A. N., Kunar, M. A., Van Wert, M. J., Hidalgo-Sotelo, B., Horowitz, T. S., & Wolfe, J. M. (2008). Why do we miss rare targets? Exploring the boundaries of the low prevalence effect. *Journal of Vision, 8*, 1–17.

Richardson, K., & Rothstein, H. (2008). Effects of occupational stress management intervention programs: A meta-analysis. *Journal of Occupational Health Psychology, 13*(1), 69–93.

Richeson, J. A., & Shelton, J. N. (2005). Thin slices of racial bias. *Journal of Nonverbal Behavior, 29*, 75–86.

Ridout, B., & Campbell, A. (2014). Using Facebook to deliver a social norm intervention to reduce problem drinking at university. *Drug And Alcohol Review, 33*(6), 667–673. doi:10.1111/dar.12141

Rideout, V. J., & Hamel, E. (2006). *The media family: Electronic media in the lives of infants, toddlers, preschoolers and their parents.* Menlo Park, CA: Kaiser Family Foundation.

Rieger, G., & Savin-Williams, R. (2012). Gender nonconformity, sexual orientation, and psychological well-being. *Archives of Sexual Behavior, 41*, 611–621.

Riggio, R. E., Zhu, W., Reina, C., & Maroosis, J. A. (2010). Virtue-based measurement of ethical leadership: The Leadership Virtues Questionnaire. *Consulting Psychology Journal: Practice and Research, 62*(4), 235–250.

Ritterband, L., Thorndike, F., Gonder-Frederick, L., Magee, J., Bailey, E., Saylor, D., et al. (2009). Efficacy of an Internet-based behavioral intervention for adults with insomnia. *Archives of General Psychiatry, 66*(7), 692–698.

Rivera, S. M., Wakeley, A., & Langer, J. (1999). The drawbridge phenomenon: Representational reasoning or perceptual preference. *Developmental Psychology, 35*, 427–435.

Rizzo, A. S., Difede, J., Rothbaum, B. O., Reger, G., Spitalnick, J., Cukor, J., & McLay, R. (2010). Development and early evaluation of the Virtual Iraq/Afghanistan exposure therapy system for combat-related PTSD. *Annals of the New York Academic of Sciences, 1208*, 114–125.

Roalf, D., Gur, R., Verma, R., Parker, W., Quarmley, M., Ruparel, K., & Gur, R. (2015). White matter microstructure in schizophrenia: Associations to neurocognition and clinical symptomatology. *Schizophrenia Research, 161*(1), 42–49.

Roberson, D. M. J., & Davidoff, J. (2000). The "categorical perception" of colors and facial expressions: The effect of verbal interference. *Memory & Cognition, 28*, 977–986.

Roberson, D. M. J., Davies, I. R. L., & Davidoff, J. (2000). Color categories are not universal: Replications and new evidence in favor of linguistic relativity. *Journal of Experimental Psychology: General, 129*, 369–398.

Roberts, B. W., & DelVecchio, W. F. (2000). The rank-order consistency of personality from childhood to old age: A quantitative review of longitudinal studies. *Psychological Bulletin, 126*, 3–25.

Roberts, B. W., Walton, K., & Bogg, T. (2005). Conscientiousness and health across the life course. *Review of General Psychology, 9*(2), 156–168.

Roberts, B., Walton, K., & Viechtbauer, W. (2006). Patterns of mean-level change in personality traits across the life course: A meta-analysis of longitudinal studies. *Psychological Bulletin, 132*(1), 1–25.

Robertson, S. I. (2001). *Problem solving.* New York: Psychology Press.

Robinson, L., Platt, B., & Riedel, G. (2011, February 16). Involvement in the cholinergic system in conditioning and perceptual memory [Electronic publication ahead of print]. *Behavioral and Brain Research.*

Robinson, S. J., & Rollings, L. L. (2011). The effect of mood-context on visual recognition and recall memory. *Journal of General Psychology, 138*(1), 66–79. doi:10.1080/00221309.2010.534405

Robinson-Cimpian, J. P., Lubienski, S. T., Ganley, C. M., & Copur-Gencturk, Y. (2014). Teachers' perceptions of students' mathematics proficiency may exacerbate early gender gaps in achievement. *Developmental Psychology, 50*(4), 1262–1281. doi:10.1037/a0035073

Roch, S. G., Woehr, D. J., Mishra, V., & Kieszczynska, U. (2012). Rater training revisited: An updated meta analytic review of frame of reference training. *Journal of Occupational and Organizational Psychology, 85*(2), 370–395. doi:10.1111/j.2044-8325.2011.02045.x

Rochlen, A., McKelley, R., & Pituch, K. (2006). A preliminary examination of the "Real Men. Real Depression" campaign. *Psychology of Men & Masculinity, 7*(1), 1–13.

Rohde, P., Stice, E. & Marti, C. N. (2015). Development and predictive effects of eating disorder risk factors during adolescence: Implications for prevention efforts. *International Journal of Eating Disorders, 48*(2), 187–198. doi:10.1002/eat.22270

Rohrer, D. (2012). Interleaving helps students distinguish among similar concepts. *Educational Psychology Review, 24*, 355–367.

Roediger, H., Agarwal, P. K., Kang, S. K., & Marsh, E. J. (2010). Benefits of testing memory: Best practices and boundary conditions. In G. M. Davies, D. B. Wright (Eds.), *Current issues in applied memory research* (pp. 13–49). New York: Psychology Press.

Rogers, J. M. (2009). Tobacco and pregnancy. *Reproductive Toxicology, 28*, 152–160.

Rogers, J., Kochunov, P., Zilles, K., et al. (2010). On the genetic architecture of cortical folding and brain volume in primates. *Neuroimage, 53*, 1103–1108.

Rollins, B. C. (1989). Marital quality at midlife. In S. Hunter & M. Sundel (Eds.), *Midlife myths* (pp. 184–194). Newbury Park, CA: Sage.

Rolls, E. T., Verhagen, J. V., & Kadohisa, M. (2003). Representations of the texture of food in the primate orbitofrontal cortex neurons responding to viscosity, grittiness, and capsaicin. *Journal of Neurophysiology, 90*, 3711–3724.

Ronaldson, A., Molloy, G. J., Wikman, A., Poole, L., Kaski, J. C., Steptoe, A. (2015). Optimism and recovery after acute coronary syndrome: A clinical cohort study [Electronic publication ahead of print]. *Psychosomatic Medicine.*

Rosch, E. H. (1973). Natural categories. *Cognitive Psychology, 4,* 328–350.

Rosch, E., & Mervis, C. B. (1975). Family resemblances: Studies in the internal structure of categories. *Cognitive Psychology, 7,* 573–605.

Rosch, E., Mervis, C. B., Gray, W., Johnson, D., & Boyes-Braem, P. (1976). Basic objects in natural categories. *Cognitive Psychology, 8,* 382–439.

Rose, A., & Swenson, L. (2009). Do perceived popular adolescents who aggress against others experience emotional adjustment problems themselves? *Developmental Psychology, 45*(3), 868–872.

Rose, A. J., Swenson, L. P., & Waller, E. M. (2004). Overt and relational aggression and perceived popularity: Developmental differences in concurrent and prospective relations. *Developmental Psychology, 40,* 378–387.

Rose, D., Wykes, T., Leese, M., Bindman, J., & Fleischmann, P. (2003). Patients' perspectives on electroconvulsive therapy: Systematic review. *British Medical Journal, 326,* 1363–1368.

Rose, N., Myerson, J., Roediger, H., & Hale, S. (2010). Similarities and differences between working memory and long-term memory: Evidence from the levels-of-processing span task. *Journal of Experimental Psychology: Learning, Memory, and Cognition, 36*(2), 471–483.

Roselli, C. E., Larkin, K., Schrunk, J. M., & Stormshak, F. (2004). Sexual partner preference, hypothalamic morphology and aromatase in rams. *Physiology and Behavior, 83,* 233–245.

Roselli, C., Reddy, R., & Kaufman, K. (2011). The development of male-oriented behavior in rams. *Frontiers in Neuroendocrinology, 32*(2), 164–169. doi:10.1016/j.yfrne.2010.12.007

Rosenhan, D. L. (1973). On being sane in insane places. *Science, 179*(4070), 250–258.

Rosenthal, R., & Fode, K. L. (1963). The effect of experimenter bias on the performance of the albino rat. *Behavioral Science, 8,* 183–189.

Rosenthal, R., & Jacobson, L. (1966). Teachers' expectancies: Determinates of pupils' IQ gains. *Psychological Reports, 19,* 115–118.

Rosenthal, R., & Jacobson, L. (1968). *Pygmalion in the classroom: Teacher expectation and pupils' intellectual development.* New York: Holt, Rinehart & Winston.

Ross, L. (1977). The intuitive psychologist and his shortcomings: Distortions in the attribution process. In L. Berkowitz (Ed.), *Advances in experimental social psychology* (Vol. 10). New York: Academic Press.

Ross, M., & Wang, Q. (2010). Why we remember and what we remember: Culture and autobiographical memory. *Perspectives on Psychological Science, 5*(4), 401–409.

Rothbart, M. K., & Bates, J. E. (2006). Temperament. In W. Damon, R. Lerner, & N. Eisenberg (Eds.), *Handbook of child psychology: Vol. 3. Social, emotional, and personality development* (6th ed., pp. 99–166). New York: Wiley.

Rothemund, Y., Ziegler, S., Hermann, C., Gruesser, Foell, J., Patrick, C. J., & Flor, H. (2012). Fear conditioning in psychopaths: Event-related potentials and peripheral measures. *Biological Psychology, 90,* 50–59.

Rotundo, M., & Sackett, P. R. (2002). The relative importance of task, citizenship, and counterproductive performance to global ratings of job performance: A policy-capturing approach. *Journal of Applied Psychology, 87*(1), 66–80.

Rouder, J. N., & Ratcliff, R. (2004). Comparing categorization models. *Journal of Experimental Psychology: General, 133,* 63–82.

Rouder, J. N., & Ratcliff, R. (2006). Comparing exemplar- and rule-based theories of categorization. *Current Directions in Psychological Science, 15,* 9–13.

Roy, B., Diez-Roux, A. V., Seeman, T., Ranjit, N., Shea, S., & Cushman, M. (2010). Association of optimism and pessimism with inflammation and hemostasis in the Multi-Ethnic Study of Artherosclerosis (MESA). *Psychosomatic Medicine, 72*(2), 134–140. PsycINFO, EBSCOhost (accessed March 20, 2015).

Rozanski, A., Blumenthal, J. A., & Kaplan, J. (1999). Impact of psychological factors on the pathogenesis of cardiovascular disease and implications for therapy. *Circulation, 99,* 2192–2217.

Rubin, D., & Wenzel, A. (1996). One hundred years of forgetting: A quantitative description of retention. *Psychological Review, 103,* 734–760.

Rushton, J., Chrisjohn, R. D., & Fekken, G. (1981). The altruistic personality and the Self-Report Altruism Scale. *Personality and Individual Differences, 2*(4), 293–302.

Rushton, J. P., & Jensen, A. R. (2005). Thirty years of research on race differences in cognitive ability. *Psychology, Public Policy, and Law, 11*(2), 235–294. doi:10.1037/1076-8971.11.2.235

Rutter, A., & Hine, D. W. (2005). Sex differences in workplace aggression: An investigation of moderation and mediation effects. *Aggressive Behavior, 31*(3), 254–270.

Ryckman, N. A., & Lambert, A. J. (2015). Unsuccessful suppression is associated with increased neuroticism, intrusive thoughts, and rumination. *Personality and Individual Differences, 73,* 88–91. doi:10.1016/j.paid.2014.09.029

Rydell, R., McConnell, A., & Beilock, S. (2009). Multiple social identities and stereotype threat: Imbalance, accessibility, and working memory. *Journal of Personality and Social Psychology, 96*(5), 949–966.

Saban, K. L., Mathews, H. L., DeVon, H. A., & Janusek, L. W. (2014). Epigenetics and social context: implications for disparity in cardiovascular disease. *Aging and Disease, 5*(5), 346–355.

Sacerdote, B. (2001). Peer effects with random assignment: Results for Dartmouth roommates. *Quarterly Journal of Economics, 116,* 681–704.

Sack, R. L., Brandes, R. W., Kendall, A. R., & Lewy, A. J. (2000). Entrainment of free-running circadian rhythms by melatonin in blind people. *New England Journal of Medicine, 343,* 1070–1077.

Sackett, P. R., Kuncel, N. R., Beatty, A. S., Rigdon, J. L., Shen, W., & Kiger T. B. (2011). The role of socioeconomic status in SAT-Grade relationships and in college admissions decisions. *Psychological Science, 23*(9), 1000–1007. doi: 10.1177/0956797612438732

Sackett, P., & Lievens, F. (2008). Personnel selection. *Annual Review of Psychology, 59,* 419–450.

Sahakyan, L., & Kelley, C. M. (2002). A contextual change account of the directed forgetting effect. *Journal of Experimental Psychology: Learning, Memory, & Cognition, 28,* 1064–1072.

Saigal, S., & Doyle, L. W. (2008). An overview of mortality and sequelae of preterm birth from infancy to adulthood. *Lancet, 371*(9608), 261–269.

Salgado, J. F. (1997). The five-factor model of personality and job performance in the European community. *Journal of Applied Psychology, 82,* 30–43.

Salgado, J. F. (2002). The Big Five personality dimensions and counterproductive behaviors. *International Journal of Selection and Assessment, 10*(1–2), 117–125.

Salgado, J., Anderson, N., Moscoso, S., Bertua, C., de Fruyt, F., & Rolland, J. (2003). A meta-analytic study of general mental ability validity for different occupations in the European Community. *Journal of Applied Psychology, 88*(6), 1068–1081.

Salo, R., Ursu, S., Buonocore, M. H., Leamon, M. H., & Carter, C. (2010). Impaired prefrontal cortical functioning disrupted adaptive cognitive control in methamphetamine abusers: An fMRI study. *Biological Psychiatry, 65,* 706–709.

Salvatore, J. E., I-Chun Kuo, S., Steele, R. D., Simpson, J. A., & Collins, W. A. (2011). Recovering from conflict in romantic relationships: A developmental perspective. *Psychological Science, 22,* 376–383.

Sanchez. J. I., & Levine, E. L. (2012). The rise and fall of job analysis, and the future of work analysis. In S. T. Fiske, Schacter, D. L., and Taylor, S. E. (eds.), *Annual Review of Psychology, 63.*

Sarchione, C., Cuttler, M., Muchinsky, P., & Nelson-Gray, R. (1998). Prediction of dysfunctional job behaviors among law enforcement officers. *Journal of Applied Psychology, 83*(6), 904–912.

Sanders, A. R., Martin, E. R., Beecham, G. W., Guo, S., Dawood, K., Rieger, G., … & Bailey, J. M. (2015). Genome-wide scan demonstrates significant linkage for male sexual orientation. *Psychological Medicine, 45*(7), 1379–1388. doi:10.1017/S0033291714002451.

Sargent, J. D., & Heatherton, T. F. (2009). Comparison of trends for adolescent smoking in movies: 1990–2007. *Journal of the American Medical Association, 301,* 2211–2213.

Saucier, G., Bel-Bahar, T., & Fernandez C. (2007). What modifies the expression of personality tendencies? Defining basic domains of situation variables. *Journal of Personality, 75*(3), 479–504.

Saus, E., Johnsen, B., Eid, J., Riisem, P., Andersen, R., &Thayer, J. (2006). The effect of brief situational awareness training in a police shooting simulator: An experimental study. *Military Psychology, 18,* s3–s21.

Savage-Rumbaugh, S., & Lewin, R. (1994). *Kanzi: The ape at the brink of the human mind.* New York: Wiley.

Savic, I., Berglund, H., Lindström, P., & Gustafsson, J. (2005, May). Brain response to putative pheromones in homosexual men. *PNAS: Proceedings of the National Academy of Sciences of the United States of America, 102*(20), 7356–7361.

Savic, I., & Lindström, P. (2008). PET and MRI show differences in cerebral asymmetry and functional connectivity between homo-and heterosexual subjects. *PNAS: Proceedings of the National Academy of Sciences of the United States of America, 105,* 9403–9408.

Savic, I., Garcia-Falgueras, A., & Swaab, D.F. (2010). Sexual differentiation of the human brain in relation to gender identity and sexual orientation. *Progress in Brain Research, 186,* 41–62.

Savin-Williams, R. C., & Cohen, K. M. (2004). Homoerotic development during childhood and adolescence. *Child Adolescent Psychiatric Clinics of North America, 13,* 529–549.

Saxe, L. (1994). Detection of deception: Polygraph and integrity tests. *Current Directions in Psychological Science, 3,* 69–73.

Schachtman, T. R., Walker, J., & Fowler, S. (2011). Effects of conditioning in advertising. In T. R. Schachtman & S. Reilly (Eds.) *Associative learning and conditioning theory: Human and nonhuman applications* (pp. 481–506). Oxford: Oxford University Press.

Schaufeli, W. B., Bakker, A. B., & Van Rhenen, W. (2009). How changes in job demands and resources predict burnout, work engagement and sickness absenteeism. *Journal of Organizational Behavior, 30*(7), 893–917.

Schaufeli, W. B., Martínez, I. M., Marques Pinto, A., Salanova, M., & Bakker, A. B. (2002). Burnout and engagement in university students: A cross-national study. *Journal of Cross-Cultural Psychology, 33*(5), 464–481.

Scheier, M. F., & Carver, C. S. (1985). Optimism, coping, and health: Assessment and implications of generalized outcome expectancies. *Health Psychology, 4*(3), 219–247.

Schenck, C. H., Lee, S. A., Bornemann, M. A., & Mahowald, M. W. (2009). Potentially lethal behaviors associated with rapid eye movement sleep behavior disorder: Review of the literature and forensic implications. *Journal of Forensic Science, 54,* 1475–1484.

Schenck, C. H., & Mahowald, M. (2002). REM sleep behavior disorder: Clinical, developmental, and neuroscience perspectives 16 years after its formal identification. *Sleep, 25,* 120–138.

Scherbaum, C. A., Goldstein, H. W., Yusko, K. P., Ryan, R., & Hanges, P. J. (2012). Intelligence 2.0: Reestablishing a research program on g in I-O psychology. *Industrial and Organizational Psychology: Perspectives on Science and Practice, 5*(2), 128–148. doi:10.1111/j.1754-9434.2012.01419.x

Schierenbeck, T., Riemann, D., Berger, M., & Hornyak, M. (2008). Effect of illicit recreational drugs upon sleep: Cocaine, ecstasy and marijuana. *Sleep Medicine Reviews, 12*(5), 381–389.

Schinka, J. A., Busch, R. M., & Robichaux-Keene, N. (2004). A meta-analysis of the association between the serotonin transporter gene polymorphism (5HTTLPR) and trait anxiety. *Molecular Psychiatry, 9,* 197–202.

Schlaug, G., Jancke, L., Huang, Y., & Steinmetz, H. (1995). In vivo evidence of structural brain asymmetry in musicians. *Science, 267,* 699–701.

Schlaug, G., Marchina, S., & Norton, A. (2009). Evidence for plasticity in white matter tracts of chronic aphasic patients undergoing intense intonation-based speech therapy. *Annals of the New York Academy of Sciences, 1169,* 385–394.

Schlaug, G., Renga, V., & Nair, D. (2008). Transcranial direct current stimulation in stroke recovery. *Archives of Neurology, 65,* 1571–1576.

Schlesinger, L. B. (2009). Psychological profiling: Investigative implications from crime scene analysis. *Journal of Psychiatry & Law, 37*(1), 73–84.

Schmader, T., Johns, M., & Forbes, C. (2008). An integrated process model of stereotype threat effects on performance. *Psychological Review, 115*(2), 336–356.

Schmidt, F. L., & Hunter, J. E. (1998). The validity and utility of selection methods in personnel psychology: Practical and theoretical implications of 85 years of research findings. *Psychological Bulletin, 124,* 262–274.

Schmidt, G. L., DeBuse, C. J., & Seger, C. A. (2007). Right hemisphere metaphor processing? Characterizing the lateralization of semantic processes. *Brain and Language, 100,* 127–41.

Schmidt, M., Sommerville, J., & Perc, M. (2011). Fairness expectations and altruistic sharing in 15-month-old human infants. *PLoS ONE, 6*(10), e23223.

Schmidt, R., & Bjork, R. (1992). New conceptualizations of practice: Common principles in three paradigms suggest new concepts for training. *Psychological Science, 3*(4), 207–217.

Schmitt, D. P., Allik, J., McCrae, R. R., Benet-Mar-tinez, V., et al. (2007). The geographic distribution of Big Five personality traits: Patterns and profiles of human self-descriptions across 56 nations. *Journal of Cross-Cultural Psychology, 38,* 173–212.

Schmolk, H., Buffalo, E. A., & Squire, L. R. (2000). Memory distortions develop over time: Recollections of the O. J. Simpson trial verdict after 15 and 32 months. *Psychological Science, 11,* 39–45.

Schneider, T. J., Goffin, R. D., & Daljeet, K. N. (2015). 'Give us your social networking site passwords': Implications for personnel selection and personality. *Personality and Individual Differences, 73,* 78–83. doi:10.1016/j.paid.2014.09.026

Schoenberger, N. E., Kirsch, I., Gearan, P., Montgomery G., Pastyrnak S., et al. (1997). Hypnotic enhancement of a cognitive behavioral treatment for public speaking anxiety. *Behavior Therapy, 28,* 127–140.

Schredl, M. (2001). Night terrors in children: Prevalence and influencing factors. *Sleep and Hypnosis, 3*(2), 68–72.

Schulz-Hardt, S., Frey, D., Luthgens, C., & Moscovici, S. (2000). Biased information search in group decision making. *Journal of Personality and Social Psychology, 78,* 655–669.

Schummers, J., & Browning, M. D. (2001). Evidence for a role for GABA(A) and NMDA receptors in ethanol inhibition of long-term potentiation. *Brain Research, 94,* 9–14.

Schwartz, B., Ward, A., Monterosso, J., Lyubomirsky, S., White, K., & Lehman, D. R. (2002). Maximizing versus satisficing: Happiness is a matter of choice. *Journal of Personality and Social Psychology, 83*(5), 1178–1197.

Scoboria, A., Mazzoni, G., Kirsch, I., & Jimenez, S. (2006). The effects of prevalence and script information on plausibility belief and memory of autobiographical events. *Applied Cognitive Psychology, 20*(8), 1049–1064.

Sedlmeier, P., Eberth, J., Schwarz, M., Zimmermann, D., Haarig, F., Jaeger, S., & Kunze, S. (2012). The psychological effects of meditation: A meta-analysis. *Psychological Bulletin, 138*(6), 1139–1171.

Segerstrom, S. C., & Miller, G. E. (2004). Psychological stress and the immune system: A meta-analytic study of 30 years of inquiry. *Psychological Bulletin, 130,* 601–630.

Seidenberg, M. S., & Pettito, L. A. (1979). Signing behavior in apes: A critical review. *Cognition, 7,* 177–215.

Seligman, M. E. P. (1971). Phobias and preparedness. *Behavior Therapy, 2,* 307–320.

Seligman, M., & Maier, S. (1967). Failure to escape traumatic shock. *Journal of Experimental Psychology, 74,* 1–9.

Selye, H. (1956). *The stress of life.* New York: McGraw-Hill.

Seppälä, E. M., Nitschke, J. B., Tudorascu, D. L., Hayes, A., Goldstein, M. R., Nguyen, D. T. H., Perlman, D., & Davidson, R. J. (2014). Breathing-based meditation decreases posttraumatic stress disorder symptoms in U.S. military veterans: A randomized controlled longitudinal study. *Journal of Traumatic Stress, 27,* 397–405.

Sergerie, K., Chochol, C., & Armony, J.L. (2008). The role of the amygdala in emotional processing: A quantitative meta-analysis of functional neuroimaging studies. *Neuroscience and Biobehavioral Reviews, 32,* 811–830.

Shad, M. U., Bidesi, A. S., Chen, L-A., Thomas, B. P., Ernst, M., & Rao, U. (2011). Neurobiology of decision-making in adolescents. *Behavioural Brain Research, 217,* 67–76.

Shallice, T. (1982). Specific impairments of planning. *Philosophical Transactions of the Royal Society of London, B, 298*, 199–209.

Shamir, B., House, R. J., & Arthur, M. B. (1993). The motivational aspects of charismatic leadership: A self-concept theory. *Organization Science, 4*, 1–17.

Sharot, T., Martorella, E. A., Delgado, M. R., & Phelps, E. (2007). How personal experience modulates the neural circuitry of memories of September 11. *PNAS: Proceedings of the National Academy of Sciences of the United States of America, 104*, 389–394.

Shechter, O. G., Durik, A. M., Miyamoto, Y., & Ha-rackiewicz, J. M. (2011). The role of utility value in achievement behavior: The importance of culture. *Personality and Social Psychology Bulletin, 37*, 303–317.

Shedler, J. (2010). The efficacy of psychodynamic therapy. *American Psychologist, 65*, 98–109.

Sherman, J. W., Kruschke, J. K., Sherman, S. J., Percy, E. J., Petrocelli, J. V., & Conrey, F. R. (2009). Attentional processes in stereotype formation: A common model for category accentuation and illusory correlation. *Journal of Personality and Social Psychology, 96*, 305–323.

Shih, M., & Sanchez, D. (2005). Perspectives and research on the positive and negative implications of having multiple racial identities. *Psychological Bulletin, 131*(4), 569-591.

Shimamura, A. P. (2014). Remembering the past: Neural substrates underlying episodic encoding and retrieval. *Current Directions in Psychological Science, 23*(4), 257–263. doi:10.1177/0963721414536181

Shoham, V., Rohrbaugh, M., Onken, L., Cuthbert, B., Beveridge, R., & Fowles, T. (2013). Redefining clinical science training: Purpose and products of the Delaware Project. *Clinical Psychological Science, 2*(1), 8–21. doi:10.1177/2167702613497931

Siegel, J. (1995). Phylogeny and the function of REM sleep. *Behavioural Brain Research, 69*, 29–34.

Siegel, J. (2005). Clues to the functions of mammalian sleep. *Nature, 437*(7063), 1264– 1271.

Siegel, S. (1984). Pavlovian conditioning and heroin overdose: Reports by overdose victims. *Bulletin of the Psychonomic Society, 22*, 428–430.

Siegel, S., Hinson, R. E., Krank, M. D., & McCully, J. (1982). Heroin "overdose" death: Contribution of drug-associated environmental cues. *Science, 216*, 436–437.

Siegler, R. S. (1992). The other Alfred Binet. *Developmental Psychology, 28*(2), 179–190.

Sih, A., Mathot, K. J., Moiron, M., Montiglio, P. O., Wolf, M., & Dingemanse, N. J. (2015). Animal personality and state-behaviour feedbacks. A review and guide for empiricists. *Trends in Ecology and Evolution, 30*, 50–60.

Simons, D. J. (2010). Monkeying around with the gorillas in our midst: Familiarity with an inattentional-blindness task does not improve the detection of unexpected events. *I-Perception, 1*(1). doi:10.1068/i0386

Silva, A. J., Paylor, R., Wehner, J. M., & Tonegawa, S. (1992). Impaired spatial learning in alpha-calcium-calmodulin kinase II mutant mice. *Science, 257*, 206–211.

Silva, M., Groeger, J., & Bradshaw, M. (2006). Attention–memory interactions in scene perception. *Spatial Vision, 19*, 9–19.

Simon, S., Khateb, A., Darque, A., Lazeyras, F., Mayer, E., & Pegna, A. (2011). When the brain remembers, but the patient doesn't: Converging fMRI and EEG evidence for covert recognition in a case of prosopagnosia. *Cortex, 47*(7), 825–838.

Simons, D. (2010). Monkeying around with the gorillas in our midst: Familiarity with an inattentional-blindness task does not improve the detection of unexpected events. *I-Perception, 1*, 3–6.

Simons, D. J., & Chabris, C. F. (1999). Gorillas in our midst: Sustained inattentional blindness for dynamic events. *Perception, 28*, 1059–1074.

Simpson, J. R. (2008). Functional MRI lie detection: Too good to be true? *Journal of the Academy of Psychology and the Law, 236*, 91–98.

Singer, M. A., & Goldin-Meadow, S. (2005). Children learn when their teacher's gestures and speech differ. *Psychological Science, 16*, 85–89.

Singh, S., Kumar, A., Agarwal, S., Phadke, S., & Jaiswal, Y. (2014). Genetic insight of schizophrenia: Past and future perspectives. *Gene, 535*(2), 97–100. doi:10.1016/j.gene.2013.09.110

Sinha, R. (2009). Modeling stress and drug craving in the laboratory: Implications for addiction treatment development. *Addiction Biology, 14*(1), 84–98.

Skerry, A. E., Lambert, E. Powell, A. J. & McAuliffe, K. (2013). The origins of pedagogy: Developmental and evolutionary perspectives. *Evolutionary Psychology, 11*(3), 550–572.

Skinner, B. F. (1948). Superstition in the pigeon. *Journal of Experimental Psychology, 38*, 168–172.

Skinner, B. F. (1985). Cognitive science and behaviorism. *British Journal of Psychology, 76*, 291–301.

Skipper, J. I., Goldin-Meadow, S., & Nusbaum, H. C. (2007). Speech-associated gestures, Broca's area, and the human mirror system. *Brain and Language, 101*, 260–277.

Skogstad, A., Aasland, M. S., Nielsen, M. B., Hetland, J., Matthiesen, S. B., & Einarsen, S. (2014). The relative effects of constructive, laissez-faire, and tyrannical leadership on subordinate job satisfaction: Results from two prospective and representative studies. *Zeitschrift Für Psychologie, 222*(4), 221–232. doi:10.1027/2151-2604/a000189

Sleigh, J., Harvey, M., Voss, L., & Denny, B. (2014). Ketamine—More mechanisms of action than just NMDA blockade. *Trends in Anaesthesia and Critical Care, 4*, 76–81.

Slotema, C. W., Blom, J. D., Hoek, H. W., & Sommer, I. E. (2010). Should we expand the toolbox of psychiatric treatment methods to include repetitive transcranial magnetic stimulation (rTMS)? A meta-analysis of the efficacy of rTMS in psychiatric disorders. *Journal of Clinical Psychiatry, 71*, 873–884.

Smalarz, L., & Wells, G. L. (2014). Confirming feedback following a mistaken identification impairs memory for the culprit. *Law and Human Behavior, 38*(3), 283–292. doi:10.1037/lhb0000078

Smith, B. W. (2004). Structural and organizational predictors of homicide by police. *Policing: An International Journal of Police Strategies and Management, 27*, 539–557.

Smith, E. S., Blass, G. R., Lewin, G. R., & Park, T. J. (2010). Absence of histamine-induced itch in the African naked mole-rat and "rescue" by substance P. *Molecular Pain, 6*, 29.

Smith, J., & Tolson, J. (2008). Recognition, diagnosis, and treatment of restless legs syndrome. *Journal of the American Academy of Nurse Practitioners, 20*(8), 396– 401.

Smith, T. B., McCullough, M. E., & Poll, J. (2003). Religiousness and depression: Evidence for a main effect and the moderating influence of stressful life events. *Psychological Bulletin, 129*, 614–636.

Smith, T. W., & Spiro, A. III. (2002). Personality, health, and aging: Prolegomenon for the next generation. *Journal of Research in Personality, 36*, 363–394.

Smither, J. W., London, M., & Reilly, R. R. (2005). Does performance improve following multisource feedback? A theoretical model, meta-analysis, and review of empirical findings. *Personnel Psychology, 58*(1), 33–66.

Snider, L. A., & Swedo, S. E. (2004). PANDAS: Current status and directions for research. *Molecular Psychiatry, 9*, 900–907.

Snook, B., Cullen, R. M., Bennell, C., Taylor, P. J., & Gendreau, P. (2008). The criminal profiling illusion: What's behind the smoke and mirrors? *Criminal Justice And Behavior, 35*(10), 1257–1276. doi:10.1177/0093854808321528

Snowden, L., Catalano, R., & Shumway, M. (2009). Disproportionate use of psychiatric emergency services by African Americans. *Psychiatric Services, 60*(12), 1664–1671. doi: 10.1176/appi.ps.60.12.1664

Snowdon, L. R. (1999). African American service use for mental health problems. *Journal of Community Psychology, 27*, 303–313.

Snyder, K. (2006). Kurt Snyder's personal experience with schizophrenia. *Schizophrenia Bulletin, 32*, 209–211.

Soto, C. J., & John, O. P. (2012). Development of big-five domains and facets in adulthood: Mean-level age trends and broadly versus narrowly acting mechanisms. *Journal of Personality, 80*, 881–914.

Sourander, A., Klomek, A. B., Ikonen, M., Lindroos, J., Luntamo, T., Koskelainen, M., Ristkari, T., & Helenius, H. (2010). Psychosocial risk factors associated with bullying and cyberbullying among adolescents: A population-based study. *Archives of General Psychiatry, 67*, 720–728.

Spanos, N., Cobb, P., & Gorassini, D. (1985). Failing to resist hypnotic test suggestions: A strategy for self-presenting as deeply hypnotized. *Psychiatry: Journal for the Study of Interpersonal Processes, 48*(3), 282–292.

Spearman, C. (1923). *The nature of intelligence and the principles of cognition.* London: Macmillan.

Spector, P. (2002). Employee control and occupational stress. *Current Directions in Psychological Science, 11,* 133–136.

Speer, A. B., Christiansen, N. D., Melchers, K. G., König, C. J., & Kleinmann, M. (2014). Establishing the cross-situational convergence of the ability to identify criteria: Consistency and prediction across similar and dissimilar assessment center exercises. *Human Performance, 27*(1), 44–60. doi:10.1080/08959285.2013.854364

Spiegel, D. (2013). Traceformations: Hypnosis in brain and body. *Depression and Anxiety, 30,* 342–352.

Spelke, E. (2005). Sex differences in intrinsic aptitude for mathematics and science? A critical review. *American Psychologist, 60*(9), 950–958.

Spelke, E. S., & Kinzler, K. D. (2007). Core knowledge. *Developmental Science, 10,* 89–96.

Spence, K. W. (1950). Cognitive versus stimulus-response theories of learning. *Psychological Review, 57,* 159–172.

Spera, S. P., Buhrfeind, E. D., & Pennebaker, J. W. (1994). Expressive writing and coping with job loss. *Academy of Management Journal, 37,* 722–733.

Sperling, G. (1960). The information available in brief visual presentations. *Psychological Monographs, 74*(11, Whole No. 498), 1–29.

Sperry, R. W. (1982). Some effects of disconnecting the cerebral hemispheres. *Science, 217,* 1223–1226, 1250.

Squire, L. R. (1986). Mechanisms of memory. *Science, 232*(4758), 1612–1619.

Squire, L. R. (1989). On the course of forgetting in very long-term memory. *Journal of Experimental Psychology: Learning, Memory, and Cognition, 15*(2), 241–245.

Squire, L. R., Wixted, J. T., & Clark, R. E. (2007). Recognition memory and the medial temporal lobe: A new perspective. *Nature Reviews Neuroscience, 8*(11), 872–83.

Staffen, W., Kronbichler, M., Aichhorn, M., Mair, A., & Ladurner, G. (2006). Selective brain activity in response to one's own name in the persistent vegetative state. *Journal of Neurology, Neurosurgery, and Psychiatry, 77,* 1383–1384.

Stahl, C., Unkelbach, C., & Corneille, O. (2009). On the respective contributions of awareness of unconditioned stimulus valence and unconditioned stimulus identity in attitude formation through evaluative conditioning. *Journal of Personality and Social Psychology, 97,* 404–420.

Stanhope, N., Cohen, G., & Conway, M. (1993).Very long-term retention of a novel. *Applied Cognitive Psychology, 7,* 239–256.

Stanton, R. D., & Nosofsky, R. M. (2013). Category number impacts rule-based and information-integration category learning: A reassessment of evidence for dissociable category-learning systems. *Journal of Experimental Psychology: Learning, Memory, and Cognition, 39*(4), 1174–1191. doi:10.1037/a0031670

Starin, E. D. (2004). Masturbation observations in Temminck's red colobus. *Folia Primatologica, 75,* 114–117.

Stark, C. E., Okado, Y., & Loftus, E. F. (2010). Imaging the reconstruction of true and false memories using sensory reactivation and the misinformation paradigms. *Learning and Memory, 17,* 485–488.

Staw, B. M., Bell, N. E., & Clausen, J. A. (1986). The dispositional approach to job attitudes: A lifetime longitudinal test. *Administrative Science Quarterly, 31,* 56–77.

Steele, C. (1997). A threat in the air: How stereotypes shape intellectual identity and performance. *American Psychologist, 52*(6), 613–629.

Steele, J. D., Christmas, D., Eliamel, M. S., & Matthews, K. (2008). Anterior cingulotomy for major depression: Clinical outcome and relationship to lesion characteristics. *Biological Psychiatry, 63,* 670–677.

Steffen, P. R., McNeilly, M., Anderson, N., & Sherwood, A. (2003). Effects of perceived racism and anger inhibition on ambulatory blood pressure in African Americans. *Psychosomatic Medicine, 65,* 746–750.

Steinberg, L. (1987). The impact of puberty on family relations: Effects of pubertal status and pubertal timing. *Developmental Psychology, 23,* 451–460.

Steinberg, L. (2007). Risk taking in adolescence: New perspectives from brain and behavioral science. *Current Directions in Psychological Science, 16,* 55–59.

Steinberg, L. (2008). A social neuroscience perspective on adolescent risk-taking. *Developmental Review, 28,* 78–106.

Sternberg, R. J., Bonney, C. R., Gabora, L., & Merrifield, M. (2012). WICS: A model for college and university admissions. *Educational Psychologist, 47*(1), 30–41. doi:10.1080/00461520.2011.638882

Sternberg, R. J., Jarvin, L., Birney, D. P., Naples, A., Stemler, S. E., Newman, T., … & Grigorenko, E. L. (2014). Testing the theory of successful intelligence in teaching grade 4 language arts, mathematics, and science. *Journal of Educational Psychology, 106*(3), 881–899. doi:10.1037/a0035833

Stevens, M. J., & Campion, M. A. (1999). Staffing work teams: Development and validation of a selection test for teamwork settings. *Journal of Management, 20,* 503–530.

Stevenson, R. J., Oaten, M. J., Caste, T. I., Repacholi, B. M., & Wagland, P. (2010). Children's response to adult disgust elicitors: Development and acquisition. *Developmental Psychology, 46,* 165–177.

Stice, E., Presnell, K., Shaw, H., & Rohde, P. (2005). Psychological and behavioral risk factors for obesity onset in adolescent girls: A prospective study. *Journal of Consulting and Clinical Psychology, 73,* 195–202.

Stinson, F. S., Dawson, D. A., Chou, P. S., et al. (2007). The epidemiology of DSM-IV specific phobia in the USA: Results from the National Epidemiologic Survey on Alcohol and Related Conditions. *Psychological Medicine, 37,* 1047–1059.

Stothart, C. R., Simons, D. J., Boot, W. R., & Kramer, A. F. (2014) Is the effect of aerobic exercise on cognition a placebo effect? *PLoS ONE 9*(10), e109557. doi:10.1371/journal.pone.0109557

Stout, J. G., Dasgupta, N., Hunsinger, M., & McManus, M. (2011). STEMing the tide: Using ingroup experts to inoculate women's self-concept and professional goals in science, technology, engineering, and mathematics (STEM). *Journal of Personality and Social Psychology, 100,* 255–270.

Strack, F., Martin, L. L., & Stepper, S. (1988). Inhibiting and facilitating conditions of the human smile: A nonobtrusive test of the facial feedback hypothesis. *Journal of Personality and Social Psychology, 54,* 768–777.

Strahan, E. J., Spencer, S. J., & Zanna, M. P. (2002). Subliminal priming and persuasion: Striking while the iron is hot. *Journal of Experimental Social Psychology, 38,* 556–568.

Strassman, R. (2001). *DMT: Spirit molecule.* Rochester, VT: Park Street Press.

Stratton, R. J., Stubbs, R. J., & Elia, M. (2003). Short-term continuous enteral tube feeding schedules did not suppress appetite and food intake in healthy men in a placebo-controlled trial. *Journal of Nutrition, 133,* 2570–2576.

Stessman, J., Rottenberg, Y., Shimshilashvili, I., Ein-Mor, E., Jacobs, J. M. (2014). Loneliness, health, and longevity. *The Journals of Gerontology. Series A, Biological Sciences and Medical Sciences, 69*(6), 744–750. doi:10.1093/gerona/glt147

Stuart, E. W., Shimp, T. A., & Engle, R. W. (1987). Classical conditioning of consumer attitudes: Four experiments in an advertising context. *Journal of Consumer Research, 14*(3), 334–349.

Stubbs, A. (2014). Reducing mental illness stigma in health care students and professionals: A review of the literature. *Australasian Psychiatry, 22*(6), 579–584. doi:10.1177/1039856214556324

Sturm, R., & Hattori, A. (2015). Diet and obesity in Los Angeles County 2007–2012: Is there a measurable effect of the 2008 "fast-food ban"? *Social Science and Medicine, 133,* 205–211.

Sturmer, S., Snyder, M., & Omoto, A. M. (2005). Prosocial emotions and helping: The moderating role of group membership. *Journal of Personality and Social Psychology, 88,* 532–546.

Substance Abuse and Mental Health Services Administration (SAMHSA). (2012). Results from the 2011 National Survey on Drug Use and Health: Mental health findings, NSDUH Series H-45, HHS

Publication No. (SMA) 12-4725. Rockville, MD: Substance Abuse and Mental Health Services Administration.

Substance Abuse and Mental Health Services Administration (SAMHSA). (2014). Results from the 2013 National Survey on Drug Use and Health: National Findings. Rockville, MD: SAMHSA.

Sulloway, F. (2007). Birth order and intelligence. *Science, 316,* 1711–1712.

Sumnall, H. R., Measham, F., Brandt, S. D., & Cole, J. C. (2010). Salvia divinorum use and phenomenology: Results from an online survey [Electronic publication ahead of print]. *Journal of Psychopharmacology.*

Sumner, J. A., Mineka, S., Zinbarg, R. E., Craske, M. G., Vrshek-Schallhorn, S., & Epstein, A. (2014). Examining the long-term stability of overgeneral autobiographical memory. *Memory, 22*(3), 163–170. doi:10.1080/09658211.2013.774021

Sundet, J. (2004). The end of the Flynn effect: A study of secular trends in mean intelligence scores of Norwegian conscripts during half a century. *Intelligence, 32,* 349.

Suomi, S. J., & Harlow, H. (1972). Social rehabilitation of isolate-reared monkeys. *Developmental Psychology, 6,* 487–496.

Swartz, M., & Swanson, J. (2004). Involuntary outpatient commitment, community treatment orders, and assisted outpatient treatment: What's in the data? *Canadian Journal of Psychiatry/La Revue Canadienne de Psychiatrie, 49,* 585–591.

Sweeny, T. D., Grabowecky, M., Suzuki, S., Paller, K. A. (2009). Long-lasting effects of subliminal affective priming from facial expressions. *Consciousness and Cognition, 18,* 929-938.

Świtaj, P., Grygiel, P., Anczewska, M., & Wciórka, J. (2014). Loneliness mediates the relationship between internalized stigma and depression among patients with psychotic disorders. *International Journal of Social Psychiatry, 60*(8), 733–740. doi:10.1177/0020764013513442

Swithers, S. E., Baker, C. R., & Davidson, T. L. (2009). General and persistent effects of high-intensity sweeteners on body weight gain and caloric compensation in rats. *Behavioral Neuroscience, 123,* 772–780.

Swithers, S. E., & Davidson, T. L. (2005). Obesity: Outwitting the wisdom of the body? *Current Neurology and Neuroscience Reports, 5,* 159–162.

Symons, C. S., & Johnson, B. T. (1997). The self-reference effect in memory: A meta-analysis. *Psychological Bulletin, 121,* 371–394.

Takahashi, Y. (1990). Is multiple personality really rare in Japan? *Dissociation, 3,* 57–59.

Talarico, J., & Rubin, D. (2003). Confidence, not consistency, characterizes flashbulb memories. *Psychological Science, 14,* 455–461.

Talmi, D. (2013). Enhanced emotional memory: Cognitive and neural mechanisms. *Current Directions in Psychological Science, 22*(6), 430–436. doi:10.1177/0963721413498893

Talmi, D., Grady, C., Goshen-Gottstein, Y., & Moscovitch, M. (2005). Neuroimaging the serial position curve: A test of single-store versus dual-store models. *Psychological Science, 16,* 716–723.

Tanaka, A., Koizumi, A., Imai, H., Hiramatsu, S., Hiramoto, E., & de Gelder, B. (2010). I feel your voice: Cultural differences in the perception of emotion. *Psychological Science, 21,* 1259–1262.

Tang, Y., Shimizu, E., Dube, G., Rampon, C., Kerchner, G., Zhuo, M., et al. (1999). Genetic enhancement of learning and memory in mice. *Nature, 401*(6748), 63–69.

Tang, Y-Y., Ma, Y., Fan, Y., Feng, H., Wang, J., Feng, S., Lu, Q., Hu, B., Lin, Y., Li, J., Zhang, Y., Wang, Y., Zhou, L., & Fan, M. (2009). Central and autonomic nervous system interaction is altered by short-term meditation. *PNAS: Proceedings of the National Academy of Sciences, 105,* 8865–8870.

Tanti, A., & Belzung, C. (2013). Neurogenesis along the septo-temporal axis of the hippocampus: Are depression and the action of antidepressants region-specific? *Neuroscience,* 234–252. doi: 10.1016/j.neuroscience.2013.08.017

Taylor, A. J., & Hort, J. (2004). Measuring proximal stimuli involved in flavour perception. In A. J. Taylor & D. R. Roberts (Eds.), *Flavor perception* (pp. 1–38). Oxford, UK: Blackwell.

Taylor, C. A., Lee, S. J., Guterman, N. B., & Rice, J. C. (2010). Use of spanking for 3-year-old children and associated intimate partner aggression or violence. *Pediatrics, 126,* 415–24.

Taylor, S. E. (2002). *The tending instinct: How nurturing is essential to who we are and how we live.* New York: Holt.

Taylor, S. E. (2006). Tend and befriend: Biobehavioral bases of affiliation under stress. *Current Directions in Psychological Science, 15,* 273–277.

Teasdale, T. W. & Owen, D. R. (2005). A long-term rise and recent decline in intelligence test performance: The Flynn effect in reverse. *Personality and Individual Differences, 39*(4), 837–843.

Tellegen, A., Lykken, D. T., Bouchard, T. J., Wilcox, K. J., Segal, N. L., & Rich, S. (1988). Personality similarity in twins reared apart and together. *Journal of Personality And Social Psychology, 54*(6), 1031–1039. doi:10.1037/0022-3514.54.6.1031

Teplin, L. A., McClelland, G. M., Abram, K. M., & Weiner, D. A. (2005). Crime victimization in adults with severe mental illness: Comparison with the National Crime Victimization Survey. *Archives of General Psychiatry, 62,* 911–921.

Terracciano, A., Abdel-Khalek, A. M., Adám, N., et al. (2005). National character does not reflect mean personality trait levels in 49 cultures. *Science, 310,* 96–100.

Tett, R. P., Jackson, D. N., & Rothstein, M. (1991). Personality measures as predictors of job performance: A meta-analytic review. *Personnel Psychology, 44,* 703–742.

Thase, M. E., & Denko, T. (2008). Pharmacotherapy of mood disorders. *Annual Review of Clinical Psychology, 4,* 53–91.

Thomas, N., Rossell, S., Farhall, J., Shawyer, F., & Castle, D. (2010). Cognitive behavioural therapy for auditory hallucinations: Effectiveness and predictors of outcome in a specialist clinic [Electronic publication ahead of print]. *Behavioural and Cognitive Psychotherapy.*

Thomas, S. B., & Quinn, S. C. (1991). The Tuskegee syphilis study, 1932 to 1972: Implications for HIV education and AIDS risk education programs in the black community. *American Journal of Public Health, 81,* 1498–1505.

Thompson, A., & Riggio, R. E. (2010). Introduction to special issue on defining and measuring character in leadership. *Consulting Psychology Journal: Practice and Research, 62*(4), 211–215.

Thoresen, C., Bradley, J., Bliese, P., & Thoresen, J. (2004). The Big Five personality traits and individual job performance growth trajectories in maintenance and transitional job stages. *Journal of Applied Psychology, 89,* 835–853.

Thoresen, C., Kaplan, S., Barsky, A., Warren, C., & de Chermont, K. (2003). The affective underpinnings of job perceptions and attitudes: A meta-analytic review and integration. *Psychological Bulletin, 129,* 914–945.

Thornicroft G. (2008). Stigma and discrimination limit access to mental health care. *Epidemiologia e Psichiatria Sociale 17,* 14–19.

Thornton, A., & Raihani, N. J. (2010). Identifying teaching in wild animals. *Learning & Behavior, 38*(3), 297–309.

Tims, M., Bakker, A., Derks, D., Rhenen, W. (2013). Job crafting at the team and individual level: Implications for work engagement and performance. *Group & Organization Management [serial online], 38*(4), 427–454. Retrieved from PsycINFO. Accessed April 11, 2015.

Tobias, M. C., O'Neill, J., Hudkins, M., Bartzokis, G., Dean, A. C., & London, E. D. (2010). White-matter abnormalities in brain during early abstinence from methamphetamine abuse. *Psychopharmacology, 209,* 13–24.

Tochigi, M., Okazaki, Y., Kato, N., & Sasaki, T. (2004). What causes seasonality of birth in schizophrenia? *Neuroscience Research, 48,* 1–11.

Todorov, A., Mandisodza, A. N., Goren, A., & Hall, C. (2005). Inferences of competence from faces predict election outcomes. *Science, 308,* 1623–1626.

Tolman, E. C., & Honzik, C. H. (1930). Degrees of hunger, reward and non-reward, and maze learning in rats. *University of California Publications in Psychology, 4241*–4256.

Tom, G., Tong, S., & Hesse, C. (2010). Thick slice and thin slice teaching evaluations. *Social Psychology of Education, 13*(1), 129–136.

Tomblin, J. B., O'Brien, M., Shriberg, L. D., Williams, C., Murray, J., Patil, S., Bjork, J., Anderson, S., & Ballard, K. (2009). Language features in a mother and daughter of a chromosome 7;13 translocation involving FOXP2. *Journal of Speech, Language, and Hearing Research, 52,* 1157–1174.

Tomko, R. L., Trull, T. J., Wood, P. K., & Sher, K. J. (2014). Characteristics of borderline personality disorder in a community sample: Comorbidity, treatment utilization, and general functioning. *Journal of Personality Disorders, 28*(5), 734–750.

Tooby, J., & Cosmides, L. (1990). On the universality of human nature and the uniqueness of the individual: The role of genetics and adaptation. *Journal of Personality, Special Issue: Biological Foundations of Personality—Evolution, Behavioural Genetics, and Psychophysiology, 58,* 17–67.

Tracy, M., Zimmerman, F. J., Galea, S., et al. (2008). What explains the relation between family poverty and childhood depressive symptoms? *Journal of Psychiatric Research, 42*(14), 1163–1175.

Trahan, L. H., Stuebing, K. K., Fletcher, J. M., & Hiscock, M. (2014). The Flynn effect: A meta-analysis. *Psychological Bulletin, 140*(5), 1332–1360. doi:10.1037/a0037173

Trajanovic, N., Radivojevic, V., Kaushansky, Y., & Shapiro, C. (2007). Positive sleep state misperception: A new concept of sleep misperception. *Sleep Medicine, 8*(2), 111–118.

Tranel, D., & Damasio, A. (1985). Knowledge without awareness: An autonomic index of facial recognition by prosopagnosics. *Science, 228,* 1453–1454.

Trinder, J. (1988). Subjective insomnia without objective findings: A pseudo-diagnostic classification? *Psychological Bulletin, 103,* 87–94.

Trivers, R. L. (1971). The evolution of reciprocal altruism. *Quarterly Review of Biology, 46,* 35–57.

Tucker-Drob, E. M., Briley, D. A., & Harden, K. P. (2013). Genetic and environmental influences on cognition across development and context. *Current Directions in Psychological Science, 22*(5), 349–355. doi:10.1177/0963721413485087

Turkheimer, E., Haley, A., Waldron, M., D'Onofrio, B., & Gottesman, I. I. (2003). Socioeconomic status modifies heritability of IQ in young children. *Psychological Science, 14,* 623–628.

Tversky, A., & Kahneman, D. (1973). Availability: A heuristic for judging frequency and probability. *Cognitive Psychology, 5,* 207–232.

Tversky, A., & Kahneman, D. (1982). The framing of decisions and the psychology of choice. *Science, 211*(4481), 453–458.

Ullman, M. T., Corkin, S., Coppola, M., Hickok, G., Growdon, J. H., Koroshetz, W. J., & Pinker, S. (1997). A neural dissociation within language: Evidence that the mental dictionary is part of the declarative memory, and that grammatical rules are processed by the procedural system. *Journal of Cognitive Neuroscience, 9,* 266–276.

Umberson, D., Pudrovska, T., & Reczek, C. (2010). Parenthood, childlessness, and well-being: A life course perspective. *Journal of Marriage and Family, 72*(3), 612–629.

Undurraga, J., & Baldessarini, R. (2011). Randomized, placebo-controlled trials of antidepressants for acute major depression: Thirty-year meta-analytic review. *Neuropsychopharmacology, 37,* 851–864.

United States Department of Health and Human Services. (2014). *The health consequences of smoking-50 years of progress: A report of the surgeon general.* Rockville, MD: Author.

University of New Hampshire (2012). Unwanted sexual experiences at UNH: 2012 study and changes over time. Retrieved from http://cola.unh.edu/sites/cola.unh.edu/files/departments/Justiceworks/use/84677USEReport.pdf

Unsworth, N., Fukuda, K., Awh, E., & Vogel, E.K. (2014).Working memory and fluid intelligence: Capacity, attention control, and secondary memory. *Cognitive Psychology, 71,* 1–26.

Urry, H. L., Nitschke, J. B., Dolski, I., Jackson, D. C., Dalton, K. M., Mueller, C. J., et al. (2004). Making a life worth living: Neural correlates of well-being. *Psychological Science, 15, 367–372.*

Valdes, S. G. (2005). Frequency and success: An empirical study of criminal law defenses, federal constitutional evidentiary claims, and plea negotiations. *University of Pennsylvania Law Review, 153,* 1709–1814.

Valkenburg, P. M., & Peter, J. (2009). Social consequences of the Internet for adolescents: A decade of research. *Current Directions in Psychological Science, 18,* 1–5.

van de Water, T. (1997). Psychology's entrepreneurs and the marketing of industrial psychology. *Journal of Applied Psychology, 82*(4), 486–499.

Van den Bussche, E., Van den Noortgate, W., & Reynvoet, B. (2009). Mechanisms of masked priming: A meta-analysis. *Psychological Bulletin, 135,* 452–477.

van der Kolk, B. A. (1994). The body keeps score: Memory and the evolving psychobiology of posttraumatic stress. *Harvard Review of Psychiatry, 1,* 253–265.

van der Sanden, R. M., Stutterheim, S. E., Pryor, J. B., Kok, G., & Bos, A. R. (2014). Coping with stigma by association and family burden among family members of people with mental illness. *Journal of Nervous and Mental Disease, 202*(10), 710–717. doi:10.1097/NMD.0000000000000189

van Hooft, E. A. J., Born, M. P. (2012). Intentional response distortion on personality tests: Using eye-tracking to understand response processes when faking. *Journal of Applied Psychology, 97*(2), 301–16.

van IJzendoorn, M., & Juffer, F. (2005). Adoption is a successful natural intervention enhancing adopted children's IQ and school performance. *Current Directions in Psychological Science, 14*(6), 326–330.

Van Le, Q., Isbell, L. A., Matsumoto, J., Nguyen, M., Hori, E., Maior, R. S., Tomaz, C., ... & Nishijo, H. (2013). Pulvinar neurons reveal neurobiological evidence of past selection for rapid detection of snakes. *PNAS: Proceedings of the National Academy of Sciences USA, 110,* 19000–19005.

van Os, J., Pedersen, C. B., & Mortensen, P. B. (2004). Confirmation of synergy between urbanicity and familial liability in the causation of psychosis. *American Journal of Psychiatry, 161,* 2312–2314.

van Praag, H. (2008). Neurogenesis and exercise: Past and future directions. *Neuromolecular Medicine, 10,* 128–140.

van Praag, H. (2009). Exercise and the brain: Something to chew on. *Trends in Neuroscience, 32,* 283–290.

van Praag, H., Lucero, M. J., Yeo, G. W., Stecker, K., Heivand, N., Zhao, C., Yip, E., Afanador, M., Schroeter, H., Hammerstone, J., & Gage, F. H. (2007). Plant-derived flavanol (−)epicatechin enhances angiogenesis and retention of spatial memory in mice. *Journal of Neuroscience, 27,* 5869–5878.

van Straten, A., & Cuijpers, P. (2009). Self-help therapy for insomnia: A meta-analysis. *Sleep Medicine Reviews, 13*(1), 61–71.

Vance, E. B., & Wagner, N. N. (1976). Written descriptions of orgasm: A study of sex differences. *Archives of Sexual Behavior, 5,* 87–98.

Vanheusden, K., Mulder, C., van der Ende, J., van Lenthe, F., Mackenbach, J., & Verhulst, F. (2008). Young adults face major barriers to seeking help from mental health services. *Patient Education and Counseling, 73*(1), 97–104.

Vanman, E. J., Saltz, J. L., Nathan, L. R., & Warren, J. A. (2004). Racial discrimination by low-prejudiced Whites: Facial movements as implicit measures of attitudes related to behavior. *Psychological Science, 15,* 711–714.

Vargha-Khadem, F., Gadian, D. G., Copp, A., & Mishkin, M. (2005). FOXP2 and the neuroanatomy of speech and language. *Nature Reviews Neuroscience, 6,* 131–138.

Vaughn, L. K., Denning, G., Stuhr, K. L., et al. (2010). Endocannabinoid signaling: Has it got rhythm? *British Journal of Pharmacology, 160,* 530–543.

Vaughn, M. G., Fu, Q., Beaver, D., DeLisi, M., Perron, B., & Howard, M. (2010). Are personality disorders associated with social welfare burden in the United States? *Journal of Personality Disorders, 24*(6), 709–720. doi:10.1521/pedi.2010.24.6.709

Verwey, M., & Amir, S. (2009). Food-entrainable circadian oscillators in the brain. *European Journal of Neuroscience, 30*(9), 1650–1657.

Vinchur, A., Schippmann, J., Switzer, F., & Roth, P. (1998). A meta-analytic review of predictors of job performance for salespeople. *Journal of Applied Psychology, 83*(4), 586–597.

Vines, B., Norton, A., & Schlaug, G. (2011). Non-invasive brain stimulation enhances the effects of melodic intonation therapy. *Frontiers in Psychology, 2*(230), 1–10. doi:10.3389/fpsyg.2011.00230

Viswesvaran, C., Schmidt, F. L., & Ones, D. S. (2005). Is there a general factor in ratings of job performance? A meta-analytic framework for disentangling substantive and error influences. *Journal of Applied Psychology, 90*(1), 108–131.

Vogel, D., Markl, A., Yu, T., Kotchoubey, B., Lang, S., & Müller, F. (2013). Can mental imagery functional magnetic resonance imaging predict recovery in patients with disorders of consciousness? *Archives of Physical Medicine and Rehabilitation, 94*(10), 1891–1898.

Vogel, D. L., Wade, N. G., & Ascheman, P. (2009). Measuring perceptions of stigmatization by others for seeking psychological help: Reliability and validity of a new stigma scale with college students. *Journal of Counseling Psychology, 56*, 301–308.

Vogel, D. L., Wade, N. G., Wester, S. R., Larson, L., & Hackler, A. H. (2007). Seeking help from a mental health professional: The influence of one's social network. *Journal of Clinical Psychology, 63*, 233–245.

Vogel, E., Woodman, G., & Luck, S. (2001). Storage of features, conjunctions, and objects in visual working memory. *Journal of Experimental Psychology: Human Perception and Performance, 27*, 92–114.

Volkow, N. D. (2010). Congressional Caucus on Prescription Drug Abuse. Retrieved November 24, 2010, from http://nida.nih.gov/Testimony/9-22-10Testimony.html

von Dawans, B., Fischbacher, U., Kirschbaum, C., Fehr, E., & Heinrichs, M. (2012). The social dimension of stress reactivity: Acute stress increases prosocial behavior in humans [Electronic publication ahead of print]. *Psychological Science*, 1–10. doi:10.1177/0956797611431576

vonFrisch, K. (1967). *The dance language and orientation of bees.* Cambridge, MA: Harvard University Press.

Vrangalova, Z., Bukberg, R. E., & Rieger, G. (2014). Birds of a feather? Not when it comes to sexual permissiveness. *Journal of Social and Personal Relationships, 31*, 91–113.

Vygotsky, L. (1978). *Mind in society: The development of higher psychological processes.* (M. Cole, V. John-Steiner, S. Scribner, & E. Soubermen, Eds.). Cambridge MA: Harvard University Press.

Wade, K., Garry, M., Read, J., & Lindsay, S. (2002). A picture is worth a thousand lies: Using false photographs to create false childhood memories. *Psychonomic Bulletin & Review, 9*, 597–603.

Waite, L. J., & Gallagher, M. (2000). *The case for marriage: Why married people are happier, healthier and better off financially.* New York: Doubleday.

Wakefield, A. J., Murch, S. H., Anthony, A., Linnell, J., Casson, D. M., Malik, M., et al. (1998). Retracted: Ileal-lymphoid-nodular hyperplasia, non-specific colitis, and pervasive developmental disorder in children. *Lancet, 351*, 637–641.

Walker, E. G., Savole, T., & Davis, D. (1994). Neuromotor precursors of schizophrenia. *Schizophrenia Bulletin, 20*, 441–451.

Walker, E. G., Shapiro, D., Esterberg, M., & Trotman, H. (2010). Neurodevelopment and schizophrenia: Broadening the focus. *Current Directions in Psychological Science, 19*, 204–208.

Wallace, J., Edwards, B., Arnold, T., Frazier, M., & Finch, D. (2009). Work stressors, role-based performance, and the moderating influence of organizational support. *Journal of Applied Psychology, 94*, 254–262.

Wallston, K. A., Wallston, B. S., & DeVellis, R. (1978). Development of the Multidimensional Health Locus of Control (MHLC) scales. *Health Education Monographs, 6*, 160–170.

Walsh, T., McClellan, J. M., McCarthy, S. E., Addington, A. M., Pierce, S. B., et al. (2008). Rare structural variants disrupt multiple genes in neurodevelopmental pathways in schizophrenia. *Science, 320*, 539–543.

Wamsley, E. J. (2014). Dreaming and offline memory consolidation. *Current Neurology and Neuroscience Reports, 14*(3), 433.

Wamsley, E., & Stickgold, R. (2010). Dreaming and offline memory processing. *Current Biology, 20*(23), R1010–R1013.

Wan, Z. Y., Zheng, X., Marchina, S., Norton, A., & Schlaug, G. (2014). Intensive therapy induces contralateral white matter changes in chronic stroke patients with Broca's aphasia. *Brain and Language, 136*, 1–7.

Wang, G. J., Volkow, N. D., Felder, C., Fowler, J. S., Levy, A. V., Pappas, N. R., Wong, C. T., Zhu, W., & Netusil, N. (2002). Enhanced resting activity of the oral somatosensory cortex in obese subjects. *Neuroreport, 13*, 1151–1155.

Wang, X., Lu, T., Snider, R. K., & Liang, L. (2005). Sustained firing in auditory cortex evoked by preferred stimuli. *Nature, 435*, 341–346.

Wansink, B., Painter, J. E., & North, J. (2005). Bottomless bowls: Why visual cues of portion size may influence intake. *Obesity Research, 13*, 93–100.

Wardell, J. D., & Read, J. P. (2013). Alcohol expectancies, perceived norms, and drinking behavior among college students: Examining the reciprocal determinism hypothesis. *Psychology of Addictive Behaviors, 27*(1), 191–196. doi:10.1037/a0030653

Ware, M. A., Wang, T., Shapiro, S. et al. (2010). Smoked cannabis for chronic neuropathic pain: A randomized controlled trial. *Canadian Medical Association Journal, 182*, E694–E701.

Wark, D. (2006). Alert hypnosis: A review and case report. *American Journal of Clinical Hypnosis, 48*(4), 291–300.

Watson, A. C., Miller, F. E., & Lyons, J. S. (2005). Adolescent Attitudes Toward Serious Mental Illness. *Journal of Nervous and Mental Disease, 193*, 769–772.

Watson, D., & Slack, A. K. (1993). General factors of affective temperament and their relation to job satisfaction over time. *Organizational Behavior and Human Decision Processes, 54*, 181–202.

Watson, J. B. (1930). *Behaviorism.* Chicago: University of Chicago Press.

Watson, J. B., & Rayner, R. R. (1920). Conditioned emotional reactions. *Journal of Experimental Psychology, 3*, 1–14.

Watson, J., & Strayer, D. (2010). Supertaskers: Profiles in extraordinary multitasking ability. *Psychonomic Bulletin & Review, 17*(4), 479–485.

Watson, M. W., & Getz, K. (1990). The relationship between Oedipal behaviors and children's family role concepts. *Merrill-Palmer Quarterly, 36*, 487–505.

Weeks, D. L., & Anderson, L. P. (2000). The interaction of observational learning with overt practice: Effects on motor skill learning. *Acta Psychologica, 104*, 259–271.

Weinsier, R. L., Hunter, G. R., Desmond, R. A., Byrne, N. M., Zuckerman, P. A., & Darnell, B. (2002). Free-living activity expenditure in women successful and unsuccessful at maintaining a normal body weight. *American Journal of Clinical Nutrition, 75*, 499–504.

Weise, D., Pyszczynski, T., Cox, C., Arndt, J., Greenberg, J., Solomon, S., et al. (2008, May). Interpersonal politics: The role of terror management and attachment processes in shaping political preferences. *Psychological Science, 19*, 448–455.

Weisman, A. G., Lopez, S. R., Ventura, J., Nuechterlein, K. H., Goldstein, M. J., & Hwang, S. (2000). A comparison of psychiatric symptoms between Anglo-Americans and Mexican-Americans with schizophrenia. *Schizophrenia Bulletin, 26*, 817–824.

Weiss, A., King, J. E., & Hopkins, W. D. (2007). A cross-setting study of chimpanzee (Pan troglodytes) personality structure and development: Zoological parks and Yerkes National Primate Research Center. *American Journal of Primatology, 69*(11), 1264.

Weiss, E., Kemmler, G., Deisenhammer, E., Fleischhacker, W., & Delazer, M. (2003). Sex differences in cognitive functions. *Personality and Individual Differences, 35*(4), 863–875.

Weitzer, R., & Tuch, S. A. (2004). Race and perceptions of police misconduct. *Social Problems, 51*, 305–325.

Wellings, K., Field, J., Johnson, A. M., & Wadsworth, J. (1994). *Sexual behaviour in Britain: The national survey of sexual attitudes and lifestyles.* Penguin: Harmondsworth.

Wells, G. L. (1984). The psychology of lineup identifications. *Journal of Applied Psychology, 14*(2), 89–103. doi:10.1111/j.1559-1816.1984.tb02223.x

Wells, G. L., & Olson, E. A. (2003). Eyewitness testimony. *Annual Review of Psychology, 54*, 277–295. doi:10.1146/annurev.psych.54.101601.145028

Wells, G. L., & Quinlaven, D. S. (2009). Suggestive eyewitness identification procedures and the Supreme Court's reliability test in light of eyewitness science: 30 years later. *Law and Human Behavior, 33*, 1–24.

Wells, G. L., Small, M., Penrod, S., Malpass, R. S., Fulero, S. M., & Brimacombe, C. E. (1998). Eyewitness identification procedures: Recommendations for lineups and photospreads. *Law and Human Behavior, 22*(6), 603–647. doi:10.1023/A:1025750605807

Wells, G. L., Steblay, N. K., & Dysart, J. E. (2015). Double-blind photo lineups using actual eyewitnesses: An experimental test of a sequential versus simultaneous lineup procedure. *Law and Human Behavior, 39*(1), 1–14. doi:10.1037/lhb0000096

Wenk, G. (2010). *Your brain on food: how chemicals control your thoughts and feelings.* Oxford, UK: Oxford University Press.

Westen, D. (1998). The scientific legacy of Sigmund Freud: Toward a psychodynamically informed psychological science. *Psychological Bulletin, 124*, 333–371.

Westen, D., Blagov, P. S., & Harenski, K. (2006). Neural bases for motivated reasoning: An fMRI study of emotional constraints on partisan political judgment in the 2004 U.S. presidential election. *Journal of Cognitive Neuroscience, 18*, 1974–1958.

Westen, D., & Bradley, R. (2005). Empirically supported complexity: Rethinking evidence-based practice in psychotherapy. *Current Directions in Psychological Science, 14*, 266–271.

Westman, M., & Eden, D. (1997). Effects of a respite from work on burnout: Vacation relief and fade-out. *Journal of Applied Psychology, 82*, 516–527.

White, A. M. (2003). What happened? Alcohol, memory blackouts, and the brain. *Alcohol Research & Health, 27*, 186–196.

White House commission on complementary and alternative medicine policy: Final report (2002). Retrieved April 9, 2015, from http://www.whccamp.hhs.gov/tc.html

White, R., & Williams, S. (2009). Amygdaloid neurosurgery for aggressive behaviour, Sydney, 1967–1977: Chronological narrative. *Australas Psychiatry, 17*, 405–209.

Whitson, J. A., & Galinsky, A. D. (2008). Lacking control increases illusory pattern perception. *Science, 322*, 115–117.

Whorf, B. L. (1973). *Language, thought, and reality: Selected writings of Benjamin Whorf,* edited by J. B. Carroll. Oxford, UK: Technology Press of MIT.

Wight, R. G., Leblanc, A. J., Lee-Badgett, M. V (2013). Same-sex legal marriage and psychological well-being: Findings from the California Health Interview Survey. *American Journal of Public Health, 103*, 339–346.

Wijdicks, E. F. (2006). Minimally conscious state vs. persistent vegetative state: The case of Terry (Wallis) vs. the case of Terri (Schiavo). *Mayo Clinic Proceedings, 81*, 1155–1158.

Willett, F., Suminski, A., Fagg, A., & Hatsopoulos, N. (2013). Improving brain–machine interface performance by decoding intended future movements. *Journal of Neural Engineering, 10*(2), 026011-026011. doi:10.1088/1741-2560/10/2/026011

Williams, J. L., Holman, D. W., & Klein, R. S. (2014). Chemokines in the balance: maintenance of homeostasis and protection at CNS barriers. *Frontiers in Cellular Neuroscience, 28*(8), 154. doi:10.3389/fncel.2014.00154.

Willingham, D. T. (2004). Reframing the mind: How Howard Gardner became a hero among educators by simply by redefining talents as "intelligences." *Education Next, 4*(3), 19–24.

Willis, J., & Todorov, A. (2006). First impressions: Making up your mind after a 100-ms exposure to a face. *Psychological Science, 17*, 592–598.

Willoughby, T., Good, M., Adachi, P., Hamza, C., & Tavernier, R. (2013). Examining the link between adolescent brain development and risk taking from a social–developmental perspective. *Brain and Cognition, 83*(3), 315–323.

Willness, C. R., Steel, P., & Lee, K. (2007). A meta-analysis of the antecedents and consequences of workplace sexual harassment. *Personnel Psychology, 60*(1), 127–162.

Wimmer, H., & Perner, J. (1983). Beliefs about beliefs: Representation and constrained function of wrong beliefs in young children's understanding of deceptions. *Cognition, 13*, 103–128.

Wing, Y., Chen, L., Lam, S., Li, A., Tang, N., Ng, M., … & Chan, P. (2011). Familial aggregation of narcolepsy. *Sleep Medicine, 12*(10), 947–951.

Winter, B., Breitenstein, C., Mooren, F. C., Voelker, K., Fobker, M., Lechtermann, A., Krueger, K., Fromme, A., Korsukewitz, C., Floel, A., & Knecht, S. (2007). High impact running improves learning. *Neurobiology of Learning and Memory, 87*, 597–609.

Winterer, G. (2010). Why do patients with schizophrenia smoke? *Current Opinion in Psychiatry, 23*, 112–119.

Witelson, S. F., Beresh, H., & Kigar, D. L. (2006). Intelligence and brain size in 100 postmortem brains: Sex, lateralization and age factors. *Brain: A Journal of Neurology, 129*(Pt 2), 386–398.

Witelson, S. F., Kigar, D. L., & Harvey, T. (1999). The exceptional brain of Albert Einstein. *Lancet, 353*, 2149–2153.

Wittchen, H. & Jacobi, F. (2005). Size and burden of mental disorders in Europe: A critical review and appraisal of 27 studies. *European Neuropsychopharmacology, 15*, 357–376.

Wobber, V., Hare, B., Maboto, J., Lipson, S., Wrangham, R., & Ellison, P. T. (2010). Differential changes in steroid hormones before competition in bonobos and chimpanzees. *PNAS: Proceedings of the National Academy of Sciences of the United States of America, 107*(28), 12457–12462.

Wolf, D., Grothe, M., Fischer, F. U., Heinsen, H., Kilimann, I., Teipel, S., & Fellgiebel, A. (2014). Association of basal forebrain volumes and cognition in normal aging. *Neuropsychologia, 53*, 54–63. doi:10.1016/j.neuropsychologia.2013.11.002

Wolfe, J., Brunelli, D., Rubinstein, J., & Horowitz, T. (2013). Prevalence effects in newly trained airport checkpoint screeners: Trained observers miss rare targets, too. *Journal of Vision,13*(3), 1–9.

Wolfe, J. M., Horowitz, T. S., Van Wert, M. J., Kenner, N. M., Place, S. S., & Kibbi, N. (2007). Low target prevalence is a stubborn source of errors in visual search tasks. *Journal of Experimental Psychology: General, 136*(4), 623–638.

Wolpe, J. (1990). *The practice of behavior therapy.* Elmsford, NY: Pergamon Press.

World Health Organization. (2014, November 1). Preterm birth. Retrieved from http://www.who.int/mediacentre/factsheets/fs363/en/

Wood, J. M., Bootzin, R. R., Rosenhan, D., Nolen-Hoeksema, S., & Jourden, F. (1992). Effects of the 1989 San Francisco earthquake on frequency and content of nightmares. *Journal of Abnormal Psychology, 101*, 219–224.

Woodberry, K. A., Giuliano, A. J., & Seidman, L. J. (2008). Premorbid IQ in schizophrenia. *American Journal of Psychiatry, 165*, 579–587.

Wright, D. (1997). Getting out of the asylum: Understanding the confinement of the insane in the nineteenth century. *Social History of Medicine, 10*, 137–155.

Wright, I. C., Rabe-Hesketh, S., Woodruff, P. W., David, A. S., Murray, R. M., & Bullmore, E. T. (2000). Meta-analysis of regional brain volumes in schizophrenia. *American Journal of Psychiatry, 157*, 16–25.

Wu, A., Ying, Z., & Gomez-Pinilla, F. (2008). Docosahexaenoic acid dietary supplementation enhances the effects of exercise on synaptic plasticity and cognition. *Neuroscience, 155*, 751–759.

Wu, L., Niu, Y., & Yang, J. (2005). Tectal neurons signal impending collision of looming objects in the pigeon. *European Journal of Neuroscience, 22*(9), 2325–2331.

Yamamoto, B. K., Moszczynska, A., & Gudelsky, G. A. (2010). Amphetamine toxicities: Classical and emerging mechanisms. *Annals of the New York Academy of Science, 1187,* 101–121.

Yamazaki, T., & Tanaka, S. (2009). Computational models of timing mechanisms in the cerebellar granular layer. *Cerebellum, 8,* 423–432.

Ybema, J. F., Smulders, P. W., & Bongers, P. M. (2010). Antecedents and consequences of employee absenteeism: A longitudinal perspective on the role of job satisfaction and burnout. *European Journal of Work and Organizational Psychology, 19*(1), 102–124.

Yoo, S. K., & Skovholt, T. M. (2001). Cross-cultural examination of depression expression and help-seeking behavior: A comparative study of American and Korean college students. *Journal of College Counseling, 4,* 10–19.

Yoon, J., Koo, B., Shin, M., Shin, Y., Ko, H., & Shin, Y. (2014). Effect of constraint-induced movement therapy and mirror therapy for patients with subacute stroke. *Annals of Rehabilitation Medicine, 38*(4), 458–466.

Yoon, P., Bastian, B., Anderson, R., Collins, J., & Jaffe, H. (2014). Potentially preventable deaths from the five leading causes of death—United States, 2008–2010. Retrieved from http://www.cdc.gov/mmwr/preview/mmwrhtml/mm6317a1.htm?s_cid=mm6317a1_w

You, J., Fung, H. H. L., & Isaacowitz, D. M. (2009). Age differences in dispositional optimism. *European Journal of Aging, 6,* 247–252.

Youyou, W., Kosinski, M., & Stillwell, D. (2015). Computer-based personality judgments are more accurate than those made by humans. *PNAS: Proceedings of the National Academy of Sciences of the United States of America, 112*(4), 1036–1040. doi:10.1073/pnas.1418680112

Zajonc, R. (2001). Mere exposure: A gateway to the subliminal. *Current Directions in Psychological Science, 10,* 224–228.

Zaleskiewicz, T., Gasiorowska, A., Kesebir, P., & Krueger, F. (2013). Saving can save from death anxiety: Mortality salience and financial decision-making. *PLoS ONE, 8*(11), e79407. doi:10.1371/journal.pone.0079407

Zeidan, F., Gordon, N., Merchant, J., & Goolkasian, P. (2010). The effects of brief mindfulness meditation training on experimentally induced pain. *Journal of Pain, 11*(3), 199–209.

Zellner, D. A., Loaiza, S., Gonzalez, Z., Pita, J., Morales, J., Pecora, D., & Wolf, A. (2006). Food selection changes under stress. *Physiology and Behavior, 87*(4), 789–793.

Zellner, D. A., Saito, S., & Gonzalez, J. (2007). The effect of stress on men's food selection. *Appetite, 49*(3), 696–699.

Zernicke, K. A., Cantrell, H., Finn, P. R., & Lucas, J. (2010). The association between earlier age of first drink, disinhibited personality, and externalizing psychopathology in young adults. *Addictive Behaviors, 35*(5), 414–418.

Zhao, H., & Seibert, S. (2006). The Big Five personality dimensions and entrepreneurial status: A meta-analytical review. *Journal of Applied Psychology, 91,* 259–271.

Zhong, C., & DeVoe, S. E. (2010). You are how you eat: Fast food and impatience. *Psychological Science, 21*(5), 619–622.

Zimmerman, F. J., & Christakis, D. A. (2005). Children's television viewing and cognitive outcomes a longitudinal analysis of national data. *Archives of Pediatrics and Adolescent Medicine, 159,* 619–625.

Credits

Photo Credits

Chapter 1 Page 2: The Everett Collection; 3 Ellie Rothnie/Alamy; 3 *r* Flirt/SuperStock; 9 Shiva3d/Shutterstock; 11 Beerkoff/Shutterstock; 13 Library of Congress Prints and Photographs Division[LC-B2-1072-12]; 13 Bettmann/Corbis; 13 AP Images; 13 Association for Psychological Science; 13 Sascha Burkard/Fotolia; 14 Pictorial Press Ltd/Alamy; 15 Mary Evans Picture Library/Alamy; 16 akg-images/Newscom; 16 Mary Evans Picture Library/Alamy; 17 *b* Classic Image/Alamy; 17 Time Life Pictures/Contributor/Getty Images; 18 Nina Leen/The Life Picture Collection/Getty Images; 21 Colin Anderson/Glow Images

Chapter 2 Page 32: LuckyBusiness/Getty Images; 36 Hawthorne Works Museum of Morton College; 42 Fabrice Beauchene/Fotolia; 45 Shutterstock; 45 Florian Franke/Corbis; 49 The National Archives and Records Administration; 52 Mona Lisa Production/Science Source; 55 Image Source/Glow Images

Chapter 3 Page 67: Anna Hoychuk/Shutterstock; 70 Martin Harvey/Alamy; 70 Creatas/Getty Images Plus; 73 The University of Western Australia; 75 Rod Williams/Nature Picture Library; 80 Martin Nemec/Shutterstock; 81 Neil Bromhall/Nature Picture Library; 83 Thinkstock/Stockbyte/Getty Images; 85 Colin Anderson/Glow Images

Chapter 4 Page 103: Tim Pannell/Corbis/Glow Images; 105 Flashon Studio/Shutterstock; 107 Nick Greening/Alamy; 108 Brian Lasenby/123RF; 110 Anthony Barnhart; 112 Eliza Snow/Getty Images; 118 Brian Prawl/Shutterstock; 118 FORGET Patrick/sagaphoto.com/Alamy; 119 The Vegetable Gardener, c.1590 (oil on panel), Arcimboldo, Giuseppe (1527–93)/Museo Civico Ala Ponzone, Cremona, Italy/Bridgeman Art Library; 119 The Vegetable Gardener, c.1590 (oil on panel), Arcimboldo, Giuseppe (1527–93)/Museo Civico Ala Ponzone, Cremona, Italy/Bridgeman Art Library; 119 PA Photos/Landov; 119 PA Photos/Landov; 121 Sketch for 'Paris, a Rainy Day', 1877 (oil on canvas), pre-restoration (see 181504), Caillebotte, Gustave (1848–94)/Musee Marmottan Monet, Paris, France/Bridgeman Images 124 ivo Gretener/Getty Images; 131 tuja66/Getty Images

Chapter 5 Page 144: PhotoAlto/Alamy; 146 Hank Morgan/Science Source; 150 Steve Prezant/Glow Images; 156 Juice Images/Glow Images; 157 Hulton-Deutsch Collection/Corbis; 158 Bikeriderlondon/Shutterstock; 163 Nathan Griffith/Alamy; 164 Advertising Archive/Courtesy Everett Collection; 164 Multnomah County Sheriff/Splash/Newscom; 166 Ted Kinsman/Science Source; 167 Owen, et al., 2006. Detecting awareness in the vegetative state. Science, vol 313, p. 1402. fig 1.; 172 Chris Gallagher/Science Source

Chapter 6 Page 177: Christina Kennedy/Alamy; 182 The Drs. Nicholas and Dorothy Cummings Center for the History of Psychology, The University of Akron; 185 The Advertising Archives/Alamy; 185 Zrc Wenn Photos/Newscom; 186 Lee O'Dell/Shutterstock; 189 Simon Hadley/Alamy; 192 Richard Goldberg/Shutterstock; 192 RisingStar/Alamy; 194 Deb Hartwell/Pearson Education; 201 Victoria Horner/Chimpanzee Sanctuary & Wildlife Conservation Trust; 201 Philip G. Zimbardo, Inc. 205 Cathy Keifer/Shutterstock; 206 From Meltzoff, A.N., & Moore, M.K. (1977). Imitation of facial and manual gestures by human neonates. Science, 198, 75–78. 206 Miles Barton/Nature Picture Library; 206 Danita Delimont Creative/Alamy; 208 Albert Bandura

Chapter 7 Page 216: Katherine Welles/Shutterstock; 218 Gilbert Iundt/Jean-Yves Ruszniewski/Corbis; 223 Kamira/Shutterstock; 227 Don Emmert/AFP/Getty Images; 233 Lori Howard/Shutterstock; 235 Matteo Malavasi/iStock/Getty Images Plus/Getty Images; 237 Dr. Elizabeth Loftus; 237 Dr. Elizabeth Loftus; 239 Dr. Kimberley Wade; 239 Dr. Kimberley Wade

Chapter 8 Page 250: Chatursunil/Shutterstock; 250 Leo/Shutterstock; 250 Al Mueller/Shutterstock; 254 Blend Images/Shutterstock; 257 AndreusK/Fotolia; 266 Manuela Hartling/Reuters; 277 *r* Nicole S. Berry, Janxin Leu; 273 Friends of Washoe; 273 Michael Nichols/National Geographic Creative

Chapter 9 Page 281: Ed Reinke/AP Images 282 Monkey Business Images/Shutterstock; 282 Luchschen/123RF; 287 Mary Evans Picture Library /Alamy; 289 Photo Researchers/Alamy; 291 Demotix/Splash News/Newscom; 295 Dan Kitwood/Getty Images Europe/Getty Images; 300 Wenn Ltd/Alamy; 302 Princeton University/KRT/Newscom; 303 Hurst Photo/Shutterstock; 303 John Dominis/Getty Images; 304 Niamh Baldock/Alamy

Chapter 10 Page 316: Leungchopan/Fotolia; 319 Doug Steley A/Alamy; 319 MedicalRF.com/Alamy.; 319 Claude Edelmann/Science Source; 322 Lee O'Dell/Shutterstock; 322 Betty Udesen/KRT/Newscom; 322 Santibhavank P/Shutterstock; 323 Cathy Melloan Resources/PhotoEdit; 323 Petit Format/Science Source; 323 Catchlight Visual Services/Alamy; 326 Roberto Westbrook/Getty Images; 327 Warner Bros. Pictures/courtesy Everett Collection; 327 Bubbles Photolibrary/Alamy; 327 Jennie Woodcock/Bubbles Photolibrary/Alamy; 327 Mauricio Jordan de Souza Coelho/ImageBroker/Glow Images; 327 OLJ Studio/Shutterstock; 327 Jim Craigmyle/Flirt/Corbis; 327 Eric Gevaert/Shutterstock; 328 Proceedings of the National Academy of Sciences; 329 Doug Goodman/Science Source; 329 Doug Goodman/Science Source; 330 Judy DeLoache; 330 Judy DeLoache; 330 Judy DeLoache; 331 Lawrence Migdale/Science Source; 333 Nolte Lourens/Shutterstock; 333 Nina Leen/The LIFE Picture Collection/Getty Images; 335 Ruth Jenkinson/DK Images; 338 Bettmann/Corbis; 338 Touchstone Television/ Album/Newscom; 341 Alex Wong/Getty Images; 343 Photos 12/Alamy; 343 AF archive/Alamy; 344 Darryl Dyck/Canadian Press; 349 Ariel Skelley/Blend Images/Alamy

Chapter 11 Page 357: Anatoly Tiplyashin/Shutterstock; 358 Mark Wilson/The Boston Globe/Getty Images; 359 Voisin/Phanie/Science Source; 361 Michele Cozzolino/Shutterstock.;

642

361 akg-images/NASA/Newscom; 362 akg-images/Newscom; 362 Image Source/Corbis 364 Lydie/SIPA/Newscom; 366 Alamy; 368 Anna Khomulo/Fotolia; 370 Alexander Tamargo/Getty Images Entertainment/Getty Images; 371 Julian W/Shutterstock; 371 Sergey Uryadnikov/Shutterstock; 372 Glow Images; 374 Alamy; 376 NJ Advance Media/Landov; 376 NJ Advance Media/Landov; 378 Walter McBride/Getty Images Entertainment/Getty Images; 379 Alamy; 382 Alamy; 383 Alamy; 384 Stock Connection Blue/Alamy; 385 Paul Ekman Group, LLC.; 385 Paul Ekman Group, LLC.; 388 Paul Ekman Group, LLC.; 388 Paul Ekman Group, LLC.; 388 Paul Ekman Group, LLC.; 388 Paul Ekman Group, LLC. 388 Paul Ekman; 388 Paul Ekman; 388 Paul Ekman; 388 Daniel Deme/WENN Photos/Newscom

Chapter 12 Page 397: Pearson Education; 407 Christopher Futcher/Getty Images; 410 AP Images; 410 Brian Zak/Sipa Press/Newscom; 412 Michael Nichols/National Geographic/Getty Images; 412 Poeticpenguin/Shutterstock; 412 Rena Schild/Shutterstock; 417 RichardBakerFarnborough/Alamy; 422 Alamy; 422 Pearson Education; 422 Image Source/Alamy

Chapter 13 Page 430: William DeShazer/MCT/Newscom; 433 Mandy Godbehear/Shutterstock; 436 UpperCut Images/Getty Images; 438 Narcissus, c.1597–99 (oil on canvas), Caravaggio, Michelangelo Merisi da (1571–1610)/Palazzo Barberini, Rome, Italy/Bridgeman Art Library; 443 Matsunaka Takeya/Aflo/Glow Images; 444 Darren Bridges Photography/Alamy; 444 David H. Lewis/Getty Images; 447 Stefanolunardi/Shutterstock; 453 Handout/Getty Images; 454 Kurt Snyder; 454 Grunnitus Studio/Science Source; 456 ImageBroker/Alamy; 458 Elaine Walker

Chapter 14 Page 466: Ambrophoto/Alamy; 468 Jerry Cooke/Contributor/Getty Images; 472 Pearson Education; 472 Pearson Education; 475 Wavebreakmedia/Shutterstock; 477 Art_man/Shutterstock; 480 Erika Schultz/Mct/Newscom; 485 Dennis Hallinan/Alamy; 490 Bettmann/Corbis; 491 Will & Deni McIntyre/Science Source; 491 Bonnie Weller/Staff/Newscom; 494 Konstantin Sutyagin/Shutterstock

Chapter 15 Page 500: Sarah Edwards/WENN Ltd/Alamy; 501 Philip G. Zimbardo, Inc.; 501 Philip G. Zimbardo, Inc. 503 Reproduced with permission. Copyright 2015 Scientific American, Inc. All rights reserved. 505 Copyright 1968 by Stanley Milgram. Copyright Renewed 1993, Alexander Milgram. From the film OBEDIENCE, distributed by Penn State Media Sales; 505 Copyright 1968 by Stanley Milgram. Copyright Renewed 1993, Alexander Milgram. From the film OBEDIENCE, distributed by Penn State Media Sales 505 Copyright 1968 by Stanley Milgram. Copyright Renewed 1993, Alexander Milgram. From the film OBEDIENCE, distributed by Penn State Media Sales; 505 Copyright 1968 by Stanley Milgram. Copyright Renewed 1993, Alexander Milgram. From the film OBEDIENCE, distributed by Penn State Media Sales; 512 Todd Bannor/Alamy; 513 Dragon Images/Shutterstock; 513 Monkey Business Images/Shutterstock; 518 Denis Closon/REX/Newscom; 520 Alamy; 521 Frank Franklin II/AP Images 522 Maximilian Weinzierl/Alamy 525 John Rowley/Stone/Getty Images; 525 Antikainen/Getty Images

Chapter 16 Page 533: stock_wales/Alamy; 538 Visions of America, LLC/Alamy; 539 James Woodson/Getty Images.; 541 Imagesource/Glow Images; 542 Cathy Yeulet/123 RF;

547 Lightwavemedia/Fotolia; 549 Photodisc/Getty Images 551 John Lund/Stephanie Roeser/Glow Images; 553 Cindy Charles/PhotoEdit; 553 Tyler Olson/Shutterstock

Chapter 17 Page 557: Glow Images 565 Kristoffer Tripplaar/Alamy; 574 Steve Prezant/Corbis/Glow Images; 575 Pressmaster/Shutterstock; 583 Richard Ellis/Alamy; 583 Chuck Kennedy/MCT/Newscom

Text Credits

Chapter 1

Text Credit page 17: Watson, J. B. (1930). *Behaviorism*. Chicago: University of Chicago Press. p. 82

Figure 1.7 "Where Professional Psychologists Work" 2007 Doctorate Employment Survey, American Psychological Association.

Figure 1.8 "Work Settings for People Earning Master's and Bachelor's Degrees in Psychology" Magaletta, P. R., Mulvey, T. A. & Grus, C. L. (2010). What Can I Do with a Degree in Psychology? Retrieved http://www.apa.org/workforce/presentations/2010-psychology-degree.pdf.

Text credit page 26: Based on "A Workout, To Go," by Tom Bolen, Head Coach, UEN Gymnastics, from *Physical Educator's Monthly*

Chapter 2

Text credit page 61: Based on "The Climate is Changing, and So Should Our Methods by Felicia Mann, PhD, from *Psychology and Public Policy Newsletter*

Chapter 3

Figure 3.1 Lilienfeld, Scott O.; Lynn, Steven J; Namy, Laura L.; Woolf, Nancy J., *Psychology: From Inquiry to Understanding*, 2nd Ed., © 2011. Reprinted and Electronically reproduced by permission of Pearson Education, Inc., New York, NY.

Text credit page 70: Dick, D. M. (2007). Identification of genes influencing a spectrum of externalizing psychopathology. *Current Directions in Psychological Science*, 16, 331–335.

Figure 3.2 Republished with permission of AAAS, from Influence of life stress on depression: Moderation by a polymorphism in the 5-HTT gene by Caspi, A., et al., *Science*, 301, 386–389. 2003; permission conveyed through Copyright Clearance Center, Inc.

Figure 3.3 © Pearson Education, Inc.

Figure 3.4 Lilienfeld, Scott O.; Lynn, Steven J; Namy, Laura L.; Woolf, Nancy J., *Psychology: From Inquiry to Understanding*, 2nd Ed., © 2011. Reprinted and Electronically reproduced by permission of Pearson Education, Inc., New York, NY.

Figure 3.5 Lilienfeld, Scott O.; Lynn, Steven J; Namy, Laura L.; Woolf, Nancy J., *Psychology: From Inquiry to Understanding*, 2nd Ed., © 2011. Reprinted and Electronically reproduced by permission of Pearson Education, Inc., New York, NY.

Figure 3.6 Lilienfeld, Scott O.; Lynn, Steven J; Namy, Laura L.; Woolf, Nancy J., *Psychology: From Inquiry to Understanding*, 2nd Ed., © 2011. Reprinted and Electronically reproduced by permission of Pearson Education, Inc., New York, NY.

Figure 3.7 Based on "The Time Course and Phases of a Nerve Cell Going from Resting to Action Potential" Adapted from Sternberg, 2004.

Figure 3.8 © Pearson Education, Inc.

Figure 3.9 © Pearson Education, Inc.

Figure 3.10 Lilienfeld, Scott O.; Lynn, Steven J; Namy, Laura L.; Woolf, Nancy J., *Psychology: From Inquiry to Understanding*, 2nd Ed., © 2011. Reprinted and Electronically reproduced by permission of Pearson Education, Inc., New York, NY.

Text credit page 85: Based on Hatsopoulos, N. G., & Donoghue, J. P. (2009). The science of neural interface systems. *Annual Review of Neuroscience*, 32, 249–266; Willett et al., 2013

Figure 3.11 © Pearson Education, Inc.

Figure 3.12 © Pearson Education, Inc.

Figure 3.13 Lilienfeld, Scott O.; Lynn, Steven J; Namy, Laura L.; Woolf, Nancy J., *Psychology: From Inquiry to Understanding*, 2nd Ed., © 2011. Reprinted and Electronically reproduced by permission of Pearson Education, Inc., New York, NY.

Figure 3.15 Lilienfeld, Scott O.; Lynn, Steven J; Namy, Laura L.; Woolf, Nancy J., *Psychology: From Inquiry to Understanding*, 1st Ed., © 2009, p. 116. Reprinted and Electronically reproduced by permission of Pearson Education, Inc., New York, NY.

Figure 3.16 Lilienfeld, Scott O.; Lynn, Steven J; Namy, Laura L.; Woolf, Nancy J., *Psychology: From Inquiry to Understanding*, © 2011. Reprinted and Electronically reproduced by permission of Pearson Education, Inc., New York, NY.

Figure 3.17 Lilienfeld, Scott O.; Lynn, Steven J; Namy, Laura L.; Woolf, Nancy J., *Psychology: From Inquiry to Understanding*, © 2011. Reprinted and Electronically reproduced by permission of Pearson Education, Inc., New York, NY.

Figure 3.18 Marieb, Elaine N.; Hoehn, Katja, *Human Anatomy and Physiology*, 7th Ed., © 2007, p.438. Reprinted and Electronically reproduced by permission of Pearson Education, Inc., New York, NY.

Figure 3.19 Lilienfeld, Scott O.; Lynn, Steven J; Namy, Laura L.; Woolf, Nancy J., *Psychology: From Inquiry to Understanding*, 2nd Ed., © 2011. Reprinted and Electronically reproduced by permission of Pearson Education, Inc., New York, NY.

Figure 3.20 Lilienfeld, Scott O.; Lynn, Steven J; Namy, Laura L.; Woolf, Nancy J., *Psychology: From Inquiry to Understanding*, 2nd Ed., © 2011. Reprinted and Electronically reproduced by permission of Pearson Education, Inc., New York, NY.

Figure 3.21 Adapted from Helm-Estabrooks, N., Nicholas M., & Morgan, A. (1989). *Melodic Intonation Therapy Program*. Austin, TX: PRO-ED.

Figure 3.22 Lilienfeld, Scott O.; Lynn, Steven J; Namy, Laura L.; Woolf, Nancy J., *Psychology: From Inquiry to Understanding*, 2nd Ed., © 2011. Reprinted and Electronically reproduced by permission of Pearson Education, Inc., New York, NY.

Text credit pages 97–98: Football Does Not Belong in Our Schools, by Lionel Matthews, city editor.

Chapter 4

Text credit page 104: Based on Galanter, E. (1962). Contemporary psychophysics. In R. Brown, E. Galanter, E. H. Hess, & G. Mandler (Eds.), *New Directions in Psychology* (p. 231). New York: Holt, Rinehart, & Winston.

Figure 4.5 Republished with permission of AAAS, from "Object Processing in the Infant Brain," by C. S. Hermann & A. D. Friederici, *Science*, 292 (5515), 165 (April 13, 2001); permission conveyed through Copyright Clearance Center, Inc.

Figure 4.8 Ciccarelli, Saundra K.; White, J. Noland, *Psychology: An Exploration*, 1st Ed., © 2010, p.79, 81, 141. Reprinted and Electronically reproduced by permission of Pearson Education, Inc., New York, NY.

Figure 4.12 Ciccarelli, Saundra K.; White, J. Noland, *Psychology: An Exploration*, 1st Ed., © 2010, p.79, 81, 141. Reprinted and Electronically reproduced by permission of Pearson Education, Inc., New York, NY.

Figure 4.14 Ciccarelli, Saundra K.; White, J. Noland, *Psychology*, 3rd Ed., © 2012, pp.96, 109. Reprinted and Electronically reproduced by permission of Pearson Education, Inc., New York, NY.

Figure 4.16 Lilienfeld, Scott O.; Lynn, Steven J; Namy, Laura L.; Woolf, Nancy J., *Psychology: From Inquiry to Understanding*, 2nd Ed., © 2011. Reprinted and Electronically reproduced by permission of Pearson Education, Inc., New York, NY.

Figure 4.17 From "Why Do We Miss Targets? Exploring the Boundaries of The Low Prevalence Effect" by A. N. Rich et al. (2008) *Journal of Vision*, 8, 1–17.

Figure 4.23 Lilienfeld, Scott O.; Lynn, Steven J; Namy, Laura L.; Woolf, Nancy J., *Psychology: From Inquiry to Understanding*, 2nd Ed., © 2011. Reprinted and Electronically reproduced by permission of Pearson Education, Inc., New York, NY.

Figure 4.24 Lilienfeld, Scott O.; Lynn, Steven J; Namy, Laura L.; Woolf, Nancy J., *Psychology: From Inquiry to Understanding*, 2nd Ed., © 2011. Reprinted and Electronically reproduced by permission of Pearson Education, Inc., New York, NY.

Figure 4.26 Lilienfeld, Scott O.; Lynn, Steven J; Namy, Laura L.; Woolf, Nancy J., *Psychology: From Inquiry to Understanding*, 2nd Ed., © 2011. Reprinted and Electronically reproduced by permission of Pearson Education, Inc., New York, NY.

Figure 4.28 "A Cochlear Implant" "Cochlear Implant" (Fig. 3.9, p. 104) from *Psychology*, 3rd edition by Saundra Ciccarelli & J. Noland White. Copyright © 2012. Printed and electronically reproduced by permission of Pearson Education, Inc., Upper Saddle River, New Jersey.

Figure 4.30 "The Sense of Kinesthesis" Figure 8.5, p. 229 from *Biological Psychology*, 10th ed. by Kalat. Copyright © 2009 by Wadsworth, a part of Cengage Learning, Inc. Reprinted by permission. http://www.cengage.com/permissions.

Figure 4.31 Ciccarelli, Saundra K.; White, J. Noland, *Psychology*, 3rd Ed., © 2012, pp.96, 109. Reprinted and Electronically reproduced by permission of Pearson Education, Inc., New York, NY.

Figure 4.32 *Psychology: From Inquiry to Understanding*, 2nd ed. by Scott O. Lilienfeld, Steven J. Lynn, Laura L. Namy, and Nancy J. Woolf. Pearson Education, Inc., 2011. Pearson adaptation derived from Ramachandran and Rogers-Ramachandran (1996). Synaesthesia in phantom limbs induced with mirrors. Proceedings of the Royal Society of London, 263, 377–386.

Figure 4.33 Figure 1 from "Mirror Therapy and Phantom Limb Pain" by B. L. Chan et al. (2007) *New England Journal of Medicine*, 357, 2206–2207.

Text Credit page 139: Based on An Open Letter to Congress By Vanessa Fowler, President, Federation of American Drivers.

Chapter 5

Figure 5.8 "The Influence of the 9/11 Terrorist Attacks on Dream Content." From Propper, R. E., Stickgold, R., Keeley, R., & Christman, S. D. (2007) Is television traumatic? Dreams, stress and media exposure in the aftermath of September 11, 2001. *Psychological Science*, 18, 334–340. American Psychological Association.

Text credit page 151: Smith, J., & Tolson, J. (2008). Recognition, diagnosis, and treatment of restless legs syndrome. *Journal of the American Academy of Nurse Practitioners*, 20(8), 396–401.

Text credit page 152: Schenck, C. H., & Mahowald, M. (2002). REM sleep behavior disorder: Clinical, developmental, and neuroscience perspectives 16 years after its formal identification. *Sleep*, 25, 120–138.

Figure 5.7 Lilienfeld, Scott O.; Lynn, Steven J; Namy, Laura L.; Woolf, Nancy J., *Psychology: From Inquiry to Understanding*, 2nd Ed., © 2011. Reprinted and Electronically reproduced by permission of Pearson Education, Inc., New York, NY.

Figure 5.10 "Meditation Reduces Negative Emotion" Figure 2 from Goldin, P. R. & Gross, J. J. (2010) Effects of mindfulness-based stress reduction (MBSR) on emotion regulation in social anxiety disorder. *Emotion*, 10 (1), 83–91. American Psychological Association.

Text credit page 161: Giacino, J., Ashwal, S., Childs, N., Cranford, R., Jennett, B., Katz, D., et al. (2002). The minimally conscious state: Definition and diagnostic criteria. *Neurology*, 58 (3), 349–353.

Table 5.3 "Application Activity: Are you Getting Enough Sleep?" Copyright © 1990–1997 by M. W. Johns. Use of the ESS by governmental agencies, as well as by organisations and individuals in a commercial or for-profit context, requires entry into a license agreement and the payment of applicable license fees. Refer to www.epworthsleepinessscale.com for further details.

Chapter 6

Figure 6.9 "Diet Soda Consumption is Associated with Increased, not Decreased Prevalence of Obesity" 6: Consumptive data for soft drinks comes from USDA Economic Research Service. Obesity prevalence data comes from National Center for Health Statistics. (Figure from Swithers Swithers, S. E., Baker, C. R., & Davidson, T. L. (2009). General and persistent effects of high-intensity sweeteners on body weight gain and caloric compensation in rats. *Behavioral Neuroscience*, 123, 772–780

Figure 6.12 Lilienfeld, Scott O.; Lynn, Steven J; Namy, Laura L.; Woolf, Nancy J., *Psychology: From Inquiry to Understanding*, 2nd Ed., © 2011. Reprinted and Electronically reproduced by permission of Pearson Education, Inc., New York, NY.

Figure 6.13 Lilienfeld, Scott O.; Lynn, Steven J; Namy, Laura L.; Woolf, Nancy J., *Psychology: From Inquiry to Understanding*, 2nd Ed., © 2011. Reprinted and Electronically reproduced by permission of Pearson Education, Inc., New York, NY.

Figure 6.15a Ciccarelli, Saundra K.; White, J. Noland, *Psychology: An Exploration*, 1st Ed., © 2010, p.79, 81, 141. Reprinted and Electronically reproduced by permission of Pearson Education, Inc., New York, NY.

Figure 6.15b "Learning without Reinforcement." Adapted from "Degrees of Hunger, Reward and Non-Reward and Maze Learning in Rats" by E. C. Tolman & C. H. Honzik, (1930), *University of California Publications in Psychology*, 4241–4256.

Text credit page 210: © Pearson Education, Inc.

Text credit page 211: John Fletcher

Text credit page 212: John Fletcher

Chapter 7

Figure 7.1 "The Atkinson-Shiffrin Model." From "Human Memory: A Proposed System and Its Control Processes" by R. C. Atkinson & R. M. Shiffrin in *The Psychology of Learning and Motivation: Advances in Research and Theory*, Vol 2 (pp. 89–195) ed. by K. W. Spence & J. T. Spence. Elsevier, 1968.

Figure 7.10 Rose, N., Myerson, J., Roediger, H., & Hale, S. (2010). Similarities and diferences between working memory and long-term memory: Evidence from the levels-of-processing span task. *Journal of Experimental Psychology: Learning, Memory, and Cognition*, 36 (2), 471–483.

Figure 7.11 Nielson, K., Yee, D., & Erickson, K. (2005). Memory enhancement by a semantically unrelated emotional arousal source induced after learning. *Neurobiology of Learning and Memory*, 84, 49–56

Text credit page 231: Friedrich Nietzsche

Figure 7.13 "Ebbinghaus's Forgetting Curve" Ebbinghaus, 1885.

Text credit page 236: Bransford, J. D., & Johnson, M. K. (1973). Considerations of some problems of comprehension. In W. Chase (Ed.), *Visual information processing* (pp. 383–438). Oxford, UK Academic.

Figure 7.15 "Schemas Affect how We Encode and Remember" Kleider, H., Pezdek, K., Goldinger, S., & Kirk, A. (2008). Schema-driven source misattribution errors: Remembering the expected from a witnessed event. *Applied Cognitive Psychology*, 22(1) 1–20.

Figure 7.17 "The Role of Eyewitness Errors in Wrongful Conviction" Reprinted by permission of The Innocence Project (http://www.innocenceproject.org).

Text credit pages 219–220: Based on Baddeley, 2012; Jonides, J., Lacey, S., & Nee, D. (2005). Processes of working memory in mind and brain. *Current Directions in Psychological Science*, 14, 2–5.

Chapter 8

Figure 8.2 "A Semantic Network Diagram for the Category 'Animal'" Based on Collins, A. M., & Quillian, M. R. (1969). Retrieval time from semantic memory. *Journal of Verbal Learning and Verbal Behavior*, 8, 240–248.

Figure 8.4 "Priming affects the Speed of Responses on a Lexical Decision Task" Figure 1, p. 1126 from "Priming the Holiday Spirit: Persistent Activation due to Extraexperimental Experiences" by J. H. Coane & D. A. Balota (2009) *Psychonomic Bulletin & Review*, 16 (6), 1124–1128.

Figure 8.8 "The Nine Dot Problem" Maier, N. F. (1930). Reasoning in humans. I. On direction. *Journal of Comparative Psychology*, 10(2), 115–143. American Psychological Association.

Figure 8.12 "Ratings of Perceived Contradictions in Political Statements" (your ?gure 2) Figure 2 from "Neural Bases of Motivated Reasoning: An fMRI Study of Emotional Constraints on Partisan Political Judgment in the 2004 U.S. Presidential Election" by D. Westen, P. S. Blagov, & K. Harenski (2006), *Journal of Cognitive Neuroscience*, 18 (11), 1947–1058.

Text credit page 261: Epley, N., & Gilovich, T. (2001, p. 392). Putting adjustment back into the anchoring and adjustment heuristic: Diferential processing of self-generated and experimenter-provided anchors. *Psychological Science*, 12, 391–396.

Figure 8.13 "Satisfaction of Maximers and Satisficers" Dar-Nimrod, I., Rawn, C. D., Lehman, D. R., & Schwartz, B. (2009). The Maximization Paradox: The costs of seeking alternatives. *Personality and Individual Differences*, 46(5–6), 631–635.

Figure 8.14 "Syntax Allows Us to Understand Language by the Organization of the Words." Adapted from *The Language Instinct* by S. Pinker, HarperCollins, 1994.

Figure 8.16 "Inheritance Pattern for the Mutated FOXP2 Gene in the KE Family" Adapted from Vargha-Khadem, F., Gadian, D. G., Copp, A., & Mishkin, M. (2005). FOXP2 and the neuroanatomy of speech and language. *Nature Reviews Neuroscience*, 6, 131–138. and Watkins et al. (2002).

Text credit page 275: Give our students a second language. By Irene Jordan, Ed.D.

Chapter 9

Text credit page 282: Neisser, U., Boodoo, G., Bouchard, T. J., Boykin, A. W., Brody, N., Ceci, S. J., Halpern, D. F., Loehlin, J. C., Perlof, R., Sternberg, R. J., & Urbina, S. (1996). Intelligence: Knowns and unknowns. *American Psychologist*, 51, 77–101.

Figure 9.4 "Sample Problem from Raven's Progressive Matrices" NCS Pearson, 1998.

Text credit page 291: Justice Kennedy, *Hall v. Florida* 572 U.S. ___ (2014)

Figure 9.7 "General Intelligence is Related to Various Outcomes" Adapted from Herrnstein, R., & Murray, C. (1994). The bell curve: Intelligence and class structure in American life. New York: Free Press.; Gottfredson, L. (1997). Why g matters : Complexity of everyday life. *Intelligence*, 24 , 79–132.

Figure 9.9a "Measuring Fluid Intelligence" from "Specific Impairments of Planning" by T. Shallice (1982), Philosophical Transcripts of the Royal Society of London B 298, 199–209. Copyright © 1982 by The Royal Society. Reprinted by permission of The Royal Society.

Text credit page 295: Gardner, H. (1983). Frames of mind: The theory of multiple intelligences. New York: Basic Books.

Figure 9.11 "Differing Perspectives on Intelligence" (Figure 1) from "Reframing the Mind: How Howard Gardner Became a Hero among Educators by Simply Redefining Talents as "'Intelligences'" by D. T. Willingham (2004), *Education Next: A Journal of Opinion and Research*, by Hoover Institution on War, Revolution, and Peace, 4 (3), 19–24.

Figure 9.12 "The Flynn Effect" from "Searching for Justice: The Discovery of IQ Gains over Time" Flynn, J. R. (1999). Searching for justice: The discovery of IQ gains over time. *American Psychologist*, 54, 5–20.

Figure 9.13 "Intelligence and Genetic Relatedness" adapted from "Intelligence: Genetics, Genes, and Genomics" by R. Plomin & F. M. Spinath. (2004). *Journal of Personality & Social Psychology*, 86 (1), 112–129.

Figure 9.15 "Birth Order and Intelligence" adapted from "Explaining the Relation between Birth Order and Intelligence" by P. Kristensen and T. Bjerkedal (2007) *Science*, Vol. 316, No. 5832: 1717–1718. Copyright © 2007 by AAAS. Reprinted by permission of AAAS.

Figure 9.17 Blackwell, L., Trzesniewski, K., & Dweck, C. (2007). Implicit theories of intelligence predict achievement across an adolescent transition: A longitudinal study and an intervention. *Child Development*, 78 (1), 246–263.

Table 9.4 Dweck, C., Chiu, C-y., & Hong, Y-y. (1995). Implicit theories and their role in judgments and reactions: A wolrd from two perspectives. *Psychological Inquiry*, 6, 267–285.

Text credit page 310–311: © Pearson Education, Inc.

Chapter 10

Figure 10.6 "Testing Conservation" Slightly adapted from figure 10.8, p. 374 in *Psychology: From Inquiry to Understanding*, 2nd ed. by Scott O. Lilienfeld, Steven J. Lynn, Laura L. Namy, & Nancy J. Woolf. Copyright © 2011. Printed and electronically reproduced by permission of Pearson Education, Inc., Upper Saddle River, New Jersey.

Figure 10.8 "Testing Infant's Understanding of Quantity" Figure 1 from "Newborn Infants Perceive Abstract Numbers" by V. Izard, C. Spann, E. S. Spelke, & A. Streri (2009), *Proceedings of the National Academy of Sciences*, 106, 10382–10385. Copyright © 2009. Reprinted by permission of PNAS.

Figure 10.9 "Measuring Attachment Styles: The Strange Situation Experiment" Slightly adapted from figure 10.17, p. 386 in *Psychology: From Inquiry to Understanding*, 2nd ed. by Scott O. Lilienfeld, Steven J. Lynn, Laura L. Namy, & Nancy J. Woolf. Copyright © 2011. Printed and electronically reproduced by permission of Pearson Education, Inc., Upper Saddle River, New Jersey.

Figure 10.10 "Piaget's Test for Egocentric Perspective in Children" Slightly adapted from figure 10.7, p. 374 in *Psychology: From Inquiry to Understanding*, 2nd ed. by Scott O. Lilienfeld, Steven J. Lynn, Laura L. Namy, & Nancy J. Woolf. Copyright © 2011. Printed and electronically reproduced by permission of Pearson Education, Inc., Upper Saddle River, New Jersey.

Figure 10.11 "Extended Brain Development" Adaptation of figure 4.25, p. 102 in *Biological Psychology*, 10th ed. by Kalat (2009, Wadsworth) after *The Prefrontal Cortex*, by J. M. Fuster (1989, Raven Press).

Figure 10.12 "What Drives Teenagers to Take Risks?" Adapted from figure 2, p. 630 in "Peer Influence on Risk-Taking, Risk Preference, and Risky Decision-Making in Adolescence and Adulthood: An Experimental Study" by M. Gardner & L. Steinberg (2005). *Developmental Psychology*, 41 (4), 652–635.

Figure 10.13 "Alzheimer's Disease Risk" From "Lifetime Risk of Dementia and Alzheimer 's Disease: The Impact of Mortality on Risk Estimates in the Framingham Study" by S. Seshadri et al. (1997) *Neurology*, 49 (6), 1498–1504. Copyright © 1997 by Wolters Kluwer Health. Reprinted by permission of Wolters Kluwer Health.

Figure 10.14 "How Alzheimer's Affects the Brain" http://www.nia.nih.gov/Alzheimers/Publications/Unraveling/Part2/changing.htm

Figure 10.16 "Emotion, Memory and Aging" "At the Intersection of Emotion and Cognition: Aging and the Positivity Effect" by L. L. Carstensen & J. A. Mikels, (2005) Current Directions in *Psychological Science*, 14 (3). Copyright © 2005 by Sage Publications. Reprinted by permission of SAGE Publications.

Chapter 11

Figure 11.4 "Obesity Map of US." http://www.cdc.gov/obesity/data/trends.html#State

Figure 11.5 "Why Have Sex?" Based on Meston, C. M. & Buss, D. M. (2007). Why Humans Have Sex. *Archives of Sexual Behavior*, 36, 477–507.

Figure 11.8 "Genetics and Sexual Orientation" Bailey & Pillard (1995), Bailey et al. (1993), Bailey et al. (2000).

Figure 11.12 "Competing Theories of Emotion" Adapted from Dr. Silvia Helena Cardosa, http://www.cerebromente.org.br/m05/mente/tub6.gif.

Figure 11.14 "How is the person in the middle of these pictures feeling?" Masuda, T., Ellsworth, P. C., Mesquita, B., Leu, J., Tanida, S., & van de Veerdonk, E. (2008). "Placing the face in context: Cultural differences in the perception of facial emotion." *Journal of Personality and Social Psychology*, 94, 365–381.

Figure 11.15 "East-West Differences in Interpreting Emotion" Masuda, T., Ellsworth, P. C., Mesquita, B., Leu, J., Tanida, S., & van de Veerdonk, E. (2008). "Placing the face in context: Cultural differences in the perception of facial emotion." *Journal of Personality and Social Psychology*, 94, 365–381.

Table 11.1 "Statistical Characteristics of Eating Disorders" From "The Prevalence and Correlates of Eating Disorders in the National Comorbidity Survey Replication" by J. Hudson, et al. (2007), *Journal of Social and Clinical Psychology*, 27 (6), 555–575. Copyright © by Elsevier. Reprinted by permission of Elsevier.

Table 11.2 "A Continuum of Sexual Orientation" From *Sexual Behavior in the Human Male*, Kinsey Institute for Research in Sex, Gender & Reproduction. Copyright 1948 by William B. Saunders. Reprinted by permission of The Kinsey Institute for Research in Sex, Gender and Reproduction.

Chapter 12

Figure 12.1 "The Big Five Personality Dimensions" After McCrae & Costa, 1987.

Figure 12.4 "The MMPI Personality Inventory" The registered trademark symbol ("R" in a circle) must follow the MMPI in line 1 and Inventory in line 1). Adapted from the MMPI-2 (Minnesota Multiphasic Personality Inventory-2) *Manual for Administration, Scoring, and Interpretation*, Revised Edition. Copyright © 2001 by the Regents of the University of Minnesota. All rights reserved. Used by permission of the University of Minnesota Press. "MMPI" and "Minnesota Multiphasic Personality Inventory" are registered trademarks owned by the Regents of the University of Minnesota.

Figure 12.5 "Personality Over the Life Span" From Roberts, B., Walton, K., & Viechtbauer, W. (2006). Patterns of mean-level change in personality traits across the life-course: A meta-analysis of longitudinal studies. *Psychological Bulletin*, 132(1), 1–25.

Figure 12.6(b) "Reciprocal Determinism and the SocialCognitive Approach" Figure 11.2, p. 394 from *Psychology: An Exploration*, 1st ed. by Saundra Ciccarelli and J. Noland White. Copyright © 2010. Reprinted and electronically reproduced by permission of Pearson Education, Inc., Upper Saddle River, NJ.

Figure 12.7 "Cultural Differences in Levels of Conscientiousness" From "The Geographic Distribution of Big Five Personality Traits: Patterns and Profiles of Human Self-Description Across 56 Nations" by D.P. Schmitt, J. Allik, R. R. McCrae, and V. Benet-Martinez (2007) *Journal of Cross-Cultural Psychology*, 38(2), 173–212. Copyright © 2007 by Sage Publications. Reprinted by permission of SAGE Publications.

Figure 12.9 "Genes and Personality" From *Genes and Environment in Personality Development* by J. C. Loehlin. Copyright © 1992. Reprinted by permission of Sage Publications, Inc.

Figure 12.10 "Genes, Serotonin, and Personality" From "Looking on the Bright Side: Biased Attention and the Human Serotonin Transporter Gene" by E. Fox, A. Ridgewell, & C. Ashwin (2009) *Proceedings of the Royal Society*, B., 276, 1747–1751. Copyright © 2009. Reprinted by permission of The Royal Society and the author.

Figure 12.13 "The Freudian Structure of Personality" Figure 14.1, p. 546 in *Psychology: From Inquiry to Understanding*, 2nd ed. by Scott O. Lilienfeld, Steven J. Lynn, Laura L. Namy, and Nancy J. Woolf. Copyright © 2011. Printed and electronically reproduced by permission of Pearson Education, Inc., Upper Saddle River, New Jersey.

Chapter 13

Figure 13.2 "Emotional Responses of Individuals with Anti-Social Personality Disorder" from "The psychopath as observer: Emotion and attention in picture processing" Adapted from Levenston, G. K., Patrick, C. J., Bradley, M. M., & Lang, P. J. (2000). The psychopath as observer: Emotion and attention in picture processing. *Journal of Abnormal Psychology*, 109 (3), 373–385.

Figure 13.2 "Emotional Responses of Individuals with Antisocial Personality Disorder" American Psychological Association (2011). http://www.apa.org/topics/suicide/signs.aspx

Figure 13.3 "Anxiety Levels are Inherited in an Animal Model" from "Selection for Contextual Fear Conditioning Affects Anxiety-Like Behaviors and Gene Expression" From "Selection for Contextual Fear Conditioning Affects Anxiety-Like Behaviors and Gene Expression" by C. A. Ponder, C. L. Kliethermes, M. R. Drew, J. Muller, K. Das, V. B. Risbrough, J. C. Crabbe, T. C. Gilliam, & A. A. Palmer (2007) *Genes, Brain & Behavior*, 6(8), 736–749. Copyright © 2007 by John Wiley and Sons. Reprinted by permission of John Wiley and Sons.

Figure 13.7 "Depression and the Brain" in "Neuroimaging and Depression: Current Status and Unresolved Issues" From "Neuroimaging and Depression: Current Status and Unresolved Issues" by I. Gotlib & J. Hamilton (2008) *Current Directions in Psychological Science*, 17, 159–163. Copyright © 2008 by Sage Publications. Reprinted by permission of SAGE Publications.

Figure 13.9 "Social Influences on Depression" from "Neighborhood Characteristics and Depression: An Examination of Stress Processes" From "Neighborhood Characteristics and Depression: An Examination of Stress Processes" by C. Cutrona, G. Wallace, & K. Wesner (2006) *Current Directions in Psychological Science*, 15 (4), 188–192. Copyright © 2006 by Sage Publications. Reprinted by permission of Sage Publications.

Table 13.3 "Varieties of Personality Disorders with Brief Descriptions of Each" Reprinted with permission from *The Diagnostic and Statistical Manual of Mental Disorders*, Fourth Edition, Text Revision (Copyright © 2000). American Psychiatric Association.

Table 13.5 "What are We So Afraid Of?" from "The Epidemiology of DSM-IV Specific Phobia in the USA: Results from the National Epidemiologic Survey on Alcohol and Related Conditions" Adaptation of Table 3 from "The Epidemiology of DSM-IV Specific Phobia in the USA: Results from the National Epidemiologic Survey on Alcohol and Related Conditions" by F. S. Stinson, et al. (2007) *Psychological Medicine*, 37, 1047–1059. Copyright © 2007 by Cambridge University Press. Reprinted with the permission of Cambridge University Press.

Chapter 14

Figure 14.1 "Who Seeks Treatment?" from "National Trends in Outpatient Psychotherapy" Adapted from Table 1 in Mark Olfson and Steven C. Marcus, "National Trends in Outpatient Psychotherapy," *American Journal of Psychiatry*, December 2010; 167: 1456–1463. Copyright © 2010. Reprinted by permission of American Psychiatric Publishing, Inc.

Figure 14.2 "Types of Treatment People Use" http://www.nimh.nih.gov/statistics/3USE_MT_ADULT.shtml.

Table 14.1 "Attitudes Toward Seeking Psychological Help" From "Attitudes toward Seeking Professional Psychological Help: A Shortened Form and Considerations for Research" by E. H. Fischer & A. Farina (1995) Journal of College Student Development, 36, 368–373. Copyright © 1995 by American College Personnel Association. Reprinted by permission.

Chapter 15

Figure 15.8 "Factors Contributing to Empathy" from "An Additional Antecedent of Empathic Concern: Valuing the Welfare of the Person in Need" Figure 1, p. 73 from Batson, C., Eklund, J., Chermok, V. L., Hoyt, J. L., & Ortiz, B. G. (2007). "An Additional Antecedent of Empathic Concern: Valuing the Welfare of the Person in Need." *Journal of Personality and Social Psychology*, 93(1), 65–74.

Figure 15.9 "Men from a Culture of Honor React More Strongly to Perceived Insults" from "Insult, Aggression, and the Southern Culture of Honor: An 'Experimental Ethnography'" Figure 2, p. 952 from "Insult, Aggression, and the Southern Culture of Honor: An 'Experimental Ethnography'" by D. Cohen, R. E. Nisbett, B. F. Bowdle & N. Schwarz (1996) *Journal of Personality and Social Psychology*, 70 (5), 945–960.

Table 15.2 "Risk Factors for Groupthink" from "The nature of social influence in groupthink: Compliance and Internalization" From McCauley, C. (1987). The nature of social influence in groupthink: Compliance and internalization. *Journal of Personality and Social Psychology*, 57, 250–260.

Table 15.3 "Attitudes Scale" adapted from "Bringing Cognitive Dissonance to the Classroom" Adapted from "Bringing Cognitive Dissonance to the Classroom" by D. M. Carkenord & J. Bullington (1993) *Teaching of Psychology*, 20(1), 41–43. Copyright © 1993 by Taylor & Francis Group. Reprinted by permission of Taylor & Francis Group, http://www.informaworld.com.

Table 15.4 "Description of Self and Others" from "Behavior as Seen by the Actor and as Seen by the Observer" Adapted from Nisbett, R. E., Caputo, C., Leganta, P., & Marecek, J. (1973). Behavior as seen by an actor and as seen by the observer. *Journal of Personality and Social Psychology*, 27 (2), 154–164.

Table 15.5 "A Self-Report Altruism Scale" (slightly adapted) From "The Altruistic Personality and the Self-Report Altruism Scale" by J. Rushton, R. D. Chrisjohn, & G. Fekken. (1981) *Personality and Individual Differences*, 2 (4), 293–302. Copyright © 1981 by Elsevier. Reprinted by permission of Elsevier.

Chapter 16

Figure 16.1 "Smoking and the Movies" from "Does watching smoking in movies promote teenage smoking?" From "Does Watching Smoking in Movies Promote Teenage Smoking?" by T. F. Heatherton & J. D. Sargent (2009) *Current Directions in Psychological Science*, 18, 63–67. Copyright © 2009 by Sage Publications, Inc. Reprinted by permission of SAGE Publications.

Figure 16.2 "Arousal and Performance" (graph depicting difficult task/easy task) From p. 39 in *Psychology*, 3rd ed. by Saundra Ciccarelli and J. Noland White. Copyright © 2012. Printed and electronically reproduced by permission of Pearson Education, Inc., Upper Saddle River, New Jersey.

Figure 16.6 "Seeing Images Where There are None" from "Lacking Control Increases Illusory Pattern Perception" From "Lacking Control Increases Illusory Pattern Perception" by J. A. Whitson & A. D. Galinsky (2008) *Science*, 322, 115–117. Copyright © 2008. Reprinted with permission from AAAS.

Figure 16.7 "Exercising Compensatory Control" from "Compensatory Control: Achieving Order Through the Mind, Our Institutions, and the Heavens" Figure 1 from "Compensatory Control: Achieving Order Through the Mind, Our Institutions, and the Heavens" by A. C. Kay, J. A. Whitson, D. Gaucher, & A. D. Galinsky (2009) *Current Directions in Psychological Science*, 18(5), 264–268. Copyright © 2009 by Sage Publications. Reprinted by permission of SAGE Publications.

Table 16.1 "Estimated Annual Deaths in the United States Due to Behavior-Related Risk Factors" from "The Preventable Causes of Death in the United States: Comparative Risk Assessment of Dietary, Lifestyle, and Metabolic Risk Factors" Derived from data noted in Danaei G, Ding EL, Mozaffarian D, Taylor B, Rehm J, et al. (2009), "The Preventable Causes of Death in the United States: Comparative Risk Assessment of Dietary, Lifestyle, and Metabolic Risk Factors." PLoS Med 6(4): e1000058. doi:10.1371/journal.pmed.1000058.

Table 16.2 "Health Costs of Tobacco Use" http://www.cdc.gov/tobacco/data_statistics/fact_sheets/fast_facts/index.htm. Retrieved June 20, 2011.

Table 16.3 "The Health Locus of Control Scale" adapted from "Development of the Multidimensional Health Locus of Control (MHLC) Scales" Adapted from "Development of the Multidimensional Health Locus of Control (MHLC) Scales" by K. A. Wallston, B. S. Wallston, & R. DeVellis (1978), *Health Education & Behavior*, 6(1), 160–170. Copyright © 1978 by Sage Publications. Reprinted by permission of SAGE Publications.

Table 16.4 "Life-Stress Inventories for the General Adult Population and for College Students" from "A Life-Stress Instrument for Classroom Use" From "A Life-Stress Instrument for Classroom Use" by M. Renner & R. Mackin (1998) *Teaching of Psychology*, 25 (1), 46–48. Copyright © 1998. Reprinted by permission of Taylor & Francis Group. http://www.informa-world.com.

Table 16.4 "Life-Stress Inventories for the General Adult Population and for College Students" from "The Social Readjustment Rating Scale" From "The Social Readjustment Rating Scale" by T. H. Holmes & R. H. Rahe (1967), *Journal of Psychosomatic Research*, 11, 213–218. Copyright © 1967. Reprinted by permission of Elsevier.

Chapter 17

Figure 17.1 "The O*NET Concept Chart" O*NET products including O*NET OnLine and O*NET Career Exploration Tools were developed by the U. S. Department of Labor. http://www.onetcenter.org/content/html.

Figure 17.2 "Conscientiousness Can Predict Job Performance" from "The Big Five Personality Traits and Individual Job Performance Growth Trajectories in Maintenance and Transitional Job Stages" From "The Big Five Personality Traits and Individual Job Performance Growth Trajectories in Maintenance and Transitional Job Stages" by C. Thoresen, J. Bradley, P. Bliese, & J. Thoresen (2004) *Journal of Applied Psychology*, 89, 835–853. American Psychological Association.

Figure 17.5 "Vacation Temporarily Relieves Burnout" from "Effects of a Respite from Work on Burnout: Vacation Relief and Fade-Out" From "Effects of a Respite from Work on Burnout: Vacation Relief and Fade-Out" by M. Westman & D. Eden (1997) *Journal of Applied Psychology*, 82, 516–527. American Psychological Association.

Figure 17.6 "Qualities Leading to Workplace Violence" from "Predicting Workplace Aggression: A Meta-Analysis" Adapted from "Predicting Work place Aggression: A Meta-Analysis" by M. Hershcovis, N. Turner, J. Barling, K. A. Arnold, K. E. Dupre, M. Sinness & N. Sivanathan (2007) *Journal of Applied Psychology*, 92 (1), 228–238. American Psychological Association.

Figure 17.7 "Assertiveness Predicts Leadership Effectiveness" from "In Search of the Right Touch: Interpersonal Assertiveness in Organizational Life" From "In Search of the Right Touch: Interpersonal Assertiveness in Organizational Life" by D. Ames (2008) *Current Directions in Psychological Science*, 17(6), 381–385. Copyright © 2008 by Sage Publications. Reprinted by permission of SAGE Publications.

Table 17.5 "A Sample Situational Judgment Test Item" From *The Psychometric History of Selected Ability Constructs* by L. C. Northrop (1998). U. S. Department of Personnel Management, Washington, DC.

Table 17.6 "Cognition Predicts Training Success and Performance" from "A Meta-Analytic Study of General Mental Ability Validity for Different Occupations in the European Community" From "A Meta-Analytic Study of General Mental Ability Validity for Different Occupations in the European Community" by J. Salgado, N. Anderson, S. Moscoso, C. Bertua, F. de Fruyt, & J. Rolland (2003) *Journal of Applied Psychology*, 88 (6), 1068–1081. American Psychological Association.

Table 17.10 "Skills and Abilities of Successful Leaders" (adapted) from "Educating the Modern Manager" From "Educating the Modern Manager" by R. Hogan & R. Warrenfeltz (2003), *Academy of Management Learning & Education*, 2 (1), 74–84. Copyright © 2003. Reprinted by permission of Academy of Management.

Name Index

Brant, A. M., 303
Brauer, J. D., 506
Braun, 79
Braz, J., 134
Brickman, A. M., 558
Brief, A., 575
Briley, 303, 403
Brion, M. J., 322
Brissette, I., 552
Brondolo, E., 538
Brophy, J. E., 514
Brotherton, 260, 261
Brown
    1958, 221
    1977, 231
    2003, 160
    2005, 73
    and Derkits, 457
Brown, B. B., 343
Browning, L., 223
    and Homes, 471
Brunell, A. B., 438
Bryant, 479
Bubic, A., 119
Buchtel, E. E., 407
Buck, L. B., 137
Buckingham, H., 269
Bukberg, R. E., 345
Bundorf, 537
Burgaleta, 294
Burger
    1999, 508
    and Caldwell, 510
Burke, B. L., 379
Burns, M., 554
Bushman, B. J., 208, 523
Buss, D., 366, 368, 413
Buston, P. M., 45

C

Cacioppo, J. T., 378, 508
Cacioppo (Mr), 538
Cacioppo (Mrs), 538
Cahill, L., 440
Cahn, B. R., 553
Cairns, B., 343
Cairns, R., 343
Cairo, 288
Calderwood, C., 109
Caldwell, D. F., 510
Calhoun, L. G., 552
Campbell, A., 502
Campion, J., 587
Cannon, M., 359
Cannon, W., 386, 544
Cao, X., 302
Capafons, A., 157
Carlson, J., 305, 306
Carlson, M. L., 128, 398
Carmichael, M. S., 370
Carmody, T. P., 158
Carre, J. M., 525
Carstensen, L. L., 349

Carston, R., 268
Carter, A. C., 168, 434
Cartwright, R., 149
Caruso, E. M., 45
Caspari, I., 269
Caspi, A., 457
Catalano, R., 470
Cattell, R., 399
Cattell, R. B., 293, 294
Cavallera, G., 148
Cave, E., 49
Ceci, S., 303, 305, 306
Cepeda, N., 204
Cesario, J., 253
Chabris, C., 110
Chaiken, 513
Chambless, D., 472, 482
Chamorro-Premuzic, T., 306, 400
Chan, B. L., 134
Charles, S. T., 349
Charron, S., 109
Chaudhari, N., 136
Chentsova-Dutton, Y. E., 168
Cheung, B. Y., 318
Cheung, F. M., 408
Choi, Y., 516
Christakis, N. A., 304, 539
Christensen, C., 359
Chuderski, 285
Church, A. T., 407
Cialdini, R., 503, 508–510, 516
Cillessen, A.H.N., 343
Clancy, S. A., 7
Clark, H., 88
Cleary, A., 156, 160
Clement, 523
Clevenger, J., 570
Coane, J., 252
Cobos, P., 387
Cohen, K. M., 345
Cohen, N. J., 379, 506, 525, 526
Cohen, S., 467, 481, 546, 547
Colagiuri, B., 186
Coleman, M. R., 161
Collins, A. M., 251
Colonna-Pydyn, C., 470
Combs, D., 455
Conde-Agudelo, A., 322
Conklin, E. L., 109
Connelly, A., 400
Connolly, J. J., 575
Copen, 344
Corballis, M. C., 91
Corkin, S., 224
Correl, J., 518
Corrigan, P., 433
Corso, P. S., 525
Cosmides, L., 71, 413
Costa, P. T., Jr., 399
Côté, S., 575
Coviello, L., 539
Cowan, 217
Cox, W. L., 379, 518

Coyle, T., 292
    and Pillow, 283
Crabbe, J., 70
Craig, I. W., 302, 524
Craik, F. I., 228, 229
Craik, F.I.M., 222
Crane, 166
Crano, 514
Creswell, 253
Creswell, J. D., 33
Critchley, H., 107
Crits-Cristoph, P., 472
Crook, M. D., 566
Crowell, S. E., 440
Crowther, S., 523
Csibra, G., 324
Cuadrado, 584
Cuijpers, P., 153
Cukor, J., 480
Cummings, D., 359
Cunningham, W. A., 517
Cutrona, C., 449

D

Dabbs, J. M., 524
Daigle, M. S., 450
Dal Cin, S., 535
Daley, T. C., 298
Damasio, A., 118
Damisch, L., 197
Danziger, N., 520
Darley, J. M., 523
Dar-Nimrod, I., 263, 264
Dastoor, S. F., 82
Daumann, J., 169
Davidoff, J., 254
Davidson, T., 187
Davis, B., 158
    and Knowles, 510, 521
Day, D., 584
Deadrick, D. L., 571
de Araujo, I. E., 360, 361
Deary, I. J., 69, 292, 302, 305
Decety, J., 522
Deci, S., 590
DeGutis, 118
Delgado, M. R., 359
DeLisi, M., 208, 454
DeLoache, J. S., 329
De Los Reyes, A., 472
Del Vecchio, W. F., 403
Demerouti, 566
Dennis, N. A., 471
Derkits, E. J., 457
Derntl, B., 524
DeRubeis, R., 472
Descartes, R., 12
DeVoe, S. E., 357
de Waal, F.B.M., 367
DeYoung, C. G., 414, 415
Diaz-Morales, J. F., 148
Dick, D. M., 70
Dick, F., 270

Subject Index